国际文化遗产保护文件选编

（2006–2017）

COLLECTIONS OF INTERNATIONAL DOCUMENTS ON CULTURAL HERITAGE PROTECTION (2006–2017)

（上册）

编译：西安市文物保护考古研究院
联合国教科文组织世界遗产中心
国际古迹遗址理事会
国际古迹遗址理事会西安国际保护中心

Xi'an Institute of Archaeology
UNESCO World Heritage Center
International Council on Monuments and Sites (ICOMOS)
ICOMOS International Conservation Center–Xi'an (IICC–X)

文物出版社

图书在版编目（CIP）数据

国际文化遗产保护文件选编：2006～2017 / 西安市文物保护考古研究院等编译. —北京：文物出版社，2020.12

ISBN 978-7-5010-7081-7

Ⅰ. ①国…　Ⅱ. ①西…　Ⅲ. ①文化遗产—保护—文件—汇编—中国　Ⅳ. ①G269.2

中国版本图书馆 CIP 数据核字（2021）第 025727 号

国际文化遗产保护文件选编（2006–2017）

编　　译：西安市文物保护考古研究院
　　　　　联合国教科文组织世界遗产中心
　　　　　国际古迹遗址理事会
　　　　　国际古迹遗址理事会西安国际保护中心

责任编辑：吕　游　李　睿
封面设计：王文娴
责任印制：陈　杰

出版发行：文物出版社
地　　址：北京市东直门内北小街 2 号楼
邮　　编：100007
网　　址：http://www.wenwu.com
经　　销：新华书店
印　　刷：宝蕾元仁浩（天津）印刷有限公司
开　　本：889mm × 1194mm　1/16
印　　张：57.75
版　　次：2020 年 12 月第 1 版
印　　次：2020 年 12 月第 1 次印刷
书　　号：ISBN 978-7-5010-7081-7
定　　价：480.00 元（全二册）

国际文化遗产保护文件选编

（2006—2017）

编纂委员会

主　　编：冯　健　景　峰

校　　译：冯　健　李同仙　周剑虹　赵凤燕

责任终校：冯　健　李同仙

翻　　译：冯　健　李同仙　周剑虹　李尔吾　巩　天
张　良　曹铭婧　陶　亮　刘一思　周晓晨
姚　逊　张竞秋　李文博　李潇潇　李　丹
祝艺苗　李娜宁　赵　戈

目　　录

CONTENTS

◎ 2011-2013 年

中华人民共和国主席习近平
在联合国教科文组织总部的演讲
Speech by H.E. Xi Jinping
President of the People's Republic of China
At UNESCO Headquarters Paris

Speech by H.E. Xi Jinping
President of the People's Republic of China
At UNESCO Headquarters
Paris, 27 March 2014

Your Excellency Madame Irina Bokova, Director-General of UNESCO,
Ladies and Gentlemen,
Dear Friends,

Good morning. It gives me great pleasure to have an opportunity of visiting the UNESCO headquarters. Let me begin by offering Madame Bokova my heartfelt congratulations on her re-election as the Director-General of the Organization and paying my sincere tribute to UNESCO for the extraordinary contribution it has made for greater exchanges and mutual learning among human civilizations.

UNESCO was born 69 years ago when the smoke of the World War against Fascism had barely dissipated. The grisly horror of war forced mankind once again to rethink on the nature of war and peace. Throughout the centuries, people have yearned for lasting peace, but war has haunted mankind every step of their progress. As we speak, many children on this planet are suffering from the horror of armed conflicts. We must do our utmost to keep war as far away as possible from mankind so that children across the world can grow up

在联合国教科文组织总部的演讲（2014年3月27日，巴黎）中华人民共和国主席习近平

尊敬的博科娃总干事，
女士们，先生们，朋友们：

大家好！有机会来到联合国教科文组织总部，感到十分高兴。首先，我谨对博科娃女士再次当选教科文组织总干事，表示衷心的祝贺！对教科文组织为推动人类文明交流互鉴做出的卓越贡献，表示诚挚的敬意！

教科文组织诞生于69年前，那时世界反法西斯战争硝烟刚刚散去。面对战争给人类带来的惨烈后果，人类又一次反思战争与和平的真谛。千百年来，人类都梦想着持久和平，但战争始终像一个幽灵一样伴随着人类发展历程。此时此刻，世界上很多孩子正生活在战乱的惊恐之中。我们必须做出努力，让战争远离人类，让全世界的孩子们都在和平的阳光下幸福成长。

happily under the sunshine of peace.

The stone wall at the entrance to the UNESCO headquarters carries the inscription of one single message in different languages: Since wars begin in the minds of men, it is in the minds of men that the defenses of peace must be constructed.

在教科文组织总部大楼前的石碑上，用多种语言镌刻着这样一句话："战争起源于人之思想，故务须于人之思想中筑起保卫和平之屏障。"

As long as the idea of peace can strike deep roots and the sail of peace can be hoisted in the minds of people all over the world, a strong defense will be built to prevent and stop war. People hoped to promote inter-civilization exchanges, equality of educational opportunities and scientific literacy in order to dispel estrangement, prejudice and hatred, and spread the seeds of the idea of peace. This is precisely why UNESCO was established in the first place.

只要世界人民在心灵中坚定了和平理念、扬起了和平风帆，就能形成防止和反对战争的强大力量。人们希望通过文明交流、平等教育、普及科学，消除隔阂、偏见、仇视，播撒和平理念的种子。这就是教科文组织成立的初衷。

The aspiration and vision as such deserve our renewed commitment. Not only so, but we must also step up inter-civilization activities in education, science, technology and culture across border, time and space to spread the seeds of the idea of peace far and wide so that they will sprout, take root and grow in the minds of the world's people, and provide the planet we share with more and more forests of peace.

这样一种期待，这样一种憧憬，是我们今天依然要坚守的。不仅要坚守，而且要通过跨国界、跨时空、跨文明的教育、科技、文化活动，让和平理念的种子在世界人民心中生根发芽，让我们共同生活的这个星球生长出一片又一片和平的森林。

Since its inception in 1945, UNESCO has faithfully lived up to its mandate and worked untiringly to enhance trust and understanding among the world's peoples and promote exchanges and mutual learning among the various civilizations. China attaches great importance to its cooperation with UNESCO, and stands ready to get more involved in its activities. As a token of its support and assistance to Africa, China has decided to increase the number of candidates for the Great Wall Fellowship program provided to African and other developing countries through UNESCO from 25 to 75 each year. We will also work with UNESCO to continue the program of Funds-in-Trust to support Africa.

自 1945 年成立以来，教科文组织忠实履行使命，在增进世界人民相互了解和信任、推动不同文明交流互鉴方面进行了不懈努力。中国高度重视同教科文组织的合作，愿意加大参与教科文组织的各项活动。为体现对非洲的支持和帮助，我们决定把通过教科文组织向包括非洲国家在内的发展中国家提供的长城奖学金名额由每年 25 人扩大为 75 人，我们还将同教科文组织一道把援助非洲信托基金的活动继续开展下去。

Ladies and Gentlemen,
Dear Friends,

Civilizations have become richer and more colorful with exchanges and mutual learning. Such exchanges and mutual learning form an important drive for human progress and global peace and development.

To promote exchanges and mutual learning among civilizations, we must adopt a right approach with some important principles. They, in my view, contain the following:

First, civilizations are colorful, and such diversity has made exchanges and mutual learning among civilizations relevant and, valuable. Just as the sunlight has seven colors, our world is a place of dazzling colors. A civilization is the collective memory of a country or a nation. Throughout history, mankind have created and developed many colorful civilizations, from earlier days of primitive hunting to the period of agriculture, and from booming industrial revolution to the information society. Together, they present a magnificent genetic map of the exciting march of human civilizations

'A single flower does not make spring, hundreds flowers full blossom in gardens bring spring to us.' If there were only one kind of flower in the world, people will find it boring no matter how beautiful it is. The Chinese civilization and other civilizations in the world are all fruits of human progress.

I have visited the Louvre Museum in France and the Palace Museum in China, both of which house millions of pieces of art treasures. They are attractive because they present the richness

女士们、先生们、朋友们!

文明因交流而多彩，文明因互鉴而丰富。文明交流互鉴，是推动人类文明进步和世界和平发展的重要动力。

推动文明交流互鉴，需要秉持正确的态度和原则。我认为，最重要的是坚持以下几点：

第一，文明是多彩的，人类文明因多样才有交流互鉴的价值。阳光有七种颜色，世界也是多彩的。一个国家和民族的文明是一个国家和民族的集体记忆。人类在漫长的历史长河中，创造和发展了多姿多彩的文明。从茹毛饮血到田园农耕，从工业革命到信息社会，构成了波澜壮阔的文明图谱，书写了激荡人心的文明华章。

“一花独放不是春，百花齐放春满园。”如果世界上只有一种花朵，就算这种花朵再美，那也是单调的。不论是中华文明，还是世界上存在的其他文明，都是人类文明创造的成果。

我参观过法国卢浮宫，也参观过中国故宫博物院，它们珍藏着千万件艺术珍品，吸引人们眼球的正是其展现的多样文明成果。文明交流互鉴不应该以独尊某一种文明或者贬损某一

of diverse civilizations. Exchanges and mutual learning among civilizations must not be built on the exclusive praise or belittling of one particular civilization. As early as over 2,000 years ago, the Chinese people came to recognize the truth behind the saying that ‘it is only natural for things to be different’ . Greater exchanges and mutual learning among civilizations can further enrich the colors of various civilizations, heighten people's enjoyment of cultural life, and open up a future with more options.

种文明为前提。中国人在2000多年前就认识到了“物之不齐，物之情也”的道理。推动文明交流互鉴，可以丰富人类文明的色彩，让各国人民享受更富内涵的精神生活、开创更有选择的未来。

Second, civilizations are equal, and such equality has made exchanges and mutual learning among civilizations possible. All human civilizations are equal in terms of value. They all have their respective strengths and shortcomings. There is no perfect civilization in the world. Nor is there a civilization that is devoid of any merit. No one civilization can be judged superior to another.

第二，文明是平等的，人类文明因平等才有交流互鉴的前提。各种人类文明在价值上是平等的，都各有千秋，也各有不足。世界上不存在十全十美的文明，也不存在一无是处的文明，文明没有高低、优劣之分。

I have visited many places in the world. The best thing I wanted to do is to learn about differing civilizations across the five continents, what make them different and unique, how their people think about the world and life and what they hold dear. I have visited Chichen Itza, a window on the ancient Maya civilization, and the Central Asian city of Samarkand, an epitome of the ancient Islamic civilization. It is my keenly-felt conviction that an attitude of equality and modesty is required if one wants to truly understand the various civilizations. Taking a condescending attitude toward a civilization can not help anyone to appreciate its essence but may risk antagonizing it. Both history and reality show that pride and prejudice are two biggest obstacles to exchanges and mutual learning among civilizations.

我访问过世界上许多地方，最喜欢做的一件事情就是了解五大洲的不同文明，了解这些文明与其他文明的不同之处、独到之处，了解在这些文明中生活的人们的世界观、人生观、价值观。我到过代表古玛雅文明的奇琴伊察，也到过带有浓厚伊斯兰文明色彩的中亚古城撒马尔罕。我深深感到，要了解各种文明的真谛，必须秉持平等、谦虚的态度。如果居高临下对待一种文明，不仅不能参透这种文明的奥妙，而且会与之格格不入。历史和现实都表明，傲慢和偏见是文明交流互鉴的最大障碍。

Third, civilizations are inclusive, and such inclusiveness has given exchanges and mutual learning among civilizations the needed drive to

第三，文明是包容的，人类文明因包容才有交流互鉴的动力。海纳百川，有容乃大。人类创造的各种文明都是劳动和智慧的结晶。每

move forward. The ocean is vast for it refuses no rivers. All civilizations are crystallization of mankind's hard work and wisdom. Every civilization is unique. Copying other civilizations mechanically or blindly is like cutting one's toes just to fit his shoes, which is not only impossible but also highly detrimental. All achievements of civilizations deserve our respect and must be treasured.

一种文明都是独特的。在文明问题上，生搬硬套、削足适履不仅是不可能的，而且是十分有害的。一切文明成果都值得尊重，一切文明成果都要珍惜。

History tells us that only through exchanges and mutual learning can a civilization be filled with vitality. If all civilizations can uphold inclusiveness, the so-called ‘clash of civilizations’ will be out of the question and the harmony of civilizations will become reality. This is like what we Chinese often say, ‘Radish or cabbage, each to his own delight.’

历史告诉我们，只有交流互鉴，一种文明才能充满生命力。只要秉持包容精神，就不存在什么“文明冲突”，就可以实现文明和谐。这就是中国人常说的：“萝卜青菜，各有所爱。”

Having gone through over 5,000 years of vicissitudes, the Chinese civilization has always kept to its original root. As the unique cultural identity of the Chinese nation, it contains our most profound cultural pursuits and provides us with abundant nourishment for existence and development. The Chinese civilization, though born on the soil of China, has come to its present form through constant exchanges and mutual learning with other civilizations.

中华文明经历了5000多年的历史变迁，但始终一脉相承，积淀着中华民族最深层的精神追求，代表着中华民族独特的精神标识，为中华民族生生不息、发展壮大提供了丰厚滋养。中华文明是在中国大地上产生的文明，也是同其他文明不断交流互鉴而形成的文明。

In the 2nd century B.C., China began working on the Silk Road leading to the Western Regions. In 138 B.C. and 119 B.C., Envoy Zhang Qian of the Han Dynasty made two trips to those regions, spreading the Chinese culture there and bringing into China grape, alfalfa, pomegranate, flax, sesame and other products. In the Western Han Dynasty, China’s merchant fleets sailed as far as to India and Sri Lanka where they traded China’s silk for colored glaze, pearls and other products. The Tang Dynasty saw dynamic interactions between China and other countries. According to historical documents, the dynasty exchanged envoys

公元前100多年，中国就开始开辟通往西域的丝绸之路。汉代张骞于公元前138年和前119年两次出使西域，向西域传播了中华文化，也引进了葡萄、苜蓿、石榴、胡麻、芝麻等西域文化成果。西汉时期，中国的船队就到达了印度和斯里兰卡，用中国的丝绸换取了琉璃、珍珠等物品。中国唐代是中国历史上对外交流的活跃期。据史料记载，唐代中国通使交好的国家多达70多个，那时候的首都长安里来自各国的使臣、商人、留学生云集成群。这个大交流促进了中华文化远播世界，也促进了各国文化和物产传入中国。15世纪初，中国明代著名航

with over 70 countries, and Chang'an, the capital of Tang, bustled with envoys, merchants and students from other countries. Exchanges of such a magnitude helped the spread of the Chinese culture to the rest of the world and the introduction into China of the cultures and products from other countries. In the early 15th century, Zheng He, the famous navigator of China's Ming Dynasty, voyaged to 'the Western Seas for seven times.', reaching many Southeast Asian countries and even Kenya on the east coast of Africa. These trips left behind many good stories of friendly exchanges between the people of China and countries along the route. In late Ming Dynasty and early Qing Dynasty, the Chinese people began to learn modem science and technology with great zeal, as the European knowledge of astronomy, medicine, mathematics, geometry and geography were being introduced into China, which helped broaden the horizon of the Chinese people. Thereafter, exchanges and mutual learning between the Chinese civilization and other civilizations became more frequent. There were indeed conflicts, frictions, bewilderment and denial in this process. But the more dominant features of the period were learning, digestion, integration and innovation.

海家郑和七次远洋航海，到了东南亚很多国家，一直抵达非洲东海岸的肯尼亚，留下了中国同沿途各国人民友好交往的佳话。明末清初，中国人积极学习现代科技知识，欧洲的天文学、医学、数学、几何学、地理学知识纷纷传入中国，开阔中国人的知识视野。之后，中外文明交流互鉴更是频繁展开，这其中有冲突、矛盾、疑惑、拒绝，但更多是学习、消化、融合、创新。

Buddhism originated in ancient India. After it was introduced into China, the religion went through an extended period of integrated development with the indigenous Confucianism and Taoism, and finally became the Buddhism with Chinese characteristics, thus making a deep impact on the religious belief, philosophy, literature, art, etiquette and customs of the Chinese people. Xuanzang (Hiuen Tsang), the Tang monk who endured untold sufferings as he went on a pilgrimage to the west for Buddhist scriptures, gave full expression to the determination and fortitude of the Chinese people to learn from other cultures. I am sure that you have all heard about the Chinese classics *Journey to the West*, which was written on

佛教产生于古代印度，但传入中国后，经过长期演化，佛教同中国儒家文化和道家文化融合发展，最终形成了具有中国特色的佛教文化，给中国人的宗教信仰、哲学观念、文学艺术、礼仪习俗等留下了深刻影响。中国唐代玄奘西行取经，历尽磨难，体现的是中国人学习域外文化的坚韧精神。根据他的故事演绎的神话小说《西游记》，我想大家都知道。中国人根据中华文化发展了佛教思想，形成了独特的佛教理论，而且使佛教从中国传播到了日本、韩国、东南亚等地。

the basis of his stories. The Chinese people have enriched Buddhism in the light of Chinese culture and developed some special Buddhist thoughts. Moreover, they also helped Buddhism spread from China to Japan, Korea, Southeast Asia and beyond.

In the course of some two thousand years and more, Buddhism, Islam and Christianity have been introduced into China successively which allowed the country's music, painting and literature to benefit from the advantages of other civilizations. China's freehand oil painting is an innovative combination of China's traditional painting and the Western oil painting, and the works of Xu Beihong and other masters have been widely acclaimed. China's Four Great Inventions, namely, paper-making, gunpowder, movable-type printing and compass, led to changes in the world, including the European Renaissance. China's philosophy, literature, medicine, silk, porcelain and tea reached the West and became part of people's daily life. *The Travels of Marco Polo* generated a widespread interest in China.

2000多年来，佛教、伊斯兰教、基督教等先后传入中国，中国音乐、绘画、文学等也不断吸纳外来文明的优长。中国传统画法同西方油画融合创新，形成了独具魅力的中国写意油画，徐悲鸿等大师的作品受到广泛赞赏。中国的造纸术、火药、印刷术、指南针四大发明带动了世界变革，推动了欧洲文艺复兴。中国哲学、文学、医药、丝绸、瓷器、茶叶等传入西方，渗入西方民众日常生活之中。《马可·波罗游记》令无数人对中国心向往之。

I assume you have all heard of China's terracotta warriors, the buried legions of Emperor Qin. After his visit to the site, President Chirac of France said that a visit to Egypt will not be complete without seeing the pyramids, and that a visit to China will not be complete without seeing the terracotta warriors. In 1987, this national treasure of China, buried underground for over two thousand years, was inscribed on the UNESCO World Cultural Heritage List. There are many more proud Chinese achievements that have been included in the World Cultural Heritage List, the World Intangible Cultural Heritage List, and the Memory of the World List. Here, I would like to express my heartfelt thanks to UNESCO for its contribution to the preservation and dissemination of the Chinese civilization.

大家都知道，中国有秦俑，人们称之为“地下的军团”。法国总统希拉克参观之后说：“不看金字塔，不算真正到过埃及。不看秦俑，不算真正到过中国。”1987年，这一尘封了2000多年的中华文化珍品被列入世界文化遗产。中国还有大量文明成果被教科文组织列入世界文化遗产、世界非物质文化遗产、世界记忆遗产名录。这里，我要对教科文组织为保存和传播中华文明做出的贡献，表示衷心的感谢！

Ladies and Gentlemen,
Dear Friends,

女士们、先生们、朋友们！

Today, we live in a world with different cultures, ethnic groups, skin colors, religions and social systems, and the people of various countries have become members of an intimate community of shared destiny.

当今世界，人类生活在不同文化、种族、肤色、宗教和不同社会制度所组成的世界里，各国人民形成了你中有我、我中有你的命运共同体。

The Chinese have long come to appreciate the wisdom of 'harmony without uniformity'. Zuo Qiuming, a Chinese historian who lived 2,500 years ago, recorded in the *Chronicle of Zuo* the following comments by Yan Ying, Prime Minister of the State of Qi during the Spring and Autumn Period: 'Achieving harmony is like preparing the pottage. Only with the right amount of water, fire, vinegar, meat sauce, salt and plum can fish and meat be cooked in delicate taste.' 'It is the same when it comes to music. Only by combining the sounds of different instruments with the right rhythm and pitch as well as tone and style can you produce an excellent melody.' 'Who can eat the soup with nothing but water in it? What ear can tolerate the same tone played repeatedly on one instrument?'

中国人早就懂得了"和而不同"的道理。生活在2500年前的中国史学家左丘明在《左传》中记录了齐国上大夫晏子关于"和"的一段话："和如羹焉，水、火、醯、醢、盐、梅，以烹鱼肉。""声亦如味，一气，二体，三类，四物，五声，六律，七音，八风，九歌，以相成也。""若以水济水，谁能食之？若琴瑟之专一，谁能听之？

There are more than 200 countries and regions, over 2,500 ethnic groups and a multitude of religions in the world today. We can hardly imagine if this world has only one lifestyle, one language, one kind of music and one style of costume.

世界上有200多个国家和地区，2500多个民族和多种宗教。如果只有一种生活方式，只有一种语言，只有一种音乐，只有一种服饰，那是不可想象的。

Victor Hugo once said, 'There is a prospect greater than the sea, and it is the sky; there is a prospect greater than the sky, and it is the human soul.' Indeed, we need a mind that is broader than the sky as we approach different civilizations. Civilizations are like water, moistening everything silently. We need to encourage different civilizations to respect one another and live together in harmony

雨果说，世界上最宽阔的是海洋，比海洋更宽阔的是天空，比天空更宽阔的是人的胸怀。对待不同文明，我们需要比天空更宽阔的胸怀。文明如水，润物无声。我们应该推动不同文明相互尊重、和谐共处，让文明交流互鉴成为增进各国人民友谊的桥梁、推动人类社会进步的动力、维护世界和平的纽带。我们应该从不同文明中寻求智慧、汲取营养，为人们提供精神

while promoting their exchanges and mutual learning as a bridge of friendship among peoples, a driving force of human progress, and a strong bond for world peace. We should seek wisdom and nourishment from various civilizations to provide support and consolation for people's mind, and work together to tackle the challenges facing mankind.

支撑和心灵慰藉，携手解决人类共同面临的各种挑战。

In 1987, 20 exquisite pieces of colored glazed wares were excavated at the underground chamber of Famen Temple in China's Shaanxi Province. These East Roman and Islamic relics were brought into China during the Tang Dynasty. Marveling at these exotic relics, I thought hard and concluded that as we approach the world's different civilizations, we should not limit ourselves to just admiring the exquisiteness of the objects involved. Rather, we should try to learn and appreciate the cultural significance behind them. Instead of satisfying ourselves with their artistic presentation of people's life in the past, we should do our best to breathe new life into their inherent spirit.

1987年，在中国陕西的法门寺，地宫中出土了20件美轮美奂的琉璃器，这是唐代传入中国的东罗马和伊斯兰的琉璃器。我在欣赏这些域外文物时，一直在思考一个问题，就是对待不同文明，不能只满足于欣赏它们产生的精美物件，更应该去领略其中包含的人文精神；不能只满足于领略它们对以往人们生活的艺术表现，更应该让其中蕴藏的精神鲜活起来。

Ladies and Gentlemen,
Dear Friends,

女士们、先生们、朋友们！

Napoleon Bonaparte once said, There are only two forces in the world, the sword and the spirit. From the point of development, the sword will always be conquered by the spirit. We should develop education more actively. Education can open people's mind, impart knowledge, and cultivate temperament. The continued process of learning will enable our people to better appreciate the value of different civilizations. In this sense, education is an effective vehicle for the continuation and creation of civilizations. We should develop science and technology more vigorously. Scientific advancement and innovation can help people understand themselves and the world and be in a stronger position to change their society for the better. The

拿破仑曾经说过，世上有两种力量：利剑和思想；从长而论，利剑总是败在思想手下。我们要积极发展教育事业，通过普及教育，启迪心智，传承知识，陶冶情操，使人们在持续的格物致知中更好认识各种文明的价值，让教育为文明传承和创造服务。我们要大力发展科技事业，通过科技进步和创新，认识自我，认识世界，改造社会，使人们在持续的天工开物中更好掌握科技知识和技能，让科技为人类造福。我们要大力推动文化事业发展，通过文化交流，沟通心灵，开阔眼界，增进共识，让人们在持续的以文化人中提升素养，让文化为人类进步助力。

continued process of exploiting nature will enable our people to master still more knowledge and skills. In this sense, science and technology are a powerful tool to make the world a better place for mankind. We should promote cultural undertakings more energetically. Cultural exchanges can help open our hearts to each other, broaden our horizon and build greater consensus among us. The continued process of cultivating people morally and intellectually will result in a higher standard of humanity. In this sense, culture is a big booster for human progress.

Ladies and Gentlemen,
Dear Friends,

女士们、先生们、朋友们！

The Chinese people are striving to fulfill the Chinese dream of the great renewal of the Chinese nation. The Chinese dream is about prosperity of the country, rejuvenation of the nation, and happiness of the people. It reflects both the ideal of the Chinese people today and our time-honored tradition to seek constant progress.

中国人民正在为实现中华民族伟大复兴的中国梦而奋斗。实现中华民族伟大复兴的中国梦，就是要实现国家富强、民族振兴、人民幸福，既深深体现了今天中国人的理想，也深深反映了中国人自古以来不懈追求进步的光荣传统。

The Chinese dream will be realized through balanced development and mutual reinforcement of material and cultural progress. Without the continuation and development of civilization or the promotion and prosperity of culture, the Chinese dream will not come true. Forefathers of the Chinese nation yearned for a world of great harmony in which people are free from want and follow a high moral standard. In the Chinese civilization, people's cultural pursuit has always been part of their life and social ideals. So the realization of the Chinese dream is a process of both material and cultural development. As China continues to make economic and social progress, the Chinese civilization will keep pace with the times and acquire greater vitality.

实现中国梦，是物质文明和精神文明均衡发展、相互促进的结果。没有文明的继承和发展，没有文化的弘扬和繁荣，就没有中国梦的实现。中华民族的先人们早就向往人们的物质生活充实无忧、道德境界充分升华的大同世界。中华文明历来把人的精神生活纳入人生和社会理想之中。所以，实现中国梦，是物质文明和精神文明比翼双飞的发展过程。随着中国经济社会不断发展，中华文明也必将顺应时代发展焕发出更加蓬勃的生命力。

A civilization carries on its back the soul of

每一种文明都延续着一个国家和民族的精

a country or nation. It needs to be passed on from one generation to the next. And more importantly, it needs to keep pace with the times and innovate with courage. As we pursue the Chinese dream, the Chinese people will encourage creative shifts and innovative development of the Chinese civilization in keeping with the progress of the times. We need to inject new vitality into the Chinese civilization by energizing all cultural elements that transcend time, space and national borders and that possess both perpetual appeal and current value, and we need to bring all collections in our museums, all heritage structures across our lands and all records in our classics to life. In this way, the Chinese civilization, together with the rich and colorful civilizations created by the people of other countries, will provide mankind with the right cultural guidance and strong motivation.

神血脉，既需要薪火相传、代代守护，更需要与时俱进、勇于创新。中国人民在实现中国梦的进程中，将按照时代的新进步，推动中华文明创造性转化和创新性发展，激活其生命力，把跨越时空、超越国度、富有永恒魅力、具有当代价值的文化精神弘扬起来，让收藏在博物馆里的文物、陈列在广阔大地上的遗产、书写在古籍里的文字都活起来，让中华文明同世界各国人民创造的丰富多彩的文明一道，为人类提供正确的精神指引和强大的精神动力。

Ladies and Gentlemen,
Dear Friends,

女士们、先生们、朋友们！

As an old Chinese poem goes, ‘When one knows vernal breeze, one will always be in spring.’ UNESCO will mark its 70th anniversary next year. I am confident that under the stewardship of Director-General Bokova, the organization will make still more achievements in its efforts to promote exchanges and mutual learning among civilizations and advance the cause of peace in the world.

“等闲识得东风面，万紫千红总是春。”明年是教科文组织成立 70 周年，我相信，在博科娃总干事领导下，教科文组织一定能为推动人类文明交流互鉴、促进世界和平谱写新的篇章。

Thank you all.

谢谢大家。

（新华网，
UNESCO 世界遗产中心）

◎ 2006—2010 年

《中国世界文化遗产保护管理办法》
The Administrative Measures for Protection and Management of World Cultural Heritage in China

Order of the Ministry of Culture (No. 41)

The Administrative Measures for the Protection and Management of World Cultural Heritages (Herein after as *the Measures*), which were deliberated and adopted at the executive meeting of the Ministry of Culture on November 14, 2006, are hereby promulgated and shall be implemented as of the date of publication.

文化部令 (第 41 号)

《世界文化遗产保护管理办法》已经 2006 年 11 月 14 日文化部部务会议审议通过，现予公布，自公布之日起施行。

Minister Sun Jiazheng

November 14, 2006

The Administrative Measures for the Protection and Management of World Cultural Heritages.

部长　孙家正

2006 年 11 月 14 日

《世界文化遗产保护管理办法》

Article 1　For the purposes of strengthening the protection and management of World Cultural Heritages, performing responsibilities and obligations of the *Convention Concerning the Protection of the World Cultural and Natural Heritage,* and inheriting the culture of the mankind, *the Measures* are formulated in accordance with *the Law of the Peoples Republic of China on Protection of Cultural Relics.*

第一条、为了加强对世界文化遗产的保护和管理，履行对《保护世界文化与自然遗产公约》的责任和义务，传承人类文明，依据《中华人民共和国文物保护法》制定本办法。

Article 2　The word ‘World Cultural Heritage’ in the *Measures* refers to cultural heritages, and the cultural heritages part of the world cultural and natural heritages which were inscribed on *the World Heritage List* by the United Nations Educational Scientific and Cultural Organization (herein after as the UNESCO).

第二条、本办法所称世界文化遗产，是指列入联合国教科文组织《世界遗产名录》的世界文化遗产和文化与自然混合遗产中的文化遗产部分。

Article 3　World cultural heritage work implements focus on the principles of protection first, rescue first, rational usage, and strengthening management to ensure the authenticity and integrity of world cultural heritage

第三条、世界文化遗产工作贯彻保护为主、抢救第一、合理利用、加强管理的方针，确保世界文化遗产的真实性和完整性。

Article 4　The National Cultural Heritage Administration shall response for national World Cultural Heritage work. It shall coordinate and solve the serious problems arising from the protection and management of World Cultural Heritages, supervise and inspect the World Cultural Heritage work where each World Cultural Heritage is located.

The local people's government at or above the county level and its cultural heritage administrative department shall, in accordance with *the Measures*, formulate management rules, implement the working methods and be responsible for the World Cultural Heritage work within its administrative area.

第四条、国家文物局主管全国世界文化遗产工作，协调、解决世界文化遗产保护和管理中的重大问题，监督、检查世界文化遗产所在地的世界文化遗产工作。

县级以上地方人民政府及其文物主管部门依照本办法的规定，制定管理制度，落实工作措施，负责本行政区域内的世界文化遗产工作。

Article 5　The local people's government at or above the county level shall integrate the operating funds for the protection and management of World Cultural Heritage into its fiscal budget. The citizens, legal persons and other organizations may establish World Cultural Heritage protection funds by ways of donations, which should be used exclusively for the protection of World Cultural Heritages. The relevant laws, administrative regulations and departmental rules should be observed in the financing, usage and management of world culture heritage protection funds.

第五条、县级以上地方人民政府应当将世界文化遗产保护和管理所需的经费纳入本级财政预算。公民、法人和其他组织可以通过捐赠等方式设立世界文化遗产保护基金，专门用于世界文化遗产保护。世界文化遗产保护基金的募集、使用和管理，依照国家有关法律、行政法规和部门规章的规定执行。

Article 6　The state shall adopt the experts consulting system for the important matters relating to the protection of World Cultural Heritages. The National Cultural Heritage Administration shall establish an experts consulting system to carry out the relevant work.

The experts consulting system for the protection of World Cultural Heritages shall be formulated

第六条、国家对世界文化遗产保护的重大事项实行专家咨询制度，由国家文物局建立专家咨询机制开展相关工作。

世界文化遗产保护专家咨询工作制度由国家文物局制定并公布。

and announced by The National Cultural Heritage Administration.

Article 7 All citizens, legal persons and other organizations have the obligation to protect the World Cultural Heritages in accordance with law.

第七条、公民、法人和其他组织都有依法保护世界文化遗产的义务。

The state encourages citizens, legal persons and other organizations to participate the World Cultural Heritages protection.

国家鼓励公民、法人和其他组织参与世界文化遗产保护。

The National Cultural Heritage Administration, local peoples' governments at and above the county level and their cultural heritage administrative departments shall offer awards to organizations and individuals who have made outstanding contributions on World Cultural Heritage protection.

国家文物局、县级以上地方人民政府及其文物主管部门应当对在世界文化遗产保护中做出突出贡献的组织或者个人给予奖励。

The provincial cultural heritage administrative department shall establish a work system for the volunteers of protection of World Cultural Heritages in the field of organize, guidance and train.

省级文物主管部门应当建立世界文化遗产保护志愿者工作制度，开展志愿者的组织、指导和培训工作。

Article 8 The protection plans of World Cultural Heritages shall be organized and compiled by the people's governments at provincial level. The institution that undertakes the task of compiling the world cultural heritage protection plan shall obtain the qualification certificate issued by The National Cultural Heritage Administration. A protection plan of World Cultural Heritages shall specify the standards and priorities for the protection of World Cultural Heritages, classify and determine the protection measures on different categories, and meet the requirements of UNESCO World Cultural Heritages protection.

第八条、世界文化遗产保护规划由省级人民政府组织编制。承担世界文化遗产保护规划编制任务的机构，应当取得国家文物局颁发的资格证书。世界文化遗产保护规划应当明确世界文化遗产保护的标准和重点，分类确定保护措施，符合联合国教科文组织有关世界文化遗产的保护要求。

If the World Cultural Heritage does not formulate the protection plan or its content does not meet the requirements of *the Measures*, a protection plan shall be formulated or be revised within one year from the date of implementation of *the Measures*.

尚未编制保护规划，或者保护规划内容不符合本办法要求的世界文化遗产，应当自本办法施行之日起 1 年内编制、修改保护规划。

A plan of World Cultural Heritages shall be submitted,via the provincial cultural heritage administrative department, to The National Cultural

世界文化遗产保护规划由省级文物主管部门报国家文物局审定。经国家文物局审定的世界文化遗产保护规划，由省级人民政府公布并

Heritage Administration for examination and approval. The plan shall be announced by the provincial people's government and be implemented upon its organization. The requirements of protection plan shall be integrated into the national economic and social development plans, overall land use plans as well as urban and rural plans of the local people's governments at and above the county level.

组织实施。世界文化遗产保护规划的要求，应当纳入县级以上地方人民政府的国民经济和社会发展规划、土地利用总体规划和城乡规划。

Article 9　The immovable cultural heritages of World Cultural Heritages shall be ratified and announced as cultural heritage protection entities according to their historic, artistic and scientific values. For any immovable cultural heritages which has not yet been ratified or announced as a cultural heritage protection entity, it shall be registered and announced by the cultural heritage administrative department at the county level.

第九条、世界文化遗产中的不可移动文物，应当根据其历史、艺术和科学价值依法核定公布为文物保护单位。尚未核定公布为文物保护单位的不可移动文物，由县级文物主管部门予以登记并公布。

The immovable cultural heritages of World Cultural Heritages shall be protected and managed accordance to *the Cultural Relics Protection Law of the People's Republic of China and the Regulation on the Implementation of the Cultural Relics Protection Law of the People's Republic of China.*

世界文化遗产中的不可移动文物，按照《中华人民共和国文物保护法》和《中华人民共和国文物保护法实施条例》的有关规定实施保护和管理。

Article 10　With regard to a cultural heritage protection entity of World Cultural Heritages, the protection range and construction control area shall be demarcated and announced according to the needs of World Cultural Heritages protection. The delineation of the protection range and construction control area shall satisfy the protection requirements for corn zone and buffer zone of World Cultural Heritages.

第十条、世界文化遗产中的文物保护单位，应当根据世界文化遗产保护的需要依法划定保护范围和建设控制地带并予以公布。保护范围和建设控制地带的划定，应当符合世界文化遗产核心区和缓冲区的保护要求。

Article 11　The provincial people's government shall put up sign and notice panels for the World Cultural Heritages. Such work will not cause any damage to World Cultural Heritage.

省级人民政府应当为世界文化遗产做出标志说明。标志说明的设立不得对世界文化遗产造成损害。

Sign or notice panels of a World Cultural Heritage shall indicate the name, corn zone, buffer zone and protection institution of the World Cultural Heritage, and shall contain a logo of the world heritage announced by the UNESCO.

世界文化遗产标志说明应当包括世界文化遗产的名称、核心区、缓冲区和保护机构等内容，并包含联合国教科文组织公布的世界遗产标志图案。

Article 12 A provincial people's government shall establish archives for the protection of World Cultural Heritages and shall, via its cultural heritage administrative department, be submitted to The National Cultural Heritage Administration for archival records.

第十二条、省级人民政府应当为世界文化遗产建立保护记录档案，并由其文物主管部门报国家文物局备案。

The National Cultural Heritage Administration shall establish national archives centre for the protection of World Cultural Heritage, and shall establish a dynamic information system for the management of World Cultural Heritages and a pre-warning system by employing high and new technologies.

国家文物局应当建立全国的世界文化遗产保护记录档案库，并利用高新技术建立世界文化遗产管理动态信息系统和预警系统。

Article 13 A provincial people's government shall determine the protection institutions for the World Cultural Heritages. The protection institution shall be responsible for the routine maintenance and monitoring of the World Cultural Heritages and shall created logs. If there are any potential risk, the institution shall undertake control measures and report it in time to local people's government at or above the county level and to the provincial cultural heritage administrative department.

第十三条、省级人民政府应当为世界文化遗产确定保护机构。保护机构应当对世界文化遗产进行日常维护和监测，并建立日志。发现世界文化遗产存在安全隐患的，保护机构应当采取控制措施，并及时向县级以上地方人民政府和省级文物主管部门报告。

The staff of a protection institution for World Cultural Heritage shall be take the employment with certificate. The key person-in-charge shall have obtained a qualification certificate issued by The National Cultural Heritage Administration.

世界文化遗产保护机构的工作人员实行持证上岗制度，主要负责人应当取得国家文物局颁发的资格证书。

Article 14 Where a World Cultural Heritage is used as a tourist area, its publicity and education roles shall be given a full play and be formulated perfect measures for the management of tourism services.

第十四条、世界文化遗产辟为参观游览区，应当充分发挥文化遗产的宣传教育作用，并制定完善的参观游览服务管理办法。

The World Cultural Heritage protection institution shall submit management measures of tourism services to the provincial cultural heritage administrative department for archival records. The provincial cultural heritage administrative department shall supervise and inspect the management the relating tourism services of World Cultural Heritage.

世界文化遗产保护机构应当将参观游览服务管理办法报省级文物主管部门备案。省级文物主管部门应当对世界文化遗产的参观游览服务管理工作进行监督检查。

Article 15　The service items set in a tourist area shall meet the requirements of World Cultural Heritage protection plan and shall be consistent with its historical and cultural attributes.

The World Cultural Heritage protection institution shall be responsible for executing the service items. The principle of openness, fairness, impartiality and giving priority to the public interests shall be observed, the rights and interests of the local residents shall be protected when the service items are executed.

第十五条、在参观游览区内，应当符合世界文化遗产保护规划的管理要求，并与世界文化遗产的历史和文化属性相协调。

服务项目由世界文化遗产保护机构负责具体实施。实施服务项目，应当遵循公开、公平、公正和公共利益优先的原则，并维护当地居民的权益。

Article 16　The cultural heritage administrative departments at all levels and the World Cultural Heritage protection institutions shall organize and carry out the investigation and research of cultural tourism, seek out and exhibit the historical and cultural values of the World Cultural Heritages, protect and utilize the intellectual property rights obtained in the work of the World Cultural Heritages.

第十六条、各级文物主管部门和世界文化遗产保护机构应当组织开展文化旅游的调查和研究工作，发掘并展示世界文化遗产的历史和文化价值，保护并利用世界文化遗产工作中积累的知识产权。

Article 17　When in emergency, which may endanger the safety of any World Cultural Heritage no matter in happens or in likely to happen, the protection institution shall immediately take necessary control measures and simultaneously report it to the local people’s government at or above the county level and to the provincial cultural heritage administrative department. The provincial cultural heritage administrative department shall, within 2 hours after it received the report, submit it to the provincial people’s government and to The National Cultural Heritage Administration.

第十七条、发生或可能发生危及世界文化遗产安全的突发事件时，保护机构应当立即采取必要的控制措施，并同时向县级以上地方人民政府和省级文物主管部门报告。省级文物主管部门应当在接到报告 2 小时内，向省级人民政府和国家文物局报告。

After received the relevant report, the provincial cultural heritage administrative department shall decide on the processing method and be responsible for the implementation. The National Cultural Heritage Administration shall supervise and inspect the in-time dispose of emergency, put forward requirements for the prevention way of the similar occurrence of emergencies, and inform the provincial people's government where the World Cultural Heritage is located about the occurrence and settlement of the emergency.

省级文物主管部门接到有关报告后，应当区别情况决定处理办法并负责实施。国家文物局应当督导并检查突发事件的及时处理，提出防范类似事件发生的具体要求，并向各世界文化遗产所在地省级人民政府通报突发事件的发生及处理情况。

Article 18 The State shall adopt the monitoring and inspection tours system for the World Cultural Heritages protection. The National Cultural Heritage Administration shall set up a monitoring and inspection tours system to carry out the relevant works.

第十八条、国家对世界文化遗产保护实行监测巡视制度，由国家文物局建立监测巡视机制开展相关工作。

The regulations on monitoring and inspection tours system for the protection of World Cultural Heritages shall be formulated and announced by The National Cultural Heritage Administration.

世界文化遗产保护监测巡视工作制度由国家文物局制定并公布。

Article 19 If the authenticity and integrity of any World Cultural Heritage is impaired due to poor protection and management, this World Cultural Heritage site shall be announced in *the Warning List of World Cultural Heritage in Danger in China* by the National Cultural Heritage Administration.

第十九条、因保护和管理不善，致使真实性和完整性受到损害的世界文化遗产，由国家文物局列入《中国世界文化遗产警示名单》予以公布。

The provincial people's government where a world cultural heritage was included in *the Warning List of World Cultural Heritages in Danger in China*, shall put forward rectification measures for the problems existing in the protection and management thereof and improve heritage's protection and management within a limited time.

列入《中国世界文化遗产警示名单》的世界文化遗产所在地省级人民政府，应当对保护和管理工作中存在的问题提出整改措施，限期改进保护管理工作。

Article 2 Anyone who violates the provisions of *the Measures* and causes damage to the world cultural heritage shall be held liable in accordance with relevant regulations.

第二十条、违反本办法规定，造成世界文化遗产损害的，依据有关规定追究责任人的责任。

Article 21　The cultural heritages inscribed on *the Tentative List of World Cultural Heritages in China* shall be protected and managed according to *the Measures*.

第二十一条、列入《中国世界文化遗产预备名单》的文化遗产，参照本办法的规定实施保护和管理。

Article 22　*The Measures* shall be implemented as of the date of promulgation.

第二十二条、本办法自公布之日起施行。

《中国世界文化遗产监测巡视管理办法》

Management Regulations on Monitoring and Inspection Tours of World Cultural Heritage in China

Management Regulations on Monitoring and Inspection Tours of World Cultural Heritage in China (here in after as *the Regulations*)

(Reviewed and approved in 20th Administration Affairs Conference of the National Cultural Heritage Administration on December 8, 2006 and implemented from December 8, 2006)

《中国世界文化遗产监测巡视管理办法》(以下简称《办法》)

(2006年12月8日经国家文物局第20次局务会议审议通过，自2006年12月8日起施行)

Article 1　In order to strengthen World Cultural Heritage protection in China，perform responsibilities and obligations as the state party of *the Convention Concerning the Protection of the World Cultural and Natural Heritage* better, we worked out the *Regulations* according with *the Law of the Peoples Republic of China on Protection of Cultural Relics* and *The Administrative Measures for Protection and Management of World Cultural Heritage in China.*

第一条、为了加强我国世界文化遗产的保护管理，更好地履行《保护世界文化和自然遗产公约》缔约国的责任和义务，依据《中华人民共和国文物保护法》和《中国世界文化遗产保护管理办法》制定本办法。

Article 2　*The Regulations* are applicable to the Chinese World Cultural Heritages and the cultural heritage part of mixed World Cultural and Natural Heritage which were inscribed on *the World Heritage List.*

第二条、本办法适用于列入《世界遗产名录》的中国世界文化遗产及世界文化与自然混合遗产中的文化遗产部分。

Article 3　The state enforces the system of three-level monitoring at the state, provincial and World Cultural Heritage sites, as well as the two-level inspection tours at the state and provincial. The monitoring includes daily monitoring, periodic monitoring and reactive monitoring. The inspection tour includes regular and irregular inspection tours.

第三条、国家对世界文化遗产实行国家、省、世界文化遗产地三级监测和国家、省两级巡视制度。监测包括日常监测、定期监测、反应性监测；巡视包括定期或不定期巡视。

The Cultural Heritage Administrative Department of State Council is responsible for working out the

国务院文物行政部门负责制订世界文化遗产监测巡视工作的方针、政策、管理制度和技

guidelines, polices, management systems and technical specifications for the monitoring and inspection tour works of World Cultural Heritage; organizing or entrusting the professional institutes to carry out the reactive monitoring; organizing regular or irregular inspection tours.

术规范；组织或委托专业机构实施反应性监测；组织定期或不定期巡视。

The provincial cultural heritage administrative department is responsible for implement periodic monitoring, reactive monitoring as well as regular or irregular inspection tours for the World Cultural Heritage within its jurisdictions.

省级文物行政部门负责对本辖区内世界文化遗产进行定期监测、反应性监测，及定期或不定期巡视。

The protection and management organization of World Cultural Heritage is responsible for the daily monitoring of World Cultural Heritage.

世界文化遗产保护管理机构负责世界文化遗产的日常监测。

Article 4　The daily monitoring includes: conservation state of major physical of cultural heritage, natural and man-made changes in its core and buffer zone, impact of surrounding development on the major physical of cultural heritage, and tourist carrying capacity etc.

第四条、日常监测的内容包括文物本体保存状况、核心区和缓冲区内的自然、人为变化、周边地区开发对文物本体的影响、游客承载量等。

The periodic monitoring includes the systematic monitoring for the World Cultural Heritage implemented by the provincial cultural heritage administrative department every five years, and the key monitoring for the World Cultural Heritage which is on *the List of World Heritage in Danger* or on *the Warning List of World Cultural Heritage in China* yearly. The systematic monitoring refers to the comprehensive monitoring for the implementation of protection planning, heritage protection, management, exhibition and publicity etc. Key monitoring includes the monitoring for the solutions and respective results of existing problems in protection.

定期监测是指省级文物行政部门每五年对世界文化遗产实行的系统监测以及每年对列入《濒危世界遗产名录》或者《中国世界文化遗产警示名录》的世界文化遗产进行的重点监测。系统监测的内容包括对保护规划执行情况、遗产保护、管理、展示、宣传等情况的全面监测；重点监测内容包括对保护存在问题采取的解决方法及成效的监测。

The reactive monitoring refers to a special monitoring as for the problems in protection and management, including monitoring the abnormal conditions or dangerous factors which threaten the heritage protection.

反应性监测是针对保护管理出现的问题进行的一种专门监测，内容包括对威胁到遗产保护的异常情况或危险因素进行监测。

Article 5　The national or provincial cultural heritage administrative department organize the regular or irregular inspection tours to the heritage sites. The inspection tours content includes

第五条、国家或省级文物行政部门组织对遗产地进行定期或不定期巡视，巡视内容包括审核监测结果，检查保护、管理状况，并提出整改要求。

reviewing the monitoring results, inspecting conditions of protection, state of management as well as raising the rectification requirements.

Article 6 The protection and management organization of World Cultural Heritage shall submit last year's daily monitoring report to the provincial cultural heritage administrative department in January every year.

第六条、世界文化遗产保护管理机构须于每年1月将上年度的日常监测报告上报省级文物行政部门。

The provincial cultural heritage administrative department shall submit the reviewed annual report of daily monitoring to The Cultural Heritage Administrative Department of State Council in March every year, and submit the regular monitoring report on time as required by The Cultural Heritage Administrative Department of State Council.

省级文物行政部门须将审核后的年度日常监测报告于每年3月上报国务院文物行政部门，并按照国务院文物行政部门的要求按时报送定期监测报告。

The Cultural Heritage Administrative Department of State Council shall publish the protection and management monitoring results of the World Cultural Heritage to public every year.

国务院文物行政部门每年向社会公布世界文化遗产保护管理监测结果。

Article 7 The national, provincial and the World Cultural Heritage protection & management organizations shall respectively compile record files of reactive monitoring, regular monitoring and daily monitoring work, and keep them properly.

第七条、国家、省、世界文化遗产保护管理机构分别对反应性监测、定期监测、日常监测工作形成记录档案，并妥善保管。

The Cultural Heritage Administrative Department of State Council shall be responsible for creating and operating the database system of protection and management record files of the World Cultural Heritage.

国务院文物行政部门负责建立并运行世界文化遗产保护管理记录档案数据库系统。

Article 8 Encourage to apply the advanced techniques to conduct monitoring with multi-disciplinary and multi-departmental cooperation for the World Cultural Heritage.

第八条、鼓励使用先进科学技术手段，对世界文化遗产开展多学科、多部门合作的监测。

The Cultural Heritage Administrative Department of State Council shall be responsible for establishing the dynamic monitoring management system of World Cultural Heritage.

国务院文物行政部门负责建设世界文化遗产动态监测管理系统。

Article 9 The authenticity and comprehensiveness of the monitoring information and data shall be guaranteed. The national and provincial administrative departments of cultural heritage shall warn the organizations and individuals whom failed to implement the monitoring work according the regulations, fail to report on time, and conceal or falsify monitoring results, and order them correct according to the law.

第九条、监测资料、监测数据的真实性、全面性必须予以保证。国家和省级文物行政部门对未按规定开展监测工作、未按时报送以及隐瞒、篡改监测结果的机构和个人予以警告并依法责令改正。

For problems found out in monitoring or inspection tours, the protection and management organizations of World Cultural Heritage shall conduct correction as required. Organizations which failing to conduct correction on schedule, The Cultural Heritage Administrative Department of State Council may include the site on *the Warning List of World Cultural Heritage in China*, or considering the conditions, on *the List of World Heritage in Danger*.

对监测巡视中发现的问题，世界文化遗产保护管理机构应按要求及时整改。未按期整改的，国务院文物行政部门可将其列入《中国世界文化遗产警示名单》或根据情况列入《濒危世界遗产名录》。

Article 10 The expense of monitoring and inspection tours work of World Cultural Heritage specified in *the Regulations* shall be disbursed from the undertaking expenses of the national, provincial and the World Cultural Heritage protection & management organizations.

第十条、本办法中规定的世界文化遗产监测巡视工作所需费用，从国家和省级文物行政部门和世界文化遗产保护管理机构的事业经费中列支。

Article 11 *The Monitoring Technical Specifications of World Cultural Heritage in China* related to the Regulations shall be formulated separately.

第十一条、与本办法相关的《中国世界文化遗产监测技术规范》另行制定。

Article 12 For the cultural heritages on *the Tentative List of World Cultural Heritage in China*, please carry out monitoring and inspection tours under *the Regulations*.

第十二条、列入《中国世界文化遗产预备名单》的文化遗产，其监测巡视工作参照本办法实行。

Article 13 *The Regulations* will take effect as of the issuing date.

第十三条、本办法自公布之日起实施。

Article 14 The National Cultural Heritage Administration is responsible for the explanation of *the Regulations*.

第十四条、本办法由国家文物局负责解释。

国际古迹遗址理事会
《文化线路宪章》
THE ICOMOS CHARTER ON CULTURAL ROUTES

THE ICOMOS CHARTER ON CULTURAL ROUTES

Prepared by the International Scientific Committee on Cultural Routes (CIIC) of ICOMOS

Ratified by the 16th General Assembly of ICOMOS, Québec (Canada), on 4 October 2008.

国际古迹遗址理事会《文化线路宪章》

国际古迹遗址理事会文化线路科学委员会制定（2008 年 10 月 4 日国际古迹遗址理事会第 16 届大会（加拿大魁北克）通过）

Preamble

As a result of the development of the sciences of conservation of cultural heritage, the new concept of Cultural Routes shows the evolution of ideas with respect to the vision of cultural properties, as well as the growing importance of values related to their setting and territorial scale, and reveals the macro-structure of heritage on different levels. This concept introduces a model for a new ethics of conservation that considers these values as a common heritage that goes beyond national borders, and which requires joint efforts. By respecting the intrinsic value of each individual element, the Cultural Route recognizes and emphasizes the value of all of its elements as substantive parts of a whole. It also helps to illustrate the contemporary social conception of cultural heritage values as a resource for sustainable social and economic development.

This more extensive notion of cultural heritage requires new approaches to its treatment within a much wider context in order to describe and protect its significant relationships directly associated with its natural, cultural and historical setting. Within this advance, the concept of the Cultural Route is innovative,

导言

“文化线路”作为文化遗产保护科学发展的成果，作为遗产保护领域的前沿概念，代表了一种影响当前文化遗产演变的新思路，以及对文化遗产背景环境和相关区域整体价值的重要性的认同趋势，同时也揭示了多层面的文化遗产的宏观结构。这个概念引入了一个新的保护标准，即这些价值是超越国界的共同遗产，需要共同努力、联合保护。在尊重每个独立要素固有价值的同时，文化线路强调，将文化遗产所有元素的价值作为整体组成部分来评估。这有助于反映当代人把文化遗产价值作为可持续的社会和经济发展资源的社会观。

在更广阔的背景中用新的方法处理更加全面的文化遗产概念，以便更准确地描述和保护文化遗产与自然、文化和历史环境间直接相关而重要的关系。在这个前提下，文化线路的概念是创新的、综合的以及多维度的。它介绍并代表了文化遗产保护理论与实践中一个有质量

complex and multidimensional. It introduces and represents a qualitatively new approach to the theory and practice of conservation of the cultural heritage.

的新方法。

Cultural Routes represent interactive, dynamic, and evolving processes of human intercultural links that reflect the rich diversity of the contributions of different peoples to cultural heritage.

文化线路反映了人类多种文化间互动的、动态的、进化的联系过程，展示了不同的人群对于文化遗产多样性的贡献。

Though Cultural Routes have resulted historically from both peaceful and hostile encounters, they present a number of shared dimensions which transcend their original functions, offering an exceptional setting for a culture of peace based on the ties of shared history as well as the tolerance, respect, and appreciation for cultural diversity that characterize the communities involved.

虽然从历史上来看文化线路形成于历史上和平交往或者敌对冲突，但如今，他们拥有的共同特质已超越其原有的功能，在共享历史、宽容、尊重和欣赏相关区域文化多样性的基础上，为和平文化提供了独特的环境。

The consideration of Cultural Routes as a new concept or category does not conflict nor overlap with other categories or types of cultural properties—monuments, cities, cultural landscapes, industrial heritage, etc.—that may exist within the orbit of a given Cultural Route. It simply includes them within a joint system which enhances their significance. This integrated, interdisciplinary and shared framework creates new relationships among them by means of an innovative scientific perspective that provides a multilateral, more complete, and more accurate vision of history. This approach stimulates not only understanding and communication among the peoples of the world, but also increases cooperation to preserve cultural heritage.

将文化线路作为一种新概念或类别，不会与现有文化遗产范畴或类型冲突或重叠，而已有的古迹遗址、城镇、文化景观和工业遗产等，也可能存在于特定文化线路之内。文化线路只是将这些联合到一个系统中，从而提升它们的价值。这种综合性的、跨学科的和共享的架构，以创新的科学视角建立起个体间新的联系，提供了一个多边的、更加完整和准确的历史图景。这一思路不仅增加世界人民间的了解与沟通，还将促进文化遗产保护的合作。

The innovation introduced by the concept of ‘Cultural Routes’ reveals the heritage content of a specific phenomenon of human mobility and exchange that developed via communication routes that facilitated their flow and which were used or deliberately served a concrete and peculiar purpose.

文化线路概念所代表的创新的思路，揭示了特定的人类迁徙和交流现象的传统内容，通过促进交流线路上的人口流动和文化往来，有意识地服务于特殊目的。一条文化线路可能是一条为此目的而特别修建的道路，也可能是整体或部分地利用原本已有的、服务于其他用途

A Cultural Route can be a road that was expressly created to serve this purpose or a route that takes advantage either totally of partially of preexisting roads used for different purposes. But beyond its character as a way of communication or transport, its existence and significance as a Cultural Route can only be explained by its use for such specific purpose throughout a long period of history and by having generated heritage values and cultural properties associated to it which reflect reciprocal influences between different cultural groups as a result of its own peculiar dynamics.

的道路。但是，除了交流或交通运输的道路功能之外，文化线路的存在和重要性唯有通过特定历史时期的特殊功能、产生的遗产价值和相关文化遗产，体现不同文化群体各自的独特动力及相互影响。

Therefore, Cultural Routes are not simple ways of communication and transport which may include cultural properties and connect different peoples, but special historic phenomena that cannot be created by applying one's imagination and will to the establishment of a set of associated cultural assets that happen to possess features in common.

因此，除了其交通运输的道路功能之外，文化线路还包括文化遗产和不同民族的联系，作为一个历史现象，它不依靠人的想象和主观意愿存在，建立起一套拥有共同特征的相关的文化资源。

Cultural Routes have sometimes arisen as a project planned a priori by the human will which had sufficient power to undertake a specific purpose (for example, the Incan and the Roman Empire Routes). On other occasions, they are the result of a long evolutionary process in which the collective interventions of different human factors coincide and are channeled towards a common purpose (such as in the Route to Santiago, the African trade caravan routes, or the Silk Route). In both cases, they are processes arising from the human will to achieve a specific objective.

有时人们为实现某一特殊目的获得大力支持会预先设计文化线路。（例如，印加和罗马帝国防线）。通常，文化线路是长期演变的结果，不同的人为因素为一个共同目标，相互作用共同干预（例如，圣地亚哥路线，非洲沙漠商路，或丝绸之路）。以上两种情况，体现了人类追求特定目标的过程。

Given the cultural richness and variety of both the interrelationships and the characteristic assets directly associated with the reason for the existence of Cultural Routes (such as monuments, archaeological remains, historic towns, vernacular architecture, intangible, industrial and technological heritage, public

鉴于直接决定文化线路存续之特色资源的内在关系和文化的丰富多样（诸如历史建筑、考古遗存、历史城镇、乡土建筑、无形遗产、工业和技术遗产、公共工程、文化和自然景观、运输工具和其他特殊知识与技能应用的实例），对文化线路遗产的研究和管理需要采用多学科

works, cultural and natural landscapes, transportation means and other examples of the application of specific knowledge and technical skills), their study and management requires a multidisciplinary approach that illustrates and reinvigorates scientific hypotheses and stimulates increased historic, cultural, technical and artistic knowledge.

视角，阐明和重振科学幻想，并不断丰富相关历史、文化、技术和艺术知识。

Objectives of the Charter

• To establish the basic principles and methods of research specific to the category of Cultural Route as they relate to other previously established and studied categories of cultural heritage assets.

• To propose the basic mechanisms for the development of knowledge about, evaluation, protection, preservation, management and conservation of Cultural Routes.

• To define the basic guidelines, principles and criteria for correct use of Cultural Routes as resources for sustainable social and economic development, respecting their authenticity and integrity, appropriate preservation and historical significance.

• To establish the bases for national and international cooperation that will be essential for undertaking research, conservation and development projects related to Cultural Routes, as well as the financing required for these efforts.

本宪章的目标

• 在建立和研究已有文化遗产类别基础上，制定针对文化线路这一特殊遗产类型的基本研究原则和方法。

• 提出发展文化线路评估、保护、保存和管理相关知识的基本机制。

• 将文化线路作为社会和经济可持续发展的资源，为其合理利用确立基本方针、原则和标准，并尊重其真实性、完整性，适当保护文化线路及其历史意义。

• 建立国家和国际合作的平台，这对开展研究、保护和发展文化线路相关项目，以及为这些活动筹集资金非常重要。

Definition

Any route of communication, be it land, water, or some other type, which is physically delimited and is also characterized by having its own specific dynamic and historic functionality to serve a specific and well determined purpose, which must fulfill the following conditions:

a) It must arise from and reflect interactive movements of people as well as multidimensional, continuous, and reciprocal exchanges of goods,

定义

无论是陆地上、海上或其他形式的交流线路，只要是有明确界限，有自己独特的动态和历史功能，服务的目标特殊、确定，并且满足以下条件的线路即可称为文化线路：

a）必须产生并反映人类的互动，和历史上各民族、国家、地区或大陆间的多维、持续、互惠的货物、思想、知识和价值观的交流；

ideas, knowledge and values between peoples, countries, regions or continents over significant periods of time;

b) It must have thereby promoted a cross-fertilization of the affected cultures in space and time, as reflected both in their tangible and intangible heritage;

b）必须在时空上促进受到影响的所有文化间的交流互惠，并反映在其有形和无形遗产中；

c) It must have integrated into a dynamic system the historic relations and cultural properties associated with its existence.

c）必须将与其存在相关的历史关系与文化特性有机融入一个动态系统中。

Defining elements of Cultural Routes: context, content, cross-cultural significance as a whole, dynamic character, and setting.

对文化线路中的元素的定义：背景、内容、整体跨文化意义、动态特征以及环境。

1. Context: Cultural Routes occur in a natural and / or cultural context upon which they exert an influence and which they help to characterize and enrich with new dimensions as part of an interactive process.

1. 背景：文化线路产生于自然或文化背景中并对其产生影响，并在互动过程中赋予其特征、丰富其新的维度。

2. Content: A Cultural Route must necessarily be supported by tangible elements that bear witness to its cultural heritage and provide a physical confirmation of its existence. Any intangible elements serve to give sense and meaning to the various elements that make up the whole.

2. 内容：文化线路必须见证文化遗产并为其存在提供必要的实体证明。所有无形要素也对构成整体的各元素给予支持和意义。

1) The indispensable physical element that determines the existence of a Cultural Route is the communication route itself as an instrument serving a project designed or arising through human activity to accomplish specific goals.

1）决定一条文化线路存在的必不可少的物质元素是交通道路本身，它或是服务于设计目标的工具，或通过人类活动实现特定目标。

2) Other basic substantive elements are the tangible heritage assets related to its functionality as a historic route (staging posts, customs offices, places for storage, rest, and lodging, hospitals, markets, ports, defensive fortifications, bridges, means of communication and transport; industrial, mining or other establishments, as well as those linked to manufacturing and trade, that reflect the technical, scientific and social applications and advances in its various eras; urban centers, cultural landscapes, sacred sites, places of worship and devotion, etc.) as

2）其他基本要素是与其历史线路功能相关的传统遗产（补给站、边境哨所、仓库、休息和寄宿地、医院、市场、码头、要塞、桥梁、交通工具、工业，矿业设施，反映不同时代科技和社会进步的其他生产和贸易设施、历史城镇、文化景观、宗教圣地、礼拜和祈祷场所等），同时还包括见证了沿线民族间交流和对话过程的无形遗产。

well as intangible heritage elements that bear witness to the process of exchange and dialogue between the peoples involved along its path.

3. Cross-cultural significance as a whole: The concept of Cultural Route implies a value as a whole which is greater than the sum of its parts and gives the Route its meaning.

1) The cultural route constitutes a cultural asset enriched by the different cultures it has fertilized and which transcends them in overall value by offering a substantial number of shared characteristics and value systems.

2) Within its overall identity, the value of its parts resides in their common, shared, multifaceted significance.

3) Its wider scale permits a cultural linking of peoples, countries, regions, and continents.

4) This breadth of scale is important from the point of view of both the territory included and of the comprehensive management of the various heritage elements included in it. At the same time the cultural diversity it implies provides an alternative to a process of cultural homogenization.

4. Dynamic character: In addition to presenting physical evidences of its historic path, along with cultural heritage elements, Cultural Routes include a dynamic factor that acts as a conductor or channel through which the reciprocal cultural influences have flowed.

1) The dynamic of a Cultural Route does not obey natural laws or casual phenomena, but rather exclusively human processes and interests, and is therefore understandable only as a cultural phenomenon.

2) This vital fluid of culture is manifested not only in material or tangible aspects, but also in the spirit and traditions making up the intangible heritage of Cultural Routes.

3) By understanding a Cultural Route as a set of dynamic elements of cultural communication

3. 整体的跨文化意义：文化线路概念所蕴含的线路整体价值，要远远大于其各个组成部分价值之和，并赋予线路真正的意义。

1）文化线路构成了一笔文化财富，得到各种文化的滋养，并且通过提供大量共有特性和价值系统，在整体价值上超越了这些文化。

2）在统一身份中，各部分的价值在于它们共有、共享和多方面的意义。

3）它在更大规模上联系了不同民族、国家、地区和大陆间的文化。

4）考虑到对其领土和包含的各种遗产要素的综合管理，更大规模很重要。同时其中包含的文化多样性也为文化同质化发展提供了另一种选择。

4. 动态特性：除了与文化遗产要素共同展现历史道路的实物证据，文化线路还包含一个动态要素，发挥引导或渠道的作用，传递相互的文化影响。

1）文化线路的动态并不遵循自然法则或偶然现象，而完全是人类行为的过程和兴趣，所以只能将其理解成一个文化现象。

2）活跃的文化交流不仅体现为物质或有形的遗产，还体现在构成文化线路无形遗产的精神和传统中。

3）通过把文化线路理解为不同民族间一系列文化交流的动态要素，我们才能将其遗产

between peoples, its cultural heritage assets can be appreciated in their true spatial and historical dimensions, which allows for a comprehensive and sustainable approach to the conservation of the Route as a whole.

资源置于真实的空间和历史范畴去理解，这也促成将线路作为整体加以全面、可持续保护的思路。

5. Setting: The Cultural Route is closely linked to its setting and forms an inseparable part of it.

1) The geographical setting has helped to shape the Cultural Route, either determining its path or influencing its development over time.

2) The territorial setting, whether natural or cultural (urban or rural), provides the framework of the Cultural Route, gives it its particular atmosphere, characterized by elements and values of both physical and intangible nature, and is fundamental for the comprehension, conservation and enjoyment of the route.

3) A Cultural Route connects and interrelates geography and very diverse heritage properties, forming a unified whole. Cultural Routes and their setting are related to their different landscapes, natural or cultural, which are but just one of their components and have their own distinctive characteristics and identity depending on the different areas and regions they pass through in their course. The different landscapes contribute to characterize the diverse sections of the Route as a whole, enriching it with their diversity.

4) The relationship with nature is especially sensitive in some sections, in others it is the relationship with the urban or rural environment, and in the areas with monuments that are isolated from other buildings (such as chapels, monasteries, fountains, bridges, boundary crosses, etc.), it is the relationship of these monuments with their landscape setting which shapes the nature of that section of the Cultural Route.

5) The protection and conservation of the Cultural Routes requires a profound knowledge of

5. 环境：文化线路与周围环境密切相关，是其不可分割的一部分。

1）地理环境对文化线路的形成起着重要作用，或决定其实际路径，或随着时间的推移不断影响着它的发展。

2）地域环境无论自然或文化环境（城市或乡村），提供了文化线路的框架，以特色的有形、无形元素和价值，赋予它独特的氛围。是理解、保护和享用文化线路的基础。

3）文化线路把多样的地理和遗产资源连接起来，形成统一的整体。文化线路及其环境与不同的自然和文化景观相关联，构成文化线路的各组成部分，并由于线路经过地区和区域的不同，而展示出各自独特的风格和特征。这些不同地段丰富多样的景观，也塑造了文化线路整体的多样性特色。

4）有些路段与自然的关系非常敏感；有些路段，与城市或乡村的环境有一定的关系。在有古迹存在的地区，如果古迹相对孤立（如小教堂、寺院、喷泉、桥梁、边界线等），则古迹与周边环境景观的关系非常重要，决定了文化线路在这一地段的性质。

5）要保存和保护文化线路，需要具备关于其周围环境的历史、自然和文化特征的广博知

the historic, natural and cultural characteristics of their surroundings. Any interventions that may be necessary must fit in with this context and respect its defining features by facilitating their understanding and not distorting the traditional landscape, whether it is natural, cultural or combined.

识。任何必要的干预都必须与背景环境相适应，促进对它的认识和理解，尊重其特征，而不能扭曲传统的自然或文化景观或混合景观。

6) A delineation of the setting must be provided for the Cultural Route, clearly marking the boundaries of a well-defined, regulated buffer zone, which should allow the material and immaterial cultural values included in it to be preserved in their full authenticity and integrity. Such protection must include the values of the different landscapes forming part of the Cultural Route and providing its characteristic atmosphere.

6）必须明确文化线路的背景环境，清楚标记已界定的缓冲区，使其中有形和无形文化价值及真实性和完整性得以全部保存。这种保护必须包括不同景观的价值，因为这些多样的景观共同构成了文化线路，并赋予它独特的魅力。

Specific indicators

具体指标

As basic differentiating indicators applicable to the category of Cultural Route, the following should be considered: the structure of the route and its physical substratum as well as historical data about its use to accomplish a specific goal; any physical structures associated with the concrete purpose and functionality of the Cultural Route; communication elements, and the existence of cultural manifestations of shared origin along (or at given points of) the route such as practices, traditions, customs, and common uses of a religious, ritual, linguistic, festival, culinary, or similar nature; reciprocal influences in music, literature, architecture, fine arts, handicrafts, scientific advances, technical and technological skills, and other material and immaterial cultural assets whose full understanding derives from the historic function of the Cultural Route.

作为用于文化线路类别的不同指标，应该考虑以下方面：线路的结构及其物质基础；为特定功能服务的历史数据；与线路使用功能相关的结构；交通元素和线路中体现的共享文化如习俗、传统、风俗和共有（或特定）的宗教、仪式、语言、节日、饮食等实践的遗存；在诸如音乐、文学、建筑、美术、手工艺、科技发展方面的相互影响，以及其他有关线路本身历史功能的有形与无形文化遗产。

Types of Cultural Routes

文化线路的类型

Cultural routes can be classified as follows:

• According to their territorial scope: local,

文化线路可以划分如下：

• 根据地域规模：地方、全国、地区、洲际

national, regional, continental, or intercontinental.

• According to their cultural scope: within a given cultural region or extended across different geographical areas that have shared or continue to share a process of reciprocal influences in the formation or evolution of cultural values.

• According to their goal or function: social, economic, political, or cultural. These characteristics can be found shared across a multi-dimensional context.

• According to their duration in time: those that are no longer used versus those that continue to develop under the influence of socio-economic, political, and cultural exchanges.

• According to their structural configuration: linear, circular, cruciform, radial or network.

• According to their natural environment: land, aquatic, mixed, or other physical setting.

和跨洲际。

• 根据文化范围：在特定的文化区域内或拓展到不同的地理区域，始终共享文化价值的形成、发展和相互影响的过程。

• 根据目标和功能：社会、经济、政治或文化的，可以发现这些特性在一个多维背景中得到共享。

• 根据延续时间：已不再使用的线路与那些在社会、经济、政治和文化交流影响下仍在发展的线路的对比。

• 根据它们的结构布局：直线的、环形的、十字形的、放射状的或网状的线路。

• 根据它们的自然环境：陆地、水上、混合或其他自然环境。

Identification, Integrity and Authenticity

Prima facie indicators

For identification and assessment purposes, the following aspects may initially be considered as prima facie, non-conclusive evidence of the existence of a Cultural Route:

—Expressions of dynamic social, economic, political, and cultural processes which have generated exchanges between different cultural groups of related areas;

—Distinguishing characteristics that are shared by different geographical and cultural areas connected by historical bonds;

—Evidences of mobility and of relationships forged between peoples or ethnic groups of different cultures;

— Specific cultural features rooted in the traditional life of different communities;

—Heritage elements and cultural practices —such as ceremonies, festivals and religious celebra-

识别完整性和真实性

· 初步指标

为了方便识别和评估，以下几个方面可作为初步的、非结论性的证据，说明文化线路的存在：

——相邻区域不同文化群体之间社会、经济、政治和文交流化进程的动态表现；

——被历史纽带联系起来的、不同地理和文化地区之间共享的鲜明特征；

——不同文化的民族或少数民族群体的迁徙及相互关系的证据；

——植根于不同社区传统文化的特定文化特征；

——特定文化和历史区域内，代表不同社区共同价值观的遗产要素和文化习俗，如仪式、

tions representative of shared values for different communities within (a) specific cultural and historic area(s)

—related to the significance and functionality of the Route.

节日和宗教庆典。

——与线路的重要意义和功能相关。

Identification process

识别程序

The process for identifying a Cultural Route will necessarily take into account its specific functionality to serve a concrete and well-determined purpose, the tangible and intangible values of its heritage dynamically generated as a results of reciprocal cultural influences, its structural configuration, its whole geographic and historic context, its natural and cultural setting, whether the latter is urban or rural, and its corresponding characteristic environmental values, its relationships to the landscape, its duration in time, and its symbolic and spiritual dimension, all of which will contribute to its identification and to the understanding of its significance.

识别文化线路有必要考虑以下多个方面：服务于明确目的的具体功能，文化相互影响带来的遗产的有形和无形价值，结构布局、完整的地理和历史环境、自然和文化环境（城市或农村环境）、相应的特色环境价值，与景观的关系、存续时间、象征和精神意义，所有这些都有助于识别和理解它的意义。

The intangible assets of a Cultural Route are fundamental for understanding its significance and its associative heritage values. Therefore, material aspects must always be studied in connection with other values of an intangible nature.

文化线路的无形遗产是理解其意义和相关遗产价值的基础，因此对有形要素的研究应与其他无形要素价值相结合。

For the purpose of its comparative evaluation, the temporal duration and historic significance of the different sections of the Route in relation to the whole should also be taken into account.

为方便比较评估，还应考虑文化线路上不同地段相对于整个线路的时间跨度和历史意义。

In the case of a living Cultural Route, the relationships and dynamic functions associated with the specific and well-determined purpose that gave rise to its existence and serves to define and identify the route should be maintained, even if the historic processes have undergone change over time and new elements have been incorporated. These new elements should be evaluated within the framework

对于仍在使用的文化线路，应维持定义和确定路线的存在、与具体目的相关的动态功能和关系，即使随着时间的推移，历史进程发生了变化，融入了新的元素。这些新元素应该在其与文化线路功能关系的框架内加以评估。有时候，有些遗产本身具有重大价值，但不是文化线路的构成部分，因而不能被视为文化线路的一部分。

of their functional relationship to the Cultural Route, and the case may occur where properties that have heritage values in themselves cannot be considered as components of the Cultural Route because they do not form part of it.

Authenticity

Every Cultural Route should fulfill authenticity criteria demonstrably and credibly expressing its value in terms of both its natural and cultural environment, and concerning both its defining elements and its distinctive features of a material and immaterial nature:

• These criteria should be applied to each section under study to assess its significance in relation to the overall meaning of the Route throughout its historical development, and to verify the authenticity of its structural layout through the vestiges of its path.

• Authenticity should also be evident in the natural and cultural context of each stretch of the Route subject to analysis and assessment, as well as in the other tangible and intangible heritage elements included within its historic functionality and its setting.

• Even if in certain sections the material traces of a Cultural Route are not clearly preserved, its existence in these areas could be shown through historiography, intangible elements and immaterial sources of information that prove their real meaning as integral components of that Route and evidence its authenticity.

• The techniques and methodologies used for the protection, conservation and management of the Cultural Routes, whether traditional or newly implemented, must respect the authenticity criteria.

Integrity

The verification of the integrity of a Cultural Route must necessarily be based on a sufficiently representative set of both tangible and intangible evidences and elements that witness to its global

真实性

每一条文化线路都要满足真实性标准，在自然、文化环境及其定义元素、有形和无形的突出特征方面，明确真实地展现自身的价值：

——这些标准应用在研究的线路中的每个部分，评估它在历史发展过程中相对于线路整体意义的重要性，并通过道路的遗迹来证实结构布局的真实性。

——应当在文化线路上各地段的自然和文化环境中，并在其历史功能和背景环境包括的其他有形和无形遗产要素中，分析评估线路的真实性。

——即使文化线路有些地段的物质痕迹没有得到切实保存，但可以通过史料文献、无形元素等非物质信息来源，证明该地段是文化线路不可分割的组成部分，并证明其存在的真实性。

——保护、保存和管理文化线路的技术和方法，不论是传统还是新型的，都必须尊重真实性标准。

完整性

确认文化线路的完整性，必须以有充分代表性的有形和无形证据和因素为基础，这些证据和因素证明该文化线路的全球意义和价值，确保完整呈现产生一条文化线路的历史进程的

significance and values as a whole and ensure the complete representation of the features and importance of the historic processes which generated the Cultural Route.

特征和重要性。

Evidences of the historic relationships and dynamic functions essential to the distinctive character of the Cultural Route should be maintained. In addition, regard must be had for whether its physical fabric and/or its significant features are in good condition and the impact of deterioration processes controlled, and whether or not the Route reflects any possible side effects of development, abandonment or neglect.

历史关系和动态功能相关证据对形成文化线路突出特色至关重要，应予以保存。此外，还必须考虑其物质构成和显著特色的保存现状是否完好，退化进程的影响是否得到控制，文化线路是否受到发展、遗弃或忽略导致的副作用的影响。

Methodology

方法论

The concept of Cultural Route requires a specific methodology for its research, assessment, protection, preservation, conservation, use and management. Given its breadth and its value as a whole, as well as its territorial dimensions, this methodology requires the establishment of a system of coordinated and integrally managed activities.

文化线路的概念需要有一套特殊的研究、保护、评估、使用和管理的方法。鉴于文化线路涵盖范围广、整体价值大以及涉及的地域层面多，这个方法论需要建立一个由相互协调、综合管理活动构成的体系。

It is essential to start with the identification both of the Route as a whole and of its individual sections, along with an inventory of the assets that comprise it and an analysis of their state of conservation which will facilitate the elaboration of a strategic plan for its preservation. This plan should necessarily include measures for raising awareness of the Route and creating interest in it among public and private entities. It also requires the formulation of coordinated measures and specific legal instruments for the protection, use and management of all of its elements as substantive parts of the value and significance of the Route as a whole.

对线路有必要进行整体和各组成部分的识别，列出构成线路的遗产清单，分析当前的保存状况，以利于制定详细的战略保护方案。该方案必须包括提升公众意识的措施，以激发公营、私营企业对文化线路的兴趣。还应制定协调措施和具体法律文书，作为线路整体价值和重要性的实质内容，以合理保护、使用和管理线路内的各构成元素。

1. Research

The study of cultural routes may extend

1. 研究

文化线路的研究可能扩展到不同的地理区

across different geographical areas, possibly widely separated from each other. It is therefore advisable to set up several research teams located at the main characteristic points of the Route under study.

域，并很可能彼此相隔甚远。因此最好在有代表性的主要地点成立几个研究小组进行研究。

The research methodology, along with the adoption of practices and the attachment of indicators for proper identification and assessment of the heritage values in the different sections of a Cultural Route, should never lose sight of the meaning of the Route as a whole, in order to avoid any loss in the meaning or historic significance of the route.

采用的研究方法，以及用来合理识别和评估文化线路不同部分遗产价值的实践和附属指标，决不忽视该文化线路的整体含义，以免丢失线路的任一意义和历史价值。

Research teams working on this cultural heritage category should be of a multidisciplinary and cooperative nature. Common working criteria should be established based on the principle of starting with an investigation of the parts, but without losing sight of the project as a whole. Similarly, common methodological instruments—standardized in advance—should be used for the collection of data. The project plan should include coordinating mechanisms that will facilitate communication and cooperation among the researchers in order to make it possible to transmit data about the work and achievements of each team.

从事这一类型文化遗产工作的研究组，应有多学科合作性。应当在从局部展开调查原则的基础上建立共同的工作标准，但时刻不忽视项目整体。也应当将事先标准化的共同方法作为数据采集的工具。项目计划中应包括协调机制，以利于研究者之间的交流与合作，使每个工作组间都可以传递自己工作成果的数据。

Researchers should keep in mind that the presence of various types of cultural heritage properties along the path of a Cultural Route does not, in and of itself, imply that they are necessarily integral components of that route or are appropriate objects of study in relation to it. The only elements that should be highlighted in the scientific investigation of a Cultural Route are those related to the specific goal of the Route and any influences arising from its functional dynamic.

研究者应当注意到文化线路上会出现不同类型的文化遗产，但这并不意味着它们一定是路线的构成部分，或与线路相关的研究对象。在对文化线路进行科学调查时，一定要强调与线路明确用途和动态功能影响相关的元素。

2. Funding

Given the scope of the tasks involved in identifying and highlighting the value of a vast Cultural Route, funding should be obtained in stages

2. 经费

鉴于认识和强调一条绵长的文化线路的价值所涉及的任务范围，经费应该分期到位，以平衡和协调研究项目，以及与文化线路各部分

that will allow for balanced, coordinated progress in the research projects as well as the preservation, use, and management projects related to its various sections. It is advisable to establish a joint estimation of the values to be preserved so as to allow the setting of a scale of priorities for action and the implementation of the corresponding strategies. This requires that funding be obtained through bilateral or multilateral cooperation agreements, as well as through the creation of bodies specifically devoted to researching and highlighting the value of the Route. Along the same lines, regional bodies whose jurisdictions coincide totally or partially with the historic path of a Cultural Route should determine how they can best gain the interest of the States involved and obtain their cooperation. It is also important to attract, if possible, the cooperation of philanthropic institutions and private donors.

相关的保护、使用和管理等项目的进度。最好是对需要保存的价值进行联合评估，以便决定优先行动和落实相关战略的范围。这就要求通过双边或多边合作协议，或设立专门研究和重视线路价值的机构来获取经费。在线路沿线，管辖权与文化线路的历史道路完全或部分重合的地区性机构，应负责决定如何最多的赢得相关国家的关注并获得合作。吸引慈善机构和私人捐款的合作也同样重要。

Protection-Assessment-Preservation/Conservation Cultural Routes and their setting require new instruments for their assessment, protection, conservation and evaluation. It is not sufficient to guarantee protection of their heritage elements on a partial or random basis. The preparation of rigorous inventories of these elements, as well as an assessment of their authenticity and integrity should take place in order to identify impacts on the values of the Cultural Route and therefore impacts on its significance. It is also necessary to control the impact of deterioration processes, and to develop a strategy to prevent the adverse effects of development and neglect. All of this requires the establishment of a system of coordinated legal measures and appropriate instruments that guarantee that the Route will be preserved and its value and significance highlighted in a holistic fashion.

3. 守卫——评估——保存——保护文化线路及其环境，要求有新的分析、保护和评估工具。仅部分或随机地保护遗产要素是不够的。应该编制详细的要素清单，并评估其真实性和完整性，确定其对文化线路价值和意义的影响。还要控制恶化进程的影响，并制定战略，避免因开发和缺乏维护带来的负面影响。需要建立一个包括协调法律措施、适当方法的系统，以确保文化线路能整体保存、呈现其整体价值和意义。在采取任何可能影响或改变文化线路意义的干预措施前，理解遗产价值至关重要。

4. Sustainable Use-Relationship to Tourist Activities

4. 可持续利用——与旅游活动的关系。

With regard to its use, a Cultural Route can be

就用途而言，文化线路可以被用于促进社

used to promote an activity of social and economic interest of extraordinary importance for stable development.

会和经济效益的活动，这对于稳定发展具有非凡的意义。

Special care should be taken to avoid confusion between the concepts of tourist routes—even including those of cultural interest—and Cultural Routes. However, it should also be recognized that a Cultural Route is a reality that can have great importance for territorial cohesion and sustainable development. From this point of view, efforts should be made to promote knowledge about Cultural Routes, along with their appropriate and sustainable use for tourism purposes, always with the adoption of appropriate measures aimed at eliminating risks. For this purpose, protection and promotion of a Cultural Route should harmoniously integrate a supplementary infrastructure for tourist activities, access routes, information, interpretation and presentation with the essential condition that it does not jeopardize the meaning, authenticity and integrity of the historic values of the Cultural Route as key elements to be conveyed to visitors.

要特别注意避免混淆旅游线路（包括有文化意义的旅游线路）和文化线路。但也应承认文化线路事实上对增强地方凝聚力和可持续发展有重要意义。因此，在加强认识文化线路的同时，将其适当和可持续地用于旅游，并采取措施规避风险。为此，保护和发展文化线路，既要配套建设旅游活动、参观路线、信息咨询、阐述和展示等基础设施，又不能损害其内涵，文化线路历史价值的真实性和完整性是要传达给参观者的最基本信息。

Tourist visits should be managed on a rational basis in accordance with prior environmental impact studies and with plans for public use and community participation, as well as control and monitoring measures intended to prevent the negative impacts of tourism.

应根据环境影响评估结果，根据公众用途和社区参与规划，采取旨在遏止旅游负面影响的控制和监督措施，合理管理旅游参观活动。

The development of a Cultural Route for tourism purposes should guarantee in any case that priority is given to the participation of the local community and to local and regional tourist companies. Every effort should be made to prevent the creation of monopolies by large international companies or by powerful companies based in the more developed countries through which the historic path of the Cultural Route passes.

以发展旅游为目的的文化线路开发，在任何情况下，当地社区及该区域的旅游公司必须优先参与。应尽力防止国际大公司和沿线较发达国家大公司的垄断。

Given the fact that a Cultural Route is an instrument for cooperation and understanding which provides a holistic reading of the encounter of cultures and civilization that form that Route, we should also keep in mind that independently of the relative importance of each one of its parts, the promotion of positive developments in each one, leads to increased interest on the Route and benefits for the other parts.

文化线路是合作与理解的工具，能全面解读组成线路的文化和文明之间的互动与交流，我们也应重视文化线路各部分的相对重要性，因为促进每一部分的积极发展都能提升公众对整个文化线路的兴趣，和其他部分的利益。

5. Management

'Understanding of Cultural Routes Significance' becomes the basic / fundamental principle associated to management of cultural routes. This implies ensuring that all activities related to their research, assessment and social dissemination of knowledge about them are carried out in a coordinated and harmonious manner. This also requires a cross coordination that guarantees the combination of policies relating to protection, preservation, conservation, territorial organization, sustainable development, use and tourism. Therefore, joint projects need to be prepared that ensure sustainable development on a national (at the provincial, regional, local level, etc.) and international scale, as well as the establishment of management tools designed to protect the Route against natural disasters and all kinds of risks which could impact on the integrity and authenticity of the Cultural Route and therefore on its significance.

5. 管理

“理解文化线路的意义”是文化线路管理的基本原则。必须以协调、和谐的方式，开展对所有文化线路的研究、评估及社会传播活动。同时也要求全面协调，确保整合文化线路的保护、保存、地区组织以可持续发展、利用和旅游等相关活动。因此，必须形成联合项目，确保国家范围（在省级、地区、当地）和国际范围内的可持续发展，同时要研发改进管理工具，保护线路免受自然灾害的影响，并规避其他各种可能影响文化线路完整性和真实性的风险。

6. Public participation

The protection, conservation, preservation, promotion and management of a Cultural Route calls for the stimulation of public awareness, and the participation of the inhabitants of the areas which share the Route.

6. 公众参与

对于文化线路的保存、保护、宣传和管理，需要激发公众意识以及沿线社区居民的参与。

International cooperation

国际合作

There are notable examples of Cultural Routes

许多文化线路途经多个国家。因此，国际

whose historic paths involve various countries. For this reason, international cooperation is essential for research, assessment, and preservation of the assets that make up international Cultural Routes.

合作对于研究、评估和保护国际文化线路的遗产非常重要。

When Cultural Routes exist which involve countries with different degrees of development, it is recommended that the more developed countries provide the means for economic, technical, and logistic cooperation as well as assistance in the exchange of information, experience, and researchers.

当文化线路存在于经济发达程度不同的国家时，建议较发达的国家提供经济、技术手段和物流合作，并协助信息、经验和专家的交流。

It is highly desirable that UNESCO and other international organizations should establish mechanisms of cooperation (financial, technical, and logistic) to help foster and implement projects related to Cultural Routes that are of interest to more than one country

强烈建议联合国教科文组织和其他国际组织建立（财政、技术和物流方面的）合作机制，来帮助开发和实施涉及多国利益的文化线路项目。

Cultural Routes should be seen as symbols of union between peoples. The historic ties developed along Cultural Routes can serve to promote projects based on renewed cooperation between peoples who shared certain values and knowledge in the past.

文化线路应当被看成民族团结的象征。文化线路沿线不同的民族曾经共享特定价值和知识，这条历史的纽带，也能够促进今天民族和社区间开展新的合作项目。

（翻译：丁援博士，同济大学国家历史文化名城研究中心）

（责任编辑：衡相锦）

国际古迹遗址理事会《文化遗产阐释与展示宪章》
THE ICOMOS CHARTER FOR THE INTERPRETATION AND PRESENTATION OF CULTURAL HERITAGE SITES

THE ICOMOS CHARTER FOR THE INTERPRETATION AND PRESENTATION OF CULTURAL HERITAGE SITES

Prepared under the Auspices of the ICOMOS International Scientific Committee on Interpretation and Presentation of Cultural Heritage Sites Ratified by the 16th General Assembly of ICOMOS, Québec (Canada), on 4 October 2008

国际古迹遗址理事会《文化遗产阐释与展示》宪章

国际古迹遗址理事会阐释与展示科学委员会协助编撰

2008 年 10 月 4 日国际古迹遗址理事会第 16 届大会（加拿大魁北克）通过。

PREAMBLE

序言

Since its establishment in 1965 as a worldwide organization of heritage professionals dedicated to the study, documentation, and protection of cultural heritage sites, ICOMOS has striven to promote the conservation ethic in all its activities and to help enhance public appreciation of humanity's material heritage in all its forms and diversity.

作为国际遗产专业组织，国际古迹遗址理事会自 1965 年成立以来，一直致力于研究、记录和保护文化遗产地，努力在工作中发扬保护遗产的职业道德，帮助公众加深理解各类型、丰富多样的人类物质文化遗产。

As noted in the Charter of Venice (1964) 'It is essential that the principles guiding the preservation and restoration of ancient buildings should be agreed and be laid down on an international basis, with each country being responsible for applying the plan within the framework of its own culture and traditions.' Subsequent ICOMOS charters have taken up that mission, establishing professional guidelines for specific conservation challenges and encouraging effective communication about the importance of

正如《威尼斯宪章》（1964）中提到的，“有必要在国际范围内协商和制定指导古建筑保护和修复的原则，并由各个国家负责在本国文化和传统的框架内实施。”国际古迹遗址理事会的本宪章承担起这一使命，针对具体的保护问题，制定专业指导准则，并鼓励世界各地对遗产保护的重要性进行有效沟通。

heritage conservation in every region of the world.

These earlier ICOMOS charters stress the importance of public communication as an essential part of the larger conservation process (variously describing it as 'dissemination,' 'popularization,' 'presentation,' and 'interpretation'). They implicitly acknowledge that every act of heritage conservation - within all the world's cultural traditions is by its nature a communicative act.

早期国际古迹遗址理事会宪章强调公众交流（也称“传播”、“推广”、“展示”和“阐释”）的重要性，因为公众交流是大规模保护过程的重要组成部分。这也间接地说明，世界所有文化传统中的各种遗产保护行为，本质上都是交流行为。

From the vast range of surviving material remains and intangible values of past communities and civilisations, the choice of what to preserve, how to preserve it, and how it is to be presented to the public are all elements of site interpretation. They represent every generation's vision of what is significant, what is important, and why material remains from the past should be passed on to generations yet to come.

在保存下来的众多物质遗存和昔日社会与文明的无形价值中，选择保护什么、如何保护以及如何向公众展示，这些都是遗产阐释的要素。这些要素体现了各个时代的人类对于：什么是重要的、为什么重要以及为什么要将过去的物质遗存传承于后世等方面的不同见解。

The need for a clear rationale, standardized terminology, and accepted professional principles for Interpretation and Presentation is evident. In recent years, the dramatic expansion of interpretive activities at many cultural heritage sites and the introduction of elaborate interpretive technologies and new economic strategies for the marketing and management of cultural heritage sites have created new complexities and aroused basic questions that are central to the goals of both conservation and the public appreciation of cultural heritage sites throughout the world:

很明显，需要制定明确的理论基础、标准化的术语和公认的解释和陈述的专业原则。近年来，许多文化遗产地大力发展阐释工作，为文化遗产地的营销和管理引进了详尽的阐释技术和新的经济战略，产生了新的复杂性，带来基本问题，这些问题是全世界文化遗产保护和公众欣赏的核心：

- What are the accepted and acceptable goals for the Interpretation and Presentation of cultural heritage sites?

——文化遗产地阐释与展示中公认的、可接受的目标是什么？

- What principles should help determine which technical means and methods are appropriate in particular cultural and heritage contexts?

——哪些原则有助于确定采用什么样的技术手段和方法，以适应特定的文化和遗产背景？

- What general ethical and professional considerations should help shape Interpretation and Presentation in light of its wide variety of specific forms and techniques?

——为形成更好的“阐释与展示”，根据多样特定的形式和技术，需要注意哪些伦理和专业？

The purpose of this Charter is therefore to define the basic principles of Interpretation and Presentation as essential components of heritage conservation efforts and as a means of enhancing public appreciation and understanding of cultural heritage sites.

因此，本宪章的目标是定义“阐释与展示”的基本原则，作为是遗产保护工作的必要组成部分，也是加深公众欣赏和理解文化遗产地的一个方法。

DEFINITIONS

定义

For the purposes of the present Charter, Interpretation refers to the full range of potential activities intended to heighten public awareness and enhance understanding of cultural heritage site. These can include print and electronic publications, public lectures, on-site and directly related off-site installations, educational programmes, community activities, and ongoing research, training, and evaluation of the interpretation process itself.

就本宪章而言，阐释：指一切可能的、旨在提高公众意识、增进公众理解文化遗产地的活动。包括印刷和电子出版物、公共讲座、现场及场外相关设施、教育项目、社区活动，以及对阐释过程本身的持续研究、培训和评估。

Presentation more specifically denotes the carefully planned communication of interpretive content through the arrangement of interpretive information, physical access, and interpretive infrastructure at a cultural heritage site. It can be conveyed through a variety of technical means, including, yet not requiring, such elements as informational panels, museum-type displays, formalized walking tours, lectures and guided tours, and multimedia applications and websites.

展示：专指在通过编辑文化遗产地阐释信息、实地参观，以及展示设施等，对阐释性内容进行精心策划地交流。可通过各种技术手段传达信息，包括（但不限于）信息板、博物馆展览、精心设计的游览路线、讲座和参观讲解、多媒体应用和网站等。

Interpretive infrastructure refers to physical installations, facilities, and areas at, or connected with a cultural heritage site that may be specifically utilised for the purposes of interpretation and presentation including those supporting interpretation via new and existing technologies.

阐释性基础设施：指在文化遗产地或与之相连的区域内，专门用于阐释与展示的，包括得到创新技术和现有技术支持的装置、设施和空间。

Site interpreters refers to staff or volunteers at a cultural heritage site who are permanently or temporarily engaged in the public communication of information relating to the values and significance of the site.

遗产地讲解员：指在文化遗产地长期或临时负责向大众讲解遗产地的价值和重要性的职员或志愿者。

Cultural Heritage Site refers to a place, locality, natural landscape, settlement area, architectural complex, archaeological site, or standing structure that is recognized and often legally protected as a place of historical and cultural significance.

文化遗产地：指公认的具有重要历史和文化意义，受到法律保护的遗迹、区域、自然景观、居民区、建筑群、考古遗址或建筑构造物等。

OBJECTIVES

目标

In recognizing that interpretation and presentation are part of the overall process of cultural heritage conservation and management, this Charter seeks to establish seven cardinal principles, upon which Interpretation and Presentation—in whatever form or medium is deemed appropriate in specific circumstances—should be based.

Principle 1: Access and Understanding
Principle 2: Information Sources
Principle 3: Attention to Setting and Context
Principle 4: Preservation of Authenticity
Principle 5: Planning for Sustainability
Principle 6: Concern for Inclusiveness
Principle 7: Importance of Research, Training, and Evaluation

由于认识到阐释与展示是整个文化遗产保护和管理过程的必要组成部分，本宪章尝试确立七项主要原则，作为根据特定情况所采取的适合各种形式或媒介的阐释与展示的基础。

原则 1：对外开放和理解
原则 2：信息源
原则 3：重视背景环境和传承
原则 4：保持真实性
原则 5：可持续性规划
原则 6：关注包容性
原则 7：研究、培训和评估的重要性

Following from these seven principles, the objectives of this Charter are to:

1. Facilitate understanding and appreciation of cultural heritage sites and foster public awareness and engagement in the need for their protection and conservation.

2. Communicate the meaning of cultural heritage sites to a range of audiences through careful, documented recognition of significance, through accepted scientific and scholarly methods

根据这七项原则，本宪章的目标是：

1. 促进公众对文化遗产地的理解和欣赏，培养公众保护文化遗产的意识并动员其积极参与。

2. 通过对文件档案的悉心研究，识别文化遗产地意义，并通过公认的科学和学术方法以及现存文化传统，向各方受众宣传文化遗产地的意义和内涵。

as well as from living cultural traditions.

3. Safeguard the tangible and intangible values of cultural heritage sites in their natural and cultural settings and social contexts.

4. Respect the authenticity of cultural heritage sites, by communicating the significance of their historic fabric and cultural values and protecting them from the adverse impact of intrusive interpretive infrastructure, visitor pressure, inaccurate or inappropriate interpretation.

5. Contribute to the sustainable conservation of cultural heritage sites, through promoting public understanding of, and participation in, ongoing conservation efforts, ensuring long-term maintenance of the interpretive infrastructure and regular review of its interpretive contents.

6. Encourage inclusiveness in the interpretation of cultural heritage sites, by facilitating the involvement of stakeholders and associated communities in the development and implementation of interpretive programmes.

7. Develop technical and professional guidelines for heritage interpretation and presentation, including technologies, research, and training. Such guidelines must be appropriate and sustainable in their social contexts.

3. 在自然和文化背景以及社会环境下，保护文化遗产地的有形和无形价值。

4. 尊重文化遗产地的真实性，传达文化遗产地的历史结构和文化价值的重要性，保护其免受侵入性展示设施、旅游压力、不准确或不恰当的阐释等危害带来的影响。

5. 通过促进公众对现行保护工作的理解、参与，通过长期维护展示设施和定期检查阐释内容，确保文化遗产地的可持续保护。

6. 鼓励利益相关者和相关团体参与阐释项目的设计和实施过程，增进文化遗产地阐释的包容性。

7. 制定、发展遗产阐释与展示的技术及专业指导方针，包括技术、研究和培训。这些指导方针必须适合社会背景并可持续利用。

PRINCIPLES

Principle 1: Access and Understanding

Interpretation and presentation programmes should facilitate physical and intellectual access by the public to cultural heritage sites.

1. Effective interpretation and presentation should enhance personal experience, increase public respect and understanding, and communicate the importance of the conservation of cultural heritage sites.

2. Interpretation and presentation should encourage individuals and communities to reflect

原则

原则 1：对外开放和理解

阐释与展示计划应方便公众接触文化遗产本体和相关知识。

1.1 有效的阐释与展示应能提升个人体验，提高公众对文化遗产地的尊重和理解，宣传保护文化遗产地的重要性。

1.2 阐释与展示应鼓励个人和团体，思考自身对遗产地的认识，帮助他们建立有意义的联

on their own perceptions of a site and assist them in establishing a meaningful connection to it. The aim should be to stimulate further interest, learning, experience, and exploration.

系，从而激发更深层次的兴趣、学习、体验和探索。

3. Interpretation and presentation programmes should identify and assess their audiences demographically and culturally. Every effort should be made to communicate the site's values and significance to its varied audiences.

1.3 阐释与展示计划应从人口统计和文化角度识别、分析其受众，力求向各方受众宣讲遗产地的价值和意义。

4. The diversity of language among visitors and associated communities connected with a heritage site should be taken into account in the interpretive infrastructure.

1.4 展示类基础设施的建设，应当考虑到参观者以及遗产地相关社区语言的多样性。

5. Interpretation and presentation activities should also be physically accessible to the public, in all its variety.

1.5 阐释与展示活动应形式多样，并能够实实在在地贴近公众。

6. In cases where physical access to a cultural heritage site is restricted due to conservation concerns, cultural sensitivities, adaptive re-use, or safety issues, interpretation and presentation should be provided off-site.

1.6 若由于保护需要、文化敏感性、改造再利用或安全考虑而限制参观，则应提供场外的阐释与展示。

Principle 2: Information Sources

Interpretation and presentation should be based on evidence gathered through accepted scientific and scholarly methods as well as from living cultural traditions.

原则 2：信息源

公认的科学和学术方法以及现存的文化传统，应作为搜集阐释与展示证据的依据。

1. Interpretation should show the range of oral and written information, material remains, traditions, and meanings attributed to a site. The sources of this information should be documented, archived, and made accessible to the public.

2.1 阐释应包括一系列源于遗产的口头和书面信息、物质遗存、传统。应对信息来源进行记录、归档，并提供给公众。

2. Interpretation should be based on a well researched, multidisciplinary study of the site and its surroundings. It should also acknowledge that meaningful interpretation necessarily includes reflection on alternative historical hypotheses, local traditions, and stories.

2.2 阐释应以对遗产地及其周边环境进行的详尽的、多学科研究为基础。也应当认识到，作为客观且有意义的阐释，有必要包括对其他历史假设、当地传统和民间传说的反思。

3. At cultural heritage sites where traditional storytelling or memories of historical participants

2.3 如果文化遗产地有传统故事或历史参与者的回忆，可为展现遗产地价值提供重要的信

provide an important source of information about the significance of the site, interpretive programmes should incorporate these oral testimonies—either indirectly, through the facilities of the interpretive infrastructure, or directly, through the active participation of members of associated communities as on-site interpreters.

息来源，则阐释计划应包含这些口头证据。传说、故事可通过展示设施间接进行展示，也可通过相关社区成员作为讲解员在现场直接讲解。

4. Visual reconstructions, whether by artists, architects, or computer modelers, should be based upon detailed and systematic analysis of environmental, archaeological, architectural, and historical data, including analysis of written, oral and iconographic sources, and photography. The information sources on which such visual renderings are based should be clearly documented and alternative reconstructions based on the same evidence, when available, should be provided for comparison.

2.4 无论由艺术家、建筑师还是由计算机建模师对遗产地进行视觉再现，应以环境、考古、建筑以及历史数据，包括书面、口头、图像材料和照片的数据分析为基础。应准确记录这些视觉表现所依据的信息来源，并应提供基于相同证据的替代重建，（如果有）以进行比较。

5. Interpretation and presentation programmes and activities should also be documented and archived for future reference and reflection.

2.5 应全面记录并保存阐释与展示方案及活动的档案以备将来的参考和反思。

Principle 3: Context and Setting

The Interpretation and Presentation of cultural heritage sites should relate to their wider social, cultural, historical, and natural contexts and settings.

原则 3：背景环境和传承

文化遗产地的阐释与展示应结合广泛的社会、文化、历史及自然的背景环境。

1. Interpretation should explore the significance of a site in its multi-faceted historical, political, spiritual, and artistic contexts. It should consider all aspects of the site's cultural, social, and environmental significance and values.

3.1 阐释应当探究遗产地在其历史、政治、精神和艺术等多层面发展的意义。应考虑遗产地文化、社会和环境意义和价值等所有方面。

2. The public interpretation of a cultural heritage site should clearly distinguish and date the successive phases and influences in its evolution. The contributions of all periods to the significance of a site should be respected.

3.2 向公众进行文化遗产地阐释，应当清晰地指出遗产地发展演变过程中经历各个时期及后续阶段的影响。应尊重各个历史时期对遗产地重要性做出的贡献。

3. Interpretation should also take into account all groups that have contributed to the historical and cultural significance of the site.

3.3 遗产阐释也要考虑对遗产地历史和文化重要性有贡献的所有群体。

4. The surrounding landscape, natural environment, and geographical setting are integral parts

3.4 遗产地周边景观、自然环境和地理背景都是遗产地历史文化重要性的必要组成部分，

of a site's historical and cultural significance, and, as such, should be considered in its interpretation.

5. Intangible elements of a site's heritage such as cultural and spiritual traditions, stories, music, dance, theater, literature, visual arts, local customs and culinary heritage should be considered in its interpretation.

6. The cross-cultural significance of heritage sites, as well as the range of perspectives about them based on scholarly research, ancient records, and living traditions, should be considered in the formulation of interpretive programmes.

因此，也应在阐释时加以考虑。

3.5 遗产的无形元素如：文化和精神传统、传说、音乐、舞蹈、戏剧、文学、视觉艺术、当地风俗和饮食文化等，在遗产地阐释过程中都应加以考虑。

3.6 在制定阐释方案时，应考虑遗产地的跨文化意义、学术研究、历史记录和现存传统为基础的各种观点。

Principle 4: Authenticity

The Interpretation and presentation of cultural heritage sites must respect the basic tenets of authenticity in the spirit of the Nara Document (1994).

1. Authenticity is a concern relevant to human communities as well as material remains. The design of a heritage interpretation programme should respect the traditional social functions of the site and the cultural practices and dignity of local residents and associated communities.

2. Interpretation and presentation should contribute to the conservation of the authenticity of a cultural heritage site by communicating its significance without adversely impacting its cultural values or irreversibly altering its fabric.

3. All visible interpretive infrastructures (such as kiosks, walking paths, and information panels) must be sensitive to the character, setting and the cultural and natural significance of the site, while remaining easily identifiable.

4. On-site concerts, dramatic performances, and other interpretive programmes must be carefully planned to protect the significance and physical surroundings of the site and minimise disturbance to the local residents.

原则 4：真实性

文化遗产地的阐释与展示必须遵守《奈良文件》（1994）中真实性的基本原则。

4.1 文化遗产的真实性是一个与人类社会和物质遗迹相关的问题。在设计遗产地阐释项目时，应当尊重遗产地的传统社会功能、当地居民及相关社区的文化习俗及尊严。

4.2 阐释与展示应宣传文化遗产地重要性、促进保护其真实性，避免对其文化价值造成不利影响或给遗产结构本身带来不可逆的变化。

4.3 所有可视的阐释设施（如问讯亭、步行路线和信息板等）必须醒目，并与遗产地的整体特点、背景环境、遗产地文化及自然价值相协调。

4.4 现场音乐会、戏剧表演和其他阐释活动必须经过精心策划，保护遗产地重要性和周边环境，对当地居民的干扰应最小化。

Principle 5: Sustainability

The interpretation plan for a cultural heritage

原则 5：可持续性

文化遗产地的阐释计划必须尊重遗产地的

site must be sensitive to its natural and cultural environment, with social, financial, and environmental sustainability among its central goals.

自然及文化环境，其核心目标应包括社会、经济及环境的可持续性。

1. The development and implementation of interpretation and presentation programmes should be an integral part of the overall planning, budgeting, and management process of cultural heritage sites.

5.1 阐释与展示项目的设计和实施，是文化遗产地总体规划、预算和管理过程的必要组成部分。

2. The potential effect of interpretive infrastructure and visitor numbers on the cultural value, physical characteristics, integrity, and natural environment of the site must be fully considered in heritage impact assessment studies.

5.2 在遗产影响评估研究中，必须全面考虑到阐释性设施和游客数量对遗产地文化价值、外部特征、完整性和自然环境的潜在影响。

3. Interpretation and presentation should serve a wide range of conservation, educational and cultural objectives. The success of an interpretive programme should not be evaluated solely on the basis of visitor attendance figures or revenue.

5.3 阐释与展示应服务于广泛的保护、教育及文化目标。阐释计划成功与否，不应单纯的以游客人数和旅游收入来衡量。

4. Interpretation and presentation should be an integral part of the conservation process, enhancing the public's awareness of specific conservation problems encountered at the site and explaining the efforts being taken to protect the site's physical integrity and authenticity.

5.4 阐释与展示应是遗产保护过程不可缺少的组成部分，它能够加深公众对遗产地面临的具体问题的认识，并更好地向公众解释为保护遗产地完整性和真实性所采取的措施。

5. Any technical or technological elements selected to become a permanent part of a site's interpretive infrastructure should be designed and constructed in a manner that will ensure effective and regular maintenance.

5.5 被确定为遗产地阐释基础设施中永久性组成部分的任何科技和技术要素，要以保证得到有效、定期维护的方式进行设计和构建。

6. Interpretive programmes should aim to provide equitable and sustainable economic, social, and cultural benefits to all stakeholders through education, training and employment opportunities in site interpretation programmes.

5.6 阐释计划的目标是：通过提供预期的教育、培训和就业机会，为遗产地所有的利益相关者带来公平的、可持续的经济、社会和文化利益。

Principle 6: Inclusiveness

The Interpretation and Presentation of cultural heritage sites must be the result of meaningful collaboration between heritage professionals, host and associated communities, and other stakeholders.

原则 6：包容性

文化遗产地的阐释与展示必须是遗产专业人士、遗产地负责机构和相关社区以及其他利益相关者之间共同进行有意义合作的结果。

1. The multidisciplinary expertise of scholars, community members, conservation experts, governmental authorities, site managers and interpreters, tourism operators, and other professionals should be integrated in the formulation of interpretation and presentation programmes.

2. The traditional rights, responsibilities, and interests of property owners and host and associated communities should be noted and respected in the planning of site interpretation and presentation programmes.

3. Plans for expansion or revision of interpretation and presentation programmes should be open for public comment and involvement. It is the right and responsibility of all to make their opinions and perspectives known.

4. Because the question of intellectual property and traditional cultural rights is especially relevant to the interpretation process and its expression in various communication media (such as on-site multimedia presentations, digital media, and printed materials), legal ownership and right to use images, texts, and other interpretive materials should be discussed, clarified, and agreed in the planning process.

6.1 在阐释与展示计划的制定过程中，应当整合学者、社区成员、遗产保护专家、政府机构、遗产地管理者和讲解员、旅游经营者和其他专业人士的多学科专业知识。

6.2 在策划遗产地阐释与展示计划时，应当注意并尊重所有者、使用者和相关社区的传统权利、责任和利益。

6.3 阐释与展示计划的扩展和修订计划应吸纳公众意见，鼓励公众参与。发表意见和观点是每个人的权利和责任。

6.4 由于知识产权和传统文化权益与遗产阐释过程及其传播媒介（如现场多媒体展示、数字媒体和印刷材料）关系密切，因此，图像、文字以及其他阐释性材料的法定所有权和使用权，均应在设计规划过程中探讨、明确并达成共识。

Principle 7: Research, Training, and Evaluation

Continuing research, training, and evaluation are essential components of the interpretation of a cultural heritage site.

1. The interpretation of a cultural heritage site should not be considered to be completed with the completion of a specific interpretive infrastructure. Continuing research and consultation are important to furthering the understanding and appreciation of a site's significance. Regular review should be an integral element in every heritage interpretation programme.

2. The interpretive programme and infrastructure should be designed and constructed in a way that facilitates ongoing content revision and/or

原则 7：研究、培训和评估

不断进行的研究、培训和评估是文化遗产地阐释工作必不可少的组成部分。

7.1 文化遗产地阐释工作不应随着具体展示设施的完工而结束。持续的研究和咨询对增进人们正确理解、评价遗产地价值起着重要作用。定期审查应是每个遗产地阐释项目中必不可少的要素。

7.2 阐释性项目和基础设施的设计和建造应便于不断的修订和扩展内容。

expansion.

3. Interpretation and presentation programmes and their physical impact on a site should be continuously monitored and evaluated, and periodic changes made on the basis of both scientific and scholarly analysis and public feedback. Visitors and members of associated communities as well as heritage professionals should be involved in this evaluation process.

4. Every interpretation programme should be considered as an educational resource for people of all ages. Its design should take into account its possible uses in school curricula, informal and lifelong learning programmes, communications and information media, special activities, events, and seasonal volunteer involvement.

5. The training of qualified professionals in the specialised fields of heritage interpretation and presentation, such as content creation, management, technology, guiding, and education, is a crucial objective. In addition, basic academic conservation programmes should include a component on interpretation and presentation in their courses of study.

6. On-site training programmes and courses should be developed with the objective of updating and informing heritage and interpretation staff of all levels and associated and host communities of recent developments and innovations in the field.

7. International cooperation and sharing of experience are essential to developing and maintaining standards in interpretation methods and technologies. To that end, international conferences, workshops and exchanges of professional staff as well as national and regional meetings should be encouraged. These will provide an opportunity for the regular sharing of information about the diversity of interpretive approaches and experiences in various regions and cultures.

7.3 应当持续监测和评估阐释与展示项目对遗产地的影响，并根据科学和学术分析以及公众的反馈信息，作定期调整。参观者、所在社区成员以及遗产专业人员都应参与到此评估过程中。

7.4 每个阐释项目都应成为各年龄段的公众教育资源。项目设计时应考虑到其可能应用在学校课程、非正式和终生学习项目、通信和信息媒体、特殊活动、大型活动中以及季节性志愿者的参与中。

7.5 在遗产地阐释与展示各个专门领域有一个关键目标，既培训合格的内容创作、管理、技术、导游和教育等领域的专业人员。此外，在遗产保护专业教学基础课中应设置阐释与展示的相关课程。

7.6 现场培训项目和课程的目标，是向相关社区、各级遗产保护和阐释工作者，宣传该领域的新发展和新成果。

7.7 国际合作及经验分享对制定和保持阐释方法与技术的标准非常必要。为此，应鼓励召开国际会议、全国和地方会议，组织专业人员研讨和交流。这些活动将为定期交流各地区、各种文化的多元化阐释、分享方法和经验提供机会。

（ICOMOS 网站）

国际古迹遗址理事会
《场所精神的保存（魁北克宣言）》
QUÉBEC DECLARATION ON THE PRESERVATION OF THE SPIRIT OF PLACE

QUÉBEC DECLARATION ON THE PRESERVATION OF THE SPIRIT OF PLACE

Adoed at Québec, Canada, October 4th 2008

场所精神的保存（魁北克宣言）

2008 年 10 月 4 日，于加拿大魁北克市通过

Preamble

Meeting in the historic city of Québec (Canada), from 29 September to 4 October 2008, at the invitation of ICOMOS Canada, on the occasion of the 16th General Assembly of ICOMOS and the celebrations marking the 400th anniversary of the founding of Québec, the participants adopt the following Declaration of principles and recommendations to preserve the spirit of place through the safeguarding of tangible and intangible heritage, which is regarded as an innovative and efficient manner of ensuring sustainable and social development throughout the world.

This Declaration is part of a series of measures and actions undertaken by ICOMOS over the course of the past five years to safeguard and promote the spirit of places, namely their living, social and spiritual nature. In 2003, ICOMOS focused the scientific symposium of its 14th General Assembly on the theme of the preservation of social intangible values of monuments and sites. In the ensuing Kimberly Declaration, ICOMOS committed itself to taking into account the intangible values (memory, beliefs, traditional knowledge, attachment to place) and the local communities that are the custodians

序文

在魁北克建城 400 年之际，应加拿大古迹遗址理事会之邀，国际古迹遗址理事会第 16 届年会于 2008 年 9 月 29 日至 10 月 4 日在历史城市魁北克举行。与会者采纳下列原则、宣言、提议，通过保护有形和无形遗产的方法，实现保护场所精神。这是全球范围内确保社会可持续发展的创新而富有实效的方法。

本宣言是过去五年国际古迹遗址理事会采取一系列措施与行动之一，以捍卫并发扬场所精神，即地方生活、社会与精神本质。2003 年，国际古迹遗址理事会召开第 14 届科学研讨会以社会无形价值的保存为主题。在随后通过的《金伯利宣言》中，国际古迹遗址理事会承诺，依照 1972 年世界遗产公约，在古迹和遗址管理中将会考虑遗产承载的无形价值（记忆、信仰、传统知识、地方情感），以及管理、保存遗址的当地社区。2005 年的《国际古迹遗址理事会西安宣言》关注保护背景环境，在保护和促进世界遗产、古迹遗址的同时更要保护遗产的实体、视觉和

of these values in the management and preservation of monuments and sites under the World Heritage Convention of 1972. The ICOMOS Xi'an Declaration of 2005 draws attention to the conservation of context, defined as the physical, visual and natural aspects as well as social and spiritual practices, customs, traditional knowledge and other intangible forms and expressions, in the protection and promotion of world heritage monuments and sites. It also calls upon a multidisciplinary approach and diversified sources of information in order to better understand, manage and conserve context. The Declaration of FozDo Iguassu, drawn up in 2008 by ICOMOS Americas, specifies that the tangible and intangible components of heritage are essential in the preservation of the identity of communities that have created and transmitted spaces of cultural and historical significance. The new ICOMOS charters on Cultural Routes and on Interpretation and Presentation, formulated after extensive consultations and presented for ratification at the present 16th ICOMOS General Assembly, also recognize the importance of intangible dimensions of heritage and the spiritual value of place. Because of the indivisible nature of tangible and intangible heritage and the meanings, values and context intangible heritage gives to objects and places, ICOMOS is currently considering the adoption of a new charter dedicated specifically to the intangible heritage of monuments and sites. In this regard, we encourage discussion and debates in order to develop a new conceptual vocabulary that takes into account the ontological changes of the spirit of place.

自然要素及社会与精神的实践、风俗、传统知识和其他无形形式和表达等背景环境。宣言同时呼吁利用多学科的方法和多元化的信息资源，让遗产背景环境得到更好的理解、管理和保护。2008 年，美洲地区的古迹遗址理事会草拟了《伊瓜苏宣言》，阐明遗产的有形与无形组成，是创立并传承遗产文化和历史意义空间的社区身份之基础。新的《国际古迹遗址理事会文化线路宪章》以及《关于阐释与展示宪章》，经过广泛磋商后送本次第 16 届年会讨论，也认同了遗产的无形维度与场所精神价值的重要性。由于有形与无形遗产不可分割的属性，和无形遗产赋予实体与场所特别的意义、价值与背景，国际古迹遗址理事会正考虑拟定保护古迹遗址无形遗产的新宪章。就这方面而言，我们鼓励通过讨论与辩论，形成一套足以解释场所精神本体论变化的新概念词汇表。

The 16th General Assembly, and more specifically the Youth Forum, the Aboriginal Forum and the Scientific Symposium, have provided an opportunity to further explore the relationship between tangible and intangible heritage, and the internal social and cultural mechanisms of the spirit

第 16 届大会，具体而言就是青年论坛、原住民论坛与科学研讨会，提供了进一步探索有形与无形遗产，及场所精神内含社会与文化机制间关系的机会。场所精神被界定为有形（建筑物、遗址、景观、路径、物件）和无形要素（记忆 、故事、书面文件、仪式、庆典、传统知

of place. Spirit of place is defined as the tangible (buildings, sites, landscapes, routes, objects) and the intangible elements (memories, narratives, written documents, rituals, festivals, traditional knowledge, values, textures, colors, odors, etc.), that is to say the physical and the spiritual elements that give meaning, value, emotion and mystery to place. Rather than separate spirit from place, the intangible from the tangible, and consider them as opposed to each other, we have investigated the many ways in which the two interact and mutually construct one another. The spirit of place is constructed by various social actors, its architects and managers as well as its users, who all contribute actively and concurrently to giving it meaning. Considered as a relational concept, spirit of place takes on a plural and dynamic character, capable of possessing multiple meanings and singularities, of changing through time, and of belonging to different groups. This more dynamic approach is also better adapted to today's globalized world, which is characterized by transnational population movements, relocated populations, increased intercultural contacts, pluralistic societies, and multiple attachments to place.

识、价值、结构、颜色、气味等）能赋予场所意义、价值、情感与神秘感的物质及精神成分。我们不是将场所与精神分离，从有形中抽离无形，视他们为相互对立的事物，而是考察两者间互动的、相辅相成的多种方式。场所精神是由各种社会角色如建筑师、管理者和使用者共同奉献，共同构建。就相关概念而言，场所精神具有多元性与动态特质，拥有多重意义及与众不同的特色，在与时俱进的同时隶属不同群体。这种更具活力的方法，也更适应今日的全球化世界。这种全球化世界的主要特色，就是跨国人口移动、搬迁、跨文化接触增加、社会多元化，以及对场所的多重依恋。

The spirit of place offers a more comprehensive understanding of the living and, at the same time, permanent character of monuments, sites and cultural landscapes. It provides a richer, more dynamic, and inclusive vision of cultural heritage. Spirit of place exists, in one form or another, in practically all the cultures of the world, and is constructed by human beings in response to their social needs. The communities that inhabit place, especially when they are traditional societies, should be intimately associated in the safeguarding of its memory, vitality, continuity and spirituality.

场所精神让人对生活，同时也对纪念物、遗址及文化景观亘古不变的特色，有较全面的了解。它为文化遗产提供了更丰富、更动态的全方位视野。场所精神以各种形式存在于全球文化之中，为满足人类社会需求而生。在此社区的群体，特别是传统社区，会密切关注并维护群体记忆、生命力、精神性、持续性。

The participants of the 16th General Assembly of ICOMOS therefore address the following Declaration

因此，国际古迹遗址理事会第 16 届大会参会者，向政府间组织、非政府组织、国家与地

of principles and recommendations to intergovernmental and non-governmental organizations, national and local authorities and all institutions and specialists in a position to contribute through legislation, policies, planning processes and management to better protecting and promoting the spirit of place.

方当局，以及所有机构与专家，提出包含下列原则与建议的宣言，从而促成通过立法、制订政策、规划过程与管理等手段，更好的保护和提升场所精神。

Rethinking the Spirit of Place

场所精神的再思考

1. Recognizing that the spirit of place is made up of tangible (sites, buildings, landscapes, routes, objects) as well as intangible elements (memories, narratives, written documents, festivals, commemorations, rituals, traditional knowledge, values, textures, colors, odors, etc.), which all significantly contribute to making place and to giving it spirit, we declare that intangible cultural heritage gives a richer and more complete meaning to heritage as a whole and it must be taken into account in all legislation concerning cultural heritage, and in all conservation and restoration projects for monuments, sites, landscapes, routes and collections of objects.

1. 了解场所精神由有形（遗址、建筑物、景观、路径、物件），与无形元素（记忆 、口头叙述、书面文件、节日、仪式、庆典、传统知识、价值、手感、颜色、气味等）构成。这些元素不仅对场所精神的形成有重大贡献，还赋予它灵魂。我们认为无形文化遗产可为遗产提供更丰富、更完整的意义，制订所有与文化遗产的相关立法，以及所有纪念物、遗址、景观、路线与收藏物品的保存与维修计划时，都必须同时考虑无形遗产。

2. Because the spirit of place is complex and multiform, we demand that governments and other stakeholders call upon the expertise of multidisciplinary research teams and traditional practitioners in order to better understand, preserve and transmit the spirit of place.

2. 由于场所精神复杂多变，为了进一步了解、保存与传递场所精神，我们要求政府与其他利益相关者，务必多向跨学科研究团队和传统从业人员请教学习。

3. Since the spirit of place is a continuously reconstructed process, which responds to the needs for change and continuity of communities, we uphold that it can vary in time and from one culture to another according to their practices of memory, and that a place can have several spirits and be shared by different groups.

3. 由于场所精神是不断重建的过程，可满足社区变化和连续性的需求，我们认同场所精神会随着时间的变化而变化，并根据记忆习惯从一种文化到另一种文化。所以同一地方可以拥有数种精神，且由不同群体共享。

Identifying the Threats to the Spirit of Place

识别对场所精神的威胁

4. Since climatic change, mass tourism, armed conflict and urban development lead to the transforma-

4. 鉴于气候变迁、众多观光者、武装冲突与城市开发，导致了社会变迁与瓦解，我们需

tion and disruption of societies, we need to better understand these threats in order to establish preventive measures and sustainable solutions. We recommend that governmental and non-governmental agencies, and local and national heritage organizations develop long term strategic plans to prevent the degradation of the spirit of place and its environment. The inhabitants and local authorities should also be made aware of the safeguarding of the spirit of place so that they are better prepared to deal with the threats of a changing world.

要更全面地了解这些威胁，加以防范，并提出持续性解决方案。我们建议政府与非政府机构、地方与国家遗址组织，必须制定长期策略性计划，避免场所精神及其环境的恶化。应指导居民与地方当局共同捍卫场所精神，让他们做好准备应对世界变迁所带来的威胁。

5. As the sharing of places invested with different spirits by several groups increases the risk of competition and conflict, we recognize that these sites require specific management plans and strategies, adapted to the pluralistic context of modern multicultural societies. Because the threats to the spirit of place are especially high amongst minority groups, be they natives or newcomers, we recommend that these groups benefit first and foremost from specific policies and practices.

5. 若一个地方由不同群体赋予其不同的精神，则面临更多的竞争与冲突的危机，我们认为需要为这些地方制定具体的管理方案与策略，以适应现代多元文化社会的背景。因为少数民族聚集地的场所精神面临更多的威胁，因此我们建议这些族群，无论土著民或外来者，首先制定具体政策和方法保障其团体利益。

Safeguarding the Spirit of Place

守护场所精神

6. Because in most countries of the world today the spirit of place, in particular its intangible components, do not currently benefit from formal educational programs or legal protection, we recommend the setting up of forums and consultations with experts from different backgrounds and resource persons from local communities, and the development of training programs and legal policies in order to better safeguard and promote the spirit of place.

6. 由于当今世上大部分国家的场所精神，尤其是其无形的元素，并未从教育计划或立法保护中受益，我们建议通过开展论坛、咨询不同领域的专家与当地资源提供者，并制定培训计划与法律政策，能够更好地守护并提升场所精神。

7. Considering that modern digital technologies (digital databases, websites) can be used efficiently and effectively at a low cost to develop multimedia inventories that integrate tangible and intangible elements of heritage, we strongly recommend their widespread use in order to better preserve, dissemi-

7. 现代数字化技术（数据资料库、网站）能以低成本、高效率的方式，通过多媒体整合了遗产的有形与无形元素。为了让场所及其精神得到比较完善的保存、宣传和提升，我们强烈建议广泛运用数字科技。这些新技术能确保场所精神文件的多样性和持续更新。

nate and promote heritage places and their spirit. These technologies facilitate the diversity and constant renewal of the documentation on the spirit of place.

Transmitting the Spirit of Place

8. Recognizing that spirit of place is transmitted essentially by people, and that transmission is an important part of its conservation, we declare that it is through interactive communication and the participation of the concerned communities that the spirit of place is most efficiently safeguarded, used and enhanced. Communication is the best tool for keeping the spirit of place alive.

9. Given that local communities are generally in the best position to comprehend the spirit of place, especially in the case of traditional cultural groups, we maintain that they are also best equipped to safeguard it and should be intimately associated in all endeavors to preserve and transmit the spirit of place. Non-formal (narratives, rituals, performances, traditional experience and practices, etc.) and formal (educational programs, digital databases, websites, pedagogical tools, multimedia presentations, etc.) means of transmission should be encouraged because they ensure not only the safeguarding of the spirit of place but, more importantly, the sustainable and social development of the community.

10. Recognizing that inter generational and trans-cultural transmission plays an important role in the sustained dissemination and the preservation of the spirit of place, we recommend the association and involvement of younger generations, as well as different cultural groups associated with the site, in policy-making and the management of the spirit of place.

传递场所精神

8. 了解场所精神主要是由人类传承，传承又是保存的重要组成部分，我们认为唯有互动沟通与相关社区的参与方能最有效的保护、利用与巩固场所精神。沟通是保持场所精神生生不息的最佳工具。

9. 鉴于当地社区，尤其是传统文化群体，对场所精神理解更深，因而最有资格保护场所精神，他们的所有努力应与保存和传承场所精神密切相关。应鼓励各种非正式（口头叙述、仪式、表演、传统经验与习惯等）与正式（教育计划、数据资料库、网站、教具、多媒体简报等）传播方法，因为这些措施不仅是保护场所精神，更重要的是保护社区与社会的可持续发展。

10. 了解到代际传承和跨文化传播对场所精神的可持续传播与保护过程至关重要，我们建议让年轻人及当地不同文化团体积极合作，参与到场所精神的立法保护和管理中。

根据吐鲁番文物网，汉唐网文章编译

资讯来源：行政院文化建设委员会 文化资产总管理处筹备处

（ICOMOS 2008年第16届年会通过之原则宣言）。

国际古迹遗址理事会
《国际考古遗址管理委员会的目标和章程》
OBJECTIVES AND PROCEDURES OF THE INTERNATIONAL COMMITTEE ON ARCHAEOLOGICAL HERITAGE MANAGEMENT

OBJECTIVES AND PROCEDURES OF THE INTERNATIONAL COMMITTEE ON ARCHAEOLOGICAL HERITAGE MANAGEMENT (ICAHM)
Eger-Xi'an Procedures of July 2008

The following rules were proposed, discussed and agreed to at the ICAHM meeting held during the 12th General Assembly in Mexico in 1999 (Willem Willems), subsequently amended to facilitate e-mail elections in 2003 (Christophe Rivet) and brought into alignment with the Eger-Xi'an principles in 2006 (Brian Egloff) and then further modified in 2008 to meet with the current revision of the Eger-Xi'an principles (Egloff).

1.The ICOMOS International Committee on Archaeological Heritage Management (hereinafter designated as ICAHM) is established in accordance with Article 14 of the ICOMOS statutes by the Executive Committee of ICOMOS on February 19, 1985.

2. The mission of ICAHM is to promote international cooperation in the field of archaeological heritage management and to advise ICOMOS on the development of archaeological heritage management programs. ICAHM shall accomplish this mission by providing a forum for the interchange of experience, ideas, knowledge, and the results of research among professionals, scientists and decision-makers,

《国际考古遗址管理委员会的目标和章程》
2008 年 7 月 埃格尔 – 西安章程

埃格尔 – 西安章程的现行版本于 1999 年在墨西哥城举行的国际考古遗址管理委员会第 12 届大会期间（威廉・威廉姆斯）提议、讨论并获通过，随后在 2003 年（克里斯多夫・雷维特主持），以电子邮件征集意见的简便方式做出修订，并于 2006 年,（布莱恩・伊格洛夫）将其纳入埃格尔 – 西安章程，2008 年,（由伊格洛夫）完成了埃格尔 – 西安章程的现行版本修订。

1. 1985 年 2 月 19 日，国际古迹遗址理事会执行委员会，根据国际古迹遗址理事会章程第 14 条，成立了国际古迹遗址理事会之国际考古遗址管理委员会。

2. 国际考古遗址管理委员会的使命是促进考古遗址管理领域的国际合作，并在开发考古遗址管理项目上向国际古迹遗址理事会提出建议。国际考古遗址管理委员会为了完成该使命，将为包括考古学家、建筑师、人类学家以及相关的政府和非政府机构管理者等各行各业的专家、学者和决策者，提供一个交流经验，理念、知识和研究成果的论坛。为了实现这个使命，

including archaeologists, architects, anthropologists and governmental and non-governmental administrators. In attaining this mission, ICAHM shall adhere to the goals and objectives of ICOMOS and the Eger-Xi'an Principles. ICAHM has decided upon the following objectives to fulfill its mission:

国际考古遗址管理委员会应遵循国际古迹遗址理事会的目标和规划，以及埃格尔－西安章程原则。国际考古遗址管理委员会经考虑后确定了以下规划：

• Promote the widest possible understanding of the importance of the archaeological heritage among the general public and government institutions.

• 最大限度地提升公众和相关政府机构对于考古遗址重要性的理解。

• Promote a systematic inventory of the world's archaeological heritage.

• 编撰全世界考古遗址的系统性目录。

• Provide expert advice to ICOMOS on world heritage matters.

• 向国际古迹遗址理事会提供有关世界遗址保护事务的专家建议。

• Develop efficient and integrated strategies for the management of the archaeological heritage for the long-term benefit of both scientists and the general public.

• 制订高效、综合的考古遗址管理的整体性战略，使公众和学者均能长期受益。

• Encourage a multidisciplinary approach to the cultural heritage.

• 鼓励在文化遗产领域的多学科交叉研究。

• Improve archaeological methods and standards among those concerned with archaeological heritage management.

• 改进与考古遗址管理有关的考古学方法和标准。

• Establish minimum standards for the training and qualification of those engaged in archaeological heritage management.

• 设定考古遗产管理从业人员的最低培训标准和资格认定标准。

• Encourage the exchange of experience and expertise in the field of archaeological heritage management.

• 鼓励考古遗址管理领域的经验交流和专家人才的交流。

3. In keeping with its international responsibilities, ICAHM has prepared the ICOMOS Charter for the Protection and Management of the Archaeological Heritage (1990)

3. 为履行相应的国际责任，国际考古遗址管理委员会起草了《国际古迹遗址理事会考古遗产保护和管理宪章 (1990)》

4. All Expert Members of ICAHM are eligible to run for an elected position. The President, Vice President and Secretary shall constitute a Bureau within the ICAHM Executive Committee and be elected by the national nominated Expert Members of ICAHM through an e-mail process verified by

4. 所有国际考古遗址管理委员会的专家成员均由选举产生。主席、副主席和秘书长组成了考古遗址国际管理委员会执行委员会下属的执行局，执行局人员由专家成员担任，并必须由成员国提名，再由国际考古遗址管理委员会专家成员采用电子邮件投票产生，并得到国际

the secretariat of an ICOMOS national committee.

古迹遗址理事会国家委员会秘书处确认。

In accordance with Article 12 of the ICOMOS Statues, the President shall be a member of the ICOMOS Advisory Committee.

根据国际古迹遗址理事会章程的第 12 条的规定，考古遗址国际管理委员会主席必须由国际古迹遗址理事会咨询委员会成员担任。

All Expert Members of ICAHM shall be eligible to elect Regional Vice-Presidents and an Administrative Secretary and Financial Secretary from among the Expert Members.

所有的国际考古遗址管埋委员会专家成员都有资格成为地区副主席、行政秘书、财政秘书的候选人。

The members of the Bureau and all elected officers, the Past Presidents and Past Vice Presidents of ICAHM, and any other member of ICOMOS selected by the ICAHM Executive Committee, shall constitute the ICAHM Executive Committee.

国际考古遗址管理委员会执行委员会由执行局的成员和所有被推选的官员、国际考古遗址管理委员会的前主席和前副主席，和其他由国际考古遗址管理委员会执行委员会选举出的国际古迹遗址理事会成员组成。

The Executive Committee is empowered to undertake the ordinary operation of ICAHM including the acceptance of members, scheduling of annual general meetings, establishment of a secretariat, maintenance of the web site and the management of conference and symposium events. If deemed necessary the entire Executive Committee can hold internal ballots to determine select positions on issues as well as put a referendum to the entire voting membership.

国际考古遗址管理委员会执行委员会被授权处理国际考古遗址管理委员会的一切日常事务，包括接纳新成员，安排每年会议，建立秘书处，维护网站和管理研讨会。必要时，整个执行委员会可以举行内部投票来决定对某些问题的看法，也可以通过全员公投来决定。

By agreement of the Executive Committee Expert Members can be appointed to those positions not filled by general election or that fall vacant.

在执行委员会专家成员们认可的情况下，选举中空缺出来的职位或因故空缺的职位，可以由委员会指定任命。

The term of office of elected officers shall be as specified in the Eger-Xi’an document.

官员的任期应遵照埃格尔 – 西安文件的说明。

5. Expert Members of ICAHM shall consist of members selected by each of the National Committees as well as members of ICOMOS that have demonstrated to the satisfaction of the ICAHM Executive Committee the following:

5. 国际考古遗址管理委员会的专家成员必须由每个国家委员会和国际古迹遗址理事会会员推选出来，必须达到国际考古遗址管理委员会执行委员会提出的要求，要求如下：

a. membership in ICOMOS.

b. competency in archaeological heritage management with a reasonable degree of professional experience,

c. sufficient educational training, and most importantly

d. willingness to participate in the activities of ICAHM.

a. 是国际古迹遗址理事会会员

b. 有一定的专业素养，胜任考古遗产管理工作

c. 需要充分的教育培训，最重要的是

d. 有参与国际考古遗址管理委员会活动的热情。

6. Associate Members of ICAHM (non voting) shall consist of members of ICOMOS who wish to build-up their interest and expertise in the field of archaeological heritage management

6. 国际考古遗址管理委员会的非正式会员（无投票权）应由热心并有志于文化遗产管理工作、并具备相关专业知识的国际古迹遗址理事会会员组成。

7. Institutional Membership will be sought and defined from case to case by the Executive.

7. 机构会员的资格认定应由执行委员会依个案酌情处理。

8. Affiliate Members (comprised of individuals who are not members of ICOMOS) and Honorary Members will be appointed by the ICAHM Executive in keeping with the Eger-Xi'an principles.

8. 附属会员（由非国际古迹遗址理事会会员个人组成）和名誉会员将由国际考古遗址管理委员会执行委员会按照埃格尔－西安章程的原则予以认定。

9. As encouraged by ICOMOS, the ICAHM Executive Committee will establish a network of corresponding members, individuals and professional institutions engaged in relevant fields of activities but not directly in heritage related activities such that they would qualify for membership in ICOMOS.

9. 在国际古迹遗址理事会的支持下，国际考古遗址管理委员会执行委员会将会建立一个会员网络平台，使任何从事相关活动但不参与文化遗产管理事务的个人和专业机构，都有资格申请加入国际古迹遗址理事会。

10. No Executive Committee member, including the President, shall remain in any single office for more than three consecutive periods of three years.

10. 包括主席在内的执行委员会成员，在其职位上不得连任三次，每次任期为三年。

11. Membership in ICAHM will be terminated under the following conditions:

a. failure to adhere to the ICOMOS Statement of Ethical Commitment, and

b. failure to participate during any triennium in the activities of ICAHM when called upon to do so.

11. 有以下情况的会员将被终止国际考古遗址管理委员会：

a. 未能遵守国际古迹遗址理事会道德承诺声明。

b. 在三年任期内未参与国际考古遗址管理委员会任何活动。

12. The Executive committee shall meet at least once a year. It shall prepare and present a report on ICAHM's activities and a list of its members to the ICOMOS Secretariat (the Secretariat) annually, a date to be announced by the Secretary General of ICOMOS. The annual report shall be submitted in accordance with a format proposed by the Secretariat.

12. 执行委员会每年至少召开一次工作会议，向国际古迹遗址理事会秘书处准备和汇报国际考古遗址管理委员会活动报告，并递交会员名单，提交的时间由秘书处秘书长决定。年度报告格式应按秘书处规定的格式准备。

13. ICAHM shall meet at least once every three years in full session preferably at the ICOMOS General Assembly. The agenda of such a meeting shall include at a minimum;

a. report on the election of officers,

b. activities of the past triennium of ICAHM,

c. balance sheet for the past triennium, and

d. program of activities for the next triennium.

13. 国际考古遗址管理委员会至少每三年要在国际古迹遗址理事会大会期间召开一次全体大会。会议的日程包括：

a. 报告官员选举情况；

b. 国际考古遗址管理委员会过去三年的活动；

c. 过去三年的资产负债情况；

d. 未来三年的活动计划。

14. The activities of ICAHM shall be financed by subsidies and grants obtained by ICAHM's own initiative from international and national bodies (including ICOMOS Committees in countries concerned); and contracts entered into by ICOMOS on behalf of ICAHM for the performance of specific tasks within its purview.

14. 国际考古遗址管理委员会活动的经费主要是委员会获得的、来自于国际和国家组织（包括国际古迹遗址理事会委员会的成员国家）的补贴和资助、捐款，国际古迹遗址理事会代表国际考古遗址管理委员会签订的协议中，已包括了在职权范围内的各项任务。

The members of ICAHM shall use the best efforts to obtain the funds necessary to ensure their own participation in ICAHM's activities.

国际考古遗址管理委员会成员要尽最大努力去获得必要的经费以便于参与委员会的活动。

15. ICAHM's activities may include the organization of meetings, the preparation of publications and the gathering and dissemination of information directly or through the UNESCO/ICOMOS International Documentation Centre in Paris. ICAHM may undertake regional activities.

15. 国际考古遗址管理委员会的活动应该包括组织会议，准备出版物，收集和传播从联合国教科文组织或国际古迹遗址理事会的国际档案中心（巴黎）直接或者间接获得的信息。委员会也可能承办地区性活动。

16. Every three years, preferably immediately following the General Assembly of ICOMOS, ICAHM shall draw up program for the forthcoming triennum. This program shall be forwarded to the

16. 每三年，在国际古迹遗址理事会大会闭幕后，国际考古遗址管理委员会应立即起草未来三年的工作规划。这个规划应在下届国际古迹遗址理事会大会召开前三个月内递交给国际

ICOMOS Secretariat at least three months prior to the General Assembly for incorporation into ICOMOS's program for the forthcoming three years.

古迹遗址理事会秘书处，以便纳入国际古迹遗址理事会未来三年的工作计划。

17. The working languages of ICAHM shall be French, Spanish and English.

17. 国际考古遗址管理委员会的工作语言包括法语、西班牙语和英语。

18. The President or other members of the ICOMOS Bureau and/or a representative of the International Centre for Conservation (Rome) shall be invited to attend all open meetings organized by ICAHM. Representatives of other organizations may be invited to attend the meetings of ICAHM.

18. 考古遗址管理委员会主席或其他国际古迹遗址理事会执行局的成员和国际保护中心（罗马）的代表都应被邀请参加委员会组织的所有公开会议。其他组织的代表也可被邀请参加委员会的部分会议。

19. It is intended that the ICAHM principles will adhere to the spirit of the Eger-Xi'an Principles.

19. 国际考古遗址管理委员会的基本原则与埃格尔－西安章程的精神相符。

Document dated 25 October 2008

文件起草于 2008 年 10 月 25 日

联合国教科文组织
《京都宣言》
UNESCO The Kyoto Declaration

Preamble

We, the participants gathered in Kyoto, on the occasion of the Closing Event of the Celebrations of the 40th Anniversary of the *World Heritage Convention*, wish to acknowledge the generous hospitality and intellectual leadership of the Japanese authorities in providing a forum to reflect on the achievements, present issues and future evolution of this unique international conservation treaty.

We reaffirm the centrality of the theme adopted by the General Assembly of the States Parties to the *Convention* and by the World Heritage Committee for this Fortieth Anniversary, namely 'World Heritage and Sustainable Development: the Role of Local Communities'. The relationship between World Heritage and local communities is indeed at the heart of the Convention and is fundamental to address the challenges currently facing all regions of the world, through increasing demographic and development pressures, global financial crises and climate change.

We recall, in this context, the outcome document of the UN Conference on Sustainable Development 'The Future We Want' (Rio de Janeiro, June 2012) and the 'Vision and Strategic Action Plan for the Implementation of the World Heritage Convention 2012-2022' adopted by the 18th General Assembly of States Parties (UNESCO, 2011); as well as the in-depth reflections and results from several expert and consultative meetings organized in all

序言

值此纪念世界遗产公约40周年大会闭幕之际，我们相聚在京都，首先感谢日本当局的盛情款待和卓越的组织能力。这次研讨会为我们提供了独一无二的、对保护条约进行回顾、反思和展望的平台，再次表达我们由衷的谢意。

我们再次重申由联合国大会缔约国和世界遗产委员会提出40周年纪念会的主题，即“世界遗产和可持续发展：地方社区的作用”。世界遗产与地方社区的关系是公约的核心，是世界各地解决当前面临各种挑战如日益增长的人口和发展压力，全球金融危机和气候变化等问题的基础。

在这个背景下，我们回顾联合国可持续发展大会的成果性文件《我们憧憬的未来》（里约热内卢，2012年6月）、在第18次联合国缔约国大会上提出的“实现世界遗产公约2012—2022愿景与行动战略规划”（联合国教科文组织，2011年）以及在《公约》40周年框架下在世界各地组织的几次专家和协商会议的深入思考和成果。

regions of the world under the framework of the 40th anniversary of the *Convention.*

Achievements of 40 years of the *World Heritage Convention*

世界遗产公约 40 年来的成就

We recognize that the *World Heritage Convention*, with its 190 States Parties, is one of the most powerful tools for heritage conservation, with a shared vision combining the protection of cultural and natural heritage of Outstanding Universal Value in one single instrument. We acknowledge the significant contribution of the *Convention* to social cohesion, dialogue, tolerance, cultural diversity and peace, through its emphasis on the common and shared importance of World Heritage for all of humankind and the promotion of international cooperation for its safeguarding.

我们必须承认，拥有 190 个缔约国的《世界遗产公约》是遗产保护最有力的方式之一，是保护文化和自然遗产的突出普遍价值的唯一共享理念。我们感谢公约对社会凝聚力、对话、宽容、文化多样性与和平等方面做出的突出贡献，它强调了民众和全人类共享世界遗产的重要性，促进了维护遗产安全的国际合作。

We also acknowledge some contributions made over time in strengthening the policies and practices of the *Convention* as a standard-setter in heritage preservation globally; the importance of youth and future generations, especially related to the *Convention*'s role in inter-generational equity; and all partners and stakeholders in heritage conservation at local, national and regional levels, including local communities and indigenous peoples, whom we acknowledge with respect and pay tribute to on this occasion.

我们也感谢那些把公约作为遗产保护工作标准指南的政策制定者和实施者的贡献；公约对于青年和子孙后代有着重要的作用，公约特别强调了代际公平；对所有当地的、国家的、地区的遗产保护工作者和利益相关者，包括当地社区和土著居民，对遗产保护所做的努力表示诚挚的敬意和谢意。

We are concerned, however, about the serious challenges confronting World Heritage properties, associated with development pressures, conflicts, man-made and natural disasters, as well as the gaps in the representativity of the World Heritage List. We also note with concern the crucial lack of technical capacity and financial resources to implement the *Convention,* particularly in the least developed and developing countries.

然而，我们不得不考虑世界遗产所面临的各种严峻的挑战，如发展压力、冲突、人为和自然灾害等，及世界遗产名录中代表性方面的差距。我们还必须注意到，在《世界遗产公约》实施过程中，特别是欠发达国家和发展中国家，技术能力和财政资源的严重不足。

A Sustainable Earth and the Role of World Heritage

We are conscious of the enormous challenges our planet is facing to in order to ensure its sustainability and of the need for a transformative change to be reflected in the post-2015 development agenda, which would take into consideration the broader picture of human progress beyond GDP.

We are convinced that a people-centred conservation of the world's cultural and natural heritage is an opportunity to provide critical learning models for the pursuit of sustainable development and for ensuring a harmonious relationship between communities and their environment. The concept of heritage is fundamental to the logic of sustainable development as heritage results from the dynamic and continuous interaction between communities and their environment. Heritage sustains and improves the quality of life of people, as reinforced in the relevant internationally recognized policies such as the Strategic Plan for Biodiversity 2011-2020 and the Aichi Biodiversity Targets, the achievement of which is beneficial to both cultural and natural heritage.

The acknowledgment and conservation of the diversity of the world's cultural and natural heritage, and the equitable sharing of the benefits deriving from its use, enhance a feeling of place and belonging, mutual respect for others and a sense of collective purpose, which contribute to the social cohesion of a community.

The Importance of the Role of Community

We reiterate the important role of communities, including local communities and indigenous peoples, in the implementation of the *World Heritage Convention,* in accordance with one of its five strategic objectives, the fifth "C" adopted in

可持续发展的地球和世界遗产的作用

我们深知为了确保地球可持续性需面对各种挑战，我们也意识到在2015年后发展议程中需要反映出革新性的变化，这些将会给人类进步带来更广阔的前景（国民生产总值除外）。

我们确信，以人为本的世界文化和自然遗产保护观念，为追求可持续发展和实现社区与自然和谐相处，提供了一个重要的学习机会。遗产概念是可持续发展的逻辑基础，遗产是动态的、持续的、社区或环境相互交融的产物。遗产能够维持和提升人类的生活品质，这在国际公认的相关政策中得到了加强，如2011–2020年生物多样性战略计划及爱知生物多样性目标，政策成果惠及文化和自然遗产。

了解并保护世界文化和自然遗产的多样性，公平分享因使用遗产而带来的收益，可以提升地区感和归属感，可以增进相互的了解，能培养集体荣誉感，这些对形成社区的社会凝聚力有巨大帮助。

社区的重要性

我们反复强调社区，即当地社区和土著居民，在实施遗产公约过程中的重要性，是2007年包含社区5“C”战略的2012–2022战略行动规划中所提及的5个战略目标之一。

2007, and the Strategic Action Plan 2012-2022.

The *Convention,* in its Article 4, places the responsibility for ensuring the identification, protection, conservation, presentation and transmission to future generations of the cultural and natural heritage with the States Parties. At the same time, if one of the aims of the *Convention* is to 'give heritage a role in the life of the community' (Article. 5), then the concerns and aspirations of communities must be centrally involved in conservation and management efforts.

《公约》第 4 条中提出，缔约国具有认定，保存、保护、展示以及向后代传递文化和自然遗产的责任。同时，如果《公约》的目标之一是“让遗产走进社区生活”（第 5 条），那么社区必须关注和参与遗产的保护和管理工作。

Only through strengthened relationships between cultural and biological diversity as a whole, integrating both tangible and intangible aspects and geared toward sustainable development, will the 'future we want' become attainable.

只有通过加强居民与遗产的联系，尊重文化多样性和生物多样性，整合有形和无形要素，实施可持续发展，才能实现“我们憧憬的未来”。

Such strengthened relationships should be grounded in a multidisciplinary and participatory approach to heritage conservation, which would integrate the consideration of social, economic and environmental dimensions, paying particular attention to vulnerable groups respecting all relevant international standards and obligations. Unless such a sustainable development perspective is integrated in the management of a World Heritage property, it will be difficult in the long run to ensure the conservation of its Outstanding Universal Value.

要加强这种紧密的联系，就必须采用多学科、共同参与的方法来保护遗产，这种方法综合考虑了社会、经济和环境等方面，特别关注弱势群体，尊重所有相关的国际标准和义务。只有将可持续发展的愿景融合到世界遗产的管理中，才能长期解决保护突出普遍价值可能存在的困难。

Thus, benefits derived from well-protected cultural and natural heritage properties should be equitably distributed to communities to foster their sustainable development and there should be close cooperation with management bodies and experts. At the same time, attention should be paid to the evolving character of cultural and social contexts relevant to World Heritage, which will inevitably

文化和自然遗产保护所获得的收益应公平地分配给每个社区，同时管理机构和专家必须密切合作，以实现遗产的可持续发展。与此同时，应当重视与世界遗产相关的文化和社会背景的演变特点，因其不可避免地导致新的利益和关切群体的出现。

lead to the emergence of new groups of interest and concerns.

This new approach and these considerations will require the building of capacities and education of relevant actors, from institutions and policy makers to heritage practitioners and communities and networks. Communities, in particular, should be empowered to harness the benefits of heritage to society through specific awareness-raising initiatives, skills-development programmes and the establishment of networks. They should be fully involved in management and conservation activities, including in reducing risks from disasters and climate change.

新方法及其考虑因素都需要对相关人员，从制度和政策的制订者到遗产从业者、社区以及网络工作者，进行能力建设和培训。特别是社区，应从利用遗产中获得好处，并通过宣传保护意识项目、技能提升项目和建立相应的网站的方式，全面参与管理和保护活动，包括减少灾害和气候变化所带来的风险。

Attention should also be given to the development of sustainable tourism as one of the sources of economic benefits and empowerment for local communities, and the appreciation of cultural diversities by visitors.

我们还应关注旅游业可持续发展的问题，它是当地社区获取经济收益的主要源泉之一，也是游客享受文化多样性的途径之一。

A Call for Action

呼吁

For forty years, the *World Heritage Convention* has embodied the global ideals and ethics of conservation. While continuing to emphasize the importance of protecting a selection of outstanding sites important for all of humankind, a holistic approach is necessary to include wider dimensions arising from new emerging challenges that threaten the foundation of our societies. The question is not only to save exceptional sites from destruction or neglect, but to demonstrate, through appropriate conservation and management, strategies and a development model based on the values of continuity.

40年来，《世界遗产公约》体现了全球性的保护理念和伦理标准。公约持续强调保护的重要性，及选择保护具有杰出价值的遗产对全人类的重要性。从全局出发，必须将威胁人类社会发展的新型挑战考虑在内。然而，我们不仅要保护被破坏或被忽视的特殊遗产，更要通过适当的保护和管理、战略和发展模式，维系遗产的价值。

To realize this Vision, the participants wish to launch an appeal to the international community with a view to:

为了实现这个理念，与会者呼吁国际社会：

mobilizing substantial financial resources for heritage conservation globally in the spirit of solidarity and cooperation; developing innovative responses to share experience, good practice and knowledge related to communities in support of World Heritage and sustainable development, including capacity building at all levels; sharing responsibility for effectively addressing threats to the world's cultural and natural heritage, and contributing to its sustainable development and collective benefits;

本着团结合作的精神，在全球筹集大量资金投入遗产保护事业；形成创新型反应机制，分享相关社区的经验、好的实践、知识，支持社区遗产保护和可持续发展；开展不同层次的能力建设；分担有效应对威胁世界文化和自然遗产的责任，实现可持续发展和维护共同利益；

taking into account World Heritage in the discussions on the post-2015 development agenda by engaging the international community-within all relevant regional and global forums-for an inclusive approach, considering environmental, cultural and socio-economic needs;

应在2015年后的发展议程中考虑世界遗产，通过相关区域和全球性的论坛吸引国际社会参与，以包容性的方法，考虑环境，文化和社会经济的需求；

enhancing cooperation and coordination among all stakeholders and ensuring effective involvement of local communities, indigenous peoples, experts and youth in conservation from the preparatory phase of the World Heritage nomination process, so that heritage conservation contributes to the sustainable development of the whole society;

加强所有利益相关者的合作和协调，确保地方社区、土著民族、专家和年轻人在申遗程序的开始阶段就参与保护活动，从而实现遗产保护对全社会可持续发展的贡献；

ensuring the sustainability of local communities through other domains such as intangible cultural heritage and cultural and creative industries, which play a crucial role and;

发挥其他领域的重要作用，如非物质文化遗产和文化创意产业等，确保社区的可持续发展。

Implementing, as a priority, the Strategic Action Plan 2012-2022 adopted by the General Assembly of States Parties to the Convention.

优先实施联合国大会上通过的“2012 — 2022战略行动计划”。

Kyoto, 8 November 2012

京都，2012年11月8日

中国大遗址保护高峰论坛
《大遗址保护西安共识》
Xi'an Consensus for Complicated Archaeological Sites' Protection

Xi'an Consensus for Complicated Archaeological Sites' Protection

In Xi'an on October 21, 2008

At the invitation of the National Cultural Heritage Administration and Shaanxi Provincial People's Government, we, representatives from Xi'an, Zhengzhou, Hangzhou, Chengdu, Luoyang, Wuxi, Yangzhou, Jingzhou, Anyang, Chaoyang and Kaifeng, attended the '*Summit Forum of Complicated Archaeological Sites' Protection*' held in Xi'an on October 21, 2008.

Centering on the theme of 'effective conservation on Complicated Archaeological Sites and promoting the harmonious development of cities', we discussed in depth in order to explore new modes for Complicated Archaeological Sites' Protection; driving health development of Complicated Archaeological Sites' Protection; promoting coordinated development of regional economy, and ensuring of public sharing of protection achievements.

It is noted that the acceleration of urbanization process brings unprecedented impacts and challenges for the cultural heritage protection, which is highly reflected in intensive conflicts between Complicated Archaeological Sites' protection and high tension of land resources, conflicts with urban construction, and the increasing disharmony with traditional protection concept and models.

大遗址保护西安共识

2008年10月21日于西安

我们，来自西安、郑州、杭州、成都、洛阳、无锡、扬州、荆州、安阳、朝阳、开封等城市的代表，应国家文物局、陕西省人民政府的邀请，参加了2008年10月21在西安举办的“大遗址保护高峰论坛”。

我们围绕“做好大遗址保护，推进城市和谐发展”的主题，就探索大遗址保护新模式，推动大遗址保护健康发展，促进区域经济协调发展，确保民众共享保护成果等内容进行了深入的探讨。

我们注意到，城市化进程的加快给文化遗产保护带来了前所未有的影响与挑战，这突出表现为大遗址保护与土地资源高度紧张的矛盾日益凸显，与城市建设的冲突日益凸显，与传统保护理念和模式的不协调日益凸显。

It is noted that from Koguryo Site, Yin-dynasty Site, Daming Palace Site, Luoyang Ancient City of Sui and Tang Dynasties, to Jinsha Site and Hongshan Site, we have been taken a series of highly effective conservation actions. With these practices, Complicated Archaeological Sites' are gradually changing from the forgotten or disorder corner of the city to the most beautiful place with the most cultural tasted space.

我们注意到，从高句丽遗址、殷墟遗址到大明宫遗址、隋唐洛阳城遗址，再到金沙遗址、鸿山遗址，都开展了一系列卓有成效的保护行动。伴随着这些实践，大遗址正在从城市中被人遗忘的角落、脏乱差的角落，逐渐转变为城市中最美丽的地方，最有文化品位的空间。

It is noted that from *the Principles for the Conservation of Heritage Sites in China,* to *Xi'an Declaration* issued by 15th general assembly of ICOMOS, to *Beijing Declaration for Urban Cultural*, the theoretical system of cultural heritage conservation in China has been matured gradually, forming distinctive Chinese protection characteristics of Complicated Archaeological Sites.

我们注意到，从《中国文物古迹保护准则》到国际古迹遗址理事会十五届大会的《西安宣言》，再到《城市文化北京宣言》，中国文化遗产保护理论体系日渐成熟，逐渐形成了大遗址保护的自身特色。

In the future, we will continue to devote our efforts to promote the harmonious development between Complicated Archaeological Sites' Protection and urban construction, implement the practices comprehensively, extensively and sustainably. Hereby, we reach the following consensus:

未来，我们将继续致力于促进大遗址保护与城市建设的和谐发展，开展全面、广泛、持续的实践。为此，我们达成以下共识：

I. Complicated Archaeological Sites are non-renewable cultural resources, and are core factors of urban cultural landscapes as well as the capital and impetus of urban sustainable development. Complicated Archaeological Sites' protection have great significance in construct urban culture, manifest urban features, maintain cultural diversity, and in safeguard the shared spiritual of Chinese nation.

一、大遗址是不可再生的文化资源，是城市文化景观的核心要素，是城市可持续发展的资本和动力。大遗址保护对建设城市文化，彰显城市特色，保持文化多样性，守望中华民族共有精神家园具有重大意义。

II. Scientifically work out the protection planning and incorporate into urban-rural development planning is the only way to optimize the urban spatial layout, allocate resources reasonably and handle the relationship between the urban construction and

二、科学编制保护规划，将其纳入城乡发展规划，是优化城市空间格局，合理配置资源，妥善处理城市建设与大遗址保护关系的必由之路。

protection of Complicated Archaeological Sites' properly.

III. Insist on the combination of government leading and public participation, insist on overall protection, continuous innovation and active exploration for new protection and usage patterns are the main guarantee to create a new situation of the Complicated Archaeological Sites' protection.

三、坚持政府主导与公众参与相结合，坚持整体保护，不断创新，积极探索保护和利用新模式，是开创大遗址保护新局面的重要保证。

IV. Deeply exploring connotation and value of Complicated Archaeological Sites; give full play to the social benefits; promote the rational development of tourism and other relevant industries to provide new growth points for the regional economy are efficient means to make Complicated Archaeological Sites' protection as an active power for urban development.

四、深入挖掘大遗址内涵和价值，充分发挥其社会效益，促进旅游等相关产业的理性发展，为区域经济提供新的增长点，是大遗址保护成为城市发展积极力量的有效途径。

V. Take people as the basis, adapt to local conditions, strengthen the environment renovation, improve urban and rural ecology, create good living environment, enhance the quality of urban life and make the protection achievements shared by the whole society, are the starting point and fundamental purpose of Complicated Archaeological Sites' Protection.

五、以人为本，因地制宜，加强环境整治，改善城乡生态，创造美好的人居环境，提高城市生活品质，让全社会共享保护成果，是大遗址保护的出发点和根本落脚点。

We shoulder not only responsible for the urban construction and development, but also for inherit and carry forward Chinese culture. We will make unremitting endeavor for the mission!

我们不但承担着城市建设与发展的职责，更肩负着传承与弘扬中华文化的重任。我们将为此不懈努力！

中国大遗址保护良渚论坛
《关于建设考古遗址公园的良渚共识》
Liangzhu Consensus on Construction of Archaeological Heritage Park

Liangzhu Consensus on Construction of Archaeological Heritage Park

[06-12-2009]

On June 12, 2009, the National Cultural Heritage Administration and Hangzhou Municipal People's Government held 'Liangzhu Forum of Complicated Archaeological Sites' Protection'. Discussions were around the theme of 'Complicated Archaeological Sites' protection and construction of archaeological heritage park', forming the following consensus for the construction of archaeological heritage park:

I. The construction of archaeological heritage park should based on the protection, presentation and usage of the heritage and its setting as well as take consideration of various functions of education, scientific research, tourism and relaxation etc, it is the product combining Complicated Archaeological Sites' protection practice in China and international cultural heritage protection concepts; also it is an effective way to strengthen heritages' protection, intensify heritages presentation and usage, which meets the actual demand of Complicated Archaeological Sites' protection at the present stage with distinctive characteristics of Chinese cultural heritage protection.

II. The archaeological heritage park, on the one hand, provides necessary space for heritage protection and research, promote the sustainable

关于建设考古遗址公园的良渚共识

[2009-06-12]

2009 年 6 月 12 日，国家文物局和杭州市人民政府共同举办了“大遗址保护良渚论坛”。论坛围绕“大遗址保护与考古遗址公园建设”的主题展开讨论，形成考古遗址公园建设的共识如下：

一、考古遗址公园立足于遗址及其背景环境的保护、展示与利用，兼顾教育、科研、游览、休闲等多项功能，是中国大遗址保护实践与国际文化遗产保护理念相结合的产物，是加强遗址保护、深化遗址展示与利用的有效途径，符合现阶段大遗址保护的实际需要，具有鲜明的中国文化遗产保护特色。

二、考古遗址公园一方面为遗址保护与研究提供了必要的空间，能够促进考古研究、遗址保护的可持续发展；另一方面借助系统化、

development of archaeological research and heritage protection. On the other hand, it depends on systematized and humanized presentation design to provide the public open and visual archaeological teaching materials with lead the public to access and to comprehend the heritage, and help the whole society to share achievements of Complicated Archaeological Sites' protection.

人性化的展示设计，为公众提供了开放和直观的考古教材，引导公众走近遗址、热爱遗址，有助于大遗址保护成果的全民共享。

III. The construction of the archaeological heritage park can effectively relieve the contradiction between cultural heritage protection and urbanization process, optimize the utilization of land resources, drive the development of relevant industries, improve the living environment further, expand and enrich the connotation of urban culture.

三、考古遗址公园建设能够有效缓解文化遗产保护与城市化进程之间的矛盾，优化土地资源的利用，带动相关产业发展，进一步改善人居环境，扩展和丰富城市文化内涵。

IV. The construction of archaeological heritage park further contributes to the theoretical research of Complicated Archaeological Sites' protection and to improve the management system of cultural heritage, which reflects the scientific development and realistic and innovative spirits.

四、考古遗址公园建设有助于进一步深化大遗址保护理论研究，完善文化遗产管理体制，是科学发展和求实创新精神的体现。

V. The construction of archaeological heritage park shall master the positioning accurately, with the fundamental purpose of protection and presentation of heritages' connotation and value, it shall target presentation methods and protection ways to form its distinctive and charm style. The construction of the archaeological heritage park shall guarantee the complete preservation of the heritage. In addition, all kinds of facilities and landscape design should be based on display heritage connotation and value.

五、考古遗址公园建设应准确把握定位，以保护展示遗址本体及其内涵和价值为根本目的，根据各自的特点，紧扣遗址内涵和价值，采取有针对性的保护展示方式，形成独特的风格和魅力。考古遗址公园建设行为应确保遗址的完整保存，各类设施及景观设计应以遗址内涵及价值的展示为前提。

VI. The construction of archaeological heritage park shall base on the ongoing archaeological work, research and protection and well conduct feasibility studies，investigation argumentation. It shall carry out overall planning and rational layout stick to the

六、考古遗址公园建设应以持续开展的考古、研究与保护工作为基础，做好可行性研究和调查论证工作，秉承科学、严谨和实事求是的态度，坚持循序渐进，统筹规划，合理布局。

scientific, rigorous and matter-of-fact attitudes as well as progressive working method.

We believed that with the in-depth development of the protection of Complicated Archaeological Sites, and the continuous exploration of the theory and practice of archaeological sites parks, the management and utilization of Chinese cultural heritage protection will definitely achieve new and greater achievements!

我们相信，随着大遗址保护工作的深入开展和考古遗址公园理论与实践的不断探索，中国文化遗产保护管理和利用工作一定能够取得新的、更大的成就！

中国大遗址保护洛阳高峰论坛
《洛阳宣言》
Luoyang Declaration

Luoyang Declaration

Background

With the rapidly development of economy and society in China, the acceleration of urbanization process brings unprecedented impacts and challenges for the cultural heritage protection, which is highly reflected in intensive conflicts between Complicated Archaeological Sites' protection and high tension of land resources, conflicts with urban construction, and increasing disharmony with traditional protection concept and models.

During the 'Luoyang Summit Forum of Great and Complicated Archaeological Sits' Protection' which was sponsored by the National Cultural Heritage Administration and Henan Provincial Government, the participants and experts of cultural heritage from Beijing, Xi'an, Hangzhou, Chengdu, Zhengzhou, Guangzhou, Changsha, Nanjing, Changchun, Luoyang, Wuxi, Yangzhou, An'yang, Kaifeng, Jingzhou, Chaoyang, Jiaxing and Ji'an, exchanged experiences and shared achievements of great and complicated archaeological sits' protection in past five years, exploring harmonious ways of great and complicated archaeological sits' protection and urban development. After careful discussion, participants approved the 'Luoyang Declaration', firstly emphasizes that the culture is the soul of a city, and great and complicated archaeological sits, as a non-renewable precious cultural resources,

洛阳宣言

背景

随着中国经济社会的快速发展，城市化进程的加快已经给文化遗产保护带来了前所未有的影响与挑战，这突出表现为大遗址保护与土地资源高度紧张的矛盾日益突出，与城市建设的冲突日显，也与传统保护理念和模式日趋不协调。

在国家文物局和河南省政府主办的“大遗址保护洛阳高峰论坛”举行期间，来自北京、西安、杭州、成都、郑州、广州、长沙、南京、长春、洛阳、无锡、扬州、安阳、开封、荆州、朝阳、嘉兴、集安等城市的代表以及文物专家，交流大遗址保护5年来取得的经验，分享成果，探索大遗址保护与城市发展的和谐之路。在与会者认真讨论后通过的“洛阳宣言”中首先强调，文化是城市的灵魂，大遗址作为不可再生的珍贵文化资源，是城市发展的积极力量。加强大遗址保护工作是践行科学发展观的重要举措，既是时代发展的必然要求，也是彰显城市特色的有效途径。

are the positive power for urban development. To strengthen great and complicated archaeological sits' protection is an important measure to execute scientific development perspective, which is the inevitable requirement of era development and an effective way to reflect the urban features.

The declaration indicates that build an archaeological heritage park at central urban and fringe area of rural-urban, could contributes to coordinate relationships between the cultural heritage protection and rural-urban economic and social development, to develop cultural tourism and relevant industries and to improve the cultural taste of a city. In order to promote the construction of archaeological heritage park, and to strengthen great and complicated archaeological sits' protection further, as well as to inherit and carry forward the excellent historic culture of China, the participants of the meeting promised that: adhere to the principles of overall planning and sustainable development, proceed from the actual conditions of heritage protection and urban development by scientific planning and orderly progress, in order to achieve a harmony and win-win result of great and complicated archaeological sits' protection and utilization. We insist the principles of giving priority to public welfare and benefiting the people, effectively maintain the public welfare of the construction of archaeological heritage park practically, and avoid *one-side* pursuit of commercialization only, and always take the protection of great and complicated archaeological sits as the starting point and objective of the work. The experts participating the meeting hold the view that inherited and carried forward from the *Xi'an Consensus for Great and Complicated Archaeological Sits' protection* and *the Liangzhu Consensus on Construction of Archaeological Heritage Park, the 'Luoyang' Declaration* clearly states the direction of great and complicated

宣言指出，当前在城市核心区和城乡接合部建设考古遗址公园，有助于协调文化遗产保护和城乡经济社会发展的关系，有助于发展文化旅游和相关产业，有助于提升城市文化品位。为推进考古遗址公园建设，进一步加强大遗址保护，传承和弘扬祖国优秀历史文化，与会城市代表承诺：坚持统筹规划、持续发展原则，从遗址保护和城市发展的实际出发，科学规划，有序推进，努力实现大遗址保护和利用的和谐共赢。坚持公益为主、惠及民众原则，切实维护考古遗址公园建设的公益性，避免片面追求商业化，始终将大遗址保护成果全民共享作为工作的出发点和落脚点。与会专家认为，这一《宣言》是对《关于大遗址保护的西安共识》和《关于建设考古遗址公园的良渚共识》的继承和发扬，明确指出了大遗址保护和考古遗址公园建设的方向，为下一步有序推进考古遗址公园建设做好了充分的准备和动员。

archaeological sits' protection and archaeological heritage park construction, which makes full preparation and mobilization for promoting the construction of the archaeological heritage park orderly in the following stage.

Full text

After Xi'an Summit Forum of great and complicated archaeological sits' protection in 2008, under the initiative of the National Cultural Heritage Administration and Henan Provincial Government, we, the representatives from Beijing, Xi'an, Hangzhou, Chengdu, Zhengzhou, Guangzhou, Changsha, Wuxi, Nanjing, Changchun, Luoyang, Yangzhou, An'yang, Kaifeng, Jingzhou, Chaoyang, Jiaxing and Ji'an gathered in Luoyang, exchanged experience, shared achievements and kept on explore the harmonious way of great and complicated archaeological sits' protection and urban development.

We realized that culture is the soul of a city, and great and complicated archaeological sits as the non-renewable precious cultural resources, are the positive power for urban development. To strengthen great and complicated archaeological sits' protection is an important measure to execute scientific development perspective, which is the inevitable requirement of era development and an effective way to reflect the urban features.

We realized that the concept of constructing the archaeological heritage park proposed in Liangzhu Forum is a theoretical innovation of cultural heritage protection and a strategic conception of protect cultural heritage actively and achieve the harmonious development of regional economy and society.

全文

我们，来自北京、西安、杭州、成都、郑州、广州、长沙、无锡、南京、长春、洛阳、扬州、安阳、开封、荆州、朝阳、嘉兴、集安等城市的代表，继2008年大遗址保护西安高峰论坛之后，在国家文物局、河南省人民政府的倡导下，相聚古都洛阳，交流经验，分享成果，继续探索大遗址保护与城市发展的和谐之路。

我们认识到，文化是城市的灵魂，大遗址作为不可再生的珍贵文化资源，是城市发展的积极力量。加强大遗址保护工作是践行科学发展观的重要举措，既是时代发展的必然要求，也是彰显城市特色的有效途径。

我们认识到，良渚论坛倡导的建设考古遗址公园的理念，是文化遗产保护理论的创新，是积极保护文化遗产、实现区域经济社会和谐发展的战略构想。

We realized that great and complicated archaeological sits' protection in central urban area encounters great challenges. And the archaeological heritage park constructed at central urban and fringe area of rural-urban, could contributes to coordinate the relationship between the cultural heritage protection and rural-urban economic and social development, develop cultural tourism and relevant industries and improve the cultural taste of a city.

我们认识到，城市核心区的大遗址保护极具挑战性；当前在城市核心区和城乡接合部建设考古遗址公园，有助于协调文化遗产保护和城乡经济社会发展的关系，有助于发展文化旅游和相关产业，有助于提升城市文化品位。

In order to promote the construction of archaeological heritage park, strengthen great and complicated archaeological sits' protection further, inherit and carry forward the excellent historic culture of China, we solemn promise:

为推进考古遗址公园建设，进一步加强大遗址保护，传承和弘扬祖国优秀历史文化，我们郑重承诺：

I. Adhere to the principles of overall planning and sustainable development, proceed from the actual conditions of heritage protection and urban development by scientific planning and orderly progress, in order to achieve a harmony and win-win result of great and complicated archaeological sits' protection and utilization.

一、坚持统筹规划、持续发展原则，从遗址保护和城市发展的实际出发，科学规划，有序推进，努力实现大遗址保护和利用的和谐共赢。

II. Adhere to the principles of government leading and multi-participation, further strengthen the leading role of the government for accurate guidance; reinforce management; mobilize social forces and masses enthusiasm to support and participate in the great and complicated archaeological sits' protection.

二、坚持政府主导、多方参与原则，进一步强化政府主导地位，正确引导，加强管理，调动社会力量和广大民众支持、参与大遗址保护的积极性。

III. Adhere the principles of giving priority to public welfare and benefiting the people, effectively maintain the public welfare of the construction of archaeological heritage park practically and avoid *one-side* pursuit of commercialization only, and always take the protection of great and complicated archaeological sits as the starting point and objective of the work.

三、坚持公益为主、惠及民众原则，切实维护考古遗址公园建设的公益性，避免片面追求商业化，始终将大遗址保护成果全民共享作为工作的出发点和落脚点。

IV. Adhere to the principles of emancipating the mind, pioneering and innovating, adjust the

四、坚持解放思想、开拓创新原则，因地制宜，积极探索考古遗址公园建设与管理的机

measures to the local conditions and actively explore the mechanism and method for the construction and management of the archaeological heritage park, expand the new situation of protection and utilization of great and complicated archaeological sits.

制和方法，开拓大遗址保护利用新局面。

The great and complicated archaeological sits' protection is under the critical period as a link between past and future has a long way to go. Let us cooperate to compose a new epic and welcome the new era of great and complicated archaeological sits' protection!

大遗址保护正处于承前启后、继往开来的关键时期，任重道远。让我们携起手来，共同谱写大遗址保护的新篇章，迎接大遗址保护的新时代！

All representatives present in the Forum In Luoyang on November 1, 2009

论坛全体代表
2009 年 11 月 1 日于洛阳

国际古迹遗址理事会
《文化遗产灾害风险管理利马宣言》
LIMA DECLARATION FOR DISASTER RISK MANAGEMENT OF CULTURAL HERITAGE

LIMA DECLARATION FOR DISASTER RISK MANAGEMENT OF CULTURAL HERITAGE
December 3rd of 2010

文化遗产灾害风险管理利马宣言
2010 年 12 月 3 日

Preamble:

Cultural heritage professionals, architects, archaeologists, structural engineers and other specialists from Peru and Japan met during the 'Symposium on Disaster Risk Management of Cultural Heritage. Sustainable Conservation of Urban Cultural Heritage in Seismic Zones'. The symposium aimed to share post disaster recovery experience and discuss the role of structural engineers and conservation architects for the protection of Cultural Heritage located in earthquake zones.

1. World is divided into seismic and non seismic areas. Earthquakes occur mainly along two big circles: the Circum Pacific seismic belt where more than 95% of seismic energy is dissipated, and the Eurasian circle. Following the introduction of international conservation charters and conservation policies, now we address the cumulative damage to cultural heritage associated with severe earthquakes prone areas.

2. Significant number of World Cultural Heritage Properties is located in these seismic areas, especially in the Circum Pacific region of Asia and Latin America, the Caribbean, Southern Europe,

前言：

来自秘鲁和日本的文物专家、建筑师、考古学家、结构工程师等专家参加了《文化遗产风险管理——地震带的城市文化遗产可持续保护》研讨会。本次研讨会旨在交流震后重建的经验，并探讨地震带文物保护区结构工程师和遗产保护专家的作用。

1. 世界分为地震带和非地震带。地震带主要分布在两个区域，环太平洋地震带和欧亚地震带，其中 95% 以上的地震发生在环太平洋地震带。随着国际保护宪章和保护政策的出台，现在我们探讨地震多发区文化遗产反复受损的问题。

2. 众多世界文化遗产位于这些地震带，尤其是环太平洋的亚洲和拉丁美洲、加勒比海以及南欧、西亚和中亚。可以预见大地震对这些地区存在着潜在危害，因此，这些地区应当采

West and Central Asia. Potential damage due to large earthquakes is foreseen in these regions. Therefore these regions need to undertake urgent measures to safeguard lives and cultural heritage from disasters;

取紧急措施保护人的生命安全，保护文化遗产免受灾害威胁；

3. Arguing safety reasons, the local authorities often demolish historic fabric after a severe earthquake. New generation of professionals should change this tendency through multidisciplinary approach aimed at sustainable protection of heritage. All cultural remains must be conserved or restored by taking into account the principles of integrity and authenticity understood in local context.

3. 出于安全考虑，大地震后，大部分地方当局会拆毁历史建筑。新一代专业人士应当通过多学科协作改变这种倾向，实现文化遗产保护的可持续性。在了解当地环境且尊重其完整性和真实性的原则上，所有文化遗存都应该被保存或修复。

4. ICOMOS National Committees are encouraged to contribute to the enrichment of the spirit of the Conservation Charters to consider the disaster mitigation on cultural heritage in seismic zone

4. 鼓励国际古迹遗址理事会国家委员会充分考虑保护宪章的精神及地震带文化遗产减灾工作。

5. Heritage conservation can be accomplished through education by organizing updated courses, seminars and training activities. Academic institutions would play an important role by including cultural heritage and tourism studies for sustainable development of heritage sites.

5. 遗产保护可以通过组织最新的课程、研讨会和培训活动完成。发挥学术机构的重要作用，把文化遗产和旅游研究纳入文化遗产的可持续发展。

6. Communication between community members and professionals from various disciplinary backgrounds, academics and authorities is necessary to explain and disseminate why restoration of heritage should be done with due respect to authenticity and integrity. Due attention should be given by journalists and other mass media professionals to spread this understanding.

6. 社区成员和来自不同学科背景、学术领域和政府机构的专业人士的交流，能够很好地帮助解释和传播在遗产修复中要尊重遗产的真实性和完整性的缘由。同样，记者和其他媒体从业人员也应当重视并宣传这一理念。

7. The responsibility of the authorities towards preparedness for the next severe earthquake needs to be stressed. Even though human life is priceless many heritage buildings at risk of collapse are also

7. 强化政府责任，为下一次强地震做好准备工作。尽管人命关天，却仍然有很多濒临倒塌的遗址建筑被用来居住、经商或用作旅游设施。

used for housing, business and/or other tourism facilities.

8. Disaster mitigation and preparedness requires a comprehensive assessment of risks to the site and its occupants and visitors. Detailed rescue and response plans should also be drawn up. For this purpose, it is mandatory to identify the carrying capacity of historic public buildings and places in order to prevent bottlenecks during disasters. Due consideration should be given to prior inspection to approve only those activities on the site that pose no risk to the life of habitants or visitors;

8. 减灾和准备工作需要对遗产点、居民和游人做全面的风险评估。应当起草详细的救援计划和应急预案。为此，需确定古建筑的承载力及位置，防止减灾中出现瓶颈。优先考虑批准那些不会影响遗址所在地居民或游人生命安全的活动。

BACKGROUND AND STATEMENTS

背景和陈述

1. *World Heritage Convention* has emphasized the responsibility of each State Party to formulate national policies for the protection of cultural heritage.

1.《世界遗产公约》强调，国家制定保护文化遗产政策是每个缔约国的责任。

2. In response to disasters, the first priority is to save human life and provide for the basic needs of victims. Next, emergency response and recovery should avoid further harm to cultural heritage;

2. 应对灾害，第一要务是抢救人的生命，向灾民提供基本生活必需品。第二，紧急抢救和修复文化遗产，避免文化遗产受到更多损害。

3. Interdisciplinary analysis and structural assessment of heritage buildings must include the use of traditional materials and technologies, if they are adequate. Considerations should be given to the deep understanding of the historical buildings and their seismic behavior through analytical or physical modeling, non destructive tests and other modern tools and to document it. Performance-based criterion complemented with strength based criterion should be considered;

3. 对古建筑的跨学科分析和结构评估，必须尽可能包括使用的传统材料和技术。通过物理模拟分析、非破坏性试验和其他现代工具和文件资料，充分了解并记录古建筑情况及它们在地震中的反应。应综合考虑性能标准和强度标准。

4. The earthquake history, especially the seismic activity in and around the heritage sites, and the impact of recent earthquakes on traditional and non-

4. 地震史，尤其是文化遗产周边的地震活动、近期地震对传统和非传统结构的影响，应当记录在册，保留以供查考。

traditional structures, should be documented and made available.

5. In order to achieve the objectives of sustainable development and risk management, recommended by the Thematic Meeting on Cultural Heritage Risk Management on Kobe during UN-WCDR in 2005, following strategic goals should be taken into account;

5. 为了实现 2005 年联合国在神户召开的减灾世界会议——《文化遗产风险管理主题会议》提出的可持续发展和风险管理的目标，必须重视以下战略目标：

Integrate cultural heritage into existing disaster reduction policies and mechanisms at the international, national and local levels including involving qualified heritage organizations and expertise;

将文化遗产包括有资格的文物组织和专家融入现有的国际、国家和地区减灾政策和机制中；

or Involve local communities in the preparation and implementation of risk management plans, and all stages of disaster recovery;

引导当地居民参与风险管理计划的准备、实施及灾后恢复的各个过程中；

Include cultural heritage as a subject to develop scientific research and technical studies, educational and training programs associated with risk management and disaster recovery, to work out such operating methods as will make the State capable of counteracting the risks that threaten cultural heritage.

将文化遗产作为一个学科，推动科学和技术研究、进行有关风险管理和灾后重建的教育和培训项目，制定使国家能够应对文化遗产风险威胁的操作方法；

ACTION RECOMMENDATIONS

行动建议

General Recommendations

总则

1. Undertake awareness-raising initiatives to involve decision-makers and local communities in the development and implementation of disaster risk reduction strategies for cultural heritage;

1. 唤醒主人翁意识，使当地居民和决策者共同参与文化遗产减灾策略的制定和实行。

2. Encourage established national and international networks of cultural heritage and disasters to promote the integration of cultural heritage protection into broader disaster management field;

2. 推动建立国家和国际的文化遗产和灾害管理网络，将文化遗产保护纳入更广阔的一体化风险管理领域。

For Intergovernmental and International Nongovernmental Organizations

International Intergovernmental and Nongovernmental Organizations concerned with cultural heritage, such as UNESCO, ICCROM, ICOMOS, ICOM, IFLA and ICA, as well as the International Committee of the Blue Shield (ICBS) and related international instruments such as the *World Heritage Convention*, should act, enhance and promote disaster risk reduction within their policies, programs, and activities;

4. Special consideration should be given to countries located in seismic areas to ensure safety in cities with living cultural heritage with due consideration to their ecological reality. Recurrent earthquakes cause cumulative damage to historic urban areas and sites. Development of new technology with necessary reinforcement that is compatible to original materials and technology and is reversible should be encouraged;

5. Include disaster risk management of cultural heritage in the scope of the assistance programs of various international development and cooperation agencies, which should also promote this policy among other multilateral development institutions to which they are a party.

For Central, Regional and Local governments

6. Governments should establish expert committees that would enable exchange of opinions to formulate coordinated policies by bringing together multidisciplinary specialists such as structural engineers, architects, archaeologists and other cultural heritage specialists. The government should also promote administrative and financial measures that are necessary to establish comprehensive disaster

政府间机构和国际非政府组织

3. 国际文化遗产相关的政府间机构和非政府组织，如联合国教科文组织，国际文物保护与修复研究中心，国际古迹遗址理事会、国际博物馆协会、国际景观建筑师联合会、国际合作总署、国际蓝盾委员会以及相关的国际公约如《世界遗产公约》，应当推进能减少灾害风险的政策、项目和活动。

4. 要特别关注处于地震带的国家，确保城市现存文化遗产的安全，适当考虑其真实的生态环境。周期性的地震使古城和古遗址不断受到破坏。应当鼓励开发具有可逆性的、可兼容原材料或原工艺的新材料和新技术，进行必要的加固。

5. 将文物灾害风险管理列入各种国际发展合作机构的援助计划，这些机构也应当在其所属的多边发展组织中促进该策略。

中央，地区和地方政府

6. 政府应建立专家委员会，组织多学科的专家，如结构工程师、建筑师、考古学家和其他文化遗产专家交流观点，形成统一意见。政府还应当采取行政和金融手段，为文化遗产及其周边环境全面设置减灾设施；

mitigation facilities for cultural heritage properties as well as their surrounding urban environment;

7. Governments should strengthen the institutional support and governance for disaster preparedness, through due regulations developed in consultation with the civil society. Public institutions, owners, and other stakeholders should be encouraged to work together in formulating policies to preserve Cultural Heritage;

7. 政府应与居民社团协商制定适当的制度，加强灾害预防制度的支持和管理。公共机构、遗产所有者和其他利益相关者应当通力合作，保护文化遗产；

8. Responsible authorities of Cultural heritage and Disaster Mitigation should jointly develop special tools for periodical inspection of structural stability of heritage buildings for their mitigation against earthquakes, in order to preserve their heritage values and use appropriates technologies that would maintain these values over time;

8. 文化遗产和减灾的相关机构为防范地震，应当共同开发出定期检测古建筑结构稳定性的工具，以保护遗产价值，并使用适当的技术长久保持遗产的价值；

9. Encourage national and international assistance to recover living heritage by including comprehensive understanding of the society in the rehabilitation programs, awareness and education activities for the inhabitants so as to improve their safety and daily life conditions;

9. 在组织对文化遗产修复的国家和国际援助项目中，鼓励社会的全面理解，开展教育活动并唤醒当地居民的文化遗产保护意识，改善居民生活状况并保证他们的安全；

10. In the context of the *World Heritage Convention* and other international instruments, adopt and implement comprehensive policies, procedures, and legal measures to integrate cultural heritage in all disaster reduction programs and to include risk management plans as part of the management system for heritage properties;

10. 在《世界遗产公约》和其他国际公约的背景下，实行全面的政策、程序和法定措施，整合所有文物减灾项目，并将风险管理计划作为文化遗产管理系统的一部分；

11. Include governmental and non-governmental cultural heritage expertise in existing and future national coordinating bodies mandated to oversee the development and implementation of disaster reduction policy, programs and actions plans;

11. 现有和未来的国家协调机构在负责监督减灾政策、方案和行动计划的制定和执行过程中，吸纳政府和非政府机构文化遗产方面的专门知识；

12. Cooperate with local administrations and provide adequate resources to ensure the adoption and implementation of consistent risk management strategies for cultural heritage assets in their territory, in particular, historic urban areas and living cultural landscapes, and their settings; including identifying, assessing and monitoring disaster risks;

12. 和当地政府合作，提供充足的资源，确保在他们的管辖范围内，对历史古城、人文景观及环境采用并持续实施一致的包括发现、评估和监测灾害风险在内的、文化遗产的风险管理策略；

13. Encourage and support civil society and non-governmental initiatives in the field of disaster reduction for cultural heritage through measures that are aimed at reducing underlying vulnerability factors;

13. 鼓励并支持民间团体和非政府机构在文化遗产减灾领域的积极性，通过此类措施减少遗产潜在的易损因素；

14. Initiate and support education and awareness campaigns to disseminate information widely for the protection of cultural heritage before, during, and after disasters; Use the knowledge, innovation and education to build a culture of disaster prevention.

14. 广泛传播保护文化遗产的知识，以便于在灾害发生前、发生中和发生后，发起并支持教育活动；并用这些知识来创新、培育和构建灾害预防的文化。

15. Central, Regional and Local governments are encouraged to promote coordination between policies for cultural heritage earthquake risk management, urban planning and disaster management for the cultural heritage properties and the surrounding environment.

15. 鼓励中央、地区和当地政府，促进并协调文化遗产地震风险管理、城市规划、文化遗产和周边环境灾害管理等政策。

For Educational/ Research Institutions

教育 / 研究机构

16. To develop training programs on repair and retrofitting aimed both, for cultural heritage professionals and emergency personnel, so as to achieve seamless integration.

16. 开展文化遗产专业修复人员和紧急维护人员培训项目，以实现无缝对接。

17. Education is the starting point to understand the importance of disaster preparedness. Therefore younger generation should be made aware of the importance of cultural heritage,

17. 教育是理解灾害预防重要性的开始。应当让年轻人意识到文化遗产的重要性，他们有保护有形及无形文化遗产的责任。

tangible and intangible and that they are responsible for its conservation.

18. Academic institutions such as universities, technical schools and research centers are encouraged to promote education and research on comprehensive disaster management of cultural heritage sites located in earthquake prone zones, and are especially encouraged to engage in international activities such as establishing networks to improve the quality of their activities by cooperating with the activities of regional cultural heritage centers.

18. 鼓励学术机构，如大学、技术学校和研究中心，全面推动地震频发地区文化遗产灾害管理的研究，尤其鼓励他们与当地文化遗产中心合作，建立全球网络系统，提升他们的活动质量。

The ‘Lima Declaration for Disaster Risk Management of Cultural Heritage’ was drafted and proposed by the professionals below, and adopted with the applause and common consent of all the participants of the International Symposium on ‘Disaster Risk Management of Cultural Heritage. Sustainable Conservation of Urban Cultural Heritage in Seismic Zones. Post-disaster recovery experience: Role of structural engineers and conservation architects’, hosted by CISMID-National University of Engineering (UNI), Ritsumeikan University (RITSDMUCH), with the support of ICOMOS-ICORP, ICOMOS Peru, which was held at the Jinnai Hall, Japan Peru Cultural Center, on 3rd December 2010.

“文化遗产灾害风险管理利马宣言”由以下专业机构提议起草，并得到与会代表的一致同意。“文化遗产灾害风险管理—地震带城市文化遗产可持续保护—灾后重建经验：结构工程师和文物保护建筑师的角色”研讨会，由国立工程大学的地震减灾研究中心，立命馆大学主办，国际古迹遗址理事会国际科学委员会，秘鲁古迹遗址理事会协办，在日本－秘鲁文化中心金奈堂，2010 年 12 月 3 日举行。

新西兰古迹遗址理事会
《保护文化遗产地—新西兰宪章》
ICOMOS New Zealand Charter for the Conservation of Places of Cultural Heritage

ICOMOS New Zealand Charter for the Conservation of Places of Cultural Heritage Value Revised 2010

新西兰古迹遗址理事会
保护文化遗产地—新西兰宪章
2010年修订

Preamble

序言

New Zealand retains a unique assemblage of places of cultural heritage value relating to its indigenous and more recent peoples. These areas, cultural landscapes and features, buildings and structures, gardens, archaeological sites, traditional sites, monuments, and sacred places are treasures of distinctive value that have accrued meanings over time. New Zealand shares a general responsibility with the rest of humanity to safeguard its cultural heritage places for present and future generations. More specifically, the people of New Zealand have particular ways of perceiving, relating to, and conserving their cultural heritage places.

新西兰保存了本土近代民族的、具有独特价值的文化遗产群。包括文化景观、文化标志、房屋及建筑、园林、考古遗址、传统保留地、纪念碑、圣地等，这些具有独特价值的宝藏随着时间的推移不断增值。新西兰和全世界人民共同承担着为当代和后代保护文物古迹的责任。更具体地说，新西兰人民有感知、认同以及保护其文物遗产的独特方式。

Following the spirit of the *International Charter for the Conservation and Restoration of Monuments and Sites (the Venice Charter-1964),* this charter sets out principles to guide the conservation of places of cultural heritage value in New Zealand. It is a statement of professional principles for members of ICOMOS New Zealand.

遵循《关于古迹遗址保护与修复的国际宪章》(《威尼斯宪章》1964年)精神，本宪章阐明了引导新西兰地方文化遗产价值保护的原则。它概括了新西兰国际古迹遗址理事会成员提出的专业性原则。

This charter is also intended to guide all those involved in the various aspects of conservation work, including owners, guardians, managers,

本宪章亦旨在指导包括所有者、监护人、管理者、开发者、规划者、建筑师、工程师、手工艺者以及建筑业业内人士、遗产从业者、

developers, planners, architects, engineers, craftspeople and those in the construction trades, heritage practitioners and advisors, and local and central government authorities. It offers guidance for communities, organisations, and individuals involved with the conservation and management of cultural heritage places.

指导顾问和当地及中央政府部门在内的所有参与保护工作各方面的人员。宪章为参与保护和管理文化遗产工作的团体、组织、个人提供指导。

This charter should be made an integral part of statutory or regulatory heritage management policies or plans, and should provide support for decision makers in statutory or regulatory processes.

宪章应成为法律或法规规定的遗产管理政策或计划不可分割的一部分，且应为决策者提供法律或法规规定的程序支持。

Each article of this charter must be read in the light of all the others. Words in bold in the text are defined in the definitions section of this charter.

宪章中各条款均应参照其他宪章。正文中加粗单词在宪章定义部分中给予解释。

This revised charter was adopted by the New Zealand National Committee of the International Council on Monuments and Sites at its meeting on 4 September 2010.

国际古迹遗址理事会新西兰委员会于 2010 年 09 月 04 日的会议通过了修订的宪章。

Purpose of conservation

保护目的

1. The purpose of conservation

The purpose of conservation is to care for places of cultural heritage value.

In general, such places:

(i) have lasting values and can be appreciated in their own right;

(ii) inform us about the past and the cultures of those who came before us;

(iii) provide tangible evidence of the continuity between past, present, and future;

(iv) underpin and reinforce community identity and relationships to ancestors and the land; and

(v) provide a measure against which the achievements of the present can be compared.

1. 保护目的

保护目的在于爱护文化遗产地价值。

一般而言，这些场所包括：

（1）自身拥有可供欣赏的永恒价值；

（2）告诉我们生活在此地的祖先的历史和文化；

（3）提供连接过去、现在和将来的实物证据；

（4）巩固和加强社区认同感及与祖先和土地间的关系；

（5）为现在的成就提供比较、对照的方法。

It is the purpose of conservation to retain and

保护的目的在于保留和揭示这些价值、保

reveal such values, and to support the ongoing meanings and functions of places of cultural heritage value, in the interests of present and future generations.

持文化遗产地的现有的意义与功能，造福后代。

Conservation principles

保护原则

2. Understanding cultural heritage value

Conservation of a place should be based on an understanding and appreciation of all aspects of its cultural heritage value, both tangible and intangible. All available forms of knowledge and evidence provide the means of understanding a place and its cultural heritage value and cultural heritage significance. Cultural heritage value should be understood through consultation with connected people, systematic documentary and oral research, physical investigation and recording of the place, and other relevant methods.

2. 理解文化遗产的价值

场所的保护基础是对有形和无形文化遗产价值的理解与欣赏。提供了所有可用的知识和证据，理解场所和文化遗产价值及重要性的方法。应通过向相关人士咨询、系统记录与口述的研究、实物调查、古迹记录和其他相关方法，理解文化遗产的价值。

All relevant cultural heritage values should be recognised, respected, and, where appropriate, revealed, including values which differ, conflict, or compete.

应承认、尊重、欣赏、展示相关文化遗产价值，包括存在的价值差异、冲突与竞争。

The policy for managing all aspects of a place, including its conservation and its use, and the implementation of the policy, must be based on an understanding of its cultural heritage value.

有关场所各方面管理的政策，包括场所的保护和使用、政策的执行，以对文化遗产价值的理解为基础。

3. Indigenous cultural heritage

The indigenous cultural heritage of tangata whenua relates to whanau, hapu, and iwi groups. It shapes identity and enhances well-being, and it has particular cultural meanings and values for the present, and associations with those who have gone before. Indigenous cultural heritage brings with it responsibilities of guardianship and the practical application and passing on of associated knowledge, traditional skills, and practices.

3. 本土文化遗产

唐加塔环努瓦（大地之子，指毛利人）的本土文化遗产与（毛利社会）瓦岛、哈甫、伊威部落群体相关。这一文化对塑造身份、提高幸福感，对当代文化有特殊的含义与价值，且与逝去的古人相关联。保护本土文化遗产同时也负责相关知识、传统技艺和习俗保护、应用和传承。

The Treaty of Waitangi is the founding document of our nation. Article 2 of the Treaty recognises and guarantees the protection of tino rangatiratanga, and so empowers kaitiakitanga as customary trusteeship to be exercised by tangata whenua. This customary trusteeship is exercised over their taonga, such as sacred and traditional places, built heritage, traditional practices, and other cultural heritage resources. This obligation extends beyond current legal ownership wherever such cultural heritage exists.

《怀唐伊条约》是新西兰立国的文献。条约第二条认同并保证对毛利人的首领制进行保护，同时授权其按惯例，由唐加塔环努瓦（大地之子）执行托管保护。执行托管惯例涉及包括圣地、传统保留地、建筑文物、传统习俗和其他文化遗产资源在内的宝藏。这一义务超出了当前法律所有权并涵盖的所有文化遗产。

Particular matauranga, or knowledge of cultural heritage meaning, value, and practice, is associated with places. Matauranga is sustained and transmitted through oral, written, and physical forms determined by tangata whenua. The conservation of such places is therefore conditional on decisions made in associated tangata whenua communities, and should proceed only in this context. In particular, protocols of access, authority, ritual, and practice are determined at a local level and should be respected.

特有的毛利人传统或文化知识，或有关文化遗产含义、价值和实践的知识均与古迹相关。毛利人传统或文化知识通过唐加塔环努瓦（大地之子）确定的口述、书面或实物形式予以保留和流传。这些古迹的保护取决于相互联系的唐加塔环努瓦（大地之子）群体的决定，且只能在此背景下进行。尤其是，有关使用、权属、惯例和习俗等协议的决定权在当地且应给予重视。

4. Planning for conservation

Conservation should be subject to prior documented assessment and planning.

4. 保护规划

保护应服从于前期的评估文件和规划。

All conservation work should be based on a conservation plan which identifies the cultural heritage value and cultural heritage significance of the place, the conservation policies, and the extent of the recommended works.

所有保护工作应以保护规划为基础，确定文化遗产的价值、意义、保护政策以及涉及的工作范围内的事务。

The conservation plan should give the highest priority to the authenticity and integrity of the place.

保护规划应以保持古迹的真实性和完整性为先决条件。

Other guiding documents such as, but not limited to, management plans, cyclical maintenance plans, specifications for conservation work,

其他指导性的文件包括但不局限于管理规划、周期性维护计划、保护工作规范、阐释说明计划、减灾规划或应急计划，这些文件均应

interpretation plans, risk mitigation plans, or emergency plans should be guided by a conservation plan.

受到保护规划指导。

5. Respect for surviving evidence and knowledge

Conservation maintains and reveals the authenticity and integrity of a place, and involves the least possible loss of fabric or evidence of cultural heritage value. Respect for all forms of knowledge and existing evidence, of both tangible and intangible values, is essential to the authenticity and integrity of the place.

5. 尊重现存的证据和知识

保护维护与揭示古迹的真实性和完整性，将有文化遗产价值的建筑或证据的潜在损失降到最低。重视所有形式的、有形和无形价值的知识及现存证据，对保护古迹的真实性和完整性意义重大。

Conservation recognises the evidence of time and the contributions of all periods. The conservation of a place should identify and respect all aspects of its cultural heritage value without unwarranted emphasis on any one value at the expense of others.

保护要承认时间证据以及所有时期的贡献。场所的保护应确定并尊重文化遗产价值的所有方面，不能无缘由地为强调某一方面价值而损失其他要素的价值。

The removal or obscuring of any physical evidence of any period or activity should be minimised, and should be explicitly justified where it does occur. The fabric of a particular period or activity may be obscured or removed if assessment shows that its removal would not diminish the cultural heritage value of the place.

应尽可能避免掩盖或拆除任何时期或活动的实物证据，如果已掩盖或拆除应保留明确证据。但如果评估显示掩盖或拆除不会降低地方文化遗产价值时，某一特定时期或活动的建筑可以被掩盖或拆除。

In conservation, evidence of the functions and intangible meanings of places of cultural heritage value should be respected.

保护中，应重视有地方文化遗产价值功能的证据和无形意义。

6. Minimum intervention

Work undertaken at a place of cultural heritage value should involve the least degree of intervention consistent with conservation and the principles of this charter.

6. 最少干预原则

对具有文化遗产价值的场所的保护性干预工作应最小化，方符合保护和本宪章原则。

Intervention should be the minimum necessary to ensure the retention of tangible and intangible values and the continuation of uses integral to those

保持最少干预确保遗产的有形和无形价值得以保留，及得到持续、完整地利用。应当避免拆除具有文化遗产价值的建筑物，避免更改其

values. The removal of fabric or the alteration of features and spaces that have cultural heritage value should be avoided.

特性和空间布局。

7. Physical investigation

Physical investigation of a place provides primary evidence that cannot be gained from any other source. Physical investigation should be carried out according to currently accepted professional standards, and should be documented through systematic recording.

7. 实地调查

对场所的实地调查将提供无法从其他渠道获得的原始证据。应根据当前公认的专业标准实施实地调查，并进行系统性记录备案。

Invasive investigation of fabric of any period should be carried out only where knowledge may be significantly extended, or where it is necessary to establish the existence of fabric of cultural heritage value, or where it is necessary for conservation work, or where such fabric is about to be damaged or destroyed or made inaccessible. The extent of invasive investigation should minimise the disturbance of significant fabric.

只有在以下情况下才能对任何时期的遗产构造实施侵入性调查：知识的显著扩展、对建立文化遗产价值现存构造必不可缺或保护工作必不可缺的步骤，或结构被破坏、毁灭或难以进入。侵入性调查应将对重要建筑物的干预降到最小的程度。

8. Use

The conservation of a place of cultural heritage value is usually facilitated by the place serving a useful purpose.

8. 利用

对文化遗产地价值的利用通常会有益于对该场所保护。

Where the use of a place is integral to its cultural heritage value, that use should be retained.

当对场所的利用是遗产价值的一部分时，应该保留此使用方式。

Where a change of use is proposed, the new use should be compatible with the cultural heritage value of the place, and should have little or no adverse effect on the cultural heritage value.

改变使用方式时，新的使用方式应当与该遗址的文化遗产价值一致，且不会对文化遗产价值造成负面影响。

9. Setting

Where the setting of a place is integral to its cultural heritage value, that setting should be conserved with the place itself. If the setting no longer contributes to the cultural heritage value of

9．环境

当遗址环境与其文化遗产价值是一个整体时，应同遗址一起受到保护。如果环境不再见证文化遗产价值，且环境重建是合理的，那么环境的任何重建应该以对该文化遗产价值全面

the place, and if reconstruction of the setting can be justified, any reconstruction of the setting should be based on an understanding of all aspects of the cultural heritage value of the place.

理解的为基础。

10. Relocation

The on-going association of a structure or feature of cultural heritage value with its location, site, curtilage, and setting is essential to its authenticity and integrity. Therefore, a structure or feature of cultural heritage value should remain on its original site.

10. 迁址

拥有文化遗产价值建筑和结构与其位置、地点、庭院及环境间的持续联系，对保持真实性和完整性至关重要。因此，具有文化遗产价值的建筑和结构应当原址保留。

Relocation of a structure or feature of cultural heritage value, where its removal is required in order to clear its site for a different purpose or construction, or where its removal is required to enable its use on a different site, is not a desirable outcome and is not a conservation process.

具有文化遗产价值建筑和结构的迁址，或因其他目的、其他建设而清除或另迁他址，均不是令人满意的结果，也不是保护性措施。

In exceptional circumstances, a structure of cultural heritage value may be relocated if its current site is in imminent danger, and if all other means of retaining the structure in its current location have been exhausted. In this event, the new location should provide a setting compatible with the cultural heritage value of the structure.

特殊情况下，如果建筑和结构在原址面临迫在眉睫的危险，且所有的措施均已无法在原址保留原建筑，则该建筑物可能会被迁移。在此情况中，新的位置环境应当与文化遗产价值的建筑物原环境相匹配。

11. Documentation and archiving

The cultural heritage value and cultural heritage significance of a place, and all aspects of its conservation, should be fully documented to ensure that this information is available to present and future generations.

11. 文件档案和建档

应当全面记录文化遗产地价值和文化遗产重要性及其保护的所有方面，确保当代和后代可以获取此信息。

Documentation includes information about all changes to the place and any decisions made during the conservation process.

文件档案应记录场所的所有变化信息和保护过程中制订的各项决定。

Documentation should be carried out to archival standards to maximise the longevity of

应按照档案标准要求整理文件，以最大限度延长该记录的寿命，并将其储存在合适的档

the record, and should be placed in an appropriate archival repository.

案库内。

Documentation should be made available to connected people and other interested parties. Where reasons for confidentiality exist, such as security, privacy, or cultural appropriateness, some information may not always be publicly accessible.

文件档案应当向相关人士和其他有关各方开放查阅。因为机密性的原因，如安全性、隐私性或文化适宜度等，公众可能无法获取某些信息。

12. Recording

Evidence provided by the fabric of a place should be identified and understood through systematic research, recording, and analysis.

12. 记录

应当通过系统性调查、记录和分析，确定并理解场所建筑物所提供的证据。

Recording is an essential part of the physical investigation of a place. It informs and guides the conservation process and its planning. Systematic recording should occur prior to, during, and following any intervention. It should include the recording of new evidence revealed, and any fabric obscured or removed.

记录是场所实地调查至关重要的一部分，为保护过程和制定规划提供信息和指导。应当在干预实施之前、期间及其后进行系统性记录。该记录包括新发现的证据和任何结构的湮没或迁移。

Recording of the changes to a place should continue throughout its life.

场所变更记录应当贯穿始终。

13. Fixtures, fittings, and contents

Fixtures, fittings, and contents that are integral to the cultural heritage value of a place should be retained and conserved with the place. Such fixtures, fittings, and contents may include carving, painting, weaving, stained glass, wallpaper, surface decoration, works of art, equipment and machinery, furniture, and personal belongings.

13. 固定附着物、陈设品及内容

应当保留、保护那些能保持文化遗产价值完整性的固定装置、陈设品及内容。此类固定装置、陈设品及内容应包括雕刻品、绘画、编织物、彩色玻璃、墙纸、表面装饰、艺术品、设备和机械、家具以及私人物品。

Conservation of any such material should involve specialist conservation expertise appropriate to the material. Where it is necessary to remove any such material, it should be recorded, retained, and protected, until such time as it can be reinstated.

此类任何物品的保护应当使用适合该物品的专业保护技术和知识。如果需要移除此类物品时，应当对此进行记录、保存和保护，直到可以恢复为止。

Conservation processes and practice

14. Conservation plans

A conservation plan, based on the principles of this charter, should:

(i) be based on a comprehensive understanding of the cultural heritage value of the place and assessment of its cultural heritage significance;

(ii) include an assessment of the fabric of the place, and its condition;

(iii) give the highest priority to the authenticity and integrity of the place;

(iv) include the entirety of the place, including the setting;

(v) be prepared by objective professionals in appropriate disciplines;

(vi) consider the needs, abilities, and resources of connected people;

(vii) not be influenced by prior expectations of change or development;

(viii) specify conservation policies to guide decision making and to guide any work to be undertaken;

(ix) make recommendations for the conservation of the place; and

(x) be regularly revised and kept up to date.

15. Conservation projects

Conservation projects should include the following:

(i) consultation with interested parties and connected people, continuing throughout the project;

(ii) opportunities for interested parties and connected people to contribute to and participate in the project;

(iii) research into documentary and oral history, using all relevant sources and repositories of knowledge;

(iv) physical investigation of the place as

保护过程和实践

14. 保护规划

基于宪章原则的保护规划应：

（1）以综合理解文化遗产地价值和对其重要性的评估为基础；

（2）包括对结构及其状况的评估；

（3）优先保护该遗址的真实性和完整性；

（4）保护包括遗址周边环境在内的整体性；

（5）保护规划应由学科专业人员编写；

（6）考虑有关人士的需要、能力及资源；

（7）不会受到先前预期改变或发展的影响；

（8）详细说明保护政策以指导决策和即将开展的工作；

（9）为遗址保护提出意见；以及

（10）定期修订并更新。

15. 保护工程

保护工程应当包含下列内容：

（1）在工程的实施过程中，保持与相关利益团体和相关人士持续的磋商；

（2）让相关利益团体和相关人士有机会参与工程和为工程做贡献；

（3）利用所有相关来源和知识储备，研究纪录和口述历史；

（4）根据情况进行场所实地调查；

appropriate;

(v) use of all appropriate methods of recording, such as written, drawn, and photographic;

(vi) the preparation of a conservation plan which meets the principles of this charter;

(vii) guidance on appropriate use of the place;

(viii) the implementation of any planned conservation work;

(ix) the documentation of the conservation work as it proceeds; and

(x) where appropriate, the deposit of all records in an archival repository.

A conservation project must not be commenced until any required statutory authorisation has been granted.

16. Professional, trade, and craft skills

All aspects of conservation work should be planned, directed, supervised, and undertaken by people with appropriate conservation training and experience directly relevant to the project.

All conservation disciplines, arts, crafts, trades, and traditional skills and practices that are relevant to the project should be applied and promoted.

17. Degrees of intervention for conservation purposes

Following research, recording, assessment, and planning, intervention for conservation purposes may include, in increasing degrees of intervention:

(i) preservation, through stabilisation, maintenance, or repair;

(ii) restoration, through reassembly, reinstatement, or removal;

(iii) reconstruction; and

(iv) adaptation.

In many conservation projects a range of processes

（5）利用所有适当方法如书写、画图及摄影进行记录；

（6）制定符合本宪章原则的保护规划；

（7）指导合理利用遗址；

（8）有计划进行保护工作；

（9）进行保护工作时的文件记录；并且

（10）适时地将所有记录存入档案库。

只有获得了法定授权后，方可实施保护工程。

16. 专业，行业和工艺技能

保护工作的各个方面应由受到过相应保护项目培训的、有经验的人员进行规划、指导、监督并执行。

采用并推广与本项目有关的所有保护条例、艺术、工艺、技术以及传统技能和实践。

17. 以保护为目的的干预程度

以保护为目的的研究、记录、评估以及规划和干预可能包括：

（1）通过加固、维护或维修进行保护；

（2）通过修复、恢复或迁移进行重建；

（3）重建；以及

（4）改造。

在多个保护项目中，可以使用一系列的流

may be utilised. Where appropriate, conservation processes may be applied to individual parts or components of a place of cultural heritage value.

程。在合适的情况下，文物保护流程序可适用于具有地方文化价值的遗产的单元或部分。

The extent of any intervention for conservation purposes should be guided by the cultural heritage value of a place and the policies for its management as identified in a conservation plan. Any intervention which would reduce or compromise cultural heritage value is undesirable and should not occur.

任何以保护为目的进行的干预，其程度应以保护规划中确定的文化遗产地价值及其管理政策准则为指导。任何可能降低或危害文化遗产价值的干预都是不可取也不应该发生。

Preference should be given to the least degree of intervention, consistent with this charter.

根据本宪章，应该优先选择最低程度的干预。

Re-creation, meaning the conjectural reconstruction of a structure or place; replication, meaning to make a copy of an existing or former structure or place; or the construction of generalised representations of typical features or structures, are not conservation processes and are outside the scope of this charter.

再创造，指根据推测、探索重建一个建筑物或场所；复建，指复制一个现有的或以前的建筑物或场所或者典型特色或建筑物的概括性代表，这些均不是保护过程，因而不在本宪章范围内。

18. Preservation

Preservation of a place involves as little intervention as possible, to ensure its long-term survival and the continuation of its cultural heritage value.

18. 保存

场所的保存，应尽可能少的涉及干预，以确保其长期生存及文化遗产价值的延续。

Preservation processes should not obscure or remove the patina of age, particularly where it contributes to the authenticity and integrity of the place, or where it contributes to the structural stability of materials.

保护过程不应掩盖或消除岁月的印记，尤其是有助于保存遗址真实性和完整性的印记，或者有助于材料结构稳定性的印记。

i. Stabilisation

Processes of decay should be slowed by providing treatment or support.

1. 加固

提供处理或支持减缓衰变过程。

ii. Maintenance

A place of cultural heritage value should be maintained regularly. Maintenance should be carried out according to a plan or work programme.

2. 维护

定期维护有文化遗产价值的场所。应按照规划或工作计划进行维护。

iii. Repair

Repair of a place of cultural heritage value

3. 维修

文化价值的遗产地维修应使用匹配或类似

should utilise matching or similar materials. Where it is necessary to employ new materials, they should be distinguishable by experts, and should be documented.

材料。必须使用新材料时，该材料应得到专家的认可并详细记录。

Traditional methods and materials should be given preference in conservation work.

保护工作中应优先选择传统方法和材料。

Repair of a technically higher standard than that achieved with the existing materials or construction practices may be justified only where the stability or life expectancy of the site or material is increased, where the new material is compatible with the old, and where the cultural heritage value is not diminished.

只有在遗址或材料的稳定性或预期寿命增加、新材料与旧材料兼容以及文化遗产价值不减退时，才可恰当选择高于现有材料或施工实践标准的维修技术。

19. Restoration

The process of restoration typically involves reassembly and reinstatement, and may involve the removal of accretions that detract from the cultural heritage value of a place.

19. 修复

修复程序通常包括重新组装和复原，以及移除可能降低文化遗产价值的添加物。

Restoration is based on respect for existing fabric, and on the identification and analysis of all available evidence, so that the cultural heritage value of a place is recovered or revealed. Restoration should be carried out only if the cultural heritage value of the place is recovered or revealed by the process.

修复以尊重现有建筑物及对现有所有证据的识别和分析为基础，恢复或彰显遗址的文化遗产价值。只有在遗址的文化遗产价值通过修复程序得到恢复或彰显时，方可进行修复。

Restoration does not involve conjecture.

修复不可依靠推测。

i. Reassembly and reinstatement

Reassembly uses existing material and, through the process of reinstatement, returns it to its former position. Reassembly is more likely to involve work on part of a place rather than the whole place.

1. 重新组装和复原

重新组装是采用现有材料，并通过复原过程，将其恢复到原来的位置。进行重新组装工作只针对遗址的一部分而不是整个遗址。

ii. Removal

Occasionally, existing fabric may need to be

2. 移除

有时，需要将现有的建筑物从遗址永久性

permanently removed from a place. This may be for reasons of advanced decay, or loss of structural integrity, or because particular fabric has been identified in a conservation plan as detracting from the cultural heritage value of the place.

移除。这可能是因为后期衰变，或者是因结构失去完整性，或保护规划已经确定因该特定建筑物的存在降低了遗址整体的文化遗产价值。

The fabric removed should be systematically recorded before and during its removal. In some cases it may be appropriate to store, on a long-term basis, material of evidential value that has been removed.

建筑物移除之前以及移除期间，应进行系统性的记录。在有些情况下，应将已移除的具有客观依据价值的材料进行长期存储。

20. Reconstruction

Reconstruction is distinguished from restoration by the introduction of new material to replace material that has been lost.

20. 重建

重建有别于修复，是使用新材料替代已经遗失的材料。

Reconstruction is appropriate if it is essential to the function, integrity, intangible value, or understanding of a place, if sufficient physical and documentary evidence exists to minimise conjecture, and if surviving cultural heritage value is preserved.

如果对遗址的功能、完整性、无形价值有充分的了解或有足够的实物和文件证据支持，最少推测或尚存的文化遗产价值得到了保护，则适合重建。

Reconstructed elements should not usually constitute the majority of a place or structure.

重建元素不应成为遗址或建筑物组成的主体。

21. Adaptation

The conservation of a place of cultural heritage value is usually facilitated by the place serving a useful purpose. Proposals for adaptation of a place may arise from maintaining its continuing use, or from a proposed change of use.

21. 改造

文化遗产地价值保护通常促进遗产地利用。遗址改造的建议是为了能保持继续使用，或者是为了用于其他用途。

Alterations and additions may be acceptable where they are necessary for a compatible use of the place. Any change should be the minimum necessary, should be substantially reversible, and should have little or no adverse effect on the cultural heritage value of the place.

必要时可以接受改建和加建以便于利用遗址。但任何改变必须严格遵循最小干预、可逆的原则，并且对遗址的文化遗产价值很少或没有不利影响。

Any alterations or additions should be compatible with the original form and fabric of the place, and should avoid inappropriate or incompatible contrasts of form, scale, mass, colour, and material. Adaptation should not dominate or substantially obscure the original form and fabric, and should not adversely affect the setting of a place of cultural heritage value. New work should complement the original form and fabric.

任何改建以及加建应与场所的原始形式和构造相配，并且应避免不适当或不相容的形式，或使用形成强烈反差的形态、规模、质量、颜色以及材料。改造不应主宰或明显掩盖原始形式和构造，并且不应对具有文化遗产价值的环境产生不利影响。新的作品只应补充原来的形状和构造。

22. Non-intervention

In some circumstances, assessment of the cultural heritage value of a place may show that it is not desirable to undertake any conservation intervention at that time. This approach may be appropriate where undisturbed constancy of intangible values, such as the spiritual associations of a sacred place, may be more important than its physical attributes.

22. 不干预

在某些情况下，文化遗产地价值的评估结果可能是，不可进行任何文物保护干预。这种方法可能适用于无形价值的持续性不受干扰，例如与圣地的精神联系，比其物理属性更重要。

23. Interpretation

Interpretation actively enhances public understanding of all aspects of places of cultural heritage value and their conservation. Relevant cultural protocols are integral to that understanding, and should be identified and observed.

23. 阐释

阐释能有效地增强公众对文化遗产地价值及其保护的各个方面的了解。相关的文化规程也是阐释的一部分，需要了解，更需要认同和尊重。

Where appropriate, interpretation should assist the understanding of tangible and intangible values of a place which may not be readily perceived, such as the sequence of construction and change, and the meanings and associations of the place for connected people.

在适当情况下，阐释应帮助了解遗址的可能不容易被感知的有形和无形价值，如系列性的建设和变更，以及遗址对于相关人物的意义和关联。

Any interpretation should respect the cultural heritage value of a place. Interpretation methods should be appropriate to the place. Physical interventions for interpretation purposes should not detract from the experience of the place, and should not have an adverse effect on its tangible or intangible values.

任何阐释都应尊重文化遗产地价值。阐释的方式应与该遗址相适应。以阐释为目标的物理干预不得贬损对场所的感受，并且不应对其有形和无形价值产生负面影响。

24. Risk mitigation

Places of cultural heritage value may be vulnerable to natural disasters such as flood, storm, or earthquake; or to humanly induced threats and risks such as those arising from earthworks, subdivision and development, buildings works, or willful damage or neglect. In order to safeguard cultural heritage value, planning for risk mitigation and emergency management is necessary.

24. 减灾

文化遗产地可能会受到自然灾害如洪水、风暴或地震、人为造成的威胁和危险如土方工程、土分化和开发、建筑工程、故意破坏或忽视而造成的风险的损坏。为了维护文化遗产的价值，应制订减灾规划和应急管理规划。

Potential risks to any place of cultural heritage value should be assessed. Where appropriate, a risk mitigation plan, an emergency plan, and/or a protection plan should be prepared, and implemented as far as possible, with reference to a conservation plan.

应对文化遗产地存在的风险进行评估。在适当情况下应提前准备制订减灾计划、应急预案或保护方案，并尽可能参照保护规划实施保护。

Definitions

For the purposes of this charter:

Adaptation means the process(es) of modifying a place for a compatible use while retaining its cultural heritage value. Adaptation processes include alteration and addition.

定义

本章程的目的：

改造是指为兼容使用，改造某个地方并同时保持其文化遗产价值的过程。改造过程包括改建及加建。

Authenticity means the credibility or truthfulness of the surviving evidence and knowledge of the cultural heritage value of a place. Relevant evidence includes form and design, substance and fabric, technology and craftsmanship, location and surroundings, context and setting, use and function, traditions, spiritual essence, and sense of place, and includes tangible and intangible values. Assessment of authenticity is based on identification and analysis of relevant evidence and knowledge, and respect for its cultural context.

真实性是指一个文化遗产地价值尚存证据和知识的可信度或真实性。相关的证据，包括外形和设计、材质和建筑物、技术和工艺、位置和周围的环境、环境和背景、用途和功能、传统、精神实质和场所感，还包括有形和无形的价值。真实性的评估应建立在对有关证据、知识的鉴定和分析之上，以及尊重其文化背景、环境的基础之上。

Compatible use means a use which is consistent with the cultural heritage value of a place, and which has little or no adverse impact on its authenticity and integrity.

兼容使用是指该用途与文化遗产地价值一致，并对其真实性和完整性只有极少或没有不良影响。

Connected people means any groups, organisations, or individuals having a sense of association with or responsibility for a place of cultural heritage value.

相关人员是指与文化场所有关或对其有责任感的团体、组织或个人。

Conservation means all the processes of understanding and caring for a place so as to safeguard its cultural heritage value. Conservation is based on respect for the existing fabric, associations, meanings, and use of the place. It requires a cautious approach of doing as much work as necessary but as little as possible, and retaining authenticity and integrity, to ensure that the place and its values are passed on to future generations.

保护是指对一个场所的理解和爱护，以保障其文化遗产价值的所有过程。保护是建立在尊重现存建筑物、社会联系、价值以及对该场所的合理使用之上。应在尽可能地减少干预以保持其真实性和完整性基础上，谨慎实施保护工作，确保把该遗产及其价值传给后代。

Conservation plan means an objective report which documents the history, fabric, and cultural heritage value of a place, assesses its cultural heritage significance, describes the condition of the place, outlines conservation policies for managing the place, and makes recommendations for the conservation of the place.

保护规划是指一个客观的报告，该报告记录着某处遗产的历史、构成和文化遗产价值，评估文化遗产价值、描述该遗产的保存状况、概述遗产管理的保护政策，并对该遗产的保护提出建议。

Contents means moveable objects, collections, chattels, documents, works of art, and ephemera that are not fixed or fitted to a place, and which have been assessed as being integral to its cultural heritage value.

内容是指不固定或不适合固定的可移动的物品、藏品、动产、文件、艺术品，以及临时用品，经评估成为文化遗产价值不可或缺的组成部分。

Cultural heritage significance means the cultural heritage value of a place relative to other similar or comparable places, recognising the particular cultural context of the place.

文化遗产重要性是指相对于其他类似或同类遗址价值，认可该遗址特定的文化背景。

Cultural heritage value/s means possessing aesthetic, archaeological, architectural, commemorative, functional, historical, landscape, monumental, scientific, social, spiritual, symbolic, technological, traditional, or other tangible or intangible values, associated with human activity.

文化遗产价值是指具有美学的、考古的、建筑的、纪念性的、功能的、历史的、景观的、古迹的、科学的、社会的、精神的、象征性的、技术的、传统的，或其他与人类活动有关的有形和无形价值。

Cultural landscapes means an area possessing cultural heritage value arising from the relationships between people and the environment. Cultural landscapes may have been designed, such as gardens, or may have evolved from human settlement and land use over time, resulting in a diversity of distinctive landscapes in different areas. Associative cultural landscapes, such as sacred mountains, may lack tangible cultural elements but may have strong intangible cultural or spiritual associations.

文化景观是指因人与环境之间关系而产生的、具有文化遗产价值的区域。文化景观可以有所设计，如花园，也可以是不同时期的人类因居住和对土地的不同使用形式，形成的不同地区、独特的景观多样性，如圣山，可能缺乏有形的文化元素，但却有着强大的无形的文化或精神联系。

Documentation means collecting, recording, keeping, and managing information about a place and its cultural heritage value, including information about its history, fabric, and meaning; information about decisions taken; and information about physical changes and interventions made to the place.

档案是指有关文化遗产地及其价值的信息的收集、记录、保管和管理，包括它的历史、构成和价值；有关管理决策的信息；以及有关文化遗址的物理变化和外界干预等信息。

Fabric means all the physical material of a place, including subsurface material, structures, and interior and exterior surfaces including the patina of age; and including fixtures and fittings, and gardens and plantings.

构成是指某遗址所拥有的有形物质，包括地下材料、建筑物、内部和外部表面的岁月印记；还包括固定装置和配件、花园和植被。

Hapu means a section of a large tribe of the tangata whenua.

Hapu 是指唐加塔环努瓦（大地之子）大部落的一部分。

Intangible value means the abstract cultural heritage value of the meanings or associations of a place, including commemorative, historical, social, spiritual, symbolic, or traditional values.

无形价值是指与某遗址有关联含义的、抽象的文化遗产价值，包括纪念性的、历史的、社会的，精神的、象征性的或传统的价值。

Integrity means the wholeness or intactness of a place, including its meaning and sense of place, and all the tangible and intangible attributes and elements necessary to express its cultural heritage value.

完整性是指场所的整体性和完好性，包括其含义和场所精神以及所有表达文化遗产价值的有形和无形属性的必要元素。

Intervention means any activity that causes disturbance of or alteration to a place or its fabric. Intervention includes archaeological excavation,

干预是指造成干扰或改变场所或建筑物的所有活动。干预包括考古发掘、对建筑结构的侵入性调查、和任何违反保护目的的干预。

invasive investigation of built structures, and any intervention for conservation purposes.

Iwi means a tribe of the tangata whenua.

Iwi 是指唐加塔环努瓦（大地之子）的一个部落。

Kaitiakitanga means the duty of customary trusteeship, stewardship, guardianship, and protection of land, resources, or taonga.

环境守护是指按惯例进行托管、管理、监护的责任，保护土地、资源或珍贵文物。

Maintenance means regular and on-going protective care of a place to prevent deterioration and to retain its cultural heritage value.

维护是指对场所实施定期和持续的保护，防止其退化，保留其文化遗产价值。

Matauranga means traditional or cultural knowledge of the tangata whenua.

Matauranga 是指唐加塔环努瓦（大地之子）的传统或文化知识。

Non-intervention means to choose not to undertake any activity that causes disturbance of or alteration to a place or its fabric.

不干涉是指选择不进行任何活动，以免对某场所或其建筑造成干扰或改变。

Place means any land having cultural heritage value in New Zealand, including areas; cultural landscapes; buildings, structures, and monuments; groups of buildings, structures, or monuments; gardens and plantings; archaeological sites and features; traditional sites; sacred places; townscapes and streetscapes; and settlements. Place may also include land covered by water, and any body of water. Place includes the setting of any such place.

场所是指新西兰任何有文化遗产价值的土地，包括以下区域：文化景观、房屋、建筑物、纪念碑、房屋群、建筑群或纪念碑群、花园及其植被、考古遗址和标志、传统保留地、圣地、城镇景观和街景以及定居点。场所可能还包括被水覆盖的土地和水域。场所包括所有古迹所处的环境。

Preservation means to maintain a place with as little change as possible.

保存是指以尽可能少的变化来维护一处场所。

Reassembly means to put existing but disarticulated parts of a structure back together.

重新组装是指将某建筑里原有的、现已脱落损坏的部分重新组装到该建筑中。

Reconstruction means to build again as closely as possible to a documented earlier form, using new materials.

重建是指使用新材料尽可能地按照早期记录的样式重新修建。

Recording means the process of capturing information and creating an archival record of the fabric and setting of a place, including its configuration, condition, use, and change over time.

记录是指撷取信息并创建档案，以记载一处建筑或场所环境包括配置、条件、利用的长期变化。

Reinstatement means to put material components of a place, including the products of reassembly, back in position.

复原是指把一处遗迹的原有材料组件，包括重新组装的成品，放到原位置。

Repair means to make good decayed or damaged fabric using identical, closely similar, or otherwise appropriate material.

修理是指使用相同、相似，或者合适材料，对腐朽的或损坏的建筑予以修补。

Restoration means to return a place to a known earlier form, by reassembly and reinstatement, and/or by removal of elements that detract from its cultural heritage value.

修复是指按已知的早期形式，重新组装和复原一处场所，或删除其中减损场所文化遗产价值的元素。

Setting means the area around and/or adjacent to a place of cultural heritage value that is integral to its function, meaning, and relationships. Setting includes the structures, outbuildings, features, gardens, curtilage, airspace, and access ways forming the spatial context of the place or used in association with the place. Setting also includes cultural landscapes, townscapes, and streetscape; perspectives, views, and view shafts to and from a place; and relationships with other places which contribute to the cultural heritage value of the place. Setting may extend beyond the area defined by legal title, and may include a buffer zone necessary for the long-term protection of the cultural heritage value of the place.

环境是指场所周围或毗邻文物古迹区、并在功能、意义和关系上与该场所形成一个整体区域。环境包括形成场所的空间背景或服务于此遗迹的建筑物、附属建筑、功能区、园林、庭院、领空、过道等。环境还包括文化景观、城镇景观和街景、视角、视轴或两处遗址间互相的双向的观光视野；能促进一处文化遗产地与其他遗迹的价值关系。环境可能超越行政管理划定的监管区域，并且可能包括一个为长期保护该地区文化遗产价值所必需的缓冲区。

Stabilisation means the arrest or slowing of the processes of decay.

稳定指停滞或减缓遗产的衰落过程。

Structure means any building, standing remains, equipment, device, or other facility made by people and which is fixed to the land.

建筑物指任何建筑、直立的遗存、设备、装置或固定在该场所的人工设施。

Tangata whenua means generally the original indigenous inhabitants of the land; and means specifically the people exercising kaitiakitanga over particular land, resources, or taonga.

唐加塔环努瓦（大地之子）广义上指在土地上生活的原始土著居民；尤其指护卫特定土地、资源或珍贵之物的人。

Tangible value means the physically observable cultural heritage value of a place, including archaeological, architectural, landscape, monumental, scientific, or technological values.

有形价值指场所中肉眼可见的、有实体的文化遗产价值，包括考古学的、建筑学的、自然景观的、纪念碑式的、科学的或者技术的价值。

Taonga means anything highly prized for its cultural, economic, historical, spiritual, or traditional value, including land and natural and cultural resources.

珍贵之物指任何因场所文化、经济、历史、精神或者传统价值而被推崇的事物，包括土地、自然和文化资源。

Tino rangatiratanga means the exercise of full chieftainship, authority, and responsibility.

酋长制指酋长的地位、权威、职责。

Use means the functions of a place, and the activities and practices that may occur at the place. The functions, activities, and practices may in themselves be of cultural heritage value.

用途指某处场所的功用，以及在此处场所中有可能进行的活动或实践。这些功能、活动和实践本身就具有文化遗产价值。

Whanau means an extended family which is part of a hapu or iwi.

家庭（Whanau）指从（毛利社会）hapu 或 iwi 次部落分离的大家庭。

ISBN 978-0-473-17116-2 (PDF)
English language text first published 1993
Bilingual text first published 1995

ISBN 978–0–473–17116–2 (PDF)
1993 年首次出版英语版
1995 年首次出版双语版

This revised text replaces the 1993 and 1995 versions and should be referenced as the ICOMOS New Zealand Charter for the Conservation of Places of Cultural Heritage Value (ICOMOS New Zealand Charter 2010).

此修订版本将替代 1993 年和 1995 年的版本，并且应作为新西兰国际古迹遗址理事会文物古迹保护章程供参阅（新西兰国际古迹遗址理事会章程 2010）。

This revision incorporates changes in conservation philosophy and best practice since 1993 and is the only version of the ICOMOS New Zealand Charter approved by ICOMOS New Zealand (Inc.) for use.

Copies of this charter may be obtained from
ICOMOS NZ (Inc.)
P O Box 90 851
Victoria Street West,
Auckland 1142,
New Zealand.

此版本包含了保护理念上的变化和自 1993 年以来的最佳实践，并且还是经新西兰国际古迹遗址理事会有限公司获得准许使用的国际古迹遗址理事会新西兰国家委员会章程的唯一版本。

本宪章版权持有
新西兰奥克兰市
维多利亚西大街 1142 号
新西兰国际古迹遗址理事会有限公司
邮箱：90 851

联合国教科文组织、国际文物保护与修复研究中心、国际古迹遗址理事会、世界自然保护联盟《世界遗产灾害风险管理》
UNESCO/ICCROM/ICOMOS/IUCN《Managing Disaster Risks for World Heritage》

Managing Disaster Risks for World Heritage
UNESCO
ICCROM
ICOMOS
IUCN

世界遗产灾害风险管理
联合国教科文组织、国际文物保护与修复研究中心、国际古迹遗址理事会、世界自然保护联盟

Original title: Managing Disaster Risks for World Heritage

原名：世界遗产灾害风险管理

Published in June 2010 by the United Nations Educational, Scientific and Cultural Organization.

联合国教科文组织，2010 年 6 月出版

About the World Heritage Resource Manual Series

关于世界遗产资源手册系列丛书

Since *the World Heritage Convention* was

自 1972 年《世界遗产公约》公布后，世界

adopted in 1972, the World Heritage List has continually evolved and is growing steadily. With this growth, a critical need has emerged for guidance for States Parties on the implementation of *the Convention.* Various expert meetings and results of Periodic Reporting have identified the need for more focused training and capacity development in specific areas where States Parties and World Heritage site managers require greater support. The development of a series of World Heritage Resource Manuals is a response to this need.

遗产名录逐渐形成并稳定增长。随着世界遗产名录中遗产数目逐渐增多，缔约国认为需要编制操作手册来确保公约的实施。各类专家会议和定期报告的结论也认为应关注特殊区域，即需要国际大力支持或世界遗产管理者能力需要培养的缔约国。世界遗产资源手册系列丛书正是为了满足这些需求。

The publication of the series is a joint undertaking by the three Advisory Bodies of the World Heritage Convention (ICCROM, ICOMOS and IUCN) and the UNESCO World Heritage Centre as the Secretariat of the Convention. The World Heritage Committee at its 30th session (Vilnius, Lithuania, July 2006) supported this initiative and requested that the Advisory Bodies and the World Heritage Centre proceed with the preparation and publication of a number of thematic Resource Manuals. The 31st (2007) and 32nd (2008) sessions of the Committee adopted the publication plan and determined a prioritized list of titles.

这一套丛书的编写由国际文物保护修复中心、国际古迹遗址理事会、世界自然遗产保护联盟等三个世界遗产委员会的顾问委员会及作为公约秘书处的联合国教科文组织世界遗产中心共同编写。世界遗产委员会在其第 30 届大会上（维尔纽斯，立陶宛共和国，2006）支持了这一动议，要求这些顾问委员会和世界遗产中心着手编制这套丛书，并按照不同的主题形成资源手册予以出版。在第 31 届（2007 年）和第 32 届（2008 年）大会上，委员会确定了出版计划并决定了系列丛书的出版顺序。

An Editorial Board consisting of members of all three Advisory Bodies and the World Heritage Centre meets regularly to decide on different aspects of their preparation and publication. For each manual, depending on the theme, one of the Advisory Bodies or the World Heritage Centre functions as the lead agency responsible for coordination, while the final production is ensured by the World Heritage Centre.

编委会成员由三个顾问委员会和世界遗产中心共同组成，编委会定期组织会议研究丛书在编制和出版过程中遇到的不同问题。对于每一部手册，根据主题不同，将由不同的顾问委员会或世界遗产中心承担领导机构的职责，负责各种协调的工作，当然，最终成果的管理权属于世界遗产中心。

The Resource Manuals are intended to provide focused guidance on the implementation of the Convention to States Parties, heritage protection authorities, local governments, site managers and local communities linked to World Heritage sites, as

编制资源手册丛书是为了给公约缔约国、遗产管理机构、当地政府、遗产管理者、与世界遗产相关的当地社区、其他在保护过程中确定的利益相关者在使用手册时提供集中的指导。本丛书希望为保护和有效管理具有代表性和可

well as other stakeholders in the identification and preservation process. They aim to provide knowledge and assistance in ensuring a representative and credible World Heritage List consisting of well-protected and effectively managed properties.

信性的世界遗产名录中遗产，提供知识和协助。

The manuals are being developed as user-friendly tools for capacity-building and awareness raising on the *World Heritage Convention.* They can be used independently for self-guided learning as well as material at training workshops, and should complement the basic provisions for understanding the text of *the Convention* itself and *the Operational Guidelines for implementation.*

这些手册将成为世界遗产中心进行能力建设和意识提升的有益工具。他们可以作为自学教材独立使用，同时也可以成为培训班的主要教材。这些教材可以使学习者能更好地理解《世界遗产公约》的主要内容以及掌握如何使用《世界遗产公约操作指南》。

The titles in this series are produced as PDF online documents which can be freely downloaded and are also available on CD-ROM.

本系列丛书将以 PDF 的形式作为网络资源，可免费下载。

List of titles:

Managing Disaster Risks for World Heritage (June 2010)

Preparing World Heritage Nominations (November 2011)

Managing Cultural World Heritage Properties (scheduled for mid-2012)

Managing Natural World Heritage Properties (scheduled for late 2012)

丛书包括：

《世界遗产灾害风险管理手册》（2010 年 6 月）

《世界遗产申报准备工作手册》（2011 年 11 月）

《世界文化遗产管理手册》（计划 2012 年中期）

《世界自然遗产管理手册》（计划 2012 年末期）

Foreword

As confirmed by the 2009 *Global Assessment Report on Disaster Risk Reduction, Risk and Poverty in a Changing Climate* (UNISDR, 2009), the number of disasters around the world increases every year. To a great extent this is due to growing exposure in terms of people and assets, in turn caused by rapid economic development and urban growth in cyclone coastal areas and earthquake-prone cities, combined with poor governance and

序

《2009 全球灾害风险减灾评估报告》、《气候变化造成的风险和贫困》（联合国国际减灾署，2009）提到近几年世界灾害逐年递增。逐年递增的灾害，在很大程度上，是因为人口和资源需求的增长、沿海地区和易发生地震地区快速的经济增长和城市化进程、再加上缺乏管理和逐渐恶化的生态环境。与此同时，气候变化伴随着频繁发生的极端天气现象在世界各地均有发生。当今，灾害成为贫困的主要原因之一，特

the decline of ecosystems. At the same time, climate change has been associated with the occurrence of more frequent and intense extreme weather events in some parts of the world. Disasters are today considered as one of the main factors contributing to poverty, especially in developing regions.

别是发展中地区。

Although heritage is usually not taken into account in global statistics concerning disaster risks, cultural and natural properties are increasingly affected by events which are less and less 'natural' in their dynamics, if not in their cause. The progressive loss of these properties as a result of floods, mudslides, fire, earthquakes, civil unrest and other hazards has become a major concern, partly because of the significant role that heritage plays in contributing to social cohesion and sustainable development, particularly at times of stress.

尽管在全球灾害威胁统计中还没有涉及遗产，但自然和文化遗产受到日益增长的、越来越不“自然”的事件的影响。影响遗产安全的灾害主要包括洪水、泥石流、火灾、地震、国内动乱和其他灾害。由于遗产在社会凝聚力和社会可持续发展中有极为重要的作用，因此对遗产的危害应该受到关注。

In the face of these challenges, the number of World Heritage properties that have developed a proper disaster risk reduction plan is surprisingly low. This is often due to a series of misperceptions. On the one hand, there is a widespread belief that disasters are events beyond human will and control, against which little can be done. On the other hand, heritage managers and policy-makers tend to concentrate their attention and resources on what they perceive as the real priorities for their properties, i.e. pressure from development and the daily wear and tear of sites as a result of slow, cumulative processes that can be 'seen'. Finally, and somewhat ironically, the vulnerability of heritage properties to disasters is normally recognized after a catastrophic event has taken place — including by the media and donor community — when it is often too late.

在面对这些挑战时，已经完成减灾规划的世界遗产少之又少。这常常是因为一系列的错觉。一方面，他们深信灾害是不受人类意愿和控制的事情，对于灾害我们能做的很少。另一方面，遗产管理和决策者趋向于把他们的经费和注意力放在他们认为应该优先处理的事情上，比如发展的压力和遗产的日常维持上，因为这些缓慢和累积的过程是可以“看到”的。最后，有点讽刺的是，遗产在灾害中的脆弱性通常是在灾害发生后才被媒体和捐助团体认识到，但为时已晚。

The reality, of course, is different. Disasters are the combined product of hazards and vulnerabilities

现实很残酷。灾害是内在的相关危害因素及复杂的缺陷相互作用的综合产物，多数不受

resulting from the complex interaction of numerous interlocking factors, many of which are very much within human control. It is therefore possible to prevent them, or at least considerably reduce their effects, by strengthening the resilience of the assets to be safeguarded. In general, moreover, the impact of a single disaster on cultural and natural properties far outstrips the deterioration caused by long-term, progressive decay and may sometimes lead to their complete obliteration. Often, therefore, disaster risks constitute the most urgent priority that heritage managers should address.

人类控制。当然通过加强遗产的自身恢复力，有可能阻止、至少减少灾害的影响，从而确保遗产安全。一般而言，单一灾害对于文化和自然遗产的破坏，远远超过了长期、持续的腐蚀过程，甚至会完全破坏遗产。因此，灾害风险是遗产管理者应该考虑的最急迫、最优先的管理事件。

An additional commonplace is the idea that heritage, in particular cultural heritage, would constitute a liability in the face of disaster, either because it requires efforts and resources for its protection — at a time when attention should be devoted to saving lives and properties — or because it adds to the risk, especially within traditional settlements where buildings do not conform to modern engineering standards of safety. Experience shows, on the contrary, that heritage if well maintained can positively contribute to reducing disaster risks. This is true not only for natural heritage resources that guarantee the proper functioning of ecosystems and the beneficial effect of their goods and services, but also for cultural heritage properties that — as a result of traditional knowledge accumulated over centuries — have proved to be resilient to disasters while providing shelter and psychological support to affected communities.

此外，遗产，特别是文化遗产，要承担面对灾害的责任，因为需要付出努力和资金来保护它——拯救生命和财产为重——特别是传统民居，因其建筑不符合现代工程的安全标准，也增加了风险。经验告诉我们，如果遗产得到很好的维护，会起到减少灾害风险的作用。这是真的，不仅因为自然遗产资源能保证生态系统功能的正常运作，保证他们服务和产品的有效成果，也因为对于文化遗产——作为世代知识积累的产物——在抵御灾害同时能够为受影响社区提供避难所和精神支持。

Recognizing these challenges, this Resource Manual prepared as part of the new World Heritage Resource Manual Series by ICCROM in collaboration with the World Heritage Centre, ICOMOS and IUCN, aims to raise the awareness of World Heritage managers and administrators of the real extent of risks associated with disasters. More importantly,

本手册是由世界遗产中心、国际古迹遗址理事会和世界自然保护联盟联合编撰的系列手册丛书中的一本，目的是让世界遗产的管理者和政府官员，在承认这些挑战基础上，真正考虑灾害风险的程度。更重要的是，从保护遗产及其作用的角度为他们提供了定义、评估和减少这些风险的、可行的方法论——充分发挥潜

it provides them with a sound methodology for identifying, assessing and then reducing these risks, with a view to preserving their heritage and ensuring that it contributes – to its full potential — to the sustainable development of their communities.

力——为社区的可持续发展。

It is hoped that this manual, used in combination with training programmes, may help to achieve the much-needed shift in attitudes that would finally lead to the building of a true culture of prevention within the heritage community, while assisting in the urgent need to prepare World Heritage properties for future disasters. As challenging as this may appear, the alternative is often the loss of our precious heritage or — where possible — long and hugely expensive reconstruction.

本手册可用于培训项目，也能帮助实现观念的迅速转变，从而最终在遗产社区中形成真正的文化防范，同时协助世界遗产形成应对灾害的能力。挑战已经出现，我们的选择常常是放弃我们珍贵的遗产——或可能的话——长期的、斥巨资的重建。

The World Heritage Centre would like to express its gratitude to ICCROM for taking the lead in this important publication, as well as to ICOMOS and IUCN for their significant contributions.

世界遗产中心在此衷心感谢在出版过程国际文物保护与修复中心所付出的努力，同时也要对国际古迹遗址理事会和世界自然保护联盟的重要贡献表达谢意。

Francesco Bandarin
Director, UNESCO World Heritage Centre

联合国教科文组织世界遗产中心主任
佛朗西斯科·邦德林

1.What is Disaster Risk Management and why is it important?

2. What does a DRM plan consist of?

3. How do you get started?

4. How do you identify and assess disaster risks?

5. How can you prevent disaster risks or mitigate their impact?

6. How do you prepare for and respond to emergencies?

7. How do you recover and rehabilitate your property after a disaster?

8. How to implement, reassess and reappraise the DRM plan?

1. 什么是灾害风险管理，为什么它如此重要？

2. 灾害风险管理规划由哪儿部分组成？

3. 从哪里入手？

4. 如何认定和评估灾害风险？

5. 如何阻止灾害风险发生或减缓灾害的影响？

6. 如何准备和应对紧急情况？

7. 灾后如何实现遗产的恢复和复原？

8. 如何实施、再评价和再评估灾害风险管理规划？

Appendix I. Glossary of relevant disaster management terms

附件 1. 与灾害管理有关的词汇表

Appendix II. Typology of hazards

Appendix III. Relevant charters and recommendations

Appendix IV. International organizations and research institutions

Appendix V. Key references and publications

附件 2. 灾害的类型

附件 3. 相关的宪章和建议

附件 4. 国际组织和研究机构

附件 5. 主要参考文献和出版物

Introduction

How this Resource Manual can help you with Disaster Risk Management

介绍

这个资源手册如何帮助你实现灾害风险管理

What are the key objectives of the Resource Manual?

资源手册的主要宗旨是什么？

• To help the managers and management authorities of cultural and natural World Heritage properties to reduce the risks to these properties from natural and human made disasters, as emphasized by the World Heritage Committee at its 2006 session (UNESCO / WHC, 2006, Section A.5, para. 19).

• To illustrate the main principles of Disaster Risk Management (DRM) for heritage and a methodology to identify, assess and mitigate disaster risks.

• To explain how to prepare a DRM plan based on this methodology.

• To demonstrate that heritage can play a positive role in reducing risks from disasters and so help to justify the conservation of World Heritage properties.

• To suggest how DRM plans for heritage properties can be integrated with national and regional disaster management strategies and plans.

• 帮助世界文化和自然遗产管理者、管理机构，降低遗产遭受自然和人为灾害的风险，这一点在世界遗产委员 2006 年大会中予以强调（UNESCO / WHC, 2006, 第 A.5 部分，第 19 段）。

• 阐释对于遗产灾害风险管理的主要原则，介绍界定、评估和削弱灾害风险的方法。

• 解释如何用以上方法准备一个灾害风险管理规划。

• 证明遗产在降低灾害风险中所发挥的积极作用，帮助证明世界遗产保护的合法性。

• 建议遗产地灾害风险规划如何与国家和地区灾害管理战略或规划衔接。

Who is the target audience?

The manual is primarily aimed at site managers, management teams and the agencies and organizations that have a direct stake in the management of a heritage property. It can also be adapted and applied by other stakeholders, depending on their mandate

目标受众是谁？

本手册的主要受众是直接负责遗产管理的遗址管理者、管理团队、机构和组织。本手册也适合其他利益相关者阅读。

and responsibilities.

What is the scope of the manual?

The manual focuses on one approach to the principles, methodology and process for managing disaster risks at cultural and natural World Heritage properties.

Considering the great variety of types of property, and many possible disaster risks, it does not attempt to be comprehensive. Disasters may result from various kinds of hazard, either natural in origin such as earthquakes and cyclones, or human-induced such as fire caused by arson, vandalism, armed conflicts or disease epidemics. The focus is on sudden catastrophic events rather than gradual, cumulative processes that can have an impact on heritage properties, such as erosion, mass tourism, drought or the spread of invasive species. Furthermore, specific technical and operational aspects (for example, how to strengthen a masonry structure against the risk from earthquake or how to set up early warning systems for a tsunami) are not covered.

The manual is concerned with planning for Disaster Risk Management at cultural heritage properties. It does not attempt to develop a general theory of cultural heritage DRM. Drawing mainly upon the available sources and published literature on DRM, it has been prepared by cultural heritage experts with some contribution from experts in the conservation of natural heritage.

How is the manual organized?

The manual is structured as a series of questions that the user might ask about preparing a DRM plan. The questions are answered by reference to a single, coherent approach to the principles, methodology and process for managing disaster risks at heritage properties. The first three sections (1 to 3) explain why DRM plans are necessary, how

手册的范围是什么？

本手册关注世界文化和自然遗产的灾害风险管理的准则、方法和过程。

考虑到遗产类型的多样性，本手册并不准备囊括全部、多种可能的灾害风险。灾害源于各种各样的灾害，既有自然的，如地震、台风，也有人为的，如因纵火而引起的火灾、恶意破坏、军事冲突和疾病流行等等。本手册是关于突然发生的灾害事件，而不是能影响遗产安全的渐进、累积过程如腐蚀、大规模的旅游、干旱或种群入侵。另外，特定的技术和操作要素（例如如何加强砖石结构抵御地震的威胁或如何建立早期的海啸预警体系）不在本手册研究范围内。

本手册注重文化遗产的灾害风险管理规划。但其目的不是发展有关文化遗产灾害风险管理的一般性理论。本手册的编写主要依赖于灾害风险管理方面现有的可用资源和已出版的文献资料。本手册由文化遗产保护专家及自然遗产保护专家共同编写。

本手册的组织结构

本手册罗列了在准备灾害风险管理规划时可能提出的系列问题，并采取将准则、方法论和灾害风险管理过程相结合的方法，逐一回答这些问题。前三章（1–3）解释了为什么需要灾害风险管理规划，它与其他管理规划如何衔接，在准备的过程中哪些人应该参与。

they relate to other management plans, and who should be involved in preparing them.

Each of the following sections (4 to 8) focuses on one step in the process of preparing a DRM plan. Throughout the manual, methodological principles are illustrated by case studies. These examples are drawn from the experience of a wide range of disaster risks, on the one hand, and from a wide range of World Heritage property types, on the other.

接下来的几章（4–8），每一章关注准备灾害风险管理规则中的一个步骤。本手册通过案例讲述了方法论原理。这些案例是从各种灾害风险实践中挑选出来的，同时也考虑到了世界遗产的不同类型。

The appendices provide a glossary of DRM terms, a typology of common hazards, and lists of relevant organizations, sources and publications useful for further reading.

附件中提供了灾害风险管理专业术语词汇表，一般灾害的类型，并列举了相关的组织、资源和出版物，为进一步了解灾害风险管理提供更多资料。

1 What is Disaster Risk Management and why is it important?

1　什么是灾害风险管理，为什么它如此重要?

1.1 Why should World Heritage site managers be concerned with DRM?

• World Heritage properties are important for national and community pride and for social cohesion. Under *the World Heritage Convention,* the States Parties sign up to the obligation of preserving World Heritage properties for future generations. Therefore managers of these properties are responsible for protecting their outstanding universal value.

• Disasters do happen, therefore it is best to be prepared to manage these unavoidable events.

• In times of disaster, an effective DRM plan can help to support vulnerable communities by preserving their heritage.

• Cultural and natural heritage can itself contribute towards reducing the effects of disasters in various ways; for example, the traditional knowledge systems embodied in physical planning and construction, local management systems and ecology, can not only prevent or mitigate the impact of disasters but also provide sufficient coping

1.1　为什么世界遗产的管理者要关注灾害风险管理？

• 世界遗产是国家和社区的骄傲，也是社区凝聚力所在，因而显得十分重要。签订《世界遗产公约》的缔约国负有保护世界遗产的责任。因此，遗产管理者有保护遗产突出普遍价值的责任。

• 当灾害发生的时候，要准备好应对不可避免事件的发生。

• 灾害发生时，有效的灾害风险管理规划将帮助那些脆弱的社区保护他们的遗产。

• 文化和自然遗产可通过各种方式降低灾害对自身的影响；例如，蕴含环境形态的规划和建筑、传统管理体系、传统社会生态学的知识体系，不仅能够防止或削弱灾害的影响，同时也能提供有效的应对机制来处理灾后状况。文化遗产在紧急情况发生后可以成为周边社区的避难港湾。

mechanisms to deal with post-disaster situations. Cultural properties can serve as safe havens for surrounding communities for their temporary relocation during emergencies.

• Earthquakes, floods, oil spills, conflict and the outbreak of disease cannot be entirely prevented but mitigation measures can effectively reduce the risk that these can present.

• 即使不能够完全阻止地震、洪水、原油泄漏、冲突和疾病的爆发，也可通过缓解措施有效的降低风险。

• Disasters can have great financial consequences: it is much more cost-effective to invest in preventive risk management planning before disaster has struck than to spend large amounts in post-disaster recovery and rehabilitation (the World Heritage Fund has only limited emergency funding available). Reducing the risk is the most effective management approach.

• 灾害对金融会有很大的影响：在灾害发生前，用于防范风险管理规划的投资，比花费大量经费用于灾后重建和修复更符合成本效益原则（世界遗产基金的应急资金份额很小）。降低风险是管理的最有效方法。

As a number of key concepts (e.g. disaster, hazard, risk) have now been introduced, the next subsection helps to define their correct usage. See also definitions in the glossary (Appendix I).

为便于正确使用一些关键概念（例如，灾害、危害、风险），下面几小结将对概念进行介绍，见词汇表中定义介绍（见附件 1）。

1.2 What is a disaster?

1.2 什么是灾害

• Disaster is defined as a serious disruption of the functioning of a community or a society causing widespread human, material, economic or environmental losses which exceeds the ability of the affected community or society to cope using its own resources (UNISDR, 2002). In this manual the definition of a disaster is extended to include its impact not only on people and property but also on the heritage values of the World Heritage property and, where relevant, its ecosystems.

• 灾害是对社区或社会功能一系列严重的破坏，它造成人类、物质、经济或环境的损失，这些损失超过了受影响社区或社会自身资源的应对能力（联合国减灾署，2002）。本手册扩展了灾害的定义，它不仅包括对人类和财产产生影响，同时也包括对世界遗产的价值及与之相关的生态系统产生影响。

• Disaster risk is a product of hazard and vulnerability. While a hazard is a phenomenon (such as an earthquake or a cyclone) which has the potential to cause disruption or damage to cultural property, vulnerability is the susceptibility or exposure of cultural property to the hazard. Whereas a hazard is the external source of a disaster,

• 灾害风险产生于潜在性和脆弱性。潜在性是指文化遗产具有遭受潜在破坏或损坏的现象（比如地震或台风），脆弱性是指文化遗产的敏感性或被暴露于自然灾害中。危害是引起灾害的外部原因，而脆弱性则是遗产自身的缺陷（与位置或具体特性有关）。必须记住危害能够引发灾害，如地震，但他们本身不是灾害（见附

vulnerability is the inherent weakness of the heritage property (due to its location or its specific characteristics). It is important to bear in mind that hazards such as earthquakes can trigger disasters although they are not disasters in themselves. (See Appendix I for definitions of these and other relevant disaster management terms.)

件 1 对于概念的定义以及其他相关的灾害管理术语）。

It is very often apparent whether a hazard is natural or human-induced, for example in the case of hurricanes or armed conflicts. However, even so-called 'natural' disasters are often the result of underlying factors resulting from human activities, such as building in flood prone areas, felling trees, or erecting non-engineered structures with no consideration for safety norms.

自然和人为的危害很容易区分，例如飓风和武力冲突。然而，即使是“自然”灾害可能也是某些人类活动所引起的，例如洪水易发区的建筑、砍伐树木或忽视安全规范搭建的非工程建筑等等。

1.3 What are the main types of hazard that may cause disasters?

1.3 哪些类型的危害能够引起灾害？

The following are some of the most common hazards that may lead to a disaster (WMO;ICSU, 2007):

- meteorological: hurricanes, tornadoes, heat-waves, lightning, fire;
- hydrological: floods, flash-floods, tsunamis;
- geological: volcanoes, earthquakes, mass movement (falls, slides, slumps);
- astrophysical: meteorites;
- biological: epidemics, pests;
- human-induced: armed conflict, fire, pollution, infrastructure failure or collapse, civil unrest and terrorism;
- climate change: increased storm frequency and severity, glacial lake outburst floods (GLOFs).

下面是可能引起灾害的最常见的危害类型（世界气象组织；国际科学理事会 2007）：

- 气象的：飓风、龙卷风、热浪、闪电、火；
- 水文的：洪水、骤发洪水、海啸；
- 地质的：火山、地震、地块运动（下沉、滑动、下滑）；
- 天体物理的：陨石；
- 生物的：传染病、害虫；
- 人类导致的：武力冲突、火灾、污染、基础设施故障或倾塌、国内动荡和恐怖行动；
- 天气变化：频繁而强烈的暴风雨及冰湖溃洪等。

Table 1 shows examples of the relationships and possible combined effect of natural and human-induced hazards.

图表 1 列出了自然灾害和人类导致灾害之间的关系以及他们联合作用的结果。

For a more comprehensive typology of hazards, see Appendix II.

更为复杂的灾害类型见附件 II。

Table 1. ***Relationships of natural hazards and human-induced hazards***

	Natural	Human-induced	Indirect / secondary
Meteorological	Hurricane Lightning Heavy precipitation		Flooding (coastal / rivers) Fire Mass movement
Hydrological (caused by high rainfall)	Flash flood Landslide / volcanic ash / lava / ice damming of a river Tsunami	Hydrological infra-structure failure (dams, levees, reservoirs, drainage systems) Coastal protection failure (sea walls)	Disease epidemic Pollution
Volcanic	Lava flows Pyroclastic flows Ash and block falls Gases	Mining-induced (e.g. mud volcano)	Lahars (mudflows) Landslides Tsunami Fire
Seismic	Faulting Transient shaking Permanent deformation (e.g. folds) Induced movement (liquefaction and mass movement)	Dam- and reservoir-induced mass movement Mining-induced Explosion / nuclear induced	Mass movement Fire Flood
Mass movement (of snow, ice, rock, soil mud, etc.) (induced by slow-acting erosion or one of the above)	Falls Slumps Slides Flows	Unstable mining / construction waste spoil heaps	

表 1　自然灾害与人类导致的灾害之间的关系

	自然的	人类导致的	直接的或次生的
气象的	飓风、闪电和暴雨		洪水（海岸或河流），火灾，地块运动
水文的（大雨形成的）	暴洪，滑坡 / 火山灰 / 熔岩 / 河流中冰坝、海啸	水利设施故障（坝、堤坝、水库和排水设施），海岸防护故障（防波堤）	流行病 污染
火山	熔岩流，火山碎屑流，泥石流，瓦斯	开矿导致的（如，火山泥开采）	火山泥流，山崩，海啸和火灾
地震引起的	断裂，瞬间摇晃，永久变形（如褶皱），引发运动（液熔和地块运动）	影响坝和水库的地块运动，采矿或核爆引发的爆炸	地块运动，火灾和洪水
地块运动（雪，冰，岩石，土壤等等）（包括缓慢的侵蚀或其中一种）	下降，陷落，下滑，流动	不稳定的开采、建筑垃圾，废石堆	

1.4 What impact may disasters have on World Heritage properties?

1.4 灾害会对世界遗产造成什么样的影响?

World Heritage properties are those defined in Articles 1 and 2 of the *World Heritage Convention* and inscribed on the World Heritage List on the basis of their outstanding universal value, which is fulfilled through meeting one or more of the ten criteria defined in *the Operational Guidelines for the Implementation of the World Heritage Convention* (UNESCO / WHC, 2008a).

世界遗产是指基于他们的突出普遍价值、满足《世界遗产公约》第1、2条要求、符合《实施遗产公约操作指南》（联合国教科文组织世界遗产中心，2008a）的10条标准中之一条或多条标准的、已列入世界遗产名录的遗产。

• All World Heritage properties can be exposed to one or more types of disaster.

• 所有的世界遗产都会遭受一种或多种类型的灾害。

• Over the last few years, natural and human-induced disasters have caused enormous losses to World Heritage properties. Examples include Bam (Islamic Republic of Iran) due to earthquake in 2003; Prambanan Temple Compounds (Indonesia) due to earthquake in 2006; the Old Town of Edinburgh (United Kingdom) due to fire in 2002; the destruction of the Bamiyan Buddhas in Afghanistan due to armed conflict and vandalism in 2001; and the Temple of the Tooth Relic in Kandy (Sri Lanka) after terrorist attack in 1998. In 2007, the Sidr cyclone in the Sundarbans (Bangladesh) led to the destruction of forest and mangroves, the drowning of fishermen and wildlife, and saltwater intrusion.

• 在过去的几年中，自然和人为灾害给世界遗产造成了巨大的损失。例如，2003年伊朗的巴姆古城受到地震的威胁，2006年印度尼西亚的普兰巴南神庙群遭受地震威胁；2002年，英国爱丁堡老城毁于大火；2001年战争和蓄意对阿富汗巴米扬大佛的破坏；1998年，恐怖袭击对康迪佛牙寺文物（斯里兰卡）的破坏。2007年，希德飓风对桑德尔本斯国家公园（孟加拉国）的森林和红树林造成了严重的破坏，甚至造成渔民和野生动物溺水以及海水侵蚀。

• Global climate change is also exposing World Heritage natural properties and the ecological systems that sustain life to increasing disaster risks (UNESCO / WHC, 2007). Additionally, climate cycles such as the El Niño — Southern Oscillation (ENSO) which is associated with drought and flood events, and climate change-associated variations in sea-level and storm or flood events may increase the probability of hazards in protected areas.

• 全球气候改变也对世界自然遗产和维持生命的生态系统造成严重的灾害威胁（联合国教科文组织世界遗产中心，2007）。另外，气候周期，例如，因干旱和洪水引起的厄尔尼诺——南方波动现象，与海平面变化和风暴或洪水有关的气候事件，都会增加危害保护区的概率。

• Climate change may also increase impacts of disasters on World Heritage cultural properties through its effects on significant underlying risk

• 气候改变会引发重大潜在的风险因素，增加了对世界文化遗产的灾害影响。例如，土壤湿度的增加会对考古遗存和历史建筑产生影响，

factors. Any increase in soil moisture, for example, may affect archaeological remains and historic buildings, thereby increasing their vulnerability to natural hazards such as earthquakes and floods.

增加了他们在自然灾害中，比如地震和洪水中的易损性。

• A hazard could potentially change, degrade or destroy the aesthetics and / or the natural balance of the ecosystem of the property or the natural phenomenon for which it has been listed. For example, the Monarch Butterfly Reserve in Mexico is entirely reliant on the annual mass migration of millions of butterflies. A disease outbreak or pollution affecting the butterfly migratory route or a fire at the forest areas where they stay at the most vulnerable time of year could destroy the outstanding universal value of this property.

• 危害可能会改变、降低或破坏遗产艺术价值、遗产区内的生态平衡及遗产得以列入名录的自然现象。例如墨西哥的金斑蝶保护区完全依赖于每年成千上万只蝴蝶的迁徙。如果在蝴蝶迁徙的时候疾病暴发或迁徙路线中受污染的影响，或森林地区的火灾等这些灾害，就会破坏遗产的突出普遍价值。

Geological and geomorphological World Heritage values are not very vulnerable to hazards. However, mass movement, earthquakes or volcanic eruptions could change the characteristics of the property and flooding could hide its values from visitors.

地质和地貌类世界遗产的价值在一般灾害面前并不十分脆弱。然而，地块运动、地震或火山喷发可能会改变这些遗产的特征，洪水会将这些特征完全淹没。

Functioning ecosystem processes are vulnerable to most hazards. Of the thirteen natural properties on the World Heritage in Danger List in 2008, eight were inscribed for their ecosystem process values. The 2004 Asian tsunami increased deforestation in the property inscribed as the Tropical Rainforest Heritage of Sumatra (Case Study 30). Conflicts in many of these areas and the resulting disappearance of key species and impacts on existing ecosystems can severely affect their long-term status of. In Manas (India), reintroduction of species is under way to restore the ecosystem after a period of conflict had resulted in heavy wildlife population losses (Case Study 29).

功能性生态系统过程在危害面前最为脆弱。2008 年，在列入濒危世界遗产名录的 13 个自然遗产中，8 个都是因为他们的生态系统过程的价值而列入。2004 的亚洲海啸，加剧了对已列入世界遗产的苏门答腊热带雨林的森林砍伐（案例 30）。这些地区性的冲突使得很多重要种群消失，同时对现存的生态系统造成影响，严重地影响了他们的长期稳定状态。在印度的玛纳斯，冲突爆发后的一段时间后，野生动物的数量严重减少，再引入的种群正在恢复生态系统（案例 29）。

Natural disasters play a significant role in shaping the character, function and outstanding

自然灾害在形成许多世界遗产的特性、功能和突出普遍价值方面，扮演了重要的角色。

universal value of many World Heritage properties. Therefore it is important to consider the extent of management interventions that would be allowable in a particular protected area to ensure that natural areas and their associated cultural features, if any, are maintained and natural processes can continue to evolve.

因此，考虑在特定的保护区允许的管理干预的程度就非常重要，它能确保自然区和与之相关的文化要素受到保护，并继续维护，自然进程才能继续进化。

• Disasters pose risks not only to the physical attributes that carry the heritage values of the property, but also to the lives of visitors, staff and local communities living on the site or in neighbouring areas, and also to important collections and documents. They can also have negative consequences for the local economy due to the loss of tourism revenues, and for the livelihoods of local people who are dependent on the property.

• 灾害形成的风险，不仅会对承载遗产价值的物质要素而且对参观者、工作人员和遗产地社区或临近区域的生命造成威胁，同样也对重要的展品和文件造成威胁。也可因丧失旅游收入对当地的经济以及依赖遗产生活的当地居民造成负面影响。

As global populations grow in number and density and are located in ever more risk-prone areas, communities are all the more vulnerable, particularly those that are poor and / or living in remote locations. Recent research has shown that in the areas adjacent to World Heritage properties, population growth is higher than the average for the rural regions in that country (Wittemyer et al., 2008). Therefore, more people may be affected by a hazard, resulting in a high disaster risk.

全球人口数量和密度的增长，以及危害多发地段社区聚落的增长都具有易损性，特别是那些生活在贫困或边远山区的居民。近些年的研究显示，毗邻世界遗产的地区人口数量的增长要高于本国其他农村区域（Wittemyer 等，2008）人口增长的平均值。因此，高灾害风险的存在，会使更多的人受到危害的影响。

• In such circumstances, site managers and management authorities are under great pressure to allow activities such as resource extraction for fuel wood, rebuilding, encroachment for agriculture and for settlement, all of which place limited management budgets under great strain.

• 在这种情况下，遗产管理者和管理机构由于管理资金有限，不得以允许在保护区内砍伐森林资源用于燃料、重建，农业和聚落侵占土地等活动。

Disasters reduce the capacity of World Heritage site managers, management authorities and rangers to monitor and enforce regulations. For example, in Comoé in Manovo-Gounda (Central African Republic), Garamba (Democratic Republic of the

世界遗产管理者、管理机构的减灾能力与监测和执行法规有关。例如，在莫克埃、马诺沃贡达（中非共和国）、刚果民主共和国瓜兰巴、尼奥科罗科巴（塞内加尔）等地的非法偷猎贸易使野生动物的数量严重下降，因为那些地方人

Congo), and Niokolo-Koba (Senegal) poaching for the illegal bushmeat trade has severely depleted wildlife populations in regions where there is little food security or few alternative livelihoods. Staff members have been unable to work in these properties due to armed rebel groups roaming across international borders in the conflict zones. This section has shown the extensive impacts that disasters can have on World Heritage properties. Section 1.5 examines how DRM aims to reduce or avoid such impacts.

们几乎没有食物保障、很少能找到替代打猎的谋生方式。又因为在这些冲突区内武装叛乱团体在国界周边游荡，因此这些地方的管理工作人员无法开展工作。这一部分介绍了灾害给世界遗产带来的负面影响。在 1.5 节中将介绍灾害风险管理的目标是如何降低或避免这样的影响。

1.5 What key principles of DRM are applied to heritage?

1.5 运用于遗灾害风险管理主要准则是什么？

• DRM aims to prevent or reduce the negative impacts of disaster on World Heritage properties. It is primarily concerned with reducing risks to the heritage values embedded in the property (authenticity and / or integrity and sustainability), but also to human lives, physical assets and livelihoods.

• 灾害风险管理的目标是阻止或减少灾害对于世界遗产的负面影响。它主要关注降低蕴含于世界遗产中遗产价值（真实性、完整性和可持续性）的风险，同样也关注人民生活、物质遗产和谋生方式的风险。

• The values for which the property was inscribed on the World Heritage List should be the foundation on which all other plans and actions are based. This will help to reduce the possibility of emergency response and recovery activities having unintended negative consequences for the property.

• 列入遗产名录的遗产价值是规划和行动依据的基础，也有助于减少可能的应急响应和恢复活动对世界遗产造成的、意想不到的负面影响。

• Various small and progressive factors may increase the vulnerability of heritage to hazards. So DRM for heritage is concerned not only with protecting the property from major hazards but also with reducing underlying vulnerability factors, such as lack of maintenance, inadequate management, progressive deterioration, or ecosystem buffering that may cause hazards eventually to become disasters.

• 各种细微的和循序渐进的因素可能会增加遗产面对危害的脆弱性。因此遗产灾害风险管理不仅要保护遗产远离主要危害，同时也要降低潜在的脆弱因素，例如，缺少日常维护、不恰当的管理、持续的恶化或生物系统减少等会引发危害并最终形成灾害。

• The risks to cultural and natural heritage that DRM must address may originate inside the property or in the surrounding environment. Therefore DRM has a significant role to play in buffer zones of World Heritage properties. Part of

• 灾害风险管理提出，文化和自然遗产的风险可能与遗产本身有关，也有可能与遗产环境有关。因此，灾害风险管理在世界遗产缓冲区中扮演了重要的角色。部分重复行动将缓冲区重新定义为新增加的保护层。基础地质调查

the iterative action may be redefining the buffer zones as an added layer of protection. Catchment areas, fire hazards and landslide probabilities based on geological surveys could help in developing appropriate risk management guidelines in the buffer zones. For example, World Heritage properties located in the dense urban fabric of the city of Kathmandu (Nepal) are at greater risk because of factors in the surrounding environment. The type of construction used in surrounding residential areas could result in impeded access to the World Heritage area in the event of an earthquake (Case Study 1).

可能发现的集水区、火灾区和滑坡区等能够帮助在缓冲区中形成适当的风险管理指南。例如，位于密集城市中的世界遗产加德满都城，受到了周边的环境要素的威胁。因为周边居民区采用的建筑类型在地震后可能会阻断进入世界遗产区的通道（例 1）。

Increased risk due to surrounding environment: earthquake risk in the World Heritage monument zones of Kathmandu Valley (Nepal)

由于周边环境而加剧的危害：加德满都谷地（尼泊尔）世界遗产纪念区的地震威胁。

The World Heritage monument zones of Kathmandu, Patan and Bhaktapur are located within a dense urban fabric in a region highly prone to earthquakes. Increasing urban pressure in Kathmandu Valley during the last few decades has resulted in a rapid transformation of the residential areas surrounding the World Heritage properties. These transformations, which include the addition of floors and the vertical subdivision of residential properties, are making them increasingly vulnerable to earthquakes. In the event of an earthquake, the access roads to the World Heritage property would be blocked, as a result of which fire services would not be able to gain access and evacuation of inhabitants and visitors would be very difficult.

加德满都的世界遗产纪念区中，帕坦古城和巴克塔普尔古城位于城市建筑密集的地区，也是地震的高发地区。在过去的几十年中，由于世界遗产周边的居民区的快速增长，加德满都谷地的城市压力剧增。这些变化，例如增加楼层和建设密集的高层居民建筑等，增加了建筑物在地震中的脆弱性。如果有地震发生，通向世界遗产的道路就会被阻断，也就是说，这个地区的消防通道就会受阻，疏散居民和游客就变得异常困难。

Source: R. Jigyasu, 2002. Reducing Disaster Vulnerability through Local Knowledge and Capacity; the Case of Earthquake Prone Rural Communities in India and Nepal, Dr. Eng. Thesis, Trondheim: Norwegian University of Science and Technology.

资料来源：R. Jigyasu, 2002. 通过地方知识和能力减少灾害的易损性，地震频发的印度及尼泊尔乡村社区案例。

特隆赫姆挪威科技大学 Dr. Eng. Thesis 著

DRM is concerned with the more positive role of using traditional knowledge and management systems in disaster mitigation as well as with passive protection. Traditional communities may not know how to respond to a major fire but they may have a specific organization for collective action in responding to a disaster. Natural heritage may also play a significant role as buffers or protection from various hazards, for example the function of mangroves in protection against coastal flooding caused by erosion or tsunami and storm surge. Functioning ecosystems also have increased capacity to store rainfall in soils, plants and wetlands during storms, thus reducing flood risk within the property and downstream of it.

灾害风险管理更多关注使用传统知识和管理系统在减灾和被动保护中扮演的积极角色。传统的社区可能不知道如何应对重大火灾，但是他们能通过组织特殊的集体行动来应对灾害。自然遗产也同样扮演着缓解或防治各种危害的重要角色，例如，红树林有抵御海啸或风暴潮引起的洪水的功能。生态系统的功能同样也能够增加土壤、植物和湿地在暴风雨中的蓄水能力，这样就降低了洪水对遗产地及其下游的威胁。

DRM should be an integral component of the management of a World Heritage property and should therefore form part of the management plan. It should also be linked to disaster management systems at local, regional and national levels. This point is further discussed in Section 2.2.

灾害风险管理应该是世界遗产管理整体和管理规划的一个组成部分。它也同当地的、区域的和国家级的灾害管理系统相关。这个内容在 2.2 章中将深入讨论。

• Various categories of cultural heritage property, such as historic buildings, historic towns and urban areas, vernacular settlements and housing, archaeological sites, historic gardens and cultural landscapes will have their own specific needs for disaster risk management. These are determined by the specific nature of each heritage type based on its scale and character (tangible and / or intangible, movable and / or immovable, living and / or uninhabited, and protected and / or unprotected).

• 各种类型的文化遗产，例如历史建筑、历史城镇和城市区域、传统民居和住宅、考古遗址、历史花园和文化景观等，对灾害风险管理都有特殊要求。这些要求由每一类遗产的规模和特性（有形和无形的、可移动和不可移动、持续使用和无人居住的、保护和未保护的）决定。

Disaster Risk Management cycle

灾害风险管理的循环周期

There are three main stages of Disaster Risk Management: before, during and after disasters (Figure 1). The preparedness activities to be undertaken before a disaster include risk assessment, prevention and mitigation measures

灾害风险管理分为三个阶段：灾害发生前、灾害发生中和灾害发生后（如图 1），预防性的活动应该在灾害发生前实施，包括风险评估、防治和缓解特殊危害的措施（维持和监控，编制和实施各种灾害管理的政策和项目）。应急

for specific hazards (maintenance and monitoring, and formulating and implementing various disaster management policies and programmes). Emergency preparedness to be undertaken before a disaster includes measures such as creating an emergency team, an evacuation plan and procedures, warning systems and drills and temporary storage.

预案应在灾前编制完成，应包括各种措施，例如建立应急团队、疏散计划和过程、预警系统、人员训练和临时仓库。

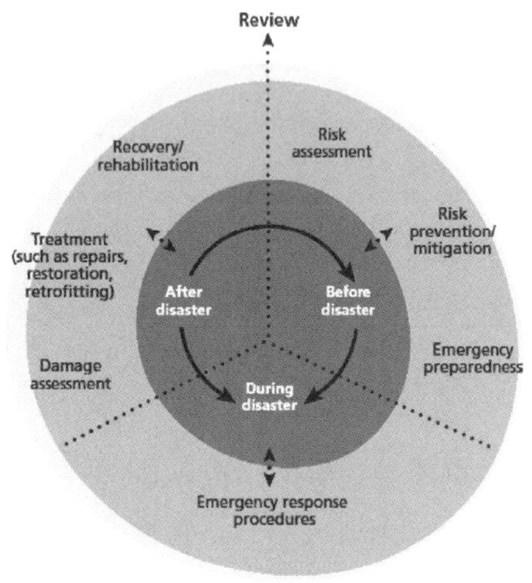

Figure 1 Disaster Risk Management cycle

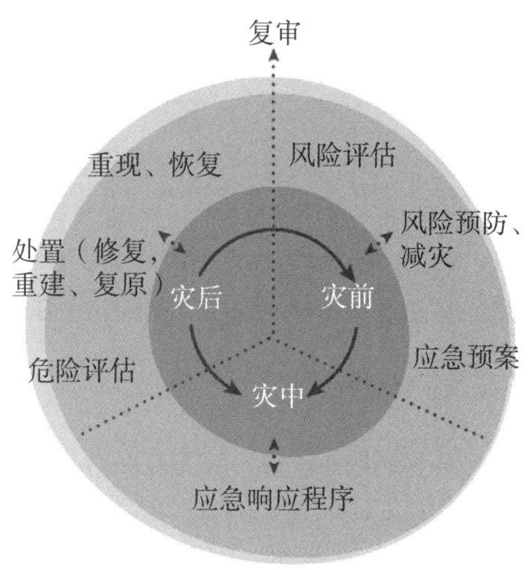

图 1 灾害风险管理的循环周期

During a disaster situation, which is usually considered to last for the first 72 hours after the incident, various emergency response procedures for saving people as well as heritage need to be developed and practised beforehand.

各种救人和拯救遗产的应急响应程序需要在灾害之前制定并经过演练。灾害发生的应急响应过程，通常在事件发生后的第一个 72 小时内。

Activities initiated after the disaster include damage assessment, treatment of damaged components of the heritage property through interventions such as repairs, restoration and retro fitting and recovery or rehabilitation activities. Note that DRM is concerned with preparedness for all these activities to be undertaken before, during and after the disaster.

灾后开始的各种活动包括对损坏程度的评估、世界遗产要素受到破坏的预防性干预措施，包括修理、修复和翻新改建、恢复或复原等活动。需要注意：灾害风险管理是为灾害发生前、中和后的各类活动作准备。

The experience of responding to and recovering from a disaster provides an opportunity to review the DRM plan for the property, based on its successes and failures. In fact, periodic communication and monitoring are essential considerations throughout the DRM cycle.

灾害应对和恢复的成败得失的经验，为我们提供了重新审视灾害风险管理规划的机会。实际上，定期的交流和监测是灾害风险管理周期中的重要环节。

The cycle is an effective tool for communicating the essential steps of DRM for cultural heritage, so it should be made available in the local language and be posted in a visible location in the site office.

循环周期图是表述文化遗产灾害风险管理基本步骤的有效工具，因此，它应该使用本地语言并张贴在遗产办公室最容易看得见的地方。

Having shown how disasters can affect World Heritage properties and reviewed some of the principles of DRM for heritage, the next step is the preparation of a DRM plan.

已经介绍了灾害如何影响世界遗产和一些灾害风险管理准则，下一步将讲解如何准备灾害风险管理规划。

2 What does a DRM plan consist of?

2 灾害风险管理规划由哪几部分组成?

2.1 What are the essential characteristics of a DRM plan?

2.1 灾害风险管理规划的基本特征是什么?

• A plan is essential for providing clear, flexible and practical guidance (rather than rigid rules) for the site manager and their team. A certain flexibility should be built into the plan from the beginning.

• 规划的本质是为遗产管理者和团队提供清晰、灵活和具有可操作性的指导（不是刚性规则）。在规划编制之初要确定规划有一定的灵活性。

• As with a generic site management plan, a DRM plan should not consist merely of a list of actions. Rather, it should describe the processes which, for different situations, should be followed by the responsible authorities in deciding and implementing the appropriate actions (see Figure 2 and refer back to Figure 1).

• 如果有通用的遗产管理规划，灾害风险管理规划不应该仅仅只罗列行动。它应该描述在不同情况下，责任机构在决定和实施适当行动时应遵循的过程（见图 1，图 2）。

• A plan should clearly state the main objectives and process of the plan, the scope, target audience and the agency(ies) responsible for its implementation.

• 应该清晰的阐释规划的主要目的、过程、范围、受众和管理机构实施职责。

• Essentially, a plan is based on identifying and assessing the main disaster risks (see Section 4) that might result in negative impacts to the heritage values of the property (as outlined in its Statement of Outstanding Universal Value), as well as to human lives and assets at the site.

• 基本上，规划的基础是对遗产价值（突出普遍价值声明中列出）、当地居民和对遗产造成负面影响的主要灾害的界定和评估（见第 4 章）。

• It then spells out the tools, techniques and implementation strategies for prevention and mitigation, emergency preparedness and response, recovery, maintenance and monitoring. These are elaborated in Sections 5 to 8 of this manual.

• 要说清楚防治或缓解、应急预案和应对、复原、维持和监控的工具、技术和实施的战略。这在本手册的 5–8 章中会有详细论述。

• The time periods and deadlines for periodic reviews of the plan should be defined.

• 应该确定规划的时限和进行定期检查的最后期限。

Depending on the nature of the property, a plan should be as comprehensive as possible. For example, if several heritage properties are located in one city or urban area, it might be advisable to have a comprehensive risk management plan for all the heritage properties in the city. The plan would establish a system for coordinating the individual plans for each property, envisaging common activities and procedures for all the properties, especially for coordination with outside agencies such as municipality, fire, police and health services.

依据遗产的特性，规划应该尽可能全面。例如，如果一个城市或城区中分布有若干个遗产，明智之举是做一个包括城市中所有遗产在内的综合性的风险管理规划。此规划应该在每个遗址单体规划之间建立一个合作机制，正视所有遗产中共同的活动和过程，特别是与其他外部机构如市政机构、消防、公安和健康服务等机构的合作。

For an example, see Case Study 2 in which the Historic Centre of Lima (Peru) requires a comprehensive plan covering all historic buildings and the surrounding area, rather than individual plans for specific buildings.

例如，利马历史中心（秘鲁）需要一个包括所有历史建筑和周边环境的综合性的规划，而不是只为具体建筑编制的单体规划（见案例 2）。

• A DRM plan can take many forms depending on the audience, for example a brochure or poster will be suitable for raising public awareness, while a report might be needed for the state agency, and a handbook / CD ROM with checklists would be more appropriate for a site manager. Whatever its format, it should be closely linked to the general management plan or system of the property (see Section 2.2). The UK National Trust's Emergency Procedures at Historic Houses is a good example of a workable plan (Case Study 3) in which concern for the welfare of the cultural heritage is placed within a larger framework of parallel concerns for life, property and the environment (see also Case Study 25 for a non-working plan).

• 一个灾害风险管理规划可以根据受众的不同采取不同的形式，例如，小册子或海报适合于提升公众意识，同时，国家机构可能需要报告的形式，而带有索引的手册或光盘可能更适合于遗产管理者。无论是什么形式，它应该与遗产的一般管理规划或系统紧密关联（见 2.2）。英国历史住宅国家信托应急程序（见案例研究 3）就是一个很好的具有可操作性的例子，应急程序将遗产作为一个具有福利的区域，它周边有很多平行的框架，包括生活、财产和环境（见案例 25，应提前熟悉的规划）。

• Copies of the DRM plan for your property should be kept securely at several locations so that these can be retrieved easily when needed, especially during a disaster.

• 为了确保安全，灾害风险管理规划的复印件应存放在若干个地点，以便在需要的时候，特别是灾害发生的时候能够便于查询。

It should be clear how the main components of a DRM plan (Figure 2) are derived from the depiction of the DRM cycle (Figure 1). Each of the main sections of this manual is concerned with one of the steps in the plan, as follows:

从灾害风险管理周期（图 1）的描述中我们抽出规划的核心要素，通过图 2 我们可以清晰了解灾害风险管理规划的主要要素是什么。这本手册的每一部分都深入研究了规划的每一步：

4. Identification and assessment: how do you identify and assess disaster risk?

4. 界定和评估：如何确定和评估灾害风险？

5. Prevention and mitigation: how do you prevent or mitigate disaster risks?

5. 防治和缓解：如何防治或缓解灾害的威胁？

6. Emergency preparedness and response: how do you prepare for and respond to emergencies?

6. 应急预案和应对：对于紧急情况该如何准备和应对？

7. Recovery: how do you recover from disasters?

7. 恢复：如何从灾害中恢原？

8. Implementation and monitoring: how do you make your plan work?

8. 实施和监测：如何实施你的规划？

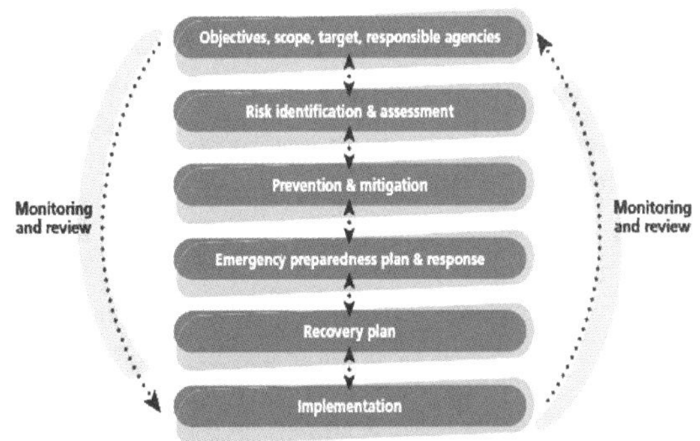

Figure 2 Main components of a Disaster Risk Management plan

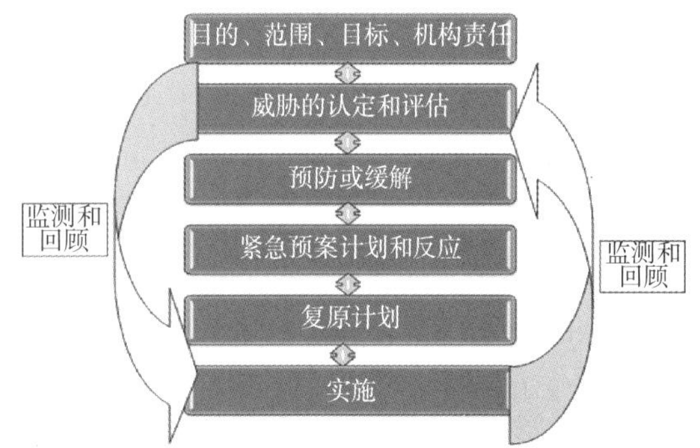

图 2 灾害风险管理规划主要要素

Before starting on a plan (Section 3), questions need to be answered about how a DRM plan relates to a site management plan, and also to larger, regional plans.

在开始编制规划之前（见第 3 章），需要回答下面一些问题：灾害风险管理规划如何与遗址管理规划关联，如何与更大的区域规划关联？

CASE STUDY 2

Need for a DRM plan to be comprehensive: Historic Centre of Lima (Peru)

案例 2

需要一个综合性的灾害风险管理规划：利马历史中心（秘鲁）

The Historic Centre of Lima was inscribed

利马历史中心作为杰出的建筑群，于 1988

on the World Heritage List in 1988 as an outstanding example of an architectural ensemble, which illustrates significant stages in human history as the capital of the Spanish dominions in South America until the mid-18th century. Around 23 per cent of the officially protected monuments are located in the historic centre, including the Convent of San Francisco, the largest of its kind in the region.

年列入世界遗产名录，这些建筑群见证了18世纪中期，西班牙人统治南美洲这一人类历史的重要阶段。有23%的官方保护纪念物分布在这个历史中心，包括了这个区域内最大建筑，圣弗朗西斯科女修道院。

The region is highly prone to earthquakes and fires which have caused significant damage to cultural heritage in the past. After a major fire in December 2001 caused by fireworks, the standards of safety inside the buildings were made very stringent. Earthquakes have also caused severe damage to the historic centre in the past; the most recent devastation occurring during the August 2007 earthquake, following which repair, restoration and reconstruction work has been initiated in several monuments. However, most of the disaster preparedness measures until now have focused on individual monuments and do not address the risks that may originate in the urban surroundings. A comprehensive risk management strategy needs to be formulated at the urban level based upon appropriate land use, transport and evacuation routes, and the installation of emergency equipment such as fire hydrants, by closely coordinating with the municipality, fire services, hospitals and other relevant urban authorities. This should be integrated with the heritage needs at the levels of individual historic buildings and of the whole urban area.

这个区域历史上是地震和火灾高发地区，过去的灾害曾经造成这个中心中很多重要建筑的严重损坏；最近一次的破坏是发生于2007年8月的地震，地震后，几处遗址的维修、修复和重建工作立即展开。然而，到目前为止，很多防治措施只是针对单体建筑的，而没有考虑到城市周边环境也会对遗产造成威胁。需要编制一个基于土地使用、交通和疏散线路、安装应急设施例如消防栓，以及与政府机构、消防局、医院和其他城市相关机构密切合作的、城市级别的综合风险管理战略。这个战略应该依据单体历史建筑和整个城区的遗址保护需求进行编制。

Source: Maria D.C.C. Perez and Patricia I.G. Yague, 2007, communication by Peruvian participants at the International Training Course on Disaster Risk Management of Cultural Heritage, Rits-DMUCH, Kyoto.

来源：Maria D.C.C. Perez and Patricia I.G. Yague, 2007，京都立命馆大学国际都市防灾研究所，秘鲁文化遗产灾害风险管理国际培训班。

CASE STUDY 3

A truly integrated approach: National Trust Emergency Procedures at Historic Houses, The National Trust for Places of Historic Interest or Natural Beauty in England developed an in-house guide in the 1980s to assist managers of National Trust Properties to ensure adequate emergency procedures. The Emergency Procedures guide was conceived as a 'working' document intended to guide staff in improving preparedness, while integrating lessons and experiences gained over time. While many organizations avoid detailed procedural manuals of this type — fearing they will not be read at the moment of emergency — the Trust suggests the critical importance of staff gaining advance familiarity with all the material in the document of relevance to their individual roles. The document is based on a core of instructions for Emergency Procedures at Historic Houses, which includes sections on policy, emergency-planning responsibilities, emergency-support team measures, immediate emergency response by emergency type, roles, staff responsibilities, communication lines and responsibilities, and salvage measures. This core is supported by a number of detailed annexes, including guidelines for establishing emergency plans at National Trust buildings, training of emergency-support teams, guidelines for rescue and protection in emergencies (specific to the materials, objects and conditions in which they are found), dealing with the press and media, general precautions for floods, and detailed descriptions of staff responsibilities for twenty-four different positions within property management hierarchies.

Source: H. Stovel, 1998, Risk Preparedness: A Management Manual for World Cultural Heritage, Rome, ICCROM, p. 69.

案例 3

一个真正的综合方法：英国历史住宅国家应急程序信托基金、英国国家历史名胜及自然美景信托基金在 20 世纪 80 年代形成了内部指南，协助国家信托遗产的管理者实施适当的应急程序。应急程序指南的最初设想是作为指导员工提高防范的“操作”文件，同时也结合了一些经验和教训。很多组织都避免细化这一类型的程序手册——害怕他们在紧急情况发生时没有办法阅读。信托基金建议，关键岗位的员工应事先熟悉和掌握这一手册，这点非常重要。指南以历史住宅的应急程序的核心指令为基础，它包括了政策、应急计划的职责、紧急团队的支援措施、突发事件的类型、任务、员工的责任、沟通路径和责任以及救援措施等几个部分。这个核心指令由若干个详细的附件支撑，包括由信托基金编制的应急计划指南、紧急支援团队的训练、在紧急情况下救助和保护指南（特别对他们发现的材料、物品和设施），应对新闻媒体、一般防洪措施、文化遗产管理中 24 种不同职位的员工职责的详细描述。

来源：H. Stovel, 1998, 风险准备：世界遗产管理手册，罗马，国际文物保护与修复研究中心 p. 69。

2.2 How is a DRM plan linked to the site management plan of a heritage property?

2.2 灾害风险管理规划如何与遗产管理规划发生关联？

One of the main challenges to the effectiveness of a DRM plan is the lack of coordination between the site management systems for the particular heritage property and the organizational set-up, policies and procedures for disaster management in the city or region in which the property is located. Therefore the DRM plan for the heritage property should be integrated with the existing plan and procedures for site management (Figure 3).

有效的灾害风险管理规划最大问题是：缺乏与特定遗产的管理体系和组织结构、与遗产所在城市或区域中灾害管理的政策和程序之间的合作。因此，遗产灾害风险管理规划应该整合现有的遗产管理的规划和程序（见图 3）。

In those cases where a comprehensive site management plan exists for a particular heritage property, the DRM plan should be well integrated with it. In cases where a site management plan does not exist, the DRM plan can stand alone but it must link to existing procedures for managing the site. In fact, formulating a DRM plan may serve as a catalyst to prepare the site management plan and can be integrated into it later.

在有综合遗产管理规划的情况下，该规划应与灾害风险管理规划整合。如果没有遗产管理规划，可以独立编制遗产灾害风险管理规划，但是需要与现存的遗产管理程序相关联。实际上，编制一个灾害风险管理规划可以促进遗产管理规划的准备，当管理规划完成后再予以整合。

When there are various stand-alone plans within a property, it is important to cross-reference them. For example, visitor use and fire management should be linked to the management plan and the larger-scale disaster risk reduction plans.

但遗产地已有多个独立存在的规划时，相互参考十分重要。例如，访客和消防管理应该与管理规划和大规模减灾计划相衔接。

An overarching general management plan is useful to ensure integration in complex sites such as serial nominations and properties that cover large areas or multiple ecosystems or physical settings.

一个包罗万象的总体规划对整合复杂遗址群十分有用，例如，涵盖多个生态系统或实体环境的、系列申报的遗产。

Figure 3 Relationship between a DRM plan and other management plan

图 3 灾害风险管理规划与其他规划的关系

The following examples demonstrate those areas in which disaster management systems or plans can be integrated with the existing site

下面的例子介绍了灾害管理系统或规划与已有的遗产管理系统或规划之间的整合：

management systems or plans:

• The Statement of Outstanding Universal Value and the boundaries of the property stated in the site management plan should be the reference points for assessing the risks to the heritage values of the property in the risk management plan.

• 在遗址管理规划中阐述的突出普遍价值声明和遗产的边界，应该作为风险管理规划中评估遗产价值威胁因素的参照点。

• The plans, maps and management plan of the area in which the property is located need to take into consideration the geology, hydrology, climate, land use, human population characteristics (such as growth and density), transport and new developments, particularly of infrastructure, industry and mining, to reduce the existing and potential risks to the site.

• 遗产所在区域的计划、地图和管理规划需要认真考虑地质、水文、气候、土地使用、人口特征（例如增长和密度），交通和新的发展，特别是基础设施、工业和矿业等因素，减少现存或潜在的威胁。

• Site maintenance and monitoring systems should take into account the equipment, techniques and strategies for prevention and mitigation of risks to the property.

• 遗产维护和监测体系应该认真考虑防治和缓解威胁的设施、技术和战略。

• The general security system of the site should also cater for the special needs that arise during emergencies.

• 一般遗址的安全体系应该同样满足紧急事件发生时的特殊需要。

• The evacuation plan for staff and visitors should require precise site documentation and mapping, which is an essential part of the site management system.

• 员工和游人的疏散计划需要精确的遗址资料和地图，这些资料和地图也是遗产管理系统的基本组成部分。

• For cultural heritage, a comprehensive inventory of movable and immovable heritage components is vital in order to identify the most valuable components (and their location) that are to be salvaged during an emergency. This inventory should be updated regularly, say every two years.

• 对于文化遗产，可移动和不可移动文物的完整清单是必不可少的，方便确定容易受损的要素及其位置，在紧急情况发生时，便于抢救。这个清单应该定期更新，如每两年更新一次。

• For natural heritage, a comprehensive inventory of the attributes of the outstanding universal value of the property for each criterion under which it has been inscribed, such as key wildlife populations or habitat distribution, should be conducted and mapped. For the protection of genetic diversity and to promote recovery of vulnerable species, breeding and reintroduction programmes may need to be put in place.

• 对于自然遗产，应该提供能够展现遗产突出普遍价值、体现遗产符合列入名录标准的遗产特性的清单和地图，例如主要的野生动物数量或栖息地分布图。保护遗产多样性、提升脆弱种群自我繁殖修复的能力和再引入项目，也应该列入清单。

• Due to the potential risk reduction roles that heritage property can play, coordination is essential

• 根据降低遗产潜在风险的原则，遗产组织与国家、地区的发展和规划机构、与国家有关

with national and regional development and planning agencies as well as with national agencies involved in disaster planning and response. For example, site managers can ensure that their national counterparts involved in hazard and disaster planning are aware of the environmental resources for the location of displaced persons (see, for example, Practising and Promoting Sound Environmental Management in Refugee / Returnee Operations, UNHCR, 2001). Without such coordinated planning, human-induced hazards can be created inadvertently during the response phase after a disaster. For example, a poor choice of location of camps for displaced people could expose them to floods and /or fire or lead to contamination of water sources. Deforestation for establishing a camp or to provide materials for shelter or energy can cause soil instability and an increased risk of landslides or flooding.

灾害规划和灾害应对机构之间的合作是必不可少的。例如，遗产管理者能够确保国家危急和灾害规划相关部门关注流散人员避难所的环境资源（见案例，实践和提升避难所合理的环境管理指南，联合国难民事务署，2001）。如果没有此类的协调规划，在灾害后的应对阶段就会在无意中形成人为灾害。例如，对于疏散人员宿营地位置的不当选择会使他们处于洪水、火灾中，也可能污染水资源。为提供修建营地、房屋的材料或获取能源而砍伐树木会造成土壤不稳定并增加了土地滑坡或洪水发生的风险。

Section 2 introduced the Disaster Risk Management cycle (Figure 1) and the three key stages of prevention / mitigation, response and recovery. These in turn form the core of the Disaster Risk Management plan, which is structured as a linear series of steps to follow in preparing a plan. However, the planning process is also cyclical in nature, with a constant feedback loop between the definition of objectives and the implementation and evaluation phases (Figure 2).

第 2 章　介绍了灾害风险管理的完整过程（图 1）和三个重要阶段，即防治或缓解、应对、恢复阶段。这些就是灾害风险管理规划的核心，准备规划应由一系列线性步骤构成。然而，规划过程在确定目标、实施和评估反馈中循环，这是它的本质特征（图 2）。

Section 3 reviews who should be in the team that prepares a DRM plan, and what resources are needed. You will then be ready to embark on the central components of a DRM plan (Sections 4 to 8).

第 3 章　评述了准备灾害风险管理规划的团队中的人员组成，需要什么样的资源，接下来准备了解灾害风险管理规划的核心要素（4–8 章）。

3. How do you get started?

3. 你该如何开始?

3.1 Who should be members of the 'core team' for preparing a plan?

3.1 哪些人应是规划准备“核心团队”的一员？

The core team should consist of the site

核心团队应包括遗产管理者或其他得到机

manager or another person designated by the authorities, along with the staff members responsible for divisions and departments such as administration, maintenance, monitoring and security. It is also very important to engage the local municipality, local government, local community leaders or elders, local scientists and researchers, the disaster management agency, police, health services, and emergency response teams (e.g. firefighters, coastguard, mountain rescue). These should be involved in the process of setting up the system and formulating the plan for disaster risk management. If there are any organized local community groups, they too should be involved in the process.

构任命的人员，以及主要责任部门的工作人员和管理、维护、监控和安全等部门的成员、当地政府、当地市政当局、当地社团领导或长者、当地科学家和研究者、灾害管理局、警察局、健康服务机构和应急应对团队（例如，消防队、海岸警备队、高山救援队等）。这些组织应该参与建立和编制系统灾害风险管理规划的过程。有组织的当地社区团队，也应该包括在这一过程中。

It is also important to involve people who could help to identify and assess risks, for example specialist professionals such as hydrologists or seismic engineers.

将具有界定和威胁评估能力的人员，例如具有水文或地震工程方面知识的专家纳入到团队中非常重要。

In some situations, conflicts of values and interests in a heritage property may arise among various stakeholders. Those persons or groups representing varied interests in the property should be identified and engaged in the process of formulating a risk management plan. On the other hand, security may be an issue if the entire plan is made public. This aspect must be considered while engaging various stakeholders in the process.

在一些情况下，在不同的利益相关者之间会形成遗产的价值和利益的冲突。应该确定代表了遗产各种利益的个人或团体，都参与到风险管理规划的编制过程中。另一方面，安全问题应该是整个公开规划中的一个因素。各类利益相关者都应该考虑安全因素。

One person should be allocated the role of representing the outstanding universal value and integrity of the property to ensure that these are fully integrated into the planning for disaster risk management. That person should reinforce the importance of these values with staff and others involved in disaster risk management.

应该有一个人承担陈述遗产突出普遍价值和完整性的任务，确保这些内容完全融合到灾害风险管理规划中。这个人应该与遗产地工作人员和其他与灾害风险有关人员一起强化遗产价值的重要性。

3.2 Who are the partners and stakeholders at local level?

• Local community leaders and organizations can play a responsible role to mobilize the community for active participation in the formulation and implementation of the plan.

• Schools, hospitals, religious groups and other formal and informal institutions may need to be approached to identify potential collaboration or information-sharing.

• Particularly in remote locations, those with access to aircraft, boats or other vehicles should be encouraged to prepare for helping in evacuation or other rescue needs.

3.3 Who are the major partners and stakeholders at national and international levels?

The State Party is the primary stakeholder responsible for protecting and managing a World Heritage property, including with respect to disaster risks. National agencies which would be the key stakeholders in formulating and implementing DRM plans for World Heritage properties include:

• Agencies responsible for the national disaster management programmes and activities (civil protection, firefighting forces, flood control engineers, health officials dealing with epidemics);

• Agencies responsible for protecting and managing cultural and natural properties;

• National hazard warning systems, such as the meteorology and seismic monitoring agencies and others involved in hazard monitoring;

• Military and police forces and volunteer groups, which should be made aware of the response plans within the property and be well trained to support their implementation if required.

Therefore, the plan should be made available to all these types of agency.

3.2　在地区层面上谁是利益相关者和合作伙伴？

• 有能力调动当地社区参与规划编制和实施的当地社区领导者和组织机构。

• 学校、医院、宗教团体和其他正式、非正式的机构，是确定的潜在合作伙伴或信息分享者。

• 需要通过飞机、轮船或其他交通设施才能到达的偏远区域，应该鼓励他们制定疏散计划或其他救援需求。

3.3　国家或国际层面上谁是主要的合作伙伴或利益相关者？

国家是保护和管理世界遗产、考虑灾害风险中最为主要的利益相关者。国家机关是世界遗产灾害风险管理规划编制和实施的核心利益相关者，国家机关应包括：

• 负责国家灾害管理项目和活动的机关（民防、消防局，防洪工程师、疾病控制机构）；

• 负责保护、管理文化和自然遗产的机构；

• 国家灾害预警系统，例如气象和地震监测机构以及其他相关的监测机构；

• 军队和警察以及一些志愿团队也应该关注遗产应急规划，必要时通过培训提高他们实施规划的能力。

因此，制定的规划应该可供以上所有类型的机构使用。

At international level, the UNESCO World Heritage Centre is the key stakeholder for the protection of World Heritage properties from disasters. Several other international agencies, research and academic institutions can play an important role in disaster prevention and response, such as ICOMOS, ICROM, IUCN and the Blue Shield through their field offices or representatives. For example, the National Committee of ICOMOS played a significant role during post-tsunami recovery of the cultural sites in Sri Lanka and successfully advocated the importance of including cultural heritage values in post-disaster recovery plans (Case Study 4).

在国际层面上，联合国教科文组织世界遗产中心是保护世界遗产远离灾害最为关键的利益相关者。其他国际机构、研究和学术机构比如国际古迹遗址理事会、国际文物保护与修复研究中心、世界自然保护联盟和蓝盾等组织的地方办公室或代表，在灾害防治和反应的过程中也扮演了重要的角色。例如，斯里兰卡古迹理事会国家委员会在海啸后文化遗产的恢复过程中扮演了重要角色，并且成功地验证了把文化遗产价值包含到灾后恢复计划中的重要性（案例 4）。

Information on ICOMOS and other relevant international organizations is given in Appendix IV.

有关国际古迹遗址理事会和其他相关国际组织的信息请参见附录 IV。

CASE STUDY 4

案例 4

How a cultural heritage NGO can help: the role of ICOMOS Sri Lanka in post-tsunami recovery.

文化遗产的非政府组织如何发挥作用：斯里兰卡古迹遗址理事会在海啸灾害后恢复过程中发挥作用。

The Indian Ocean tsunami on 26 December 2004 caused heavy destruction of the rich cultural property located in the maritime provinces of Sri Lanka. Among the heritage components that were damaged were some of the oldest religious buildings still in use, a range of secular buildings with a blend of architectural styles ranging from the local vernacular to Portuguese, Dutch and British influences, and traditional fishing villages and unique ecosystems.

2004 年 12 月 26 日印度洋的海啸对位于斯里兰卡滨海诸省的文化遗产造成了严重的破坏。在这些被严重破坏的遗产中，包括了至今仍在使用的最老的宗教建筑、一系列带有混合建筑形式的不朽建筑、当地独特建筑、受葡萄牙、荷兰和英国影响的建筑，以及传统的渔村和稀有的生态系统。

ICOMOS Sri Lanka, though a small group, was in action soon after the tsunami-most members had seen the devastation within twenty-four hours of the event and a few even had had first-hand experience. Thus the National Committee decided to

斯里兰卡古迹遗址理事会的小团队在海啸发生后立刻行动，大部分成员在 24 小时内查看了毁坏状况，少数人因此掌握了第一手经验。这时，国家委员决定至少开展一项文化遗产调查，他们也深知在这个危机时刻没有其他组织能够

carry out at least a survey of the cultural properties, knowing that no other party would undertake such a study during that time of crisis.

承担这样的责任。

As planners were going to be preparing development proposals for the affected areas, ICOMOS Sri Lanka issued a public statement within a week of the incident appealing to officials to recognize the cultural properties and to save them from destruction. This had the desired effect when the Sri Lankan Government agreed to allow cultural sites and monuments, along with hotels and structures relating to the fishing industry, to be permitted to remain within the newly declared buffer zone from the coastline. ICOMOS then undertook the arduous task of carrying out a survey of the cultural properties affected by the tsunami. To be meaningful, it had to be carried out as quickly as possible and the results passed to the planners to incorporate in development proposals. The support of local universities was also mustered under the supervision of ICOMOS

当规划者开始准备编制受影响地区的发展计划时，斯里兰卡古迹遗址理事会在海啸发生后的一个星期内发布了一个公告，恳求政府认定文化遗产并从灾害中拯救它们。值得称赞是斯里兰卡政府同意在新划定的海岸线缓冲区内，把与渔业相关的旅馆和建筑作为文化遗址和纪念物予以保留。国际古迹遗址理事会开始执行调查被海啸破坏的文化遗产的艰巨任务。这项任务执行的非常快，调查结果被提供给规划者去编制新的发展规划。在国际古迹遗址理事会的监管下，当地的大学也参加了这项工作。

Source: P. Wijeratne, 2008,Post-tsunami redevelopment and the cultural sites of the maritime provinces of Sri Lanka, in H. Meir and T. Will(eds), Heritage at Risk: Cultural Heritage and Natural Disasters, ICOMOS.

来源：P. Wijeratne, 2008, 斯里兰卡沿海城市 H. Meir and T. Will(eds) 海啸后再发展及文化遗址，遗产风险：文化遗产和自然灾害，国际古迹遗址理事会。

3.4 What human, technical and financial resources are needed?

• Additional human resources to support the core team would include professionals from the fields of conservation and disaster risk management. Other specialist professionals such as meteorologists, climatologists, seismic engineers, hydrologists, public health experts, epidemiologists, and sociologists, etc. can also provide valuable inputs.

• Technical resources would include tools and equipment necessary to undertake various measures

3.4 需要什么样的人、技术和财政资源？

• 支持核心团队的人力资源应该包括来自于保护和灾害风险管理的专家。具有其他专业知识的人员，例如，气象学、气候学、地震工程师、水文学，和公共健康等学科的专家、流行疾病学专家和社会科学家等等都能提供有用的帮助。

• 技术资源应该包括：实施对遗产及其各要素评估、布置降低危害措施时所需要的工具和

for assessing and reducing disaster risks to the property and its various components. For example, extinguishers, hydrants and smoke detectors make up the equipment necessary for fire prevention. Someone who can help in identifying these would be useful as part of the planning team.

设施。例如，灭火器、消防栓和烟雾探测器等火灾防治的基本设施。那些能够协助使用这些设备的人也应该作为规划团队的一部分。

• Financial resources required for the development of the plan will depend on the nature and extent of the property and its vulnerability to various hazards. A preliminary survey is required to assess the scope of work on the basis of which estimates for the projects and activities can be prepared.

• 编制规划所需要的财政资源取决于遗产的特性、范围以及面对各种灾害的脆弱性。需要以初步调查为基础，评估项目和活动工作范围。

• The planning team should make every effort to develop plans that can be implemented within the available resources. However, a plan may include estimates for which essential resources may be found afterwards. Local and national funding should cover all core budget requirements.

• 规划团队应全力以赴在利用资源的基础上编制规划。然而，一个规划应该包括找到基本的预算资源。当地和国家财政应该支付所需要的核心预算。

• All kinds of inventories, including lists of staff members, heritage components of the property and equipment likely to be damaged as a result of a disaster, need to be prepared and made easily accessible.

• 需要准备各种类型的清单，包括工作人员、遗产构成要素和灾害中易损设备的清单等，并方便查询。

• Frequently, the resources needed to respond to and recover from disaster cannot be provided by the local site management agency. In these cases there will be a need for assistance from the local government and disaster management agencies and even greater attention from the state and national governments. With a broader agency and stakeholder response comes the need to educate those involved in the guidelines forming part of the DRM plan for the cultural heritage property, including special considerations for the protection of heritage values.

• 最后，灾害应对和灾后恢复的资金不应该由当地遗产管理机构提供。这种情况下，需要获得当地政府和灾害管理机构的协助，并得到国家政府的高度关注。其他机构和利益相关者应参与各种灾害风险管理规划指南形式的教育活动，包括对遗产价值保护的特殊关注。

Sections 1 and 2 have reviewed why a plan is needed and what it can do. Section 3 has indicated who should be involved in preparing and implementing it. We are now ready to discuss the central

第 1、2 章介绍了为什么要编制规划和如何编制规划。第 3 章指明谁将参与到规划的编制和实施过程。下来我们准备讨论灾害风险管理规划应该包括的核心要素。

components of a DRM plan.

Sections 4 to 8 address a different step in the plan (Figure 2), starting with how to identify and assess disaster risks.

第 4 至 8 章将介绍规划的不同步骤（图 2），首要步骤是如何认定和评估风险。

4 How do you identify and assess disaster risks?

4 如何认定和评估灾害风险

Section 4 reviews what information is needed in order to identify risks (4.1), then analyses potential risks (risk assessment, 4.2) to see how they can be reduced by means of good planning and management (4.3).

第 4 章介绍了认定风险必需的信息是什么（4.1），紧接着分析潜在的风险（风险评估，4.2），最后要看看如何通过好的规划或管理降低风险（4.3）。

Case studies are used to illustrate important points. The DRM cycle remains fundamental to the discussion (Figure 1).

案例分析用来解释重要观点。灾害风险管理周期是讨论的基础（图 1）。

4.1 What kind of information do you need to identify disaster risks to your property?

The following categories of information are essential:

• The particular attributes (tangible as well as intangible) that carry the outstanding universal value and justify the criteria for inscription of the property on the World Heritage List. Statements on authenticity and integrity are also very helpful. This information should normally be available to the site manager. *The Operational Guidelines* and other important information on *the World Heritage Convention* are available online from http://whc.unesco.org/.

• The factors and processes that, for each of the possible hazards affecting the property, may result in damage or deterioration. The probability of occurrence of each hazard should also be assessed.

• Geographical information on the location of the property, its boundaries, its buffer zone, its immediate surroundings, access, topography, etc.

4.1 认定遗产灾害风险需要哪些信息？

下面是必要信息类型：

• 承载了遗产突出普遍价值和遗产符合列入世界名录标准的特殊属性（有形和无形的）。真实性和完整性声明同样也很有用。这些信息可以从遗产管理者处获得。操作指南和其他世界遗产公约中的重要信息可在网站上获取：http://whc.unesco.org/。

• 威胁遗产安全、导致遗产破坏或彻底毁坏的每一种可能的危害要素和过程。对每一种危害发生的可能性也要进行评估。

• 遗产位置、边界和缓冲区、周边环境、通道和地形等地理信息。

•Geological, hydrological, and meteorological information on the nature of the climate, soil, fault lines (if any), water table, surface water such as a river, etc.

• 地质的、水文的、气象的信息，例如气候特征、土壤、断层带（如果有）、地下水、地表水如河流等等。

• Thematic maps of the area or region in which the property is located, such as a hazard vulnerability map. A series of generalized maps that describe the major hazards (or natural disaster hot spots) that would probably affect World Heritage properties in given regions may also be useful. These are generally available from the principal national, regional or local agencies responsible for disaster management. They are best utilized by either including a set of maps that display the location of World Heritage properties along with known natural disaster hot spots, or by providing a web link to these types of map in the plan. A good source of information on natural disaster hots pots is *the World Bank Disaster Risk Management Series* (Dilley et al., 2005).

• 标注有这个地区或区域遗产位置的专题地图，例如灾害脆弱性地图。一些描述能够影响特定区域内主要危害世界遗产安全的一般性地图（或自然灾害热点图）可能也会有帮助。这些地图一般可以从国家、地区或当地负责灾害的机关获得。最好既包括展示世界遗产位置、已知自然灾害热点的一系列地图，也包括规划中各种类型地图的网站链接。自然灾害热点的最好的有用信息资源是世界银行灾害风险管理丛书（Dilley et al., 2005）。

Specialized maps such as cultural heritage risk maps at national or area level, if available, can also be useful. A geographical information system (GIS) is a useful application to prepare such thematic maps. The Risk Map of Cultural Heritage in Italy is an important project that illustrates a systematic attempt at national level to map the vulnerability to risk of cultural heritage (Case Study 5).

如果可以使用特殊的地图，例如国家层面或地区层面的文化遗产风险地图，将对规划十分有帮助。地理信息系统是准备专题地图非常有用的工具。意大利的文化遗产风险地图是一个重要的项目，它尝试从国家层面上构建一个系统，用地图表示文化遗产的脆弱性及危害（案例 5）。

• Information on the history of different disasters affecting the area or the property itself, obtained from historical records and from specific agencies dealing with different types of disaster.

• Inventories and the current status of existing management systems and disaster preparedness equipment and facilities in the property, such as for shelter, evacuation and rescue. Hazard-specific equipment should also be evaluated, e.g. the

• 区域或遗产遭受过的不同灾害的历史信息，可以从历史档案和处理不同类型灾害的特殊机构中获得。

• 防治设备和设施清单，例如庇护、疏散和现有管理系统的现状、遗产急救的设施和设备。灾害特殊设备，例如，应付洪水、火灾、滑坡、污染和流行病传播等事件的不同需求的设施，应进行专门评估。

different needs for floods, fires, landslides, pollution events and disease epidemics.

• The existing relevant institutions and the community within and around the property.

• The physical planning (land use, transport, infrastructure) of the area in which the property is located. This is available through local planning documents such as a master plan or regional plan.

• The condition of roads for potential evacuation.

• Local and traditional knowledge systems relevant to disaster risk reduction.

• A complete and easily accessible directory of agencies that will take action.

CASE STUDY 5

Preparing hazard vulnerability maps: Risk Map of Cultural Heritage in Italy.

This initiative by the Istituto Centrale per il Restauro is aimed at preparing urgent preventive measures by taking into consideration the environmental and human conditions of Italian cultural heritage. The project has been developed over several phases. The first stage involved gathering data on the environmental risks to which cultural heritage is exposed, in order to draw up thematic maps for various natural factors such as earthquakes, volcanoes, floods or air pollution; and human factors such as theft, vandalism or tourist pressures. Information gathered from municipal databases concerning the distribution of cultural heritage was integrated to identify the areas most exposed to risk factors. The second phase involved, first, detailed catalogue of various cultural heritage properties and their vulnerability, and second, detailed analysis of related conditions such as stone deterioration and impact of environmental pollution. The purpose is to verify over time the actual nature and rate of decay in order to improve the predictive accuracy of risk mapping.

• 遗产内或遗产周边社区已存在的相关研究机构。

• 遗址所在区域的环境形态规划（土地使用、道路、基础设施）。这些信息可以从当地规划部门档案资料中找到，例如总体规划或地区规划。

• 用于疏散的道路状况信息。

• 与减灾有关的当地或传统知识体系。

• 完整和可访问的行动机构的目录。

案例 5

准备危害脆弱性地图：意大利文化遗产风险地图。

由意大利修复中心提议的这个项目，目的是在考虑意大利文化遗产环境和人类近况的基础上，准备紧急防治措施。项目完成经过了几个阶段。第一阶段包括收集遗产所处环境的风险资源信息，以便能够画出包含各种自然要素的主题地图，自然要素包括地震、火山、洪水和空气污染；以及与人有关的要素如盗取、故意破坏或旅游压力。信息收集来源于多个与文化遗产分布有关的数据库，根据信息整合并确定这些危害要素最容易爆发的地区。第二阶段，先对各种类型的文化遗产和他们的脆弱性详细编目，然后，详细分析相关的条件，例如石头风化和环境污染影响。这样做的目的是核实遗产实际特性和衰变的速率，从而提升风险地图预测的准确性。最后，生成地图，利用计算机把文化遗产分布、认定的文化遗产脆弱性以及与他们相关的威胁因素等所有这些要素都合成标示在图上。

The final phase involved generation of a computer-based synthesis of the distribution and vulnerability of the cultural heritage properties identified and their associated risk factors, all represented in map form.

Source: Details of the project, with maps (http://www.uni.net/aec/).

来源：项目详细信息和地图见（http://www.uni.net/aec/）。

Where little historical data are available or where monitoring gaps occur, the best available data should be used and can be amplified through ‘triangulation’, i.e. the use of multiple sources. Local knowledge can supply valuable qualitative data to help with verification.

如果可用的历史数据较少或监测数据有出入，应该使用最好的数据并通过“三角剖分”法将其扩大化，例如，使用多重资源的时候。地方知识可作为珍贵的定性数据，对核查很有帮助。

During emergency response, the data collected are valuable in improving future response and allowing lessons to be learned.

应急响应期间的数据收集有利于提高将来的应急响应，吸取经验和教训。

Note: It is very important to make a clear distinction between natural hazards and disasters, as this relates to the degree of management intervention that is appropriate for a given World Heritage property. Your ability to prevent harm or loss of heritage values as a result of natural processes may be limited. So the response and recovery actions must be careful studied. The general view that static natural or cultural heritage features can be maintained in a changing environment is being replaced with an understanding that some alterations to these values cannot be avoided. Therefore assessing disaster risks will become increasingly complex as these properties experience both gradual and sometimes catastrophic affects of climate change.

注意：分清自然危害和灾害十分重要，因为这与管理干预的程度直接关联。防止因自然危害而引发的、损伤遗产价值的措施极为有限。因此应对和恢复行动必须要认真研究。一般认为“静态的自然或文化遗产特征在改变的环境中能够维持不变”这一观念已经被“遗产价值的有些改变是不可避免”的认知所替代。因为遗产正在经历缓慢的气候变化可能导致的突发性灾害，所以评估灾害风险变得越来越复杂。

CASE STUDY 6

Communication with the public when a natural hazard is not a disaster: natural processes in Kamchatka (Russian Federation).

案例 6

当自然灾害发生时与公众的交流：在堪察加半岛的自然进程（俄罗斯联邦）。

Recognized for all four natural heritage criteria including its outstanding geological processes, the Kamchatka World Heritage site contains twenty-nine active volcanoes. In June 2007, a landslide choked the river flowing through the Valley of Geysers in the Kronotsky Nature Preserve. This blockage submerged many of the valley's geysers. At one point the dam of rock, gravel and ice was estimated to be 4.5 million m3.

堪察加半岛世界遗产包括了 29 座活火山，因其杰出的地理进程，符合自然遗产的四条标准。2007 年 6 月，山体滑坡阻塞了流经克罗诺斯基自然保护区间歇泉河谷的河水。它的阻塞使得很多河谷的间歇泉淹没在水面以下。有一段时期，大坝中的岩石、碎石和冰块估计达到 450 万立方米。

The Valley of Geysers is a tourist attraction and the landslide and subsequent flooding of the valley attracted worldwide media attention and concern about damage to the protected area. However, the event simply represented a natural part of the ongoing processes operating within the property. Site managers can benefit from communicating clearly with the media and public about such events which, while sudden and possibly shocking, represent opportunities for increasing awareness on natural processes.

间歇泉谷地是旅游胜地，滑坡和瞬间的洪水立刻引起世界范围媒体的注意，他们关注保护区的破坏状况。然而，事件只代表了遗产自然形成进程的一部分。遗产管理者从与公众和媒体的交流中获益，因为公众在感到突然和震惊的同时，增加了认识自然进程的机会。

However such events do create a need for assessment of possible increased hazards to human life. In the case of this landslide, important measures include assessment and monitoring of risks and communication to ensure that tourists, researchers and people living downstream are aware of the risk of sudden flooding if the dam were to breach.

然而，这类事件也增加了灾害对人类生活影响的评估。在上述滑坡的案例中，最重要的措施包括评估、监测危害和与公众交流，以确保游客、研究人员和生活在下游的居民意识到，因大坝崩塌所引起洪水可能会对他们造成的威胁。

4.2 How do you analyse the factors that may cause disaster risks to your property?

4.2 如何分析能够引起遗产灾害风险的要素？

The factors that may cause disaster risks to the property can be analysed through the following steps (Figure 4):

能够引起遗产灾害风险的要素可以通过以下几步分析（图 4）。

Analysis of factors

• Listing all the natural and human-induced hazards that expose the property to disaster

分析要素

• 罗列所有能够在遗产上产生的自然和人为灾害，包括具有潜在灾害性影响的基本灾害，

risks. These would include primary hazards with potentially disastrous impact, such as earthquakes, as well as slow and progressive secondary hazards, or underlying risk factors, such as changes in natural vegetation due to rising ground water or changes in ground water quality due to pollution. In the case of cultural properties, secondary hazards might be the growth of vegetation on monuments and dampness from rising ground water.

例如地震；也包括缓慢和逐步形成的次生灾害，或潜在的风险因素，例如自然植被的改变会导致地下水位上升、改变地表水的质量、甚至造成污染。对于文化遗产，次生灾害则可能是在遗址本体上生长的植被和来自于地下水的潮气。

(Note that, although the focus here is hazards such as earthquakes and cyclones that have the potential to unleash disasters, secondary hazards that increase disaster vulnerability cannot be overlooked).

（注意：尽管此处关注的是灾害，例如地震、飓风具有能够引发潜在灾害的可能，但也不可忽视因次生灾害而增加的脆弱性。）

• Identifying the processes that might, in combination with a primary hazard, cause disaster risk to the property. These processes can be identified on the basis of:

• 认定过程应包括确定主要危害、威胁遗产安全的主要原因，这些过程可基于以下条件进行：

– evaluating the performance of existing management systems and disaster preparedness measures;

– 评估现有管理系统和灾害防治措施的效果；

– analyzing the potential negative impacts of existing damage and deterioration patterns or phenomena, or present irreversible interventions, activities or physical planning which could contribute towards increasing the vulnerability of the property to various hazards. This can be done using various tools, and may also involve the local community, as in the Disaster Imagination Exercise described in Case Study 7.

– 分析已存在的破坏和劣化模式或现象、目前不可逆的干预活动或实际环境规划的负面影响。这些负面影响降低了遗产抵御各种灾害的能力，增加了遗产的脆弱性。这可以通过各种工具实现，同时也要有当地社区的参与，如案例 7 所描述的。

– analyzing the underlying risk factors relating to the surrounding environment that increase the property's vulnerability. These factors may be physical, social, economic or institutional, as well as attitudinal. The physical vulnerability may be at the structural or material level. Each property should identify its specific indicators of vulnerability to be assessed for change over time. For example, the World Heritage monument zones that are located in the dense urban areas of Kathmandu, Patan and Bhaktapur (Nepal) are highly vulnerable in terms

– 分析可能增加遗产脆弱性、与环境相关的潜在威胁因素。这些因素可以是物质的、社会的、经济的或研究机构的，或态度上的。物理易脆性可能是结构上的或物质层面上的。应确定每一个遗产的特殊易脆性指标，从而实施评估。例如，世界遗产区位于加德满都、帕坦和巴克塔普尔（尼泊尔）的城市密集区内，具有很高的脆弱性，表现在灾害中建筑结构的脆弱性和出入通道的脆弱性（例 1）。

of their structural weakness as well as accessibility during disasters (Case Study 1).

– analyzing the potential negative effect of poor restoration done in the past. For example, according to some experts, investigation at the Prambanan Temple Compounds (Indonesia) following the June 2006 earthquake revealed that the extensive damage to the main stone temples was due principally to the reinforced concrete understructure that was introduced into the temples during prior restoration. Similar reasons were also cited by experts in explaining the damage to Bam Citadel in the Islamic Republic of Iran following the 2003 earthquake there (see also Case Study 27 on Bam).

– 分析过去不恰当的修复带来的潜在负面影响。例如，根据一些专家对于普兰巴南神庙（印度尼西亚）的调查，2006 年 6 月的地震对石建的寺庙有大面积的损坏，这些损坏形成的原因是因为在早期的修复过程中使用了钢筋混凝土结构。相同的，在专家解释伊朗巴姆古城因 2003 年地震破坏的原因时，也认为造成破坏的主要原因是在维修的过程中使用了钢筋混凝土结构。（见案例 27）。

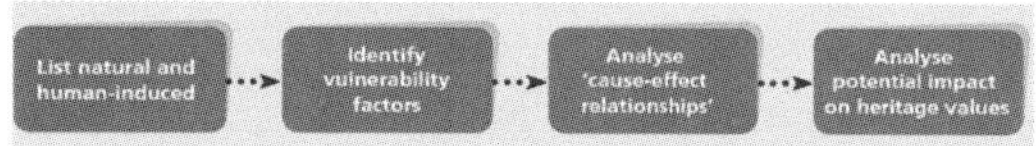

Figure 4 Risk Analysis Process

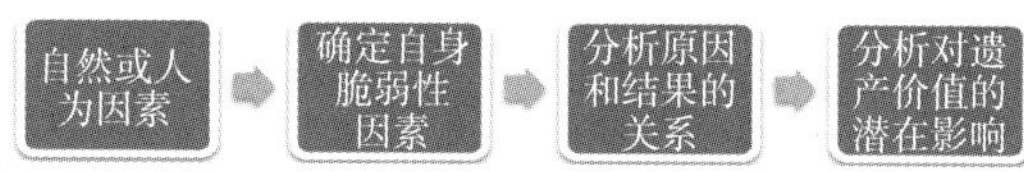

图 4 风险分析过程

– analyzing the 'cause-effect' relationships between various primary hazards and underlying risk factors that increase the property's vulnerability and expose it to disaster risk and clarify the way these interlock. Several secondary hazards (or factors) may increase the vulnerability of a property to a primary hazard. For example, secondary hazard agents such as termites and vegetation affecting a historic building may be caused by a primary hazard, such as heavy rainfall due to improper drainage and lack of maintenance. This might in turn weaken the structure of the property, making it more vulnerable to earthquake (primary hazard). At the same time, a solution to a specific hazard may increase a property's vulnerability with respect to another hazard. For example, conservation guidelines for mortars developed because of a greater incidence of flash-storms may not be appropriate in terms of earthquake resistance (Figure 5).

– 分析各种基本灾害与潜在威胁因素之间的"原因——结果"关系，这些可能增加遗产自身的脆弱性，并置遗产于灾害风险之中，需清楚确定他们的内在联系。许多次生灾害（或因素）也会增加遗产自身抵抗基本灾害的脆弱性。例如，次生灾害如白蚁和植被对历史建筑的影响，又例如大雨或缺少维护而造成排水系统不畅，都会增加基本灾害的危害性，造成遗产的结构在地震中更加脆弱。同时，特殊灾害的解决方案可能增加遗产自身应付其他灾害的脆弱性。例如，保护指南中混凝土的应用能防止高频率的闪电风暴，但不适合防震（表 5）。

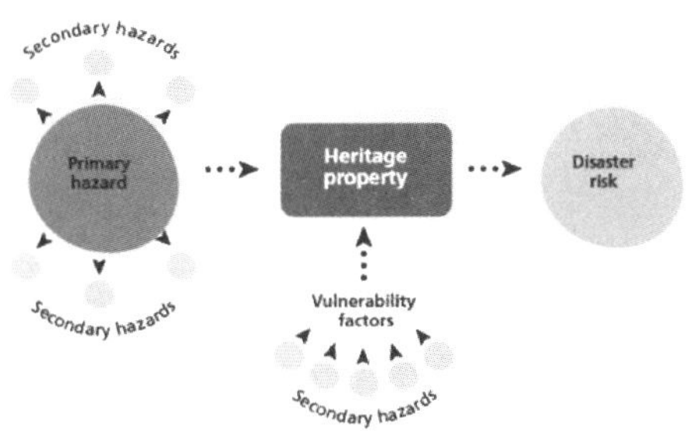

Figure 5 Relationship between hazard, vulnerability and disasters

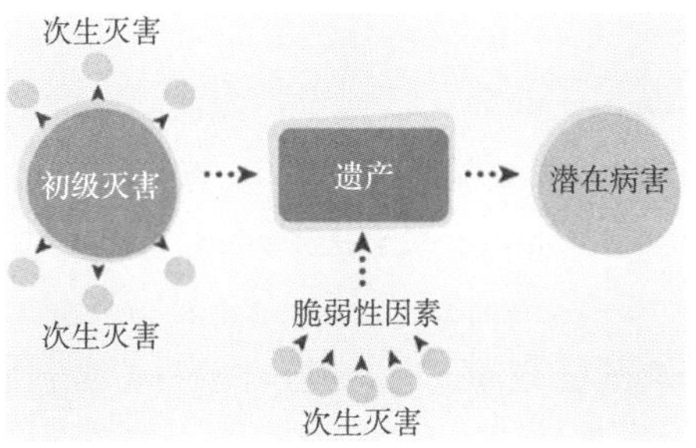

图 5　灾害，自脆性和灾害的关系

CASE STUDY 7

Disaster Imagination Exercise: a method of community-based risk assessment of post-earthquake fire in historic urban areas.

案例 7

灾害想象练习：针对历史城区震后发生火灾的、以社区为基础（本位）的风险评估法。

The Disaster Imagination Exercise is an effective tool for analyzing disaster risks to cultural heritage located in urban areas by engaging the local community. The first step of this exercise is to obtain an appropriate base map of the area and fix it on a table under a transparent sheet. Based on preliminary research, legends are decided for important heritage buildings, safety areas, fire risk areas, and water sources such as hydrant, cistern, warehouse, etc. Essential areas that need to be saved in case of a fire should be decided, including cultural heritage buildings and community facilities. As the next step, the participants should imagine the scenario when a serious earthquake hits the area causing the disruption of the city water and electricity network, and subsequently mark the water resources that need electricity, for example normal hydrants, wells with pumps, etc. This should be followed by a discussion on possible earthquake damage such as road blockage, building collapse based on the hazard maps and site inspection. Next, the participants should imagine the scenario that a fire breaks out around the heritage buildings as a result of the earthquake, and consequently mark places such as restaurants where fire is likely to occur. They should try to figure out ways of

灾害想象法是对位于城区的遗产、由当地社区参与管理的文化遗产灾害风险评估的有效分析方法。练习的第一步是获得该区域的基本地图，把它固定在桌上，其上覆盖透明纸。基于初步的研究，在地图上标上重要遗产建筑、安全区、火灾威胁区和水资源分布，例如消防栓、蓄水池和仓库等等。先确定火灾中需要抢救的重要区域，如文化遗产建筑和社区设施。下一步，参与者应该想象当发生严重地震后，城市的供水和供电网络会受到严重的破坏，之前标识的水资源点都需要用电，例如普通的消防水龙头、井水需要用泵，等等。接下来要讨论的是基于灾害地图和遗产，地震可能造成的破坏，如道路阻断、建筑物坍塌。接下来，参与者应该想象遗产周边建筑因地震而引起的火灾，之前标识的地方如餐馆可能会发生火灾。他们应该指出哪一条线路可为消防人员提供可用的水资源、考虑水资源的距离、运送的方式、人力资源需求等等。练习的最后一步，基于距离、清晰路线和灵活性的原则，应标识出过火区域可能影响的遗产，从建筑遗产中抢救出来的珍宝的运送路线也应该进行讨论。这个练习所得出来的结论对制订历史城区灾害风险预案很有帮助。

firefighting by tracing the route by which usable water can be delivered to the affected site, taking into account the distance of the source, means of delivery, human resources needed, etc. As the last step of this exercise, the spread area around the fire site should be marked by a big circle and routes for salvaging treasures from heritage buildings should be discussed, based on considerations such as distance, clear route and feasibility. The findings of this exercise should be used to make proposals for disaster risk preparedness in historic urban areas.

Source: Okubo Takeyuki, 2007, Research Center for Disaster Mitigation of Urban Cultural Heritage, Ritsumeikan University, Kyoto.

来源：Okubo Takeyuki, 2007, 减少都市文化遗产灾害，京都立命馆大学。

Writing disaster scenarios

描述灾害情景

The next step involves writing disaster scenarios, i.e. predictions of what the situation is likely to be at a specified time following the disaster (e.g. after one week, or after one month). Scenarios are constructed on the basis of assumptions derived from information about the current and the proposed activities and projects in the area, the management systems in place, and the vulnerability of the property to various hazards that has been previously assessed.

下一步应该描述灾害情景，例如，预测在灾害后的特定时间段的情况应该是什么样的（例，灾后一周，灾后一个月）。情景构建应基于先前评估的一些信息，如当前和计划的活动和项目、当地管理系统信息、遗产自身对于各种灾害的脆弱性信息等等。

The development of alternative scenarios helps in assessing different possibilities and their potential impacts on heritage resource components. Scenarios are explained as narratives — as progressive sequences of events affecting each other, thereby unfolding a particular situation. Scenario planning is indeed a creative exercise, aimed at playing with various existing and potential variables in a particular context. The scenarios will have different scopes and natures, depending on whether:

描述可能发生的场景有助于评估不同的可能性和他们对遗产资源要素的潜在影响。场景可被认为是叙述——有相互影响的、进行中的序列事件，以及对特殊情景的展开。情景规划是真实的创造性练习，目的在于在特定的背景下考虑各种已有的或潜在的变量。这个情景可以有不同的范围和特点，取决于：

• the disaster is caused by one extreme hazard

• 灾害是否是由极端的危害引起（主要危

(primary hazard), such as a cyclone;

• the disaster is followed by other hazards, for example an earthquake is followed by fire as in the case of the Kobe (Japan) earthquake in 1993;

• the disaster takes place when two or more hazards act simultaneously or in close association, creating a cumulative effect, as in the case of the Indian Ocean tsunami when an earthquake led to massive tsunami waves that caused heavy damage in an area affected by civil unrest, only to be followed by looting and arson.

害），如飓风；

• 灾害之后是否还有其他危害，例如地震之后可能会伴有火灾，就像 1993 年日本神户地震；

• 灾害发生，无论是两个或更多危害同时发生、还是一个紧接着一个发生，都会产生累积效果。例如，印度洋海啸，当地震引起大规模的海啸潮，造成城镇的重创后，紧接着城市发生动荡、抢劫和纵火。

Disaster risk scenarios need to take into consideration different variables that are specific to the nature of the property and the kind of risks to which it is exposed. For example, the oil spill model developed for Banc d’Arguin National Park in Mauritania (Case Study 8) covers a number of risks to which the property is exposed but a review identified additional issues in implementing risk reduction measures.

灾害风险情景需要认真考虑不同的变量，这些对分析遗产的自然属性和各类威胁因素特别重要。例如，在毛里塔尼亚的班克达尔金国家公园（案例 8）开发的漏油模型，包含了遗产可能面临的多种威胁因素，但有评论认为应该增加实施减灾措施的专题。

Useful questions to ask: What is the state of conservation of the entire property, a section of it, or specific heritage components? What could be the potential impacts of the disaster scenarios on various heritage components of your site? How do these affect the heritage values (notably the outstanding universal value and the tangible / intangible, movable / immovable attributes that support the criteria used for inscription) of the property and the associated conditions of authenticity and / or integrity?

还有一些问题对描述场景也有帮助，如整个、部分或遗产特殊要素的保护状态是什么？灾害对于遗产各个组成要素的潜在影响有哪些？这些威胁如何影响遗产的价值（特别是突出普遍价值及有形或无形的、可移动不可移动等使遗产符合列入名录标准的特性）？与遗产相关的真实性和完整性状况如何？

CASE STUDY 8

Developing a contingency plan for oil spill risk reduction in Banc d’Arguin (Mauritania).

案例 8

为班克达尔金国家公园编制降低漏油威胁的应急方案。

Maritime oil exploitation and transport in Mauritania’s coastal waters pose a risk to the Banc

在毛里塔尼亚的沿海水域进行海上石油的开采和运输，对世界遗产——保护生态进程和

d'Arguin National Park, a World Heritage site protected for its ecosystem process and biodiversity. Petrochemical extraction and transport outside the boundaries of the World Heritage site pose a threat to marine and coastal species, habitat and water quality through the risk of currents carrying oil spills and pollution into the property.

多样性的班克达尔金国家公园形成威胁。世界遗产区范围外石化产品的提取和运输会对海洋和沿海鱼类种群、栖息地和水质造成威胁，特别是输油管道的泄漏和污染，对遗产的威胁更大。

Although the State Party of Mauritania has signed the major conventions relating to marine pollution prevention and safety MARPOL (1973/1978) and Oil Spill Response (1990), there is still no National Oil Spill Response Plan, designated Oil Spill Response Authority, or experience in dealing with oil spills. However, the Government of Mauritania, with support from the Banc d'Arguin Foundation (FIBA) and IUCN, has been engaging with Woodside, a company involved in oil exploration and extraction in the offshore waters of Mauritania. A panel of independent experts on the impact of the petrochemical industry has also been established to provide oversight.

尽管毛里塔尼亚政府已经签订了防止海洋污染和海洋安全的公约，如防止船舶污染国际公约（1973/1978）和溢油应急（1990）公约，但仍没有制定国家溢油应急规划，确定溢油的管理权，或进行溢油处理的演练。毛里塔尼亚政府在班克达尔金基金会和世界自然保护联盟支持下，与负责石油开采和提炼的伍德赛德公司合作，成立了独立的专家团队负责石化工业影响分析及监督工作。

Woodside has conducted an Environmental Impact Assessment (EIA) to assess the social and environmental impact of its oil extraction activities. Part of the EIA included the modeling of currents and potential oil transport from its area of extraction. The Netherlands Commission for Environmental Assessment, at the request of the Government of Mauritania, also conducted a review of the EIA and made particular comments on the oil spill modeling and Oil Spill Contingency Plan, part of the Woodside Environmental Management Plan.

伍德赛德公司指导了一次环境影响评估，以评判原油提炼活动对周边环境和社区的影响。此次环境影响评估包括了原油从开采地到提炼地的现有和潜在的运输模式。在毛里塔尼亚政府的要求下，荷兰环境评估委员会，对此次环境影响评估进行了评价，并对漏油模式和溢油应急性计划给出了特殊的评估。溢油应急性计划是伍德赛德制订的环境管理规划的一部分。

Although an oil spill model is essential for pollution risk analysis and to aid oil spill management, it is critical that the variables of the model and its assumptions are sufficiently robust to provide reliable oil spill scenarios. Such variables

尽管溢油模式是污染风险分析和协助石油溢油管理的基础，对溢油模式变量的假设也十分重要，它提供了可靠的描绘溢油场景的依据。这些变量包括海底水深测量、湍流、潮汐运动、风力、地球自转引起的对流及大规模的漂移流。

include seabed bathymetry, turbulence, tidal motion, wind-driven and geostrophic convection currents and large-scale drift currents. The independent review confirmed that the model was suitable but raised several concerns: the model was based only on extraction from the existing Chinguetti site; and did not include scenarios for extraction at other locations or the effect of oil transport. Also, the limited expertise in the national government agencies limits the capacity of the responsible agencies to use and interpret the model and associated technical information independently. The oil spill model is an important tool for the Oil Spill Contingency Plan as a response should incorporate the following factors:

在独立评价后，要确定合适的模型，同时也要注意以下几点：模型仅以已开采的欣盖提油田为基础；没有包括评估从其他位置抽取或运输原油的影响因素。同样，国家政府机构的有限演练限制了这些机构独立使用和解释模型及相关技术信息的能力。溢油模型是溢油应急计划中最为重要的工具，作为应对方案，它应该和以下几个因素联合使用：

• Volume of oil spill: which clean-up measures are suitable given the volume of the spill?

• 溢油体积：大体积的漏油需要采用哪一种清理措施？

• Expected drift and dispersal: is the spill likely to drift towards the Banc d'Arguin or other vulnerable areas?

• 预期漂移或扩散：漏油漂移的方向是班克达尔金公园还是其他脆弱地区？

• Seasonal variation in species distribution: are migrant birds or other wildlife present and therefore more vulnerable?

• 种群分布的季节性变化：迁徙候鸟或其他野生动物是否在此区域，它们是否更易受伤害？

• Stationing of response equipment: where should vacuum-cleaning ships be distributed to optimize response prior to pollutants reaching the shore?

• 定点安置的反应设施：怎么分配、布置清油船以达到最优化？

• Location of floating production, storage and offloading systems (FPSO) that receive crude oil from deep-water wells and store it in their hull tanks: have protection screens been installed around the FPSO?

• 从深井抽取的原油和储藏罐的浮式生产、储存和接受卸油系统的位置：在浮式生产、储存和接受卸油系统周围有没有安装保护屏？

• Low vulnerability sites: are there areas where oil spills can be allowed to disperse or land without significant harm?

• 低脆弱性遗产：这个区域的漏油允许扩散么？或对土地会不会有严重的伤害？

A World Heritage site manager should engage with private companies and relevant government agencies to ensure that risk reduction measures are developed to protect the outstanding universal

一个世界遗产的管理应该引入私人公司和相关的政府机构，确保形成降低风险的措施，并能够保护世界遗产的突出普遍价值及其完整性。

values and integrity of the property.

4.3 How can you evaluate disaster risks and prioritize risk reduction measures / strategies?

Disaster risks can be evaluated by assessing the level of risk on the basis of the following criteria：

A. The probability of a particular disaster scenario occurring in your property. The probability might be:

• high, as in the case of heavy rainfall in a temperate climate;

• medium, as in the case of extreme weather events in the tropics;

• low, as in the case of an earthquake that may happen once every fifty years.

The probability is expressed as a ratio, e.g. 1 in 100 (see Case Study 9, which is explained below).

B. The severity of the consequences of the disaster scenario on the property and its components, including people, property, livelihoods; also other physical attributes in which heritage values of the property are embedded, such as landscapes and infrastructure, the disruption of human activities, the loss of traditional knowledge, etc. (in physical, social, cultural and economic terms). A consequence is the direct effect of an event, incident or accident and can be expressed as a health effect (e.g. death, injury, exposure), a property loss in economic terms or number of structures damaged, and an environmental effect. Consequences might be evaluated in the following terms:

• catastrophic or severe;

• mild;

• gradual;

• no consequence.

These can be numerically expressed in relative terms on a scale of 0 to 1, where 0 stands for no

4.3 如何评估灾害风险，最好的降低风险的措施或战略是什么？

灾害风险可以先通过评估风险等级来进行，风险等级的评估应基于以下准则：

A. 遗产发生特定灾害场景的概率。这个概论可分为：

• 高，例如温带气候的暴雨；

• 中等，如热带地区的极端天气事件；

• 低，如 50 年可能发生一次的地震。

概率表示的是比例，例如，百分之一（见案例 9，下面将详细解释）

B. 遗产及其构成要素，包括居民、财产和生计等受灾的严重程度；以及展现遗产价值的其他物质特性，如景观和设施、人类活动的分布、传统知识的损失等等（从物质、社会、文化和经济的角度考虑）。结果是事件、事变和事故直接的影响，也可以是对健康的影响（如，死亡、受损、暴露），或者经济上财产损失或对建筑物破坏、以及对环境影响。结果可以从以下几个方面评估：

• 灾害的程度或严重程度；

• 温和的；

• 渐进的；

• 没有结果。

可以用 0 到 1 的数值表示相关的级别，0 表示没有结果，1 就表示灾害性结果。

consequence and 1 for catastrophic consequences.

The consequence in terms of 'loss of value' represented by the relative impact on various attributes associated with specific values of the property. Within a single property, some attributes could be absolutely essential and irreplaceable to convey the outstanding universal value, whereas others, although important, could be less crucial or more easily restored.

"价值损失"的结果代表对与遗产价值相关的、各种属性的相对影响。对于一个单体遗产，一些属性是其突出普遍价值独一无二、无可替代的证据，而另一些属性，尽管也很重要，但是重要性要低一些，或容易修复。

The consequence on values would be higher in the former case, less in the latter. Therefore one of the factors for risk evaluation could be developed by devising a recovery index for attributes that can be restored.

价值影响结果可能在前一种情况高，在后一种情况低。因此，可以将属性设计成复原指数，即将能否修复作为风险评估的一个因素。

The level of risk to the site for a particular scenario is assessed vis-à-vis the probability, severity of consequence on people, lives and livelihoods, and potential loss of values (Figure 6).

确定特定的遗产风险等级方案的相对概率，评估灾害后果对人类、生活和社区及失去潜在价值的严重性。

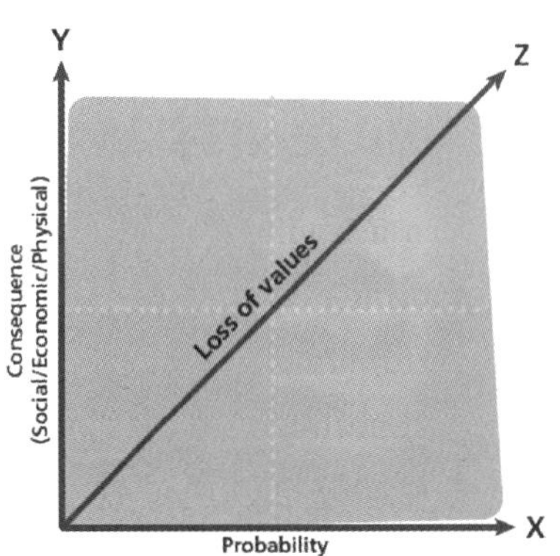

Figure 6 Analysis of the level of risk

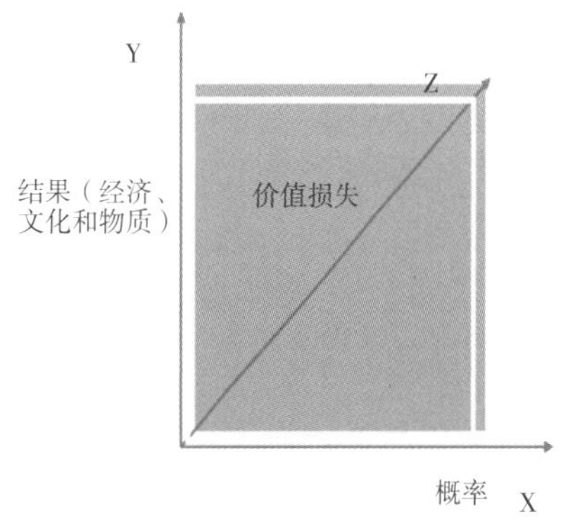

图 6 风险等级分析

For example, an earthquake affecting a dense urban fabric with rich cultural heritage will represent a scenario with low probability, high physical, social and economic consequences and high loss of value, and therefore a high level of risk; whereas the same earthquake affecting open farm land with no habitation and cultural heritage may represent a scenario of low probability, low physical, social and economic consequences and

例如，地震发生在文化遗产资源丰富、密高度的城市，代表了低概率，高物质、高社会和经济结果、高价值损失的情况，可以认为是高等级风险；然而，同等级地震发生在没有居民和文化遗产的农耕地上，则代表了低概率，低物质、低社会和经济结果甚至可能没有价值损失的场景，则可以被认为是低等级风险。

probably no loss of value, and therefore low level of risk.

To take another example, minor seepage of water from the roof in a significant historic building, due to improper drainage, may cause extensive damage to exquisitely painted ceilings. This would represent a scenario with high probability, with low consequences in physical and economic terms but high consequences for the values represented by the painted ceiling. On the other hand, continual leakage of rainwater through cracks in the roof of an outhouse of little heritage significance, located in an area with a high frequency of rainfall, may represent a high probability or high-consequence scenario in physical terms with a not-so-high loss of value.

再看其他例子。重要历史建筑中因不适当的排水设施而引起房顶上的轻微渗水，可能会对天花板上的精美绘画造成了重大损失。这代表了高概率、低物质、低社会和经济结果、高价值损失（天花板上的壁画带来的损失）的一种情况。另一种情况，位于暴雨高发区的厕所屋顶裂隙，雨水的持续渗漏对遗产重要性几乎没有影响，这就代表了高概率，或高物质结果，却没有价值损失的情况。

Various quantitative and qualitative tools can be used to assess the level of risk to heritage sites. One such quantitative tool has been developed for assessing the risk to museum collections (Case Study 9).

在遗产风险级别评估中可以使用各种定量和定性工具。其中一种定量工具用于博物馆藏品的风险评估（案例 9 ）。

CASE STUDY 9

Quantitative expression of risk: the ABC risk assessment scales for museum collections.

案例 9

风险量化表示：博物馆藏品的 ABC 风险评估。

The probability of disaster and its consequence can also be quantified using mathematical principles. For example, if the probability (say ‘A’) of severe museum fires was 5 museums over a period of 50 years in a country with 2,000 museums, then the probability for each museum is 5 / (50 x 2,000), which means there is 1 chance in 20,000 of fire each year or 1 in 200 every 100 years. The consequence on the museum collections(say ‘B’) can be quantified in terms of percentage of collection that is affected in a museum, for example, loss of all or most of the collection can be quantified

灾害概率和结果可以通过数学原理量化。例如，如果近 50 年内，2000 座博物馆中有 5 座博物馆发生过的严重的火灾被确认为概率（称之为 A），那么每个博物馆可能发生严重火灾的概率是 5/(50x2000)，也就是说，每一年在 2 万个博物馆中有 1 个博物馆可能发生火灾，或在 100 年中，每 200 个博物馆有 1 个博物馆可能发生火灾。博物馆藏品的结果（B）可以从对博物馆藏品影响的比例去定量，例如，藏品的全部或大部分损失，定量为 100%，而微乎其微的损失份额定量为 0.01%。同样每一个受影响的藏品价值损失的比例（称为 C），完全或几乎完全的

as 100 per cent while a mini scale fraction of loss may be just 0.01 per cent. Similarly, the percentage of value lost in each affected object (say ‘C’) can be quantified as 100 per cent for total or almost total loss of value in each affected object while mini scale loss of value in each affected object can be 0.01 per cent. According to ABC risk assessment scales, the magnitude of risk to museum collections will thus be the sum total of the three indicators ‘A’, ‘B’ and ‘C’.

价值损失可以定量为100%，微乎其微的损失可认为是0.01%。根据ABC风险评估尺度，博物馆藏品的危害等级将通过“A”“B”“C”三个指数之和确定。

Source: S. Michalski, 2007, ICCROM-CCI-ICN Reducing Risks to Collections Course, Sibiu, Romania.

来源：S. Michalski, 2007, ICCROM–CCI–ICN降低风险系列课程，罗马尼亚锡比乌。

The prioritization of risk reduction measures may depend on several factors:

• Although the risk level of a disaster scenario may be quite high, the mitigation measures may need to be optimized if the available or promised resources are limited.

• Prioritization for disaster reduction may sometimes have to wait in the face of the immediate conservation needs of a property, such as repair of a severely damaged structure.

• Prioritization also depends on the costs and benefits associated with both implementation and maintenance stages. This is linked to the availability of human and financial resources.

• Another factor in the prioritization of risk reduction measures is the effect that the proposed measure may have on risks to one heritage component at the cost of reducing the risk to another component, to visitors and staff, or to the environment.

减灾措施的优先等级由以下几个元素决定：

• 尽管灾害的危害等级可能会很高，如果可利用或承诺的资金有限，应最优先考虑缓解措施。

• 减灾的优先级有时候可能需要等到遗产出现保护需求的时候才能确定，例如，维修严重破损的构筑物。

• 优先权应根据实施和维持阶段的花费和收益而定，这与人力和财力资源直接相关。

• 减灾措施优先权的其他因素还包括，计划措施可能对威胁遗产的一个要素产生作用，但可能对另一个要素造成威胁，如对参观者、员工或者是环境的威胁。

Section 4 has reviewed what information is needed in order to identify risks (4.1), analysed potential risks (4.2) and seen how they can be reduced by prioritizing them, making use of three general criteria (4.3). The concept of probability

第4章 介绍了确定威胁需要什么信息（4.1），分析潜在威胁（4.2），优先选择的方法是什么，确定了三个有用的基本准则（4.3）。也简单介绍了概率的概念以及风险可以通过量化表达的理念。

and the idea that risk can be expressed quite simply in quantitative terms were introduced.

Section 5 reviews the measures that can be adopted to prevent disaster risks or at least to mitigate their impact. Again, a number of case studies illustrate what can be done.

第 5 章 介绍防止、至少减缓灾害风险影响应采取的措施。在本章中会详细介绍很多相关案例。

5.How can you prevent disaster risks or mitigate their impact?

5 如何阻止灾害风险发生或减缓他们的影响?

5.1 What measures can you adopt to prevent or mitigate disaster risks?

5.1 能采取什么样的措施阻止或减弱灾害威胁?

Disaster risks can be prevented or mitigated by:

• preventing hazards such as fires and theft; or

• mitigating the impact of hazards such as earthquakes and flooding; or

• reducing the vulnerability of the property and its environs; or

• training the staff in self-protection strategies.

灾害风险能够通过以下途径阻止或减弱：

• 阻止灾害比如火灾和失窃；或

• 减弱灾害带来的影响，例如地震或洪水，或

• 降低遗产的易损性或他们的环境，或

• 培训员工的自我保护战略。

The prevention and mitigation measures require coordination among various staff members and departments responsible for managing the property as well as contact with outside agencies and experts in relevant fields.

需要负责遗产管理的各个员工和不同部门之间的通力合作实施阻止或减弱措施，同时也要联络外部机构和相关领域的专家。

Specific equipment might be required to prevent or reduce the impact of hazards on the property. The cost-effectiveness of this equipment needs to be assessed on the basis of various factors such as available resources and staffing.

需要准备特殊设备防止或降低灾害影响。该设备的成本效益需要以对各种因素包括可用资源和人员配置进行评估为基础。

Different measures, techniques and strategies for mitigating disaster risks to heritage sites are illustrated here by case studies. These include:

• Urban and regional planning measures in and around a property, which address disaster risks to the property itself and its immediate environs. The

通过案例解释减弱遗产灾害威胁的不同措施、技术和战略，可概括为：

• 对遗产或其周边城市或区域的规划措施，重点阐述了遗产及其周边环境的灾害风险。应将遗产的特殊规划项目整合到现有的城市或区

need to integrate heritage within existing urban or regional plans and specific planning projects has already been emphasized (Section 2.2) as part of the discussion on the relationship of a DRM plan to other management plans. A good example of this linkage is provided by the regional projects that were designed to avoid flooding of the Historic City of Ayutthaya (Thailand), following the 1995 disaster (Case Study 10; see also Case Study 14 for another response to flooding of a heritage area, involving planning measures at the urban scale).

域规划中，这部分内容在讨论灾害风险管理规划与其他管理规划的关系章节（2.2）中已经强调过了。关于区域规划与灾害风险管理规划完美结合的案例，将介绍历史城市大城府防洪的地区计划（见案例10，及案例14其他遗产区对洪水的反应，包括了城镇级别的规划措施）。

• Strategic decisions based on detailed studies such as the impacts of climate change and of changes in the ecosystem. This may involve the strategic restoration of a previous ecosystem (Case Study 11).

• 依据详细研究例如气候和生态圈改变的影响，做出的战略决定。将包括对此前原有生态系统的战略修复（案例11）。

• Various tools may be used by site managers to mitigate disaster risks in protected areas. In the Galápagos Islands (Ecuador) the management of invasive species through eradication and the imposition of strict controls is crucial to the mitigation of the risk of endemic species loss (Case Study 12).

• 遗产管理者在保护区内使用的各种减灾方法。在加拉帕戈斯群岛（厄瓜多尔）对于入侵种群的管理，通过消灭和严格控制入侵种群的方法降低了地方种群消失的危害（案例12）。

• Analysis of the flood damage in summer 2002 suggested that restoration of the floodplain ecosystem that was once much more extensive would aid in flood mitigation of the Danube region in South-Eastern Europe (Case Study 11).

• 通过对2002年夏季洪水危害的分析得出以下结论，广泛恢复以往泄洪区的生态系统，有利于减弱欧洲东南部多瑙河流域洪水的威胁（案例11）。

• Successful mitigation measures were taken in the face of a predicted El Niño event and possibly accelerated erosion of the earth-construction remains at Peru's Chan Chan Archaeological Zone (Case Study 16).

• 成功的减灾措施被用于预测厄尔尼诺现象，这一现象可能加速对秘鲁昌昌考古区域土遗址的侵蚀（案例16）。

• Mitigation measures can also include changes to the management of the property and definition of buffer zones.

• 减灾措施同样也包括改变对遗产的管理和对缓冲区的划定。

• Technical measures for protecting the site from the impact of specific natural disasters. The type of measures would depend on the nature of the property and the main disaster risk to which it

• 用于因特殊自然灾害影响而对遗产实施的保护性技术措施。措施的类型应该根据遗产特性和主要灾害威胁决定。以威尼斯为例，这里经常爆发季节性的洪水，需要复杂的技术解决

is exposed. In the case of Venice, which is exposed to regular flooding, a sophisticated technological solution has led in turn to ecosystem regeneration (Case Study 13).

方案进而引导生态圈的再生（案例 13）。

Proposed measures should depend on the nature of the risk while taking into account their potential impact on the values of the property. It is paramount that the proposed intervention should have minimal impact on the values, authenticity and integrity of the property (see Section 5.2 and Case Study 17 on Kobe, Japan).

拟议措施应该针对危害的特性，要考虑他们对遗产价值潜在的影响。最好的干预措施应该对遗产价值、真实性和完整性的影响限度最低（见 5.2 节和案例 17，神户，日本）。

Planned measures, moreover, should not be seen in isolation but would need to be integrated with other existing planning frameworks. In the case of Grimma (Germany), a technical solution to prevent flooding of the city had to be revised to take account of much broader concerns of planning and public reaction (Case Study 14).

计划措施不应是孤立的，应与其他已有的规划框架整合在一起分析。在格里马（德国）案例中，考虑到规划和公众的反应，对一个预防城市洪水的技术方案进行了修改（案例 14）。

• Disaster risks can also be mitigated to a great extent through effective monitoring systems. Thus the risk of glacial lake outburst floods in Sagarmatha National Park (Nepal) has been reduced by monitoring glacial lakes and by introducing early warning systems (Case Study 15).

• 有效的监测系统在很大程度上可以减轻灾害风险。因此，在萨加玛塔国家公园（尼泊尔）冰川湖遭到突发洪水的威胁时，通过监测冰川湖泊和引入预警系统等措施，减弱了洪水造成的灾害（案例研究 15）。

CASE STUDY 10

Integrating heritage in urban and regional planning: risk preparedness for the Historic City of Ayutthaya (Thailand).

案例 10

整合城市和区域规划中的遗产：历史名城大城府（泰国）的风险预案。

Over ten ancient towns and several archaeological sites and monuments were flooded due to incessant heavy rainfall during several weeks in 1995. Many historic sites were damaged, and some buildings collapsed. The main cause of increasing flood intensity in historic areas of Ayutthaya was the lack of effective land-use control, causing

1995 年，由于连续数周的暴雨，阿瑜陀耶大城府历史城区数十个古老城镇、几个考古遗址、纪念遗址遭到了洪水的威胁。许多历史古迹遭到破坏，一些建筑物倒塌。此次洪水强度加大的主要原因是缺乏有效的土地使用控制，原有的自然泄洪道和滞洪区被开发成了功能性的城市区，导致自然泄洪的渠道被毁。事实上，

many natural floodways and retention areas to be destroyed and developed as functional urban areas. In fact, traditional flood prevention systems using water gates and dykes had been effective in Ayutthaya for centuries until they suffered deterioration and destruction in recent years. As a preventive measure for such devastating floods in the future, several projects were formulated at regional level. These included construction of dams and reservoirs, grass plantation along the banks of major rivers, floodwater retention projects, dredging of waterways and removal of water weeds. Revitalization of ancient city moats, walls and gateways was proposed to prevent future floods.

几个世纪以来，使用水闸和堤坝的传统防洪系统已有效地保护了大城府，直到它们近年来遭受破坏。作为防治未来毁灭性洪水的措施，在区域内已陆续形成了几个项目。这些项目包括建造水坝和水库、恢复主河流两侧的植被、防洪工程项目、疏通河道和去除水中杂草等，建议修复古城的护城河、城墙和闸道以防止将来的水患。

Site plans were also prepared for monuments in lower areas outside the city to be protected by dams and drainage systems.

遗产计划也准备让处于城外低洼区的遗迹得到大坝和排水系统的保护。

Source: K. Ronarit, 1997, Risk Preparedness for Cultural Properties: a Case Study on the Old Cities of Bangkok and Ayutthaya, Kobe/Tokyo International Symposium on Risk Preparedness for Cultural Properties.

来源 K. Ronarit, 1997, 文化遗产风险防范：曼谷及阿瑜陀耶老城保护，神户 – 东京文化遗产风险防范研讨会。

CASE STUDY 11

Flood mitigation through ecosystem restoration: the Danube in south-eastern Europe

案例 11

通过恢复生态系统缓解洪水的威胁：欧洲东南部的多瑙河流域。

In Europe, floods are the most common type of natural disaster, threatening lives and livelihoods and incurring great cost. In summer 2002, 100 people lost their lives through flooding of the Danube. The estimated cost of the flooding was €10 billion in Germany, €3 billion in Austria and €2 billion in the Czech Republic. In 2005 many villages in Romania and Bulgaria were destroyed by flash floods along the Danube. In 2006 up to 30,000 people were displaced in the Danube Basin and at least ten people died, and millions of hectares of

在欧洲，洪水是最常见的自然灾害类型，威胁着生命和生计，也造成了巨大的经济损失。2002 年夏天，有 100 人在多瑙河的洪水中丧生，据估计在洪水治理上的花费，德国 100 亿欧元，奥地利 30 亿欧元，捷克共和国 20 亿欧元。2005 年，多瑙河沿岸的罗马尼亚和保加利亚的许多的村庄被洪水破坏。2006 年，累计有 30000 人在多瑙河盆地流离失所，至少 10 人死亡，数百万公顷的农田被淹，庄稼颗粒无收。估计总损失超过 5 亿欧元。

agricultural land were flooded, destroying crops. The overall damage was estimated at over half a billion euros.

Studies of satellite images and geographical information systems concluded that the direct cause of flooding was rapid snow melt and heavy rains. However, the restriction of the floods to former floodplains demonstrated that the underlying causes of the disaster were poor planning and investment, allowing industry, agriculture and property to be located on the high-risk Danube floodplain. More than 80 per cent of the former natural floodplain in the Danube Basin has been lost in the last 150 years due to such measures. The Danube Delta World Heritage site is one of the few remaining areas along the lower and middle Danube which still contains large natural floodplain ecosystem complexes capable of mitigating the flood risk. Flood research and models suggest that if natural processes were restored in the most affected areas, the water level would be 40 cm lower during flooding events.

从卫星图像和地理信息系统的研究中可知，快速融雪和暴雨是形成洪水的直接原因。然而，灾害的根源是对泄洪区泛滥平原（河滩地）规划不完善和资金不足，允许在高风险的多瑙河泛滥平原上修建工业、农业和建筑物。由于上述原因，在过去的 150 年中，在多瑙河盆地上已有超过 80% 的自然泛滥平原消失。多瑙河三角洲世界遗产是多瑙河中下游现存的、能够降低洪水威胁的自然泄洪泛滥平原生态系统之一。洪水研究和模型表明，如果在受洪水影响最严重的地区实施恢复自然生态系统，在洪水期间水位将降低 40 厘米。

Recent studies based on climate models predict that intensity and frequency of flooding will increase in the future. While climate change is difficult to address directly, mitigation through ecological restoration of floodplains, including reconnecting side channels and widening of the riverbed upstream of settlements, would reduce flood risks by restoring ecological functions. These measures would provide additional ecosystem services including provision of wood, reed, fish, drinking water, nutrient reduction and storage. A network of existing and new protected areas including Srebarna Nature Reserve World Heritage site (Bulgaria), Ramsar Sites, Biosphere Reserves and National and Nature Parks is being developed to help the restoration and protection of the Danube floodplain.

基于气候模型预测的研究显示，未来洪水的强度和频率将会增加。虽然气候变化很难直接解决，但通过生态系统修复如缓解冲积平原，包括重新连接两侧旁通渠和扩宽定居点上游的河床等措施，恢复生态功能，减少洪水威胁。这些措施将提供额外的生态系统服务，包括提供木材、芦苇、鱼、饮用水、养分还原和存储。现有的网络和新的保护区，包括斯雷巴那世界遗产自然保护区（保加利亚）、国际重要湿地、生物圈保护区和国家自然公园等，已被用来恢复和保护多瑙河泄洪泛滥平原。

Site managers have a variety of tools available to increase the role of their protected areas in flood mitigation. Materials are available from various international programmes and conventions such as the Ramsar Convention's Wetlands Risk Assessment Framework, and the World Meteorological Organization's Disaster Risk Reduction Programme.

遗产的管理人员使用各种各样的措施来缓解保护区的洪水泛滥。资料可通过各种国际项目和公约，如湿地公约、湿地风险评估框架和世界气象组织的减少灾害风险的计划等获取。

CASE STUDY 12

Mitigation through ecosystem recovery: invasive species eradication in the Galápagos Islands (Ecuador).

案例 12

通过恢复生态系统实现减弱灾害威胁：在加拉帕戈斯群岛（厄瓜多尔）消灭入侵的物种。

Introduced species facilitated by lack of effective control and quarantine measures threaten the endemic species of the Galápagos Islands World Heritage site. By 1900, 112 introduced species had already been identified and by 2007 the number had risen to 1,321. In 2006, a survey showed that the approximately 500 native plant species, of which about 180 are endemic, were outnumbered by the 748 introduced plants. More than half of the 180 species of endemic plants in the Galápagos are now threatened, according to the IUCN Red List of Threatened Species. Invasive and introduced species may lead to the extinction of native plants. Overgrazing from goats can remove entire ecosystems from islands, as well as prevent regeneration after disturbance. Grazing is believed to be responsible for one plant extinction on Santiago Island, and has a knock-on effect on other species.

由于缺乏对引入的物种有效的协调控制和检疫措施，威胁到加拉帕戈斯群岛世界遗产的特有物种。1900 年，已确认引进的物种达 112 种，到 2007 年这一数字已上升到 1321 种。2006 年的一项调查表明，在这个地区大约有 500 多种本地植物，其中约 180 种是当地特有的，而引入植物的数量多达 748 种。根据世界自然保护联盟濒危物种名录，在加拉帕戈斯群岛的 180 种特有植物均被列入濒危名录，其中超过一半的特有植物正受到威胁。其他物种的侵入和引进可能会导致本地物种、植物的灭绝。山羊过度放养破坏了海岛上整个生态系统，包括干扰生态系统再生。在圣地亚哥岛，放牧被认为是一种植物灭绝的重要原因，并对其他物种产生连锁效应。

Initial attempts to manage invasive species failed due to lack of monitoring and lack of systematic planning. On Santiago Island a pig eradication programme took thirty years and over 18,000 pigs were removed in all, the last one in November 2000. The programme has allowed turtle, tortoise, nesting birds and many plant species to recover. It also took thirty years to eradicate goats from the Island of Pinta, where they were introduced

由于缺乏监督和系统规划，最初管理外来物种入侵的尝试失败了。在圣地亚哥岛禁止养猪的计划花了 30 年，超过 18000 头猪被全部迁移，2000 年 11 月最后一头猪迁出后，猪在岛上彻底根除。该计划让乌龟、海龟、筑巢的鸟类和许多动植物物种的得以恢复。他们还用了 30 年时间，禁止在平塔岛养山羊，自 1950 年山羊引入后，到 20 世纪 70 年代，原生植被系统已被摧毁。最初计划 1971—1982 年间外迁 41000

in 1950 and had devastated native vegetation by the 1970s. The initial programme from 1971–82 removed 41,000 goats but the lack of monitoring and regular visits meant that the island was twice wrongly declared free of the animals. During the successful 1999–2003 programme over 56,000 goats were removed. In response to the severity of the threat to the natural heritage of the Galápagos from feral animals, the Charles Darwin Foundation (a conservation NGO) has carried out extensive research. A Global Environment Facility (GEF)-funded Invasive Species Project, including the goat eradication component Project Isabella, was jointly conceived between the Galápagos National Parks Service and the Charles Darwin Foundation. At a cost of more than US$18 million, goats and donkeys were removed through an intensive eradication programme. The effectiveness of the project was greatly aided by the use of a geographical information system (GIS). This database aided the project management and monitoring during the project and in the analysis of results.

头山羊，但缺乏监控和定期回访，岛上两次陷入动物失控状况。在1999—2003项目中，超过56000头山羊被成功迁移。为了应对野生动物对加拉帕戈斯群岛自然遗产的严重威胁，查尔斯·达尔文基金会（民间保护组织）实施了一系列的研究。由全球环境基金资助的入侵物种迁移项目，包括伊莎贝拉山羊外迁项目，也是加拉帕戈斯群岛国家公园和查尔斯·达尔文基金会的共同构想。一个成本超过1800万美元的强制外迁项目，彻底迁出了山羊和驴子。地理信息系统的使用对该项目的有效实施提供了极大地帮助。在项目实施和结果分析期间，这个数据库对项目管理和监控极有帮助。

Prevention of introductions is the first and most cost-effective method of addressing risk from invasive species. Had procedures been in place decades ago to prevent introduction of invasive species, the widespread loss of native species and cost of eradication in the Galápagos could have been avoided. Identifying and blocking pathways for entry of any species, rather than species-based prevention, is the most efficient way to concentrate efforts. For the Galápagos the main entry points are aircraft and ships (tourist and cargo). The Global Invasive Species Programme identifies three major possibilities to prevent further invasions:

禁止通告是解决入侵物种风险首选和最有效的方法。禁止引入外来物的通告程序在这个地方已实施了几十年了，避免了本土物种的消失，也降低了在加拉帕戈斯群岛根除入侵生物物种的成本。确定和阻塞外来物种的入侵通道，而不是以物种预防为基础，是最有效的集中精力的方法。加拉帕戈斯群岛的主要的入侵通道是飞机和船只（旅游和货物）。全球入侵物种项目确定了三个主要的可能性来防止外来生物进一步的入侵：

• interception based on regulations enforced with inspections and fees;

• treatment of material suspected to be contaminated with non-indigenous species;

• 依据法规实施检查并收取一定费用，达到拦截的目的；

• 治理能引起污染的非本土物种；

• prohibition of particular commodities in accordance with international regulations. There is also a need to assess the risk of deliberate introduction of non-indigenous species.

• 根据国际法规，禁止特定商品进口。还要对引入非本土物种的风险进行审慎的评估。

With increasing entry points to the Galápagos and rising visitation and immigration rates, the role of the government in enforcing prevention and management policies is key. Although protocols and policies have been adopted, implementation is hampered by low capacity and training on the importance of invasive introduction risk reduction activities.

随着进入加拉帕戈斯人口和参观、移民率不断增加，政府在加强防治和管理政策上扮演了关键的角色。尽管逐步采用相关协议和政策，但实施减少入侵风险的重要活动依然因人员能力低下和缺少培训而受到阻碍。

CASE STUDY 13

Mitigation through flood control and environmental regeneration: Venice (Italy).

案例 13

通过洪水控制和环境再生削弱影响：威尼斯（意大利）。

Following the disastrous flooding of 4 November 1966, Italy launched an action plan to save Venice by developing and approving special laws for the city, making sizeable sums and resources available, setting up special procedures and instruments for the historic city and its lagoon. The government commissioned Consorzio Venezia Nuova to find a definitive solution to the serious problem of increasingly frequent high tides in the Venice Lagoon Basin. The solution (called MOSE) adopted to counter exceptional flooding is the outcome of a lengthy process, which called for research, experimentation, the construction of mathematical and physical models and careful monitoring of various aspects of the project. This system, in case of exceptionally high tides, will allow the temporary closure by a number of mobile floodgates of the three entrances that link Venice Lagoon to the Adriatic. Three floodgates will be attached to the sea floor at the three entrances of the lagoon. They are called mobile because under normal conditions, they remain filled with water and

1966 年 11 月 4 日灾害性的洪水后，意大利发起了一个通过编制和批准专门法律来拯救威尼斯的行动计划，动用巨额资金和可用资源，设置特殊的程序和工具以满足历史城区和泄洪的需求。政府委托新威尼斯协会寻找最终方案，解决威尼斯盆地越来越频繁的威尼斯泻湖涨潮这一威胁城市的严重问题。方案 (称为 MOSE) 通过研究、试验、建立数学和物理模型、仔细监测各方面内容，计算出可能发生异常洪水的时段。当出现异常的潮汐时，这个系统将暂时关闭连接威尼斯水城与亚得里亚海三个入口中的移动闸门。三个闸门附着在海底的三个泻湖入口处。他们被称为移动的是因为在正常情况下，他们仍然充满了水，安放在位于海底的一个特殊的套管中。一个铰链系统连接在闸门的这些套管装置上，当潮汐水位超过预先设定的水位时，既超过 110 厘米 (大约一年发生 7 次)，压缩空气被泵压到闸门中，清空其中的水，这样闸门上升到水面，阻止潮汐涌入。负责这个项目的新威尼斯协会已经将闸门扩展到覆盖保卫海岸、岛屿和居住区域，并实施了重要泻湖区域部分土地的生态学修复和再生，防止再次

rest on the seabed in a special casing. A system of hinges attaches the floodgates to these structures, and when tide levels above 110 cm are expected (which happens about seven times a year), compressed air is pumped into the floodgates, emptying them of water. This causes them to rise to the surface and block the in-flowing tide. The responsibility of Consorzio Venezia Nuova has been extended to cover a vast range of consolidation work to defend the shores, islands and inhabited zones, and to undertake the morphological restoration and regeneration of significant parts of the lagoon territory, and its protection against pollution. The quantity and quality of this complex range of projects, supported by a modern and sophisticated information service, including a data bank on the transformation of the lagoon environment, have led to the creation of the most important programme of environmental protection, recovery and management ever undertaken in Italy.

的污染。这个复杂项目的数量和质量得到现代、先进的信息服务系统支撑，包括一个有关泻湖环境转化的数据库，这个项目成为意大利有史以来实施的环境保护、恢复和管理最重要项目。

Source: Quaderni Trimestrali, 2002, Safeguarding Venice and its Lagoon – Atlas of Works, Ministry of Infrastructures and Transport, Venice Water Authority.

来源：Quaderni Trimestrali, 2002, 维护威尼斯泻湖及防护工程——阿特拉斯的作品，威尼斯水利局基础设施和运输部。

CASE STUDY 14

Integrating flood protection measures with historic urban area planning: Grimma (Germany).

案例 14

历史城镇规划与防洪措施相结合：格里马（德国）。

Grimma, a small historic city situated on a terrace in the Mulde River valley in Germany, has an unusually well preserved setting in the river landscape, with a largely intact medieval city wall still bordering the river bank. The city was one of the worst affected of the many places in Saxony that were flooded in August 2002.

格里马是坐落在德国穆尔德河河谷台地上历史悠久的城市，有一处不同寻常、保护完好的沿河景观带，基本保存完好的中世纪城墙与河岸相邻。2002 年 8 月的洪水，淹没了萨克森的很多地方，格里马安全受到了最严重威胁。

Comprehensive flood protection concepts for all the bigger rivers in Saxony and their catchment

在萨克森的所有大的河流和集水区开始形成整体防洪概念，大坝管理机构开始准备并形

areas were prepared by the Dam Authority and form the basis for planning in Grimma. An initial, technically oriented proposal for Grimma was promptly rejected by both the city council and the permit authority. The citizens were confronted with the prospect of being blocked off from the river by a monolithic concrete wall stretching 1,200 m and rising about 3 m. It was obvious that realization of this proposal would inevitably involve severe and irreversible damage, not only to the river landscape but also to the functional and aesthetic qualities of the city, particularly the historic fabric and the visual experience of the architectural heritage. As a result it was agreed that flood protection in historic urban areas must be seen as part of a complex planning process that needs to be integrated with other related activities, such as town planning and urban design, historic preservation, environmental protection and design, local economy and infrastructure, recreation and tourism. The following guiding principles were adopted for positioning the flood protection measures:

成了格里马规划的基础。起初技术性的格里马规划遭到了议会和权威机构的拒绝。公众从河岸上看到的景色被一道长约1200米，高3米的整体式混凝土墙遮挡。很明显，提议的实施将不可避免地对河流景观及其功能、美感，特别是对建筑遗产的历史机理和视觉体验造成严重、不可逆转的损害。因此，历史城区的防洪必须被作为复杂规划过程的一部分，需要与其他相关活动如城市规划和城市设计、历史文物保护、环境保护和设计、当地的经济和基础设施、娱乐和旅游相结合。防洪措施设计的指导原则如下：

• No protective wall would be planned in front of public buildings; instead their own exterior walls would be structurally retrofitted to meet flood protection requirements. Shutters would be installed to seal windows and doors in case of flooding.

• 在公共建筑前不设计防护墙；而是改造建筑自身外墙的结构以满足防洪要求。应安装卷帘来密封门窗以防洪水。

• For historic buildings in private ownership, where integration of the protective wall into the building was not possible for legal reasons, the flood wall would be placed directly in front and adapted like a facing.

• 对于私有的历史建筑，法律不强制要求修建统一的防护墙，防洪墙设置应像屏障一样直接阻拦洪水。

• In the open spaces between buildings, the flood wall would be clearly set back.

• 建筑物之间的开放空间，防洪墙应明显后缩。

• A special solution had to be developed for the city wall in order to harmoniously integrate the new flood wall in the historic waterfront ensemble.

• 需采取特殊的解决方案让新的防洪墙与历史滨水区的体系整体和谐。

Source: T. Will, 2008, Integrating technical flood protection and heritage conservation planning

来源：T. Will, 2008, H. Meir and T. Will (eds)) 整合格里马萨克森防洪技术和遗产保护规划，

for Grimma, Saxony, in H. Meir and T. Will (eds), Heritage at Risk: Cultural Heritage and Natural Disasters, ICOMOS.

国际古迹遗址理事会《遗产风险：文化遗产和自然灾害》。

CASE STUDY 15

Mitigation through monitoring and early warning systems: glacial lake outburst floods in Sagarmatha National Park (Nepal).

案例 15

通过监测和早期预警系统降低灾害威胁：萨加玛塔国家公园（尼泊尔）的冰湖溃洪。

Global climate change, both natural and anthropogenic, causes the melting of most mountain glaciers around the world. Glacier melting leads to the formation and rapid expansion of glacial lakes. The moraine banks of such lakes are made of loose deposits that may collapse when the lakes fill up or when avalanches fall into the lakes — leading to sudden and violent flooding in the downstream valleys. Any floods of this sort, referred to as glacial lake outburst floods (GLOFs), can have disastrous consequences for the population and biodiversity of the entire downstream region. In the eastern Himalayan region, more than fifteen major GLOFs have been recorded since 1995.

因自然与人为原因和全球气候变化，造成世界各地大多数山地冰川开始融化。冰川融化会导致冰川湖泊迅速膨胀。这种湖泊的冰碛石河岸是由松散的沉积物形成，当湖泊满溢或雪崩落入湖泊时可能会造成河岸垮塌——导致突然和猛烈的洪水冲向下游河谷。这类洪水，被称为冰湖溃洪（GLOF），给整个下游地区的人口和生物多样性带来灾害性的后果。在东喜马拉雅地区，自 1995 年以来，已记录了超过 15 个冰湖溃泄。

In the Khumbu region of Sagarmatha National Park (Nepal), three major GLOFs occurred in 1977, 1985 and 1998. The 1977 flood destroyed park facilities and a tourist lodge located along the riverbeds. The 1985 flood killed at least twenty people, washed away houses, cultivated land and livestock, and completely destroyed a hydropower station, trails and bridges along its 90 km downstream impact zone.

在萨加玛塔国家公园的昆布地区（尼泊尔），发生了三次冰湖溃泄事件，分别在 1977 年，1985 年和 1998 年。1977 年的洪水摧毁了坐落在河床上的公园设施和旅游小屋。1985 年的洪水造成至少 20 人死亡，冲走了房屋、耕地和牲畜，完全摧毁一个水电站，下游 90 公里的范围内道路和桥梁受到了严重影响。

An effective monitoring and early warning system, embedded in an appropriate risk preparedness strategy, can greatly reduce the loss of life and property caused by GLOFs downstream of potentially dangerous glacial lakes. A 2002 inventory of glaciers and glacial lakes by ICIMOD

在适当的风险防范战略中规划了一个有效的监测和预警系统，它可以大大减少位于冰湖泄洪下游的生命和财产的损失。2002 年由国际山地组织和联合国环境规划署发布冰川和冰湖的名录，确定了在尼泊尔 2323 个冰川湖中有 20 个具有潜在的危害。世界冰川监测机构提供了

and UNEP identified twenty of the 2,323 glacial lakes in Nepal as potentially dangerous. The methods of the World Glacier Monitoring Service provide state-of-the-art guidance for effective monitoring of glaciers and glacial lakes.

有效监测冰川和冰川湖的最先进的方法。

Appropriate monitoring and early warning systems include the use of remote-sensing tools, over flight reconnaissance with small-format cameras, and telecommunication and radio broadcasting systems integrated with on-site installed hydrometeorological and geophysical instruments.

适当的监测和早期预警系统中使用了遥感工具、小型相机空中勘测、无线通信和无线电广播系统、并在现场安装水文气象和地球物理仪等设施。

In many instances, sudden and violent flooding may also be prevented by artificially draining potentially dangerous glacial lakes. Such a strategy has been implemented at the Tsho Rolpa Lake in the western part of Sagarmatha National Park. The lake was storing approximately 90–100 million m3 water held back by a 150 m tall moraine. A breach in this moraine would have caused at least a third of the lake to flood the valley. This threat led to collaborative action by the Government of Nepal with international partners. The 1998–2002 GLOF management project drained the lake, lowering its water level by 3 m, and installed early warning systems in villages downstream.

在许多情况下，人工排水可以防治冰川湖突发和猛烈的洪水。这样的战略在萨加玛塔国家公园西部的 Tsho Rolpa 湖得以实施。这个湖受到了高达 150 米的冰碛石的阻碍，存储了大约 9 千万—1 亿立方米的水。如果冰碛石出现缺口，那么至少有三分之一的湖水将形成洪水，淹没河谷。在这种威胁下，尼泊尔政府与国际合作伙伴协同行动。通过 1998—2002 年的冰湖泄洪管理项目，实施了湖泊排水工程，将湖泊的水位降低了 3 米，并在下游的村庄安装了早期预警系统。

The lowering of the water level reduced the risk of flooding and associated loss of life and property by 20 per cent. However, complete GLOF prevention at this lake would require further draining, perhaps as much as 17 m.

降低水位同时也降低了的洪灾风险，并减少了 20% 的生命和财产损失。然而，要完成这个湖的冰湖泄洪可能需要进一步的排水，水面应该至少再下降 17 米。

Sources:

Case Studies on Climate Change and World Heritage, 2007, UNESCO World Heritage Centre/ UK Department of Culture, Media and Sport.

International Centre for Integrated Mountain

来源：

气候变化和世界遗产案例研究，2007，联合国教科文组织世界遗产中心 / 英国文化、媒体和体育部。

国际山地综合发展中心（ICIMOD）（http://

Development (ICIMOD) (http://www.icimod.org/).

ICIMOD Publications on Climate Change and Responses

(http://books.icimod.org/index.php/search/subject/2).

ICIMOD / UNEP. Inventory of Glaciers, Glacial Lakes and Glacial Lake Outburst Floods Monitoring and Early Warning Systems in the Hindu Kush-Himalayan Region Nepal. United Nations Environment Programme

(http://www.rrcap.unep.org/glofnepal/guide/movie.html).

World Glacier Monitoring Service

(http://www.geo.unizh.ch/wgms/).

CASE STUDY 16

Mitigation in the face of a potential El Niño event and climate change: Chan Chan Archaeological Zone (Peru).

The vast and fragile site of Chan Chan in Peru was added to the List of World Heritage in Danger in 1986, the same year that it was inscribed on the World Heritage List. Its earthen structures are particularly vulnerable and thus quickly damaged by natural erosion as they become exposed to the environment, and therefore require continuous conservation efforts and substantial ancillary measures. Besides erosion, intense precipitation is damaging the base of the earthen structures, leading to greater humidity in the lower parts of the buildings, an increase in salt contamination of the structures and the growth of vegetation such as reeds. This phenomenon is due to the combined effect of changes in the irrigation technology for extensive mono-cultures in the area and the reduction of the use of water as the local population now obtains freshwater from a new system. Climate change poses an additional source of stress on this site and intense precipitations during the 1997–98

www.icimod.org/）。

国际山地综合发展中心关于气候变化和响应的出版物（http://books.icimod.org/index.php/search/suject/2）。

国际山地综合发展中心 / 联合国教科文组织。在尼泊尔兴都库什—喜马拉雅地区的冰川，冰川湖泊和冰湖溃洪监测和早期预警系统的详细名录。联合国环境规划署（http://www.rrcap.unep.org/glofnepal/guide/ movie.html）。

世界冰川监测服务机构（http://www.geo.unizh.ch/wgms/）。

案例 16

面对潜在的厄尔尼诺现象和气候改变的缓解措施：昌昌考古遗址区（秘鲁）。

1986 年，巨大而脆弱的秘鲁昌昌遗址，在列入世界遗产名录的同年也列入了濒危世界遗产名录。暴露在自然环境中的土构建筑异常脆弱，在自然侵蚀下迅速毁坏，需要持续的保护工作和大量的辅助措施。除了侵蚀，强烈的降水破坏了土构建筑的基础，增加了建筑底部及较低部分的湿度和含盐量，这些加速了建筑的侵蚀和植被如芦苇的生长。这种现象是当地改变了广泛而单一的灌溉技术和当地人使用新的淡水资源系统而减少用地下水的综合效应。气候变化是额外压力，在这个遗址，1997—1998 年的冰雹也明显的导致了地下水位提升。

events have also significantly contributed to the increase in groundwater level.

In September 1997, an emergency assistance fund was allocated to implement immediate measures to protect the most significant and vulnerable parts of Chan Chan against the devastating impacts of the El Niño event that was projected to occur in 1998. Consequently, the impacts on the site were relatively modest, which shows that the protective measures were effective. Long-term adaptation is also under way, with the reinforcement and stabilization of foundations and structures for the main buildings and the urban heritage surrounding the Huachaque of the Tschudi Palace. These works are carried out combining the use of traditional materials and skills with modern engineering techniques.

1997 年 9 月，运用紧急援助基金对最重要、最脆弱的昌昌遗址实施了直接的保护措施，遏制 1998 年发生的厄尔尼诺现象可能对遗址毁灭性的影响。结果是，由于有效的防护措施，使得这次厄尔尼诺现象对于遗址的影响相对有限。正在实施长期保护措施以加固和稳定主要建筑及提驻狄宫周围的华查克城的基础和结构。保护工作中结合了传统材料、传统技术与现代工程技术。

Source: Case Studies on Climate Change and World Heritage, 2007, UNESCO World Heritage Centre/UK Department of Culture, Media and Sport.

来源：世界遗产气候变化案例分析 2007, 联合国教科文组织世界遗产中心、英国文化媒体体育部。

5.2 How can you make sure that risk prevention and mitigation measures do not have an unintended impact on the heritage values of your property?

5.2　如何确定风险防范和缓解措施不会对遗产价值造成意外影响？

The risk prevention and mitigation measures should ideally have no impact on the heritage values, authenticity and integrity of a cultural or natural property. However, strengthening or retrofitting might be necessary if the property is highly vulnerable to hazards such as earthquakes or cyclones. For example, the various approaches to interventions that were adopted in the aftermath of the earthquake in Kobe (Japan) in 1993 took into account the need to avoid, wherever possible, any impact on the cultural values of affected cultural

风险防范和缓解措施不应影响文化或自然遗产的属性、价值、真实性和完整性。然而，如果遗产极易遭受灾害的威胁，如地震或飓风的威胁，必要时应进行加固或翻新改装。例如，1993 年神户大地震之后，日本开始考虑采取各种措施，避免地震对文化遗产文化价值的影响（案例研究 17）。

heritage properties (Case Study 17).

Measures such as installing hydrants or water pressure mechanisms, widening narrow streets in historic urban areas (or dirt tracks in natural sites) to accommodate emergency vehicles can have a detrimental effect on the outstanding universal value of a heritage property. Moreover, emergency activities such as flood control, fire prevention, and humanitarian relief efforts can lead to resettlement areas being selected at the expense of protected areas, for example within national parks. Site managers should ensure their involvement or availability for consultation on strategic decisions during the emergency response period of a catastrophic event. The location of camps for displaced peoples is critical as they can expose a protected area to greatly increased pressure on resources, as happened in Virunga National Park (Democratic Republic of the Congo).

安装消防栓或水压装置，拓宽历史城市的狭窄街道（或自然遗址的泥土小道）以确保应急车辆畅通无阻等措施，避免对遗产的突出普遍价值造成负面影响。此外，如防洪、防火、和人道主义救援等应急活动，可能会把保护区变成暂时的安置地，例如，把国家公园作为安置地。在灾害事件应急期战略决策中应该确保遗址管理者的有效参与。为流离失所的人选择设立营地的位置至关重要，因为他们可能使保护区暴露在巨大的压力之下，如发生在维龙加国家公园的事情（刚果民主共和国）。

Among risk reduction activities, caution is needed before applying fire-retardant chemicals to historic structures if the potential reaction of the building materials and paintings, for example, is not known during extreme heat conditions in the case of fire.

在降低风险的活动中，在历史建筑物中应谨慎使用阻燃化学品，因为我们还不能确定当火灾发生时，极度高温的情况下，阻燃化学品对建筑物或绘画有什么样的潜在影响。

It is important to consider, furthermore, that the various stakeholders may perceive impacts differently. For example, reduced tourism would be seen as a negative economic impact by some but could also inadvertently lead to the recovery of water supplies, because fewer tourists would mean reduced water consumption.

认识到不同利益相关者对风险影响的不同反应十分重要。例如，减少旅游可能会对经济产生的负面影响，但游客减少意味着水资源消耗减少，可能无意中有利于恢复水的供应。

On the other hand, reduced tourism might also lead to increased poaching as people involved in the tourism industry seek alternative income-generating activities to those lost through the decline in tourism.

另一方面，游客数量减少可能使参与旅游业的居民为了寻找替代性的收入而增加非法狩猎行为，以弥补因游客数量减少带来的收入损失。

Reviews to prevent any unintended impact of risk-reduction activities should be incorporated throughout the planning cycle.

对于防止任何因减灾活动而产生的意想不到的影响的评述，应该贯穿整个规划周期。

CASE STUDY 17

Principles for repair and restoration of damaged cultural properties: Kobe (Japan) following the 1993 earthquake.

案例 17

修理和修复文化遗产的准则：1993 年神户大地震。

When repairing and restoring cultural properties following an earthquake, accurate identification of their state of damage and appropriate retrofitting measures for improving their seismic resistance as well as retaining their heritage values are essential considerations. Following the great Hanshin-Awaji earthquake in 1993, a special committee was constituted to examine the repair policies for cultural properties, which required large-scale repairs and complex seismic retrofitting measures. The committee members comprised architectural historians, specialists in structural studies and repair engineers. The person in charge of cultural assets in the administration managed the committee. The topics discussed by the committee included:

- analysis of earthquake damage to buildings;
- evaluation of the seismic resistance of cultural properties according to the results of structural diagnosis;
- the structural reinforcement needed when seismic resistance is found to be insufficient;
- examination of proposals on retrofitting methods incorporating new techniques designed so that the values of the cultural property are not damaged, using wherever possible non-destructive testing.

地震发生后，修理和修复文化遗产时应考虑，准确识别他们受损害程度，并采取适当的改造措施，以提高其耐震性，从而保持他们的传统价值。1993 年阪神地震后，成立了文化遗产维修政策的特别委员会，检查文化遗产需要的大规模维修和复杂的抗震措施。委员会成员由建筑历史学家、结构研究专家和修复工程师组成。由文化遗产管理机构的负责人管理委员会。委员会讨论的议题包括：

- 分析地震对建筑物的损坏；
- 根据结构诊断的结果，评估文化遗产的减震措施；
- 发现抗震稳定性不够时，对结构进行加固；
- 尽可能使用无损检测，测试被建议纳入改造的新方法、新技术是否会对文化遗产的价值产生影响。

The cultural properties were divided into those that could be visited by the public and those where entry was prohibited. The committee determined the approaches for retrofitting in the following order of

文化遗产可以分为两类，一类是允许公众参观的，一类是不允许的。委员会决定的改造方法按照下列顺序选择：

priority:

(1) Additions using traditional techniques and traditional materials, e.g. reinforcement of roofs with palm tree rope.

（1）使用传统方法和传统材料安装加固，例如，使用棕榈树绳捆扎屋顶。

(2) Additions using traditional techniques and those derived from them, and traditional and modern materials, e.g. reinforcement by carbon-fibre sheet.

（2）使用传统技术或源自传统的技术，以及传统和现代的材料安装加固，例如使用碳纤维薄板加固房顶。

(3) Additions using modern techniques and modern materials, e.g. inserting an iron frame in the structure for load sharing.

（3）使用现代技术或现代材料安装加固，例如，在结构中嵌入钢铁构架减轻负重。

(4) Replacements using modern techniques and modern materials, e.g. through base isolation of the structure.

（4）使用现代技术和现代材料更换部件，例如更换建筑物的基础隔离层。

Source: Y. Murakami, 2006, Risk Management of Cultural Assets. Based on the Experience of the Great Hanshin Earthquake.

来源：Source: Y. Murakami,2006, 阪神大地震中文化遗产风险管理经验。

5.3 How can traditional knowledge systems for disaster mitigation help protect your property from disasters? Can you integrate these into the plan?

5.3 传统减灾的知识体系如何帮助遗产抵御灾害？能把他们加到保护规划中吗？

Traditional knowledge systems for disaster mitigation may take one of several forms:

减灾的传统知识体系能够表现为一种或多种形式：

• Indigenous management systems: in Kathmandu valley, Guthi lands are jointly owned by the community for fulfilling various social and religious functions. The returns from these lands provide resources for the maintenance and repair of historic temples, especially after disasters.

• 本土管理系统：在加德满都山谷，由拥有的古蒂平原社区履行各种社会和宗教职能。从这些土地获得收益提供了维护和修理的历史寺庙的资金，特别是灾后重建。

• Indigenous monitoring systems: in Shirakawa Village (Japan), the community members share responsibility for going around the village daily to inspect any possible risk of fire. While on inspection they call out reminders of the need to be vigilant.

• 本土的监控体系：在白河村（日本），社区成员分担了日常巡查村落、防止火灾风险的责任。通过巡查提醒大家加强警惕。

• Traditional skills and techniques in building construction and periodic maintenance. Analysis of those constructions that had a higher rate of survival in the Kashmir and Gujarat earthquakes showed

• 在建筑施工和定期保养过程中可使用传统技能和技术。在克什米尔和古吉拉特邦地震中，传统建筑结构有较高的幸存率，这表明传统施工技术有助于提高建筑物的抗震性能（案例研究 18）。

how traditional construction techniques often conferred a good earthquake resistance on buildings (Case Study 18).

• Local ecological relationships and indigenous planning systems may also contribute to sustainability and thus prevent disasters such as floods. For example, in Majuli Island in Assam (India), a large river island with unique local ecology, the vernacular housing in the area using locally available bamboo and constructed on stilts has evolved as a sensitive response to local factors, notably floods that inundate the island on a regular basis. The light bamboo structure enables easy dismantling and relocation, in the event that the area is affected by floods.

• 当地生态关系和本土规划系统可持续发展也有利于防止洪水等灾害。例如，阿萨姆邦（印度）马居利岛，是具有当地独特的生态的河中岛，岛屿经常被洪水淹没，使用竹子和在高脚柱上建造房屋（类似于干栏式建筑）等传统建筑已演变为应对当地易发洪水的措施，特别是定期淹没岛屿的洪水。当洪水发生时，竹结构建筑较轻，容易拆除和搬迁。

• If such traditional knowledge systems exist, every effort should be made to integrate these into the DRM plan of a heritage property.

• 如果存在以上传统知识系统，应尽一切努力将这些元素融入遗产灾害风险管理规划中。

CASE STUDY 18

Traditional knowledge systems: earthquake-resistant construction in Kashmir and Gujarat.

案例 18

传统知识体系：克什米尔和古吉拉特邦的抗震建筑。

On close inspection of earthquake-prone regions of Kashmir and Gujarat, we discover several examples of good-quality traditional constructions that survived the devastating earthquakes of 2005 and 2001 respectively. During the Kashmir earthquake, the traditional structures built using local building techniques of Taq (timberlaced masonry-bearing wall) and Dhajji Dewari(complete timber frame with one wythe of masonry forming panels within the frame), in part or in whole, performed much better than many poorly built 'modern' structures. Although there were many cracks in the masonry infill, most of these structures did not collapse, thereby preventing loss of life. Also some vernacular constructions such as wooden log houses, and those employing the use of well-laid masonry with through-stones and well-

在对克什米尔和古吉拉特邦地震多发地区的考察过程中，我们发现高质量的传统建筑，在 2005 年和 2001 年毁灭性的地震中保存下来。在克什米尔地震中，使用当地 Taq 建筑技术（砖木结构的墙壁）和 Dhajji Dewari 技术（完整的木构架中用单砖砌墙作为支撑）建造的传统建筑，比许多简陋的“现代”建筑要保存的好得多。尽管在墙体的填充部分有许多裂缝，但大多数建筑并没有坍塌，从而防止了生命伤亡。还有些乡土建筑如原木房子，和采用石质高压砌体和精心设计的拱、桁架、子母榫和露台，倚靠木质的托梁，在地震中发挥了巨大的作用。在地震多发的古吉拉特邦的喀奇地区，Bhungas 的传统聚落建筑经受住了地震威胁，他们的圆形结构，对于抵抗地震横波十分有利。用抹灰篱笆墙的建筑结构，特别是再用木头加固墙体的建筑能十分有效地抵御地震。很多古吉拉特邦

designed arches, trusses, tongue-and-groove joints and balconies resting on projecting wooden joists performed well in the earthquake. The traditional dwellings of the earthquake-prone Kutch region in Gujarat, the Bhungas, have also withstood the earthquakes, thanks to their circular form, which is very good at resisting lateral earthquake forces. Moreover, wattle and daub constructions, especially where wood is used as reinforcement for the wall, have proved to be very effective. Many traditional structures in Gujarat built prior to the 1950s had floor joists extending through the rubble stone walls to support the balconies. These types of structures were more successful in stabilizing the walls than those where joists terminated in pockets and performed much better during the 2001 quake.

的传统建筑修建于20世纪50年代以前，用搭建在的碎石墙上的楼板托梁来支撑阳台。这一类型建筑的墙体比把托梁放在凹槽中更加稳定，在2001年的地震中这一类建筑很好地保存下来。

Sources: R. Jigyasu, 2002, Reducing disaster vulnerability through local knowledge and capacity, Dr.Eng. thesis, Trondheim, Norwegian University of Science and Technology.

来源：R. Jigyasu, 2002, 通过地方知识和能力减低易损性灾害 挪威特隆赫姆科技大学 Dr.Eng. thesis,

6 How do you prepare for and respond to emergencies?

6 如何准备和应对紧急情况

Section 5 answered questions about reducing disaster risk or mitigating the impact of disasters. Several case studies showed that disaster risk can be reduced or mitigated. The importance was stressed of adopting and implementing measures that, as far as possible, will not diminish the heritage values of the property. Moreover, there may exist local traditional knowledge of disaster vulnerability that can be built into a DRM plan.

第5章回答了如何降低灾害威胁或缓解灾害影响的问题。从很多个案例我们可以看出灾害风险是可以降低或缓解的。重要的是强调采取和实施有效的措施时尽可能地不要降低遗产的价值。更重要的是，现存的有关抵御灾害脆弱性的传统知识，应列入地灾害风险管理规划中。

Section 6 is concerned with the response phase of the DRM cycle (Figure 1, and refer also to the plan structure in Figure 2), after the hazard event has occurred. It answers questions about the risks that may be encountered immediately following

第6章将关注灾害发生后，灾害风险管理周期中的对应部分（图1，及图2规划结构）。这部分将回答灾害发生后立刻面对的风险是什么（6.1）和应急响应团队的角色、责任（6.2）。通过案例分析，了解在遗产上的应急行动有

the disaster (6.1) and the roles and responsibilities of the emergency response team (6.2). Examples are given, by means of case studies, of emergency response actions at properties (6.3) and of how a property itself can contribute to an emergency response (6.4).

哪些（6.3）？遗产本身对应急响应有什么帮助（6.4）。

6.1 What risks might be encountered during the first 72 hours after the disaster?

6.1 在灾后72小时会发生什么样的威胁？

An emergency period normally lasts for around 72 hours after the hazard event such as an earthquake and flooding. The emergency may itself create new kinds of risk:

• Theft of collapsed or damaged fragments or movable objects in the property.

• Flooding may cause contamination through pollution and mould growth.

• Risks arising from the surrounding environment or habitat.

• Insensitive actions by relief agencies or by volunteers (due to lack of awareness), such as pulling down damaged structures of heritage value or destroying the indigenous vegetation in the name of 'life safety'. During fire control, additional damage to the heritage property may be caused by the water used for extinguishing the fire.

• Risk of making inappropriate damage assessment of heritage property due to a lack of prior knowledge or experience.

• Confusion due to lack of coordination and preparedness.

无论是地震还是洪水，灾后72个小时都被认为是最危险的时间段。突发事件本身可能引发新的威胁：

• 哄抢遗产建筑物倒塌或破坏后碎片，哄抢遗产中的可移动文物。

• 因洪水造成污染或因霉菌生长而产生的污染。

• 因周边环境或栖息地而引起的危害。

• 救援机构或志愿者（由于缺乏知识）的无知行为，如拆除能体现遗产价值的受损结构或以“生命安全”为由破坏原生植被。在火势得到控制后，用于救火的水也会造成遗产的额外损害。

• 因为缺少风险知识或经验而对遗产进行不恰当的、有损害的评估。

• 因缺少协调和准备而造成的混乱。

The emergency protection measures undertaken during the crucial first 72 hours following the Friuli earthquake of 1976 in Italy managed to save buildings that might otherwise have been demolished and replaced, and also allowed them to withstand a major aftershock four months later (Case Study 19).

1976年意大利弗留利地震，在关键的72小时内实施紧急保护措施，拯救了可能被拆除和更换的建筑物，并使之经受住四个月后的大余震（案例研究19）。

CASE STUDY 19

Saving structures of heritage value: emergency protection following the 1976 earthquake in Friuli (Italy).

Before it was damaged during the 1976 Friuli earthquake, the main street in the historic town of Gemona was narrow and twisting. Set between the cathedral and the Palazzo Comunale, the street was flanked by a covered arcade on both sides. Along one side, the buildings were aligned in one plane facing the street with continuous elevation. The two end buildings suffered considerable damage from the earthquake and, as their upper stories rested on arches, the condition in which they remained was alarming. The earthquake provoked the collapse of a good portion of the street elevation and the displacement of the end column. Demolition was considered. However, after convincing the local authorities that there was a way to protect the street, using salvaged wooden beams with the help of engineers, the displaced end corner was shored up, thus saving the building from demolition. Emergency measures aimed at filling the gaps in the wall and the supporting arches with brick masonry. Closing the openings in the bearing wall increased the area of load transmission. A second measure was to improve and enlarge the preliminary wood shoring at the end of the displaced corner. Finally, bracing between the damaged structure and the buildings across the street created continuity of support between the city blocks and reduced the number of 'end buildings' or gaps within the fabric of the city. The street was left in this condition until, four months later, a major aftershock hit the area, causing large amounts of damage and destruction. The emergency measures protected the damaged structures from the second seismic shock.

Source: D. del Cid, 1990, Emergency Protection to Damaged Structures.

案例 19

拯救具有遗产价值的建筑：1976 年意大利弗留利地震后的应急保护。

在 1976 年弗留利地震受损之前，历史小镇杰莫纳的主要街道狭窄，曲折。在大教堂和市政厅之间景色宜人，街道两侧分布着拱廊。建筑物基本平齐，临街面连续升高。两端建筑在地震中受到了严重破坏，毗连拱廊的建筑上部结构的稳定性仍然令人担忧。地震引起沿街建筑立面彻底损毁，端柱移位。在这种情况下已考虑全部拆迁。幸好，当地政府被说服采用紧急措施保护街道，在工程师的帮助下利用回收的木梁，支撑起移位的角端柱，拯救了建筑。紧急措施旨在填补墙上的缝隙和用砖砌墙体支撑拱廊，填充承重墙的豁口，增加墙的负荷力。第二个措施是改善和扩大基础的木建筑支撑。最后，是改善受损建筑和街对面的建筑之间的支撑，形成了城市街区和顶端建筑间、城市建筑缺口间连续支撑。街道一直保持这种情景。四个月后，大余震再次袭击了该地区，导致大面积的损失和破坏。幸好，紧急措施使受损建筑在第二次余震中保存下来。

来源：D. del Cid, 1990, 受损结构的紧急保护。

6.2 What should be the roles and responsibilities of the emergency response team members in your property?

• The emergency response team should consist of members or groups who together cover the following responsibilities:

– coordinator;

– safety and security;

– administration and finance;

– spokesperson for the media;

– cultural heritage (to include building and maintenance, and salvage of collections or fragments);

– natural heritage (to include evacuation, community liaison, national disaster relief liaison relocation of injured or rare animals, restoration and reintroduction of vegetation cover and wildlife).

• The team should be well aware of the roles and responsibilities shared by each member and group and undertake regular drill and simulation exercises to test their operational effectiveness. There should be a provision for a back-up in case a member is not able to perform their function for unavoidable reasons. The value of a clear command structure established as part of a contingency response plan was demonstrated when the World Heritage site of Dorset and East Devon Coast (United Kingdom) was exposed to a potential environmental catastrophe (Case Study 21). The site manager played an important role in the environmental advisory group as part of the coordinated response that was already in place prior to the incident.

This team should have strong links with the emergency response systems of the larger area in which the property is located. These would comprise police, health services, fire services and the municipality or local government and its planning departments. Initiating these links may in turn encourage the emergency services to undertake

6.2 应急团队成员应该发挥什么样的作用和承担什么样的责任？

• 应急团队成员应该由共同承担以下责任的成员或团队组成：

– 协调人；

– 安全与保障；

– 管理和财政部门

– 媒体发言人；

– 文化遗产（包括建设和维护、抢救文物和碎片）；

– 自然遗产（包括疏散、社区联络、国家救灾联络，搬迁受伤珍稀动物、恢复植被和放归野生动物）。

• 团队应该很清楚每个成员及团队整体的角色和职责，进行定期训练和模拟演习来测试计划的实施效果。万一某成员因无法避免的原因不能够执行任务，应该有后备人员顶替。建立一个有效的指挥机构是应急反应计划的一部分。在世界文化遗产的多塞特郡和东德文郡海岸（联合王国）遭受潜在的环境灾害中，就体现出指挥机构的重要性（案例 21）。在事件发生前，作为协作反应的一部分，遗产管理者在环境咨询组织中扮演了重要角色。

这个团队与遗产所在区域的应急系统有很强的联系。应急系统包括警察、医疗服务、消防服务和市政当局或当地政府和规划部门。而保持积极联系，反过来也鼓励了对遗产实施特别的急救服务措施。京都城市消防部门（案例研究 20）和美国国家公园服务是这方面的典范。

special measures for heritage properties. The initiatives of the City Fire Department in Kyoto (Case Study 20) and the US National Park Service are exemplary in this regard.

• The team should establish links with the local community and volunteers by raising awareness through the media, both before and during the emergency.

• 无论是灾前还是灾后，团队应该建立与当地社区和志愿者的沟通渠道，并通过媒体提高他们的保护意识。

CASE STUDY 20

Preventive measures for heritage sites taken by municipal services: Kyoto City Fire Department (Japan).

案例 20

市政管理实施遗产预防措施：京都城市消防局。

Kyoto City has more than 2,000 cultural assets spanning 1,200 years of history. Seventeen of these have been given World Heritage status as the Historic Monuments of Ancient Kyoto. Fires due to carelessness and arson have resulted in the loss of many cultural assets in the past. Establishing fire prevention measures is there for every important for preserving these vital assets.

在 1200 年的历史过程中，京都形成了超过 2000 处文化遗产。有 17 座建筑是作为古都历史纪念群的组成要素，被列入世界文化遗产。由于粗心和纵火引起的火灾导致很多文化遗产丧失。因此，建立防火措施对保留这些遗产非常重要。

The Civil Rescue System for Cultural Assets was set up by the Kyoto City Fire Department so that custodians of these assets, local residents, and related organizations such as the Fire Department and Volunteer Fire Corps are able to collaborate to protect cultural assets from fire. The activities of the department include:

京都城消防部门建立了文化遗产的民事救援体系，便于遗产保管人、当地居民以及相关的组织，比如消防部门和志愿消防总队能够合作，以便于在火灾中保护文化遗产。组织的活动包括：

Installation in cultural heritage sites of state-of-the art equipment and systems for fire prevention and control such as alarms, fire extinguishers, indoor and outdoor fire hydrants, water guns and lightning conductors. On-site inspections by the fire officers. Erection of notice boards prohibiting open-air fires and smoking. Fire drills are organized by the department to ensure that people respond promptly and appropriately in an emergency,

在文化遗产地安装先进的防火和控制设备及系统，如警报、灭火器、室内和室外消防栓、水枪和避雷针。消防人员负责现场巡查。安装禁止明火和吸烟的公告牌。由消防部门组织消防演习，以确保人们在紧急情况下，对扑灭火灾、搬移文物藏品或人身安全救护迅速做出适当的反应。住在文化遗产附近的居民都要参与培训，从而创建一个文化遗产本地居民的救援系统。消防队员自愿指导当地居民，增强他们

whether by putting out a fire at its onset, removing cultural objects, or leading people to safety. The residents living near the cultural assets participate in the training to create a local cultural asset residents' rescue system. The firefighters voluntarily provide guidance to the local residents to enhance their disaster fighting capabilities. In order to make fire prevention facilities readily available during emergency situations, the custodians of the cultural assets voluntarily carry out periodic inspection as well as maintenance and control.

抵御灾害的能力。为了确认防火设施在紧急情况下可以使用，文化遗产保管人应主动进行定期检查、维护和控制。

Source: Flyer, 2007, Kyoto City Fire Department, Kyoto, Japan.

来源：Flyer, 2007, 京都消防局，日本京都

CASE STUDY 21

Coordinated emergency response: Dorset and East Devon Coast (United Kingdom).

案例 21

应急反应的协作体制：多塞特郡和东德文郡的海岸（英国）。

Successful emergency response requires a timely and efficient coordinated response. In the event of a ship in difficulty at sea, effective intervention at an early stage can prevent severe consequences.

成功的应急响应需要及时和有效的协调反应。如果一艘船在海上遇到困难，早期有效的干预可以预防严重的后果。

In January 2007, the container ship MSC Napoli was beached off the Dorset and East Devon coast to prevent an environmental catastrophe. If left to drift in one of the world's busiest shipping channels, the ship and its cargo could have caused additional accidents or sunk with the loss of the full cargo and a large tonnage of fuel oil. The national Coastal Pollution Clearance Plan was used to respond to the impact on the shore. The Salvage Control Unit of the UK Maritime and Coastguard Agency assessed the beaching and monitored the MSC Napoli, directing the response operation when cargo was unexpectedly released.

2007 年 1 月，MSC 那坡里号集装箱船被搁浅在多塞特郡和东德文郡的海岸，以防止发生环境灾害。如果任由轮船漂移到世界上最繁忙的航道上，可能导致额外的事故：轮船及其全部货物——燃油一起沉没。全国沿海污染清理计划是用来应对对海岸的各种影响。英国海事和海岸警备局的打捞控制部，负责评估和监测 MSC 那坡里号的动态，指导货物意外泄漏后可采用的应急措施。

An established generic emergency planning

建立一个通用的应急反应计划，应采取多

response was adapted to outline the multi-agency working arrangements and deal with pollution from the vessel. A command structure was detailed in the Dorset response contingency plan that included the following roles: Overall Incident Commander, On Shore Strategic Co-ordinating Group, On Shore Dorset (Tactical Response located in the Dorset Emergency Centre), On Shore Devon, Salvage Control Unit, Marine Response Centre, Incident Environment Group (environmental advice), and Control Room (incident notification and call out).

单位合作的形式，安排和处理来自船舶海运的污染。在多塞特郡应急反应计划中有详细的指挥结构，包括以下角色：整体事件指挥官、岸上战略协调小组、岸上多塞特（战略响应中心位于多塞特应急响应中心）、岸上德文郡、救助控制部门、海洋应急中心、环境事故部门（提供环境建议）和控制室（事件通知和地图标注）。

Those involved in the emergency response were aided by the response arrangements set out in the UK national contingency plans of the Maritime and Coastguard Agenda, and at the local level in the County Emergency Plans and Coastal Oil and Chemical Pollution Clearance Plans maintained by Dorset and Devon County Councils. A specific response strategy was developed focused on public safety, limiting access to polluted shorelines, controlling unauthorized removal of property washed ashore, mobilizing ‘spotters’ to track pollutants and containers, and collecting and collating pollution and debris information into GIS.

参与应急响应的团体得到英国国家海上应急计划和海岸警卫队发布的应急安排的帮助和指导，并按县级应急计划，由多塞特郡和德文郡议会分别通过沿海石油和化学污染清理计划的指导，形成一个特定的响应策略以关注公共安全、限制进入污染海域、管理未经许可搬运货物上岸、动员“观察者”追踪污染物和货物、收集和整理污染物和残片信息并输入到全球地理信息系统中。

During the emergency response the Dorset and East Devon Coast World Heritage site was represented on the environmental advisory group established to advise on all aspects of incident response. In communication with the clean-up crews, the site manager provided advice on appropriate clean up techniques, access and vehicle use, waste disposal and storage to avoid environmental damage. Rangers from the property acted as ‘spotters’ along the shore, helping to track pollution, ship debris and cargo, and clean up oiled birds. The successful and smooth response to the incident was made possible by the experience and training of those involved. The emergency plan is

在应急响应过程中，成立了代表多塞特郡和东德文郡海岸世界文化遗产的环境咨询小组，为事件提供全方位的建议。在与清理人员沟通后，遗产管理者为清理提出了技术性建议，如道路和车辆使用、废弃物的处理和保存，以避免破坏环境。来自于遗产的管理者充当岸边“观察者”，帮助跟踪污染物、船舶残骸和货物，并清洗被油污污染的鸟类。经验丰富和训练有素人员的参与是成功和平稳的应对事件的关键。日常针对应急计划的训练，在真实事件发生的数小时内发挥作用，熟悉计划、沟通流程和决策文件，亦可作为保险索赔的重要依据。独立机构负责具体培训现场工作人员，例如处理被油污污染的鸟类。参与当地复原力论坛并通过

subject to a regular exercise in real time to practise the first hours of an incident and be familiar with the plan, communication processes and documentation of decisions which can be important for later insurance claims. Individual organizations provide specific training to their site staff, for example in handling oiled birds. Involvement in the Local Resilience Forum and experience gained through emergency planning activities meant that plans and protocols could be quickly adapted, thus saving the World Heritage property and marine and coastal ecosystem from significant damage.

紧急计划活动获得经验，这些都意味着可以及时调整计划和协议，从而拯救世界遗产和沿海生态系统遭受重大损害。

Planning and preparation is key to success in responding to an emergency. Events happen quickly and systems need to be in place to take effective decisions and get the response happening on the ground. Coordinated communication is essential, along with a clear and consistent message to the public. A site manager will not be able to respond to a major incident alone and should be part of a coordinated response. It is important to find out if plans already exist because otherwise the protected area staff may not be involved and the values of the property may not be taken into account in an emergency response.

计划和准备是成功应对紧急情况的关键所在。事件发生后需要迅速、系统的实地决策和立即实施应急措施。必须进行协调沟通，同时向公众传达清晰、一致的信息。单靠遗产管理者无法单独应对重大事件，他们应该是响应协调体系的一部分。提前确定应急计划是非常重要的环节，否则保护区工作人员可能不能参与应急行动，在应急响应中可能就不会考虑遗产的重要价值。

Sources:

http://www.cabinetoffice.gov.uk/ukresilience.aspx

http://www.devon.gov.uk/multi_agency_debrief_v5.0.pdf JoeuDnkleyc

来源：

http://www.cabinetoffice.gov.uk/ukresilience.aspx

http://www.devon.gov.uk/multi_agency_debrief_v5.0.pdf

6.3 What can you do to improve emergency preparedness in your property?

6.3 如何提高遗产的应急准备？

Develop a plan and procedures for evacuating people by answering the following questions:

– Will you aim to move people out of the property or collect them in one place within the site

在编制疏散人群的计划和过程时，应回答以下问题：

– 要把人群撤离到遗产区以外还是把他们集中在遗产的某一个位置（取决于遗产的特性和

(this depends on the nature of the property and its location)?

位置）?

– Which is the shortest exit route for pedestrians (one that has the least potential impact on the values of the property)?

– 行人撤离的最短路径是哪条（对遗产价值潜在影响最小的）?

– What movement patterns do you envisage for emergency vehicles such as a fire engine or ambulance?

– 为紧急车辆如消防车或救护车设计什么样的移动路径?

– How will you balance evacuation needs with minimizing the risk of theft (of cultural items) during the emergency? (Opening too many access points may provide opportunities for thieves.)

– 在紧急情况下，如何平衡疏散要求和最小盗窃风险（文化遗产）之间的关系?（开放太多出口会为盗窃提供机会。）

– How will you ensure the security of people and heritage properties during emergency response?

– 在应急反应的过程中，该如何确保生命和财产安全。

Install general emergency equipment, e.g. emergency alarm systems, specific equipment for flood, fire prevention and mitigation, but only after formulating a comprehensive strategy based on the main risks, the location of the property, and available resources and expertise. The Environmental Water Supply System in Kyoto (EWSS) is an inspiring example of how this can be achieved (Case Study 22).

在综合考虑主要灾害、遗产位置、现有资源及专业知识基础上形成整体战略后，再配备、安装日常的应急设备，如应急预警系统、防洪的特殊设备、阻止或缓解火灾的设备。京都的环境供水系统（EWSS）是实现以上方案的典型案例。

CASE STUDY 22

Preventing post-earthquake fire: Environmental Water Supply System in Kyoto (Japan).

案例 22

预防地震后的火灾：京都的环境供水系统（日本）。

Post-earthquake fire caused serious damage after the Great Hanshin Awaji earthquake of 1993. This was largely due to breakdown of a modern electricity-driven infrastructure, which led to a lack of water for fire fighting. Based on this experience, the Environmental Water Supply System (EWSS) has been developed for Kyoto by harnessing various kinds of water resources for maintaining the water supply at any time, and in adequate quantity to enable firefighting.

1993 年，阪神大地震后火灾对城市造成严重损害。这很大程度上是因为现代电力驱动的基础设施遭到严重破坏，导致消防用水严重缺乏。根据这一经历，开发出京都环境供水系统（EWSS），管理各种水资源，随时维持水的供应，提供充足的消防用水。

The EWSS development plan is evaluated on the basis of:

(1) identification of possible sources of water supply and their location;

(2) estimation of reserved amount of water based on the existing water system and the development measures;

(3) calculation of the reserved amount of water against the recommended amount.

基于以下内容对环境供水系统发展规划进行了评价：

（1）确定可能的供水资源及其位置；

（2）基于现有的水系，评估水资源的储存量，研发对策；

（3）计算现有水量以及需要水量。

The requirements of water and necessary fire extinction systems are calculated on the basis of the scale of fire. For a small fire, water stored in tubs, ponds or a river would suffice for use by the citizens. However, fires at the scale of a house or neighbor hood area would require large amounts of water for a longer period of firefighting, using hydrants and water sources such as wells, ponds or rivers.

根据火灾规模的大小，计算水的需求量和必要的灭火系统。对于小火，储存在浴缸、池塘或河流中的水将满足公民使用。然而，一座房子或邻近地区的火灾需要大量的水，时间也较长，就要使用消防栓和其他水源如水井、池塘或河流。

The Sannei-zaka Historical Preservation District in the Ancient Kyoto World Heritage site was selected as the pilot case study area. The EWSS system at this site uses an existing natural water source from a small dam at an elevation of 80 m with natural gravity for water pressure. User-friendly hydrants and sprinkler nozzles are placed at strategic positions in the district to deliver usable firefighting water for the citizens. Some cisterns have also been added as back-up to this system. The concept of EWSS effectively contributes towards a sustainable environment.

京都世界遗产内的产宁坂历史保护区被选为案例研究区域。在这个遗址中环境供水系统使用了现有的天然水源：一个海拔 80 米小水坝，利用自然重力增加水的压力。便携消防栓和喷水灭火器被放置在战略位置，为本区公民提供灭火用水。一些蓄水池也被添加到这个系统作为备用。环境供水概念为保持可持续的环境提供了帮助。

Source: K. Toki and T. Okubo, 2005, Protection of Wooden Cultural Heritage from Earthquake Disaster, Proceedings of Meetings on Cultural Heritage Risk Management, World Conference on Disaster Reduction, Rits-DMUCH, Kyoto, pp. 94–102.

来源：K. Toki and T. Okubo, 2005, 地震灾害中木结构文化遗产的保护，文化遗产风险管理会议，世界减灾大会，京都协议 pp. 94－102。

Consider setting up alarm systems, special

考虑建立预警系统、特殊的安全警戒线，

security cordons and coordination between the site staff and security.

及遗址员工和安保之间的协调。

Prepare maps of the property indicating specific features such as utility mains, fire exits, fire extinguishers, etc.

准备有特殊标识的遗产地图，例如标明实用电源、消防通道，灭火器等的位置。

Communicate the emergency plan and procedures to visitors, staff and local residents by easily readable handbooks, manuals, drawings and signage, and by organizing awareness-raising activities such as seminars and exhibitions.

通过使用简单易读的手册、说明书、图纸和标识、组织能提高应急意识的研讨会和展览等活动，使游客、员工、当地民众了解应急计划和步骤。

The initiatives of the City Government of Vigan (Philippines) illustrate the range of activities that can be undertaken through proactive efforts involving both municipal services and the public (Case Study 23). The management plan for Cousin Island Special Reserve in the Seychelles also demonstrates a systematic approach to emergency preparedness, recovery and response and was successfully put to the test in a cyclone in 2002 (Case Study 24).

维甘（菲律宾）市政府的举措，说明了通过市政服务和公共服务积极活动得以实现的范围（案例研究 23）。塞舌尔的库森岛特别保护管理计划也展示了一个应急准备、恢复和响应的系统化方法，并经受了 2002 年飓风的考验（案例研究 24）。

CASE STUDY 23

Emergency preparedness initiatives: City Government in the Historic Town of Vigan (Philippines).

案例 23

应急行动：历史城镇维甘（菲律宾）的市政府。

The Historic Town of Vigan was inscribed on the World Heritage List in 1999 for its unique cultural and historical significance as an exceptionally intact and well-preserved example of a European trading town in East and South-East Asia. However, the town is located in a region highly prone to earthquakes and volcanoes, and its historic buildings are highly vulnerable to fires. The City Government has undertaken several initiatives to improve the emergency preparedness for such natural disasters. An Emergency Response Handbook for the Historic District has been prepared under the administration of the mayor. The town has a well equipped Fire

1999 年，历史城镇维甘作为唯一一处位于东亚及东南亚、保存完好、具有文化和历史重要性的、欧洲式样的贸易小镇被列入世界遗产名录。然而，小镇位于地震和火山多发地区，火对历史建筑有很大的威胁。当地政府开始实施若干项目提升对自然灾害的应急准备能力。在该市市长的监管下制定了历史街区的应急反应手册。城市中的消防部门设备精良，消防人员全天候待命，特别是在夜间和节日。

Department and fire fighters conduct round-the-clock monitoring patrols, especially at night and during festivals.

The local community is involved in emergency preparedness through the City Fire Volunteer Brigade. Several activities are conducted as part of Vigan's annual observance of the National Disaster Consciousness Month in July. These include prioritizing emergency response measures in the various offices of the City Hall, retraining the City Fire Volunteer Brigade, crowd control and fire drill at the City Hall, installation of signage at tsunami safe places and warning sirens. In 2007, the City Government also handed over new fire suits to the personnel of the Bureau of Fire Protection.

通过加入城市防火志愿者大队，当地居民参与了应急准备工作。每年 7 月是维甘国家防灾月，当地会组织很多活动。包括市政厅各种办公室按优先次序的应急响应措施、城市防火志愿大队训练、人群控制和市政大厅的消防演习、在安全的地方安装海啸预警标识牌和警报等。在 2007 年，市政府也给消防局人员提供了新的防火配置。

Source: Official Website of Vigan City (www.vigancity.gov.ph), 2007, final presentation by Glen Concepcion, city disaster action officer and city environment and natural resources officer, City of Vigan, and Eric Quadra, architect, LGU Vigan, at the International Training Course on Disaster Risk Management of Cultural Heritage, Rits-DMUCH, Kyoto.

来源：维甘市政府官网 (www.vigancity.gov.ph), 2007, 维甘市灾害行动和环境自然资源主任 Glen Concepcion、维甘市政府建筑师 Eric Quadra 的最终报告，在京都，立命馆大学历史都市防灾研究所的国际文化遗产灾害管理培训课上展示。

Case study 24

Risk awareness and training as part of management plan: natural heritage of Cousin Island (Seychelles).

案例 24

塞舌尔库森岛自然遗产管理规划之风险意识提升和培训。

The management of Cousin Island Special Reserve in the Republic of Seychelles has included disaster mitigation as part of its management plan since 1999, including restoration of native vegetation and prevention of invasive species. The programme for emergency planning, preparedness and response has included the establishment of contingency plans to prevent disasters that could impact the Marine Protected Area management

自 1999 年起，在塞舌尔共和国库森岛特别保护区管理中，把减灾作为其管理规划的一部分，包括恢复本土植被及预防外来物种入侵。应急预案、准备和反应包括制定应急计划，通过遵守严格的船舶维修制度、消除潜在危险、替换过时的材料，防止可能影响海洋保护区管理系统的灾害。建立了应急会议点，维护了直升机紧急降落点。

system by following a strict boat maintenance protocol and removing potential hazards and obsolete materials. Emergency meeting points have been established and emergency helicopter landing sites are maintained.

Since designation in 1968 and management by Bird Life International and more recently by Nature Seychelles, the values of Cousin Island have been greatly restored, with thick native forest covering the entire island. This mitigates against erosion, landslides and fires. Risk awareness and management on the island include maintaining boats and engines in top condition and keeping replacement parts, removing potential hazards, trimming trees near trails and infrastructure, fireproofing fuel stores with bunding and sitting buildings beyond the high-water mark.

自 1968 年国际鸟组织类生活组织对它实施管理，到最近由自然塞舌尔接管，库森岛的遗产价值已逐步恢复，浓密的原始森林覆盖整个岛屿。恢复的植被抵御了侵蚀、山体滑坡和火灾等风险。小岛的风险意识和管理包括保持船只、引擎的最佳状态、并维护更换零件、消除潜在的危害因素、修剪步行道和基础设施周边的树木，在防火燃料仓库前筑堤，在高水位线之上为建筑选址。

Cousin Island is also covered by various forms of insurance, including third-party liability, staff disability or death, and damage to buildings, the hulls of boats and mooring buoys. A small fund has also been established to deal with emergency situations resulting from events such as cyclones. In 2002, the fund was used to help repair infrastructure and rehabilitate the ecosystems.

库森岛也包括各种形式的保险，包括第三方责任、员工伤残或死亡、建筑物受损、船体全损险和定泊浮标险等。同时还成立了一个小型基金会处理紧急情况下产生各种事件，如飓风等。2002 年，该基金被用来帮助维修基础设施和恢复生态系统。

In addition, staff received training in first aid, firefighting and safety at sea. A health and safety manual is readily accessible, and all staff carry mobile telephones. A designated helicopter landing pad is available for emergency evacuations, as well as special tools for helicopter-related accidents.

此外，员工接受急救、消防和海上安全培训。便于使用的健康和安全手册人手一册，所有工作人员携带移动电话。备有直升机的专用停机坪可用于紧急疏散，同时也备有处理直升机事故的特殊工具。

Sources: Nirmal Jivan Shah, Chief Executive, Nature Seychelles, Center for Environment and Education, Roche Caiman, Mahe,Seychelles (nature@seychelles.net).

来源：Nirmal Jivan Shah, 首席执行官，塞舌尔自然部，环境与教育中心，罗切凯曼马赫主席，塞舌尔，（nature@seychelles.net）。

The success of management plans such as that for Cousin Island depends on their design but especially on their being implemented. If, for whatever reasons, a DRM plan cannot be implemented, a high level of risk can continue with no mitigation measures being taken. The Historic Sanctuary of Machu Picchu in Peru provides an example of a Disaster Prevention and Mitigation Plan that has so far failed to be implemented. Among a number of factors inhibiting its implementation is the lack of local awareness of the high-risk situation (Case Study 25).

成功的管理规划例如库森岛的规划依赖于设计，但更主要的是规划的实施。无论什么原因，如果灾害风险管理规划不能实施或没有实施减缓措施，高风险就会一直存在。秘鲁的马丘比丘印加历史保护区的遗址是未能落实灾害防治和缓解计划的实例。妨碍计划实施的根本原因是当地缺乏高风险意识（案例 25）。

CASE STUDY 25

Having a plan is not enough: lack of risk reduction in the Historic Sanctuary of Machu Picchu (Peru).

案例 25

仅有规划是不够的：缺少减灾意识的马丘比丘印加遗址。

The economic and social impact of disasters is well documented and such impacts can be closely dependent on effective management of a protected area, particularly when it attracts large numbers of visitors. The Historic Sanctuary of Machu Picchu earns the highest revenue in Peru (WCMC,2005), and was visited by some 1.8 million tourists in 2007. However, the World Heritage property, the local population, and visitors are threatened by landslides, disease, building failure and fire. With such high visitor numbers a natural hazard has the potential to cause loss of life, and a negative impact not only on the local economy and management of the World Heritage site. Despite the identification of risks and repeated warnings from experts since at least 1989, no systematic disaster risk reduction strategy was in place in Machu Picchu in 2008.

灾害对于经济和社会的影响早已记录在案，这些影响可以依赖保护区的有效管理，特别是吸引众多游客时。印加遗址马丘比丘，是秘鲁收入最高的遗产（世界保护监测中心 ,2005），在 2007 年，游客人数超过了 180 万。但世界遗产、当地居民和游客都受到滑坡、建筑物倒塌和火灾的严重威胁。自然灾害多发的遗产地会对众多参观者的生命安全造成潜在威胁。尽管自 1989 年后，危害种类已经确定，也不断地受到专家的警告，直到 2008 年，马丘比丘遗址才有了系统的减灾防灾战略。

Due to the site's topographical and climatic characteristics, landslides are a risk in the citadel, along the rail line, on the vehicle sector and in the sector of Machu Picchu Village. Accelerated glacial

鉴于遗址所在的地形地貌和气候特征，山体滑坡始终威胁着城堡、铁路沿线、部分公路路段以及马丘比丘村落一带。加之自 1998 年起，冰川融化加速也增加了这个地区发生山体滑坡

regression since 1998 has further increased the occurrence and risk of landslides. Given the high population density in the area, rapidly increasing, and the high visitor and day labourer rates, the risk of loss of life and property from landslides is high.

的次数。鉴于这个地区的居民密度高且人口数量仍在增长，高游客流量加上工作人员，因山体滑坡造成人员伤亡和财产损失的危害性依旧很高。

The World Heritage Committee, on the basis of missions carried out by UNESCO, IUCN and ICOMOS and information received, has repeatedly expressed its concerns over the lack of implementation of a Natural Disaster Mitigation Plan. Several factors have been preventing the implementation of risk reduction measures:

根据联合国教科文组织、世界自然保护联盟和国际古迹遗址理事会所执行的任务和收集到的信息，世界遗产委员会不断的表达他们对于当地缺少自然灾害减缓规划的关注，他们指出，以下几个因素阻碍了减灾措施的实施：

• Low risk awareness among the local population, who have little experience of managing risk.

• 当地居民的低风险意识，他们几乎没有灾害管理的经验。

• The National Institute for Natural Resources has released a Disaster Prevention and Mitigation Plan for the Machu Picchu Town Centre, and has drawn up evacuation, diffusion and drill maps; but application is limited by little awareness of the plan; scant drills; lack of awareness of the risk especially by tourists and workers; vendors and tourist service areas blocking the escape routes; and so on.

• 国家资源研究所已经公布了马丘比丘中心城市灾害防治及缓解规划，也草拟了疏散方案，散发和张贴了地图，但是由于几乎没有人关注这个规划尤其是游客和员工缺乏风险意识，旅游商店和旅游服务设施阻塞了逃生路线等等，所以效果甚微。

• There is no allocation for the Disaster Prevention and Mitigation Plan in the official Management Plan budget for the World Heritage site.

• 灾害的防治和缓解规划没有纳入官方的世界遗产管理规划的预算中。

• The existing Risk Preparedness Plan has not been used to prevent uncontrolled construction in Machu Picchu Village and new roads and bridges have been built in a geologically unstable area that is subject to landslides.

• 现有的预防性规划没能用于规划马丘比丘村庄新建筑的建设，新建桥梁和道路也都位于容易遭受滑坡威胁的地质不稳定区域。

Protected area managers should ensure that budgets include sufficient funds to implement Disaster Prevention and Mitigation Plans. Additional factors that can prevent effective risk reduction include weaknesses in the governance system such as lack of integrated planning, EIA studies and risk mapping.

保护区管理者应该确定，在其财政预算中应包括实施灾害防治和缓解规划需要的资金。影响实施有效减灾措施的其他因素还包括脆弱的治理体制，例如缺乏整体规划、缺乏环境影响评估研究和缺乏风险地图等。

Sources: UNESCO / IUCN, 2007, World Heritage Monitoring Mission report to Machu Picchu.

(http://whc.unesco.org/archive/2007/).

来源：联合国教科文组织、世界自然保护联盟，2007，马丘比丘世界遗产监测报告。（http://whc.unesco.org/archive/2007/）。

Ensure that signage for emergency evacuation is legible and placed at strategic locations. It should show the location of extinguishers, hydrants, first-aid boxes, etc. using universally recognized symbols. For emergency actions to save or salvage heritage components, fragments or complete collections in the property, train a team in salvage, immediate storage and treatment, depending on the nature of the fragments or collection. Good documentation and safekeeping at various locations is critical for careful inventorying and identification of objects during the salvage operation. Create a directory of contacts that should be easily accessible for unexpected emergencies. The directory should be regularly reviewed and updated.

确定摆放紧急疏散标识的位置应清晰醒目，标识应该包括灭火器、消防栓、急救箱等等的位置，并使用国际通用标识。应训练一只专门的救援队伍，用于遗产组件、部件或完整藏品的应急抢救行动，并及时根据部件和藏品的特性直接存储和处理。在抢险过程中，各处遗址档案和安全防护对清查保护藏品和鉴定文物十分重要。建立通讯录，实现在不可预见紧急情况下的各种联系。通讯录应该经常更新。

6.4 How can your property contribute positively to the emergency response?

6.4 遗产在应急反应中有什么积极的贡献?

A heritage property can contribute positively to emergency efforts in a variety of ways:

遗产能从不同角度影响应急反应的效果：

Designated areas for emergency evacuation within the property can also be used for providing temporary shelter, if the nature of the property allows and such activities do not damage the outstanding universal value of the property. For example, Kiyomizudera, Nijo Castle and other temple sites within the dense urban fabric of Kyoto can be important areas for temporary refuge in case of disasters caused by earthquake or fire. The same is true of Lal Bagh Fort Complex within Dhaka city in Bangladesh.

在不损坏遗产的突出普遍价值前提下，允许在遗产中设定应急疏散区域或提供临时的庇护所。例如，日本京都清水寺，二条古城堡和其他寺院遗址位于京都高密度的城市中，可以作为地震或火灾引起的灾害时的重要临时避难场所。孟加拉国达卡市的拉尔巴格堡花园遗址发挥过同样的作用。

Traditional knowledge systems for emergency warning or response may exist in the area where

遗产区域还可能保存着紧急预警和响应的传统知识体系。例如，在安达曼群岛生活的部

the property is located. For example, the Andaman Islands tribes had the indigenous knowledge that when the sea recedes, they should also recede, and this knowledge saved their lives during the Indian Ocean tsunami. In the Kathmandu valley, the temple bells on the roof of Pagoda temples are rung in warning in the event of an earthquake.

落的传统认知中，当海潮减弱时，他们也应该后退。这种知识在印度洋海啸中拯救了他们的生命。在加德满都山谷，寺庙屋顶宝塔的钟声敲响则警告可能会发生地震。

Existing social networks in the community or among religious bodies can be used for creating effective teams of volunteers that can contribute towards emergency response. For example, in the Kiyomizudera temple complex in Kyoto, the network of local communities living around the site has been effectively utilized to create a disaster response team of volunteers. As the site manager you should therefore identify the ways in which your site can contribute to disaster risk reduction and integrate these into your management plan and into the overall DRM plan for the area. This will strengthen your position within the community and support possible requests for funding conservation activities.

社区或宗教团体中的现有社交网络对创建有效的志愿者团队很有帮助，这些志愿者可以参与各种应急措施。例如位于京都的清水寺建筑群，遗址周边的当地社区生活网络被有效地利用起来，并创建了一支灾害应急志愿者团队。作为遗产管理者，需要找到有效减少本遗产点灾害风险的办法，并将其整合到遗产管理规划及整个地区的灾害风险管理规划中。这样能强化遗产管理者在社区中的地位及在保护活动中得到资金支持。

Section 6, concerned with the response phase of the DRM cycle, has reviewed the risks that may be encountered immediately following a disaster (Section 6.1) and the roles and responsibilities of the emergency response team (6.2). Several case studies have shown how site managers can undertake emergency response actions (6.3) and how the property itself can contribute to an emergency response (6.4).

第 6 章，关注了灾害风险管理循环中的应急反应阶段，回顾了灾害发生后可能出现的风险（6.1），应急小组的主要角色和任务（6.2）。多个案例介绍了遗产管理者如何实施应急反应行动（6.3），最后介绍了遗产本身对应急响应的贡献。

Section 7 considers the Recovery phase of the DRM cycle (Figure 1; see also Figure 2).

第 7 章，考虑灾害风险管理循环中恢复阶段（图 1 及图 2），

7. How do you recover and rehabilitate your property after a disaster?

7 灾后如何实现遗产的恢复和复原?

Section 6 has reviewed what actions a site

第 6 章 回顾了遗产管理在灾害风险管理

manager should take in the Response phase of the DRM cycle (Figure 1). Section 7 covers the following phase, Recovery, which asks questions about new risks that might arise following a disaster (7.1) and how to assess damage to the property (7.2). It then asks how the sustainability of long-term recovery can be ensured (7.3) and how heritage sites themselves can play a larger role in DRM (7.4).

循环反应阶段应该采取的行动。第 7 章包括下面的阶段：如何恢复，是关于灾害后可能出现的新的风险（7.1），如何评估遗产的损坏程度（7.2）。然后如何确定长期的可持续的恢复（7.3）和遗产本身如何在灾害风险管理中扮演重要角色（7.4）。

7.1 What new risks might your property be exposed to after a disaster? The following kinds of risks may be a consequence of a disaster:

7.1 在灾害以后遗产会暴露在什么样的危害下？以下的危害可能是由灾害引起的：

General

常规的

Damage to the property's outstanding universal value during emergency response activities.

在应急响应行动中遗产的突出普遍价值遭到破坏。

Damage or pressure caused by displaced peoples, particularly regarding camps of displaced peoples, their associated infrastructure and their waste and energy requirements.

因流离失所的居民所形成的破坏和压力，特别是成为疏散居民营地后，对相关基础设施、垃圾废弃物和能源需求。

Encroachment.

侵入

Pressure of development and illegal or uncontrolled development.

发展压力，特别是非法或不受控制开发的压力。

For people

对于人

Injury, mortality or displacement of staff that can reduce capacity for security, monitoring and enforcement.

员工受伤，死亡或流离失所会降低安全、监控和执法的能力。

Loss of livelihood sources linked to the property.

丧失与遗产相关的生活来源。

For cultural sites

对于文化遗产

Looting and theft.

抢劫和偷盗。

Enhanced rate of deterioration of damaged wood or stone.

受损木头或石头腐蚀度增加。

Risk of the loss of authenticity or of falsification through reconstruction.

真实性损失或重建过程中被篡改的风险。

Water damage from firefighting.

消防用水对遗产的破坏。

For natural sites (and some cultural landscapes)

对于自然遗产（及部分文化景观）

Outstanding universal value and integrity degraded through habitat loss and poaching.

Pollution from waterborne debris and contaminated watercourses.

Encroachment.

Pressure of development and illegal or uncontrolled development.

栖息地的减少和非法狩猎会降低遗产的突出普遍价值和完整性。

来自于水中碎屑的污染和受污染河道的污染。

侵入及侵蚀。

发展压力，特别是非法及不受控制开发的压力。

For existing management systems

Site level office buildings and equipment may be damaged.

Site level staff may be affected.

Risks relating to the type of hazard.

Hurricanes and tornadoes can lead to storm surge, which can cause flooding.

Earthquakes may cause a tsunami, fire and landslides.

Many of the longer-term impacts of a hazard, such as debris fields, obstructed watercourses, or large areas of damaged historic structures, may persist for months or even years after the event. The recovery and rehabilitation of larger natural and cultural sites will therefore require resources well beyond those of the local World Heritage property, necessitating integration with the state or national incident command system for recovery from large-scale disasters.

对现有管理系统

遗产地办公室和设备会遭到破坏。

遗产地管理员工会受到影响。

与某一类型危害相关的风险。

飓风和龙卷风会导致风暴潮，形成洪水。

地震可能引起海啸、火灾、山体滑坡。

许多危害造成长期影响，例如土地沙化，河道阻塞，或大面积的历史建筑损毁，可能会在灾后持续数月、数年。较大的自然和文化遗产恢复和修复，耗费的资金远远超过当地的世界遗产的预算，需要整合到国家应急事故指挥系统中，方可共同完成修复任务。

7.2 What are the essential questions when assessing damage to your property?

7.2　当评估遗产的破坏程度时，最基本的问题是什么？

If the property is affected by a major disaster,

如果重大灾害对遗产产生了影响，你应该

you should ask the following questions:

How many people were present at the time of the event?

Which components of the property and its surroundings should you inspect for damage?(e.g. historic building, landscape element, archaeological site, etc.)

Which aspect of each component should you inspect? (i.e. structural stability, material damage, loss of authenticity or integrity, environmental setting, etc.)

What tools should you use and how do you inspect the various components of your site?(i. e. formats for recording, documentation and inspection).

Who will be responsible for inspection?

What emergency actions should you consider for the cultural property to prevent further damage (such as scaffolding, enclosing certain areas, disconnecting gas and electricity supply, prohibiting transit).

What short-term recovery activities should you undertake and in what order of priority?

It is important to follow a systematic process of damage assessment, taking into account the local context and the resources available. Thus, a strict methodology was developed for costing the war damage to historic buildings in Croatia, based on three different methods depending on the information available (Case Study 26). Similarly, damage recording sheets were developed by the Republic of Montenegro for movable and

提出以下问题：

事件发生时有多少人在场？

应该检测哪些易损坏的遗产要素和环境？（例如历史建筑、景观要素、考古遗址等等）。

每一个遗产要素的哪些因素需要检测？（例如建筑稳定性、材料损坏、真实性或完整性损失、环境背景等等）。

应该使用什么样的工具，以及该如何检测各种要素？（例如记录的形式，档案文件和检查）。

谁负责检查？

为了防止文化遗产的进一步破坏，你认为应该采取什么样的应急行动？（例如搭脚手架、封闭某些地区、切断天然气和电力供应、禁止通行）。

针对短期恢复应该采取什么样的行动？如何排定他们的优先顺序？

破坏评估应遵循系统过程，还要考虑当地的文化背景和可用的资金。这样，依赖可用信息资源，基于三个不同的方式，为核算毁于战火的克罗地亚历史建筑成本开发了一套严格的方法（案例 26）。用类似的方法，黑山共和国为被毁坏的可移动文物和不可移动文物编制了档案登记（Feilden，1987 pp.81–6）。

immovable cultural property (Feilden, 1987, pp. 81–6).

The team assessing the damages to the property must be able to give orders for carrying out these actions. This would be helpful in saving lives as well as heritage components of the property.

评估遗产受到破坏的团队必须能发布实施行动的命令。这样同样有助于挽救生命和遗产要素。

CASE STUDY 26

Methodology for damage assessment: post-war reconstruction of Vukovar (Croatia).

案例 26

受损评估的方法：战后重建武科瓦尔（克罗地亚）。

The listing and assessment of war-inflicted damage on monuments located in Vukovar's historic urban complex was performed under Section 5 of the *War Damage Assessment Act*. As materials, structures and construction techniques of monuments hardly correspond to those described by the 'Standard Calculation', a special typology of historic building elements was elaborated under a special clause, for the needs of listing and assessing war-inflicted damage on these monuments. The Act envisages three costing methods to be applied to the listing, assessment and calculation of war-inflicted damage on monuments:

根据《战争损失评估法》第 5 章的内容，对位于武科瓦尔历史城区遗产在战争冲突中受到的损坏进行了登记和评估。遗产的材料、结构和建造技术几乎不能用现有的“标准计算”方法来描述，因此为登记和评估遗产在战争的损失，开发了详细阐述历史建筑元素的特殊方案。该方案采用三种成本核算方法，用于登记、评估和计算战争对古迹造成的破坏：

Bill of quantities; where the necessary documentation of the historic buildings is available.

工程量清单：需要提供历史建筑必要的资料。

Overall assessment method; where it is not possible to apply a bill of quantities either due to lack of documentation or difficulty in recognizing original building elements. The method consists of establishing the aggregate floor area and the appropriate current building cost per unit of gross floor area for each monument.

总体评估方法：因为缺乏建筑资料或原有建筑要素已难以辨识，而无法提供工程量清单。该方法包括：确定遗产总体建筑面积和当前适合每处单体遗产建筑面积的成本。

Building elements method: by applying this method, damage caused to individual building elements and their respective shares in total building

建筑构件法：通过使用这种方法，评估单体建筑构件损失，并对其在总建筑成本中各自所占的份额进行估算。

costs are assessed.

Thus calculated, war damage amounts were then in each individual case added to the real cost incurred by the preventive technical protection and urgent preventive measures undertaken.

因此计算出，遗产战争损失总额是，每一个单个建筑预防保护技术加上实施紧急预防措施后所产生的实际费用之和。

Source: Vukovar Reconstruction Challenge, 1997, Republic of Croatia, Ministry of Development and Reconstruction, Zagreb.

来源：Vukovar 重建的挑战 , 1997, 克罗地亚共和国，萨格勒布，发展与重建部。

7.3 What measures will help ensure that the long-term recovery process is sustainable？

7.3　什么样的措施能够帮助确保可持续的、长期的复原过程?

After the disaster phase is over, long-term measures need to be formulated to ensure that the property is rehabilitated at the earliest and is protected from future disasters. Lessons learned from the disaster should help in reviewing existing risk management systems. The following aspects need to be reviewed or be put in place for effective recovery:

在灾后阶段，需要形成长期的措施以确定遗产恢复到原有状态，并能抵御未来的灾害。从灾害中获取的教训可以帮助我们评估现有的风险管理系统。为完成有效恢复，以下几个因素应该得到复查或落实到位：

Links with the social and economic rehabilitation of the property and its surrounding area. For example, the number of visitors to Bam Citadel (Islamic Republic of Iran) following the 2003 earthquake did not diminish, and so a number of measures were taken early on to facilitate their visits (Case Study 27).

恢复遗产及其周边环境相关的社会和经济的联系。例如，2003 年地震后，因为在重新对外开放前采取了一系列的便利措施，所以参观巴姆古城（伊朗伊斯兰共和国）的游客数量并没有减少（案例 27）。

CASE STUDY 27

Visitor-friendly measures during post-earthquake recovery: Bam 2003 (Islamic Republic of Iran)

案例 27

震后恢复的方便游客的参观措施：巴姆 2003（伊朗伊斯兰共和国）。

A disastrous earthquake on 26 Decembe2003 caused severe damage to the Citadel (Arg) and other historic buildings in the city of Bam. After the earthquake, the rescue and restoration of the rich

2003 年 12 月 26 日，灾难性地震对位于巴姆城的城堡和其他历史建筑造成了严重的破坏。地震以后，拥有丰富文化遗产的巴姆城的救援和修复工作，需要一个复杂管理规划。

cultural heritage of Bam needed a comprehensive management plan.

Therefore various studies and practical interventions were carried out, of which the most important related to the experience of crisis management. The planning phase during the crisis lasted six months, starting immediately after the earthquake. One of the actions initiated during this phase was to establish a visitor passage (pathway).

因此，实施了各种前期研究和实践干预，其中最为重要的是与危机管理实践相关的内容。在震后开始了持续 6 个月的危机规划部分。规划阶段的行动之一是修建游客通道。

This was already taken into consideration in the early days after the earthquake and later acquired a renewed importance after the debris from the bazaar had been removed and signs to show the boundaries and roads had been fixed. The earthquake did not reduce the number of visitors. In fact, their number gradually increased. The particular condition of the citadel after the earthquake attracted a number of enthusiasts and experts. Therefore, a temporary wooden passageway for visitors was constructed through the debris. This structure was a great help in visitor safety and provided access for experts to the various parts of the citadel. Guides were also deputed to control and guide the visitors.

在地震发生后的最初几天，已经考虑到这一点，随后清理市场残存物、设置固定的边界和道路标识这一动议，重新变得重要起来。地震并没有减少游客量。实际上，游客的数量还在逐步增加。地震后城堡的特殊状态吸引了大量的狂热者和专家。因此，在废墟中修建了临时的木质参观通道确保游客的安全，同时也为专家进入城堡各个部分提供了入口。委派导游员负责控制和指导游客。

Moreover, blocking the street in front of the citadel and turning it into a pedestrian urban centre was one of the actions taken for the convenience of visitors. Besides making a park in this area, a space was also allocated for the exhibition of ceramic shards discovered during the removal of the debris, so that visitors could be well informed of the archaeological activities and phases of documentation of the archaeological finds in the citadel.

此外，把城堡前面拥堵的街道变成城镇步行中心是方便游客的一大举措。除了在这个区域建立停车场外，也留出空间用于展览在清理遗址废墟时发现的陶片，这样参观者就可以更好地了解城堡的考古活动，以及考古发现各个阶段的文档记录。

Source: A. Vatandoust, E.M. Taleqani and M. Nejati, 2008, Risk management for the recovery project of Bam's cultural heritage, in H. Meir and T.

来源：A. Vatandoust, E.M. Taleqani and M. Nejati, 2008, H. Meir and T. Will (eds) 巴姆文化遗产修复的风险管理项目：风险中的遗产：文化遗产和

Will (eds), Heritage at Risk: Cultural Heritage and Natural Disasters, ICOMOS.

自然灾害，国际古迹遗址理事会。

Approaches to restoration, reconstruction and rehabilitation of the property following the disaster and how they link to issues such as identity and utility of the property. Debate over the reconstruction of Bryggen in Norway following the 1955 fire, for example, brought out constraints but also opportunities that had not previously existed (Case Study 28).

灾后遗产面临着采用何种修复、重建和复原方法及如何辨别和利用遗产等相关议题。例如，1995 年，挪威大火后布吕根的重建带来前所未有的严格限制，也带来前所未有的机遇（案例 28）。

• Review of cultural heritage legislation and policy, and disaster management if necessary.

• Review of site management systems if necessary.

• Assessment of human resources available or needed, e.g. volunteers.

• 必要时全面检查文化遗产法律和政策，和灾害管理规划。

• 必要时检查遗产管理体系。

• 评估可用的和需要的人力资源，例如志愿者。

Stakeholder involvement and community participation. In the case of Manas Wildlife Sanctuary (India), the local Bodo community has effectively participated in post-conflict recovery efforts which may contribute also to avoidance of future conflict (Case Study 29).

引入利益相关者和社区参与。在玛纳斯自然保护圣殿（印度），当地波多（Bodo）社区有效的参与到冲突后修复工作中，这也避免了未来的冲突（案例 29）。

Regular discussions with stakeholders and the local community are important for keeping these groups involved during recovery and rehabilitation and for their understanding the importance of restoring the lost cultural or natural heritage values of the World Heritage property.

与利益相关者和当地社区的常规讨论是非常重要的，让这些团队参与到修复或复原的工作中，对帮助他们理解为何要修复受损的世界自然或文化遗产重要价值也十分关键。

• Educational and awareness-raising activities: following the Indian Ocean tsunami, the tropical rainforest of Sumatra were under threat of deforestation to meet the need for timber to undertake massive reconstruction activities, emphasizing the need for awareness raising among local populations (Case Study 30).

• 教育和认识提升行动：在印度洋海啸之后，苏门答腊热带雨林遇到了森林砍伐的威胁，而砍伐森林原木是为了满足大规模重建活动的需求，所以应强化居民的保护意识（案例 30）。

• Introduction of a monitoring system and process.

• 引入监控系统和程序。

CASE STUDY 28

Options for post-fire reconstruction: the case of Bryggen in Bergen (Norway).

The disastrous fire in 1955 totally destroyed half of the then preserved area of Bryggen, a primarily residential area, which is inscribed on the World Heritage List. The discussion on reconstruction dates to 1976–77, when the question was reopened on the future of this site. The possibility of reconstruction was evaluated on the basis of documentation of the burnt-down area, which were mainly the measured drawings. Their assessment was based on their degree of completeness, accuracy, degree of mutual verification between two or more sets of drawings and conditions of preservation at the time of measuring. The amount of daylight that could be brought in and the views from the buildings were also considered as influencing factors. For example, it was found that rebuilding a neighbouring yard to the former height would reinstate the former poor daylight situation and so create problems for the use of preserved buildings. Limitations in town plan and neighbourhood were also considered. For example, some of the limitations laid down in the town plan were dispensable. The prescribed building line along the harbour was based on outdated plans for an underground bus terminal, and could be adjusted to the former front line.

Building regulations gave clear restrictions in terms of fire security on the use of wood in the new buildings. According to the earlier standards, there had to be an 8 m open-air gap or fireproof panels between buildings. However, if the wood in the reconstructed building was covered by fireproof panels or laminated, more ground area could be achieved, which could help in supplying escape routes. The buildings in the site also had

案例 28

火灾后重建的选择：俾尔根市的布吕根镇（挪威）。

1955 年的火灾使一半的布吕根保护区受到严重的破坏，其中列入世界遗产名录的主要住宅区域遭到严重破坏。1976–1977 年研究这个遗产的未来时，开始了关于重建的讨论。在被烧毁区域现有档案文件，主要是测量图纸的基础上，评估重建的可能性。他们的评估是根据这些图纸的完整度、精确度、两组或多组图纸相互验证的程度、图纸测量时候的保存条件进行的。确定采光时长以及建筑的景观等都是应该考虑的影响因素。例如，如果按原高度重建毗邻的院子，那么采光条件就跟原来的一样差，这就带来保护建筑使用的新问题。城市规划和街区也同样需要考虑限制性。城市规划中一些限制性规定现在变的可有可无。例如，原有的海港的建筑基线是根据废弃的地下巴士站规划的，可修改为更早的基线。

建筑规定中明确提出，为了消防安全，严格限制新建筑中木构建的使用。根据以前的标准，在建筑之间应该有 8 米的开放带或防火通道。然而，如果在重建的过程中，用防火板或防火层覆盖木材，会有更多的空间可以用作逃生通道。遗址上的建筑还有基础问题。在海平面下修建地下室，由于浮力和施工的问题而变得异常昂贵。因此，打基桩就被认为是处理地基最现实的方法。重建不仅为改善遗址的灾害

foundation problems. The building of cellars was very expensive due to buoyancy and construction problems below sea level. Therefore piles were considered as the only realistic method for the foundations. Reconstruction thus provided an opportunity not only to improve the risk preparedness of the site but also to make changes to suit contemporary needs that would not otherwise have been possible.

准备提供了机会，同时也为满足当代的需求提供了机会。

Source: H.J. Hansteen, 1992, International Symposium on the Fire Protection of Historic Buildings. Central Office of Historic Monuments and Sites, Norway; Norwegian Institute of Technology; ICOMOS International Wood Committee Norway, Tapir Publishers.

来源：H.J. Hansteen, 1992, 历史建筑防火研讨会，挪威历史纪念物和遗址中心办公室，挪威科技研究院，挪威古迹遗址理事会国际木材委员会 Tapir 出版社。

CASE STUDY 29

Involving local communities in post-conflict recovery: Manas Wildlife Sanctuary (India).

案例 29

社区参与到冲突后的遗产恢复行动中：玛纳斯野生动植物的殿堂（印度）。

Dealing with insurgency has been a significant feature in the management of Manas Wildlife Reserve in Assam (India) during the period from 1986 to 1993. Infrastructure necessary for management, patrols and research were destroyed including the range headquarters, offices and anti-poaching camps, roads and bridges. Periodic fighting continued until 2000. In 2003 the Bodo Territorial Council was established and accorded semi-autonomous powers, leading to improved relations between the World Heritage site and the surrounding Bodo communities.

从 1986 年到 1993 年，处理盗猎是阿萨姆邦马纳斯（印度）野生动物保护区的一项重要任务。冲突造成包括总部区域、办公室和反盗猎营地、道路和桥梁等基础设施所需的管理、巡逻和研究所被毁。周期性的斗争一直持续到 2000 年。2003 年，波多（Bodo）领土委员会成立并拥有半自治的权力，因此改进了世界遗产和波多社区之间的关系。

During this period, biodiversity loss occurred through encroachment, overgrazing, poaching and logging. Rhinos are now extinct, tiger population status is unknown but depleted, and buffalo are largely semi-domesticated through cross-breeding with domestic cattle. Although the park infrastructure

在此期间，因物种入侵、过度放牧、偷猎和伐木等原因造成遗产区生物多样性丧失。犀牛已经灭绝、老虎目前的状态未知，但肯定是数量减少，大部分水牛与家养牛杂交，成为半驯化牛。虽然公园基础设施遭受了相当大程度的损害，但在人迹罕至的地区，栖息地基本保存完好。

suffered considerable damage, the habitat in the inaccessible parts of the Sanctuary is largely intact.

Policies for recovery have been essentially based on the involvement of the Bodo people in the management of the region and through the leadership of the Bodo Territorial Council. Former poachers have become guards, tourism initiatives have been developed and the potential benefits of Manas and its wildlife for improved economic development through tourism revenue are acknowledged by local people. The national initiative IRV2020 has funded anti-poaching camps which are staffed with forest personnel and ninety rotating volunteers from the local Bodo community, some of whom are ex-poachers motivated by tourism initiatives and awareness of the increased revenue these could bring. The young volunteers also receive an allowance and food. The Bodo community owns a small eco-friendly tourism camp run by the Manas Maozigendri Ecotourism Society. Home Stays with local Bodo families is another initiative targeting the adventure traveller. The Bodo Territorial Council is playing an important role in restoring the Manas Wildlife Sanctuary through promotion of tourism as an industry for the 45,000 resident villagers around the property.

复苏政策实质上由波多领土委员会领导，波多人参与管理。以前的偷猎者成为守卫者、倡导开发旅游项目可以改善经济，对玛纳斯当地人以及它的野生动物均有潜在好处。国家IRV2020计划资助了反盗猎营地，营地配有护林人员和九十位转为志愿者的当地波多人，而他们中的一些人以前是盗猎人，通过参与旅游计划，不但提高了意识，同时也增加了收入。年轻的志愿者因参与了这个活动得到了津贴和食品。波多社区目前拥有一个小型环保旅游营地，由玛纳斯 Maozigendri 生态旅游协会管理运行。当地另一个计划是针对爱冒险的旅游人士的波多家庭寄宿。波多领土委员会在恢复玛纳斯野生动物保护区中扮演了重要的角色，它将旅游业作为遗产区 45000 位居民的共同产业予以推动。

The Bodo Territorial Council is also taking a strong positive lead in the protection of the Manas Wildlife Sanctuary and is currently providing most of the funding for the management of the property. This significant and positive change to the status of the property should allow recovery of the degraded wildlife populations and forests over the next few years if sufficient additional support and training is obtained. To prevent a return to the problems experienced in the past, the factors that led to the initial situation need to be understood and avoided in the future. Maintaining social stability

在保护玛纳斯野生动物的过程中，波多领土委员会也采取强有力的积极领导，提供了遗产保护的绝大部分资金。遗产保护状况有如此有效而积极的改变，如果在接下来几年有充分的外部支持和培训，退化的野生动物数量和森林就可能得到恢复。为了防止重蹈覆辙，需要理解导致最初状况产生的因素，才能在未来避免同样问题。通过实施旅游计划来维护社会稳定和减少贫困，目前看来是可行的，但需要更多国家与联邦资金的预算分配，提供急需的培训，让波多人民在能力建设、教育和世界遗产价值保护意识提高等方面获利，从而为保护遗

and reducing poverty through local initiatives are currently helpful, but more formalized budget allocation with federal and state funding would provide much-needed training for capacity-building, education and raising awareness of the benefits of World Heritage status to the Bodo people and thus ensuring a more sustainable peaceful future for the property and its biodiversity.

产及其生物多样性提供一个可持续的、更和平的未来。

Sources: UNESCO World Heritage Committee, 1992

(http://whc.unesco.org/archive/repcom92.htm#manas).

UNESCO / IUCN, 2008, Monitoring Mission Report

(http://whc.unesco.org/en/list/338/documents/).

http://www.iisd.org/pdf/2002/envsec_conserving_overview.pdf

WWF Species Programme 2008

(http://www.panda.org/about_wwf/what_we_do/species/news/index.cfm?uNewsID=129761).

http://www.pubmedcentral.nih.gov/articlerender.fcgi?artid=2002516

来源：联合国教科文组织世界遗产委员会，1992

（http://whc.unesco.org/archive/repcom92.htm#manas）

UNESCO/ 世界自然保护联盟，2008，监测任务报告

（http://whc.unesco.org/en/list/338/documents/）。

http://www.iisd.org/pdf/2002/envsec_conserving_overview.pdf

世界自然基金会 2008 物种计划

（http://www.panda.org/about_wwf/what_we_do/species/news/index.cfm?uNewsID=129761）.

http://www.pubmedcentral.nih.gov/articlerender.fcgi?artid=2002516

CASE STUDY 30

Deforestation as a secondary risk: post-tsunami rainforest in Sumatra (Indonesia).

案例 30

砍伐森林引发次生灾害：海啸后苏门答腊岛的雨林（印度尼西亚）。

Protected areas can mitigate the impact of a disaster and are often more resilient than modified ecosystems are to natural hazards; however, they also suffer from secondary risks. When communities and infrastructure are devastated by a sudden event, resources within a protected area can provide much needed fuel, food and materials for reconstruction. World Heritage managers should be aware of their role and the measures that can be taken to support local communities without degrading the values and integrity of their World Heritage site.

保护区可以缓解灾害的影响，也使灾后生态系统更具有恢复力；然而，他们却遭受着次生灾害的威胁。突发事件摧毁了社区和基础设施，只有保护区能提供燃料、食品和建筑材料等资源。世界遗产管理者应该意识到他们的角色，应该采取既不降低世界遗产价值和完整性，又能协助当地社区恢复重建的措施。

The tsunami that hit South-East Asia on 26 December 2004 did not directly affect the ecosystem of the Gunung Leuser National Park (GLNP), part of the Tropical Rainforest Heritage of Sumatra; however, the human resources and infrastructure of the national park and the nature conservation agency responsible for the management of conservation areas adjacent to the GLNP were heavily impacted. A wedge of coastline and existing infrastructure up to 6 km inland was devastated. The Nature Conservation Agency Aceh (BKSDA-A) Office in Banda Aceh, the provincial capital of Nanggroe Aceh Darussalam (NAD), and several GLNP resort offices along the western coast of Aceh were destroyed. The capacity to protect and manage the property was seriously affected as many victims worked for government and conservation NGOs, including more than 150 staff in the forestry agencies. The destruction of housing and infrastructure of local communities was estimated to require 8.5 million m3 of timber to build 123,000 houses. This placed great pressure on local and national governments to allow logging within the property. Illegal logging was widespread due to the extreme needs of the local communities, compounded by the reduced capacity to protect the property. In Aceh, increased deforestation degraded the GLNP and the surrounding forests, causing further risk to vulnerable communities through increased flash floods and landslides.

2004 年 12 月 26 日，袭击亚洲东南部的海啸对贡努列尤择国家公园的生态系统和苏门答腊部分热带雨林并没有造成直接的影响；然而，国家公园的基础设施和人力资源，以及与贡努列尤择国家公园相关的、负责保护区保护工作的自然保护机构受到了重创。一段凸出的海岸线以及岛上长约 6 公里的基础设施完全被摧毁。位于南格罗亚齐达鲁萨兰的省府，班达亚齐的亚齐自然保护机构办公室、贡努列尤择国家公园在亚齐西海岸的保护办公室全部损毁。灾害造成服务于政府和非政府保护组织的员工包括 150 个森林管理员的伤亡，使得保护和管理遗产的能力受到严重的影响。据估计受损的当地社区房屋和基础设施需要 850 万立方米木料，需建 123,000 间房屋。远远超出地区和国家政府允许的、在保护区内的采伐量。由于社区对木材的极度需求，再加上保护能力的减弱，非法砍伐极为普遍。在亚齐，剧增的森林砍伐使贡努列尤择国家公园和它周边的森林急剧减少，也使脆弱的社区面临洪水或山体滑坡的威胁。

WWF Indonesia helped to raise awareness of the extent of forest destruction after the tsunami. Through the efforts of the Environment Minister, plans to exploit the GLNP were rejected and alternative solutions for reconstruction were sought through international assistance. The Government of Spain supported a two-year UNESCO/ PHKA project aiming to mitigate post-tsunami environmental threats to the national park and adjacent conservation areas.

世界自然基金会印尼分会，在海啸后帮助人们认识到森林过度砍伐的危害。通过环境部的努力，拒绝了开发贡努列尤择国家公园的计划，取而代之以通过寻求国际援助进行重建的解决方案。西班牙政府支持的、为期 2 年的、联合国教科文组织及印尼自然资源保护组织项目，旨在减轻海啸后环境对国家公园和相邻保护区的威胁。

Resisting the pressure to exploit protected areas during the recovery phase of a disaster requires protected area managers to raise awareness among local communities, businesses and politicians and to work closely with aid agencies and NGOs. Education, training and awareness raising should be ongoing so that emergency response includes the advice of the property management (see also Case Study 21 on the Dorset and East Devon Coast).

灾后恢复阶段，保护区管理人员顶着层层压力，提高保护区当地的社区、企业和政客的保护意识，与援助机构和非政府组织密切合作。应该持续进行教育、培训和提高保护意识，以便在危急时刻按遗产管理方的建议进行应急反应（参见案例研究21的多塞特和东德文郡海岸）。

Sources: UNESCO / IUCN, 2006, TRH Sumatra Monitoring Mission Report

(http://whc.unesco.org/en/list/1167/documents/).

Flora and Fauna International, Rapid Response Facility

(http://www.fauna-flora.org/rrf.php)

WWF Indonesia (www.wwf.or.id/).

Leuser Foundation

(http://www.leuserfoundation.org/)

© UNESCO /

来源：联合国教科文组织、世界自然保护联盟，2006，TRH苏门答腊监测任务报告。

（http://whc.unesco.org/en/list/1167/documents/）.

国际动植物协会快速反应机制

（http://www.fauna-flora.org/rrf.php）

印度尼西亚世界野生动物基金（www.wwf.or.id/）.

勒赛尔基金

（http://www.leuserfoundation.org/）.

联合国教科文组织版权

7.4 How can heritage property play a more proactive role in post-disaster recovery and rehabilitation?

7.4 在灾后恢复和复原的过程中如何发挥遗产的积极作用？

Heritage property can play a more proactive role in recovery and rehabilitation by:

• using traditional skills and capacities for post-disaster rehabilitation.

• providing evidence of the local way of life, technologies and sources of livelihood that should be used when undertaking post-disaster reconstruction. In this respect, much can be learned from past mistakes (Case Study 31).

• recognizing that cultural and natural heritage as a source of identity can contribute to the psychological recovery of disaster victims.

• using local coping mechanisms through traditional social networks to promote recovery.

遗产在灾后恢复和复原的过程中能发挥以下的积极作用：

• 在灾后重建中使用传统技术和技能。

• 提供当地生活方式、技术和生计资源的证据用于灾后重建，在这方面，从过去的失误中可以学到很多知识（见案例31）。

• 认同文化和自然遗产资源，对灾民的心理康复发挥积极作用。

• 采用地方性应对机制，通过传统的社区网络促进灾后重建工作。

CASE STUDY 31

Impact of reconstruction following Dhamar earthquake (Yemen).

Following the Dhamar earthquake in 1982, the Yemeni Government emphasized the tender (contractor built) approach to reconstruction by relocating villages, rather than the self-help or repair approaches. The cultural dimension of reconstruction was overlooked, which in many cases led to total rejection of the new settlements by local people. Residents did not think of these settlements as permanent homes, as they failed to offer the advantages of their original village. In some cases, new settlements within an acceptable distance were actually competing with the old ones, as they were neither close enough to merge with the original village, nor far enough away to establish a new centre. Another physical factor seen to have a marked effect on acceptance of the new settlements was their distance from agricultural land. Moreover, the architecture of the new houses was urban and had no link with the local lifestyle. A prototype house layout produced by the Executive Office was later adopted by all types of contractors. The unit was repeated in its thousands by different contractors on different sites, using the same technology of reinforced concrete. As a result, those houses that were inhabited had been substantially altered, extended or changed in some way, or in a number of cases used for functions other than accommodation (storage or animal byres). Also most of the subsequent additions to houses did not have earthquake-safe features because of the inability to follow the introduced technology.

Source: S. Barakat, 1993, Rebuilding and Resettlement, 9 Years Later. A case study of the contractor built reconstruction in Yemen, following the 1982 Dhamar earthquake, York, UK, Institute of

案例 31

扎马尔省（也门）震后重建的影响。

1982 年，在扎马尔省地震之后，也门政府强调采用承包商招标异地重建的方法，而不是原址自救或修复。由于重建中忽视了文化层面，当地居民完全拒绝新的定居点。因为新的定居点没有原来村落的优势，居民不认可新定居点为永久的家园。新定居点距他们原始村落仍有一段距离，无法合并，而这段距离也不足以形成一个新的中心。另一个显著影响居民接受新定居点的客观因素是，新定居点与耕种土地之间的距离更远。并且，新房屋的建筑形式适合于城镇，不符合当地的生活习惯。所有的承包商按执行办公室提供标准的房屋布局建房。不同的承包商按同样建筑形式，同样的钢筋混凝土技术，在不同的地点修建了数以千计相似的房屋。结果是，居民都得进行改造、扩充。大多数情况，这些建筑的不只是居住（变成了储藏室或牲口棚）。另外，增建的附属设施因为没有按照推荐的技术进行施工，不具备抗震的能力。

来源：S. Barakat, 1993,9 年后的重建与再安置，1986 年也门扎马尔震后重建案例研究，英国约克郡约克大学高级建筑研究学院，战后重建和发展工作报告 No. 2。

Advanced Architectural Studies, University of York. Post-War Reconstruction and Development Unit Working Paper No. 2.

8. How to implement, reassess and reappraise the DRM plan.

8 如何实施、重新评价和评估灾害风险管理规划。

8.1 How do you implement and monitor the DRM plan for your property?

8.1 如何实施和监测遗产灾害风险管理规划？

An action plan is needed to implement the DRM plan and then to monitor it. Appropriate implementation and monitoring mechanisms form part of the DRM plan.

• The action plan should consist of the following:

– various activities or projects;

– time-frame for their implementation;

– financial resources required;

– existing and additional human resources;

– identification of agency(ies) responsible for implementation.

• Periodic review based on the effectiveness of the plan after implementation and in the light of the experience of an emergency, if any has happened.

在实施灾害风险管理规划时应制定行动计划，然后监督计划的实施。适宜的实施和监测机制是灾害风险管理规划的一部分。

• 行动计划应该包括以下内容：

– 各种活动和项目；

– 实施的时间期限；

– 需要的资金；

– 现有和额外的人力资源；

– 确定具体负责实施的部门。

• 在计划有效实施后可根据紧急情况的经验（如果发生过），进行定期复审。

8.2 How do you train and build local capacity for implementing and monitoring the plan?

• Undertake training and capacity-building on the use of emergency equipment such as fire extinguishers, and emergency simulations in cooperation with external agencies such as fire services.

• Organize regular emergency simulation drills, awareness-raising activities, short publications for visitors, etc. It is crucial to perform simulation drills periodically. A simulation exercise at the archaeological site of Pompeii (Italy) attracted some fifty volunteers to be trained in the event of an emergency at the site or in local museums (Case Study 32).

8.2 如何训练和构建当地实施和监测计划的能力？

• 与外部机构如消防部门等合作，对如何使用灭火器等应急设备，进行应急模拟培训和能力建设。

• 组织常规的应急模拟训练、宣传活动、为游客准备简短的出版物等等。定期的模拟演练十分必要。在庞贝考古遗址（意大利）模拟训练中，50多个志愿者参与遗产地或当地博物馆组织的、应对发生紧急情况的培训。

Involving volunteers in emergencies requires linking them to regular maintenance programmes and simulation exercises.

CASE STUDY 32

Training through simulation exercises: salvaging cultural heritage in Pompeii (Italy).

The Archaeological Areas of Pompei, Herculaneum and Torre Annunziata, near Naples (southern Italy), is a UNESCO World Heritage site. The Vesuvius volcanic eruption in AD 79 covered the city with ash and therefore preserved almost the entire Roman city. However, the site is still exposed to many risks, such as volcanic eruptions, earthquakes and the ever-present risk of fire. An artifact emergency plan was therefore developed by the chief archaeologist, Prof. Guzzo, with the support of a consultant and a team of local volunteers. The assistance of volunteers was deemed necessary due to the large number of artifacts in storage and the lack of in-house human resources. Volunteers can be really helpful only if they are suitably trained. Therefore a training course was set up in 2007 and suitable candidates were found through a major public relations push. Eventually over fifty volunteers, many from the local university, took part in a three-day training course, with practical demonstrations carried out by the archaeologists from the Ministry of Cultural Heritage and Activities. The topics illustrated during the training course included the techniques of calling to action and dressing for emergency situations, arriving on site and moving around, handling delicate artifacts such as pottery, statues, frescoes, iron, glass and bronze objects, classifying artifacts during salvage, setting up initial space for cleaning and packing salvaged objects pending further professional restoration. A full-scale drill in the coordinated presence of the security guards, fire officers, archaeologists, first-

当志愿者参与到紧急情况训练时，需要定期对他们进行相关项目培训或模拟演练。

案例 32

通过模拟训练，进行抢救庞贝古城文化遗产的培训（意大利）。

庞贝古城，赫库兰尼姆和托雷安农齐亚塔考古遗址区，位于那不勒斯（意大利南部），是著名的文化遗产。公元前 79 年，维苏威火山爆发，火山灰将整座城市覆盖，因此也把几乎整座古罗马时代的城市完整的保存下来。然而，这个遗址依旧暴露在火山喷发、地震和火灾隐患等诸多威胁下。首席考古学家古佐教授制定的艺术品应急计划，获得当地顾问和志愿者的支持。由于遗址存有大量的艺术品，同时又缺乏有效的人力资源，因此获得志愿者的协助非常重要。只有持续接受训练的志愿者才能真正发挥作用。2007 年，在主要公共关系的推动下，选拔了志愿者的候选人，并开设了培训课程。最终 50 多个志愿者，其中大部分来自于当地大学，参加了为期三天的课程培训，来自文化遗产和活动部的考古专家做了现场演示。训练课程主题包括接受行动命令、紧急情况下的包装、到达现场后巡视周边，搬运陶器、雕像、壁画、铁、玻璃和青铜等精致工艺品，不同类别艺术品的抢救等技术，以及建立清洗和包装文物空间，以便进一步的专业修复。现场的保安、消防人员、考古学家、急救人员和全体训练有素的志愿者团队进行了一次全方位的合作演习，并取得了良好的效果。此后，模拟演习计划每隔六个月实施一次。在赫库兰尼姆，奥普隆蒂斯和博斯科雷尔博物馆也实施了模拟演习，设置不同的场景（火灾、爆炸装置等等，有没有游客正在参观）以提高参与人员的基本技能。

aid crew and the full team of trained volunteers was carried out with favourable results. Thereafter, a regular simulation drill was planned at six-month intervals. The simulation drill was repeated in Herculaneum, Oplontis and the Boscoreale Museum, with different scenarios (fire, explosive device, and so on, with and without visitors present) in order to improve the basic skills of the personnel involved.

Source: A. Biasiotti, UNESCO Consultant on Security for Cultural Heritage, 2007.

来源：A. Biasiotti，联合国教科文组织文化遗产安全顾问，2007。

Appendix I

附件 1

Glossary of relevant disaster management terms

与灾害管理有关的词汇表

Climate change: a change in climate which is attributed directly or indirectly to human activity that alters the composition of the global atmosphere and which is in addition to natural climate variability observed over comparable time periods (United Nations Framework Convention on Climate Change; http://unfccc.int/).

气候改变：观测到的可比时间段内、非自然气候变化造成的，而是由人类活动直接或间接地改变全球大气组成所导致的气候改变（联合国气候变化框架公约 http://unfccc.int/）。

Disaster: A serious disruption of the functioning of a community or a society causing widespread human, material, economic or environmental losses which exceeds the ability of the affected community or society to cope using its own resources (http://www.unisdr.org).

灾害：严重干扰社区或社会的功能，造成大量人员、材料、经济和环境的损失，这些损失超过了社区或社会利用现有资源应对灾害的能力（www.unisdr.org）。

Emergency: An unforeseen combination of circumstances or the resulting state that calls for immediate action (Merriam Webster Online Dictionary, www.m-w.com).

紧急情况：需要立即采取应对行动的、各种不可预见的情况和状态（韦氏在线词典，www.m–w.com）。

Hazard: Any phenomenon, substance or situation, which has the potential to cause disruption or damage to infrastructure and services, people,

危害：任何潜在的、能破坏基础设施、服务、威胁生命财产安全、造成环境混乱的现象、物质或状况（Abarquez and Murshed, 2004）。

their property and their environment (Abarquez and Murshed, 2004).

Mitigation: Taking action in the time frame before a disaster to lessen post-event damage to lives and property. In risk management, many hazards such as earthquakes cannot be reduced, but the risk from that hazard can be reduced, or mitigated, for example by constructing earthquake-resistant buildings, or shelves that prevent objects from sliding off. The former is structural mitigation, the latter is non-structural.

缓解：在灾害发生前采取的减轻灾害对生命和财产伤害的行动。在风险管理中，许多灾害如地震风险无法减少，但可以降低或者缓解，例如建造具有抗震能力的建筑、搭建防止物品滑落的架子。前者是结构性的缓解，后者是非结构化的缓解。

Prevention: Measures taken to reduce the likelihood of losses. Ideally, these measures would seek to reduce losses to zero, but this often is not possible.

预防：用于降低可能性损失的措施。理想上这些措施能将损失降低为零，但实践中多无法实现。

Key question: How much prevention do you need to undertake?

核心问题：你需要实施多少预防措施。

Recovery: The process of returning the institution to normal operations, which may also involve the repair and restoration of the building or site.

恢复：恢复机构的正常运行状态，也包括对建筑物和遗址的维修和修复。

Response: The reaction to an incident or emergency to assess the damage or impact to the site and its components, and actions taken to prevent people and the property from suffering further damage.

紧急应对：评估遗址或构成要素因偶然或紧急情况，受到损坏或影响的程度，并采取行动防止人和财产遭受进一步的破坏。

Risk: The chance of something happening that will have an impact upon objectives. (Emergency Management Australia, 2000).

风险：会影响目标的事件发生的机会（澳大利亚应急管理中心，2000）。

Vulnerability: The susceptibility and resilience of the community and environment to hazards. ‘Resilience’ relates to ‘existing controls’ and the capacity to reduce or sustain harm. ‘Susceptibility’ relates to ‘exposure’ (Emergency Management Australia, 2000).

脆弱性：社区或环境对于灾害的敏感性和恢复力。“恢复力”与“现有的控制”有关，是减少或承受伤害的能力。“敏感性”与“暴露”或接触有关（澳大利亚应急管理中心，2000）。

World Heritage property: World Heritage properties are those defined in Articles 1 and 2 of the World Heritage Convention and inscribed on the World Heritage List on the basis of their outstanding universal value, which is fulfilled through meeting one or more of criteria(i)–(x) in the Operational Guidelines for the Implementation of the World Heritage Convention (UNESCO / WHC, 2008a).

世界遗产：世界遗产是指满足《世界遗产公约》第 1 和 2 条的定义，其突出普遍价值符合《实施世界遗产公约操作指南》(i) – (x) 标准中的一个或多个标准，得以列入世界遗产名录的遗产（联合国教科文组织世界遗产中心，2008a）。

Appendix II

附件 2

Typology of hazards

1. Meteorological

a. storm

i. high precipitation

ii. strong wind

iii. cyclone/ hurricane/ typhoon

iv. tornado/hail storm

v. ice storm

vi. dust storm

vii. wave action (at sea / lake)

b. fire induced by lightning / static, spontaneous coal /peat combustion

c. drought

d. heat wave

e. high sea-surface temperature

It is also important to be aware of the effect of climate cycles such as the El Niño Southern Oscillation and North Atlantic Oscillation, and the effect of other cycles on predictable variations in risk of certain events such as drought, storm frequency, increased rainfall, etc.

灾害的类型

1. 气象灾害

a. 风暴

ⅰ. 降水量大

ⅱ. 风力强

ⅲ. 旋风、台风、飓风

ⅳ. 龙卷风和冰雹风暴

ⅴ. 冰暴

ⅵ. 沙尘暴

ⅶ. 波浪潮（海洋或湖）

b. 因闪电或静态的、煤 / 泥炭自燃引起的火灾

c. 干旱

d. 热浪

e. 海面温度过高

注意气候周期的影响，例如厄尔尼诺南部涛动和北大西洋涛动，其他周期预测变化影响所带来的风险，如干旱、长期的风暴、持续的暴雨等等。

2. Hydrological

a. flood

i. precipitation flood – inadequate drainage or infiltration

ii. flash flood

iii. river or lake flood

iv. mass movement dam

2. 水文灾害

a. 洪水

ⅰ. 降水洪水，因排水不畅或下渗不足引起的洪水

ⅱ. 山洪

ⅲ. 河或湖洪水

ⅳ. 溃坝

v. storm surge

b. tsunami

3. Geological / geomorphological

a. volcanic

b. seismic

c. mass movement (land and sea)

d. erosion (river bank / coast line / reef)

4. Biological

epidemics (human, animal, or plant and human-animal transferable diseases)

b. pest infestations

c. algal blooms

d. rapidly spreading weeds or nuisance plants

e. coral bleaching event

5. Astrophysical

a. space weather

b. meteorite impact

6. Human-induced

a. fire (land clearance, arson, accident, drainage of peat soils)

b. pollution (health, e.g. food poisoning, disease)

i. nuclear/ radioactive accident

ii. waste mass movement (unstable spoil heap)

iii. air pollution toxic fire or explosion or leak

iv. water pollution failure or leak / spill → wildlife, plant mortality, disease

1. toxic

2. radioactive / nuclear

3. organic waste

4. sediment

c. Violence-and conflict-induced human and wildlife mortality and ecosystem destruction

i. disease

1. rapid-acting: Ebola fever, H5N1, SARS, cholera, rabies

ⅴ. 风暴潮

b. 海啸

3. 地质、地貌灾害

a. 火山

b. 地震

c. 板块运动（大陆和海洋）

d. 侵蚀（河岸、海岸线、礁石）

4. 生物灾害

a. 流行病（人、动物、植物或人－动物传播的疾病）

b. 虫害

c. 赤潮

d. 迅速蔓延杂草或有害的植物

e. 珊瑚白化

5. 天体物理灾害

a. 太空天气

b. 陨石冲击

6. 人类引起的灾害

a. 火灾（土地清理、纵火、事故、泥炭土壤的排水）

b. 污染（健康，例如食物中毒，疾病）

ⅰ. 核或辐射事件

ⅱ. 废弃物移动（不稳定的废石堆）

ⅲ. 污染空气的、含有有毒物质的火灾或爆炸或泄漏

ⅳ. 水污染或泄漏——野生动物、植物死亡或疾病

1. 有毒的

2. 放射性或核污染的

3. 有机废弃物

4. 沉淀物

c. 暴力和冲突引起的人员和动物伤亡和生态系统的破坏

ⅰ. 疾病

1. 快速传播：埃博拉热、H5N1 流感病毒、非典、霍乱、狂犬病；

2.gradual capacity loss and social disintegration → HIV/AIDS

ii. human wildlife / conflict

1. poaching, wildlife massacres, species extinction → pest outbreaks

2. wildlife stampedes, predator attacks

iii. large-scale population dislocation or relocation

1. rapid loss of vegetation cover →flood, mass movement, human/wildlife conflict

2. soil or water contamination →disease, pest outbreak

3. heavy hunting/ poaching →increased human-wildlife conflict or pest outbreak

iv. illegal activities and violence, e.g. illegal drug trade

v. Warfare

1. explosives (nuclear or other)

2. biological warfare agents

3. firearm use

4. landmines

d. Gas flaring

e. Infrastructure failure

i. water pollution (algal blooms, coral bleaching, pest infestation, disease epidemic)

ii. dam or levee failure, flood

iii. coastal protection (wall, artificial beach) failure flood and erosion

iv. mass movement (e.g. waste slumps)

f. Mining-induced

i. seismic activity and mass movement

ii. volcanic activity and mud volcano

iii. mass movement

iv. climate change and rainfall variation, e.g. mountain-top mining

7. Climate change

a. sea-level rise

b. melting permafrost

c. rainfall pattern change

2. 免疫能力丧失或社会解体→艾滋病毒、艾滋病

ⅱ. 人类、野生动物冲突

1. 偷猎，灭绝野生动物物种的屠杀，→害虫爆发

2. 野生动物入侵，食肉动物的攻击

ⅲ. 大规模的人口迁徙

1. 迅速的植被损失→洪水，块体移位，人类或野生动物冲突

2. 土壤或水污染→疾病，爆发害虫病

3. 过度的狩猎和偷盗→加剧人与野生动物之间的冲突，或爆发害虫病

ⅳ. 非法活动或暴力行为，如非法毒品买卖

ⅴ. 战争

1. 爆炸（核）

2. 生化战争

3. 使用武器

4. 地雷

d. 天然气燃烧

e. 基础设施故障

ⅰ. 水污染（赤潮、珊瑚白化、害虫感染、疾病流行）

ⅱ. 溃堤溃坝，洪水

ⅲ. 防海堤（墙、人工海滩）溃塌，洪水和侵蚀

ⅳ. 物质运动（如废弃物倒塌）

f. 采矿引起的灾害

ⅰ. 地震活动和块体移位

ⅱ. 火山活动和泥火山

ⅲ. 块体移位

ⅳ. 气候变化与降水变化，例如山顶采矿

7. 气候变化

a. 海平面上升

b. 冻土融化

c. 降雨模式改变

d. increased storm severity or frequency

e. desertification

d. 增加风暴的严重性或频率

e. 沙漠化

Appendix III

附件 3

Relevant charters and recommendations Convention concerning the Protection of the World Cultural and Natural Heritage, UNESCO, 1972.

http://whc.unesco.org/archive/convention-en.pdf

相关的宪章和建议

《保护世界文化和自然遗产公约》，联合国教科文组织，1972。

http://whc.unesco.org/archive/convention-en.pdf

Final Recommendations of the International Course on Preventive Measures for the Protection of Cultural Property in Earthquake Prone Regions, Skopje, Yugoslavia, 1985.(Stovel, ICCROM, 1998)

《关于地震多发带文化遗产预防措施国际课程的最终建议》，斯科普里，南斯拉夫，1985（Stovel 国际文物保护与修复研究中心，1998）。

Conclusions and Recommendations of the International Workshop on Structural and Functional Rehabilitation of Housing in Historic Buildings in Seismic Regions, Mexico City, 1986. (Stovel, ICCROM, 1998)

《地震带重建历史建筑房屋、结构和功能的结论和建议》，国际研讨会墨西哥城。

（Stovel，国际文物保护与修复研究中心，1998）。

Council of Europe, Committee of Ministers, Recommendation No. R(93)9 of the Committee of Ministers to Member States on the Protection of the Architectural Heritage against Natural Disasters, adopted by the Committee of Ministers on 23 November 1993 at the 503rd Meeting of the Ministers' Deputies. (ICOMOS Heritage at Risk, H@R, 2008)

欧洲委员会、部长委员会在 1993 年 11 月 23 日第 503 届部长代表会议上的第 R（93）9 号建议，号召成员国抵御自然灾害、保护建筑遗产（国际古迹遗址理事会遗产面临风险，H@R，2008）。

Declaration of Quebec, Ist National Summit on Heritage and Risk Preparedness, Quebec City, Canada, 1996. (Stovel, ICCROM, 1998)

《魁北克宣言》，第一届遗产和风险防范峰会，魁北克城，加拿大，1996（Stovel，国际文物保护与修复研究中心，1998）。

The Kobe/Tokyo Declaration on Risk Preparedness for Cultural Heritage, Kobe/Tokyo International Symposium on Risk Preparedness for Cultural Properties, 1997. Radenci Declaration,

《神户 / 东京文化遗产风险防范宣言》，文化遗产风险防范神户 / 东京国际研讨会，1997。

Blue Shield Seminar on the Protection of Cultural Heritage in Emergencies and Exceptional Situations, Radenci, Slovenia, 12–16 November 1998. http://www.ifla.org/VI/4/admin/emergcy.htm

《拉登齐宣言》，紧急情况和异常情况中保护文化遗产的蓝盾研讨会，Radenci，斯洛文尼亚 ,1998 年 11 月 12 日至 16 日。http://www.ifla.org/VI/4/admin/emergcy.htm

Declaration of Assisi by ICOMOS Scientific Committee for the Analysis and Restoration of Structures of Architectural Heritage, 1998. (Stovel, ICCROM, 1998)

阿西西声明，国际古迹遗址理事会科学委员会，分析和恢复建筑遗产结构，1998。（Stovel，国际文物保护与修复研究中心，1998)

Torino Declaration. Resolutions of the First Blue Shield International Meeting, Torino, Italy,

2004.http://www.ifla.org/VI/4/admin/torino-declaration2004.pdf

《都灵宣言》。第一届蓝盾国际会议决议，意大利都灵，2004 年。http://www.ifla.org/VI/4/admin/torino–declaration2004.pdf

Kyoto Declaration 2005 on the Protection of Cultural Properties, Historic Areas and their Settings from Loss in Disasters (adopted at the Kyoto International Symposium 2005 'Towards the Protection of Cultural Properties and Historic Urban Areas from Disaster' held at Kyoto Kaikan on 16 January 2005); http://www.international.icomos.org/xian2005/kyoto-declaration.pdf

《保护文化遗产和历史城市地区远离灾害的 2005 京都议定书》，（2005 年"保护文化遗产和历史城市地区远离灾害"京都国际研讨会采纳，2005 年 1 月 16 日京都会馆举行）；http://www.international.icomos.org/xian2005/kyoto–declaration.pdf

Recommendations of the UNESCO/ICCROM/Agency for Cultural Affairs of Japan – Thematic Meeting on Cultural Heritage Risk Management, World Conference on Disaster Reduction, Kobe, 2005.

http://australia.icomos.org/wp-content/uploads/Japan-recommendations.pdf

建议联合国教科文组织 / 国际文物保护与修复研究中心 / 日本文化事务代理专题会议，"文化遗产风险管理、灾后恢复国际会议"（神户，2005）。

http://australia.icomos.org/wp–content/uploads/Japan–recommendations.pdf

UNESCO / WHC. 2006. Strategy Document for Reducing Risks from Disasters at World Heritage Properties. World Heritage Committee, 30th Session, Vilnius, Lithuania, 8–16 July 2006. http://whc.unesco.org/download.cfm?id_document=6525

联合国教科文组织、世界遗产中心。2006 年。《减低世界遗产灾害风险战略文件》。世界遗产委员会会议，立陶宛，维尔纽斯第 30 届，2006 年 7 月 9 日 –18 日。http://whc.unesco.org/download.cfm?id_document=6525

Declaration on the Impact of Climate Change on Cultural Heritage, International Workshop on

《气候变化对文化遗产影响声明》，气候变化对文化遗产影响的国际会议，新德里（印度），

Impact of Climate Change on Cultural Heritage, New Delhi (India), 22 May 2007. (ICOMOS News, June 2008)

2007 年 5 月 22 日（国际古迹遗址理事会新闻，2008 年 6 月）。

Appendix IV

附件 4

International organizations and research institutions

国际组织和研究机构

A. International organizations concerned with the cultural and natural sectors

A. 文化和自然部分的国际组织

• International Centre for the Study of the Preservation and Restoration of Cultural Property (ICCROM) is an intergovernmental organization dedicated to the conservation of cultural heritage. ICCROM aims at improving the quality of conservation practice as well as raising awareness about the importance of preserving cultural heritage. It contributes to preserving cultural heritage through five main areas of activity: training, information, research, cooperation and advocacy. For details visit http://www.iccrom.org. ICCROM, in cooperation with ICOMOS and the UNESCO World Heritage Centre, published Risk Preparedness: A Management Manual for World Cultural Heritage (Stovel, 1998). Furthermore, with assistance from the World Heritage Centre, ICCROM developed a set of training materials which have been tested in a number of countries. Risk management components have also been incorporated into various training programmes (King and Wijesuriya, 2008).

• 国际文物保护和修复研究中心（ICCROM）是一个政府间的组织，致力于保护文化遗产。国际文物保护和修复研究中心旨在提高保护实践的质量，同时也提高对保护文化遗产重要性的认识。它对保护文化遗产领域突出贡献表现在五个主要方面的活动：培训、信息、研究、合作和倡导。详情见其与国际古迹遗址理事会和联合国教科文组织世界遗产中心合作，公开出版的《风险准备：世界文化遗产管理手册》http://www.iccrom.org。ICCROM（Stovel，1998）。此外，它协助世界遗产中心，国际文物保护和修复研究中心形成了一系列的训练材料，已在各国使用。风险管理要素已经加入到各种训练项目中。

• International Committee of the Blue Shield (ICBS): The Blue Shield is the cultural equivalent of the Red Cross. It is the symbol specified in the 1954 Hague Convention for marking cultural sites to give them protection from attack in the event of armed conflict. It is also the name of an international committee set up in 1996 to work to protect the world's cultural heritage

• 蓝盾国际委员会（ICBS）：蓝盾与红十字会有文化相同性。1954 年，海牙公约规定，它是保护文化遗产免受武装冲突攻击的象征标志。它也是 1996 年成立的国际委员会名称，这个组织负责保护世界文化遗产免受战争和自然灾害影响的工作。蓝盾国际委员包括博物馆和档案、历史估计和图书馆、汇集的知识、经验与国际网络的五个专家组织处理文化遗产。详见 http://

threatened by wars and natural disasters. The ICBS covers museums and archives, historic sites and libraries, bringing together the knowledge, experience and international networks of the five expert organizations dealing with cultural heritage. For details visit http://www.ifla.org/blueshield.htm

www.ifla.org/blueshield.htm

• International Council on Monuments and Sites (ICOMOS) is an association of professionals throughout the world that works for the conservation and protection of cultural heritage places. It is the only global non-government organization of this kind, which is dedicated to promoting the application of theory, methodology, and scientific techniques to the conservation of the architectural and archaeological heritage. For details contact; http://www.icomos.org. ICOMOS members and committees have been developing activities, publications and cooperation to enhance prevention or adapting broad conservation principles to the reality of heritage sites located in risk areas (Bumbaru, 2008).

• 国际古迹遗址理事会（ICOMOS）：是一个负责文化遗产保护和保管的专业协会。它是全球唯一的非政府组织，致力于提高理论、方法和科学技术在建筑和考古遗址的保护。详见 http://www.icomos.org。国际古迹遗址理事会成员及委员会组织各种活动，出版和合作，以确保规则的采用，以及灾害的预防（Bumbaru, 2008）。

• International Council on Museums (ICOM) is devoted to the promotion and development of museums and the museum profession at an international level. ICOM is a nongovernmental organization with around 21,000 members in 146 countries, many of which have World Heritage sites with museums. http://www.icom.org

• 国际博物馆协会（ICOM）致力于博物馆提升和发展，国际水平的博物馆职业管理。国际博物馆协会是非政府组织，在 146 个成员国已有 21000 成员，很多都是世界遗产中的博物馆（http://www.icom.org）。

• International Union for Conservation of Nature (IUCN) helps the world to find pragmatic solutions to the most pressing environment and development challenges. It supports scientific research, manages field projects all over the world and brings governments, non-governmental organizations, United Nations agencies, companies and local communities together to develop and

• 世界自然保护联盟（IUCN）帮助世界寻找环境压力和发展挑战中，自然遗产实际的解决方案。它支持全世界科学研究、管理野外项目和带来政府，非政府组织，联合国代理，公司，和社区一起形成和实施政策，法律和最好的实践。详见：http://www.icom.org

implement policy, laws and best practice. For details visit http://www.iucn.org

UNEP World Conservation Monitoring Centre (UNEP-WCMC) is a collaboration between the United Nations Environment Programme, the world's foremost intergovernmental environmental organization, and WCMC 2000, a UK-based charity. http://www.unep-wcmc.org.

• 联合国环境规划署世界保护监测中心（UNEP–WCMC）与联合国环境规划署协作，是世界最重要的政府间环境组织，世界保护监测中心 2000，一个以英国为基地的慈善机构。

Regional organizations. There are several regional organizations, both inter-governmental as well as non-governmental, which can provide their expertise for the protection of cultural and natural heritage from disasters and also recovering from these.

地区组织、政府间和非政府的地区组织，他们能提供文化和自然遗产预防灾害和恢复的帮助。

The Asian Disaster Preparedness Centre (ADPC; http://www.adpc.net/) based in Bangkok and the Asian Disaster Reduction Centre (ADRC; http://www.adrc.asia/) in Kobe are two such organizations actively working in the area of disaster management.

亚洲灾害预防中心，位于巴格达

（ttp://www.adpc.net/），

神户世界减灾中心

（http://www.adrc.asia/）是这样两个负责这些地区的灾害管理的组织。

Cultural Heritage without Borders (CHwB; http://www.chwb.org/bih) is a Swedish non-governmental organization that lends international support to cultural heritage at risk of being destroyed whether as a result of natural disasters, war or neglect because of poverty or political and social conditions. It has been very active in emergency rescue and recovery of cultural heritage damaged due to war in South-East Europe.

• 无国界文化遗产组织（CHwBhttp://www.chwb.org/bih）是瑞士非政府组织，对因自然灾害、战争或因贫困或政治或社会条件的忽略，造成的对文化遗产破坏风险提供的国际间支持。该组织对东南欧洲文化遗产在战争中遭到的破坏实施了有效的紧急救助和恢复。

• Academic and research institutions: Various institutions are engaged in research and training in this area or related disciplines. One such institution is the Research Center for Disaster Mitigation of Urban Cultural Heritage at Ritsumeikan University, Kyoto, which has started a UNESCO Chair Programme on Cultural Heritage Disaster Risk

• 学术和研究机构：从事遗产领域研究和训练或相关规则。城市文化遗产缓解灾害研究中心，日本立命馆大学，东京，已经开始了文化遗产灾害风险管理联合国教科文组织主席项目。详见 http://www.rits–dmuch.jp/en/unesco.html

Management. For details visit http://www.rits-dmuch.jp/en/unesco.html

B. International organizations concerned with the disaster management sector

B. 关注灾害管理的国际性组织

• Food and Agriculture Organization of the United Nations. http://www.fao.org

• 联合国粮食与农业组织 http://www.fao.org

• Humanitarian agencies and NGOs with emergency support roles in the region

(e.g. Médecins Sans Frontières, Flora and Fauna International) (Rapid Response Facility).

• 紧急支援的地区间人道主义组织和非政府组织。

（e.g. Médecins Sans Fronti è res, Flora and Fauna International）

• United Nations Environment Programme Post-conflict and Disaster Branch.

http://www.unep.org/conflictsanddisasters/

• 联合国环境项目冲突后和害后部。

http://www.unep.org/conflictsanddisasters/

• Where relevant, international and United Nation agencies such as UN Peacekeeping forces, UNHCR and others involved in refugee management.

• 与之相关的国际和联合国机构还有，联合国维和部队，联合国难民事务高级专员和其他救援管理组织。

• World Health Organization for epidemics.

http://www.who.int/csr/en/

• 世界流行病防治健康中心。

http://www.who.int/csr/en/

• World Meteorological Organization.

http://www.wmo.int

• 世界气象组织。

http://www.wmo.int

Appendix V
Key references and publications

附件 5　参考文献和出版物

Publications on Disaster Risk Management of heritage properties

遗产灾害管理文献

Feilden, B. 1987. Between Two Earthquakes; Cultural Property in Seismic Zones.

Rome /Los Angeles, ICCROM/Getty Conservation Institute.

Feilden, B. 1987.《两次地震》间：罗马洛杉矶地震带的文化遗产国际文物保护与修复研究中心 / 盖悌保护研究所。

Feilden, B.M. and Jokilehto, J. 1993, 2nd ed. 1998. Management Guidelines for World Cultural

Feilden, B.M. and Jokilehto, J. 1993, 2nd ed. 1998.《世界文化遗产管理指南》，罗马，国际文

Heritage Sites.Rome, ICCROM.

物保护与修复研究中心。

Getty Conservation Institute. Online Bibliography for Museum Emergency Programme.

http://gcibibs.getty.edu/asp/

盖蒂保护研究所博物馆应急计划在线参考文献。

http://gcibibs.getty.edu/asp/

ICOMOS. Risk Preparedness; Heritage at Risk. Bibliography. Paris, UNESCO-ICOMOS Documentation Centre.

http://www.international.icomos.org/centre_documentation/bib/riskpreparedness.pdf

国际古迹遗址理事会。《风险准备，遗产面临的风险》，参考文献，巴黎 联合国教科文组织，国际古迹遗址理事会文件中心。

http://www.international.icomos.org/centre_documentation/bib/riskpreparedness.pdf

Jigyasu, R. and Masuda, K. 2005. Proceedings; Cultural Heritage Risk Management. World Conference on Disaster Reduction Kyoto; Research Center for Disaster Mitigation of Urban Cultural Heritage, Ritsumeikan; Kyoto, Japan.

Jigyasu, R. and Masuda, K. 2005.《文化遗产风险管理》京都国际文化遗产风险管理减灾大会，日本京都立命馆大学都市文化遗产减灾研究中心。

Meir, H. and Will, T. (eds). 2008. Heritage at Risk: Cultural Heritage and Natural Disasters.Paris, ICOMOS.

Meir, H. and Will, T. (eds). 2008.《遗产面临的风险和自然灾害》，巴黎，国际古迹遗址理事会。

Menegazzi, C. 2004. Cultural Heritage Disaster Preparedness and Response. Proceedings of International Symposium held at Salar Jung Museum, Hyderabad, India, 23–27 November 2003. Paris, ICOM. http://icom.museum/disaster_preparedness_book/copyright.pdf

Menegazzi, C. 2004.《文化遗产灾害预防和应急反应》国际研讨会会议记录，在印度尼西亚海德拉巴撒拉族荣格博物馆，2003 年 11 月 23—27 日，巴黎，国际博物馆协会。http://icom.museum/disaster_preparedness_book/copyright.pdf

Michalski, S. 2004. Care and preservation of collections. In: P. Boylan (ed.), Running a Museum, A Practical Handbook. Paris, ICOM, pp. 51–91.

Michalski, S. 2004. 藏品保护和保管 . In: P. Boylan (ed.),《博物馆运行实践手册》，巴黎，国际博物馆协会 , pp. 51–91。

Spenneman, D. and Look, D. (eds.) 1998. Disaster Management Programs for Historic Sites. Proceedings of a Symposium organized by the US National Park Service, Western Regional Office, San Francisco, in collaboration with the Western Chapter of the Association for Preservation Technology, 27–29 June 1997, San Francisco.

Spenneman, D. and Look, D. (eds.) 1998. 历史遗址灾害管理项目，研讨会会议记录，由美国国家公园西区旧金山办公室与技术保护协会西部分会联合举办，1997 年 6 月 27–29, 旧金山 Stovel。

Stovel,

H. 1998. Risk Preparedness: A Management Manual for World Cultural Heritage.Rome, ICCROM. http://www.iccrom.org/pdf/ICCROM_17_RiskPreparedness_en.pdf

H. 1998. 风险预防：世界文化遗产管理手册，罗马，国际文物保护与修复研究中心。http://www.iccrom.org/pdf/ICCROM_17_RiskPreparedness_en.pdf

UNESCO. 1983. Desirability of adopting an international instrument on the protection of the cultural heritage against natural disasters and their consequences. Report of the Director General. http://unesdoc.unesco.org/images/0005/000560/056088eo.pdf

联合国教科文组织。1983. 希望采用国际手段保护文化遗产抵抗自然灾害影响，执行主席报告。http://unesdoc.unesco.org/images/0005/000560/056088eo.pdf

UNESCO/WHC 2007. Case Studies on Climate Change and World Heritage. Case Studies on Climate Change and World Heritage, 2007, UNESCO World Heritage Centre/UK Department of Culture, Media and Sport.

http://unesdoc.unesco.org/images/0015/001506/150600e.pdf

联合国教科文组织 / 世界遗产中心 2007. 气候变化对世界遗产影响案例研究，2007, 联合国教科文组织 / 英国文化媒体体育部。

http://unesdoc.unesco.org/images/0015/001506/150600e.pdf

UNESCO / WHC. 2008a. Operational Guidelines for the Implementation of the World Heritage Convention. Paris, UNESCO World Heritage Centre.

联合国教科文组织 / 世界遗产中心 . 2008a. 世界遗产公约操作指南，巴黎，联合国教科文组织 / 世界遗产中心。

UNESCO / WHC. 2008b. Policy Document on the Impacts of Climate Change on World Heritage Properties. Paris, UNESCO World Heritage Centre.

http://whc.unesco.org/en/CC-policy-document/

联合国教科文组织 / 世界遗产中心 . 2008b. 关于气候变化对世界遗产影响的文件，巴黎 联合国教科文组织 / 世界遗产中心。

http://whc.unesco.org/en/CC-policy-document/

UNHCR. 2001. Practicing and Promoting Sound Environmental Management in Refugee / Returnee Operations. Papers presented at an international workshop, Geneva, Switzerland,22–25 October.

http://www.unhcr.org/406c34174.html

联合国难民署 . 2001. 实践和促进难民管理及遣返的良好环境，瑞士日内瓦国际会议论文，10 月 22–25 日。

http://www.unhcr.org/406c34174.html

Waller, R. 2003. Cultural Property Risk Analysis

Waller, R. 2003. 文化遗产风险模式，发展和

Model, Development and Application to Preventive Conservation at the Canadian Museum of Nature. Gutenberg Studies in Conservation 13,Gutenberg Act Universitatis Gothoburgensis.

预防保护运用，加拿大自然博物馆，古腾堡保护研究 13，古腾堡全局行动。

Wittemyer, G., Elsen, P., Bean, W.T., Coleman, A., Burton, O. and Brashares, J.S. 2008. Accelerated Human Population Growth at Protected Area Edges. Science. No: 321,pp.123-126.

Wittemyer, G., Elsen, P., Bean, W.T., Coleman, A., Burton, O. and Brashares, J.S. 2008. 保护区边缘人口增长，科学 No: 321,pp.123–126。

Publications relating to Disaster Risk Managemen Abarquez, I. and Murshed, Z. 2004. Field Practitioners' Handbook, Community-based Disaster Risk Management. Bangkok, Asian Disaster Preparedness Centre.

与灾害管理相关的出版物

Abarquez, I. and Murshed, Z. 2004. Field 从业人员手册：社区基础上的灾害风险管理，曼谷，亚洲灾害预防中心。

Barakat, S. 1993. Rebuilding and Resettlement, 9 Years Later. A case study of the contractor built reconstruction in Yemen, following the 1982 Dhamar earthquake, York,UK, Institute of Advanced Architectural Studies, University of York. Post-War Reconstruction and Development Unit Working Paper No. 2.

Barakat, S. 1993 年，9 年后的重建与再安置，1986 年也门扎马尔震后重建案例研究，英国约克郡约克大学高级建筑研究学院，战后重建和发展工作报告 No. 2。

Berz, G., Kron, W., Loster, T., Rauch, E., Schimetschek, J., Schmieder, J., Siebert, A.,Smolka, A., and Wirtz, A. 2001. World map of natural hazards – a global view of the distribution and intensity of significant exposures, Natural Hazards, Vol. 23, Nos 2–3, pp. 443–65.

http://www.ingentaconnect.com/content/klu/nhaz/2001/00000023/F0020002/00280052

Berz, G., Kron W., Loster, T., Rauch, E.Schimetschek, J., Schmieder, J., Siebert, A.,Smolka, A., and Wirtz, A. 2001. 世界自然灾害全球分布和重大风险强度图，世界自然灾害 Vol. 23, Nos 2–3,pp. 443–65。

http://www.ingentaconnect.com/content/klu/nhaz/2001/00000023/F0020002/00280052

CARE /IUCN/WWF. Alert.Joint publication on earthquake-related environmental issues.Crisis Response Centre, World Wildlife Fund.

美国援外合作署 / 世界自然保护联盟 / 世界自然基金会 . Alert. 地震联合发布——相关环境问题，应急反应中心，世界野生动物基金。

del Cid, D. 1990. Emergency Protection to Damaged Structures.

del Cid, D. 1990. 受损结构紧急保护，

Dilley, M., Chen, R.S., Deichmann, U., Lerner-Lam, A.L. and Arnold, M. 2005. Natural Disaster Hotspots: A Global Risk Analysis. Washington DC, World Bank.

http://www.preventionweb.net/english/professional/publications/v.php?id=1100

Emergency Management Australia. 2000. Emergency Risk Management Applications Guide. Dickson, ACT, Australian Emergency Manuals Series. http://www.ema.gov.au

FEMA. Region II Hazard Mitigation Plan Tool Kit: Risk Assessment. Washington DC, Federal Emergency Management Agency.

http://www.fema.gov/about/regions/regionii/toolkit_risk.shtm

IADB. 1999. Reducing Vulnerability to Natural Hazards: Lessons learned from Hurricane Mitch. A Strategy Paper on Environmental Management. Stockholm, Sweden, 25–28 May.

Inter-American Development Bank.

http://www.iadb.org/regions/re2/consultative_group/groups/ecology_workshop_1.htm

IDNDR-ESCAP. 1999. Water Hazards, Resources and Management for Disaster Prevention: A Review of the Asian Conditions. IDNDR 1991-1999, IDNDR-ESCAP Regional Meeting for Asia: Risk Reduction & Society in the 21st Century, Bangkok, 23–26 February.

http://www.unescap.org/enrd/water_mineral/disaster/watdis4.htm

New South Wales Government. 1990. Coastline Hazards, NSW Coastline Management Manual, Appendix C.

http://www.environment.gov.au/coasts/publications/nswmanual/appendixc6.html

Dilley, M., Chen, R.S., Deichmann, U., Lerner–Lam, A.L. and Arnold, M. 2005.《自然灾害热点：全球风险分析》，华盛顿特区世界银行。

http://www.preventionweb.net/english/professional/publications/v.php?id=1100

澳大利亚风险管理 . 2000.《应急风险管理指南》，澳大利亚迪克森法，紧急系列手册。www.ema.gov.au

联邦应急管理局《Ⅱ类地区减灾计划工具，风险评估》，华盛顿特区，FEMA。

http://www.fema.gov/about/regions/regionii/toolkit_risk.shtm

美洲防务委员会 1999.《减少自然灾害程度：应对飓风的经验教训》，瑞典斯德哥尔摩环境管理战略文件，美洲发展银行 5 月 25–28。http://www.iadb.org/regions/re2/consultative_group/groups/ecology_workshop_1.htm

国际减灾十年—亚洲太平洋地区经济与社会管理委员会 1999.《水灾，防灾资源和管理：亚洲国情回顾》，国际减灾十年 1991–1999 国际减灾十年—亚洲太平洋地区经济与社会管理委员会亚洲区域会议：21 世纪社会减灾，曼谷，2 月 23–26。

http://www.unescap.org/enrd/water_mineral/disaster/watdis4.htm

新南威尔士政府，1990，海岸灾害，《新南威尔士海岸管理手册》，附件 . C。

http://www.environment.gov.au/coasts/publications/nswmanual/appendixc6.html

NOAA. About the Marine Modeling and Analysis Branch Hazard Map. Washington DC, National Oceanic and Atmospheric Administration.

http://polar.ncep.noaa.gov/mmab/hazard.about.html

美国国家海洋大气局，《关于航海模式和灾害地图分支分析》，华盛顿特区，国家海洋大气局。

http://polar.ncep.noaa.gov/mmab/hazard.about.html

OAS. Natural Hazard Risk Reduction in Project Formulation and Evaluation. Washington DC, Organization of American States.

http://www.oas.org/dsd/publications/Unit/oea66e/ch02.htm

美洲国家组织《自然灾害减灾项目制定和评估》，华盛顿特区美洲国家组织。

http://www.oas.org/dsd/publications/Unit/oea66e/ch02.htm

Tear Fund. Mainstreaming Disaster Risk Reduction: a Tool for Development Organisations.

Teddington, UK, Christian Action with the World's Poor.

http://www.unisdr.org/HFdialogue/download/tp2-Tearfund-Mainstreaming-drr.pdf

德爱基金，《主流灾害减灾，组织发展工具》，英国特丁郡，基督与世界穷人同在。

http://www.unisdr.org/HFdialogue/download/tp2–Tearfund–Mainstreaming–drr.pdf

UNEP. Resource Kit.Geneva, United Nations Environment Programme.

http://www.unep.org/tools/default.asp?ct=er

联合国环境规划署．资源工具，日内瓦，联合国环境规划署。

http://www.unep.org/tools/default.asp?ct=er

UNISDR. 2002. Terminology of Disaster Risk Reduction. Geneva, United Nations International Strategy for Disaster Reduction.

http://www.unisdr.org/eng/library/lib-terminology-eng%20home.htm

联合国国际减灾战略，《减灾术语》，日内瓦联合国国际减灾战略 2002。

http://www.unisdr.org/eng/library/lib–terminology–eng%20home.htm

UNISDR. 2009. Risk and Poverty in a Changing Climate.Global Assessment Report on Disaster Risk Reduction.

http://www.preventionweb.net/english/hyogo/gar/report/index.php?id=9413

联合国国际减灾战略，2009.《气候变化中的风险和贫困全球减灾评估报告》。

http://www.preventionweb.net/english/hyogo/gar/report/index.php?id=9413

University of Colorado. Natural Hazards. Disaster Research. University of Colorado at Boulder, United States.

http://www.colorado.edu/hazards/dr/currentdr.html

科罗拉多大学，《自然灾害》，《灾害研究》，美国博尔德科罗拉多大学。

http://www.colorado.edu/hazards/dr/currentdr.html

WMO. Disaster Risk Reduction (DRR) Programme. Geneva, World Meteorological Organization.

http://www.wmo.int/pages/prog/drr/

世界气象组织，《减灾 (DRR) 项目》，日内瓦世界气象组织。

http://www.wmo.int/pages/prog/drr/

Web links on early warning

Epidemic and Pandemic Alert and Response, World Health Organization.

http://www.who.int/csr/en/

早期预防的相关网站

传染病流行预警及反应，世界卫生组织。

http://www.who.int/csr/en

Global Outbreak Alert and Response Network, World Health Organization.

http://www.who.int/csr/outbreaknetwork/en/

全球疫情警报和反应网，世界卫生组织。

http://www.who.int/csr/outbreaknetwork/en/

Humanitarian Early Warning Service, Inter-Agency Standing Committee developed by the World Food Programme.

http://www.hewsweb.org/

人道主义早期预警服务，联合国粮食计划署政府间委员会。

http://www.hewsweb.org/

Rapid Response Facility, Flora and Fauna International.

http://www.fauna-flora.org/rrf.php

国际动植物种群快速反应机制。

http://www.fauna–flora.org/rrf.php

Severe Weather Information Centre, World Meteorological Organization.

http://severe.worldweather.wmo.int/

恶劣天气信息中心，世界气象组织。

http://severe.worldweather.wmo.int/

United Nations International Strategy for Disaster Reduction.

http://www.unisdr.org

联合国国际减灾战略。

http://www.unisdr.org

国际古迹遗址理事会
《在世界遗产公约框架下宗教遗产保护的基辅声明》
Kyiv Statement on the Protection of Religious Properties within the Framework of the World Heritage Convention

Kyiv Statement on the Protection of Religious Properties within the Framework of the World Heritage Convention

《在世界遗产公约框架下宗教遗产保护的基辅声明》

1. The main objective of the Kyiv Seminar 2010 on the Role of Religious Communities in the Management of World Heritage Properties was to explore ways of establishing a dialogue between all stakeholders, and to explore possible ways of encouraging and generating mutual understanding and collaboration among them in the protection of religious World Heritage properties.

1.“2010年宗教社区在世界遗产管理中的作用之基辅研讨会”，主要目标是探索在所有的利益相关者之间进行对话的方法；并寻求在保护宗教世界遗产上鼓励他们之间相互理解和合作的方法。

2. The stakeholders would include religious communities, which can comprise believers, traditional and indigenous peoples, as well as States Party authorities, professionals and experts in relevant fields, property owners, funding bodies and other interested partners.

2. 利益相关者应包括宗教社区即信徒、传统住户和土著居民，国家管理层、相关领域的专业人员和专家、遗产所有者、资助机构和其他有兴趣的合作者。

3. The participants of the Seminar welcomed the International Year for the Rapprochement of Cultures, proclaimed by the United Nations General Assembly, as a valuable tool for the mutual exchange of experiences and dialogue between cultures aiming to foster respect for each others' beliefs.

3. 研讨会参会人员迎来了联合国大会的“国际文化和睦年”，作为有效的经验交流和文化对话的工具，培养彼此间对不同信仰的相互尊重。

They furthermore:

Recognized the role played by religious communities in the creation, maintenance, and continuous shaping of sacred places, and the custodial role played

此外：

认识到宗教社区在遗产圣地创建、维护、形成、延续过程中扮演的角色，和在“活态”遗产发展进化过程中一直承担着保管者的角色。

by them in caring for these as living heritage.

4. Reaffirmed the vital further role of religious communities in conveying, expressing and sustaining spiritual identity, meaning and purpose to human life, considering that these offer significant opportunities in a fast developing and globalizing world, as well as presenting serious challenges.

4. 再次确认宗教社区在传播、表达和维持精神特质、对人类生活的意义和目的方面有更重要的作用，为快速发展和全球化，提供重大机遇同时也带来了严峻挑战。

5. Stressed that culturally and environmentally sustainable management of such heritage should be the responsibility of all stakeholders concerned, and that mutual acceptance and respect will bring different and complementary perspectives to shared cultural and spiritual values.

5. 强调对宗教社区文化和环境的持久管理是所有利益相关者的责任，相互接纳和彼此尊重，将为社区共享文化和精神价值带来不同而互补的视角。

6. Recalled that the protection of religious heritage represents a special challenge and opportunity that needs to be addressed in the effective implementation of the World Heritage Convention, and noted that living religious places have often been placed on UNESCO's World Heritage List specifically for their religious and spiritual significance; in other cases, religious properties and sacred places can be an integral part of larger ensembles, such as historic cities, cultural landscapes and natural sites. The significance of such sites and the interests of associated religious communities should be duly recognized in sustainable management processes.

6. 回顾对宗教遗产的保护，展现了在有效实施《世界遗产公约》中的特殊挑战与机遇，注意到那些依然进行宗教活动的场所，因其特殊的宗教和精神意义，通常已经列入联合国教科文组织的世界遗产名录；另一方面，宗教遗产和圣地通常是更大的遗产例如历史城区、文化景观或自然遗产不可分割的部分。此类遗址的重要意义和相关宗教社区的利益，在可持续管理过程中得到认可。

7. Emphasized that the continuing nature of religious heritage calls for dialogue and mutual understanding between the religious communities concerned and all other stakeholders, who must work together to preserve the significance of cultural, mixed and natural heritage sites associated with the sacred.

7. 强调宗教遗产自然延续的特性，要求在相关宗教社区和所有利益相关者之间保持对话和相互理解，共同努力保护与圣地相关的文化、混合和自然遗产的重要性。

8. Considered it particularly timely to define an Integrated Strategy for the development of a

8. 认为应及时确定一项综合战略，以便在所有利益相关者的协作和密切协调下，制定一

World Heritage Thematic Programme on religious heritage in collaboration and close coordination between all stakeholders, and that this Programme should create an action plan for the protection of religious heritage world-wide aimed at enhancing the role of communities and the avoidance of misunderstandings, tensions, or stereotypes.

项关于宗教遗产的世界遗产专题方案，因而在全球范围内制定宗教遗产保护行动计划，旨在加强社区的作用，避免误解、紧张或成见。

9.Recognized the need to raise awareness of all stakeholders of the importance of the management of religious places in order to enable mutual understanding and acceptance of the World Heritage significance and specificity of each heritage place, and its associated spiritual and religious values.

9. 认识到需要提升全体利益相关者对宗教遗产管理重要性的认识，以便于相互理解和接受世界遗产中每个地方遗产的重要性和独特性，以及与之相关的精神和宗教价值。

10. In furtherance of this, and taking into account the resolution 17 GA 9 of the States Parties to the World Heritage Convention, they called for the establishment of integrated and interactive training programmes in the management of religious places in cooperation with the Advisory Bodies, ICCROM, ICOMOS and IUCN, aimed at helping representatives of religious communities to enhance and share their managerial skills.

10. 为促成这一目标，并考虑到《世界遗产公约》缔约国大会 17 届 9 号决议，呼吁宗教社区与咨询团队如国际文物保护与修复研究中心、国际古迹遗址理事会、世界自然保护联盟等组织合作，建立综合、互动的宗教遗产管理培训项目，旨在帮助宗教团体代表加强和分享他们的管理技能。

Concluded that safeguarding religious heritage of outstanding universal value for future generations requires new forms of action, and that the Kyiv seminar formed the start of a new ongoing process, and an opportunity to establish a platform for dialogue and shared knowledge among all communities involved in the preservation of our common heritage.

结论，为了替子孙后代保护好宗教遗产的突出普遍价值，需要采用新的行动方式，基辅研讨会形成一个全新的发展进程和机会，为所有参与保护我们共同遗产的社区，建立一个对话和分享知识的平台。

Kyiv, 5 November 2010

2010 年 11 月 5 日
基辅

◎ 2011—2013 年

联合国教科文组织、国际古迹遗址理事会《巴黎宣言》
UNESCO/ICOMOS Paris Declaration

Preamble

The 1150 participants from 106 countries gathered in Paris at the UNESCO headquarters at the invitation of France from 28 November to 1 December 2011 on the occasion of the 17th General Assembly of the International Council on Monuments and Sites (ICOMOS) adopt this of Principles and Recommendations on the relationship between heritage and development, to be viewed as an asset to heritage conservation, to the dissemination of its inherent values, and to the cultural, social and economic development of communities. This declaration and the recommendations are addressed to stakeholders involved in heritage conservation, development and tourism, and more especially to States, local authorities, international institutions, the United Nations agencies and UNESCO in particular, as well as to relevant civil society associations.

This Declaration forms part of a series of initiatives and actions that have been undertaken by ICOMOS over many years in order to promote a development process that incorporates tangible and intangible cultural heritage as a vital aspect of sustainability, and gives a human face to development. Of particular note is the ICOMOS conference held at Moscow and Suzdal in Russia (1978), on the theme of 'The Protection of Historical Cities and Historical Quarters in the Framework of Urban Development'. One of its sub-themes was 'Historical Monuments as a

序言

应法国的邀请，来自 106 个国家的 1150 位代表，于 2011 年 11 月 28 日至 12 月 1 日，参加了在联合国教科文组织巴黎总部召开的国际古迹遗址理事会第十七届全体大会，通过了关于遗产传承与发展的一系列原则和建议，将其视为遗产保护、遗产内在价值传播、社区文化、社会以及经济发展的资本。本宣言和建议主要面向与遗产保护、发展和旅游相关的利益相关者，特别是各个国家、地方政府、国际机构、联合国各个组织尤其是联合国教科文组织，以及相关的民间团体。

国际古迹遗址理事会多年来一系列的举措和行动，旨在促成一个发展进程，把有形与无形文化遗产作为人类可持续发展核心组成部分。本宣言是这些努力的成果之一。特别值得一提的是，1978 年国际古迹遗址理事会在俄罗斯莫斯科和苏兹达尔举办的“城市发展框架下的历史城市和历史城区的保护”专题研讨会，其中一个子论题是“支持社会经济发展的历史古迹”，这表明早在 33 年前，国际古迹遗址理事会就已经开始思考遗产保护与发展之间的关系。在国际古迹遗址理事会第六届全体大会（意大利）上，

Support to Economic and Social Development', which shows that, 33 years ago, our organization had already begun to reflect on the relationship between heritage and development. The scientific symposium entitled 'No Past, No Future', at the Sixth General Assembly of ICOMOS in Italy and the scientific symposium on 'The Wise Use of Heritage' held in Mexico in 1999 further explored the subject. The work and reports of Nara (1997), Xi'an (2005) and Quebec (2008) helped to develop the heritage concepts of 'authenticity', 'context' and 'spirit of place'. An important step has been the work of ICOMOS in developing Charters that have become international benchmarks, especially for UNESCO and its Member States. Of particular note are the ICOMOS International Cultural Tourism Charter developed in 1977 and updated in 1999, the ICOMOS Charter on Cultural Routes adopted by ICOMOS in 2008 and the ICOMOS Charter for the Interpretation and Presentation of Cultural Heritage Sites, which was also adopted in 2008.

名为“没有过去就没有未来”及1999年在墨西哥召开的题为“明智利用遗产”的科学研讨会，进一步探讨了这一论题。之后的奈良（1997年）、西安（2005年）和魁北克（200 8年）研讨会和宣言也逐步丰富了遗产保护的相关理念，包括真实性、背景环境以及场所精神等。国际古迹遗址理事会的主要成就之一就是在起草遗产保护宪章中发挥核心作用，这些宪章已经成为国际上，尤其是联合国教科文组织及其缔约国通用的重要参考，特别是《国际文化旅游宪章》（1977年发布，1999年修订）、《文化线路宪章》（2008年发布）以及《文化遗产阐释与展示宪章》（2008年通过）。

Why this theme?

选择该主题的原因

The effects of globalization on societies are manifested in the attrition of their values, identities and cultural diversity, and of their tangible and intangible heritage, in the broadest sense. Therefore, the relationship between development and heritage must be examined.

全球化对社会价值观的影响广泛反映在价值、身份、文化多样性以及减弱的有形和无形遗产上。因此，必须深入检查遗产与发展之间的关系。

Concerns revolving around heritage and development are also echoed in the theme that UNESCO has chosen to celebrate the 40th anniversary of the World Heritage Convention in Kyoto in 2012, 'World Heritage and Sustainable Development the Role of Local Communities'.

2012年，联合国教科文组织在日本京都庆祝世界遗产公约40周年的活动中，选择了传承与发展关系作为主题，关注“地方社区对世界遗产和可持续发展的作用”。

This aims first to measure the effects of globalization on communities and heritage. It will then identify the actions needed not only to

这首先是衡量全球化对社区和遗产影响。其次，确认目前我们的行动不仅要保护遗产，也要确保利用、推广和提高其经济、社会和文化

protect heritage, but also to ensure that its use, its promotion and enhancement, and its economic, social and cultural value are harnessed to the benefit of local communities and visitors. Finally, it will assess the ability of heritage and its inherent values to inspire and to build tomorrow's societies, curbing the negative effects of globalization.

价值，造福当地社区和游客。最后，将评估遗产能力及其内在价值，以激励和建设未来社会，从而遏制全球化的负面影响。

Rising to the Challenge

应对挑战

As various aspects of development threaten to degrade and destroy heritage and its inherent values, it is necessary to take up the challenge of conserving this fragile, crucial and non-renewable resource for the benefit of current and future generations.

各方面的发展可能破坏和毁灭遗产及其内在价值，因此我们必须主动迎接挑战，保护这一脆弱、关键而不可再生的资源，造福当代和后代。

It is now widely agreed that heritage — with its value for identity, and as a repository of historical, cultural and social memory, preserved through its authenticity, integrity and 'sense of place' — forms a crucial aspect of the development process.

人们普遍认为遗产及其内在价值是满载着历史、文化和社会记忆的储存库，充满了真实性、完整性和“地方感”，是发展进程中的核心要素。

The challenge of integrating heritage and ensuring that it has a role in the context of sustainable development is to demonstrate that heritage plays a part in social cohesion, well-being, creativity and economic appeal, and is a factor in promoting understanding between communities.

整合遗产并确保其在可持续发展中发挥作用的挑战，是展现遗产在社会凝聚力、福祉、创造力和经济吸引力方面的作用，是促进社区间理解的一个因素。

In the light of over 150 papers and the debates that they inspired, the participants witnessed how heritage, in the widest sense of the term, can make valuable contributions and provide far-reaching and constructive guidance in response to the issues raised by development. These inputs are drawn together in the principles and recommendations that the General Assembly wishes to bring to the attention of States, and through them, to the international community, as The Paris Declaration.

经过大会上 150 个主题演讲及相关讨论，参与者了解了广义上遗产价值的贡献，为应对发展中遇到的问题，提出长期和建设性的指导原则，大会汇聚所有能引起相关国家及国际社会关注的问题，形成《巴黎宣言》，作为本届大会通过的原则和建议。

Culture, the fourth pillar of sustainable development

The Johannesburg World Summit on Sustainable Development (2002) recognized cultural diversity as the fourth pillar of sustainable development, alongside the economic, social and environment pillars. The definition of development in Article 3 of the UNESCO Universal Declaration on Cultural Diversity (2001) corresponds closely to the role in the development process that we would like to give heritage, interpreted in its broadest sense: 'development, understood not only in terms of economic growth, but also as a means to achieve a more satisfactory intellectual, emotional, moral and spiritual existence'.

Resolution 65/166 on Culture and Development, adopted by the United Nations General Assembly in February 2011, as proposed by the Director General of UNESCO, has further strengthened awareness of the prominent role that culture plays in development, noting '... that culture [of which heritage forms a part] is an essential component of human development … providing for economic growth and ownership of development processes.'

Declaration of the Symposium

The participants of the 17th General Assembly address this Declaration to intergovernmental organizations, national and local authorities and all institutions and specialists, and recommend the following actions:

1-Heritage and Regional Development

Controlling and Redistributing Urban Development

—To preserve historic districts and encourage their restoration and regeneration;

—To establish and direct work on regeneration

文化，可持续发展的第四大支柱

主题为可持续发展的约翰内斯堡峰会（2002年）认为，文化多样性是经济、社会和环境外可持续发展的第四大支柱。此外，联合国教科文组织《世界文化多样性宣言》（2001年）的第三条对发展的定义，最符合遗产在发展进程中的角色，广泛描述为："对发展的认识不仅是经济增长，也是获得知识、情感、道德、精神存在的方式"。

根据联合国教科文组织总干事的建议，2011年2月，联合国大会通过了关于"文化与发展"的65/166号决议，进一步认识到文化对发展的作用"……文化（遗产是其中一部分）是人类发展的基本组成……有助于推动经济增长和掌控发展进程"。

研讨会宣言

第17届大会与会者，向政府间组织、国家、地方当局、所有机构和专家发布了本宣言，建议采取以下行动：

1- 文化遗产和区域发展

控制和重新分配城市发展

——保护历史区域，鼓励对其修复和重建；

——为建立和指导城市重建工作，增加城

and increased urban densification, promoting a harmonious, balanced and coherent approach to street and plot layout, streetscapes, massing and height of urban developments, and reclaiming urban wastelands and peripheral urban zones, in order to recreate multifunctional, landscaped urban neighbourhood; restoring the concept of urban boundaries.

市容纳度，探寻城市发展中道路、地块布局、街景、城市发展中的建筑体量和高度之间和谐、平衡和连贯的方法，恢复开垦城市荒地和外围区域，以重塑多功能和风景优美的城市居民区，恢复城市边界的概念。

—To promote balanced planning and development in order to ensure the most appropriate allocation of activity zones, including educational, cultural, tourism and leisure facilities.

——促进均衡的规划和发展，以确保在活动区域中恰当配置教育、文化、旅游和休闲设施。

Revitalising Towns and Local Economies

—To encourage the selective retention and reuse of built heritage in towns and rural villages in order to foster socio-economic regeneration; increase the density of urban cores to contain the anarchic spread of new buildings;

—To support the maintenance of traditional agricultural and craft activities to preserve skills and expertise and provide employment for local communities;

—To maintain and bring back into use local, sustainable, traditional energy production techniques, and develop new sources of energy production, with a view to economic and energy security.

振兴城镇和当地经济

——鼓励选择性保留和再利用位于城镇和偏远乡村的建筑遗产，以促进社会经济的复兴；增加城市核心区的容纳度，遏制新建筑物的无序扩张；

——支持传统农业和手工业的持续发展，保护传统技艺和专业知识，同时为当地社会提供就业机会；

——从经济和能源安全角度，维持和恢复当地的、可持续的、传统的能源生产技术，同时发展新的能源技术。

Preserving Space

—To preserve open spaces, which are non-renewable; to maintain rural landscapes and the organization and scale of their agriculture and forests; to conserve indigenous plant and aquatic heritage; to protect geological and archaeological heritage, groundwater and ecosystems;

—To maintain regional and local communication networks (railway heritage, roads, navigable waterways) to transport people and goods, and to ensure the provision of local services; to promote alternative modes of transport;

保留空间

——保留不可再生的开放空间，保持乡村景观，维持农业和森林的组织和规模；保护本土植物和水生物种；保护地质和考古遗产，保护地下水资源和生态系统；

——维护人员、物资的区域和地方交通运输网（铁路遗产、道路、航道、水路），确保提供地方交通服务；推广其他交通方式；

—Preserve rural heritage, ensuring its appropriate reuse while maintaining integrity of spatial distribution and functional elements; strictly limit urban sprawl and place conditions on the right to build, stipulating that development should respect the historic landscape and traditional settlement patterns.

——保存乡村文化遗产，在维持其空间分布和功能要素的完整性同时确保适当的再利用；严格建设用地条件和限制城市扩张，规定发展需以尊重历史环境和传统居住格局为前提。

2-A Return to the Art of Building

2- 回归建筑艺术

Conservation

—To conserve built heritage, whether urban or rural, prestigious or vernacular, which is of high quality, including original materials, design and construction, architecture, the maintenance of original functions, and integration into the physical and socio-cultural environment;

—To adapt new uses and functions to existing heritage, rather than the reverse, and to help users of historic buildings to adjust their expectations of modern living standards;

—Recall that 'architectural and landscape heritage is unique, and as such may require flexibility in the application of standards and regulations which do not meet its needs. A moratorium should be instituted immediately in order to bring on board the advice of experts and specialists, and should continue until they have developed specific and appropriate approaches, and the transitional measures have been adopted.' (ICOMOS - Paris, November 2000);

—To bring back traditional building skills and best practice as evidence of competence to undertake restoration work;

—To adapt methods of performance assessment and analysis of structures, thermal properties and safety to heritage requirements, and not vice versa;

—To take the necessary measures to ensure that, under normal safe working conditions, traditional construction materials continue to be produced, and that traditional tools are used appropriately in the

保护

——保护高质量的建筑遗产，不管其位于城市还是乡村，知名的还是本土的，包括保持建筑的原材料、原设计和原建造方式、维持原来功能，并确保遗产融入自然和社会文化环境。

——新的用途和功能要适应现存的遗产，而不是遗产适应新功能。帮助历史建筑的使用者调整他们对于当代生活标准的期望。

——重申“建筑和景观遗产是独特的，对不符合其本身要求的标准和规章需要灵活应用，首先立即暂停执行，其次采纳专家和专业人士的意见，并采取过渡措施直至制定了具体和适当的办法”（国际古迹遗址理事会 - 巴黎，2000 年 11 月）。

——能重新采用传统的建造技术和最佳实践，是有能力参与修复工作的资格证据。

——使结构、热性能和安全性的性能评估和分析方法符合遗产要求，不可反其道而行。

——采取必要措施确保在正常安全的工作条件下，继续生产传统的建筑材料，并在修复历史建筑时适当用传统工具。

restoration of historic structures.

Inspiring Innovative Architecture

—Traditional historic buildings are a treasury of architectural experience. They are an inexhaustible universal source of inspiration for modern and innovative architecture, in terms of materials, construction methods, layout and design, contributing to a high quality of life.

鼓励创新建筑

——传统的历史建筑是建筑经验的宝库，尤其在材料、施工方法、布局和设计上，是现代建筑和创新建筑取之不尽的灵感源泉，帮助人们提高生活的品质。

3-Tourism and Development

3. 旅游与发展

Heritage and the Challenge of Tourism: What Strategies, What Tools?

为迎接文化遗产和旅游业的挑战：采用何种策略和何种工具？

—To raise awareness and build the capacity of conservation professionals and site managers appropriately to address issues associated with tourism and development; to raise awareness of the fragility and value of heritage among tourism professionals, tour-operators, hotel and cruise companies.

——要提高保护意识，加强专业保护人士及遗产管理者的能力建设，从而适当地解决相关旅游及发展的问题；帮助提升旅游从业者、运行商、酒店和旅游公司人员对遗产价值及遗产的脆弱性认识。

—To involve all stakeholders in the creation of management plans for heritage sites, tourist destinations, urban centers and regions, addressing the following questions: what kind of tourism, for whom, and for what reason? To develop management plans that build on the specific cultural, historical, environmental, aesthetic and memory values to be preserved, on the 'spirit of place', as well as building on a long-term vision for the sustainable development of tourism as agreed by all the stakeholders.

——让所有的利益相关者参与编制有关遗址、旅游目的地、城市中心和当地遗产的管理计划，解决下列问题：什么类型的旅游？为谁设计的旅游？为什么开展旅游？要编制符合特定文化、历史、环境、美观、记忆的管理计划，在“地方精神”和征得所有利益相关者同意基础上，制定旅游业长期、可持续发展的愿景。

—To develop management tools for collecting data on tourism, for the evaluating of the role of heritage and its enhancement in the context of tourism development; to assess the cost of the degradation of heritage values and heritage assets; to ensure the long term preservation of the cultural and economic resource; to encourage heritage, tourism

——开发管理工具，收集有关旅游资料数据、评估遗产在旅游发展中的作用、提升遗产、评估遗产价值和遗产资产退化的成本；确保长期保护文化和经济资源；鼓励对遗产、旅游和发展的影响进行评估；形成可靠的旅游管理培训。此外，在地方社区、地方、国家和国际旅游公司间，建立一套能在保护成本与遗产管理成本之间合理配置遗产旅游收入的方法。

and development impact assessments; to develop training in responsible tourism management. In addition, to establish methods to achieve the fair distribution of heritage tourism — related revenues, between the costs of conservation and of heritage management, local communities, and local, national and international tourism companies.

Can Tourism Development be Sustainable?

—To link and integrate conservation and preservation of heritage into the core of the development of cultural tourism. To preserve the cultural resource as a fundamental asset of long term tourism development, especially, in developing countries and the least developed countries (LDC).

—To put authenticity at the heart of the development of cultural tourism and the growth of interpretation and communication strategies; to promote interpretation based on sound research and inventories, avoiding manufactured 'travels in hyper-reality' that are crudely derived from heritage values.

—To help local communities take ownership of their heritage and related tourism projects. To encourage their empowerment and their participation in heritage conservation, in the planning process and in decision making. Local participation, drawing on local perspectives, priorities and knowledge, is a pre-condition of sustainable tourism development.

可持续的发展旅游

——要把保护和保存文化遗产作为文化旅游发展的核心。特别是在发展中国家和欠发达国家，应将文化遗产作为旅游长期发展的基本资产。

——应把真实性作为文化旅游和交流、阐释和发展战略的核心；在合理的科研基础上，提升阐释效果，避免只靠简单提取遗产价值而制造出来的“超现实旅游”。

——帮助当地社区取得遗产和相关旅游项目的所有权。鼓励并授权他们自主参与文物保护、规划和决策的过程。从当地的角度考虑，注重地方参与是旅游业可持续发展的先决条件。

Encouraging Local Communities to take Ownership of Heritage and Tourism Development

—To educate young people, especially at school, and the wider population about their heritages, and the inherent historical, cultural and social values that give meaning and a sense of the past.

—To make use of modern media in order to disseminate knowledge about heritage, which will create a sense of pride and a desire to become involved in its protection and enhancement.

鼓励当地社区全身心投入遗产和旅游业的发展

——教育年轻人，尤其是学生和一般大众，了解当地遗产、固有的历史及文化和社会价值相关知识，让他们了解历史的意义和历史感。

——利用现代媒体普及遗产知识，营造大众自豪感，让大众渴望参与并增强保护意识。

—To encourage communities' engagement, as stakeholders, in the cultural heritage and tourism sectors and to foster creativity, personal development and an entrepreneurial spirit.

——鼓励社区作为利益相关者参与文化遗产和旅游，培养创造力、鼓励个人发展和创业精神。

—To encourage a dialogue between local and indigenous communities and visitors so as to contribute to cultural exchange, to spread the social, cultural and human values of heritage and to interpret them in a way that is scientifically, historically and socially accurate.

——鼓励地方、原住民社区和游客之间的对话，为文化交流做贡献，传播遗产的社会、文化和人文价值，并用精确、科学、历史和社会的方式诠释遗产及其价值。

4-Heritage and Economics

4. 遗产和经济

Fostering a Better Understanding of the Economic Impact of Heritage Conservation

更好的理解遗产保护对经济的影响

—To better understand the economic and social impact of maximising the value of heritage, which is an asset to development;

——最大化的理解遗产价值对经济和社会影响，将其作为一种更好的发展资产；

—To collate existing research and to undertake further detailed studies, in collaboration with relevant institutions, and to disseminate the results widely;

——与相关机构合作整理当前的研究成果，开展更详细的研究并广泛推广研究成果；

—To develop research on the contribution of heritage to sustainable development and on the relationship between investment and development; to study the relationships between heritage, creativity and development, and to identify performance indicators;

——研究遗产与可持续发展的贡献、投资与发展之间关系；研究遗产、创造力及发展之间的关系，并确定性能指标；

—To consider how multi-faceted heritage might best be managed, in order to pass it on to future generations, and to ensure that it contributes to development in mobile and dynamic societies.

——多方面考虑遗产管理，以利于传给后代，并确保在易变和动态社会中，遗产对发展的贡献。

Promoting the Long Term Impacts of Heritage on Economic Development and Social Cohesion

促进遗产对经济发展和社会凝聚力的长期影响

Studies show that heritage can be a tool in regional development, but it is not used consistently: it must become a goal of development policies;

研究表明，虽然遗产不一定始终能加以利用，但作为区域发展的工具，它必须成为发展政策的目标；

—Place people at the heart of policies and projects; emphasis that ownership of heritage strengthens the social fabric and enhances social

——人是政策和项目的核心，强调遗产所有权，加强社会结构和增强社会福利；在开发和改进的初级阶段就应接受当地社区的建议；

well-being; involve local communities at a very early stage in development and enhancement proposals; raise awareness, particularly among young people; develop training for professionals;

提高意识，尤其是年轻人的保护意识；开展专业的培训；

—Take into account the direct effects, tourism benefits, and the financial leverage of heritage to enhance the appeal and creativity of regions; take care that economic imperatives respect those of the conservation of tangible and intangible heritage; ensure particularly that the economic returns of heritage benefit primarily its maintenance and enhancement, and also local communities;

——考虑遗产的直接影响，旅游收益和财务杠杆作用，提升区域的吸引力和创造力；考虑经济上遵守有形和无形文化遗产保护要求；尤其是确保经济效益用于遗产的基本维持和价值提升，同样也要提升当地社区；

—Pay particular attention to the restoration of urban and industrial heritage, especially in historic and major city centers, as a way to combat poverty in developing countries.

——注意到恢复城市和工业遗产，特别是位于历史中心和城市中心的遗产，可作为发展中国家应对贫困的一种方法。

Developing the Economic Impact of Heritage

—Remind public authorities that they are the guardians of the public interest and responsible for the legal protection of heritage in the face of pressure on land; give priority to restoring rather than demolishing heritage;

遗产对经济发展的影响

——提醒政府当局，他们是公众利益的监护人，负责对遗产实施法律保护，在遗产面临用地压力时，应优先修复而不是拆除遗产；

—Place heritage at the heart of overall development strategies, setting goals for economic and social benefits to ensure that the development of heritage rewards local communities in terms of employment, the flow of finance, and well-being; the cultural, creative and craft industries associated with the enhancement of heritage assets contribute to the improvement of living conditions;

——将遗产放在整体发展战略的核心位置，制定经济和社会利益目标，以确保遗产发展，推动当地社区的就业、资金流动和福祉；提升与传统资产相关的文化、创意和工艺产业，为改善生活条件做出贡献；

—Implement policies for protection, planning, financing and management, adapted over time so that change respects the authenticity of heritage and contributes to sustainable development; sharing experience on best practice.

——随着时间推移，逐步完善保护、规划、融资和管理政策的实施，以尊重遗产真实性的方式进行变化、并为可持续发展作贡献；分享最佳实践经验。

5-Stakeholders and Capacity Building

5. 利益相关者和能力建设

The role of local communities and raising

社区角色和提升利益相关者意识

stakeholder awareness

Local people, civil society, and elected local and national officials will play a key role in the design and implementation of heritage as a driver of development, and, through raised awareness of heritage, they will have ownership of the development process. Information campaigns to raise awareness will enable civil society to recognize and take ownership of heritage and harness these values in sustainable development.

在设计和发挥遗产作为社会发展驱动力的方面，当地居民、社会团体、当选的地方和国家官员扮演关键的角色，并通过提高遗产保护意识来管控发展的过程。提升遗产保护意识的宣传活动会让民间团体认识遗产并获取遗产开发的所有权，并在可持续发展中利用其价值。

Professional training

The key stakeholders in heritage conservation in development — architects, conservators, heritage managers, development planners, investors and tour operators — require training and capacity building.

专业培训

需要对遗产保护中关键的利益相关者如建筑师、保护者、遗产管理者、开发规划者、投资者和旅游经营者等人进行培训，加强能力建设。

The legal framework

Heritage protection in the context of development also involves the creation and continual revision of institutional and legal frameworks at a local, national and international level (World Heritage Convention). Above all, these frameworks need to be implemented on the ground. The frameworks will involve consultation following the procedures of democratic governance and participatory planning, resulting in a good level of understanding and acceptance which will assist in their effective implementation.

法律框架

在发展的背景下的遗产保护同样包括在地方、国家和国际层面(《世界遗产公约》)创建和不断修订制度和法律框架。最重要的是，框架要确实得到实行。这些框架经过民众参与管理和制定规划的程序后进行协商，将得到民众更好的理解和接受，并得到有效实施。

Research

Research institutes, universities, expert advisory organizations such as ICOMOS and intergovernmental organizations such as UNESCO need to strengthen their research programs and studies. These initiatives will involve the field monitoring of analytical tools used to assess the physical performance of built heritage, measuring the economic value of heritage, evaluating the impact of cultural tourism on employment and regional wealth, and investigating

研究

研究机构、大学、专家咨询机构等如国际古迹遗址理事会、和政府间组织如联合国教科文组织，需要加强他们的研究项目和学习。这些方案应涉及用于评估建筑遗产物理性能的现场监测的分析工具，测算遗产的经济价值，评估文化旅游对区域就业、财富、调查条件、遗产保护投资风险和机遇的影响，使遗产成为经济和金融发展的伙伴。

the conditions, risks and opportunities of investing in heritage protection, bringing together economic and financial development partners.

Cooperation

ICOMOS could strengthen its cooperation and partnerships with national and international institutions carrying out work on heritage and development, including UNESCO. ICOMOS is actively involved in UNESCO's World Heritage Tourism Programme and UNESCO's Recommendation on the relationship between heritage conservation and sustainable tourism.

合作

在遗产与发展工作中，国际古迹遗址理事会要加强自身与国家和国际机构，包括联合国教科文组织的合作和伙伴关系。国际古迹遗址理事会积极参与联合国教科文组织世界遗产旅游项目和遗产保护与旅游的可持续发展的相关建议。

国际古迹遗址理事会《关于保护与管理历史城市、历史城镇与都市区域的瓦莱塔原则》ICOMOS Valletta Principles

From the '*Valletta Principles*'
towards the Safeguarding and Management of Historic Cities, Towns and Urban Areas.

《关于保护与管理历史城市、历史城镇与都市区域的瓦莱塔原则》

Dr. Sofia Avgerinou Kolonias
Professor of National Technical University of Athens
President of CIVVIH-ICOMOS
ICOMOS Executive Committee member

撰文：索菲亚·阿维吉利诺·科洛尼亚斯博士
雅典国家技术大学教授，国际古迹遗址理事会历史村镇科学委员会理事长，国际古迹遗址理事会执行委员会成员。

Historical background

历史背景

In addition to *the International Charter for the Conservation and Restoration of Monuments and Sites*, the Second International Congress of Architects and Technicians of Historical Monuments that took place in Venice, under the auspices of UNESCO, the 31st of May 1964, formulated, in its eight resolution, a request for the protection and revival of historical centers. This decision constituted the starting point of the efforts made by ICOMOS for the adoption of a policy for the protection and restructuring of historical towns. In the twenty years' period following the Venice Congress, ICOMOS elaborated the views expressed in the Charter, according to the developments in the debate and practice for the protection and conservation of monuments and sites.

除《国际古迹保护与修复宪章》之外，1964年5月31日联合国教科文组织赞助的、在威尼斯召开的第二届国际历史建筑专家与建筑师会议，在其第八号决议中提出了历史中心的保护和复兴的要求。这份决议是制订历史城镇保护和重建政策所做出的众多努力的起点。在威尼斯会议后的许多年间，根据对古迹遗址保存和保护的辩论和实践的发展，对宪章中所表达的观点进行了详尽的阐述。

The first texts drafted by 1980 were submitted to, and, afterwards, elaborated by, CIVVIH

1980年前起草的第一批文件被提交给了国际古迹遗址理事会历史村镇科学委员会，在经

International Committee on Historic Towns and Villages), following a debate with the National and Scientific Committees of ICOMOS, which had, in the meanwhile, been established in 1982. Subsequently, CIVVIH proposed *the Charter for the Conservation of Historic Towns* that was adopted in 1987 by the General Assembly of ICOMOS in Washington, DC. The Charter remained loyal to the objectives set out in the '*Recommendation Concerning the Safeguarding and Contemporary Role of Historic Areas*' (Warsaw -Nairobi, 1976) of UNESCO. However, without being a sole repetition of the Declaration, its Articles contain both its philosophical view and its practical objectives.

过与成立于1982年的国家科学委员会的辩论之后，对这些文件进行了详尽的阐述。随后，提出了《历史城镇保护宪章》，于1987年在华盛顿特区的全体大会上通过。宪章仍然忠于《关于历史城镇保护及其当代功能的建议》（华沙－内罗毕，1976年）中所设定的目标，但是其中的条款并不是对《建议》的简单重复，而是包含了其自身的哲学观点和实用目标。

The Charter was pioneering at the time it was adopted by ICOMOS. It supported the fundamental principle of sustainability, i.e. that the next generations should receive everything we have inherited from the previous ones. It also adopted, as a fundamental principle, the connection of growth to social development and the adaptation of historic towns to modern life. The Charter proposed methods and tools to the specialists and to those deciding upon the future of historic towns. It also made an appeal that younger generations and wider society should be mobilized to protect historic towns. Towns are created during the history of mankind and are shaped to the extent that human societies evolve. The urban phenomenon has currently acquired a global character but the towns still preserve their particular features. The rapid changes in the context of a globalized reality are instrumental in the future of historic towns. CIVVIH has been monitoring and discussing for the last fifteen years, in the scientific meetings and symposiums it organizes, the changes taking place in the modern world and their impacts on historic towns. Furthermore, it has been accepted that the main modifications consist in greater awareness

《宪章》获国际古迹遗址理事会通过时还是很先进的。它秉承可持续发展的基本原则，既我们应该把从前辈那里继承的一切传递给我们的后代。《宪章》还将成长与社会发展之间的联系，以及历史城镇应当根据现代生活进行调整作为一项基本原则。《宪章》为专家以及决定历史城镇未来的人提供了一些方法和工具，同时还呼吁应当发动年轻一代以及更广泛的社会人士参与保护历史城镇。城镇是人类历史的产物，随着人类社会的进化而形成。当前都市已经有全球化趋势，但是城镇仍然保留着它们独有的特征。全球化背景下城市的飞速变迁也推动着历史城镇未来的发展。历史村镇科学委员会15年来一直致力于组织科学会议和论坛，以监测和探讨现代社会的变迁以及它们对历史城镇的影响。此外，他们还认为，主要的改变包括提高对无形价值、社会经济因素、环境因素以及历史遗产层面问题的认识，而不仅仅是城市整体规模。历史村镇科学委员会一致承认并同意，将遗产看作是一种基本资源以及城市生态系统的一部分，这一点极为重要。必须尊重这一认识，以确保城镇及规模的和谐发展。

of intangible values, socio-economic factors, environmental factors, as well as the issue of historical heritage on a territorial level and not only on an urban ensemble scale. CIVVIH recognized and agreed that, in this sense, the understanding of heritage as an essential resource, part of the urban ecosystem, is fundamental. This understanding must be respected in order to ensure a harmonious development of the town and its territory.

Within the framework of reflection which is underway on an international level, on urban conservation, by the organizations charged with the conservation and enhancement of heritage, and in a period of great changes in the political (governance, decentralization), economic (globalization of markets and production modes), cultural (reinforcement of identities facing the globalization) and social field (migration towards big cities, movements of populations etc.), CIVVIH started considering the need to update *the Washington Charter*.

在这政治（治理、权力下放）、经济（市场和生产模式全球化）、文化（全球化特征的强化）和社会（向大城市移民、人口流动，等等）领域均面临重要变革的历史时期，由负责保护和促进遗产的组织，在国际层面开展的针对城市保护而进行反思的框架内，历史村镇科学委员会着手考虑修订《华盛顿宪章》。

Development

发展

In May 2005, roughly at the time that the experts' conference organized by UNESCO in Vienna adopted *the Vienna Memorandum on Historical Urban Landscapes* (HUL), CIVVIH, during its annual meeting in Istanbul, Turkey, and the scientific symposium on the preservation of historic centers in large metropolitan areas, examined the problems affecting historic centers and the possibility for preservation and promotion guidelines. Finally, CIVVIH decided to update the approaches and considerations developed in *the Washington Charter and the Nairobi Recommendation.*

2005 年 5 月，大约是在维也纳举行的专家会议通过《维也纳历史城市景观备忘录》的同时，在土耳其伊斯坦布尔的年会和关于保护大都市地区历史中心的科学论坛上，历史村镇科学委员会考察了影响历史中心的问题，以及出台保护和推广指南的可能性。最后，历史村镇科学委员会决定，对《华盛顿宪章》和《内罗毕建议》中的方法和考虑事项加以修订。

In April 2007, during the Annual Meeting in Helsinki, Finland, CIVVIH noted the great sensitivity on themes regarding the quality of

2007 年 4 月，历史村镇科学委员会在芬兰赫尔辛基年会期间，注意到关于景观质量课题的高度敏感性，以及出台必要的城市规划工具

landscape that has brought to light the necessity for urban planning instruments and for management and control plans in order to hinder interventions liable to alter the areas' identity.

和管理及控制计划，以阻止可能改变地区身份的干预行为。

In May 2009, a CIVVIH work meeting took place in Athens, Greece. It unanimously decided to keep the initial form of *the Washington Charter* — as it constitutes a 'historic text'. The new document would offer proposals and strategies for managing the inevitable changes in the development of historic cities intended not only for professionals, but also for local management bodies, so that stakeholders can specify it and adapt it to the particularities of the urban phenomenon in each geographical region, taking into consideration all preceding theoretical texts.

2009 年 5 月，历史村镇科学委员会在希腊雅典举行工作会议。与会人员一致决定，保留《华盛顿宪章》的最初形式，因为它构成了一份“历史文件”。新文件必须参考之前的所有理论文本，为管理历史城市发展过程中出现的不可避免的变化，向专家和地方管理机构提供建议和策略，以便于一般利益相关者能够将其具体化，根据各个地理区域的城市现象的具体特征进行调整。

In April 2010, during the Annual CIVVIH Meeting in Valetta, a whole day was dedicated to the systematic discussion and common formulating of the CIVVIH proposal. The document was adopted (in French and English version) by the majority of the members, as was the title. Afterwards, consultation was carried out on the ICOMOS doctrinal text with the National and International Scientific Committees and, finally, the document was adopted by the 17th International Meeting of ICOMOS in Paris, France, in November 2011.

2010 年 4 月，在历史村镇科学委员会瓦莱塔年会期间，与会人员花了一天的时间，专门进行系统性的讨论，并共同拟订建议书。这份文件得到了绝大多数成员的赞同（法语和英语版本）。随后，国际古迹遗址理事会国家和国际科学委员会共同讨论会议文件，并于 2011 年 11 月在法国巴黎的第 17 届国际会议上通过。

At this point, I have to thank very much, on behalf of CIVVIH, all colleagues who took part in the drawing up of *the Valetta Principles*. However, I have to thank, in particular, Elvira Petroncelli, who took the initiative to propose this document and who, along with Alvaro Gomez Ferrer Bayo, have elaborated its first version that constituted the basis for the discussion within the context of CIVVIH. Moreover, I would like to thank all colleagues who, during the long and difficult consultation process

在这里，我必须要代表历史村镇科学委员会对所有参与起草《瓦莱塔原则》的同仁表示衷心的感谢。其中，我尤其需要感谢的是艾尔维拉 · 佩特罗西里，是他倡议提出这份文件，并与阿尔瓦罗戈梅兹 · 菲雷 · 巴约一道，编写出了第一版文稿，作为历史村镇科学委员会展开讨论的基础。除此之外，我还要感谢从 2010 年夏天到第 17 届全体大会期间整个漫长而艰难的磋商过程中，支持我的所有同事，帮助我作为历史村镇科学委员会代表，于 2010 年 10 月

from summer 2010 to the 17th General Assembly, have supported me and helped me respond, as a representative of CIVVIH, to the demanding debate with the National and International Scientific Committees and the Advisory Committee in October 2010 in Dublin.

在都柏林，按要求完成国家和国际科学委员会以及顾问委员会委员们答辩。

The Valetta Principles were based on the corpus of reference documents, so as to define the new challenges and take into consideration the significant evolution in the definitions and methodologies in the matter of safeguard, conservation and management of historical towns and urban areas. The notion of sustainable development has gained such importance that many directives on architectural planning and intervention are based on no demolition policy and, rather, on the preservation of the urban heritage limited resources.

《瓦莱塔原则》在汇集众多参考文献的基础上，定义了在保护、保存和管理历史城镇和城区的事务中所面临的新挑战，并将相关定义和方法的重大沿革也纳入了考虑范围。可持续发展的观念尤为重要，很多关于建筑规划和干预的指导性文件，都是建立在不拆除以及保护有限的城市遗产资源这一政策的基础上。

The main objective of *the Valetta Principles* was to propose principles and strategies applicable to the interventions in historical towns and areas. These should safeguard the values of historical towns and their setting, as well as their integration in the social, cultural and economic life of our times.

《瓦莱塔原则》的主要目标，是提出适用于历史城镇和城区干预的原则和策略。这些原则应当保护历史城镇及其背景的价值，并使之与当代社会、文化和经济生活整合。

This is important in order to guarantee respect towards the historical tangible and intangible values of the heritage, and towards the environment, as well as the quality of life of their inhabitants.

这些原则对于确保尊重遗产的有形和无形历史价值、环境以及居民生活品质都具有重要的意义。

The messages of the *Valetta Principles* are proven to be actual and significant.

事实证明，《瓦莱塔原则》所传递的信息真实而重要。

Therefore, even though the first version of the document was drafted in French and in English (which are the working languages of CIVVIH) and edited by the ICOMOS France and ICOMOS UK, respectively, the colleagues of CIVVIH have

因此，尽管本文件的第一版是以法语和英语（两种工作语言）起草并由法国和英国分别编辑，所有同事很快就认可了这份文件，并积极地参与其传播。第一个翻译版本为西班牙语，由维克多·萨利纳和安吉拉·罗贾斯主持，伊

rapidly embraced the document and engaged in its diffusion. The first translation was made to Spanish on the initiative of Victor Salinas and Angela Rojas, with the participation of the colleagues in the Ibero-American Sub Committee of CIVVIH (CIHIB). Subsequently, the document was translated to Russian, thanks to Olga Sevan and Vladimir Krogius, and to Greek, thanks to Eleni Maistrou, with the assistance of the students of the Post-Graduate Studies' Programme on the Protection of Monuments of the National Technical University of Athens. I have also been informed that a translation is being elaborated in Polish by Danuta Klosek-Kozlowska and in Hebrew by Giora Solar.

比利亚美洲国家小组委员会的同事参与完成。随后，这份文件又被翻译为：俄语——由奥尔加·西万和弗拉蒂米尔·克罗杰斯翻译；希腊语，由艾林·梅斯特罗及雅典国立技术大学古迹保护研究生项目的学生协助翻译。同时，我还听说由达努塔·克洛塞科—克孜罗斯卡主持的波兰语和由吉奥拉·索拉主持的希伯来语翻译也正在进行之中。

Main issues

However, CIVVIH is a group of sensitive and restless experts who do not stop worrying about the new challenges driving discussion relating to the heritage of historic towns. The shuffle in the second post-war period brought significant changes and transformations in historic towns. However, the most rapid and intense ones, as well as strong and special phenomena in the context of the globalized modern reality, have taken place in the last decade, constantly changing the data.

Nevertheless, there are certain issues relating to historic towns that remain actual, such as:

• The impact of de-industrialization caused by the changes in the global allocation of jobs, which intervenes in the economic basis of towns and urban areas, creates empty spaces or building potential that remains inactive, waiting for new uses.

• Enhancement of interventions in devaluated historic districts and historic centers, resulting in the abandonment of traditional vocational activities, the change in their social and economic basis and the emergence of gentrification.

主要课题

然而，历史村镇科学委员会由一群极具敏锐感知力和忧患意识的专家组成，他们永远都在思虑新的挑战，推动与历史城镇遗产相关的讨论。第二次世界大战以后的洗牌给历史城镇带来了大规模的变化和变革。然而，在全球化背景下，过去十年发生了快速和激烈的变化，包括重大特殊现象，使得相关数据不断地变化。

尽管如此，关于历史城镇的部分课题至今仍然是真实存在的，比如：

• 由于全球化就业分配变化所导致的去工业化的影响，干扰了城镇和城区的经济基础，造成了不复活跃、正在等待新用途的潜在的空置空间或建筑。

• 由于增加了对于正在丧失价值的历史城区和历史中心的干预，导致传统职业活动的消亡、社会和经济基础的改变以及中产阶级化的出现。

• The tourist attraction arising in most cases of enhanced and designated historic towns and districts.

• The generalized trend for commercialization, through which historic towns are urged to elaborate new policies with a view to become increasingly attractive in order to cope with global competition.

• Migration, from and to modern towns and urban areas, is an additional major phenomenon that is due to the economic and political conditions and constitutes a decisive factor of developments in modern reality.

• Mega-constructions housing the services of the globalized economy, which appear in historic towns and urban areas, transforming the historic urban landscapes.

• The risks of unexpected natural disasters, such as earthquakes and any kind of acts of God, as well as the negative impact of the financial crisis, social and political conflicts, which intensify in the context of the globalized modern reality. Modern towns and urban areas are complex phenomena that have resulted from the historical stratification of cultural values imprinted in their wider natural environment. Nowadays, the urban phenomenon, much more so in the historic urban areas, cannot be diagnosed without reference to all physical and cultural, tangible and intangible parameters, through which their particular identify is shaped:

• the natural environment, as determined by the particular climatic parameters, the geomorphology, the topography, the subsoil;

• the built-up environment, as shaped through time by man, along with its particular morphological features, the variety of volumes and intermediate free spaces;

• the local economy and society, where the singular economic relations and practices, expertise, existence patterns and life styles of the different social groups are shaped. Within the context of the modern, global debate on spatial management

• 在大多数受到重视及列入世界遗产名录的历史城镇和城区，旅游观光开始增加。

• 商业化趋势的大潮，迫使历史城镇拟订新的政策，增加自身的吸引力，以适应全球化竞争。

• 现代化城镇和城区移民的搬进和搬出则是另一个由于经济和政治条件所导致的重大现象，构成了现代社会发展的决定性要素。

• 服务于全球化经济的巨型建筑出现在历史城镇和城区，改变了城市的历史景观。

• 难以预料的自然灾害的风险，比如地震以及任何自然灾害，以及财政危机、社会和政治冲突的消极影响，在全球化背景下日益强化。现代城镇和城区的复杂现象，产生于更广泛自然环境和历史层面上的文化价值烙印。当今时代，尤其是在历史城区，如果不参照所有物质和文化、有形和无形的参数，不了解形成其特殊性的特征，就无法真正诊断城市现象：

• 自然环境由气候、地形学、地貌学、底层土等特殊参数决定；

• 建筑环境是随着时间的推移被人类塑造出来人工环境、特殊的地貌特征、各种形态和作为媒介的自由空间；

• 地方经济和社会，形成不同的社会群体和独特的经济关系和实践规范、专业技术、生存模式和生活方式。在关于现代空间管理全球辩论的背景下，出现了在新的经济和社会框架内，以可持续发展为目标的、对城市空间整体规划

and planning, the need for integrated strategies for planning urban space, towards the direction of sustainable development, within the new economic and social frameworks created, emerges. In addition to the citizens' participation, modern tools are required to enable the implementation of these interventions in the new emerging economic and social contexts. Diagnostic methods, able to identify the particular cultural identity and authenticity of the heritage of historic towns and urban areas, must be used. Lastly, urban development mechanisms exploiting, apart from everything else, the traditional local expertise, must be proposed.

的战略需要。除了公民的参与之外，还需要现代化的工具，在新兴经济和社会背景下实施这些干预手段。必须采用能够识别出历史城镇和城区遗产的、特殊文化特征和真实性的诊断方法。最后，在其他技术之外，还必须提出能够利用本地传统专业技术的城市发展机制。

Future Dynamics

Towns and urban areas are currently called to undertake the role of organizer for the economy and to evolve into centers of economic activity, innovation and culture. Nowadays, the relation of heritage and culture with sustainable development is not questioned. Moreover, these are considered to be necessary components of sustainability. Within this context, culture and heritage stand out as the main objectives for sustainable urban development. On the other part, the request that historic towns and urban areas should preserve their authenticity, highlight and promote their particular identity, seems to be more actual than ever.

Currently, there are many examples of mainly historic towns where the culture and, more specifically, cultural industry already constitute the basis of interventions and initiatives for their revival, development and, lastly, promotion. Cultural activities of any kind stand for a significant part in the life of these towns. Cultural identity is highlighted and cultural heritage, as well as any cultural activity, is capitalized. However, the symbolic capital, formed in conjunction with the

未来动态

城镇和城区目前承担着经济组织者的角色，正逐步演变成经济活动、创新和文化中心。当今世界，遗产和文化与可持续发展的关系毋庸置疑。除此之外，它们还是可持续发展的必要组成部分。在这一背景下，文化和遗产成为城市可持续发展的主要目标。另一方面，对于历史城镇和城区应当保存其真实性，也迫切要求突出和促进其特殊特征。

目前，很多主要历史城镇的文化，准确地说文化产业，是复兴、发展以及推广等干预和行动计划的基础。各种类型的文化活动成为这些城镇生活的重要组成部分。文化身份被强调，文化遗产与其他文化活动一样被资本化。文化遗产在日益商业化的趋势下成为象征性资产，为历史城镇的生活赋予了新的条件，在这一背景下，人们开始寻求新的政策来提升其竞争力。从创意经济开始，出现一种新趋势，将文化遗产和文化作为最重要的工具之一，用于城市政

increasing trend for commercialization of the cultural heritage, imposes new terms on the life of historic towns, in the context of which new policies are searched for improving their competitiveness. Starting from the creative economy, a new trend for urban policy, urban planning, revival, development and, lastly, promotion of these towns emerges, using cultural heritage and culture among its most important tools. At this point, serious dilemmas and fragile balances are recorded and must be discussed upon by CIVVIH.

策、城市规划以及城镇的复兴、发展和推广。历史村镇科学委员会必须记录并讨论这种严重的困境及脆弱的平衡。

Therefore, this debate has not moved very far from its starting point! Connecting protection to economic and social development, within the context of sustainability, and adaptation of historical towns and urban areas to modern life is still the main task. However, the fact that historic towns are urged, through the aforementioned procedures, to increase their competitiveness, affects their main qualities, such as their identity, integrity, authenticity, which are, on the other part, both the basic elements for their being designated cultural heritage and strict prerequisites for their preservation. CIVVIH, being fully aware that the changes currently observed in the life of towns and urban areas take place rapidly, within the multidimensional modern environment, will continue being concerned with, and make its recommendations, in view of, the main developments and challenges.

因此，这场辩论并没有远离其最初的出发点。当前的主要任务仍然是，在可持续发展的背景下，将遗产保护与经济和社会发展联系起来，根据现代生活的需要改造历史城镇和城区。然而，历史城镇通过上述过程被迫提升竞争力这一事实，已经影响到了它们的主要品质，比如身份认同、完整性和真实性。另一方面，这些品质是历史城镇成为文化遗产的基础元素，也是它们得到保护的严格的先决条件。历史村镇科学委员会深知，城镇和城区生活，在目前多维度现代化环境下正在发生的飞速变化，还将继续成为人们关注的课题，于是根据当前的主要发展和挑战提出了自己的建议。

The Valletta Principles: the paradigm of change and research of a convergence among culture and different experiences prof. arch. Elvira Petroncelli.

《瓦莱塔原则》：融合不同文化和经验的变革和研究案例。撰文：艾尔维拉·佩特罗西里教授。

Introduction

导言

I am glad to have the opportunity to briefly show the more significant elements of *'The Valletta Principles for the Safeguarding and Management of*

我很高兴能够借此机会，简要地阐述《关于保护与管理历史城市、历史城镇与都市区域的瓦莱塔原则》这份文件中的一些重要元素，

Historic Cities, Towns and Urban Areas' document and the spirit that has marked, during the years, the drawing up of this document. I was given the duty by the International Committee on Historic Towns and Villages (CIVVIH) to take care of the writing, in a first phase together with Alvaro Gomez Ferrer. In fact I had the opportunity to conceive the structure and I have worked with perseverance during the last 6 years to succeed in doing a bilingual (French and English) document, in an informal and/or official manner shared, in its writing process, by CIVVIH and International ICOMOS members.

以及多年以来在编写这份文件的过程中所体现出来的精神。我曾受国际历史城镇和乡村委员会委派，与阿尔瓦多·戈梅兹·菲雷一道，负责这份文件第一阶段的撰写工作。事实上，我还曾参与了整个结构的构思，在过去六年我一直持续不懈地从事这一工作，正式和非正式的与历史村镇科学委员会和国际古迹遗址理事会成员合作，成功发布了这份文件的双语（法语和英语）文本。

Perhaps it is opportune to add that the CIVVIH, besides having supported the debate during every annual meeting, in particular in May 2009 has organized a joint working meeting in Athens. Moreover to give a new relevance to the work, during the annual meeting in Narni, a Sub-Committee on Charter was set up and I was nominated President.

值得一提的是，除了每次年度会议辩论提供的支持之外，2009 年 5 月还在雅典组织了一次联合工作会议。除此之外，为了给这一工作提供新的支持，在纳尔尼年会期间，还成立了一个与宪章有关的小组委员会，我被任命为这个小组委员会的主席。

The document published here was voted for and adopted in Paris on November 28th 2011 during the XVII General Assembly of ICOMOS .

今天所发布的这份文件于 2011 年 11 月 28 日在巴黎举行的第 17 届全体大会上投票通过。

There were moments of lively debate during the writing of this document. Indeed we also have to note that this debate has been very profitable because it has lead the CIVVIH to reflect, in a very ample manner, on the problems of historic towns, in general, and on the policy for safeguarding this precious historic-social and cultural heritage. The followed procedures to make the document official — dissemination in the ICOMOS National Committees and International Scientific Committees and the approval in occasion of the General Assembly — I think have had the merit to promote reflections on different cultural contexts, inducing among others to calibrate the use of many words and concepts.

在撰写这份文件的过程中，曾经发生过很多激烈的辩论。事实上，我们必须要说，这些辩论非常有益，因为它们充分反思历史城镇的问题，以及保护这些宝贵的历史、社会和文化遗产的政策。后来在国家委员会和国际科学委员会所进行正式传播并通过全体大会审批等程序，也有力地促进了我们针对不同的文化背景进行反思，引导很多词汇和概念的使用。

In relation to the CIVVIH annual meeting — that took place in Istanbul in May 2005 — and the debate developed during the Scientific Colloquium on 'The preservation of historic centers in large metropolitan areas', the CIVVIH decided to start a wide reflection on *the Washington Charter* (1987), or rather on the historic towns and their issues, with the objective to define criteria for their safeguarding and development.

鉴于2005年5月在伊斯坦布尔举行的年会以及"关于大型都市历史中心的保护科学讨论会"期间所发生的辩论，决定对《华盛顿宪章》（1987年），或者说是对历史城镇及其相关课题，展开广泛的反思，以定义保护和发展的标准。

A first hypothesis of revision was presented by Alvaro and in Helsinki (April, 2007). This consisted of little changes and completions, in relation to the original Charter, discussed during the annual meeting of our Committee. The necessity emerged strongly, from this discussion, to opt for a more radical revision:

—giving a clearer structure to the new document;

—introducing new topics that were not dealt with in *the Washington Charter* (among which: intangible values, identity and spirit of places);

—revising some concepts and issues about tourism, mobility, new architectures, etc.;

—taking into account some issues that were well expressed by the Nairobi Recommendations.

我和阿尔瓦多在赫尔辛基（2007年4月）提交了第一份修订设想，对原来的《宪章》做出了一些小的改动和完善，但在委员会年度会议讨论中，我们发现迫切需要进行更大规模的修订：

—为新文件赋予更清晰的结构；

—引入《华盛顿宪章》中没有触及的新课题（包括：无形价值、身份认同以及场所精神）；

—修订关于旅游、交通、新建筑等概念和问题；

—将《内罗毕建议》中充分阐述过的部分问题纳入考虑范围。

Indeed, in a first moment the idea was to set up a sort of update and revision of *the Washington Charter*, also on the basis of a rich corpus of documents which during the years were produced. In a short time, on the contrary, we realize as every document is the child of its historic-cultural context and, if we don't wont to diminish its value, in relation to the current situation it is more opportune to work for the definition of 'principles' for safeguarding and management of the historic cities, towns and urban areas.

事实上，刚开始的想法只是想对《华盛顿宪章》以及这些年丰富的文件资料进行某种程度的更新和修订。很快，我们就意识到，从历史文化背景来看，每一份文件都还很不成熟，如果我们不想减弱其价值，从当前的形势来看，最好是先定义保护和管理历史城镇和城区的"原则"。

Starting from these considerations, a first draft in July 2007 was drawn up following the instructions which emerged in Helsinki. Many

带着这些考虑，我们在2007年7月根据赫尔辛基会议指示，起草了第一稿。很多人都通过电子邮件给我发来了对文件第一稿的看法和

people have sent me lots of general opinions and useful comments on the contents of the draft by e-mail which have been very meaningful. The document in the new structure took in consideration specific remarks on the contents, but always considering their validity in different international contexts. I think it is interesting to underline how the need for a new document has transformed progressively in a sort of bottom-up process. Indeed, as Jean Louis Luxen has said, a new document '… should be the final step of a long process of collective work and consultation …'. That's why it was very important to settle on an organization for sharing the set up of the document, according to the decisions made in the Executive Committee for the doctrinal text (ICOMOS ADCOM 2009/10).

有用的建议，这些看法和建议具有重要的意义。这份采用了全新结构的文件在吸纳初稿内容和这些具体建议的同时，更多地考虑了不同国际背景下的适用性。有意思的是，对新文件的需求，是由下而上逐渐发展而来的。事实上，正如让·路易·路克森所说，一份新的文件“……必须是集体工作和磋商讨论这一漫长进程的最后一步……”。因此，这是根据执行委员会的决议（2009/10 国际古迹遗址理事会 ADCOM）成立一个组织并共同确立一个理论性文件的重要原因。

The Document

There is no doubt that a connection with the previous *Washington Charter* has persisted in a strong way, also if the formulation and many of the topics faced are wholly new. However, the Charter of 1987 was an important starting and comparison point. For this reason it was chosen to extrapolate some issues, enriching them with new considerations.

If that could be considered as a starting point, I would also like to underline as there is no doubt that the new Document is the outcome of an ever so rich debate, not only for the liveliness of those who have taken part, but as much for their solid stock of experiences on the field. Therefore the Document, even if for choice it has formulations in general terms, hides a big concreteness of contents.

The first strongly discussed and shared idea was to set a document without references to a specific context: it was opportune to enounce general principles, valid in variegated physical

文件

毫无疑问，这份文件与之前的《华盛顿宪章》有着深厚的渊源，而整个构思和所面临的很多课题却都是全新的。但 1987 年的《宪章》是一个重要的开始和参照点。因此，我们选择了对部分议题进行扩写，加入新的元素，使其更加丰富。

如果说原文件只是一个起点，我想要强调的是，新文件无疑是前所未有的丰富辩论的结晶，不仅凝聚了所有参与者的活力，同时也凝聚了他们在各自领域的丰富经验。因此，这份文件即使看上去选择了公式化的表述方式，但却隐藏着大量丰富的内容。

第一个引发激烈讨论的共同观点，是起草一份不指向任何具体背景的文件：阐明在各种物质和文化背景下均有效的总体原则。第二个目标则更具野心，是创作一份不针对任何具体

and cultural contexts. The second aim, perhaps ambitious, was to create a document not addressed to a specific class of goods (for example those for which there is *a Statement of Outstanding Universal Value* (So OUV)): the Document has to represent an indisputable universal reference point, useful for the definition of types of intervention types in historic centers of any size and value. The matured experience in relation to the World Heritage List (WHL) and to all of its definition process-well expressed also in the '*Operational Guidelines for the Implementation of the World Heritage Convention*' — had to allow us to point out different issues and needs. This is not to say though, that we would argue and deal with in the same way contexts that aren't expression of integrity or of exceptional values.

类别的文件（比如《突出普遍价值声明》）：这份文件必须代表的是毫无争议的普遍参照点，用于界定针对任何规模和价值的历史中心的干预类型。与世界遗产名录及其所有定义过程相关的成熟经验（这些经验在《关于实施世界遗产公约的操作指南》中有很好的介绍），让我们得以甄别出不同的问题和需要。然而，这并不意味着我们应该以同样的方式去辩论和处理并不能够表现完整性或特殊价值的背景。

In fact sometimes we forget that what has matured according to the safeguarding and exploitation policies for the World Heritage (WH) finds justification in the exceptional of the good and it isn't always possible to use the same standard for all the so-called historic heritage.

事实上，我们有时会忘记，根据成熟的世界遗产保护和开发政策，再好的事情也会出 现特殊的例外，我们不能将同样的标准套用于所有的历史遗产。

Now, then, it is strong awareness of the great value of historic tangible or intangible so-called minor heritage, that man takes part in its making, by his slow and constant daily action. Every person agrees with its invaluable value, prescind from its exception, as testimony of a gradual cultural process. The conviction that this 'process' doesn't have to be interrupted and undergo extraneous transformations, today induces us to look at this heritage as a indisputable reference, to which we need to be reconnected. In particular, we are faced with the breaks and the confusions that the introduction of exogenous elements to the cultural heritage of a community induces on the life and relation systems of the whole community.

因此，人们现在要做的，就是在缓慢而持续的日常活动中，深刻认识到即便是微小遗产也拥有巨大的有形或无形价值。作为一个循序渐进的文化进程，每个人都不要忘记其特殊性，认识到它不可估量的价值。今天，对于不必打断这一“进程”并接受外部改造的信念，让我们得以将遗产看作是一个无可争议的参照物，需要我们重新建立联系。尤其是，当一个社区的文化遗产引入外部元素后，我们整个社区生活和关系系统将面临破坏和困惑。

The imposition of not appropriate bonds could cause the interruption also of the natural development process of this heritage. These processes, when they are an expression of definite socio-cultural needs, form significative and valuable testimonies. It is not by chance that in the Document, in defining what we have to consider for 'historic towns and urban areas', it is specified that they '...are spatial structures that express the evolution of a society and of its cultural identity... form part of daily human life'.

强加的不恰当的联系可能会中断遗产的自然发展进程。当这些进程代表着明确的社会文化需求的时候，它们是遗产有意义、有价值的证明。因此，在界定我们必须将“历史城镇和城区”的某一特性纳入考虑范畴的时候，文件明确指出它们“……是表达一个社会及其文化身份的沿革的空间结构……构成人类日常生活的一部分。”

Saying that, it is possible to say that during numerous meetings, drawings up and exchanges, the discussion has ended by getting to the heart of the matter, three issues that are considered fundamental:

a) changes and evolution which register the urban areas, in general, and the historic towns, in particular, in relation to the quick innovative processes that pervade culture, behaviors and economy today;

b) possible criteria to suggest for the intervention in historic towns and urban areas;

c) methodological matters and more opportune strategies to adopt.

可以说，正是在无数次的会议、起草和交流之中，我们的讨论最终抵达了问题的核心。其中最为重要的三个问题分别是：

a）记录一般城市地区以及历史城镇变化和沿革，尤其是当今时代盛行的文化、社会行为和经济普遍存在的快速创新进程；

b）建议了干预历史城镇和城区的可能标准；

c）应当采取的方法和更适宜的策略。

Thus the Document, beyond the two parts which could be considered as an introduction (Preamble Definitions), or rather considered important but like a frame, it is structured on a canonical formula: 'analysis-diagnosis', 'definition of reference principles', 'definition of the possible interventions and actions'.

因此，除了被看作是序言或者是重要框架的两个部分（“序言”和“名词解释”）之外，这份文件都是通过一种规范格式来组织的：“分析——诊断”、“定义参考原则”、“定义可能发生的干预和行为”。

Probably it is also opportune to specify that the decision to set up a document like 'principles', besides being in reference to the decisions made for doctrinal texts, also depends on the goal: to write a text of guidelines not only for professionals, but also for local management bodies. Not by

值得说明的是，除了根据相关决定编写类似“原则”的文件之外，这样的文件还有一个目标：为专业人士、地方管理机构编写一份指导性文件。绝非偶然，基础目标就是更广泛的传播这些年来已经成熟的主要课题以及这一领域的不同经验。“前言”部分在国际范围内面关

chance, the bottom goal was to allow a greater diffusion of the main matured issues during the years and of the different experiences on the field. The Preamble, in prime, intends to pay attention to the current situation of change, at world level, which has repercussions in the economic, social, environmental and cultural context. The change, if on one hand comes nearly to lacerate the historic centers, on the other hand represents a characteristic and unavoidable feature of the present historic situation, which could admit possible governance forms. The globalization of markets and the innovation of process and product, in general, induce substantial transformations in the political governance and in the way of life. They lead us to shape new social demands, as behaviour which could have the effect to alter in a irrevocable way the identity and also the historic-cultural heritage.

注经济、社会、环境和文化背景下的变化形势及其产生的影响。这些变化在一方面近乎破坏了历史中心，另一方面却代表了当前历史形态特有的、不可避免的特征，接受可能的管理形式。总的来说，市场的全球化以及工艺和产品的创新激发了政治管理和生活方式的重大变革。这些变革让我们发现新的社会需求，认识到这种行为可能以不可逆转的方式改变身份认同和历史文化遗产。

The numerous epochal transformations, which we are living, induce a general sense of bewilderment, especially if we try to think about our future. Now the present doesn't appear as the outcome of the slow evolving of the past, but very often becomes a 'fait accompli'：its appearance leads us to lose both the memory of the past and the imagination of the future. The extraordinary expansion of the space — became accessible for everybody by a system of transport and communication inconceivable until some decades ago — determines an unshakable contraction of the time, crushed by the immediateness.

我们目前正经历的无数划时代的变革，引发了一种整体的迷惘感，尤其是在我们思考未来的时候。现在，不再是过去的缓慢演进的结果，而是经常成为“既成事实”：它的出现，让我们失去了对过去的记忆，以及对未来的想象。意想不到的空间扩张（在数十年前还无法想象的交通和通信系统使每个人都可以进入该空间），使毫无弹性的时间，被瞬间挤压。

The wide role given to the variable 'time' leads us to emphasize the dimension of the present with precise effects, on one hand, on the ways to look to the past, on the other hand, on ways to build the future. It is also according to these considerations that it seems opportune to consider the problems and perspectives for the historic towns and urban areas, and to trace the outline of policies to adopt in

可变的“时间”被赋予了广泛的角色，让我们强调当下确切影响的维度，一方面回顾过去，一方面着眼建设未来。正是出于这些考虑，我们更应该思考历史城镇和城区的问题和前景，关注对它们的正确利用和可持续发展，制定相关的政策大纲。在辩论期间，有一个问题以非常激烈的方式凸显出来：必须要对相关术语加以定义，作为参照让其在所有社区共同使用。因

relation to their right exploitation and sustainability. During the course of the debate a problem comes out in a very strong way: it was the need to insert definitions which could be shared, as referential terms, in all the communities. The importance to have a clear and uni-vocal terminology has immediately leads us to give space to the section definitions, trying after to make the text slimmer and unambiguous.

为有一个清晰而意义明确的术语表很重要，我们立即决定编辑“名词解释”部分，使文本更加简洁和明确。

The numerous documents that have been produced until now-that often we can say are at a ‘regional’ level, also if in a national or continental scale, for example-and the lexicon which was being structured (which often has caused many problems for the translation in the different idioms) have contributed to produce a large number of difficulties in the conceptual and operative field. Perhaps two terms are useful as a more meaningful example: ‘conservation’ and ‘safeguarding’. *The Washington Charter* has utilized unconditionally the word ‘conservation’ which, especially in the Anglophone context, has had the upper hand nourishing an absence of clearness and precision. *The Washington Charter*, without offering a punctual definition of the word, has utilized it over and over again. *The previous Recommendation of Nairobi* (1976), instead, had re-conducted the ‘conservation’ inside ‘safeguarding’ and in this sense introduced an exact definition of the latter. At this point, we can easily imagine the debate which, in fact, was beginning to develop about this issue, also because over time the positions are always enlarging. Therefore the definition given to the word ‘safeguarding’ in 1976, recovered in this new document, is the fruit of what has already been expressed in previous official documents. Not by chance we have decided to recover the richness of this word, as regards to a reduction which had got the upper hand.

在迄今为止所出台的无数文件中——可以说，这些文件一般都是在“地区”层面，比如说在国家或洲的层面，词汇的组织方式（通常会在不同俗语的翻译中引发很多问题）给概念和操作领域带来了诸多困难。比如这两个词：“保护conservation”和“safeguarding保护”。《华盛顿宪章》无条件地使用了“保护conservation”一词，这个词的使用更为广泛，尤其是在英语语境下，但却严重缺乏清晰和准确的定义。但是，《华盛顿宪章》并没有特别对这个词加以解释，只是反复使用而已。之前的《内罗毕建议》（1976年）却将“保护conservation”纳入到了“safeguarding保护”这个语意下，并对后者进行了准确的定义。看到这里，我们已经可以很容易想象这中间会发生的辩论。事实上，关于这个问题争论的确已经开始出现，随着时间的推移，形势正愈演愈烈。因此，1976年《内罗毕建议》对“safeguarding保护”一词的定义是在之前的官方文件中已经进行过的定义的汇总。我们决定恢复这个词的丰富含义，以期减少另一个已经占据上风的词语的使用。

It is in my opinion that, in reading our Document, special attention has to be paid to the words inserted in Part 1, because they are the result of shared approaches at a wide scale and of a precise adopted lexicon. Therefore in this section the choice of the explained 'terms' isn't casual, but indeed in the viewpoint to appreciate what matured in the experience of the UNESCO WHL, and not only there. As it is possible to perceive by the title, having first of all tried to define the outstanding values of the contexts which the Document is focused, it seemed us the best way to allow the comprehension of their peculiar richness and their characteristics, and to emphasize the elements to consider primarily.

我建议，在阅读这份文件的时候，应该特别关注第1部分所使用的词汇，因为它们是我们经过大范围的共同工作，对很多语汇进行精确修订后的成果。因此，在这一部分，对于解释“术语”的选择是基于联合国教科文组织世界遗产中心及其他组织成熟经验成果，而不是随心所欲的。正如标题所示，这一部分首先尝试着定义文件所关注的突出价值，这也让我们理解遗产特殊的丰富性和特征，以及突出强调需要首要关注的元素的最佳方法。

I am persuaded that all the Document and what is around the current, always stronger need, to have exact and stable points of reference are connected to the way in which our society lives today. This is almost swallowed up by the rapid processes of change in which it is involved. It is for this reason that the topic reflected on in Part 2 is the continuous and widespread process of change which we are living and which permeates not only our activity, but also our way of life, relationships and actions.

我相信，整个文件以及当前更强烈需求，是获取与我们当今社会的生活方式相关的准确而稳定的参照点。我们正在经历的快速变化进程几乎吞没这一切。因此，第2部分所思考的课题，正是我们正在经历的持续而普遍的变化进程，这一过程不仅影响我们的活动，同时也渗透到我们的生活方式、关系和行为之中。

Today man runs the risk to be absorbed by the events, to lose control of one's own actions, to wander without targets and aims, to become a 'splinter' at the mercy of events or of dark minds.

今天，人们正面临着被各种突发事件吞没的风险，失去对自身行为的控制，毫无目的地游荡在这个世界上，被突发事件或黑暗意识撕成“碎片”。

Man cannot destroy its history and culture, the result of the thought and action of many generations. From being the craftsman and thinking subject he cannot begin to have a secondary role: he has to become the steersman again 'Change, when appropriately managed, can be an opportunity to improve...'.

人类不能摧毁自己的历史和文化，它们是世世代代思想和行为的成果。人类不能让自己从艺术和思考的主体沦为次要的角色：必须要再次成为掌舵者。“变化，得到适当管理，就能成为进步的契机……”。

It is in that meaning that the Document, in this important Part, introduces, in a certain way, punctual considerations on different Aspects of Change, with the aim to point out the wide range of the issues and the challenges that we have faced. The analysis, handled in a certain sense, as well as the diagnosis, which it is possible to deduce, have the aim to goad us into recovering positiveness and proactive behaviors.

正是出于这一原因，本文件在这个重要部分以某种方式介绍了关于不同“变化方面”的严肃思考，以期能够指出这个问题所涉及的广泛领域，以及我们所面临的挑战。文件中以某种方式进行的分析和诊断（推论），正是为了激励我们恢复主动精神和积极行动。

To begin from these considerations it seemed a way to solicit and promote a wider awareness of the different issues on the table, as well as allowing to pave the way for the individuation and set up of ‘intervention criteria’. So, in a certain way, we had aimed to detail the different ambit in which it is possible to register the impact of the actual process of change. The aim was not so much to understand the various effects, as to outline possible forms of response to spur and induce.

从这些考虑来看，似乎是一个征求和促进人们对当前不同问题的普遍认识的一种解决方式，同时也为个性化和建立“干预标准”铺路。因此，从某种意义上来说，我们必须尽可能详尽地在不同范围内，找出实际变革进程的影响。我们的目标并不只是了解各种影响，而是要描述应对刺激和诱因的可能形式。

Without doubt ‘Part 3’ (Intervention Criteria) represents the heart of the Document. The joint effort had addressed to define a system of elements and attributes that today couldn’t be ignored and unbroken. Values, Quality, Quantity, Coherence, Balance and compatibility, Method and scientific discipline, Governance, Time, Multi-disciplinarity and Cooperation, Cultural diversity form almost the focus which are assuming new appearances and nerve-centre meanings. Therefore it is important to pay particular attention to them, with the aim to consider in the best way the significance and value to give them. This has allowed us, later, to refer to them in writing the Proposals and Strategies. These have the aim to point out the elements to which we have to pay a particular attention today, as well as on which we have to base our policy choices.

毫无疑问，第3部分（干预标准）是整份文件的核心所在。大家共同努力，定义了一系列在今天不能被忽视的、完整的元素和特质。价值、品质、数量、一致性、平衡性和匹配性、方法和科学训练、管理、周期、多学科及其合作、文化多样性等构成了整个文件的焦点，有神经中枢的意义，呈现出全新的面貌。因此，我们需要特别关注这些部分，找到赋予它们意义和价值的最佳方式。这可以让我们在撰写“提议和策略”的时候以它们为参照。这几个部分指出了我们当前必须要特别关注的元素，以及进行政策抉择的基础。

Some criteria pose the different issues in a very

有的标准以极具创新的方式提出了不同的

innovative way. Thus, highlighting the issue Time, for example, or 'Cultural diversity has become ineluctable, just having pointed out the previous positions.

问题。因此，就此前立场而言，不可避免要重点讨论“周期”或者“文化多样性”等问题。

In the same way 'Part 4' (Proposal and Strategies), dealing with a necessary clearing up of the 'Elements to be preserved' - enlarging the concepts that were already expressed in the Washington Charter-works out possible 'principles' to propose in relation to the issues often at the heart of the debate. Without doubt the objective was to enlarge, as much as possible, the horizon on issues which could be defined over time in a more or less punctual manner.

同样，第 4 部分（提议与策略），对“有必要保留的元素”进行了整理——扩展了《华盛顿宪章》中已经阐述过的概念——针对辩论的时候经常出现的核心问题，提出相关的“原则”。毫无疑问，这份文件的目标是，拓展问题的范围，但随着时间的推移，定义方式要尽可能精确。

Facing to the necessity to define in a clean and clear way articulated guidelines, it was fundamental to guarantee an adequate generality of the propositions.

在需要以简洁清晰的方式阐述指导方针时，重点是确保这些主张具有足够的普遍性。

It is for this reason that it seemed opportune to pay attention to some topics in a specific way: from 'New functions', to 'Contemporary architecture', 'Public space', 'Facilities and modifications', 'Mobility', 'Tourism', 'Risks', 'Energy saving', 'Participation', as far as considering the tools utilized at present ('Conservation Plan' and 'Management Plan'). The Document, as it is also specified in the 'Follow Up', has to be considered as a work in progress and so it '... can be updated in the light of the evolution of the issue discussed'. However it is easy to understand as the matter is strongly susceptible to the definition of new cultural and scientific approaches, above all in virtue of the evolution of the life and relation systems. The flexibility that we have to give to the possibilities of action cannot be considered, on the other hand, as a sign of weakness and instability. We have to consider it as a mark of capacity to visit again and replace the reading of the historic-cultural contexts,

因此，我们需要以一种特别的方式关注以下课题：从新功能、到当代建筑、公共空间、设施和修改、交通、旅游、风险、节约能源、参与；以及对目前所使用的工具的思考（保护规划、管理计划）。正如“跟进工作”这部分所指出，这份文件应当被看作是一个持续进行的工作，“……可以根据所讨论的问题不断更新。”然而，它又很容易理解，因为事件很容易受到新的文化和科学方法的定义的影响，主要是生活及相关系统的进化。另一方面，不能认为我们灵活采取行动是虚弱和不稳定的信号。我们必须要将其看作是回顾并修正解读历史文化背景能力的一种标志，一种在历史证据和未来资产之间寻求恰当平衡的研究。事实上，我认为这就是我们处理这份文件应该秉持的精神。

a research to look for a correct equilibrium between historic evidence and future assets. In fact, I believe this is the spirit in which we have to approach the Document.

In this way it will be possible to better understand the message transmitted to us by who was before us. Not by chance, the aphorism of Bernardo de Chartres is very effective: we are dwarfs who walk on the shoulders of giants. The giants are our past, our experiences, our memories. Staying 'on their shoulders', we can see further, catch sight of our future moments. It is positive to be men who look to the future, but it is also fundamental to have the awareness of our past and present. We will be better only when we understand completely 'the memory and history of who was before us'. So we could build, stone after stone, a new society.

如此方能更好地理解前人所传递给我们的讯息。正如贝尔纳多·德·沙特尔的格言所说：我们是行走在巨人肩膀上的侏儒。这个巨人是我们的过去、我们的经验、我们的记忆。站在“巨人的肩膀上”，我们可以看得更远，看向未来。能够心怀未来固然是积极的，认识过去和现在是根本。我们能够全面认识“前人的记忆和历史”，我们才能更上一层楼。这样才能一块一块地垒起一个全新的社会。

New Policies and Intervention Criteria for the Safeguarding and Management of Historic Cities, Towns and Urban Areas arch. Marialuce Stanganelli

保护和管理历史城镇和城区的新政策和干预标准。

撰文：考古学家玛利亚鲁斯·斯坦加内里

New issues and new risks for HC

遗产保护的新问题和新风险

During the 25 years gone by from the Washington Charter, town and historic cities have undergone epoch-making changes. All over the world urbanization is going along at a speed never reached before, the problem of sustainability of transformations has arisen urgently: new phenomena such as climate change increase old problems such as natural risks and heighten the dyscrasia of the present city such as energy dissipation and traffic, considered as ones of the main causes of greenhouse gases. Towns, and in particular, historic cities, are increasingly subjected to new economic and social pressure produced by the growing globalization, the spreading of mass tourism and the intensive real estate exploitation. The historic cities, whose

在《华盛顿宪章》颁布后的25年间，历史城市和城镇经历了划时代的变革。整个世界全球化的速度前所未有，变革的可持续性问题也迅速凸显出来：气候变化等新现象也进一步强化自然风险等老问题，同时也使得能源消耗和交通拥堵导致的恶性温室效应等现代城市问题更加恶化。城镇，尤其是历史城市，正面临由于全球化的日益增长、大众旅游业的扩张以及房地产的过度开发所带来的全新的经济和社会压力。很多重要性和价值已获得认可的历史城市正遭遇严重掠夺：旅游的压力、服务业不加控制的发展以及将手工业和地方小企业置于生死存亡境地的大企业的扩张，使得这些场所正面临着全面的灾难。这些影响历史城市的全新问题和风险，要求我们重新定位保护和维护规

importance and value are acknowledged, have been greatly exploited causing a total devastation of the places due to tourism pressure, uncontrolled expansion of service industry and spreading of big holdings which put craft activities and small local businesses in a critical position. The new problems and risks affecting the historic cities ask for a re-orientation of the practices on safeguard and conservation. From these issues the need for a new document has arisen. This would be capable of facing the big risks that the transformation of ancient space according to the current requirements entails.

范。对新文件的需要也由此应运而生。这份文件应该能够处理由于按照当前要求改造历史城镇空间所带来的巨大风险。

Change as opportunity

The basic subject of the Valletta Principles is the Change that, in the present context, affects the whole society. For a long time in the theory of historic heritage conservation, change and subsequent transformations have been considered as a threat for conservation, since they produce irreversible alterations to the existing historic heritage. *The Washington Charter* had already pointed out that the transformations within the historic cities are necessary in order to adapt those contexts to the present ways of living and keep them alive. Then, the action for the safeguarding of Historic cities should not only entail protection and preservation, but also consider the need for supporting economic growth and actions capable of assuring an harmonious adaptation of the historic contexts to the present life. *The Valletta Principles* improve and strengthen those concepts stressing the importance of change and management of change in the new framework of principles, tools and actions for the safeguard of historic cities. As an active part of contemporary life, the historic cities are subjected to change, and this can have both negative and positive impacts. The effects of change depend

变化就是机会

《瓦莱塔原则》的基本主题是处理当前背景下给整个社会带来影响的变化。在历史遗产保护的进程中，有很长一段时间，变化和随之而来的变革都被看作是对保护的威胁，因为它们会对现存的历史遗产造成不可逆转的改变。《华盛顿宪章》已经指出，历史城市的变革必须适应当今生活方式和保存它们的生命力。因此，保护历史城镇的行为就不仅只是促进保护和维护，还要考虑为确保历史背景与现代生活和谐相容的经济成长和行为提供必要的支持。《瓦莱塔原则》改善和强化了这些概念，强调了变化以及在全新的历史城镇保护原则、工具和行为框架下改变管理方式的重要性。作为当代生活积极的组成部分，历史城镇一定会经历变化，这一变化可能同时具有消极和积极的影响。变化的影响取决于对变革进程的管理方式。事实上，如果对变革进程管理不善，就可能导致状况恶化，失去有形和无形价值。与此同时，变革管理缺失也可能导致历史城镇遭遇遗弃和衰败。

on the way in which the transformation process is managed. Indeed, if the process of transformation is managed in a bad way, it could lead to deterioration and loss of tangible and intangible values, as well as the absence of transformations could lead to desertion and decay of the historical cities.

At present, changes are increasingly influenced by external powers that seldom take inhabitants needs into account. In several historic centers placed in urban areas, the process of built heritage regeneration and improvement has produced bad effects due to the great increase in the cost of buildings that has made it difficult to buy a house not only for the economically weaker classes, but also for the middle classes. The recovery and improvement of built heritage have often taken place neglecting the social and cultural safeguarding of the places. Therefore the original inhabitants have been substituted by new social classes and shops and traditional craft activities have been replaced by financial services, franchising and big trade holdings, fostering a process of global homologation of historic cities that show the same activities, the same shops and the same products all over the world. Consequently the economic activities placed in a historic city are not linked to the local economy of the district, but are influenced by the global economy. Also the small historic cities, improved and developed, have faced risks produced by too fast and too drastic changes. Indeed, the excessive exploitation of historic cities as tourist resources can transform the small historic cities into empty boxes destined for the free time of tourist crowds: the replacement of the local shops with tourist services, the loss of traditional activities (craft, agriculture, fishing and so on) and the crumbling of identity characteristics could made these historic cities unsuitable for the every day's life of the inhabitants who have moved away.

当今时代，这些变化越来越受到外部力量的影响，很少考虑本地居民需要。在拥有多个历史中心的城区，由于建筑成本增加给建筑遗产翻新和修缮过程造成困难，也使工薪阶层乃至中产阶级难圆住房梦。由此引发诸多不良影响，使得修复和修缮建筑遗产时通常会忽视对场所的社会和文化保护。因此，原来的居民会被新的社会阶层和商铺所取代，传统的手工业活动被金融服务、特许经营商店和大型贸易公司所取代，导致历史城市出现全球同质化的过程，全世界都是同样的活动、同样的商店和同样的产品。历史城市的经济活动不再与该地区的地方经济有关，而是受到全球经济的影响。同样，经过修缮和开发的小型历史城市也面临着快速和激烈的改变所带来的风险。事实上，历史城市作为旅游资源被过度开发的现象，也可能将小型历史城市变成用来填补旅游大军闲暇时光的空壳：旅游服务商店取代本地商店，传统活动消失（手工业、农业、渔业等等），身份认同消失，使得这些历史城市不再适合居民的日常生活，于是他们也随之搬离。

On the contrary, the lack of change, the staying out of contemporary life has often caused the progressive abandonment of several minor historic cities that, in a situation of economic slackening, see their population ageing and their heritage starting to decay without maintenance. In big cities, the historic centers which have not been recovered and enhanced, become marginalized areas prone to building blight and social decay, where there are often problems of segregation of immigrants and lower classes.

相反，缺乏变化和远离当代生活通常也会使不少小型历史城市逐渐被遗弃。随着经济停滞，人口老化，遗产也会因为缺乏维护而被毁弃。在大型城市，没有被修复和加固的历史中心会逐步边缘化、建筑荒芜、社会腐化，通常会出现移民和低收入阶层相互隔离的状况。

Starting from the above-said assumptions, all the document aims at defining modalities and policies for managing change and turning it into an opportunity. ‘Change as opportunity’ represents one of the key concepts of the document: in a turbulent age, such as the present one, change cannot be avoided, but it should be directed and oriented so that safeguard interventions in historic cities could become the opportunity to increase the citizens’ quality of life, improve the quality of natural environment and reduce the vulnerability to the natural and man-made disasters. Therefore change must be managed to guarantee both sustainable development and conservation.

从上述假设开始，整个文件都力求定义管理这些变化的形式和政策，将变化变成机会。“变化就是机会”是本文件的一个重要概念：在风云变幻的年代，比如当今时代，变化不可避免，但是可以加以引导，让对历史城市的保护干预手段成为一个机会，提高公民生活品质、改善自然环境的质量、提升对自然和人为灾难的抵抗力。因此，我们必须对变化加以管理，确保遗产可持续发展和保护并驾齐驱。

In defining the criteria of intervention to manage change in the best way, the document points out, among others (such as consistency, balance, quality, compatibility and so on), two factors taking part to change vulnerability: quantity and time. The changes impact, in fact, disregards the scale and is influenced by time: many little changes could produce great transformations while the speed of change defines the strength of the impact. Changes carried out too fast can have negative effects on the integrity of tangible and intangible values which characterize the historic city.

在定义以最佳方法管理变化的干预标准时，文件指出，除了诸多其他因素之外（比如连续性、平衡、品质、匹配性等等），有两个因素可以改变脆弱性：数量和时间。事实上，变化的影响与规模无关，而是与时间有关：很多小改变可以累积成为巨大的变革，变化的速度也决定了影响的强度。变化速度太快，会消极影响构成历史城市特征的有形和无形价值的完整性。

New dimensions for safeguarding actions

In the Valletta principles change is considered from a multi-dimensional point of view: spatial, temporal, multi-scale and intangible. Accordingly, the document suggests a new and different approach to historic urban areas; an approach that extends its scope of investigation to the surrounding urban, natural and landscape context and adds new ways of understanding historical spaces based on the perception, identity and, in broad terms, on intangible values. The intangible dimension is one of the most innovating elements of the new document, which promotes a cultural approach that acknowledges the existence and importance of intangible and symbolic values that characterize the historic city and territory. The preservation of intangible values is as important as the conservation of built environment, because they help to define a live and culturally prolific environment.

That typology of approach was already implied in *the Quito Charter* in 1977 where the historic centers were defined as 'to dos aquellos a sentamien to shumanos vivos, fuertemente condicionados por una estructura física provenientedel pasado, reconocibles como representativos de la evolución deun pueblo' (Carta de Quito, 1977). According to this statement, an historic centre is identified by the presence of a social and cultural living core and not only by an historic-architectural heritage. Also *the Washington Charter* quotes, among the quality to be preserved, the spiritual elements that express the historic features of a place. *The Valletta Principles* develop this concept further by investigating all its implications, because at present the elements mainly at risk are the intangible ones: the traditional activities, retail trade, craft, cultural traditions, all those things that define the spirit of places. It is not by chance that in the section 'definitions' of

维护行为的新维度

《瓦莱塔原则》对变化展开了多维度的思考：空间、时间、多规模、无形。据此，文件建议对历史城区采取一种全新的方法；这种方法将调查范围拓展到了城市周边、自然和景观背景，在感知、身份认同（更广义地说）和无形价值基础上增加理解历史空间的全新方法。无形维度是本文件最具创新性的元素之一，它推出了一种文化方法。这种方法承认标志历史城市和城区特点的无形和象征价值的存在和重要性。保存无形价值与保护建筑环境同样重要，因为它们有助于我们定义一个生动而具有丰富文化内涵的环境。

这一类方法已经在1977年的《基多宪章》中有过暗示。《基多宪章》对历史中心的定义是“所有仍然活跃的、深受过去的物理结构影响的、代表某一地区人口进化过程的人类聚居地”。根据这一声明，历史中心的身份认同存在于社会和文化生活内核中，而不仅仅是历史建筑遗产中。同样，《华盛顿宪章》也指出，在需要被保存的品质中，精神元素才能真正表现一个场所的历史特征。《瓦莱塔原则》进一步发展了这一概念，深入研究了这一改变背后的所有内涵，因为目前最大风险的元素都是无形元素：如传统活动、零售业、手工业、文化传统，这些都是构成场所精神的东西。正因为这个原因，本文件“名词解释”一部分也提到了场所的精神，这个概念由诺贝格—舒尔兹提出，相关报告请查看最近对《魁北克宣言》（2008年）的重新阐释。根据这一解释，场所精神与身份认同概念和空间的产生密切相关：“精神创造了空间，同时空间也构成了精神《瓦莱塔原则 1.g》)。因而，

the document there is the reference to the spirit of places, the concept worked out by Norberg-Shulz, here reported in the latest re-interpretation of *the Quebec Declaration* (2008). In this definition the spirit of places is strictly connected with the concept of identity and with the production of spaces: 'the spirit creates the space and at the same time the space constructs and structures this spirit' (Valletta Principles, 1g). So there is a strict correspondence among spaces, buildings and the culture and lifestyles that produced them. As a consequence, in the new document the spirit of places becomes the element to be referred to in order to build new spaces of contemporary architecture in historical contexts.

在空间、建筑和它们赖以产生的文化及生活方式之间有着严格的相关性。因此，在新文件中，场所精神是在历史背景下建设全新当代建筑空间时需要参考的元素。

The loss of identity is one of the main threat that the historic cities have to face at present. Gentrification, replacement of traditional activities with new ones, too great an influx of tourists wear away the identity of places and transform historic cities in mono-functional areas oriented to satisfy leisure needs and not suitable to live. This situation would reduce the historic city to 'a consumer product for mass tourism'. The essence of identity can be found in the relationship between space and community. City and its spaces are constituted both by buildings and people who live there everyday. The link between inhabitants and their space of life is developed through the memory of little and great events, related to daily needs or to exceptional events. The sense of identity is created when the relationship between space and time is consolidated inside the memory of the population, then urban spaces gain more meanings and can produce several forms of individual and collective identity. 'The identities are built and consolidated by stratification of uses and meanings, which settle in the places according to the evolution of the community's ways of living and cannot be artificially created by simply reproducing buildings, spaces or man-

身份认同的失落是历史城市当前不得不面对的主要威胁之一。中产阶级化、传统活动被新活动所取代、旅游者的大量涌入等这一切使得场所身份逐渐弱化，将历史城市变成以满足休闲需求为目的的单一功能区，不再适合日常生活。这一状况可能会将历史城市变成“大众旅游的消费品”。在空间与社区的关系中，可以发现身份的本质。城市及其空间由建筑和每天生活在建筑中的人共同构成。居民与生活空间之间的联系，乃是通过一些与每日生活需要或意外事件相关的大大小小活动的记忆构成。当空间与时间之间的关系在人们的记忆中得到固化，城市空间就能获得更多的意义，发展出几种形式的个体和集体身份认同。“身份认同是通过用途和意义的分层来构建和巩固，是根据不同社区生活方式的演化积淀而来，不能靠简单地复制建筑、空间或人工元素人为地创造出来”。相应地，个人和集体认同形式的延续性也为空间赋予了活力，因为人们找到了日常使用和占据这些空间的动机，社区就会照顾这些空间，因为这是他们日常生活的参照点。持续的维护对于历史城市的保护至关重要。

made elements.'Accordingly, the permanence of individual and collective forms of identity makes spaces alive because population finds motivations for using and occupy them daily, then communities take care of these spaces since they are point of reference of their everyday life. The continuous maintenance is essential for the safeguard of historic cities.

The way in which identities are formed and change reveals two of the most frequent problems that can occur in breaking former balances: time and quantity. The speed with which a change takes place is crucial for defining the impact on the pre-existent structure 'excessive speed of change can adversely affect the integrity of all the values of a historic town'. The excessive speed denies the sedimentation of usages and meanings which is the basis of the process of construction and transformation of identities, in so doing, there is the risk of destroying the existing identities without creating new ones. Identity is the product of a slow process of sedimentation and incorporation of external stresses and internal reactions that happens over a long space of time. So, identity of places has to be considered a dynamical entity: as time goes by it changes, enriching or impoverishing itself depending on the path taken, but, in any case, it needs a long time and gets lost in processes that are too fast. Identity is lost, by example, in areas where sudden gentrification occurs, or where land usage is switched fast. In these cases the physical space is left as a tangible reminder of a culture that has disappeared, and part of his appeal is wasted together with part of its intrinsic beauty. No identity can be created in a short time: identity is linked to the maturity of a city, i.e. to the quality that a urban environment gets through the passing of time, by subsequent modifications and implementations.

身份认同形成和改变的方式揭示了打破原有平衡时最容易出现的两个问题：时间和数量。变化发生的速度对原有结构的影响至关重要。“快速变化可能对历史城镇所有价值的完整性造成负面影响”。过快的速度否认了以身份构成和转化进程为基础的用途和意义的沉淀，造成破坏现有身份认同、却不能创建新的身份认同的风险。身份认同是外部压力和内部反应长期积淀和合并的产物。因此，场所身份认同是动态的实体：随着时间的推移发生改变，并因不同的方法变得丰富或贫瘠。但是，在任何情况下，都需要很长的时间，如果这个进程太快，就可能会迷失方向。比如，一个地区突然出现中产阶级化现象，或者是土地使用转换太快，就容易出现身份迷失。在这些情况下，物质空间只是对消失的文化的有形提醒，它的吸引力和内在魅力已经被废弃了。任何身份都不能在短期内创建：身份与城市的成熟度密切相关，例如，城市的品质必须是城市环境经过长期持续地改造和实施的成果。

The same consideration can be applied to the quantity of changes, not only big changes have shocking effects on existing balances, but often many little accumulated changes mark a decisive turning point. According to that, in the criteria of interventions of *the Valletta Principles* it is stressed the need for controlling those two parameters. The elements that contribute to build the identity of places and their spirit should be identified and safeguarded as they help determine a live environment, giving sense to the existing building layout. Identity safeguarding requires participation as unavoidable strategy in the safeguarding of historic places. The essence of identity consists in the relationship between space and community, therefore it asks for an active behaviour of the social component. Indeed, any initiative is doomed to failure because only promoting the construction of 'meaningful project', it is possible to help determine forms of identity acknowledgment. Therefore 'mutual understanding, based on public awareness, and the search for common objectives between local communities and professional groups, is the basis of the successful conservation, revitalization and development of historic towns'.

同样的考虑也适用于数量的变化，不仅巨大的变化会强烈影响现有的平衡，众多小变化积聚起来也可能成为决定性的转折点。因此，《瓦莱塔原则》的干预标准特别强调必须控制这两个参数。应当甄别和保护有助于建立场所身份及其精神的元素，因为它们有利于决定生活的环境，使现有的建筑布局有意义。保护身份认同需要公众参与，这是保护历史场所必要的策略。身份认同的本质在于空间与社区之间的关系，要求社会各组成部分之间有积极的行为。事实上，只有促进“有意义的项目”的建设行动，才有助于确定身份认同的形式，否则只能是失败的活动。因此，“基于公众意识的相互理解，以及在当地社区与专业团体之间寻求共同目标，才是成功让历史城镇获得保护、重新散发活力并得以发展的基础”。

New scales for safeguard action

保护行为的新层面

Change and its transformations have to be assessed according to the several dimensions of change: scalar, perceptive, temporal, functional. Historic cities are an integral part of a broader (territorial and landscape) context that should be considered as an indissoluble part of it. The safeguard of historic cities and other historic areas should be an integral part of a general territorial understanding, which cannot be divided from the overall urban structure.

变化和变革必须通过几个变化维度来加以评估：数量、感知、时间、功能。历史城市是更广泛的（地域和景观）环境不可或缺的一部分。对历史城市及其他历史城区的保护也应当成为认识整个地域的不可或缺的一部分，不能将其从城市的整体构造中剥离出来。

It is essential to consider historical cities as a part of the surrounding landscape and ecosystem.

一定要将历史城市看作是周边景观和生态系统的一部分。针对历史城市的传统方法通常

The traditional approach to historic cities usually preferred the investigations on buildings and spaces that formed them, the new document suggests to widen investigations analyzing the relationships between historic space and the surrounding urban, natural and landscape context. The historical cities are not special or autonomous ambit but belong to a wider (urban too) environment and are subject to the quality of their context.

更倾向于研究构成它们的建筑和空间，新的文件则建议扩展研究范围，对历史空间和城市周边、自然和景观背景之间的关系加以分析。历史城市并不是特殊或自治的领域，而是属于一个更广泛的环境（包括整个都市），具有与其环境一样的品质。

Nevertheless the enjoyment of a historic city is not focused on single elements, but it often refers to a global view, in which the main role is played by the relationships among the objects and by the role that each element has in defining the overall spatial layout. Then each object should be set inside the system of multi-dimensional relationships it has with the context, highlighting the role of visual perception as a reading tool for urban spaces and revealing the 'other', symbolic and intangible, values which produce the spatial, material and formal characteristics. Topography, morphology, natural resources have always constituted primary relationship factors for the historical context.

不过，欣赏历史城市不能只关注单独的元素，而是关注对象之间的整体关系，以及每一个元素在整体空间布局的作用。然后，将每一个对象放置在与环境相关的多维度系统之中，将视觉感知作为读取城市空间的工具，揭示其空间、品质和形式特征和“其他”的无形价值。地形、地貌、自然资源总是形成、影响历史环境的主要因素。

Localization and urban development planning of an area depend on topography of places. The relationship between urban layout and natural context has produced several variations through which an ideal pattern of city, due to a particular historic age or functional need, has been developed in order to better adapt to the site configuration. Besides, the relationship with the natural resources of the area helps define culture and sense of possession of a community. The material characterizing the architecture of places issues from the natural context, and the surrounding natural landscape represents the scenic context where the buildings develop. The historic urban space is often based on the visual use of surrounding natural scenario: views, sudden

一个城市的定位和城市发展规划取决于当地的地形。城市规划布局与自然背景之间的关系发生一些变化，又因特殊的历史时代或功能需要，方能发展出理想的城市模式，更好地适应场所的格局。此外，厘清当地自然资源的关系有助于界定社区的文化和归属感。代表地方建筑特征的材料来自自然背景，周围的自然景观则代表了建筑的景观背景。历史城市空间通常都建立在对周边自然场景的视觉应用的基础上：景观、观景台和景观路都是历史城市的常用词汇。所以，不仅要维护历史城市，同时也要维护周边环境；《原则》通过两个概念阐明了这一需要：背景和缓冲区。背景指的是历史城区周边区域，是构成历史城市的不可分割的整体，因为它能密切感知历史城市及生活方式。

sights on panoramic areas, panoramic viewpoints and scenic roads belong to the daily vocabulary of historic city. For those reasons it is not only the historic cities that must be safeguarded but also the surrounding environment; this need is stated in the 'Principles' by two concepts: setting and buffer zone. The first one defines the area surrounding an historic city that forms with it an indissoluble unity, since it is connected with the way in which historic city is perceived and lived. The buffer zone is an outside area aimed at protecting the historic city and its setting against the impacts of changes occurring in the surrounding areas, considering both physical, social and visual impacts. The safeguarding of historic heritage should be therefore considered according to different scales: regional scale, urban scale and district ones.

缓冲区是外围区域，旨在为历史城市及其背景提供保护，使其免于受到周边地区所发生的变化，包括物理的、社会的和视觉上的影响。因此，历史遗产的保护应该从以下不同层面来加以思考：地方层面、城市层面和区域层面。

A new way of perceiving historic space

The safeguard project must be related to the many different ways of perceiving historic context. *The Valletta Principles* consider the experience of the space, which take place at different perceptive levels, as the focus of the planning action. According to this new approach the perceptive experience of historic urban space seems complex and space is seen as part of a variegated sequence where different perceptive feelings follow each other (hot, cold, breezy, light, comfortable) producing an emotional space experience. Along urban corridors there is the alternation of historic references, contrasting experiences, a sudden passage from close to open spaces,from winding roads to straight ones, from light to dark.

感知历史空间的新方式

保护项目必须与感知历史背景的不同方式相关。《瓦莱塔原则》将感知不同层面的空间体验看作是规划行动的核心。根据这一最新方法，历史城市空间的感知体验看上去很复杂，空间似乎是一个斑驳序列的一部分，不同的感知情绪此起彼伏（热、冷、微风、光、舒适），创造出一种感情空间体验。城市走廊总是交替出现各种历史参照物、经验对比：从封闭转向开阔空间、从蜿蜒小径到笔直大道以及从光明到黑暗的变化。

Visual perception is a central experience for enjoying historic urban spaces and has to be analyzed and safeguarded both in the global views (panoramas, skylines, view-lines) and in the single roads and views. The visual *Arnheim, Rudolph*, The dynamics

视觉感知是享受城市历史空间的核心体验，必须同时从整体视角（全景、天际线、视线）和单一方法和视角去加以分析和保护。见鲁道夫·阿内海姆，建筑形式动力学，美国加利福尼亚大学出版社，1977。视觉感知目标通常

of architectural form, University of California Press, USA,1977 perception is often targeted to the possibility of understanding spaces and finding one's way about. Historical cities are rich in reference elements such as towers, bell towers, domes and other peculiar building elements. These elements give direction, orientation and rhythm to urban space representing also stops along the path. Sometimes the orientation is originated by the relationship between layout and natural elements (like the sea, a river, a slope). In further cases the references are built through the light, driving the path from shaded inner spaces to large and sunny spaces that open onto unexpected scenic views. In the perception of the historic urban spaces one of the main characteristics is shape. The shape has not to be confused with the geometric form from which it is independent. In an historical urban space the shape is originated by the proportions of spaces and the relations with the surrounding buildings. Where the size of the open space is too large and the outlines slightly defined, the shape is no more recognizable and the space seems empty. The perceptive emptiness could be defined as the quality of an area whose spatial characteristics are not controlled by the surrounding objects. Where distances among buildings are too big and it become impossible to make out any relationship between them, then the middle space appears empty and shapeless as well as where relationships among the buildings surrounding an open space do not exist or are clashing among them, then the outlines are not able to impose a structural organization to the open space. The balance between open spaces and built-up areas should be then investigated in-depth and checked when new interventions and new uses are expected. New interventions must 'respect for historical values, patterns and layer' and 'consistent with the spatial organization of the historic area and respectful of its traditional morphology'.

要理解空间和找到自己的方法。历史城市多有塔楼、钟楼、穹顶和其他特殊建筑等参照元素。这些元素为城市空间赋予了方向、定位和节奏，同样也代表着道路上的站点。有的时候，定位来自空间格局与自然元素（比如海洋、河流和山坡）之间的关系。还有些情况下，这些参照点是通过光来建造的，沿着一条路从遮蔽的内部空间走向阳光充沛的大空间，能看到意想不到的景观。在感知历史城市空间的时候，一个主要的特征就是形。不能将外形与几何形式相混淆，两者是相互独立的。在一个历史城市空间内，空间及其与周围建筑之间的比例关系决定外形。当开阔空间的规模太大，边际线不够清晰的时候，外形就无法辨识，空间似乎就是空的。我们所感知到的空间可以用于界定一个地区的特性，其空间特征不受周边物体的控制。当建筑物之间的距离太远，无法在其之间建立任何关系时，中间就是空的、无形的，当环绕开阔空间的建筑之间没有关联的或者是相互冲突时，就无法为开阔的空间营造边际线。应当深入考察开阔空间与建筑区域之间的平衡，并检查想要进行的新干预和增加的新用途。新的干预必须“尊重历史价值、形式和层次”，并“与历史区域的空间组织保持一致，尊重其传统地形”。

In the whole document there is the concern for safeguarding not only spaces but also the ways of perceiving them. ‘Perspectives, views, focal points and visual corridors are integral parts of the perception of historic spaces’.

整份文件既关注对空间的保护，也关注对空间感知方式。“视角、视野、焦点和视觉带是历史空间感知不可或缺的一部分”。

Public spaces have to be considered not only as a resource for circulation,but also as places ‘for contemplation, learning and enjoyment of the town’.

公共空间不仅是流通的资源，也是供“城镇居民沉思、学习和欣赏”的场所。

The new that goes on

新的延续

The question of new architecture and activities is argued in this context. The transformation of the historic space according to the modern requirement simply the need for functional and, where necessary, spatial renewal. In the present debate on historical centers, a crucial topic is represented by the ways and tools of intervention and transformation. Historical centers, apart from giving witness to past ages and artistic events, are the physical representation of a defined cultural tradition of a community. They are the result of long cumulative historical processes belonging to a peculiar place and a particular community. Hence, they are unrepeatable and irreplaceable. At the same time, like any other urban area, they expresses social, economic and environmental needs that must be satisfied trough urban changes.

文件在这个背景下讨论了新建筑和活动的问题。根据现代要求改变历史空间，需要重新定义功能以及（在必要的情况下）空间。在目前关于历史中心的辩论中，一个至关重要的课题就是干预的方式和变革的工具。除了见证历史和艺术事件之外，历史中心也定义一个社区文化传统的物理表征。它们是历史进程在某个特定地方和特定社区长期积累的结果。因此，它们是不可重复和不可替代的。与此同时，和很多其他城区一样，它们还表现了必须通过城市变迁来满足的社会、经济和环境需求的进程。

In these contexts, the accomplishment of each new building inspired to contemporary architecture often raises controversy and disagreements. Starting from the opinion that historical centers are live environments, it is impossible to pursue a total preservation without denying to this same urban areas the possibility of an evolution. The set up of guidelines to steer the planning and the insertion of these new buildings is a complex task. Even

在这些背景下，每一幢当代建筑的落成，都会激发论战和分歧。从历史中心就是生存环境这个观点可知，我们不能在否认城区进化情况下去寻求整体保护。制订一个指导方针用来指导、规划和建设新建筑是一个复杂的任务，因为当代社会并没有一个共同的美学标准，或者是另一套可供抉择的原则。

because contemporary society has not an aesthetic criterion share or another principle able to address choices.

As it is well known, aesthetic criterion's change depending on time and cultural pattern. It is likely that every aesthetic concept is originated by an intelligibility need. Everything that is possible to read, understand and decode following its own way to perceive reality and contemporary life is considered beautiful. Then the obstacles in understanding contemporary transformation of historic environments could be due to the objective difficulty that the contemporary man feels facing a reality interpreted more and more as extremely complex. In this context contemporary life and contemporary city seems a chaotic assembly of things having all the same value. It becomes difficult to distinguish from the whole, to separate, to create hierarchies since we have not a code to understand reality and its entities. Without a rule, an analytical paradigm, every element seems to have the same weight, the observation becomes a fortuitous activity and assessment and evaluation become extremely subjective. Within a pluralist culture, like the contemporary one, there are no paradigmatic knowledge systems: the decline of the technical, systematic and elitist knowledge and the contextual recognizing of pluralist, non-specific, non-technical cognitional processes has brought to the refusal of privileged point of view and the denial of hierarchies in the description of the elements. This creates a situation where it is difficult to set up concrete design guidelines.

众所周知，美学标准变化取决于时间和文化模式。每一种美学概念都源于可理解的需求。每一种按照自己的方式去认识、理解和解读现实和当代生活的概念都很美。当代人们理解历史环境变迁的障碍，可能是由于当代人面对现实的客观困难，被解释的越来越复杂。在这一背景下，当代生活和当代城市似乎只是杂乱而等价的东西。因为我们没有解读现实及其实体的代码，我们很难从整体中分离出个体，创造出层次。没有了规则，也就是没有分析的模式，似乎每一个元素的权重都相等，观察成为一种偶然的活动，评估和评价也变得极端主观化。在当今时代的多元文化下，不存在范例式的知识体系：没落的技术、系统和精英知识，以及认可多元化的、非特定的、非技术认知过程的语境，导致了人们在对元素的描述中拒绝承认特权观点和否定社会等级制度，增加了我们建立具体的设计指南的难度。

The last decade has seen the rise of the phenomenon of the iconic architectural works created by the so called 'star architects'. These works sometimes are created regardless of the city's existing character and inherited values and have generated an opposition critical movement: '[These architects] threaten to

在过去十多年，出现了由所谓的“明星建筑师”设计标志性建筑的现象。这些作品有时候没有考虑到城市现有的个性和传承价值，引发了激烈的反对运动：“这些建筑师出于自身目的一味寻求建筑创新，极有可能污染现有的历史城市景观……这种只是为了吸引眼球的设计

contaminate the existing historic townscape in a search for architectural novelty for its own sake. … this kind of design works towards confrontation, or dissociation instead of harmonization, in order to attract attention'.

只会带来冲突或分裂，而不是和谐……"。

Different attempts have been made to find rules, key concepts, standard parameters to address new buildings in historical context. Until now the main solution has been the call for 'continuity' with the past for the designers. Different formulas have been proposed as 'innovation in continuity', 'innovation by preserving'. But history of architecture has shown us many times the importance of the moments of breaks and cuts with the past, when there is a full innovative interpretation of the context conditions. Many methodologies proposed for new building impact assessment consist of identifying a list of positive categories and a list of negative ones to assess undesired effect. Nevertheless, as showed by Cullen, the wise use of discordances, intrusions, discontinuities can create intense emotional and dramatic effects. Ackerman examining the Laurenziana Library of Michelangelo noticed the dramatic effectiveness of the staircase which breaks into the entrance hall as an intrusion.

人们曾做出很多不同的尝试，试图找到在历史背景下去解读新建筑的规则、主要概念、标准参数。直到现在，主要的解决方案都是呼吁设计者与过去建立"连续性"。人们也提出了不同的方案，比如"延续性创新"、"保护中创新"。但是，当对环境条件进行全面创新的诠释时，建筑史无数次向我们展示了打破旧俗的重要性。很多方法论建议，在评估新建筑的影响的时候，应该同时列出积极和消极的影响，并对未曾预料到的影响加以评估。尽管如此，正如库伦所指出，明智地使用不一致、插入或间隔可以创造出强烈的情感和戏剧效果。在考察米开朗基罗的洛伦佐图书馆时，阿克曼注意到了在门厅中突兀矗立的楼梯所带来的戏剧性效果。

As a result, it could be said that it is impossible to classify what is always positive and what is absolutely negative, to exclude or forbid anything without forcing attitudes and falling into ordinary pattern. Anyway it has to be possible to find a right way between formal camouflage and the self-referencing of many buildings of contemporary architecture.

因此，我们可以说，我们其实并不能绝对划分积极或消极的影响，或不带情感、不落俗套的排除或禁止任何东西。尽管如此，我们可以在很多当代建筑作品的条理性修饰和自我定位中找到合适的方法。

The document finds this way calling the designers to establish a dialectic, better than continuity, relationship with the existing context: contemporary architecture should 'have a clear

文件找到了一种方法，呼吁设计者与现有环境建立一种超越延续性的对话关系：当代建筑可以"与现有的建筑及其环境的发展模式建立一种清晰的关系。"对话关系必须建立在与现

relation with existing architecture and the development patterns of its context'. Dialectic relationship must be based on coherence with the existing spatial layout and other intervention criteria quoted:

—respect of tangible and intangible values;

—preservation of fundamental spatial, environmental, social, cultural and economic balance.

有空间布局保持一致的基础上，其他干预标准还有：

—尊重有形和无形价值；

—保护基本的空间、环境、社会、文化和经济平衡。

New architectures should be coherent with spatial organization of historical settlements in order to avoid, on the one hand, homologation of shapes and forms and, on the other hand, the negative effects of an architecture unrelated to existing context such as disfigurement, break of continuity, fragmentation, bewilderment, extraneousness. Coherence must regard both spatial, visual and functional asset of the historic city.

新建筑必须与历史聚居区的空间布局连贯一致，一方面是为了避免外形和形式的同质化，另一方面是为了避免与现有背景不相关的建筑可能带来的负面效果，比如外形损毁、破坏连续性、断裂、混乱、异域化。一致性必须要考虑到历史城市的空间、视觉和功能利用。

Within this kind of framework every position could be possible, provided that it is aware. This awareness must be acquired through the knowledge of rules and basic principles which have lead to the transformation and change of places, through the knowledge of what are the tangible and intangible elements which represent and describe the spirit of the places. The study of shapes, relationships among spaces, visual and perceptive balances, materials, colours and connections among particular and general, the analysis of symbols and meanings, of intangible elements, must bused to identify ways of intervention consistent with the values of historical centers.

在这类框架下，只要有认识就有可能落到实处。获得这个认识的基础是了解指导场所变革和变化的规则和基本原则，了解代表和描述场所精神的有形和无形元素。必须通过对外形、空间关系、视觉和感知的平衡、材质、颜色、个体与整体之间的联系的研究，以及对无形元素的符号和内涵的分析，来选择与历史中心价值观一致的干预方式。

The same attention must be paid to the introduction of new activities, these must be compatible with the character of historic towns and should not compromise traditional activities. Then number of users, length of utilization, compatibility with other activities and traditional practices must be

在引进新活动时，也要注意与历史城镇的特点相适应，不得牺牲传统活动。在引进新活动之前，必须要考虑使用者的数量、使用的时间长度、与其他活动以及传统规范的兼容性。

considered,before introducing a new one.

Conclusions

To sum up change as opportunity means:

—to get the best of change ;

—to take the chance of reducing old problems ;

—to take the advantage from global dynamics for improving local situation.

The transformation of ancient space according to the present needs entails big risks that are often produced by a bad management of change, which otherwise could have positive impacts. The whole Valletta document stresses the twofold role that some phenomena, such as tourism, can play. The latter is positive, on the one hand, because it promotes economic development and keeps a historic city alive, on the other hand it can become a devastating event in causing the loss of identity and depriving the historic cities of meanings transforming them into mere attractions. The needs of a tourist market can be actually incompatible with those of people living permanently in the historic cities and, generally, ungoverned economic development can have as a result the disappearance of traditional economic activities and the increase in land revenues, which underlie the processes of gentrification. That is the reason why *the Valletta Principles* point out that tourist activity should be based on the respect for local cultures and traditional activities, and the tourism impact should be assessed and governed within the management plans. An excessive tourist flow can be dangerous for the safeguarding of historic areas.

Change cannot be avoided, but has to be addressed to sustainability targets, so it can become the cue for improving the pre-existent dyscrasia such as the existence of practices and uses of spaces being

结语

总的来说，将变化作为机会意味着：

——得到最好地变化；

——借机减少老问题；

——利用全球动态优势改善地方形势。

按照现有需求改造古代空间风险巨大，改造的积极影响往往被错误管理消除。整个瓦莱塔文件都在强调这些现象的双刃剑作用，比如说旅游业：一方面旅游业有促进经济发展，让历史城市保持活力的积极影响。另一方面，它又可能导致城市身份认同的消失、剥除历史城市的内涵、将它们变成纯粹的旅游景点，成为灾难性的事件。旅游市场的需求与长期在历史城市生活的居民的需求可能并不相容，而且，通常，没有监管的经济发展可能会导致传统经济活动的消失，增加土地收入，引发中产阶级化现象的出现。因此，《瓦莱塔原则》指出，旅游活动应当以尊重本地文化和传统活动为基础。管理规划应当评估和监管旅游业的影响。过高的客流量可能会威胁到对历史社区的保护。

变化不可避免，但是必须坚持可持续发展的目标，所以变化可以改善目前存在的不良状况，比如改进与历史价值的保护不相容的行为和空间使用方法。《华盛顿宪章》已经讨论了交

incompatible with the safeguard of historic values. The question of traffic and its scarce compatibility with the structural characteristics of historic cities has been already faced by the *Washington Charter,* which asked for an adequate control, for planning parking areas and for forbidding the penetration of main motorways inside the city. Over the years the problem of urban traffic has increased and the ways and strategies to face it have changed. The invasion of cars in spaces previously destined for pedestrians has caused decay and decrease in the quality of life in our cities. Rather than actions based only on planning transport infrastructure, the document suggests working out an integrated system of urban mobility where the priority is given to pedestrians and cyclists by means of a network of public transportation at low environmental impact. To achieve that, the use of car has to be drastically discouraged also by reducing parking areas.

通与历史城市结构缺少兼容性的问题，要求适当控制停车场规划，禁止主要高速公路深入到城市内部。多年以来，城市交通问题日益严重，必须改变应对交通问题的方法和策略。汽车侵占人行道空间，降低城市生活品质。文件建议在规划交通基础设施的实践基础上，设计出一个城市交通综合系统，通过公共交通网络减少对环境的影响，优先考虑行人和自行车一族。要实现这一点，就必须大力减少汽车的使用，从而减少停车场的建设。

Finally the document encourages to take advantage of global changes in order to address better the transformations on local scale, like in the case of climate change. The historic cities are more vulnerable to climate change than the modern urban centers, since the obsolescence of buildings is added to the fragility of urban tissue. The high level of world attention to this problem leads to in-depth investigative strategies including actions to improve energy efficiency and to reduce pollutants. Then 'the aim should be to take advantage of strategies arising from growing global awareness of climate change and to apply them appropriately to the challenges of safeguarding historic towns'.

最后，文件还鼓励利用全球变化，更好地应对局部变化，比如气候变化。与现代城市中心相比，历史城市对气候变化更敏感，因为陈旧的建筑物增加了城市肌理的脆弱性。全世界对这一问题都高度重视，人们开展了不少深度调查的战略，包括改善能源效率和减少污染等行为。这样做的"目标是，把全球对气候变化认识所产生的策略，恰当地应用到保护历史城镇的挑战中去。"

To protect intangible values as well as the tangible ones, to give more importance to the way the historic spaces are enjoyed and perceived, to widen the scale of safeguard action, to accept new

保护遗产的无形和有形价值，更加重视欣赏和感知历史空间的方式，扩大保护行为的规模，在不牺牲现有价值的前提下接纳新的元素——这些就是《瓦莱塔原则》主要保护战略

elements without compromising the existing values, these could be synthesized as the main objectives of the safeguard strategy 'change as opportunity' identified by *the Valletta Principles* to face the many threats attacking historic cities in the contemporary age.

的目标，"把变化作为机遇"，应对当今时代历史城市所遭遇的众多威胁。

Document history

The Valletta Principles for the safeguarding and management of historical cities, towns and urban areas.

Adopted by CIVVIH, April 10, 2010

文件历史

关于维护与管理历史城镇与城区的瓦莱塔原则。

历史村镇科学委员 2010 年 5 月 10 日通过。

Background

May 2005: During the annual meeting of the CIVVIH (Istanbul-Turkey). and the scientific conference on 'The preservation of historic centers in large metropolitan areas' the problems affecting historic centers and the possibility for preservation and promotion guidelines was examined. CIVVIH decided to reconsider *the Washington Charter*

March 2006: During the Annual Meeting and the first reunion of the Mediterranean sub-committee of the CIVVIH (Patras-Greece), the discussion focused on the first considerations basis: a) change and evolution in historic cities and urban zones b) intervention criteria c) methodological aspects.

April 2007: The debate moved outside the borders of CIVVIH — like for instance the considerations on the *Vienna Memorandum and HUL*. The Annual Meeting at Helsinki decided a new version of a Charter for historic cities. The great evolution noted on an urban scale and the newly found sensitivity on themes regarding the quality of landscape brought to light the necessity for urban planning instruments and

背景

2005 年 5 月：在历史村镇科学委员 会年会（土耳其，伊斯坦布尔）及"保护城市历史中心"科学会议期间，考察了影响历史中心的问题以及保存和推广行动指南的可能性，决定对《华盛顿宪章》加以重新考虑。

2006 年 3 月：在历史村镇科学委员会年会和首次地中海小组委员会联合会（希腊，帕特拉斯）期间，对下列核心问题展开了讨论：a）历史城市和城市区域的变迁；b）干预标准；c）方法论问题。

2007 年 4 月：历史村镇科学委员会的辩论范围延伸，思考了比如关于《威尼斯备忘录》和历史城镇景观的问题。赫尔辛基年会决定针对历史城市出台一个新版的宪章。城市层面上的重大沿革，以及与景观质量相关的最新敏感性发现，彰显出制订城市规划工具、阻止改变地区身份的管理控制计划等干预手段的必要性。

for management and control plans in order to hinder interventions liable to alter the areas' identity.

July 2007: A first draft of the new document. This kind of update of the previous *Washington Charter* stresses the meaning of certain strategic words, reminds the basic questions and gives the principles and intervention methods.

2007年7月：出台了新文件初稿。这份文件对之前的《华盛顿宪章》加以修订，重点讨论了某些战略词汇的意义，重申了一些基本问题，提出了一些原则和干预方法。

April 2008: During the second reunion of the Mediterranean sub-committee of CIVVIH (Corfu), the new version of the document was largely debated. The proposed and approved structure was that of a《*Charter for the protection of historic cities and urban zones in a changing world*》.

2008年4月：在地中海小组委员会第二次联合会议（科孚岛）期间，对新版文件展开了广泛的辩论。决定沿用《关于在一个不断变化的世界保护历史城市和城区的宪章》的结构。

September 2008: The document was presented and revised at the 16th ICOMOS General Assembly (Québec) during a special workshop.

2008年9月：文件于第16届全体大会（魁北克）期间在一次特别研讨会上发布并修订。

May 2009: The document was reorganized in the form of guidelines, in view of a more universal document for the CIVVIH a work meeting of CIVVIH-ICOMOS took place at Athens-Greece, aiming at updating the Charter of Historic Cities, 22 years after its voting, and to formulate guidelines addressed to experts concerning the protection of Historic Cities. It was unanimously decided to keep the initial form of *the Charter of Historic Cities*— as it constitutes a 'historic text' — and to write a text of guidelines to complete and take into consideration all preceding theoretical texts, not only for professionals, but also for local management bodies. Starting from general principles, it would offer proposals and strategies for managing the inevitable changes in the development of historic cities (new environmental technologies, new infrastructure, new developments, etc.). The directives text formulated by Elvira Petronel and Alvaro Gómez-Ferrerwas reformulated. A committee was formed for the elaboration of the

2009年5月：基于在希腊雅典举行的工作会议提出的需要一份更通用的文件的要求，文件按行动指南的要求进行了重新组织。此次会议的目标是在22年后首次对《历史城市宪章》重新加以修订，拟订出针对历史城市保护的专家行动指南。全体与会人员决定，保留《历史城市宪章》原来的形式——因为它构成了"历史文本"，补充及吸纳之前的所有理论文本，——并撰写一份不仅针对专业人士，同时也针对地方管理机构的行动指南。从总体原则开始，为管理历史城市发展过程中出现的不可避免的变化，提供建议和策略（新的环境技术、新的基础设施、新的发展等等）。对艾尔维亚·佩特罗西里和阿尔瓦多·戈梅兹—菲雷拟订的指导性文件进行重拟。成立一个委员会，负责最终文本的编写。

final text。

June 2009: On the occasion of the Annual CIVVIH Meeting at Narni, a first version of the document was presented. The new Bureau elected assigned Elvira Petroncelli with the Presidency of the Sub-Committee on Charters.

2009 年 7 月：文件第一版在纳尔尼年会期间发布。选举新的工作小组，任命艾尔维亚·佩特罗西里为宪章小组委员会主席。

July-August 2009: ICOMOS-Hellenic grouped all observations and incorporated them in the French and English version of the text.

2009 年 7—8 月：希腊古迹遗址理事会整理所有观察报告，并整合到英语和法语文本中。

November 2009: During the Mediterranean Sub-Committee meeting at Edirne (Turkey), the document was revised, in reference to the decisions made for the doctrinal texts (ICOMOS ADCOM 2009/10) in the Executive Committee meeting at Malta.

2009 年 11 月：在埃迪尔内（土耳其）的地中海小组委员会会议期间，参照马耳他执行委员会针对理论性文件（ICOMOS ADCOM 2009/10）的决议对文件进行了修订。

December 2009: A new version of the document was sent to the Committee charged with drafting the observations and the text was then sent (February2010) to all CIVVIH members for commentaries and observations.

2009 年 12 月：新文本送达负责起草意见和建议的委员会，供全体历史城镇科学委员会委员观察评论。

April 2010: During the Annual CIVVIH Meeting at Valetta, one day was dedicated to the systematic discussion and common formulating of the CIVVIH proposal. The document was adopted (in English and French version) by the majority of members, as was the title. Versions in Spanish and in Italian will also be drafted.

2010 年 4 月：历史村镇科学委员会在瓦莱塔年会期间，用一整天的时间进行了系统性的讨论，共同拟订建议书。文件（英语和法语版本）及其标题获得了绝大多数成员的通过。也即将起草西班牙语和意大利语版本。

October 2010: The document was presented and discussed during the Advisory Committee's meeting at Dublin. Following the Committee's proposal and the corresponding decisions of the Executive Committee, all observations that had reached the CIVVIH until the 22/10/2010 were incorporated in the text.

2010 年 10 月：文件在都柏林顾问委员会会议期间公布并讨论。根据委员会的提议以及执行委员会的相应决议，在 2010 年 10 月 22 日之前提交给历史村镇科学委员 会的所有观察报告，都被整合到了文本中。

January 2011: The updated document was passed through the ICOMOS International Secretariat for linguistic editing for French and English towards the relevant committees of the French and English ICOMOS. Through this Secretariat, the CIVVIH sent the updated and edited text to all International Scientific Committees and National Committees of ICOMOS so as to receive their observations.

2011 年 1 月：修订后的文件获得国际古迹遗址理事会秘书处的通过，提交法国和英国相关委员会进行法语和英语编辑。通过这个秘书处，将修订和编辑后的文本发送给了所有国际科学委员会和国家委员会，以获得他们的观察报告。

February 2011 By the set date of 21/02/2011, the committee had received the observations of the International Scientific Committees and the ICOMOS National Committees; these observations were finally incorporated in the text submitted to the Executive Committee for examination in view of its meeting on the 12th and 13th March 2011, which will determine whether this final draft should go forward for adoption by the 17th General Assembly of ICOMOS in November of 2011. In accordance with the procedure for the adoption of an ICOMOS doctrinal text, the final draft has to be approved by the Executive Committee at its meeting in Dublin if it is to go forward for adoption by the next General Assembly. The Executive Committee finally opined that this final draft should go forward for adoption by the 17th General Assembly of ICOMOS in November of 2011. Many thanks to: ICOMOS Secretariat for its support on the communication level, ICOMOS France and UK Committees for their linguistic support, all colleagues who had the good will to participate and intervene in our scientific dialogue and particularly the Editing Committee of our colleague Prof. Elvira Petroncelli for the coordination.

2011 年 2 月：按规定，委员会把 2011 年 2 月 21 日之前收到的国际古迹遗址理事会国际科学委员会和国家委员会的观察报告，整合到最终文本之中，在 2011 年 3 月 13 日前 12 次会议期间提交给执行委员会检查，以决定是否将这个最终版本提交给 2011 年 11 月的第 17 届全体大会通过。根据理论性文件通过流程，如果要将文件提交下一次全体大会通过，就必须将终稿提交给执行委员会都柏林会议审批。执行委员会最终认为，终稿可以在 2011 年 11 月提交第 17 届大会通过。衷心感谢：秘书处在沟通方面的支持，法国和英国委员会对语言的修改，以及所有参与和干预科学对话的同事，尤其是我们的同事艾尔维亚·佩特罗西里教授的编辑委员会所做出的协调工作。

The Valletta Principles for the Safeguarding and Management of Historic Cities, Towns and Urban Areas

关于维护与管理历史城镇与城区的瓦莱塔原则

Adopted by the 17th ICOMOS General

第 17 届全体大会于 2011 年 11 月 28 日通过

Assembly on28 November 2011

Preamble

Humanity today must confront a number of changes. These changes concern human settlements, in general, and historic towns and urban areas in particular. The globalization of markets and methods of production cause shifts in population between regions and towards towns, especially large cities. Changes in political governance and in business practices require new structures and new conditions in towns and urban areas. These are also necessary to counteract segregation and social rootlessness as part of attempts to reinforce identity.

Within what is now an international framework of reflection on urban conservation, there is an ever increasing awareness of these new demands. The organizations charged with the conservation of heritage and the enhancement of its value need to develop their skills, their tools, their attitudes and, in many cases, their role in the planning process.

CIVVIH (ICOMOS-International Committee on Historic Towns and Villages) has therefore updated the approaches and considerations contained in *the Washington Charter* (1987) and *the Nairobi Recommendation* (1976), based on the existing set of reference documents. CIVVIH has redefined the objectives, attitudes and tools needed. It has taken into consideration the significant evolution in definitions and methodologies concerning the safeguarding and management of historic towns and urban areas.

The modifications reflect a greater awareness of the issue of historic heritage on a regional scale rather than just confined to urban areas; of intangible values such as continuity and identity; of traditional land use, the role of public space in communal

前言

当今时代，人类必须应对众多变化。这些变化与人类聚居地尤其是历史城镇和城区有关。市场和生产方式的全球化，导致了地区之间以及城镇的人口向城市，尤其是大城市迁移。政治监管和商业规范的变化，也要求城镇和城区建立新的结构和条件。除此之外，还要消除种族隔离和社会漂泊感，作为强化身份认同的部分手段。

在当前城市保护的国际反思框架下，人们正越来越多地认识到这些新的要求。负责遗产保护并提高其价值的组织需要发展他们的技能、工具和态度，在很多情况下，还包括他们在规划进程中的作用。

因此，国际历史村镇委员会（国际古迹遗址理事会）根据现有的一系列参考文件，对《华盛顿宪章》（1987 年）和《内罗毕建议》（1976 年）中所列出的方法和关注事项进行了修订。重新界定了目标、态度和所需的工具，将历史城镇和城区保护和管理相关的定义和方法的重大变革，纳入了考虑范畴。

这些修订内容反映了对区域范围内不限于城市中的历史遗产问题更广泛的认识：如对延续性和身份认同等无形价值的认识；传统土地使用的认识；公共空间在社区互动中的作用；以及其他社会经济因素比如融合和环境因素的

interactions, and of other socioeconomic factors such as integration and environmental factors. Questions around the role of landscape as common ground, or conceptualizing the townscape, including its topography and skyline, as a whole, seem more important than before. Another important modification, particularly in fast growing cities, takes into account the problems of large-scale developments, which alter the traditional lot sizes that help to define historic urban morphology.

影响等问题的认识。围绕景观的作用作为共同点或将城市景观整体概念化（包括地貌与天际线）的问题，也变得前所未有的重要。另一个重要的修订内容，尤其是在快速发展的城市，则将大规模发展问题纳入了改变传统场所规模、确定历史城市形态的考虑范畴。

In this sense, it is fundamental to consider heritage as an essential resource, as part of the urban ecosystem. This concept must be strictly respected in order to ensure harmonious development of historic towns and their settings.

从这个意义上来说，将遗产看作是一种基本资源，看作是城市生态系统的一部分至关重要。要确保历史城镇及其背景的和谐发展，就必须严格尊重这一概念。

The notion of sustainable development has gained such importance that many directives on architectural planning and interventions are now based on policies designed to limit urban expansion and to preserve urban heritage.

可持续发展的观念也变得更加重要，当前很多有关建设规划和干预指导文件，都以限制城市扩张和保护城市遗产的政策为基础。

The main objective of this document is to propose principles and strategies applicable to every intervention in historic towns and urban areas. These principles and strategies are meant to safeguard the values of historic towns and their settings, as well as their integration into the social, cultural and economic life of our times.

这份文件的主要目标是，提出适用于历史城镇和城区的每一个干预行为的原则和策略。这些原则和策略旨在保护历史城镇及其背景的价值，以及它们与当今时代的社会、文化和经济生活的融合。

These interventions must ensure respect for tangible and intangible heritage values, as well as for the quality of life of inhabitants.

这些干预活动必须尊重遗产有形和无形价值，以及居民生活品质。

This present document for the safeguarding of historic towns and urban areas and their settings, is divided into four parts:

1-Definitions

a-Historic towns and urban areas

这份关于维护历史城镇和城区及其背景的文件被分为四个部分：

1– 名词解释

a– 历史城镇与城区

Historic towns and urban areas are made up of tangible and intangible elements. The tangible elements include, in addition to the urban structure, architectural elements, the landscapes within and around the town, archaeological remains, panoramas, skylines, view-lines and landmark sites. Intangible elements include activities, symbolic and historic functions, cultural practices, traditions, memories, and cultural references that constitute the substance of their historic Value. Historic towns and urban areas are spatial structures that express the evolution of a society and of its cultural identity. They are an integral part of a broader natural or man made context and the two must be considered inseparable. Historic towns and urban are as living evidence of the past that formed them. Historical or traditional areas form part of daily human life. Their protection and integration into contemporary society are the basis for town-planning and land development

历史城镇和城区由有形和无形元素构成。除城市结构外，有形元素包括：建筑元素、城镇内外的景观、考古遗迹、全景图、天际线、视线和地标性场所。无形元素包括：构成它们的历史价值的实质的活动、象征和历史功能、文化行为、传统、记忆和文化参照物。历史城镇和城区是表现一个社会及其文化特征变革的空间结构。它们是更广泛的自然或人造背景不可或缺的组成部分，两者不可分割。历史城镇和城区是历史构成的生动证据。历史或传统地区构成了人类日常生活的一部分。对它们的保护及其与当代社会的融合，构成了城镇规划和土地发展的基础。

b-Setting

Setting means the natural and/or man-made contexts (in which the historic urban heritage is located) that influence the static or dynamic way these areas are perceived, experienced and/or enjoyed, or which are directly linked to them socially, economically or culturally.

b– 环境

环境是指自然或人造背景（历史城市遗产所处的环境）对以静态或动态方式感知、体验和欣赏历史城市的影响，或者是对与它们有直接联系的社会、经济或文化的影响。

c-Safeguarding

The safeguarding of historic towns and urban areas, and their surroundings, includes the necessary procedures for their protection, conservation, enhancement and management as well as for their coherent development and their harmonious adaptation to contemporary life.

c– 保护

历史城镇和城区及其周边环境的保护包括维护、保存、提升和管理的必要程序、可持续发展和适应当代和谐生活的必要程序。

d-Protected urban area

A protected urban area is any part of a town that represents a historical period or stage of development of the town. It includes monuments

d– 保护城区

受保护的城区是城镇中任何代表城镇某一个历史时期或发展阶段的部分，包括：纪念碑和真正的城市结构，这些地方建筑表现了场所

and authentic urban fabric, in which buildings express the cultural values for which the place is protected.The protection may also include the historical development of the town and support its characteristic civic, religious and social functions.

之所以被保护的文化价值。保护可能还包括城镇的历史发展，并支持历史城区特有的城市、宗教和社会功能。

e-Buffer zone

A buffer zone is a well-defined zone outside the protected area whose role is to shield the cultural values of the protected zone from the impact of activities in its surroundings. This impact can be physical,visual or social.

e– 缓冲区

缓冲区是位于保护区外围的一个清晰划定的区域，其作用是为保护区的文化价值提供屏障，使其免于受到周边活动的影响。这个影响可以是物质的、视觉的或社会的。

f-Management Plan

A Management Plan is a document specifying in detail all the strategies and tools to be used for heritage protection and which at the same time responds to the needs of contemporary life. It contains legislative, financial, administrative and conservation documents, as well as Conservation and Monitoring Plans.

f– 管理规划

管理规划是一份文件，该文件详尽地列出所有可用于遗产保护的战略和工具，同时也反映当代生活的需求，包括法律、财务、行政和管理文件，同时也包括保护和监管计划。

g-Spirit of place

Spirit of place is defined as the tangible and intangible, the physical and the spiritual elements that give the area its specific identity, meaning, emotion and mystery. The creates the space and at the same time the space constructs and structures this spirit (*Quebec Declaration*, 2008).

g– 场所精神

场所精神是赋予一个地区特定身份、内涵、情感和神秘性的有形和无形的、物质的和精神的元素。精神创造了空间，同时，空间也构造了精神，并赋予其结构（《魁北克宣言》，2008 年）。

2-Aspects of Change

Historic towns and urban areas, as living organisms, are subject to continual change. These changes affect all the elements of the town (natural, human, tangible and intangible) change, when appropriately managed, can be an opportunity to improve the quality of historic towns and urban areas on the basis of their historical characteristics.

2– 变化要素

历史城镇和城区要素作为生命的有机体，总是不断经历变化。这些变化会影响到城镇的所有元素（自然、人工、有形和无形）。变化如果管理得当，可以成为根据历史特征提升历史城镇和城区品质的机会。

a-Change and the natural environment

The Washington Charter has already focused

a– 变化与自然环境

《华盛顿宪章》已经关注了与自然环境变化

on the problems linked to changes in the natural environment: 'Historic towns (and their settings) should be protected against natural disasters and nuisances such as pollution and vibration sin order to safeguard the heritage and for the security and well-being of the residents'. (*Washington Charter*). In historic towns and urban areas, change should be based on respect for natural balance, avoiding the destruction of natural resources, waste of energy and disruption in the balance of natural cycles.

相关的问题："为了保护遗产并为了居民的安全与安居乐业，应保护历史城镇（及其背景）免受自然灾害、污染和噪音的危害"（《华盛顿宪章》）。在历史城镇和城区，变化应当建立在尊重自然平衡的基础上，避免破坏自然资源、浪费能源和打破自然循环的平衡。

Change must be used to: improve the environmental context in historic towns and urban areas; improve the quality of air, water and soil; foster the spread and accessibility of green spaces; and to avoid undue pressure on natural resources. Historic towns and their settings must be protected from the effects of climate change and from increasingly frequent natural disasters.

变化应被用于：改善历史城镇和城区的环境背景；改善空气、水和土壤质量；鼓励拓展绿色空间及其可亲近性；避免给自然资源造成不恰当的压力。应保护历史城镇及其环境免受气候变化以及日益频繁的自然灾害的影响。

Climate change can have devastating consequences for historic towns and urban areas because, in addition to the fragility of the urban fabric, many buildings are becoming obsolete, requiring high levels of expenditure to tackle problems arising from climate change. The aim should be to take advantage of strategies arising from growing global awareness of climate change and to apply them appropriately to the challenges of safeguarding historic towns.

气候变化可能给历史城镇和城区带来灾难性的影响，除了城市结构的脆弱性之外，很多建筑正遭到废弃，需要花费大量的资金去处理气候变化所导致的问题。我们的目标是，利用全球对气候变化日益提升的认识而形成策略，并恰当地把这些策略用于维护历史城镇的挑战。

b-Change and the built environment

On the subject of modern architecture, the *Washington Charter* states: 'The introduction of contemporary elements in harmony with the surroundings should not be discouraged since such features can contribute to the enrichment of an area'. The introduction of contemporary architectural elements must respect the values of the site and its setting. It can contribute to the enrichment of the town, bringing alive the value of urban continuity. The basis of appropriate

b- 变化与建筑环境

关于现代建筑，《华盛顿宪章》指出："应当引入而不应打击与周围环境和谐的现代元素，因为，这些元素能为这一地区增添光彩。"引进现代建筑元素时必须尊重古迹及其环境价值。这些元素可以为城镇增添光彩，并延续城市的价值。从空间、视觉、无形和功能角度来说，对建筑恰当的干预是对历史价值、模式和层次的尊重。新建筑必须与历史区域的空间组织连贯一致，尊重传统地貌，同时又能恰当地表现当时当地的建筑潮流。无论采取何种风格和表现

architecturally interventions in spatial, visual, intangible and functional terms should be respect for historical values, patterns and layers. New architecture must be consistent with the spatial organization of the historic area and respectful of its traditional morphology while at the same time being a valid expression of the architectural trends of its time and place. Regardless of style and expression, all new architecture should avoid the negative effects of drastic or excessive contrasts and of fragmentation and interruptions in the continuity of the urban fabric and space. Priority must be given to a continuity of composition that does not adversely affect the existing architecture but at the same time allows a discerning creativity that embraces the spirit of the place. Architects and urban planners must be encouraged to acquire a deep understanding of the historic urban context.

方式，所有新建筑都必须避免戏剧性、过度对比以及割裂和打破城市结构和空间带来的负面效果。新建筑必须优先考虑城市结构的延续性，既不能给现有建筑造成负面影响，又具有敏锐的创造力，并蕴含场所精神。建筑师和城市规划师必须对城市历史背景有深入的理解。

c-Change in use and social environment

The loss and/or substitution of traditional uses and functions, such as the specific way of life of a local community, can have major negative impacts on historic towns and urban areas. If the nature of these changes is not recognized, it can lead to the displacement of communalities and the disappearance of cultural practices, and subsequent loss of identity and character for these abandoned places. It can result in the transformation of historic towns and urban areas into areas with a single function devoted to tourism and leisure and not suitable for day-to-day living. Conserving a historic town requires efforts to maintain traditional practices and to protect the indigenous population. It is also important to control the gentrification process arising from rent increases and the deterioration of the town or area's housing and public space. It is important to recognize that the process of gentrification can affect communities and lead to the loss of a place's live ability and,

c– 用途和社会环境的变化

传统用途和功能比如某个地方社区的特定生活方式的丧失或被替代，可能对历史城镇和城区造成巨大的负面影响。如果不能认识这些变化的本质，就可能导致社区的迁移和文化活动消失，这些被遗弃的场所也会随之失去身份和个性。还可能导致历史城镇和城区变成只从事休闲旅游的单一功能区，不再适合日常生活。保护历史城镇时需要采取措施保持传统活动，保护本地原住民。另一个重要的问题就是控制由于租金上涨，以及城镇和城区房屋和公共空间的恶化带来的住宅高档化进程。重要的是认识到住宅高档化进程可能影响社区，导致场所失去可居住性，并最终丧失个性。保留每一个场所的特色传统文化和经济多样性至关重要。历史城镇和城区正面临着成为大众旅游消费品的风险，这可能导致它们丧失真实性和遗产价值。因此，必须审慎管理新活动，避免运输冲突或交通拥堵造成的次生负面影响。

ultimately, its character. Retention of the traditional cultural and economic diversity of each place is essential, especially when it is characteristic of the place. Historic towns and urban areas run the risk of becoming a consumer product for mass tourism, which may result in the loss of their authenticity and heritage value. New activities must therefore be carefully managed to avoid secondary negative effects such as transport conflicts or traffic congestion.

d-Change and intangible heritage

The preservation of intangible heritage is as important as the conservation and protection of the built environment. The intangible elements that contribute to the identity and spirit of places need to be established and preserved, since they help in determining the character of an area and its spirit.

d- 变化和无形遗产

无形遗产的保护与建筑环境的保存、保护一样重要。需要认识和保存构成场所身份和精神的无形元素，因为它们有助于决定一个地区和场所的个性和精神。

3-Intervention Criteria

3- 干预标准

a-Values

All interventions in historic towns and urban areas must respect and refer to their tangible and intangible cultural values.

a- 价值

对历史城镇和城区的所有干预活动都必须尊重并参考其有形和无形文化价值。

b-Quality

Every intervention in historic towns and urban areas must aim to improve the quality of life of the local residents and the quality of the environment.

b- 质量

对历史城镇和城区的每一个干预活动都必须以改善当地人的生活质量以及环境质量为目标。

c-Quantity

An accumulation of changes could have a negative effect on a historic town and its values. Major quantitative and qualitative changes should be avoided, unless they will clearly result in the improvement of the urban environment and its cultural values. Changes that are inherent to urban growth must be controlled and carefully managed to minimize physical and visual effects on the

c- 数量

变化的累积可能对历史城镇及其价值造成负面影响。应避免重大的量变和质变，除非它们能够明显地改善城市环境及其文化价值。应控制和审慎管理城市增长中固有的变化，尽量减少对城市景观和建筑结构的物理和视觉影响。

townscape and architectural fabric.

d-Coherence

On ‘coherence’ article 3 of *the Nairobi Recommendation* states: ‘Every historic area and its surroundings should be considered in their totality as a coherent whole whose balance and specific nature depend on the fusion of the parts of which it is composed and which include human activities as much as the buildings, the spatial organization and the surroundings. All valid elements, including human activities, however modest, thus have significance in relation to the whole which must not be disregarded’. Historic towns and urban areas as well as their settings must be considered in their totality. Their balance and nature depend on their constituent parts. However, the safeguarding of historic towns and urban areas must be an integral part of a general understanding of the urban structure and its surroundings. This requires coherent economic and social development policies that take historic towns into account at all planning levels, whilst always respecting their social fabric and cultural diversity.

d– 一致性

关于“一致性”，《内罗毕建议》第条指出：“每一历史地区及其周围环境应从整体上视为一个相互联系的统一体，其协调性及特性取决于它的各组成部分的联合，这些组成部分包括人类活动、建筑物、空间结构及周围环境。因此一切有效的组成部分，包括人类活动，无论多么微不足道，都对整体具有不可忽视的意义。”历史城镇和城区及其背景都应被看作是一个统一体。它们的平衡和性质取决于其构成成分。然而，保护历史城镇和城区，必须是整体认识城市结构及其周边环境的必要部分。这需要采取连贯一致的经济和社会发展政策，将历史城镇纳入到所有规划层面的思考之中，同时尊重它们的社会结构和文化多样性。

e-Balance and compatibility

The safeguarding of historic towns must include, as a mandatory condition, the preservation of fundamental spatial, environmental, social, cultural and economic balances. This requires actions that allow the urban structure to retain the original residents and to welcome new arrivals (either as residents or as users of the historic town), as well as to aid development, without causing congestion.

e– 平衡和兼容性

历史城镇的保护必须将维护空间、环境、社会、文化和经济的基本平衡作为必要条件。这需要采取一定的行动，在城市结构中保留原住民，欢迎新来者（无论是作为居民还是历史城镇的使用者），同时还要在不造成拥堵的情况下帮助发展交通。

f-Time

The speed of change is a parameter to be controlled. Excessive speed of change can adversely affect the integrity of all the values of a historic

f– 时间

变化的速度是需要控制的参数。变化速度过快可能给历史城镇所有价值的完整性造成负面影响。在可行性研究和规划文件中，必须纳

town. The extent and frequency of intervention must be embedded in and compatible with feasibility and planning documents and studies,as well as adhering to transparent and regulated intervention procedures.

入与之兼容的干预活动的范围和频率，同时遵守透明而有控制的干预流程。

g-Method and scientific discipline

'Knowledge of the history of a historic town or urban area should be expanded through archaeological investigation and appropriate preservation of archaeological findings'. (*Washington Charter*) The safeguarding and management of a historic town or urban area must be guided by prudence, a systematic approach and discipline, in accordance with the principles of sustainable development. Safeguarding and management must be based on preliminary multidisciplinary studies, in order to determine the urban heritage elements and values to be conserved. It is imperative to have a profound knowledge of the site and its setting to inform any safeguarding action. Continuous monitoring and maintenance is essential to safeguard a historic town or urban area effectively. Proper planning requires up-to date precise documentation and recording (context analysis, study at different scales, inventory of component parts and of impact, history of the town and its phases of evolution, etc.). Direct consultation and continuous dialogue with the residents and other stakeholders is indispensable because the safeguarding of their historic town or area concerns them first and foremost.

g- 方法和科学训练

“应通过考古调查和适当展出考古发掘物，拓展历史城镇和城区的历史知识”（《华盛顿宪章》）。应以审慎的、系统性的方法和态度指导历史城镇或城区的保护和管理，遵循可持续发展原则。保护和管理必须建立在展开多学科研究的基础上，确定需要保护的城市遗产元素和价值。必须深入学习古迹及其背景蕴含的深厚知识，为保护行动提供资料。持之以恒的监测和维护是有效保护历史城镇或城区的重要措施。正确的规划要求有最新的精确文件和记录（背景分析、不同规模的研究、组成部分和影响的清单、城镇历史及其演变阶段等）。必须与居民和其他利益相关者直接磋商和持续对话，因为历史城镇或城区的维护首先与他们有关。

h-Governance

Good governance makes provision for organizing broad orchestration among all stakeholders: elected authorities, municipal services, public administrations, experts, professional organizations, voluntary bodies, universities, residents, etc. This is essential for the successful safeguarding, rehabilitation and sustainable development of historic towns and urban areas. Participation by

h- 监管

良好的监管规定要组织所有利益相关者：如选举机构、市政服务、公共管理、专家、专业组织、志愿机构、大学、居民等等的广泛参与。这对于历史城镇和城区的成功维护、恢复和可持续发展至关重要。可以通过信息传播、意识提升和培训来推动居民的参与。传统的城市监管系统应当审查文化和社会多样性的所有方面，建立新的民主机构，以满足新的现实需

the residents can be facilitated through distributing information, awareness raising and training. The traditional systems of urban governance should examine all aspects of cultural and social diversity, so as to establish new democratic institutions to suit the new reality. Procedures for urban planning and safeguarding historic cities must provide sufficient information and time for residents to give fully informed responses. Safeguarding needs to be encouraged and financial measures put in place, in order to facilitate partnerships with players from the private sector in the conservation and restoration of the built environment.

要。在城市规划、保护历史城市的流程中，必须为居民提供足够的信息和时间，以获得充分的反馈。必须鼓励并采取恰当的财务措施，维护、推动私人所有者参与建筑环境保护和修复方面的合作。

i-Muti-disciplinarity and cooperation

'Planning for the conservation of historic towns and urban areas should be preceded by multidisciplinary studies.' (*Washington Charter*) From the beginning of preliminary studies, the safeguarding of historic towns should be based on an effective collaboration between specialists of many different disciplines, and undertaken with the cooperation of researchers, public services, private enterprises and the broader public. These studies should lead to concrete proposals that can be taken up by political decision-makers, social and economic agents and residents.

i– 多学科合作

“在做出保护历史城镇和城区规划之前必须进行多学科研究”（《华盛顿宪章》）。从早期研究开始，历史城镇的保护就必须以众多不同学科的专家间的有效合作为基础，在研究者、公共服务机构、私营企业和广大工作人员的合作下开展。这些研究应当提出明确的建议，供政治决策者、社会和经济机构及居民采纳。

j-Cultural diversity

Within the context of urban conservation planning, the cultural diversity of the different communities that have inhabited historic towns over the course of time must be respected and valued. It is essential to establish a sensitive and shared balance in order to maintain their historical heritage in the fullness of its cultural diversity.

j– 文化多样性

在城市保护规划的背景下，必须尊重和重视历史上居住在历史城镇的不同社区的文化多样性。建立敏感的、共享的平衡是保护历史遗产、维护丰富的文化多样性的重要举措。

4-Proposals and Strategies

a-Elements to be preserved

1-The authenticity and integrity of historic

4– 建议和策略

a– 需要保存的元素

1– 作为其最基本的特征，历史城镇的真实

towns, whose essential character is expressed by the nature and coherence of all their tangible and intangible elements, notably: a-Urban patterns as defined by the street grid, the lots, the green spaces and the relationships between buildings and green and open spaces; b-The form and appearance, interior and exterior, of buildings as defined by their structure, volume, style, scale, materials, colour and decoration; c-The relationship between the town or urban area and its surrounding setting, both natural and man-made; (*Washington Charter*) d-The various functions that the town or urban area has acquired over time; e-Cultural traditions, traditional techniques, spirit of place and everything that contributes to the identity of a place;

性和完整性是通过所有有形和无形元素和一致性表现出来的，尤其是：a.——通过街道、街区、绿地以及建筑和绿地及空地之间的关系分割所定义的城市格局；b.——建筑物内部或外观形式，包括规模、大小、风格、建筑、材料、色彩以及装饰；c.——城镇和城区与周围环境的关系，包括自然的和人工的（《华盛顿宪章》）；d.——城镇或城区随着时间的推移而发展出来的各种功能；e.——文化传统、传统技巧、场所精神以及有助于决定场所身份的一切；

2-The relationships between the site in its totality, its constituent parts, the context of the site, and the parts that make up this context;

2- 场所作为一个整体与其组成部分、环境及其背景组成部分之间的关系；

3-Social fabric, cultural diversity;

3- 社会结构，文化多样性；

4-Non-renewable resources, minimizing their consumption and encouraging their reuse and recycling.

4- 不可更新的资源，将资源的消耗降至最低，鼓励重复和循环使用。

b-New functions

'New functions and activities should be compatible with the character of the historic towns or urban area.' (*Washington Charter*) The introduction of new activities must not compromise the survival of traditional activities or anything that supports the daily life of the local inhabitants. This could help to preserve the historical cultural diversity and plurality, some of the most valuable elements in this context. Before introducing a new activity, it is necessary to consider the number of users involved, the length of utilization, compatibility with other existing activities and the impact on traditional local practices. Such new functions must also satisfy the need for sustainable development, in line with the concept

b- 新功能

"新的功能和活动应该与历史城镇和城区的特征相适应"（《华盛顿宪章》）。引进新活动不能破坏传统活动的生存或者破坏那些支持本地居民日常生活的活动。这有助保护历史文化的多样性这一最有价值的元素。在引进新活动之前，有必要考虑涉及的用户数量、使用范围、与其他现有活动是否兼容，以及对地方传统活动的影响。这些新功能必须满足可持续发展的需要，与历史城镇作为一个独特的不可替代的生态系统的概念一致。

of the historic town as a unique and irreplaceable ecosystem.

c-Contemporary architecture

When it is necessary to construct new buildings or to adapt existing ones, contemporary architecture must be coherent with the existing spatial layout in historic towns as in the rest of the urban environment. Contemporary architecture should find its expression while respecting the scale of the site, and have a clear rapport with existing architecture and the development patterns of its context. 'Analysis of the urban context should precede any new construction not only so as to define the general character of the group of buildings but also to analyse its dominant features, e.g. the harmony of heights, colors, materials and forms, constants in the way the facades and roofs are built, the relationship between the volume of buildings and the spatial volume, as well as their average proportions and their position. Particular attention should be given to the size of the lots since there is a danger that any reorganization of the lots may cause a change of mass which could be deleterious to the harmony of the whole' (*Nairobi Recommendation* article 28). Perspectives, views, focal points and visual corridors are integral parts of the perception of historic spaces. They must be respected in the event of new interventions. Before any intervention, the existing context should be carefully analyzed and documented. View cones, both to and from new constructions, should be identified, studied and maintained. The introduction of a new building into a historical context or landscape must be evaluated from a formal and functional point of view, especially when it is designated for new activities.

c– 当代建筑

如果必须要建造新建筑，或者是改造现有建筑，新建筑必须要与历史城镇现有的空间规划以及整个城市环境保持一致。当代建筑应在尊重场所规模、与现有建筑及其背景的发展模式和谐一致的前提下，找到自己的表达方式。“应特别注意对新建筑物制定规章并加以控制，以确保该建筑能与历史建筑群的空间结构和环境协调一致。为此，在进行任何新建项目之前，应分析城市的来龙去脉，其目的不仅在于确定该建筑群的一般特征，而且在于分析其主要特征，如：高度、色彩、材料及造型之间的和谐、建筑物正面和屋顶建造方式的衡量、建筑面积与空间体积之间的关系及其平均比例和位置。特别应注意基址的面积，因为存在着这样一个危险，即基址的任何改动都可能带来整体的变化，对整体和谐不利”（《内罗毕建议》第 28 条）。视角、景观、焦点和视觉带都是历史空间认知不可或缺的部分。在采取新的干预活动时必须予以尊重。在采取任何干预活动之前，应对现有背景进行仔细的分析和档案整理，应甄别、研究和维护从周围看向新建筑及由新建筑看向周围环境的视野视角。应从正式的功能性的角度评估在历史背景或景观中引入新建筑的行为，尤其是当其涉及新活动的时候。

d-Public space

Public space in historic towns is not just an

d– 公共空间

历史城镇中的公共空间不仅是重要的流通

essential resource for circulation, but is also a place for contemplation, learning and enjoyment of the town. Its design and layout, including the choice of street furniture, as well as its management, must protect its character and beauty, and promote its use as a public place dedicated to social communication. The balance between public open space and the dense built environment must be carefully analyzed and controlled in the event of new interventions and new uses.

资源，也是供城中居民思考、学习和欣赏的场所。其设计和布局，包括街道设施的选择及其管理都必须保护其个性和魅力，促进其作为社会交流的公共场所的使用。在采取新的干预行为和增加新的用途时，必须仔细分析和控制公共空地与建筑密集环境之间的平衡。

e-Facilities and modifications

Urban planning to safeguard historic towns must take into consideration the residents' need for facilities. The integration of new facilities into historic buildings is a challenge that local authorities must not ignore.

e– 设施和改造维护

历史城镇的城市规划必须考虑居民必要的设施。将新设施整合到历史建筑中是地方政府机构不容忽视的挑战。

f-Mobility

'Traffic inside a historic town or urban area must be strictly controlled by regulations.' (*Washington Charter*) 'When urban or regional planning provides for the construction of major motorways, they must not penetrate a historic town or urban area, but they should improve access to them.' (Washington Charter) Most historic towns and urban areas were designed for pedestrians and slow forms of transport. Gradually these places were invaded by the car, causing their degradation. At the same time, quality of life has reduced. Traffic infrastructure (car parks, subway stations, etc) must be planned in ways that will not damage the historic fabric or its environment. A historic town should encourage the creation of transport with a light footprint. It is important to encourage pedestrian circulation. To achieve this, traffic should be drastically limited and parking facilities reduced. At the same time, sustainable, nonpolluting public transport systems need to be introduced, and soft mobility promoted. Roadways should be studied and planned to give

f– 活动

“历史城镇和城区内的交通必须加以控制”（《华盛顿宪章》）。“城市或区域规划中做出修建主要公路的规定时，这些公路不得穿过历史城镇或城区，但应改善进出历史城镇或城区的交通”（《华盛顿宪章》）。大多数城镇和城区的交通形式都是为行人和缓慢交通方式设计。这些地方逐渐被机动车入侵，导致景观退化，与此同时也降低了居民的生活质量。交通基础设施（停车场、地铁站等）的规划不能破坏城镇历史结构或其环境。历史城镇应鼓励开设轻便的交通方式。特别鼓励步行交通。要做到这一点，应大幅度限制交通，减少停车设施。与此同时，还需要引入可持续发展的无污染的公共交通系统，推广轻便、机动的交通。应研究和规划道路，优先考虑人行道。停车场最好位于保护区外，如果有可能，最好位于缓冲区外。应规划地下设施（比如地铁）以避免破坏历史或考古结构或其环境。主要高速公路网络必须避开保护区和缓冲区。

priority to pedestrians. Parking facilities should preferably be located outside protected zones and, if possible, outside buffer zones. Underground infrastructure, such as subways, must be planned so as not to damage historic or archaeological fabric or its environment. Major highway networks must avoid protected areas and buffer zones.

g-Tourism

Tourism can play a positive role in the development and revitalization of historic towns and urban areas. The development of tourism in historic towns should be based on the enhancement of monuments and open spaces; on respect and support for local community identity and its culture and traditional activities; and on the safeguarding of regional and environmental character. Tourism activity must respect and not interfere with the daily life of residents.

Too great an influx of tourists is a danger for the preservation of monuments and historic areas. Conservation and management plans must take into account the expected impact of tourism, and regulate the process, for the benefit of the heritage and of local residents.

h-Risks

'Whatever the nature of a disaster affecting a historic town or urban area, preventative and repair measures must be adapted to the specific character of the properties concerned.' (*Washington Charter*) Conservation plans offer an opportunity to improve risk preparedness and to promote environmental management and the principles of sustainability.

i-Energy saving

All interventions in historic towns and urban areas, while respecting historic heritage characteristics, should aim to improve energy efficiency and to reduce

g– 旅游业

旅游业可以给历史城镇和城区的发展和复兴带来积极影响。历史城镇的旅游业发展应该以为遗址及开阔空间增添光彩为基础；尊重和支持本地社区的身份认同及其文化和传统活动；维护地区和环境特征。旅游活动还必须尊重而不是干扰居民的日常生活。太多旅游者涌入可能给遗址和历史城区的保护带来危险。

制定保护和管理计划时必须考虑旅游业可能带来的影响，并本着对遗产和本地居民有利的原则，规范相关流程。

h– 风险

“不管影响历史城镇或城区的灾害的性质如何，必须针对有关遗产的具体特性采取预防和维修措施”(《华盛顿宪章》)。保护计划应提供机会，改善风险准备、推动环境管理和可持续原则。

i– 节约能源

对历史城镇和城区的所有干预活动，都应在尊重历史遗产个性的基础上，以提高能源效率和减少污染为目标。应增加可再生能源的使

pollutants. The use of renewable energy resources should be enhanced. Any new construction in historic areas must be energy efficient. Urban green spaces, green corridors and other measures should be adopted to avoid urban heat islands.

用。历史城区的任何新建筑都应尊重能源效率。应采用城市绿地、绿化带及其他措施，避免城市热岛。

j-Participation

'The participation and the involvement of the residents —and all local interest groups — are essential for the success of the conservation programme and should be encouraged. The conservation of historic towns and urban areas concerns their residents first of all.' (Washington Charter, article 3). Planning in historic urban areas must be a participatory process, involving all stakeholders. In order to encourage their participation and involvement, a general information programme should be set up for all residents, beginning with children of school age. The actions of conservation associations must be encouraged, and financial measures put in place, to facilitate the conservation and restoration of the built environment. Mutual understanding, based on public awareness, and the search for common objectives between local communities and professional groups, is the basis of the successful conservation, revitalization and development of historic towns. Information technology enables direct and immediate communication. This allows for active and responsible participation by local groups. Authorities must be encouraged to take an interest in the safeguarding of historic towns and urban areas, in order to establish financial measures which will enable management and improvement plans to succeed.

j– 参与

“居民的参与对保护计划的成功起着重大的作用，应加以鼓励。历史城镇和城区的保护首先涉及它们周围的居民”(《华盛顿宪章》，第3条)。所有利益相关者都必须参与历史城区规划的过程。为了鼓励参与，应设计从学龄儿童开始的、与所有居民沟通的一整套计划。必须鼓励保护协会等行为，采取恰当的财政措施，推动建筑环境的保护和修复。基于对公共意识的共同认知以及地方社区与专业团体对共同目标的追求，是成功保护、复兴和发展历史城镇的基础。信息技术可以促进直接和即时的沟通，有利于本地团体积极、负责的参与。必须鼓励政府机构对维护历史城镇和城区的兴趣，建立完善的、能够促进管理和改善计划的财务措施。

k-Conservation Plan

'The conservation plan should aim at ensuring a harmonious relationship between historic urban areas ...' (*Washington Charter* article 5).

k– 保护规划

“保护规划的目的旨在确保历史城镇和城区作为一个整体的和谐关系”(《华盛顿宪章》，第5条)。

It covers both tangible and intangible elements, in order to protect a place's identity without impeding its evolution.

The principal objectives of the conservation plan 'should be clearly stated as should the legal, administrative and financial measures necessary to attain them.' (*Washington Charter article 5*)

A conservation plan must be based on urban planning for the whole town, including analysis of archaeological, historical, architectural, technical, sociological and economical values. It should define a conservation project, and be combined with a management plan and followed by permanent monitoring.

The conservation plan must determine the terms, rules, objectives and outcomes of any changes. It 'should determine which buildings— and spaces — must be preserved, which should be preserved under certain circumstances and which, under quite exceptional circumstances, might be expendable.'(*Washington Charter*). Before any intervention, existing conditions should be rigorously documented.

The conservation plan must identify and protect the elements contributing to the values and character of the town, as well as the components that enrich and/or demonstrate the character of the historic town and urban area. The proposals in the conservation plan must be articulated in a realistic fashion, from the legislative, financial and economic point of view, as well as with regard to the required standards and restrictions.' The Conservation Plan should be supported by the residents of the historic area.' (Washington Charter article5).

When there is no conservation plan, all necessary conservation and development activities in a historic town must be carried out in accordance with the principles and objectives of conservation and enhancement.

保护规划应涵盖有形和无形元素，在不阻碍沿革的前提下保护场所身份。

保护规划的主要目标“应该明确说明达到上述目标所需的法律、行政和财政手段”(《华盛顿宪章》，第 5 条)。

保护规划必须建立在对整个城镇的城市规划的基础上，包括对考古、历史、建筑、技术、社会和经济价值的分析。规划应指定保护项目，并结合一份管理计划和后续的持久监测。

保护规划应决定遗址任何变化的条件、规则、目标和结果。“应该决定哪些建筑物必须保存，哪些在一定条件下应该保存以及哪些在极其例外的情况下可以拆除”(《华盛顿宪章》)。在采取任何干预行动之前，应全面的记录该遗产地的现状。

保护规划必须指明并保护构成城镇价值和特征的元素，以及丰富并展现历史城镇和城区特征的要素。保护规划中的建议必须以实际可行的方式从法律、财务和经济角度，根据所需要的标准和限制，清晰地阐述出来。“保护规划应得到该历史地区居民的支持”(《华盛顿宪章》，第 5 条)。

如果该区域尚没有保护规划，则必须按照保护和提升的原则和目标，进行历史城镇中所有必要的保护和发展活动。

I-Management Plan

An effective management system should be devised according to the type and characteristics of each historic town and urban area, and their cultural and natural context. It should integrate traditional practices, and be co-ordinated with other urban and regional planning tool sin force. A management plan is based on the knowledge, conservation and enhancement of tangible and intangible resources. Therefore it must:

• determine the cultural values;

• identify stakeholders and their values;

• identify potential conflicts;

• determine conservation targets;

• determine legal, financial, administrative and technical methods and tools;

• understand strengths, weaknesses, opportunities and threats;

• define suitable strategies, deadlines for the work, and specific actions.

• The production of such a management plan should be a participatory process. In addition to the information provided by local authorities, officials, field survey and detailed documentation, the Plan should include, as an appendix, the conclusions from stakeholder discussions and an analysis of the conflicts arising in these inherently contradictory debates.

I– 管理计划

应根据每一个历史城镇和城区的类型和特征及其文化和自然背景，设计有效的管理系统。管理计划应整合传统活动，并与当前正在使用的、其他的城市和地区规划工具协调。管理计划是建立在对有形和无形资源的了解、保护和提升的基础上。因此，管理计划应：

• 决定文化价值；

• 指明利益相关者及其价值；

• 指明潜在冲突；

• 决定管理目标；

• 决定法律、财政、行政和技术方法和工具；

• 了解优势、劣势、机会和威胁；

• 定义恰当的策略、工作期限和具体行动。

• 制定管理计划应该是一个广泛参与的过程。除了地方政府机构、官员、现场调查和详尽的档案所提供的资料外，计划还应该在附录中放入利益相关者的讨论结果，以及对内在的，产生冲突的矛盾讨论结果的分析。

Follow up

These recommendations are the outcome of collaborative work by CIVVIH, which intends them as a contribution to the wider discussions being led by ICOMOS. This is an open source document that can be updated in the light of the evolution of the issues discussed.

后续工作

上述建议是历史村镇科学委员会共同劳动的结果，也是国际古迹遗址理事会对所主持的大范围讨论的一点贡献。这是一份开放的资源文件，可以随着话题讨论的发展而不断更新。

CIVVIH

The International Committee on Historic Towns and Villages (CIVVIH) was established in

国际历史村镇委员会

国际历史村镇委员会成立于 1982 年。委员会致力于处理有关历史村镇规划和管理的问题。

1982. The Committee deals with questions relevant to the planning and management of historic towns and villages. Its membership is made of experts who have different professional backgrounds related to historic town preservation. We come from ICOMOS member countries all over the world to share their knowledge and experience with colleagues practicing in the field.

委员会成员由与历史城镇保护相关的、不同专业背景的专家组成，愿与来自全球的国际古迹遗址理事会成员国、与致力于这个领域的所有同事分享我们的知识和经验。

CIVVIH EXECUTIVE President:
Sofia AVGERINOU KOLONIAS, Greece

Vice Presidents:
Nils AHLBERG, Sweden / Michel BONNETTE, Canada

Secretary General:
Michal FIRESTONE, Israel

Members:
Samir ABDULAC, France
Nur AKIN, Turkey
Danuta KLOSEK KOZLOWSKA, Poland
Michel VAN DER MEERSCHEN, Belgium

Co-opted members:
Saleh LAMEI, Egypt
Yu FUKUKAWA, Japan
David LOGAN, Australia
Paolo MOTTA, Italy

Honorary members:
Alvaro GOMEZ-FERRER BAYO, Spain

Krysztof PAWLOWSKI, Poland
Nevzat ILHAN, Turkey
Ray BONDIN, Malta
Tamas FEJERDY, Hungary
Vladimir KROGIUS,Russia

国际历史村镇委员会执行主席
Sofia AVGERINOU KOLONIAS, 希腊；

副主席：
Nils AHLBERG, 瑞典；
Michel BONNETTE, 加拿大；

秘书长：
Michal FIRESTONE, 以色列；

委员：
Samir ABDULAC, 法国；
Nur AKIN, 土耳其；
Danuta KLOAEK KOZLOWSKA, 波兰；
Michel VANDER MEERSCHEN, 比利时；

增选委员：
Saleh LAMEI，埃及；
Yu FUKUKAWA, 日本；
David LOGAN, 澳大利亚；
Paolo MOTTA, 意大利；

荣誉委员：
Alvaro GOMEZ–FERRER BAYO, 西班牙；

Krysztof PAWLOWSKI, 波兰；
Nevzat ILHAN, 土耳其；
Ray BONDIN, 马耳他；
Tamas FEJERDY, 匈牙利；
Vladimir KROGIUS, 俄罗斯；

Coordinator on the Valletta Principles:

Elvira Petroncelli

THE VALLETTA PRINCIPLES FOR THE SAFEGUARDING AND MANAGEMENT OF HISTORICAL CITIES, TOWNS AND URBAN AREAS • Adopted by CIVVIH, April 10, 2010

ISBN: 978-960-93-4331-2

creation by：George Tsitoumis

《瓦莱塔原则》协调员：

Elvira Petroncelli,

关于保护与管理历史城市、历史城镇与都市区域的瓦莱塔原则，2010 年 4 月 11 日通过

ISBN: 978–960–93–4331–2

撰稿：George Tsitoumis

本文中英文均由世界遗产中心提供。

国际古迹遗址理事会
《产业遗产保护的都柏林原则》
The Dublin Principles（2011）

Joint ICOMOS – TICCIH Principles for the Conservation of Industrial Heritage Sites, Structures, Areas and Landscapes

国际古迹遗址理事会及国际产业遗产保护委员会关于产业遗产、结构、区域和景观保护的共同原则

《The Dublin Principles》

Adopted by the 17th ICOMOS General Assembly on 28 November 2011

《都柏林原则》

国际古迹遗址理事会第 17 届大会 2011 年 11 月 28 日通过

Preamble

前言

Around the World, a great diversity of sites, structures, complexes, cities and settlements, areas, landscapes and routes bear witness to human activities of industrial extraction and production. In many places, this heritage is still in use and industrialization is still an active process with a sense of historical continuity, while in other places it offers archaeological evidence of past activities and technologies. Besides the tangible heritage associated with industrial technology and processes, engineering, architecture and town—planning, it includes many intangible dimensions embodied in the skills, memories and social life of workers and their communities.

世界上存在着丰富多样的遗址、建筑物、复合式建筑群、城市、定居点、地区、景观和线路，承载着人类进行工业开采和生产的证据。在很多地方，这类遗产仍在使用中，工业化一直是延续该地区历史的活跃进程，而在其他地方，这类遗产提供了过去活动和技术的考古证据。除了与工业技术、过程、工程、建筑学和城镇规划等有关的有形遗产外，工业遗产还包括工人的技能、记忆、社会和社区生活方式等无形遗产。

The global process of industrialization observed over the past two centuries constitutes a major stage of human history, making its heritage particularly important and critical to the Modern World. Precursors and beginnings of industrialization can be recognized in many parts of the world well back into ancient times through active or archaeological sites,

近两个世纪来，全球工业化进程是人类历史上重要阶段，这使得产业遗产对现代社会尤为重要并成为关键。通过世界各地仍在使用中的产业遗产及考古活动，可追溯确认古代工业化的早期进程，这类进程和遗产案例也成功吸引了我们的注意力。然而，对我们的目标而言，这类共同原则的主要利益与现代工业革命的共

and our attention extends to any examples of such process and its heritage. However, for our purposes, these joint principles' primary interests coincide with the common notions of the Modern Era Industrial Revolution, marked by distinctive and dedicated production, transportation and power—generating or harnessing processes and technologies, trade and commercial interactions, and new social and cultural patterns.

同概念是一致的，其特征是独特且专用的产品、运输系统、动力设备、工艺流程和技术、贸易和商业互动以及社会和文化的新方式。

The industrial heritage is highly vulnerable and often at risk, often lost for lack of awareness, documentation, recognition or protection but also because of changing economic trends, negative perceptions, environmental issues or its sheer size and complexity. Yet, by extending the life-cycle of existing structures and their embodied energy, conservation of the built industrial heritage, can contribute to achieving the goals of sustainable development at the local, national and international levels. It touches the social as well as the physical and environmental aspects of development and should be acknowledged as such.

产业遗产很脆弱，常因缺乏认知、文献资料、识别或保护而处于危险之中，也受经济趋势变化、消极观念、环境问题、遗址本身的规模和复杂性的影响。但为了延长遗址现存结构的生命周期及发掘其自身能量，要保护已建成的产业遗产，以利于实现区域、国家及国际性可持续发展的目标。这触及发展中的社会、物质、环境开发因素以及对这些因素的认知。

Over the past decades, growing research, international and interdisciplinary cooperation as well as community initiatives have greatly contributed to a better appreciation of the industrial heritage and increased collaboration between stewards, stakeholders and professionals. This progress has benefited from the development of a corpus of international references and guidelines by ICOMOS — the International Council on Monuments and Sites, and the implementation of international recommendations and instruments such as the World Heritage Convention adopted by UNESCO in 1972. In 2003, The International Committee for the Conservation of Industrial Heritage (TICCIH) adopted its *Nizhny Tagil* Charter for the Industrial Heritage, a first international

在过去的几十年间，随着研究的不断深入，国际及跨学科的合作以及社区主动参与，极大地促进了对产业遗产的理解，并加深了管理者与利益相关者、专业人士之间的合作。这个进程也受益于执行国际古迹遗址理事会制定的国际参考文献和指导方针以及执行其他国际规范和文献，如联合国教科文组织在1972年通过的《世界遗产公约》。2003年，国际产业遗产保护委员会通过了旨在保护产业遗产的《下塔吉尔宪章》，作为第一个指导该领域国际保护的参考文本。

reference text of such recognition to guide protection and conservation in the field.

Acknowledging the particular nature of the industrial heritage and the issues and threats affecting it as a result of its relation to the contemporary economic, legal, cultural and environmental contexts, ICOMOS and TICCIH wish to expand their cooperation by adopting and promoting the dissemination and use of the following Principles to assist in the documentation, protection, conservation and appreciation of industrial heritage as part of the heritage of human societies around the world.

国际古迹遗址理事会和国际工业遗产保护协会认识到工业遗产的特殊性质、存在的问题和面临的威胁，以及对当代经济、法律、文化和环境背景的关系和影响，希望通过扩大合作，采纳和促进以下原则的传播和使用，以及记录、保护、修复、赏鉴等方式对待产业遗产，使其成为全球人类社会遗产的一部分。

1. Definition: The industrial heritage consists of sites, structures, complexes, areas and landscapes as well as the related machinery, objects or documents that provide evidence of past or ongoing industrial processes of production, the extraction of raw materials, their transformation into goods, and the related energy and transport infrastructures. Industrial heritage reflects the profound connection between the cultural and natural environment, as industrial processes — whether ancient or modern — depend on natural sources of raw materials, energy and transportation networks to produce and distribute products to broader markets. It includes both material assets —immovable and movable, and intangible dimensions such as technical know— how, the organisation of work and workers, and the complex social and cultural legacy that shaped the life of communities and brought major organizational changes to entire societies and the world in general.

1. 定义：产业遗产由遗址、结构、复合建筑群、区域、景观及相关的机械、物体或文献记载提供的证据组成，记载过去或仍在使用的各种工业生产过程、原材料的采集、原料到成品的转化以及与能源和运输相关的基本设施。产业遗产的生产过程反映了文化与自然环境间的深厚联系 ---- 无论是古代还是现代，依靠自然资源提供的原材料、能源及运输网络使产品生产和销售有更广阔的市场。它包括不可移动及可移动的有形资产，还包括技术，工作及工人的组织形式、形成的社区生活模式、复杂的社会文化遗产等无形资产，影响着整个社会和世界的变革。

2. Industrial heritage sites are much diversified in terms of their purpose, design and evolution over time. Many are representative of processes, technologies as well as regional or historical conditions while others constitute outstanding achievements of global influence. Others are

2. 产业遗产遗址因其目的、设计随时间演变而形式多样。许多遗址是过程、技术和区域或历史条件的代表，另外一些则是影响世界的先进成就。还有一些由复杂多样的操作或系统构成，其各个部分是相互依赖的，并在不同历史阶段有不同的新技术频繁出现。产业遗产的

complexes and multiple site operations or systems whose many components are interdependent, with different technologies and historical periods frequently present. The significance and value of industrial heritage is intrinsic to the structures or sites themselves, their material fabric, components, machinery and setting, expressed in the industrial landscape, in written documentation, and also in the intangible records contained in memories, arts and customs.

意义和价值在于遗址本身及其建筑物、原料、部件、机械系统及环境，并以工业景观、书面文献和记忆、艺术或风俗及无形形式得以表达。

I- Document and understand industrial heritage structures, sites, areas and landscapes and their values

Ⅰ、记录遗址、区域、景观及其价值。

3. Researching and documenting industrial structures, sites, landscapes and the related machinery, equipment, records or intangible aspects is essential to their identification, conservation, and the appreciation of their heritage significance and value. Human skills and knowledge involved in old industrial processes are a critically important resource in conservation and must be considered in the heritage evaluation process.

3. 通过研究和记录工业建筑物、遗址、景观和相关的机械、设备、记录或无形方面的要素，来识别、保护和欣赏其遗产意义和价值。古老工业进程中所包含的人类技术和知识，是非常重要的遗产保护资源，必须同时在遗产评估过程中得到充分考虑。

4. Researching and documenting industrial heritage sites and structures must address their historical, technological and socio-economical dimensions to provide an integrated base for conservation and management. It requires an interdisciplinary approach supported by interdisciplinary research and educational programmes to identify the significance of industrial heritage sites or structures. It should benefit from a diversity of sources of expertise and information including site surveys and recording, historical and archaeological investigation, material and landscape analysis, oral history and/or research in public, corporate or private archives. Research and preservation of documentary records, company archives, building plans, and specimens

4. 研究和记录产业遗产、建筑物，必须解决他们的历史、工艺和社会经济方面的问题，以便为保护和管理提供综合基础。它需要跨学科方法和多学科研究教育项目的支持，以辨别产业遗产或建筑物的重要性。它将受益于丰富多样的专业知识和信息，包括对遗址的现场调查、记录、历史和考古调查、材料和景观分析、口头历史及对公众、企业或私人档案的研究。鼓励研究和保护文件记录、公司档案、建筑图纸、工业产品标本等。对文献的评估、评价要由能确定遗产意义的相关行业的专家执行。相关社区和其他利益相关者也应参与整个评估工作。

of industrial products should be encouraged. The evaluation and assessment of documents should be undertaken by an appropriate specialist in the industry to which they relate to determine their heritage significance. The participation of communities and other stakeholders is also an integral part of this exercise.

5. Thorough knowledge of the industrial and socioeconomic history of an area or country or their links to other parts of the world is necessary to understand the significance of industrial heritage sites or structures. Single industry context, typology or regional studies, with a comparative component, aimed at key industrial sectors or technologies are very useful in recognizing the heritage values inherent in individual structures, sites, areas or landscapes. They should be accessible and searchable by the public, scholars as well as managers.

5. 只有充分了解一个地区或国家的工业和社会经济历史及其与世界其他部分的联系，方可了解当地产业遗产或建筑物的重要性。单一的工业背景下，对产业遗产进行类型学或区域性元素对比，特别是针对关键工业部门或技术对比研究，是认识蕴含在产业遗产、建筑物、地区、景观中的遗产价值的有效手段。这些信息应该是易于被公众、学者及管理者检索的。

II-Ensure effective protection and conservation of the industrial heritage structures, sites, areas and landscapes

Ⅱ、确保有效保护、维护产业的遗产、建筑物、遗址、区域及景观

6. Appropriate policies, legal and administrative measures need to be adopted and adequately implemented to protect and ensure the conservation of industrial heritage sites and structures, including their machinery and records. These measures have to address the close relation between the industrial heritage, industrial production and the economy, in particular with respect to rules for corporations and investments, trades or intellectual property such as patents, and standards applicable to active industrial operations.

6. 需要充分采用并实施适当的政策、法规和管理措施保护和修复产业遗产、建筑物，包括其机器装置和记录。这些措施必须解决产业遗产、工业产品和经济之间的密切联系，特别是企业和投资、贸易或知识产权规则诸如专利、适用于现行行业操作的标准等方面。

7. Integrated inventories and lists of structures, sites, areas, landscapes their setting and associated objects, documents, drawings and archives or intangible heritage should be developed and used as part of these effective management and

7. 完整的建筑物、遗址、区域、景观、环境和相关对象、文件、图纸、档案或无形遗产的目录和清单，将作为有效管理、保护、保护政策及保护措施的一部分，加以开发和利用。法律认可、适当的保护管理方法，是确保维持产

conservation policies and protection measures. These should benefit from a legal recognition, adequate conservation and management to ensure that their significance, integrity and authenticity are maintained. In the case of industrial heritage identified through fortuitous discovery, temporary protection should be granted to allow time necessary for proper heritage documentation and research.

业遗产的重要性、完整性和真实性的措施。对于偶然发现并确定的工业遗产，应给予临时保护，留出必要的时间进行适当的遗产记录和研究。

8. In the case of active industrial structures or sites of heritage significance, it must be recognized that their continued use and function might carry some of their heritage significance and provide adequate conditions for their physical and economic sustainability as a living production or extraction facilities. Their specific technical characteristics and features need to be respected while implementing contemporary regulations such as building codes, environmental requirements or risk reduction strategies to address hazards of natural or human origin.

8. 对于具有重要历史意义的仍在使用中的工业结构或场所，必须认识到他们持续使用及功能中蕴含的遗产意义，并提供适当的条件使其生产和开采设备能适应物质及经济的可持续发展。要尊重他们独特的技术特点和特征，以适应实施当代标准如建筑法规、环境要求、采取减灾策略及应对自然或人类灾害的需要。

9. Protection measures should apply to buildings and their contents since completeness or functional integrity is especially important to the significance of industrial heritage structures and sites. Their heritage value may be greatly jeopardized or reduced if machinery or other significant components are removed, or if subsidiary elements which form part of a whole site are destroyed. Legal and administrative frameworks should be developed to enable authorities to respond quickly to the closure of operating industrial heritage sites and complexes to prevent removal or destruction of significant elements such as machinery, industrial objects or related records.

9. 保护措施适用于建筑物及其内部，因为建筑和功能的完整性对产业遗产的建筑物和遗址有重要的意义。拆除机械设备及其他重要的组件或者破坏构成遗产整体的某个部分会极大地损害或降低遗址的遗产价值。应设立合法的行政管理框架（机构），使当局能快速反应，阻止对产业遗产及附属物的操作，阻止移动或破坏遗产重要元素如机械系统、工业物件或相关记录。

III-Conserve and maintain the industrial heritage structures, sites, areas and landscapes

Ⅲ、保护、维护产业遗产上的建筑物、遗址、区域及景观

10. Appropriate original or alternative and

10. 选择原始、适当或替代的方式使用产业

adaptive use is the most frequent way and often the most sustainable way of ensuring the conservation of industrial heritage sites or structures. New uses should respect significant material, components and patterns of circulation and activity. Specialist skills are necessary to ensure that the heritage significance is taken into account and respected in managing the sustainable use of these industrial heritage sites and structures. Building codes, risk mitigation requirements, environmental or industrial regulations, and other standards should be implemented in an adapted way to take heritage dimensions into account when they are enforced through physical interventions.

遗产，是对产业遗产或其建筑结构最常见也最具可持续性的保护。遗产的新用途应以尊重其重要材料、组件、流通方式和活动模式为基础。在对这些产业遗产和建筑结构进行管理及可持续使用时，必须考虑和尊重专业技能，以确保遗产的意义。当对遗产进行物理干预时，必须考虑遗产规模，并同时采取符合建筑规范、减灾要求、环境或工业法规及其他标准的方式实施。

11. Wherever possible, physical interventions should be reversible, and respect the age value and significant traces or marks. Changes should be documented. Reverting to a previous known state may be acceptable under exceptional circumstances for educational purposes, and must be based on thorough research and documentation. Dismantling and relocating are only acceptable in extraordinary cases when the destruction of the site is required by objectively proved overwhelming economic or social needs.

11. 应尽可能采用可逆性物理干预措施，尊重其时代价值和重要轨迹、标记。认真记录所有的改变和干预。以宣传教育为目的的特殊情况下，可以以深入的研究和翔实的文献为基础，按以前状况复原遗址。在特殊情况下，即遗址客观上已经严重影响经济和社会发展的需求时，方可进行拆除或搬迁。

12. In case of prospective redundancy, decommissioning, and / or adaptation of industrial heritage sites or structures, the processes should be recorded including, for example, where components have to be demolished and machinery has to be removed. Their material form as well as their functioning and location as part of the industrial processes should be exhaustively documented. Oral and /or written stories of people connected with work processes should also be collected.

12. 必须详细记录对于产业遗产或建筑物未来进行废弃、关闭或改造的整个过程，如，哪些部分被拆卸，或哪些机械被迁移。他们的物质形式、功能和位置，作为工业化进程的一部分，必须有详细记录。还应收集与该进程相关人物的口头和有记载的故事。

IV-Present and communicate the heritage dimensions and values of industrial structures, sites,

Ⅳ、诠释与传达工业建筑物、遗址、区域和景观的遗产规模和价值，提高公众和企业意

areas and landscapes to raise public and corporate awareness, and support training and research

识，并支持相关的培训和研究。

13. The industrial heritage is a source of learning which needs to be communicated in its multiple dimensions. It illustrates important aspects of local, national and international history and interactions over times and cultures. It demonstrates the inventive talents related to scientific and technological developments, as well as social and artistic movements. Public and corporate awareness and understanding for the industrial heritage are important means for its successful conservation.

13. 产业遗产是进行多维度知识学习、交流的源泉。它表述了该遗址在地方、国家和国际历史上重要地位，以及跨时间、跨文化的相互作用。它论证了人类在科学技术发展、社会和艺术相关活动中的创造性。公众和企业的认知是成功保护产业遗产的重要手段。

14. Programmes and facilities such as visits of active industrial heritage sites and the presentation of their operations as well as the stories and intangible heritage associated with their history, machinery and industrial processes, industrial or city museums and interpretation centers, exhibitions, publications, websites, regional or trans-boundary itineraries should be developed and sustained as means to raise awareness and appreciation for the industrial heritage in the full richness of its meaning for contemporary societies. These should ideally be located at the heritage sites itself where the process of industrialization has taken place and can be best communicated. Wherever possible, national and international institutions in the field of research and conservation of heritage should be empowered to use them as educational facilities for the general public and the professional communities.

14. 提供相关活动和设施，如参观仍在使用的遗产、展示其操作过程、与遗产历史、机械系统、行业发展进程相关的故事、无形遗产等，以及行业或城市博物馆及介绍、阐释中心、展览、出版物、网站、区域或跨区域旅行线路等方法，提高当代社会对产业遗产认识和欣赏，充分了解其对当代社会的意义。这些活动的理想地点是设在工业化进程发生的遗产点上，并与遗产点有最好的沟通。条件允许时，授权国家或国际的遗产保护研究机构，利用产业遗产作为公众和专业团体接受教育的场所。

联合国教科文组织世界遗产中心《关于历史城镇景观的建议书》

UNESCO Recommendation on the Historic Urban Landscape

Recommendation on the Historic Urban Landscape

关于历史城镇景观的建议书

The General Conference,

Taking note of the final report on the elaboration of a standard-setting instrument on the historic urban landscape in the form of a recommendation (report – 36 C/23; recommendation – 36 C/23 Annex), recognizing the significance of the historic urban landscape approach as an innovative way to preserve heritage and manage historic cities.

大会，

以建议书的形式拟定关于制定历史城市景观标准性文件的最终报告（报告 –36 C/23 号文件；建议书 –36 C/23 号文件的附件），认识到历史城镇景观方法作为一种保存遗产和管理历史名城的创新方式，具有重要意义。

1. *Commends* the international partner organizations that have contributed to the review process and supported UNESCO over the last six years in its task of establishing principles and guidelines for the conservation of the historic urban landscape in support of Member States and local communities;

1. 感谢合作的国际组织在文件审查过程中做出的贡献，并在过去的 6 年里，一直支持联合国教科文组织、帮助缔约国和当地社区，制定保护历史城市景观的原则和指导方针；

2. *Recommends* that Member States take the appropriate steps to: adapt this new instrument to their specific contexts, disseminate it widely across their national territories, facilitate its implementation through the formulation and adoption of supporting policies, and monitor its impact on the conservation and management of historic cities;

2. 建议缔约国采取适当的措施，以便这份文件：能适应当地的具体需要；在缔约国内的广泛宣传；通过制订和采纳各种支持性政策来促进本文件的实施；监测本文件对历史名城的保护和管理的影响；

3. *Also recommends* that Member States and relevant local authorities identify within their specific contexts the critical steps for implementing the historic urban landscape approach, which may

3. 建议缔约国和有关地方当局根据当地的具体情况，确定推行历史城镇景观方法的关键步骤，其中可能包括：

include the following:

(a) to undertake comprehensive surveys and mapping of the historic cities' natural, cultural and human resources;

（a）对历史城镇的自然、文化和人文资源进行综合调查和测绘工作；

(b) to reach consensus using participatory planning and stakeholder consultations on what values to protect for transmission to future generations, and to determine the attributes that bear these values;

（b）通过参与性规划及与利益相关者磋商，确认哪些价值需要保护并传承，并确定承载这些价值的属性特征；

(c) to assess the vulnerability of such attributes to socio-economic pressures and the impacts of climate change;

（c）评估这些特征在社会经济压力和气候变化影响下的脆弱性；

(d) to integrate urban heritage values and their vulnerability status into a wider framework of city development, which shall provide indications of areas of heritage sensitivity which require careful attention to planning, design and implementation of development projects;

（d）将城市遗产价值和它们的脆弱性纳入更广泛的城市发展框架，并应在规划、设计和实施开发项目时，标明需要特别注意的遗产敏感区域；

(e) to prioritize actions for conservation and development;

（e）对保护和开发行动排定优先顺序；

(f) to establish the appropriate partnerships and local management frameworks for each of the projects identified for conservation and development, as well as to develop mechanisms for the coordination of the various activities between different actors, both public and private;

（f）为每个得到确认的保护和开发项目，建立适当的伙伴关系和当地管理框架，为公共和私营部门不同行动者间的各种活动制定协调机制；

4. Decides to adopt the Recommendation on the Historic Urban Landscape, as approved on 27 May 2011 at the Intergovernmental Meeting of Experts on the Historic Urban Landscape (category II) at UNESCO Headquarters, which is annexed to this resolution.

4. 2011 年 5 月 27 日在教科文组织总部召开的关于历史城镇景观的政府间专家会议上（II 类）通过本决议《关于历史城镇景观的建议》，见附件。

ANNEX

Recommendation on the Historic Urban Landscape, including a glossary of definitions.

附件

关于历史城镇景观的建议书，包括定义汇编。

Preamble

前言

The General Conference,

Considering that historic urban areas are among

大会

考虑到历史城区是我们共同的文化遗产最

the most abundant and diverse manifestations of our common cultural heritage, shaped by generations and constituting a key testimony to humankind's endeavors and aspirations through space and time.

为丰富和多样的表现方式之一，是一代又一代的先辈所缔造的，是通过空间和时间来证明人类的努力和抱负的关键证据。

Also considering that urban heritage is for humanity a social, cultural and economic asset, defined by an historic layering of values that have been produced by successive and existing cultures and an accumulation of traditions and experiences, recognized as such in their diversity.

还考虑到城市遗产对人类来说是一种社会、文化和经济资产，其特征是历史文化和现有文化所创造的价值在历史上的层层积淀，以及传统和经验的累积，这些都体现在其多样性中。

Further considering that urbanization is proceeding on an unprecedented scale in the history of humankind, and that throughout the world this is driving socio-economic change and growth, which should be harnessed at the local, national, regional and international levels.

进一步考虑到城市化正以人类历史上前所未有的规模和速度向其推进，并且在全世界推动社会经济的变革和发展，应从地方、国家、地区和国际各级层面对城市化加以利用。

Recognizing, the dynamic nature of living cities,

承认鲜活的城市动态特性。

Noting, however, that rapid and frequently uncontrolled development is transforming urban areas and their settings, which may cause fragmentation and deterioration to urban heritage with deep impacts on community values, throughout the world.

但注意到时常失控的、高速发展的、变化中的城区及其环境，可能正在导致全球城市遗产的分散化和恶化，对社区价值观产生深刻的影响。

Considering, therefore, that in order to support the protection of natural and cultural heritage, emphasis needs to be put on the integration of historic urban area conservation, management and planning strategies into local development processes and urban planning, such as, contemporary architecture and infrastructure development, for which the application of a landscape approach would help maintain urban identity.

考虑到要支持保护自然遗产和文化遗产，就必须强调把历史城区的保护、管理及规划战略纳入地方发展进程和城市规划中，例如，在发展当代建筑和基础设施时，采用历史城市景观方法有助于保持城市的特征。

Also considering that the principle of sustainable

考虑到可持续发展原则规定要保护现有资

development provides for the preservation of existing resources, the active protection of urban heritage and its sustainable management is a condition sine qua non of development.

源，而积极保护城市遗产及其可持续管理是发展的一个必要条件。

Recalling that a corpus of UNESCO standard-setting documents, including conventions, recommendations and charters exists on the subject of the conservation of historic areas, all of which remain valid.

忆及教科文组织为保护历史区域的问题而制定的一系列标准性文件，包括各项公约、建议书和宪章，所有这些文件仍然有效。

Also noting, however, that under processes of demographic shifts, global market liberalization and decentralization, as well as mass tourism, market exploitation of heritage, and climate change, conditions have changed and cities are subject to development pressures and challenges not present at the time of adoption of the most recent UNESCO recommendation on historic areas in 1976 (Recommendation concerning the Safeguarding and Contemporary Role of Historic Areas).

注意到由于人口结构变化、全球市场的自由化和分散化、大规模旅游、对遗产的市场开发以及气候变化等一系列过程，情况已经发生了变化，城市承受着发展的压力和挑战，这些压力和挑战在 1976 年教科文组织通过《关于保护历史或传统建筑群及其在现代生活中的作用的建议》时并不存在。

Further noting the evolution of the concepts of culture and heritage and of the approaches to their management, through the combined action of local initiatives and international meetings, which have been useful in guiding policies and practices worldwide.

还注意到通过地方倡议和国际会议的联合行动，文化和遗产的概念及其管理方式都发生了变化，这些地方倡议和国际会议有益于指导世界各地的政策和实践用。

Desiring to supplement and extend the application of the standards and principles laid down in existing international instruments.

希望补充和拓展现有国际文件中标准和原则的适用范围。

Having before it proposals concerning the historic urban landscape as an approach to urban heritage conservation, which appear on the agenda of the 36th session of the General Conference as item 8.1, *having decided* at its 35th session that this issue should be addressed by means of a recommendation to Member States,

收到了第三十五届会议上向缔约国提出的“关于把历史城镇景观作为城市遗产保护方法的建议”，该建议书在第三十六届会议的 8.1 议程项目中通过并进行处理。

1. *Adopts*, this 10th day of November 2011, the present Recommendation on the Historic Urban Landscape;

1. 兹于 2011 年 11 月 10 日通过了《关于历史城市景观的建议书》；

2. *Recommends* that Member States adopt the appropriate legislative institutional framework and measures, with a view to applying the principles and norms set out in this Recommendation in the territories under their jurisdiction;

2. 建议缔约国采纳适当的法律框架和措施，以期在其辖区内执行本《建议书》中确立的原则和标准；

3. *Also recommends* that Member States bring this Recommendation to the attention of the local, national and regional authorities, and of institutions, services or bodies and associations concerned with the safeguarding, conservation and management of historic urban areas and their wider geographical settings.

3. 还建议缔约国要求地方、国家和地区当局及有关保护、维护和管理历史城区及其广泛地理环境的机构、部门、社团及协会，重视本《建议书》。

Introduction

引言

1. Our time is witness to the largest human migration in history. More than half of the world's population now lives in urban areas. Urban areas are increasingly important as engines of growth and as centers of innovation and creativity; they provide opportunities for employment and education and respond to people's evolving needs and aspirations.

1. 我们的时代见证了历史上大规模的人类迁徙。如今，全世界超过一半的人口生活在城市地区。作为发展的动力、创新和创造的中心，城市地区变得越来越重要；城市提供的就业和教育机会，满足人们逐步进化的需求和向往。

2. Rapid and uncontrolled urbanization, however, may frequently result in social and spatial fragmentation and in a drastic deterioration of the quality of the urban environment and of the surrounding rural areas. Notably, this may be due to excessive building density, standardized and monotonous buildings, loss of public space and amenities, inadequate infrastructure, debilitating poverty, social isolation, and an increasing risk of climate-related disasters.

2. 然而，无节制的快速城市化进程常常导致社会和空间的四分五裂、城市及周边田园环境的急剧恶化。显然，造成恶化的原因可能是建筑物密度过大、建筑物趋向标准化、单调化、缺少公共场所、缺乏便利设施、基础设施不足、严重的贫困现象、社会隔离及气候灾害风险因素增加等。

3. Urban heritage, including its tangible and

3. 在提高城区的宜居性、在不断变化的全

intangible components, constitutes a key resource in enhancing the live ability of urban areas, and fosters economic development and social cohesion in a changing global environment. As the future of humanity hinges on the effective planning and management of resources, conservation has become a strategy to achieve a balance between urban growth and quality of life on a sustainable basis.

球环境中促进经济发展和社会融合方面，城镇遗产（包括有形遗产和无形遗产），是一种重要的资源。由于人类的未来取决于有效的规划和资源管理，城市遗产保护成为在可持续的基础上，实现保持城市发展与生活质量之间平衡的战略。

4. In the course of the past half century, urban heritage conservation has emerged as an important sector of public policy worldwide. It is a response to the need to preserve shared values and to benefit from the legacy of history. However, the shift from an emphasis on architectural monuments primarily towards a broader recognition of the importance of the social, cultural and economic processes in the conservation of urban values, should be matched by a drive to adapt the existing policies and to create new tools to address this vision.

4. 在过去的半个世纪里，城镇遗产保护成为全世界公共政策的重要部分，满足了维护共同价值观和从历史遗存中获益的需要。然而，维护城市价值时要转变观念，不仅要强调建筑遗址，还要更广泛地承认其在社会、文化和经济进程中的重要作用，需要努力调整现行政策，并为实现城市遗产保护的理念创造新的工具。

5. This Recommendation addresses the need to better integrate and frame urban heritage conservation strategies within the larger goals of overall sustainable development, in order to support public and private actions aimed at preserving and enhancing the quality of the human environment. It suggests a landscape approach for identifying, conserving and managing historic areas within their broader urban contexts, by considering the interrelationships of their physical forms, their spatial organization and connection, their natural features and settings, and their social, cultural and economic values.

5.《建议书》提到要更好地设计城镇遗产保护战略，并将其纳入可持续发展的更广泛的整体目标内，以支持旨在维持和改善人类环境质量的政府行动和私人行动。《建议书》通过考虑城市遗产的自然形状、空间布局的组织和联系、自然特征和环境，以及社会、文化和经济价值的相互联系，为在城市大背景下识别、保护和管理历史区域提出了一种景观方法。

6. This approach addresses the policy, governance and management concerns involving a variety of stakeholders, including local, national, regional, international, public and private actors in the urban development process.

6. 这一方法涉及政策、治理和管理方面要关心的问题，包括各利益相关者，包括地方、国家、地区、国际各级参与城市发展进程的政府和私人行动者。

7. This Recommendation builds upon the four previous UNESCO recommendations concerning heritage preservation, and recognizes the importance and the validity of their concepts and principles in the history and practice of conservation. In addition, modern conservation conventions and charters address the many dimensions of cultural and natural heritage, and constitute the foundations of this Recommendation.

7.《建议书》借鉴了以前教科文组织公布的四份与遗产保护有关的建议，承认其概念和原则在保护历史和实践中的重要性和有效性。此外，现代保护公约和宪章涉及文化和自然遗产的许多方面，为《建议书》奠定了基础。

I. Definition

I. 定义

8. The historic urban landscape is the urban area understood as the result of a historic layering of cultural and natural values and attributes, extending beyond the notion of 'historic centre' or 'ensemble' to include the broader urban context and its geographical setting.

8. 历史城镇景观是文化和自然价值及属性在历史上层层积淀而产生的城市区域，超越了“历史中心”或“整体”的概念，包括更广泛的城市背景及其地理环境。

9. This wider context includes notably the site's topography, geomorphology, hydrology and natural features, its built environment, both historic and contemporary, its infrastructures above and below ground, its open spaces and gardens, its land use patterns and spatial organization, perceptions and visual relationships, as well as all other elements of the urban structure. It also includes social and cultural practices and values, economic processes and the intangible dimensions of heritage as related to diversity and identity.

9. 上述更广泛的背景主要包括遗址的地形、地貌、水文和自然特征；建成环境，不论是历史上的还是当代的；地上、地下的基础设施；空地和花园、土地使用模式和空间安排；认知和视觉的联系；以及城市结构的所有其他要素。背景还包括遗产的社会和文化习俗、价值观、经济进程以及与多样性和独特性等无形遗产。

10. This definition provides the basis for a comprehensive and integrated approach for the identification, assessment, conservation and management of historic urban landscapes within an overall sustainable development framework.

10. 定义在一个可持续发展的大框架内，以全面、综合的方式，为识别、评估、保护和管理历史城市景观打下了基础。

11. The historic urban landscape approach is aimed at preserving the quality of the human environment, enhancing the productive and

11. 历史城镇景观方法旨在维持人类环境的质量，在承认其动态特性的同时提高城市空间的生产效用和可持续利用，以及促进社会和功

sustainable use of urban spaces, while recognizing their dynamic character, and promoting social and functional diversity. It integrates the goals of urban heritage conservation and those of social and economic development. It is rooted in a balanced and sustainable relationship between the urban and natural environment, between the needs of present and future generations and the legacy from the past.

能方面的多样性。该方法结合了城镇遗产保护目标与社会和经济发展目标，根植于在城市环境与自然环境之间、今世后代的需要与历史遗产之间的、平衡而可持续的关系。

12. The historic urban landscape approach considers cultural diversity and creativity as key assets for human, social and economic development, and provides tools to manage physical and social transformations and to ensure that contemporary interventions are harmoniously integrated with heritage in a historic setting and take into account regional contexts.

12. 历史城镇景观方法将文化多样性和创造力看作是促进人类发展、社会发展和经济发展的重要资产，它考虑地区环境，并提供了一种工具，用于管理自然和社会方面的变化，确保当代干预行动与历史背景下的遗产和谐地结合。

13. The historic urban landscape approach learns from the traditions and perceptions of local communities, while respecting the values of the national and international communities.

13. 历史城镇景观方法在尊重国内和国际社会价值观的同时，也借鉴地方社区的传统和看法。

II. Challenges and opportunities for the historic urban landscape

Ⅱ. 历史城镇景观面临的挑战和机遇

14. The existing UNESCO recommendations recognize the important role of historic areas in modern societies. These recommendations also identify a number of specific threats to the conservation of historic urban areas, and provide general principles, policies and guidelines to meet such challenges.

14. 现有的教科文组织《建议》，承认历史城市区域在现代社会中的重要作用。这些《建议》还明确了历史城区保护面临的一些特殊威胁，并提出了应对这些挑战的一般性原则、政策和准则。

15. The historic urban landscape approach reflects the fact that both the discipline and practice of urban heritage conservation have evolved significantly in recent decades, enabling policy-makers and managers to deal more effectively with new challenges and opportunities. The historic urban landscape approach supports communities in

15. 历史城镇景观方法反映了一个事实，即城镇遗产保护之科学和实践在最近几十年里发生了显著的变化，使得政策制定者和管理者能够更有效地应对新的挑战和机遇。城镇景观方法支持社区在寻求发展和适应求变的同时，保留与其历史、集体记忆和环境有关的特征和价值。

their quest for development and adaptation, while retaining the characteristics and values linked to their history and collective memory, and to the environment.

16. In the past decades, owing to the sharp increase in the world's urban population, the scale and speed of development, and the changing economy, urban settlements and their historic areas have become centers and drivers of economic growth in many regions of the world, and have taken on a new role in cultural and social life.

16. 过去几十年里，由于世界城市人口激增、城市规模扩大和高速发展、不断变化的经济，使城市居住区及其历史区域在世界许多地区成为经济增长的中心和驱动力，在文化和社会生活中发挥着新的作用。

As a result, they have also come under a large array of new pressures, including:

因此，城市区域也承受着各种各样的新压力，包括：

Urbanization and globalization

城市化和全球化

17. Urban growth is transforming the essence of many historic urban areas. Global processes have a deep impact on the values attributed by communities to urban areas and their settings, and on the perceptions and realities of their inhabitants and users. On the one hand, urbanization provides economic, social and cultural opportunities that can enhance the quality of life and traditional character of urban areas; on the other hand, the unmanaged changes in urban density and growth can undermine the sense of place, the integrity of the urban fabric, and the identity of communities. Some historic urban areas are losing their functionality, traditional role and populations. The historic urban landscape approach may assist in managing and mitigating such impacts.

17. 城市发展正在改变许多历史城区的本质。全球进程对社区、城区及其环境的价值、对居民和用户的世界观和他们的现实生活产生了深刻的影响。一方面，城市化提供了能够改善生活质量和城区传统特征的经济、社会和文化机遇；另一方面，城市密度和规模增长等无节制的改变会损害地方感、城市结构的完整性、以及社区的特性。一些历史城区正在丧失功能、传统作用和人口。历史城镇景观方法可以帮助控制和减轻这样的影响。

Development

发展

18. Many economic processes offer ways and means to alleviate urban poverty and to promote social and human development. The greater availability of innovations, such as information technology and sustainable planning, design and

18. 许多经济进程提供了减轻城市贫困、促进社会和人类发展的途径和手段。信息技术以及可持续的规划、设计和建筑方法等新事物的进一步普及能够改善城市区域，从而提高生活质量。如果通过历史城镇景观方法进行妥善管理，

building practices, can improve urban areas, thus enhancing the quality of life. When properly managed through the historic urban landscape approach, new functions, such as services and tourism, are important economic initiatives that can contribute to the well-being of the communities and to the conservation of historic urban areas and their cultural heritage while ensuring economic and social diversity and the residential function. Failing to capture these opportunities leads to unsustainable and unviable cities, just as implementing them in an inadequate and inappropriate manner results in the destruction of heritage assets and irreplaceable losses for future generations.

服务和旅游等新功能可以在经济方面发挥重要的积极作用，增进社区的福利，促进对历史城区及其文化遗产的保护，同时确保城市经济和社会的多样性以及居住的功能。如果不能把握这些机遇，那么城市就失去了可持续性和宜居性，对城市不恰当和不合时宜开发会损毁历史城市遗产，给子孙后世造成不可挽回的损失。

Environment

环境

19. Human settlements have constantly adapted to climatic and environmental changes, including those resulting from disasters. However, the intensity and speed of present changes are challenging our complex urban environments. Concern for the environment, in particular for water and energy consumption, calls for approaches and new models for urban living, based on ecologically sensitive policies and practices aimed at strengthening sustainability and the quality of urban life. Many of these initiatives, however, should integrate natural and cultural heritage as resources for sustainable development.

19. 人类居住区不断地适应气候和环境的变化，包括灾害所导致的变化。然而，当前变化的强度和速度对我们复杂的城市环境构成了挑战。出于对环境，尤其是水和能源等资源消费的担心，在加强城市生活的可持续性和质量、重视生态的政策和措施的基础上，城市生活需要采取新的方式和模式。不过，应统筹考虑所有这类举措，把保护自然遗产和文化遗产作为促进可持续发展的资源。

20. Changes to historic urban areas can also result from sudden disasters and armed conflicts. These may be short lived but can have lasting effects. The historic urban landscape approach may assist in managing and mitigating such impacts.

20. 突发的灾害和武装冲突也可能改变历史城区。这些灾害和冲突过程可能是短暂的，但会产生持久影响。历史城镇景观方法可以帮助控制和减轻这样的影响。

III. Policies

Ⅲ. 政策

21. Modern urban conservation policies, as

21. 现有国际建议和宪章中所反映的现代城

reflected in existing international recommendations and charters, have set the stage for the preservation of historic urban areas. However, present and future challenges require the definition and implementation of a new generation of public policies identifying and protecting the historic layering and balance of cultural and natural values in urban environments.

市保护政策，为维护历史城区创造了条件。然而，为了应对现在和未来的挑战，需要拟定和执行一批新的公共政策，以识别和保护城市环境中的历史性积淀和平衡其文化和自然价值。

22. Conservation of the urban heritage should be integrated into general policy planning and practices and those related to the broader urban context. Policies should provide mechanisms for balancing conservation and sustainability in the short and long terms. Special emphasis should be placed on the harmonious, integration of contemporary interventions into the historic urban fabric. In particular, the responsibilities of the different stakeholders are the following:

(a) Member States should integrate urban heritage conservation strategies into national development policies and agendas according to the historic urban landscape approach. Within this framework, local authorities should prepare urban development plans taking into account the area's values, including the landscape and other heritage values, and features associated therewith;

(b) Public and private stakeholders should cooperate, inter alia, through partnerships to ensure the successful application of the historic urban landscape approach;

(c) International organizations dealing with sustainable development processes should integrate the historic urban landscape approach into their strategies, plans and operations;

(d) National and international non-governmental organizations should participate in developing and disseminating tools and best practices for the implementation of the historic urban landscape approach.

22. 应将保护城镇遗产纳入一般性政策规划和实践，或纳入与更广泛的城市背景相关的政策规划和实践。政策应提供短期和长期的平衡、保护与可持续性的机制。应特别强调具有历史意义的城市结构与当代干预行动之间的协调整合。尤其是，各方利益相关者负有下述责任：

（a）缔约国应按照历史城镇景观方法，将城镇遗产保护战略纳入国家发展政策和议程。在这一框架内，地方当局在拟定城市发展计划时，应考虑区域价值，包括景观及其他遗产的价值及其相关特征；

（b）公共和私营部门的利益相关者尤其应开展伙伴关系的合作，以确保成功实施历史城市景观方法；

（c）涉及可持续发展进程的国际组织应将历史城市景观方法纳入其战略、计划和行动；

（d）国内和国际非政府组织应参与制定和传播城市景观实施方法的工具，并采用城市景观的最佳方法。

23. All levels of government — local, regional, national/federal, — aware of their responsibility — should contribute to the definition, elaboration, implementation and assessment of urban heritage conservation policies. These policies should be based on a participatory approach by all stakeholders and coordinated from both the institutional and sectorial viewpoints.

23. 各级政府（地方、地区国家、联邦）应清楚自己的责任，为定义、拟定、执行和评估城市遗产保护政策做出贡献。这些政策基础方针应是所有利益相关者参与，并且在机构和部门间加以协调。

IV. Tools

Ⅳ. 工具

24. The approach based on the historic urban landscape implies the application of a range of traditional and innovative tools adapted to local contexts. Some of these tools, which need to be developed as part of the process involving the different stakeholders, might include:

(a) Civic engagement tools should involve a diverse cross-section of stakeholders, and empower them to identify key values in their urban areas, develop visions that reflect their diversity, set goals, and agree on actions to safeguard their heritage and promote sustainable development. These tools, which constitute an integral part of urban governance dynamics, should facilitate intercultural dialogue by learning from communities about their histories, traditions, values, needs and aspirations, and by facilitating mediation and negotiation between groups with conflicting interests.

(b) Knowledge and planning tools should help protect the integrity and authenticity of the attributes of urban heritage. They should also allow for the recognition of cultural significance and diversity, and provide for the monitoring and management of change to improve the quality of life and of urban space. These tools would include documentation and mapping of cultural and natural characteristics. Heritage, social and environmental impact assessments should be used to support

24. 基于历史城镇景观的方法，意味着应用一系列适应当地环境的传统工具和创新工具。这些工具，作为开发程序的一部分，需涉及不同利益相关者，包括：

（a）公民参与工具，应让各方面的利益相关者参与进来，并赋予他们确定其所属城区重要价值的权力，形成反映城区多样性的愿景，确立目标，达成保护遗产和促进可持续发展的一致行动。作为城市治理的一个动态组成部分，这些工具应通过借鉴各个社区的历史、传统、价值观、需要和愿望以及促进相互冲突的不同利益群体间的调解和谈判，为跨文化对话提供便利。

（b）知识和规划工具，应有助于维护城镇遗产属性的完整性和真实性。这些工具还应考虑到对文化意义及多样性的认识，并规定对变化进行监督和管理以改善生活质量和城市空间的质量。这些工具将包括记录、测绘文化特征和自然特征。应利用遗产评估、社会评估和环境评估，在可持续发展框架内支持决策工作。

and facilitate decision-making processes within a framework of sustainable development.

(c) Regulatory systems should reflect local conditions, and may include legislative and regulatory measures aimed at the conservation and management of the tangible and intangible attributes of the urban heritage, including their social, environmental and cultural values. Traditional and customary systems should be recognized and reinforced as necessary.

（c）监管制度，应反映当地条件，包括旨在维护和管理城市遗产的有形和无形特征如社会、环境和文化价值的立法措施和监管措施。必要时应承认和加强传统和习俗。

(d) Financial tools should be aimed at building capacities and supporting innovative income-generating development, rooted in tradition. In addition to government and global funds from international agencies, financial tools should be effectively employed to foster private investment at the local level. Micro-credit and other flexible financing to support local enterprise, as well as a variety of models of partnerships, are also central to making the historic urban landscape approach financially sustainable.

（d）财务工具，旨在能力建设和支持植根于传统的、能创造收入的创新发展模式。除了政府资金和来自国际机构的全球资金，应有效利用财务手段来促进地方一级的私人投资。支持地方事业的小额贷款和其他灵活融资以及各种合作模式，在财务方面对保护历史城镇景观方法的可持续性，具有重要作用。

V. Capacity-building, research, information and communication

V. 能力建设、研究、信息和传播

25. Capacity-building should involve the main stakeholders: communities, decision-makers, and professionals and managers, in order to foster understanding of the historic urban landscape approach and its implementation. Effective capacity-building hinges on an active collaboration of these main stakeholders, aimed at adapting the implementation of this recommendation to regional contexts in order to define and refine the local strategies and objectives, action frameworks and resource mobilization schemes.

25. 能力建设应包含主要的利益相关者：社区、决策者以及专业人员和管理者，以促进对历史城镇景观方法及其实施的理解。有效的能力建设取决于这些主要的利益相关者的积极配合，以便根据区域环境因地制宜地落实本《建议书》，制定和完善地方战略和目标、行动框架以及资源筹备计划。

26. Research should target the complex layering of urban settlements, in order to identify values, understand their meaning for the communities,

26. 应针对城市复杂的居住层次进行研究，以认定价值，理解其对社区的意义，并全面展示给游客。应鼓励学术机构、大学机构以及其

and present them to visitors in a comprehensive manner. Academic and university institutions and other centres of research should be encouraged to develop scientific research on aspects of the historic urban landscape approach, and cooperate at the local, national, regional and international level. It is essential to document the state of urban areas and their evolution, to facilitate the evaluation of proposals for change, and to improve protective and managerial skills and procedures.

他研究中心，对历史城镇景观方法的方方面面开展科学研究，并在地方、国家、地区和国际各个层面开展合作。重要的是翔实记录城区的状况及其演变，以评估改革提案，改进保护和管理的技能及程序。

27. Encourage the use of information and communication technology to document, understand and present the complex layering of urban areas and their constituent components. The collection and analysis of this data is an essential part of the knowledge of urban areas. To communicate with all sectors of society, it is particularly important to reach out to youth and all under-represented groups in order to encourage their participation

27. 鼓励利用信息和通信技术来记录、了解和展示城区组成部分及其复杂的层次现象。收集和分析这些数据是城区知识的一个重要部分。加强与社会各阶层进行沟通，尤其是青年和所有代表人数不足的群体的沟通，以鼓励其参与。

VI. International cooperation

Ⅵ. 国际合作

28. Member States and international governmental and non-governmental organizations should facilitate public understanding and involvement in the implementation of the historic urban landscape approach, by disseminating best practices and lessons learned from different parts of the world, in order to strengthen the network of knowledge-sharing and capacity-building.

28. 各缔约国、国际政府和非政府组织，应通过传播从世界不同地方汲取的最佳做法和经验教训，促进公众理解和参与实施历史城镇景观方法，以加强知识共享网络和能力建设。

29. Member States should promote multinational cooperation between local authorities.

29. 缔约国应促进地方当局之间的多国合作。

30. International development and cooperation agencies of Member States, non-governmental organizations and foundations should be encouraged to develop methodologies which take into account the historic urban landscape approach and to

30. 应鼓励各缔约国、非政府组织以及基金会等国际开发合作机构，考虑、制定历史城镇景观方法，并使其与城区的援助计划和项目相协调。

harmonize them with their assistance programmes and projects pertaining to urban areas.

APPENDIX

Glossary of definitions

Historic area/city (from the 1976 Recommendation)

'Historic and architectural (including vernacular) areas' shall be taken to mean any groups of buildings, structures and open spaces including archaeological and paleo-ecological sites, constituting human settlements in an urban or rural environment, the cohesion and value of which, from the archaeological, architectural, prehistoric, historic, aesthetic or socio-cultural point of view are recognized. Among these 'areas', which are very varied in nature, it is possible to distinguish the following in particular: prehistoric sites, historic towns, old urban quarters, villages and hamlets as well as homogeneous monumental groups, it being understood that the latter should as a rule be carefully preserved unchanged.

Historic urban area (from the ICOMOS Washington Charter)

Historic urban areas, large and small, include cities, towns and historic centers or quarters, together with their natural and man-made environments. Beyond their role as historical documents, these areas embody the values of traditional urban cultures.

Urban heritage (from European Union research report No. 16 (2004), Sustainable development of Urban historical areas through and active Integration within Towns – SUIT)

附件

定义词汇

历史区域 / 城市（引自教科文组织 1976 年《建议书》）

“历史建筑区域（包括具有民间风格的）是指自然和生态环境中的任何建筑群、架构和空地的集合体，包括考古和古生物遗址，它们是人类在城市或农村环境中的居住地，其聚合力和价值从考古、建筑、史前、历史、美学或社会文化角度得到承认。在这些性质千变万化的“区域”中，特别是可以辨别的以下几类：史前遗址、历史名城、古老的城市街区、乡村和小村庄以及同类纪念性建筑群，把小心谨慎地保持纪念性建筑群的原貌作为一项规则。

历史城区（引自国际古迹遗址理事会，《华盛顿宪章》）

历史城区，无论大小，包括城市、城镇和历史中心或街区及其自然和人工环境。除了起着历史文献的作用，这些区域还体现了传统城市文化的价值。

城镇遗产（引自欧盟第十六号报告（2004 年）：通过积极整合城市内部实现城市历史区域的可持续发展 – 缩写 SUIT）

Urban heritage comprises three main categories:

A. Monumental heritage of exceptional cultural value;

B. Non-exceptional heritage elements but present in a coherent way with a relative abundance;

C. New urban elements to be considered (for instance):

• The urban built form;

• The open space: streets, public open spaces;

• Urban infrastructures: material networks and equipment.

Urban conservation

Urban conservation is not limited to the preservation of single buildings. It views architecture as but one element of the overall urban setting, making it a complex and multifaceted discipline. By definition, then, urban conservation lies at the very heart of urban planning.

Built environment

The built environment refers to human-made (versus natural) resources and infrastructure designed to support human activity, such as buildings, roads, parks, and other amenities.

Landscape approach (from the International Union for Conservation of Nature – IUCN, and the World Wildlife Fund – WWF)

The landscape approach is a framework for making landscape-level conservation decisions. The landscape approach helps to reach decisions about the advisability of particular interventions (such as a new road or plantation), and to facilitate the planning, negotiation and implementation of activities across a whole landscape.

Historic urban landscape

(see definition in paragraph 9 of the Recom-

城市遗产包括三大类：

A. 具有特殊文化价值的遗迹；

B. 并不独特但以相对连贯的方式呈现历史遗留的元素；

C. 应考虑新的城市要素（例如）：

• 城市建成结构。

• 开放空间：空地、街道、公共空地。

• 城市基础设施、重要网络和设备。

城市保护

城市保护不只是单个建筑物的保护。城市保护是把建筑看作整个城市环境的一个要素，把它作为一个复杂和多面的学科。顾名思义，城市保护是城市规划的核心。

建成环境

建成环境指的是用于支持人类活动的人造的（对应于天然的）资源和基础设施，例如建筑物、道路、公园以及其他福利设施。

景观方法（引自世界保护自然联盟和世界自然基金会）

景观方法是做出景观保护决定的框架。景观方法有助于明智决定具体的干预行动（例如新修道路或种植人工林），能够为整个景观活动的规划、协商和执行提供便利。

历史城镇景观

（见《建议书》第9段：定义）

mendation)

Setting (from the ICOMOS Xi'an Declaration)

The setting of a heritage structure, site or area is defined as the immediate and extended environment that is part of, or contributes to, its significance and distinctive character.

Cultural significance (from the ICOMOS Australia Burra Charter)

Cultural significance means aesthetic, historic, scientific, social or spiritual value for past, present or future generations. Cultural significance is embodied in the place itself, its fabric, setting, use, associations, meanings, records, related places and related objects. Places may have a range of values for different individuals or groups.

环境（引自国际古迹遗址理事会《西安宣言》）

遗产建筑物、遗址或历史区域的环境被定义为其直接环境和延伸环境，该环境是其重要性和独特性的组成部分，或是形成其重要性或独特性的原因之一。

文化重要性（引自国际古迹遗址理事会澳大利亚《巴拉宪章》）

文化重要性指的是过去、现在或未来的人类美学、历史、科学、社会或精神价值。文化意义蕴涵于地方本身，蕴涵于其结构、环境、用途、联系、含义、记录、相关地方和相关对象。场所，对不同的人或群体而言可能具有一系列的价值。

联合国教科文组织
《实施世界遗产公约愿景与战略计划》
Strategic Action Plan and Vision

Reflection of the Future of the World Heritage Convention

World Heritage 18 GA

Distribution Limited WHC-11/18.GA/11 Paris, 1 August 2011

Original: English/French

UNITED NATIONS EDUCATIONAL, SCIENTIFIC AND CULTURAL ORGANIZATION EIGHTEENTH SESSION OF THE GENERAL ASSEMBLY OF STATES PARTIES TO THE CONVENTION CONCERNING THE PROTECTION OF THE WORLD CULTURAL AND NATURAL HERITAGE

Paris, UNESCO Headquarters

7-9 November 2011

Item 11 of the Provisional Agenda: Future of the World Heritage Convention

第十八届联合国缔约国全体大会 WHC-11/18.GA/11

巴黎，2011 年 8 月

原文：英语或法语

巴黎，联合国教科文组织总部，第十八届《关于保护世界文化与自然遗产公约》缔约国大会

2011 年 11 月 7 日 – 9 日

第 11 项临时议程：《世界遗产公约》的未来

SUMMARY

In conformity with Decision 35 COM 12A (UNESCO, 2011), this document provides the Strategic Action Plan and Vision as developed by the World Heritage Committee through a working group established as a consultative body at its 33rd (Seville, 2009), 34th (Brasilia, 2010) and 35th (UNESCO, 2011) sessions respectively and was finalized subsequently by the Chair of the working group in cooperation with the World Heritage Centre.

概要

经过在第 33 届大会上（塞尔维亚，2009）世界遗产委员成立的一个作为咨询主体的工作组，以及 34 届大会（巴西利亚，2010）、和 35 届大会（联合国教科文组织，2011）的讨论，形成了 35 届大会的 12A 决议（联合国教科文组织，2011），最终工作组主席与世界遗产中心共同合作，完成了《战略行动计划和愿景》的终稿。

The Committee recommended furthermore that ‘the 18th session of the General Assembly takes

委员会建议“第十八届缔约国大会应将 WHC-11/35.COM/12A、WHC-11/35.COM/12B、

note of documents WHC-11/35.COM/12A, WHC-11/35.COM/12B, WHC-11/35.COM/12C, WHC-11/35.COM/12D and WHC-11/35.COM/INF.7C, as part of a summary of the work undertaken in relation to the reflection on the future of the Convention.' These documents are available at http://whc.unesco.org/en/sessions/35COM/documents/. All decisions on the 'Reflection of the Future of the World Heritage Convention' (35 COM 12A to 35 COM 12E) are available in the Decisions Report of the 35th session of the World Heritage Committee at http://whc.unesco.org/en/sessions/35COM *Draft Resolution: 18 GA 11*, see Point 11. Future of the *World Heritage Convention* WHC-11/18.GA/11, p.2

WHC–11/35.COM/12C、WHC–11/35.COM/12D、WHC–11/35.COM/INF.7C 等文件作为能够体现《公约》的未来工作的概要”。文件查询网址 http://whc.unesco.org/en/sessions/35COM/documents/。所有“关于《世界遗产公约》未来的反思”的决议（35 届大会文件 12A 至 12E）已收在世界遗产委员会 35 届大会决议报告中，查询网址为 http://whc.unesco.org/en/sessions/35COM：见 18 届大会决议草案 11，第 11 条《世界遗产公约的未来》WHC–11/18.GA/11, p.2

Strategic Action Plan for the Implementation of the World Heritage Convention 2012-2022

《2012–2022 年实施世界遗产公约的战略行动计划》

1. Our Vision for 2022

International cooperation and shared responsibility through the *World Heritage Convention* ensures effective conservation of our common cultural and natural heritage, nurtures respect and understanding among the world's communities and cultures, and contributes to their sustainable development.

1. 2022 愿景

通过《世界遗产公约》要求的国际合作和责任分担，将更有效的保护我们共同的文化和自然遗产，在全世界培育社区和文化之间的相互尊重和理解，同时也为可持续发展做出贡献。

2. Our Mission since 1972

To identify, protect, conserve, present and transmit to future generations the world's outstanding cultural and natural heritage (cf. Art. 4)

2. 1972 年以来我们的使命

自 1972 年以来我们的使命是认定、保存、保护、展示和传承世界杰出的文化和自然遗产（cf.Art.4）。

3. Our pledge to cooperation

Through cooperation, we seek: A sustainable environment in which States Parties are encouraged, supported and assisted by the international community to fully meet their obligations and enjoy their rights under the *World Heritage Convention.*

3. 我们合作的承诺

通过合作，我们追求：国际社会鼓励、支持和协助缔约国，在《世界遗产公约》的框架下可持续履行义务和享有其权利的环境。

Local, national and international communities,

地方、国家和国际社会，无论是现在还是

both now and in the future, which feel a connection to, engage with and benefit from the world's natural and cultural heritage.

将来，都将因为联系、参与了世界自然和文化遗产而获益匪浅。

A World Heritage List that is a credible, relevant and representative selection of the world's most outstanding heritage sites.

世界遗产名录是对世界上最杰出遗产可信的、有意义的和最具代表性的选择。

A World Heritage system which remains transparent, equitable, accountable and efficient in an ever-changing world.

世界遗产体系在不断变化的世界中依然保持透明、公平、负责和高效。

4. Our World Heritage Goals 2012-2022

Goal 1: The Outstanding Universal Value of World Heritage sites is maintained;

Goal 2: The World Heritage List is a credible selection of the world's most outstanding cultural and natural heritage;

Goal 3: Heritage protection and conservation considers present and future environmental, societal and economic needs;

Goal 4: World Heritage maintains or enhances its brand quality;

Goal 5: The Committee can address policy and strategic issues;

Goal 6: Decisions of statutory meetings are informed and effectively implemented.

4. 2012–2022 世界遗产的目标

目标 1：维护世界遗产的突出普遍价值；

目标 2：世界遗产名录是对世界上最杰出的文化和自然遗产的有公信力的选择；

目标 3：遗产的保护和保存应考虑到当前和未来的环境、社会和经济需求；

目标 4：维持或提升世界遗产的品牌质量；

目标 5：委员会应提出政策和战略议题；

目标 6：公布并有效执行法定会议的决议。

4.1 Background

The 1972 *Convention concerning the Protection of the World Cultural and Natural Heritage* has proved to be a remarkably visionary instrument for safeguarding the world's heritage. Following significant achievements over four decades, the context in which the Convention operates has changed and the very success of the Convention has led to an increasing scale and complexity of operations.

4.1 背景

1972 年《关于保护世界文化和自然遗产公约》，已经为保护世界遗产提供了非常有远见的方法。实施公约 40 年来所取得的重要成果使公约执行的背景发生变化，公约的成功实施使其范围不断扩大，操作也更为复杂。

This Strategic Action Plan seeks to ensure that the *World Heritage Convention maintains* its status as a credible international mechanism for the identification and conservation of the

《战略行动》计划旨在维持《世界遗产公约》作为认定和保护世界上文化和自然遗产这一值得信赖的国际机制的地位。寻求利用公约的优势，协助委员会适应新环境和最大限度的认定、

world's cultural and natural heritage. It seeks to use the strengths of the Convention to assist the *Committee* to adapt to a new context and maximise the identification, protection, conservation, and presentation of World Heritage and its transmission to future generations.

保存、保护和展示世界遗产并予以传承。

In 2008, the World Heritage Committee (Decision 32 COM 10) decided to reflect on nearly forty years of achievement. The *Futures Process* was characterised by its spirit of creativity, cooperation and open participation by all members of the World Heritage community.

2008年，世界遗产委员会决定（第32号决议）回顾了40年来的成就。世界遗产团体的全体成员认为《未来进程》的特征是创造性、合作精神和世界遗产社区所有成员的公开参与。

A website (http://whc.unesco.org/en/futureofthe convention/) enabled all States Parties to participate, including through submissions. A workshop on the Future of the *Convention* was held in February 2009 at UNESCO headquarters to identify global strategic issues, key challenges, trends and opportunities facing the Convention. The report of the workshop (WHC-09/33.COM/14A) was conveyed to both the World Heritage Committee at its 33rd session (Seville 2009) and the 17th session of the General Assembly. Resolution 17 GA 9 mandated priorities for action and called for this Strategic Action Plan. States Parties hosted expert workshops on mandated priorities. *The Strategic Action Plan for the Implementation of the World Heritage Convention: 2012–2022* was reviewed by the 34th (Brasilia 2010) and 35th sessions (UNESCO 2011) of the World Heritage Committee.

缔约国意见和建议可通过（http://whc.unesco.org/en/futureoftheconvention/）网站发表。有关《公约的未来》的研讨会于2009年2月在联合国教科文组织的总部召开，会议的议题包括全球战略、《公约》面临的核心挑战、趋势和机会。有关研讨会的报告精神在世界遗产委员会（WHC–09/33.COM/14A）第33届大会（塞尔维亚，2009）和第17届缔约国大会予以传达。17届大会上的决议9（17 GA9）确定了行动的优先权并呼吁实施《战略行动计划》。缔约国有权优先举办专家会议。世界遗产委员会在第34届（巴西利亚2010）和35届大会（联合国教科文组织2011）上审议了《2012–2022实施遗产公约的战略行动计划》。

4.2 Situation analysis

The submissions to and discussion at the February 2009 workshop on the Future of the *Convention* identified the following strengths and weaknesses and the perceived opportunities and threats to the implementation of the *World Heritage Convention:*

4.2 形式分析

2009年2月研讨会上提交并讨论了《公约的未来》，确定了《公约》优势和不足，以及实施《世界遗产公约》面临的机会和挑战：

STRENGTHS 40 years of operation ； An intergovernmental agreement with strong consensus; Near universal membership, including wide range of members from developing and developed countries.	WEAKNESSES Slow to enact change; Emphasis on inscription as an end in itself; Differing interpretations of the Convention, Outstanding Universal Value and management standards by States Parties, Advisory Bodies and the secretariat; Reduced technical basis for decision making; Increasing Committee, Advisory Body and secretariat workloads.
OPPORTUNITIES Part of the UN family and able to strengthen relations with other international instruments; Heritage as a driver for sustainable development; Able to improve structures, plans and practices for business; Can harness civil society support; New technology enables faster and more efficient awareness raising and knowledge sharing.	THREATS Pressure on budget from near universal membership and global economic slowdown; Emerging competitor organizations / lists and brand confusion; Political, economic, environmental and social pressures on heritage sites.

优势 已经实施 40 年； 具有高度共识的政府间协议； 会员国遍布全球，来自于发展中和发达国家。	不足 改变很缓慢； 遗产列入名录被作为最终目的； 缔约国、咨询机构和秘书处对公约、突出普遍价值和管理标准有不同解释； 简化了决策的技术基础； 增加了委员会、咨询机构和秘书处的工作量。
机会 作为联合国大家庭的一员，和国际上其他组织有很密切联系； 遗产成为可持续发展的动力； 能够提升业务结构、规划和实践； 可以获得公众的支持； 新技术使保护意识和知识共享更快速、有效。	挑战 会员国受到财政压力和全球经济下滑影响； 新兴竞争对手、组织的不同名录和品牌，造成混乱； 遗产地面临的政治、经济、环境和社会压力。

5 Revisiting the 5Cs

The Committee has set a number of key long-term strategic directions. These are encapsulated in the Strategic Orientations adopted in Santa Fe (1992) to mark the 20th anniversary of the Convention and the 'Cs' outlined in the Budapest Declaration on World Heritage (adopted in 2002 to mark the 30th anniversary of the Convention and reaffirmed and added to in 2007).

5 重新审视 5C 战略

委员会提出了一系列的长期战略方向。1992 年，在圣达菲举行的纪念《公约》实施 20 周年大会中采纳了包含“C”系列战略方针的《世界遗产布达佩斯宣言》（2002 年作为公约 30 周年的典型成果采纳，2007 年得到重新确认和采用）。

The Committee agrees that it is essential to:

委员会认为它是以下战略的根本：

Strengthen the credibility of the World Heritage List, as a representative and geographically balanced testimony of cultural and natural properties of outstanding universal value	Ensure the effective Conservation of World Heritage properties universal value	Promote the development of effective capacity building measures for the understanding and implementation of the World Heritage Convention and related instruments	Increase public awareness, involvement and support for World Heritage through communication	Enhance the role of communities in the implementation of the World Heritage Convention

增强世界遗产名录作为文化和自然遗产突出普遍价值的代表性和地理均衡性的公信力。	确保对世界遗产价值的有效保护。	提升和发展能力建设以便有效理解和实施世界遗产公约及相关条约。	通过交流，增强公众参与和支持世界遗产的意识。	提升社区在实施世界遗产公约中的作用。

Participants in the Futures process reaffirmed the primacy of the 5Cs, and also agreed to the need to update how they are implemented.

《未来进程》的参与者高度肯定了的“5C”，同时也同意在实施的过程中需要不断地更新战略。

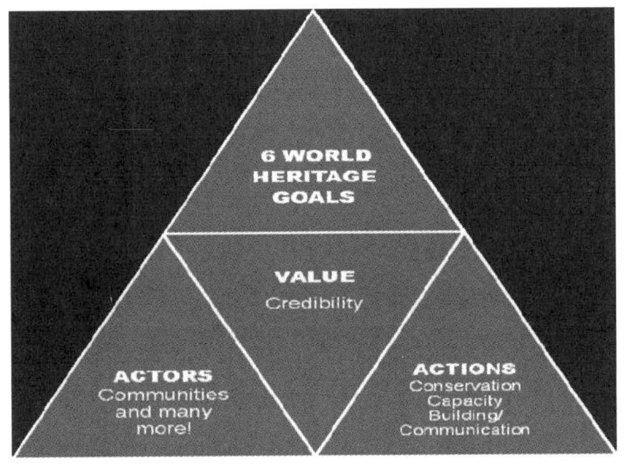

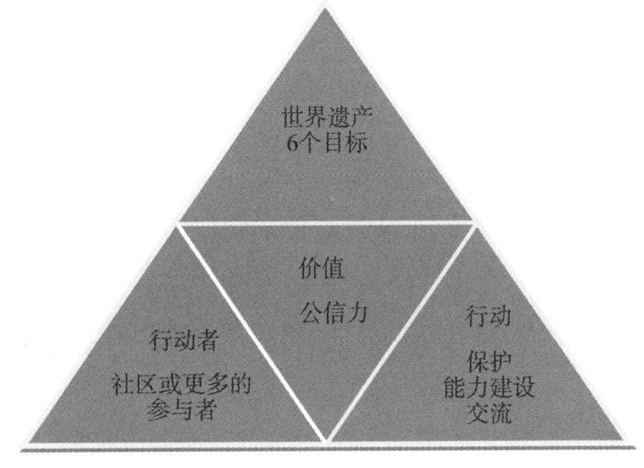

6 A Future value: The World Heritage system has ‘Credibility’

Credibility is the central quality or value that we seek for the World Heritage system as a whole and results from a renewed focus on conservation, awareness raising, engaging communities, building the capacity of all actors within the system and performing core functions efficiently and effectively. The desired reputation or identity of the *World Heritage Convention* — its credibility — was a key focus of the Futures Process.

6　未来的价值：作为具有“公信力”的世界遗产系统

公信力是我们整个世界遗产体系所追求的核心质量和价值，是我们重新注重保护、提高认识、让社区参与、提高所有行动者的能力以及高效和有效地履行核心职能的结果。《世界遗产公约》的声誉或身份——公信力——是《未来进程》的核心要素。

7 Future Goals: Defining priorities and desired outcomes

The Futures Process sought to assist in structuring the work of the Convention. It identified World

7　未来目标：确定优先权和预期成果

《未来进程》旨在协助建立《公约》的工作框架。在未来10年，它将通过确定世界遗产

Heritage Goals, priorities and desired outcomes to consolidate and build upon the existing strengths of the *World Heritage Convention* over the next ten years. Implementation arrangements, including time-frames, financial and human resources required, roles and responsibilities and indicators of progress are to be developed under an Implementation Plan.

目标、优先权和预期成果来稳固和增强《世界遗产公约》的现有优势。在实施计划的指导下，完成安排与实施时间框架、财政和人力资源需求、角色和责任等进程中的指标。

8. Future Actors: Engaging Communities

The *World Heritage Convention* is implemented through a wide and ever-expanding network of actors. Each has an important role to play in shaping policies, driving management practices, building capacity and expanding awareness of cultural and natural heritage. The traditional actors—States Parties, the Committee, Secretariat and Advisory Bodies continue to need encouragement, support and assistance to meet their obligations under the *Convention*, but it is also important to ensure that local, national and international communities feel a connection to, engage with and benefit from the world's natural and cultural heritage.

8. 未来行动者：社区的参与

《世界遗产公约》是通过广泛和不断扩展的行动者网络实施的。每一个行动者都是形成政策、推动管理实践、能力建设和提升文化和自然遗产保护意识方面的重要角色。应继续鼓励、支持和协助《公约》的传统行动者包括缔约国、委员会、秘书处和咨询机构继续履行他们的义务，确保当地、国家和国际社会感受到与世界自然和文化遗产的联系，参与世界自然和文化遗产的管理并从中获益。

9 Future Actions: Conservation, Capacity Building and Communication

The World Heritage system includes both core activities mandated under the *Convention* and what might be termed corporate or operational activities. The ongoing credibility of World Heritage relies upon maintaining the conservation of cultural and natural heritage sites, increased capacity building and improved communication.

9 未来行动：保护、能力建设和交流

世界遗产体系包括公约授权的核心活动和被称为合作或运作的活动。世界遗产持续的公信力依赖于保持维护文化和自然遗产，提高能力建设和增进交流。

Inscription on the World Heritage List is not the end of the process, but a part of the responsibility to ensure that World Heritage is effectively protected and managed for the benefit of current and future generations. There are clear synergies between this primary conservation task of the *World Heritage Convention* and sustainable development principles.

将遗产列入世界遗产名录不是进程的终点，而是确保世界遗产得到有效的保护和管理，造福于今世后代。在主要的保护任务和可持续发展原则之间，世界遗产名录有很明显的协同作用。

Conservation and communication are complementary tasks. For World Heritage, increased awareness and knowledge of World Heritage objectives can increase commitment to conserve, engage with and support cultural and natural heritage sites. Each World Heritage property communicates the value and quality of the *World Heritage Convention* and should operate as a standard bearer for other heritage places.

保护和交流的任务相辅相成。对世界遗产而言，深化对世界遗产目标的认识和了解，可以强化保护、参与、支持文化和自然遗产的承诺。每一个世界遗产都传达了世界遗产公约的价值和品质，应该成为保护其他遗产地的标杆。

The Future's Process emphasized the need for greater dialogue on Tentative Lists, the preparation of nominations, evaluation processes and inscription, as well as on conservation and monitoring activities. Similarly, there is a clear need to develop skills and knowledge on the implementation of the *Convention* to ensure a World Heritage system which remains transparent, equitable, accountable and efficient in an ever-changing world.

《未来进程》强调，需要在准备预备名录、准备申报文件、评估和列入名录过程、同时在保护和监测活动过程中进行更多的对话。同样的，也需要发展实施《公约》的技能和知识，从而确保世界遗产体系在不断变化发展的世界中，保持透明、公平、负责和高效。

Strategic Action Plan for the Implementation of the World Heritage Convention 2012-2022

	Priority	Outcomes
World Heritage Goal 1: The Outstanding Universal Value of World Heritage sites is maintained		
1.1	Statements of Outstanding Universal Value	Statements of Outstanding Universal Value are the basis for protection and management
1.2	Monitoring mechanisms	Focus monitoring mechanism and resources on critical conservation issues while allowing States Parties time to implement recommendations
1.3	Conservation requirements	Requirements for conservation of Outstanding Universal Value are implemented transparently and consistently
1.4	Training and research	Capacity needs of communities and agencies to address conservation are met, including those identified through Periodic Reporting
1.5	Mitigation of serious threats	Requirements for removal from the List of World Heritage in Danger or World Heritage List are clear and applied consistently
World Heritage Goal 2: The World Heritage List is a credible selection of the most outstanding world's cultural and natural heritage		
2.1	Strategy for Representative, balanced, and credible World Heritage List	Activities under the Global Strategy for a representative, balanced and credible World Heritage List reflect agreed priorities and are consistent with the Convention
2.2	Nominations	Inscriptions on the World Heritage List fully meet requirements set out in the Operational Guidelines

续表

	Priority	Outcomes
World Heritage Goal 3: Heritage protection and conservation considers present and future environmental, societal and economic needs		
3.1	Sustainable development	Increased consideration of sustainable development through connecting conservation to communities
World Heritage Goal 4: World Heritage maintains or enhances its brand quality		
4.1	Awareness raising	World Heritage is widely recognized as the highest standard of heritage and conservation
4.2	Publie image	World heritage value, credibility and quality widely know and under stood.
World Heritage Goal 5: The Committee can address policy and strategic issues		
5.1	Inclusive and systematic policy development	Time is allowed to address strategic and policy issues in a consultative and systematic manner
5.2	Coordination with related instruments	Increased synergy with UNESCO's broader objectives and programmes and other relevant international instruments
World Heritage Goal 6: Decisions of statutory meetings are informed and effectively implemented		
6.1	Decision making	Decisions are informed, consistent and implemented
6.2	Workload	Reduced workload while maintaining quality
6.3	Secretariat support	Strengthened secretariat support to the Committee
6.4	Budget	Decisions are costed, reporting considers all sources of funding and funding reflects agreed priorities
6.5	Implementation Plan	Actions under the Strategic Action Plan are linked to priorities and available budget, and outcomes monitored and reviewed

实施世界遗产公约 2012–2022 战略行动计划

	优先权	成果
世界遗产目标 1：维持世界遗产的突出普遍价值		
1.1	突出普遍价值声明	突出普遍价值声明是保护和管理遗产的基础。
1.2	监测机制	把监测机制和资源重点放在关键的保护问题上，允许缔约国有时间实现承诺。
1.3	保护要求	保护突出普遍价值的要求应得到透明、一致的实施。
1.4	培训和研究	社区和机构的保护能力应达到需求，包括定期报告中确定的需求。
1.5	削弱、降低严重威胁的影响	从《世界遗产名录》或《濒危世界遗产名录》中除名的要求需清晰和一致。
世界遗产目标 2：世界遗产名录是世界上最杰出文化和自然遗产的可信选择。		
2.1	具有代表性、平衡性和公信力的世界遗产名录战略	根据具有代表性、平衡性和公信力世界遗产名录全球战略开展的活动，反映了商定的优先权，与《公约》相符。
2.2	申报	列入世界遗产名录的遗产需完全满足《操作指南》中所提出的要求。

续表

	优先权	成果
世界遗产目标 3：遗产保存和保护应考虑当前和未来的环境、社会和经济需求		
3.1	可持续发展	将保护责任与社区相联系，增加了对可持续发展的考虑。
世界遗产目标 4：维持或提升世界遗产的品牌质量		
4.1	意识提升	世界遗产是广泛公认的最高等级的遗产保护。
4.2	公众形象	世界遗产的价值、公信力和品质得到广泛认识和理解。
世界遗产目标 5：委员会应提出政策和战略议题		
5.1	兼容和系统的政策发展	有时间通过咨询和系统的方法，处理战略和政策议题。
5.2	与相关机构的合作	逐步加强与联合国教科文组织其他更多目标、项目和其他相关国际组织的协作。
世界遗产目标 6：法定会议决议的公布和有效实施		
6.1	通过决议	决议是公开的、贯彻始终的，并得到执行。
6.2	工作负荷	减小工作负荷同时保持质量。
6.3	秘书处支持	秘书处对委员会强有力的支持。
6.4	财政	计算决定的成本，报告中考虑所有资金来源，资金反映商定的优先权。
6.5	实施计划	战略行动计划下的行动与优先权和现有预算相关，监测和审查实施成果。

10 Implementation and review of the Strategic Action Plan

10 战略行动规划的实施和监督

This plan is a living document.

本规划是动态文件。

The World Heritage Centre, working with the Advisory Bodies, will develop an Implementation Plan to ensure the goals and objectives identified are realized, to be updated biennially. The Implementation Plan should include a business planning section to review the financial impact of proposed activities and to assess options for funding actions included within the Implementation Plan. It should draw upon inter alia:

世界遗产中心与咨询机构将联合编制一个实施规划，以确保实现既定的目标和目的，本规划每两年更新一次。实施规划应该包括业务规划章节以审核准备执行活动中的财务影响，并评估在实施计划中融资行为的期权。它应该包括：

• The Independent Evaluation by the UNESCO External Auditor on the Implementation of the Global Strategy for a credible, representative and

• 联合国教科文组织外聘审计师对《具有代表性、平衡性、公信力的世界遗产名录全球战略》和《合作保护倡议》（PACT）的执行情况进

balanced World Heritage List and the Partnerships for Conservation Initiative (PACT);

行独立评估；

• The World Heritage Capacity Building Strategy;

• 世界遗产能力建设战略；

• The Disaster Risk Reduction Strategy;

• 减少灾难风险的战略；

• The Policy on the Impacts of Climate Change on World Heritage sites;

• 气候改变对世界遗产影响的策略；

• The recommendations of expert group meetings held on:

• 推荐举办以下专家会议：

1. global state of conservation challenges for World Heritage properties;

1. 全球局势对保护世界遗产的挑战；

2. decision-making procedures of the statutory organs of the *World Heritage Convention*;

2.《世界遗产公约》法定机关的决策程序；

3. improvements to the 'upstream processes' prior to consideration of nominations by the World Heritage Committee;

3. 在考虑向世界遗产委员会提交申报文件前，优先推荐"上游程序"的水平；

4. the relationship between the *World Heritage Convention*, conservation and sustainable development.

4.《世界遗产公约》、保护和可持续发展之间的关系。

The role of the Advisory Bodies, through the provision of technical support and access to expert networks, will be central to supporting implementation of the Strategic Action Plan.

咨询机构提供技术支持、利用专家网络，是支持并执行《战略行动计划》的核心。

Outcomes against the Strategic Action Plan will be reported to the General Assembly of States Parties. This will ensure that activities undertaken under the framework of the Strategic Action Plan are linked to agreed priorities and budget allocations and will provide an opportunity for States Parties to retest Committee priorities, check progress and where necessary, revise priorities and the allocation of resources.

《战略行动计划》的执行成果要向缔约国大会汇报。在《战略行动计划》框架下，确保项目实施的优先权和预算分配，也可以给缔约国提供机会重新评估委员会的优先权、检查进程，必要时重新配置优先权和资源。

The Secretariat's annual report to the World Heritage Committee should also be adapted to follow this structure.

秘书处应按下面的框架向世界遗产委员会提交年度报告。

It is expected that the Committee will review the activities under each goal on a two-yearly

委员会计划在两年一次的基础上，检查每一个目标的活动进程，收集缔约国反馈的信息，

basis to receive feedback from members, discuss objectives and activities, set timeline for their implementation and ensure the highest standards of delivery.

讨论目标和活动，确定时间表并确保最高的执行标准。

11 Draft Resolution

11 决议草案

Draft Resolution 18 GA 11

决议草案 18 GA 11

The General Assembly,

缔约国大会

1. Having examined Document WHC-11/18. GA/11 and Document WHC-11/18.GA/INF.11,

1. 审议了 WHC–11/18.GA/11 和 WHC–11/18GA/INF.11 等文件；

2. Recalling Decisions 35 COM 12A, 35 COM 12B, 35 COM 12C, 35 COM 12D, and 35 COM 12E adopted by the World Heritage Committee at its 35th session (UNESCO, 2011),

2. 回顾了世界遗产委员会在 35 届大会上采纳的（联合国教科文组织，2011）35 COM 12A, 35 COM 12B, 35 COM 12C, 35 COM 12D 和 35 COM 12E 等决议；

3. Adopts the Vision and Action Plan and requests the World Heritage Centre to disseminate it widely;

3. 采纳了愿景和行动规划，并要求世界遗产中心广泛宣传；

4. Recalls the request by the 35th session of the World Heritage Committee to the World Heritage Centre and the Advisory Bodies to develop a draft Implementation Plan for consideration by the World Heritage Committee at its 36th session in 2012;

4. 回顾了 35 届世界遗产委员会要求世界遗产中心和咨询机构拟定的实施计划草案，并于 2012 年提交 36 届委员会讨论审议。

5. Welcomes the activities proposed by States Parties to the Convention for the 40th anniversary and encourages all States Parties and partner organizations to promote the anniversary and sponsor further events to reach out to the broader public;

5. 欢迎缔约国关于纪念世界遗产公约 40 周年活动的提议，鼓励所有缔约国和合作组织促进和赞助更多的周年活动，使更多的民众接触世界遗产。

6. Also requests that an updated report of activities on the 40th anniversary of the World Heritage Convention be included on the World Heritage Centre web-page and be provided for information to the World Heritage Committee at its 36th session in 2012.

6. 要求在世界遗产中心的网站上及时更新世界遗产公约 40 周年活动信息，同时向世界遗产委员会第 36 届大会（2012）提供相关信息。

国际古迹遗址理事会
《世界文化遗产影响评估指南》(2011)
Guidance on Heritage Impact Assessments for Cultural World Heritage Properties

Guidance on Heritage Impact Assessments for Cultural World Heritage Properties

A publication of the International Council on Monuments and Sites, January 2011

ICOMOS, 49-51 rue de la Fédération 75015 Paris, France

In collaboration with the World Heritage Centre

《世界文化遗产影响评估指南》(2011 年 1 月)

国际古迹遗址理事会出版

国际古迹遗址理事会,

49–51 rue de la Fédération 75015

法国巴黎

与世界遗产中心合作

Purpose

To offer guidance on the process of commissioning HERITAGE IMPACT ASSESSMENTS (HIAs) for World Heritage (WH) properties in order to evaluate effectively the impact of potential development on the Outstanding Universal Value (OUV) of properties.

目标

为有效的评估潜在发展对遗产突出普遍价值的影响,为世界遗产的遗产影响评估过程提供指导。

The guidance is addressed at managers, developers, consultants and decision-makers and is also intended to be relevant to the World Heritage Committee and States Parties. The concept of OUV underpins the whole World Heritage Convention and all activities associated with properties inscribed on the List.

指南适用于管理者、开发者、顾问人员和决策者,同时也适用于世界遗产委员会及缔约国。突出普遍价值的概念是《世界遗产公约》和所有有关遗产列入《世界遗产名录》活动的基础。

The World Heritage Convention, for the protection of World's Cultural & Natural Heritage, which came into being in 1972, recognizes properties of 'Outstanding Universal Value' which are part of the 'world heritage of mankind as a

《世界遗产公约》,即《关于保护世界文化和自然遗产公约》制定于 1972 年,认可具有"突出普遍价值"的遗产是"作为人类整体的世界遗产"的一部分,值得"保护和传承"。此类遗产被来自 21 个缔约国的代表组成的世界遗产委

whole' and deserve 'protection and transmission to future generations'. Such properties are recognized through inscription on the World Heritage list by the World Heritage Committee, which consists of representatives from 21 States Parties.

员会认可并列入《世界遗产名录》。

Their OUV is fixed by the World Heritage Committee at the time of inscription and since 2007 has been encapsulated in a Statement of OUV. OUV thus defines the thinking at the time of inscription and is non-negotiable. The World Heritage Convention is ratified by States Parties, who agree to conserve properties on their territories that are seen to be of OUV, and thus contribute towards protecting the shared heritage of humanity. This means that OUV needs to be sustained over time through the protection of attributes that are seen to convey OUV.

世界遗产委员会在遗产列入名录时，已确定了他们的突出普遍价值，自 2007 年以来，突出普遍价值成为遗产声明的一部分。突出普遍价值一旦确定就不可更改。缔约国批准《世界遗产公约》，保护其领土范围内遗产的突出普遍价值，为保护人类共同的遗产做出贡献。这意味着，为确保突出普遍价值的持久不变，就需要保护能够传递突出普遍价值的遗产属性。

World Heritage sites are thus single heritage assets with an international value that has been clearly articulated. Not everything within them contributes to OUV, but those attributes that do must be appropriately protected.

世界遗产地是能够清晰阐述国际价值的、单一的传统资产。并非遗产的所有属性都能体现突出普遍价值，但是那些体现突出普遍价值的属性必须得到适当的保护。

This guidance sets out a methodology to allow HIAs to respond to the needs of World Heritage sites, through considering them as discrete entities and evaluating impact on the attributes of OUV in a systematic and coherent way. The Guidance was developed following an international workshop organized by ICOMOS in Paris in September 2009.

这一指南制定了遗产影响评估的方法，使国际机构对世界遗产地的需求做出反应，将它们视为独立实体从而系统、连贯的评价对突出普遍价值属性的影响。该指南于 2009 年 9 月在巴黎国际古迹遗址理事会大会上制定。

Contents

目录

c) Tools, resources and capacities needed to undertake an HIA.

c）实施遗产影响评估所需工具、经费和能力。

2 Suggested HIA procedures

2-1 Introduction

2-2 Understanding what needs to be undertaken before starting an HIA

2 建议的遗产影响评估程序

2–1 简介

2–2 了解进行遗产影响评估前的准备工作

3 Data and documentation

3 数据和文档

4 Methods and approaches appropriate to the property — optimizing available tools, techniques and resources

4 适当的方法和途径——充分利用现有的工具、技术和资源

5 A defendable system for assessing/evaluating impact

5 评价 / 评估影响中的防范系统

6 Can impacts be avoided, reduced, rehabilitated or compensated — mitigation?

6 能够避免、减少、修复或弥补、缓解影响吗？

7 Deliver an evaluation that is helpful to States Parties, the Advisory Bodies and the World Heritage Committee, and relevant to the World Heritage context in general and specific properties in particular

7 提交的评估应对缔约国、咨询机构、世界遗产委员会、世界遗产相关背景以及具体遗产有帮助。

Appendix 1: Heritage Impact Assessment Process

附录 1：遗产影响评估的过程

Appendix 2: Scoping Report Contents

附录 2：报告的内容范围

Appendix 3A: Example Guide for assessing value of heritage assets

附录 3A：案例：传统遗产的遗产价值评估

Appendix 3B: Example Guide for assessing magnitude of impact

附录 3B：案例：评估影响程度指南

Appendix 3C: Example Inventory Entry

附录 3C：录入条目案例

Appendix 4: Heritage Impact Report Contents

附录 4：遗产影响报告书内容

1 Background

In recent years the UNESCO World Heritage Committee has addressed considerable numbers of State of Conservation Reports related to threats to World Heritage properties from various forms of large-scale development. These developments include roads, bridges, tall buildings, 'box' buildings (e.g. malls), inappropriate, a contextual or insensitive developments, renewals, demolitions and new infrastructure typologies like wind farms, as well as land-use policy changes and large scale urban frameworks. The Committee has also examined threats from excessive or inappropriate tourism. Many of these projects have had the potential to impact adversely on the appearance, skyline, key views and other different attributes that contribute to Outstanding Universal Value (OUV).

In order for the ICOMOS and the Committee to evaluate satisfactorily these potential threats, there is a need to be specific about the impacts of proposed changes on OUV. While heritage impact assessment exists in many countries, these seem less reliably used in the World Heritage context.

Where formal evaluations are undertaken, many of these make use of procedures for environmental impact assessment (EIA). Whilst there is merit at looking at the experience of EIA, this is not likely to be immediately useful without some adaptation. EIA frequently disaggregates all the possible cultural heritage attributes and assesses impact on them separately, through discrete receptors such as protected buildings, archaeological sites, and specified view-points with their view cones, without applying the lens of OUV to the overall ensemble of attributes. A more global approach to the site is required, one directly linked to the expression of the site's OUV.

1 背景

近年来，联合国教科文组织世界遗产委员会处理了大量的、有关各种形式的大规模开发威胁到世界遗产保护的报告。大规模的发展包括修建道路、桥梁、高楼、“箱体”建筑（例如购物中心）；不当的、盲目的发展、更新、破坏以及新的基础设施建设比如风力发电厂，还有土地使用政策的变化和大规模的城市建设等等。委员会还审查了过度的、不当的旅游威胁。其中大部分项目对遗产景观有潜在的不利影响，例如影响了遗产外观、天际线、核心景观等有利于展现遗产的突出普遍价值的属性。

为了让国际古迹遗址理事会和委员会圆满地完成对潜在威胁的评估，需要具体说明预期变化对突出普遍价值造成的影响。当前许多国家都进行遗产影响评估，但在世界遗产背景下，这些影响评估似乎都不可靠。

正式进行评估时，许多都是借用环境评估的程序。尽管环境评估的程序有可借鉴之处，但在没有调整的情况下尽量不要直接使用。通常，环境影响评估要分解文化遗产所有属性，并对各部分、个体要素例如受保护的建筑物、考古遗址、指定的特殊景观点及其视野等受到的影响分别评估，而不是评估突出普遍价值所有属性。对于遗址的评估需要一种全球化的方法，一种直接表达相关遗产突出普遍价值的方法。

EIA therefore often produces disappointing results when applied to cultural World Heritage properties as the assessment of impacts is not clearly and directly tied to the attributes of OUV. Cumulative impacts and incremental changes (adverse) may also more easily pass undetected. The recent work done to assess the impacts of the proposed bridge on the World Heritage site of the Middle Rhine Valley is an example of this problem.

当我们用环境影响评估的方法进行世界遗产评估时，因为影响评估方法与体现突出普遍价值的遗产属性之间没有明确和直接的关系，结果往往令人失望：容易忽略不利因素影响的积累和增量造成的改变。近期评估的莱茵河谷中游在建桥梁对世界遗产造成的影响，正是此类问题的一个例子。

Currently, there are limited formal tools for identifying receptors and for assessing impact and few examples of excellence for Heritage Impact Assessment (HIA) undertaken for cultural WH properties. However, progress in 3D virtual representations and digital tools open new means to operate HIA.

目前，用于确定评估受体和评估影响的正式工具十分有限，较好的世界文化遗产影响评估案例也屈指可数。然而，3D虚拟技术和数字工具的开发利用为遗产影响评估提供了新的方法。

a) World Heritage context within which HIA are undertaken World Heritage properties need to be seen as single entities that manifest OUV.

a）在世界遗产背景下进行遗产影响评估时，应把突出普遍价值作为一个整体。

Their OUV is reflected in a range of attributes, and in order to sustain OUV it is those attributes that need to be protected. Thus the HIA process needs to consider the impact of any proposed project or change on those attributes, both individually and collectively, rather than on a standard range of receptors.

遗产的突出普遍价值是通过一系列属性反映的，保护这些属性就是维护其突出普遍价值。因此，在遗产影响评估过程中，需要考虑实施任何的项目或变化对这些属性个体和整体所造成的影响，而不是只考虑标准范围内对受体的影响。

The development of Statements of OUV (So OUV) for all World Heritage properties, a requirement set out in the Operational Guidelines for the implementation of the World Heritage Convention (UNESC0, 2008) paragraph 154-5, should assist through setting out clearly the attributes that reflect OUV and the links between them. The examination of integrity and authenticity is also a useful starting point.

《世界遗产公约实际操作指南》（2008年，联合国教科文组织颁布）第154–155条明确提出，所有世界遗产都应该提交突出普遍价值声明，这样可以帮助我们清晰列出突出普遍价值的属性以及它们之间的联系。这一点也有助于检查遗产的完整性和真实性。

In terms of assessing the effect of any impact on OUV, concepts such as 'limits of acceptable change' and 'absorption capacity' are being discussed, although there is no consensus yet on the usefulness of these concepts, or on how to operationalize them. There is also no consensus on how to revive heritage value that has been eroded.

在评估任何因素对突出普遍价值的影响方面，对“可以接受的有限变化”和“吸收能力”等概念如何用于实践，目前还没有达成共识，对于如何恢复被侵蚀的遗产价值，也没有达成共识。

Numerous visual assessment tools have been adapted to the assessment of impacts of proposed developments on the OUV of various World Heritage properties, especially those located within dynamic urban contexts, but so far these have rarely been linked to a more in-depth assessment of impact on all the attributes of OUV. There are also new tools on recording and mapping intangible heritage and multiple layers of attributes that have not been exploited for use in WH properties.

许多视觉评估工具经过调整用于评估各类对世界遗产突出普遍价值，尤其是处于动态发展的城市环境中的遗产价值的影响，但目前为止，对遗址突出普遍价值所有属性几乎没有进行相关的、深入的影响评估。当前也有一些新的记录和绘制无形遗产及其多层次属性的工具，但尚未在世界遗产领域应用。

World Heritage properties are very diverse, as are the potential impacts. Although development of new tools is potentially useful, for the foreseeable future, impact assessment processes need to be able to access a variety of existing tools, without relying entirely on any one of them.

世界遗产的特性多种多样，潜在影响也很大。尽管开发新型工具可能会有用，但在可预见的未来，影响评估过程需要多种工具，而不是依赖于其中任何一个单一工具。

The 2nd cycle of the World Heritage Periodic Reporting should provide ICOMOS with a new data set relevant to this issue. The goal to have So OUVs for all World Heritage properties by 2012 will also be an important underpinning of the guidance provided by ICOMOS.

《世界遗产定期报告》的第二个周期应向国际古迹遗址理事会提供有关问题的新数据。2012年的目标是完成所有世界遗产的突出普遍价值声明，这也将成为国际古迹遗址理事会提出指导方针的重要基础。

b) The diverse regulatory, planning and management contexts

b）监管、规划、管理环境的多样性

Neither EIA nor HIA are mandated in many countries and there is often no national regulatory framework within which they can operate. The capacity of heritage authorities varies globally and

许多国家没有环境影响评估和遗产影响评估，也没有确保实施评估的国家监管规章制度。全世界遗产管理当局的能力不同，一些国家的政府机构中，遗产管理当局很弱势。一些国家

some are not strong within the national government structures. In some countries there are strong environmental systems that provide a basis for EIA, but the heritage elements (including World Heritage) are underdeveloped or non-existent. In others, HIA are undertaken but the identified 'triggers' for their use are often basic (usually in the form of lists of activities) or age.

虽然有强劲的环境体系作为环境影响评估基础，但是遗产元素（包括世界遗产）开发不充分或根本不存在。另一些国家，虽然实施了遗产影响评估，但实施的“诱因”，通常是基本的（通常是名录中所列活动形式）或阶段性的。

This guidance aims to support the use and influence of HIAs, even where there are few legal structures that support the EIA/HIA processes. Industry codes of practice should be influential in ensuring that HIA processes occur, and that the methods employed meet internationally recognized standards of practice. However, in many countries specific sectors considered to be of national interest are permitted to override EIA or HIA requirements.

虽然环境影响评估和遗产影响评估的过程少有法律结构支持，但本指南旨在支持、使用和影响遗产价值评估。行业规范的使用方法应当在实施遗产影响评估过程中发挥作用，且符合国际公认的规范。然而，许多国家为了国家利益而忽视了特定行业的环境评估与遗产评估要求。

Management plans for WH properties are potentially very important. They should be well anchored in planning arrangements at national, regional and local levels, and although embedded in national systems of protection in different ways, could be utilized more to define how change will be assessed.

世界遗产的管理规划是非常重要的。它们应该被视为国家、区域和地区级规划安排不可或缺的部分，以不同方式纳入国家保护体系中，这比定义什么样的改变需要进行评估更为有用。

The sustainable development of WH properties is extremely important, including the protection of OUV elements. If the management plan is sufficiently robust and has undergone a thorough consultation process in its development, it should be possible to implement cooperative approaches to potential problems within the framework of the plan. Potential threats should be anticipated in the management system in a property specific way — not 'one size fits all'. Conservation policies embedded in the management system may also be used as a measure to assess potential adverse impacts.

世界遗产的可持续发展包括保护突出普遍价值要素都很重要。如果管理规划稳健有效，并在规划制定过程中进行了充分的咨询讨论，那么可以在规划框架内采取合作式方法解决潜在问题。应以特殊方式预见管理系统中存在的潜在威胁，而不是“一刀切”。管理系统中的保护政策也可作为评估潜在不利影响的方法。

A large number of World Heritage properties do not have a well-functioning management system (for some even where there is a management plan). This is an underlying issue for many properties selected for State of Conservation reporting.

大部分世界遗产没有一个运行完善的管理系统（有些仅有一个管理规划）。这是许多缔约国保护报告中提及的一个根本问题。

c) Tools, resources and capacities needed to undertake a HIA

c）实施遗产影响评估所需工具、资源和能力

State of the art techniques are possible in many countries, but in many others, the levels of skills, knowledge and resources are quite basic. This guidance attempts to be applicable to all situations. The skills required to do a HIA, using modern IT based and highly technical tools are only held by a limited number of people. These can be very helpful, particularly in complex situations, but HIA should not depend on them. On the other hand, diffusion of new HIA tools should be encouraged when their efficiency is proven.

许多国家可以使用先进技术，但另外一些国家只有基础的技术、知识、资源。该指南试图满足所有情况。仅有少数人使用现代信息技术和高科技工具进行遗产影响评估。这些技术对实施遗产影响评估当然有用，特别是对于复杂的环境，但遗产影响评估不应当依赖它们。另一方面，新的遗产影响评估工具的功效得到证实时，应该鼓励新工具的推广。

In some cases, the level of analysis undertaken is very deep and expensive to produce but the outcome is difficult to understand and to operationalise. A key issue is identifying the optimum resources to get the job done, and not requiring more than is necessary.

在某些方面，所做的分析等级高、花销大，但分析结果却难以理解和运作。所以关键问题是确定完成工作所需的最佳资源，而不是占用资源越多越好。

Training of managers and staff at World Heritage properties and in the approvals agencies of all levels of government within a country will be important in order to ensure that the commissioning process for HIA is appropriate and that full and effective use is made of the output.

对世界遗产和国内各级政府审批机构的管理人员和工作人员进行培训非常重要，将确保遗产影响评估实施过程的恰当性和高效性。

The backgrounds and professional skills of those who conduct HIA are diverse, but training and capacity-building will often be needed. Single professionals cannot always do a total HIA — there is most often a need to bring together an HIA team with the specific analytical skills needed for a

虽然实施遗产影响评估人员的背景和专业技能各不相同，但是日常培训和能力建设必不可少。专业人士个人无法完成整个遗产影响评估，对特殊项目或特殊遗址，通常需要一个具有特殊分析技能的遗产影响评估团队。一些专业的环境管理机构可提供档案和其他工具。在

particular project or site. A number of professional environmental management institutions provide archiving and other tools. In some circumstance opportunities for partnerships could be explored.

一些情况下，应建立合作机制。

Although proposals for WH nominations should make sure adequate data and documentation are in place, and that realistic and relevant monitoring arrangements are in use, there is often a lack of baseline documentation.

尽管申报世界遗产时建议提供充足的数据和资料，也安排了实时的、相关的监测，但却常常缺乏基线资料。

Good documentation does not require a Geographic Information System (GIS), although this has been a powerful and useful tool where it is available. All approaches need to be systematic and follow rational guidelines.

好的资料并不需要借助地理信息系统，尽管这是一个强大且实用的工具。所有方法需要系统化且有合理的指导。

2 Suggested procedures for Heritage Impact Assessment

2 建议的遗产影响评估程序

2-1 Introduction

2-1-1 This section is intended to help to States Parties, heritage managers and decision-makers or others in managing their WH properties in circumstances where some form of change may affect the Outstanding Universal Value (OUV) of those sites. Change may be adverse or beneficial, but both need to be assessed as objectively as possible, against the stated OUV as reference point.

2–1 简介

2–1–1 本节目的在于帮助缔约国、遗产管理者、决策者或其他人，在遇到可能影响遗产突出普遍价值的变化时，管理遗产。变化可能是不利的，也可能是有利的，这些变化可能影响突出普遍价值，因此要进行客观的评估。

2-1-2 The guidance is a tool to encourage managers and decision-makers to think about key aspects of heritage management and to make decisions based on evidence within the framework of the 1972 World Heritage Convention. It is also designed to encourage potential developers or other agents of change to consider key factors at an appropriate time and at an appropriate level of detail. Heritage Impact Assessments (HIAs) may also be useful in the general management of cultural WH properties by collating

2–1–2 本指南是鼓励管理者和决策者在1972年《世界遗产公约》的基础上，考虑遗产管理的重要因素、做出合理决定的工具。同时也鼓励潜在开发商和其他的代理人，在适当时间和适当程度考虑关键环节的细节。在特定时间完成遗产影响评估，对整理一般文化遗产管理资料，也有一定的帮助。

information at a given point in time.

2-1-3 There are many ways of assessing impact on heritage assets, some formalized in law, some very technical and sophisticated, others less so. This guidance sets down some principles and options. But whatever route is chosen, the assessment must be 'fit-for-purpose' — suitable for the WH property and for the changes proposed, and suitable to the local environment. It must provide the evidence on which decisions can be made in a clear, transparent and practicable way.

2–1–3 有很多方法会影响遗产的评估，有些以法律形式，有些技术性强还复杂，有些比较简单。该指南规定了一些原则和选项。但无论选择哪种途径，评估必须"与目的相适应"，适合世界遗产及其可能的变化，并适应当地环境，能为清晰、透明和实践性的决策提供依据。

2-1-4 In any proposal for change there will be many factors to be considered. Balanced and justifiable decisions about change depend upon understanding who values a place and why they do so. This leads to a clear statement of a place's significance and with it the ability to understand the impact of the proposed change on that significance.

2–1–4 任何计划实施的项目都需要考虑很多因素。那些理解、重视地方价值及原委的人，方可为有关项目做出合理、平衡的决定。这就要求我们对这个遗产的重要性有清晰的声明，并有能力了解计划中的变化对遗产重要性的影响。

2-1-5 In the case of WH properties, their international significance is established at the time of inscription and defined as their Outstanding Universal Value (OUV). States Parties undertake to retain and guard this OUV through protecting and conserving the attributes that convey OUV. The Statement of Outstanding Universal Value (So OUV) which sets out why a property is deemed to have OUV and what the attributes are that convey OUV will be central to the HIA. Every reasonable effort should be made to eliminate or minimise adverse impacts on significant places. Ultimately, however, it may be necessary to balance the public benefit of the proposed change against the harm to the place. It is therefore also important to know who benefits from the proposed change and for what reasons. In such cases the weight given to heritage values should be proportionate to the significance of the place and the impact of the change upon it. WH properties defacto are seen to have global value and thus logically have a higher significance

2–1–5 对于世界遗产，它们的国际重要性，即突出普遍价值在申报时已经确定。各缔约国通过保存和保护能传递遗产突出普遍价值的属性来维持和保护突出普遍价值。该声明包括遗产为何具有突出普遍价值，哪些属性能够证明遗产具有突出普遍价值，而这些属性正是遗产评估的核心内容。每个合理可行的解决方案都应当尽量消除或减少不利因素对遗产价值的影响。最终，拟定的变化，要在公众获得利益和对遗产的破坏之间寻找平衡。因此，了解拟定变化的受益人和受益原因十分重要。在这种情况下，遗产价值的权重应该和遗产地的重要性及变化对遗产的影响成比例。事实上世界遗产被认为是具有世界性价值，因而从逻辑上来说比国家级或地方级别的遗产具有更高的重要性。

that national or local heritage value.

2-1-6 Where change may affect the OUV of a WH property, consideration of the cultural [and/ or natural] heritage attributes should be central to planning any proposal and should be presented early on in any general assessment (such as an Environmental Impact Assessment — EIA). Managers and decision makers should consider whether the heritage conservation needs should be given greater weight than competing uses and developments. A key consideration is the threat or risk to the WH status and this should be clearly addressed in the HIA report.

2–1–6　如果变化会对世界遗产的突出普遍价值产生影响，则关注文化、自然遗产的属性应该是所有项目规划的核心，应该在所有评估的早期提出（例如环境影响评估）。与竞争性发展利用相比，管理者和决策者应该更重视遗产保护的需求。关键是要考虑到对世界遗产状况的威胁或风险，这点应当在遗产影响评估报告中写明。

2-1-7 Where statutory environmental impact assessments apply, the cultural heritage sections must take account of this ICOMOS guidance where the EIA relates to a WH property. An HIA undertaken as part of an EIA in these circumstances is not additional to normal EIA requirements, but uses a different methodology which clearly focuses on OUV and attributes that convey that OUV. The HIA should be summarized early on in the Environmental Statement, and the full technical HIA report should be included as a technical appendix. The requirements should be made clear at the planning or scoping stage. ICOMOS and the World Heritage Centre will encourage States Parties to ensure that HIAs in line with this guidance are undertaken in line with best practice. Where cultural heritage sections of EIAs clearly do not focus on the attributes of OUV, they would not meet desired standards in managing change at WH properties.

2–1–7　法定的环境影响评估申请，如果涉及世界遗产，那么文化遗产评估的部分应借鉴国际古迹遗址理事会的这份指南。这种情况下，遗产影响评估是环境影响评估的一部分，而不是正常环境影响评估的补充，且使用的是不同的方法，更注重对遗产突出普遍价值及能表达其突出普遍价值属性的影响进行评估。遗产影响评估应当早于环境评估声明，完整的技术性遗产影响评估报告应当包括技术附录。应明确要求规划范围。国际古迹遗址理事会和世界遗产中心，鼓励缔约国确保按本指南进行遗产影响评估，并选择相应的最佳实践方式。如果环境影响评估中的文化遗产评估部分不重视对突出普遍价值及其属性的评估，就达不到世界遗产管理标准。

2-2 Understanding what needs to be undertaken before starting an HIA

2–2　了解进行遗产影响评估前的准备工作

2-2-1 The assessment process is in essence very simple:

• What is the heritage at risk and why is it important – how does it contribute to OUV?

2–2–1　评估过程本质很简单：

• 遗产面临的风险是什么，为什么重要？它如何展现突出普遍价值？

• How will change or a development proposal impact on OUV?

• How can these effects be avoided, reduced, rehabilitated or compensated?

• 拟定的改变或发展建议对突出普遍价值有何影响？

• 该如何避免、降低、修复或补偿这些影响？

2-2-2 The overall process is summarized in Appendix 1, but key elements include early and continued consultation with all relevant parties and agreement on the scope and expectations of the HIA before work commences. It is also important to identify possible negative impacts very early in the process, in order to inform both the development design and the planning process in a pro-active rather than reactive manner.

2–2–2　附录 1 中总结了评估的全过程，关键要素包括：与相关各方早期和持续的协商、工作开始前对遗产影响评估的范围和期望达成一致。在评估过程早期找出可能存在的负面影响同样重要，以便在开发设计和规划过程中积极主动，而不是被动应对。

2-2-3 The basis for management and decision making is a good understanding of the WH property, its significance and OUV, its attributes and its context. The Management Plan will often be the important first step in building an ability to have clear and effective impact assessments. Establishment of baseline data about the WH property and its condition is critical.

2–2–3　管理和决策的基础是很好地理解世界遗产、它的重要性和突出普遍价值、遗产属性和相关环境。管理规划往往是制定明确有效的影响评估极为重要的第一步。遗产现状是建立世界遗产基线数据库的关键。

2-2-4 The starting point for any heritage assessment, once an initial development proposal or change of use is identified, should be to set out the scope of work necessary for an HIA which will provide the evidence for decision making. Early consultation with relevant parties, including any affected community, is important. The HIA may also be useful in collating information about WH properties not otherwise easily accessible. HIA is a useful cooperative tool for all stakeholders.

2–2–4　一旦提出了初步的发展计划或改变方案，就应该确定必要的遗产评估范围，以便为决策提供依据，这就是遗产评估的起因。早期与有关各方（包括受影响的社区）的协商是评估的重要的部分。遗产影响评估对收集不宜获取的、与遗产相关的信息也有帮助。遗产影响评估是利益相关者之间最有效的合作方式。

2-2-5 A Scoping Report (or HIA brief) should be agreed with all relevant parties — the State Party, regional or local government, heritage advisers or managers, local communities or others as necessary. The scoping report should make it clear what is

2–2–5　研究范围报告（或遗产影响评估简短报告）应取得所有利益相关者——缔约国、地区或地方政府、遗产顾问或管理者、当地社区或其他必要相关者的认可。范围报告清晰确定了做什么、为什么做、怎么做、何时做及预期

to be done, why and how, when and what are the expected outputs. It is important to include an agreed calendar between all stakeholders and the development programme (Appendix 2)

效果。必须与利益相关者和项目开发商共同协商达成一致，确定时间表（见附录 2）。

2-2-6 The Scoping Report should provide an outline description of the WH property and set out its OUV. It should have an outline of the proposed change or development including the need for change or development, a summary of the conditions present on the site and its environs, details of any alternative development being considered, an outline methodology and terms of reference for the HIA. The methodology should include organizations or people to be consulted, determining, for example, who are stakeholders and who is part of a heritage community related to the site, details of the baseline information to be collected including methods and appropriate study areas, likely sensitive heritage receptors and proposed survey and assessment methodology. It is also important at this stage to identify whether the proposed development is within a WH property or within a buffer zone or within the setting of the property but outside both. A Scoping Report should be used to flag large or critical impacts — the full HIA Report can then assess any positive reaction in terms of the altered development.

2–2–6 范围报告应该包括世界遗产的概要，并阐述其突出普遍价值。还应该拟定改变和发展意向包括需求、遗产现状及其环境的概要、已考虑的替代发展的细节、遗产影响评估的方法概要和职权范围。方法论应当包括确定需要协商的个人或组织，例如，谁是利益相关者，谁是遗产地相关社区的组成部分。基础信息的详述包含方法和适当研究领域，如可能很敏感的遗产受体，提议的调查和评估方法。同样重要的是，在此阶段要确定：拟定发展实施的区域是在遗产区、缓冲区或二者之外的遗产景观范围内。范围报告应重点标记大范围或重要的影响因素——完整的遗产影响评估报告应可以评估任何开发和改变所带来的积极反应。

2-2-7 The Scoping Report should also give (as far as is practicable) a clear indication of what knowledge exists about the site and where lacunae exist— how good is the information base and what level of confidence may be placed on the assessment. This should be followed through in the actual assessment itself.

2–2–7 范围报告也应当明确指出（尽可能地）对遗产现有认识及对其缺陷的理解 ---- 基础信息库的准备情况如何，评估的可信度多高。这些应该在实际评估中贯彻到底。

2-2-8 It is not only big developments that need an assessment of impact. WH properties may also be vulnerable to changes of policy which could have

2–2–8 不仅仅是大型发展项目才需要作影响评估。世界遗产也可能因政策变化引发严重后果——例如土地用途改变、城市规划政策的

significant consequences — for example changes in land use and urban planning policies. Tourism infrastructure and increased visits may have unintended consequences. Major archaeological excavations could also adversely affect the OUV of properties, though possibly compensating by the gaining of knowledge.

变化等。旅游基础设施和游客量增长可能带来意想不到的后果。重要的考古发掘也可能对突出普遍价值属性造成不利影响，尽管会以获取知识为补偿。

2-2-9 It is also important at this stage to ensure that organizations or individuals undertaking the HIA are suitably qualified and experienced, and that their expertise matches the demands of the site, its material and intangible content, its OUV and the nature and extent of the proposed changes. Single professionals can rarely do a total HIA, and the composition of the HIA team — heritage professionals and all other necessary competences — is crucial: the team will need specific analytical skills for a particular project or site. Opportunities for partnerships could be explored. This may also bring benefits in terms of developing capacity for HIA, and in developing and sharing best practice.

2–2–9 在这一阶段，要确保进行遗产影响评估的组织或个人有适当的资格和经验，以及拥有与遗址、物质和无形内容的要求、与遗产突出普遍价值、性质和提出的修改程度相匹配的专业知识。专业人士个人难以独立完成完整的遗产影响评估，组成一个遗产影响评估团队——由遗产专家和具有其他专业能力的人组成——的关键是：对特定项目或遗产有特殊分析技能的团队。应该创造更多的合作机会以利于遗产影响评估的能力建设、发展和分享最佳实践经验。

3 Data and documentation

3 数据和文档

3-1 There are no agreed minimum standards for inventories, data review or condition surveys, though it may in due course be useful to define these. Such matters need to be proportionate to the property and its management needs. It is desirable that the HIA documentation stage is as comprehensive as possible, including developing an archive.

3–1 尚未商定关于调查清单、数据审查或状况调查的最低标准，尽管制定最低标准有利于评估过程。标准应与遗产及管理需求相适应。档案收集和梳理、包括建档阶段的遗产影响评估应尽可能全面。

3-2 For WH properties the core documentation is the Statement of OUV and the identification of attributes that convey OUV. Hence this guidance concentrates on identifying impact on attributes that convey that OUV. However, the HIA should collect and collate information on all aspects and attributes of the cultural heritage within the agreed study area,

3–2 对于世界遗产来说，其核心档案是突出普遍价值声明、确定能传达突出普遍价值的遗产属性。因此，本指南关注于对能传达突出普遍价值的遗产属性的影响。然而，对商定的文化遗产评估应当收集并整理相关要素和属性的资料，充分理解遗产的历史沿革、背景、环境、和其他适当的价值（例如国家的和地方性

so that the historical development of the property, its context, setting and where appropriate other values (for example national and local) can be fully understood.

的价值）。

3-3 It is useful, if not essential, to document and manage the collection of data. Assessment processes can be very lengthy and data sources may require periodic 'refreshment'. When data sources are in a state of flux or the timetable for assessment is lengthy, it may be necessary to agree a 'data freeze' so that the HIA team can compare like with like information.

3–3 对收集的数据进行归档和整理非常有用。评估过程可能非常漫长，数据资源可能需要定期“更新”。当数据资源不稳定，或是评估时间很长时，需要商讨“数据冻结”，便于遗产影响评估团队找到适宜的数据进行比较研究。

3-4 Inventories should be included in the HIA reports, as tables or gazetteers in appendices to the main text. Underpinning archives of material and information collected should be retained for future use and properly referenced, including location and accessibility. Good documentation does not require sophisticated techniques such as GIS or complex databases; it needs a common sense, systematic and consistent approach which is suitable to the needs of the property.

3–4 遗产影响评估报告应包括正文、附录的图表或地名表的调查清单。应当保存档案材料和收集的信息，包括存储位置和可访问性，以便日后使用或检索。好的档案需要满足遗产的常识性、系统性和一致性，并不需要像地理信息系统或综合数据库那样复杂的技术。

3-5 In more complex cases, more sophisticated approaches could be considered. However, the use of databases and GIS, or 3D-modelling, changes the way in which HIAs are undertaken. The systems allow assessment to be a far more iterative process, and as a result HIA can be more effectively fed back into the design processes. But this also allows for more 'what if' scenarios to be requested of the HIA team. The scoping report would need to set down the principles for this iteration so that the HIA team can work effectively.

3–5 情况复杂时，应使用更精细的方法。不过，使用数据库、地理信息系统、三维建模改变了遗产影响评估的方式。该系统通过反复运算进行遗产影响评估，从而为设计拟定变化方案的过程反馈信息。但是，这也要求遗产影响评估团队有更多的设想。应事先按反复运算的原则提出范围报告，便于遗产影响评估团队更有效地工作。

4 Methods and approaches appropriate to the property — optimizing available tools, techniques and resources

4 适当的方法和途径——充分利用现有的工具、技术和资源

4-1 The collection of information during HIA should consider all potential sources of data.

4–1 遗产影响评估，在收集信息过程中应当考虑所有潜在的数据资源。技术措施包括案

Techniques will include desk study or historical research, and site visits to check condition, authenticity and integrity, sensitive viewpoints and so on. They may include terrain modelling, or inter-visibility modelling to predict impacts on heritage assets. It is necessary to capture and explain in clear text evidence of both tangible and intangible heritage attributes, and wherever possible to relate the latter to the physical features which embody them.

头研究、历史研究和实地调查评估，真实性和完整性、敏感视角评估等等。应当通过地形模型、可通视模型等方式预测遗产的影响。找到并以文字说明所有有形和无形遗产属性的证据，并尽可能地让物质形态与其所蕴含的无形遗产特性相关联。

4-2 Field studies are also generally essential to ensure that the HIA is robust. Techniques should be linked to the development proposal and could include non intrusive evaluation or field testing by topographic survey, geophysical survey, virtual 3D scale models or more intrusive methods such as artifact collection, scientific survey, test pitting or trial trenching. In some circumstances the collection of oral histories or evidence may also be valid and useful.

4–2　实地调查研究是确保遗产影响评估有序进行的重要方式。与评估发展意向相关的技术包括非干扰性评价、实地地形勘测、测量、地理勘探、虚拟三维模型或其他非侵入式方法，如收集工件、科学调查、勘探或试掘。在某些情况下，收集口述历史或证据也有效且有用。

4-3 The data collection must enable the heritage attributes to be quantified and character rised, and allow their vulnerability to proposed changes to be established. It is also necessary to look at the interrelationship/s between discrete heritage resources, in order to understand the whole. There is often a relationship between a material aspect and an intangible aspect which must be brought to the fore.

4–3　收集数据必须量化遗产的属性并表现其特征，并确定遗产承受变化最大的能力。同时，为了全面了解遗产，有必要深入了解分散的遗产资源之间的相互关系。首先就要弄清楚有形和无形要素之间的关系。

4-4 Collection of information during the HIA is an iterative process which can often lead to the emergence of alternatives and options for the development proposal.

4–4　在遗产影响评估期间收集信息是一个反复运算的过程，常常需要准备替代或备选的发展计划。

4-5 Understanding the full meaning of the OUV of a WH property (and other values of heritage) is a crucial part of the HIA process. The

4–5　遗产影响评估过程的关键是理解世界遗产突出普遍价值的全部内涵（和遗产其他的价值）。对影响的总体意义（总体影响）的评价，

evaluation of the overall significance of the effect (overall impact) is a function of the heritage value and assessment of scale of changes and impact.

是对遗产价值和变化规模及影响程度的评价。

4-6 When describing WH properties, it is essential to start by describing the attributes of OUV. This is the 'baseline data' against which impacts must be measured, and includes both tangible and intangible aspects. A statement of condition may be useful for each key attribute of OUV.

4–6 在描述世界遗产时，最好从描述体现突出普遍价值的遗产属性开始。这是衡量影响的"基线数据"，包括有形和无形的各种要素。现状声明可能对每一个突出普遍价值的关键属性都很有用。

4-7 However, while the So OUV is an essential starting point, sometimes they are not detailed enough in terms of attributes to be directly useful to impact assessment work. Each property will need to be assessed and where necessary, the attributes may need to be more specifically defined during the HIA process.

4–7 然而，虽然突出普遍价值声明是重要起点，有时因为属性的描述不详细不能直接用于遗产影响评估工作。在评估过程中，每个属性都需要被评估，必要时可在遗产影响评估中更具体的定义属性。

4-8 Such definition of attributes should not seek to re-define the So OUV, but to describe the attributes in a way which assists decision-making on the proposed change. It should be noted that OUV is defined at the time a WH property is inscribed on the WH List and cannot be changed without a re-nomination which goes through a full evaluation process.

4–8 这种属性定义不是要重新定义突出普遍价值声明，只需要通过一种对属性的描述，协助决策即可。应该指出的是，突出普遍价值在世界遗产被列入《世界遗产名录》时就已经确定，不得改变，除非经过全面评估后需再次申报。

4-9 The production of location or themed maps or plan views is almost always needed to demonstrate the findings and issues raised. Spatial rendering is useful to show the disposition of attributes, the relationships between the attributes (which may be processes), and the associations attributes have such as visual, historical, religious, communal, aesthetic or evidential. It is necessary to link the attributes back to the components of the So OUV in a clear and readable manner, which does not oversimplify but retains cultural or other

4–9 生产地点、主题地图、规划意见总是用来说明调查结果和问题。空间渲染有助于显示属性的分布、属性间的关系（也可以是过程）或与属性相关的视觉、历史、宗教、社区、审美、证据等。必须用清晰可读的方式把属性与突出普遍价值声明联系起来，不过分简化，但在综述声明或表格中保持文化或其他复杂要素。然而，遗产影响评估团队不应过分依赖地图，人们对于一个地方的体验是立体的——需要根据遗产地面实际情况检查空间关系。

complexities in synoptic statements or in grams. HIA teams should, however, be wary of too much reliance on maps, as our human experience of places is in 3D — ground-truth is always required to check spatial relationships.

4-10 One option for assessing value is set out in Appendix 3A. In this system the value of heritage attributes is assessed in relation to statutory designations, international or national, and priorities or recommendations set out in national research agendas, and ascribed values. Professional judgement is then used to determine the importance of the resource. Whilst this method should be used as objectively as possible, qualitative assessment using professional judgement is inevitably involved. The value of the asset may be defined using the following grading scale:

- Very High
- High
- Medium
- Low
- Negligible
- Unknown

4–10 附件3A中提供一种价值评估的方法。在这一体系中，遗产属性的价值是根据法定名称、国际或国家的研究议程中确定的优先事项或建议以及已认定的价值进行评估，然后用专业判断来确定资源的重要性。为了能让评估尽可能的客观，不可避免的要用到专业判断的定性评估。遗产价值可使用以下的分级标准：

- 非常高
- 高
- 中
- 低
- 微不足道
- 未知

4-11 In the HIA Report there should be a clear and comprehensive text description of individual and/or groups of heritage attributes, which sets out their individual and/or collective condition, importance, inter-relationships and sensitivity, and possibly also an indication of capacity for change. This should be accompanied by appropriate mapping to aid the reader. All heritage elements should be included, but the components contributing to the WH property's OUV will be particularly relevant and may merit a further detailed section. A detailed inventory should be included in supporting appendices or reports so that the reader may check the assessment of each element. An example is included in Appendix 3C.

4–11 遗产影响评估报告应当用清晰而全面的文字，陈述遗产的个体或整体属性，其中含有个体或整体条件、重要性、内在联系和敏感度，如果可能，提供承受变化的能力的指标。可以通过适当的图表帮助读者理解。所有的遗产元素都应当包含在内，但应特别关注与世界遗产突出普遍价值相关的属性，需要做更详细的描述。详细的文本应有附录或报告支持，以便读者随时检索每个要素的评估。实例详见附录3C。

5 A defendable system for assessing/evaluating impact

5-1 Effects on cultural heritage attributes from development or other changes may be adverse or beneficial. It is necessary to identify all changes on all attributes, especially those attributes which give the property its OUV, on which this guidance concentrates. It is also important to identify the scale or severity of a specific change or impact on a specific attribute — as this combination is what defines the significance of the impact, otherwise called ‘significance of effect’.

5-2 There is sometimes a tendency to see impacts as primarily visual. While visual impacts are often very sensitive, a broad approach is needed as outlined in the ICOMOS Xi’an Declaration. Impacts take many forms — they may be direct and indirect; cumulative, temporary and permanent, reversible or irreversible, visual, physical, social and cultural, even economic. Impacts may arise as a consequence of construction or operation of the proposed development. Each needs to be considered for its relevance to the HIA.

5-3 Direct impacts are those that arise as a primary consequence of the proposed development or change of use. Direct impacts can result in the physical loss of part or all of an attribute, and/or changes to its setting — the surroundings in which a place is experienced, its local context, embracing present and past relationships to the adjacent landscape. In the process of identifying direct impacts care must be taken of the development technique of gaining approvals by just avoiding direct impact — impacts which just ‘miss’ physical resources can be just as negative to a single resource, a pattern, ensemble, setting, spirit of place etc.

5 评价、评估影响可控系统

5–1 开发或其他变化对文化遗产属性带来的影响有利有弊。本指南目的是必须确定所有属性上的所有变化，尤其是那些对遗产突出普遍价值有贡献的属性。同样重要的是，确定特殊变化对遗产特性影响的规模及程度或对特定属性的影响也很重要——因这个组合确定了影响的重要性，即所谓的“影响的重要性”。

5–2 有一种倾向认为主要对视觉有影响。因为视觉影响很敏感，在国际古迹遗址理事会的《西安宣言》中提到了广义的方法。影响有很多种形式——直接、间接、累积的、短期或长期的，可逆和不可逆、视觉的、物质的、社会和文化、甚至是经济的影响。影响可体现在拟定方案的实施过程、运营中。每种影响都要考虑与遗产影响评估的关系。

5–3 直接影响是拟定发展或改变用途所产生的主要结果。直接影响可能会造成遗产部分或整体属性的有形损失，改变了它的环境——历史形成的周边环境、地方文脉、现今和过去与相邻环境的联系。在确定直接影响的过程中，必须注意用获得批准的开发技术来避免直接影响——“缺少”物质资源可能对个体资源、模式、组合、环境、地区精神等等方面有负面影响。

5-4 Direct impacts resulting in physical loss are usually permanent and irreversible; they normally occur as a consequence of construction and are usually confined within the development footprint. The scale or magnitude of these impacts will depend on the proportion of the attribute affected, and whether its key characteristics or relation to OUV would be affected.

5–4 直接影响造成的有形损失，通常是永久且不可逆转的；这种情况通常由施工造成，一般局限在发展范围内。这些影响的程度或规模取决于受影响的属性所占比例以及主要特征或与突出普遍价值相关的属性是否受到影响。

5-5 Direct impacts that affect the setting of an attribute may occur as a consequence of construction or operation of the development scheme and may have an effect some distance from the development. Assessment of impacts on setting refers to perceptible visual and aural (noise) effects that can be appreciated at a given time. Such impacts may be temporary or permanent, reversible or irreversible depending on the extent to which the cause of the impact can be removed. Impacts may also be transient where occurrence is sporadic or of limited duration, for example, related to hours of operation or the frequency of passage of vehicles.

5–5 对遗产属性的直接影响可能是发展计划的建设与运行的结果，并对开发有一定距离的影响。环境影响评估是指在规定时间内可感知的视觉和听觉（噪声）影响。这种影响可能很短，也可能永久，可能是可逆的，也可能是不可逆的，这取决于影响因素能否消除。影响可能偶然、瞬间发生，或在一段时间发生，例如，与操作的时间或车辆通行的频率有关。

5-6 Indirect impacts occur as a secondary consequence of construction or operation of the development, and can result in physical loss or changes to the setting of an asset beyond the development footprint. For example, construction of related infrastructure such as roads or power lines that are required to support the development. Facilitated impacts should also be considered which may be further actions (including by third parties) which are made possible or facilitated by the development.

5–6 间接影响是建设或开发的次要后果，是导致开发范围内物质实体损失或遗产环境改变的影响。例如，为开发而进行的相关基础设施的建设，如建设道路、电力线路等。还应考虑有利于发展的影响，包括可能促使第三方采取进一步行动造成的影响。

5-7 Scale or severity of impacts or changes can be judged taking into account their direct and indirect effects and whether they are temporary or permanent, reversible or irreversible. The

5–7 可根据影响是直接、间接、暂时性的还是永久性、可逆的还是不可逆的，来判断影响或变化的规模或严重程度。也应该考虑个别影响的累积效应。在不考虑遗产价值的情况下

cumulative effect of separate impacts should also be considered. The scale or severity of impact can be ranked without regard to the value of the asset as:

- No change
- Negligible change
- Minor change
- Moderate change
- Major change

影响及其程度可以分为以下几类：

- 没有变化
- 变化可忽略不计
- 小的改动
- 适度调整
- 重大变化

5-8 The scale or severity of impact can be ranked without regard to the value of the asset. This can be summarized for each attribute described using the following descriptors. As change or impacts may be adverse or beneficial, there is a nine-point scale with 'neutral' as its centre point:

- Major beneficial
- Moderate beneficial
- Minor beneficial
- Negligible beneficial
- Neutral
- Negligible adverse
- Minor adverse
- Moderate adverse
- Major adverse

5–8 可以不考虑资产的价值而对影响的规模或严重程度进行排序。描述每个属性的变化可以参考下列的术语。由于变化或影响有弊有利，这里分九个不同程度，以“中性”作为分界点：

- 高度获利
- 中度获利
- 轻度获利
- 有利处可忽略不计
- 中性
- 不利处可忽略不计
- 轻微不利
- 中度不利
- 高度不利

VALUE OF HERITAGE ASSET	SCALE & SEVERITY OF CHANGE/IMPACT				
For WH properties Very High-attributes which Convey OUV	No Change	Negligible change	Minor change	Moderate change	Major change
	SIGNIFICANCE OF EFFECT OR OVERALL IMPACT (EITHER ADVERSE OR BENEFICIAL)				
	Neutral	Slight	Moderate/ Large	Large/very Large	Very Large

遗产价值	变化 / 影响的规模或严重程度				
	没有变化	变化可忽略不计	小的改动	适度调整	重大变化
对于高度传达世界遗产突出普遍价值的属性	作用或整体影响的重要性（无论是不利的还是有利的）				
	中性	轻微	中度 / 大	大 / 非常大	巨大

For other heritage assets or attributes	SIGNIFICANCE OF IMPACT (EITHER ADVERSE OR BENEFICIAL)				
Very High	Neutral	Slight	Moderate/ Large	Large/very Large	Very Large
High	Neutral	Slight	Moderate/ Slight	Moderate/ Large	Large/Very Large
Medium	Neutral	Neutral/Slight	Slight	Moderate	Moderate/ Large
Low	Neutral	Neutral/Slight	Neutral/Slight	Slight	Slight/ Moderate

对于遗产其他价值或属性	影响的重要性（无论是不利的还有有利的）				
巨大	中性	轻微	中度 / 大	大 / 非常大	巨大
高大	中性	轻微	中度 / 轻微	中度 / 大	大 / 巨大
中度	中性	中性 / 轻微	轻微	中度	中度 / 大
低	中性	中性 / 轻微	中性 / 轻微	轻微	轻微 / 中度
可忽略不计	中性	中性	中性 / 轻微	中性 / 轻微	轻微

5–9 For example:

• Total demolition of a key building which is the main conveyance of OUV for a WH property to make way for a new road would be a major adverse effect or overall major adverse impact.

• Removal of a later road from the immediate vicinity of a key building which conveys OUV and which is not directly related to its OUV attributes would be a major beneficial effect or overall impact.

5-10 The table above is a summary to aid assessment of impact. The HIA Report will need to show the assessment for each OUV attribute — for example in a simple table—and demonstrate how the results for each individual or collective heritage attribute have been obtained. This should include qualitative as well as quantitative evaluation.

5-11 Proposals should be tested against existing policy frameworks and the management plan for the property and surrounding area. The compatibility of the scale, pattern, use, etc should be tested according to the attributes of the property that convey

5–9 例如：

• 为修新道路完全拆除一个突显世界遗产突出普遍价值的关键建筑，对遗产而言是一个重大不利影响或整体重大不利的影响。

• 移除一条后人所修、与突显突出普遍价值的关键建筑紧邻的道路，这与突出普遍价值属性并无直接关联，但对关键建筑或遗产整体产生了有利影响。

5–10 上面的汇总表格有助于影响评估。遗产影响评估报告需要体现对突出普遍价值每个属性的评估——例如：在一个简单的表格中——显示已获得的遗产每个各体或整体属性的评估结果。包括定性和定量的评估。

5–11 建议使用现有的遗产政策框架和周边环境管理规划进行测试。应根据传达突出普遍价值和其他价值属性测试规模、格局、用途等兼容性。也应测试诸如视线、建筑类型、体积、外观、沉降形式、功能用途和持久性等相

OUV and other assets. Issues such as sight lines, architectural type, volumes and surface appearances, settlement form, functional uses and persistence through time etc might be relevant. In all this, it is necessary to match the attributes of the development to the attributes of the site, so that development is complementary and even enhancing to the property.

关问题。所有开发的属性必须和遗产属性相匹配，这样才可以使开发与遗产互补，提升遗产价值。

5-12 Changes arising from developments must also be assessed for their impact on integrity and authenticity. The property should have baseline statements regarding integrity and authenticity at the time of inscription, or at the time the retrospective So OUV was undertaken [paragraphs 79-88 in Operational Guidelines]. The relationship between attributes of OUV, authenticity and integrity needs to be understood and needs to be shown to be understood in the HIA report. Authenticity relates to the way attributes convey OUV and integrity relates to whether all the attributes that convey OUV are extant within the property and not eroded or under threat.

5–12 必须评估开发变化对真实性和完整性影响。遗产在申报或回顾突出普遍价值声明时就有真实性和完整性基础描述 [操作指南第 79–88 段]。应该理解遗产突出普遍价值、真实性和完整性之间的关系，并体现在遗产影响评估报告中。真实性与遗产突出普遍价值的属性传达方式有关，完整性与传达突出普遍价值的属性在遗产区内的分布有关，不可受到削弱或威胁。

5-13 Benefits and dis-benefits — or adverse effects — must be very carefully considered. There are a range of benefits and dis-benefits, and the question of who receives the benefits (or misses out through the benefits) is important. Often the property itself and the associated communities do not receive the benefits flowing from development. Financial consequences of the assessment are also important and often directly influence decisions. The analysis must reveal rather than disguise these complexities. The conservation of the property should be counted within the benefits of a project, so that projects that are supportive of conservation can be weighted more than those that do not.

5–13 必须仔细考虑影响的利弊。影响利弊有一定范围，谁从影响中获利（或利益损失）是很重要的问题。通常遗产本身和相关社区并未从开发中获益。评估的财务结论也是很重要的，往往直接影响决策。分析必须揭示这些影响，而不是掩饰他们的复杂性。有利于遗产保护的因素应当列入开发项目，这样可以保证支持保护的项目所占份额更大。

6 Can impacts be avoided, reduced, rehabilitated or compensated —mitigation?

6 可以避免、减少、修复或弥补 – 缓解影响吗?

6-1 Impact assessment is an iterative process.

6–1 影响评估是一个需要反复的过程。数

Results of data collection and evaluation should be fed back into the design process for the development, or proposals for change or for archaeological investigation.

据收集和评估的结果应在开发设计过程、改革意向或考古调查中得到反馈。

6-2 Conservation is about managing sustainable change. Every reasonable effort should be made to avoid, eliminate or minimise adverse impacts on attributes that convey OUV and other significant places. Ultimately, however, it may be necessary to balance the public benefit of the proposed change against the harm to the place. In the case of WH properties this balance is crucial.

6–2　保护是对可持续改变的管理。一切合理的努力应该避免或减少对传达突出普遍价值属性和其他遗产属性的不利影响。归根结底，要平衡拟定变化带来的对公众利益和对遗产的破坏。对世界遗产来说，找到这个平衡至关重要。

6-3 HIA should include proposed principles and where possible proposed methods to mitigate or offset the effects of a development proposal or other agent of change. This should include consideration of other options for the development including site selection/location, timing, duration and design. The HIA should indicate fully how the mitigation is acceptable in the context of sustaining OUV, including the authenticity and integrity of the WH property. Available guidance in the Operational Guidelines on periodic reporting should be consulted to help this process.

6–3　遗产影响评估应包括建议的原则和可能情况下建议的方法，以减轻或补偿开发意向或其他代理人的变化造成影响。应包括考虑开发的其他选项，涵盖选址、地点、时间、期限和设计等。遗产影响评估应充分说明在维持突出普遍价值及其真实性和完整性的前提下，如何接受风险缓解措施。应当参照《操作指南》定期报告的有关指导完善整个过程。

6-4 It may be appropriate to undertake further consultation at this stage before finalising the HIA.

6–4　在确定最终的遗产影响评估之前应进行深入的磋商。

7 Deliver an evaluation that is helpful to States Parties, the Advisory Bodies and the World Heritage Committee, and relevant to the World Heritage context in general and specific properties in particular

7　进行有助于缔约国、咨询机构、世界遗产委员会的评估，并与世界遗产总体情况、特定遗产相关。

7-1 Appendix 4 sets out a guide to the contents of an HIA report. It is a matter of expert judgement, following suitable consultation and scoping to define exacted requirements.

7–1　附录 4 提供遗产影响评估报告的具体内容指南。须经过适当的协商和范围界定，确定严格的要求，进行专业的判断。

7-2 The HIA report should provide the evidence on which decisions can be made in a clear, transparent and practicable way. The level of detail needed will depend on the site and proposed changes. The Statement of OUV will be central to the evaluation of the impacts and risk to the property.

7–2 遗产影响评估报告是做出明确、透明和可操作性决策的依据。所需资料的详细程度取决于遗产地和拟定变化。突出普遍价值声明将是遗产影响和风险评估的核心。

7-3 The HIA report will need to show:

7–3 遗产影响评估报告需要有以下内容：

• A comprehensive understanding of the WH property and its OUV, authenticity and integrity, condition, context (including other heritage attributes) and interrelationships;

• An understanding of the range of impacts arising from the development or other proposal for change;

• An objective evaluation of those impacts (beneficial and adverse) on the heritage elements and in particular on the site's OUV, integrity and authenticity;

• An assessment of the risk posed to the retention of OUV and the likelihood that the property may be in potential or actual danger;

• A statement of heritage benefits which may arise from proposals including better knowledge and understanding and awareness-raising;

• Clear guidelines as to how impact can be mitigated or avoided;

• Supporting evidence in the form of a suitably detailed inventory of attributes of OUV and other heritage assets, impacts, survey or scientific studies, illustrations and photographs.

• 对世界遗产及其突出普遍价值、真实性和完整性、现状、环境（包括其他遗产属性）、内在联系的全面理解；

• 对拟定开发或其他改变造成影响范围的理解；

• 对遗产要素产生的影响（有利和不利），尤其对遗产的突出普遍价值、完整性和真实性要素的影响进行的客观评估；

• 对维持突出普遍价值潜在或现有的威胁进行影响评估；

• 可给遗产带来收益的发展意向声明，例如提高人们的认知、更好地掌握和理解知识；

• 如何减轻或避免不利影响的清晰指南；

• 提供支持性证据的清单，包括突出普遍价值和其他遗产属性、影响、调查或科学研究、插图和照片等。

7-4 The HIA Report will need to have a non-technical summary clearly setting out all relevant matters, a detailed text description and analysis and a text summary of the results of the evaluation of impact accompanied by tables to assist the reader.

7–4 遗产影响评估报告需要有一个非技术性的总结，清楚列明所有相关事宜，把影响评估结果做一份详细的文字说明、分析、附带表格，以帮助读者。

Appendix 1: Heritage Impact Assessment Process Stages of HIA

- Initial development and design
- Early consultation
- Identify and recruit suitable organizations to undertake works
- Establish study area
- Establish scope of work
- Collect data
- Collate data
- Characterize the heritage resource, especially in identifying attributes that convey OUV
- Model and assess impacts, direct and indirect
- Draft mitigation — avoid, reduce, rehabilitate or compensate
- Draft report
- Consultation
- Moderate the assessment results and mitigation
- Final reporting and illustration — to inform decisions
- Mitigation
- Dissemination of results and knowledge gained

附录 1：遗产影响评估的过程

- 初始开发和设计；
- 早期咨询；
- 遴选和招聘合格的组织承接项目；
- 确立研究区域；
- 确定工作范围；
- 收集数据；
- 校勘数据；
- 描述遗产资源特性，尤其是能传达突出普遍价值的属性；
- 直接和间接影响的模式和评估；
- 消除——避免、减少、修复或弥补影响的草案；
- 报告草案；
- 咨询协商；
- 修正评估结果和消除影响；
- 最终报告和插图——告知决定；
- 消除影响；
- 传播取得的成果和知识。

Appendix 2: Scoping Report Contents

At the outset of any proposed impact assessment it is desirable to agree the scope of the work needed so that the work is 'fit-for-purpose' and will enable decision to be made. Early consultation is essential.

附录 2：报告内容范围界定

在开始任何提议的影响评估报告工作时，应商定工作范围，以确保工作“与目的相一致”，也有助于做出决定。早期咨询至关重要。

The scope should be agreed with all relevant parties, including the State Party, regional or local government or its agencies, any statutory consults and local community representatives and the public. In some cases it may be also desirable to consult with the WHC or its advisers, ICOMOS or IUCN. The 'developer' is responsible for producing the scoping report.

工作范围应获得利益相关者的认可，包括缔约国、地区或地方政府或其代理机构、法定咨询机构和当地社区代表以及公众。在某些情况下，还包括咨询世界遗产中心及其咨询机构：国际古迹遗址理事会或世界自然保护联盟。“开发商”负责确定范围报告。

Its contents should include

报告内容应包括：

- An outline description of the proposed

- 概括拟定的改变或发展意向，尽可能的描

change or development, providing as much detail as is available at the time of writing;

述细节；

• A summary of the conditions present on the site and its environs, based on information collated to that point in time;

• 根据收集信息的时间点，编写遗产现状和周围环境的概要；

• The Statement of Outstanding Universal Value

• 突出普遍价值的声明；

• Details of how alternatives to changes are being considered;

• 考虑拟定变化替代方案的详细信息；

• Outline methodology and terms of reference for the HIA as a whole;

• 概括整个遗产影响评估方法和职权范围；

• The organizations/people consulted and to be consulted further;

• 已咨询的组织或个人，以及须进一步磋商的组织或个人；

• A topic by topic assessment of the key impacts of the development; this should include: -details (as known) of the baseline conditions; -consideration of the potential effects of the development where overall impacts or effects are not considered to be significant, a justification of why they should be 'scoped out' of the HIA; -where overall impacts are considered to be potentially significant, details of the baseline information to be collected (including methods and appropriate study areas), likely sensitive heritage receptors in particular those related to attributes of OUV and proposed survey and assessment methodology.

• 对开发中的主要影响逐一做专题评估，应包括：——已知的基线条件的详细信息；——考虑开发中潜在的、被认为不重要的整体影响和效果，提出他们被"排除"在评估范围之外的理由；——如果认为总体影响具有潜在的重大意义，则应收集基线资料的细节（包括方法和适当研究领域），敏感的尤其是与突出普遍价值属性相关的遗产受体，并提出调查和评估方法。

• A negotiated calendar covering the whole process, including deadlines for reporting and consultation.

• 整个评估过程的磋商日程，包括报告和咨询的最后期限。

Appendix 3A: Example Guide for Assessing Value of Heritage Assets

附录 3A：遗产价值评估的指导案例

HIAs for WH properties will need to consider their international heritage value and also other local or national values, and priorities or recommendations set out in national research agendas. They may also need to consider other international values which are reflected in, for example, international natural heritage designations.

世界遗产的遗产影响评估既要考虑它们的国际遗产价值、地方或国家价值，还要考虑国家研究议程规定的优先事项或建议。可能还需要考虑反映遗产的其他国际价值，比如世界自然遗产。

Professional judgement is used to determine the importance of the resource. The value of the asset may be defined using the following grading scale:

专业判断以确定遗产资源的重要性。遗产价值可以分为以下级别：

• Very High
• High
• Medium
• Low
• Negligible
• Unknown potential.

• 非常高
• 高
• 中
• 低
• 细微影响
• 潜在未知

The following table is not intended to be exhaustive.

下表并不全面。

Grading	Archaeology	Built heritage or Historic Urban Landscape	Historic landscape	Intangible Cultural Heritage or Associations
Very High	Sites of acknowledged international importance inscribed as WH property. Individual attributes that convey OUV of the WH property. Assets that can contribute significantly to acknowledged international research objectives.	Sites or structures of acknowledged international Importance inscribed as of universal importance as WH property. Individual attributes that convey OUV of the WH property. Other buildings or Urban landscapes of re-cognised International importance.	Landscapes of acknowledged International importance inscribed as WH Property. Individual attributes that convey OUV of the WH property. Historic landscapes of international value, whether designated or not. Extremely wellpreserved historic landscapes with Exceptional coherence, time-depth, or other critical factors.	Areas associated with Intangible Cultural heritage activities as evidenced by the national register. Associations with particular innovations, technical or scientific developments or movements of global Significance. Associations with particular individuals of global importance
High	Nationally-designated archaeological monuments protected by the State Party's laws. Undesignated sites of the quality and importance to be designated. Assets that can contribute significantly to acknowledged national research objectives.	Nationally-designated structures with standing remains. Other buildings that can be shown to have exceptional qualities in their fabric or historical associations not adequately reflected in the listing grade. Conservation Areas containing very important buildings. Undesignated structures of clear national importance.	Nationally-designated historic landscape of outstanding interest. Undesignated landscapes of outstanding interest. Undesignated landscapes of high quality and importance, and of demonstrable national value. Well preserved historic landscapes, exhibiting considerable coherence, time-depth or other critical factors.	Nationally-designated areas or activities associated with globally-important intangible cultural heritage activities. Associations with particular innovations, technical or scientific developments or movements of national significance. Associations with particular individuals of national importance.

续表

Grading	Archaeology	Built heritage or Historic Urban Landscape	Historic landscape	Intangible Cultural Heritage or Associations
Medium	Designated or undesignated assets that can contribute significantly to regional research objectives.	Designated buildings. historic (unlisted) buildings that can be shown to have exceptional qualities or historical associations. Conservation areas containing buildings that contribute significantly to its historic character. Historic townscape or built-up areas with important historic integrity in their buildings, or built settings.	Designated special historic landscapes. Undesignated historic landscapes that would justify special historic landscape designation. Landscapes of regional value. Averagely well preserved historic landscapes with reasonable coherence, time-depth or other critical factors.	Areas associated with intangible cultural heritage activities as evidenced by local registers. Associations with particular innovations or developments of regional or local significance. Associations with particular individuals of regional importance
Low	Designated or undesignated assets of local importance. Assets compromised by poor preservation and/or poor survival of contextual associations. Assets of limited value, but with potential to contribute to local research objectives.	'Locally listed' buildings. Historic (unlisted) buildings of modest quality in their fabric or historical associations. Historic townscape or built-up areas of limited historic integrity in their buildings, or built settings.	Robust undesignated historic landscapes. Historic landscapes with importance to local interest groups. Historic landscapes whose value is limited by poor preservation and/or poor survival of contextual associations.	Intangible cultural heritage activities of local significance associations with particular individuals of local importance poor survival of physical areas in which activities occur or are associated
Negligible	Assets with little or no surviving archaeological interest.	Buildings or urban landscapes of no architectural or historical merit; buildings of an intrusive character.	Landscapes little or no significant historical interest.	Few associations or ICH vestiges surviving
Unknown potential	The importance of the asset has not been ascertained.	Buildings with some hidden (i.e.inaccessible) potential for historic significance.	n/a	Little is known or recorded about ICH of the area

级别	考古	文物建筑或城市历史景观	历史景观	无形文化遗产或相关领域
非常高	具有国际公认的重要性，已列入世界遗产名录的遗址。 能传达世界遗产突出普遍价值的单个属性。 遗产对国际研究目标有公认的重要贡献。	遗址或建筑具有国际公认的重要性，已列入世界遗产名录。 能传达世界遗产突出普遍价值的单个属性。 其他具有公认的国际重要性的建筑物或城市景观。	景观具有国际公认的重要性，已列入世界遗产名录。 能传达世界遗产突出普遍价值的单个属性。 具有国际价值的历史景观，无论是否列入世界遗产名录。 保存完好的历史景观，具有非常好的连贯性、时间深度或其他关键因素。	国家登记过的无形文化遗产活动的相关领域。 与特别创新技术、科学发展或有全球意义的活动相关。 与全球重要性有关的特殊个体。
高	得到缔约国法律保护的，国家认可的考古遗址。 遗产质量和重要意义有待认可的遗址。 遗产对国际研究目标有公认的重要贡献。	国家认可的、依然存在的建筑。 建筑结构的卓越品质或历史关联性在世界遗产名录上未得到充分反映的建筑类型。 保护区内已有的非常重要的建筑。 未得到认可的、明显具有国家重要性的建筑。	国家认可的有杰出价值的历史景观。 未认可的、有杰出价值的景观。 未认可的具有高价值和重要性的景观，且有显而易见的国家价值。 保存完好的历史景观，显示相对连贯性、时间深度或其他关键因素。	国家认可的与世界重要无形文化遗产活动相关的区域或活动。 与特别创新技术或科学发展或具有国家意义的运动有关。 与国家重要性有关的特殊个体。
中	对区域研究目标有重要贡献的、得到认可或未认可的遗产。	得到认可建筑。具有卓越品质或历史关联性的历史建筑（名录外）。 保护区内对历史风貌有重要贡献的建筑。 历史城镇景观或建成区里历史完整性重要的建筑或构筑物。	得到认可的特殊历史景观。 未认可的历史景观中有特征值得得到认可的特殊历史景观。 有地区价值的景观。 保存完好的历史景观，有合理的连贯性、时间深度或其他关键因素。	得到地方认可的、与无形文化遗产活动相关的区域。 与区域或地区意义相关的、特别是与创新技术或科学发展。 与地区重要性有关的特殊个体。
低	具有重要地区价值的认可或未认可的遗产。 因保存不当或周边环境不佳，而使价值受损的遗产。 价值有限，但对当地研究目标有贡献潜力。	“地方名录”中的建筑。 建筑结构和历史关联、有中等特殊价值的历史（未列入名录）建筑。 历史城镇景观或建成区里历史完整性有限的建筑或构筑物。	坚固但未认可的历史景观。 对当地利益群体很重要的历史景观。 因保护不周或管理不善而价值有限的历史景观。	有地区重要性的无形文化遗产活动。 与地区重要性有关的特殊个体。 与物质环境恶劣的区域的无形遗产活动相关。
细微影响	遗产少有或根本没有考古意义。	建筑或城市景观没有建筑或历史价值；建筑风格是侵入式的建筑（外来建筑风格的建筑）。	小或没有重要历史意义的景观。	与无形遗产少有关系。
未知潜在影响	未确定遗产的重要性。	建筑物隐蔽（即人迹罕至）但有潜在历史重要性。	[此栏不适用]	鲜为人知或少有记录的区域的无形文化遗产。

Appendix 3B: Example Guide for assessing magnitude of impact

Impact Grading	Archaeological attributes	Built heritage or Historic Urban Landscape attributes	Historic landscape attributes	Intangible Cultural Heritage attributes or Associations
Major	Changes to attributes that convey OUV of WH properties. Most or all key archaeological materials, including those that contribute to OUV such that the resource is totally altered. Comprehensive changes to setting.	Change to key historic building elements that contribute to OUV, such that the resource is totally altered. Comprehensive changes to the setting.	Change to most or all key historic landscape elements, parcels or components; extreme visual effects; gross change of noise or change to sound quality; fundamental changes to use or access; resulting in total change to historic landscape character unit and loss of OUV.	Major changes to area that affect the ICH activities or associations or visual links and cultural appreciation.
Moderate	Changes to many key archaeological materials, such that the resource is clearly modified. Considerable changes to setting that affect the character of the asset.	Changes to many key historic building elements, such that the resource is significantly modified. Changes to the setting of an historic building,such that it is significantly modified.	Change to many key historic landscape elements, parcels or components; visual change to many key aspects of the historic landscape; noticeable differences in noise or sound quality; considerable changes to use or access; resulting in moderate changes to historic landscape character.	Considerable changes to area that affect the ICH activities or associations or visual links and cultural appreciation.
Minor	Changes to key archaeological materials, such that the resource is slightly altered. Slight changes to setting.	Change to key historic building elements, such that the asset is slightly different. Change to setting of an historic building, such that it is noticeably changed.	Change to few key historic landscape elements, parcels or components; slight visual changes to few key aspects of historic landscape; limited changes to noise levels or sound quality; slight changes to use or access; resulting in limited change to historic landscape character.	Changes to area that affect the ICH activities or associations or visual links and cultural appreciation.
Negligible	Very minor changes to key archaeological materials, or setting.	Slight changes to historic building elements or setting that hardly affect it.	Very minor changes to key historic landscape elements, parcels or components; virtually unchanged visual effects; very slight changes in noise levels or sound quality; very slight changes to use or access; resulting in a very small change to historic landscape character.	Very minor changes to area that affect the ICH activities or associations or visual links and cultural appreciation.
No change	No change.	No change to fabric or setting.	No change to elements, parcels or components; no visual or audible changes; no changes in amenity or community factors.	No change

附录 3B ：案例：评估影响程度指南

影响级别	考古属性	文物建筑或城市历史景观属性	历史景观属性	无形文化遗产属性或相关领域
主要影响	改变了能传达世界遗产突出普遍价值的属性。完全改变大多数或所有关键考古材料，包括对突出普遍价值有贡献的所有资源。环境完全改变。	改变了对突出普遍价值有贡献历史建筑的关键要素，遗产资源完全改变。环境完全改变完。	改变了大多数或全部历史景观关键元素、地块或组成部分；极端的视觉效果，总体改变噪音或音质；改变根本用途或到访线路；造成历史景观特色单元完全改变，并丧失突出普遍价值。	对区域的重大改变影响了无形文化遗产活动或视觉衔接、文化欣赏。
中等影响	改变了关键考古要素，使得资源有清晰改动。重要环境变化影响遗产特性。	改变了许多历史建筑关键元素，资源有显著的修改。对历史建筑环境的改变较大。	改变了历史景观一些关键元素、地块或组成部分；改变历史景观关键视觉部分；明显改变噪音或音质；对用途或访问途径的重大变动；造成历史景观特色重大变化。	区域变化影响了无形文化遗产活动或视觉衔接、文化欣赏。
细微影响	轻微改变了关键考古要素，资源有轻微变化。	轻微改变历史建筑关键元素，不受环境影响。	轻微改变了历史景观关键元素、地块或组成部分；几乎不影响视觉效果，噪音或音质上有细微变化；用途或到访线路有细微变化；造成历史景观特色非常小的改变。	区域里有细微变化，并细微影响无形文化遗产活动或视觉衔接、文化欣赏。
没有变化	没有变化。	其结构或环境没有变化。	历史景观元素、地块或组成部分没有变化；视觉和听觉效果上没有变化；设施和社区因素没有变化。	没有变化。

Appendix 3C: Example Inventory Entry

附录 3C ：录入清单条目案例

The following list gives a suggested set of data fields which could be used in supporting tables or inventories which collate information on an individual or group of heritage assets.

下表是建议的数据库，用于收集单个或整体的遗产信息时，核对和录入数据。

Unique Identity number
Asset name
Location (map reference)
Type of asset (burial mound, church, fort, landscape, ICH etc)
Date
Statutory designation (e.g. on national or local register, WHS)
Brief description
Condition
Authenticity
Integrity

唯一的身份编号
遗产名称
地点（参考地图）
遗产类别（古墓葬、教堂、堡垒、景观、无形文化遗产等）
日期
遗产法定级别（如：列入国家或地方名单或世界遗产）
概述
现状
真实性
完整性

Inter-relationships (list)

Sensitivity

Importance (Very high, high,)

Development magnitude of impact — construction (Major, Moderate, Minor, Negligible, No change)

Development significance of effect — construction (Major beneficial, Moderate beneficial, Minor beneficial, Negligible beneficial; No Change, Negligible adverse, Minor adverse, Moderate adverse, Major adverse).

Operational magnitude of impact (as above) .

Operational significance of effect

内在联系（列表）

脆弱性

重要性（非常高，高）

发展的影响程度——解释（主要的、中等的、次要的、细微影响的、没有变化的）

发展对重要性的影响——解释（主要有利的、适当有利的、中度有利的、益处可忽略不计、没有变化、可忽略不计的不利影响、中度不利影响、主要不利影响）

操作过程影响的程度（如上述）

操作过程对重要性的影响

Appendix 4: Heritage Impact Report Contents

附录 4：遗产影响报告的内容

The HIA Report should provide the evidence on which decisions can be made in a clear, transparent and practicable way. The level of detail needed will depend on the site and proposed changes. The Statement of OUV will be central to the evaluation of the impacts and risk to the site.

遗产影响评估报告是做出清晰、透明和具有可操作性的决策的依据。所需资料的详细程度将取决于遗产地和拟定变化。突出普遍价值声明是评估遗产影响和风险评估的核心内容。

The report should include:

• the proper name of the WH property,

• its geographical coordinates,

• the date of inscription,

• the date of the HIA report,

• the name of the organization or entities responsible for preparing the HIA report,

• for whom it was prepared, and

• a statement on whether the report has been externally assessed or peer-reviewed.

该报告应包括：

• 世界遗产的正确名称，

• 地理坐标，

• 列入名录时间，

• 遗产影响评估报告完成时间，

• 负责编制遗产影响评估报告的组织或机构名称，

• 为何人准备的报告，

• 一份关于该报告是否经过外部评估或同行评审的声明。

Outline report contents

报告内容概述：

1. Non-technical summary – must contain all key points and be usable alone.

2. Contents

3. Introduction

1. 非技术性总结——必须包括所有关键点，并可以单独使用；

2. 内容

3. 概要

4. Methodology
• Data sources
• Published works
• Unpublished reports
• Databases
• Field Surveys
• Impact Assessment Methodology
• Scope of Assessment
• Evaluation of Heritage Resource
• Assessment of Scale of Specific Impact and Change
• Evaluation of Overall Impact
• Definition of the Assessment Area

4. 方法论
• 数据资源
• 已发布的成果
• 未公布的报告
• 数据库
• 实地调查
• 影响评估的方法
• 评估范围
• 遗产资源的评估
• 具体影响或变化范围的评估
• 总体影响的评估
• 评估区域的界定

5. Site history and description –

Key in this section will be the Statement of OUV, and a description of the attributes which convey OUV and which contribute to the Statements of authenticity and integrity.

5. 遗址历史和描述——

本节的关键是突出普遍价值声明，和能传达突出普遍价值的、有助于真实性和完整性声明的属性的描述。

This section should also include any nationally or locally designated sites, monuments or structures as well as non-designated sites. It should set out the historical development of the study area, and describe its character, such as the historic landscape, including field patterns, boundaries and extant historic elements of the landscape and cultural heritage. It should describe the condition of the whole and of individual attributes and components, physical characteristics, sensitive viewpoints and intangible associations which may relate to attributes. This should focus on areas affected in particular but must include a description of the whole.

本节还包括国家或当地认可的遗址、纪念碑或建筑物，遗迹或未认可定的遗址。它应包括研究区域的历史沿革、描述它的属性：如历史景观包括场地结构图、边界、现存的历史景观和文物古迹的元素。它应当描述整体和个体的属性及组成部分、实体特性、敏感视点和涉及属性的无形遗产。其重点应放在受影响的特别区域，但必须包括整体描述。

6. Description of changes or developments proposed

6. 对变化和拟定发展的描述

7. Assessment and evaluation of overall impact of the proposed changes

This part should set out an assessment of

7. 拟定变化整体影响的评估和评价。

这部分应具体评估变化对能传达突出普遍

specific changes and impacts on the attributes of OUV and other heritage assets. It should include a description and assessment of the direct or indirect impacts, including physical impacts, visual, or noise, on individual heritage attributes, assets or elements and associations, and on the whole. Impact on OUV should be evaluated through assessment of impact on the attributes which convey the OUV of the site. It should consider all impacts on all attributes; professional judgement is required in presenting the information in an appropriate form to assist decision-making.

价值及其他遗产价值的属性的影响。它应当包括对直接及间接影响的描述和评估，包括描述和评估对单个遗产属性、遗产价值、元素和及相关的实体、视觉、噪音的影响，以及对整体的影响。对能传达遗产突出普遍价值属性的影响所做的评估，是评估对突出普遍价值影响的基础。它应当考虑对所有属性的全部影响；以适当的形式提交信息协助决策时，需要专业判断。

It should also include an evaluation of the overall significance of effect — overall impact — of the proposals for development or change on individual attributes and the whole WH property. This may also need to include an assessment of how the changes may impact on the perception of the site locally, nationally and internationally.

它还应该包括对整体重要性影响的评价——整体影响的评估——拟定发展或改变对个别属性和整个遗产价值的影响。这可能还需要评估这些变化将如何影响本地、国内甚至是国际遗产。

8. Measures to avoid, to reduce or to compensate for impacts — Mitigation Measures

Such measures include both general and site or asset-specific measures and cover：

• those needed before the development or change proceeds (such as archaeological excavation),

• those needed during construction or change (such as a watching brief or physical protection of assets) and

• any post-construction measures during the operation of any proposed change or development (such as interpretation or access measures, awareness-building, education, reconstruction proposals),

• proposals to disseminate information, knowledge or understanding gained by the HIA and any detailed desk, field or scientific studies.

8. 用来避免、减少或补偿影响的措施——缓解措施

这些措施包括一般以及遗址或遗产专用措施，包含：

• 开发或改变过程开始前的需求（如考古发掘）；

• 建设期间或变化时的需要（如观察简报或对遗产实体的保护）；

• 拟定开发或改变过程的施工后措施（如阐释或到访参观方法、意识建设、教育、重建建议）；

• 传播由遗产影响评估和案头细节研究、实地调查、科学研究获得的信息、知识或理解的相关建议。

9. Summary and Conclusions, including

• A clear statement on effects on the Outstanding

9. 总结和结论，包括：

• 关于对世界遗产地的突出普遍价值及其完

Universal Value of the WHS, its integrity and authenticity,

整性和真实性影响的明确声明；

• The risk to the Inscription of the site as a WH property,

• 影响遗产申报世界遗产的风险；

• Any beneficial effects, including better knowledge and understanding and awareness-raising.

• 任何有益的影响，包括更好的知识和了解，意识提升。

10. Bibliography

10. 参考书目

11. Glossary of terms used

11. 所用术语词汇表

12. Acknowledgement and authorship

12. 致谢和版权

13. Illustrations and photographs showing for example

• Location and extent of sites, including buffer zones

• Any study area defined

• Development or proposals for change

• Visual or inter-visibility analyses

• Mitigation measures

• Key sites and views

13. 插图和照片清单

• 遗址的位置和范围，包括缓冲区；

• 定义研究区域；

• 拟定的开发和改变计划；

• 视觉或相互通视的分析；

• 缓解措施；

• 关键遗址和景观。

14. Appendices with detailed data, for example

• Tables of individual sites or elements, summary description and summary of impacts

• Desk studies

• Field study reports (such as geophysical survey, trial evaluation, excavation)

• Scientific studies

• List of consultants and consultation responses

• The scoping statement or project brief.

14. 详细数据的附录，例如：

• 遗址个体或元素、概括描述和总结影响的表格；

• 案头研究；

• 实地调查报告（如地理调查、实验评估、发掘）；

• 科学研究；

• 咨询者名单和咨询回复；

• 范围声明或项目简介。

联合国教科文组织世界遗产中心
《佛罗伦萨景观宣言》(2012)
UNESCO FLORENCE DECLARATION ON LANDSCAPE

FLORENCE DECLARATION ON LANDSCAPE, 2012

Final Declaration of the UNESCO International Meeting on ‘The International Protection of Landscapes’ held in Florence on September 19-21, 2012 on the occasion of the 40th Anniversary of the World Heritage Convention

2012 佛罗伦萨景观宣言是 2012 年 9 月 19 日到 21 日，为纪念《世界遗产公约》40 周年，联合国教科文组织在佛罗伦萨举行的“景观的国际保护”国际研讨会的最终宣言。

The participants to the meeting that has reunited over 30 experts of all countries. the representatives of UN Agency (UNESCO FAO, UNCCD, UNEP). relevant international intergovernmental bodies, centers and international associations (ICCROM, EUI UNU，ICOMOS，IFLA, ICQHS，ITKI, IPSI, LHP), national and non-governmental organizations, universities, local administration.

来自各国的 30 余名专家参加了这次会议，代表包括联合国机构 (如联合国教科文组织、联合国粮食及农业组织、联合国防治荒漠化公约、联合国环境规划署)、相关国际政府间机构、中心和国际协会 (如国际文物保护与修复研究中心、欧洲大学学院、联合国大学、国际古迹遗址理事会、国际景观设计师联合会、国际暗渠灌溉系统与历史性水利建筑中心、国际传统知识研究所、国际和平与安全研究所、活态的历史项目)，国家和非政府组织、大学、地方管理机构。

• Thanking the organizers for having convened a meeting on the International Protection on Landscapes;

• 感谢主办方召开了景观国际保护会议；

• Having examined and discussed the challenges of today;

• 研究和讨论当今挑战；

• Expressing their deep concern for the degradation of Landscapes worldview due to industrialization, rapid urbanization, intensification of agricultural processes and other threats and risks caused by the global change;

• 表达他们对于因工业化带来的世界性景观退化的深切关注及对城市化快速发展、集约化农业生产和全球变化带来的威胁和风险的关注。

• Acknowledging landscape as the expression of the relationship between people and environment which, over time, has created and still creates harmonic life conditions and wealth;

• 确认景观作为人和环境关系的表达，随着时间的推移，创造了并仍在创造着和谐的生活条件和财富；

• Recognizing the importance of the landscape as an educational tool to promote knowledge and raise awareness of cultural diversity, identity and responsibility;

• Considering that the landscape is a common good, the right to the landscape is a human necessity;

• Aware that it is impossible to protect landscapes ignoring the local and traditional knowledge that have generated them and whose loss destroys a heritage of know-how usable for appropriate and innovative solutions;

• Acknowledging that international resolutions recognize intrinsic aspects of the landscape, such as adaptive management and a holistic approach between social, economic and aesthetic elements as possible answers to the global challenges;

• Taking into account the request of local communities and administrative representative to preserve the landscape for better living conditions based on global sharing opportunities and common goals;

• Recalling the Rio+20 outcome document 'The feature we want' and the upcoming revision of the Millennium Developments Goals;

• Taking note of numerous initiatives at the international, national and local levels, addressing landscape management in the context of sustainable development within the United Nations system;

• Affirming the importance of safeguarding and improving landscapes for:

1. The quality of daily life and cultural identity；
2. Enhancing wellbeing；
3. Reacting in an adaptive and participatory way to risk and catastrophes；
4. Combating desertification, land degradation and draught, preserving biological diversity and mitigating the effects of climate change;
5. Promoting work opportunities, food security, environmental protection and community resilience;
6. Promote social and economic sustainable

• 认识到景观作为一种教育工具，对推广知识，提高文化多样性、身份和责任意识的重要性；

• 考虑到景观是一种共同利益，景观权是人类的必需品；

• 意识到保护景观不能忽视对孕育了景观的当地和传统知识的保护，因为这种忽视也会破坏适当的和创新解决方案所依赖的传统专有技术；

• 承认国际决议认可的景观内在本质，如适当的管理以及社会、经济和美学元素，可用于应对全球性挑战的整体分析方法；

• 考虑当地社区和行政代表的要求，在全球共享机遇和共同目标下，保护景观并改善生活条件；

• 回顾里约 20+ 峰会成果文件“我们想要的未来”和即将修订的千年发展目标；

• 注意到在联合国可持续发展范围内，国际、国家和地方层面有关处理景观管理问题的众多倡议；

• 肯定了保护和改善景观有以下重要性：

1. 生活质量和文化认同；
2. 提高福利；
3. 以适当的参与方式应对风险和灾难；
4. 防治荒漠化、土地退化和干旱，维护生物多样性和减轻气候变化的影响；
5. 促进工作机会、粮食安全、环境保护和社区的恢复力；
6. 通过扩展景观的空间界限和概念边界，

development by extending the spatial boundaries and conceptual frontiers of the landscape

促进社会和经济的可持续发展；

7. Recognizing the value of traditional knowledge and practices as the basis for balanced technological and innovative development programme.

7. 认识到，传统知识和实践的价值，是平衡发展技术和创新发展计划的基础；

8. Promoting participatory and bottom-up programmes together with activities based on local knowledge ;

8. 促进参与性、自下而上的项目及以当地知识为基础的活动；

9. Empowering communities and institutions in decision-making processes;

9. 授予社区和机构参与决策过程的权利；

10. Fostering the respect for human rights, including the rights of communities to ensure their livelihood and preserve their resources, identity and belief's;

10. 培养对人权的尊重，包括尊重社区的权利，以确保社区生活，维护社区资源、身份和信仰；

11. Encouraging the respect of the sites, and decision processes that safeguard communities and people;

11. 鼓励尊重景观所在地、保护社区和人民的决策过程；

12. Preserving diversity, tangible and intangible heritage assets;

12. 维护有形和无形遗产的多样性；

13. Ensuring the ecosystems' continuity in providing services to communities;

13. 确保生态系统向社区提供服务的可持续性；

Call upon intergovernmental agencies and secretariats responsible for United Nations programmes and international conventions together with non-governmental organizations concerned to:

呼吁负责联合国项目和国际公约的政府间机构和秘书处及相关非政府组织，共同关注以下事项：

• strengthen the global awareness on the need to safeguard and improve landscapes as an integral element of sustainable development processes;

• 加强全球保护和改善景观意识，将其作为可持续发展进程必要组成部分；

• Share information and make expertise available ;

• Establish effective partnership ;

• 分享信息和提供专业知识；

• 建立有效的伙伴关系；

Further call upon the Intergovernmental Agencies and Programmes, including the pertinent UNESCO Centers and Chairs to create a Working Group to foster the coordination between the existing international instrument and programmes in order to promote international, national and local polices aimed at linking safeguarding and improvement of landscapes;

进一步呼吁政府间机构和项目，包括教科文组织相关中心和主席，创建一个工作组，以促进、协调现有国际文件和方案，促进国际、国家和地方保护和改善景观的政策；

Support immediate national and local government initiatives for the protection of landscapes;

支持国家和当地政府立即行动以保护景观；

Request the creation of international forum on 2013 for the safeguard of landscapes as a tool for sustainable development with the aim of advancing proposals for the reflection on the Post-2015 International Development Agenda and to start relevant international mechanism.

要求于2013年建立一个保护景观的国际论坛作为可持续发展的工具，目的在于推动对2015年后的国际发展议程的反思，并启动相关的国际机制。

International Bodies

ICCROM—International Centre for the Study of the Preservation and Restoration of Cultural Property

EUI—European University Institute

UNU—United Nations University

ICOMOS—International Council on Monuments and Sites

IFLA—The International Federation of Landscape Architects

ICQHHS—International Center on Qanats And Historic Hydraulic Structures

ITKI—International Traditional Knowledge Institute

IPSI—International Peace and Security Institute

LHP—Living History Project

国际机构：

国际文物保护与修复研究中心

欧洲大学学院

联合国大学

国际古迹遗址理事会

国际景观设计师联合会

国际暗渠灌溉系统和历史性水利建筑中心

国际传统知识研究所

国际和平与安全研究所

活态的历史项目

中国《世界遗产无锡倡议“世界遗产：可持续发展”》(2012)

Wuxi Proposal of 'World Heritage: Sustainable Development'

Wuxi Proposal of 'World Heritage: Sustainable Development' (2012)

In April 2012, while the 40th anniversary for *the Convention Concerning the Protection of the World Cultural and Natural Heritage* which was issued by UNESCO, the 7th Wuxi Forum of *China Cultural Heritage Protection was* held successfully in Wuxi. More than 100 participants in relative fields from domestic and abroad gathered together, conducted fully discussion and profound exchanges on the epoch theme of 'World Heritage: Sustainable Development'.

Participants presented at the meeting had reviewed the development process of world heritage and believed that:

I. As a state party of the *Convention*, China implements the relevant obligations practically and carries out the work actively in identification, protection and inheritance of the World Cultural Heritage, and achieves great outcomes. The precious heritages comprehensive representing China's long history and cultural diversity, with their outstanding universal value which had been inscribed in the World Heritage List and kept them under proper conservation and scientific utilization. *The Convention* has promoted the development of cultural heritage protection in China, and in addition,

“世界遗产：可持续发展”无锡倡议

2012年4月，第七届中国文化遗产保护无锡论坛成功召开。时逢联合国教科文组织《保护世界文化和自然遗产公约》诞生40周年，百余名中外业界代表共聚一堂，围绕“世界遗产：可持续发展”这一时代主题展开充分讨论和深入交流。

回顾世界遗产事业的发展历程，与会代表认为：

1. 作为《公约》缔约国，中国切实履行相关义务，在识别、保护和传承世界文化遗产方面积极开展工作，取得了良好的成效，使一批全面代表了中国悠久历史和多元文化、具有全球突出普遍价值的宝贵遗产纳入世界遗产保护范畴，并得以妥善保存和科学利用。《公约》促进了中国文化遗产保护事业的发展，而中国同行践行《公约》的行动又对人类文化遗产保护事业做出了积极贡献。

Chinese efforts to implement the *Convention* have made positive contributions to the protection of human cultural heritage.

II. Under cities and provinces government's guidance and social participation, the World Cultural Heritages had carried out relevant research and practice carefully; strive improved the protection management level; advanced with times and kept up the pace with the economic and social development; actively explored the development path that adapts to its own characteristics and needs, played a model role of promotion and demonstration in the field of the cultural heritage of China.

2. 作为世界文化遗产，各地在政府指导和社会多方参与下，认真开展相关研究和实践，努力提高保护管理水平，与时俱进，紧跟经济社会发展步伐，积极探索适应自身特点和需求的发展道路，逐步实现着对中国文化遗产事业的推动和示范作用。

III. At present, Chinese World Cultural Heritage Protection is facing unprecedented opportunities as well as a series of universal internationally pressures and challenges from the economic construction, climatic change, natural disaster, environmental change and tourism development etc. We saw the existing threats and realized the severity situation, regarded that we should take the sustainable development of world heritage as the major issue and core mission in the future.

3. 当前，中国的世界文化遗产保护迎来了前所未有的机遇，但同样面临着一系列来自经济建设、气候变化、自然灾害、环境改变、旅游发展等带有国际普遍性的压力和挑战，我们看到了威胁的存在，意识到了形势的严峻，我们将把实现世界遗产可持续发展作为今后的重大课题和核心任务。

Hereby, the participants in the forum call on the following proposals:

I. Pay close attention to the protection and sustainable development of the world heritage; raise the public awareness. Let the masses know the history and value of the heritage; make the tourists respect the rare and fragile property of the heritage; let the city maintain a healthy environment and sufficient space for the heritage; make the society understand and support all efforts to protect the world heritage.

为此，论坛代表共同发出以下倡议：

1. 密切关注世界遗产的保护和可持续发展，提高公众意识。让百姓了解遗产的历史和价值，让游客尊重遗产珍稀而脆弱的属性，让城市维护遗产健康的环境和充足的空间，让社会理解和支持为保护世界遗产所做出的各种努力。

II. Consolidate the social resources and strength widely to achieve the multidisciplinary and multi-industry cooperation for the development of world

2. 广泛整合社会资源和力量，实现世界遗产保护发展的跨学科、跨行业联手。让法律为其建立严明的保障，让规划为其统筹保护与发

heritage protection. Establish strict and impartial guarantee relying on laws; implement protection and development depending on planning; provide efficient measure by means of science and technology; strengthen the prevention ability counting on monitoring; strive for wide publicity participation.

展，让科技为其提供高效的手段，让监测为其增强防范的能力，让宣传为其争取广泛的参与。

III. Build the positive interaction between the community development and heritage protection actively to achieve mutually beneficial. Encourage the communities to participate and to become the major force of protection and development in heritage protection, conservation and utilization. Promote the protection of heritage sites in order to benefit the community livelihood, enrich the community culture, adjust the industrial structure of community and improve the community image. Drive the community development to expand financial resources increasing participants, building the platform for the exchange and discussion as well as creating good order and environment for the heritage protection.

3. 积极构建社区发展与遗产保护的良性互动，实现共生共济。鼓励社区参与遗产保护和利用，成为保护与发展的重要力量；促进遗产地保护惠及社区民生、丰富社区文化、调整社区产业结构、提升社区形象；推动社区发展为遗产保护扩大经费来源，壮大人员队伍，搭建交流研讨平台，营造良好秩序环境。

IV. Give full play to the leading role of the government and arouse the local administration departments' enthusiasm effectively. The local government of the world heritage sites, as the responsibility main body of protection, conservation and management, the site management organizations as the responsibility subjects of management, shall conduct heritage protection and conservation activities positively while defending the heritage safety and dignity as their own responsibility, performing the heritage conservation plan as their own task as well as achieving the heritage value and expanding the heritage influence as their own honor, and do their utmost to protect and inherit the world heritage.

4. 充分发挥政府的主导作用，有效调动地方管理部门积极性。各世界遗产地政府作为保护管理的责任主体，各遗产地管理机构作为保护管理的执行实体，应当积极开展遗产保护各项行动，以捍卫遗产安全和尊严为己责，以落实遗产保护规划措施为己任，以实现遗产价值、扩大遗产影响为己荣，为保护和传承世界遗产不遗余力。

The mentioned content is the heartfelt wish of all the participants in the forum. We will start with

以上为论坛全体代表的心声，我们将从自身做起，并呼唤社会各界人士加入这一行列，

ourselves and call on all societies to join us with cooperative to prompt the sustainable development of world heritage in China and circulate Chinese civilization to the future generations!

共同努力，推动中国的世界遗产可持续发展，实现中华文明的永续流传！

The 7th Wuxi Forum of China Cultural Heritage Protection

April 11, 2012

第七届中国文化遗产保护无锡论坛

2012 年 4 月 11 日

中国国家文物局
《考古遗址公园规划》
National Cultural Heritage, Administration of China, Plan of National Archaeological Heritage Park

Chapter I General Principles

Article 1 The requirement is formulated for standardize the content and depth of the Plan. National Archaeological Heritage Park (hereinafter as the Plan)

Article 2 The Plan is applicable to the complicated archaeological sites which really need to build a National Archaeological Heritage Park (hereinafter as Heritage Park). The Plan should be pursuant to the cultural heritage conservation & protection plan and meet its principles and requirements of presentation design, and is the technical document for construction and management of the heritage park.

Article 3 Basis on scientific preservation of the heritage, the Plan should explain the value of the heritage fully and accurately, evaluate relevant social, economic, and environmental conditions, determine positions, construction objectives and contents of the heritage park.

Article 4 The Plan should comply with laws and regulations concerning cultural heritage conservation & protection and related industries; technical specifications and be in coordinate with the local national economy and social development plan, master land-use plan as well as other related plans.

第一章　总则

第一条　为规范国家考古遗址公园规划（以下简称规划）的内容和深度，制定本要求。

第二条　规划适用于确需建设国家考古遗址公园（以下简称遗址公园）的大遗址。规划必须以文物保护规划为依据，符合文物保护规划中展示规划的原则和要求，是遗址公园建设与管理的技术性文件。

第三条　规划应在科学保护遗址的基础上，充分、准确阐释遗址的价值，评估相关社会、经济和环境条件，确定遗址公园的定位、建设目标、内容等。

第四条　规划须遵守文物保护的法律法规和相关行业技术规范，并与地方国民经济与社会发展规划、土地利用总体规划等相关规划相协调。

Article 5 The preparation of the Plan should be completed by a Grade A qualification unit in survey & design of the cultural heritage conservation projects (plan category) or other related Grade A qualification unit such as urban and rural plan, architectural engineering design, landscape design, jointly with archaeological excavations qualification unit which engaged in archaeological work at the site.

第五条 规划编制工作需由具有文物保护工程勘察设计（规划类）甲级资质单位，或城乡规划、建筑工程设计、风景园林工程设计等相关甲级资质单位，与在该遗址从事过考古工作的考古发掘资质单位共同完成。

Article 6 The Plan achievements mainly include plan description, plan drawing and attachment.

第六条 规划成果主要包括规划说明、规划图纸及附件。

Chapter II Plan Description

第二章 规划说明

Article 7 The Plan's description should be basis on the scientific evaluation that to explain the principle, objective and ideas of the Plan, illuminate various plan contents in accurate, clear, scientific and standardized words and in consistent with the Plan drawing. Generally included followings:

7.1 Overview;

7.2 Resource condition and status analysis;

7.3 Overall design;

7.4 Specialized plan;

7.5 Node design;

7.6 Investment estimation.

第七条 规划说明应在科学评估的基础上说明规划的原则、目标和思路，对各项规划内容进行阐述，文字表达应准确、清晰、科学、规范，并与规划图纸保持一致。一般应包括如下内容：

7.1 概述；

7.2 资源条件与现状分析；

7.3 总体设计；

7.4 专项规划；

7.5 节点设计；

7.6 投资估算。

Article 8 The content of general overview include:

8.1 Heritage overview: include the title, location, time, nature, scope, heritage compositions and historical evolution;

8.2 Preparation reference: include relevant laws and administrative regulation, departmental regulations and normative documents, technical standards and specifications, archaeological and scientific research achievements and related plans, etc.;

8.3 plan scope: state the extent and acreage of plan and the extent and acreage of heritage park;

第八条 概述内容包括：

8.1 遗址概况：应包括遗址名称、位置、时代、性质、范围、遗存构成和历史沿革等；

8.2 编制依据：应包括有关法律与行政法规、部门规章与规范性文件、技术标准和规范、考古与科研成果以及相关规划等；

8.3 规划范围：应说明规划范围和面积、遗址公园范围和面积；

8.4 plan objective: specify positions and construction objectives of the heritage park;

8.5 plan principle: put forward principles in terms of archaeology, protection, research, utilization and management and other different levels focusing on the Plan objective.

Article 9 The content of resource conditions and present situation analysis should include:

9.1 Cultural heritage resources: define its value and attributes, and evaluate the value carrier's preservation, protection status and utilization conditions of valuable attributes and other cultural heritage resource conditions within the heritage park.

9.2 Regional location conditions: evaluate the urban and rural regional location relationship and surrounding traffic conditions of the heritage park.

9.3 Social conditions: evaluate social and economic conditions, humanity resource conditions, local government policies and financial support, present situation of land-use, and land tenure administration, etc. where the heritage park was belonging.

9.4 Environmental conditions: evaluate regional natural resources, ecological environment, landscape, construction status in the site, as well as infrastructure conditions and public health conditions, etc. where the heritage park was belonging.

9.5 Archaeological and scientific research conditions: evaluate the history, status, and research achievements of the site's archaeological work, and the relationship between existing archaeological working plans and the construction of the heritage park.

9.6 Management conditions: evaluate the implementation of the heritage conservation & protection and management plan, system or mechanism of management and operation, construction of related conservation and management facilities, public exhibition and visitors services, etc.

9.7 Related plan analysis: analyze the relationship between the heritage park plan and cultural

8.4　规划目标：应明确遗址公园定位及建设目标；

8.5　规划原则：应围绕规划目标，从考古、保护、研究、利用、管理等不同层面提出具有针对性的原则。

第九条　资源条件与现状分析内容包括：

9.1　文物资源：明确遗址的价值与价值载体，评估价值载体的保存、保护状况及利用条件，以及遗址公园范围内其他文物资源条件。

9.2　区位条件：评估遗址公园与所在区域的城乡区位关系、外部交通条件等情况。

9.3　社会条件：评估遗址公园所在区域的社会经济条件、人文资源条件、地方政府政策与资金支持、土地利用现状、土地权属管理等情况。

9.4　环境条件：评估遗址公园所处区域的自然资源、生态环境、景观风貌、场地内建设现状、基础设施条件与公共卫生条件等。

9.5　考古和科研条件：评估考古工作历史、现状、研究成果，以及现有考古工作计划和遗址公园建设之间的关系。

9.6　管理条件：评估遗址保护规划实施、管理运营体制机制、相关保护与管理设施建设、开放展示与游客服务等情况。

9.7　相关规划分析：分析遗址公园规划与文物保护规划的关系，分析遗址公园所在区域

heritage preservation plan, analyze the regional economic and social development plan, master land-use plan and the urban master plan, etc. of the area where the heritage park is located.

的国民经济与社会发展规划、土地利用总体规划、城市总体规划等涉及遗址公园规划范围的建设、管理要求和规定。

Article 10 The overall design include:

10.1 System plan of interpretation and presentation including interpretation, presentation plan and its structure, etc.

10.1.1 plan of interpretation and presentation: on the basis of existing exhibition principle and content of the cultural heritage preservation plan, a valuable interpretation framework should be constructed in according with the resource condition and status analysis, and determine the object, position, theme, content and method of interpretation and exhibition.

10.1.2 Interpretation and presentation structure: based on the plan of interpretation, construct the spatial display relationship, including partition, exhibition streamline and important node, etc.

10.2 Overall layout of heritage park

Including function zone, traffic organization and facilities distribution, etc.

10.2.1 Function zone: in general, the function zone should include heritage display zone, management service zone and reserve zone, etc, and refine as appropriate. Where there are important natural and social resources in The Plan area, related special resources display zone could be designated so as to satisfied the requirements of related industries management plan and harmonies with the heritage display zone. In which:

1) Heritage display zone is an area focused on the function of heritage display, and is limited to the attributes distribution area where spatial location, shape and structure and connotation were identified basicly.

2) Management & service zone is an area focused on management & operation and public

第十条 总体设计内容包括：

10.1 阐释与展示体系规划

包括阐释与展示策划、阐释与展示结构等内容。

10.1.1 阐释与展示策划：应在文物保护规划中已有展示原则和内容的基础上，根据资源条件与现状分析构建价值阐释框架，确定阐释与展示的对象、定位、主题、内容、方法等。

10.1.2 阐释与展示结构：应根据阐释与展示策划，构建展示空间关系，包括展示分区、展示流线、重要节点等。

10.2 遗址公园总体布局

包括功能分区、交通组织、设施分布等内容。

10.2.1 功能分区：一般应包括遗址展示区、管理服务区、预留区等，并可酌情细化。规划区域内具有重要自然、人文社会资源的，可划定专门的相关资源展示区。相关资源展示区应符合相关行业规划保护要求，并与遗址展示区相协调。其中：

1）遗址展示区：是以遗址展示为主要功能的区域，仅限于空间位置、形制和内涵基本明确的遗迹分布区域。

2）管理服务区：是集中建设管理运营、公共服务等设施为主的区域，一般应置于遗址保

service facilities, and which in general was placed outside of heritage preservation zone.

护范围之外。

3) Reserve zone is an area where archaeological survey work is inadequate or temporarily unsuitable for display. Keep the area in its original state for protection, any construction project which may disturbing the heritage itself or its landscape should be forbidden.

3）预留区：是考古勘测工作不充分或暂不具备展示条件的区域。预留区内以原状保护为主，不得开展干扰遗址本体及景观环境的建设项目。

10.2.2 Traffic arrangement: adhere the minimum interference principle and according to interpretation and presentation structure, the traffic system should be reasonably reflect overall layout of the heritage and organize traffic system to guarantee the accessibility to the heritage display zone, and service quality of the heritage park. Strictly control size of exit, evacuation square and parking lots of the heritage park, and properly handle the relation between the new road network and the heritage. The road in the heritage park should not to be too wide, and paving materials such as asphalt should be used with caution to avoid over modernization and artificial.

10.2.2 交通组织：应坚持最小干预原则，根据阐释与展示结构，合理体现遗址整体布局并组织交通系统，保证遗址展示区的可达性和遗址公园服务质量。应严格控制遗址公园内入口、集散广场与停车场的规模，妥善处理新建路网与遗址的关系。遗址公园内道路不宜过宽，铺装材质应慎用柏油等现代材料，避免过于现代化和人工化。

1) Designed visitors' main, secondary and special exits, and designed the location, layout or scale of evacuation square and parking lots both inside and outside the exits.

1）应进行出入口设计，确定游人主、次和专用出入口，及出入口内外集散广场与停车场的位置、布局与规模要求。

2) the road network design should give priority to heritage layout and road system, and according to the requirement of activities content, visitors capacity and management, to arrange specific route, classification & grading and traffic facilities, and define the structure and paving features of the road.

2）路网设计应优先考虑遗址布局和道路体系，并根据各分区的活动内容、游人容量和管理需要确定具体路线、分类分级、交通设施配备，明确道路形制与铺装特色等。

3) The main road should have the function of tour guiding, and identify the direction in easy. Garden path in the area where visitors concentrated substantially should be clear, smooth and convenient for distributing.

3）主要道路应具有引导游览的作用，易于识别方向。游人大量集中地区的园路要做到明显、通畅、便于集散。

10.2.3 Facilities distribution: should follow the principle of meeting the minimum functional requirements, strictly control the quantity and scale of the facilities and weaken design to keep

10.2.3 设施分布：应以满足最低功能需求为原则，严格控制设施数量和规模，淡化设计，确保遗址本体和周边环境的真实性和完整性。应落实策划阶段所需展陈、标识、管理设施，并

the authenticity and integrity of the heritage and surrounding environment. Presentation, identification and management facility as required should be implement at the plan stage, and reasonably allocate the public service facilities in conjunction with visitors requirement, and determine the quantity, scale and location of various facilities reasonably.

结合游客需求合理配置公共服务设施，合理确定各类设施的数量、规模与位置。

1) Presentation facilities: include on-site protection facilities, heritage museum or presentation hall, and archaeological workstation, etc. according to the actual requirement of cultural heritage protection and management plan, select reasonably display plan and arrange presentation buildings & structures and other presentation facilities; the architectural style of the facilities should be concise and in coordination with the heritage and the surroundings; the display of important nodes should be according to the local condition; on-site museum or exhibition hall, archaeological workstation, on-site display buildings and other structures should be strictly controlled in mass, scientifically calculated specific construction technical and economic indicators according to the functional requirement.

1）展陈设施：可包括现场保护展示设施、遗址博物馆或陈列馆、考古工作站等。应根据实际保护展示需求及文物保护规划要求，合理选择展示方式并设置展示建构筑物等展示设施；设施建筑风格应简洁，与遗址本体和周边环境相协调；重要节点的展示方式应因地制宜；遗址博物馆或陈列馆、考古工作站、遗迹现场展示等建构筑物应严格控制体量，根据功能需求科学测算具体的建筑技术经济指标。

2) Interpretive/information infrastructure: include information panels and interpretive panels, etc. In accordance with the requirements of the interpretation and display system in the relevant plan, organize and arrange display methods and setting; clearly identify content, positions, ways and patterns of the system etc. The logo should be identifiable and harmonize with the environment.

2）标识设施：包括标识牌、解说牌等。应根据相关规划中的阐释与展示体系要求，配合展示方式组织与展陈设施设置，明确标识系统的阐释内容、标识位置、方式与样式等。标识样式应具有可辨识性，并与环境相协调。

3) Management facilities: include heritage park management center, management rooms, safety protection facilities, etc. Management facilities should be taken into account as a whole in conjunction with the on-site museum or exhibition hall and other exhibition facilities as well as public service, the quantity and scale of the facilities should be strictly controlled. According to the management

3）管理设施：可包括遗址公园管理中心、管理用房、安全防护设施等。管理设施应结合遗址博物馆或陈列馆等展陈设施、公共服务设施统筹考虑，严格控制设施数量和规模。应根据遗址公园管理需要，合理确定管理设施的功能、位置、体量、建筑风格等。

needs of the heritage park, the function, location, volume and architectural style of management facilities should be reasonably determined.

4) Public service facilities: may include the visitor service center, booths, toilets, landscape pavilion, parking lot, transfer station, garbage can, and seats, etc. The visitors capacity, construction scale or service requirements of the heritage park should following the principle of meeting the minimum functional requirements, while determine the type, quantity, location and scale of the public service infrastructures.

4）公共服务设施：可包括游客服务中心、商亭、厕所、观景亭、停车场、换乘点、垃圾桶、座椅等。应根据游客容量、遗址公园建设规模和服务需求，以满足最低功能需求为原则，确定公共服务设施的种类、数量、位置与规模等。

10.3 Overall landscape control

Include spatial layout of landscape, buildings and structures style control, and modeling of public environment, etc.

10.3 总体景观控制

包括景观空间布局、建构筑物风貌控制、公共环境塑造等。

10.3.1 spatial layout of landscape: should master and extract landscape features on the whole to meet the evolving rules of the heritage and features of natural resources surrounding so that to prevent excessive artificial and to distinguish it from general city park. The overall spatial structure of the heritage park should be planned according to the distribution characteristics of the ruins.

10.3.1 景观空间布局：应从总体上把握、提炼符合遗址演变规律的景观特征，以及遗址周边自然资源特色，防止过度人工化，并区别于一般城市公园。应按照遗迹的分布特征规划遗址公园整体空间架构。

10.3.2 Buildings and structures style control: should put forward control requirements such as the style, mass, scale, facade and architectural concept of the buildings and structures etc.

10.3.2 建筑物风貌控制：应提出建筑物的风格、体量、规模、立面及建筑语汇等控制要求。

10.3.3 Modeling of public environment: should put forward necessary control requirement and design principle of the environmental facilities, and the control requirements of overall atmosphere, visitor order and various business in the heritage park.

10.3.3 公共环境塑造：应提出必要的环境设施的控制要求和设计原则，以及遗址公园整体氛围、游客秩序、园内各类经营行为的控制要求。

Article 11 Special plan contents should include:

According to the specific situation of the park, establish necessary specialized plan content which may include archaeological and study implementation scheme, management and operation plan, infras-

第十一条 专项规划内容包括：

根据公园具体情况，制定必要的专项规划内容，可包括考古与研究实施方案、管理运营规划、基础设施规划、竖向规划、综合防灾规划等，专项规划内容应遵循文物保护规划的原

tructure plan, vertical plan, and comprehensive disaster prevention plan, etc. specialized plan should follows the principles and requirements of the cultural heritage protection plan, minimize the impact on the heritage itself and the surroundings as possible, comply with related professional laws, regulations, standards and specifications.

则和要求，尽量减少对遗址本体和周边环境的影响，并符合相关专业法规、标准及规范。

11.1 Archaeological and study implementation scheme

11.1 考古与研究实施方案

Archaeological and study implementation scheme should take the heritage park as the main working area to define archaeological work's target, task and research subject etc. in the heritage park plan.

考古与研究实施方案，应以遗址公园为主要工作区域，明确遗址公园规划范围内的考古工作目标、任务、研究课题等。

11.2 Management and operation plan

11.2 管理运营规划

Include management framework of the heritage park, operation mode and publicity & education plan.

包括遗址公园管理架构、遗址公园运营模式、宣传教育计划。

11.2.1 Management framework of the heritage park: based on the full communication with the relevant administrative departments of the park, formulate goals, strategy and structure of operation management, and define the organize, personnel and system and other ideas of the management mechanism of the heritage park.

11.2.1 遗址公园管理架构：应在与遗址公园所在地相关行政管理部门充分沟通的基础上，制定遗址公园运营管理的目标、战略和架构，明确遗址公园管理机构的设置、人员、制度等构想。

11.2.2 Operation mode of the heritage park: should define the operation subject and operation system. Conducting visitors and market analysis, put forward supporting proposals for construction, maintenance, operation funds as well as benefits (social and economic comprehensive benefits).

11.2.2 遗址公园运营模式：应明确运营主体和运营机制，进行游客与市场分析，对遗址公园建设、运营维护资金来源与回报（社会、经济综合效益）提出保障建议。

11.2.3 Publicity and education plan: should define goal, source and theme of publicity and education; formulate staffs' professional training scheme, and define the training modes and team building goal etc.

11.2.3 宣传培训计划：应明确宣传教育的目标、资源、主题等；制定工作人员的专业培训方案，明确培训方式和团队建设目标等。

11.3 Infrastructure plan

11.3 基础设施规划

In case of the heritage park which occupied a larger scope, with complex constructions and more reconstruction of infrastructure pipeline network,

如遗址公园范围较大、建设情况复杂并对原有基础设施管网改造较多，应根据实际情况补充道路建设、电力电讯、给排水等基础设施

should according to the actual situation, supplement special plans for road construction, electric power and telecommunication, water supply and drainage and other infrastructure facilities. Following the principle of meeting the minimum functional requirements, various special plan should be in compliance with corresponding technical standards and specifications in order to minimize the impact of the transformation of infrastructure on the heritage and the surroundings. Infrastructure pipeline should keep away from archaeological heritage in order to avoid influencing landscape.

专项规划。各专项规划应符合相应技术标准和规范，以满足最低功能需求为原则，尽量减少基础设施改造对遗址本体和周边环境的影响。基础设施管线应避开考古遗迹，主要设施应避免影响景观。

11.4 Vertical plan

According to the burial depth, protection requirement of the heritage, and on-site natural condition, construction features and application requirements of the heritage park, under the circumstances of keeping the original land-form, and indicate control point elevation of the site, drainage slope and slope aspect, etc. measure and calculate the earthwork balance.

11.4 竖向规划

应根据遗址埋藏深度、遗址护要求、遗址公园场地自然状况、建设特点和使用需求等，在尽量保持原有地形地貌的情况下，标明场地控制点标高、排水坡度、坡向，测算土方平衡等。

11.5 Comprehensive disaster prevention plan

Where the safety protection of the heritage is complex, a comprehensive disaster prevention plan should formulated according to the actual disaster factors, including flood control, anti-earthquake, fire protection, guard against theft and lightning protection plan, etc. in terms of main disaster factors and according to relevant standards, reasonably confirm disaster prevention control and mitigation standards, put forward prevention measures and contingency plan.

11.5 综合防灾规划

遗址安全防范情况复杂的，应根据实际灾害因素制定综合防灾规划，包括防洪、防震、防火、防盗、防雷规划等。并根据主要灾害因素，按照相关标准合理确定灾害防治和避险的标准，提出防治措施及应急预案。

Article 12 Nodes deign should include:

12.1 Design the conceptual scheme under the guidance of overall design and select important nodes of the heritage park scientifically. The node selection should include main site display nodes, landscape nodes, main entrances and exits, important traffic nodes and important facilities, etc.

12.2 Conceptual design of the node should

第十二条 节点设计内容：

12.1 应在总体设计的指导下，科学选择遗址公园重要节点进行概念性方案设计。节点选择应包括遗址公园主要遗址展示节点、景观节点、主要出入口、重要交通节点、重要设施等。

12.2 节点概念性设计应包括节点总平面设

include the general plan design of nodes, 3D image display and construction control requirements, etc.

计、三维形象示意、建设控制要求等。

Article 13 Investment estimation should include:

According to the Plan, put forward the investment estimation for implementation of relevant projects in the heritage park.

第十三条 投资估算内容：

根据规划内容，提出遗址公园相关项目实施的投资估算。

Chapter III plan drawings

第三章 规划图纸

Article 14 plan drawing and content:

14.1 Regional-location drawing: Indicate the location of the heritage park administrative areas in different country, province, city, and different jurisdictions involved.

14.2 Heritage park area map: delineate the heritage park area and plan scope on the standard topographic map, and clarify the boundaries and coordinate points.

14.3 Remains distribution drawing: according to the latest archaeological outcomes, indicate various remains distribution of the heritage and their relationship with planned scope of the heritage park.

14.4 Cultural heritage resources analysis drawing: classify or grade the protection, conservation and utilization status of the cultural heritage resources which can be expressed by series of drawings. If there are any other cultural heritage resources existing within the scope of the heritage park, relevant cultural heritage resources analysis map can be draw.

14.5 Regional-location condition analysis drawing: indicate the external traffic condition, surrounding environment condition and surrounding infrastructure distribution which can be expressed by series of drawings.

14.6 Social conditions analysis drawing: indicate the distribution and status of the relevant social resources around the heritage park and spatial

第十四条 规划图纸与内容：

14.1 区位图：标明遗址公园所在地在国家、省、市等不同行政辖区的位置、所涉及的行政区划关系。

14.2 遗址公园范围图：在标准地形地图上划定遗址公园范围及规划范围，明确边界和坐标点。

14.3 遗存分布图：根据最新考古工作成果标明遗址的各类遗存分布情况，及其与遗址公园规划范围的关系。

14.4 文物资源分析图：分类或分级表达文物资源保存、保护和利用现状，可通过系列图纸表达。遗址公园范围内如有其他文物资源的，可绘制相关文物资源分析图。

14.5 区位条件分析图：标明遗址公园的外部交通条件、周边环境情况、周边基础设施分布等，可通过系列图纸表达。

14.6 社会条件分析图：标明遗址公园所处区域周边相关社会资源分布、现状及与遗址间的空间关系。

relationship with the heritage.

14.7 Environmental conditions analysis drawing: indicate the natural resource distribution, land-form features and buildings, roads, vegetation and other environmental elements around the heritage park.

14.8 Present land-use drawing: indicate the land use status within the Plan scope and provide the present land use balance sheet.

14.9 Archaeological and scientific research condition analysis drawing: indicate the area where the archaeological work has been developed, the previous archaeological outcomes, and the area where archaeological work is excavated and its implementation plan.

14.10 Management condition analysis drawing: indicate the current protection zone scope of the heritage, though series of drawings express various implemented plan measures, distribution and scale of the existing management and exhibition facilities, public exhibition area and visitors service infrastructures, etc.

14.11 Related plan analysis drawing: indicate other relevant plan involved in this area and relevant requirements about the heritage park and the construction projects which are planned to implement, etc.

14.12 Interpretation and presentation plan drawing: according to presentation and interpretation system plan, express interpretation and presentation structure and indicate the exhibition zone, exhibition streamline and important nodes distribution.

14.13 General layout drawing: on the base of accurate marking of present situation of the archaeological heritage, clearly express the main plan content within the Plan scope of the heritage park, such as main display object, traffic and facility distribution, etc.

14.14 Functional zone drawing: indicate the location, scope and area of heritage exhibition , management service zone, reserve zone and other

14.7 环境条件分析图：标明遗址公园所处区域周边自然资源分布，地貌特征，以及建筑、道路、植被等环境要素。

14.8 土地利用现状图：标明规划范围内的土地利用现状，提供现状用地平衡表。

14.9 考古和科研条件分析图：标明已开展考古工作的区域、历次考古工作成果、待开展考古工作的区域和实施计划。

14.10 管理条件分析图：标明遗址现行保护区划范围、已实施的各类规划措施、现有管理和展示设施分布与规模、开放展示区域与游客服务设施等，可通过系列图纸表达。

14.11 相关规划分析图：标明本区域涉及的其他相关规划以及涉及遗址公园的相关要求、计划实施的建设项目情况等。

14.12 阐释与展示规划图：根据展示与阐释体系规划，表达阐释与展示结构，标明展示分区、展示流线及重要节点分布。

14.13 总平面图：在准确标识考古遗址现状的基础上清晰表达遗址公园规划范围内的主要规划内容，如主要展示对象、道路交通、设施分布等。

14.14 功能分区图：标明遗址公园的遗址展示区、管理服务区、预留区等功能分区的位置、范围、面积。

function zones.

14.15 Presentation and interpretation system design drawing: series of drawings indicate the exhibition streamline of the heritage park, organization and distribution of various display methods, distribution of exhibition facilities such as museum, distribution and pattern of various panels or logos which can be expressed through a series of drawings.

14.15 展示与标识系统设计图：标明遗址公园展示流线、各类展示方式组织与分布、博物馆等展示设施分布、各类标识分布与样式，可通过系列图纸表达。

14.16 Traffic arrangement plan drawing: on the basis of accurate addressing of various remains, indicate the location of primary, secondary and special exits and entrances, scope and scale of parking lots and evacuation square both inside and outside of exits and entrances, distribution of various levels of roads and provision of traffic facilities.

14.16 交通组织规划图：在准确表达各类遗迹的基础上，标明遗址公园的主、次及专用出入口位置，停车场、出入口内外集散广场范围及规模，各级道路分布及交通设施配备。

14.17 Facilities distribution drawing: indicate the location and scale of various facilities.

14.17 设施分布图：标明各类设施的位置与规模。

14.18 Landscape spatial layout drawing: express analysis process of cultural characteristics of landscape and characteristics of natural resources, and indicate the integral spatial framework of the heritage park.

14.18 景观空间布局图：表达景观文化特征及自然资源特色分析过程，标明遗址公园整体空间架构。

14.19 Landscape control drawing of buildings and structures: express buildings and structures landscape control from style, mass, size, facade and architectural concept, which can be illustrated by pictures.

14.19 建构筑物风貌控制图：从风格、体量、规模、立面及建筑语汇等方面表达建构筑物景观风貌控制，可以图片示意。

14.20 Public environment landscape diagram: express the control requirement and design principle on important environmental facilities (interpretation panel, sculptures, sanitation facilities and advertisement, etc.), night-lighting and green landscape by landscape diagram.

14.20 公共环境景观示意图：通过景观示意图表达对重要环境设施（标识设施、雕塑小品、环卫设施、广告等）、夜景照明、绿化景观的控制要求和设计原则。

14.21 Special plan diagram: according to specific plan of heritage park, mapped archaeological and study implementation scheme drawing, management and operation plan drawing, infrastructure plan drawing, vertical plan design, comprehensive disaster prevention plan drawing and other special plan

14.21 专项规划图：根据遗址公园规划具体情况，可分别绘制考古与研究实施方案图、管理运营规划图、基础设施规划图、竖向规划图、综合防灾规划图等专项规划图纸，图纸要求应符合相关专业标准及规范。

drawings separately, and the requirements of the drawings should be in compliance with relevant professional standards and specifications.

14.22 Node design drawing: map the node general layout and 3D image schematic general. Such drawings should clearly indicate all contents of nodes designed, and the protection, presentation measures and construction control requirements should be indicated in the node.

14.22　节点设计图：绘制节点总平面图、三维形象示意总图，图纸应清晰表达节点设计的全部内容，遗址展示节点应注明遗址本体保护与展示措施及建设控制要求。

14.23 Aerial view and 3D drawing for expression of design intention: overall aerial view of the heritage park; aerial view or human visual effect drawing of important nodes; image diagrams of exhibition facilities, supporting facilities and other buildings; and other image diagrams such as sculptures, sanitation facilities.

14.23　鸟瞰图及表达设计意向的三维示意图：遗址公园全景鸟瞰图；重要节点鸟瞰或人视效果图；展示设施、配套设施等建筑的形象示意图；雕塑小品、环卫设施等的形象示意图。

Article XV plan drawing requirements:

15.1 Operational scale of the general plan should be determined according to the actual area, and in principle, the general plan should be mapped on the basis of the topographic map with precision no less than 1∶1000. The proportional scale of general plan should be 1∶500—1∶2000.

15.2 The proportional scale of node design plan should be 1∶100—1∶500.

15.3 The title, scale, north arrow, legend, name of plan unit and drawing time should be marked in the Plan drawing.

第十五条　规划图纸绘制要求：

15.1　规划总平面图应根据实际面积决定可操作的比例尺度，原则上应在不小于1∶1000精度地形图基础上绘制，总平面图比例尺为1∶500—1∶2000。

15.2　节点设计平面图比例尺为1∶100—1∶500。

15.3　规划图纸中需标注图名、比例尺、指北针、图例、规划单位名称、绘制时间。

Chapter IV Annex

Article XVI The Annex of The Plan should generally include:

16.1 Previous archaeology and research achievements.

16.2 Relevant documents or requirements of the local governments concerning the project approval, construction and management of the heritage park.

第四章　附件

第十六条　规划附件一般包括：

16.1　以往考古与研究成果。

16.2　地方政府关于遗址公园立项、建设与管理的相关文件或要求。

16.3 Summary content of the Plan include; implemented protection projects, completion reports, related requirements and stipulations of related plans such as local land-use, urban and rural construction, major infrastructure construction; general cultural heritage management plan drawing which has been approved and published, marked the Plan scope of the heritage park, the relationship between zoning and cultural heritage protection division, diagram for measures for cultural heritage protection and presentation plan drawing.

16.3 保护规划摘要内容，已实施的保护工程及竣工报告，所在地土地利用、城乡建设、重大基础设施建设等相关规划的有关要求和规定等内容；已批复公布的遗址文物保护规划总图，并标注遗址公园规划范围、分区与文物保护区划的关系，文物保护措施图、展示规划图。

国际文化遗产保护文件选编

（2006-2017）

COLLECTIONS OF INTERNATIONAL DOCUMENTS ON CULTURAL HERITAGE PROTECTION (2006-2017)

（下册）

编译：西安市文物保护考古研究院
联合国教科文组织世界遗产中心
国际古迹遗址理事会
国际古迹遗址理事会西安国际保护中心

Xi'an Institute of Archaeology
UNESCO World Heritage Center
International Council on Monuments and Sites (ICOMOS)
ICOMOS International Conservation Center-Xi'an (IICC-X)

文物出版社

国际文化遗产保护文件选编

（2006—2017）

编纂委员会

主　　编：冯　健　景　峰

校　　译：冯　健　李同仙　周剑虹　赵凤燕

责任终校：冯　健　李同仙

翻　　译：冯　健　李同仙　周剑虹　李尔吾　巩　天
张　良　曹铭婧　陶　亮　刘一思　周晓晨
姚　逊　张竞秋　李文博　李潇潇　李　丹
祝艺苗　李娜宁　赵　戈

目　录

CONTENTS

联合国教科文组织世界遗产中心《世界遗产申报准备工作手册》(2011) Preparing World Heritage Nominations (Second edition, 2011)

Original Title: Preparing World Heritage Nominations (Second edition, 2011)

文件原名：世界遗产申报准备工作手册（2011 年第二次修订）

Published in November 2011 by the United Nations Educational, Scientific and Cultural Organization.

联合国教科文组织 2011 年 11 月发布。

The designations employed and the presentation of material in this publication do not imply the expression of any opinion whatsoever on the part of UNESCO, ICCROM, ICOMOS and IUCN concerning the legal status of any country, territory, city or area or of its authorities, or concerning the delimitation of its frontiers or boundaries.

本出版物中采用的名称和材料编制方式，并不代表联合国教科文组织、国际文物保护与修复研究中心、国际古迹遗址理事会、世界自然保护联盟等组织对有关任何国家、领地、城市、地区及其当局的法律地位，或关于边界或分界线的规定表达任何意见。

The UNESCO World Heritage Centre, ICCROM, ICOMOS, IUCN and other participating organizations disclaim any errors or omissions in the translation of this manual from the original version in English, or from primary errors in any of the data interpreted within it.

对本手册英文版在翻译过程中出现的任何错误、遗漏或数据解释中的任何错误，联合国教科文组织世界遗产中心、国际文物保护与修复研究中心、国际古迹遗址理事会、世界自然保护联盟和其他参与组织，不承担相关责任。

This manual is a second edition. The first edition, Edition 2010, took as a reference *The Operational Guidelines for the Implementation of The World Heritage Convention (2008)*. This manual is based on the new version of The Operational Guidelines (2011).

本手册为第二版。2010 年第一版是 2008 年修订《实施世界遗产公约操作指南》的参考资料。本手册以 2011 年《操作指南》为基础。

Free non-profit use/reproduction of this manual

鼓励免费、非营利性使用或复制本手册，

is encouraged, always quoting the original source.

ICCROM
Via di San Michele 13
I-00153 Rome
Italy
Tel: +39 06 585-531
Fax: +39 06 585-53349
E-mail: iccrom@iccrom.org
http: //www.iccrom.org

ICOMOS
49-51, Rue de la Fédération
75015 Paris
France
Tel: +33 (0) 1 45 67 67 70
Fax: +33 (0) 1 45 66 06 22
E-mail: secretariat@icomos.org
http: //www.icomos.org

IUCN
Rue Mauverney 28
1196 Gland
Switzerland
Tel: +41 (22) 999-0000
Fax: +41 (22) 999-0002
E-mail: worldheritage@iucn.org
http: //www.iucn.org

UNESCO World Heritage Centre
7, Place de Fontenoy
75352 Paris 07 SP
France
Tel: +33 (0) 1 45 68 18 76
Fax: +33 (0) 1 45 68 55 70
E-mail: wh-info@unesco.org
http: //whc.unesco.org

ISBN 978-92-3-001029-4

以保证其引用的原真性。

国际文物保护与修复研究中心（ICCROM）
Via di San Michele 13
I–00153 Rome
Italy
Tel：+39 06 585–531
Fax：+39 06 585–53349
E–mail：iccrom@iccrom.org
http：//www.iccrom.org

国际古迹遗址理事会（ICOMOS）
49–51，Rue de la Fédération
75015 Paris
France
Tel：+33（0）1 45 67 67 70
Fax：+33（0）1 45 66 06 22
E–mail：secretariat@icomos.org
http：//www.icomos.org

世界自然保护联盟（IUCN）
Rue Mauverney 28
1196 Gland
Switzerland
Tel：+41（22）999–0000
Fax：+41（22）999–0002
E–mail：worldheritage@iucn.org
http：//www.iucn.org

联合国教科文组织世界遗产中心（UNESCO WHC）
7，Place de Fontenoy
75352 Paris 07 SP
France
Tel：+33（0）1 45 68 18 76
Fax：+33（0）1 45 68 55 70
E–mail：wh–info@unesco.org
http：//whc.unesco.org

ISBN 978–92–3–001029–4

Cover photo: uKhahlamba/Drakensberg Park, South Africa

© OUR PLACE - The World Heritage Collection

• www.ourplaceworldheritage.com

Graphic design: RectoVerso

With the support of Ireland

Preparing World Heritage Nominations •

Second edition, 2011

封面照片：uKhahlamba/德拉肯斯堡公园，南非，

© 我们的地方 – 世界遗产集

• www.ourplaceworldheritage.com

平面设计：RectoVerso

《申报世界遗产准备工作手册》编辑过程中得到爱尔兰的支持

• 2011 年第二版

1. About the World Heritage Resource Manual Series

Since *The World Heritage Convention* was adopted in 1972, the World Heritage List has continually evolved and is growing steadily. With this growth, a critical need has emerged for guidance for States Parties on the implementation of the Convention. Various expert meetings and results of Periodic Reporting have identified the need for more focused training and capacity development in specific areas where States Parties and World Heritage site managers require greater support. The development of a series of World Heritage Resource Manuals is a response to this need.

The publication of the series is a joint undertaking by the three Advisory Bodies of The World Heritage Convention (ICCROM, ICOMOS and IUCN) and the UNESCO World Heritage Centre as the Secretariat of the Convention. The World Heritage Committee at its 30th session (Vilnius, Lithuania, July 2006) supported this initiative and requested that the Advisory Bodies and the World Heritage Centre proceed with the preparation and publication of a number of thematic Resource Manuals. The 31st (2007) and 32nd (2008) sessions of the Committee adopted the publication plan and determined a prioritized list of titles.

An Editorial Board consisting of members of

1. 关于世界遗产资源系列手册

自 1972 年《世界遗产公约》通过后，《世界遗产名录》逐渐形成，遗产数目稳定增长。随着《世界遗产名录》中遗产数目逐渐增多，缔约国认为需要编制操作手册来确保公约的实施。各类专家会议和定期报告的结论也认为，需要关注特殊地区的人才培训和能力发展，缔约国对世界遗产的管理，也需要国际上大力支持。为满足这些需求，《世界遗产资源系列手册》应运而生。

这一套丛书由国际文物保护与修复研究中心、国际古迹遗址理事会、世界自然保护联盟等三个《世界遗产公约》的咨询机构，和作为《公约》秘书处的联合国教科文组织世界遗产中心共同编写。世界遗产委员会在第 30 届大会上（维尔纽斯，立陶宛共和国，2006）通过了这一倡议并要求这三家咨询机构和世界遗产中心着手准备编制这套丛书，并按照不同的主题，形成资源手册予以出版。第 31 届（2007 年）和第 32 届（2008 年）大会上，委员会确定了出版计划并决定了系列丛书的出版顺序。

编委会成员由三个咨询机构和世界遗产中

all three Advisory Bodies and the World Heritage Centre meets regularly to decide on different aspects of their preparation and publication. For each manual, depending on the theme, one of the Advisory Bodies or the World Heritage Centre functions as the lead agency responsible for coordination, while the final production is ensured by the World Heritage Centre.

心共同组成，编委会组织定期会议，研究在准备和出版过程中遇到的不同问题。对于每一部手册，根据主题不同，由一个咨询机构或世界遗产中心担任领导机构的职责，负责各种协调工作。最终成果由世界遗产中心确定。

The Resource Manuals are intended to provide focused guidance on the implementation of the Convention to States Parties, heritage protection authorities, local governments, site managers and local communities linked to World Heritage sites, as well as other stakeholders in the identification and preservation process. They aim to provide knowledge and assistance in ensuring a representative and credible World Heritage List consisting of well-protected and effectively managed properties.

《资源手册》为公约的缔约国、遗产管理机构、当地政府、遗产地管理者、与世界遗产相关的当地社区和其他利益相关者，在确定和保护遗产过程中提供指导意见。本丛书提供的知识和协助，有助于确保《世界遗产名录》的代表性和可靠性，让列入名录的遗产得到妥善保护和有效管理。

The manuals are being developed as user-friendly tools for capacity-building and awareness raising on The World Heritage Convention. They can be used independently for self-guided learning as well as material at training workshops, and should complement the basic provisions for understanding the text of *the Convention* itself and *The Operational Guidelines* for implementation.

这些手册将成为世界遗产中心能力建设和意识提升的有益工具。他们既可作为自学教材独立使用，也可以成为培训班的主要教材。这些教材可以帮助自学者更好的理解《世界遗产公约》和《操作指南》的主要内容。

The titles in this series are produced as PDF online documents which can be freely downloaded.

本手册 PDF 格式文件可在网上免费下载。

List of titles:

Managing Disaster Risks for World Heritage (June 2010)

Preparing World Heritage Nominations

Managing Cultural World Heritage

Managing Natural World Heritage

丛书包括：

世界遗产地灾害风险管理手册

（2010 年 6 月）

世界遗产地申报准备工作手册

世界文化遗产地管理手册

世界自然遗产地管理手册

Forward

In a constantly changing world, in which conservation challenges emerge on a daily basis, the capacity for adaptation is one of the main assets of *The World Heritage Convention*. Whereas the text of the Convention is essentially immutable, its *Operational Guidelines*, the provisions through which the principles of the Convention are implemented, allow for the integration and evolution of new concepts and processes. The latest revision of *The Operational Guidelines* (August 2011) addresses not only these new ideas, but also reflects, our growing collective experience.

Detailed analysis of all nomination files of properties inscribed on *the World Heritage List*, carried out at the end of the 1990s, revealed a situation that could have jeopardized the credibility of *the Convention*. Elements as essential as the boundaries of the inscribed property were often unknown or unclear. Nominations were made up of a few pages containing fairly generic information. With such limited documentation, even the protection and management of the inscribed property could have been compromised.

These shortcomings warranted an improved nomination process. A completeness check of nominations was introduced in 1999. Until then, nominations were automatically transmitted to the Advisory Bodies without a prior check of their content by the Secretariat. Consequently, for a large number of nomination files for properties inscribed between 1978 and 1998, the documentation available is basically inadequate with regard to conservation.

When a revised version of *The Operational Guidelines* came into force in 2005, a completeness check and a new and more detailed and annotated

序

随着社会的变迁，文化遗产保护所面临的挑战也日新月异，适应能力是《世界遗产公约》应具备的重要条件之一。公约内容没实质有变化，其《操作指南》，即关于《公约》原则具体实施的规定，却形成和发展了新的概念及进程。最新版本的《实施世界遗产公约操作指南》（2011 年 8 月）不但表达了这些新思想，而且也反映长期以来获得的经验。

通过对 20 世纪 90 年代末以来入围《世界遗产名录》的申遗文本的详细分析，揭示了对公约的信任危机。像遗产范围这样的核心组成部分在“遗产申报”文本中常常表述不清楚或者不为人知，只有寥寥几张纸。这些信息模糊、不全的文件甚至影响了相关已列入名录的遗产的保护和管理工作。

因为存在种种问题，必须改善遗产申报过程。1999 年，对遗产申报过程进行了全面审视。此前，没有要求提前把申遗文本交给秘书处检查，而是自动提交给顾问委员会。结果，在 1978—1998 年间的大量申遗文本中，有关遗产保护的信息都不够充分。

2005 年，《操作指南》的修订版正式公布，一个经过完整审核的、全新的、更详细的、有注释的申遗文本格式得到世界遗产委员会认可。

format for nominations were officially endorsed by the World Heritage Committee. Since 1999, the overall improvement of the quality and depth of information in nominations has substantially reinforced the World Heritage inscription process. In addition, it has helped to strengthen the implementation of the Convention, notably by enhancing and facilitating monitoring of the state of conservation of inscribed properties.

自1999年起，申遗文本中有关遗产信息描述的质量和深度得到改善，大大加强了世界遗产申报进程，增强了公约的实施力度，特别是增强并改善了对世界遗产保护状况的监测。

Along with increasingly comprehensive requirements, the preparation of nominations has become an important, but rather complex process which requires a good understanding of the various requirements. The participation of local people in the nomination process is also essential to enable them to have a shared responsibility with the State Party in the maintenance of the property, and has to be strongly encouraged.

由于申报要求变得日益全面、复杂，准备申遗文本成为一个异常重要、复杂的过程，需要深入了解各种要求。在遗产申报过程中，当地居民的参与具有重要的意义，有利于他们日后与缔约国共同进行遗产维护，必须大力支持。

The nomination document, along with the Advisory Bodies' evaluation, is the principal basis on which the Committee considers the inscription of properties on *the World Heritage List*. This document may be compared with an agreement between the State Party concerned and the international community, in which the former commits itself to protect and manage an identified property on its territory while the latter pledges support and assistance. Just like any agreement, the nomination should be accurate, informative and complete. If this is not the case, ensuring the fulfillment of the agreement between the State Party and the international community and the effective implementation of *The World Heritage Convention* become very difficult. For this reason, it is of great importance to provide to States Parties a manual for the preparation of nominations, in the form of a user-friendly guide, including information on various steps of the process.

申报材料和咨询机构的评估意见是世界遗产委员会考虑这些遗产地能否列入《世界遗产名录》最根本的依据。将这份文件和相关国家与国际社会的协议相比较，前者注重对本土申报遗产的管理和保护状况的描述，而后者更关注国际社会给予的协助和支持承诺。就像所有的协议一样，申遗文本必须要信息充足、内容准确和完整。否则，难以保证缔约国和国际社会之间有效实施、履行协议和《世界遗产公约》。鉴于此，为缔约国提供易于使用的、包含各申报程序和步骤的申报指南，成为一项非常重要的工作。

As a consequence of the greater prominence and recognition accorded to World Heritage, there is a growing range of interests and motivations behind seeking World Heritage inscription. So, while the feasibility of new procedures like the 'Upstream Processes' is currently being tested, the value of this manual is evident when looking at the increasing interest of States Parties in developing nominations, which present new justifications for Outstanding Universal Value, and the emergence of new themes to support nominations. Further, explanatory notes and practical guidance are necessary given the growing complexity of nominated properties, as is evident, for instance, in the increasing number of nominations of transnational serial sites, including some that are transcontinental in scope.

世界遗产越来越得到关注和认可，申报背后的利益和动机也越来越多。在测试“上游程序”等新程序的可行性同时，随着缔约国的遗产申报利益因素日益增加，对世界遗产的突出普遍价值有了新的认知，或出现了支持遗产申报的新主题，此时这本手册的价值是十分明显的。此外，遗产申报的过程越来越复杂，跨国、跨洲的系列遗产申报逐渐增加，本手册解释、注释作用和实用指导更为明显。

This Resource Manual has been produced with the above needs in mind, thanks to the invaluable help of the Advisory Bodies and a number of experts in the field. We hope that it will prove to be an effective tool to supplement the text of *The Operational Guidelines* in the preparation of successful nominations to help ensure the protection of World Heritage.

Kishore Rao
Director, UNESCO World Heritage Centre

感谢咨询委员会和专家们给予的无限的帮助，本《资源手册》的编写考虑了上述需求。我们希望这本手册可以成为实施《操作指南》的有效工具，也可以帮助缔约国成功申报遗产，从而确保对世界遗产的保护。

基紹尔·饶
联合国教科文组织
世界遗产中心主任

Contributors

Coordinating author
Duncan Marshall

IUCN authors
Tim Badman
Bastian Bomhard
Pedro Rosabal

ICOMOS authors
Duncan Marshall
Susan Denyer

编委会成员

主编：
邓肯·马歇尔

世界自然保护联盟作者
蒂姆·巴德曼，
巴斯蒂安·博姆哈德，
佩德罗·罗萨巴尔

国际古迹遗址理事会作者：
邓肯·马歇尔，
苏珊·丹尼尔

Paul Dingwall

保罗·丁沃尔

Reviewers/other contributors

审核、其他编著者：

Alessandro Balsamo
Gwenaëlle Bourdin
Kristal Buckley
Angel Cabeza
Claudine Déom
Regina Durighello
Phyllis Ellin
Nicolas Faucherre
Zhan Guo
Tilman Jaeger
Luba Janikova
Qiong Lu
Zhou Lv
Webber Ndoro
Christophe Rivet
Michael Turner
Gamini Wijesuriya

亚历山德罗·巴尔萨莫
格温内勒·布尔丹
克里斯朵·巴克利
安杰尔·卡贝扎
克劳丁·德奥姆
瑞吉娜·杜里格哈罗
菲莉斯·埃琳
尼古拉斯·福谢尔
郭旃
蒂尔曼·耶格
卢巴·珍妮科瓦
陆琼
吕舟
韦伯·恩杜罗
克里斯托夫·里维特
迈克尔·特纳
加米尼·维杰苏里亚

Other contributors relating to the previous draft natural and cultural nominations resource manuals, which are the basis for this combined manual, are as follows:

此前参与自然文化遗产申报手册草案的其他相关作者：

Natural nominations
Reviewers
World Heritage Centre
Alessandro Balsamo, World Heritage Centre
Guy Debonnet, World Heritage Centre
Marc Patry, World Heritage Centre
Kishore Rao, World Heritage Centre
Mechtild Rössler, World Heritage Centre
Peter Stott, former World Heritage Centre

自然遗产申报
审核
来自世界遗产中心：
亚历山罗德·巴尔萨莫
盖伊·德博内
马克·帕特里
基绍尔·饶
梅希特·罗斯勒
彼得·斯托特（前雇员）

ICCROM
Joe King, ICCROM
Gamini Wijesuriya, ICCROM

来自国际文物保护与修复研究中心：
乔·金
加米尼·维杰苏里亚

IUCN
Tarek Abdulhawa, IUCN
Delwyn Dupuis, IUCN
Elery Hamilton-Smith, IUCN
Kari Lahti, IUCN
Josephine Langley, IUCN
Georgina Peard, IUCN
Pedro Rosabal, IUCN
David Sheppard, IUCN
Kumiko Yoneda, IUCN

来自世界自然保护联盟：
塔雷克・阿卜杜勒哈瓦
德尔文・杜普伊斯
埃莱依・汉密尔顿・史密斯
卡里・拉赫蒂
约瑟芬・兰利
乔治娜・皮尔德
佩德罗・罗萨巴尔
大卫・谢帕德
库米克・耶内德

WCPA
Jim Barborak, WCPA
Stephanie Eissing, WCPA
Vinod Mathur, WCPA

来自世界保护区委员会：
吉姆・巴尔博克
斯蒂芬妮・艾星
维诺德・马瑟

Cultural nominations

文化遗产申报（国际古迹遗址理事会）：

Conception

Bénédicte Selfslagh, ICOMOS

策划

班尼迪克特・塞尔芙斯拉

Contributors
Gwenaëlle Bourdin, ICOMOS
Michel Cotte, ICOMOS
Regina Durighello, ICOMOS
Jukka Jokilehto, ICOMOS

撰稿
格温内勒・布尔丹
米歇尔・科特
瑞吉娜・杜里格哈罗
尤卡・约基莱赫托

Reviewers
World Heritage Centre
Alessandro Balsamo, World Heritage Centre
Mechtild Rössler, World Heritage Centre
Anne Lemaistre, World Heritage Centre

审核：
来自世界遗产中心：
亚历山罗德・巴尔萨莫
梅希特・罗斯勒
安妮・勒梅斯特

ICOMOS
Kristal Buckley, ICOMOS
Alfredo Conti, ICOMOS
Susan Denyer, ICOMOS
Nobuko Inaba, ICOMOS
Jukka Jokilehto, ICOMOS

来自国际古迹遗址理事会：
克里斯朵・巴克利
阿尔弗雷多・康蒂
苏珊・丹尼尔
稻叶信子
尤卡・约基莱赫托

Edward Matenga, ICOMOS
Bénédicte Selfslagh, ICOMOS

爱德华·马腾赫
班尼迪克特·塞尔芙斯拉

UNESCO World Heritage Centre coordination
Vesna Vujicic-Lugassy
Laura Frank

世界遗产中心协调人
韦斯娜·武伊契奇－鲁戈什
劳拉·弗兰克

Context

正文

Foreword by Kishore Rao, Director of UNESCO World Heritage Centre

序　联合国教科文组织世界遗产中心主任　基绍尔·饶　撰稿

Contributors

投稿人

Preface by ICOMOS and IUCN

前言　国际古迹遗址理事会和世界自然保护联盟

Introduction
Context and overview of the Resource Manual
Cooperation between States Parties
Who is the Resource Manual for?

介绍
资源手册正文及概述
缔约国间的合作
哪些人使用资源手册？

1 World Heritage background
1.1 Getting informed
1.2 Overview of the World Heritage nomination process
1.3 Illustrations of World Heritage concepts

1. 世界遗产背景
1.1　信息获得
1.2　世界遗产申报程序概述
1.3　世界遗产概念解读

2 Preparation
2.1 Existing information on the property
2.2 Setting up a team
2.3 Participation of local people and other stakeholders
2.4 Staging the preparation of a nomination and suggested key stages

2. 准备
2.1　遗产现状信息
2.2　建立团队
2.3　当地民众及其他利益相关者的参与
2.4　开始申报准备及确定关键步骤

3 Defining and understanding the property
3.1 Potential Outstanding Universal Value, attributes and boundaries
3.2 Extra tips

3. 定义和理解遗产
3.1　潜在突出普遍价值，特性及边界
3.2　特别建议

Preface

Preparing World Heritage Nominations has been compiled by ICOMOS and IUCN and provides additional guidance on preparing nominations to the World Heritage List for natural, cultural and mixed properties.

前言

国际古迹遗址理事会和世界自然保护联盟汇编《世界遗产申报准备工作手册》，为那些准备列入《世界遗产名录》的自然、文化和自然文化混合遗产提供进一步指导。

The manual is based on the version of *The Operational Guidelines for the Implementation of The World Heritage Convention dated* August 2011 and seeks to complement it. Anyone with a serious interest in preparing a World Heritage nomination should obtain a copy of the latest version of The *Operational Guidelines* and become familiar with its content.

手册是对 2011 年 8 月版的《实施世界遗产公约操作指南》的补充。任何有兴趣准备遗产申报的人都应该得到最新版本的《操作指南》，并熟知指南内容。

In particular, the manual seeks to support States Parties in implementing *The World Heritage Convention* and to provide guidance and knowledge that will help to ensure a credible *World Heritage List* of well-managed properties of Outstanding Universal Value. As requested by the World Heritage Committee and States Parties, it is an attempt to support States Parties at any early stage of the research process — upstream of the point at which a nomination is submitted for formal evaluation — as the Advisory Bodies evaluating

本手册为支持缔约国运用《世界遗产公约》，帮助缔约国更好的管理世界遗产的突出普遍价值，提供特别指导和知识，从而确保名录的公信力。根据世界遗产委员会和缔约国的要求，作为评估申遗文本的咨询委员会，国际古迹遗址理事会和世界自然保护联盟不能直接参与遗产申报的准备工作，本手册尝试帮助缔约国在正式提交遗产申报文件进行评估的初期阶段，就开展上游程序研究工作。所以，我们希望通过这个手册，能帮助缔约国仔细地考虑遗产申报过程的意义，实施必要的措施以确保遗产申

nominations, ICOMOS and IUCN, cannot work directly on the preparation of specific nominations. However, it is hoped that the manual will help States Parties to carefully consider the implications of proceeding with World Heritage nominations and take the necessary steps to ensure that the effort is worthwhile for both the conservation of the property and the well-being of local communities and other local stakeholders.

报成功，以便既能保护遗产，也能为当地居民和利益相关者带来福祉。

Lack of preparation time is the biggest enemy of successful nominations. Far too many are prepared against unrealistically short time frames. It can take at least a year to set up appropriate support mechanisms and gather material, and a further year to write the nomination text and consult stakeholders. When research is needed, protection has to be achieved, and new management systems put in place and documented, so the process might take much longer. If the aim is a successful nomination that leads to inscription on the World Heritage List and long-term conservation and presentation of the property, a realistic time frame should be allowed. Too often, lack of adequate preparation time leads to deferred or referred nominations, which is frustrating for States Parties, the World Heritage Committee and the Advisory Bodies. Sometimes political commitments are made which set an unrealistic time frame for preparing a nomination, resulting in a nomination dossier which is inadequate and not ready for evaluation.

准备时间不足是遗产申报成功的劲敌。有些遗产甚至预备根据一个不现实的短期时间表进行遗产申报。建立适当的支持机制和收集基础资料至少需要一年的时间，编写申遗文本并与利益相关者协商达成协议也需要一年的时间。如果还需考虑进一步研究、了解保护措施的成效、运行新的管理系统和收集整理相关档案等事情，将会需要更长的时间准备申报。如果遗产申报成功的目的是遗产列入《世界遗产名录》并且得到长时间保护和展示，就应该准备一个合理而实际的时间表。有很多因为缺少足够的准备时间而被推迟列入或发还待议的申报实例，这样的结果是缔约国、世界遗产委员会和咨询委员会都不愿意看到。有些时候，因政治承诺的原因，制定了不切实际的遗产申报准备时间表，致使申遗文本材料内容不全面，委员会无法进行评估。

This manual brings together current knowledge and available resources to help States Parties to compile nominations for properties. It seeks to highlight and explain in straightforward terms those parts of *The Operational Guidelines* that are relevant to World Heritage nominations. Additionally, clear guidance is given on the overall approach to preparing nominations, on preparatory

本手册将目前遗产申报的最新知识和可利用的资源汇集在一起，帮助缔约国编制申遗文本。本书力求简明扼要的解释和说明《操作指南》中与遗产申报相关的各个部分。此外，对于遗产申报的整体方法，例如一个遗产在决定申报之前的预备工作、在申遗文本中必须包含的关键内容等，本书中将会有系统的论述。本手册没有涵盖文件中需要的所有内容，只是根

work needed before a decision is taken to nominate a property, and on the critical elements to be included in a nomination dossier. The manual does not however cover all aspects of a dossier, but identifies those aspects that, in the experience of the Advisory Bodies, are often not comprehensively prepared in many nominations.

据咨询委员会的经验，提出了此前诸多申遗文本中准备不够充分的部分问题。

Publication is supported by the World Heritage Fund and the Department of Environment, Heritage and Local Government of Ireland. Funding and volunteer support from ICOMOS, IUCN and their networks is gratefully recognized.

本书的出版得到世界遗产基金会和爱尔兰环境、遗产部门以及当地政府的大力支持。同时，国际古迹遗址理事会和世界自然保护联盟也为本书的编撰提供了大量的人力物力支持。特此鸣谢。

ICOMOS and IUCN hope that the advice in this manual proves useful and welcome feedback on any suggested improvements.

国际古迹遗址理事会和世界自然保护联盟希望本书的内容对缔约国有帮助，同时也希望缔约国提出意见和建议，便于我们改正提高。

Context and overview of the Resource Manual

资源手册的内容和综述

The aim of this Resource Manual is to help States Parties to achieve good quality World Heritage nominations.

编写资源手册丛书的目的是为了帮助缔约国高质量完成世界遗产申报工作。

The World Heritage Convention and The *Operational Guidelines for the Implementation of The World Heritage Convention* (latest version dated August 2011) are key documents and can be found on the World Heritage Centre website. *The Operational Guidelines* are crucial to understanding the way The World Heritage Convention works. The manual should be used in conjunction with the most recent version of *The Operational Guidelines* - which are revised from time to time by the World Heritage Committee. The guidelines should be read before this manual, and carefully consulted throughout the process of preparing nominations.

《世界遗产公约》和《实施世界遗产公约操作指南》(简称《操作指南》)，2011 年 8 月版本（2013 年 6 月修订）是世界遗产委员会的核心文件，可在世界遗产中心的网站上免费下载。《操作指南》是了解《世界遗产公约》运作方式的重要工具。本手册应该和最新版本的《操作指南》联合使用（世界遗产委员会根据需要不断修订《操作指南》)，在使用手册前，应通读《操作指南》，并在整个遗产申报准备的过程中查阅参考。

Definitive advice on *the Operation* and requirements of *The World Heritage Convention* is

《操作指南》中决定性意见和《世界遗产公约》的要求，在《公约》和《操作指南》的内

contained in the Convention text itself and in *The Operational Guidelines*. This manual does not replace *The Operational Guidelines* in any way but provides additional guidance. In all cases, *the Convention* and *Operational Guidelines* remain the primary references. The text of *The World Heritage Convention* (available in Arabic, Chinese, English, French, Hebrew, Portuguese, Russian and Spanish) and *The Operational Guidelines* (in English and French) are available from the UNESCO World Heritage Centre and on its website (http: //whc.unesco.org/).

容中都有所表现。因此，《手册》不能替代《操作指南》，只能作为《操作指南》的辅助和补充。任何情况下，遗产申报的首选参考文献依旧是《公约》和《操作指南》。《世界遗产公约》（提供阿拉伯语、中文、英语、法语、希伯来语、葡萄牙语、俄语和西班牙语版本）和《操作指南》（英语和法语）可以在世界遗产中心及其官网上找到。（http ：//whc.unesco.org/）

There are many different ways to prepare a nomination. The diversity of administrative structures and cultures are necessarily reflected in the nominations. It is not appropriate to give ‘recipes’ or to recommend a preferred working method for preparing nominations. There are many different good ways of doing so. Nevertheless the Advisory Bodies consider that there are a few underlying basic principles which should underpin all good nominations to ensure that the most appropriate properties are nominated, properties are represented as effectively as possible within nominations, and the nomination process itself contributes to protection, conservation and effective management of natural and cultural heritage.

准备申报世界遗产有许多不同的方法。行政机构和文化的多样性都会对遗产申报形成一定的影响。给遗产申报提供“秘方”或推荐最佳的工作方式都是不合适的，因为遗产申报有多种不同的好方法。不过，咨询委员会认为，好的遗产申报方法应该遵循几条最为根本的原则，从而确保选择最适合的遗产列入遗产名录，同时，遗产申报过程本身也对自然和文化遗产的保存、保护和有效管理产生积极的影响。

There are many similarities, but also significant differences, between the preparation of cultural heritage nominations and natural heritage nominations. Accordingly several sections of this manual apply specifically to either cultural or natural heritage properties. Note however the differentiation that was formerly made between the cultural and natural criteria no longer exists.

虽然申报世界文化遗产和自然遗产的过程存在着很多相似之处，但他们之间也有明显的差别。鉴于此，本书的部分章节侧重自然遗产申报，另一部分章节侧重文化遗产申报。需要注意的是，早期划分文化遗产和自然遗产的标准已经不复存在。

The concept of ‘Outstanding Universal Value’ underpins *The World Heritage Convention*. It is the touchstone for all inscribed properties. The

“突出普遍价值”的概念是《世界遗产公约》根基，也是遗产列入名录的检验标准。遗产申报的最根本目的是要说清楚遗产是由哪些部分

basic purpose of nominations is to say what a property consists of, why it demonstrates potential Outstanding Universal Value, and how this value will be sustained, protected, conserved, managed, monitored and communicated.

构成的，它是如何证明潜在的突出普遍价值的，以及用什么样的方法可以维持、保存、保护、管理、监测和向公众转达这些价值。

This manual seeks to:

本书的内容包括：

- stress the importance of understanding the World Heritage nomination system;
- highlight and explain in simple terms key World Heritage concepts;
- emphasize the importance of the team in preparing a nomination;
- provide a better understanding of the scope of work in preparing a nomination;
- provide information and tips on understanding the property; and
- provide tips on preparing the nomination file to help to clarify The Operational Guidelines.

- 强调并了解世界遗产申报体系的重要性；
- 强调并以简明的术语解释世界遗产的相关概念；
- 强调遗产申报准备工作中团队的重要性；
- 明确遗产申报准备工作的范畴；
- 提供理解遗产的信息和技巧；
- 提供准备申遗文本的建议，以帮助阐释《操作指南》。

The manual also provides some advice on proposals for an extension to an existing World Heritage property, as a significant extension is treated as a new nomination.

本手册对扩展已列入《世界遗产名录》的遗产组成部分也具有参考作用，因为意义重大的扩展等同于一个新的遗产申报项目。

Cooperation between States Parties

缔约国之间的合作

The World Heritage Convention explicitly promotes international cooperation in achieving the goals of *the Convention*. The process of preparing nominations to the World Heritage List provides many opportunities for such cooperation, including:

- technical and financial assistance provided by one State Party to another;
- development of trans-boundary/transnational nominations;
- research to develop a sound comparative analysis; and
- assisting with the international peer review of

《世界遗产公约》希望通过国际间的合作实现《公约》的目标。遗产申报过程提供了许多这样的合作机会：

- 提供缔约国之间的资金和技术协助；
- 开展跨境或跨国遗产申报；
- 进行深入的比较分析研究；
- 在正式提交申遗文本前，提供一个机会让

nominations prior to formal lodgement.

World Heritage nominations should not be viewed as a competition between States Parties as this would be contrary to the entire spirit of The *World Heritage Convention*.

文本先接受国际同行的评议。

世界遗产申报不是缔约国之间的竞争，这种认知有悖于《世界遗产公约》的宗旨。

Who is the Resource Manual for?

资源手册的使用人群

This manual is primarily for all those who are involved in developing World Heritage nominations for properties. It may also prove useful for the preparation of Tentative Lists, and for other heritage listing activities.

本手册适用于参与世界遗产申报工作的工作人员。同时它也能为准备申报预备遗产名录或申报其他遗产名录工作的人员提供帮助。

In addition, it will be of interest to:

- States Parties including federal and national levels;
- heritage protection/protected area agencies;
- non-governmental organizations (NGOs);
- local governments;
- local communities;
- institutions;
- persons giving training workshops or courses on the development of World Heritage nominations; and
- concerned individuals.

The manual is designed to be a tool for:

- self-guided learning;
- training workshops; and
- briefing and educating.

另外，本书还适宜于以下人群：

- 包括联邦和国家层面的缔约国；
- 遗产保护或保护区的管理机构；
- 非政府组织；
- 当地政府；
- 当地社区；
- 研究机构；
- 参与世界遗产申报培训班或课程的个人；
- 相关个人；

本书可作为工具书用于：

- 自学指导；
- 培训班；
- 简介和教育。

1. World Heritage background

1. 世界遗产的背景

Key message: Be well prepared and organized to develop a nomination.

关键信息：认真准备和组织申报

1.1 Getting informed

1.1 获取信息

Introduction

概要

Preparing a World Heritage nomination can be one of the most satisfying and rewarding of

遗产申报工作是所有参与人员获得满足感和实践经验的最好方法之一。遗产申报的准备

experiences for those involved. The preparation of a nomination provides a chance to:

• understand and present a property to the international community;

• critically review the known values of a property and assess its relationship to global natural and cultural themes — to locate the property in the broad sweep of natural history, human history, culture and development;

• compare the property on an international level with other potentially similar properties;

• test, challenge and improve the adequacy of the property's protection, conservation and management, including the protection of its setting;

• engage and support communities and stakeholders in the protection, conservation and management of a property; and

• recognize the range of interests in a property, sometimes including conflicting interests, and seek ways of effectively addressing the various interests.

工作提供了如下机会：

• 向国际社会展示了解遗产；

• 全面回顾遗产已知价值、评估遗产与全球自然和文化主题的关系——在自然历史、人类历史、文化和发展的广阔的视野下定位遗产；

• 在国际上与其他潜在的、类似遗产进行比较研究的机会；

• 检验、挑战和提高遗产保存、保护和管理的机会（包括遗产环境的保护）；

• 吸引和支持社区、利益相关者参与保存、保护和管理遗产等工作；

• 梳理遗产的利益范围，有时包括利益冲突，寻求平衡各方利益的方法。

Some possible benefits from World Heritage status are:

• providing an opportunity for the State Party and for the local community to celebrate the property as one of the most important natural and cultural places on Earth;

• the property often becomes a flagship for the national protected area/site system, including a deeper recognition and better protection for heritage in the life of the community;

• international interest in World Heritage often provides a stimulus for international cooperation and joint efforts to ensure the protection of the property;

• providing opportunities to mobilize funding and support, including from donors, and the World Heritage Fund; and

• providing techniques and practices for protection, conservation and management that can

世界遗产的身份所带来的收益有：

• 为缔约国和当地社区提供一个宣传该遗产成为世界上最重要的自然或文化地的机会；

• 列入《世界遗产名录》的遗产常常成为一个国家的保护区或保护体系的标志，包括唤起公众加深对遗产的认知和更好的保护遗产；

• 国际对世界遗产的关注常常会提供国际合作的机会，共同努力完成遗产的保护工作；

• 提供筹措资金和获得资金支持的机会，包括来自捐赠、世界遗产基金会的资金；

• 提供把保存、保护技术和管理实践应用于国家和当地遗产的机会。

be applied to national and local heritage properties.

Developing a World Heritage nomination involves a journey that takes time and effort. Preparing a nomination usually involves at least two years' work — sometimes many years. Being well prepared and organized for developing a nomination will keep this time and effort to a minimum. On the other hand, a lack of preparation often extends the time and multiplies the effort.

完成一个世界遗产的申报过程是一次需要花费时间和努力的行程。准备申报常常需要至少二年、甚至更长的时间。有效的、好的准备和组织将会缩短遗产申报时间，节省精力。而缺少准备工作常常会延长时间并需要付出成倍的努力。

The character of the nominated property can also influence the time and effort required. For example, a well-researched cultural monument or site can require a much less complicated and less time-consuming nomination process than, for example, a large multi-use natural property, a historic town, a cultural landscape or a cultural route. In the latter cases, the stakeholders are also generally multiplied, resulting in a more complicated management system or plan. In other cases, time may be needed to provide an adequate thematic context, if a relevant thematic study is not already available.

申报遗产的特性也会影响遗产申报所需的时间和付出的努力。例如，申报一个有很好研究基础的文化文物或遗址，与那些用途多、规模大的自然遗产、历史城镇、文化景观或文化线路相比，用时更短，程序更简单。对于后者而言，由于利益相关者更多更复杂，他们需要的管理体系或者规划也更为复杂。如果遗产没有进行相关的专题研究，那么还要花费时间完成相关研究工作，以充分确立遗产地在该类别遗产中的地位。

World Heritage nominations are fundamentally concerned with the potential Outstanding Universal Value of properties. The nomination process should not be primarily motivated by perceived economic development opportunities.

申报世界遗产时关注的核心是遗产蕴含的突出普遍价值。所有获得经济发展机会不应该成为遗产申报的主要动机。

A World Heritage nomination is also just the start of a much longer journey towards the improvement of conservation processes at all levels. If a nomination is successful, World Heritage inscription commits the State Party to the ongoing care of the property to ensure its Outstanding Universal Value is protected, conserved and managed for all time.

申报世界遗产只是全面提升遗产保护漫漫征程的第一步。如果申报成功，世界遗产所在国就将长久地担负起保存、保护和管理遗产突出普遍价值的责任。

Case study
Timing to prepare a nomination

Canal du Midi (France) — This property was inscribed in 1996 after a two-year process to prepare the nomination. The short time frame is a considerable achievement given the long length of the property (360 km) and large number of communities involved. Elements which were important in achieving a relatively short time frame included:

- the quick establishment of an effective steering committee and scientific committee;
- committee members were intellectually and practically ready and able to develop the nomination;
- the various communities fully supported the nomination;
- funding for preparing the nomination was quickly arranged;
- the local offices of national ministries contributed fully and effectively;
- an effective coordinator was appointed and accepted by the many stakeholders;
- good basic information was readily available at the start of the process;
- drafting the nomination was collectively understood as an intellectual exercise aiming at excellence, not as a bureaucratic task of completing a form; and
- the various government agencies worked cooperatively and effectively in favour of the nomination.

案例研究
准备申报的时间

米迪运河（法国）——遗产在经过两年的准备后，1996 年列入《世界遗产名录》。鉴于遗产的长度（360 公里）和涉及众多的社区，在短短两年内完成遗产申报无疑是一个巨大的成功。在相对较短的时间内实现遗产成功申报的原因有以下几点：

- 迅速成立了有效的指导委员会和科学委员会；
- 委员会成员有准备遗产申报的知识和能力；
- 各社区全力支持遗产申报；
- 遗产申报资金快速到位；
- 国家部委下属机构对当地全力而有效的帮助；
- 高效且同时得到不同的利益相关者认可和接受的协调机制；
- 准备充足的基础信息为开展遗产申报工作奠定了良好的基础；
- 全体成员都认为编写遗产申报文件草案是一种力求完美的学术实践，而不仅仅是走程序完成填表任务；
- 政府的各个管理机构通力完成申遗工作。高效合作。

Key message: Understand the recommended documents before starting a nomination.

关键信息：在开始准备遗产申报文件之前全面了解推荐的参考资料

Learning about World Heritage - important documents

了解世界遗产—重要文件

An important first step in being well prepared is to become well informed about the World Heritage

遗产申报准备工作的最重要的一步就是掌握丰富的世界遗产知识体系，遗产申报过程和

system, processes and other information specifically relevant to the property to be nominated.

其他与遗产申报遗产相关的特殊信息，都应该包含在这个体系中。

A list of recommended reference documents which should be understood is below. Many of these are available through the internet or otherwise in hard copy from the relevant organizations. Contact details can be found at the end of the manual.

下面是推荐的参考文档。这些文档可以在网络下载或从其他相关组织得到。具体联络方式本可以手册结尾处找到。

The bibliography at the end of this manual also contains many other worthwhile references.

本手册后记的参考书目也包含其他许多有价值的参考文献。

Important reference World Heritage documents General	Comments
World Heritage Convention (formally Convention concerning the Protection of the World Cultural and Natural Heritage, 1972)	The Convention provides the fundamental framework for the World Heritage system. It provides key definitions concepts, organizational structures and processes - including those relating to nominations. Available in Arabic, Chinese, English, French, Hebrew, Portuguese, Russian and Spanish: http: //whc.unesco.org/en/conventiontext/ (English web page) http: //whc.unesco.org/fr/conventiontexte/ (French web page)
Operational Guidelines for the Implementation of The World Heritage Convention (WHC.11/01, August 2011)	The main guidance on the implementation of The World Heritage Convention is set out in The Operational Guidelines, which detail procedures for a range of key World Heritage processes, including nomination processes. The Operational Guidelines also include a list of recommended documents to read in the bibliography. These should also be carefully examined, as some documents will be especially relevant to certain nominations. The latest and past versions of The Operational Guidelines are available at: http: //whc.unesco.org/en/guidelines/ (English web page) http: //whc.unesco.org/fr// (French web page)
Decisions and the Summary Record of recent World Heritage Committee meetings	An important source of information about the views of the World Heritage Committee can be found in the decisions and summary records of recent Committee meetings. http: //whc.unesco.org/en/sessions/ (English web page) http: //whc.unesco.org/fr/sessions/ (French web page)
World Heritage List	The World Heritage List contains properties inscribed by the World Heritage Committee for their Outstanding Universal Value. The List is an important source because it may identify properties in other countries which are comparable to the property being considered for nomination. If so, this will be useful information to consider in the comparative assessment part of the nomination dossier. http: //whc.unesco.org/en/list/ (English web page) http: //whc.unesco.org/fr/list/ (French web page)
Tentative Lists of other States Parties	These are lists of properties which might be of World Heritage value. The Tentative Lists are important because they may identify properties in other countries which are comparable to the property being considered for nomination. If so, this will be useful information to consider in the comparative assessment part of the nomination dossier. http: //whc.unesco.org/en/tentativelists/ (English web page) http: //whc.unesco.org/fr/listesindicatives/ (French web page)

续表

Important reference World Heritage documents General	Comments
Thematic studies,	Thematic studies, where these exist, provide a very important information source to help with nominations. If there is a thematic study relevant to the property proposed for nomination, then the study will be of great assistance in preparing the comparative analysis part of the nomination dossier. In some cases, States Parties have prepared specific thematic analyses as part of the process of developing a nomination dossier. Thematic studies for cultural properties which are available from ICOMOS can be found at www.icomos.org/studies/. Thematic studies for natural properties which are available from IUCN can be found at www.iucn.org. In addition, there may be other thematic studies, and research should be undertaken to identify any studies relevant to the property to be nominated.
Report of the World Heritage Global Strategy Natural and Cultural Heritage Expert Meeting, 25 to 29 March 1998, *Amsterdam, The Netherlands* (UNESCO World Heritage Centre / Government of the Netherlands, 1998)	This report contains useful background information as well as conclusions and recommendations regarding Outstanding Universal Value. http: //whc.unesco.org/archive/amsterdam98.pdf
Natural heritage references	
Outstanding Universal Value-Standards for Natural World Heritage, A Compendium on Standards for Inscriptions of Natural Properties on the World Heritage List (IUCN, 2008b)	This report prepared by IUCN reviews past World Heritage Committee inscription decisions relating to natural properties. It provides a compendium of relevant material and decisions, compiled into a guidance manual, giving clear precedents on how to interpret and apply discussions of Outstanding Universal Value, in terms of nominations to the World Heritage List. http: //data.iucn.org/dbtw-wpd/edocs/2008-036.pdf
Cultural heritage references	
The World Heritage List: Filling the Gaps - An Action Plan for the Future (ICOMOS, 2005a)	This ICOMOS analysis of cultural properties on the World Heritage List and Tentative Lists is a contribution to the further development of the Global Strategy for a credible, representative and balanced World Heritage List. The analysis is a work in progress by ICOMOS and considers the typological, regional, chronological and thematic representations on the lists. A key aim was to identify under-represented categories of properties on the World Heritage List. Consulting this study will assist in the development of the comparative analysis for a nomination. In general, under-represented categories are more likely to succeed compared with well or over-represented categories. http: //www.international.icomos.org/world_heritage/gaps.pdf (English web page) http: //www.international.icomos.org/world_heritage_fre/whlgaps.htm (French web page)
Compendium on Standards for the Inscription of Cultural Properties to the World Heritage List (ICOMOS, 2008)	This report prepared by ICOMOS reviews past World Heritage Committee inscription decisions relating to cultural properties. It provides a compendium of relevant material and decisions, compiled into a guidance manual, giving clear precedents on how to interpret and apply discussions of Outstanding Universal Value, in terms of nominations to both the World Heritage List and the List of World Heritage in Danger. http: //whc.unesco.org/en/sessions/32COM/documents/ (see WHC.08 /32.COM /9)

续表

Important reference World Heritage documents General	**Comments**
Thematic and Regional Bibliographies prepared by the ICOMOS Documentation Centre	Many of these bibliographies are relevant to cultural properties, including those on: *Modern Heritage Properties (19th and 20th Centuries) on the World Heritage List* *World Heritage Rock Art Sites* *World Heritage Cultural Landscapes* *World Heritage Urban Sites* *World Heritage Hominid Sites* *World Heritage in Africa* *World Heritage in Asia and Pacific* *Patrimonio Mundial en América Latina y Caribe* *World Heritage in Arab States* *Industrial and Technical Heritage in the World Heritage List http: //www.international.icomos.org/centre_documentation/bib/index.hthml*
International Charter for the Conservation and Restoration of Monuments and Sites (The Venice Charter 1964) (ICOMOS,1965)	*This Charter is one of the key guiding documents for the conservation of cultural heritage properties.* *http: //www.international.icomos.org/charters.htm (English web page)* *http: //www.international.icomos.org/chartes.htm (French web page)*

重要参考文件	注释
综合参考	
《世界遗产公约》（保护世界文化与自然遗产公约），1972	《公约》提供了世界遗产体系的基本框架。公约提供了与遗产申报相关的重要的定义、概念、组织结构和程序。 提供阿拉伯、中、英、法、希伯来、葡萄牙、俄和西班牙语的版本：http ：//whc.unesco.org/en/conventiontext/（英文） http ：//whc.unesco.org/fr/conventiontexte/（法文）
《实施世界遗产公约操作指南》（2011.8）	是使用《世界遗产公约》的主要指南，详细叙述了包括申报在内的一系列与世界遗产相关的操作过程。 《操作指南》在其参考书目中推荐了一些需要仔细研读的、与特定遗产申报程序相关的文件。 最新版本和以前版本的《操作指南》在以下网站下载。 http ：//whc.unesco.org/en/guidelines/（英文） http ：//whc.unesco.org/fr//（法文）
近期世界遗产委员会的决议和会议记录刚要	记录世界遗产委员会员会观点的重要信息来源，记录最近的世界遗产委员会员会的决议和会议记录纲要等。 http ：//whc.unesco.org/en/sessions/（英文） http ：//whc.unesco.org/fr/sessions/（法文）
《世界遗产名录》	《世界遗产名录》收录了世界遗产委员会选择的具有突出普遍价值的遗产。名录使申报遗产得以与已列入遗产名录其他国家的类似遗产进行比较。因此，名录将成为各国准备申遗文本时进行比较评估的重要资源。 http ：//whc.unesco.org/en/list/（英文） http ：//whc.unesco.org/fr/list/（法文）

续表

重要参考文件	注释
各个国家的《预备名录》	《预备名录》中的遗产可能具有世界遗产的价值。《预备名录》可以确定拟申报的遗产与其他国家的遗产是否相似，因此十分重要。因此，《预备名录》的信息可以用来进行比较分析。 http：//whc.unesco.org/en/tentativelists/（英文） http：//whc.unesco.org/fr/listesindicatives/（法文）
专题研究	专题研究为遗产申报提供了重要的信息资源。如果对预备申报的遗产进行了相关的专题研究，研究成果将对准备申遗文本的比较分析部分提供重要的帮助。 在某些情况下，缔约国完成详细的专题分析，可作为遗产申报过程中编制申遗文本的一个必要组成部分。 文化遗产的专题研究见国际古迹理事会官网。www.icomos.org/studies/. 自然遗产的专题研究见世界自然保护联盟官网。www.iucn.org. 此外，还有其他的专题研究，应加以甄别，确定其与欲申报遗产相关的研究。
《自然和文化遗产全球战略专家会议报告》，1998 年 3 月 25–29，阿姆斯特丹，荷兰（联合国教科文组织世界遗产中心 / 荷兰政府）	这份报告包括有用的背景资料，同时也包括突出普遍价值的研究结论和介绍。 http：//whc.unesco.org/archive/amsterdam98.pdf
自然遗产参考资料	
《突出普遍价值—世界自然遗产标准》，《自然遗产列入世界遗产名录的标准纲要》（世界自然保护联盟，2008b）	这个报告由世界自然保护联盟提供，回顾了世界遗产委员会有关自然遗产申报的决议。它提供了相关材料和决议的纲要并编入手册丛书，提供了如何利用以前的实例来解说和讨论待申报遗产的突出普遍价值。 http：//data.iucn.org/dbtw–wpd/edocs/2008–036.pdf
文化遗产参考资料	
《世界遗产名录：填补空白——未来行动计划》（ICOMOS，2005a）	国际古迹理事会对《世界遗产名录》和《预备名录》中的文化遗产进行了分析，进一步为建立一个可信的、具有代表性和平衡性的《世界遗产名录》的全球战略做贡献。咨询分析是国际古迹理事会正在进行的一项工作，划分了遗产名录中的遗产类型、区域、年代和专题。研究的主要目的是要确定在《世界遗产名录》中哪类遗产的份额偏低。本研究将对申报过程中的比较分析研究提供帮助。一般而言，份额偏低的遗产类型，要比数量较多、份额较高的遗产类型申报成功的可能性更大。 http：//www.international.icomos.org/world_heritage/gaps.pdf（英文）http：//www.international.icomos.org/world_heritage_fre/whlgaps.htm（法文）
《文化遗产世界遗产名录的标准纲要》（ICOMOS，2008）	国际古迹理事会对世界遗产委员会将文化遗产列入名录时所形成的决议进行了系统的回顾，并形成了报告。这个报告提供相关材料和决议纲要并编入手册丛书，提供了如何利用以前的实例来解说和讨论遗产的突出普遍价值，特别是申报《世界遗产名录》和列入《濒危世界遗产名录》。 http：//whc.unesco.org/en/sessions/32COM/documents/（见 WHC.08 /32.COM /9）
国际古迹理事会文献中心已有的专题或区域性的文献	文献中心有许多关于文化遗产的参考文献，包括： 《〈世界遗产名录〉中的当代遗产（19–20 世纪）》；《世界遗产中的岩画艺术遗产》；《世界遗产中的文化景观》；《世界遗产中的城市遗产》；《世界遗产中的原始人类遗址》；《非洲的世界遗产》；《亚太地区的世界遗产》；《拉美及加勒比地区世界遗产》；《阿拉伯国家的世界遗产》；《世界遗产中的工业和技术遗产》。 http：//www.international.icomos.org/centre_documentation/bib/index.html
《修复和保护文物和遗址的国际宪章》（威尼斯宪章，1964 年）ICOMOS 1965 年	《威尼斯宪章》是文化遗产保护领域的最基础的指导性文件之一。http：//www.international.icomos.org/charters.htm（英文） http：//www.international.icomos.org/chartes.htm（法文）

Learning about World Heritage — the work of the World Heritage Committee

了解世界遗产——世界遗产委员会的工作

Key massage: Send a representative of the nomination team to World Heritage Committee meetings.

从遗产申报团队中选派代表参加世界遗产委员会大会

It is very helpful to have some familiarity with the work of the World Heritage Committee. This can be achieved partly through an understanding of *The World Heritage Convention* and The *Operational Guidelines*. As noted above, reviewing the decisions and the Summary Record of recent World Heritage Committee meetings will also help.

了解世界遗产委员会的工作有利于申报。掌握《世界遗产公约》和《操作指南》可以部分了解委员会工作内容。而全面回顾近年来遗产委员会会议形成的决议和会议记录纲要，也有助于理解委员会的工作。

In addition, it is very beneficial if a representative of the team preparing the nomination is included in the National Delegation sent to World Heritage Committee meetings. Watching the proceedings of the Committee provides an important insight into its work, especially the deliberations about nominations and state of conservation matters.

此外，遗产申报团队派一个成员跟随国家代表团参加世界遗产委员会会议，有益于理解委员会的工作。亲历委员会的议程，特别是审议申遗文本和评估保护现状，能深入了解委员会的工作。

***The World Heritage Convention* at a glance**

《世界遗产公约》概览

The World Heritage Convention is an international treaty between Member States of the United Nations. It seeks to identify, protect, conserve, present and transmit to future generations cultural and natural heritage of Outstanding Universal Value. Specific criteria and conditions, defined in *The Operational Guidelines* of *the Convention*, are used to identify properties for inclusion on the World Heritage List.

《世界遗产公约》是联合国各成员国之间的国际性条约。它是为了认定、保存、保护、展示文化和自然遗产具有的突出普遍价值，并将其传递给后代而签订的合约。《操作指南》中具体条款、条件和定义，用来确定哪些遗产可以列入《世界遗产名录》。

The Convention sets out the duties of States Parties in identifying potential sites and their role in protecting and preserving them. By ratifying *the Convention*, each country pledges to conserve not only the World Heritage sites situated on its

《公约》明确了缔约国有识别潜在遗产的责任，并应承担保存、保护这些遗产的责任。加入公约后，缔约国不但有保护本国世界遗产的义务，亦有保护本国其他遗产的责任。《公约》鼓励缔约国将自然和文化遗产的保护列入地区

territory, but also to protect its national heritage. The States Parties are encouraged to integrate the protection of the cultural and natural heritage into regional planning programmes, set up staff and services at their sites, undertake scientific and technical conservation research, and adopt measures which give this heritage a function in the day-to-day life of the community.

发展规划中，设置遗产管理机构，实施科技保护研究，同时采取措施让遗产与遗产地居民的日常生活能够和谐共生。

It explains how the World Heritage Fund is to be used and managed and under what conditions international financial assistance may be provided.

《公约》解释了世界遗产基金的使用和管理模式，以及在何种情况下提供国际资金援助。

The Convention stipulates the obligation of States Parties to report regularly to the World Heritage Committee on the state of conservation of their World Heritage properties. These reports are crucial to the work of the Committee as they enable it to assess the conditions of the sites, decide on specific programme needs and resolve recurrent problems.

《公约》规定缔约国有义务定期向遗产委员会报告本国世界遗产的保护状况。这个报告对于委员会的工作十分重要，可以根据报告对遗产的保护状态进行评估，决定是否需要开展专项行动，解决经常出现的问题。

It also encourages States Parties to strengthen the appreciation of the public for World Heritage properties and to enhance their protection through educational and information programmes.

《公约》还鼓励缔约国通过教育和宣传活动帮助公众欣赏世界遗产，从而加强遗产保护。

The World Heritage Convention is rooted in the recognition that cultural and natural heritage is among the priceless and irreplaceable assets, not only of each nation, but of humanity as a whole. The loss, through deterioration or disappearance, of any of these most prized properties constitutes an impoverishment of the heritage of all the peoples of the world. Parts of that heritage, because of their exceptional qualities, can be considered to be of Outstanding Universal Value (often referred to as OUV) and as such worthy of special protection against the dangers which increasingly threaten them.

《世界遗产公约》植根于认定自然或文化遗产不仅是每个国家，而且是整个人类的无价和不可替代的财富。遗产遭到破坏、进行性恶化或消失，对全人类而言，都是一场灾难。遗产具有特殊、独一无二的的特性，被认为是遗产的突出普遍价值（简称 OUV），需要通过特殊的保护措施来抵御对其突出普遍价值日益严重的威胁。

To ensure, as far as possible, the proper identification, protection, conservation and presentation of the world's heritage, member States of UNESCO adopted *the Convention concerning the Protection of the World Cultural and Natural Heritage* known as *The World Heritage Convention* in 1972. *The Convention* has established the World Heritage Committee and a World Heritage Fund, and both have been in operation since 1976. The World Heritage Committee has developed *The Operational Guidelines* for the Implementation of *The World Heritage Convention* which provide the official guidance on the implementation of *the Convention*, revised as necessary by the Committee. To achieve the mission of *the Convention* to identify, protect, conserve, present and transmit to future generations cultural and natural heritage of Outstanding Universal Value, the World Heritage Committee manages a list of properties which have met the requirements of the Convention, called the World Heritage List.

为尽可能确保世界遗产的认定、保存、保护和展示工作顺利开展，联合国教科文组织成员国1972年通过了《保护世界文化和自然遗产公约》。依据《公约》，1976年成立了世界遗产委员会和世界遗产基金。世界遗产委员会编制了《实施世界遗产公约操作指南》，作为履行《公约》的官方指导性的文件，并根据需要对《指南》适时进行修改。为了实现《公约》认定、保存、保护、展示文化和自然遗产突出普遍价值并将其传递给后代的任务，世界遗产委员会把达到《公约》要求的遗产纳入一个名录并加以管理，这个名录就是《世界遗产名录》。

Criteria and conditions for the inscription of properties on the World Heritage List have been developed to evaluate properties and to guide States Parties in their protection and management. For a property to be inscribed on the World Heritage List it must be accepted by the World Heritage Committee as being of Outstanding Universal Value. A nomination document provides the basis for the World Heritage Committee to evaluate whether a property meets the requirements of *the Convention*, and in particular whether it is of Outstanding Universal Value. The Operational Guidelines specify the key tests that the World Heritage Committee applies to decide whether a property is of Outstanding Universal Value:

• the Committee considers a property as having Outstanding Universal Value if the property meets one or more of the World Heritage criteria (Operational Guidelines, Paragraph 77); and

世界遗产委员会规定了将遗产列入《世界遗产名录》的标准和条件，以评估遗产是否具有突出普遍价值，并指导缔约国保护和管理世界遗产。当遗产具有世界遗产委员会认可的突出普遍价值时，遗产才能列入《世界遗产名录》。申遗文本是世界遗产委员会评估遗产是否符合公约要求，特别是是否具有突出普遍价值的基础资料。《操作指南》具体说明世界遗产委员会为裁定遗产是否具有突出普遍价值而采用关键指标：

• 委员会认为当遗产满足了一个或多个世界遗产标准时，就具有突出普遍价值（《操作指南》，77段）；

• to be deemed of Outstanding Universal Value, a property must also meet the conditions of integrity and/or authenticity, and must have an adequate protection and management system to ensure its safeguarding (Paragraph 78).

• 具有突出普遍价值的遗产必须要满足真实性和完整性的条件，同时必须有适宜的保护和管理体系来确保遗产的安全（《操作指南》，78段）。

When a property inscribed on the World Heritage List is threatened by serious and specific dangers, the Committee considers placing it on the List of World Heritage in Danger. When the Outstanding Universal Value of the property which justified its inscription on the World Heritage List is destroyed, the Committee considers deleting the property from the World Heritage List. The current World Heritage List and the List of World Heritage in Danger are available on the UNESCO World Heritage website (whc.unesco.org).

当列入《世界遗产名录》遗产的突出普遍价值受到严重威胁时，委员会将决定把遗产列入《濒危遗产名录》。如果遗产的突出普遍价值遭到破坏，委员会会把遗产从名录中删除。目前的《世界遗产名录》和《濒危世界遗产名录》在联合国教科文组织世界遗产中心官网可以查询。（whc.unesco.org）

The Convention is governed by the World Heritage Committee, which is responsible for deciding whether or not to inscribe a nominated property on the World Heritage List. The work of the World Heritage Committee is supported by a Secretariat, the UNESCO World Heritage Centre, and by three recognized Advisory Bodies — ICCROM (International Centre for the Study of the Preservation and Restoration of Cultural Property), ICOMOS (International Council on Monuments and Sites), and IUCN (International Union for Conservation of Nature).

世界遗产委员会负责实施《公约》，并决定一个申报的遗产能否列入遗产名录。世界遗产委员会的工作由其秘书处即联合国教科文组织遗产中心负责，并得到三个咨询机构——国际文物保护与修复研究中心、国际古迹遗址理事会、世界自然保护联盟的支持和协助。

IUCN is the Advisory Body responsible for evaluating properties nominated for their natural values, while ICOMOS is responsible for evaluating properties nominated for their cultural values.

世界自然保护联盟作为咨询机构负责对申报的自然遗产的价值进行评估，与此同时，国际古迹遗址理事会负责对申报的文化遗产价值进行评估。

World Heritage and other conservation instruments

世界遗产和其他保护方式

While *The Operational Guidelines of the Convention* call for a balanced, representative and

《操作指南》提倡建立一个具有平衡性、代表性和可信性的《世界遗产名录》，其目的不是

credible World Heritage List, it was never intended that the List should ensure complete representivity of all the Earth's numerous ecosystems and habitats, or of the world's entire cultural heritage, which is the role of national, regional and other international protected area/site systems and instruments.

要囊括地球上众多的生物系统和生活环境或世界上所有的文化遗产，而是在国家、地区及其他国际保护区或遗址中发挥保护系统和工具的作用。

It is important in this context to consider World Heritage properties in relation to other types of protected areas and sites. This relationship is expressed in the following diagram developed by UNEP-WCMC and IUCN for natural heritage. It shows the relationship of World Heritage properties to other protected area types and systems in terms of relative global numbers and the application of Outstanding Universal Value as the key measure for assessing which protected areas should be on the World Heritage List. The diagram also highlights the importance of all protected areas for ecosystem, landscape and species conservation, to provide a full representation of the natural features of the Earth.

在这样的背景下考虑世界遗产与其他种类的保护区和遗址间的关系十分重要。联合国环境规划署——世界保护监测中心、世界自然保护联盟共同绘制的自然遗产示意图做出说明。图表从全球遗产数量、以突出普遍价值为标准来评估保护区能否列入世界遗产的角度，解释了世界遗产与其他类型的保护区之间的关系。该图高度强调所有保护区对生态系统、景观和种群保护的作用，展示地球的自然特性。

As noted in the diagram there are a series of other intergovernmental (Ramsar sites, Biosphere Reserves, Geo-Parks) and regional designations that are available to enhance the protection of a number of natural protected areas, but World Heritage status should only be for properties that have the potential to meet the test of Outstanding Universal Value as defined in *The Operational Guidelines*. A key issue for States Parties at the earliest stages of considering World Heritage potential should be to also consider the alternatives, and ideally develop a connected and coordinated approach to using the full range of international, regional and national instruments available to recognize, protect and conserve their protected areas and national heritage.

如图所示，一系列政府间（国际重要湿地名录、生物圈保护区、地质公园）和地区性的保护区，有利于提高自然保护区的保护，但是想列入《世界遗产名录》，遗产必须具备符合《操作指南》要求的、潜在的突出普遍价值。对于缔约国而言，最初阶段的核心议题是，在考虑申报潜在世界遗产的同时，也要考虑替代性的选择，建立一个理想的联络和合作方法，全面使用国际、地区和国家的措施去认识、保存和保护他们的保护区及本土遗产。

While the range of international and regional conservation instruments for cultural properties

尽管缔约国之间和地区间的文化遗产保护设施范围可能有限，但是对于保护理念却有完

may be more limited, the principles expressed are generally the same.

全一致的表达。

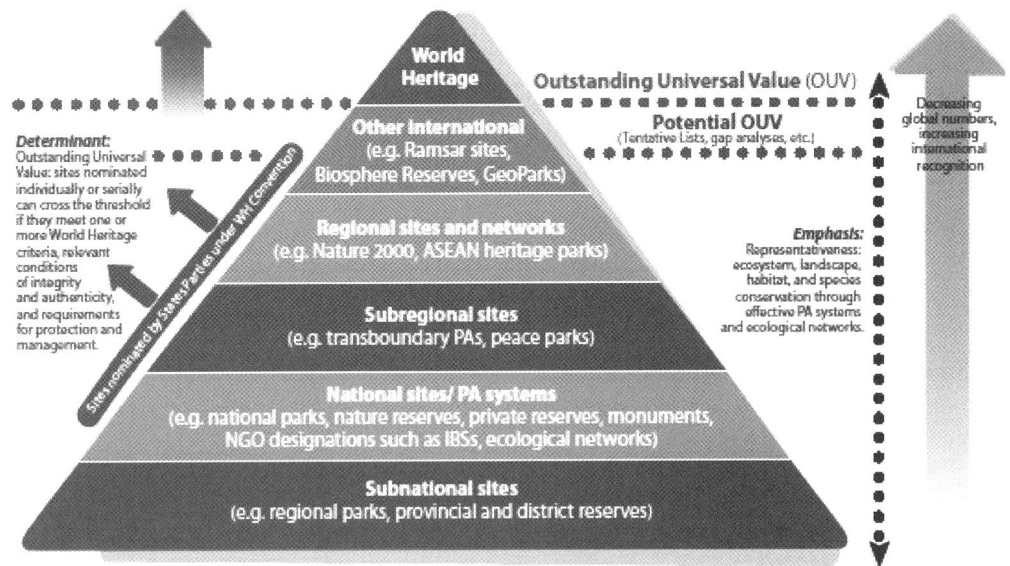

Relationship of World Heritage sites to other types of protected areas (PAs) in terms of Outstanding Universal Value versus representativeness as key determinants

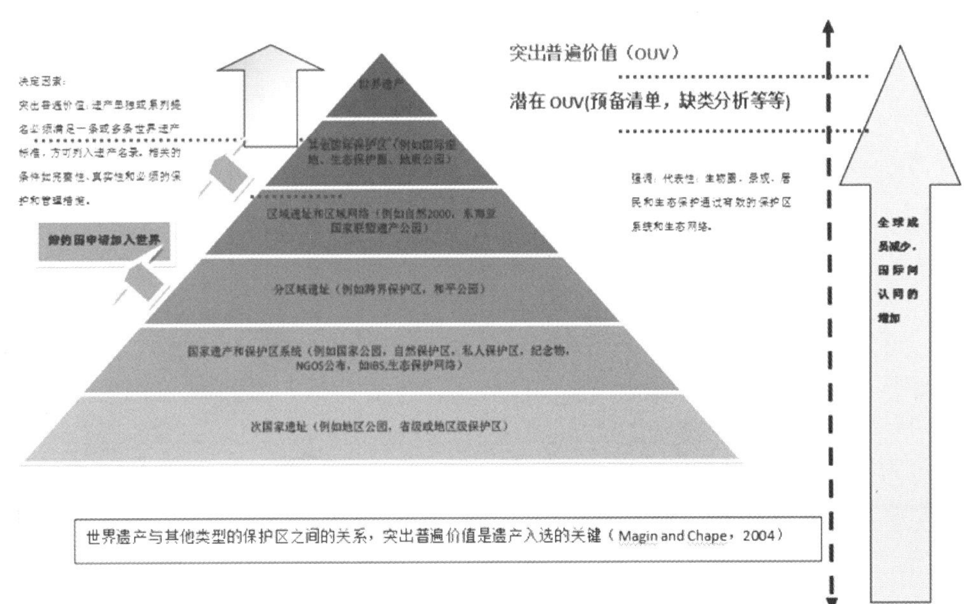

世界遗产与其他类型的保护区之间的关系，突出普遍价值是遗产入选的关键（Magin and Chape，2004）

1.2 Overview of the World Heritage nomination process

1.2 世界遗产申报过程综述

The processes of nomination and inscription of properties on the World Heritage List are at the core of *The World Heritage Convention*, and are a critical responsibility for States Parties to *the Convention*.

遗产申报和列入《世界遗产名录》的过程是《世界遗产公约》的核心内容，也是缔约国的重要责任，这个责任包括了三个关键区域：

These responsibilities cover three key areas:

• preparation of Tentative Lists;

• preparation of nominations; and

• effective management of properties that are inscribed to protect, conserve and manage their Outstanding Universal Value.

• 准备《预备名录》；

• 准备申遗文本；

• 有效的遗产管理体系以保存、保护和管理已列入名录的遗产的突出普遍价值。

The process of inscription is summarized in the diagram below, alongside the different responsibilities of the State Party and the World Heritage Committee.

列入遗产名录的过程概述如下，缔约国和世界遗产委员会有不同的责任。

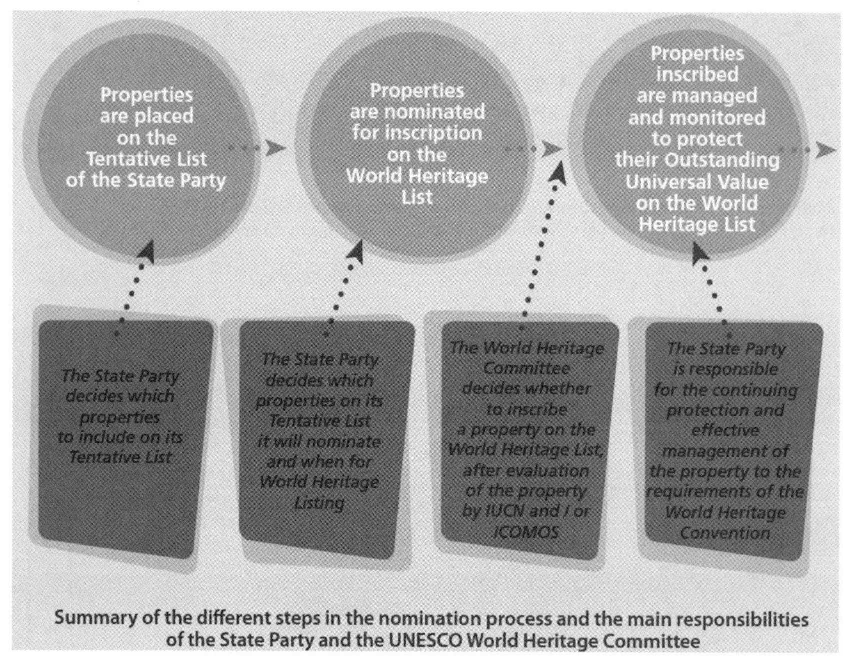

Summary of the different steps in the nomination process and the main responsibilities of the State Party and the UNESCO World Heritage Committee

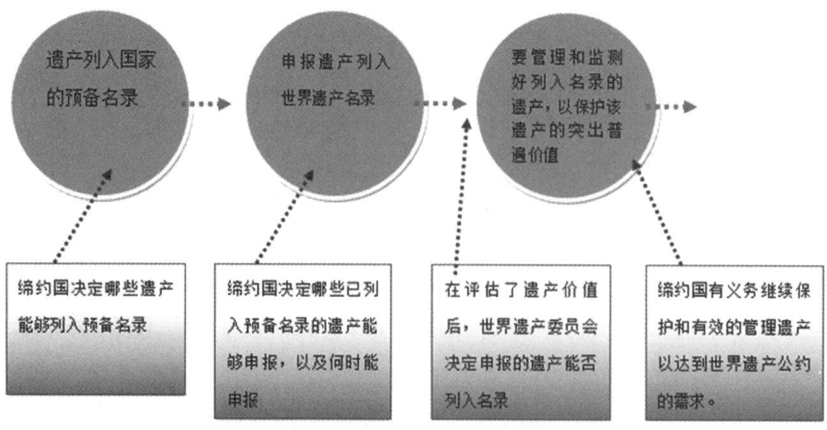

申遗过程的不同步骤概要以及缔约国和UNESCO 世界遗产委员会的主要责任

Only countries that have signed *The World Heritage Convention* can submit nominations for properties within their territory to be considered for inclusion on the World Heritage List. Key elements in the nomination process are summarized as follows.

只有签订了《世界遗产公约》的缔约国才能申报本国的遗产列入下列名录：

Tentative List

《预备名录》

The first step a country must take is to make an 'inventory' of its important natural and cultural heritage sites located within its boundaries which are considered to be cultural and/or natural heritage of potential Outstanding Universal Value, and therefore suitable for inscription on the World Heritage List (see Chapter II.C of *The Operational Guidelines*). This 'inventory' is known as the Tentative List, and includes properties that a State Party may decide to submit for inscription in the next five to ten years. Tentative Lists are not expected to be exhaustive of all possible properties. They may be updated at any time, and States Parties are encouraged to re-examine and resubmit their Tentative List at least every ten years.

缔约国的第一项工作是要制定本国的遗产清单，包括境内具有潜在的突出普遍价值的、适合列入《世界遗产名录》的、重要的自然和文化遗产遗址（见《操作指南》第二章）。这个清单被称为《预备名录》，本国在未来五到十年预备申报的遗产都应该列入《预备名录》。《预备名录》并不期望能囊括所有可能的遗产。《预备名录》需要实时更新，鼓励缔约国至少每十年更新一次他们的《预备名录》。

Tentative List Submission formats are provided in *The Operational Guidelines*, including a special format for serial transnational and trans-boundary properties.

《预备名录》提交格式已在《操作指南》中列出，包括系列的、跨国或跨境遗产的特殊格式。

States Parties should submit Tentative Lists to the World Heritage Centre, at least one year prior to the submission of any nomination.

缔约国应该至少提前一年将《预备名录》提交给世界遗产中心，方可提出遗产申报。

Why are Tentative Lists important?

为什么《预备名录》如此重要?

The World Heritage Committee cannot consider a nomination for inscription on the World Heritage List unless the property has already been included on the State Party's Tentative List.

世界遗产委员会在决定申报遗产能否列入遗产名录时，不考虑没有列入国家《预备名录》的遗产。

• They allow for preliminary consultation, collaboration and agreement in relation to properties with potential for World Heritage status among relevant stakeholders, including federal, national, regional and local governments, property owners and/or managers, local communities, the private sector and NGOs such as the local committees/ representatives of ICOMOS and IUCN. This process might usefully include a study or studies involving such stakeholders.

•《预备名录》可以让潜在世界遗产的利益相关者之间达成初步的磋商、合作和协议，利益相关者包括联邦政府、国家政府、地区政府和当地政府、遗产所有者和管理者、遗产地所属社区、私人组织和非政府组织如地方委员会、国际古迹遗址理事会和世界自然保护联盟等非政府组织代表。利益相关者参与将对一项或多项遗产研究过程有所裨益。

• They help States Parties to carry out preliminary studies to identify natural and cultural heritage properties of potential global importance.

• 能够帮助缔约国开展初步研究，确定自然或文化遗产潜在的国际重要性。

• They help States Parties to identify needs in management and measures for protection, allowing for input from natural and cultural heritage experts where necessary.

• 能够帮助缔约国确定遗产的管理需求和保护方法，必要时可以采纳专家意见。

• They are useful planning tools for the States Parties, the World Heritage Committee, World Heritage Centre and Advisory Bodies to indicate future potential nominations.

• 是缔约国、世界遗产委员会、世界遗产中心和咨询团队提出未来的、潜在的遗产申报最有用的规划工具。

• They are a useful resource in undertaking a comparative analysis as part of the process to develop a nomination.

• 是遗产申报过程中进行比较研究时重要的可用资源。

Nomination dossier

申遗文本

By preparing a Tentative List and selecting properties from it, a State Party can plan when to present each nomination dossier for a particular property. The World Heritage Centre offers advice and assistance to the State Party in preparing this dossier, which needs to be as comprehensive as possible, making sure the necessary documentation and maps are included. The nomination is submitted to the World Heritage Centre to check it is complete. Once a nomination file is complete the World Heritage Centre sends it to the appropriate Advisory Body/Bodies for evaluation.

通过准备《预备名录》，从中选出拟申报遗产，缔约国能够计划提交申遗文本的时间。世界遗产中心可以为缔约国准备的文本提供意见和协助，文本应该尽可能全面，确保包含必要的文件和地图。申遗文本应提交给世界遗产中心以确定其完整性。世界遗产中心确定了申遗文本的完整性后，会转交给合适的咨询机构进行评估。

Selection criteria

To be included on the World Heritage List, sites must be of Outstanding Universal Value and meet at least one of ten criteria, as well as the relevant conditions of integrity and authenticity and requirements for protection and management. The World Heritage criteria are explained in *The Operational Guidelines for the Implementation of The World Heritage Convention* which, besides the text of the *Convention*, is the main working tool on World Heritage. The criteria are also discussed in more detail on late pages of this manual.

The criteria are regularly revised by the Committee to reflect the evolution of the World Heritage concept itself.

Limitation on the number of nominations to be submitted and evaluated

States Parties should be aware of decisions taken by the World Heritage Committee which have the effect of limiting the number of nominations that may be submitted, and also limiting the number of nominations that may be considered at a meeting of the Committee.

An ongoing priority for the Committee is the desirability of achieving a reasonable balance between the numbers of cultural heritage and natural heritage properties included in the World Heritage List.

Timetable

The Operational Guidelines provide a detailed timetable for the submission and evaluation of nominations, which is binding on States Parties and the Advisory Bodies (Paragraph 168). The key

选择标准

列入《世界遗产名录》的遗产必须具有突出普遍价值，并且至少满足十条标准中的一条，同时，也需要满足完整性、真实性以及保护和管理需求等相关条件。《操作指南》是《世界遗产公约》重要的运行工具，并对世界遗产标准进行了解释。标准在本手册中将有更详细的讨论。

委员会定期修改准则以反映世界遗产概念本身的变化。

限制提交和评估申报遗产的数量

缔约国应该了解世界遗产委员会关于限制申报遗产数量的决定，即限制委员会每次会议讨论的申报遗产数量。

委员会会继续实行优先战略，以保持遗产名录中自然遗产与文化遗产的合理平衡。

时间表

《操作指南》提供了一个提交和评估申遗文本的详尽的时间表，这个时间表对于缔约国和咨询机构（168 段）都有约束力。最后截止日期绝对不可协商。

deadlines are absolute and non-negotiable.

Advisory Bodies

A nominated property may be independently evaluated by one or both of the two Advisory Bodies mandated by *The World Heritage Convention:* ICOMOS (International Council on Monuments and Sites) for cultural properties and IUCN (International Union for Conservation of Nature) for natural properties. The third Advisory Body is ICCROM (International Centre for the Study of the Preservation and Restoration of Cultural Property), an intergovernmental organization which provides the Committee with expert advice on conservation and monitoring of cultural sites, as well as on training and capacity-building activities.

咨询机构

根据《公约》要求，申报遗产将由世界遗产委员会授权的一个或两个咨询机构独立或共同评估，国际古迹遗址理事会负责评估文化遗产部分，世界自然保护联盟负责评估自然遗产部分。第三个评估机构是国际文物保护与修复研究中心，它是政府间组织，为委员会提供文化遗产保护和监测方面的专家建议，同时也承担培训和能力建设等任务。

World Heritage Committee

Once a property has been nominated and evaluated, it is up to the intergovernmental World Heritage Committee to make the final decision on its inscription. Once a year, the Committee meets to decide which properties will be inscribed on the World Heritage List. In addition to inscribing a property or deciding not to inscribe, the Committee can also defer or refer the nomination and request further information on a property from the relevant State Party.

世界遗产委员会

一旦遗产经过了申报和评估，作为政府间组织的世界遗产委员会将决定遗产能否列入名录。每一年世界遗产委员会都会确定哪些遗产可以列入《世界遗产名录》。除了做出遗产是否列入名录的决定外，委员会还可以做出延迟和退回申报的决议，以要求相关缔约国补充更多遗产信息。

World Heritage Centre

The World Heritage Centre (WHC) is the Secretariat of *The World Heritage Convention* and the focal point and coordinator within UNESCO for all matters relating to World Heritage. WHC provides assistance to States Parties throughout the preparation of nominations in different ways,

世界遗产中心

世界遗产中心是《世界遗产公约》的秘书处、联络处和协调处，是处理世界遗产事务、负责与联合国教科文组织协调的机构。世界遗产中心通过不同方式协助缔约国的遗产申报准备工作，例如，提供成功申报的案例、提供管理和法律条款、帮助选择适当的地图、对于不

among others it provides examples of successful nominations, of management and legislative provisions, helps in identifying appropriate maps, gives more specific guidance for nominating different types of properties, such as cultural landscapes, towns, canals, and heritage routes or for nominating serial and trans-boundary properties. In cooperation with the Advisory Bodies and other institutions, WHC organizes specific workshops on issues linked to the preparation of nominations. The Centre also provides comments and guidance when States Parties submit draft nominations to the Secretariat. The Centre updates the World Heritage List and database. When an official nomination is submitted, WHC checks the file for completeness and if the nomination is considered as complete, the Centre transmits the file to the appropriate Advisory Body, while, if the nomination is considered incomplete, the Centre gives guidance to the State Party on how to complete it.

同类型的遗产如文化景观、城镇、运河和遗产线路或跨国、跨境系列申报等提供更多的特别指导。世界遗产中心还与咨询机构和其他研究机构合作，举办各类与准备申报遗产相关的、特殊议题的研讨会。中心还会评议和指导缔约国提交的申遗文本草案。中心负责《世界遗产名录》和数据库的更新工作。收到缔约国提交的正式申遗文本后，中心对文本的完整性进行审查，并把符合完整性要求的文本转交给适当的评估机构，同时，如果认为申遗文本不够完整，中心将指导申报国进一步完善他们的文件。

1.3 Illustrations of World Heritage concepts

1.3 世界遗产相关概念说明

This section provides illustrations of some key World Heritage concepts including definitions, criteria and different types of properties.

本节将对世界遗产的一些重要概念进行解释和说明，包括其定义，标准和遗产分类。

Definitions—cultural and natural heritage, mixed properties

定义——文化、自然和混合遗产

Key message: Be clear about the category of cultural heritage being nominated.

关键信息：明确文化遗产申报的种类

CULTURAL HERITAGE

文化遗产

The World Heritage Convention defines cultural heritage as:

• monuments: architectural works, works of monumental sculpture and painting, elements or structures of an archaeological nature, inscriptions,

《世界遗产公约》对于文化遗产的定义如下：

• 纪念物：从历史、艺术或科学角度看具有突出普遍价值的建筑物、碑雕和碑画、具有考古性质的成分或结构、铭文、洞窟以及联合体；

cave dwellings and combinations of features, which are of Outstanding Universal Value from the point of view of history, art or science;

• groups of buildings: groups of separate or connected buildings which, because of their architecture, their homogeneity or their place in the landscape, are of Outstanding Universal Value from the point of view of history, art or science;

• 建筑群：从历史、艺术或科学角度看，在建筑式样、分布、与当地景观的一致性等方面，具有突出普遍价值的独立或连接的建筑群；

• sites: works of man or the combined works of nature and man, and areas including archaeological sites which are of Outstanding Universal Value from the historical, aesthetic, ethnological or anthropological point of view (Article 1).

• 遗址：从历史、审美、人种学或人类学角度看具有突出普遍价值的人类和自然工程以及考古遗址等（第一条）。

Some properties might satisfy more than one of these definitions (e.g. be both a monument and group of buildings).

一些遗产的定义可以是多重的，满足以上若干条件（例如既是文物又是建筑群）。

This definition was developed in 1972 and concepts of cultural heritage have expanded since that time. Nonetheless, the definition has been interpreted very broadly to embrace the diversity of cultural heritage.

文化遗产的定义形成于 1972 年，随着时间的推移，文化遗产的概念也在不断地扩大。定义得到非常广泛的解读，以囊括当前文化遗产的多样性。

The Operational Guidelines offer additional definitions regarding cultural landscapes, historic towns and town centers, heritage canals and heritage routes (Annex 3). Cultural landscapes are also discussed further in the following section.

此外，《操作指南》中又提供了文化景观、历史城镇、中心城镇、遗产运河和文化线路等定义（附件 3）。有关文化景观的讨论将在下文中展开。

Some examples of listed properties below give a sense of the scope of cultural heritage (text and illustrations for these definitions are drawn from the UNESCO World Heritage website).

将介绍一些已列入的文化遗产案例来说明它的范畴（文字和插图摘自联合国教科文组织世界遗产中心网站）。

Minaret and Archaeological Remains of Jam (Afghanistan)

查姆回教寺院尖塔和考古遗存（阿富汗）

An architectural work and archaeological site. The 65m Minaret of Jam is a graceful, soaring

建筑物和考古遗址，高 65 米的查姆回教寺院尖塔是一个高耸的、优雅的建筑，修建于 12

structure, dating back to the 12th century. Covered in elaborate brickwork with a blue tile inscription at the top, it is noteworthy for the quality of its architecture and decoration, which represent the culmination of an architectural and artistic tradition in this region. Its impact is heightened by its dramatic setting, a deep river valley between towering mountains in the heart of Ghur province.

世纪，外墙以精美雕刻的方砖砌成，在塔顶装饰有刻字的蓝色琉璃瓦，是当地传统建筑工艺和装饰艺术巅峰之作，具有极高的价值。古尔省高山峡谷这引人注目的环境，为古塔增添了更多吸引力。

Sukur Cultural Landscape (Nigeria)

苏库尔文化景观（尼日利亚）

Sukur Cultural Landscape, with the Palace of the Hidi (chief) on a hill dominating the villages below, the terraced fields and their sacred symbols, and the extensive remains of a former flourishing iron industry, is a remarkably intact physical expression of a society and its spiritual and material culture.

苏库尔文化景观，包括位于高山上的希迪宗庙遗址、下面的村庄、梯田和他们神圣符号，保存了大量早期铁器制造业繁荣时期的遗存，表现了他们的社会、精神和物质文明。

Old Town of Lijiang (China)

丽江古城（中国）

A group of buildings. The Old Town of Lijiang, which is perfectly adapted to the uneven topography of this key commercial and strategic site, has retained a historic townscape of high quality and authenticity. Its architecture is noteworthy for the blending of elements from several cultures that have come together over many centuries. Lijiang also possesses an ancient water supply system of great complexity and ingenuity that still functions effectively today.

建筑群。丽江古城是完美适应谷地地形的商业和战略要地遗产，它完整、真实地保持了历史城镇景观。几个世纪来它的建筑融合了若干不同的文化元素。丽江还拥有古代复杂的、独创的供水体系并沿用至今。

Zollverein Coal Mine Industrial Complex in Essen (Germany)

埃森市的关税同盟煤矿工业遗址群（德国）

A group of buildings and industrial archaeological site. The Zollverein industrial complex in Land Nordrhein-Westfalen consists of the complete infrastructure of a historical coal-mining site, with some 20th-century buildings of outstanding architectural merit. It

一组建筑群和工业考古遗址。位于北莱茵－威斯特法伦的关税同盟工业区，遗址群包括了早期的全套的采煤设备，也包括具有 20 世纪独特特征的建筑。它是采煤业发展演进的杰出物质代表，也见证了当地基础采矿业在过去 150

constitutes remarkable material evidence of the evolution and decline of an essential industry over the past 150 years.

年的兴衰。

Cueva de las Manos, Río Pinturas (Argentina)

A monument/work of monumental painting and site. The Cueva de las Manos, Río Pinturas, contains an exceptional assemblage of cave art, executed between 13, 000 and 9, 500 years ago. It takes its name (Cave of the Hands) from the stencilled outlines of human hands in the cave, but there are also many depictions of animals, such as guanacos (Lama guanicoe), still commonly found in the region, as well as hunting scenes. The people responsible for the paintings may have been the ancestors of the historic hunter-gatherer communities of Patagonia found by European settlers in the 19th century.

平图拉斯河　洛斯马诺斯岩画手印洞穴（阿根廷）

文物及岩画遗址。平图拉斯河洛斯马诺斯岩画手印洞穴包含了从 13000 到 9500 年前创造的一系列不可思议的洞穴艺术。遗址因洞窟中刻画了人类手印所以得名（手印洞穴），当然洞窟中也描绘了很多当地动物的形象，例如产于南美安第斯山脉的、现在依旧常见的南美骆，以及打猎的情景。负责绘画的人群可能是 19 世纪被欧洲移民发现的、在草原上以采集、狩猎为生的巴塔哥尼亚民族的祖先。

Hiroshima Peace Memorial (Genbaku Dome) (Japan)

The Hiroshima Peace Memorial (Genbaku Dome) was the only structure left standing in the area where the first atomic bomb exploded on 6 August 1945. Through the efforts of many people, including those of the city of Hiroshima, it has been preserved in the same state as immediately after the bombing. Not only is it a stark and powerful symbol of the most destructive force ever created by humankind, it also expresses the hope for world peace and the ultimate elimination of all nuclear weapons.

广岛和平纪念公园（核爆圆顶，日本）

广岛和平纪念公园（核爆圆顶）是在 1945 年 8 月 6 日原子弹爆炸后唯一保留下来的建筑。在原子弹爆炸后，通过很多人包括原广岛市民的努力，这个建筑遗址按原子弹爆炸后的惨状被保留下来。它不仅仅是人类创造力造成的巨大破坏的象征，同时也表达了渴望维护世界和平、永远消除核武器的期望。

Botanical Garden (Orto Botanico), Padua (Italy)

A site/work of man. The world’s first botanical garden was created in Padua in 1545. It still preserves its original layout — a circular central plot, symbolizing the world, surrounded by a ring

帕多瓦植物园（意大利）

人类工程遗址。世界上最早的植物园 1545 年修建于帕多瓦。目前始终保存了它的原始格局——象征世界的中心点的、被一系列水道所包围的圆形土地。还有后期增加的元素包括建

of water. Other elements were added later, some architectural (ornamental entrances and balustrades) and some practical (pumping installations and greenhouses). It continues to serve its original purpose as a centre for scientific research.

筑（装饰过的入口和栏杆）和一些实用设施，如泵水装置和暖房。目前仍保持着它科学研究的原始功能。

NATURAL HERITAGE

自然遗产

The World Heritage Convention defines natural heritage as:

• natural features consisting of physical and biological formations or groups of such formations, which are of Outstanding Universal Value from the aesthetic or scientific point of view;

• geological and physio-graphical formations and precisely delineated areas which constitute the habitat of threatened species of animals and plants of Outstanding Universal Value from the point of view of science or conservation;

• natural sites or precisely delineated natural areas of Outstanding Universal Value from the point of view of science, conservation or natural beauty (Article 2).

《世界遗产公约》对于自然遗产的定义如下：

• 从审美或科学角度看具有突出普遍价值的、由物理和生物结构或这类结构群组成的自然地域；

• 从科学或保护角度看具有突出普遍价值的地质和自然地理结构以及明确划为受威胁的动植物栖息地；

• 从科学、保护或自然美角度看具有突出的普遍价值的天然名胜或边界描述明确的自然区域。（第 2 条）。

A few examples of listed properties below give a sense of the scope of natural heritage.

通过列举《世界遗产名录》中的自然遗产来说明它的范畴。

Sagarmatha National Park (Nepal)

萨加玛塔国家公园（尼泊尔）

Sagarmatha is an exceptional area with dramatic mountains, glaciers and deep valleys, dominated by Mount Everest, the highest peak in the world (8, 848 m). Several rare species, such as the snow leopard and the lesser panda, are found in the park. The presence of the Sherpas, with their unique culture, adds further interest to this site.

萨迦玛塔国家公园是由高山、冰川和深谷组成的独一无二的区域，世界最高峰珠穆朗玛峰（8848 米）矗立其中。很多稀有物种，例如雪豹、小熊猫等生活于公园中。在这个区域生存的夏尔巴人及其独特的文化为这个遗址增添了魅力。

Ilulissat Icefjord (Denmark)

伊路利萨特冰湾（丹麦）

Located on the west coast of Greenland, 250 km north of the Arctic Circle, Greenland's Ilulissat

位于格陵兰岛西岸，北极圈以北 250 公里，格陵兰岛的伊路利萨特冰湾是瑟梅格库亚雷哥

Icefjord is the sea mouth of Sermeq Kujalleq, one of the few glaciers through which the Greenland ice cap reaches the sea. is one of the fastest (19 m per day) and most active glaciers in the world. It annually calves over 35 km^3 of ice, i.e. 10 per cent of the production of all Greenland calf ice and more than any other glacier outside Antarctica. Studied for over 250 years, it has helped to develop our understanding of climate change and icecap glaciology. The combination of a huge ice-sheet and the dramatic sounds of a fast-moving glacial ice-stream calving into a fjord covered by icebergs makes for a dramatic and awe-inspiring natural phenomenon.

的海口，是格陵兰岛冰冠中少数入海的冰川之一。瑟梅格库亚雷哥是世界上移动最快（19 米／天）最活跃的冰川。年平均裂冰量达 3 5 立方公里，占格陵兰岛裂冰量的 10%，是南极洲之外裂冰量最多的冰川。250 年来的冰川学研究和发现，对于我们了解此区域气候变迁和冰盖起到重要作用。巨大的冰盖和快速流动的冰川一起，撞击着冰山覆盖的峡湾发出的巨响，形成神奇且令人惊叹的自然现象。

Joggins Fossil Cliffs (Canada)

Joggins Fossil Cliffs, a 689 ha palaeontological site along the coast of Nova Scotia (eastern Canada), have been described as the ‘coal age Galápagos’ due to their wealth of fossils from the Carboniferous period (354 to 290 million years ago). The rocks of this site are considered to be iconic for this period of the history of Earth and are the world’s thickest and most comprehensive record of the Pennsylvanian strata (dating back 318 to 303 million years) with the most complete known fossil record of terrestrial life from that time. These include the remains and tracks of very early animals and the rainforest in which they lived, left in situ, intact and undisturbed. With its 14.7 km of sea cliffs, low bluffs, rock platforms and beach, the site groups remains of three ecosystems: estuarine bay, floodplain rainforest and fire prone forested alluvial plain with freshwater pools. It offers the richest assemblage known of the fossil life in these three ecosystems with 96 genera and 148 species of fossils and 20 footprint groups. The site is listed as containing outstanding examples representing major stages in the history of the Earth.

乔金斯化石崖（加拿大）

乔金斯化石崖沿新斯科舍（加拿大东部）海岸线分布，是占地 689 公顷的古生物化石遗址。鉴于这个地区有石炭纪形成的丰富化石而被称为“成煤纪的加拉帕戈斯”（354—290 百万年前）。这一遗址的岩石被认为是地球形成历史上该时期的标志，是世界上宾夕法尼亚地层（3.18–3.03 亿年前）最厚、最全面的化石记录，完整记录并展现已知的、那时的地球生物化石。这里原封不动的保存了极早期动物和雨林的化石和遗存。在 14.7 公里长的海崖，分布有低矮的绝壁，岩石台面和海滩，这个遗址群保留了三种生态系统：河湾、漫滩上的热带雨林和丛生的草木，及易着火的、淡水湖泊分布的冲积平原。这里是三个生态系统生物化石的最丰富的聚合体，包括了 96 个属，148 种生物的化石和 20 组足迹。这个遗址因提供了代表地球历史发展主要阶段的杰出证据而被列入名录。

Malpelo Fauna and Flora Sanctuary (Colombia)

Located c. 500 km off the coast of Colombia, the site includes Malpelo island (350 ha) and the surrounding marine environment (857, 150 ha). This vast marine park, the largest no-fishing zone in the Eastern Tropical Pacific, provides a critical habitat for internationally threatened marine species, and is a major source of nutrients resulting in large aggregations of marine biodiversity. It is in particular a 'reservoir' for sharks, giant grouper and billfish, and is one of the few places in the world where sightings of the short-nosed ragged-toothed shark, a deep water shark, have been confirmed. Widely recognized as one of the top diving sites in the world, due to the steep walls and caves of outstanding natural beauty, these deep waters support important populations of large predators and pelagic species (e.g. aggregations of over 200 hammerhead sharks and over 1, 000 silky sharks, whale sharks and tuna have been recorded) in an undisturbed environment where they maintain natural behavioural patterns.

马尔佩洛岛动植物保护区（哥伦比亚）

马尔佩洛岛距哥伦比亚海岸500公里，包括马尔佩洛岛（350公顷）和周围的海洋环境（857150公顷）。这个巨大的海洋公园是太平洋东部最大的热带禁渔区，为国际上受威胁的海洋生物提供了唯一的栖息地，同时它也为多样性海洋生物的聚集提供营养来源。它是鲨鱼、鞍带石斑鱼和长嘴鱼的保育区，同时它也是世界上少数能看到短鼻锯齿鲨鱼、深水鲨鱼的海域。同时它有着陡峭崖壁和迷人洞穴，是世界公认的、风景优美的最佳潜水遗址，深水区域为大型食肉鱼类和浮游生物提供了没有污染的生存生活环境，可以维持他们天然行为模式（例如这里生活200多头双髻鲨、超过1000头丝鲨，鲸鲨和金枪鱼）。

Great Barrier Reef (Australia)

The Great Barrier Reef is a site of remarkable variety and beauty on the north-east coast of Australia. It contains the world's largest collection of coral reefs, with 400 types of coral, 1, 500 species of fish and 4, 000 types of mollusc. It also holds great scientific interest as the habitat of species such as the dugong ('sea cow') and the large green turtle, which are threatened with extinction.

澳大利亚大堡礁

大堡礁是澳大利亚东北海岸风景美丽多变的遗址。它包含了世界上最大的珊瑚礁群，有400种珊瑚，1500种鱼和4000种软体动物。同时，它也是研究濒临灭绝的生物，例如儒艮（海牛或称美人鱼）和大型绿龟生活习性的科研场所

Virunga National Park (Democratic Republic of the Congo)

Virunga National Park (covering an area of 790,000 ha) comprises an outstanding diversity of

维龙加国家公园（刚果共和国）

维龙加国家公园（790000公顷），是杰出的具有多样性的生物栖息地，包含了从湿地、草

habitats, ranging from swamps and steppes to the snowfields of Rwenzori at an altitude of over 5,000 m, and from lava plains to the savannahs on the slopes of volcanoes. Mountain gorillas are found in the park, some 20,000 hippopotamus live in the rivers, and birds from Siberia spend the winter there.

原、到海拔超过 5000 米高的鲁文佐里山上的雪山，从火山岩浆平原到火山坡上的大草原。在公园中还发现了山地大猩猩的踪影，20000 只河马生活在河谷，成千上万只来自于西伯利亚的候鸟在此过冬。

MIXED PROPERTIES

混合遗产

The Operational Guidelines define mixed properties as those which satisfy part or the whole of the definitions of both cultural and natural heritage laid out in Articles 1 and 2 of *the Convention* (Paragraph 46).

《操作指南》中对于混合遗产的定义如下：只有同时部分满足或完全满足《公约》第 1 条和第 2 条关于文化和自然遗产定义的遗产才能认为是“文化和自然混合遗产”。

Examples of listed mixed properties are given below.

混合遗产的实例如下。

Tikal National Park (Guatemala)

蒂卡尔国家公园（危地马拉）

In the heart of the jungle, surrounded by lush vegetation, lies one of the major sites of Mayan civilization, inhabited from the 6th century BC to the 10th century AD. The ceremonial centre contains superb temples and palaces, and public squares accessed by means of ramps. Remains of dwellings are scattered throughout the surrounding countryside.

这处最为重要的玛雅文明遗址，坐落在丛林的中心地区，周围环绕着繁密的植被，是公元前 6 世纪到 10 世纪玛雅人主要的居住场所。祭祀中心由宏伟的宗庙、宫殿和进入公共广场的斜坡构成。周边的村落中还零散地保留着一些聚落遗址。

Tassili N’Ajjer (Algeria)

阿杰尔塔西利（阿尔及利亚）

Located in a strange lunar landscape of great geological interest, this site has one of the most important groupings of prehistoric cave art in the world. More than 15, 000 drawings and engravings record the climatic changes, the animal migrations and the evolution of human life on the edge of the Sahara from 6, 000 BC to the first centuries of the present era. The geological formations are of outstanding scenic interest, with eroded sand-stones

该遗址地质价值极高，地形奇特类似月球表面，是世界上最重要的史前洞穴艺术群之一。超过 15000 副绘画和雕刻记录了从公元前 6000 年到公元初几个世纪，撒哈拉沙漠边缘地区气候的变化、动物的迁徙、人类生活的进化。受到风蚀的砂岩形成了变化万千的“石林”，使这里的地质层成为杰出的自然景观。

forming ‘forests of rock’.

Definitions of cultural heritage

文化遗产的界定

MONUMENTS

纪念物

The formal definition in *the Convention* is provided above under Cultural Heritage. Some examples of listed properties which are monuments are given below.

公约中对于文物的正式定义是在文化遗产概念下提出的。名录中关于文物的遗产的实例如下。

Statue of Liberty (United States)

自由女神雕像（美国）

A work of monumental sculpture. Made in Paris by the French sculptor Bartholdi, in collaboration with Gustave Eiffel (who was responsible for the steel framework), this towering monument to liberty was a gift from France on the centenary of American independence in 1886. Standing at the entrance to New York Harbour, it has welcomed millions of immigrants to the United States ever since.

纪念性塑像作品。由法国雕塑家巴尔托迪与古斯塔夫·埃菲尔（负责钢铁框架）合作雕刻完成。1886年法国将其作为美国独立百年纪念的礼物送给美国，安放在纽约港口，代表美国迎接了数百万移民。

Taj Mahal (India)

泰姬陵（印度）

An architectural work. An immense mausoleum of white marble, built in Agra between 1631 and 1648 by order of the Mughal emperor Shah Jahan in memory of his favourite wife, the Taj Mahal is the jewel of Muslim art in India and one of the universally admired masterpieces of World Heritage.

建筑遗产。这座白色大理石的大型陵墓建筑，1631–1648年修建于阿格拉，是印度莫卧儿帝国皇帝沙贾汗为了纪念他最爱的妻子而下令修建的，泰姬陵是穆斯林艺术在印度的璀璨结晶，也是全世界公认的杰出的世界遗产之一。

GROUPS OF BUILDINGS

建筑群

The formal definition in *the Convention* is provided above under Cultural Heritage. *The Operational Guidelines* also offer a definition of groups of urban buildings in the context of historic towns and town centers (Annex 3). Some examples

公约中对于建筑群的正式定义是在文化遗产概念下提出的。《操作指南》中也在历史城市和城市中心的界定中提到了建筑群的定义（见附件3）。遗产名录中典型的建筑群介绍如下。

of listed properties which are groups of buildings are below.

Ksar of Ait-Ben-Haddou (Morocco)

阿伊特本哈杜堡（摩洛哥）

The ksar, a group of earthen buildings sur the defensive walls, which are reinforced by cornrounded by high walls, is a traditional pre-Saharan habitat. The houses crowdtogether withiner towers. Ait-Ben-Haddou, in Ouarzazate province, is a striking example of the architecture of southern Morocco.

阿伊特本哈杜堡，是四周高墙环绕的生土建筑，是前撒哈拉沙漠居民的传统民居。在城墙内密集分布了多座房屋，城墙四角的角楼起到了加固城墙的作用。位于瓦尔扎扎特省的阿伊特本哈杜堡是摩洛哥南部传统建筑的典型代表。

Megalithic Temples of Malta (Malta)

马耳他巨石神庙（马耳他）

Seven megalithic temples are found on the islands of Malta and Gozo, each the result of an individual development. The two temples of Ggantija on the island of Gozo are notable for their gigantic Bronze Age structures. On the island of Malta, the temples of Hagar Qin, Mnajdra and Tarxien are unique architectural masterpieces, given the limited resources available to their builders. The Ta'Hagrat and Skorba complexes show how the tradition of temple-building was handed down in Malta.

七座巨石神庙修建在马耳他岛和戈佐岛上，每一座都是独立的建筑。其中在戈佐岛的两座吉甘提亚神庙建筑是繁荣的青铜时代杰出的代表性建筑。在马耳他岛上的其他建筑，哈加因、姆那拉及塔尔西安神庙都是利用马耳他群岛极有限的资源修建的、独一无二的杰出代表性建筑。塔哈格拉特和斯克尔巴建筑群展示了在马耳他建造寺庙传统的传承。

SITES

遗址

The formal definition in *the Convention* is provided above under Cultural Heritage. *The Operational Guidelines* also provide guidance regarding certain property types (Annex 3).

公约中对于遗址的正式定义是在文化遗产概念下提出的。《操作指南》中也提供了认定此类遗产的指南（附件 3）。

Some examples of listed properties which are sites are given below.

遗产名录中关于遗址的实例如下。

Site of Palmyra (Syrian Arab Republic)

帕尔米拉古城遗址（阿拉伯叙利亚共和国）

An archaeological site. An oasis in the Syrian

考古遗址。位于大马士革的东北部叙利亚

desert, north-east of Damascus, Palmyra contains the monumental ruins of a great city that was one of the most important cultural centers of the ancient world. From the 1st to the 2nd centuries, the art and architecture of Palmyra, standing at the crossroads of several civilizations, married Graeco-Roman techniques with local traditions and Persian influences.

沙漠中的绿洲，帕尔米拉古城是古代最重要文化中心之一，如今仍有大量建筑物遗存。城市修建于公元 1—2 世纪，当时帕尔米拉古城是多种文化交汇的中心，这里的艺术和建筑是希腊、罗马、当地传统技术和波斯技术融合的结晶。

Taxila (Pakistan)

塔克希拉考古遗址（巴基斯坦）

An archaeological site. From the ancient Neolithic tumulus of Saraikala to the ramparts of Sirkap (2nd century BC) and the city of Sirsukh (1st century AD), Taxila illustrates the different stages in the development of a city on the Indus that was alternately influenced by Persia, Greece and Central Asia and which, from the 5th century BC to the 2nd century AD, was an important Buddhist centre of learning.

考古遗址。从新石器时代萨莱卡拉的古墓到锡尔凯波时期的（公元前 2 世纪）壁垒，再到公元 1 世纪的锡尔苏克古城，塔克希拉作为当时的佛教学习中心，展现了从公元前 5 世纪到 2 世纪，印度河流域的城市发展不同时期受到波斯、希腊和中亚地区文化交替影响的不同阶段。

CULTURAL LANDSCAPES

文化景观

The Operational Guidelines define cultural landscapes as cultural properties which represent the 'combined works of nature and of man' as designated in Article 1 of *the Convention* (Paragraph 47).

《操作指南》中对于文化景观的定义是能够代表人类与自然相结合的文化遗产（见公约第一条，《操作指南》第 47 段）。

There is no single World Heritage criterion for cultural landscapes and it is conceivable that any of the cultural criteria might be used in justifying the Outstanding Universal Value of a cultural landscape.

没有单一的世界遗产标准可以定义文化景观，但任何可以用于判定文化遗产突出普遍价值的文化标准，同时都适用于文化景观。

There are three main types of cultural landscape:

- landscapes designed and created intentionally by people;
- organically evolved landscapes; and
- associative landscapes (see *Operational Guidelines*, Annex 3).

文化景观有三种类型：

- 由人类有意设计和创造的景观；
- 有机进化的景观；
- 关联性景观。（见《操作指南》，附件 3）

Many properties exhibit more than one of these types and they may be overlapping.

很多遗产有不止一个类型特征，或者说，这些类型是重叠的。

This is a dynamic aspect of *the Convention*, and the concepts are being increasingly elaborated, as are the management approaches, etc.

这是《公约》中的动态组成部分，并且概念在不断完善，管理方法等等也在不断完善。

ICOMOS has produced a thematic bibliography on World Heritage Cultural Landscapes which is available at http: //www.international.icomos.org/centre_documentation/bib/index.html.

国际古迹遗址理事会提供的世界遗产文化景观专题在线参考文献：http：//www.international.icomos.org/centre_documentation/bib/index.html.

Examples of the three types of cultural landscape are provided below.

三种类型的文化景观实例如下。

A designed landscape: Vat Phou and Associated Ancient Settlements within the Champasak Cultural Landscape (Lao People's Democratic Republic)

The Champasak Cultural Landscape, including the Vat Phou Temple complex, is a remarkably well-preserved planned landscape more than 1, 000 years old. It was shaped to express the Hindu vision of the relationship between nature and humanity, using an axis from mountain top to river bank to lay out a geometric pattern of temples, shrines and waterworks extending over some 10 km. Two planned cities on the banks of the Mekong River are also part of the site, as well as Phou Kao mountain. The whole represents a development ranging from the 5th to 15th centuries, mainly associated with the Khmer Empire.

设计类的景观：占巴塞文化景观中的瓦普庙和相关古民居（老挝共和国）

占巴塞文化景观，包括瓦普寺庙遗址群，修建于1000年前，是经过设计的、完好保存的景观。占巴塞文化景观，以山顶至河岸为轴心，在方圆10公里的范围内，整齐而有规划地建造了一系列庙宇、神殿和水利设施，完美表达了古代印度文明中天人关系的文化理念。占巴塞文化景观还包括湄公河两岸的两座文明城市和普高山，体现了公元5世纪到15世纪以高棉帝国为代表的老挝文化发展概况。

An organically evolved landscape: Rice Terraces of the Philippine Cordilleras (Philippines)

有机进化的景观：菲律宾科迪勒拉山系的水稻梯田

For 2, 000 years, the high rice fields of the Ifugao have followed the contours of the mountains. The fruit of knowledge handed down from one generation to the next, and the expression of sacred traditions and a delicate social balance, they have

两千年来，伊富高人的高产稻田沿着科迪勒拉山山坡修建。丰富的种植经验代代相传，表达了神圣的传统和微妙的社会平衡，他们创造了人类与环境协调共生的美丽景观。

helped to create a landscape of great beauty that expresses the harmony between humankind and the environment.

An associative landscape: Uluru-Kata Tjuta National Park (Australia)

关联性景观：乌卢鲁卡塔曲塔国家公园（澳大利亚）

This park, formerly called Uluru (Ayers Rock — Mount Olga) National Park, features spectacular geological formations that dominate the vast red sandy plain of central Australia. Uluru, an immense monolith, and Kata Tjuta, the rock domes located west of Uluru, form part of the traditional belief system of one of the oldest human societies in the world. The traditional owners of Uluru -Kata Tjuta are the Anangu Aboriginal people.

这个公园，以前称为乌卢鲁（爱尔斯岩——欧加山）国家公园，展现了独特的地质构造，位于澳大利亚中心的红色砂岩平原。乌卢鲁，巨大的独体巨石，卡塔曲塔，位于乌卢鲁西部的穹顶椭圆形巨石，构成了全球最古老的人类社会的传统信仰体系的一部分。乌卢鲁卡塔曲塔国家公园传统所有者是阿南古土著居民。

Definitions of natural heritage

自然遗产的定义

NATURAL FEATURES CONSISTING OF PHYSICAL AND BIOLOGICAL FORMATIONS OR GROUPS OF SUCH FORMATIONS

由物质和生态群系构成的，或一类群系的组合群的自然地域。

The formal definition in *the Convention* is provided above under Natural Heritage. Some examples of listed properties are provided below.

正式的定义在《公约》中已经提及。遗产名录中的自然遗产实例如下。

South China Karst (China)

中国南方喀斯特地形（中国）

The South China Karst region extends over a surface of half a million km^2 lying mainly in Yunnan, Guizhou and Guangxi provinces. It represents one of the world's most spectacular examples of humid tropical to subtropical karst landscapes. The stone forests of Shilin are considered superlative natural phenomena and a world reference with a wider range of pinnacle shapes than other karst landscapes with pinnacles, and a higher diversity of shapes and changing colours. The cone and tower karsts of Libo, also

中国南方的喀斯特地形占地超过50万平方公里，分布在云南省、贵州省和广西壮族自治区。它是世界上潮湿的热带到副热带地区喀斯特景观的杰出代表。云南石林被认为是世界级的参照标准，其尖塔形石峰比其他喀斯特区域分布更广，同时形态和色彩也更加丰富多彩。荔波县的椎体和塔形的喀斯特地貌同样也是世界各类喀斯特的典型代表，形成了独具特色的美丽的景观。武隆喀斯特因具有世界最大的灰岩坑、自然桥和洞穴而列入世界遗产名录。

considered the world reference site for these types of karst, form a distinctive and beautiful landscape. Wulong Karst has been inscribed for its giant dolines (sinkholes), natural bridges and caves.

Volcanoes of Kamchatka (Russian Federation)

堪察加半岛火山群（俄国）

This is one of the most outstanding volcanic regions in the world, with a high density of active volcanoes, a variety of types, and a wide range of related features. The six sites included in the serial designation group together the majority of volcanic features of the Kamchatka peninsula. The interplay of active volcanoes and glaciers forms a dynamic landscape of great beauty. The sites contain great species diversity, including the world's largest known variety of salmonoid fish and exceptional concentrations of sea otter, brown bear and Steller's sea eagle.

这是世界上最突出的活火山区域之一，活火山密度高，各种火山种类繁多，分布广泛。由六个遗址群组成的系列遗址区共同展现了堪察加半岛火山遗产奇观。活火山和冰川相互作用形成了美丽而生机勃勃的景观。遗址还有丰富多样的种群，有世界现存最大的、种类最多的鲑亚目鱼群和大量的水獭、棕熊和虎头海雕。

GEOLOGICAL AND PHYSIOGRAPHICAL FORMATIONS AND PRECISELY DELINEATED AREAS WHICH CONSTITUTE THE HABITAT OF THREATENED SPECIES OF ANIMALS AND PLANTS

地质和自然地理形态，划分明确的濒危动植物种群聚集区

The formal definition in *the Convention* is provided above under Natural Heritage. Some examples of listed properties are provided below.

在《公约》中有自然遗产的正式定义。名录中自然遗产典型如下。

Okapi Wildlife Reserve (Democratic Republic of the Congo)

獾㹢狓野生动物保护区（刚果共和国）

The Okapi Wildlife Reserve occupies about one fifth of the Ituri forest in the north-east of the Democratic Republic of the Congo. The Congo River basin, of which the reserve and forest are a part, is one of the largest drainage systems in Africa. The reserve contains threatened species of primates and birds and about 5, 000 of the estimated

獾㹢狓野生动物保护区占据了位于刚果共和国东北部的伊图里雨林面积的五分之一。保护区和雨林是刚果河盆地的重要组成部分，拥有非洲最大的灌溉系统。保护区内生活着受威胁的灵长类动物和鸟类种群，30000 只野生獾㹢狓中大约有 5000 只生活在这个区域。保护区有美轮美奂的景观，包括伊图里河和埃普鲁河上的

30, 000 okapi surviving in the wild. It also has some dramatic scenery, including waterfalls on the Ituri and Epulu rivers. The reserve is inhabited by traditional nomadic Mbuti and Efe hunters.

瀑布。保护区内还居住着传统的穆布提人和埃费猎人。

Lagoons of New Caledonia: Reef Diversity and Associated Ecosystems (France)

新喀里多尼亚泻湖：多样性的暗礁和与之适应的生态系统（法国）

This serial site comprises six marine clusters that represent the main diversity of coral reefs and associated ecosystems in the French Pacific Ocean archipelago of New Caledonia and one of the three most extensive reef systems in the world. These lagoons are of exceptional natural beauty. They feature an exceptional diversity of coral and fish species and a continuum of habitats from mangroves to seagrass with the world's most diverse concentration of reef structures. The Lagoons of New Caledonia display intact ecosystems, with healthy populations of large predators, and a great number and diversity of big fish. They provide habitat to a number of emblematic or threatened marine species such as turtles, whales or dugongs whose population here is the third largest in the world.

这个系列遗产包含了六个海洋生物群落，他们代表了位于法属太平洋群岛的新喀里多尼亚多样的珊瑚礁和与之相关的生态系统，也展现了地球上最大的三个暗礁群之一。这些泻湖是自然界最美的景观。有多种多样的海洋生物如珊瑚和鱼群，成片的红树林和海草以及世界上最密集的珊瑚群。新喀里多尼亚的泻湖展现了保存完好的生态系统，大量的掠食动物群和大量大型鱼类种群保持着健康的数量。这个系列遗产为典型的濒危海洋生物如乌龟、鲸鱼提供了栖息地，这里儒艮数量排名世界第三。

NATURAL SITES OR PRECISELY DELINEATED NATURAL AREAS OF OUTSTANDING UNIVERSAL VALUE FROM THE POINT OF VIEW OF SCIENCE, CONSERVATION OR NATURAL BEAUTY

从科学、保护和自然美的角度具有突出普遍价值的自然遗产或定义明显的自然保护区

The formal definition in *the Convention* is provided above under Natural Heritage. Some examples of listed properties are provided below.

在公约中已提到自然遗产的定义，下面对名录中部分自然遗产进行介绍。

Grand Canyon National Park (United States)

大峡谷国家公园（美国）

Carved out by the Colorado River, the Grand Canyon (nearly 1,500 m deep) is the most spectacular

因科罗拉多河的切割而形成的大峡谷（深1500米）是世界上最壮观的峡谷景观。位于亚

gorge in the world. Located in the State of Arizona, it cuts across the Grand Canyon National Park. Its horizontal strata retrace the geological history of the past 2 billion years. There are also prehistoric traces of human adaptation to a particularly harsh environment.

利桑那州，横穿大峡谷国家公园。大峡谷的水平层次结构展示了20亿年来地球的地质学变迁。这里也有史前人类适应这种特殊恶劣环境的遗存。

Ha Long Bay (Viet Nam)

下龙湾（越南）

Ha Long Bay, in the Gulf of Tonkin, includes some 1,600 islands and islets, forming a spectacular seascape of limestone pillars. Because of their precipitous nature, most of the islands are uninhabited and unaffected by a human presence. The site's outstanding scenic beauty is complemented by its great biological interest.

下龙湾，位于北部湾，包括1600座岛屿和小岛，形成了石灰岩柱矗立的奇特海景。鉴于这里环境险峻，因而大多数岛礁无人居住，人类生活也没有对它造成影响。遗址区风景宜人，同时是多种生物的栖息地。

Glossary of key concepts

核心概念词汇表

OUTSTANDING UNIVERSAL VALUE (OUV)

突出普遍价值

The World Heritage Convention was established to recognize 'sites of Outstanding Universal Value' which are part of the heritage of humankind as a whole, which deserve protection and transmission to future generations, and which are important for the whole of humanity.

《世界遗产公约》的目的是为了认可"遗产的突出普遍价值"，因其是全人类遗产的组成部分，值得我们去保护并传递给未来，同时对于整个人类而言也具有重要的作用。

The Operational Guidelines define Outstanding Universal Value as being cultural and/or natural significance which is so exceptional as to transcend national boundaries and to be of common importance for present and future generations of all humanity (Paragraph 49).

《操作指南》对于突出普遍价值的定义是：罕见的、超越了国家界限的、对全人类的现在和未来均具有普遍的重要意义的文化和自然价值。（《操作指南》49段）

This definition is understood through the criteria for the inscription of properties on the World Heritage List. The criteria are discussed below.

通过对列入《世界遗产名录》标准的分析，可以加深我们对突出普遍价值的理解。

To be deemed of Outstanding Universal Value,

如果认定一个遗产具有突出普遍价值，那

a property must also meet the conditions of integrity and/or authenticity and must have an adequate protection and management system to ensure its safeguarding (*Operational Guidelines*, Paragraph 78, see also sections on integrity and authenticity in Section II.E).

么它必须符合完整性和真实性的条件，同时还要有足够的保护和管理体系确保遗产的安全（《操作指南》78段，在完整性和真实性的章节中也有详细论述，第二部分.E）

Outstanding Universal Value is:

• the main focus of the nomination;

• what is evaluated;

• why a property is inscribed on the World Heritage List; and

• what needs to be sustained through protection, conservation and management.

突出普遍价值是：

• 申报的主要核心；

• 是评估的对象；

• 是遗产能够列入《世界遗产名录》的原因；

• 需要通过保存、保护和管理加以维持。

Since 2007, the World Heritage Committee has adopted a Statement of Outstanding Universal Value at the time a property is inscribed on the World Heritage List, and there are processes in place to create such statements for the many properties inscribed before this practice was started. These Statements are now central to the Committee's work and encapsulate why each inscribed property is considered to be of Outstanding Universal Value, how it satisfies the criteria and the requirements for authenticity, integrity, protection and management.

自从2007年，世界遗产委员会要求，在遗产列入《世界遗产名录》时必须要有突出普遍价值的声明，并为此前已列入《世界遗产名录》的很多遗产如何编制《突出普遍价值声明》规定了相关程序。这些声明，包括每项已列入的遗产为什么具有突出普遍价值、概述其突出普遍价值及其如何达到标准，如何满足真实性、完整性和保护管理需求等，已成为委员会工作的重心。

The Statement of Outstanding Universal Value (So OUV) over-arches the whole life of a property.

突出普遍价值声明（以下简称So OUV）是整个遗产的灵魂所在。

Once adopted by the World Heritage Committee, the So OUV is also the reference point for:

• monitoring by the State Party and property manager;

• Periodic Reporting;

• Reactive Monitoring and State of Conservation Reporting;

• inscription on the List of World Heritage in Danger; and

• possible deletion of a property from the

一旦世界遗产委员会接受了突出普遍价值声明，它将成为以下工作评判的标准：

• 缔约国和遗产管理机构对遗产的监测；

• 定期报告；

• 反应性监测与保护状况报告；

• 列入《濒危世界遗产名录》；

• 可能从《世界遗产名录》中除名。

World Heritage List.

Themes and thematic frameworks are important in understanding Outstanding Universal Value. See Report of the World Heritage Global Strategy Natural and Cultural Heritage Expert Meeting (UNESCO World Heritage Centre/Government of the Netherlands, 1998) and The World Heritage List: Filling the Gaps - An Action Plan for the Future (ICOMOS, 2005a).

理解突出普遍价值的主题或主题框架十分重要，参考《世界自然和文化遗产全球战略专家会议的报告》（联合国教科文组织世界遗产中心及荷兰政府 1998 年报告）和《世界遗产名录：填补空白—未来行动计划》（国际古迹遗址理事会，2005a）。

As noted above, Outstanding Universal Value is a special category of cultural and/or natural significance. There are other levels of heritage value, such as local or national heritage value. Throughout this manual the use of the terms value or significance should be understood in the context provided - often it will be Outstanding Universal Value but sometimes they may refer to other levels of heritage such as national or local heritage.

如上所述，突出普遍价值是自然和文化遗产的特殊重要属性。遗产还有其他层面的价值，比如说地区或国家层面的遗产价值。本手册所提及的价值或重要性常常是指突出普遍价值，但是有些时候也指不同层面的遗产价值，比如国家、地区层面的遗产价值等。

ATTRIBUTES OR FEATURES

属性或特性

Attributes are aspects of a property which are associated with or express the Outstanding Universal Value. Attributes can be tangible or intangible. *The Operational Guidelines* indicate a range of types of attribute which might convey Outstanding Universal Value, including:

• form and design;
• materials and substance;
• use and function;
• traditions, techniques and management systems;
• location and setting;
• language, and other forms of intangible heritage;
• spirit and feeling (Paragraph 82).

属性是能展现突出普遍价值或与突出普遍价值相关的遗产组成部分。属性可以是有形的也可以是无形的。《操作指南》中指出能够揭示突出普遍价值的属性组成部分包括以下几类：

• 形式和设计；
• 材料和物质；
• 用途和功能；
• 传统、技术和管理体系；
• 位置和环境；
• 语言和其他无形遗产；
• 精神和感知（82 段）。

This list is for guidance. It is essential that the

这几条是判断特征的指南。认定遗产属性

attributes identified for a property should flow from the Statement of Outstanding Universal Value and the justification for the criteria.

的基础应该是突出普遍价值声明和适用标准。

Attributes must be identified as they are vital to understanding authenticity and integrity, and are the focus of protection, conservation and management.

属性的定义对于了解遗产的真实性和完整性也极为重要，同时它也是开展保存、保护和管理工作的关键。

For natural properties, it is more common to speak of 'features', although the word attributes is sometimes used. Examples of attributes for natural properties could include:

• visual or aesthetic significance;

• scale of the extent of physical features or natural habitats;

• intactness of physical or ecological processes;

• naturalness, and intactness of natural systems;

• viability of populations of rare species; and

• rarity.

对于自然遗产，可用特征一词，但通常会以属性代替。自然遗产的属性应该包括：

• 观赏性或艺术价值；

• 自然特征或天然栖息地的规模；

• 物理和生态进程的完整性；

• 自然系统的自然性、完整性；

• 稀有物种的生存能力；

• 稀有性。

BUFFER ZONE

缓冲区

Buffer zones are clearly delineated area (s) outside a World Heritage property and adjacent to its boundaries which contribute to the protection, conservation, management, integrity, authenticity and sustainability of the Outstanding Universal Value of the property.

缓冲区是具有明显边界、位于世界遗产范围之外、并与遗产直接衔接的区域，这个区域对保存、保护、管理遗产，体现遗产完整性、真实性，维持遗产的突出普遍价值有着重要的作用。

Although buffer zones are not regarded as part of the inscribed property, their boundaries and relevant management approaches should be evaluated, approved and formally recorded at the time they are proposed by a State Party.

尽管缓冲区并不是世界遗产的正式组成部分，但是缔约国在准备申报遗产时，应该对缓冲区的界限和与之相关的管理模式，进行评估、核准和正式记录。

Where buffer zones are defined, they should be seen as an integral component of the State Party's commitment to the protection, conservation

划定缓冲区也是缔约国对保存、保护和管理世界遗产承诺的一个重要组成部分。缓冲区应该反映出不同类型和等级的保存、保护和管

and management of the World Heritage property. The functions of the buffer zone should reflect the different types and levels of protection, conservation and management needed to protect the attributes that sustain the Outstanding Universal Value of the World Heritage property.

理工作，这些工作是保护遗产的突出普遍价值的组成部分。

Some examples of buffer zones are provided on late pages where the requirements for defining such zones are discussed. A useful reference on buffer zones is World Heritage and Buffer Zones, International Expert Meeting on World Heritage and Buffer Zones, Davos, Switzerland, 11-14 March 2008 (Martin and Piatti, 2009).

本文例举了一些缓冲区的实例，讨论有关缓冲区的要求。有关缓冲区的参考文献包括《世界遗产和缓冲区国际专家会议》，达沃斯，瑞士，2008 年 3 月 11–14 日。（Martin and Piatti，2009）

COMPARATIVE ANALYSIS

比较分析

The comparative analysis explains the importance of the nominated property both in its national and international context. In order to do this, the property should be compared with similar properties, whether on the World Heritage List or not. The comparison should outline the similarities the nominated property has with other properties and the reasons that make the nominated property stand out.

比较分析解释了申报遗产在本土和国际上的重要性。为此，遗产应该与相似的遗产（无论该相似遗产是否已列入遗产名录）进行比较。比较时应该罗列出申报遗产与其他遗产的相似之处，同时也要指出申报遗产比其他遗产更胜一筹的原因。

The comparative analysis is discussed in more detail later.

有关比较分析的讨论见后文。

PROPERTY

遗产

The property is the land or sea area which has Outstanding Universal Value.

遗产是指具有突出普遍价值的陆地或海洋区域。

The term ‘core zone’ was formerly used to describe the property. However, it is now out of date and should not be used. All references should be made to the ‘property’.

以往习惯用核心区来描述遗产。然而，现在核心区这个词已经过时了，不再使用。以后，所有文献中将用遗产这个词替代。

SETTING

环境

Where the setting is a part of, or integral to, the Outstanding Universal Value of a property, then it should be part of the inscribed property, or in some cases, such as extensive views, part of the buffer zone. Where the setting may assist in the appreciation of the Outstanding Universal Value, but does not contribute to the Outstanding Universal Value, then it is desirable that it be incorporated in the buffer zone or otherwise protected.

遗产环境是体现遗产突出普遍价值的重要组成部分，也是遗产列入名录时完整性的重要组成部分，比如广阔的视野也应该是缓冲区的组成部分。环境助于提升遗产的突出普遍价值，但不一定具备突出普遍价值，应该纳入缓冲区或以其他方式加以保护。

The ICOMOS Xi'an Declaration on the Conservation of the Setting of Heritage Structures, Sites and Areas notes,

在国际古迹遗址理事会《保护建筑遗产、遗址和遗产区环境的西安宣言》里提到（2005b）:

The setting of a heritage structure, site or area is defined as the immediate and extended environment that is part of, or contributes to, its significance and distinctive character.

古建筑、古遗址和历史区域的周边环境指的是紧靠古建筑、古遗址和历史区域的和延伸的、影响其重要性和独特性或是其重要性和独特性组成部分的周围环境。

Beyond the physical and visual aspects, the setting includes interaction with the natural environment; past or present social or spiritual practices, customs, traditional knowledge, use or activities and other forms of intangible cultural heritage aspects that created and form the space as well as the current and dynamic cultural, social and economic context.

除了实体和视角方面的含义之外，周边环境还包括与自然环境之间的相互关系；所有过去和现在的人类社会和精神实践、习俗、传统的认知或活动，创造并形成了周边环境空间中的其他形式的非物质文化遗产，以及当前活跃发展的文化、社会、经济氛围。

The concept and requirements relating to settings are discussed further.

关于环境的定义以及需求在后文将会详细讨论。

Relationship between natural, cultural and mixed properties, and the special case of cultural landscapes

自然、文化和混合遗产的关系，以及文化景观特案

It is important not to confuse mixed properties and cultural landscapes. Mixed properties are inscribed under both at least one of criteria (i) to (vi)

分清混合遗产和文化景观这两类遗产十分重要。混合遗产必须要同时满足标准（1）到（6）的其中一条，及标准（7）至（10）的至少

and at least one of criteria (vii) to (x), because they meet both criteria independently. The Outstanding Universal Value of cultural landscapes arises not from their cultural or natural qualities assessed independently but from the inter-relationship between culture and nature. Cultural landscapes are identified under the cultural criteria. Such properties often have natural values, but usually not at the level to justify inscription under natural criteria. In the cases where they do, the property will be inscribed as a mixed site and a cultural landscape. This set of relationships is theoretically explained in the diagram below.

一条，既混合遗产必须同时满足自然遗产和文化遗产的标准。文化景观的突出普遍价值不是分别评估遗产的自然或文化属性，而是评估遗产内在的文化与自然之间相互联系。文化景观应符合文化遗产的评价标准。尽管这些遗产常常同时具有自然价值，但是其自然价值没有达到自然遗产评估标准的要求。这种情况下，遗产既以混合遗产又以文化景观的类型列入名录。他们之间的理论关系在下面图表中将详细论述。

For some mixed properties the natural values and cultural values are integrated and co-dependent. In other cases, the values may not be co-dependent but simply share the same geographic location.

对于某些混合遗产，其自然价值和文化价值相互融合，相互依存。在另一些情况下，这些价值并不相互依存，只是简单的分布于同一地理位置。

Mixed properties
Meet at least one cultural and one natural criterion
Natural properties
Properties in this part of the diagram meet one or more of the natural criteria (vii-x) only
Natural properties
Mixed properties
Cultural properties
Cultural landscapes
Cultural properties
Properties in this part of the diagram meet one or more of the cultural criteria (i-vi) only
Some **cultural landscapes** can also be **mixed sites**. They are identified as cultural landscapes under the cultural criteria, but their natural values are also sufficient to meet one of the natural criteria
Cultural landscapes are inscribed under the cultural criteria, representing the combined works of nature and man

World Heritage criteria

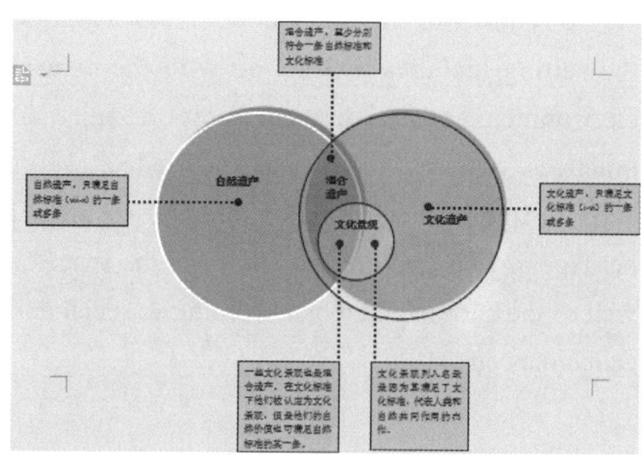

World Heritage criteria

世界遗产标准选择

Key message: Choose only relevant criteria that demonstrate Outstanding Universal Values.

关键信息：选择相关的标准来论证突出普遍价值

There are ten criteria for World Heritage inscription identified in *The Operational Guidelines* (Paragraph 77). Criteria (i) to (vi) relate to cultural

在《操作指南》中列出了10条界定世界遗产的标准（77段），标准1到6是国际古迹理事会评估文化遗产的标准，标准7到10是世界

properties, and are therefore assessed by ICOMOS, and the remaining criteria (vii) to (x) relate to natural properties and are assessed by IUCN. While many properties may only meet some natural or cultural criteria, mixed properties will meet some natural as well as some cultural criteria. Nominations of mixed properties are evaluated by both IUCN and ICOMOS.

自然保护联盟评估自然遗产的标准。多数自然或文化遗产仅仅能满足相关标准的一条或几条，混合遗产则要同时满足至少一条自然标准和一条文化标准，并由世界自然保护联盟和国际古迹理事会共同评估。

Examples of properties which meet the criteria are provided below (text and illustrations for these examples are drawn from the UNESCO World Heritage website).

遗产符合标准的实例如下。（下面的描述内容和解释均摘自世界遗产网站）

Criterion (i) : represent a masterpiece of human creative genius

In other words, this criterion relates to an outstanding example (perhaps the peak or a landmark example) of a style evolved within a culture, having:

• a high intellectual or symbolic endowment; and

• a high level of artistic, technical or technological skills.

标准（1）人类创造精神的杰作；

换句话说，这一标准与某一文化类型遗产演化的典范相关（可能是巅峰或里程碑之作），具有：

• 高智慧或天才的象征；

• 高水平的艺术、工艺和技术技巧。

Uniqueness is not, on its own, sufficient to justify inscription. The property must be considered in a broader cultural-historical context, and its value assessed in relation to this context.

就其本身而言，唯一性不足以让遗产列入名录。必须在广泛的文化历史背景下进行遗产考量，在对其价值进行评估时也要考虑它的历史文化背景。

The World Heritage List is a list of properties, not a list of people. So, for example, under criterion (i) what is required is a masterpiece of human creative genius. The World Heritage List does not list geniuses but it can list their masterpieces. Similarly, it does not list the body of work of a genius, but it may list the masterpiece that has Outstanding Universal Value or a series of masterpieces that has Outstanding Universal Value as a whole.

《世界遗产名录》是遗产名录而不是人类名录。因此，例如，在标准（1）下需要的是展现人类创造天赋的杰作。《世界遗产名录》也不是天才的名录，但是可以记录天才们的杰作。同样的，它也不是天才作品本身的名录，它是具有突出普遍价值杰作的名录，或者是一系列具有突出普遍价值杰作的名录。

Not all masterpieces have known architects or designers. Some prehistoric structures have become icons for the creativity and technical sophistication of prehistoric peoples for instance; in other cases the collective works of a community can be deemed to have achieved the status of a masterpiece — even though they were perhaps not intended when built to be more than functional. Some industrial structures are also seen to have risen above the functional and utilitarian to embody creativity to the point of genius.

并不是所有杰作的建筑师或设计师，都为人所知。例如，一些史前建筑已经成为史前人类创造力和技术成熟度的标志。此外，社区集体的作品也可以被认为具有杰作性质——即使当初建造时实用性多于艺术性，而一些工业建筑也因其本身的实用功能和独特作用成为人类创造的杰作。

EXAMPLE

Sydney Opera House (Australia)

案例

悉尼歌剧院（澳大利亚）

Inaugurated in 1973, the Sydney Opera House is a great architectural work of the 20th century that brings together multiple strands of creativity and innovation in both architectural form and structural design. A great urban sculpture set in a remarkable water scope, at the tip of a peninsula projecting into Sydney Harbour, the building has had an enduring influence on architecture. The Sydney Opera House comprises three groups of interlocking vaulted 'shells' which roof two main performance halls and a restaurant. These shell-structures are set upon a vast platform and are surrounded by terrace areas that function as pedestrian concourses. In 1957, when the project of the Sydney Opera House was awarded by an international jury to Danish architect Jørn Utzon, it marked a radically new approach to construction.

悉尼歌剧院 1973 年正式落成，作为 20 世纪伟大的建筑物，体现了建筑形式和结构设计的创造力和创新性。伟大的城市雕塑构建了一个独一无二的、从半岛的顶端延伸到悉尼海港的水景，这个建筑对以后的建筑设计产生长远的影响。悉尼歌剧院由三组咬合的贝壳状穹顶组成，其中两个是歌剧院的主要演出厅的屋顶，一个是餐厅的屋顶。这些贝壳状穹顶架设在一个大平台上，环绕四周的露台区域作为人行道。1957 年，国际评审团把悉尼歌剧院项目授予设计师丹麦的约恩·乌特松，因其代表了全新的建造方法。

Criterion (ii) : exhibit an important interchange of human values, over a span of time or within a cultural area of the world, on developments in architecture or technology, monumental arts, town-planning or landscape design

标准（2）：体现一段时期内或世界某一文化区域内人类价值观的相互交流，对建筑、技术、古迹艺术、城镇规划或景观设计的发展，产生重大影响；

The key phrase in this criterion is 'interchange

在这个标准中最重要的短语是“人类价值

of human values'. What ICOMOS evaluates is whether the physical assets of a property, in terms of architecture, technology, monumental arts, town-planning or landscape design can be said to relate to an interchange of ideas — and this can be interpreted in several different ways:

观的相互交流”。国际古迹理事会评估的内容是看遗产的物质形态（比如建筑、技术和古迹艺术、城市设计或景观设计）是否与人类思想观念的相互交流相关。这项标准可以从多方面解读：

• the property may be the embodiment of an idea or concept imported from another region or area and which transformed subsequent creativity in the original region, the recipient region or otherwise;

• 遗产能够展现从其他地区输入的观念或想法，同时持续改变输出区域、输入区域及其他地区的创造力；

• alternatively, the property may itself have prompted the interchange of human values through inspiring ideas that influenced other areas; and

• 其二，遗产激发的创意影响了其他领域的思想，从而促使人类价值观的相互交流；

• thirdly, there could have been a two-way flow of ideas, with the property displaying some sort of cultural fusion or local adaptation that could be deemed to be emblematic in some way.

• 第三，观念传播是双向流动的，遗产可以体现文化融合和地方性适应，某种程度上有象征意义。

In all cases the interchange of human ideas or influences needs to have prompted a response, which can be said to be outstanding in terms of the influence it had at the time and/or subsequently on people or society.

在所有情况下，人类理念的交流或影响都会有所反应，会给当时或后世人们和社会带来突出影响。

In many properties, the influences or interchanges refer to the tangible dissemination of ideas important in the history of art, architecture or urban design, or the history of technology, all as embodied in the attributes of the property.

对多数遗产而言，影响或交换是指艺术史、建筑史、城市设计史或技术发展史等重要理念的有形传播，这些都体现在遗产的属性中。

As interchange in and between human societies and cultures is commonplace, this criterion requires that the interchange and the values/influence are substantial and important in their impact on the recipient culture. The transfer of a minor cultural aspect, or the transfer of a value which had little impact, are insufficient.

人类社会和文化之间的交换司空见惯，这个标准的要求对于接受文化交换或价值和影响有实质的、重要的效果。次要文化组成部分的转变或影响不大的文化或价值转变影响都不足以影响这一标准。

In addition, the values or influence interchanged

此外，价值的交换或影响必须在拟申报的

must be manifest in some way in the nominated property, through being embodied in the attributes of the property. An interchange of human values or influence with no manifestation in the property is not a good argument for inscription.

遗产中以某种方式展现，并通过遗产属性表现出来。如果人类价值的交换或影响在遗产中没有体现，则不能成为列入遗产名录的依据。

Using this criterion to justify a well-preserved example of a type of property is not generally appropriate, and is best argued under other criteria.

一般来说不适合使用本标准判断一类遗产是否得到好的保护，使用其他标准申报可能更为适合。

EXAMPLE

Samarkand - Crossroads of Cultures (Uzbekistan)

案例

撒马尔罕—文化交汇点

The historic town of Samarkand is a crossroad and melting pot of the world's cultures. Founded in the 7th century BC as ancient Afrasiab, Samarkand had its most significant development in the Timurid period from the 14th to the 15th centuries. Ensembles in Samarkand such as the Bibi Khanum Mosque and Registan Square played a seminal role in the development of Islamic architecture over the entire region, from the Mediterranean to the Indian subcontinent.

历史城镇撒马尔罕是世界多元文化的交汇点和大熔炉。撒马尔罕始建于公元前 7 世纪，古称阿佛洛西亚，在 14 到 15 世纪的帖木儿帝国时期得到重要发展。撒马尔罕的建筑群，比如撒马尔罕比比哈内姆大清真寺和列基斯坦广场等，对伊斯兰建筑在整个区域（从地中海地区到印度次大陆）发展，有重要作用。

Also inscribed under criteria (i) and (iv).

遗产列入名录还符合标准（1）和（4）。

Criterion (iii) : bear a unique or at least exceptional testimony to a cultural tradition or to a civilization which is living or which has disappeared

标准（3）：能为延续至今或业已消逝的文明或文化传统提供独特的、至少是特殊的见证；

In contrast to criterion (ii), this criterion considers processes — cultural traditions that have, normally over a long period of time, defined a way of life or civilization in a geo-cultural region. Such traditions may still be living and vibrant, or may have atrophied in which case the testimony is their memorial. The traditions may be ways of building, spatial planning, or urban patterns. Alternatively, the traditions may be intangible but with precise tangible results — such as for instance rock art

与标准（2）形成鲜明的对比，这个标准更强调过程——文化传统是对地理文化圈长时间形成的生活或文明的一个定义。这样的传统可能至今仍充满生机，也可能已经开始衰退，遗产见证了文化传统的记忆。传统可以通过建筑物、空间规划或城市布局得以展现。此外，传统也可以是无形的，但常常以有形形式表现出来——例如能够反映传统文化的理念和组成部分岩画艺术。

images which can reflect ideas or aspects of cultural traditions.

The key words are ‘exceptional testimony’. The testimony is the evidence of a cultural tradition or civilization and must clearly be found in the nominated property.

该标准的核心词汇是“特殊的见证”。见证就是传统文化或文明的证据，并且这些证据在申报的遗产中可以清晰地发现。

The cultural tradition or civilization must be understood in the context of Outstanding Universal Value. They must express ‘issues of universal nature common to or addressed by all human cultures’ (World Heritage Expert Meeting, Amsterdam, 1998). That is, the cultural tradition or civilization cannot merely relate to issues which are only important to the specific culture.

传统文化或文明必须要在突出普遍价值的背景下理解。他们必须表达“全世界共同的文化特性或讨论全人类共有话题”（世界遗产专家会议，阿姆斯特丹，1998 年）。也就是说，文化传统或文明不能仅对特殊文化有重要地作用。

A civilization might normally be expected to have lasted for a substantial period, to have an organized character or unifying qualities, and to involve a relatively substantial group of people. Relatively short-lived societies, groups lacking an organized character or unifying qualities, or very small groups may not necessarily be regarded as civilizations.

通常而言，文明在很长一段时间，有组织性或统一性、有大量的人群参与。相对而言，短暂的社会，缺乏组织性或统一性或很小的集团都不能认为是文明。

EXAMPLE
Historic Centre of Macao (China)

Macao bears a unique testimony to the first and longest-lasting encounter between the West and China. From the 16th to the 20th centuries, it was the focal point for traders and missionaries, and the different fields of learning. The impact of this encounter can be traced in the fusion of different cultures that characterize the historic core of Macao.

Also inscribed under criteria (ii), (iv) and (vi).

案例
澳门历史中心（中国）

澳门是第一个也是持续时间最长的、中国和西方文化交融的独特见证。从 16 到 20 世纪，这里是商人和传教士的聚集区，也是不同文化的学习地。不同文化交融在澳门历史街区的物质特性中都有所体现。

同时，遗产还符合标准（2）（4）和（6）。

Criterion (iv) : be an outstanding example of a type of building, architectural or technological ensemble or landscape which illustrates (a) significant stage (s) in human history

标准 4：是一种建筑、建筑学或整体技术、景观的杰出范例，展现人类历史上一个（或几个）重要阶段；

This criterion relates to the outstanding nature of the typology of a property, nominated in the context of the defined typology illustrating one or more significant stages in history.

本标准涉及遗产地在某一类型方面杰出性质，申报的遗产在该类型中展现了历史上的一个或几个重要阶段。

The essence of this criterion is that the property must in some way demonstrate that it is associated with a defining moment or moments — or significant stage (s) in human history. The property may have been prompted by that moment, or may reflect its impact. The historical moment needs to be deemed to be of outstanding importance, as do its repercussions. The stages may relate to political or economic history, or equally to artistic or scientific history, which had far-reaching consequences.

本标准的基础是必须通过一些方式证明遗产与一个或多个确定的时间或人类历史发展的重要阶段相关。遗产是那个发展时刻的见证者或者反映了它的重要影响，要能体现这个历史时刻的特有影响的突出重要性。这个阶段可能和政治或经济发展史相关或与艺术史、科学史相关，且产生深远的影响。

The property must illustrate a significant stage in human history, in an outstanding way. Such a stage needs to be assessed in a regional and global context, and the stage must be important in that context. An important stage in just the history of one country is insufficient unless there is a substantial regional or global impact. There is also a time dimension to a stage. A stage should be defined in terms of cultural history and the patterns of continuity and change in that history. Artificial time periods (e.g. 18th century) are not, in themselves, a satisfying definition. A meaningful time period should be a defined period which is important and recognized within a cultural context.

遗产必须以突出的方法阐明人类历史发展这一重要阶段。这一阶段需要在地区和全球的范围内进行评估，这点很重要。一个国家的历史上的一个重要阶段，如果没有对周边地区或全球都持续产生影响，就不认为其具有突出普遍价值。这个阶段也有时间跨度。可以根据文化史及在历史上的延续方式和变化形式，来确定其时间跨度。人为界定的时间（比如 18 世纪）无法符合本准则的规定。有意义的时间跨度应该是文化背景下重要的、确定的、被认可的时期。

The criterion should thus be used in relation to significant ‘prototypes’ or strongly representative examples of a defined type of property.

因此，该标准可用于重要的“原型”或某类特定遗产的杰出代表。

This criterion is not meant to encourage or allow the inscription of an example of every type of building, ensemble or landscape in the world — even if it is an outstanding example.

本标准并不是鼓励或允许将世界上每种形式的建筑、建筑群或景观的实例都列入名单——即便它是杰出的实例。

ICOMOS has developed a number of studies on property types such as railways, canals, rock art and bridges to enable the objective assessment of some types of nominated properties (see http: //www.icomos.org/studies/). There are also a number of helpful thematic and regional bibliographies compiled by the ICOMOS Documentation Centre available online (http: //www.international.icomos.org/centre_documentation/bib/index.html).

国际古迹遗址理事会对不同类型的遗产进行了专题研究，例如铁路、运河、岩画艺术和桥梁，以便对申报遗产的类型进行客观的评估（见 http：//www.icomos.org/studies/）。国际古迹遗址理事会官网的档案中心提供了大量有用的其他专题研究报告和区域性参考书目。（http：//www.international.icomos.org/centre_documentation/bib/index.html）

EXAMPLE

Rideau Canal (Canada)

案例

里多运河（加拿大）

The Rideau Canal is an extensive, well preserved and significant example of a canal which was used for a military purpose linked to a significant stage in human history — that of the fight to control the north of the American continent.

里多运河是大型的、保存完好的运河的一个重要实例，它因军事目的而修建，与控制北美大陆的战争这一重要的人类历史阶段有关。

The nominated property includes all the main elements of the original canal together with relevant later changes in the shape of watercourses, dams, bridges, fortifications, lock stations and related archaeological resources. The original plan of the canal, as well as the form of the channels, has remained intact. The Rideau Canal has fulfilled its original dynamic function as an operating waterway without interruption since its construction. Most of its lock gates and sluice valves are still operated by hand-powered winches.

申报遗产包括原运河所有组成部分、后期水路、河道、坝、桥、防御工事、闸坝等组成部分及相关考古资源的变化。运河的原始布局，河道的形式都原封未动。里多运河自建成以来就是一条持续使用的水路，至今依旧发挥着控制航道的作用，从未受到干扰。大多数的闸门和水闸阀门仍用手动绞盘进行控制。

Also inscribed under criterion (i).

里多运河列入《世界遗产名录》还符合标准（1）。

Criterion (v) : be an outstanding example of a traditional human settlement, land-use, or sea-use

标准（5）：是传统人类居住地、土地使用或海洋开发的杰出范例，代表一种（或几种）

which is representative of a culture (or cultures), or human interaction with the environment especially when it has become vulnerable under the impact of irreversible change

文化或人类与环境的相互作用，特别是当它面临不可逆变化的影响而变得易于损坏；

Traditional settlements may be urban or rural. Similarly, land-use does not just apply to rural occupations. The key aspect of this criterion is that the property must represent a particular culture or cultures and that representivity needs to be outstanding in some way. It is sometimes assumed that the emphasis in this criterion is on the impact of irreversible change — in that a property that is vulnerable to irreversible change is therefore of outstanding value. This is not the case. However, the vulnerability can mean that what formerly was plentiful has become scarce, and what is left is now rare, possibly the only surviving example of a type of settlement or land-use.

传统的居住地可以在城镇，也可以在乡村。同样的，土地使用不单指农村用地。这个标准的核心组成部分是遗产必须代表某一种（或多种）特殊的文化，而这个代表性必须在某些方面非常杰出。有时会设定本标准的重点是因不可逆转的改变而产生的影响——既遗产是因遭受到不可逆转的改变而具有了突出价值。事实并非如此。脆弱性是指以前丰富的后来变得稀有了、遗留至今的更少、可能成为某类居住地或土地使用方式的唯一幸存的范例了。

The key phrase is 'land-use'. There must be some reasonably long period of time associated with the settlement or use in order for it to be considered traditional.

关键词“土地使用方式”。说明这种居住地或土地的使用方式，必须经过相当长的一段时间，才能被认为是传统的。

The settlement or use must also be an outstanding representation of a culture or human interaction with the environment. That is, the settlement or use must be important within the life of the culture, or the human interaction must have universal relevance.

居住地或土地使用方式必须能够突出代表文化或人类与自然相互作用。也就是说，居住地或土地使用方式对文化生活十分重要，或者与人类的互动作用有普遍的相关性。

ICOMOS has developed a number of global thematic studies such as on vineyard landscapes, or regional thematic studies, to provide objective support for the assessment of some types of settlements or landscapes (see http: //www.icomos.org/studies/).

国际古迹理事会完成了很多全球性的专题研究，例如，葡萄园文化景观，或者区域性专题研究，从而为评估某些类型的居住地和景观提供客观的帮助。见（http：//www.icomos.org/studies/）。

EXAMPLE

Agave Landscape and Ancient Industrial Facilities of Tequila (Mexico)

案例

龙舌兰景观和古代特基拉工业设施（墨西哥）

The 34, 658 ha site, between the foothills of the Tequila Volcano and the deep valley of the Rio Grande River, is part of an expansive landscape of blue agave, shaped by the culture of the plant used since the 16th century to produce tequila spirit and for at least 2, 000 years to make fermented drinks and cloth. Within the landscape are working distilleries reflecting the growth in the international consumption of tequila in the 19th and 20th centuries. Today, the agave culture is seen as part of national identity. The area encloses a living, working landscape of blue agave fields and the urban settlements of Tequila, Arenal and Amatitan with large distilleries where the agave 'pine - apple' is fermented and distilled. The property is also a testimony to the Teuchitlan cultures which shaped the Tequila area from AD 200-900, notably through the creation of terraces for agriculture, housing, temples, ceremonial mounds and ball courts.

一个位于特基拉火山山脚和里奥格兰德河的河谷之间、面积为34658公顷的遗址，是广袤的令人震惊的蓝色龙舌兰生产地的一部分，从16世纪开始因使用植物酿造龙舌兰酒而形成的龙舌兰文化，2000多年来人们一直用龙舌兰酿酒和染织布料。该景观内仍有很多酿酒厂在生产，反映了19—20世纪国际上不断上升的对龙舌兰酒的消费需求。目前，龙舌兰文化被认为是墨西哥国家身份的一部分。至今这个区域依然是蓝色龙舌兰种植基地、周边环绕着特基拉地区、阿雷纳尔市及阿玛提坦市的几个大型仍在使用的龙舌兰发酵、蒸馏、酿造工厂等景观。该遗产地还包括塔栖兰文化时期的考古遗址，见证了形成于公元200-900年特基拉地区的龙舌兰酒文化，如开垦梯田促进农业发展、修建房屋、庙宇和用于举行仪式的土台及球场。

The overall landscape of fields, distilleries, haciendas and towns is an outstanding example of a traditional human settlement and land-use which is representative of a specific culture that developed in Tequila.

上述景观如种植园、酿造厂、大庄园和城镇是人类传统聚集地和土地使用的杰出案例，代表了特基拉地区龙舌兰特殊文化的发展。

Also inscribed under criteria (ii), (iv) and (vi).

同时也符合标准（2），（4），（6）。

Criterion (vi) : be directly or tangibly associated with events or living traditions, with ideas, or with beliefs, with artistic and literary works of outstanding universal significance. (The Committee considers that this criterion should preferably be used in conjunction with other criteria.)

标准6：与具有突出的普遍意义的事件、生活传统、观点、信仰、艺术或文学作品有直接或有形的联系。（委员会认为本标准最好与其他标准一起使用）；

Most of the other criteria involve intangible

多数标准都涉及某种无形关联——例如历

associations of one sort or another — such as historical events, political leaders, wars and conflict, or ideas in town planning or structural innovations, but they concern the tangible impacts of these associations. This criterion by contrast relates to associations that may not have a tangible impact within the property, but nevertheless can be clearly and directly demonstrated. For instance, a mountain or landscape may be sacred or inspirational; a property may have inspired painters, artists or musicians; or the property may be associated with some sort of event that is itself of outstanding importance.

史事件、政治领袖、战争和冲突，或城市规划的理念，或结构创新等，但主要关注的是这些关联的实际影响。相比之下，该标准涉及的关联可能不会对遗产本身产生实质性影响，但是仍然可以清楚、直接地展示着无形影响。例如，一座山脉或一种文化景观可能很神圣或成为精神象征；一处遗产也可能激发画家、艺术家和音乐家的灵感，或者一处遗产与某些本身就具有突出普遍价值的事件相关联。

The starting point for justifying this criterion must be that the events, traditions, ideas, beliefs or artistic or literary works are of outstanding universal significance. Then the way these events, traditions, ideas, beliefs or artistic or literary works are demonstrated directly or tangibly in the property needs to be set out.

要证明这一标准的基础是，这些相关事件、传统、理念、信仰或艺术或文学作品本身，具有重要的突出普遍价值。然后需要阐明这些事件、传统、理念、信仰或艺术或文学作品在遗产中直接或实际的展示方式。

Bearing in mind that *The World Heritage Convention* is about properties, this criterion may only be used if the physical aspects of the property are of Outstanding Universal Value, it preferably satisfies at least one other criterion, and it can be protected for agreed attributes that convey Outstanding Universal Value.

时刻铭记《世界遗产公约》所关注的是遗产，只有遗产的物质遗存本身具有突出普遍价值，同时遗产最好符合至少一项其他标准，确保遗产的突出普遍价值得到保护时，方适用本标准。

The World Heritage List does not inscribe events, traditions, ideas, beliefs and artistic or literary works in themselves, but it may inscribe properties which are directly and tangibly associated with these. For example, where a religion or movement is of outstanding universal significance and is directly or tangibly reflected in a property, then this may be a good case for inscription. However, the List cannot include every temple, shrine or church of the major world

《世界遗产名录》并不是事件、传统、理念、信仰、艺术或文学著作的名录，但很多遗产列入名录都与这些有直接或明确的关联性。例如，一处遗产的突出普遍意义是直接且明白反映了在这里发生的宗教或运动，那么该遗产应该列入名录。但是，名录不能包括与世界主要宗教有关的所有庙宇、神殿或教堂。列入名录的遗产必须是直接或有形联系的杰出代表。

religions. A property must be an outstanding example of direct or tangible associations.

In addition, more weight has been given to associations with the birthplace or principal place in a particular religion, than to places used to diffuse such faith in a particular context.

另外，与某种宗教的发源地或圣地相关的地区，比如宗教的传播区域，在特殊背景下更能体现这种杰出的代表性。

Note that while a few exceptional cases exist, *The Operational Guidelines* clearly indicate that this criterion should be used in conjunction with other criteria, rather than alone.

虽然在名录中少有这样的范例，《操作指南》中也明确提出本标准要和其他标准联合使用，不能单独使用。

EXAMPLE

Struve Geodetic Arc (Belarus, Estonia, Finland, Latvia, Lithuania, Republic of Moldova, Norway, Russian Federation, Sweden and Ukraine)

案例

斯特鲁维地理探测弧线（白俄罗斯、爱沙尼亚、芬兰、拉脱维亚、立陶宛、摩尔多瓦共和国、挪威、俄罗斯联邦、瑞典和乌克兰）

The measuring of the arc and its results are directly associated with scientific inquiry about the shape and size of the world. It is linked with Sir Isaac Newton's theory that the world is not an exact sphere.

对这个弧线的测量及结果直接与对地球的形状和大小的科学调查息息相关。它与艾萨克·牛顿爵士关于地球并不是一个正球体的理论相关联。

Also inscribed under criteria (ii) and (iii).

同时满足标准（2）和（3）。

Criterion (vii) : contain superlative natural phenomena or areas of exceptional natural beauty and aesthetic importance

标准（7）：绝妙的自然现象或具有罕见自然美和美学价值的地区；

Two distinct ideas are embodied in this criterion. The first, 'superlative natural phenomena', can often be objectively measured and assessed (e.g. deepest canyon, highest mountain, largest cave system, highest waterfall, etc.).

在这个标准中表达了两个有明显区别的概念。第一个"绝妙的自然现象"通常指能够得到客观测量和评估（如最深的峡谷、最高的山峰、最大的洞穴系统、最高的瀑布等）。

The second concept, that of 'exceptional natural beauty and aesthetic importance', is harder to assess. This criterion applies to natural properties which are seen as having exceptional natural beauty and

第二个概念是"具有无可比拟的自然美或审美重要性"，对这部分的评估比较困难。本标准适用于那些看起来就具有无可比拟的自然美或审美重要性的自然遗产。现在有很多科学方

aesthetic importance. There are many intellectual approaches to concepts of the beauty and aesthetics of natural areas. While no one approach is recommended, adopting one or more recognized approaches is essential. Merely asserting these qualities without a robust supporting argument is insufficient. The application of this criterion should not be confused with the recognition of the aesthetics of cultural properties and cultural landscapes that is currently expressed through the use of the cultural criteria.

法用来评估自然区域的秀美，但是缺少一个公认的方式，因此采取一种或多种被认可的方法至关重要。缺乏有力证据支持则不足以判定其秀美。应用这个标准时不能与其他识别文化遗产或文化景观的美学标准混淆。

In addition, the nature of this criterion is that the types of properties that are proposed for inscription will have comparable sites distributed on a worldwide, rather than regional basis, so standards applied under this criterion are expected to meet a global standard of proof. This fact distinguishes the application of the aesthetic element of this criterion from those factors relevant to the consideration of cultural landscapes. Evaluation in relation to this aspect is based on comparison with properties previously inscribed by the World Heritage Committee under this criterion and, to the extent possible, it also involves a comparison of measurable indicators of scenic value. The comparison with properties already listed under this criterion, and the World Heritage Committee and IUCN past practice in its use are also further important elements in considering its appropriateness.

另外，本标准的本质是为所申报的遗产提供全球性的比较对象，而不仅仅是地区性的。所以，根据此项标准申报的遗产应当符合全球性标准。这样就把使用美学组成部分这一判断标准与文化景观中相关的组成部分区分开。使用本标准进行这一评估时，应与那些根据此项标准已列入名录的遗产进行对比研究，同时也要与可量化的景观价值进行比较研究。而与根据本标准已列入名录的遗产进行比较研究，以及世界遗产委员会和世界自然保护联盟过去经验及惯例，也是进一步考虑其适用性的重要因素。

IUCN intends to develop further thematic advice on the application of this criterion for delivery to the World Heritage Committee in 2012. IUCN has also noted that the application of criterion (vii) has also normally been considered in conjunction with at least one other natural criterion.

世界自然保护联盟有意对本标准开展更深层次的专题研究，并于 2012 年将研究成果递交世界遗产委员会。世界自然保护联盟同时注意到，标准（7）通常要和其他至少一条自然遗产标准共同使用。

EXAMPLE

Monarch Butterfly Biosphere Reserve (Mexico)

The 56,259 ha biosphere reserve lies within rugged forested mountains about 100 km north-west of Mexico City. Every autumn, millions, perhaps a billion, butterflies from wide areas of North America return to the site and cluster on small areas of the forest reserve, colouring its trees orange and literally bending their branches under their collective weight. In the spring, these butterflies begin an eight-month migration that takes them all the way to Eastern Canada and back, during which time four successive generations are born and die. How they find their way back to their overwintering site remains a mystery.

案例

帝王蝶生物圈保护区（墨西哥）

保护区的面积为56259公顷，位于距墨西哥城西北约100公里密林丛生的崎岖山区中。每年秋天，数百万、甚至数亿只蝴蝶从北美大陆回到这个保护区，聚集在森林保护区的一个小块林地内，大量蝴蝶把树装扮成橘色，把枝条压弯。春天，这些蝴蝶开始长达8个月的迁徙，到达加拿大东部地区，然后返回，并在这个过程中，繁衍了四代蝴蝶。因而他们如何回到这个过冬的栖息地始终是个难解的谜。

Criterion (viii) : be outstanding examples representing major stages of Earth's history, including the record of life, significant ongoing geological processes in the development of landform, or significant geomorphic or physiographic features

标准（8）：是地球演化史中重要阶段的突出例证，包括生命记载、地貌演变中的重要地质过程或显著的地质、地貌特征；

The assessment framework for this criterion is global, reflecting both the global distribution of geomorphological features and the worldwide perspective required to encompass the representation of the 4.6 billion years of Earth history, address the evolution of life on Earth, as well as the changes in the geography of the planet. Properties where discoveries have led to radical changes in our understanding of Earth history and geological processes are considered, rather than very narrow ranging and highly specialized features. In view of the specialized nature of some geological nominations, IUCN takes advice from geological experts. This criterion involves four distinct, although closely linked, natural elements relevant to geological and geomorphological science, as follows.

这个标准的评估框架是全球性，既反映了全球分布的地形地貌特性，也反映了全球视野下地球46亿年历史，展现地球上生物进化，同时也反映我们星球地理变化。那些能够改变人类理解地球历史和地质演变过程的重大发现的遗产地，才会纳入考虑范围，仅具有很小的范围和特殊性质是不够的。对那些特殊性质的地质遗产申报，世界自然保护联盟将咨询地质专家的意见。本标准涉及关于地质、地形地貌科学不同的、但紧密相关的四个方面自然组成部分：

• Earth's history: This subset of geological features includes phenomena that record important events in the past development of the planet such as the record of crustal dynamics, the genesis and development of mountains, plate movements, continental movement and rift valley development, meteorite impacts, and changing climate in the geological past. Properties that may be considered for inscription on the World Heritage List under this category would primarily involve major discoveries that have led to our overall understanding of earth processes and forms as revealed by rock sequences or associations, rather than fossil assemblages.

• 地球历史：这一子类地质遗产包括记录星球形成过程中重要事件的现象，比如记录地壳运动、山脉的隆起和发展、板块移动、大陆漂移和大裂谷的形成、陨石撞击、不同地质时期的气候变化等。根据这一标准而列入遗产名录的遗产主要是能够更好地帮助我们理解地球形成和发展过程，例如岩石顺序和组合的重大发现，而不是化石集合的重大发现。

• The record of life: This subset includes palaeontological (fossil) sites. For evaluating such nominations IUCN has developed a checklist (see box below).

• 生命的记录：这一子类包括古生物学（化石）遗址。为了评估这类申报遗产，世界自然保护联盟编制了评估检查表（见下表）。

• Significant ongoing geological processes in the development of landform: Geomorphological properties record current geological processes and their relationship to landform and landscapes (or physiography). This subset of criterion (viii) features represents active geomorphological processes such as those associated with glaciers, mountains, deserts, active volcanoes, rivers and deltas, island and coasts.

• 地貌演变中重要的地质过程：地貌遗产记录地质过程和与之相关的地貌或景观（或自然地理学）。符合标准（8）的这一子类遗产代表了常见的地形地貌的形成过程，例如有关冰川、山脉、沙漠、活火山、河流、三角洲和海岸的形成的证据。

Significant geomorphic or physiographic features: This subset includes landform that are the products of active processes, and is intimately linked with the consideration of processes listed above. This group also includes features resulting from earlier or longstanding periods of activity, such as relicts glacial landform, extinct volcanic systems and karst features. These features may sometimes also be considered in relation to the application of criterion (vii), in view of the aesthetic quality of some spectacular landforms.

重要的地形或地貌特征：这一子类包括了运动过程的结果即各种地貌，并且这类遗产与上述过程紧密相关。这一子类也包括早期或长期存在的活动地貌的产物，例如冰川地貌，死火山体系或喀斯特地形。这一类遗产常常与符合标准（7）的遗产有密切的关系，能从审美的角度欣赏壮丽的地貌。

IUCN fossil site evaluation checklist

世界自然保护联盟化石遗址评估检查表

1. Does the site provide fossils which cover an extended period of geological time: i.e. how wide is the geological window?

2. Does the site provide specimens of a limited number of species or whole biotic assemblages: i.e. how rich is the species diversity?

3. How unique is the site in yielding fossil specimens for that particular period of geological time: i.e. would this be the 'type locality' for study or are there similar areas that are alternatives?

4. Are there comparable sites elsewhere that contribute to the understanding of the total 'story' of that point in time/space: i.e. is a single site nomination sufficient or should a serial nomination be considered?

5. Is the site the only main location where major scientific advances were (or are) being made that have made a substantial contribution to the understanding of life on Earth?

6. What are the prospects for ongoing discoveries at the site?

7. How international is the level of interest in the site?

8. Are there other features of natural value (e.g. scenery, landform, vegetation) associated with the site: i.e. does there exist within the adjacent area modern geological or biological processes that relate to the fossil resource?

9. What is the state of preservation of specimens yielded from the site?

10. Do the fossils yielded provide an understanding of the conservation status of contemporary taxa and/or communities: i.e. how relevant is the site in documenting the consequences to modern biota of gradual change through time?

IUCN has undertaken a global thematic study on geological World Heritage (Dingwall et al., 2005). The study provides further guidance on this criterion, and enables further consideration

1. 这个遗址保存的化石是否能代表地质年代中的一个较长的时期，即，地质构造期有多长？

2. 这个遗址展现的是数量有限的种群的样本、还是生物组合的样本：即，种群的多样性有多丰富？

3. 这个遗址出土的化石样本对于特定的地质时代是否独特：即，这里是不是进行研究的“典型地点”、是否存在相似区域可供选择？

4. 在理解这个时期或空间“故事”时是否有类似的遗产：例如，申报单个遗产就能充分表现还是需要申报系列遗产才能说明整个“故事”。

5. 这个遗址是不是唯一的、对理解地球生命有实质性贡献的、科学研究有重大进展地方？

6. 这个遗址发掘的前景如何？

7. 国际上对该遗址的兴趣度多高？

8. 是否存在与这个遗产相关的其他自然价值（例如，景观、地貌和植被）：即，毗邻区域是否存在与此化石资源相关的、当代的地貌或生物进化过程？

9. 在这个遗址采集的标本，其保存状态怎么样？

10. 此处发现的化石是否有助于理解当代生物种群或群落的保护状态？即，遗址是否能记录现代生物随着时间逐步变化的进程。

世界自然保护联盟已经实施了关于地质类世界遗产的全球专题研究（丁沃尔等，2005）。研究为本标准提供了进一步的指导，也扩大了与《世界遗产名录》相关的13类不同地质遗产

of the scope of the World Heritage List in relation to thirteen different thematic groups of geological properties.

的专题研究的范围。

EXAMPLE

Wadi Al-Hitan (Whale Valley) (Egypt)

案例

鲸鱼谷（埃及）

Wadi Al-Hitan, Whale Valley, in the Western Desert of Egypt, contains invaluable fossil remains of the earliest, and now extinct, suborder of whales, Archaeoceti. These fossils represent one of the major stories of evolution: the emergence of the whale as an ocean-going mammal from a previous life as a land-based animal. This is the most important site in the world for the demonstration of this stage of evolution. It portrays vividly the form and life of these whales during their transition. The number, concentration and quality of such fossils here is unique, as is their accessibility and setting in an attractive and protected landscape. The fossils of Al-Hitan show the youngest archaeocetes, in the last stages of losing their hind limbs. Other fossil material in the site makes it possible to reconstruct the surrounding environmental and ecological conditions of the time.

鲸鱼谷位于埃及的西部沙漠，保留很多无价的，古老的，现在已经灭绝的亚目鲸鱼——古鲸亚目的化石。这些化石展现了一个重要的生物进化过程：鲸鱼从陆生动物进化为海洋哺乳动物的过程。这是世界上展现这一生物进化阶段最重要的遗址。它生动的描绘了这些鲸鱼在进化过程中的形态和生活。这些化石的数量，密集度和质量是世界上绝无仅有的，并且此处风景秀丽，交通便利，化石得到良好保护。鲸鱼谷的化石为我们展示了最年轻的古鲸后肢转化为鳍最后阶段的原始状态。遗址中的其他化石可帮助我们恢复当时周边的环境和生态条件。

Criterion (ix) : be outstanding examples representing significant ongoing ecological and biological processes in the evolution and development of terrestrial, fresh water, coastal and marine ecosystems and communities of plants and animals

标准（9）：突出代表了陆地、淡水、海岸和海洋生态系统及动植物群落演变、发展的生态和生理过程。

The assessment of this criterion depends on the scientific knowledge and understanding of earth's ecosystems and the ecological and biological processes associated with their dynamics. To assess this criterion in an objective manner, IUCN and partners have developed a number of global thematic studies such as on forests, wetlands,

本标准的评估需要掌握和理解有关地球生态系统、及与其动态相关的生态、生物进化过程方面的科学知识。为了能客观的评价本标准，世界自然保护联盟及其合作伙伴启动了大量全球专题研究，例如森林、湿地、海洋和海岸区域、高山、小岛生态系统和北方森林地区的研究。他们可作为本标准评估的指导性

marine and coastal areas, mountains, small island ecosystems and boreal forests. These have guided the evaluation of this criterion. These studies can be found at http: //www.iucn.org/about/work/programmes/wcpa_worldheritage/

文件。这些研究成果在网站中可以免费下载。http：//www.iucn.org/about/work/programmes/wcpa_worldheritage/

EXAMPLE

Rain-forests of the Atsinanana (Madagascar)

案例

阿钦安阿纳雨林（马达加斯加岛）

The Rainforest of the Atsinanana comprise six national parks distributed along the eastern part of the island. These relict forests are critically important for maintaining ongoing ecological processes necessary for the survival of Madagascar's unique biodiversity, which reflects the island's geological history. Having completed its separation from all other land masses more than 60 million years ago, Madagascar's plant and animal life evolved in isolation. The rain-forests are inscribed for their importance to both ecological and biological processes as well as their biodiversity and the threatened species they support. Many species are rare and threatened, especially primates and lemurs.

阿钦安阿纳雨林包括沿半岛东部分布的6个国家自然公园。这些森林遗存对于维持马达加斯加岛独特的生物多样的生态进化过程极为重要，也反映了马达加斯加岛的地质历史。马达加斯加岛于6000万年前与大陆分离隔绝，岛上植物和动物因而独立进化。阿钦安阿纳雨林被列入遗产名录，一方面源于它对生态和生物进化过程的重要作用，另一方面是因为能保护其生物多样性和濒危物种。这里有很多受到威胁和濒临灭绝的物种，特别是灵长类动物和狐猴类。

Also inscribed under criterion (x).

同时还符合标准（10）。

Criterion (x) : contain the most important and significant natural habitats for in situ conservation of biological diversity, including those containing threatened species of Outstanding Universal Value from the point of view of science or conservation

标准（10）：是生物多样性原址保护的最重要的自然栖息地，包括从科学和保护角度看，具有突出的普遍价值的濒危物种栖息地。

There are a range of tools available to help assess this criterion, including the IUCN Red List, centers of Plant Diversity, Endemic Bird Areas of the World, Conservation International's Biodiversity Hotspots, and WWF's Global 200 Ecoregions for Saving Life on Earth. The bibliography of this manual provides a list of references regularly

评估符合这一标准的遗产的可用工具较多，包括世界自然保护联盟公布的《濒危物种红皮书》、《植物多样性中心》、《世界地方鸟类保护区》、《国际生态多样性保护热点地区》、世界自然全球基金会《拯救地球生命的200个生态区》。本手册结尾的参考文献提供了一个定期更新的、可查阅此类资料的目录。

consulted in this regard.

Additional information on the application of these global classification systems can be found in the *Background Paper for the Special Expert Meeting of the World Heritage Convention: The Concept of Outstanding Universal Value* (Cameron, 2005).

此外，国际分类系统应用指南在《世界遗产公约特别专家会议的背景文件：突出普遍价值的概念》中可以找到。（Cameron，2005）。

EXAMPLE
Socotra Archipelago (Yemen)

案例
索科特拉群岛（也门）

Socotra Archipelago, in the northwest Indian Ocean near the Gulf of Aden, is 250km long and comprises four islands and two rocky islets which appear as a prolongation of the Horn of Africa. The site is of universal importance because of its biodiversity with rich and distinct flora and fauna: 37 per cent of Socotra's 825 plant species, 90 per cent of its reptile species and 95 per cent of its land-snail species do not occur anywhere else in the world. The site also supports globally significant populations of land and sea birds (192 bird species, 44 of which breed on the islands while 85 are regular migrants), including a number of threatened species. The marine life of Socotra is also very diverse, with 253 species of reef-building corals, 730 species of coastal fish and 300 species of crab, lobster and shrimp.

索科特拉群岛，在印度洋西北侧，靠近亚丁湾附近，250公里长，包括了四个海岛和两个岩石小岛，是“非洲之角”的延伸。该遗址有多种生物群和动物群所形成的生态多样性。因而具有全球重要性：索科特拉岛825种植物的37%，以及90%的爬行动物和95%的陆地蜗牛种群，在地球的其他区域没有发现。岛屿上还栖息了全球大部分的陆地和海洋鸟类，包括很多受威胁的种群（192种鸟类，其中44种在岛上留居繁衍，85种定期迁徙）。索科特拉岛的海洋生物也多种多样，拥有253种珊瑚礁，730种鱼类，300种螃蟹，龙虾和虾。

Key message: Be clear about the type of property being nominated.

关键信息：明确申报遗产的类型

Serial and trans-boundary properties

系列和跨界遗产

Properties inscribed on the World Heritage List are typically single land areas located within the borders of a single State Party. The property might be large as in the case of some landscapes such as Vat Phou and Associated Ancient Settlements

列入《世界遗产名录》的遗产一般是位于单一国界内的单一区域。遗产可以面积很大，例如位于老挝的占巴塞文化景观（39000公顷）。遗产也可以很小，如日本的广岛核爆圆顶和平纪念碑（0.4公顷）。遗产也可以是自然、文化

within the Champasak Cultural Landscape, in the Lao People's Democratic Republic (39, 000 ha). On the other hand the property might be quite small, an example being the Hiroshima Peace Memorial (Genbaku Dome) in Japan (0.4 ha). Properties can also be natural, cultural or mixed.

和混合遗产。

In addition, there are a number of special types of properties:

- trans-boundary properties;
- serial properties; and
- serial transnational properties (*Operational Guidelines*, Paragraphs 134-39).

此外，遗产还有很多类型：

- 跨境遗产；
- 系列遗产；
- 系列跨国遗产（《操作指南》，134–39段）。

These special types of properties are discussed below. In all cases, the rationale behind the selection of components for inclusion in the nominated property must be clearly understood and explained (see pages 76-79). A useful reference on serial properties is *Nominations and Management of Serial Natural World Heritage Properties - Present Situation, Challenges and Opportunities* (Engels et al., 2009).

这些特殊遗产类型将会在下文讨论。一般情况，要清楚理解和解释选择遗产组成部分进行申报的基本原理。对系列遗产研究有帮助的参考文献是《世界自然系列遗产申报和管理——现状、挑战和机会》（恩格：尔斯等，2009）。

TRANS-BOUNDARY PROPERTY

跨境遗产

These properties are a continuous land or sea area which extends across the borders of two or more adjoining States Parties.

跨境遗产跨越两个或多个毗邻国家的陆地或海洋区域。

The advantages of trans-boundary properties include the ability to incorporate in a single property all of the area and attributes which convey Outstanding Universal Value, irrespective of current political boundaries. Such properties may help to reflect and encourage international and peaceful cooperation on the shared heritage of countries.

跨境遗产的优势是，将能够传达突出普遍价值的所有地区和特征归纳为一类遗产，而与当前的政治国界无关。这样的遗产能够帮助反映和鼓励所有共享该遗产的国家间的和平合作。

Preparing a nomination, and ongoing protection and management can require additional effort because

因为需要对不同国家机构间的安排进行协调和合作，系列遗产申报的准备及持续的保护

of the need for coordination and cooperation between the institutional arrangements of different countries. There may be differences in protection and management mechanisms available in each country, as well as differences in the availability of resources for site management, presentation and conservation. To address such issues, *The Operational Guidelines* recommend a joint management committee or similar body to advise on the management of the property.

和管理工作需要各国付出更多的努力。每个国家的保护和管理机制都有差异，同时，这些遗址的管理、展示和保护也各有不同。为了能够协调解决这些问题,《操作指南》建议成立一个联合的管理委员会或相似组织，为跨境遗产的管理提供指导。

In addition, the state of conservation between components on either side of a border may differ, creating a challenge for future management of the overall property.

此外，各国境内对遗产组成部分的保护状况有所不同，未来各国将面临遗产整体管理的挑战。

EXAMPLES

Muskauer Park/Park Muzakowski (Germany and Poland)

案例

穆斯考尔公园（德国和波兰）

A landscaped park of 559.9 ha astride the Neisse River and the border between Poland and Germany, it was created by Prince Hermann von Puckler-Muskau from 1815 to 1844. Blending seamlessly with the surrounding farmed landscape, the park pioneered new approaches to landscape design and influenced the development of landscape architecture in Europe and America. Designed as a 'painting with plants', it did not seek to evoke classical landscapes, paradise, or some lost perfection, instead using local plants to enhance the inherent qualities of the existing landscape. This integrated landscape extends into the town of Muskau with green passages that formed urban parks framing areas for development. The town thus became a design component in an Utopian landscape. The site also features a reconstructed castle, bridges and an arboretum.

GERMANY POLAND

Identification of the property 1: 25 000

占地 559.9 公顷的景观公园跨越尼斯河，位于波兰和德国边界，由赫尔曼·冯·普克勒·穆斯考大公于 1815–1844 年创建。公园采用一种新的景观设计方法，使之与周围的耕作农场完美融合，对欧洲和美洲的景观设计发展产生了深远的影响。设计就像用“植物绘画”，它并不试图唤起人们对传统景观、乐园或某些失落的完美事物的追求，而是用本地植物来提升现有景观的内在质量。这种综合景观形成的绿色通道一直延伸到穆斯考镇，形成城市公园并界定了发展范围。这个城镇也成为乌托邦景观的设计组成部分。遗产也包括一些重建的城堡、几座桥梁和一个植物园。

德国、波兰

遗产认定 1 图：25000

EXAMPLES

Mosi-oa-Tunya/Victoria Falls (Zambia and Zimbabwe)

These are among the most spectacular waterfalls in the world. The Zambezi River, which is more than 2 km wide at this point, plunges noisily down a series of basalt gorges and raises an iridescent mist that can be seen more than 20 km away.

案例

莫西奥图尼亚瀑布（维多利亚瀑布）（赞比亚和津巴布韦）

这里拥有世界上极为壮观的瀑布群。2 公里宽的赞比西河流经此地，河流呼啸着冲入玄武岩峡谷，水雾形成的彩虹在 20 公里以外也能看见。

SERIAL PROPERTY

Serial properties are a series of individual or discrete components/areas which are not contained within a single boundary. Components may be quite close or geographically remote, but all components are within a single country. Transnational serial properties are discussed below.

Serial properties will include two or more component parts related by clearly defined links:

a) Component parts should reflect cultural, social or functional links over time that provide, where relevant, landscape, ecological, evolutionary or habitat connectivity.

b) Each component part should contribute to the Outstanding Universal Value of the property as a whole in a substantial, scientific, readily defined and discernible way, and may include, among other things, intangible attributes. The resulting Outstanding Universal Value should be easily understood and communicated.

c) Consistently, and in order to avoid an excessive fragmentation of component parts, the process of nomination of the property, including the selection of the component parts, should take fully into account the overall manageability and coherence of the property.

and provided it is the series as a whole — and

系列遗产

系列遗产由一系列独立或不相邻的组成部分或区域组成，他们并未处于同一个区域中。这些组成部分间距离可能很近也可能很远，但是所有的组成部分分布在一个国家中。跨境系列遗产将在后文讨论。

系列遗产包括两个或多个有清晰的关联性的组成部分：

a）组成部分应反映文化、社会或功能的历史变迁，反映景观、生态圈，栖息地等组成部分间的关联性。

b）每一组成部分应该通过物质、科学性、易界定和易辨识的方式，对遗产整体的突出普遍价值有所贡献，同时可能包括其他无形的贡献。由此体现的突出普遍价值应该容易理解和交流。

c）坚持一点，为了避免组成部分过度分割，系列遗产的申报过程，包括组成部分的选择，应充分考虑遗产整体的可管理性和一致性。

必须是系列遗产整体，而不是其独立的组

not necessarily the individual parts of it — which are of Outstanding Universal Value. (Operational Guidelines, Paragraph 137)

成部分具有突出普遍价值。(《操作指南》137 段）

In some cases, the discrete components/areas might be within a single buffer zone.

在一些情况下，不相连的组成部分独立或区域可能在同一个缓冲区内。

A serial property can overcome the temptation to try and create a single boundary encompassing all the components, thereby including large areas that have no attributes of Outstanding Universal Value.

系列遗产要克服试图划定一个统一的边界以包含所有组成部分的诱惑，否则，可能会将很多没有突出普遍价值的遗产包含在这个大区域中。

Such an approach can make the nomination more complicated because of the range of discrete areas to be included, as each has to be addressed within the nomination dossier. In addition, protection, conservation and management can be more complex because different mechanisms may apply to the different discrete components, even when they are within the same country. To address such issues, The Operational Guidelines note that coordinated management of the separate components is essential.

因为遗产的每个零散区域必须完成独立的申遗文本，所以像这样统一的边界包括了过多的区域，会使得申报过程更加复杂。此外，即便是在同一个国家中，由于不同区域有不同的管理机制，使得保存、保护和管理会更加复杂。《操作指南》指出，协调管理各个组成部分是解决这个问题的基础。

In some cases, a serial property approach may be inappropriately adopted in order to unreasonably draw component boundaries which are too restrictive. As noted elsewhere, the values, authenticity and integrity should determine the appropriate boundaries and the application of the serial approach.

在一些情况下，采用系列遗产方法可能不适合于确定遗产边界，因为限制太多，也不合理。在其他章节中提示过，应通过价值、真实性和完整性来确定适当的遗产边界，这个方法同样适用于系列遗产。

EXAMPLES

Baroque Churches of the Philippines (Philippines)

案例

菲律宾巴洛克风格的教堂（菲律宾）

These four churches (monuments), the first of which was built by the Spanish in the late 16th century, are located in Manila, Santa Maria, Paoay and Miagao. Their unique architectural style is a

这个系列遗产由分别位于马尼拉，圣玛丽亚、帕瓦伊和米亚高四个城市的四座教堂（文物）组成，其中最早的一个教堂是由西班牙人修建于 16 世纪晚期。然后中国和菲律宾工匠们

reinterpretation of European Baroque by Chinese and Philippine craftsmen.

重新解读和阐释了欧洲的巴洛克风格，形成了他们独特的建筑风格。

EXAMPLES

Australian Fossil Mammal Sites (Australia)

案例

澳大利亚哺乳动物化石遗址（澳大利亚）

Riversleigh and Naracoorte, situated in the north and south respectively of eastern Australia, are among the world's ten greatest fossil sites. They are outstanding examples representing major stages of Earth's history, including the record of life, particularly the middle to late Tertiary evolution of mammals in Australia (Riversleigh) and an outstanding record of terrestrial vertebrate life spanning the last 170, 000 years (Naracoorte), and significant ongoing geological processes.

里弗斯利和纳拉库特，分别位于东澳大利亚的南部和北部，是世界上的十大化石遗址之一。他们是代表地球历史主要阶段的杰出范例，记录了生命的进程，特别是澳大利亚哺乳动物在第三纪中晚期的进化（里弗斯利），同时记录陆生脊椎动物在过去170000年的进化（纳拉库特）和重要的地质演化过程。

SERIAL PROPERTY/TRANSNATIONAL

跨国系列及遗产

A serial property/transnational is another form of serial property but in this case components are located in more than one country.

跨国系列遗产是系列遗产的另一种形式，因为构成遗产的各组成部分分布在多个国家。

The advantages and problems of such a property are similar to those outlined for trans-boundary properties and serial properties.

跨国系列遗产与跨界遗产和系列遗产具有相似的优势和问题。

EXAMPLES

Stone Circles of Senegambia (Gambia and Senegal)

案例

塞内甘比亚石圈（冈比亚和塞内加尔）

The site consists of four large groups of stone circles that represent an extraordinary concentration of over 1, 000 monuments in a band 100 km wide along some 350 km of the River Gambia. The four groups, Sine Ngayène, Wanar, Wassu and Kerbatch, cover ninety-three stone circles and numerous tumuli, burial mounds, some of which have been excavated to reveal material that suggest dates between the 3rd century BC and 16th century AD. Together the stone circles of laterite pillars and

这个遗产由四组巨石圈构成，它展示了沿着冈比亚河，在长350公里，宽100公里的范围内密集分布的超过1000处的文物。这四个石圈群，赛内迦叶纳、瓦那尔、瓦苏和科尔巴切还涵盖了93个石圈、很多坟墓和坟丘，根据对其中一些墓葬的考古发掘，这些遗址的年代跨越公元前3世纪到公元16世纪。用红土、石柱子围起来的石圈和与之相关的坟丘，是形成于1500年前大型的神圣祭祀景观。它体现了一个繁荣、组织严密的悠久社会。

their associated burial mounds present a vast sacred landscape created over more than 1, 500 years. It reflects a prosperous, highly organized and lasting society.

EXAMPLES

Uvs Nuur Basin (Mongolia and Russian Federation)

Uvs Nuur Basin (1,068,853 ha) is the northernmost of the enclosed basins of Central Asia. It takes its name from Uvs Nuur Lake, a large, shallow and very saline lake, important for migrating birds, waterfowl and seabirds. The site is made up of twelve protected areas representing the major biomes of eastern Eurasia. The steppe ecosystem supports a rich diversity of birds and the desert is home to a number of rare gerbil, jerboa and marbled polecat. The mountains are an important refuge for the globally endangered snow leopard, mountain sheep (argali) and the Asiatic ibex.

The figure below illustrates the theoretical differences between these various types of property.

案例

乌布苏湖盆地（蒙古和俄罗斯联邦）

乌布苏湖盆地（1,068,853 公顷）是中亚最北部封闭式的盆地。盆地因乌布苏湖而得名，乌布苏湖是巨大的淡盐水湖，是迁徙的候鸟、水鸟和海鸟的重要栖息地。遗址由 12 个保护区组成，代表了欧亚大陆东部主要的生物群系。草原生态系统为丰富多样的鸟类的栖息提供了有利的支持，沙漠是罕见的沙鼠、跳鼠和虎鼬的家园，山区成为世界濒危动物如雪豹、山羊和亚洲野生山羊的重要庇护场所。

下图从理论上阐释了的各类遗产的不同。

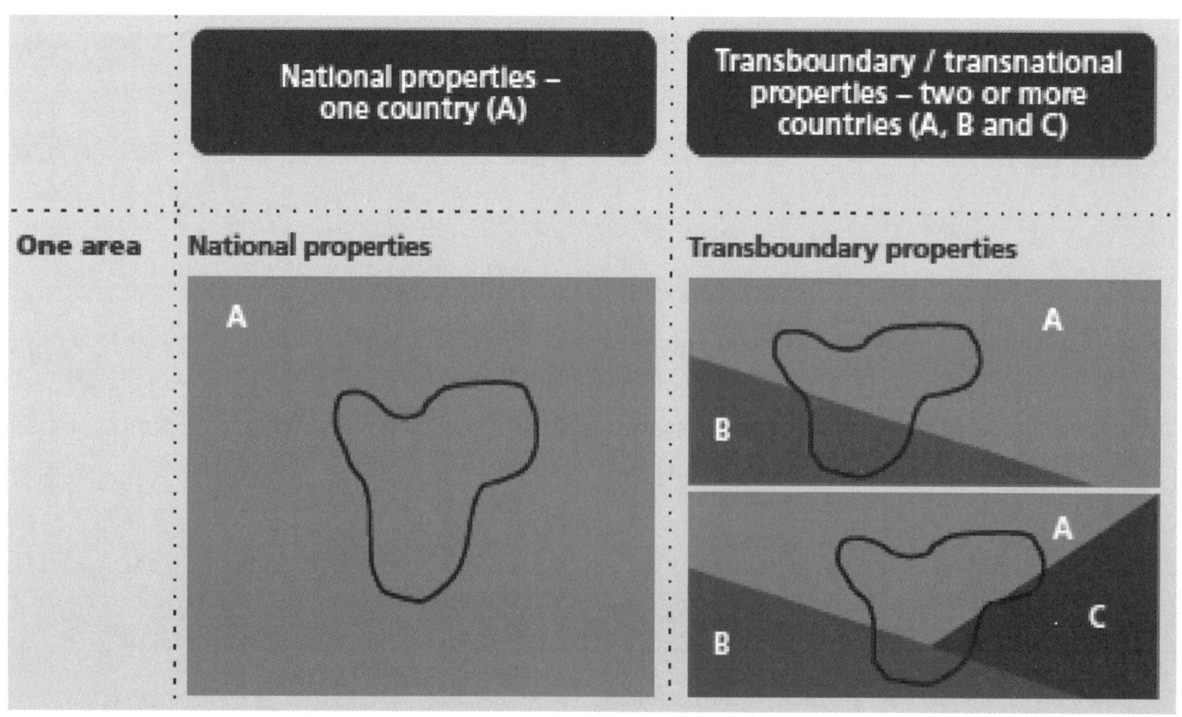

More than one area: serial properties	Serial national property	Serial transnational property (some potential configurations)
	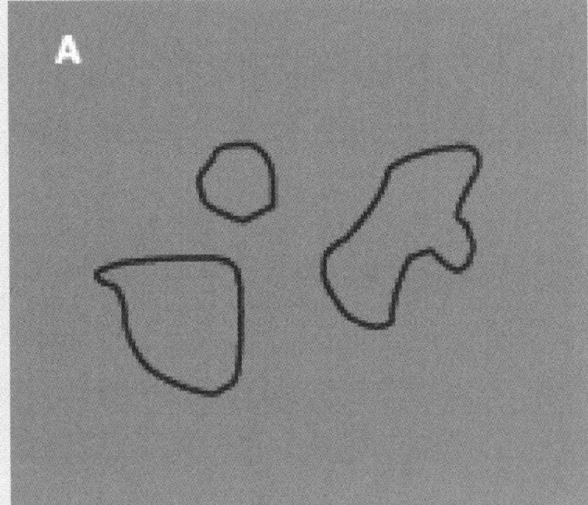	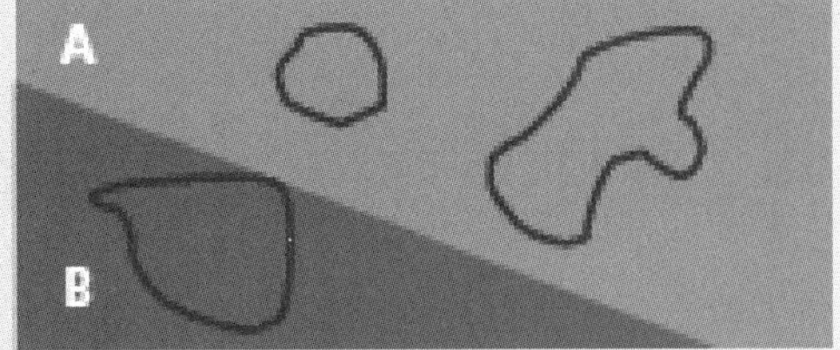 A linked series of components, each entirely within one country.
		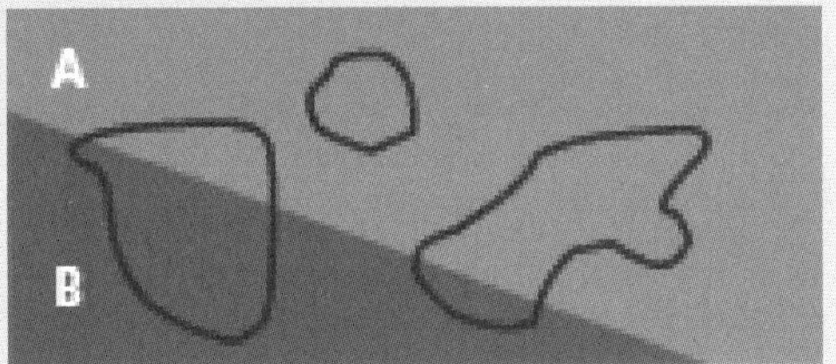 A linked series of components, some of which are shared between more than one country.
		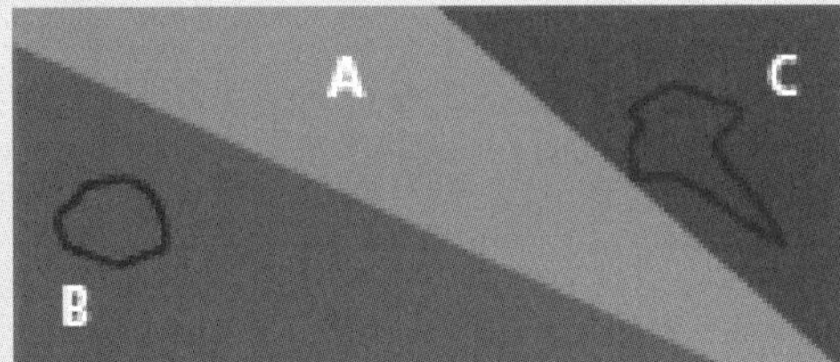 Serial properties may include components in countries that do not have a shared border, although such examples are unusual and currently only found in cultural properties (e.g. Struve Geodetic Art, and Frontiers of the Roman Empire World Heritage properties). The example series above has component parts in countries B and C, but not in country A.

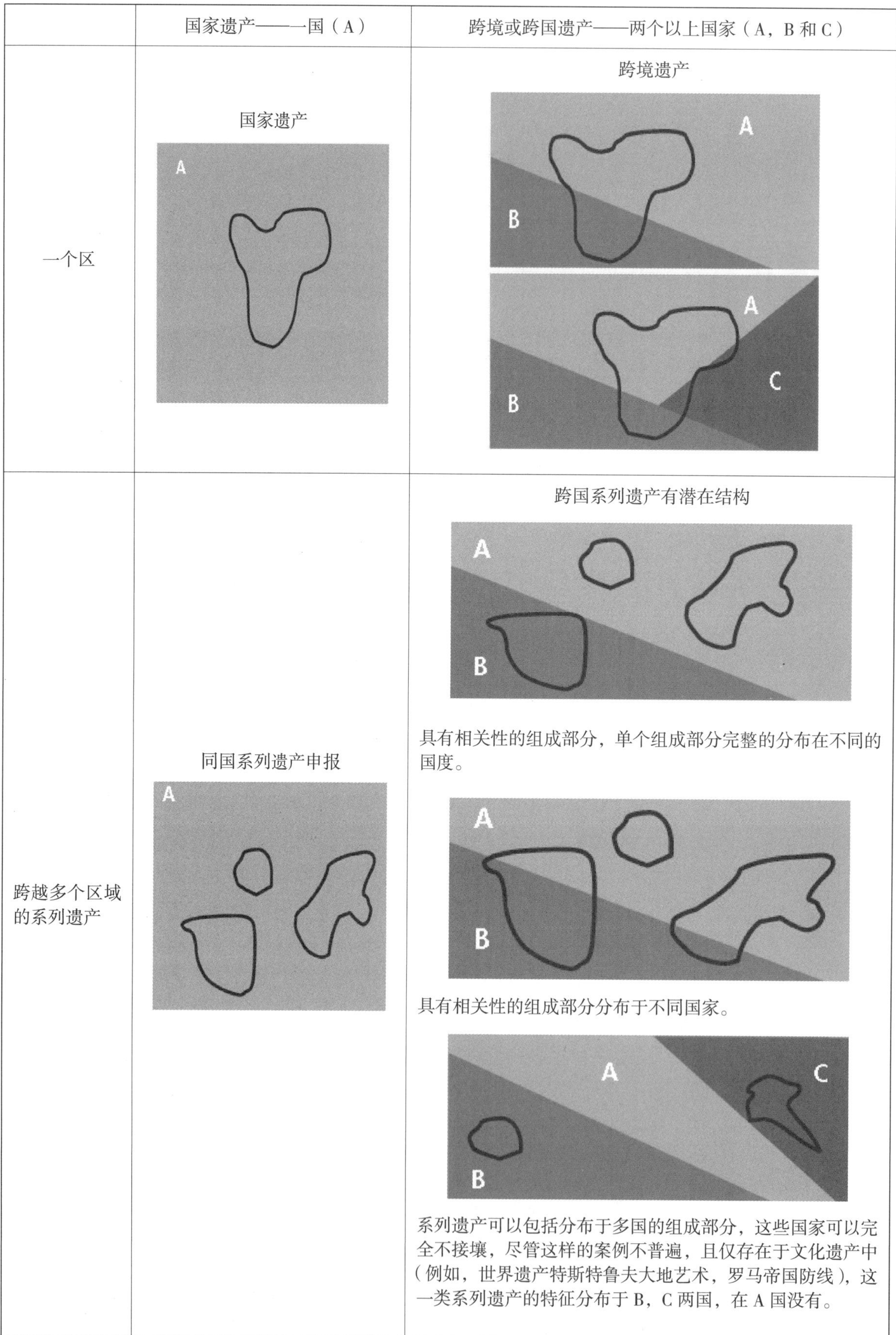

	国家遗产——一国（A）	跨境或跨国遗产——两个以上国家（A，B 和 C）
一个区	国家遗产	跨境遗产
跨越多个区域的系列遗产	同国系列遗产申报	跨国系列遗产有潜在结构 具有相关性的组成部分，单个组成部分完整的分布在不同的国度。 具有相关性的组成部分分布于不同国家。 系列遗产可以包括分布于多国的组成部分，这些国家可以完全不接壤，尽管这样的案例不普遍，且仅存在于文化遗产中（例如，世界遗产特斯特鲁夫大地艺术，罗马帝国防线），这一类系列遗产的特征分布于 B，C 两国，在 A 国没有。

2 Preparation

A successful World Heritage nomination requires careful preparation. Part 2 contains advice regarding:

• existing information about the property which will help with the nomination, and what further research is needed;

• setting up and resourcing the nomination team; and

• staging the nomination process, and what the key stages are.

As noted in the introduction to this manual, there are many different ways to prepare a nomination and it is not appropriate to offer 'recipes' or to recommend a preferred working method. There are many different good ways of preparing nominations. Nevertheless the advice provided here is intended to offer basic principles and guidance to assist States Parties as they establish a working method.

Key message: Gather and review existing relevant information and identify any gaps.

2.1 Existing information on the property

It is important to consider what relevant information already exists on the property which will help with the nomination.

For almost every property, work is needed to bring together all the material that is often scattered in many different places — in the case of cultural properties this will include oral history, published archaeological evidence, conservation history, tourism data, planning regulations, and so on. For most properties there is usually a need to undertake some sort of research, either because none exists,

2 准备

遗产申报成功必须要有细致的准备工作，第二部分将包括以下几条建议：

• 收集与遗产相关的、能够帮助遗产成功申报的信息并需要进一步研究的内容；

• 寻找资金支持并组建遗产申报团队；

• 把遗产申报过程阶段化并确定核心阶段。

在本手册的介绍中提到，准备遗产的申报有不同的方式，没有最适合的申报“妙方”，也不推荐具体的工作方法。准备申报有很多种好方法。因此，在这里只提供基本的准则和指南，帮助缔约国确立自己的申报方式。

关键信息：收集审核已有信息，明确差异

2.1 遗产现有的信息资源

理清已有的遗产信息资源中哪些与申报相关，这对申报工作十分重要。

对大多数遗产而言，都需要完成零散资料的收集汇总工作——如果是文化遗产，这些资料包括口头历史、考古出版物、保护历史、旅游数据、规划和规定等等。无论是否做过遗产研究，遗产申报都需要开展专题研究工作，以便对已有的研究成果进行补充和更新。

or to supplement or update what has already been achieved.

As a preliminary to a nomination it is helpful to assemble what is known and whether more work is needed on:

作为申报工作的初期阶段，收集现有的信息，并了解是否需要进行下列工作：

• research — is existing research relevant to the nomination adequate or is more needed to articulate the values and to understand the global and cultural contexts of the property's history and attributes?

• 研究——与申报遗产相关的已有研究是否充足，或是否需要对价值进行深入的研究，理解在全球和文化的视野下遗产的历史和特性？

• inventories — what inventories documenting the property exist and is further work needed to complete or update them?

• 清单——建立遗产已有档案的清单，决定是否需要展进一步完善或更新档案。

• documentation — referring to the many categories of information required in the nomination format — what exists to be able to complete the nomination and what more might be needed?

• 档案——根据《申遗文本格式》需要的各种类型的信息——这些档案是否能满足编制申遗文本的需要，还可能会使用哪些档案？

• stakeholder analysis — who needs to be involved in the nomination, including who lives or has direct relationships with the property? What are the social, economic and political realities of the property?

• 利益相关者分析——在申报过程中可能会牵扯哪些人的利益，包括居住在遗产内或与遗产有直接联系的人？遗产区域的社会、经济和政治现状如何？

There are cases where the World Heritage Committee has referred or deferred nominations because of a lack of research to support the nominations.

世界遗产委员会对那些缺乏必要的遗产研究支持的申遗文本，做出延迟待议或重新递交申遗文本的决议。

Key message: Involve stakeholders and experts in the team.

关键信息：团队中应包括专家和利益相关者

2.2 Setting up a team

2.2　建立团队

Nomination team

遗产申报团队

Preparing a World Heritage nomination usually requires a team approach because of the complexity of the task, the range of key stakeholders, and the range of expertise required.

由于准备申报世界遗产是一项复杂的工作，涉及核心利益相关者的范围大，所需专业知识的范畴广，需要采取团队工作的方法。

Important information and advice will be

与申报遗产相关的利益相关者往往掌握了

held by a range of stakeholders associated with the nominated property. It is usually helpful to compile a list of key stakeholders, as a first step to forming a team. These might include or represent the site owner /manager, State Party, national heritage agencies, local authorities, other government agencies, local communities, indigenous peoples, universities, researchers and academics, local businesses, tourism operators, NGOs and user groups (e.g. fishermen, forest users, recreational users, researchers). The National Committees of ICOMOS may also be a useful resource for cultural nominations. The range of contributors should reflect the range of values of the nominated property, and ideally should include experts who have some understanding of the property in an international context. These stakeholders and experts should be part of or represented on the nomination team, or at least have direct access and input to the work of the team. The team membership should have some flexibility to take account of the possibility of emerging interests.

重要的信息和建议。作为组建队伍的第一步，必须编制核心利益相关者名单。该名单应该包括遗产的所有者、管理者、国家、国家遗产管理机构，地方政府、其他政府机构、当地社区、土著人群、高校、研究人员和学者、本地企业、旅游业从业者、非政府组织和用户团体组织（例如，渔民、森林使用者、娱乐设施用户、研究人员）。国际古迹理事会国家委员会是文化遗产申报的有用资源。团队参与者范围应该反映出申报遗产的价值范围，理想的团队还应包括能够从国际视野理解遗产价值的专家们。这些利益相关者与专家，应该是遗产申报团队的一部分或是团队中的代表，或者至少能够直接参与团队的工作。考虑到可能出现的利益，团队的成员应该具有一定的灵活性。

The participation of local people in the nomination process is essential to enable them to have a shared responsibility with the State Party in caring for the property and to ensure proper use is made of local knowledge, and to ensure that the local situation regarding issues such as perception and resource use is understood.

当地人员必须参与申报准备过程，以便他们能够与国家共同承担保护遗产的责任并合理利用地区知识，更好理解当地情况，比如对遗产的充分认识和对资源更好的使用。

It is a usually essential to identify a single project leader who can take responsibility for managing the complete nomination process and delivering the final document.

确定一个项目总负责人非常重要，因为此人要负责管理整个遗产申报过程和提交最终文件。

Key message: A good, focused and well-resourced team can greatly help a nomination.

关键信息：专注而资源丰富的团队能极大促进遗产申报

The team can be important in many ways,

团队在很多方面都发挥重要的作用，包括

including fostering support at local, national and international levels for the nomination and for long-term protection, conservation and management of the property.

在当地、国家和国际上促进遗产申报，以及对遗产的长期保存，保护和管理等方面的支持。

In some cases it may be useful to have a small core team to work on the nomination itself, and a larger reference group to support the work. Teams usually work well if they are well led, have the right membership, are focused on their task, and have a clear and realistic work plan with milestones. Individual team members may have specific roles which should be clearly understood (e.g. expert in a particular field, community representative, editor, etc.).

在某些情况下，组建一个小型的核心团队专注申报工作本身，同时需要大量相关团队支持这份工作。当团队有好的领导，有专注于工作的成员，有清晰可行的工作计划和阶段性目标时，团队的工作将事半功倍。团队的成员分工明确，解决不同类型的问题（例如，特殊领域的专家、社区代表、编辑等等）。

It may be helpful to establish a specialist technical or scientific group to support the development of the Statement of Outstanding Universal Value within the nomination team. An example of such a group is discussed below.

在遗产申报团队中确定一个技术或科技小组，专门研究突出普遍价值声明的内容，对遗产申报过程也十分有利。对于组建这样的团队后文有实例介绍。

For many properties, the nomination process provides the first opportunity for such people to collaborate as a group. This is equally true for the range of natural and cultural properties — including national parks, urban areas, cultural landscapes, archaeological heritage or monuments. The nomination process requires the property to be considered from many different standpoints, such as science, history, archaeology, landscape, conservation, management, social structures, tourism, planning, business, development and regulation. If these dimensions are to be well integrated in the nomination and then in the protection, conservation and management of the property, it helps to construct a dialogue between the various parties who can represent these aspects.

无论是自然遗产还是文化遗产（包括国家公园、城镇区域、文化景观、考古遗产或文物古迹），申报过程都为上述团体或个人提供了一次通力合作机会。申报过程也需要从不同的角度，例如科学、历史、考古、景观、保护、管理、社会形态、旅游、规划、商贸、发展和立法等方面对遗产进行考虑。如果在遗产申报的过程中能把这些方面很好的整合在一起，再与保存、保护和管理工作进行整合，这将有助于在各方代表间建立对话关系。

There is no ideal team structure or method for

目前，并没有一个理想的团队结构或方法

producing a successful nomination. Nonetheless, there are many good examples which can be considered.

能够确保遗产申报成功。但是，有些可供参考的有效的实例。

In summary, key tips for structuring a team:

构建团队的关键点：

• compile a list of key supporters or stakeholders (e.g. site owner/manager, State Party, national heritage agencies, local authorities, local communities, indigenous populations, tourism operators, universities and experts);

• 编写主要支持者或核心利益相关者名单（例如，遗址所有者、管理者、缔约国、国家遗产管理机构、地方政府、当地社区、土著人群、旅游管理者、高校和专家等）；

• check that the range of knowledge and expertise within the team reflects the range of values, ideally have some understanding of the property in an international context, and have useful networks for obtaining wider advice;

• 核对团队中是否有拥有、掌握评价遗产价值必备的专业知识和技能的人员，最为理想的是。有能从国际视野中理解遗产的人员，建立起能够获取广泛信息和建议的可用网络。

• be flexible about team membership to take account of the possibility of emerging interests, however it is preferable to retain a continuing editor;

• 考虑到可能出现的利益影响，团队的成员应该具有一定的灵活性，但最好保证有一个编辑人员能够参与申报的全过程。

• consider creating a small core team to work on the nomination itself, and a larger reference group to support the work; and

• 遗产申报过程最好建立一个小型的核心团队，同时要获得更多团队的参与支持。

• ensure that the team is clearly led, has the right membership, has a clear task, and has a clear and realistic work plan with milestones.

• 确认团队有明确的领导、有合适的成员、清楚的任务、目标清晰而现实的工作计划表。

It is important to stress the need for a realistic work plan — a rushed nomination is not likely to be satisfactory and is more likely to have problems during evaluation.

强调制定切合实际、目标明确的工作计划——仓促的申报难以令人满意，而且评估时更容易出现问题。

Checklist: Some important skills to consider for the nomination team

备忘录：遗产申报团队人员应该具有的重要技能

• An understanding of *The World Heritage Convention* and *The Operational Guidelines*, and the ability to interpret the information within them.

• 了解《世界遗产公约》和《操作指南》，有能力阐释他们的内容；

• The ability to research and understand information on other properties on the World

• 有研究和理解与已列入《世界遗产名录》中的类似遗产信息进行价值比较的能力，以及

Heritage List with comparable values, and to understand and evaluate past reports and decisions of the World Heritage Committee and its Advisory Bodies.

• The ability to:

—bring together and understand information about the nominated property and its values, including scientific information;

— manage a range of inputs from scientists, experts and local stakeholders;

— research, understand and evaluate the values of other properties with comparable values on a global basis;

— distinguish between significant and insignificant facts in defining the most significant values of the property;

— document findings in concise and accurate statements, with clear supporting information; and

— challenge interpretations and values credited to the property to ensure that statements made are accurate and well supported.

• Because of the working languages of the *Convention* a technically qualified translator might be needed to translate the nomination and ensure the quality and accuracy of the information and arguments.

• Skills in management planning, implementation and presentation should be part of the core team, in order to link the nomination to the management of the property, and reflect the management plan or system that will form part of the nomination.

理解和评估世界遗产委员会和咨询机构提供的以往报告和决议的能力。

• 具有以下能力：

——收集和理解申报遗产的信息和价值，包括科技信息的能力；

——管理来自科学家、专家和当地利益相关者的一系列信息；

——全球范围内研究、理解和评估用以比较的其他类似遗产价值的能力；

——在评价遗产重要性过程中能够区分重要和非重要组成部分的能力；

——精确记录调查结果，提供明确的信息支持能力；

——质疑现有的对遗产及其价值的理解，确保声明阐述准确，能很好支撑遗产价值的能力；

• 鉴于公约的工作语言，必须由高水平、合格的翻译人员翻译申遗文本，确保对信息和讨论翻译的质量和准确性。

• 核心团队应具有制定管理规划、实施和展示的技能，把遗产管理与遗产申报相结合，管理规划或管理体系作为重要组成部分，必须反映在申遗文本中。

Resources

The nomination team and process will need adequate resources and funding to support the work. Early in the process, the level of resources and funding should be estimated, and sources identified and confirmed to provide this support.

资源

组建申遗团队和遗产申报过程的相关工作需要大量的资源和资金的支持。在遗产申报的早期阶段，应该提前对资源和资金的需求进行评估，确定提供支持的渠道。

The most important sources of funding are likely to be provided within the State Party, however for eligible properties and countries there may be some scope to seek assistance from the World Heritage Fund (see whc.unesco.org/en/funding or whc.unesco.org/fr/fonds). There is also a growing number of regionally focused organizations which might have scope to provide support such as the African World Heritage Fund (www.awhf.net) and the Pacific World Heritage Fund (currently being established). The African World Heritage Fund can assist with financial assistance for preparing nominations, as well as information and technical support. Assistance could also be sought from specific subject interests and even sponsorships.

对多数遗产而言，资金的最重要来源是国家，然而对于一些符合条件的遗产或相关国家，可以寻求世界遗产基金会资助（见 see whc.unesco.org/en/funding or whc.unesco.org/fr/fonds）。有越来越多的地区性组织可以对特定区域的遗产给予支持，比如非洲世界遗产基金会（www.awhf.net）和太平洋世界遗产基金会（筹建中）。非洲世界遗产基金会能够为遗产申报提供财务、信息和技术支持。在主体利益相关者、甚至在赞助商那里也能获得一定的援助。

In some nominations the role of NGOs can also be important in relation to both funding and the skills required.

在某些申报项目中，非政府组织在经费和技术上提供了很大帮助。

Another important issue to be addressed in the development of a nomination is the ongoing resources to support the sustainable protection, conservation and management of the property.

另一个与遗产申报过程相关的重要议题是现有的、支持遗产可持续保存、保护和管理的资源。

Possible role of the team after inscription

遗产列入名录后遗产申报团队的作用

Submission of a nomination and subsequent inscription are not the end of the process. While this manual focuses on the nomination of properties, it is worthwhile considering the possible role that the team brought together for the nomination might play in the long-term protection, conservation, management and monitoring of the property. The nomination team might, possibly with some changes, play an important and ongoing role after inscription regarding these aspects.

提交了申遗文本并成功列入《世界遗产名录》不代表整个过程结束了。当然这个手册仅关注遗产的申报过程，但为了遗产申报而组建的团队随后还要在长期的遗产保存、保护、管理和监测等工作中继续发挥作用。在遗产列入名录后，遗产申报团队仍然会在以上领域继续发挥重要的作用。

World Heritage properties succeed in the long

世界遗产在社会和政府有效的支持下方能

term if they are effectively supported and integrated with wider social and governmental structures. The nomination process is the time to identify and put in place such support mechanisms, if these do not already exist. An ongoing team approach to protection, conservation and management can be one such mechanism.

取得长久成功。如果这些支持尚未确立，遗产申报的过程就是这些支持体系形成和付诸实施的过程。团队发挥保存，保护和管理作用，是这个机制的重要组成部分。

2.3 Participation of local people and other stakeholders

2.3 当地居民或其他利益相关者的参与

The Operational Guidelines stress at several points the need to promote the participation of local people and other stakeholders in World Heritage generally, and there are specific references to such participation in the case of nominations. This can include property owners, site managers, local and regional governments, local communities, NGOs and other interested parties.

《操作指南》中多次强调要鼓励当地居民和利益相关者参与世界遗产管理，申报过程中也专门要求利益相关者包括遗产所有者、遗址管理者、当地或地区政府、当地社区、非政府组织和其他对遗产保护有兴趣的团体参与。

The reasons for this approach are many but include the need to develop a shared understanding of the nominated property and shared responsibility for its future. Successful integrated management is not likely if stakeholders are not involved and do not participate.

让公众参与遗产保护的原因很多，但是最重要的是要公众能够分享遗产的价值，并共同承担遗产保护的责任。成功的综合管理应引入利益相关者，并让他们参与遗产的管理。

Such participation should be a priority from the start of the process and all the way through the preparation of a nomination. This participation should also continue after the nomination as well, as part of the ongoing management of the property.

应在准备遗产申报时考虑公众和利益相关者的参与，而且他们要自始至终参与遗产申报过程。并在申报工作完成后，作为一个重要组成部分持续地参与遗产管理工作。

2.4 Staging the preparation of a nomination and suggested key stages

2.4 分阶段申报遗产，确定重要阶段

Key message: Consider staging the nomination process

关键信息：考虑分阶段遗产申报

For many properties it can be very helpful

对于很多遗产，在其列入《预备名录》后，

to address the nomination as at least a two-stage process, which follows some time after the preparation of a Tentative List. The first stage is to:

• identify the potential Outstanding Universal Value of the property;

• ensure that this is justified through a comparative analysis; and

• make sure adequate protection, conservation and management is provided.

将整个遗产申报过程分成至少两个阶段，可能更有助于申报工作的完成。第一阶段：

• 确定遗产潜在的突出普遍价值；

• 通过比较分析后确定突出普遍价值的合理性；

• 确保遗产得到足够的保存、保护和管理。

In this first stage, the nomination team would be created, and all the work in Part 3 of this manual would be undertaken.

在第一阶段，应该组建遗产申报团队，并陆续展开本手册第 3 部分中包含的所有工作。

When this stage has been completed, the writing of the nomination dossier can then be started as the second stage. This second stage involves the work described in Part 4.

当这一阶段完成后，应进入第二阶段：编写申遗文本，第二阶段的具体工作将在第 4 部分详细论述。

Even if the work is undertaken as a single project, it is often preferable to consider two phases to the work. Attempting to write the nomination before the potential Outstanding Universal Value has been defined can lead to too much emphasis being given to description and history, and insufficient emphasis to the core part of the nomination — why the property has potential Outstanding Universal Value and how it is to be sustained.

即便是一个单一项目，最好也分成两个阶段。在没有总结出潜在的突出普遍价值时就开始编写申遗文本，可能会导致过分强调遗产的描述和历史，而忽略论证遗产申报的核心内容：为什么遗产具有潜在的突出普遍价值？及如何维护这些价值？

Staging the nomination process can also have advantages by spreading the funding needed across the two stages.

分阶段申报遗产也有利于不同阶段的资金分配。

3. Defining and understanding the property

3. 确定和理解遗产

A thorough understanding of the property is vital to developing a successful nomination. Part 3 offers advice on developing a good understanding of the property, especially relating to key aspects

对遗产的全面理解是遗产成功申报的必备条件。第三部分内容对如何充分了解遗产，特别是对与申报相关的核心内容的理解提供了一些建议。

which are central to the nomination.

3.1 Potential Outstanding Universal Value, attributes and boundaries

Knowledge of the property

As noted in Section 2.1, as a preliminary to a nomination it is helpful to assemble existing information and documentation and to decide whether further work is needed on:

• research — is existing research relevant to the nomination adequate or is more research needed?

• inventories — what inventories documenting the property exist and is further work needed to complete or update them?

• documentation — referring to the many categories of information required in the nomination format — what exists to be able to complete the nomination and what more might be needed?

• stakeholder analysis — who needs to be involved in the nomination, including who lives or has direct relationships with the property? What are the social, economic and political realities of the property?

Identifying and defining potential Outstanding Universal Value

The fundamental part of the nomination dossier is demonstrating why a property should be considered to have potential Outstanding Universal Value. Ideally, this is set out when a property is put on the Tentative List (see *Operational Guidelines*, II.C). However, more detailed work is often undertaken as an early task in developing a nomination. This detailed work can be summarized as follows.

3.1 潜在的突出普遍价值，特征和边界

遗产的相关知识

在2.1节中我们已经提到，收集整理已有的信息和档案资料是遗产申报第一步，然后确定需要进一步开展的工作，包括：

• 研究——现有的、与申报遗产相关的研究是否充足；是否需要进一步研究；

• 清单——建立遗产现有档案的清单，决定是否需要开展进一步的工作以完善或更新档案；

• 档案——指申遗文本中需要的各种类型的信息——这些档案是否能满足编制遗产申报文本的需要，还需要补充什么档案？

• 利益相关者分析——哪些人会参与遗产申报，哪些人居住在遗产内或何人会与遗产有直接的联系？遗产区域的社会、经济和政治现状如何？

识别和确定潜在的突出普遍价值

申遗文本的基本内容就是要证明为什么遗产具有潜在的突出普遍价值。最好在遗产列入《预备名录》时，就已经清楚阐述了突出普遍价值（见《操作指南》，Ⅱ.C）。然而，遗产申报的最初阶段常要开始更为详尽的价值研究。包括以下内容：

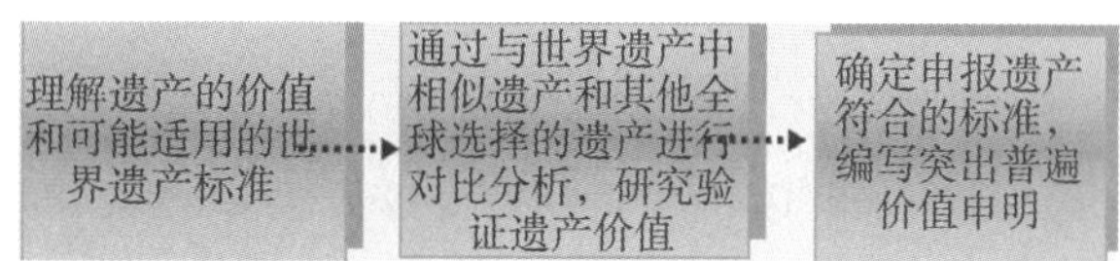

Outstanding Universal Value is why the property is considered to be so significant as to justify recognition on the World Heritage List. Outstanding Universal Value underpins the whole *World Heritage Convention*.

突出普遍价值是遗产得以列入遗产名录的重要原因。突出普遍价值是加强《世界遗产公约》的基础。

Outstanding Universal Value is the value agreed by the World Heritage Committee as reflecting why a property is seen to have international significance — it is not about national or local value.

突出普遍价值是世界遗产委员会认同的价值，说明为什么遗产价值不只限于本国或本地，而是具有国际意义。

A good knowledge and understanding of the property and its condition are essential to identifying its potential Outstanding Universal Value and the attributes that convey this value.

充分了解和理解遗产的环境是确定遗产潜在突出普遍价值的基础，同时传达该价值的属性。

Indeed, until potential Outstanding Universal Value has been set out and justified, it is not possible to develop many other aspects of the nomination such as:

• defining the boundaries, which should be drawn to reflect the extent of attributes that convey potential Outstanding Universal Value; and

• being clear about protection, conservation, management and presentation/promotion of the attributes that convey the potential Outstanding Universal Value.

实际上，只有提出和确定潜在的突出普遍价值，才有可能完成遗产申报其他方面的内容，例如：

• 划定遗产边界，包括能体现遗产突出普遍价值的所有组成部分的分布范围；

• 对能够体现遗产突出普遍价值的所有组成部分进行保存、保护、管理和展示、宣传。

Identifying and defining values is a mixture of knowledge and methodology. It is usually helpful to structure this process initially to bring out as far as possible all the values of the property, with a view to establishing which of these might provide the basis for supporting a World Heritage nomination.

认定和确定突出的普遍价值既要知识也要方法。尽早完成识别遗产所有价值的过程，确定其中能支持遗产申报的价值。

Key message: It is vital to clearly understand the Outstanding Universal Value.

关键信息：理解遗产突出普遍价值至关重要

This definition of values should eventually be set out in a relatively short text which will form part of the Statement of Outstanding Universal Value for the nomination (the statement is separately discussed below). This text should be a brief synthesis, not necessarily in distinct sections, setting out:

• an evocation of the property and what it consists of — a word picture for those who do not know it, its character and especially for cultural properties, its meaning and 'stories' associated with it;

• why the property could be considered to be of potential Outstanding Universal Value; and

• a summary of the attributes that convey the potential Outstanding Universal Value of the property.

应该简短表述已确定的遗产价值，最终成为遗产《突出普遍价值声明》的一部分（声明将单独讨论）。文字必须简明扼要，不需要分段落，要能说明：

• 遗产的精髓和构成——用文字描绘遗产，让那些不知道遗产的人，能够清晰的了解遗产的特性是什么，它的意义和与之相关的故事有哪些；

• 为什么遗产被认为具有潜在的突出普遍价值；

• 能表达潜在的突出普遍价值特征的概要。

It thus encapsulates the whole rationale for the nomination and proposed inscription.

因此囊括了遗产申报列入《世界遗产名录》的所有理论基础。

At the end of the nomination process, this short paragraph can be used by UNESCO on the World Heritage Center's website, if the property is inscribed, as the description that allows viewers to understand what the property is, as well as why it is significant.

最后，如果遗产列入名录中，联合国教科文组织会在世界遗产中心的网站上使用这段简短的话介绍遗产，让公众能够知道遗产是什么，为什么重要。

Key message: Facts do not replace good arguments.

关键信息：事实不可替代充分论证

Various research frameworks might be developed to help understand the values of the property. Potentially useful cultural frameworks include thematic, chronological-regional and typological frameworks, elaborating those found in *The World Heritage List: Filling the Gaps — An Action Plan for the Future (ICOMOS, 2005a)*. In the case of natural properties, see *The World Heritage List:*

各种研究架构对理解遗产的价值都有帮助。一般而言，文化遗产的研究框架包括按年代顺序——区域——类型分类的专题研究：在《世界遗产名录：填补空白——未来的行动指南》中对这方面研究有详细说明。对于自然遗产，见《世界遗产名录：确定自然遗产的潜在突出普遍价值指南和今后的重点》（世界自然保护联盟，2006）。例如，如果在进行特殊主题研究的

Guidance and Future Priorities for Identifying Natural Heritage of Potential Outstanding Universal Value (IUCN, 2006). For example, if research into a specific theme found that it was of universal relevance, and the property is strongly related to the theme, then the research would be useful in exploring the values of the property.

过程中发现它有全球性普遍意义，并且拟申报的遗产与这个主题紧密相关，那么这个研究的成果就是价值比较评估的基础资料。

Identification of the meaning and relative value of a cultural property should start with the identification of the themes, then proceed to the chronological—regional assessment, and finally define the typology to be proposed, whether for a monument, a group of buildings, or a site.

确定文化遗产的意义和价值应该从确定主题入手，按时间顺序——地域进行评估，最终确定申报的类型，既选择：按文物古迹、按建筑群还是按遗址进行申报。

In addition to an assessment of cultural values, Outstanding Universal Value also includes tests relating to integrity and authenticity, protection and management. These other factors are discussed separately below.

此外，评估文化遗产价值（无论是文物古迹、建筑群还是遗址）和突出普遍价值也应该包括对与之相关的真实性、完整性、保护和管理等组成部分进行评判。这些组成部分将在下面分别讨论。

A failure to make a convincing case for potential Outstanding Universal Value is one of the main reasons for the failure of nominations. Some common problems include:

• the failure to strike a reasonable balance in the definition of significance (or in the case of a cultural property, its ‘story’ or ‘narrative’) so that it is neither too broad to be able to be clearly defined (such as a story of freedom or memory) nor too narrow (such as a specific type of hospital or castle, a particular type of geological phenomenon, or a value for one particular species);

• the tendency to assert Outstanding Universal Value as a list of qualities that are brought together in a property, without defining any overall significance;

• justifying the proposed inscription of a property in terms of national or regional interest alone (and, for example, the related significance and symbolism);

申报失败的重要原因之一，是无法充分论述遗址潜在的突出普遍价值。普遍存在的问题包括：

• 未能在定义意义上取得合理的平衡（在文化遗产中，它的故事或叙述），不是故事太广博了难以清晰界定（自由和记忆的故事），就是范围太狭小（比如特殊类型的医院、城堡、特殊类型的地质现象或某一物种的价值）；

• 评估遗产突出普遍价值时只罗列遗产的特性，却没有总体定义遗产的重要性；

• 仅从国家或地区的角度对遗产能否能列入名录进行评判（例如，与某个重要事件相关，或是某事的重要象征）；

• general claims being put forward for a property, for instance as the 'crossroads of cultures', 'a unique site', without the provision of detailed justification why the property meets one or more of the World Heritage criteria. Uniqueness does not automatically equate with Outstanding Universal Value;

• the idea that presenting evidence of all periods from the Stone Age to the present day necessarily adds up to a demonstration of Outstanding Universal Value for a cultural property; and

• lack of a comparative analysis established in relation to the appropriate global /geo-cultural framework.

• 简单定义遗产，例如作为“文化交融十字路口”，“独特的遗产”，却没有详尽的论证为什么遗产符合一条或多条价值标准。独特性绝不能自动等同于突出普遍价值；

• 应把代表各个时期（从石器时代到如今）主要观念的证据融汇到一起，以证明文化遗产的突出普遍价值；

• 缺少与全球或地域文化框架相关的比较分析研究。

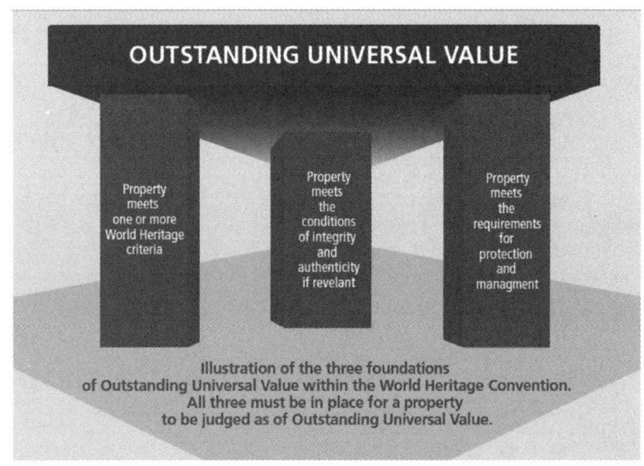

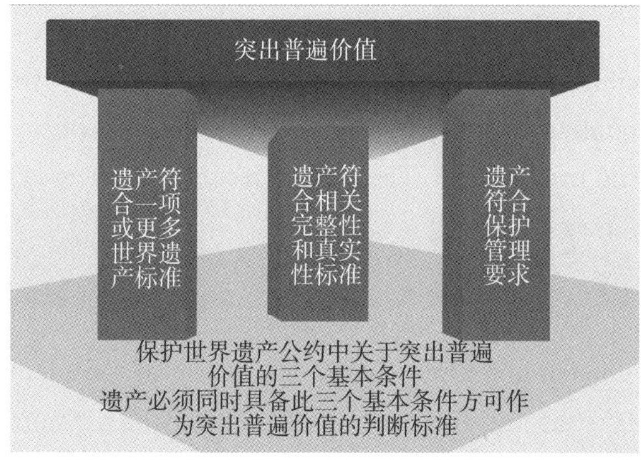

While the focus of the nomination must be on potential Outstanding Universal Value, properties will invariably have local and national values as well. These other levels of value should also be understood. These other values are part of the natural and cultural richness of the property, and the harmonious protection, conservation and management of all values is an objective of good conservation practice. Understanding local values means consulting local people, especially indigenous peoples where they are present. Local people are a primary source of information about local values. A useful reference is *Linking Universal and Local Values: Managing a Sustainable Future for World Heritage* (de Merode et al., 2004).

当然，申报关注的是遗产潜在的突出普遍价值，但这并不影响遗产同时具有当地和国家层面的价值。对于遗产其他层面的价值也应该深入的理解，也是遗产的自然和人文财富的一部分，良好保护行动的目标是协调保存、保护和管理遗产的所有价值。了解当地价值就要考虑到当地居民需求，特别是现在居住在遗产地中的本土居民。当地居民是遗产地区价值信息的主要来源。《联系普遍价值与当地价值：管理世界遗产的可持续的未来》是很有用的参考文献。（德梅罗德等，2004）。

Case Study
Layers of cultural values

Robben Island (South Africa)

Robben Island has been World Heritage listed for the following reasons.

Criterion (iii) : The buildings of Robben Island bear eloquent testimony to its sombre history.

Criterion (vi): Robben Island and its prison buildings symbolize the triumph of the human spirit, of freedom, and of democracy over oppression.

The management of the island has the challenge of addressing a complex layering of values arising from changing usage over time. The property has been:

• a refreshment site for Dutch sailors;

• a sanatorium/isolation hospital for lepers and the chronically ill in the 19th century;

• a prison for some pre-colonial leaders during the frontier/occupation wars;

• a military site during the Second World War; and

• an apartheid prison from the 1960s

Identifying attributes and features

World Heritage properties are places that convey their Outstanding Universal Value.

Cultural value may relate to intangible qualities such as social structure, economic needs and political context, in space as well as time. It may relate to famous events, persons or works of art, literature, science or music. However, the *World Heritage Convention* is a property based convention — properties themselves are inscribed on the List, not ideas or people as such, however great their global influence. Listed properties are required to demonstrate Outstanding Universal

案例
文化价值的层次

罗宾岛（南非）

罗宾岛列入《世界遗产名录》基于以下几个原因。

标准（3）：罗宾岛的建筑是罗宾岛灰暗历史的无可辩驳的实证。

标准（6）：罗宾岛及其监狱建筑是人类精神、自由和民主战胜专治的象征。

管理小岛的最大挑战是如何统一不同时期、因用途不断更改而形成的、复杂的多层次价值。遗产曾经是：

• 荷兰水手的补给场所；

• 19 世纪的麻风病和慢性病的疗养院或隔离医院；

• 边境战争或殖民占领时期关押前领导人的监狱；

• 第二次世界大战军事遗址；

• 自 20 世纪 60 年代起成为种族隔离监狱。

确定遗产属性和特点

世界遗产是能够表达突出普遍价值的地方。

遗产的文化价值可能与某一时间、某一地点的无形组成部分，比如，社会结构、经济需求和政治背景密切相关，也可能和著名的事件、名人、艺术品、文学作品、科学和音乐相关。然而，《世界遗产公约》是基于遗产的公约——是遗产列入名录，而不是影响全球的理念或名人等列入名录。列入名录的遗产需要通过他们的属性证明突出普遍价值。

Value through their attributes.

Having considered what the potential Outstanding Universal Value of a natural or cultural property might be, it is essential to consider the attributes, more commonly called features for natural properties, which convey the potential Outstanding Universal Value and allow an understanding of that value.

考虑自然或文化遗产潜在的突出普遍价值时，必须了解、传达遗产潜在普遍价值的属性，在自然遗产中我们称之为特性，他们能够体现遗产的潜在的突出普遍价值，并有助于对突出普遍价值的理解。

These attributes will be the focus of protection and management actions, and institutional arrangements, and their disposition will inform the boundary of the property.

这些属性是保护和管理行动、机构安排的核心，他们的分布是划定遗产边界的依据。

Attributes might be physical qualities or fabric but can also be processes associated with a property that impact on physical qualities, such as natural or agricultural processes, social arrangements or cultural practices that have shaped distinctive landscapes. For natural properties they can be specific landscape features, areas of habitat, aspects relating to environmental quality (such as intactness, high/pristine environmental quality), scale and naturalness of habitats, and size and viability of wildlife populations.

这些属性可能是遗产的物理特性或组织构造，也可能是与遗产相关的、影响其物理特性的过程，例如能够形成独特景观的自然或农业过程、社会安排或文化实践。对于自然遗产而言，属性可以是特定的景观特征、栖息地，与环境质量有关的方面（例如完整性、高级、原始环境质量），栖息地的规模和自然性，以及野生动物种群的规模和生存力。

A useful technique for complex properties or properties, and in particular cultural properties, with a complex layering of attributes is to map the important attributes and the values they convey. This mapping can assist with understanding the relationship between attributes, but it can also highlight conflicts or management issues, and it is essential for the delineation of boundaries.

对于复杂的、特别是具有复杂层次的文化遗产，最实用的方法就是，用图表揭示其重要属性及其所承载的价值。这个图表将帮助我们理解属性之间的关系，当然也会凸显冲突或管理中的议题，但它是划定遗产边界的基本依据。

In the case of extensions to properties, the attributes of the original nomination are examined and consideration is given to how these might be exemplified, extended, complemented or amplified

扩展遗产时，需要重新检查原始申报的属性，考虑在证明、延伸、补充或扩大的遗产的属性同时，如何保持相同的突出普遍价值。

by the attributes of the proposed extension, while bearing the same Outstanding Universal Value.

Key message: Only use criteria which are well supported.

关键信息：仅使用得到充分论证的评判标准

Checking potential Outstanding Universal Value against World Heritage criteria and identifying appropriate criteria

按照世界遗产标准检验潜在的突出普遍价值，并确定适用的标准

An integral part of the process of demonstrating potential Outstanding Universal Value is to justify one or more of the World Heritage criteria (listed in Section 1.3 of this manual).

证明遗产具有潜在突出普遍价值过程的重要环节之一，就是要证明遗产符合一个或多个世界遗产标准（在本手册 1.3 中有介绍）。

There should be a clear and logical connection between the Statement of Outstanding Universal Value and the selection of criteria. If this connection is not clear then this could indicate that the selection of criteria is not appropriate for the property, and the need for reconsideration. Poor application of the criteria can be an obstacle to the evaluation and successful inscription of a property.

突出普遍价值声明与选择的标准之间应该有合理、清晰的关联。如果他们之间的关联不清楚，那就说明选择的标准对遗产不适合，需要考虑重新选择。选用不恰当的标准将会影响遗产的评估及遗产列入名录。

Only one criterion needs to be satisfied for a property to be inscribed on the World Heritage List (although in the case of criterion (vi), the Committee considers that it should preferably be used in conjunction with other criteria). There is no necessity or particular advantage in trying to nominate a property under as many criteria as possible if they are not well supported by the research and documentation of specific value and attributes. Including weakly argued criteria does not help a nomination. In addition, using many criteria can have implications for the amount of research needed to support the property, for the comparative analysis, for boundaries and other aspects of the nomination.

遗产只要满足一条标准就能够列入《世界遗产名录》（即便是标准（6），委员会认为该标准最好与其他标准一起联合使用）。申报的遗产如果没有特殊价值和属性研究的文件支持，即使符合多条标准也不具有特殊的优势。选择没有充分论证的标准对申报没有帮助。此外，使用多条标准需要更多的比较研究，并影响遗产保护范围和与遗产申报相关其他的组成部分的划定。

The text must go beyond merely asserting that the selected criteria are satisfied, and it must explain why the property justifies each of the criteria. It should also identify the attributes or features that convey the potential Outstanding Universal Value.

申遗文本的内容不仅仅是符合标准的声明，它还必须要解释为什么遗产符合该条标准。文本同时也要明确展示潜在突出普遍价值的属性或特性。

For example, with criterion (ii), avoid saying that the property demonstrates an important interchange of human values without explaining what that interchange is and how it can be perceived through the attributes.

例如，标准（2），提及遗产展现了重要人类价值的相互交换时，就要解释交换的内容是什么，以及该交换如何通过遗产属性得到证明。

Similarly for criterion (iii), the reasons why the property constitutes unique or exceptional testimony should be detailed and the attributes conveying this testimony must be identified.

同样的，在使用标准（3），阐释为什么遗产具有唯一或独特的证据时，应该详细的论证，并且明确提出能够展现这一证据的属性。

Any justification of these criteria needs to explain not only whether ideas are important (such as an interchange of values or exceptional testimony) but whether the property has attributes that reflect these ideas, and whether and how the ideas can be appreciated or experienced in some way at the property.

使用任何一个标准都需要有详细的解释，无论这个观念是否重要（例如价值交换或独特证据），或者遗产的属性是否反映这些观念，遗产是否及如何展现这些观念等。

In the case of criterion (vii), exceptional natural beauty and aesthetic importance must be supported by clear evidence and rigorous intellectual analysis. Merely asserting that a property has exceptional natural beauty and providing attractive photographs is inadequate.

在使用标准（7）时，无可比拟的自然美或审美重要性都需要有清晰的证据和严谨的分析。仅仅断言遗产具有无可比拟自然美且提供具有吸引力的照片完全不能满足论证的需要。

Criterion (ix) requires ‘outstanding examples representing significant ongoing ecological and biological processes...’ and this must be demonstrated in a global scientific/thematic context. Accordingly the context should be clear, and the reasons why the property is an outstanding example in this context should be detailed.

标准（9）要求“代表重要的生态演化和生物进化过程的杰出范例”并得到全球科学、专题研究文本的证明。背景必须要清晰，要详细论述该背景下遗产是杰出典范的原因。

Regarding extensions, the assessment of criteria is carried out in relation to the criteria used for the inscription of the original nomination and how they might apply to the proposed extension. The same criteria should be justified for the original nomination and the proposed extension. For a small extension, the proposed area might amplify some of the attributes of the original nomination but not all of them, although it might be concluded that the original criteria are still valid as the overall spread of attributes is still sufficient for justification. Different or new attributes might also be identified within the proposed extension but they should bear the same values as those already recognized as outstanding. An extension would not normally add new values to the original nomination. However a State Party might take the opportunity of nominating an extension to put forward for evaluation new criteria for the combined original property and its extension. In this case, the nomination dossier must encompass the whole property and provide justification for any new criteria.

对于扩展遗产的评估标准，首先考虑最初申遗文本中提出评估标准及如何将这些标准运用于申报扩展遗产，因为申报扩展遗产要和最初申报使用同样的标准。对于一个小型的扩展，拟申报区域可能强化了原遗产一些属性，但并不是全部，据此可以认为原来标准依然适用，且所有属性仍能展现遗产的重要性。在此过程中，准备扩展的遗产会出现不同的或新的属性，但他们仍应该展现已得到认可的遗产价值。通常情况下，拓展项目不会给原遗产增加新的价值。然而，缔约国应该争取利用扩展申报的机会，为原遗产和扩展遗产整体提出新的评估标准。在这种情况下，申遗文本必须包含所有的遗产，并为评估新的适用标准提供详细论证。

Assessing authenticity

评估真实性

Two of the other important requirements specified in *The Operational Guidelines* relate to the authenticity and integrity of the nominated property. Authenticity only applies to cultural properties and to the cultural aspects of ‘mixed’ properties.

《操作指南》中另外两个重要的要求就是遗产的真实性和完整性。真实性仅仅适用于文化遗产和混合遗产中的文化因素。

Authenticity is about the link between attributes and potential Outstanding Universal Value. That link needs to be truthfully expressed so that the attributes can fully convey the value of the property.

真实性是遗产属性和潜在突出普遍价值之间的纽带。必须如实表达这个纽带才能通过遗产属性全面展现遗产的价值。

The Nara meeting of 1994 clearly set out the way, ‘Our ability to understand these values

1994 年的奈良会议清晰的阐述了真实性的内容，“在某种程度上，我们理解遗产的价值是

depends, in part, on the degree to which information sources about these values may be understood as credible or truthful' (UNESCO World Heritage Centre, 1994, p. 94).

依赖于与价值相关的信息资源的可信或真实程度。”（联合国教科文组织世界遗产中心，1994，94 页）。

The Operational Guidelines state that 'properties may be understood to meet the conditions of authenticity if their cultural values (as recognized in the nomination criteria proposed) are truthfully and credibly expressed through a variety of attributes' (Paragraph 82).

《操作指南》明确提出“如果申报遗产文化价值的各个组成特征（申报时我们确定的标准）是真实可信的，我们就认为遗产符合了真实性的要求。”（82 段）

The Operational Guidelines suggest that the following types of attribute might be considered as conveying or expressing Outstanding Universal Value:

• form and design;
• materials and substance;
• use and function;
• traditions, techniques and management systems;
• location and setting;
• language and other forms of intangible heritage; and
• spirit and feeling.

《操作指南》提出遗产突出普遍价值应在下面的几种属性中得以体现：

• 形式和设计；
• 材料和内容；
• 使用和功能；
• 传统，技术和管理系统；
• 位置和环境；
• 语言或其他形式的无形遗产；
• 精神与感知。

Case study

An example of these attributes relating to the Tombs of Buganda Kings at Kasubi (Uganda) are as follows:

案例

卡苏比布干达国王的王陵的真实性乌干达：

Form and design

The spatial organization of the Kasubi Tombs site — representing the best extant example of a Baganda palace/architectural ensemble.

Materials and substance

The four royal tombs within the Muzibu Azaala Mpanga, the main building, and the use of materials — wood, thatch, reed, wattle and daub.

Use and function

形式与设计：

卡苏比王陵遗址的空间布局——展现了现存最完美的布干达宫殿及建筑组合的实例。

材料和内容：

在慕子布、阿兹拉姆潘喀的四个皇家陵墓，主要建筑和使用的材料——木材、茅草、苇、荆条和篱笆墙都保持了真实性。

使用和功能：

Religious use — it is a major spiritual centre for the Buganda and is the most active religious site in the kingdom — including cultural/religious practices and rituals.

Traditions, techniques and management systems

Traditional management — the site continues to be managed in a traditional manner through a complex system of responsibilities. Traditions — cultural/religious practices and rituals.

Location and setting

The original location and surviving rural setting — including the agricultural part of the site which continues to be farmed in a traditional manner.

Language and other forms of intangible heritage

Religious use — it is a major spiritual centre for the Buganda and is the most active religious site in the kingdom, including a place where the Kabaka and his representatives carry out important rituals relating to Buganda culture. Such use involves cultural/religious practices and rituals.

Spirit and feeling

The built and natural elements of the Kasubi Tombs site are charged with historical, traditional and spiritual values. These are a combination of physical attributes, such as buildings and plans, and intangible attributes such as cultural processes. In 2010, one building — the most important architecturally — of the extensive 26 hectare Kasubi Tombs site was damaged by fire. Commitments have been made to reconstruct the damaged building.

For each property the attributes that have been identified as conveying the potential Outstanding Universal Value should be considered for the way they might be said to 'truthfully' convey or express that value. For example, for an urban area it

宗教功能——是布干达地区重要的精神中心，是王国举办最重要宗教活动的场所——包括文化和宗教习俗和仪式。

传统，技术和管理体系：

传统管理——遗址一直使用复杂的责任系统、以传统方式进行管理。传统——文化或宗教活动和仪式。

位置和环境：

原始地点和保存下来的乡村环境——包括遗址区内的农业，仍旧按照传统的方式进行耕作。

语言和其他无形遗产。

宗教功能——是布干达地区重要的精神中心，是王国举办最重要宗教活动的场所，包括卡帕卡及其众议员进行与布干达文化相关的、重要宗教仪式的场所，这样的使用包括了文化、宗教活动和仪式。

精神和感知：

卡苏比皇陵遗址的建筑和自然组成部分展现了历史的、传统的和精神的价值。它包括了物质属性，例如建筑和规划，也包括了无形属性例如文化过程。在2010年，其中的一个建筑——在建筑史上最为重要的建筑——占地面积达26公顷的卡苏比墓被火焚毁。已承诺重建被焚毁建筑。

对每一个遗产，展现突出普遍价值的属性是真实展现或表达价值的方式。例如，在城镇区域，其建筑、空间规划、传统和分布于遗产内社区的社会经济、环境结构等被认为是表达遗产价值的组成部分。

might be appropriate to consider structures, spatial plans, as well as traditions and socio-economic — environmental structures of the living communities that populate the property, and which allow it to express its value.

Authenticity is therefore a measure of how well attributes convey potential Outstanding Universal Value. Authenticity can be compromised if the attributes are weak — communities cease to thrive, buildings collapse, traditions disappear, and so on.

真实性是衡量遗产特性如何展现突出普遍价值的一种方法。如果遗产的属性展现遗产价值的能力较差，遗产的真实性也会受到牵连——造成社区不再繁荣、房屋倒塌、传统消失等等。

In the case of archaeological sites, authenticity is judged according to the ability of the archaeological remains to truthfully convey their meaning. In many cases, conjectural reconstruction might hinder this process and compromise authenticity. Similarly, while reconstruction of incomplete buildings and structures can be justified in some circumstances, this can also impact on their ability to truthfully convey meaning.

对于考古遗址，需要通过考古遗存能否如实传达他们含义和意义来判定其真实性。在很多情况下，推测性的重建隐藏了这一判断过程，削弱了真实性。同样的，在某种情况下，对不完整建筑或构筑物的重建都会影响遗产如实表达意义的能力。

A statement of authenticity needs to set out the ability of a property to convey its potential Outstanding Universal Value through the way its attributes convey their value truthfully (credibly, genuinely) (Operational Guidelines, Paragraphs 79-86).

真实性声明需要陈述通过遗产属性所体现的真实价值（可信的、真正的），展现它潜在突出普遍价值的能力。(《操作指南》，79–86 段)。

Examples of some questions which might be used in the assessment are provided in the following table. These attributes and questions should not be adopted without critically reviewing the potential Outstanding Universal Value and attributes of the nominated property, and the latter should structure this assessment. Uncritically adopting the following table as a standard recipe may create problems for the nomination.

下表中列出了评估真实性过程中可能出现的一些问题。如果未能对所申报遗产潜在的突出的普遍价值及其特征进行批判性审查（评估的重要组成部分），则不可采用这些属性和问题。在遗产申报过程中不加辨别的采用下表作为审查标准，就会产生很多的问题。

Attribute	Examples of assessment questions
For all attributes	• Given that authenticity must be judged within the cultural context to which the property belongs, what is that cultural context? • Does the attribute credibly and truthfully convey the potential Outstanding Universal Value of the property? • Can the potential Outstanding Universal Value be understood because the attributes are believable and honestly portray the value? • To what degree is the value present in or expressed by the attributes? • What were the original characteristics of the property's cultural heritage and how have these changed through time? • Have changes in the attributes reduced the ability to understand the value of the property? • Has the property been reconstructed to any degree? If so, was this based on complete and detailed documentation? Was there any conjecture used in the reconstruction? It is noted that reconstruction can sometimes be part of the value.
Form and design	• Has the form or design been changed and, if so, to what extent? It is noted that sometimes change is part of the value. • Is the form or design accurate in all respects?
Materials and substance	• Have the materials, fabric or substance been changed or replaced? If so, to what extent? • Have repairs been carried out using materials traditional to the culture?
Use and function	• Who does the use or function relate to? • Does the use or function continue, or have they been changed, and why? • Has the intensity of use or function changed? • How robust are the societal mechanisms which support the use or function?
Traditions, techniques and management systems	• Who do the traditions, techniques or management systems relate to? • How robust are the societal mechanisms which support the traditions, techniques or management systems? • Are the traditions, techniques or management systems changed or changing, and why? • Has the strength of traditions, techniques or management systems changed, and why? • Have repairs been carried out using methods traditional to the culture?
Location and setting	• Has the location or setting changed and, if so, why and to what extent? Note: Assessing these attributes requires a clear understanding of the boundaries of the property and its appropriate setting, or will have a direct impact on the definitions of the boundaries.
Language, and other forms of intangible heritage	• Who are the people who use the language or are keepers/custodians/practitioners of the intangible heritage? • Do the language or other forms of intangible heritage continue, or have they been changed, and why? • Has the extent of use of language or other forms of intangible heritage declined, and why? • How robust are the societal mechanisms which support the language or other forms of intangible heritage? • How viable is the population which use the language or other forms of intangible heritage? What factors threaten their viability?
Spirit and feeling	• In whom does the spirit or feeling reside? • Does the spirit or feeling continue, or have they changed, and why? • Has the extent of appreciation of the spirit or feeling declined? • How robust are the societal mechanisms which support appreciation of the spirit or feeling? • How viable is the population which appreciate the spirit or feeling?

属性	评估过程中存在问题
对于所有的属性	假定真实性必须在遗产具有的、特定的文化背景下进行判断，那么文化背景是指什么？ 遗产属性是否能可信的、真实地展现遗产潜在的突出普遍价值？ 是否因为属性可信、诚实的描绘价值，就能理解潜在的突出普遍价值。 遗产属性蕴含或表现遗产价值的程度有多大？ 什么是文化遗产原来的特征，这些特征如何随着时间变迁的？ 遗产属性的变化是不是会降低我们理解遗产价值的能力？ 遗产是否进行了任何程度的重建？如果有，重建是否根据完整和详细的档案资料进行？重建的过程中是否有推断或猜想？有些时候，重建是价值的一部分。
形式和设计	形式和设计是否发生了改变，如果发生了改变，改变程度多大？有人认为改变有时也是价值的一部分。 是不是形式和设计的所有组成部分都是精确的？
材料和内容	是否遗产的材料、构筑物或内容已经被改变或被替换了？如果有，程度有多大？ 是否实施了维修？维修的材料是否是传统文化的一部分？
使用和功能	使用或功能与何人有关系？ 使用和功能是否有延续性，是否发生变化，如果有，为什么？ 遗产或功能的强度是否发生了变化？ 支持使用或功能的社会体制的繁荣程度如何？
传统，技术和管理体系	传统，技术或管理体系与何人相关？ 支持传统、技术和管理体系的社会体制的繁荣程度如何？ 传统、技术或管理体系是否已经或正在发生变化，为什么？ 是否使用了本文化中传统的方法进行维修？
位置和环境	遗产的位置和环境是否发生了变化，如果发生变化，原因是什么，变化的程度有多大？ 注意：评估这些特性需要对遗产的边界和它所适宜的环境有清晰的了解，或者说它将直接影响划定遗产边界。
语言，和其他无形遗产	使用该语言或无形遗产的管理者、保管者或参与人是谁？ 该语言和其他形式的无形遗产是否持续使用，如果他们有所改变，改变的原因是什么？ 该语言或其他无形遗产的使用范围是否缩小了，为什么？ 支持该语言和其他无形文化遗产的社会体制的繁荣程度如何？ 使用这种语言或其他形式的无形遗产的人群有多少？什么因素威胁了他们的生存？
精神和感知	精神或感知属于哪些人？ 这种精神和感知是否一直存在，有没有改变，为什么改变？ 对于这种精神和感知欣赏程度有没有削弱？ 支持精神和感知的社会体制的繁荣程度如何？ 欣赏这个精神与感知的人群的生存能力如何？

It is not necessary within the nomination to consider attributes irrelevant to the potential Outstanding Universal Value of the property.

在申报过程中，不必考虑与申报遗产潜在的突出普遍价值不相关的属性。

Case study

Authenticity and integrity for cultural properties

案例

文化遗产的真实性和完整性

Aflaj Irrigation Systems of Oman (Oman)

阿曼坎儿井灌溉系统（阿曼）

The collection of Aflaj irrigation systems

阿夫拉贾坎儿井灌溉系统代表了3000个仍

represents some 3, 000 still-functioning systems in Oman. Ancient engineering technologies demonstrate long-standing, sustainable use of water resources for the cultivation of palms and other produce in extremely arid desert lands. Such systems reflect the former total dependence of communities on this irrigation and a time-honoured, fair and effective management and sharing of water resources, underpinned by mutual dependence and communal values.

在继续使用的灌溉系统。古代的工程技术展示了在极度干旱的荒漠，长期、持续使用的水资源系统种植棕榈和其他作物。这反映了历史上当地社区完全依赖灌溉系统，对水资源的有效管理和共享，相互依赖和共同的价值支持了这一系统。

Initially, only a portion of each Aflaj system was nominated — from the mother well to the Sharia. Those parts of the system in the settlements, serving the needs of the community through the provision of water for cooking, washing and agriculture, were added to the nomination and the property now reflects the integrity of the whole Aflaj system.

最初，只把从母井到沙利亚这一段列入申报，后来把位于村落中为社区成员提供烹调、洗涮和农业灌溉等功能的其他水系统部分，增加到遗产申报中，使得阿夫拉贾坎儿井遗产的完整性得以展现。

Case study
Historic Monuments of Ancient Nara (Japan)

案例
古代奈良的历史文物（日本）

The level of authenticity of the various properties included in the property is high. Japanese conservation principles have ensured that replacement of damaged or degraded architectural elements has respected the materials and techniques used by the original builders. There has been some in site reconstruction on the Nara Palace Site. The continuity of traditional architecture in Japan and the substantial amount of data recovered by archaeological excavation has ensured that the reconstructed buildings have a high level of authenticity in design and materials.

遗产所涵盖的各类遗产有高度的真实性。日本的保护准则已经明确提出必须用原来建造者所使用的、原来的材料和工艺，替代建筑中受损或退化的构件。奈良皇宫在原址重建。日本传统建筑的持续性和考古发掘过程中发现的大量重要材料，保证了重建建筑在设计和材料方面有极高的真实性。

The same assessment applies to the garden reconstructions. The only reconstruction that might be considered to involve a significant element of conjecture is that of the Suzaku (south gate). Much of the constructional and decorative details depend upon archaeological evidence and that

同样的评估用于园林的重建。在朱雀门（南门）的重建过程中最可能用到推测。大部分重要构件的构造和装饰细节都依赖于考古证据和残存的同时代的建筑结构。

from surviving structures from the same period elsewhere.

Assessing integrity

评估完整性

Integrity is required for both natural and cultural properties.

Integrity is a measure of the completeness or intactness of the attributes that convey Outstanding Universal Value. Accordingly a clear understanding of the potential Outstanding Universal Value is required before it is possible to consider the integrity of the property.

自然遗产和文化遗产都应具有完整性。

完整性是对能够展现突出普遍价值属性的完全性和无缺性进行的判定。在确定遗产是否具有完整性之前，应清晰理解突出普遍价值。

The Operational Guidelines, in Paragraph 88, set out the need to assess, the extent to which the property:

• includes all elements [attributes] necessary to express its Outstanding Universal Value;

• is of adequate size to ensure the complete representation of the features and processes which convey the property's significance.

• suffers from adverse effects of development and/or neglect.

《操作指南》的第 88 段指出评估遗产的要求：

• 所有组成部分（属性）表现突出普遍价值的程度；

• 遗产规模是否足够完整的展现特性，或遗产重要进程是否得到完整展现；

• 开发对于遗产的负面影响的程度有多大。

The key words are 'wholeness', 'intactness' and 'absence of threats'. These can be understood as follows:

• Wholeness: all the necessary attributes are within the property.

• Intactness: all the necessary attributes are still present — none are lost or have been significantly damaged or have decayed.

• Absence of threats: none of the attributes are threatened by development, deterioration or neglect.

关键词包括"完全"，"没有损伤"和"不存在威胁"。可理解为：

• 完全：所有必要的属性都包括在遗产中；

• 没有损伤：从古至今，所有必须地属性都存在——没有消失或损坏严重或已衰退。

• 不存在威胁：没有一个属性受到发展、恶化或疏忽的威胁。

The Operational Guidelines provide specific guidance in relation to the various World Heritage criteria, which is important to understand (Paragraphs 89-95).

《操作指南》对各类世界遗产标准提供了详尽的说明，这个对于理解遗产的完整性十分重要。（89–95 段）。

A statement of integrity needs to set out how the collection of features, processes and/or attributes that convey potential Outstanding Universal Value are contained within the boundaries, that the property does not have substantial parts that have lost their values, or where none of the relevant features or attributes are present, and that the property exhibits a satisfactory state of conservation and its values are not threatened. There should always be a logical and scientific basis for the selection of the area to be nominated.

完整性的声明需要说明：遗产区范围是否足以展现突出普遍价值的特性、过程或属性，遗产重要价值是否存在丧失的情况或虽有丧失但没有影响到相关的属性或特性，遗产保护状态是否令人满意、遗产价值是否受到了威胁。这些都是选择申报区域的逻辑和科学的依据。

Assessing the state of conservation of aspects of the property that are not related to the potential Outstanding Universal Value is not required in a World Heritage nomination. Similarly, introducing other concepts of integrity not relating to World Heritage or the values under consideration should be avoided.

不需要评估与遗产潜在突出普遍价值无关的其他组成部分的保存状态，因其不是申报世界遗产的必须条件。同样的，也应尽量避免介绍与世界遗产或价值整体性无关的其他概念。

Key message: Integrity and authenticity are different aspects of the Outstanding Universal Value of a property.

关键信息：真实性与完整性从不同方面体现遗产的突出普遍价值

Examples of questions useful in the assessment of integrity are:

- Are the key features and attributes of the property that carry potential Outstanding Universal Value whole or intact?
- Does the property include all the elements necessary to express its potential Outstanding Universal Value?
- Is the property of adequate size to ensure the complete representation of the features and processes which convey its significance?
- What is the condition of the key features and attributes of the property, and are they well conserved/in good condition?
- In the case of cultural landscapes, historic towns or other living cultural properties, are the

可用于完整性评估中的提问包括：

- 承载遗产潜在突出普遍价值的所有特性和属性是否完整无缺？
- 遗产是否包含了所有能表现遗产突出普遍价值的组成部分？
- 遗产展示出的规模是否足以体现遗产的重要特性和过程？
- 核心特性或属性的现状如何，是否得到了保护或处于良好的保存状态？
- 对于文化景观，历史城镇和其他活态的文化遗产，其具有显著特色的过程、关系和动态

processes, relationships and dynamic functions essential to their distinctive character maintained and in a robust state?

功能是否得到有效维持并处于健康状态？

• In the case of natural properties, are the processes, relationships and dynamic functions essential to physical features (e.g. landform, habitats) maintained, in a robust state and recognized at a scale appropriate to their operation?

• 对于自然遗产，他们物质特性（如地貌，栖息地）的过程、关系和动态功能是否得到维持，遗产是否处于健康活跃状态，其范围是否在管理机构的权限内？

• Does the property suffer from the adverse effects of development, neglect or any other degrading process?

• 遗产是否受到开发的负面影响，是否被忽略或受到其他退化进程的影响？

• Are any processes causing deterioration under control?

• 是否导致退化的进程都得到了有效控制？

Several of these questions relate to the boundaries of the property. If the necessary elements are not included, or the property is not of adequate size, then the boundaries should be reconsidered to address these issues. While it may be convenient to determine boundaries on the basis of administrative arrangements or property ownership, this may not always be suitable for the potential Outstanding Universal Value of the property. Administrative convenience should not be the primary consideration in establishing the boundaries of the nominated property.

这些问题中有一些是与遗产的边界相关。如果必要组成部分不在边界内，或遗产的规模不充分，就应该重新考虑划定边界以解决这些问题。虽然以行政管理或遗产所有权为依据来确定遗产的边界比较方便，但可能不适用于遗产潜在的突出普遍价值。行政管理的便利不应是考虑划定遗产范围主要的因素。

It may be possible to argue that the condition of integrity is met by a property that is representative of a wider landscape, habitat, geological system or cultural system. However, it will be important to show that the boundaries have a logical basis for distinguishing the nominated property from the wider area, and that the property is distinctly of potential Outstanding Universal Value when considered in relation to the wider area.

有人认为，遗产具有典型代表性的广阔的景观、栖息地、地理系统或文化遗产体系就符合完整性条件。但是遗产边界的划定应有合理的逻辑，以便识别出申报的遗产区域明显比周边广阔地域更具有潜在突出普遍价值。

For some properties with complex landscapes, values or processes, it might be possible to map the attributes that carry potential Outstanding Universal

对于具有复杂景观、价值或过程的遗产，可以通过在地图上标注的方法，确定能展现潜在突出普遍价值属性的逻辑边界。将遗产所有价

Value to show where a logical boundary might lie. This is a meaningful way to demonstrate integrity by showing that the boundaries of the property adequately encompass all its values.

值都包含在遗产边界内是描述遗产完整性的有效方法。

In the case of natural and cultural properties, human use is both permissible and compatible with World Heritage listing, provided it is sustainable, and compatible with the values of the property. It is important to critically evaluate the condition of the property within the nomination document, and to explain honestly and openly any areas where there are human or other impacts on the condition of the property.

对自然和文化遗产，人类对遗产的利用更能证明其遗产价值符合名录要求的可持续性和兼容性。依据申遗文本对遗产状态进行批判性评估，开诚布公的解释人们活动或其他组成部分对遗产保存状态的影响，也十分重要。

In some cases, elements might be geographically disconnected and remote from one another, and creating one large boundary is not appropriate. This is a situation where a serial nomination may be more appropriate.

在一些情况下，遗产的组成部分可能在地理上相距甚远，完全不适合划定一个很大范围的遗产边界。在这种情况下应采用系列申报的方法。

Comparative analysis

比较分析

The purpose of the comparative analysis is to ascertain, first, whether there is scope in the World Heritage List for the inclusion of the nominated property, and second, to demonstrate that there are no comparable properties in the same geo-cultural area (cultural properties) or globally (natural properties) with similar values that might be nominated in the future. The geo-cultural area varies according to the values expressed by the property and might be defined at the regional level or worldwide.

比较分析的目的是为了确定：首先，拟申报的遗产要素在《世界遗产名录》是否已有体现；其次，证明在相同的地理文化区域（文化遗产）中，全球（自然遗产）范围内未来没有带有类似价值的相似遗产进行申报。地理文化区根据遗产所表现的价值可能有所不同，应该在区域或世界范围遗产内进行界定。

The starting point of the analysis is to define what combination of potential Outstanding Universal Value and the related features and attributes are being compared. That is, what is the particular significance of the property, and how is

比较分析的出发点是明确突出普遍价值的特性或属性组合方式。也就是说，遗产的特殊重要性表现在什么地方，如何证明？

this manifested?

Comparisons should be drawn with properties expressing the same values as the nominated property, and within a defined geo-cultural area (cultural properties) or globally (natural properties). Therefore the values need to be clearly defined and, in the case of cultural properties, the geo-cultural framework should be determined according to these values. In some cases the geo-cultural framework may be global.

对比分析应在特定的地理文化区（文化遗产）或全球范围内（自然遗产）、能表达相同价值的遗产之间进行。因此，遗产的价值应该明确，对于文化遗产，应该确定基于这些价值的地理文化范畴。有些时候，其范畴可能是全球性的地理文化圈。

In the case of natural properties, the comparative analysis needs to be of global scope, thus comparing the property with similar properties that exist in other regions of the world and not only with properties of the region in question. For example, a desert environment in Africa should not only be compared with deserts elsewhere in Africa, but all other deserts in the world.

对于自然遗产，比较分析要在全球范围内进行，用以比较的遗产可能处于世界的其他地区，而不是仅与本区域内的遗产比较。例如，位于非洲的沙漠环境不仅应该和非洲地区的沙漠相比，同时也要和世界上其他区域的沙漠相比。

For a serial nomination, the comparative analysis for the whole property is based on the same principles as for a property with a single component. The potential Outstanding Universal Value and the related features and attributes of the whole property, that is the series, should be compared with other properties to demonstrate that, first of all, there is room on the World Heritage List and, secondly, there are no other similar serial properties that might be nominated. There is however a second part to the comparative analysis for serial properties and that relates to the choice of components. The nomination needs to set out the rationale for choosing the components, in terms of comparing them with other similar components and justifying the choice made.

对于系列遗产，整个遗产的比较分析准则与单个遗产比较分析准则相同。在遗产中，与潜在的突出普遍价值相关的特性或属性应是系列的，应该和其他展现相同价值的遗产进行比较，首先是与《世界遗产名录》中的遗产进行比较；其次，确定没有其他相似的系列遗产在进行申报。系列遗产比较分析的第二部分是选择相关组成部分。申报时需要说明选择这些组成部分的原因，通过与相似组成部分的比较来证明本选择的正确性。

The first task is to ascertain whether this combination of values and attributes is already

比较分析首先要证明相同价值和属性组合是否已经存在于《世界遗产名录》中。这一任

represented on the World Heritage List. This is done by comparing the nominated property with other similar properties already inscribed. At the end of this task, a conclusion should be drawn.

It might happen that there are no properties already inscribed on the World Heritage List that could be compared with the nominated property. However, the aim of the comparative analysis is not to demonstrate that the property is unique, but that it has an exceptionally strong claim to be of Outstanding Universal Value in a defined context.

Changes over time to World Heritage criteria

In making comparisons with existing World Heritage properties, it is important to note there have been changes to the World Heritage criteria over time. Prior to 2005 the criteria were set out as two separate lists of cultural criteria (i-vi) and natural criteria (vii-x). With the adoption of revised *Operational Guidelines* in 2005, and since then, only one set of ten criteria now exists. The relationship between the old and new numbering of the system is shown in the table below.

	Cultural criteria	Natural criteria
Operational Guidelines pre-2005	(i) (ii) (iii) (iv) (v) (vi)	(i) (ii) (iii) (iv)
Operational Guidelines post-2005	(i) (ii) (iii) (iv) (v) (vi)	(viii) (ix) (vii) (x)

Note that the relative order of the four old natural criteria has changed in the new list, and the former natural criterion (iii) now comes before the other former natural criteria (i, ii and iv) in the current Operational Guidelines. Further, the precise wording of the criteria has changed over time, with the most significant amendments being made in 1992. It is important to bear this in mind when making comparisons between properties inscribed before and after this time.

The next task is to consider whether, in the

务需要在申报遗产与已列入名录相似遗产的比较过程中完成，并给出一个明确的结论。

可能会出现名录中没有相似遗产能与申报遗产进行对比的情况。然而，比较分析的目的不是要说明该遗产的独一性，而是要证明该遗产具有突出普遍价值。

世界遗产标准的改变

与已有的世界文化遗产进行比较时，需要注意世界遗产标准随着时间在改变。在 2005 年以前，标准分为两个部分，标准（1–6）适用于文化遗产，标准（7–10）适用于自然遗产。自 2005 年采用了新版本的《操作指南》后，只存在十条标准。新的编号变化的联系见下表。

	文化准则	自然准则
2005 年以前的《操作指南》	(i)(ii)(iii)(iv)(v)(vi)	(i)(ii)(iii)(iv)
2005 年以后的《操作指南》	(i)(ii)(iii)(iv)(v)(vi)(vii)(viii)(ix)(x)	

注意：在新版的指南中，自然遗产标准的顺序发生了变化，前版自然标准的（3）现在在其他标准（1、2 和 4）之前。此外世界遗产标准的措词越来越准确，1992 年对此进行了重要的修正。切记，在对 2005 年前后列入遗产名录的遗产进行比较分析时，应重点关注这个变化。

比较分析的另一任务是考虑在相同的地理

future, other similar properties could be nominated from within the same geo-cultural region or, where appropriate, from other parts of the world. The nominated property needs to be compared with other known examples based on the selected values and attributes. Again a conclusion should be drawn as to how it compares with other properties and why, if there are other similar properties, the nominated property should be seen as the best exemplar or representative, or whether in the future other properties might join it as a serial nomination.

文化圈或世界的其他地区，将来是否会有相似的遗产申报。申报遗产应根据价值和属性选择已知的遗产进行比较。另外，应该对如何与其他遗产做出比较和为什么要比较给出结论，如申报遗产应该比其他同类的遗产更具有代表性和榜样，未来是否有其相似的遗产作为系列遗产进行申报。

Comparisons by typology or comparing only elements of the property with other elements of other properties are considered not to be relevant unless they relate directly to the claimed values.

仅进行类型比较或将遗产组成部分与其他遗产的其他组成部分比较是不够的，除非这些组成部分与价值声明直接相关。

Authenticity and integrity are an important part of the comparative analysis. Among comparable properties, some might have greater or lesser authenticity and integrity, and this will influence potential Outstanding Universal Value.

真实性和完整性是比较分析的重要部分。在用于比较分析的遗产中，有些可能具有较高的真实性和完整性，有些可能较低，这些会影响潜在的突出普遍价值。

At the end of the comparative analysis, it should be possible to position the nominated property with respect to properties already inscribed on the World Heritage List, and with respect to the body of similar properties within the defined geo-cultural area (cultural property) or globally (natural property). The analysis should show that there is room on the List for the nominated property and that there are no other similar properties that could be nominated.

在比较分析的最后，与已列入名录的遗产或相同地理文化圈（文化遗产）或全球（自然遗产）的遗产比较后，确定申报遗产的地位。分析证明申报遗产在《世界遗产名录》中仍属缺项，可以列入，同时也应说明没有相似遗产会进行申报。

Sources of information about comparable properties might be found in:

• the World Heritage List;

• nomination dossiers, Advisory Body/ies evaluations, and past World Heritage Committee decisions for comparable properties already on the World Heritage List;

比较分析的遗产可供选择的资源包括：

•《世界遗产名录》；

• 申遗文本，咨询机构的评估报告，世界遗产委员会对以往已列入名录的类似遗产的决议；

• information on properties which have not been recommended for inscription, as these help to identify the threshold or level of importance that is expected to meet the claim for Outstanding Universal Value;

• 未提出申报的遗产的信息，这些信息可能有助于提高申报遗产的突出普遍价值的阈值或重要性等级；

• Tentative Lists of the same country and other countries;

• 本国或其他国家遗产的《预备名录》；

• *The World Heritage List: Filling the Gaps — An Action Plan for the Future* (ICOMOS, 2005a), for cultural properties;

• 文化遗产的《世界遗产名录：填补空白——未来行动计划》（国际古迹遗址理事会，2005a）；

• IUCN and ICOMOS thematic studies;

• 世界自然保护联盟和国际古迹理事会的专题研究；

• World Database on Protected Areas (www.wdpa.org), for natural properties;

• 世界自然遗产保护区数据库（www.wdpa.org），

• inventories prepared by other expert organizations (such as Docomomo or TICCIH); and

• 其他专家团体提供的各种目录（例如国际工业遗址保护协会或国际现代建筑记录与保护组织）；

• other research reports and literature, or as provided by relevant international experts.

• 其他研究报告和论文，或其他国际专家提供的相关文献。

Online references for many of these sources are listed in Section 1.1 of this manual.

网上的资源信息在本手册的 1.1 中已详细罗列。

Another useful source of information is national and international experts working in fields relating to the property. Using international experts, in addition to the best national experts, in preparing or reviewing the comparative analysis can be highly valuable in developing the nomination. The earlier such an analysis is done in the process the better, and in principle such an analysis could usefully be done for sites on the Tentative Lists of States Parties to the Convention in order to assist the setting of priorities for future nominations.

其他有用的信息资源，包括遗产相关领域国内、国际专家的研究成果。准备申遗文本时邀请本国最好的专家和国际专家共同审查比较分析的结果很重要。比较分析开始的越早，越有益于遗产申报工作，原则上说，应将缔约国《预备名录》上的遗产都进行比较分析，这样有利于确定遗产申报的先后次序。

Key message: Have the analysis peer-reviewed by international experts.

关键信息：国际专家组开展比较分析

Example of using an expert group to develop the comparative analysis

利用专家组进行比较分析的实例

In some cases, especially for natural

在一些情况下，特别是自然遗产，利用专

properties, the use of an expert group to develop the comparative analysis is the preferred method, as outlined below.

家组进行比较分析是最合适的方法：

1. A property that would be the subject of a new nomination should be clearly classified in relation to:

• the theme, geo-cultural context and bio-geographic provinces that it represents. This classification should be based on the information provided in the analysis of the World Heritage List and Tentative Lists prepared by IUCN and ICOMOS, for example terrestrial wetlands, deserts, marine and coastal areas, rock art, bridges, cultural landscapes, etc.; and

• specific World Heritage criteria, which should be used to provide the framework for the geo-cultural area (cultural property) or global (natural property) comparative analysis that follows.

1. 确定遗产将要申报世界遗产时，应该先进行分类：

• 该遗产代表的主题、地理文化背景和生物地理区。这种分类应该以世界自然保护联盟和国际古迹遗址理事会提供的《世界遗产名录》和《预备名录》的分类为基础，例如陆地、湿地、沙漠、海洋和海岸线区域，岩画、桥梁、文化景观等；

• 确定具体的世界遗产标准，并据此确定地理文化圈（文化遗产）内或全球范围内（自然遗产）比较分析的框架。

2. Based on how the nominated property is classified, the State Party should put together an expert group, formed by specialists on those themes, geo-cultural context and biogeographic provinces represented by the nominated property. Such an expert group should be formed by national specialists and ideally should include international experts who can assist in maintaining a global perspective throughout the whole analysis. The Advisory Bodies can provide suggestions on international experts if requested by States Parties. This group should include the experts involved in the initial identification and agreement of the values of the property, but should also ideally involve experts who can take an international perspective from outside the country and region concerned. Such opinion can be obtained by e-mail and correspondence as an alternative to taking part in meetings.

2. 基于申报遗产的分类，缔约国应该组建一个专家组，由申报遗产所代表的主题、文化地理圈和生态地理研究的专家组成。这样的团队应有国内专家，最好还有能从全球视野下进行对比分析的外国专家。如果缔约国要求的话，咨询机构可推荐国际专家提供建议和意见。这个团队应该包括能确定和认同遗产价值的专家，同时最好包括能够站在相关国家和地区之外的国际角度上提出帮助的专家。这些理念可以通过电子邮件或参加国际会议得以实现。

3. The expert group should identify a full range of properties that should provide the basis for comparative analysis. Important sources of information to select this list are noted above.

3. 确定遗产整体范围，这是专家组比较分析的基础。用于比较的重要信息的来源见上文所述。

4. The expert group should then obtain as much information as possible — both quantitative and qualitative — for both the nominated property and similar properties that will be subject to the comparative analysis, in order to assess how the nominated property ranks in comparison. The entry point for information gathering and for the comparative analysis should be the criteria under which the property is likely to be nominated. The comparative analysis does not necessarily need to be a long descriptive document, provided there is a clear indication of the sources of information that it relies on. The analysis could be reflected in a consolidated table. *The Operational Guidelines* make it clear that it is relevant to discuss the relative state of conservation of different properties within a comparative analysis. Properties that are of comparable importance but in poor condition, or without effective protection and management, may be regarded as having a weaker claim to potential Outstanding Universal Value compared with a property in good condition and with a high standard of protection and management.

4. 专家组应该尽可能保质保量的获取申报遗产和用于比较分析的相似遗产的更多信息，从而确定申报遗产在比较遗产中的级别。比较分析信息收集的切入点应该是遗产所符合的标准。比较分析不需要长篇大论，只需要明确指证所依赖的信息资源。分析内容可在综合的表格中体现。《操作指南》明确指出，必须讨论不同遗产的相对保护状态。虽然申报遗产具有很重要的价值，但如果该遗产保护状态较差或缺乏有效的保存和管理，却选择与保存状态较好、保护和管理标准高的遗产进行比较，反而会削弱申报遗产的突出普遍价值。

5. The expert group should prepare the final comparative analysis based on its research and discussions, including conclusions about the nominated property (see also the discussion about conclusions below).

5. 专家组应根据他们的研究和讨论结果，准备比较分析报告，包括对申报遗产的最终结论。（见下文讨论结果章节）

As noted above, various research frameworks might help to understand the values of the property, including thematic, chronological-regional and typological frameworks. Comparable properties would be part of such research frameworks.

如上所述，各种研究体系包括按专题、按年代顺序——按区域和类型的研究均有助于理解遗产价值。相似遗产应该是比较研究工作体系的组成部分。

In some cases, there may be no existing information or study on which to base a comparative analysis, or the information is too limited. One option is to undertake the research necessary to provide this information, or to encourage other reputable and relevant experts or organizations to do this work. It is often better if such experts or organizations are independent of the nomination, and have international credibility. This may involve additional cost.

在一些情况下，可能缺乏资料或相似的比较研究，或者信息资源十分有限。可选择启动必要研究以提供这些信息，或者鼓励其他卓越或相关的专家或组织进行研究。如果这些专家或组织能够独立于遗产的申报工作之外、具有国际的公信力可能更好。当然也可能会增加额外的费用。

While different languages may be a problem in accessing information for the comparative analysis from other countries, this must be overcome. It is not intellectually or practically acceptable that a body of information highly relevant to the comparative analysis is ignored simply for this reason.

在对不同国家的遗产进行比较分析时，必须克服语言障碍。如果因语言问题而忽略大量与比较分析高度关联的信息，这样的选择在理论上和操作过程中均不可接受。

The comparative analysis is a vital part of understanding the potential Outstanding Universal Value of a property, and feeds in to the process of identifying such value.

比较分析是理解潜在突出普遍价值最重要的一步，也会影响遗产价值的认定过程。

The comparative analysis must draw conclusions. Thorough and objective comparative analyses greatly contribute to successful nominations. The result of the comparative analysis may lead to three different outcomes:

比较分析必须得出结论。完整的、客观的比较分析对遗产申报大有作为。比较分析结果会导致三种不同的效果：

• the property ranks highly when compared with similar properties and can fill a critical gap on the World Heritage List, and the State Party should go ahead with its nomination process;

• 在与类似遗产的比较分析过程中，该遗产处于较高的等级，同时填补了《世界遗产名录》的主要空白，缔约国应继续遗产申报进程；

• the property ranks at a low level when compared with similar properties and it does not fill any gap on the World Heritage List, and the State Party may wish to carefully reconsider the nomination of the property; or

• 在与其他遗产的比较分析过程中，该遗产的等级较低，也没有填补世界遗产的任何空白，这时缔约国应该认真考虑是否要继续申报这个遗产；

• the property ranks at the same level of importance as other similar properties. This may

• 该遗产属性与其他类似遗产同样重要。这就说明遗产的潜在突出普遍价值较弱或临界。

also indicate that the case for potential Outstanding Universal Value is relatively weak or a borderline case. If there are only a small number of other high-ranking sites, then this might indicate the potential to enlarge or link the concept to other properties in a serial and/or transnational nomination.

如果高等级的遗址数量很少，就应考虑扩大遗产范围或将申报遗产与其他遗产联系起来，进行系列申报或跨国申报。

For extensions, specific attention is paid to the comparative analysis included in the original nomination dossier — how the proposed extension compares with the original nomination, and how the values of the original nomination are articulated in the proposed extension.

对于扩展遗产，应该特别关注原始申遗文本中的比较分析——如何将扩展的申报项目与原始申报项目比较，扩展项目与原始申报项目的价值存在怎样的关联性。

In conclusion, some key principles to be considered in preparing a comparative analysis are:

- The analysis should be as rigorous and objective as possible, and should always maintain a broad scope, keeping aside issues of national pride which could distort the objectivity of the analysis (e.g. 'this is the best heritage property in the country');
- It should be supported by the best scientific information available both at the national and international levels. Grey literature, such as unpublished reports and management documents, can be used as long as copies of the articles and publications are referenced in the nomination dossier;
- Thematic studies should be referred to where they exist, but as background context for the development of a full analysis. Relevant thematic studies cannot be ignored;
- Global assessments on conservation priorities for natural properties are very useful and can provide valuable information on the importance of a property (such as, for natural properties, *Conservation International's Biodiversity Hot spots* or *WWF's 200 Ecoregions*). However, they have not been specifically prepared to respond to the

总之，在准备比较分析时应牢记如下核心准则：

- 分析应该尽可能的严谨和客观，应该具有较宽的范围，避免因为国家自豪感而扰乱分析的客观性。（例如，“这是我们国家最好的遗产”）；
- 比较分析应得到国内或国际上最好的科研信息支撑。灰色文献如没有公开发表的报告和管理文件，只能作为申遗文本引用的文章和出版物的副本使用；
- 现有专题研究可作为比较分析的背景文件，应注明出处，不能忽略相关的专题研究成果。
- 自然遗产的优先保护排序对全球性评估遗产十分有用，能为遗产的重要性分析提供有用的信息（例如，自然遗产、《国际生物多样性保护热点》或世界自然基金会的《全球200个生物区》）。然而，这些信息并不是专门为分析潜在突出普遍价值而准备。为了准备比较分析，建议优先使用全球性的评估，以确定该遗产等

question of potential Outstanding Universal Value. For the purpose of preparing a comparative analysis it is recommended to give priority to the use of global assessments that can assist in defining how unique a property is at the global level; and

级及其在全球的独特性；

• When the first draft of the comparative analysis is completed, it is highly recommended to share it with other leading national and international experts to obtain additional information and feedback, and to verify its findings. The Advisory Bodies can provide advice, on request from States Parties, on key leading experts that could provide relevant input or a peer review. The first draft should be identified as a milestone in the overall nomination process.

• 比较分析的初稿完成后，建议征求其他国内、国际一流专家意见，从而获得更多的信息和反馈，并对信息和反馈进行查证。咨询机构在缔约国的要求下，推荐核心专家提供相关的信息或同行之间的评议。初稿的完成应该被认为是整个遗产申报过程的一个里程碑。

The comparative analysis is often a weak component of nominations, and this jeopardizes the success of the nomination. Common problems include:

比较分析常常是遗产申报过程中最弱的一环，且会影响遗产申报成功。问题出在以下几点：

• lack of objectivity in the analysis;

• 缺乏客观的分析；

• not making a determined effort to look for comparable properties beyond the same geo-cultural area (cultural property) or globally (natural property);

• 在寻找相同地理文化圈（文化遗产）或全球遗产（自然遗产）的比较对象时没有全力以赴；

• only using the World Heritage List and Tentative Lists as a source of information about comparable properties;

• 仅将《世界遗产名录》和《预备名录》上的遗产作为比较对象；

• comparing the nominated property with obviously less important properties to increase the apparent importance of the nominated property;

• 以为用重要性较弱的遗产与申报遗产进行比较，能提升申报遗产的重要性；

• comparing the nominated property with listed properties that are entirely different; and

• 用已列入名录但类型完全不同的遗产与申报遗产进行比较；

• basing the analysis on less important aspects of properties or irrelevant attributes, rather than on the potential Outstanding Universal Value and the specific related attributes.

• 以遗产非重要组成部分或关联性不大的属性为基础进行比较分析，而不是以潜在突出普遍价值和与之紧密相关的属性进行分析。

If the results of the comparative analysis are not robust and convincing, the intention to nominate a property should be reconsidered.

如果比较分析的结果不充分也不令人信服，就应该重新考虑该遗产的申报。

Case study

Preparation of a detailed thematic analysis by a State Party

Thematic research can make a vital contribution to a comparative analysis. For references to thematic studies see Section 1.1 of this manual.

While thematic studies are prepared by ICOMOS, a State Party might prepare a thematic analysis which is thorough and more detailed than usual, specifically to assist with the nomination of a particular property. Examples of this are:

• a thematic study of pastoralism around the Mediterranean was prepared by France following workshops involving other countries;

• Sacri Monti of Piedmont and Lombardy (Italy) — a comprehensive thematic study was prepared at the time of its inscription;

• the nomination of Liverpool — Maritime Mercantile City (United Kingdom) included a comparative study which was effectively a thematic study (see below);

• the nomination of Le Morne Cultural Landscape (Mauritius) also included a thematic analysis relating to resistance to slavery;

• and the nomination for the Protective town of San Miguel and the Sanctuary of Jesús Nazareno de Atotonilco (Mexico) included a comparative analysis which was effectively a thematic study on colonial towns in Latin America and the Caribbean, and suggests a regionally relevant framework.

案例分析

缔约国准备详细的专题分析

进行比较分析时，专题研究的作用很重要。相关的专题研究参考资料见 1.1.

相比国际古迹遗址理事会进行的专题研究，申报国准备的专题分析通常更全面更细致，特别有助于特殊遗产的申报。例如：

• 法国在与其他国家召开研讨会之后进行了关于地中海地区畜牧业的专题研究；

• 在开始皮尔蒙蒂和伦巴第圣山（意大利）申请列入遗产名录时，进行了全面的专题研究；

• 利物浦申报世界遗产时对海运商城（英国）专题研究中包括了有效的比较研究（见下文）：

• 莫纳山文化景观遗产申报（毛里求斯）包括与抵抗奴隶制相关的主题分析；

• 申报圣米格尔防卫城镇和纳萨雷诺德阿托托尼尔科耶稣教堂（墨西哥）遗产时，比较分析包括在拉丁美洲和加勒比海殖民城市的专题研究，并提出了一个相关区域框架。

Comparative analysis

Liverpool — Maritime Mercantile City (United Kingdom)

The comparative analysis for this property is a

比较分析

利物浦——海运商城（英国）

这个遗产的比较分析是一个好的案例，原

good example because it:

• describes the important theme within which the property needs to be assessed, that is as a port in the British Empire, and also as a European port of emigration;

• begins with a comparison with other ports in the UK, and considers the attributes relevant to the claims for potential Outstanding Universal Value such as size, tonnage, the nature and period of the shipping operations and infrastructure, and economic relationship to the host city. Issues of authenticity and integrity are an important part of these comparisons;

• examines comparable ports in Europe and other iconic ports to support the claim for Liverpool. Again, these ports are considered in terms of the relevant potential Outstanding Universal Value as well as issues of integrity and authenticity; and

• considers existing World Heritage sites, including both those which are specifically listed as ports and those which incidentally include ports, again looking at relevant Outstanding Universal Value.

The conclusion in the nomination dossier reads,

'Internationally, no other major port was so solely focused on trade and commerce, and no other port expressed the wealth, ambition and power of the British Empire, or any other empire, like Liverpool. Ports on the World Heritage List tend to be older or longer-lived than Liverpool, but none currently captures the values and historical significance expressed by Liverpool's urban landscape. As it did in the 18th, 19th and early 20th centuries, Liverpool still stands apart from all other comparable ports. Especially in the degree of survival of its port infrastructure and historic urban landscape.'

因如下：

• 表述了遗产需要评估的重要内容，它作为大英帝国的海港，也是欧洲国家移民出境的重要港口；

• 分析之初，将之与英国的其他港口进行比较，分析了与潜在突出普遍价值有关的遗产特性如规模、吨位，自然环境和各个历史时期船只的运营、基础设施及其与主要城市之间的经济关系。真实性和完整性也是这些比较分析的重要部分。

• 与欧洲的海港和其他标志性的海港比较，支持利物浦申报的潜在突出普遍价值。另外，在分析海港相关潜在突出普遍价值同时，也分析了其真实性和完整性；

• 与已列入遗产名录的遗产进行比较，包括作为海港列入名录的，以及因包含海港遗产组成部分而列入名录的，对突出普遍价值相关的组成部分进行比较。

申遗文本中比较研究的结论如下：

“在国际上，除外利物浦港，没有其他主要的海港只关注贸易和商业，也没有其他海港能向利物浦港一样展现了大英帝国或其他帝国的财富、抱负和权利。《世界遗产名录》中有的海港比利物浦更古老的，使用时间更长，但是没能超出利物浦从城市景观角度表达的价值和历史重要性。从 18 到 20 世纪，利物浦与其他海港相比始终鹤立鸡群，特别是它保留的海港设施和城镇历史景观。”

Miguasha National Park (Canada)

For natural properties of geological significance the most comprehensive comparative analysis so far undertaken is that for Miguasha Park in Canada, a fossil site of Devonian age. The innovative, science based methodology used is regarded by IUCN as a model approach worthy of wider adoption and adaptation in the process of evaluating natural sites. A threefold method was used, as follows:

• Establish assessment criteria: The basis for identifying the criteria was the checklist of ten questions developed by IUCN for evaluating the palaeontological significance of fossil sites, together with the nine recommended criteria of Wells (1996) for establishing the World Heritage standing of a fossil site.

• Select key sites to be evaluated: From bibliographic research and consultation with other experts, a total group of sixty-one Devonian vertebrate fossil sites was selected from throughout the world. This total was then reduced to fifteen sites by eliminating all sites that failed to meet at least one of five qualifying standards in terms of their fossil context.

• Conduct score-based assessment: the fifteen chosen sites were each assessed against the criteria, using a scoring system that awarded either an arbitrary score or an absolute score based on actual numbers of fossil elements.

米瓜莎国家公园（加拿大）

迄今为止最全面的比较分析是具有地质重要性的自然遗产米瓜莎国家遗址公园——泥盆纪时代的化石遗址。世界自然保护联盟认为其创新的、基于科学的、评估自然遗产的方法，值得借鉴和推广。它使用了三重证据法：

• 建立评估标准：以世界自然保护联盟提出的、有关自然遗产认定的。作为评估具有化石遗址的古生物学重要性的 10 大问题、结合威尔斯认定世界遗产化石遗产应具备的 9 个标准，进行评估；

• 选择重要遗址进行评估；经过研究书目和咨询其他专家意见，在全球范围内选择了 61 个泥盆纪脊椎动物遗址比较名单，然后从中删除无法符合 5 条标准至少之一条的遗址，最终仅剩余 15 个遗址；

• 进行评估，评出分值：依据标准，利用评分系统对 15 个遗址进行分别评估，评分系统根据化石元素的实际数量评出任意分值或绝对分值。

Key message: A draft Statement of OUV should be clear before work on the rest of the nomination starts.

关键信息：编制申遗文本前，应完成突出普遍价值声明草案

Writing a Statement of Outstanding Universal Value

编写突出普遍价值声明

It is highly recommended that a robust and rigorous Statement of Outstanding Universal Value

首先提醒，在编制申遗文本之前，应先完成编写有效而严谨的突出普遍价值声明的工作。

to be prepared well in advance of the process of actually writing the nomination dossier. Successful nominations require such a statement. If a clear and compelling statement cannot be developed, it may be that the property is a questionable candidate for World Heritage inscription, and that the proposed nomination should be reconsidered.

一个成功的申报过程需要这样的声明。如果没有清晰和完整的声明，遗产可能就成为有问题的候选者，那么就应该重新审视这个申报遗产。

The various parts of the nomination process discussed above are intended to help arrive at the point where the relevant World Heritage criteria can be confirmed and a Statement of Outstanding Universal Value can be prepared. To summarize:

- potential Outstanding Universal Value should have been defined, and the features and attributes that convey it are identified;
- appropriate World Heritage criteria should have been selected based on the understanding of potential Outstanding Universal Value;
- if appropriate, the question of whether the property is a serial nomination should have been answered, and the selection of the components should have been justified based on the potential Outstanding Universal Value;
- authenticity and integrity should have been assessed and described; and
- a thorough and objective comparative analysis should have been completed.

以上我们所提及的各部分内容都是为了证实申报遗产符合世界遗产的哪条标准，我们可以在此基础上准备突出普遍价值声明。总结如下：

- 潜在的突出普遍价及承载这些价值值特性或属性应该已经确定；
- 理解遗产的潜在突出普遍价值，选定适当的世界遗产标准；
- 如果标准适当，则确定该遗产是否需要申报系列遗产，所选出来的遗产组成部分均符合潜在突出普遍价值的检验标准；
- 已完成了真实性和完整性的评估和描述；
- 已经完成全面而客观的比较分析。

Using this body of information, a check should be made that the proposed criteria are still appropriate for the property. Again, make sure that the chosen criteria are well supported by strong evidence and sound argument.

运用上面的信息时，需要核实该遗产采用的标准是否适合，是否有强有力的证据和合理的讨论支撑。

This information should also be used to write a Statement of Outstanding Universal Value. Writing the statement may lead to some reconsideration of the criteria to be used. This should be accepted as part of the normal refinement process for the

这些信息同样要用于编写突出普遍价值声明。撰写突出普遍价值时会再次核对使用标准。这是完成申报的一个常规精炼的过程。

development of the nomination.

A Statement of Outstanding Universal Value should respect the following format (two A4 pages maximum, see annex 10 of *The Operational Guidelines*) :

突出普遍价值声明最好按以下形式提供（最多 A4 纸 2 页，见《操作指南》的附件 10）：

• Brief synthesis:

• 概述：

- Summary of factual information (what the property consists of, and the geographical and historical context, 150 words maximum);

——概括性的描述遗产信息（遗产构成，地理位置和历史背景，150 个字）；

- Summary of qualities (values, attributes, 150 words maximum);

——概括遗产品质（价值，属性，150 个字）；

• Justification for criteria (values and attributes which manifest them, and why the property justifies each proposed criterion, 200 words maximum for each criterion);

• 陈述采用的标准（如何体现价值和属性，以及遗产为什么能够符合选定的标准，每一条标准最多 200 字）；

• Statement of integrity (all properties) at the date of drafting/inscription (the way the attributes or features of the property that convey potential Outstanding Universal Value may be said to be all in place and within the boundaries of the property, 200 words maximum);

• 完整性声明起草或发布的日期（所有遗产）（所有能表达潜在突出普遍价值的属性和特性应该都在遗产区的范围内，最多 200 字）；

• Statement of authenticity (the statement is only needed for properties nominated under criteria i-vi) at the date of drafting/inscription (whether the attributes that carry potential Outstanding Universal Value truthfully reflect the value, 200 words maximum);

• 真实性声明起草或发布日期（本声明只有在运用标准 1–6 时才需提供，承载潜在突出普遍价值的属性是否真实的反映遗产价值，最多 200 字）

• Requirements for protection and management necessary to maintain potential Outstanding Universal Value (how the protection and management arrangements, both systems and plans, are robust enough to carry forward the protection and management of the property in a way that sustains potential Outstanding Universal Value) (protection and management are discussed below) :

• 对维持潜在突出普遍价值的保护和管理要求（保护和管理是如何安排的，维持潜在突出普遍价值的保护和管理体系和规划是否足够严谨）（保护和管理将在下文进行细致讨论）：

— Overall framework (200 words maximum);

——工作的整体框架（最多 200 字）；

—Specific long-term expectations — the key issues that require long-term attention (for

——对未来的展望——需要长期关注的核心问题（例如，主要威胁因素，能力和资金维

example protection from key threats, maintenance of capacity and finance, maintenance of community support, 150 words maximum).

护，社区支持的维持，最多 150 个字）。

Key message: Actively review the draft Statement of OUV throughout the process.

关键信息：在整个过程中主动回顾突出普遍价值声明

In the case of statements prepared retrospectively for pre-2007 inscriptions, slightly different guidance is appropriate. The integrity and authenticity components should reflect the situation at the time of inscription, if such information is available.

对于准备编写 2007 年以前列入名录遗产的声明，与我们上面所提到的表述形式略有不同。如果要提供完整性和真实性组成部分信息时，应该反映遗产列入名录时的情况。

The Statement of Outstanding Universal Value is one of the most difficult and important tasks in writing a good nomination and it requires careful consideration. The statement should be:

- a powerful description of the potential Outstanding Universal Value to inform future protection, conservation, management and monitoring. The statement should be capable of explaining the property's value and attributes to decision-makers, politicians and the general public;
- the strongest statement of value that can be made for the property, and a description of the attributes that convey the value;
- a robust justification of the chosen criteria;
- concise — sufficient to convey information about the most important features of the property; and
- written to engage a wide range of people, and if possible avoid jargon and specialized language.

编写优秀的突出普遍价值声明是申遗文本最重要也是最困难的一个步骤，需要仔细考量。突出普遍价值声明应该具有以下特点：

- 权威性描述突出普遍价值，说明将来需要的保存、保护、管理和监测。声明应该能够向决策者，官员和普通民众解释遗产的价值和属性；
- 是针对遗产价值最有力的声明，以及对传达该价值的属性的描述；
- 有力的证明所选择的世界遗产标准；
- 简明而充分的传达有关遗产重要特性的信息；
- 为广泛人群编写，如果可能的话尽量避免术语和专业语言。

The work of developing the Statement of Outstanding Universal Value can also establish a shared understanding among all those involved in the nomination process about the potential value of the property. This statement also underpins all sections of the nomination dossier — the description, justification, conservation, protection,

突出普遍价值声明的编写工作也让参与遗产申报过程的工作人员能够全面的了解遗产的价值。这个价值声明同样是申遗文本相关描述、理由、阐释、保护、保存、管理和监测等其他部分的基础。

management and monitoring.

After the statement has been drafted, stakeholders and relevant experts should be consulted and their comments sought on the statement. The aim is to get widespread agreement to the statement. It may be necessary to allow a period of consultation to ensure this agreement.

当突出普遍价值声明草案完成后，利益相关者和专家应该进行进一步的探讨，征求意见并加以完善。这样做的目的是为了能让更多人赞同声明。开展的咨询活动应有一定的延续时间，从而确保得到更多人的认可。

While the statement might be reasonably final at this point, except for the parts on protection and management, further work on the nomination and other consultations might lead to useful revisions. This is quite normal and should be accepted as part of the process of developing a robust statement.

在这个时候，除了保存和管理的部分，声明基本完成，进一步的申报工作和其他咨询工作对完善声明很有益处。这些都应该作为编写严谨声明的重要组成部分。

In the case of new serial nominations, the Statement should address the standard requirements, noted above, for the property as a whole. Summary information relevant to the whole property should be provided, where possible, rather than essentially similar information for each of the components of the serial. Nonetheless, there may also be reasons to note exceptions or specific key information relevant to one or only a few components.

对于新的系列遗产申报，声明应该到达上面我们所说的标准要求。应提供与整个遗产群相关的概要信息，而不是系列遗产每个组成部分的描述信息。尽管如此，仍然允许描述一个或多个组成部分的具体或特殊信息。

Where a component is proposed for addition to an existing inscribed serial property, an existing Statement of Outstanding Universal Value may be adequate to encompass the addition without change, or minor change may be needed to reflect the additional component. Where a minor change is required or no statement exists, this should be revised/prepared in accordance with the requirements of the World Heritage Committee. Guidance on the preparation of retrospective Statements of Outstanding Universal Value have also been prepared by the World Heritage Centre and the Advisory Bodies to guide this process. In either case, the statement should reflect significant

对于准备将某处遗产扩展到已列入名录的系列遗产，原有的突出普遍价值声明已包含了新增遗产部分，不需要另作修改，或仅做微调以反映新添遗产的价值。如果有细微的修改或者该遗产没有突出普遍价值声明，应根据世界遗产委员会的各项要求做出相应的修改。世界遗产中心和咨询团队将指导及审核准备突出普遍价值声明的过程。无论如何，声明应该反映新属性的重要性而不是提出新的价值，价值仍然是世界遗产委员会先前通过的价值，不得改变。如果拟增加新的、不同的价值，那就必须准备新的申报程序（《操作指南》，166 段）。

new attributes but not new values. The values must be those previously agreed by the World Heritage Committee. In the case of proposed additional or different values, a new nomination must be prepared (*Operational Guidelines*, Paragraph 166).

In the case of an extension to an existing property, either the existing Statement of Outstanding Universal Value for the original property will be revised to reflect significant new attributes, but not new values, or a new statement will be prepared for the whole property.

扩展遗产时，应重新修正遗产的原突出普遍价值声明，以反映新组成部分的重要性，但不是增添新价值，也不是为整个遗产编写一个新的声明。

Case Study

Statement of Outstanding Universal Value Chief Roi Mata's Domain (Vanuatu)

案例

马塔王酋长领地（瓦努阿图）突出普遍价值声明

The continuing cultural landscape of Chief Roi Mata's Domain, Vanuatu, has Outstanding Universal Value as an example of a landscape representative of Pacific chiefly systems. This is reflected in the interaction of people with their environment over time in respecting the tangible remains associated with Roi Mata and being guided by the spiritual and moral legacy of his social reforms. The landscape reflects continuing Pacific chiefly systems and respect for this authority through tabu prohibitions on use of Roi Mata's residence and burial that have been observed for over 400 years and structured the local landscape and social practices. The landscape memorializes the deeds of Roi Mata who still lives for many people in contemporary Vanuatu as a source of power and inspiration.

瓦努阿图国的持续文化景观，作为太平洋主要系统景观的代表，具有突出的普遍价值。通过保留在领地上的有形遗存，景观反映了在与环境之间的互动关系中，人们尊重与马塔王酋长相关联的有形遗存，并受到其社会改革的精神和道德遗产的引导。此处景观反映出持续存在的太平洋首领制度，特别是马塔居民通过禁止使用马塔王的住处和墓地等宗教限制的方式，表示对其所有权利的尊重，这种禁忌已有400多年的历史，构成了当地的景观和社会习俗。景观纪念了马塔王酋长的功绩，作为力量和精神的象征，他始终活在当代瓦努阿图人们的心中。

Criterion (iii) : Chief Roi Mata's Domain is a continuing cultural landscape reflecting the way chiefs derive their authority from previous title holders, and in particular how the tabu prohibitions on the use of Roi Mata's residence and burial site have been observed for 400 years and continue to

标准（3）：马塔王酋长领地是反映历任酋长在继位后，如何延续他们权威的文化景观，特别是马塔居民如何通过宗教禁忌保护已保存了400多年的马塔王住处和墓地不被打扰，尊重当地景观和社会习俗。

structure the local landscape and social practices.

Criterion (v) : Chief Roi Mata's Domain is an outstanding example of a landscape representative of Pacific chiefly systems and the connection between Pacific people and their environment over time reflected in respect for the tangible remains of the three key sites associated with Roi Mata, guided by the spiritual and moral legacy of his social reforms.

标准（5）：马塔王酋长领地是代表太平洋主要系统景观的杰出代表，也是反映太平洋居民和他们生存环境之间关系的典型代表。随着时间的推移，这种联系反映在尊重与马塔王有关的三个关键遗址上及尊重马塔王社会改革所带来的精神和道德遗产的影响上。

Criterion (vi) : Chief Roi Mata's Domain still lives for many people in contemporary Vanuatu, as a source of power evident through the landscape and as an inspiration for people negotiating their lives.

标准（6）：马塔王酋长作为一种力量和精神的象征活在当代瓦努阿图居民的心中，影响着当代人的生活。

The authenticity of Chief Roi Mata's Domain lies in the continuing association of the landscape with the oral traditions of Roi Mata, continuity of chiefly systems of authority and customary respect for the tangible remains of his life evident in the continuing tabu prohibitions on these places.

马塔王酋长领地的真实性表现在与景观和马塔王相关地口头传说、首领权利制度的延续性、当地长期存在的宗教禁忌、保存有形遗产、尊重传统习俗中。

The legal protection of the nominated areas and their buffer zones are adequate. The overall management system for the property is adequate, involving both traditional management through the chiefly system and tabu prohibitions and government legislation for protection of the site. The management system involves the local community and government administrative bodies. The integrity of the site is thus maintained.

遗产区和缓冲区有充足合法的保护体系。整个系统的管理工作适当，包括首领制度的传统管理，也包括宗教禁忌和当地政府的法制管理。管理体系中包括了当地社区和政府管理机构。遗产的完整性得以维持。

Jeju Volcanic Island and Lava Tubes (Republic of Korea)

济州火山岛和熔岩洞（韩国）

Jeju Volcanic Island and Lava Tubes is a coherent serial property comprising three components. The unequalled quality of the Geomunoreum lava tube

济州火山岛和熔岩柱是相关的系列遗产，由 3 个部分组成。无可比拟的龙头岩溶洞系统，及其他两处火山展现的多样性和可接近性等特

system and the exhibition of diverse and accessible volcanic features in the other two components demonstrate a distinctive and important contribution to the understanding of global volcanism.

性，对理解全球火山系统有重要作用。

Criterion (vii) : The Geomunoreum lava tube system, which is regarded as the finest such cave system in the world, has an outstanding visual impact even for those experienced with such phenomena. It displays the unique spectacle of multi-coloured carbonate decorations adorning the roofs and floors, and dark-coloured lava walls, partially covered by a mural of carbonate deposits. The fortress-like Seongsan Ilchulbong tuff cone, with its walls rising out of the ocean, is a dramatic landscape feature, and Mount Halla, with its array of textures and colours through the changing seasons, waterfalls, display of multi-shaped rock formations and columnar-jointed cliffs, and the towering summit with its lake-filled crater, further adds to the scenic and aesthetic appeal.

标准（7）：被认为是世界上最好的龙头岩溶洞系统，即便是对已参观过此类景观的人员也会产生极强的视觉影响。它展示了由五颜六色碳酸盐岩柱装饰的溶洞洞顶和地面，碳酸盐沉积物覆盖在黑色熔岩墙壁形成独一无二的奇特图案。成山日出峰的凝灰锥如坚实堡垒一般的峭壁，从海底升出，是不可思议的景观特征，汉拿山随季节变化的纹理和色彩、瀑布、千姿百态的岩石造型和竹节状的悬崖，以及火山口的湖泊，高耸的峰顶，更加增添风景的美感。

Criterion (viii) : Jeju has a distinctive value as one of the few large shield volcanoes in the world built over a hot spot on a stationary continental crust plate. It is distinguished by the Geomunoreum lava tube system, which is the most impressive and significant series of protected lava tube caves in the world and includes a spectacular array of secondary carbonate speleothems (stalactites and other decorations), with an abundance and diversity unknown elsewhere thin a lava cave. The Seongsan Ilchulbong tuff cone has exceptional exposures of its structural and sedimentological characteristics, making it a world-class location for understanding surtseyan-type volcanic eruptions.

标准（8）：济州岛具有更为显著的价值，它作为世界上少有的面积较大的盾状火山，是在大陆板块上形成的热点。它杰出的令人永生难忘的龙头岩熔岩系统，包括了一系列壮观的次生碳酸盐钟乳石（钟乳石和其他装饰品），多样的熔岩洞，在其他区域难得一见。成山日出峰的凝灰锥具有特殊的结构和独特的沉积岩特征，成为研究舒赛岩型火山喷发的最佳地点。

The property is well managed and resourced, with a management plan in place for the period 2006-2010 and resources for its implementation.

在 2006–2010 的保护管理规划的指导下，对遗产实施了有序的管理，并有充足的资金支持。管理的核心议题包括避免农业对地下环境

Key management issues include avoiding potential agricultural impact on the underground environment and managing the high number of visitors to the property. There is potential for further extension of the property to include other significant lava tube systems and volcanic features of Jeju.

的潜在影响，以及管理高密度的游客。此遗产范围可能会扩大，包括其他重要的熔岩洞窟群和展现济州岛火山特性的景观。

Serial nominations

系列申报遗产

Serial nominations involve two or more separate component parts, which together are of potential Outstanding Universal Value (see definitions in Section 1.3 of this manual).

系列申报包括两个或多个独立的组成部分，这些组成部分整体，具有潜在的突出普遍价值（见 1.3 定义部分）。

In the case of a serial nomination, the potential Outstanding Universal Value of the series of components is fundamental and must be justified. In addition, there must be a very clear rationale for the selection of the components, and this rationale must be based on the potential Outstanding Universal Value and the attributes and features that the components demonstrate.

对于系列遗产，系列组成部分的潜在的突出普遍价值是基础，需要逐步证明。此外，选择组成部分应确定清晰的准则，该准则必须符合组成部分所表达的、潜在的突出普遍价值和属性或特征。

The comparative analysis must justify the selection of the components, as well as demonstrate that the series as a whole is of potential Outstanding Universal Value.

比较分析必须要证实选择的组成部分的合理性，同时要证明系列遗产整体具有潜在的突出普遍价值。

Components which are not strongly or clearly related to the potential Outstanding Universal Value of the nominated property should not be included.

与潜在的突出普遍价值关系不大或不够清晰的组成部分，不应该包括在系列申报遗产中。

In principle, all components of a potential serial nomination should be indicated in the nomination dossier, even if only the first component/s is/are being nominated at this time. *The Operational Guidelines* permit the initial nomination of part of a series, with other components to be added at a later time (Paragraphs 137-39). The other intended components of the series should be clearly indicated

基本上，系列申报的所有要素都应该在申遗文本中有所涉及，即便本次只申报一个要素。《操作指南》允许初次只申报系列遗产的一部分，遗产的其他组成部分在后期逐步增加（137–139 段）。其他可能加入系列遗产的组成部分应在申遗文本中说明和清晰表述。

and described.

Information should be provided about whether the separate components of the property are functionally linked, and if there is an overall management framework for all components.

同时要提供遗产各部分相关信息，说明他们是否具有功能上的关联性，以及遗产的各个组成部分是否都在整体保护管理框架内。

An important principle in relation to serial nominations is that they are evaluated against the same set of criteria, requirements for integrity, authenticity and management as are all other nominations. They also have the same requirements for geo-cultural area/global comparative analysis in establishing the basis for inscription.

对于系列遗产而言，最重要的一个原则就是他们都是以同一套遗产标准以及相同的真实性，完整性和管理要求进行评估。在确定申报遗产的基础时，要求采用同样的地理文化区域或全球背景的比较分析。

A further important principle is that any serial nomination represents a single nomination to the World Heritage List. Thus the serial sites are inscribed as a single property, and are treated accordingly. If the values of one part of a serial property are threatened such that it is proposed to be placed on the List of World Heritage in Danger, the entire property is inscribed on the List of World Heritage in Danger. This applies to all serial properties including those which are only in one country as well as transnational properties.

另一个重要的准则就是：任何一个系列申报遗产在《世界遗产名录》中仅作为一个遗产。也就是说系列遗址被看作单个遗产申报，也按单个遗产对待。如果系列遗产一个组成部分的价值受到威胁，那么将拖累整个系列遗产全部被列入濒危遗产名录。这条准则适用于全部的系列遗产，无论它位于一个国家境内还是跨国系列遗产。

A useful reference on serial properties is *Nominations and Management of Serial Natural World Heritage Properties — Present Situation, Challenges and Opportunities (Engels et al., 2009).*

对系列遗产申报有帮助的参考文献是“自然世界遗产系列申报和管理——现状、挑战和机遇”（Engels 等，2009 年）

Case Study

Serial site — Melaka and George Town, Historic Cities of the Straits of Malacca (Malaysia)

案例（3 图）

系列遗产——马六甲和乔治城，马六甲海峡上的历史城镇（马来西亚）

Melaka and George Town, historic cities of the Straits of Malacca, have developed over 500 years of trading and cultural exchanges between East and West in the Straits of Malacca. The

马六甲和乔治城，马六甲海峡上的历史城镇，见证马六甲海峡 500 年来东西方文化和商贸交换。亚洲和欧洲对于这个城市的影响，赋予了城镇具有特殊的多文化融合的特性，这些

influences of Asia and Europe have endowed the towns with a specific multicultural heritage that is both tangible and intangible. With its government buildings, churches, squares and fortifications, Melaka demonstrates the early stages of this history originating in the 15th-century Malay sultanate and the Portuguese and Dutch periods beginning in the early 16th century. Featuring residential and commercial buildings, George Town represents the British era from the end of the 18th century. The two towns constitute a unique architectural and cultural townscape without parallel anywhere in East and Southeast Asia. Inscribed under criteria (ii), (iii) and (iv).

特性通过有形和无形遗产得以展现。马六甲城的政府建筑、教堂、广场、防御工事展现了15世纪以来马来苏丹政权、和16世纪早期葡萄牙统治时期、荷兰统治时期的城市景象。乔治城具有特色的住宅和商铺代表了18世纪晚期大英帝国统治时期的景象。两个城市的独特建筑和文化城市景观在东亚或东南亚绝无仅有。符合标准（2）（3）（4）。

Case study
Serial site - Berlin Modernism Housing Estates (Germany)

The property consists of six housing estates that testify to innovative housing policies from 1910 to 1933, especially during the Weimar Republic, when the city of Berlin was particularly progressive socially, politically and culturally. The property is an outstanding example of the building reform movement that contributed to improving housing and living conditions for people with low incomes through novel approaches to town planning, architecture and garden design. The estates also provide exceptional examples of new urban and architectural typologies, featuring fresh design solutions, as well as technical and aesthetic innovations. Bruno Taut, Martin Wagner and Walter Gropius were among the leading architects of these projects which exercised considerable influence on the development of housing around the world. Inscribed under criteria (ii) and (iv).

案例
系列遗产——柏林现代主义住宅小区（德国）

遗产由六个住宅小区组成，反映1910–1933年特别是在魏玛共和国时期的房屋政策变化，当时柏林市社会、文化和政治发展迅速。遗产是当时建筑改革运动的杰出典范，希望通过在城市规划、建筑和园林设计中采取新的方法，改善低收入人群的居住和生活条件。遗产为新城镇、新建筑形式、新的设计提供了解决方案，同时也是艺术和技术革新的独一无二的例证。布鲁诺·陶特，马丁·瓦格纳和沃尔特·格罗皮乌斯是设计这些项目的著名建筑师，他们的实践活动对全世界住宅建设发展产生了极为深远的影响。符合标准（2）（4）。

Serial site - South China Karst (China)

The South China Karst region extends over a surface of half a million km^2 lying mainly in Yunnan, Guizhou and Guangxi provinces. It represents one of the world's most spectacular examples of humid tropical to subtropical karst landscapes. The stone forests of Shilin are considered superlative natural phenomena and a world reference with a wider range of pinnacle shapes than other karst landscapes with pinnacles, and a higher diversity of shapes and changing colours. The cone and tower karsts of Libo, also considered the world reference site for these types of karst, form a distinctive and beautiful landscape. Wulong Karst has been inscribed for its giant dolines (sinkholes), natural bridges and caves. Inscribed under criteria (vii) and (viii). The map to the right shows only part of the serial property.

系列遗产——中国南方的喀斯特地形（中国）

中国南方喀斯特覆盖了五十万平方公里，主要位于云南省、贵州省和广西壮族自治区，有着多样的喀斯特地形地貌。这个世界遗产目前包含荔波、石林和武隆喀斯特。中国南方喀斯特是湿润的热带至亚热带的喀斯特地貌最壮观的代表。石林喀斯特是世界自然奇观和世界性参照标准。同其他喀斯特地貌相比，石林喀斯特的石峰更加丰富多彩，形状和颜色也更富于变化。荔波喀斯特的特点是锥形和塔形地貌，构成了独特、美丽的风景，同样是同类型喀斯特地貌的世界级标准。武隆喀斯特有天生桥、天坑地缝、落水洞等立体喀斯特景观。符合标准（7）（8）。

Key message: The boundary must encompass the Outstanding Universal Value.

关键信息：边界必须包含突出普遍价值

Establishing a robust boundary encompassing the potential Outstanding Universal Value

准确划定边界，包含潜在突出普遍价值

The boundary proposed for the property must encompass all the attributes and features that convey its potential Outstanding Universal Value. A boundary which includes areas not related to the potential Outstanding Universal Value is not appropriate. On the other hand, excluding areas which do have attributes or features that convey potential Outstanding Universal Value is also a problem.

遗产所划定的边界必须包含能展现突出普遍价值的所有属性和特性。边界不应包含与潜在突出普遍价值无关的区域。另一方面，将能表达潜在突出普遍价值的属性或特性排除在边界外也同样是个问题。

It is important to remember that nominated properties must pass a series of tests. The property must:

- have Outstanding Universal Value;

一定要记住申报遗产要经历一系列的检验，遗产必须：

- 具有突出普遍价值；

• meet the requirements for authenticity and integrity; and

• be protected and well managed.

All these factors influence the boundaries of a property.

The mapping of attributes and features suggested earlier is a useful starting point for working out the appropriate boundaries.

For cultural properties, where a nomination includes a number of important elements, such as the buildings of a historic town, it is sometimes better to nominate a single area or zone for inscription which includes all these components, rather than having a number of isolated components. As always, the rationale for the boundary chosen is important, and in these situations a single nominated area may be quite justifiable.

In some cases, elements or areas of conservation significance might be geographically disconnected and remote from one another, and creating one large boundary is not appropriate. This is a situation where a serial nomination may be more suitable.

In some cases part of the property may not be protected or well managed. If the part of the property is a necessary or essential element of the property, then adequate protection and management must be achieved if the nomination is to succeed. This may require the nomination process to be suspended while such protection and management is negotiated or otherwise developed.

Defining the boundary is a part of conflict management and prevention, and requires stakeholder involvement. This is a critical land-

• 满足真实性和完整性的要求；

• 得到很好的保护和管理。

所有这些因素都对划定遗产的边界产生影响。

在前面我们提到要绘制遗产属性或特性列表，这对划定遗产区的边界十分有益。

对于文化遗产，它的申报包括了许多重要因素，例如历史城镇的建筑群，有时申报成一个包含了诸多组成部分单独的地区或区域，比申报多个不相连的组成部分更容易成功。一般而言，选择边界划定准则十分重要，在这种情况下，申报一个单独区域可能更适合。

有时，具有保护价值的组成部分或区域在地理上可能各不相连甚至相距甚远，保持一个大的遗产边界反而不合适。此时更适合系列申报。

有时遗产的某个部分可能没有得到保护或管理。如果此部分是整体遗产的必要或关键组成部分，那么想要申报成功就必须先给以充分的保护和管理。此时也许要暂停申报进程，先行商讨、重新制定保护和管理方案。

划定遗产边界能预防和控制冲突，需要利益相关者参与。这是与遗产保存、保护和管理相关的、重要的土地使用决策过程，也是利益

use decision relating to the protection, conservation and management of the property, and thus a very important moment for stakeholder involvement and communication.

相关者参与和交流的重要时刻。

There should be an explicit rationale or explanation for the chosen boundary, and this should be included in the integrity section of the nomination dossier.

在划定边界时应有明确的理由或解释，应该是申遗文本中完整性章节的一部分。

In summary:

概括如下：

• the property boundaries must encompass the attributes necessary to meet the condition of integrity, that is a complete and intact set of attributes that convey potential Outstanding Universal Value;

• 遗产边界必须要包含能够证明完整性的所有属性，它应该包括一系列全面、完整的属性并能够表达遗产的潜在突出普遍价值；

• boundaries must be logical and defensible in relation to the identification of attributes that convey the value of the property;

• 边界必须能逻辑、辩证地表达遗产价值的各种相关属性；

• boundaries must be clearly defined in relation to the legal protection and management of the property;

• 边界必须以对遗产的法律保护和管理清晰的界定为根据；

• boundaries should be readily identifiable if they are to be useful for management. They will often be based on physical features and sometimes on natural features. Effective boundaries may also be based on human-made features such as roads, which may often be critical features in relation to management. However, more care is needed with using such features to ensure that the area enclosed meets the condition of integrity;

• 边界应该容易辨识，利于开展管理工作。边界常常以遗产的物质特性或自然特性为基础划定。有效的边界有时也可以是人为的特征物，比如道路，它可能是与管理相关的关键节点。然而，在使用人为设施作为界限时应该确定这个区域符合了完整性的条件；

• good-quality mapping of boundaries is essential; and

• 高质量的地图是划定边界的基础；

• it is also essential that the establishment of boundaries (including zoning schemes) within a nominated property is carried out in conjunction with defining the management priorities and requirements for the property, and with effective stakeholder engagement. This is to create a strong link between this process and protection, conservation and management.

• 划定申报遗产的边界需要与确定管理优先次序和遗产要求联合起来，并且应有利益相关者参与。划定遗产边界与申报过程、遗产保存、保护和管理有着密切的关联性。

Boundaries

Renaissance Monumental Ensembles of Úbeda and Baeza (Spain)

The property was nominated as parts of two historic towns. In the end, the property was limited to just the Renaissance palaces in both cases. The justification was changed to state that these represented the introduction of Renaissance civic architecture and ideas to Spain, from where these were transferred to Latin America via architectural treatises.

边界

文艺复兴时期的不朽的建筑群——乌贝达和巴埃萨（西班牙）

这个申报遗产包括两个独立的历史城镇。最终，遗产只限定为这两个地区文艺复兴时期的宫殿。列入理由也变为阐释这些宫殿是西班牙文艺复兴时期建筑和理念的代表，并且此建筑形式后来传到拉丁美洲。

Historic Centre of Macao (China)

The original nomination was limited to twelve buildings, leaving out some important examples in the belief that it was better not to have too many examples. Fortunately, the main street had retained its integrity in a reasonable manner. So it was possible to redefine the property including the street and the principal urban squares with relevant buildings.

澳门历史中心（中国）

最初的申报仅限于12座建筑，当初认为包含太多范例不好，而将一些重要范例排除。幸运的是，通过合理的方法保持了主要街道完整性。因此，重新界定的遗产就包括了街道、主要的城区广场以及相关建筑。

Bam and its Cultural Landscape (Islamic Republic of Iran)

The original serial nomination essentially proposed only the citadel and some ruined listed buildings. Following consultations, the character of the nomination changed from a serial nomination to a cultural landscape. This was because it had become clear that the water management system and the oasis lifestyle were of great importance.

巴姆古城和文化景观（伊朗）

原先的系列申报包含了古城堡和一些损坏的建筑。在召开咨询会议时，改系列申报为文化景观申报。因为在研究的过程中，他们确认了水资源的管理体系和绿洲的生活方式才是最为重要的。

Centennial Hall in Wroclaw (Poland)

The original nomination was for the Centennial Hall building and nothing else. However, as a result of an ICOMOS mission, it was agreed that

弗罗茨瓦百年厅（波兰）

最初申报只是百年厅的建筑。然而国际古迹遗址理事会代表现场考察后，建议将与弗罗茨瓦百年厅同期规划的展示区域纳入申报范围。

the exhibition zone which had been planned at the same time with the Centennial Hall should also be included. The buffer zone was also extended to provide more protection to the whole area.

缓冲区也相应扩大以提供更多的保护。

Soltaniyeh (Islamic Republic of Iran)

The original proposal included the mausoleum, the surrounding vernacular village and some minor religious or funeral monuments. As a result of the evaluation, the boundaries were redesigned limiting the property to the mausoleum and the archaeological remains of the small citadel. The rest of the village with the monuments was included as the buffer zone. Surrounding this, there is also a landscape protection area which covers the grassland, one of the reasons why the Ilkhanid Mongols once built their capital in this location.

苏丹尼叶城（伊朗）

最初的申报遗产包括了陵墓，周边村落和一些小的宗教或殡葬纪念地。评估后重新划定边界，仅限定陵墓和周边小城堡等考古遗存。村落其他部分放到了缓冲区内。周边还设立草原景观保护区，解释了蒙古伊卡哈尼德人建都于此的原因。

Pitons, cirques and remparts of Reunion Island (France)

The original nomination included a range of settled areas and did not include all of the most important areas of endemic vegetation of this island environment. A revised nomination rationalized the boundary to link with a newly created National Park, while establishing effective buffer zone arrangements to include adjoining areas of settlement. The result is a site that both includes the most important areas of natural landscape on the Island, and is clearly linked to the protection and management that has been established, thus ensuring effective conservation.

留尼汪岛上的双峰山、冰斗及山脊盆地（法国）

最早的申报仅包括一些定居地区，却没有包括能够展现岛屿环境的特有植被。修改后申报的遗产边界与新创建的国家公园联系起来，同时将附近区域的居住点纳入缓冲区进行有效管理。调整的结果是这个遗址即包括岛屿上重要的自然景观区，也与已确立的保护管理相关联，以确保有效保护。

The Dolomites (Italy)

An initial nomination of the Dolomites comprised a serial nomination of twenty-seven component parts which was deferred, and the

多洛米蒂山区（意大利）

最初申报的多洛米蒂山区包括了由 27 个组成部分构成的系列遗产，这个项目被推迟待议，建议缔约国重新整合遗产，只保留了能体现景

State Party was advised to refocus the nomination with a reduced number of components to convey the landscape and aesthetic values of the area at a landscape scale. A revised series including nine component parts was prepared supported by a clear comparative analysis, and was inscribed on the World Heritage List in 2009.

观和景观审美价值的部分。重新进行的系列申报，经过仔细的比较分析后，确定了9个组成部分，这个遗产在2009年列入遗产名录。

Buffer zones

缓冲区

Every World Heritage property needs protection and management arrangements for activities outside the property, including their immediate setting. Buffer zones are one commonly used means to achieve this protection, conservation and management. However a buffer zone is not always a requirement if, as outlined in *The Operational Guidelines*, there are also legal, regulatory and other methods available to protect the property from wider threats (Paragraph 104). These may include recognition in land-use plans or development regulations, or ensuring landscape level connectivity between protected areas. Countries may have different mechanisms in this regard.

每一个世界遗产都需要有对遗产区外的活动进行保护和管理的安排，包括遗产周边的环境。缓冲区是非常普遍的一种遗产保存、保护和管理方法。但在《操作指南》要求中，如果通过法律、法规或其他措施保护遗产不受外来威胁的侵害（104段），缓冲区并不是必备条件。这些措施包括已公布的土地使用规划或发展规划，或确保保护区景观的连续性。不同的国家有不同的保护机制。

It should be clearly understood that the buffer zone does not form part of the World Heritage property but is there to assist in its protection, conservation and management. Buffer zones in protecting the immediate setting of a property can thus contribute to protecting authenticity and integrity. For example, this might be the case for a temple that is aligned to a mountain in the distance, and where that alignment is partly in the buffer zone.

需要清楚地知道缓冲区并不是世界遗产的组成部分，只是协助遗产保存、保护和管理。保护遗产周边的缓冲区能够更好地保护遗产的真实性和完整性。例如，与远处高山结合在一起的寺庙，结合部分就应该是缓冲区的一部分。

While buffer zones are not of Outstanding Universal Value, they are seen as critically related to the protection, conservation and management of the nominated property. Attributes or features that are

虽然，缓冲区不能展现遗产的突出普遍价值，但他们与申报遗产的保存，保护和管理关系密切。能够体现潜在突出普遍价值的属性，或特性应该包括在申报遗产边界内，而不能作

part of the case for potential Outstanding Universal Value should be included within the boundary of the nominated property, and not proposed as part of the buffer zone.

为缓冲区的一部分。

Although a buffer zone is not part of the inscribed World Heritage property, the buffer zone boundaries are formally registered at the time of inscription of a property, or at the time modifications are approved by the World Heritage Committee. The buffer zone is an integral component of the State Party's commitment to the protection, conservation and management of the property. As such any buffer zone should be part of the overall management system for the property, and it should be clear how those responsible for managing the property are also able to provide input to and influence the management of activities in any buffer zone.

尽管缓冲区部分不是世界遗产，但是在遗产列入名录时缓冲区的边界或遗产委员会批准的遗产范围修正也要记录在案。缓冲区是缔约国承诺保存、保护和管理遗产不可分割的组成部分。因此，缓冲区应该是整个遗产管理体系的一部分，同时应明确遗产地管理者有权对缓冲区的管理活动提出意见，施加影响。

The process of defining the buffer zone can be an important opportunity to involve stakeholders in understanding the property and working together for its long-term protection, conservation and management.

确定缓冲区的过程是利益相关者参与理解遗产价值，与管理者一起共同保存、保护和管理遗产的绝佳机会。

Buffer zones may be neutral areas which include no qualities relating to the nominated property. On the other hand they may be areas which include physical and other qualities (e.g. economic, legal, functional, visual or environmental) that support those in the nominated property. They might contain the physical approach to the property, and can play an important role in defining views in and out of the nominated area. Their role can include protection of the wider natural system that supports the property (such as a river catchment), or may relate to the management of visitor pressures or industrial use (such as the inclusion of adjacent roads and car parks that lead

缓冲区既可以是一个与申报遗产特性无关的中性区域，也可以是一个对遗产有实质性支撑作用的（如经济、法律、功能、视觉或环境）区域。他们有通向遗产区的道路，对确定遗产内外的景点起着至关重要的作用。这些作用包括保护支撑遗产价值的更宽泛的生态系统（例如河流流域），或与游客压力或工业利用管理相关（例如邻近遗产区的公路和通向遗产区的停车场）。

to the property).

The features and values of a buffer zone are therefore not included in the assessment of Outstanding Universal Value but may be relevant to the assessment of whether a nominated property meets requirements for integrity, authenticity, protection and management.

在突出普遍价值的评估中不包括缓冲区的价值和特性，但是在评估申报遗产是否符合完整性、真实性、保护和管理要求时，将会涉及缓冲区。

Consideration needs to be given as to whether the immediate setting of the property is understood and can be readily defined, or whether more work is needed to define it.

需要考虑与遗产直接相关的周边环境是否得到了足够的理解、已经认定或是否需要实施更多的研究来认定周边环境。

Issues that can influence the buffer zone boundary include:

• characteristics of the potential Outstanding Universal Value;

• management requirements of the property;

• character of known or foreseeable threats or impacts;

• important views to or from the property;

• existing character of the potential buffer zone;

• ownership, resource use, management and protection (including legislation) within the potential buffer zone.

能够影响缓冲区边界的问题包括：

• 潜在突出普遍价值的特性；

• 遗产管理的需求；

• 已知或可预测特殊威胁或影响因素；

• 遗产周边重要的景点；

• 将要划定的缓冲区已有的特性；

• 将要划定的缓冲区所有者、资源使用、管理和保存（包括法律）。

A

Buffer zones may provide for a range of functions, uses or activities which are different to those within the property.

缓冲区与遗产区的保护要求有所不同，可以具有一系列的功能、用途或开展一系列的活动。

Key message: buffer zone with no protection or formal recognition is not effective.

关键信息：没有保护的和正式认可的缓冲区是无效的

While buffer zones for cultural properties are frequently determined on the basis of visual impact, there can be other bases for or influences on choosing a buffer zone (e.g. acoustic impact and hydrology).

文化遗产的缓冲区经常根据视觉效果来划定，缓冲区的划定还有其他的依据和影响因素（例如，听觉效果和地理水文特征）。

As with the property boundary, there should be an explicit rationale or explanation for the chosen buffer zone boundary, relating to the protection, conservation and management of the property values. This rationale should be provided in the protective designation section of the nomination dossier. The relationship between the function, extent, protection, conservation and management of the buffer zone and the property needs to be made clear. Protection, conservation and management of the buffer zone and property should be integrated. Where responsibility for the protection, conservation and management of the property and its buffer zone is split between different agencies, the commitment of and coordination between these agencies should be described.

就如遗产区一样，划定与保存、保护和管理遗产价值相关的缓冲区，也应有一个明确的理由或解释。这个理由应该在申遗文本中的保护级别这个章节中提出。应该明晰缓冲区与遗产区的功能、范围、保存、保护和管理之间的关系。遗产区和缓冲区的保存、保护和管理应结合起来。如果对遗产及其缓冲区的保护、保存和管理责任是由不同机构承担的，这些机构的义务以及机构之间的协作应描述清楚。

Although the concept of buffer zones arises as a measure to protect the World Heritage property, which can include restrictions, well-designed buffer zones can also have an important role in providing benefits for local communities and others, consistent with the protection, conservation and management of values, and also to enhance sustainable use. The buffer zone may contain farm land or be the location for tourism support activities such as food outlets and accommodation which are run by the local community. The nomination should give emphasis to this aspect.

尽管缓冲区概念是作为世界遗产保护的一种手段，严谨的、规划良好的缓冲区会让当地社区或其他团体受益，从而在保护、保存和管理遗产价值，提高可持续利用等方面发挥重要作用。缓冲区内可以包括农田，也可以设置支持各项旅游活动的设施，比如，由当地社区运营管理的食品小卖部或者住宿场所。申报时对这些因素应予以强调。

In addition, buffer zones can play an important role in social, cultural and economic exchanges which are vital for the survival of the property and its values. Protection, conservation and management should be carefully designed to recognize and sustain these supporting processes for the property. Similarly, buffer zones should not unreasonably isolate the property from its longstanding social, cultural and economic context, turning the buffer zone into a ‘museum’ or tourist zone.

此外，缓冲区在社会，文化和经济交流方面扮演着重要的角色，这种交流对遗产及其价值的存续至关重要。应该精心设计保存、保护和管理措施，确认和维持这些重要性。同样，缓冲区不应该隔绝遗产和它所依赖的社会、文化和经济文脉，变成一个“博物馆”或旅游区。

The following steps should be noted in establishing a buffer zone, although their order could vary:

• analyse the potential Outstanding Universal Value, integrity and characteristics of the property to define the external issues and relationships;

• also analyse the potential positive opportunities to establish more effective protection, conservation, management and benefits from sustainable use within the buffer zone;

• consider the legal provisions relevant to the implementation of the buffer zone, such as national law and local legislation/regulations;

• ensure effective implementation and mechanisms in relation to the functions of the buffer zone; and

• delineate the buffer zone based on these analyses and considerations, and with particular regard to the protection of the Outstanding Universal Value of the property from external threats (for serial properties, there may need to be different buffer zones for different component parts of the property).

在划定缓冲区的过程中应包括以下几个步骤，他们的顺序可以随意调节：

• 分析遗产潜在的突出普遍价值、完整性及其特性，确定外部因素及与遗产的关系；

• 分析潜在的、建立有效保存、保护和管理的机会，提高缓冲区可持续利用带来的收益；

• 考虑制定与缓冲区有关的法律规定，例如国家法律和当地法规和条例；

• 确定与缓冲区功能相关的各种机制的有效实施；

• 基于以上的分析和考虑，划定缓冲区的界限，特别要考虑突出普遍价值不受外部威胁（对于系列遗产，遗产的不同组成部分需划定多个不同的缓冲区）。

If the protective arrangements relating to the buffer zone do not yet exist, the timescale for achieving protection could influence the nomination process and timetable for submission. The protective arrangements should be operational before the nomination is submitted.

如果与缓冲区相关的保护措施不到位，则到位需要的时间可能影响申报过程和提交文本的时间表。保护措施应该在提交申遗文本前开始实施。

Buffer zones have been found to be effective if the concept is already included in legislation for the territory containing the property. Accordingly, it is desirable that States Parties move to recognize the concept of buffer zones in their legal systems, if this is not already the case.

已经证实，有法律认可的缓冲区均十分有效。尚未将缓冲区的概念纳入法律体系中的缔约国应加快立法。

While buffer zones are one important way to offer additional protection to the immediate area

缓冲区是对遗产区周边环境提供进一步保护的重要的方法，还需要提出其他相关的方法

around the nominated property, other mechanisms may be needed to address protection of the wider setting. There is also the possibility of synergies with other conservation instruments such as conventions, programmes and initiatives that provide alternative and complementary protection for heritage.

扩大保护范围。缓冲区与其他保护活动，如其他公约、会议、计划等活动相结合，作为遗产保护备选和补充方法，将会事半功倍。

There is a special case with buffer zones for properties where the potential Outstanding Universal Value is underground. In such cases a buffer zone may not be needed.

关于缓冲区有一个特殊的案例，即遗产的突出的普遍价值是存在于地下。此时可能不需要缓冲区。

Buffer zones

Central University City Campus of the Universidad Nacional Autónoma de México (UNAM) (Mexico)

缓冲区

墨西哥国立自治大学城核心校区（墨西哥）

The ensemble of buildings, sports facilities and open spaces of the Central University City Campus of the Universidad Nacional Autónoma de México (UNAM), was built from 1949 to 1952 by over sixty architects, engineers and artists who were involved in the project. As a result, the campus constitutes a unique example of 20th-century modernism integrating urbanism, architecture, engineering, landscape design and fine arts with references to local traditions, especially to Mexico's pre-hispanic past. The ensemble embodies social and cultural values of universal significance and is one of the most important icons of modernity in Latin America.

墨西哥国立自治大学城的建筑群、体育设施和露天空间，建于1949–1952年，60个建筑学家、工程师和艺术家共同参与。校园具有20世纪现代主义风格，是融合了城市化、建筑、工程和景观设计、艺术、结合当地墨西哥前西班牙时期传统的唯一实例。这个建筑群具有普遍的社会和文化价值，是拉丁美洲现代主义最重要的标志之一。

In the case of this property, the buffer zone was revised in order to provide more effective protection for its setting.

为了更有效地保护遗产的环境，对此项遗产的缓冲区进行了调整。

Humberstone and Santa Laura Saltpeter Works (Chile)

The initial delineation of the buffer zone was considered too schematic and it was requested that the buffer zone be revised to reflect the landscape of the property.

亨伯斯通和圣劳拉的硝石采石场（智利）

最初划定的缓冲区被认为太过形式化，要求调整缓冲区使其能够反映遗产的景观。

Mount Huangshan (China)

The buffer zone of Mount Huangshan serves to protect the property, and to slow down or prevent impacts from outside the site by a variety of means including: providing a migration corridor for wildlife, limiting certain land-uses that could create impacts, providing tourism infrastructure, and supporting management of additional scenic localities, outside the World Heritage property, to reduce pressures on the property itself.

黄山（中国）

黄山的缓冲区起到保护遗产的作用，采取各种措施降低或阻止、外部因素对遗产的影响，包括为野生动物提供迁徙廊道，限制可能造成影响的土地用途，提供旅游服务设施，并支持对遗产区以外的其他景点进行管理以减少外界环境对遗产的压力。

Crac des Chevaliers and Qalat Salah El-Din (Syrian Arab Republic)

In the case of the Fortress of Saladin, the buffer zone was extended across the valley, taking account of the potential archaeological interest of the area and a decision on cable car access.

十字军堡和喀拉特萨拉丁城堡（阿拉伯叙利亚共和国）

对十字军堡和喀拉特萨拉丁城堡，考虑到这个区域可能有潜在的考古价值以及要建造索道，决定将缓冲区扩大至整个山谷。

St Kilda (United Kingdom)

For the physical cultural heritage on the islands, the sea in itself serves as a protection area around the islands, and therefore a formally defined additional buffer zone was not found to be necessary.

圣基尔达岛（英国）

对于岛上的物质文化遗产而言，岛屿四周的海洋本身就是保护区，因此没必要再正式划定缓冲区。

Kuk Early Agricultural Site (Papua New Guinea)

The buffer zone is only on two sides of the property. It has been determined to protect the upstream hydrology of the property and its archaeological remains.

库克早期农业遗迹（巴布亚新几内亚）

缓冲区位于遗产的两侧，旨在保护遗产上游的水文系统和考古遗存。

Wider setting

In addition to the property and its buffer zone, it can be very important, to consider a further area outside of these — the wider setting for the property. For some properties, the wider setting

广袤的环境

除了遗产及其缓冲区，遗产周边广袤的环境也十分的重要。对于一些遗产，环境是对视野特征或遗产属性产生重要影响的区域。

is an area that may be important for the visual characteristics or attributes of the property.

As noted above, the wider setting might also play an essential role in protecting the authenticity and integrity of the property.

如上所述，广袤的环境对保护遗产的真实性和完整性至关重要。

Examples of development or changes within the wider setting which can adversely impact on the potential Outstanding Universal Value of a property include visually prominent items such as tall buildings or wind farms. These might be a considerable distance from the property and yet could compromise the way the property is understood through the relationship to its setting.

因周边环境的发展或改变对遗产潜在突出普遍价值可能造成负面影响，包括肉眼可见的突兀项目，例如高楼或风电场。虽然这些项目可能远离遗产，但它们与环境的关系却会妨碍对遗产的理解。

In some situations the wider setting and the buffer zone may be the same, in other cases the wider setting may be much larger. A rationale for the extent of the wider setting should be provided, noting this is not formally required by *The Operational Guidelines*.

在一些情况下，广袤的周边环境和缓冲区可能一致，有时周边环境比缓冲区大很多。划定遗产周围环境的边界也要有理有据。同时，应注意在《操作指南》中并未要求遗产环境的范围。

A useful reference on the issue of settings includes the *Xi'an Declaration on the Conservation of the Setting of Heritage Structures, Sites and Areas (ICOMOS, 2005b).*

有关遗产环境问题可参考《关于保护建筑遗产、遗址和周边环境的西安宣言》。（ICOMOS，2005b）

The extent of the wider setting should be indicated on a map or maps as part of the nomination dossier, and the wider setting should be discussed in the description section of the nomination.

应该在图中标识环境的范围，或专门绘制一张环境范围图作为申遗文本附件，环境在申遗文本的遗产概述的章节中予以讨论。

Issues with the setting of a property

遗产环境的问题

UNESCO-ICOMOS reactive monitoring mission to the Old and New Towns of Edinburgh (United Kingdom)

联合国教科文组织——国际古迹遗址理事会反应性监测活动：新旧爱丁堡（英国）

Experts from the World Heritage Centre and

2008 年，世界遗产中心和国际古迹遗址理

ICOMOS undertook a reactive monitoring mission in 2008 to examine development projects affecting the Old and New Towns of Edinburgh (United Kingdom), inscribed on the World Heritage List in 1995.

事会的专家，对 1995 年列入遗产名录的新旧爱丁堡进行反应性监测，审查各开发项目对该遗产的影响。

Undertaken at the request of the World Heritage Committee, the mission particularly focused on the Calton gate development.

在世界遗产委员会的要求下，委员会特别关注爱丁堡老城卡尔敦门的发展。

The experts reviewed the overall situation of the Old and New Towns of Edinburgh with regard to their state of conservation in their wide urban context, integrity and authenticity. They also looked at how current construction projects, including high-rise developments, affect the Outstanding Universal Value, that is the exceptional qualities for which the property was inscribed on the World Heritage List.

专家在考虑了大的城市背景下的保护状态、真实性和完整性的基础上，对新旧爱丁堡的整体状况进行了评估。他们也考察了目前的建设项目、包括开发高层建筑等对突出普遍价值的影响，而突出普遍价值是遗产列入名录的显著特征。

With representatives of the national and local authorities, institutions, organizations and other stakeholders, the experts reviewed measures to protect the landscape of the historic urban area. Besides Calton gate, the experts reviewed the impact of outline proposals for Leith Docks, St James Centre, Haymarket and other projects on the property. The mission also discussed opportunities for enhanced conservation and management.

专家们与国家和当地管理机构、研究机构、组织和其他利益相关者代表一起审核、评估历史城镇景观的保护方法。除了卡尔敦门，专家还对利思码头、圣詹姆斯中心、哈马肯特（Haymarket）和其他项目进行了影响评估。专家组还讨论了加强遗产保护和管理的契机。

The World Heritage site was designated in recognition of Edinburgh's standing as the capital of Scotland since the 15th century. The World Heritage Committee recognized two distinct areas: the Old Town, dominated by a medieval fortress; and the neoclassical New Town, whose development from the 18th century onwards had a far-reaching influence on European urban planning. The harmonious juxtaposition of these two contrasting historic areas, each with many important buildings,

因自 15 世纪以来爱丁堡作为苏格兰的首都，而列入《世界遗产名录》，世界遗产委员会认可其中两个截然不同的区域：中世纪城堡占主导地位的旧城和 18 世纪以来受到欧洲城市规划影响而发展起来的新古典主义风格的新城。风格迥异的两个历史区域和谐共存，每个都有独特风格的建筑，赋予城市独特魅力和突出普遍价值。

is what gives the city its unique character and Outstanding Universal Value.

Present state of conservation—threats or pressures

Threats to or pressures on the potential Outstanding Universal Value of the nominated property are an important consideration in the assessment process. *The Operational Guidelines* mention four such factors — development, environmental, natural disasters and visitors/ tourism. Accordingly, the information provided about the state of conservation of the nominated property should be realistic, supported by evidence, and not overstated on the one hand or understated on the other. For example, claims that a property is in good condition must reflect reality, and substantial threats should not be ignored or downplayed. In addition, trends are vital to understand the situation — good and improving is dramatically different to good and deteriorating. A key task of the evaluation mission which visits the nominated property is to check and report on threats, including looking for evidence of threats which have not been reported.

Information on threats should only include those which are reasonable to predict or expect for a particular property, or which have been previously raised. For example, highly unlikely threats do not need to be addressed.

Nonetheless, accurate and frank information about such threats must be provided. A growing problem is the inscription of properties which are shortly afterwards reporting threats which were not documented in the nomination. For this reason, it is desirable to keep the World Heritage Centre informed of any new development projects or other

保护现状——威胁和压力

申报遗产潜在突出普遍价值所面临的威胁和压力应该是评估过程中着重考虑内容。《操作指南》中提到了四个组成部分——发展、环境、自然灾害和旅游压力。申报遗产有关保护状况的信息必须真实客观，证据充足，不能夸大其词也不能轻描淡写。例如，如果这个遗产处于良好的状态，就必须得到真实的反映，不应忽略威胁或对实质性的威胁轻描淡写。此外，了解保护状态的发展趋势也很重要——“保护良好同时逐步改善”与“保护良好但正日益恶化”是截然不同的状态。申报项目的现场考察团的关键任务就是要检查和报告没有列入申遗文本的威胁因素，包括寻找威胁的证据。

威胁信息不仅要合理预测和预期对于特殊遗产有影响的信息，还包括过去曾经出现过的威胁的信息。但不太可能出现的威胁不需要说明。

无论如何，必须如实提供相关威胁的信息。日益突出的问题是遗产刚列入名录就提交了关于遭受威胁的报告，且此威胁信息在申遗文本中没有记录。鉴于此，如果在评估过程中有新的开发项目或出现其他变化，应及时通知世界遗产中心。

changes that arise during the evaluation process.

Protection

Nominated properties should have good legal and/or traditional protection. Ideally the property should have the best available protection in a given jurisdiction and context, and sometimes this will include layers of legislative and other protection.

Legal and traditional protection are not mutually exclusive mechanisms and they can often work successfully together to achieve a layered approach to protection. In many cases legal protection is necessary to provide a suitable and supported context for traditional protection, particularly where threats are present.

A nomination for a property which does not have satisfactory protection will fail to achieve World Heritage inscription.

A clear definition of the tangible and intangible attributes which convey the potential Outstanding Universal Value is essential in achieving good protection, conservation and management of the property, as these are what need to be protected in order to sustain potential Outstanding Universal Value.

Key message: Protection must be effective.
Useful questions include:

• Will the potential Outstanding Universal Value be maintained or enhanced by the protection?

• Is protection long term?

• In the case of traditional protection, are the community mechanisms underpinning the protection robust?

• Is protection provided at all necessary levels

保护

申报遗产应该受到法律或传统的保护。理想状况是，遗产在相关的区域内，得到最佳的保护，包括不同级别的立法保障和其他保护。

法律和传统保障体系并不是相互排斥的机制，他们常常成功合作而形成多层次的保护方法。在出现威胁的情况下，法律保障为传统保障体系提供了适当的支持和环境。

申报遗产没有令人满意的保障体系时，将导致申报失败。

清楚界定能够展现遗产突出普遍价值的有形遗产和无形遗产，是实现有效保存、保护和管理遗产的基础，也就是明确我们需要保护什么，才能维护遗产突出普遍价值。

关键信息：遗产保护必须有效。
有用的问题包括：

• 通过遗产保护是否维护或加强遗产潜在突出普遍价值?

• 遗产保护是否具有长效性?

• 传统保护情况下，社区机制是否提供更有效的保护?

• 是否在所有层面上都有保护（如，传统、

(e.g. traditional, local, regional, national)?

• Is the property protected from development or change that might have negative impacts on values, integrity or authenticity?

• Is protection effectively implemented?

• Is protection periodically audited/monitored to assess effectiveness?

• Is the approach to protection fully integrated with overall conservation and management?

Protection needs to apply to both the property and its buffer zone, although different measures may apply to the different areas. Protecting the value of the property should not be at the expense of any heritage within the buffer zone.

Significant visual qualities of the wider setting should also be protected and managed.

Whether adequate protection is in place needs to be examined very early in the nomination process. This is because developing such protection may take considerable time (e.g. pre - paring new legislation), and this timing could impact on the timetable for the overall nomination process.

Case study

Traditional protection - cultural property - Tomb of Askia (Mali)

The dramatic 17 m pyramidal structure of the Tomb of Askia was built by Askia Mohamed, the Emperor of Songhai, in 1495 in his capital Gao. It bears testimony to the power and riches of the empire that flourished in the 15th and 16th centuries through its control of the trans-Saharan trade, notably in salt and gold. It is also a fine example of the monumental mud-building traditions of the West African Sahel. The complex, including the

当地、区域、国家的）？

• 是否已经消除保护措施中可能会对遗产价值及完整性和真实性产生负面影响的发展或改变因素？

• 保护措施是否有效实施？

• 是否通过定期审计或监测来评估保护措施的效果？

• 保护措施能否与整体保护和管理相融合？

遗产区和缓冲区都应得到保护，尽管在不同地区可能使用不同的方法。保护遗产价值的同时不能牺牲缓冲区内的任何遗产。

还应保护和管理遗产周边环境内重要的视觉组成部分。

在申报的起始阶段，就应审查保护措施是否充分。因为制定保护措施往往要很长时间，甚至要草拟一个新法律，因而会影响申报过程的时间表。

案例

传统保护——文化遗产——阿斯基亚王陵（马里）

17 米高的、金字塔结构的阿斯基亚王陵是桑海帝国国王、阿斯基亚 · 穆罕默德的陵墓，1495 年修建于桑海的首都加奥。它是 15–16 世纪帝国权利和财富的象征，这一时期帝国因控制跨越撒哈拉地区的贸易特别是盐和黄金而繁荣。它也是西非荒漠草原地区土构建筑传统的典型代表。遗址包括了金字塔形的陵墓、两层的穆斯林建筑、穆斯林公墓和加奥作为桑海王朝首都时期修建的开阔广场，这些都是在阿斯

pyramidal tomb, two flat-roofed mosque buildings, the mosque cemetery and the open-air assembly ground, was built when Gao became the capital of the Songhai Empire and after Askia Mohamed had returned from Mecca and made Islam the official religion of the empire.

基亚·穆罕默德从麦加回来钦定伊斯兰教为国教并将加奥定为首都后建造。

The site is effectively under a traditional form of protection. The management is under the supervision of an association set up by the prefect of Gao in 2002. This consists of representatives of all the key stakeholders including the imam, the muezzin, and representatives of the Regional Agency for Arts and Culture in Gao, and the Regional and Local Commissions for Safeguarding Cultural Heritage. The association has no statutory basis but has strong moral authority by virtue of the involvement of the Imam and the Chief of Songhai.

遗产在传统的保护体系下得到有效的保护。2002 年，在加奥行政官员协助下建立管理协会。它由所有的利益相关者组成，包括教长、宣礼员、当地文化艺术管理机构的代表，当地的文化遗产保护委员会的代表。这个团体没有法律地位，但因有教长和桑海酋长参加而具有很强的道德权威。

Traditional protection - natural property - East Rennell (Solomon Islands)

传统保护——自然遗产——东伦内尔岛（所罗门群岛）

East Rennell makes up the southern third of Rennell Island, the southernmost island in the Solomon Island group in the western Pacific. Rennell, 86 km long by 15 km wide, is the largest raised coral atoll in the world. The site includes approximately 37, 000 ha and a marine area extending 3 nautical miles out to sea. A major feature of the island is Lake Tegano, which was the former lagoon on the atoll. The lake, the largest in the insular Pacific (15, 500 ha), is brackish and contains many rugged limestone islands and endemic species. Rennell is mostly covered with dense forest, with a canopy averaging 20m in height. Combined with the strong climatic effects of frequent cyclones, the site is a true natural laboratory for scientific study. It is under customary land ownership and management.

东伦内尔岛是伦内尔岛南部三岛之一，位于所罗门群岛最南部。伦内尔岛 86 公里长、15 公里宽，是世界上最大的珊瑚环礁岛。遗址包括大约 37000 公顷及周边 3 海里的海区。这个岛最主要的特色就是特加诺湖，它以前是环状珊瑚岛的泻湖。特加诺湖是太平洋岛上最大的泻湖，面积为 15500 公顷，是咸水湖，包括很多奇形怪状的石灰岩岛屿和当地特有的物种。伦内尔岛被高达 20 米的浓密森林所覆盖。由于频繁飓风气候的影响，该遗产是科学研究的天然实验场。这个岛屿遵循传统的土地公有和统一管理。

Key message: The management plan/system must be effective

Management

A principal focus of management of a World Heritage property is the attributes and features which are associated with or convey the potential Outstanding Universal Value of the property. The aim is to ensure that the value, authenticity and integrity of the property are sustained for the future through managing the attributes. Accordingly, the Statement of Outstanding Universal Value is a key reference for management.

Management of the potential Outstanding Universal Value of the property also needs to be delivered in a holistic way that is also relevant to the conservation needs of the property as a whole, and has regard to all its values.

Nominated properties should demonstrate that they have an adequate management plan or documented management system to define their management arrangements. If neither of these is in place, it is important to set realistic time-frames for their development, and this may impact on the nomination timetable. Suitable management arrangements should also exist for the buffer zone and the setting for the property.

A nomination for a property which does not have satisfactory management at the time of nomination may struggle to achieve World Heritage inscription.

The Operational Guidelines include a provision indicating a nomination may be accepted without a management plan or documented system being fully in place (Paragraph 115). However, this is not

关键信息：有效的管理规划或体制

管理

世界遗产管理的核心内容是能展现潜在突出普遍价值的属性和特性。管理的目的是为了能够永久确保遗产的价值、真实性和完整性。鉴于此，突出普遍价值声明是管理的重要参考文件。

遗产的潜在突出普遍价值的管理需要全方位的实施，包括遗产及其价值的整体保护。

应证明申报项目已经拥有充分的管理规划或有文可依的管理体制，对其管理做出了规定。如果这两样都没有，就应该设立一个切实可行的时间表来制定管理规划或建立管理体制，这将影响遗产申报时间表。应对缓冲区和遗产环境也做出适当的管理安排。

遗产在申报时仍没有令人满意的管理体制，遗产难以实现成功申报。

《操作指南》中不提倡没有充分的管理规划或有文可依的管理体制的遗产进入申报程序（115 段）。有效的、正在实施的管理规划或有文可依的管理体制，将提高遗产申报成功的机会。

desirable. Having an effective management plan or documented system in operation greatly improves the chances of a nomination succeeding.

There is no particular preference for a management plan or a management system, and in some cases both may be available. The key issue is whether the management plan or system is effective and adequate. In some cultures, for example, management plans may be generally unknown, there is no experience with them, and their effectiveness would be highly uncertain. Nonetheless, an adequate management system may well exist, and be appropriate to manage the nominated property. In other cultures, management plans are well established mechanisms and should be in place.

指南没有特别指明要制定管理规划或建立管理系统，在一些情况下，二者可以并存。核心问题是管理规划或管理体系是否有效，是否充分满足保护的需要。例如在一些文化中，人们没有编制管理规划或相关经验，规划有效性也完全不确定。但是，有一套适合遗产管理的完善的管理体制。而在另一些文化中，管理规划则是长期行之有效的机制，应予以实施。

The management of a property should have a realistic vision for the medium to long-term future of the property, including the changes and challenges that could arise from inscription in the World Heritage List. Such changes and challenges may be considerable.

管理一个遗产应该有中长期的、切合实际的预测，包括列入《世界遗产名录》后的机遇和挑战。这种变化和挑战可能是巨大的。

Management plans and documented systems should be put forward as tried and tested arrangements rather than ‘paper’ plans that will be implemented in the future. There should be an intimate connection between key sections of the nomination (such as state of conservation and monitoring) and the information and programmes set out in any management plan for the property.

管理规划和管理体制应该是得到认可的、可靠的、经过考验和检验，是将来可能实施的规划，而不是“纸上谈兵”的规划。申报的关键环节（例如保护和监测状况），应该与管理规划中的信息和方案一致。

As part of any management plan or system, a mechanism to undertake impact assessments for proposed changes, developments or interventions is essential.

在管理规划或体制中必须有对规划中提出的改变、开发或干预项目进行评估的机制。

Sometimes the management of a property

有时，遗产的管理要依赖于若干个管理规

will rely on a number of management plans or documented systems. It is important to demonstrate that these various plans or systems provide an integrated or complementary and effective management outcome relative to the potential Outstanding Universal Value. This situation often arises where the property, its buffer zone and broader setting are managed by different agencies, or when several local authorities are involved.

划或管理体制。这些规划和体制对潜在的突出普遍价值实施了整体的或互补的、有效的管理。当缓冲区和周边区域由不同管理机构负责管理时，或当若干个地方政府参与管理时，容易出现这种多个管理规划或管理体制并存的情况。

Tourism management is often a major issue for World Heritage properties given the great interest by people in visiting properties, the potentially large scale of visitation, and the need to provide information about a property as well as other visitor facilities. The specific effects of World Heritage listing on visitor numbers vary, and should be specifically anticipated.

由于世界遗产对公众有极大的吸引力，大批的潜在游客可能会参观遗址，同时需要提供更多的遗产信息和服务设施，因此，旅游管理也是世界遗产管理的重要议题。世界遗产身份会对游客数量产生特殊的不同影响，对此应按实际情况做专门的预测分析。

Tourism management consistent with and sympathetic to the protection, conservation and management of potential Outstanding Universal Value must be addressed as part of the nomination. In many cases, a separate tourism management plan is prepared for properties — integrated with the general property management plan or system. Such tourism management plans must be implemented and effective.

在申遗文本中，旅游管理应与潜在突出普遍价值的保障体系、保护和管理协调一致。在一些情况下，会编制该遗产独立的旅游管理规划，作为该遗产管理规划或管理体系整体的一部分。这样的旅游管理规划必须有效落实。

For natural properties, a separate IUCN resource manual on management plans for World Heritage properties has been prepared (IUCN, 2008a). A resource manual for cultural properties is planned as part of the series of World Heritage Resource Manuals to be prepared by the UNESCO World Heritage Centre and the Advisory Bodies.

对于自然遗产，世界自然保护联盟已经独立编制了《世界遗产管理规划资源手册》（世界自然保护联盟，2008a）。文化遗产的资源手册作为世界遗产资源手册的一部分，由世界遗产中心和相关的咨询机构正在编制中。

Time is needed to put in place appropriate plans or documentation, and to demonstrate that these work, before the nomination is submitted.

在提交申遗文本之前必须花费一定的时间，制定适当的规划或编制适当的文件，同时需要证明这些规划或文件的有效性。这些工作的实

Achieving this could have a considerable influence on the timetable for the nomination process. Getting the management arrangements in place before the nomination is submitted is to the long-term benefit of the conservation of the property, and to all owners and stakeholders.

施会对确定遗产申报时间表带来影响。制定的管理安排在提交文本时已经实施，对于保护遗产、遗产所有者和利益相关者意义深远。

Useful questions include:

• Does the management plan/ system specify how the potential Outstanding Universal Value will be sustained through protection and conservation?

• Is the management plan/system practically effective in achieving on-ground conservation outcomes?

• In the case of multiple plans or systems, are these integrated or complementary to achieve effective outcomes?

• Does the management plan or system have priority over other types of plans or systems (e.g. tourism, development and regional economic plans)?

• Do stakeholders in the property have a shared understanding of the property?

• Does the management plan/system include a cycle of planning, implementation, monitoring, evaluation and feedback?

• Are the impacts of trends, changes and proposed interventions monitored and assessed?

• Are sustainable development principles integrated into the management?

• Does the management plan/system involve stakeholders, especially property owners and managers, and is there strong support for the plan/ system?

• Is the plan/system adequately resourced, both at the moment and into the future?

• Is there adequate finance and business planning to meet current and future needs of the nominated property?

• Does the plan/system include relevant

有用的问题包括：

• 管理规划或体制是否详细说明了如何通过保护和管理，维系了遗产突出普遍价值？

• 管理规划或体制是否有效的实现了实地保护？

• 在多规划、多体制的情况下，这些规划是否相互结合、互相补充从而实现了保护的效果？

• 管理规划或体制是否比其他规划或体制具有优先权（如旅游规划、发展规划和区域经济规划）？

• 利益相关者是否也了解遗产？

• 管理规划和体制是否包括了规划、应用、监测、评估和反馈的完整过程？

• 对于遗产动态、改变和计划性的干预活动是否进行了监测和评估？

• 可持续发展的理念是否贯穿到管理工作中；

• 管理规划或体制是否有利益相关者、特别是遗产所有者和管理者的参与，他们是否强烈支持该规划或体制；

• 管理规划或体制近期及远期资金支持是否充足？

• 申报遗产的财务和经营计划是否足以满足现在和将来的需求？

• 管理规划或体制是否包含了相关能力建设？

capacity-building?

• Does the plan/system provide a transparent description of how the system actually functions?

• Does the management plan include risk preparedness?

• Is the management system fully integrated with the protection of the property?

• 管理规划或体制是否对制度的实际运作进行了透明的阐述？

• 管理规划是否包括了风险防范机制？

• 管理体制是否与保护保障相结合？

In this context, stakeholders may include local people, indigenous peoples, property owners and managers, governments at all levels, commercial interests including tourism, and NGOs.

在这样的背景下，利益相关者应该包括当地居民、土著居民、遗产所有者和管理者、各级地方政府、包括旅游在内的商业团体和非政府组织。

In the case of serial or trans-boundary/transnational nominations, a priority should be to ensure that adequate protection and management for each component is in place and working effectively. There should also be a management system at the level of the whole property that should ensure communication and coordination between all component parts in relation to, at least:

• the harmonization of management of all the component parts to meet a set of shared objectives of conserving potential Outstanding Universal Value;

• the identification of and response to threats to the property; and

• the coordination of monitoring and reporting, in particular in relation to the requirements of The World Heritage Convention.

系列跨国或跨境申报，先决条件是遗产每个构成组成部分得到有效的保护和管理。针对遗产整体应该建立一个管理体制，负责各个组成部分至少在以下方面的沟通和协作：

• 协调对各个组成部分的管理以实现保护潜在突出普遍价值的共同目标；

• 确定威胁因素，制定相应的应急措施；

• 协调监测和报告，特别是世界遗产委员会要求提供的报告。

The management system for a serial or trans-boundary/transnational property should regularly review and reinforce where feasible the coordinating mechanisms to increase the cohesion and effectiveness of its management as a World Heritage property, and respond to changes that affect its component parts.

应该定期审查和加强系列或跨国遗产的协调管理体制，以提高对其作为一处遗产地进行管理时的协调性和效率，并有效应对会对遗产各个组成部分产生影响的变化。

It must be clear how coordinated management

要对如何实现遗产地各个组成部分之间协

is to be achieved for the separate components, especially where different managers and management systems may apply. Coordinated management must be effective.

调管理有清楚的认识，特别是对不同的管理机构采用不同的管理体制的协调管理，协调管理必须有效。

It is not necessary to create a specific management authority for the property if the existing management plans or systems are working well. However, where existing mechanisms are inadequate, new specific mechanisms may be needed but they must be effective.

如果现有的管理规划或管理体系运作良好，就没有必要为该遗产建立一个特殊的管理机构。但如果现有的机制无法满足管理的需求，则需要建立一个新的专门的机制，并确保这个机制必须有效。

Case Study

案例

The Loire Valley between Sully-sur-Loire and Chalonnes (France)

位于叙利－沙洛纳－夏龙纳之间的卢瓦尔河谷

The Loire Valley is an outstanding cultural landscape of great beauty, containing historic towns and villages, great architectural monuments (châteaux), and cultivated lands formed by many centuries of interaction between their population and the physical environment, primarily the River Loire itself.

卢瓦尔河谷是卓越的文化景观，包括了美丽的景色、历史城镇和村镇、雄伟的古建筑（城堡）、和很多世纪以来人类开垦的土地，这是人类与自然环境（主要是卢瓦尔河）相互作用协和发展的产物。

The French Government decided in 1994 to implement a ten-year master plan for the coherent planning and management of the Loire Valley (Plan Loire Grandeur Nature). This covers the protection of the environment and the economic development of the area. It is operated in close collaboration with the relevant organizations and institutions — territorial collectivities, economic agencies and associations. In addition, responding to a recommendation made during the evaluation of the property, a Steering Committee was established to oversee the management of the area, with representation from the government authorities and institutions involved.

1994 年，法国政府决定实施一个为期十年的总体规划来规划和管理卢瓦尔河谷。这个规划中包括了该区域的环境保护和经济发展。这个规划由相关的组织和机构联合实施——集体土地、经济管理局和相关部门。此外，根据遗产评估时的决议，建立一个由政府部门和相关机构成员组成的指导委员会监督整个区域的管理。

Nomination dossier as a contribution to property management

In addition to the role of the nomination dossier as documenting the case for World Heritage inscription, the nomination can also contribute to the ongoing management of the nominated property. This contribution can arise because:

• the nomination includes information about the condition of the property and a series of commitments for future protection, management and monitoring;

• World Heritage status has the potential to change and benefit a property, and the implications of this status need to be properly addressed in the nomination, such as, for example, in relation to increased visitation or growing tourism pressures after possible inscription;

• the nomination, including the proposed management arrangements, will be closely analysed during the evaluation process. Changes to the property and its management may be proposed which need to be negotiated and understood by the State Party and the various stakeholders;

• the potential for World Heritage status can be a powerful means of engaging stakeholders in the management and protection of the property, in particular if the potential benefits can be conveyed to them as a reason to take part. Equally, some stakeholders may perceive World Heritage status as a threat, and their views and concerns will need to be properly taken into account during the development of the nomination; and

• the nomination will provide key baseline data against which the state of conservation of the property can be measured in future years.

申遗文本对遗产管理的贡献

申遗文本是申报世界遗产的档案资料，对持续性的日常管理有所帮助，帮助的原因如下：

• 申遗文本包括了遗产现状的信息和一系列有关未来保护、管理和监控的承诺；

• 世界遗产的身份对遗产会带来潜在改变和收益，这个身份带来的影响在申遗文本中应予以描述，例如遗产如果申报成功将带来游客数量的剧增，旅游压力增加等；

• 申遗文本，包括了在评估过程中认真考虑的、拟实施的管理安排。遗产的改变和对改变的管理，需要缔约国和多方利益相关者协商完成；

• 世界遗产身份是让利益相关者参与到遗产的管理和保护过程的最有力的方法，特别是他们可以从参与保护与管理中获利时。同时，一些利益相关者可能认为世界遗产身份是一种威胁，他们的这些看法和忧虑在申报过程中也应予以关注；

• 申遗文本将提供重要的基础数据，可以作为将来衡量遗产保护状态的基本数据。

Monitoring

An integral part of good management is to

监测

良好管理的一个必不可少的组成部分就是：

monitor a range of key factors which will give an indication about the current situation of the property, its state of conservation and its likely future. Monitoring provides valuable information for the property manager — it can show that protection, conservation and management are achieving their goals or that changes need to be made. Monitoring of a World Heritage property should focus on Outstanding Universal Value, including integrity, protection and management, and authenticity for cultural properties. Again, the Statement of Outstanding Universal Value is a key reference for monitoring.

对一系列能够说明遗产当前状况、其保存现状及将来情况等关键因素进行监测。通过监测为遗产管理者提供遗产的保护、保存和管理是否已经达到既定目标或者是否需要改进等宝贵的信息。世界遗产监测的核心是突出普遍价值，包括完整性、保护和管理、文化遗产的真实性。同时突出普遍价值是监测的关键依据。

Monitoring is often inadequately addressed in nominations.

在申遗文本中监测的说明往往不够充分。

The World Heritage system also includes formal Periodic Reporting whereby inscribed properties are subject to monitoring reports every six years (see *Operational Guidelines,* V). A well-developed monitoring system for a property will help with Periodic Reporting.

世界遗产体系也包括了正式的定期报告（当遗产列入名录后），定期报告实际上就是每六年提交一次的监测报告（见《操作指南》5）。建立一个行之有效的监测系统将有助于编写定期报告。

The nomination dossier should include key indicators which will be used to measure and assess a range of factors, including the state of conservation of the property. These indicators need to be related to the attributes that convey potential Outstanding Universal Value, to ensure that these attributes are protected, conserved and managed in order to sustain potential Outstanding Universal Value.

申遗文本应该包括测量和评估组成部分包括遗产保存现状的重要指标。这些指标要与体现潜在突出普遍价值的属性相关，确保这些属性能够得到很好的保存、保护和管理从而长久维持潜在的突出普遍价值。

Monitoring should be undertaken regularly, according to a time-frame which is appropriate to the character of the property. The regularity of monitoring will depend on the robustness or fragility of attributes and their susceptibility to change.

监测应该根据与遗产特性相适应的时间表定期进行。监测频率应根据遗产属性的健康或脆弱程度，以及变化的敏感度决定。

An important issue is who undertakes monitoring as this can influence the real or apparent credibility of the monitoring results. In general, monitoring will have greater credibility if undertaken in a transparent way by relevant experts who are independent.

谁来实施监测是一个重要的议题，将会影响监测结果的真实性和可信度。一般而言，如果由相对独立的专家以高度透明的方法进行监测，监测结果就具有较高的可信度。

A useful general reference is *Monitoring World Heritage, World Heritage Papers 10* (UNESCO World Heritage Centre/ICCROM, 2004).

《世界遗产监测，世界遗产期刊 10》（UNESCO，世界遗产中心 /ICCROM，2004）是有用的参考文献。

For natural sites a range of management effectiveness tools have been developed which can assist the monitoring process. These include the *Enhancing Our Heritage Toolkit, Assessing Management Effectiveness of Natural World Heritage Sites* (Hockings et al., 2008). There are also some simpler management effectiveness tools that are also relevant. IUCN can provide further advice on these if required.

对于自然遗产，目前已有一系列有效的管理工具可用于监测。这包括《遗产强化工具包：评估自然世界遗产管理的有效性》（霍金斯等，2008）。还有一些简单有效的管理工具，如果需要的话，世界自然保护联盟可提供进一步的建议。

Key message: Examples of other nomination dossiers and processes may be helpful.

关键信息：有帮助的申遗文本和申遗过程案例

3.2 Extra tips

3.2 其他建议

Review successful nomination dossiers and processes

参考成功的申遗文本和过程

It may be helpful at the start of preparing a nomination to examine examples of nomination dossiers for successful properties. Recent dossiers are probably better than older examples as standards and expectations have changed over time. Also, examples of properties in some way similar to the proposed property may be useful.

在准备申报之初，研究成功列入遗产名录的申遗文本是很好的参考。新近提交的文件比早年更有帮助，因为标准和要求在不断地改变。同样的，与申报遗产类型相似的遗产可能对申报的帮助更大。

The dossiers for directly comparable properties should be very carefully examined as part of the comparative analysis (see earlier pages).

应该仔细研究可直接用于比较分析的申遗文本（见前文）。

Dossiers of properties inscribed since 1998 are available at:

- http: //whc.unesco.org/en/list/ (English web page)
- http: //whc.unesco.org/fr/list/ (French web page)

自 1998 年以来列入名录的遗产的申遗文本可在以下网站中直接下载。

http：//whc.unesco.org/en/list/（英），

http：//whc.unesco.org/fr/list/（法）

Having looked at the dossier, look also at the Advisory Body evaluation (s) for important clues about the quality of the dossier, its strengths and possible weaknesses. These evaluations are also available at the above web pages.

在参考申遗文本时，也应该参考咨询机构对文本的评价，以便了解对于申遗文本质量的要求、这些文本的优缺点。这些评价文件在以上网站也可找到。

Beyond this documentation, it may be possible to obtain useful information from other States Parties about the process undertaken to prepare a nomination. Otherwise, discussions with States Parties responsible for a recent successful nomination may prove helpful.

除了这些文件，还可以从其他缔约国那里获得一些有关申报过程的有用信息。除此之外，与最近成功申报的缔约国进行讨论也很有帮助。

It is important to stress that examples of successful nominations or nomination processes should not be uncritically adopted as a template for the proposed nomination. Each nomination and each State Party have particular circumstances which will result in a unique nomination and process which cannot simply be copied from elsewhere.

还需要强调的是，不应盲目照搬成功的遗产申报或申报过程作为自己的模板。每一个申报遗产，每一个缔约国都有特殊背景环境，因此每个申报的项目和过程也就具有独特性和不可复制性。

4. Writing and preparing the nomination file

4. 编写和准备申遗文本

Once a Statement of Outstanding Universal Value has been developed, a robust and defensible boundary defined, protection, conservation and management is in place, and key stakeholders support the preparation of the nomination, the second stage is to prepare the nomination dossier.

一旦突出普遍价值声明编制完成，确定了恰当的遗产边界，保存、保护和管理到位，核心利益相关者也支持申报的准备工作，就可以开展申报工作的第二步，准备申遗文本。

4.1 General tips

4.1 总体建议

Who should write the nomination

谁来编写申遗文本

It is essential that the nomination is clear and

申报文件的目标、其中所含的信息、观点

consistent in terms of its purpose, information, arguments and conclusions. Bringing in an expert consultant to write a nomination might be seen as the quickest and simplest way to achieve inscription. Such an approach can work well if the expert understands World Heritage and the property, but this is not a requirement for the production of a good nomination.

和结论应当清晰一致，这是非常重要的。组织专家咨询团队来编写申遗文本是实现申报最快最简单的方法。如果专家能够全面了解世界遗产和拟申报的遗产，这个方法很有效。但是，这并不是准备一个好的申遗文本的必要条件。

In the case of many properties, the experience of local staff working together on a nomination, perhaps with some guidance from external specialists, can have considerable long-term benefits. These benefits include allowing a good understanding to develop of the values of the property, its needs, constraints and opportunities, and providing continuity with the protection, conservation and management of the property after it has been considered for inclusion in the World Heritage List. For properties that are inscribed on the World Heritage List, there are obvious benefits arising from having a local team well versed in the values and the future requirements for conservation, protection and management.

对于大多数遗产而言，当地遗产工作者在来自外部的专家的指导下，共同准备申遗文本，可能会带来相当长远的益处，包括很好地了解遗产价值的开发，遗产的需要、局限性以及带来的机会，使该遗产在通过列入《世界遗产名录》的审查之后能够得到持续的保护、保存和管理。对于已经列入《世界遗产名录》的遗产来讲，组建一支由对遗产价值及遗产将来的保存、保护和管理要求非常精通的当地人士组成的团队带来的好处是显而易见的，且符合遗产保护长远要求。

The nomination should be written in clear and fluent English or French. Where one of these languages is not the fluent language of the nomination team or writer, it may be wise to write the nomination in the native language of the nomination team, and then have the final nomination translated into fluent English or French. Poorly translated nominations can lead to confusion and problems during its evaluation.

申遗文本要求用清楚流利的英语或法语编写，如果申报团队或编写者不能流利的使用这两个语言的任何一种，用母语编写是较为明智的选择，再将定稿的申遗文本翻译成流利的英语或法语。如果翻译水平较差，可能会在评估的过程中造成误解和问题。

It may be very helpful to develop a glossary of terms in the local language to overcome misunderstandings.

用母语编制专业术语表可能有助于避免误解。

Purpose of nomination

申报目的

A World Heritage nomination is, in essence, the official application form for World Heritage

本质上，世界遗产申报是以官方申请的形式获得世界遗产身份。申遗文本是缔约国提交

status. It is an official document that is submitted to UNESCO by the relevant State Party, or two or more States Parties in the case of transnational nominations.

给联合国教科文组织的官方文件。而对于跨国申报来讲，则需要由两个或多个缔约国共同提交。

The purpose of the nomination dossier is to set out as clearly as possible:

- what the property consists of and how it is documented;
- why it has potential Outstanding Universal Value;
- the state of conservation and the factors affecting the property; and
- how the property is to be protected, conserved, managed, presented and monitored in relation to its potential Outstanding Universal Value.

申遗文本的目的要尽可能的阐释清楚：

- 遗产由哪儿部分组成和他们是如何被记录的；
- 为什么该遗产具有潜在的突出普遍价值；
- 该遗产保护现状和影响遗产的因素有哪些：
- 遗产的潜在突出普遍价值是如何得到保存、保护、管理、解说和监测。

The nomination is the basis for the evaluation of the property for the World Heritage List and subsequent decision by the World Heritage Committee whether or not to inscribe it on the World Heritage List.

申遗文本是评估遗产是否列入遗产名录的基础资料，世界遗产委员会在评估文本后决定遗产是否列入遗产名录。

Key message: All sections of a nomination must relate to OUV.

关键信息：申遗文本的每部分都应与突出普遍价值相关

Sequence for preparing a nomination

申遗文本准备的顺序

The sequence or order for preparing a nomination is important. It is essential to follow this sequence, while realizing it is an iterative process, involving continued communication and engagement with stakeholders:

- carry out relevant background research;
- work on a comparative analysis;
- prepare the Statement of Outstanding Universal Value, including criteria, authenticity and integrity;
- define relevant attributes;
- define appropriate boundaries;

文本的准备顺序十分重要。一般情况下要与利益相关者反复进行交流和磋商后，确定以下顺序：

- 进行相关的背景资料研究；
- 进行比较分析；
- 准备突出普遍价值声明，包括遗产的适用标准、真实性和完整性；
- 确定相关属性；
- 确定适当的遗产边界；

• prepare the description;

• prepare the history; and

• complete the remaining parts of the nomination format.

• 编制遗产概述；

• 编制历史沿革；

• 完成格式文件的其他部分。

The order of the format required by *The Operational Guidelines* for nomination dossiers is not necessarily the most logical way to proceed, and it can lead to over-long dossiers where the justification of the potential Outstanding Universal Value and demonstration of the criteria are the least satisfactory parts.

按照《操作指南》要求的格式的顺序编写申报材料不一定最合理，而且可能导致申遗文本过长，不能很好证明遗产具有突出的普遍价值，也不能很好证明其所适用标准。

Some parts of the nomination dossier are much easier to complete than others, and often these get the most attention. For example, the description and history sections are often extensive because information is readily available and the text is straightforward to prepare.

申遗文本的有些部分比较容易完成，也更受重视。例如，申报材料中的“概述”和“历史沿革”部分通常都占有很大的篇幅，因为与此相关的信息是现成的，而易于编制完成。

Basic outline of the suggested sequence for preparing a nomination

Carry out relevant background research

Develop comparative analysis

Prepare the draft Statement of Outstanding Universal Value and identify criteria

Define relevant attributes

Assess authenticity and integrity

Define appropriate boundaries

Prepare description

Prepare history

Complete remaining nomination dossier

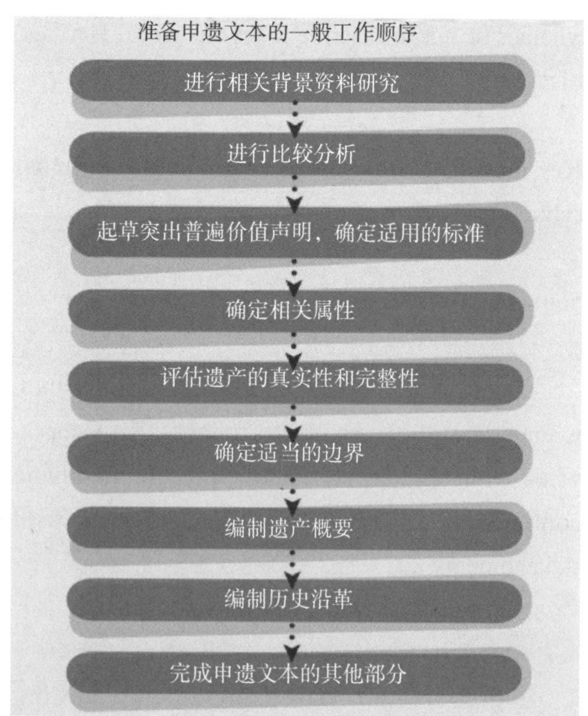

However, it is often the case that these sections are insufficiently related to potential Outstanding Universal Value, possibly because they have been

然而，因为这些章节在确定遗产的突出普遍价值之前已提前准备好，因而没有充分体现与突出普遍价值的联系。此时递进式的工作方

prepared before the values have been identified. An iterative approach is essential. For example, historical research may well be undertaken before the identification of values but the history may subsequently need to be revised to improve its relevance to the values.

式很重要。例如，在确定遗产价值之间可以先开展历史沿革的研究，但是随后还要不断修改以加强它与确定价值之间的联系。

As stressed above, it is recommended that the potential Outstanding Universal Value be identified first and then the remaining sections written to relate specifically to the values. The description needs to explain the physical attributes that convey the potential Outstanding Universal Value, and the history should explain how the property developed its attributes and their value.

正如上文所述，建议首先确定潜在的突出普遍价值，之后编写其他各章节就能使其与价值密切相关。遗产概述需要解读与遗产潜在突出普遍价值相关的、具体属性，而历史沿革应该解释遗产的属性和价值如何形成和演变。

Executive Summary

《执行摘要》

The first part of every nomination dossier is an Executive Summary. This is a key element of the dossier that sets out the essence of the nomination.

申遗文本的第一部分应该是执行摘要，这是文本的核心组成部分，也是制定文本的精髓。

Having undertaken the tasks outlined in Part 3 of this manual, at least to a reasonable draft stage, use this information to write a draft Executive Summary. It is suggested that the Executive Summary should at least be drafted early in the process of actually writing the nomination dossier, so that the key messages that the nomination is aiming to transmit can be set out very clearly. This will then help the dossier to remain tightly focused on what is really important.

这一部分要完成的任务在本手册的第三部分已经列出，至少要在起草阶段就利用这些信息草拟《执行摘要》。《执行摘要》在编写申遗文本前完成，即使只是草稿，这样就能清楚表述编制申遗文本目的。编制文本时就能牢牢地抓住核心内容。

As the nomination progresses, the Executive Summary can be revised in the light of new information or findings. Again, this can helpfully keep the process focused.

随着申报过程的推进，《执行摘要》可以根据新的信息或发现不断修改，这将有助于申报过程中突出重点程序。

The information presented in the Executive Summary should correspond with the information

在《执行摘要》中所提及的信息应该与申遗文本中涉及的信息一致。

presented in the main text of the nomination.

Key message: Examples of other nomination dossiers and processes may be helpful.

关键信息：参考其他申遗文本或申报过程会有所帮助

Presentation of nomination dossier

申遗文本的形式

The nomination needs to:

• clearly define the proposed boundaries of the property;

• describe the property;

• outline its history;

• demonstrate its significance and why it is thought to demonstrate potential Outstanding Universal Value;

• show how it can satisfy one or more criteria;

• explain its state of conservation and how it is documented and monitored;

• set out how in the long term its potential Outstanding Universal Value will be sustained through legal protection and management of attributes that convey its value, and who will be involved in that process; and

• how its value will be presented or interpreted to visitors and others.

申遗文本包括：

• 明确合理的遗产边界；

• 进行遗产描述；

• 记录历史沿革；

• 证明遗产重要性和为什么遗产具有潜在的突出价值；

• 说明遗产如何符合一条或多条标准；

• 解释遗产的保存现状及其记录和监测情况；

• 陈述遗产的潜在突出普遍价值如何通过法律保护和长期管理得到传递，谁将会参与这个过程；

• 如何向参观者展示或阐释遗产的价值。

The length and complexity of nomination dossiers is not an indication of how good they are in fulfilling their purpose. Nomination dossiers need to be well targeted to achieve their purpose, but they need not be enormously lengthy, and long nominations can often be counter productive by not giving a sufficiently focused presentation of the property. Nor do they have to be lavishly prepared in terms of design, illustrations and printing. There is no need for elaborate packaging.

申遗文本的长度和复杂程度并不意味着它能很好地完成使命。申遗文本目标明确，不需要很长的文字，冗长而重点不明确的申遗文本，反而影响申报。不要把准备时间浪费在设计、插图、打印和精美的包装上。

The focus of the nomination dossier should be on its contents rather than on expensive or glossy presentation. Nonetheless, some attention

申遗文本的核心应该是它的内容而不是华丽的外观，适当注意文本的形式能使读者迅速了解文本，掌握各章节的内容。

to presentation can help readers to understand the dossier quickly, and to navigate between sections.

In order to keep the dossier as manageable as possible, it is suggested that detailed material is put in annexes, leaving the main text for setting out the key messages and ensuring that these are not obscured by too much detail. Detailed information in an annex can be referenced in the main text. However, succinct and meaningful answers must be provided within the main text of the nomination dossier, and it is not appropriate to merely provide a reference to an annex. Annexes should also be carefully selected to include only information that is clearly relevant to the nomination. It is not helpful to include a lot of unnecessary information in annexes, but rather select the essential information that is required to support the information summarized in the nomination. Large numbers of unnecessary annexes can make a nomination more difficult to evaluate and hinder the presentation of clear arguments for potential Outstanding Universal Value.

为了让文本尽可能的简洁明了，建议将详细的资料放在附录中，从而突出关键信息，不因细节掩盖了主题。附件中的详细信息可在文本正文中引用，为读者提供简洁明了的答案，而不应仅仅提示读者去参考附件内容。附件中仅挑选与申报有明确关系的信息。附件中过多无用信息反而隐藏了原本清晰的潜在突出普遍价值的阐释参数，使申报评估更困难，且妨碍遗产突出的普遍价值的表达。

Those writing the dossier should always have in mind the key messages of what the property is, why it has potential Outstanding Universal Value and how this value is to be conserved, protected, managed and presented. This is to ensure that these key messages are not buried by detailed information.

在编写文本的时候，一定要牢记文本的核心内容：申报的遗产是什么，为什么他们具有突出普遍价值以及如何保护、保存、管理和阐释这些价值。如此方可保证这些关键信息不被冗长无用的细节所淹没。

The Operational Guidelines require a certain number of copies of the nomination to be provided depending on the type of property (see Paragraph 132.10). In all cases, the hard copies and electronic copies should be identical, even if one copy is considered to be the original. In addition to one copy being retained by the World Heritage Centre, other copies are distributed to the Advisory Bodies

《操作指南》要求，根据遗产类型的不同，准备不同数量的申报材料评估。（见 132 段，10）。所有情况下，打印版材料和电子版材料应当完全一致，尽管只有一份是原版。由于世界遗产中心会保存一份材料，其他则分发给各个咨询机构进行评估，所以，每份材料的信息必须完全一致，这一点非常重要。同时还要注意《操作指南》中关于文件的格式的要求。（132 段）

for assessment, and it is important that exactly the same information is provided in each copy. Note also the requirements in *The Operational Guidelines* about the format for the dossier (Paragraph 132).

The finalization and formal signing of the nomination should be publicly celebrated rather than treated as a mere technicality.

申遗文本定稿并正式签字不应仅视为一个技术细节，而应该让公众知晓。

Additional guidance is provided below.

额外指导见下文。

Printed documents

打印文档

• Documents should be clearly printed, well organized and laid out in standard format. If in doubt keep the layout simple and clear, and use a small number of fonts.

• 文档应该清晰打印，按照标准格式组织和安排。保证版式设计简单清晰，尽可能使用较少的的字体类型。

• Use pictures and diagrams to illustrate the property and its issues where possible — choose illustrations and pictures that make clear points about the property and its values, integrity or management issues.

• 使用图表阐释遗产和与他们相关的问题——选择能够清晰解释遗址和价值、完整性或管理问题的插图和图片。

• Choose a selection of images that illustrate the full range of aspects of a property, and avoid repetition where possible.

• 选择的图像能充分说明遗产的各个组成部分，避免重复。

• Documentation must be presented in either English or French. It is a good idea to make sure that a final draft nomination is reviewed by someone with a high standard of either language to make sure it is clearly written and intelligible.

• 文件必须用英语或法语。申遗文本完稿后最好由精通英语或法语的人审核一遍，这样能确保表述清晰和明确。

• The World Heritage nomination format does not lend itself to the creation of publications with widespread or public appeal, as it is too technical. It is therefore recommended that nomination documents be supplemented by the preparation of more popular documentation after inscription.

• 世界遗产申报文件格式本身技术性很强，不宜公开出版以满足公众需求。因此建议该遗产列入《世界遗产名录》之后，编制更为通俗的文件作为对申报文件的补充。

• Remember that the priority is the quality of the case and arguments within the nomination, and not its presentation. A poor case that is presented in a beautiful book is still a poor argument for

• 记住最重要的是申报材料的重点是项目和论据的质量，而不是它的表现。缺乏论据但外观精美的申遗文本对申遗帮助不大。

inscription.

• Some nominations are provided in an elaborate and special box. While packaging the information in a box can be practically convenient, it is the quality of the information which is important, not the quality of the packaging.

• Print enough nomination documents to meet the needs of relevant stakeholders.

• Nomination documents should be well distributed and visible among local stakeholders, and should be accessible. It is a good idea to distribute free copies to local stakeholders, and if a cover price is charged it should be at a level that does not put the publication out of reach of relevant stakeholders.

• Providing a free copy of a nomination document is a good way to thank those who have contributed.

• Typical print runs for nomination documents range from less than a hundred to several thousand. Depending on the needs of stakeholders and other interested parties, it may be wise to wait until after the decision of the World Heritage Committee before undertaking large print runs for wide distribution. Nonetheless, at least some copies of the nomination will be needed soon after it is finalized.

• 一些申遗文本被放在精美和特别的盒子里提交。存放文件的盒子应该便于使用，但信息的质量是关键，盒子的质量无关紧要。

• 打印足够份数的申遗文本以满足利益相关者需求。

• 申遗文本应便于当地利益相关者查阅。最好给当地利益相关者免费发放复印件，如果要收取一定的费用，则不应超过利益相关者能够承受的水平。

• 提供免费的申遗文本复印件给参与者是表达感谢最好的一种方式。

• 申遗文本的印刷数量从少于100册到上千册。应等到遗产委员会做出决议后，根据利益相关者和其他利益团队的需要再加大印刷量。尽管如此，申遗文本终稿完成后就必须准备复制一些。

Electronic documents

• An electronic version of the nomination document is required for every nomination, including annexes.

• The electronic version should be produced from the file that forms the printed document, so that the format and page numbering are identical. The information must be identical between printed and electronic copies.

• It is recommended to provide Microsoft Word and Adobe PDF files.

• The nomination dossier is usually reviewed

电子文档

• 每一个申报遗产都需要准备电子版申遗文本，包括附件；

• 电子版应该与打印文件完全一致，保证格式和页码完全相同。电子版和打印版的所有信息都必须一致。

• 电子文件需要提供微软 Word 和 Adobe PDF 两个版本。

• 在咨询委员会评估的过程中，会有很多专

by many experts in the overall process undertaken by the Advisory Bodies. This means providing a copy to these experts, often in electronic form. Accordingly, the resolution of electronic documents needs to be sufficient for experts to be able to examine the detail of images such as photographs and maps. Poor quality images are of no use. If in doubt, provide the highest resolution images, especially in the case of maps and historical images.

家评估申遗文本。也就是说，要向这些专家提供文件，通常是电子版。因此，需要高分辨率电子版让专家能够审查照片和地图等图像细节。低分辨率的图像毫无用处。如果不确定，则提供最高分辨率的图像，特别是地图和历史影像。

• Otherwise, think about the file size of the document, and in particular avoid using unnecessarily large image files. Scale images to suit the resolution of the document — very large/high-quality images are not usually necessary in A4 documents. Also reduce the overall file size using the option available in producing the PDF version. Images that should remain as large files/high quality can be annexed and provided as a separate file. In the case of large files, it is also suggested that a text-only version be provided as well as a text and image version. If a text-only version is provided, include the images (including maps) as separate files.

• 另外，考虑到文件的大小，避免使用不必要的过大照片。照片的大小要与文档分辨率适应——A4 纸的文档不需要太高质量的图片。使用 PDF 文档时也可用工具来压缩整个文件的容量。高分辨率的大图片文件可作为附件独立提交。如果文件较大，还建议在提交图文并茂的文件的同时，提供一份纯文字文件。如果提供的是纯文字文件，图片和地图应该作成独立文件提交。

• Avoid unusual fonts unless it is possible to embed them within the document. Such fonts may not work on other computers.

• 避免使用非常规的字体，除非这些字体可以嵌入文档。因为这些字体在其他计算机中可能无法正常显示。

• It is a good idea to establish a website to ensure availability of an electronic version of the World Heritage nomination.

• 建议建立网站并提供可用的申遗文本的电子版。

• Any additional supporting information should be copied onto CD.

• 其他附加的支持信息应该刻录在 CD 中。

Annexes

附件

• The main nomination document should be able to stand alone in conveying the arguments for inscription, and all the key requirements in relation to integrity, authenticity, protection and management of the property. Additional information can be usefully included in annexes. However caution should be taken in using annexes, and the

• 申报文件正文应当能够独立传达申请列入《世界遗产名录》的论据，符合对遗产完整性、真实性、保护和管理等相关要求。其他的一些有用信息可包括在附件中。然而，制作附件时必须谨慎，附件信息必须能清晰高质的支持申遗文本正文的所有关键信息。关键信息应该在主要文件而不是附件中出现。

focus should be on ensuring the main nomination document includes all the essential information and that it is clear and of high quality. Essential information should not be included in annexes but should be in the main document.

• Very large annexes of supporting information should be avoided if possible. It is recommended that only information that genuinely adds value to the information already summarized in the nomination should be included in annexes. Avoid adding documents to the annexes simply for the sake of completeness.

• 应该避免特别大的附件。再次提醒，只有在申遗文本概况中已有、能直接增加遗产申报价值的信息，才能作为附件。避免为了完整性而任意添加附件。

• The nomination should specifically mention the relevance of material that is included in annexes. It is generally impractical for the Advisory Bodies to circulate large amounts of annexed material to evaluators and reviewers. So key information should always be referred to directly in the nomination document. The Advisory Bodies cannot be expected to find key information if it is deeply buried in large annexes.

• 申报文件应当具体说明附件所包含资料的相关性。对于咨询机构而言，对大量的附件材料进行评估和查询不切实际。关键信息应该在申遗文本正文中直接体现。不要期望咨询机构在庞杂的附件材料中找到深埋在附件里的关键信息。

• Annexes should also be submitted in an electronic version.

• 附件材料也要提交电子版。

Maps

地图

• The quality and clarity of maps provided as part of the nomination is often an issue in terms of their usefulness for understanding the property. The requirements for maps are discussed in the Section 4.2.

• 高质量、清晰的地图是申遗文本的组成部分，是理解遗产的重要手段。对于地图的要求将在 4.2 节中讨论。

• In addition, the following two examples of maps help to show what is required for cultural and natural properties.

• 此外，下面两张地图样例将展示文化和自然遗产对于地图的要求。

The most common reason for incompleteness of nominations are issues linked to the identification of the property, especially regarding the maps provided, and it is very helpful to note six key requirements for adequate maps:

认为申遗文本不完整的最常见的理由是遗产的辨识部分、特别是与地图有关，一个高质量的地图应该包括以下六个组成部分：

• Choose the proper typology of map depending on the category of property to be represented - topographic maps for large properties, and cadastral plans for smaller properties.

• The proposed boundary lines should be as thin as possible yet still easily seen. Colours should not cover topographic elements, and thin yet visible lines are preferable to clearly define the boundaries. The main identification map (s) should only contain the lines identifying the proposed nominated property and its buffer zone (if any).

• The map should have a coordinates grid or show the coordinates of a series of identified points.

• It is important to choose the appropriate scale. Natural properties and cultural landscapes are normally better identified with 1: 50, 000 scale topographic maps, and it does not matter if more than one map is needed to show the whole property. For other cultural properties, usually cadastral plans are the best option. For single monuments, the scale should not be less than 1: 2, 000. In addition, a bar and numerical scale should be shown on all maps.

• The map should carry a clear caption only identifying the boundary lines of the proposed nominated property and its buffer zone (if any) (see second dot point above). The main identification map should not carry information on other zones of protection, in order to avoid any confusion. The caption should use the terminology of *The Operational Guidelines* — do not use terms such as ‘protection zone’, ‘conservation area’, ‘historic district’, etc.

• The maps and plans submitted, including the caption, should be either in English or French.

EXAMPLE OF MAPS

Map of a cultural property

This fictional example shows one of the most

• 不同类型的遗产应选择不同类型的地图——大遗产使用地形图，小遗产使用地籍图。

• 划定的边界线在可识别的情况下要尽可能的细，其颜色不能覆盖地形图的内容，标明遗产的边界的细线最好清晰可辨。遗产认定的主要地图应该包括申报的遗产区线条和缓冲区线条（如果有缓冲区）。

• 地图应该有坐标网格或者标注有辨识点的坐标。

• 应选择适当比例的地图。自然遗产和文化景观最好是 1：50000 的地形图，可用多幅地图展现完整的遗产范围。对于其他类型如文化遗产，地籍图是最佳选择，对于单独的文物，比例不能小于 1：2000。另外，在所有的地图上都应该有图形和数字比例尺。

• 申报遗产在地图上应该有明确的边界线和缓冲区界线（如有，参见上文第二点）。用于遗产辨认的主要地图中不应该包括其他保护区域的信息，以免让人误解。地图名称应该使用《操作指南》中提到的专业术语——不要使用如保护区、保存区、历史街区这样的名词。

• 所提交的地形图和地籍图，包括图例都应当采用英语或法语。

地图案例

文化遗产的地图

这个虚构的文化遗产地图是最普通的类型

common types of cultural property in which the boundaries run through an urban area. The map clearly distinguishes the proposed nominated property and its buffer zone. There are no other lines showing other protection zones which may lead to confusion. The scale of the map (cadastral), along with the appropriate thickness of the lines showing the boundaries (a line which is too thick loses precision), provides the required level of detail to establish whether a given point (building, block, street, etc.) is within or outside the proposed boundaries. Also, the presence of the scale-bar and a clear caption which uses the appropriate definitions ('nominated property' and'buffer zone') and language (the language on the maps should be the same as used in the nomination text) ensure the clarity of the proposed boundaries. Finally, while a coordinate grid is not necessary in the case of cadastral maps, it is essential in all other kinds.

之一，遗产的边界穿越了市区。地图清晰的界定了遗产区和缓冲区。在地图中没有会引起混淆的其他保护区的界线。这张地图比例尺恰当（地籍图），遗产的边界线条粗细适当（如果线太粗就会失去精确度），按要求提供的细节用于确定某个给定的点的位置（建筑、街区、街道等等）在遗产区内还是在遗产区外。同时，在地图中使用恰当定义的清晰图例（遗产区和缓冲区）和清晰明确语言（地图上标注的语言应该和申遗文本中所用的语言一致）标注比例尺。最后，所有类型的地形图必须具备坐标网，地籍图除外。

Map of a natural property

This example relates to the Jeju Volcanic Island and Lava Tubes (Republic of Korea) and shows the case of a serial natural property. The topographic map carries a coordinate grid, scale-bar, a clear caption, and the lines showing the proposed boundaries are not too thick yet clearly visible. Very importantly, the topographic elements (such as roads, rivers, mountains, villages, etc.) are all visible and identifiable on the map. The boundaries should always be marked with lines, and the proposed areas should not be covered with uniform colours that hide the details of the topographic elements present on the map.

自然遗产地图

以系列自然遗产济州火山岛和熔岩洞（韩国）为例。地形图上标有坐标网、比例尺、清晰的图例、遗产区边界线粗细适宜清晰。最为重要的是，地形图上的地形内容（道路、河流、村庄、山脉等）都可以在地图上清楚辨识。边界均用线条标示，遗产区不能用统一的颜色覆盖，以免遮蔽地形内容。

Note: These examples have been reduced in size for this manual. In the nomination dossier, the maps should be produced at a size to enable details to be understood.

注：为了便于手册编写，地图的尺寸已经缩小。在申遗文本中，地图的大小应该以能够显示细节为准。

Key message: Be realistic about the time needed to prepare a nomination

Timetable for preparing the nomination and submission

Writing nominations often takes longer than anticipated. Although it is understood that once a decision has been taken to submit a nomination, all those involved wish to achieve that as quickly as possible, nevertheless timescales must be realistic. As set out above, adequate time needs to be allowed for preliminary processes before writing begins. For the writing process, time should also be allowed for adequate consultations and checking, and for assembling suitable maps and illustrations.

Take into account the fact that often ensuring adequate protection, conservation and management need extra time. Similarly, there is often a lack of readily available information for the comparative analysis, especially about comparable properties in other countries.

A reasonable contingency time should also be built into the process to cope with things that go wrong.

Key message: Do not rush to submit a nomination before it is ready.

The Advisory Bodies often note that nominations appear rushed, without all elements fully worked through prior to submission. This is a common reason underlying recommendations from ICOMOS and IUCN for nominations to be deferred or referred back to the State Party for additional work. In such situations, the haste to submit the nomination can actually lengthen the time taken to achieve a successful inscription.

关键信息：注意准备遗产申报需要的时间应切合实际

准备申报和提交文本的时间表

编写申遗文本需要的时间往往比预期的要长。一旦决定提交申遗文本，所有参与人都希望尽快完成，但是时间表必须切合实际。如上所述，动笔前的准备过程需要充足的时间。文本的编写过程中，也需要给咨询、校对、收集合适的地图和插图留时间。

要考虑到，确保遗产的保存、保护和管理到位也需要时间。同样，收集比较分析的可用信息也需要大量的时间，特别是从其他国家找寻类似遗产信息，收集相关信息也需要时间。

同时应该留出一段灵活的时间，用来纠正错误。

关键信息：在申遗文本没有准备好之前，不用急于提交

咨询机构常常注意到，申遗文本准备仓促，未能在提交申报文件之前处理好所有相关因素。国际古迹遗址理事会和世界自然保护联盟常常由于这个原因会建议延迟申报，或将其退回缔约国加以完善，在这种情况下，仓促提交申报材料反而会延长成功申报所需的时间。

The aim should be to send everything at the same time and not in stages. Although supplementary material can be submitted after the main dossier has been accepted, this should be in response to any requests from the Advisory Bodies or any unforeseen, or occasionally planned, circumstances.

所有的文件应同时提交而不是分阶段进行。尽管可以在接受主要文件后提交补充材料，但仅限于咨询机构提出的新要求或未能预见的、突发情况或未能列入计划的情况。

It is also desirable that nominations are not sent at the last moment before the deadline for submission. The deadline for submissions is absolute. Nominations can be submitted at any time well before the deadline.

申遗文本最好不要在截止日期的最后一刻才提交。要严格遵守提交的最后期限。申遗文本可在截止日期前之任何时间提交。

The Operational Guidelines provide that States Parties may voluntarily submit draft nominations to the World Heritage Centre for comment on completeness by 30 September of each year (Paragraph 127). This is a very useful opportunity for States Parties to have aspects of the nomination checked prior to final submission. A well-planned nomination process should include this step. However, it should be noted that the assessment of the World Heritage Centre is advisory and only relates to the completeness of the nomination. It is not a comment on the possible strength of the case for potential Outstanding Universal Value which is only assessed by IUCN and/or ICOMOS after a completed nomination is accepted.

《操作指南》提出，缔约国可以在每年的 9 月 30 日（第 127 条）前自愿向世界遗产中心提交申遗文本的草稿，对文件的完整性进行咨询。缔约国可以在提交最终文本前利用这一难得的机会，对其各部分内容进行审查。一个好的申报过程应该包含这一步。然而，世界遗产中心的咨询评估只是建议和意见，也只针对文本的完整性而不评判潜在突出普遍价值的强弱。国际古迹遗址理事会和世界自然保护联盟在收到了完整的申遗文本后，才评估突出普遍价值。

4.2 Nomination format

4.2 申报材料的格式

Key message: Carefully read the explanatory notes as well as the additional advice.

关键信息：仔细阅读解释条款和其他建议

The World Heritage Committee has approved an official format for World Heritage nominations and the latest version of this information must always be followed when submitting a nomination (see *Operational Guidelines*, Annex 5). The format is designed to provide the World Heritage

世界遗产委员会提供了申报世界遗产的正式格式，当提交申遗文本时，必须要关注最新版本的格式信息（《操作指南》，附件 5）。按正式格式提交是保证向世界遗产委员会提交的申报项目内容统一，且符合标准。官方标准格式中包含注释，对每一部分的要求进行了说明。

Committee with consistent information about nominated properties, to the specified standard. The official format includes a commentary on what is required in each section.

It is important to note that the World Heritage Committee will only examine nominations that are regarded as complete at the deadline for submission. Therefore only complete nominations are forwarded to IUCN and/or ICOMOS for evaluation. Incomplete nominations are returned without further consideration to the State Party, they must be completed and resubmitted, and then will be reconsidered at least one year later. Paragraph 132 along with Annex 5 of *The Operational Guidelines* set out what constitutes a complete nomination.

世界遗产委员会只对格式完整的、在截止日期前提交的文件进行审查。只有完整的申遗文本才会转交给世界自然保护联盟和国际古迹遗址理事会进行评估。不完整的申遗文本将退还缔约国，必须得到进一步完善后方可重新提交，推迟至少一年的时间后方再次考虑。在《操作指南》附件 5 第 132 段中明确定义了完整的申遗文本所应当包括的内容。

Key message: It is essential that all sections of the nomination format are completed.

关键信息：必须确定申遗文本所有部分都按格式完成

This section of the manual provides a copy of the existing World Heritage nomination format together with additional advice or tips for key sections.

本章将提供世界遗产申报版式和各部分应该注意的问题、提示和建议。

Check for the latest version of the official format for nominations at the World Heritage website (whc.unesco.org) or contact the World Heritage Centre.

可在世界遗产网站上找最新的申报格式，或直接与世界遗产中心联系。

Executive Summary

《执行摘要》

This information, to be provided by the State Party, will be updated by the Secretariat following the decision by the World Heritage Committee. It will then be returned to the State Party confirming the basis on which the property is inscribed on the World Heritage List

执行摘要的信息应该由缔约国提供，在世界遗产委员会做出决议后，由秘书处更新。然后反馈给缔约国，作为遗产列入《世界遗产名录》的基本依据。

Existing nomination form INFORMATION HEADING	Existing nomination form EXPLANATORY NOTES	Additional advice
		• The information in this Executive Summary should be the same as that provided in the main part of the nomination itself. • The Executive Summary should provide a clear and concise overview of what is being nominated and why. • It should be short and concise, *between one and three pages*, and should not include long descriptive text. • New text should not be written for the Executive Summary. The Statement of Outstanding Universal Value should be the same as that under Section 3b of the nomination, for example. If these sections are well written within the nomination they should not require shortening for the Executive Summary.
State Party		
State, province or region		
Name of property		
Geographical coordinates to the nearest second		
Textual description of the boundary(ies) of the nominated property		The maps provided with the nomination and the textual description should together show unambiguously the location of the boundary of the property and also any buffer zones defined. It is not always necessary to describe the entire boundary but to give a general description of how it is defined. For example: • The boundaries of the nominated property are those of the <property name> National Park / cultural site. A buffer zone of 1–5 km surrounds the nominated property following natural features, including the River <name> to the south and south-east, the limit of the <name> forest reserve to the north, and the coastline to the low-tide mark to the west and south. • The boundaries of the serial transnational nominated property are those of the <name> National Park (country A), <name> Conservation Area (country A) and <name> Strict Nature Reserve (country B). • The nominated property includes four islands of the <place name> archipelago and the surrounding waters for 12 nautical miles from the low-tide mark of each Island.

Existing nomination form INFORMATION HEADING	Existing nomination form EXPLANATORY NOTES	Additional advice
A4 (or 'letter') size map of the nominated property, showing boundaries and buffer zone (if present)	Attach A4 (or 'letter') size map	This is the map that will be used in the Advisory Body's evaluation report, in the presentation to the World Heritage Committee. Therefore, it must be correct and easy to read. Some key points to remember are that the map should: • be A4 (or 'letter') size to facilitate its use as noted above; • be an extract from a topographic map; • clearly show the entire nominated property, and its buffer zone, using different coloured, clearly visible lines for the nominated property and for the buffer zone(s); • have a clear caption in English or French (depending on the language of the nomination) referring specifically to the 'nominated property' and naming component sites in the case of serial properties; and • have a clearly marked scale indicating size and distance. It may be helpful to have a small box (general location map) in the corner of the main map showing the general location within the country(ies) concerned. For serial properties that cannot adequately fit on one A4 page, a number of A4 size maps should be provided to include: • one map showing the entire property, the location and distance between each component; and • one or more maps showing each individual component and its buffer zone. The map(s) should be included in the Executive Summary and not referred to or attached later in the document or as an annex. • More detailed topographical and other maps are to be included in other sections of the nomination document.
Criteria under which property is nominated (itemize criteria) (see Paragraph 77 of the *Operational Guidelines*)		• The criteria for which the property is being nominated should simply be listed together with a short statement of not more than 100 words per criteria.

Existing nomination form INFORMATION HEADING	Existing nomination form EXPLANATORY NOTES	Additional advice
Draft Statement of Outstanding Universal Value (text should clarify what is considered to be the Outstanding Universal Value embodied by the nominated property, approximately 1-2 page format)	According to the paragraph 155, the Statement of Outstanding Universal Value should be composed of: a. Brief synthesis b. Justification for Criteria c. Statement of Integrity (for all properties) d. Statement of authenticity for properties nominated under criteria (i) to (vi) e. Requirements for protection and management See format in Annex 10	• This statement should be the same as that under Section 3.3 of the nomination document. • The statement should be concise and sufficient to convey information about the most important features of the property. More detail can be provided in sections 3.1.a-3.1.e.
Name and contact information of official local institution / agency	Organization: Address: Tel: Fax: E-mail: Web address:	• The details sought should at least be for the lead agency contact point for the nomination in the State Party. • Details of the lead agency contact points at other levels within the State Party may also be provided (e.g. provincial or local governments). • For a serial national property, one lead contact agency should be cited. For transnational properties, each lead national agency should be cited.

现有的申报形式 标题	现存的申报形式 填报须知	其他建议
		在《执行摘要》中的提供信息要与申遗文本正文一致； 《执行摘要》应该清晰准确的说明申报遗产是什么，为什么要申报； 报告要短小精炼，一般在 1–3 页，不得用较长的文字描述； 新的文本内容不要出现在《执行摘要》中。突出普遍价值声明应该和文本中的第 3b 节相一致，如果这个章节在申遗文本上写的很好很长，在《执行摘要》中也不需要删减。
缔约国		
国家，省或区		
遗产名称		
地理坐标（到秒）		
申报遗产边界描述		申报文件中用地图和文字描述一起来显示明确的遗产区边界、缓冲区边界的位置。通常不需要描述所有遗产区范围，只需要一般性的说明边界是如何确定的。例如： 遗产区边界是某某遗产、自然公园和文化遗址的边界，缓冲区为遗产区外扩 1–5 公里，包括了一些自然特性，如南侧和东南侧到某某河，北部到某某森林保护区边缘，西部和南部到低海潮水位线。 系列跨国遗产的遗产区是某某自然公园（国家 A），某某保护区（国家 A），某某自然保护区（国家 B）的界限。 遗产区包括某群岛的 4 个小岛及周边 12 海里的水域（从每个岛的低潮水位线算起）

续表

现有的申报形式标题	现存的申报形式填报须知	其他建议
遗产区地图应为 A4（或“信纸”）大小，展现遗产区和缓冲区边界（如果有）	附 A4（或信纸）大小地图	这地图将用于咨询机构的评估报告和在世界遗产委员会上作说明时。因此，这张图必须准确易读。制图时应该牢记以下组成部分： • 使用 A4 大小纸张，以便用于上述用途； • 使用地形图作为底图； • 清楚的展示整个遗产区和缓冲区，遗产区和缓冲区使用不同颜色和清晰可见的线来标识； • 有清晰的图例（英语或法语），明确提及遗产区，系列申报中应标明遗产各组成部分； • 有明显的比例尺，注明遗址尺寸和距离， • 如果能在地图（总体位置图）的一角留出一个小框，用来说明该遗产在所涉及的一个（或多个）国家中的整体位置，将很有用； 如果系列遗产不能调整到一张 A4 纸大小的图上，可以采用多张 A4 纸大小地图，其中提供以下信息： • 有一张整个遗产的示意图，要标明每个组成部分的位置和距离， • 一张或多张图标明单个组成部分区和缓冲区， • 地图应该包括在《执行摘要》中，不能见于以后章节，也不能做成附件。 • 更多详细的地形图或其他地图应该包括在申报文件的其他章节中。
申报标准（分项标准）（见《操作指南》77 段）		• 罗列遗产的申报标准，每条标准都应简单描述，但字数不超过 100 字
突出普遍价值声明草案（正文应该证明遗产所具备的突出普遍价值，最多2页）	根据第 155 段，突出普遍价值声明应该包括： a. 简要概述 b. 标准论证 c. 完整性声明（所有遗产） d. 真实性声明（符合标准 Ⅰ 到 Ⅵ 的遗产） e. 保障和管理的必要条件见附件 10	这个声明应该和申报文件 3.3 章完全一致。 声明应该准确充分的表达遗产最为重要的组成部分信息。详见章节 3.1a–3.1e
当地官方研究或管理机构的名称和联系方式	机构名称： 地址： 电话： 传真： 网址：	• 详细信息应包括缔约国负责申报事宜机构的联络信息。 • 也需要提供其他层次机构的联系信息详情（省级或当地政府）。 • 国内系列遗产，应该有一个主要联系机构。对于跨国遗产，要提供每一个国家主要联系机构的详细信息。

Properties for inscription on the World Heritage List

Note: In preparing the nomination, States Parties should use this format but delete the explanatory notes.

Existing nomination form NOMINATION FORMAT	Existing nomination form EXPLANATORY NOTES	Additional advice
1. Identification of the property	Together with Section 2, this is the most important section in the nomination. It must make clear to the Committee precisely where the property is located and how it is geographically defined. In the case of serial nominations, insert a table that shows the name of the component part, region (if different for different components), coordinates, area and buffer zone. Other fields could also be added (page reference or map number, etc.) that differentiate the several components.	• This section of the nomination document provides factual information about the location and size of a nominated property. It should be short and concise. Particular attention should be given to the maps provided.

Existing nomination form NOMINATION FORMAT	Existing nomination form EXPLANATORY NOTES	Additional advice
1.a Country (and State Party if different)		• The country (or countries in the case of transboundary or transnational properties) that is nominating the property should simply be named. No information about the country is required.
1.b State, province or region		• The state(s), province(s) or region(s) within which the nominated property lies should be named or listed. In the case of transboundary or transnational properties, include the country beside each state, province or region listed.
1.c Name of property	This is the official name of the property that will appear in published material about World Heritage. It should be concise. Do not exceed 200 characters, including spaces and punctuation. In the case of serial nominations (see Paragraphs 137–140 of the *Operational Guidelines*), give a name for the ensemble (e.g. Baroque Churches of the Philippines). Do not include the name of the components of a serial nomination, which should be included in a table as part of 1.d and 1.f.	• The name of the property should make sense in terms of any existing local or national name for the property, and the character / values of the property. It may be better to use a recognized name rather than an invented one. • Remember that the name will be used in promotion of the property in the future. • The name of the property should be concise and not exceed 200 characters, including spaces and punctuation. • Consultation at the national and local levels may be necessary to ensure that local language, culture and tradition are taken into consideration. • In some cases, two joined names are chosen (e.g. Te Wahipounamu – South West New Zealand, and uKhahlamba / Drakensberg Park). • For serial properties, one overall name should be chosen (e.g. Three Parallel Rivers Protected Areas, Tropical Rain - forest Heritage of Sumatra, Canadian Rocky Mountain Parks). • For transboundary or transnational properties, the name of the property must be agreed by both countries concerned, e.g. Uvs Nuur Basin (Mongolia and Russian Federation), and High Coast / Kvarken Archipelago (Finland and Sweden). • It is preferable not to use the names of many separate components but rather a name that captures the values of the whole property.
1.d Geographical coordinates to the nearest second	In this space provide the latitude and longitude coordinates (to the nearest second) or UTM coordinates (to the nearest 10 metres) of a point at the approximate centre of the nominated property. Do not use other coordinate systems. If in doubt, please consult the Secretariat. In the case of serial nominations, provide a table showing the name of each component part, its region (or nearest town as appropriate), and the coordinates of its centre point. Coordinate format examples: N 45° 06′ 05″ W 15° 37′ 56″ or UTM Zone 18 Easting: 545670 Northing: 4586750	

ID No.	Name of the component part	Region(s) / District(s)	Coordinates of the Central Point	Area of Nominated component of the Property (ha)	Area of the Buffer Zone (ha)	Map N°
001						
002						
003						
Etc.						
			Total area (in hectares)	ha	ha	

Existing nomination form NOMINATION FORMAT	Existing nomination form EXPLANATORY NOTES	Additional advice
1.e Maps and plans, showing the boundaries of the nominated property and buffer zone	Annex to the nomination, and list below with scales and dates: (i) An original copy of a topographic map showing the property nominated, at the largest scale available which shows the entire property. The boundaries of the nominated property and buffer zone should be clearly marked. Either on this map, or an accompanying one, there should also be a record of the boundaries of zones of special legal protection from which the property benefits. Multiple maps may be necessary for serial nominations (see table in 1.d). The maps provided should be at the largest available and practical scale to allow the identification of topographic elements such as neighbouring settlements, buildings and routes in order to allow the clear assessment of the impact of any proposed development within, adjacent to, or on the boundary line. Care is needed with the width of boundary lines on maps, as thick boundary lines may make the actual boundary of the property ambiguous. Maps may be obtained from the addresses shown at the following Web page http://whc.unesco.org/en/mapagencies If topographic maps are not available at the appropriate scale, other maps may be substituted. All maps should be capable of being geo-referenced, with a minimum of three points on opposite sides of the maps with complete sets of coordinates. The maps, untrimmed, should show scale, orientation, projection, datum, property name and date. If possible, maps should be sent rolled and not folded. Geographic Information in digital form is encouraged if possible, suitable for incorporation into a GIS (Geographic Information System). In this case the delineation of the boundaries (nominated property and buffer zone) should be presented in vector form, prepared at the largest scale possible. The State Party is invited to contact the Secretariat for further information concerning this option.	• The maps and plans (drawings) required for cultural heritage properties depend on the type of property and its history. They must portray aspects of the potential Outstanding Universal Value in some way. • The scale, detail and resolution of maps and plans should be sufficient to enable boundaries to be related to features, and for the context of the property to be easily understood. • Stylized maps with minimal schematic information do not meet the requirements. Large-scale topographic maps or cadastral plans (for cultural properties) are usually ideal, even if these are used as the base for information overlaid on top. • Where features of the property are indicated on maps / plans or in the written text, a consistent naming or coding system should be used to enable easy cross-reference between the map / plan and the written text. That is, a feature name used on a map should be the same as that used in the text. The language used on maps or plans should be either English or French. • It is recommended a map be provided identifying the location of the country (maximum A4 or 'letter' size). • It is recommended the location map of the property within the country be a maximum A4 or 'letter' size. • In addition, it is recommended a topographic map or a cadastral plan (for cultural properties) showing the entire nominated property, its boundaries and the buffer zone (maximum A4 or 'letter' size) be provided. This is the same map to be used in the Executive Summary. • It is essential that an original topographic map or a cadastral plan (for cultural properties) showing the nominated property, its boundaries and the buffer zone to the largest scale possible be provided. • Important features referred to in the text should be highlighted on maps or plans at a suitable scale, but not on the main map showing the proposed boundaries. • Where original base maps / plans are in colour, then colour versions should also be provided. • It is very important to prepare a good caption for the map showing the boundaries. The caption should identify

Existing nomination form NOMINATION FORMAT	Existing nomination form EXPLANATORY NOTES	Additional advice
	(ii) A location map showing the location of the property within the State Party. (iii) Plans and specially prepared maps of the property showing individual features are helpful and may also be annexed. To facilitate copying and presentation to the Advisory Bodies and the World Heritage Committee A4 (or "letter") size reduction and a digital image file of the principal maps should be included in the nomination text if possible. Where no buffer zone is proposed, the nomination must include a statement as to why a buffer zone is not required for the proper protection of the nominated property.	the *nominated property* and its *buffer zone* (if any) using the terminology of the *Operational Guidelines*. These boundaries should be clear and not confusing, such as with other linework on the map. • In the case of some serial nominations, a location plan showing all components of the nomination should be provided, as well as individual location plans for components to enable components to be related to their surrounding region. For serial properties that cannot adequately fit on one A4 page, a number of A4 size maps should be provided to include: (i) one map showing the entire property, the location and distance between each component; and (ii) one or more maps showing each individual component and its buffer zone. • For serial national and transnational properties an original topographical map clearly marking the boundaries should be provided for each component of the property. • In the case of nominations proposing an extension to an existing property, it is useful to have a map showing the location of the original property in comparison to the location of the proposed extension. • Additional maps to illustrate specific values, features or issues can be provided in other sections, *not* the identification section, including: - Geological map – for properties nominated under criterion (viii); - Vegetation map – for properties nominated under criteria (ix) and (x); - Species distribution map – for properties nominated under criteria (ix) and (x); - Infrastructure or infrastructure proposals (e.g. road and road building, dams, future development, etc); and - Access map – to show major access routes within and adjacent to the property. • The basic maps in A4 size identifying the location and boundaries of the property should be included in the main document. Additional maps should usually be included in the annexes, be clearly marked and referred to in the text. A list of maps and where to find them should be included in Section 1.e. • A good way to present maps is in A3 size, folded over to fit within an A4 size document.

Existing nomination form NOMINATION FORMAT	Existing nomination form EXPLANATORY NOTES	Additional advice
		• Maps should also be included in electronic form on an attached CD. • Topographic maps are essential for the nomination to be complete for non-urban properties. In the same way, cadastral plans are crucial for urban properties. Nominations which only include drawings, including computer drawn maps, will lead to a nomination being considered incomplete. • Any setting for the property (beyond the buffer zone) should also be indicated on a relevant map(s). See pages 85–86 of this manual.
1.f Area of nominated property (ha) and proposed buffer zone (ha) **Area of nominated property: _______ ha** **Buffer zone _______ ha** **Total _______ ha**	In the case of serial nominations (see Paragraphs 137–140 of the *Operational Guidelines*), insert a table that shows the name of the component part, region (if different for different components), coordinates, area and buffer zone. The serial nomination table should also be used to show the size of the separate nominated areas and of the buffer zone(s).	
2. Description		• It is recommended that this section of the nomination is completed after finalizing Section 3 – the justification for inscription. The description should expand on the justification for inscription and include the information and evidence supporting the conclusions which should be summarized in the justification, as well as other information that provides a complete picture of the nominated property. However care is needed that the description remains focused and is not too long.
2.a Description of property	This section should begin with a description of the nominated property at the date of nomination. It should refer to all the significant features of the property. In the case of a cultural property this section will include a description of whatever elements make the property culturally significant. It could include a description of any building or buildings and their architectural style, date of construction, materials, etc. This section should also describe important aspects of the setting such as gardens, parks, etc. For a rock art site, for example, the description should refer to the rock art as well as the surrounding landscapes. In the case of an historic town or district,	• The description should focus on those things which are associated with the potential Outstanding Universal Value of the property, as well as providing some general overview of the property. • The description should be sufficient to understand what has potential Outstanding Universal Value and its important characteristics. • A comprehensive, lengthy description of everything about the property is not necessary. • If the description is complex and very lengthy, it may be desirable to provide a summary description, with the detailed description included in an annex. • The description should focus on the nominated property whose boundaries

Existing nomination form NOMINATION FORMAT	Existing nomination form EXPLANATORY NOTES	Additional advice
	it is not necessary to describe each individual building, but important public buildings should be described individually and an account should be given of the planning or layout of the area, its street pattern and so on. In the case of a natural property the account should deal with important physical attributes, geology, habitats, species and population size, and other significant ecological features and processes. Species lists should be provided where practicable, and the presence of threatened or endemic taxa should be highlighted. The extent and methods of exploitation of natural resources should be described. In the case of cultural landscapes, it will be necessary to produce a description under all the matters mentioned above. Special attention should be paid to the interaction of man and nature. The entire nominated property identified in Section 1 (Identification of the property) should be described. In the case of serial nominations (see Paragraphs 137–140 of the *Operational Guidelines*), each of the component parts should be separately described.	are identified in the previous section. Description of elements outside the property could be offered, if relevant in some way, but the description of such elements is best presented separately (e.g. by means of a subtitle such as 'Description of relevant elements outside the property'). • Any setting for the property (beyond the buffer zone) should be discussed in this section. See pages 85–86 of this manual.
2.b History and development	Describe how the property has reached its present form and condition and the significant changes that it has undergone, including recent conservation history. This should include some account of construction phases in the case of monuments, sites, buildings or groups of buildings. Where there have been major changes, demolitions or rebuilding since completion they should also be described.	• As with the description, the history should focus on providing the story relevant to the potential Outstanding Universal Value of the property, as well as providing some general historical context for the property. • A comprehensive, lengthy history of everything about the property is not necessary. Such information can be included in an annex if necessary, or simply referenced. • It may be important to place the story of the property in a world historical context, in which case some information should be provided. This may be summarized rather than detailed at length. • Referencing the history is usually very important, as claims may rely on other sources of information which should be properly referenced and supportable. • In the case of the development history of the property, it is often very helpful to provide diagrams illustrating stages in development. For example, in the case of a town of mixed age buildings, it is

Existing nomination form NOMINATION FORMAT	Existing nomination form EXPLANATORY NOTES	Additional advice
	In the case of a natural property, the account should cover significant events in history or pre-history that have affected the evolution of the property and give an account of its interaction with humankind. This will include changes in the use of the property and its natural resources for hunting, fishing or agriculture, or changes brought about by climatic change, floods, earthquake or other natural causes. Such information will also be required in the case of cultural landscapes, where all aspects of the history of human activity in the area need to be covered.	helpful to have illustrations showing which buildings relate to which historical period as discussed in the text. • Other illustrations, such as maps, engravings or historical photographs can be used in the text. Ideally, these illustrations should help to explain some aspect of the story relating to the potential Outstanding Universal Value.
3. Justification for inscription [1]	The justification should be set out under the following sections. This section must make clear why the property is considered to be of 'Outstanding Universal Value'. The whole of this section of the nomination should be written with careful reference to the requirements of the *Operational Guidelines*. It should not include detailed descriptive material about the property or its management, which are addressed in other sections, but should convey the key aspects that are relevant to the definition of the Outstanding Universal Value of the property.	The text in the following sections 3.1.a-3.1.e should contain more detailed information to support the text provided in the Draft Statement of Outstanding Universal Value.
3.1.a Brief synthesis	The brief synthesis should comprise (i) a summary of factual information and (ii) a summary of qualities. The summary of factual information sets out the geographical and historical context and the main features. The summary of qualities should present to decision-makers and the general public the potential Outstanding Universal Value that needs to be sustained, and should also include a summary of the attributes that convey its potential Outstanding Universal Value, and need to be protected, managed and monitored. The summary should relate to all stated criteria in order to justify the nomination. The brief synthesis thus encapsulates the whole rationale for the nomination and proposed inscription.	This text should contain more detailed information to support the text provided in the Draft Statement of Outstanding Universal Value.
3.1.b Criteria under which inscription is proposed (and justification for inscription under these criteria)	See Paragraph 77 of the *Operational Guidelines*. Provide a separate justification for each criterion cited.	• See pages 60–61 of this manual. • The justification prepared under each criterion should be useful text in preparing the Statement of Outstanding Universal Value below.

Existing nomination form NOMINATION FORMAT	Existing nomination form EXPLANATORY NOTES	Additional advice
	State briefly how the property meets those criteria under which it has been nominated (where necessary, make reference to the 'description' and 'comparative analysis' sections of the nomination, but do not duplicate the text of these sections) and describe for each criterion the relevant attributes.	• The justification is really the argument why the property meets a criterion. • This text should contain more detailed information to support the text provided in the Draft Statement of Outstanding Universal Value.
3.1.c Statement of Integrity	The statement of integrity should demonstrate that the property fulfils the conditions of integrity set out in Section II.D of the *Operational Guidelines*, which describe these conditions in greater detail. The *Operational Guidelines* set out the need to assess the extent to which the property: • includes all elements necessary to express its Outstanding Universal Value; • is of adequate size to ensure the complete representation of the features and processes which convey the property's significance; • suffers from adverse effects of development and/or neglect (Paragraph 88). The *Operational Guidelines* provide specific guidance in relation to the various World Heritage criteria, which is important to understand (Paragraphs 89–95).	• See pages 61–67 of this manual. • The rationale for the property boundary should be provided in this section. • This text should contain more detailed information to support the text provided in the Draft Statement of Outstanding Universal Value.
3.1.d Statement of Authenticity (for nominations made under criteria (i) to (vi))	The statement of authenticity should demonstrate that the property fulfils the conditions of authenticity set out in Section II.D of the *Operational Guidelines*, which describe these conditions in greater detail. This section should summarise information that may be included in more detail in section 4 of the nomination (and possibly in other sections), and should not reproduce the level of detail included in those sections. Authenticity only applies to cultural properties and to the cultural aspects of 'mixed' properties. The *Operational Guidelines* state that 'properties may be understood to meet the conditions of authenticity if their cultural values (as recognized in the nomination criteria proposed) are truthfully and credibly expressed through a variety of attributes' (Paragraph 82). The *Operational Guidelines* suggest that the following types of attributes might	• See pages 61–67 of this manual. • This text should contain more detailed information to support the text provided in the Draft Statement of Outstanding Universal Value.

Existing nomination form NOMINATION FORMAT	Existing nomination form EXPLANATORY NOTES	Additional advice
	be considered as conveying or expressing Outstanding Universal Value: • form and design; • materials and substance; • use and function; • traditions, techniques and management systems; • location and setting; • language and other forms of intangible heritage; • spirit and feeling; and • other internal/external factors.	
3.1.e Protection and management requirements	This section should set out how the requirements for protection and management will be met, in order to ensure that the Outstanding Universal Value of the property is maintained over time. It should include both details of an overall framework for protection and management, and the identification of specific long term expectations for the protection of the property. This section should summarise information that may be included in more detail in section 5 of the nomination document (and also potentially in sections 4 and 6), and should not reproduce the level of detail included in those sections. The text in this section should first outline the framework for protection and management. This should include the necessary protection mechanisms, management systems and/or management plans (whether currently in place or in need of establishment) that will protect and conserve the attributes that carry Outstanding Universal Value, and address the threats to and vulnerabilities of the property. These could include the presence of strong and effective legal protection, a clearly documented management system, including relationships with key stakeholders or user groups, adequate staff and financial resources, key requirements for presentation (where relevant), and effective and responsive monitoring. Secondly this section needs to acknowledge any long-term challenges for the protection and management of the property and state how addressing these will be a long-term strategy. It will be relevant to refer to the most significant threats to the property, and to vulnerabilities and negative changes in	• This text should contain more detailed information to support the text provided in the Draft Statement of Outstanding Universal Value.

Existing nomination form NOMINATION FORMAT	Existing nomination form EXPLANATORY NOTES	Additional advice
	authenticity and/or integrity that have been highlighted, and to set out how protection and management will address these vulnerabilities and threats and mitigate any adverse changes. As an official statement, recognised by the World Heritage Committee, this section of the Statement of Outstanding Universal Value should convey the most important commitments that the State Party is making for the long-term protection and management of the property.	
3.2 Comparative Analysis	The property should be compared with similar properties, whether on the World Heritage List or not. The comparison should outline the similarities the nominated property has with other properties and the reasons that make the nominated property stand out. The comparative analysis should aim to explain the importance of the nominated property both in its national and international context (see Paragraph 132 of the *Operational Guidelines*). The purpose of the comparative analysis is to show that there is room on the List using existing thematic studies and, in the case of serial properties, the justification for the selection of the component parts.	• See pages 67–73 of this manual.
3.3 Proposed Statement of Outstanding Universal Value	A Statement of Outstanding Universal Value is the official statement adopted by the World Heritage Committee at the time of inscription of a property on the World Heritage List. When the World Heritage Committee agrees to inscribe a property on the World Heritage List, it also agrees on a Statement of Outstanding Universal Value that encapsulates why the property is considered to be of Outstanding Universal Value, how it satisfies the relevant criteria, the conditions of integrity and (for cultural properties) authenticity, and how it meets the requirements for protection and management in order to sustain Outstanding Universal Value in the long-term. Statements of Outstanding Universal Value should be concise and are set out in a standard format. They should help to raise awareness regarding the value of the property, guide the assessment of its state of conservation and inform protection and management. Once adopted by the Committee, the Statement of Outstanding Universal Value is displayed	• See pages 73–76 of this manual.

Existing nomination form NOMINATION FORMAT	Existing nomination form EXPLANATORY NOTES	Additional advice
	at the property and on the UNESCO World Heritage Centre's website. The main sections of a Statement of Outstanding Universal Value are the following: a. Brief synthesis b. Justification for criteria c. Statement of integrity (for all properties) d. Statement of authenticity (for properties nominated under criteria i to vi) e. Requirements for protection and management.	
4. State of conservation and factors affecting the property		
4.a Present state of conservation	The information presented in this section constitutes the base-line data necessary to monitor the state of conservation of the nominated property in the future. Information should be provided in this section on the physical condition of the property, any threats to the OUV of the property and conservation measures at the property (see Paragraph 132 of the *Operational Guidelines*). For example, in a historic town or area, buildings, monuments or other structures needing major or minor repair works, should be indicated as well as the scale and duration of any recent or forthcoming major repair projects. In the case of a natural property, data on species trends or the integrity of ecosystems should be provided. This is important because the nomination will be used in future years for purposes of comparison to trace changes in the condition of the property. For the indicators and statistical benchmarks used to monitor the state of conservation of the property see Section 6 below.	• Information about the state of conservation should be realistic and not overstated or understated. Remember that the evaluation mission will visit the property and check on these aspects. • Measures to protect the condition of a property must relate not only to features but also to the dynamic processes that contribute to the evolution of a property, in order to maintain the integrity of all relevant attributes. • Where the state of conservation is complex, diagrams or annotated maps / plans may be useful in conveying this information. For example, in a town the condition of buildings may vary widely. Similarly, the extent of threats or conservation measures may be best portrayed using annotated maps/plans. • This section should address the current situation of the property. Potential or future threats should be addressed in Section 4.b.
4.b Factors affecting the property	This section should provide information on all the factors which are likely to affect or threaten the OUV of a property. It should also describe any difficulties that may be encountered in addressing such problems. Not all the factors suggested in this section are appropriate for all properties. They are indicative and are intended to assist the State Party to	• Note particularly the explanatory note which indicates that not all factors are relevant for all properties. Where factors are irrelevant, this should be simply explained without an attempt to address the factor in detail. • This section should address potential or future threats to the Outstanding Universal Value of the property. Current

Existing nomination form NOMINATION FORMAT	Existing nomination form EXPLANATORY NOTES	Additional advice
	identify the factors that are relevant to each specific property.	threats should be addressed in 4.a. • Threats should only be those which are reasonable to predict or expect for a particular property, or which have been previously raised. • Nonetheless, accurate and frank information about such threats must be provided.
(i) Development pressures (e.g. encroachment, adaptation, agriculture, mining)	Itemize types of development pressures affecting the property, e.g. pressure for demolition, rebuilding or new construction; the adaptation of existing buildings for new uses which would harm their authenticity or integrity; habitat modification or destruction following encroaching agriculture, forestry or grazing, or through poorly managed tourism or other uses; inappropriate or unsustainable natural resource exploitation; damage caused by mining; the introduction of exotic species likely to disrupt natural ecological processes, creating new centres of population on or near properties so as to harm them or their settings.	
(ii) Environmental pressures (e.g. pollution, climate change, desertification)	List and summarize major sources of environmental deterioration affecting building fabric, flora and fauna.	• Sources of deterioration should only be listed if they are actually present and having a major impact.
(iii) Natural disasters and risk preparedness (earthquakes, floods, fires, etc.)	Itemize those disasters which present a foreseeable threat to the property and what steps have been taken to draw up contingency plans for dealing with them, whether by physical protection measures or staff training.	• The estimated frequency of such disasters and the likely scale of impact should be indicated. • Risk preparedness should be designed and resourced to meet the frequency and scale of impact. • Risk preparedness should deal with pre-disaster preparations, as well as response measures during and after the disaster. • The information sought should be summarized with references to other documents (e.g. contingency / disaster plans).
(iv) Responsible visitation at World Heritage sites	Provide the status of visitation to the property (notably available baseline data; patterns of use, including concentrations of activity in parts of the property; and activities planned in the future). Describe projected levels of visitation due to inscription or other factors. Define the carrying-capacity of the property and how its management could be enhanced to meet the current or expected visitor numbers and related	• The method for determining the carrying capacity should be briefly described. • The basis for predicting future visitor numbers should be outlined. • A realistic estimate of future visitor numbers is required, taking special note of the impact of World Heritage inscription. Inscription can often result in a substantial increase in visitor numbers. • Evidence should be presented or referenced to support conclusions about the capacity to absorb current or predicted future visitor numbers without adverse

Existing nomination form NOMINATION FORMAT	Existing nomination form EXPLANATORY NOTES	Additional advice
	development pressure without adverse effects. Consider possible forms of deterioration of the property due to visitor pressure and behaviour including those affecting its intangible attributes.	effects. A simple assertion is insufficient. In the case of current numbers, has there been any monitoring of impacts which can be referenced? • Is there a visitor / tourism management plan for the property? Is it appropriate and effective? • The desired conditions for the visitor / tourist experience(s) to be described include the messages, techniques, qualities of the experience, and amenities available. This information might normally be included within a visitor / tourism management plan. A summary of key points from this plan may be included in the nomination dossier, and the plan annexed to the dossier. • Visitor / tourist numbers should be the latest annual numbers. • A property may not have different areas or zones, in which case the visitor / tourist numbers should simply be for the whole property.
(v) Number of inhabitants within the property and the buffer zone **Estimated population located within:** **Area of nominated property ________** **Buffer zone ________** **Total ________** **Year ________**	Give the best available statistics or estimate of the number of inhabitants living within the nominated property and any buffer zone. Indicate the year this estimate or count was made.	
5. Protection and management of the property	This section of the nomination is intended to provide a clear picture of the legislative, regulatory, contractual, planning, institutional and/or traditional measures (see Paragraph 132 of the *Operational Guidelines*) and the management plan or other management system (Paragraphs 108–18 of the *Operational Guidelines*) that is in place to protect and manage the property as required by the World Heritage Convention. It should deal with policy aspects, legal status and protective measures and with the practicalities of day-to-day administration and management.	• See pages 87–91 of this manual. • Effective protection is essential for World Heritage properties, and the nomination must demonstrate how this is both provided and implemented on the ground. • An effective management plan or documented system is expected at the time of nomination. • The principles of sustainable tourism management can be found in *Managing Tourism at World Heritage Sites: a Practical Manual for World Heritage Site Managers, World Heritage Manuals 1* (Pedersen, 2002).

Existing nomination form NOMINATION FORMAT	Existing nomination form EXPLANATORY NOTES	Additional advice
5.a Ownership	Indicate the major categories of land ownership (including state, provincial, private, community, traditional, customary and non-governmental ownership, etc.).	• In the case of complex properties, this information may best be provided in a table and portrayed in an annotated map / plan.
5.b Protective designation	List the relevant legal, regulatory, contractual, planning, institutional and/or traditional status of the property: For example, national or provincial park; historic monument, protected area under national law or custom; or other designation. Provide the year of designation and the legislative act(s) under which the status is provided. If the document cannot be provided in English or French, an English or French Executive Summary should be provided highlighting the key provisions.	• In addition to a list, this information may be usefully portrayed in an annotated map / plan for complex properties. • The rationale for the boundary of the buffer zone should be provided in this section.
5.c Means of implementing protective measures	Describe how the protection afforded by its legal, regulatory, contractual, planning, institutional and/or traditional status indicated in Section 5.b actually works.	• There can be a considerable difference between the theoretical protection available and the actual protection achieved. Information about the actual situation is most important and should be provided. • Evidence to support any claims should also be referenced.
5.d Existing plans related to municipality and region in which the proposed property is located (e.g. regional or local plan, conservation plan, tourism development plan)	List the agreed plans which have been adopted with the date and agency responsible for preparation. The relevant provisions should be summarized in this section. A copy of the plan should be included as an attached document as indicated in Section 7.b. If the plans exist only in a language other than English or French, an English or French Executive Summary should be provided highlighting the key provisions.	• The status of the plans should also be indicated, along with an appraisal of their effectiveness. • In addition, information should be provided about whether such plans are consistent with the protection, conservation and management of the property. • The geographic or other scope of the plans should be indicated (e.g. does a plan deal with the whole of the property or only a certain part?).
5.e Property management plan or other management system	As noted in Paragraph 132 of the *Operational Guidelines*, an appropriate management plan or other management system is essential and shall be provided in the nomination. Assurances of the effective implementation of the management plan or other management system are also expected. Sustainable development principles should be integrated into the management system. A copy of the management plan or documentation of the management system shall be annexed to the	• See pages 89–91 of this manual. • Evidence of the effectiveness of the management plan / system should be provided, not simply assurances or assertions. • The management plan / system must primarily manage for the protection and conservation of the potential Outstanding Universal Value. • The management plan / system must deal with the real-world circumstances of the property, especially problems and issues.

Existing nomination form NOMINATION FORMAT	Existing nomination form EXPLANATORY NOTES	Additional advice
	nomination, in English or French as indicated in Section 7.b. If the management plan exists only in a language other than English or French, an English or French detailed description of its provisions shall be annexed. Give the title, date and author of management plans annexed to this nomination. A detailed analysis or explanation of the management plan or a documented management system shall be provided. A timetable for the implementation of the management plan is recommended.	• In the case of serial or transnational properties, or complex properties with multiple plans / systems, the complementarity of the plans / systems should be demonstrated. Coordinated management of the separate components should be documented.
5.f Sources and levels of finance	Show the sources and level of funding which are available to the property on an annual basis. An estimate could also be given of the adequacy or otherwise of resources available, in particular identifying any gaps or deficiencies or any areas where assistance may be required.	
5.g Sources of expertise and training in conservation and management techniques	Indicate the expertise and training which are available from national authorities or other organizations to the property.	• An indication should be given of the actual expertise and training which are used at the property, in addition to that which may be available. • Expertise and training may exist within the dedicated management agency for the property, as well as from other organizations. • An appraisal should be given of the suitability and capacity of the expertise and training to meet the specific needs of the property.
5.h Visitor facilities and infrastructure	The section should describe the inclusive facilities available on site for visitors and demonstrate that they are appropriate in relation to the protection and management requirements of the property. It should set out how the facilities and services will provide effective and inclusive presentation of the property to meet the needs of visitors, including in relation to the provision of safe and appropriate access to the property. The section should consider visitor facilities that may include interpretation/explanation (signage, trails, notices or publications, guides); museum/exhibition devoted to the property, visitor or interpretation centre; and/or potential use of digital technologies and services (overnight accommodation; restaurant; car parking; lavatories; search and rescue; etc.).	• An appraisal should be given of the suitability and capacity of the facilities to meet the specific needs of the property. • Any conflicts between these facilities and the protection and conservation of the property should be noted.

Existing nomination form NOMINATION FORMAT	Existing nomination form EXPLANATORY NOTES	Additional advice
5.i Policies and programmes related to the presentation and promotion of the property	This section refers to Articles 4 and 5 of the World Heritage Convention regarding the presentation and transmission to future generations of the cultural and natural heritage. States Parties are encouraged to provide information on the policies and programmes for the presentation and promotion of the nominated property.	• Only summary information is required. • Such policies and programmes might be incorporated in an interpretation plan or similar. • Information about resourcing for programmes and the effectiveness of policies and programmes should be provided. • Do the programmes actually present and promote the potential Outstanding Universal Value? • Are there conflicts between presentation / promotion and protection / conservation?
5.j Staffing levels and expertise (professional, technical, maintenance)	Indicate the skills and qualifications available needed for the good management of the property, including in relation to visitation and future training needs.	• Are the staffing levels adequate? • Are these skills and training appropriate to the values of the property?
6. Monitoring	This section of the nomination is intended to provide the evidence for the state of conservation of the property which can be reviewed and reported on regularly so as to give an indication of trends over time.	
6.a Key indicators for measuring state of conservation	List in table form those key indicators that have been chosen as the measure of the state of conservation of the whole property (see Section 4.a above). Indicate the periodicity of the review of these indicators and the location where the records are kept. They could be representative of an important aspect of the property and relate as closely as possible to the Statement of Outstanding Universal Value (see Section 2.b above). Where possible they could be expressed numerically and where this is not possible they could be of a kind which can be repeated, for example by taking a photograph from the same point. Examples of good indicators are the: (i) number of species, or population of a keystone species on a natural property; (ii) percentage of buildings requiring major repair in a historic town or district; (iii) number of years estimated to elapse before a major conservation programme is likely to be completed; (iv) stability or degree of movement in a particular building or element of a building; (v) rate at which encroachment of any kind on a property has increased or diminished.	• The indicators must relate to the potential Outstanding Universal Value, and not simply be something that can be measured.

Existing nomination form			Additional advice
Indicator	Periodicity	Location of records	

Existing nomination form NOMINATION FORMAT	Existing nomination form EXPLANATORY NOTES	Additional advice
6.b Administrative arrangements for monitoring property	Give the name and contact information of the agency(ies) responsible for the monitoring referenced in 6.a.	
6.c Results of previous reporting exercises	List, with a brief summary, earlier reports on the state of conservation of the property and provide extracts and references to published sources (for example, reports submitted in compliance with international agreements and programmes, e.g. Ramsar, MAB).	• In the case of problems noted or a poor state of conservation, the current situation or corrective action taken should be briefly indicated. • If there are still problems or a poor state of conservation, this should be reported in Section 4 above.
7. Documentation	This section of the nomination is the checklist of the documentation which shall be provided to make up a complete nomination.	
7.a Photographs and audiovisual image inventory and authorization form	States Parties shall provide a sufficient number of recent images (prints, slides and, where possible, electronic formats, videos and aerial photographs) to give a good general picture of the property. Slides shall be in 35 mm format and electronic images in jpg format at a minimum of 300 dpi (dots per inch) resolution. If film material is provided, Beta SP format is recommended for quality assurances. This material shall be accompanied by the image inventory and photograph and audiovisual authorization form as set out below. At least one photograph that may be used on the public web page illustrating the property shall be included. States Parties are encouraged to grant to UNESCO, in written form and free of charge, the non-exclusive cession of rights to diffuse, to communicate to the public, to publish, to reproduce, to exploit, in any form and on any support, including digital, all or part of the images provided	• Images should portray the potential Outstanding Universal Value of the property, as well as its context.

Existing nomination form NOMINATION FORMAT	Existing nomination form EXPLANATORY NOTES	Additional advice
	and license these rights to third parties. The non-exclusive cession of rights does not impinge upon intellectual property rights (rights of the photographer / director of the video or copyright owner if different) and that when the images are distributed by UNESCO a credit to the photographer / director of the video is always given, if clearly provided in the form. All possible profits deriving from such cession of rights will go to the World Heritage Fund.	

Existing nomination form								Additional advice
ID No.	Format (slide / print / video)	Caption	Date of photograph (mo/yr)	Photographer / director of video	Copyright owner (if different from photographer / director of video)	Contact details of copyright owner (name, address, tel / fax, and e-mail)	Non-exclusive cession of rights	

Existing nomination form NOMINATION FORMAT	Existing nomination form EXPLANATORY NOTES	Additional advice
7.b Texts relating to protective designation, copies of property management plans or documented management systems and extracts of other plans relevant to the property	Attach the texts as indicated in Sections 5.b, 5.d and 5.e above.	
7.c Form and date of most recent records or inventory of property	Provide a straightforward statement giving the form and date of the most recent records or inventory of the property. Only records that are still available should be described.	
7.d Address where inventory, records and archives are held	Give the name and address of the agencies holding inventory records (buildings, monuments, flora or fauna species).	
7.e Bibliography	List the principal published references, using standard bibliographic format.	

Existing nomination form NOMINATION FORMAT	Existing nomination form EXPLANATORY NOTES	Additional advice
8. Contact information of responsible authorities	This section of the nomination will allow the Secretariat to provide the property with current information about World Heritage news and other issues.	
8.a Preparer **Name:** **Title:** **Address:** **City, province / state, country:** **Tel:** **Fax:** **E-mail:**	Provide the name, address and other contact information of the individual responsible for preparing the nomination. If an e-mail address cannot be provided, the information must include a fax number.	
8.b Official local institution / agency **8.c Other local institutions**	Provide the name of the agency, museum, institution, community or manager locally responsible for the management of the property. If the normal reporting institution is a national agency, please provide that contact information. List the full name, address, telephone, fax and e-mail addresses of all museums, visitor centres and official tourism offices who should receive the free *World Heritage Newsletter* about events and issues related to World Heritage.	
8.d Official web address **http://** **Contact name:** **E-mail:**	Please provide any existing official web addresses of the nominated property, indicate if such web addresses are planned for the future with the contact name and e-mail address.	
9. Signature on behalf of the State Party	The nomination should conclude with the signature of the official empowered to sign it on behalf of the State Party.	

遗产申请列入世界遗产名录

注：在准备申遗的过程中，缔约国应该使用这个表格，但是要将填报须知这一部分删除。

现有申报形式 申报标题	现存的申报形式填报须知	其他建议
1. 遗产识别	和第二部分一样，这是申报文件最为重要的章节，必须让委员会清楚的了解遗产的位置和地理学界限。对于系列申报遗产，应该插入表格，说明遗产组成部分名称、区域（如果组成部分分布于不同区域时）、坐标、遗产区和缓冲区。其他一些组成部分也可以添加在表中（页码索引或地图序号等），这样易区分多个组成部分。	申报文件的这一部分提供有关遗产位置和大小的真实信息。应该短小精炼。特别需要注意的是应该提供地图。
1.a 国家（如果有不同的缔约国）		• 申报遗产国家的名字（或对于跨国或跨境申报应该是所有国家）不需要提供其他的信息。
1.b 州，省或区		• 应该分别罗列遗产所在州，省或区名称。对于跨国或跨境申报的遗产，应详细列出所在州，省或区，还应列出国家名称。
1.c 遗产名称	这是遗产的官方名称，将出现在与世界遗产有关的公开出版物上，文字准确。不要超过200 个字，包括空格和标点。 对于系列申报（见《操作指南》137–140 段），提出总名称（例如，菲律宾巴洛克风格的教堂）。不需罗列系列遗产每个组成部分的名称，它们应该在表 1.d 和 1.f 中。	最好使用已经公认地区或国家中遗产的名称，而不要新创一个。 • 牢记这个名字会用于将来遗产的宣传。 • 遗产的名称应该简洁准确，不要超过 200 个字符，包括空格和标点符号。 • 需要在地区或国家级咨询讨论，确定名字是否考虑了当地语言，文化和传统。 • 在一些情况，选用两个以上名字联合表达一个遗址。（比如，蒂瓦希普纳穆 – 新西兰西南部地区，和夸特兰巴山脉 / 德拉肯斯堡山公园）。 • 对于系列遗产，应选用总体名称（如三江并流保护区，苏门答腊热带雨林遗产，加拿大落基山国家公园）。 • 对于跨国或跨境遗产，所有参与国都必须同意申报遗产的名称，（例如乌布苏湖盆地，蒙古和俄罗斯联邦），高海岸瓦尔肯岛（芬兰和瑞士） • 最好不要使用多个组成部分名字的组合，建议使用能表达整个遗产价值的名称。
1.d 地理坐标（精确到秒）	此处提供的是遗产区中心点的经纬度坐标（精确到秒）或墨卡托 UTM 投影分度带坐标系统（精确到 10 米），不要在使用其他坐标系统。如果有疑问，请与秘书处联系。 系列申报遗产，以表格的形式说明遗产名称、每一个组成部分部分的区域（离得最近的城镇），和中心点坐标。 坐标格式：N 45° 06’ 05" W 15° 37’ 56" 或 UTM Zone 18 东：545670 北：4586750	

续表

序号	组成部分名称	地区、区域	中心点地理坐标	各组成部分遗产区面积（公顷）	缓冲区面积（公顷）	地图编号
001						
002						
003						
004						
005						
006						
总面积（公顷）				公顷	公顷	

现有申报表格申报格式	现有申现有申报表格填报须知	其他建议
1.e 地图和规划，显示遗产区和缓冲区的边界	申报文件的附件，比例和日期如下： （i）能够以最大比例展现整个遗产区原貌的地形图。应清晰划定遗址区和缓冲区的边界。此图及其附图上都应该标识对遗产有益的具有特殊法律效力的保护区的边界。系列申报遗产可使用多张地图（见表 1.d）。应该使用能够看清楚地形图上组成部分，如临近的村落、建筑和道路的最大比例地图，便于评估对申报遗产周边，临近地区或边界有影响的因素。 应该注意地图上边界线条的宽度，过粗的边界线条会导致对遗产边界辨认模糊。 地图可以从以下网站上获取。http：//whc.unesco.org/en/mapagencies 如果没有合适比例地形图，可是使用其他地图替代。所有的地图应该包含	• 文化遗产需要提交的地图或规划图（图表）由其类型和历史决定。必须能描绘遗产潜在的突出普遍价值。 • 地图和规划图的比例、细节和分辨率应该满足与遗产特性相关的边界划定的需要，而且要容易了解遗产周边的环境。 • 风格独特但信息量很少的地图不符合要求。最好用大比例的地形图或地籍图（文化遗产）作为底图，标注相关信息。 • 遗产特性应标识在图上或用文字表述，应该使用统一的名称和编码系统便于在地图和文本之间互相印证。也就是说，地图上使用的名称应该和文本中使用的名称一致。地图上使用的语言应该是法语或英语。 • 建议用一张地图标明缔约国所在地（最大 A4 或信纸的大小）。 • 标明遗产在缔约国内所处位置的地图不超过最大 A4 或信纸的大小。 • 此外，建议提供地形图或地籍图（文化遗产）显示整个遗产、遗产边界和缓冲区边界（最大 A4 或信纸大小），执行摘要中应使用同一份地图。

续表

现有申报表格 申报格式	现有申现有申报表格填报须知	其他建议
1.e 地图和规划，显示遗产区和缓冲区的边界	地理参照物，最起码在地图上有三个点，点点相对，组成完整的坐标系统。地图不能缩减，应有比例尺、方位、投影、数据、遗产名称和日期，如果可能的话，地图应该卷成轴状，不要折叠。 鼓励提供数字地理信息以纳入地理信息（GIS）系统。在这种情况下，（遗产区和缓冲区）边界线应该用矢量的形式提供，尽量准备大比例的地图。如有问题，相关详情缔约国可与秘书处联系。 （ii）区位图应显示该遗产在申报国的具体位置， （iii）可用标有遗产个体特性的规划图或特别地图，应该包含在附件中。 为了便于复制和向咨询机构和世界遗产委员会展示，地图应缩为 A4 纸大小，如果可能的话， 基础地图的电子图像应该包含在申遗文本中。 如果申报遗产没有划分缓冲区，申遗文本必须说明为什么不需要缓冲区也能保证遗产得到的适当保护。	• 尽可能提供大比例的地形图或地籍图（文化遗产），包括整个遗产、遗产边界和缓冲区边界。 • 在文本中提到的重要的特性应该用比例适当的地图显著标识，而不是在遗产边界的主地图上标识。 • 如果原始底图是彩色的，也应该提供彩色版本。 • 在有边界标识的地图上应该有清晰的图例系统，图例应该用《操作指南》中提供的、界定遗产区和缓冲区的专业术语。图上边界线应该清晰不与其他线条混淆。 • 对于系列遗产申报，应该在区位图上显示遗产所有组成部分的位置，同时各组成部分单独的区位图应该能展现其与周边环境的关系。对于系列遗产，在一张 A4 图上可能无法展示详细信息，可以提供若干张 A4 的图纸，包括：（1）一张标有遗产情况的总区位图，包括位置和各组成部分之间的距离；（2）一张或多张图标识每个组成部分的遗产区和缓冲区。 • 对于国内系列遗产和跨国遗产，应该提供地形图原件，清晰标识每个各组成部分的界线。 • 对于扩展项目，需要提供既有原遗产又有遗产扩展部分的区位图。 • 可以提供其他地图来说明遗产的具体价值、特性或问题，包括： ——地质图—用于依据标准（8）申报的遗产； ——植被图—用于依据标准（9）和（10）申报的遗产； ——物种分布图—用于依据标准（9）和（10）申报的遗产； ——基础设施或基础设施规划图（如道路和建设中的道路、大坝、未来发展等等）； ——交通图—遗产区内主要道路和与相邻区域的道路； • 标有遗产位置和边界的 A4 大小的基础地图应该包括在正文中。其他地图常常作为附件，清晰界定的、并在文字内容中提供参考。在表 1.e 项中应该能找到地图一览表，说明各图所处的位置； • A3 大小的地图最好折成 A4 大小放置在文件中； • 所有地图应该提供电子版，随文件刻录在 CD 中； • 对于非城市遗产，完整的地形图是申报遗产的关键。同样的，地籍图对城市遗产很重要。只有图表及电子绘图的申遗文本，不是完整文件。 • 遗产的环境（缓冲区之外）应该在相关的图纸上有所标示。见前文。
1. f 遗产区和缓冲区面积（公顷）____ 遗产区面积 ____ 公顷 ____	对于系列申报遗产（见《操作指南》137–140 段），可插入表格，显示组成部分名称、地区、坐标、（不同组成部分处于不同地域）遗址区和缓冲区。	

续表

现有申报表格申报格式	现有申现有申报表格填报须知	其他建议
缓冲区面积 ______ 公顷 ______ 总面积 ______ 公顷 ______	系列申报遗产表也可显示各个申报去和缓冲区规模。	
2. 概述		• 建议本部分在完成第 3 部分——列入理由后再编写。概述应详细描述列入理由，包括申报原因及支持结论的信息和证据，以及其他能够表现遗产全貌的信息。需要注意的是描述要凝练，不能太长。
2.a 遗产描述	本节在描述申报遗产区的情况时，应该提及遗产所有重要特性。 对于文化遗产，本部分将包括能够证明遗产因为哪些组成部分而具有重要意义。应该包括建筑或建筑群、其建筑风格、建造时间、材质等等。同时也包括一些重要的环境，比如公园、花园等等。例如一个岩画遗址，遗产描述应提及岩画艺术本身及周边景观。对于历史城镇或历史街区，不需要描述每个单体建筑，但应该逐个描述重要的公共建筑、本区域的规划和布局、街道格局等等。 对于自然遗产，概述应该包括物质属性、地质情况、栖息地、物种及种群数量、其他重要的生物特性和过程。应该提供实用的物种清单，特别是濒危物种和地方特有物种。应描述自然资源开发的范围和方法。 对于文化景观，它要描述的内容包括上面提到自然或文化遗产应描述的所有内容。特别关注人和自然的互动关系。 应该描述第一部分确定的整体遗产区。对于系列遗产（见《操作指南》137-140 段），各构成部分应该分开描述。	• 与突出普遍价值有关的内容应作为重点进行描述，同时概况性描述遗产。 • 描述应该清晰说明遗产的突出普遍价值是什么，它有哪些重要特征。 • 不需要全面、冗长的描述所有方面。 • 如果描述过于复杂冗长，最好能提供描述概要，详细的描述资料可作为附件。 • 描述重点是已确定边界的申报遗产区。尽量避免描述遗产区以外的组成部分，除非与遗产有一定的相关性，对于遗产区以外描述最好分开（例如，遗产区外相关因素的描述等副标题形式）。 • 遗产的环境（缓冲区外）应该在这节中讨论（见前文）。
2.b 历史和发展	描述遗产如何发展到今天的形状和条件、遗产经历的重大改变、包括近期的保护历程。 对于文物、遗址、建筑或建筑群应包括不同建筑阶段的描述。建成后，哪个部分有变化、破坏或重建都应该有记录。 对于自然遗产，概要应该包括历史上或史前时期与遗产有关的重要事件，及遗产与人类的关系。包括遗产使用方式及用于狩猎、捕鱼或农业的自然资源，或因气候改变、洪水、地震或其他自然因素带来的变化。 文化景观中也要求提供这些信息，以及该区域与人类活动史的所有方面。	• 历史描述应该着重介绍与突出普遍价值有关的情况，介绍遗产有关的历史背景。 • 不需要冗长的描述有关遗产历史的所有事件。这个信息可以作为附件，或简单提及。 • 在世界历史背景下讲述遗产历史更重要，需要提供相关信息。这一部分概述，不必冗长而详细。 • 注明历史情况出处通常非常重要，来自其他资源的信息应该有相关的文献或实例支持。 • 遗产的历史沿革，提供图解形式更有助于掌握各个阶段的发展脉络。例如，融合了不同时代历史建筑的城镇，插图有助于解释哪些建筑与文字中的哪段历史时期相关。 • 其他的插图，如地图、雕刻或历史照片都可在文字中，这些插图对解读与遗产突出普遍价值相关的各方面有帮助。

续表

现有申报表格申报格式	现有申现有申报表格填报须知	其他建议
3. 列入理由（见 132 及 133 段.）	理由应该分为以下几部分陈述。 这部分必须让人们清楚了解遗产为什么具有突出普遍价值。 这部分文件的编写应该仔细参考《操作指南》的要求。这一部分不需要详细论述遗产及管理有关信息，这些内容将在其他章节安排，但是需要介绍那些与确定突出普遍价值有关的核心组成部分。	• 3.1a–3.1e 中的内容应该包括更多详细信息以支持突出普遍价值声明草案的内容。
3.1.a 概述	概述应该包括（1）事实信息概述（2）遗产性质概述。真实信息陈述包括地理和历史背景及主要特性。遗产性质应向决策者和公众阐释需要维持的潜在突出普遍价值，也包括表现突出普遍价值属性，及对其进行保护，管理和监测的描述。概述中还包括所有依据标准的阐述。概述要把遗产申报和建议列入的所有原理都囊括进来。	这部分内容应该包括更多详细信息以支持突出普遍价值声明。
3.1.b 遗产列入依据的标准（选择这些标准的理由）	见《操作指南》77 段 分别说明引用每一个标准的理由。 简述该项遗产如何满足申报标准，（如果需要，参照描述和比较分析章节，但不要复制整章内容）描述与每一个标准相符的属性。	• 见本指南前文。 • 每一个标准的论述理由对准备突出普遍价值声明很有帮助。 • 清晰证明遗产为什么符合这条标准。 • 这部分内容应该包括更多详细信息以支持突出普遍价值声明草案。
3.1.c 完整性声明	完整性声明应该描述遗产符合了《操作指南》第 II.D 中完整性的条件，指南中对条件有详细的论述。 《操作指南》提出需要评估遗产的符合以下各项标准的程度： ——包括能表现突出普遍价值的所有组成部分； ——遗产范围是否完整地代表了能体现遗产价值的特性和过程； ——受到发展或忽略带来的负面影响（88 段）；《操作指南》提供与各个世界遗产标准相关的重要指导，需要重点理解（89–95）。	• 见本指南前文。 • 应该在本节论述遗产边界确定的原因。 • 文本中应该包括更多详细信息来支持突出普遍价值声明草案。
3.1.d 真实性声明（针对申报标准为（i）到（vi）的遗产）	真实性声明应该描述遗产满足真实性的条件（在《操作指南》II.D 中有详细论述）。 这一部分应该高度概况申遗文本第四部分中详细论述的信息（在其他章节也有涉及），其他章节已有的信息就不需要赘述。 真实性只适用于文化遗产和混合遗产中文化部分。 《操作指南》中指出“如果遗产的文化价值（正如申报标准所描述的内容）通过它的属性真实的，可信的传递出来，遗产就符合真实性的要求（82 段）。” 《操作指南》建议下面的属性类型应该被认为能够表达突出普遍价值：	• 见本指南前文。 • 本部分内容应该更多详细信息支持突出普遍价值声明草案。

续表

现有申报表格申报格式	现有申现有申报表格填报须知	其他建议
3.1.d 真实性声明（针对申报标准为（i）到（vi）的遗产）	•形式和设计 •内容和材料 •用途和功能 •传统，技术和管理系统 •位置和环境 •语言和其他形式的无形遗产 •精神和感知 •其他内在和外部组成部分。	
3.1.e 保护和管理需求	这一章将陈述遗产如何满足保护和管理的要求，以确保长期维持遗产的突出普遍价值。它应该包括保护和管理工作的详细描述，和明确长期对遗产保护工作。 本章高度概括应在第5部分详述的内容（同时，第4，6章中也会涉及），其他章节已有的信息就不需要赘述。 本节内容首先应描绘保护和管理工作框架。这部分包括必要的保障机制，管理体系或管理规划（无论是正在实施的，还是需要建立的），以保存或保护能够展现遗产突出普遍价值的属性，应对威胁因素或遗产自身的缺陷。应该包括目前有效的法律保障体系、记录清晰的管理系统、与核心利益相关者、使用群体间的沟通，人员与财政资源、展示的要求、有效和有针对性的监测。 第二，本部分需要确定保护和管理遗产面临的长期挑战，阐述如何通过长期战略迎接挑战。这里需要强调威胁遗产真实性和完整性的脆弱性和负面的变化？要提出保护和管理如何控制威胁、并降低负面影响。 作为世界遗产委员会认可的正式的声明，关于突出普遍价值声明要重申缔约国对于长期保护和管理遗产的承诺。	•本部分内容应该更多详细信息支持突出普遍价值声明草案。
3.2 比较分析	遗产应该与类似遗产进行比较（无论是否已经列入遗产名录）。比较时应该概述该项遗产与其他遗产之间的类似点，以及该遗产更胜一筹的原因。比较分析的目标是解释申报遗产的在本国或国际背景下的重要性（见《操作指南》132）。 比较分析的目的是利用现有的专题研究，显示显示其列入名录的合理性，对系列申报而言，则是选择这些组成部分的理由。	•见本指南前文。
3.3 提议的突出普遍价值声明	突出普遍价值声明是世界遗产委员会在遗产列入名录是采纳的官方声明。当世界遗产委员会同意将遗产列入名录，也表示赞同突出普遍价值声明。这个声明囊括了为什么遗产具有这样的突出普遍价值、如何符合相关标准的、完整性和真实性、保护和管理如何满足长期保护遗产的突出普遍价值的需求。	•见本指南前文。

续表

现有申报表格申报格式	现有申现有申报表格填报须知	其他建议
3.3 提议的突出普遍价值声明	突出普遍价值应该简洁精确，遵循标准格式。应有助于提高对遗产价值的公众认识，指导现状评估和保护管理。 一旦被委员会采纳，该声明将在遗产点和世界遗产中心的网站上公布。 突出普遍价值声明包括以下几个部分： a）简要概述； b）符合标准的理由； c）完整性声明（所有遗产）； d）真实性声明（符合（1）到（4）的标准的遗产； e）保护和管理要求。	• 见本指南前文。
4. 保存状态和影响遗产的因素		
4.a 遗产保存现状	本章信息是未来监测保护状态的基础数据。本章应提供遗产自然条件、威胁遗产突出普遍价值的因素和保护遗产的方法（见《操作指南》132 段） 例如，一个历史城镇或地区，需要对其建筑群、古迹及其他建筑大大小小的维修，近期或将来的维修，如维修的规模，持续的时间等进行记等。 对于自然遗产，提供物种演化群趋势的数据或整个生物系统完整的数据。因为在今后若干年仍将继续使用，比较并跟踪遗产变化的痕迹。 对于监测遗产保护状态指标和统计基点见第六部分。	• 遗产保护状态的信息应该真实，不要夸大其词或轻描淡写。谨记评估考察团会到现场考察并检查这些组成部分。 • 保护遗产本体状况的方法必须与遗产特性有关，同时与遗产进化动态过程有关，从而维持遗产的完整性。 • 如果遗产的保存状况复杂，可采用表格或注释图、平面图的形式解释。例如，一个城市建筑的保护状况可能情况各异。同样，也可以用注释图或平面图的方式描述遗产面临的威胁或保护措施。 • 本节应该描述遗产目前的保护状态。潜在的威胁因素应在 4.b 内提出。
4.b 影响遗产的因素	本节提供威胁或影响遗产突出普遍价值所有因素的信息。同时也提出在解决这些问题时遇到的困难。本章提到的所有因素并不都适合于所有遗产。他们只是标识性的，以协助缔约国确认与各自遗产相关的因素。	• 注意所提及的影响因素并不适应于所有遗产。如果因素没有相关性，那么说明要简单，不必详细。 • 这一部分应该指出潜在或未来威胁突出普遍价值的因素。当前的威胁因素应在 4.a 中提出。 • 威胁指合理预期的具体遗产可能面临的，或者是以前曾经出现过的威胁。 • 此外，应该提供威胁因素的准确和真实的信息。
（1）发展压力（例如，侵占、改建、农业、采矿）	详细列举影响遗产发展压力的类型，例如：破坏压力、重建压力或新建建筑压力；已存在建筑的再利用、新的利用方式可能破坏遗产的真实性或完整性；因农业、林业或放牧扩张而造成栖息地的改造或破坏，对自然资源不适当或不可持续的开发；因采矿而引起的破坏、引进破坏自然生态过程的外来物种、在遗产上或周边形成一个新的栖息地、对遗产或环境产生影响。	

续表

现有申报表格 申报格式	现有申现有申报表格填报须知	其他建议
（2）环境压力（污染，气候变化，沙漠化）	列举并概况影响建筑结构、动植物环境恶化的根源。	• 只需列举确实存在，并产生主要影响的环境恶化。
（3）自然灾害和危险预防	逐条列举可能对遗产产生威胁的灾害，在应急预案中详细列出处理的步骤和方法，以及是否采取了物理保护方法或开展了员工培训。	• 应评估这些灾害的频率，指出可能的影响范围。 • 准备与灾害频率和影响范围相符灾害预防预案和资金配备。 • 灾前准备、设计灾害预防预案，以及灾难发生中、发生后的应急机制。 • 信息来源应该概况，并参考其他文件（如，应急、灾害规划）。
（4）世界遗产的游客数量	提供遗产参观状况分析（提供可用的基线数据；使用模式、包括遗产活动的分布区域、未来的活动计划）。 预计遗产列入名录后游客数量或其他因素。确定遗产的承载能力，如何提高管理水平以满足目前或期望的游客数量，以及发展压力所带来的负面影响。 考虑遗产可能因参观压力或游客行为造成的恶化，包括对无形属性的影响。	• 简单介绍确定承载能力的方法。 • 罗列预测未来参观者数量的依据。 • 要估计未来参观者数量，应特别关注列入遗产名录后的影响。列入名录可能会带来游客数量的持续增长。 • 提供证据证明遗产具有容纳能力，未来游客数量不会对遗产产生负面影响，简单的评估是不充分的。应提及是否监测了现有的人数对遗产的影响。 • 遗产是否有有效而适当旅游管理规划？ • 描述旅游实践的设施条件，包括信息、技术、活动的质量、便利设施。这些信息应该包括在旅游管理规划中。该规划的关键点概况应包括在申报文件中，规划应作为附件提交。 • 参观旅游人数应是最新的年游客数量。 • 如果遗产没有在不同的区域，则游客数量应该是整个遗产的人数。
（5）遗产区和缓冲区居民人数 估计遗产区内的人口：__________ 遗产区：_______ 缓冲区：_______ 合计：_________ 年份：_________	给出遗产区和缓冲区居民的统计数据或估计数据。标明人数统计或估测统计的年份。	
5. 遗产的保护和管理	这部分需要提供用于遗产保护和管理的法律、法规，契约、规划、制度和传统方法（《操作指南》132段）确立管理规划或其他管理系统，按世界遗产委员会要求保护管理该遗产（见《操作指南》108-18段）。它涉及政策、法律地位、保护方法和日常行政管理实施情况。	• 见本手册前文。 • 世界遗产必须得到有效保护，文件中应该详细说明如何提供和实施这些保障。 • 在本章论述有效的管理规划和或其他管理体制。 • 可持续的旅游管理的原则见：世界遗产的旅游管理：世界遗产实践管理手册，世界遗产手册1（2002，佩德森）

续表

现有申报表格 申报格式	现有申现有申报表格填报须知	其他建议
5.a 遗产所有人	列举主要类型的土地所有人（包括国家、省市、个人、社区、传统、约定俗成和非政府所有者，）	• 鉴于遗产的复杂性，这部分信息最好以表格或通过带有注释的地图 / 平面图表现。
5.b 保护称号	罗列遗产相关的法律、法规、契约、规划、制度或传统地位。例如国家或省级公园、历史文物、国家法律或传统保护区，或其他的保护称号。 提供获取各种称号的时间或立法年代。 如果这些文件不能提供英语或法语版本，应提供英语或法语版的《执行摘要》并将重要条文醒目提示。	• 对于复杂遗产可添加清单，使用带有注释的地图或平面图标示。 • 提供划定遗产区和缓冲区的依据。
5.c 实施保护措施的方法	描述 5.b 所列法律、法规、契约、规划、制度或传统地位实现保护的具体方法。	• 理论上的保护与实在保护成果的不同可能有差异，信息应包含目前的实际情况。 • 提出的任何主张都应该有证据支持。
5.d 遗产所在区域内与市政和区域相关的现有规划（地区规划，保护规划，旅游发展规划）	罗列已公布的规划、公布时间及规划机构。相关的条款应该在本节中概况。规划的副本（如 7.b 所示）应该作为附件。 如果现有规划语言不是英语或法语，需要有英语或法语的《执行摘要》，重要条文应该醒目提示。	• 应该说明规划的地位，以及评估规划的实施效果。 • 此外，应该提出这些规划是否与遗产保存，保护和管理一致。 • 应该说明规划地理或其他的范围（例如，规划是针对整个遗产区还是仅是一部分）。
5.e 遗产管理规划或其他管理系统	《操作指南》132 段指出，一个适宜的管理规划或其他管理系统是申报的基础，需要在申报文件中明确申明。也要提交保证管理规划或管理体系有效运作的系统。可持续发展的原则应该运用在管理系统中。 管理规划或有关管理系统的文件（如 7.b 所示）应该作为附件提供。 如果规划使用其他语言编写，那么相关条约的英语或法语版本应作为附件。申报遗产的名称、日期和规划编制单位附加在申报文件后面。 应该提供有关管理规划或成文管理系统的详细的分析或解释。 建议提供管理规划实施时间表。	• 见前文。 • 应提供管理规划或体制有效运作的证据，而不是简单的保证和声明。 • 管理规划或系统必须包括那些保存和保护突出普遍价值的主要管理措施。 • 管理规划或体制必须能解决遗产现实环境下所存在的问题。 • 对于系列和跨国遗产，或有多个规划或体系的复杂遗产，应该说明这些规划或体系的互补性。独立组成部分的协作管理应该有文可依。
5.f 来源和资金水平	提供每年资金来源和资金水平。可以提供估计的数据或其他可用资金，确定不足的数额及其他可能需要的赞助。	
5.g 来自专业的知识保护与管理技术的培训	指出国家当局或其他组织提供的有关遗产专业知识和培训。	• 除了未来可能得到的专业知识和相关培训以外，还应描述目前正在遗产地发挥作用的专业知识和相关培训； • 遗产的指定管理机构可以具备这些专业知识并提供培训，其他组织也能进行这项工作； 应当评估上述专业知识和相关培训的适用性和能力是否符合遗产具体要求。

续表

现有申报表格 申报格式	现有申现有申报表格填报须知	其他建议
5.h 旅游设施和基础设施	这一章应该描述遗产已有的旅游设施，解释他们是否与遗产保护和管理要求一致。需要陈述这些设施和服务如何提供有效的服务和展示以满足参观者需求，包括提供安全、适当的到达和进入遗产地的形式。旅游设施应该包括阐释系统（标识、参观线路、注意事项、出版物和导游）； 博物馆展厅、游客中心，或者使用的数字技术或服务（住宿、餐饮、停车场、卫生间、研究和救护中心）	• 评估相关设施能否满足遗产特殊需要。 • 设施与遗产保存、保护出现冲突时，应予以说明。
5.i 与展示和宣传遗产相关的政策和项目	这一部分引用了与展示和传承文化遗产相关的《世界遗产公约》第四和五条。鼓励缔约国提供与展示和提升遗产形象相关的政策和项目信息。	• 只需要概要性的信息。 • 这些政策和项目要与阐释规划一致或相似。 • 应该提供关于项目的资金信息和政策信息。 • 项目是否切实的提升或展现了遗产的潜在突出普遍价值？ • 遗产的展示或提升计划是否与遗产的保存与保护相冲突。
5.j 员工的水平和技能（专业，技术，维修）	好的管理需要员工有一定的技能和资格，包括旅游和未来培训的需求。	• 员工配备是否充足。 • 现有的技能和培训是否对遗产的价值保护有所帮助。
6. 监测	这一部分提供了缔约国保护遗产证据，是缔约国提到和报告的日常监测活动的见证，以明确遗产保护趋势指标。	
6.a 衡量保护状态的核心指标	表中所列出的核心指标与衡量遗产保护状态相关（见 4.a）。说明定期检查指标和这些指标记录的存放地点。他们代表了与遗产突出普遍价值有密切关系的重要因素（见 2.b）。指标可用数字表示，不能用数字的话，以可重复方式出现，例如在同一点拍摄的照片。好的指标包括： a）自然遗产的物种数量，关键物种种群的数量； b）历史城镇或街区中建筑物需要大修的比例； c）预计完成主要保护项目所需时间； d）特殊建筑或建筑构建的稳定性或活动程度；对遗产侵蚀的消长速度；	指标必须与潜在的突出普遍价值相关，而不仅仅是那些可用测量的数据。

申报形式			其他建议
指标	周期（频率）	记录保存的位置	

现有申报表格申报格式	现有申现有申报表格填报须知	其他建议
6.b 遗产监测的行政安排	提供负责遗产监测机构（如第 6.a 条所示）的名称和联系信息。	
6.c 早期活动的结果	早期遗产保护状态报告概要，提供报告摘要和参考文献（比如，根据国际协议和方案，如《拉姆萨湿地公约》,《人与生物圈计划》,提交的报告）。	• 这一部分关注有问题或较差的保存状态，在此提供现状说明或即将采取的改善行动。 • 如果保存状态存在问题仍未得到改善，这个问题就应该在本报告的第 4 部分详细说明。
7. 文献	这一部分是提供一个完整的申报文件所需要的文献清单。	
7.a 照片和试听图像库和授权书	缔约国应该提供足够数量的近期影像（打印、幻灯片、电子版、录像和航拍片）以展现遗产的概貌。 幻灯片应该是 35mm 的，电子图片使用 jpg 格式，最小分辨率为 300dpi，如果提供短片，最好是 Beta SP 格式以确保影片的质量。 这些材料应该存放在影片库中，包括照片、试听授权书。 在公开的网页中至少要有一张申报遗产的照片。 上述权利转让不得侵犯知识产权（摄影师 / 录像导演以及其他所有人的权利），另外，教科文组织在发行图像时，如果表格中有明确的说明，教科文组织通常会提供摄影师 / 录像导演的姓名。 因转让版权而获得的所有收益将纳入世界遗产基金会。	• 影像应该能够描述潜在突出普遍价值及其背景环境。

申报形式								其他建议
序号	格式（幻灯片、印刷品，视频录像）	图片说明	拍摄时间	拍摄者	版权所有人（如果不是拍摄者）	版权所有人的联系信息，姓名，住址，电话，传真，email	非排他性权利转让	

现有申报表格 申报格式	现有申现有申报表格填报须知	其他建议
7.b 与保护规划文本、管理规划或成文管理制度的复印件或与遗产保护相关的其他规划的摘要	按照 5.b，5.d 和 5.e 的要求，附加在文本的最后	
7.c 最近记录或遗产的详细目录的日期和形式，	用简单的语句表明最近记录或遗产的详细目录的日期和形式。只需要提及手头可用的记录。	
7.d 清单，记录和档案保存的地点	提供保存清单，记录和档案的单位的名称和地址。	
7.e 参考文献	列出主要的出版参考文献，用标准的参考文献格式。	
8. 主管单位联系方式	秘书处可通过该联系方式把世界遗产的最新消息和其他相关事宜通知给遗产负责机构。	
8.a 填表人 姓名： 职务： 城市，省（州）： 国家： 电话： 传真： 电子邮箱：	提供申报材料编纂人员的姓名、地址和其他联系信息。如果没有电子邮箱，联系信息中必须包括传真号码。	
8.b 当地官方机构	提供负责遗产管理的地方机构、博物馆、组织、社区或管理人员的姓名。如果是国家机关提供常规报告，请提供该国家机关的联系方式。	
8.c 其他当地机构	列出应接收免费《世界遗产时事通讯》（讨论关于世界遗产的事件和议题）的所有博物馆、游客中心和官方旅游办公室的全称、地址、电话、传真和电子邮件地址。	
8.d 官方网址 http：// 联络人姓名： 电子邮箱：	请提供申报遗产的现有官方网站。说明今后是否计划设立该类网站，并提供联系人姓名和电子邮件地址。	
9 代表国家签名	申报材料末尾应由缔约国的正式授权代表签字。	

Key message: Have the nomination peer reviewed

关键信息：同行评估申遗文本

4.3 Extra tips

4.3 其他建议

Review and revision

复审和修订

Having completed the nomination there are a number of useful steps that can help to ensure a good product:

• review and, if necessary, revise the Executive Summary to ensure it is consistent with the main nomination text;

• check the whole nomination to ensure the key messages are addressed and clearly expressed;

• have the nomination edited for consistency and style, especially if different parts of the nomination have been prepared by different authors. However, make sure important content is not lost or distorted;

• have the draft nomination peer reviewed, including by someone not closely involved with the property, and by someone who does not know anything about the country or its heritage. Address any questions raised by these reviews; and

• check the completeness of the nomination in accordance with Paragraph 132 of the Operational Guideline

在完成了申遗文本后，以下几步能帮助进一步完善申遗文本。

• 必要时，复审和修订《执行摘要》，确保与申遗文本一致；

• 检查申遗文本全文，确定关键信息表述清晰且前后一致，无遗漏；

• 对申遗文本进行编辑，确保形式和风格的一致性，特别是由不同作者准备了不同部分的申遗文本。确定重要的内容没有遗漏或歪曲；

• 申遗文本草案进行独立审核，包括邀请与遗产没有密切关系的专家同行，或对该缔约国或该遗产毫不了解的专家，解决在评议过程中发现的问题；

• 根据《操作指南》第 132 段的内容检查文本的完整性。

serial nominations

系列申报

In the case of serial nominations, the amount of information to be included can be considerable as this is multiplied by the number of components which are part of the series (e.g. descriptions of each component). Including too much information can make the nomination difficult to read or understand.

系列申报遗产由有一定数量的构成组成部分，因此它的信息量是单个组成部分的申报的信息量数倍。信息量过大会对申遗文本的阅读和理解造成困难。

Achieving the right balance of key information

掌控每个遗产关键信息量的平衡是一个挑战。

about each component is the challenge.

One option is to provide only summary information in the body of the nomination, with more detailed component information included in annexes referenced in the main text

一个选择是提供整个遗产概要信息，而单个构成部分的详细信息在完整文本的附件中。

5 Evaluation process

5. 评估过程

5.1 General

5.1 一般过程

Following submission of the nomination dossier, with all the required copies, the evaluation process begins.

在提交了申遗文本和所有需要的副本之后，评估过程就开始了。

The first step is a check by the World Heritage Centre to ensure the completeness of the dossier. If it is considered to be incomplete, it will not be forwarded to the Advisory Bodies for evaluation, and must be completed for submission in the following year or later.

评估的第一步是由世界遗产中心检查申遗文本的完整性。如果文本不完整，不会被送到咨询机构进行评估，缔约国必须补充完整，并在来年或以后再次提交。

If the nomination is complete, it will be forwarded to the relevant Advisory Body (ies) for evaluation. During this process, the Advisory Bodies will evaluate whether or not the nominated property has potential Outstanding Universal Value, if it meets the conditions of integrity and/or authenticity, and meets the requirements for protection and management. Details of the ICOMOS and IUCN evaluation procedures are provided in Annex 6 of *The Operational Guidelines,* and these are also described below.

如果文本完整，将转送到相应的评估机构进行评估。在评估的过程中，评估机构将评估申报遗产是否具有突出普遍价值、是否符合了完整性、真实性的条件、是否达到了保障和管理的要求。国际古迹理事会和世界自然保护联盟评估的过程在《操作指南》的附件 6 中有详细的介绍，下面也有一定描述。

After an evaluation by the Advisory Bodies but before consideration of a nomination by the World Heritage Committee, the Advisory Bodies can send questions or request information from a State Party by 31 January of the year in which the nomination will be considered by the Committee (*Operational*

在评估机构完成遗产评估后、未交世界遗产委员会讨论前，咨询机构可以向遗产申报国提出质疑或要求提供更多的信息，以便遗产委员会能在当年的 1 月 31 日以前讨论。（见《操作指南》149 段）。

Guidelines, Paragraph 149).

This information must be sent by 28 February for it to be considered by the Advisory Bodies. *The Operational Guidelines* formally prevent the Advisory Bodies from considering any information which is sent after this date.

这些信息必须在当年的 2 月 28 日前送达咨询机构。《操作指南》中明确规定，咨询机构对任何晚于该日期送达的相关信息不予考虑。

States Parties are also able to write to the Chairperson of the Committee, before the Committee meeting, pointing out any factual errors in the Advisory Bodies' evaluation (*Operational Guidelines*, Paragraph 150).

缔约国也可以在委员会会议召开前写信给委员会主席，指出评估机构在评估中发现的事实性错误（《操作指南》，150 段）。

It is important for States Parties to inform the World Heritage Centre about any developments affecting a nominated property during the evaluation. Such information may have an important impact on the evaluation.

在评估过程中，缔约国应及时向世界遗产中心告知任何开发对于遗产的影响。这些信息将对评估产生重要影响。

The World Heritage Committee makes the decision about whether or not to inscribe a property. In making this decision, the Committee is assisted by a recommendation from the relevant Advisory Body (ies).

世界遗产委员会决定是否将申报遗产列入遗产名录。在做出决定的过程中，遗产委员会将会听取相关评估机构的建议。

5.2 IUCN evaluation process

5.2 世界自然保护联盟评估过程

In carrying out the technical evaluation of nominations IUCN is guide d by *The Operational Guidelines* of the Convention. The evaluation process is carried out over the period of one year, from the receipt of nominations by IUCN in April and the submission of the IUCN evaluation report to the World Heritage Centre in May of the following year. The process involves the following steps.

在《操作指南》的指导下，世界自然保护联盟对申报遗产实施技术性评估。评估的过程大概需要 1 年时间，世界自然保护联盟的评估从 4 月拿到申遗文本开始，到第二年的 5 月提交评估报告给世界遗产中心止。评估过程包括以下几步：

1. Data assembly. A standardized data sheet is compiled using the nomination document, the World Database on Protected Areas and other

1. 数据整合。使用申遗文本、国际保护区数据库和其他相关的参考资料编辑标准化的信息清单。

available reference material.

2. External review. The nomination is sent to independent experts knowledgeable about the property or its natural values, including members of WCPA, other IUCN specialist commissions and scientific networks or NGOs working in the region (typically up to 100-150 external reviewers contribute each year).

2. 外部评审。申遗文本将送给了解遗产或自然价值的独立专家，包括世界自然保护区委员会成员、在该地区工作的其他世界自然遗产委员会成员、科技工作者或当地非政府组织的工作人员（一般而言，外部专家每年有 100–150 人）。

3. Field mission. Missions involving one or more IUCN and external experts evaluate the nominated property on the ground and discuss the nomination with the relevant national and local authorities, local communities, NGOs and other stakeholders. Missions usually take place between May and November. In the case of mixed properties and certain cultural landscapes, missions are jointly undertaken with ICOMOS.

3. 现场考察。考察团包括一个或多个世界自然保护联盟的成员和外部专家，对申报遗产进行实地评估并与相关国家和当地政府，当地社区，非政府组织和其他利益相关者对申遗文本进行讨论。现场考察的时间通常是 5 月到 11 月，如果是混合遗产或特定的文化景观，现场考察将与国际古迹理事会联合进行。

4. IUCN World Heritage Panel Review. The IUCN World Heritage Panel meets at least once per year, usually in December at IUCN Headquarters in Switzerland to examine each nomination. A second meeting or conference call is arranged as necessary, usually in the following March. The Panel intensively reviews the nomination dossiers, field mission reports, comments from external reviewers, the property data sheets and other relevant reference material, and provides its technical advice to IUCN and recommendations for each nomination. A final report is prepared and forwarded to the World Heritage Centre in May for distribution to the members of the World Heritage Committee.

4. 世界自然保护联盟世界遗产专家小组审议。世界自然保护联盟世界遗产专家小组审议会议至少每年一次，通常是 12 月在瑞士联盟的总部召开，评议每一个申报遗产。必要时会在下一年的 3 月召开第二次会议。专家小组集中评议申遗文本、现场考察报告、外部专家评估意见、遗产信息清单和其他相关的参考资料、向世界自然保护联盟提供对每一个申报遗产的专业的技术建议。准备最终报告并与 5 月提交最终报告给世界遗产中心，供其分发给世界遗产委员会的各个委员国。

5. Final recommendations. IUCN presents, with the support of images and maps, the results and recommendations of its evaluation process to the World Heritage Committee at its annual session in June or July, and responds to any questions. The World Heritage Committee makes the final decision on whether or not to inscribe the property on the World Heritage List.

5. 最终的建议。世界自然保护联盟在每年 6 月或 7 月的年会上，要通过图像和地图资料、相关问题的回应等向世界遗产委员会阐释他们评估的结果和建议。世界遗产委员会做出最后决议是否将遗产列入《世界遗产名录》。

It should be noted that IUCN seeks to develop and maintain a dialogue with the State Party throughout the evaluation process to allow the State Party every opportunity to supply all the necessary information and to clarify any questions or issues that may arise. For this reason, there are three occasions at which IUCN may request further information from the State Party. These are as follows.

应该注意，世界自然保护联盟致力于发展和维持与缔约国的对话，整个评估过程允许缔约国利用每一次机会提供必要的信息和澄清可能产生的各类问题和议题。鉴于此，联盟会在三种情况下要求缔约国提供更多信息：

• Before the field mission — IUCN sends the State Party, usually directly to the person organizing the mission in the host country, a briefing on the mission, in many cases raising specific questions and issues that should be discussed during the mission. This allows the State Party to properly prepare in advance.

• 在现场考察之前——联盟将派人到缔约国，简要介绍考察任务，包括在考察过程中可能会讨论的特殊问题或议题。这样可让缔约国提前准备。

• Directly after the field mission — Based on discussions during the field mission, IUCN may send an official letter requesting supplementary information before the IUCN World Heritage Panel meets in December, to ensure that the Panel has all the information necessary to make a recommendation on the nomination.

• 现场考察后——基于现场考察期间的讨论，联盟可能会发出官方信件要求缔约国在12月的联盟专家专家小组会议之前补充信息，以确保专家小组会议得到所有必须的、评估申报遗产全部的信息。

• After the IUCN World Heritage Panel — if the Panel finds some questions are still unanswered or further issues need to be clarified, a final letter will be sent to the State Party requesting supplementary information by a specific deadline. That deadline must be adhered to strictly in order to allow IUCN to complete its evaluation.

• 在世界自然保护联盟世界遗产专家小组会议之后——如果专家小组会议发现一些问题未能答复或需要进一步澄清，会最后一次要求缔约国必须在十二月召开会议之前提供相关信息。必须严格遵守截止日期以确保世界自然联盟有充足的时间完成评估。

Note: If the information provided by the State Party at the time of nomination and during the mission is adequate, IUCN does not request supplementary information. It is expected that supplementary information will be in response to specific questions or issues, and should not include

注意：如果缔约国在提交文本时已提交了充足的信息，联盟将不会要求补充信息。补充的信息是针对特殊问题或议题，而不是修改申遗文本或提供大量新信息

completely revised nominations or substantial amounts of new information.

In the technical evaluation of nominated properties, the Udvardy bio-geographical province concept is used for comparison of nominations with other similar properties. This method makes comparisons of natural properties more objective and provides a practical means of assessing similarity at the global level. At the same time, World Heritage properties are expected to contain special features, habitats and faunistic or floristic peculiarities that can also be compared on a broader biome basis. It is stressed that the bio-geographical province concept is used as a basis for comparison only and does not imply that World Heritage properties are to be selected solely on this criterion. In addition, global priority setting systems, such as Conservation International Biodiversity Hotspot, WWF Ecoregions, Birdlife International Endemic Bird Areas, IUCN/WWF centers of Plant Diversity and the IUCN/SSC Habitat Classification, and the 2004 IUCN/UNEP-WCMC Review of the World Heritage Network are used to identify properties of global significance. The guiding principle is that World Heritage properties are only those areas of Outstanding Universal Value.

在对申报遗产进行专业评估的过程中，将使用乌德瓦尔第生物地理系统的概念，对申报遗产与其他相似遗产进行比较。这个方法使得自然遗产有了在全球层面评估相似遗产的可行性方法。同时提供含具体特性、栖息地和动物植物群，这些要和更为广泛的动植物群系进行比较，使世界遗产的比较更加客观。需要强调的是乌德瓦尔第生物地理系统概念是作为比较的基础，而不是世界遗产的遴选标准。此外全球领先的环境系统，例如，《国际生物多样性保护热点》、世界自然基金会《拯救地球生命的200个全球生物区》、《国际鸟类联盟：地方性鸟类栖息地》、世界自然保护联盟/世界自然基金会的植物多样性中心以及世界保护自然联盟/物种存续委员会的栖息地分类，和2004年世界自然保护联盟/联合国环境规划署世界保护监测中心的世界遗产网络审查，都可以用来确定具有全球意义的遗产。世界遗产指导原则是：世界遗产只能是具有的突出普遍价值的遗产。

Finally, the evaluation process is aided by the publication of some twenty reference volumes on the world's protected areas published by IUCN, UNEP-WCMC and several other publishers. These include:

最后，评估过程参考了由世界自然保护联盟、联合国国际规划署、世界保护监测中心或其他出版商出版的关于世界保护区参考以下20种文献，他们包括：

- reviews of Protected Area Systems in Africa, Asia and Oceania;
- a four-volume directory of Protected Areas of the World;
- a six-volume Global Biodiversity Atlas series;

- 《非洲、亚洲和大洋洲保护区制度》的评论；
- 世界遗产保护区（4卷）目录；
- 《全球生物多样性地图集》系列（6卷）

• a three-volume directory of centers of Plant Diversity;

• a three-volume directory of Coral Reefs of the World; and

• a four-volume synthesis on A Global Representative System of Marine Protected Areas.

These documents together provide system-wide overviews which allow comparison of the conservation importance of protected areas throughout the world.

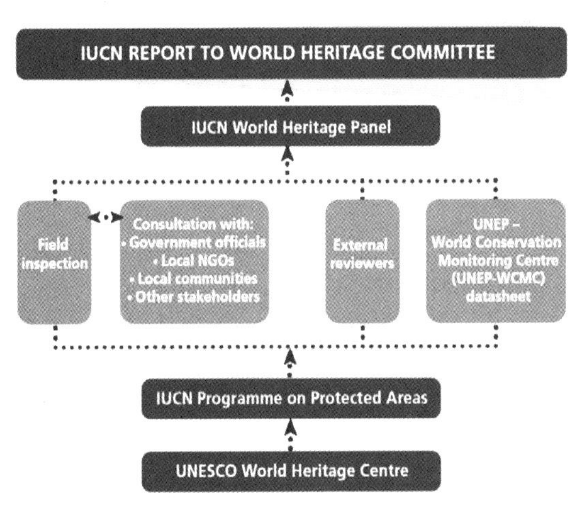

• 《植物多样性中心》（3 卷）目录；

• 《世界珊瑚礁》（3 卷）目录；

• 《海洋保护区全球代表性制度》（4 卷）。

这些文件组合起来提供了一个系统的概述，可以用于比较全球范围内保护区域保护的重要性。

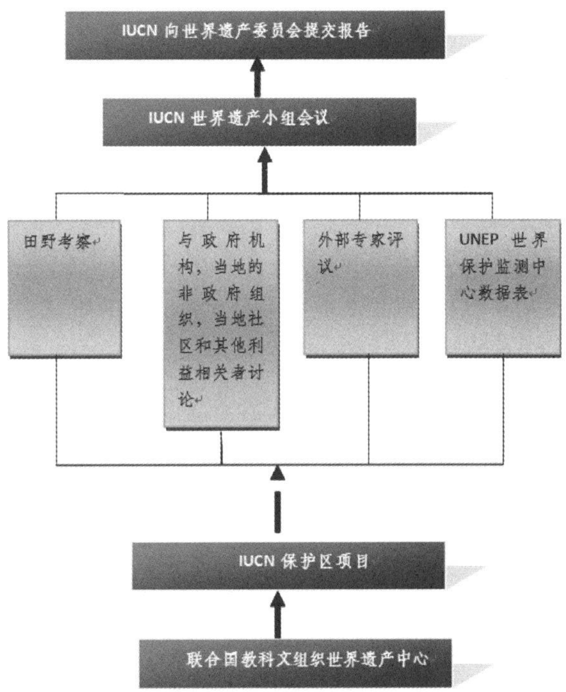

5.3 ICOMOS evaluation process

In carrying out its evaluation of nominations of cultural properties, ICOMOS (International Council on Monuments and Sites) is guided by The Operational Guidelines (see Paragraph 148).

The evaluation process (see figure on page 125) involves consultation of the wide range of expertise represented by the membership of ICOMOS and its National and International Committees, as well as the many other specialist networks with which it is linked. Members are also sent on expert missions to carry out confidential on-site evaluations. This extensive consultation results

5.3 国际古迹遗址理事会评估过程

国际古迹遗址理事会《操作指南》负责对文化遗产的评估。（148 段）

评估过程（见下表）包括广泛咨询国际古迹遗址理事会成员、各国国际委员会的专家意见，还包括其他很多相关网络专家意见。这些成员也会作为专家组成员前往遗产地实施秘密的现场评估。理事会根据大量的咨询工作准备详细的建议，并在年度会议上提交给世界遗产委员会。

in the preparation of detailed recommendations that are submitted to the World Heritage Committee at its annual meetings.

Choice of experts

There is a clearly defined annual procedure for the submission of properties to the World Heritage List. Once new nominations have been checked for completeness by the UNESCO World Heritage Centre, the nomination dossiers are then delivered to ICOMOS, where they are handled by the ICOMOS World Heritage Secretariat. The first action involved is the choice of the experts who are to be consulted. This involves two separate groups. First, there are those who can advise on the Outstanding Universal Value of the nominated property. This is essentially a 'library' exercise for specialist academics, and may sometimes involve non-ICOMOS members, in cases where there is no adequate expertise within the ICOMOS membership on a specific topic: an example is the occasional nomination of fossil hominid sites, where the services of specialist palaeontologists are required.

The second group of experts comprises those with practical experience of the management, conservation and authenticity aspects of individual properties, who are required to carry out site missions. The process of selecting these experts makes full use of the ICOMOS network. The advice of International Scientific Committees and individual members is sought, as is that of specialist bodies with whom ICOMOS has partnership agreements, such as the International Committee for the Conservation of the Industrial Heritage (TICCIH), the International Federation of Landscape Architects (IFLA), and the International Committee for the Documentation and Conservation

专家的选择

世界遗产申报有明确规定的年度程序。一旦申遗文本的完整性已通过了世界遗产中心审查，申遗文本将由世界遗产中心秘书处转交国际古迹遗址理事会。第一步是遴选咨询专家。这些专家分为两部分，一部分是能够对申报遗产的突出普遍价值提出建议的专家。这一工作对专家而言就是“图书馆”式活动，这个评估有时可由非国际古迹遗址理事会会员承担，因为国际古迹遗址理事会的成员中没有足够的特定主题的专家：比如申报原始人类化石遗址的遗产时，就需要有古生物学家作为专家。

第二个团队的专家包括对管理、保护和单个遗产真实性组成部分评估有实战经验的专家，他们将承担现场考察的任务。选择这些专家时要有效利用国际古迹遗址理事会专家数据库。将考虑国际科学委员会和个人成员建议，也将考虑与国际古迹遗址理事会有合作协议的专业团队，例如国际工业遗址保护委员会、国际园林建筑师联合会和国际现代建筑记录与保护组织等机构专家的建议。

of Monuments and Sites of the Modern Movement (Docomomo).

Site missions

In selecting experts to carry out on-site evaluation missions, the policy of ICOMOS is wherever possible to choose someone from the region in which the nominated property is located. Such experts are required to be experienced in heritage management and conservation: they are not necessarily high academic experts in the type of property. They are expected to be able to talk to site managers on a basis of professional equality and to make informed assessments of management plans, conservation practices, visitor handling, etc. They are provided with detailed briefings, which include copies of the relevant information from the dossiers. The dates and programmes of their visits are agreed in consultation with States Parties, who are requested to ensure that ICOMOS evaluation missions are given a low profile so far as the media are concerned. ICOMOS experts submit their reports in confidence to the Executive Committee on practical aspects of the properties concerned, and premature publicity can cause embarrassment both to ICOMOS, the State Party concerned, and to the World Heritage Committee.

现场评估

选择专家实施现场评估时，国际古迹遗址理事会的政策是，尽可能从遗产地选择专家实施遗产评估。要求专家具有遗产管理和保护工作的实际经验：不必是某一遗产类型的顶级专家。希望他们基于专业，平等的基础上与遗产管理者直接对话，同时有充足的知识对遗产的管理规划、保护措施、旅游管理等进行评估。相关人员向专家详细介绍情况，并提供与申报材料相关的信息。现场考察的时间可以与缔约国协商并达成一致，国际古迹遗址理事会的遗产实地评估要求低调进行，最好不要惊动媒体。国际古迹遗址理事会专家秘密向执行委员会提交关于遗产实际存在问题的报告，因为过早的传播遗产信息可能会给国际古迹遗址理事会、缔约国和世界遗产委员会造成不必要的麻烦。

World Heritage Panel

The two types of report (cultural assessment and site mission report) that emerge from these consultations are received by the ICOMOS Secretariat in Paris, and from them a draft evaluation is prepared. This contains a brief description and history of the property, summaries of its legislative protection, management and state of conservation, comments on these aspects, and draft recommendations to the World Heritage

世界遗产专家小组会议

位于巴黎的国际古迹遗址理事会秘书处将收到两份的报告（文化评估和遗产地现场考察报告），根据他们的内容，开始准备评估草案。这包括遗产简要描述和历史沿革、立法保护、管理和保护状态概要，对于这些事项的评论、以及提交给世界遗产委员会的建议。评估草案将提前提交给国际古迹遗址理事会世界遗产专家小组，届时将召开2–3天会议。专家小组会议的成员是执行委员会成员，他们来自世界各

Committee. Draft evaluations are then presented to a two or three-day meeting of the ICOMOS World Heritage Panel. The Panel comprises the members of the Executive Committee, who come from all parts of the world and possess a wide range of skills and experience. The Executive Committee members are supplemented by experts in certain categories of heritage that figure on the annual list of nominations but which are not represented on the Committee. Depending on the characteristics of the nominations received, ICOMOS might also invite representatives of TICCIH and Docomomo to join the Panel.

地，具有专业技能和知识。此外，年度申报列表中的遗产类型超出执行委员会专业范畴时，还需要请相应类别的遗产专家进行补充。根据申报遗产的特点，国际古迹遗址理事会可能会要求国际工业遗址保护委员会和国际现代建筑记录与保护组织的代表参加专家小组会议。

The Panel works under conditions of confidentiality, guided by the ICOMOS Policy Document (available from the ICOMOS website). Each nominated property is the subject of a 10-15 minute illustrated presentation by a representative of ICOMOS, followed by discussion. Following the objective and exhaustive examination of the nominations, the collective recommendations of ICOMOS are prepared, and the evaluations are revised and printed, for presentation to the World Heritage Committee.

专家小组会议在国际古迹遗址理事会政策文件的指导下召开。国际古迹遗址理事会的代表对每一个申报遗产进行 10–15 分钟的简要陈述，接下来进行讨论。通过客观和耗时的检查，国际古迹遗址理事会将形成一致意见，修改后打印评估报告，提交给世界遗产委员会。

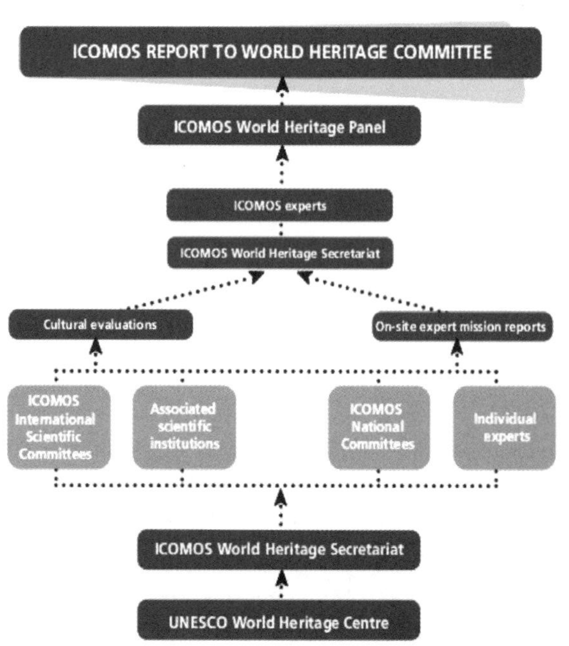

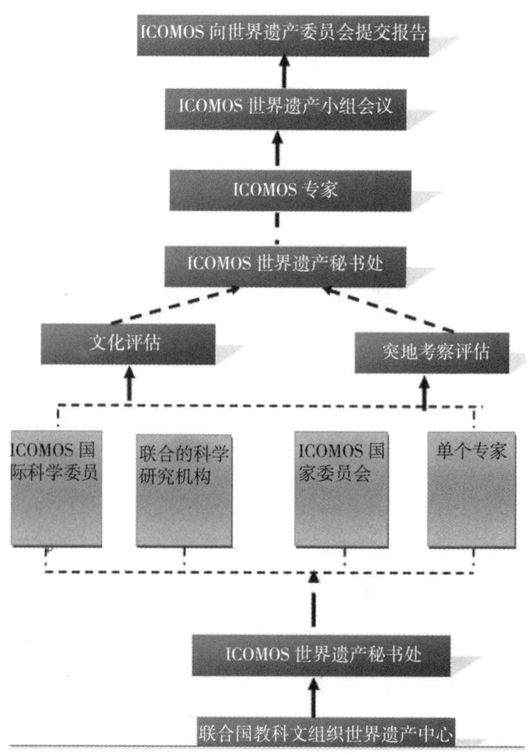

Bibliography

参考文献

General

总目录

Badman, T., Bomhard, B. and Dingwall, P. 2008. World Heritage Nominations for Natural Properties: A Resource Manual for Practitioners. Gland, Switzerland, IUCN.

Badman，T.，Bomhard，B.and Dingwall，P.2008.《世界自然遗产申报手册》瑞士，格兰德，世界自然保护联盟

Cameron, C. 2005. Background Paper for the Special Expert Meeting of the World Heritage Convention: The Concept of Outstanding Universal Value. Kazan, Republic of Tatarstan, Russian Federation.

cmsdata.iucn.org/downloads/kazan_abs_english.pdf

Cameron，C.2005.《世界遗产公约》特殊专家会议背景文件:《突出普遍价值的概念》喀山，俄罗斯联邦鞑靼斯坦共和国

cmsdata.iucn.org/downloads/kazan_abs_english.pdf

de Merode, E., Smeets, R. and Westrik, C. 2004. Linking Universal and Local Values:

Managing a Sustainable Future for World Heritage. Paris, UNESCO World Heritage Centre. (World Heritage Papers 13.)

http: //whc.unesco.org/en/series/ (English web page)

http: //whc.unesco.org/fr/series/ (French web page)

de Merode，E.，Smeets，R.and Westrik，C.2004.《连接一般价值与地方价值，管理未来永续的世界遗产》巴黎，联合国教科文组织世界遗产中心（世界遗产论文 13.）

http ：//whc.unesco.org/en/series/（英语界面）

http ：//whc.unesco.org/fr/series/（法语界面）

Dingwall, P., Weighell, T. and Badman, T. 2005. Geological World Heritage: A Global Framework. Gland, Switzerland, IUCN.

Dingwall，P.，Weighell，T.and Badman，T.2005.《全球世界遗产：全球框架》瑞士，格兰德，世界自然保护联盟

Engels, B., Ohnesorge, B. and Burmester, A. (eds). 2009. Nominations and Management of Serial Natural World Heritage Properties — Present Situation, Challenges and Opportunities.

Proceedings of a workshop organized by the German Federal Agency for Nature Conservation (BfN) in cooperation with the UNESCO World Heritage Centre and IUCN,

Engels，B.，Ohnesorge，B.and Burmester，A.（eds）.2009.《系列自然遗产的申报和管理——现状，挑战和机遇》。

2008 年 11 月 26–30 日由德国联邦自然保护机构与联合国教科文组织世界遗产中心及世界自然保护联盟合办的研讨会论文

November 26-30 2008.

Hockings, M., James, R., Stolton, S., Dudley, N., Mathur, V., Makombo, J., Courrau, J. And Parrish, J. 2008. Enhancing Our Heritage Toolkit, Assessing Management Effectiveness of Natural World Heritage Sites.

Hockings, M., James, R., Stolton, S., Dudley, N., Mathur, V., Makombo, J., Courrau, J.and Parrish, J.2008 年,《优化遗产管理工具包。评估世界自然遗产管理的有效性》。

ICOMOS. 1965. International Charter for the Conservation and Restoration of Monuments and Sites (The Venice Charter 1964). Paris, ICOMOS.

http: //www.icomos.org/venice_charter.html

1965 年国际古迹遗址理事会,《国际古迹遗址理事会宪章》(威尼斯宪章), 巴黎

http：//www.icomos.org/venice_charter.html

ICOMOS. 2005a. The World Heritage List: Filling the Gaps - An Action Plan for the Future. Paris, ICOMOS.

http: //www.international.icomos.org/world_heritage/gaps.pdf (English web page)

http: //www.international.icomos.org/world_heritage_fre/whlgaps.htm (French web page)

2005a, 国际古迹遗址理事会,《世界遗产公约》:《填补空白——未来行动计划》, 巴黎

http：//www.international.icomos.org/world_heritage/gaps.pdf（英语界面）

http：//www.international.icomos.org/world_heritage_fre/whlgaps.htm（法语界面）

ICOMOS. 2005b. Xi'an Declaration on the Conservation of the Setting of Heritage Structures, Sites and Areas.

http: //www.international.icomos.org/charters/xian-declaration.pdf

2005b, 国际古迹遗址理事会,《关于保护古迹遗址及其周边环境的西安宣言》

http：//www.international.icomos.org/charters/xian−declaration.pdf

ICOMOS. 2008. Compendium on Standards for the Inscription of Cultural Properties to the World Heritage List.

whc.unesco.org/en/sessions/32COM/documents/

2008, 国际古迹遗址理事会,《文化遗产列入《世界遗产名录》标准纲要》

whc.unesco.org/en/sessions/32COM/documents/

IUCN. 2000. World Heritage and Mining.

http: //unesdoc.unesco.org/images/0012/001231/123112e.pdf

2000. 世界自然保护联盟。《世界遗产和采矿业》

http：//unesdoc.unesco.org/images/0012/001231/123112e.pdf

IUCN. 2003. World Heritage in the Boreal Zone. Available at the IUCN website.

2003. 世界自然保护联盟。

《北极地区的文化遗产》见世界自然保护联

盟网站

IUCN. 2004. Review of the World Heritage Network: Biogeography, Habitats and Biodiversity: A Contribution to the Global Strategy for World Heritage Natural Sites. Available at the IUCN website.

2004. 世界自然保护联盟。《世界遗产网络回顾，生物地理学、栖息地和生物多样性，全球战略对世界自然遗产的贡献》见世界自然保护联盟网站

IUCN. 2005a. Enhancing the IUCN Evaluation Process of World Heritage Nominations: A Contribution to Achieving a Credible and Balanced World Heritage List. Available at the IUCN website.

2005a. 世界自然保护联盟。《强化申报世界遗产自然评估程序：对取得可信而平衡的世界遗产的贡献》见世界自然保护联盟网站

IUCN. 2005b. World Heritage Thematic Study for Central Asia: A Regional Overview.
Available at the IUCN website.

2005b. 世界自然保护联盟。《世界遗产中亚专题研究：区域概述》见世界自然保护联盟网站

IUCN. 2006. The World Heritage List: Guidance and Future Priorities for Identifying Natural Heritage of Potential Outstanding Universal Value. Available at the IUCN website.

2006. 世界自然保护联盟。《〈世界遗产名录〉：指导和未来重点识别自然遗产的潜在的突出普遍价值》见世界自然保护联盟网站

IUCN. 2007. Harmonisation of Tentative Lists in Central, Eastern and South-Eastern Europe. Available at the IUCN website.

2007. 世界自然保护联盟。《和谐的中欧、东欧和东南欧预备名录》见世界自然保护联盟网站

IUCN. 2008a. Management Planning for Natural World Heritage Properties, A Resource Manual for Practitioners, interim version. IUCN Programme on Protected Areas. (IUCN World Heritage Studies 5.) Available at the IUCN website.

2008a. 世界自然保护联盟。《自然遗产管理规划，参与者资源手册临时版》世界自然保护联盟保护区项目（世界自然保护联盟世界遗产研究 5）见世界自然保护联盟网站

IUCN. 2008b. Outstanding Universal Value - Standards for Natural World Heritage, A Compendium on Standards for Inscriptions of Natural Properties on the World Heritage List. Available at the IUCN website.

2008b. 世界自然保护联盟。《突出普遍价值——自然遗产标准，自然遗产列入世界遗产目录标准纲要》见世界自然保护联盟网站

IUCN. 2008c. World Heritage and Protected Areas. Available at the IUCN website.

2008c. 世界自然保护联盟。《世界遗产和保护区》见世界自然保护联盟

网站

IUCN. 2008d. World Heritage Caves and Karst. Available at the IUCN website.

2008c. 世界自然保护联盟。
《世界洞窟及喀斯特地形遗产》见世界自然保护联盟网站

IUCN. 2009. Serial Natural World Heritage Properties. Available at the IUCN website.

2009. 世界自然保护联盟
《系列自然遗产》见世界自然保护联盟网站

Jokilehto, J. 2008. The World Heritage List. What is OUV? Defining the Outstanding Universal Value of Cultural World Heritage Properties. Paris, ICOMOS. (Monuments and Sites XVI.) http: //www.international.icomos.org/publications/index.html

Jokilehto，J.2008.《《世界遗产名录》，何为突出普遍价值？世界文化遗产突出普遍价值的辨别》，巴黎，国际古迹遗址理事会（古迹遗址）

http：//www.international.icomos.org/publications/index.html

Magin, C. and Chape, S. 2004. Review of the World Heritage Network: Biogeography, Habitats and Biodiversity. IUCN/UNEP-WCMC.

Magin，C.and Chape，S.2004.《世界遗产网络回顾，生物地理学、栖息地和生物多样性》世界自然保护联盟、联合国环境署－世界保护监测中心

Martin, O. and Piatti, G. (eds). 2009. World Heritage and Buffer Zones, International Expert Meeting on World Heritage and Buffer Zones, Davos, Switzerland, 11-14 March 2008.

Paris, UNESCO World Heritage Centre. (World Heritage Papers 25.)

http: //whc.unesco.org/en/series/ (English web page)

http: //whc.unesco.org/fr/series/ (French web page)

Martin，O.and Piatti，G.（eds）.2009.《世界遗产和缓冲区专家会议》瑞士达沃斯，2008年3月11–14日。巴黎，联合国教科文组织世界遗产中心（世界遗产论文25）

http：//whc.unesco.org/en/series/（英语界面）

http：//whc.unesco.org/fr/series/（法语界面）

Pedersen, A. 2002. Managing Tourism at World Heritage Sites: a Practical Manual for World Heritage Site Managers. Paris, UNESCO World Heritage Centre. (World Heritage Manuals 1.)

http: //whc.unesco.org/en/series/ (English web page)

http: //whc.unesco.org/fr/series/ (French web page)

Pedersen，A.2002《世界遗产旅游管理，世界遗产管理者手册》巴黎，联合国教科文组织世界遗产中心（世界遗产手册1）

http：//whc.unesco.org/en/series/（英语界面）

http：//whc.unesco.org/fr/series/（法语界面）

UNESCO. 1972. Convention concerning the Protection of the World Cultural and Natural Heritage. (World Heritage Convention).

http: //whc.unesco.org/en/conventiontext/ (English web page)

http: //whc.unesco.org/fr/conventiontexte/ (French web page)

1972 年，联合国教科文组织

《保护世界自然和文化遗产公约》(《世界遗产公约》)

http：//whc.unesco.org/en/conventiontext/（英语界面）

http：//whc.unesco.org/fr/conventiontexte/（法语界面）

UNESCO. 2003. Convention for the Safeguarding of Intangible Cultural Heritage.

http: //www.unesco.org/culture/ich/index.php?lg=en&pg=00022 (English web page)

http: //www.unesco.org/culture/ich/index.php?lg=fr&pg=00022 (French web page)

2003 年，联合国教科文组织

《保护非物质文化遗产公约》

http：//www.unesco.org/culture/ich/index.php？ lg=en&pg=00022（英语界面）

http：//www.unesco.org/culture/ich/index.php？ lg=fr&pg=00022（法语界面）

UNESCO World Heritage Centre. Tentative Lists.

http: //whc.unesco.org/en/tentativelists/ (English web page)

http: //whc.unesco.org/fr/listesindicatives/ (French web page)

联合国教科文组织世界遗产中心《预备名录》

http：//whc.unesco.org/en/tentativelists/（英语界面）

http：//whc.unesco.org/fr/listesindicatives/（法语界面）

UNESCO World Heritage Centre. World Heritage List.

http: //whc.unesco.org/en/list/ (English web page)

http: //whc.unesco.org/fr/list/ (French web page)

联合国教科文组织世界遗产中心《世界遗产名录》

http：//whc.unesco.org/en/list/（英语界面）

http：//whc.unesco.org/fr/list/（法语界面）

UNESCO World Heritage Centre. 1994. Nara Document on Authenticity.

http: //www.international.icomos.org/charters/nara_e.htm

(Also reproduced as Annex 4 of Operational Guidelines.)

1994 年，联合国教科文组织世界遗产中心《奈良真实性文件》

http：//www.international.icomos.org/charters/nara_e.htm（见《操作指南》附件 4）

UNESCO World Heritage Centre. 2005. Vienna Memorandum on World Heritage and Contemporary Architecture - Managing the Historic Urban Landscape.

2005 年，联合国教科文组织世界遗产中心《维也纳世界遗产和当代建筑——历史性城市景观管理备忘录。》

whc.unesco.org/archive/2005/whc05–15ga–

whc.unesco.org/archive/2005/whc05-15ga-inf7e.doc

inf7e.doc

UNESCO World Heritage Centre. 2011. Operational Guidelines for the Implementation of The World Heritage Convention.

http: //whc.unesco.org/en/guidelines/ (English web page)

http: //whc.unesco.org/fr// (French web page)

2011 年，联合国教科文组织世界遗产中心《实施〈世界遗产公约〉操作指南》

http：//whc.unesco.org/en/guidelines/（英语界面）

http：//whc.unesco.org/fr//（法语界面）

UNESCO World Heritage Centre/Government of the Netherlands. 1998. Report of the World Heritage Global Strategy Natural and Cultural Heritage Expert Meeting, 25 to 29 March 1998, Amsterdam, the Netherlands.

1998 年，联合国教科文组织世界遗产中心及荷兰政府《1988 年世界自然和文化遗产战略会议报告》1998 年 3 月 25–29 日，阿姆斯特丹，荷兰。

UNESCO World Heritage Centre/ICCROM. 2004. Monitoring World Heritage. (World Heritage Papers 10.)

http: //www.international.icomos.org/world_heritage/gaps.pdf (English web page)

http: //www.international.icomos.org/world_heritage_fre/whlgaps.htm (French web page)

2004 年，联合国教科文组织世界遗产中心及国际文物保护及修复研究中心《世界遗产监测》

http：//www.international.icomos.org/world_heritage/gaps.pdf（英语界面）

http：//www.international.icomos.org/world_heritage_fre/whlgaps.htm（法语界面）

Additional sources of information for global comparative analyses for natural properties and the review and update of Tentative Lists

对全球自然遗产比较分析和和《预备名录》初步审查的附加信息来源

IUCN Technical and Thematic Studies

世界自然保护联盟技术和专题研究

• The World's Greatest Natural Areas: an indicative inventory of natural sites of World Heritage Quality (1982).

• 世界上最伟大的自然领域：世界自然遗产的质量指标清单（1982）

• Earth's Geological History: a contextual framework for assessment of World Heritage fossil site nominations (1994).

• 地球地质史：评估化石遗址申报世界遗产背景框架（1994）

• A Global Overview of Wetland and Marine Protected Areas on the World Heritage List

•《世界遗产名录》中全球湿地和海洋保护区的概述（1997）

(1997).

• A Global Overview of Forest Protected Areas on the World Heritage List (1997).

•《世界遗产名录》中全球森林保护区概述（1997）

• A Global Overview of Human Use of World Heritage Natural Sites (1997).

• 全球人类利用世界自然遗产概述（1997）

• A Global Overview of Protected Areas on the World Heritage List of Particular Importance for Biodiversity (2000).

•《世界遗产名录》中全球特别保护区概述（2000）

• Which Oceanic Islands Merit World Heritage Status? (1991).

• 海洋岛屿在世界遗产中有何优势地位?（2000）

• Report of the Working Group on Application of The World Heritage Convention to Islands of the Southern Ocean (1992).

•《世界遗产公约》在南极洋岛屿应用的工作组报告（2000）

• Future Directions for Natural World Heritage Sites in East and Southeast Asia. Filling the Biome Gaps: a thematic approach to achieving biodiversity conservation through World Heritage, Les Molloy (2000).

• 自然世界遗产在东亚和东南亚未来的发展方向．填充生物群系差距：通过专题研究的方法实现世界遗产生物多样性保护 Les Molloy（2000）

• Potential Natural World Heritage Sites in Europe, Lars-Erik Esping (1998).

• 欧洲潜在的世界自然遗产 Lars–Erik Esping（1998）

• A Global Representative System of Marine Protected Areas, World Bank/IUCN, 4 vols (1995).

• 全球海洋保护区代表系统，世界银行及世界自然保护联盟，4 卷（1995）

Reports from selected regional meetings and UNESCO World Heritage initiatives to identify potential natural World Heritage sites

• 精选区域会议和联合国教科文组织关于识别潜在自然世界遗产的报告项目

• Task force to select a global inventory of fossil sites (1991).

• 全球化石类遗产选择小组（1991）

• Nordic World Heritage - proposals for new areas for the UNESCO World Heritage List (1996).

• 北欧世界遗产—联合国教科文组织《世界遗产名录》新区域（1991）

• Identification of potential World Heritage sites in Arab countries (1999).

• 阿拉伯国家潜在世界遗产辨别（1999）

• Tropical forests (Berastagi meeting report, 1998).

• 热带森林（贝拉斯塔基会议报告，1998）

• Identification of World Heritage properties in the Pacific (1999).

• 太平洋区域世界遗产辨别（1999）

• Regional workshop on the nomination of World Heritage sites, Mozambique (2000).

• 申报世界遗产区域研讨会，莫桑比克（2000）

• Seminar on natural heritage in the Caribbean, Suriname (2000).

• 加勒比海自然遗产研讨会，苏里南（2000）

• Central Asian meeting (2000).

• 中亚会议（2000）

• Karst sites in East and South East Asia (2001).

• 东亚及东南亚喀斯特遗产（2001）

• Alpine Arc meetings (2000-2001).

• 高山弧会议（2000–2001）

• Tropical marine and coastal sites (Viet Nam workshop, 2002).

• 热带海洋和海岸遗产（越南研讨会，2002）

• Boreal forest protected areas (Russian Federation, October 2003).

• 北方森林保护区（俄罗斯联邦，2003 年 10 月）

References

BirdLife International. 1998. Endemic Bird Areas of the World: Priorities for Biodiversity Conservation. Cambridge, UK, BirdLife International.

BirdLife International. 2000. Threatened Birds of the World. Barcelona/Cambridge, Lynx Edicions/ BirdLife International.

Hillary, A., Kokkonen, M. and Max, L. (eds). 2003. Proceedings of the World Heritage Marine Biodiversity Workshop. Paris, UNESCO World Heritage Centre. (World Heritage Papers 4.)

参考文献

国际鸟类联盟：1988 年世界禽类区域流行病：重点保护生物多样性。英国剑桥，国际鸟类联盟

国际鸟类联盟：2000 年世界濒危禽类，巴塞罗那及剑桥，Lynx Edicions 及国际鸟类联盟

Hillary，A.，Kokkonen，M.and Max，L.（eds）. 2003.《世界遗产海洋生物多样性研讨会》，巴黎，联合国教科文组织世界遗产中心，（世界遗产论文 4）

ICOMOS. 2004. ICOMOS Analysis of the World Heritage List and Tentative Lists and Follow-Up Action Plan. Paris, ICOMOS.

2004 年《国际古迹遗址理事会《世界遗产名录》和《预备名录》分析及后续行动计划》，巴黎，国际古迹遗址理事会

IUCN. 1997. World Heritage Special Issue. PARKS, Vol. 7, No. 2.

1997 年世界自然保护联盟《世界遗产的特殊问题》公园卷 7，2

IUCN. 2004. The World Heritage List: Future Priorities for a Credible and Complete List of Natural and Mixed Sites. Gland, Switzerland, IUCN Protected Areas Programme.

2004 年世界自然保护联盟《《世界遗产名录》：未来重点是一个可信而完整的自然和混合遗产名录》瑞士格兰德，世界自然保护联盟保护区项目

Miklos, D. F. and Udvardy, M. 1975. A Classification of the Biogeographical Provinces of the World - Prepared as a contribution to UNESCO's Man and the Biosphere Programme. Morges, Switzerland, IUCN. (Occasional Paper No. 18.)

Miklos，D.F.and Udvardy，M.1975.《世界的生物地理学范围分类——为联合国教科文组织人与生物圈项目准备》瑞士莫尔根斯，世界自然保护联盟（不定期刊第 18 期）

Smith, G. and Jakubowska, J. 2000. A Global Overview of Protected Areas on the World Heritage List of Particular Importance for Biodiversity. Cambridge, UK, UNEP World Conservation Monitoring Centre.

Smith，G.and Jakubowska，J.2000.《全球世界遗产尤其是生物多样性的保护区概览》

英国剑桥，联合国规划署世界保护监测中心

Thorsell, J., Ferster Levy, R. and Sigaty, T. 1997. A Global Overview of Wetland and Marine Protected Areas on the World Heritage List. Gland, Switzerland, IUCN Natural Heritage Programme.

Thorsell，J.，Ferster Levy，R.and Sigaty，T.1997.《〈世界遗产名录〉中全球湿地和海洋保护区概述》，瑞士格兰德，世界自然保护联盟自然遗产项目

Thorsell, J. and Hamilton, L. 2002. A Global Overview of Mountain Protected Areas on the World Heritage List. Gland, Switzerland, IUCN Protected Areas Programme.

Thorsell，J.and Hamilton，L.2002.《世界遗产名录》中全球山脉保护区概述》，瑞士格兰德，世界自然保护联盟自然遗产项目

Thorsell, J. and Sigaty, T. 1997a. A Global Overview of Forest Protected Areas on the World Heritage List. Gland, Switzerland, IUCN Natural Heritage Programme.

Thorsell，J.and Sigaty，T.1997a.《世界遗产名录》中全球森林保护区概述》瑞士格兰德，世界自然保护联盟自然遗产项目

Thorsell, J. and Sigaty, T. 1997b. Human Use of World Heritage Natural Sites: A Global Overview. Gland, Switzerland, IUCN Natural Heritage Programme.

Thorsell，J.and Sigaty，T.1997b.《《世界遗产名录》中全球人类利用自然的保护区概述》瑞士格兰德，世界自然保护联盟自然遗产项目

UNEP-WCMC. 1992. Global Biodiversity: Status of the Earth's Living Resources. London, / World Conservation Monitoring Centre.

联合国规划署世界保护监测中心《全球生物多样性：地球生物资源的状态》伦敦，Chapman & Hall 及世界保护监测中心

UNEP-WCMC. 2004. Review of the World Heritage Network: Biogeography, Habitats and Biodiversity. Cambridge, UK, UNEP World Conservation Monitoring Centre

联合国规划署世界保护监测中心《回顾世界遗产遗产：生物地理学、栖息地和生物多样性》，英国剑桥，联合国规划署世界保护监测中心

Wells, R. T. 1996. Earth's Geological History: A Contextual Framework for Assessment of World Heritage Fossil Site Nominations. Gland, Switzerland, IUCN Natural Heritage Programme.

联合国规划署世界保护监测中心《地球的地质历史：评估申报世界遗产背景框架下的化石遗址》瑞士格兰德，世界自然保护联盟自然遗产项目

WWF/IUCN. 1994. centers of Plant Diversity: A Guide and Strategy for their Conservation - Volume 1. 3 vols. Cambridge, UK, IUCN Publications Unit.

世界野生动物基金会，世界自然保护联盟《植物多样性中心：指导和保护策略 – 卷 1.3》英国剑桥世界自然保护联盟出版社

◎ 2017 年

联合国教科文组织《实施〈世界遗产公约〉操作指南》(2017) The Operational Guidelines for the Implementation of the World Heritage Convention

Chapter number	**章节**
ACRONYMS AND ABBREVIATIO	缩略语
I. INTRODUCTION	I. 引言
I.A The Operational Guidelines	I.A《操作指南》
I.B The World Heritage Convention	I.B《世界遗产公约》
I.C The States Parties to the World Heritage Convention	I.C《世界遗产公约》缔约国
I.D The General Assembly of States Parties to the World Heritage Convention	I.D《世界遗产公约》缔约国大会
I.E The World Heritage Committee	I.E 世界遗产委员会
I.F The Secretariat to the World Heritage Committee (the World Heritage Centre)	I.F 世界遗产委员会秘书处（世界遗产中心）
I.G The Advisory Bodies to the World Heritage Committee:	I.G 世界遗产委员会咨询机构
- ICCROM	- 国际文物保护和修复研究中心
- ICOMOS	- 国际古迹遗址理事会
- IUCN	- 世界自然保护联盟
I.H Other organizations	I.H 其他组织
I.I Partners in the protection of World Heritage	I.I 保护世界遗产的合作伙伴
I.J Other Conventions, Recommendations and Programmes	I.J 其他公约、建议和方案
II. The World Heritage List	II.《世界遗产名录》
II.A Definition of World Heritage	II.A 世界遗产的定义
- Cultural and Natural Heritage	- 文化和自然遗产
- Mixed Cultural and Natural Heritage	- 文化和自然混合遗产
- Cultural landscapes	- 文化景观
- Movable Heritage	- 可移动遗产
- Outstanding Universal Value	- 突出的普遍价值

II.B A Representative, Balanced and Credible World Heritage List	II.B 具有代表性、平衡性和可信性的《世界遗产名录》
- The Global Strategy for a Representative, Balanced and Credible World Heritage List	- 构建具有代表性、平衡性、可信性的《世界遗产名录》的《全球战略》
- Other measures	- 其他措施
II.C Tentative Lists	II.C《预备名录》
- Procedure and Format	- 程序和格式
- Tentative Lists as a planning and evaluation tool	-《预备名录》作为规划与评估工具
- Assistance and Capacity-Building for States Parties in the preparation of Tentative Lists	- 在缔约国编撰《预备名录》过程中提供的协助和能力建设
II.D Criteria for the assessment of Outstanding Universal Value	II.D 突出的普遍价值的评估标准
II.E Integrity and/or authenticity	II.E 完整性和 / 或真实性
- Authenticity	- 真实性
- Integrity	- 完整性
II.F Protection and management	II.F 保护和管理 •
- Legislative, regulatory and contractual measures for protection	- 立法、规范和契约性的保护措施
- Boundaries for effective protection	- 确保有效保护的边界
- Buffer zones	- 缓冲区
- Management systems	- 管理体制
- Sustainable use	- 可持续利用
III. PROCESS FOR THE INSCRIPTION OF PROPERTIES ON THE WORLD HERITAGE LIST	III. 列入《世界遗产名录》的程序
III.A Preparation of Nominations	III.A 申报准备
III.B Format and content of nominations	III.B 申报文件的格式和内容
1. Identification of the Property	1. 遗产的辨认
2. Description of the Property	2. 遗产描述
3. Justification for Inscription	3. 列入理由
4. State of conservation and factors affecting the property	4. 保护状况和影响因素
5. Protection and Management	5. 保护和管理
6. Monitoring	6. 监测
7. Documentation	7. 文件
8. Contact Information of responsible authorities	8. 负责机构的联系信息
9. Signature on behalf of the State Party	9. 缔约国代表签名
10. Number of printed copies required	10. 要求打印的附件数量（含地图附件）

(including maps annexed)

11. Paper and electronic format

12. Sending

III.C Requirements for the nomination of different types of properties

- Transboundary properties

- Serial properties

III.D Registration of nominations

III.E Evaluation of nominations by the Advisory Bodies

III.F Withdrawal of nominations

III.G Decision of the World Heritage Committee

- Inscription

- Decision not to inscribe

- Referral of nominations

- Deferral of nominations

III.H Nominations to be processed on an emergency basis

III.I Modifications to the boundaries, to the criteria used to justify inscription or to the name of a World Heritage property

- Minor modifications to the boundaries

- Significant modifications to the boundaries

- Modifications to the criteria used to justify inscription on the World Heritage List

- Modification to the name of a World Heritage property

III.J Timetable - overview

IV. PROCESS FOR MONITORING THE STATE OF CONSERVATION OF WORLD HERITAGE PROPERTIES

IV.A Reactive Monitoring

- Definition of Reactive Monitoring

- Objective of Reactive Monitoring

- Information received from States Parties and/or other sources

- Decision by the World Heritage Committee

IV.B The List of World Heritage in Danger

- Guidelines for the inscription of properties

11. 纸质和电子格式

12. 递送

III.C 各类遗产申报的要求

- 跨境遗产

- 系列遗产

III.D 申报登记

III.E. 咨询机构评估

III.F 撤销申报

III.G 世界遗产委员会的决定

- 列入名录

- 决定不予列入

- 发还待议的申

- 推迟申报

III.H 紧急受理的申报

III.I 修改世界遗产的边界、原列入标准或名称

- 边界细微调整

- 边界重大修改

-《世界遗产名录》所依据标准的修改

- 世界遗产名称的更改

III.J 时间表——总表

IV. 世界遗产保护状况的监测程序

IV.A 反应性监测

- 反应性监测的定义

- 反应性监测的目标

- 来自缔约国和 / 或其他渠道的信息

- 世界遗产委员会的决定

IV.B《濒危世界遗产名录》

- 列入《濒危世界遗产名录》的指导原则

on the List of World Heritage in Danger

- Criteria for the inscription of properties on the List of World Heritage in Danger

- 列入《濒危世界遗产名录》的标准

- Procedure for the inscription of properties on the List of World Heritage in Danger

- 列入《濒危世界遗产名录》的程序

- Regular review of the state of conservation of properties on the List of World Heritage in Danger

- 对于《濒危世界遗产名录》上遗产保护状况的定期检查

IV.C Procedure for the eventual deletion of properties from the World Heritage List

IV.C《世界遗产名录》中遗产彻底除名的程序

V. PERIODIC REPORTING ON THE IMPLEMENTATION OF THE WORLD HERITAGE CONVENTION

V. 有关《世界遗产公约》实施情况的《定期报告》

V.a Objectives

V.A 目标

V.B Procedure and Format

V.B. 程序和格式

V.C Evaluation and follow up

V.C 评估和后续工作

VI. ENCOURAGING SUPPORT FOR THE WORLD HERITAGE CONVENTION

VI. 鼓励对《世界遗产公约》的支持

VI.A Objectives

VI.A 目标

VI.B Capacity-building and research

VI.B 能力建设与研究

- The Global Training Strategy

- 全球培训战略

- National training strategies and regional co-operation

- 国家培训策略和区域性合作

- Research

- 研究

- International Assistance

- 国际援助

VI.C Awareness-raising and education

VI.C 提高认识与教育

- Awareness-raising

- 提高认识

- Education

- 教育

- International Assistance

- 国际援助

VII. THE WORLD HERITAGE FUND AND INTERNATIONAL ASSISTANCE

VII. 世界遗产基金和国际援助

VII.A The World Heritage Fund

VII.A 世界遗产基金

VII.B Mobilization of other technical and financial resources and partnerships in support of the World Heritage Convention

VII.B 调动其他技术及财务资源，展开合作，支持《世界遗产公约》

VII.C International Assistance

VII.C 国际援助

VII.D Principles and priorities for International Assistance

VII.D 国际援助的原则和优先顺序

VII.E Summary table

VIIE 总表

VII.F Procedure and format

VII.F 程序和格式

VII.G Evaluation and approval of International Assistance

VII.G 国际援助的评估和核准

VII.H Contractual Arrangements

VII.H 合同协议

VII.I Evaluation and follow-up of International Assistance

VII.I 国际援助的评估和后续跟踪

VIII. THE WORLD HERITAGE EMBLEM

VIII. 世界遗产标志

VIII.A Preamble

VIII.A 前言

VIII.B Applicability

VIII.B 适用性

VIII.C Responsibilities of States Parties

VIII.C 缔约国的责任

VIII.D Increasing proper uses of the World Heritage Emblem

VIII.D 增加对世界遗产标志的正确使用

- Production of plaques to commemorate the inscription of properties on the World Heritage List

制作遗产列入《世界遗产名录》纪念章

VIII.E Principles on the use of the World Heritage Emblem

VIII.E 世界遗产标志的使用原则

VIII.F Authorization procedure for the use of the World Heritage Emblem

VIII.F 使用世界遗产标志的授权程序

- Simple agreement of the national authorities

- 国家权威机构的初步认定

- Agreement requiring quality control of content

- 要求对内容进行质量控制的协议

- Content Approval Form

- 内容审批格式

VIII.G Right of States Parties to exert quality control

VIII.G 缔约国政府有权进行质量控制

IX. INFORMATION SOURCES

IX. 信息来源

IX.A Information archived by the Secretariat

IX.A 秘书处存档的信息

IX.B Specific Information for World Heritage Committee members and other States Parties

IX.B 世界遗产委员会成员国和其他缔约国的详细信息

IX.C Information and publications available to the public

IX.C. 向大众公开的信息和出版物

ANNEXES

附件

1. Model Instrument of Ratification/Acceptance and Accession

1. 接受 / 正式批准，登记入册的模式

2A. Tentative List submission format

2A.《预备名录》提交格式

2B. Tentative List submission format for Serial, Transnational and Transboundary Future Nominations

2B. 适用于系列、跨国或跨境遗产申报的《预备名录》提交格式

3. Guidelines on the inscription of specific types of properties on the World Heritage List

3. 特定遗产列入《世界遗产名录》指南

4. Authenticity in relation to the *World Heritage Convention*

4.《保护世界文化与自然遗产公约》相关的真实性

5. Format for the nomination of properties for inscription on the World Heritage List

5. 申报列入《世界遗产名录》的文本格式

6. Evaluation procedures of the Advisory Bodies for nominations

6. 咨询机构对申报材料的评估程序

7. Format for the Periodic Reporting on the application of the *World Heritage Convention*

7.《世界遗产公约》实施的定期报告的格式

8. International Assistance Request Form

8.《国际援助申请表》

9. Evaluation criteria of the Advisory Bodies for International Assistance requests

9. 专家咨询机构评估国际援助申请的标准

10. Statement of Outstanding Universal Value

10.《突出普遍价值声明》

11. Modifications to World Heritage properties

11. 对世界遗产的修改

12. Form for the submission of Factual Errors in the Advisory Bodies Evaluations

12. 咨询机构提交事实性错误格式

13. Format for the submission of State of Conservation Reports by the States Parties

13. 缔约国提交保护状况声明格式

14. Table of uses of the World Heritage Emblem

14. 世界遗产标识使用表

SELECT BIBLIOGRAPHY ON WORLD HERITAGE

世界遗产相关的参考书目

ACRONYMS AND ABBREVIATIONS

缩略语

DoCoMoMo International Committee for the Documentation and Conservation of Monuments and Sites of the Modern Movement

现代主义建筑保护与记录国际委员会

ICCROM International Centre for the Study of the Preservation and Restoration of Cultural Property

国际文物保护与修复研究中心

ICOMOS International Council on Monuments and Sites

国际古迹遗址理事会

IFLA International Federation of Landscape Architects

国际景观设计师联合会

IUCN International Union for Conservation of Nature and Natural Resources

世界自然保护联盟（前国际自然及自然资源保护联盟）

IUGS International Union of Geological Sciences

国际地质科学联合会

MAB Man and the Biosphere programme of

联合国教科文组织人与生物圈计划

UNESCO

NGO Non-governmental organization 非政府组织

TICCIH International Committee for the Conservation of the Industrial Heritage 国际工业遗产保护委员会

UNEP United Nations Environment Programme 联合国环境规划署

UNEP-WCMC World Conservation Monitoring Centre (UNEP) 世界保护监测中心（联合国环境规划署）

UNESCO United Nations Educational, Scientific and Cultural Organization 联合国教育、科学及文化组织

I. INTRODUCTION

Ⅰ.引言

1. *The Operational Guidelines for the Implementation of the World Heritage Convention* (hereinafter referred to as *the Operational Guidelines*) aim to facilitate the implementation of *the Convention* concerning the *protection* of the World Cultural and Natural Heritage (hereinafter referred to as *'the World Heritage Convention' or 'the Convention'*), by setting forth the procedure for:

1.《实施〈世界遗产公约〉操作指南》（以下简称《操作指南》）旨在促进《保护世界文化和自然遗产公约》（以下简称《世界遗产公约》或《公约》）的实施，并具体为开展下列工作设置相应的程序：

a) the inscription of properties on the World Heritage List and the List of World Heritage in Danger;

a）将遗产列入《世界遗产名录》和《濒危世界遗产名录》；

b) the protection and conservation of World Heritage properties;

b）世界遗产的保护和保存；

c) the granting of International Assistance under the World Heritage Fund; and

c）世界遗产基金提供的国际援助；

d) the mobilization of national and international support in favor of *the Convention.*

d）调动国家和国际力量为《公约》提供支持。

2. *The Operational Guidelines* are periodically revised to reflect the decisions of the World Heritage Committee.

2.《操作指南》将会定期修改，以体现世界遗产委员会的最新决策。

The historical development of *the Operational Guidelines* is available at the following Web address: http: //whc.unesco.org/en/guidelineshistorical

《操作指南》的发展历程可参见以下网址：*http：//whc.unesco.org/en/guidelineshistorical*

3. The key users of the *Operational Guidelines* are:

3.《操作指南》主要使用者：

a) the States Parties to the *World Heritage*

a）《世界遗产公约》的缔约国；

Convention;

b) the Intergovernmental Committee for the Protection of the Cultural and Natural Heritage of Outstanding Universal Value, hereinafter referred to as 'the World Heritage Committee' or 'the Committee';

c) the UNESCO World Heritage Centre as Secretariat to the World Heritage Committee, hereinafter referred to as 'the Secretariat'

d) the Advisory Bodies to the World Heritage Committee ;

e) site managers, stakeholders and partners in the protection of World Heritage properties.

b）保护具有突出的普遍价值的文化和自然遗产政府间委员会，以下简称“世界遗产委员会”或“委员会”；

c）联合国教科文组织世界遗产中心作为世界遗产委员会秘书处，以下简称“秘书处”；

d）世界遗产委员会的咨询机构；

e）负责保护世界遗产的遗产地管理人员、利益相关者和合作伙伴。

I.B The *World Heritage Convention*

I.B《世界遗产公约》

4. The cultural and natural heritage is among the priceless and irreplaceable assets, not only of each nation, but of humanity as a whole. The loss, through deterioration or disappearance, of any of these most prized assets constitutes an impoverishment of the heritage of all the peoples of the world. Parts of that heritage, because of their exceptional qualities, can be considered to be of 'Outstanding Universal Value' and as such worthy of special protection against the dangers which increasingly threaten them.

4. 无论对各国还是对全人类而言，文化和自然遗产都是不可估价且无法替代的财产。这些最珍贵的财富，一旦遭受破坏或消失，都是对世界各族人民遗产的一次浩劫。一些遗产具有独一无二的特性，因而认为具有“突出的普遍价值”，需加以特殊的保护，以消除日益威胁遗产安全的各种危险。

5. To ensure, as far as possible, the proper identification, protection, conservation and presentation of the world's heritage, the Member States of UNESCO adopted the *World Heritage Convention* in 1972. The *Convention* foresees the establishment of a 'World Heritage Committee' and a 'World Heritage Fund'. Both the Committee and the Fund have been in operation since 1976.

5. 为了尽可能保证对世界遗产的认定、保存、保护和展示，联合国教育、科学及文化组织成员国于 1972 年通过了《世界遗产公约》。《公约》提出建立世界遗产委员会和世界遗产基金，二者自 1976 年开始运行。

6. Since the adoption of the *Convention* in 1972, the international community has embraced the concept of 'sustainable development'. The

6. 自从 1972 年《公约》通过以来，国际社会全面接受了“可持续发展”这一概念。保存、保护自然和文化遗产就是对可持续发展的巨大

protection and conservation of the natural and cultural heritage are a significant contribution to sustainable development.

贡献。

7. The *Convention* aims at the identification, protection, conservation, presentation and transmission to future generations of cultural and natural heritage of Outstanding Universal Value.

7.《公约》旨在认定、保存、保护、展示具有突出的普遍价值的文化和自然遗产，并将其代代相传。

8. The criteria and conditions for the inscription of properties on the World Heritage List have been developed to evaluate the Outstanding Universal Value of properties and to guide States Parties in the protection and management of World Heritage Properties.

8. 已制定遗产列入《世界遗产名录》的标准和条件，以评估遗产是否具有突出的普遍价值，并指导缔约国保护和管理世界遗产。

9. When a property inscribed on the World Heritage List is threatened by serious and specific dangers, the Committee considers placing it on the List of World Heritage in Danger. When the Outstanding Universal Value of the property which justified its inscription on the World Heritage List is destroyed, the Committee considers deleting the property from the World Heritage List.

9. 当《世界遗产名录》上的某项遗产受到了严重的特殊威胁时，委员会将考虑将该遗产列入《濒危世界遗产名录》。遗产列入《世界遗产名录》的突出普遍价值受到破坏时，委员会将考虑把该遗产从《世界遗产名录》上移除。

I.C The States Parties to the *World Heritage Convention*

I.C《世界遗产公约》缔约国

10. States are encouraged to become party to the *Convention*. Model instruments for ratification/acceptance and accession are included as Annex 1. The original signed version should be sent to the Director-General of UNESCO.

10. 鼓励各国家加入《公约》，成为缔约国。附件 1 收录了批准及接受公约和正式加入公约的文书范本。签署后的文书原件应呈递联合国教育、科学及文化组织总干事。

11. The list of States Parties to the *Convention* is available at the following Web address:

http: //whc.unesco.org/en/statesparties

11.《公约》各缔约国名单可参见以下网址：

http ：//whc.unesco.org/en/statesparties

12. States Parties to the *Convention* are encouraged to ensure the participation of a wide variety of

12. 鼓励《公约》缔约国保证各利益相关者，包括遗产管理者、当地和地区政府、当地社区、

stakeholders, including site managers, local and regional governments, local communities, non-governmental organizations (NGOs) and other interested parties and partners in the identification, nomination and protection of World Heritage properties

非政府组织（NGO）、其他相关团体和合作伙伴，参与世界遗产的认定、申报和保护。

13. States Parties to the *Convention* should provide the Secretariat with the names and addresses of the governmental organization (s) primarily responsible as national focal point (s) for the implementation of the *Convention*, so that copies of all official correspondence and documents can be sent by the Secretariat to these national focal points as appropriate. A list of these addresses is available at the following Web address:

http: //whc.unesco.org/en/statespartiesfocalpoints

13.《公约》各缔约国应向秘书处提供作为国家实施《公约》协调中心的政府机构的名称和地址，以便秘书处发送各种官方信函和文件。这些机构的地址列表可参见以下网址：

http：//whc.unesco.org/en/statespartiesfocalpoints

States Parties are encouraged to publicize this information nationally and ensure that it is up to date.

鼓励《公约》各缔约国公开以上信息并保证不断更新。

14. States Parties are encouraged to bring together their cultural and natural heritage experts at regular intervals to discuss the implementation of the Convention. States Parties may wish to involve representatives of the Advisory Bodies and other experts as appropriate.

14. 鼓励缔约国定期召集文化、自然遗产专家讨论《公约》的执行情况。缔约国可酌情邀请咨询机构代表或其他专家参与讨论。

15. While fully respecting the sovereignty of the States on whose territory the cultural and natural heritage is situated, States Parties to *the Convention* recognize the collective interest of the international community to cooperate in the protection of this heritage. States Parties to the *World Heritage Convention*, have the responsibility to: (2016)

Article 6 (1) of the World Heritage Convention.

a) ensure the identification, nomination, protection, conservation, presentation, and transmission to future generations of the cultural

15. 在充分尊重文化和自然遗产所在国主权的同时，《公约》各缔约国也应该认识到，合作开展遗产保护工作符合国际社会的共同利益。《世界遗产公约》各缔约国有责任做到以下几点：

《世界遗产公约》第 6（1）

a）保证在本国境内文化和自然遗产的认定、申报、保护、保存、展示以及代代相传，并在其他国家提出请求时就以上事宜提供帮助；

and natural heritage found within their territory, and give help in these tasks to other States Parties that request it;

Article 4 and 6 (2) of the World Heritage Convention.

b) adopt general policies to give the heritage a function in the life of the community;

Article 5 of the World Heritage Convention.

c) integrate heritage protection into comprehensive planning programmes;

d) establish services for the protection, conservation and presentation of the heritage;

e) develop scientific and technical studies to identify actions that would counteract the dangers that threaten the heritage;

f) take appropriate legal, scientific, technical, administrative and financial measures to protect the heritage;

g) foster the establishment or development of national or regional centres for training in the protection, conservation and presentation of the heritage and encourage scientific research in these fields;

h) not take any deliberate measures that directly or indirectly damage their heritage or that of another State Party to the Convention;

Article 6 (3) of the World Heritage Convention.

i) submit to the World Heritage Committee an inventory of properties suitable for inscription on the World Heritage List (referred to as a Tentative List);

Article 11 (1) of the World Heritage Convention.

j) make regular contributions to the World Heritage Fund, the amount of which is determined by the General Assembly of States Parties to the *Convention*;

Article 16 (1) of the World Heritage Convention.

k) consider and encourage the establishment of national, public and private foundations or

《世界遗产公约》第4条和第6（2）条。

b）制定、通过旨在赋予文化和自然遗产合理功能，使其在社会生活中发挥一定作用的总体政策；

《世界遗产公约》第5条。

c）将遗产保护纳入整体规划；

d）建立负责遗产保存、保护和展示事务的机构；

e）开展科学和技术研究，找出威胁本国遗产的危害的并找出消除方法；

f）采取适当的法律、科学、技术、行政和财政措施来保护遗产；

g）促进建立或发展有关保存、保护和展示文化和自然遗产的国家或地区培训中心，并鼓励这些领域的科学研究；

h）不得故意采取任何可能直接或间接损害本国或其他缔约国领土内遗产的措施；

《世界遗产公约》第6（3）条

i）向世界遗产委员会递交一份关于本国领土内适于列入《世界遗产名录》的遗产清单（称为《预备名录》）；

《世界遗产公约》第11（1）条。

j）定期向世界遗产基金缴款，缴款额度由公约缔约国大会决定；

《世界遗产公约》第16（1）条。

k）考虑和鼓励设立国家、社会以及私立基金会或协会，促进保护世界遗产的募捐；

associations to facilitate donations for the protection of World Heritage;

Article 17 of the World Heritage Convention.

l) give assistance to international fund-raising campaigns organized for the World Heritage Fund;

Article 18 of the World Heritage Convention.

m) use educational and information programmes to strengthen appreciation and respect by their peoples of the cultural and natural heritage defined in Articles 1 and 2 of the *Convention*, and to keep the public informed of the dangers threatening this heritage;

Article 27 of the World Heritage Convention.

n) provide information to the World Heritage Committee on the implementation of the *World Heritage Convention* and state of conservation of properties; and

Article 29 of the World Heritage Convention. Resolution adopted by the 11th General Assembly of States Parties (1997)

16. States Parties are encouraged to attend sessions of the World Heritage Committee and its subsidiary bodies.

Rule 8.1 of the Rules of Procedure of the World Heritage Committee.

I.D The General Assembly of States Parties to the *World Heritage Convention*

17. The General Assembly of States Parties to the *World Heritage Convention* meets during the sessions of the General Conference of UNESCO. The General Assembly manages its meetings according to its *Rules of Procedure*, available at the following Web address:

http: //whc.unesco.org/en/garules

Article 8 (1), of the World Heritage Convention, Rule 49 of the Rules of Procedure of the World Heritage Committee.

《世界遗产公约》第 17 条。

l）对世界遗产基金的国际募款运作给予协助；

《世界遗产公约》第 18 条。

m）通过教育和宣传活动，努力加强本国公民对公约第 1 和 2 条中所确定的文化和自然遗产的理解和尊重，并使公众广泛了解遗产面临的威胁；

《世界遗产公约》第 27 条。

n）向世界遗产委员会递交报告，详述《世界遗产公约》的实施情况和遗产的保护状况；

《世界遗产公约》第 29 条。1997 年第十一届缔约国大会通过《决议》。

16. 鼓励本公约缔约国参加世界遗产委员会及其附属机构的各届会议。

《世界遗产委员会议事规则》第 8.1 条。

I.D《世界遗产公约》缔约国大会

17. 大会在联合国教科文组织大会常会期间召开。缔约国大会根据《议事规则》组织会议，相关内容可参见以下网址 http：//whc.unesco.org/en/garules

《世界遗产公约》第 8（1）条，《世界遗产委员会议事规则》第 49 条。

18. The General Assembly determines the uniform percentage of contributions to the World Heritage Fund applicable to all States Parties and elects members to the World Heritage Committee. Both the General Assembly and General Conference of UNESCO receive a report from the World Heritage Committee on its activities.

18. 大会确定适用于所有缔约国的统一缴费比例，并选举世界遗产委员会成员。缔约国大会和联合国教科文组织大会都将收到世界遗产委员会关于各项活动的报告。

Articles 8 (1), 16 (1) and 29 of the World Heritage Convention and Rule 49 of the Rules of Procedure of the World Heritage Committee

《世界遗产公约》第 8（1）条、第 16（1）条和第 29 条;《世界遗产委员会议事规则》第 49 条。

I.E The World Heritage Committee

I.E 世界遗产委员会

19. The World Heritage Committee is composed of 21 members and meets at least once a year (June/July). It establishes its Bureau, which meets during the sessions of the Committee as frequently as deemed necessary. The composition of the Committee and its Bureau is available at the following Web address: http: //whc.unesco.org/en/committeemembers

19. 世界遗产委员会由二十一个成员国组成，每年至少召开一次会议（六月或七月）。委员会设有主席团，通常在委员会常会期间召集开会。委员会及其主席团的组成可参见以下网址：

http：//whc.unesco.org/en/committeemembers

The World Heritage Committee can be contacted through its Secretariat, the World Heritage Centre.

可以通过世界遗产中心，即世界遗产委员会秘书处，与委员会取得联系。

20. The Committee manages its meetings according to its *Rules of Procedure*, available at the following Web address:

http: //whc.unesco.org/committeerule

20. 世界遗产委员会根据《议事规则》召开会议，可参见以下网址：

http：//whc.unesco.org/committeerules

21. The term of office of Committee members is six years but, in order to ensure equitable representation and rotation, States Parties are invited by the General Assembly to consider voluntarily reducing their term of office from six to four years and are discouraged from seeking consecutive terms of office.

21. 世界遗产委员会成员任期六年。然而，为了保证世界遗产委员会公正的代表性和轮值制，大会建议缔约国自愿考虑将任期从六年缩短到四年，不鼓励连任。

Article 9 (1) of the World Heritage Convention.

《世界遗产公约》第 9（1）条

Article 8 (2) of the World Heritage Convention and the Resolutions of the 7th (1989), 12th (1999) and 13th (2001) General Assembly of States Parties to the World Heritage Convention

《世界遗产公约》第 8（2）条和《世界遗产公约》缔约国第七届（1989 年）、第十二届（1999 年）及第十三届（2001 年）大会决议。

22. A certain number of seats may be reserved for States Parties who do not have a property on the World Heritage List, upon decision of the Committee at the session that precedes the General Assembly.

Rule 14.1 of the Rules of Procedure of the General Assembly of States Parties.

22. 根据委员会在大会前一届会议中达成的决议，为尚无遗产列入《世界遗产名录》的缔约国保留一定数量的席位。

《缔约国大会议事规则》第 14.1 条

23. Committee decisions are based on objective and scientific considerations, and any appraisal made on its behalf must be thoroughly and responsibly carried out. The Committee recognizes that such decisions depend upon:

a) carefully prepared documentation;

b) thorough and consistent procedures;

c) evaluation by qualified experts; and

d) if necessary, the use of expert referees.

23. 委员会的决定基于客观和科学的考虑，为此进行的任何评估工作都应该得到彻底和负责的贯彻。委员会认识到这类决定取决于以下几个方面：

a）认真编撰的文献资料；

b）全面、统一的程序；

c）资深专家的评估；

d）必要时，启用专家仲裁。

24. The main functions of the Committee are, in co-operation with States Parties, to:

a) identify, on the basis of Tentative Lists and nominations submitted by States Parties, cultural and natural properties of Outstanding Universal Value which are to be protected under the *Convention* and to inscribe those properties on the World Heritage List;

Article 11 (2) of the World Heritage Convention.

b) examine the state of conservation of properties inscribed on the World Heritage List through processes of Reactive Monitoring (see Chapter IV) and Periodic Reporting (see Chapter V);

Articles 11 (7) and 29 of the World Heritage Convention.

24. 委员会的主要职能是与缔约国合作开展下述工作：

a）认定根据缔约国递交的《预备名录》和申报文件，按照《公约》实施保护的具有突出的普遍价值的文化和自然遗产，并把这些遗产列入《世界遗产名录》；

《世界遗产公约》第 11（2）款

b）通过反应性监测（参见第Ⅳ章）和定期报告（参见第Ⅴ章）审查已经列入《世界遗产名录》的遗产的保护状况。

《世界遗产公约》第 11（7）条和第 29 条）。

c) decide which properties inscribed on the World Heritage List are to be inscribed on, or removed from the List of World Heritage in Danger;

Article 11 (4) and 11 (5) of the World Heritage Convention.

d) decide whether a property should be deleted from the World Heritage List (see Chapter IV);

e) define the procedure by which requests for International Assistance are to be considered and carry out studies and consultations as necessary before coming to a decision (see Chapter VII);

Article 21 (1) and 21 (3) of the World Heritage Convention.

f) determine how the resources of the World Heritage Fund can be used most advantageously to assist States Parties in the protection of their properties of Outstanding Universal Value;

Article 13 (6) of the *World Heritage Convention*

g) seek ways to increase the World Heritage Fund;

h) submit a report on its activities every two years to the General Assembly of States Parties and to the UNESCO General Conference;

Article 29 (3) of the World Heritage Convention and Rule 49 of the Rules of procedure of the World Heritage Committee.

i) review and evaluate periodically the implementation of the *Convention*;

j) revise and adopt the *Operational Guidelines*.

25. In order to facilitate the implementation of the *Convention*, the Committee develops Strategic Objectives; they are periodically reviewed and revised to define the goals and objectives of the Committee to ensure that new threats placed on World Heritage are addressed

c）决定《世界遗产名录》中的哪些遗产应该列入《濒危世界遗产目录》或从中移除；

《世界遗产公约》第11（4）条和第11（5）条。

d）决定是否应将一项遗产从《世界遗产名录》上移除（参见第Ⅳ章）；

e）制定关于申请国际援助的审议程序，在做出决定之前，进行必要的研究和磋商（参见第Ⅶ章）；

《世界遗产公约》第21（1）条和第21（3）条。

f）决定如何发挥世界遗产基金资源的最大优势，帮助缔约国保护遗产的突出的普遍价值；

《世界遗产公约》第13（6）条。

g）设法增加世界遗产基金；

h）每两年向缔约国大会和联合国教科文组织大会递交一份活动报告；

《世界遗产公约》第29（3）条和《世界遗产委员会议事规则》第49条。

i）定期审查并评估《公约》的实施情况。

j）修改并通过《操作指南》。

25. 为了促进《公约》的实施，委员会制定了战略目标，并对这些目标定期审查和修改，确保有效应对世界遗产面临的新威胁。

effectively.

The first 'Strategic Orientations' adopted by the Committee in 1992 are contained in Annex II of document WHC-92/CONF, 002/12

1992 年委员会通过的第一份《战略目标》刊登在文件 WHC–92/CONF，002/12 附件 II 中。

26. The current Strategic Objectives (also referred to as 'the 5 Cs') are the following:

26. 目前的战略目标（简称为"5C"）是：

In 2002 the World Heritage Committee revised its Strategic Objectives. The Budapest Declaration on World Heritage (2002) is available at the following Web address: http: //whc.unesco.org/en/budapestdeclaration

2002 年世界遗产委员会修订的战略目标。《布达佩斯世界遗产宣言》（2002 年）可参见以下网址：

http：//whc.unesco.org/en/budapestdeclaration

1) Strengthen the Credibility of the World Heritage List;

1）提升《世界遗产名录》的可信度；

2) Ensure the effective Conservation of World Heritage Properties;

2）确保对世界遗产的有效保护；

3) Promote the development of effective Capacity-building in States Parties;

3）促进各缔约国有效的能力建设；

4) Increase public awareness, involvement and support for World Heritage through Communication.

4）通过交流增强大众对世界遗产的认识、参与和支持；

5) Enhance the role of Communities in the implementation of the *World Heritage Convention*.

5）加强社区在实施《世界遗产公约》中的作用。

Decision 31 COM 13B

第 31 COM13B 决定

I.F *The Secretariat to the World Heritage Committee (World Heritage Centre)*

I.F 世界遗产委员会秘书处（世界遗产中心）

UNESCO World Heritage Centre

联合国教科文组织世界遗产中心

7, place de Fontenoy
75352 Paris 07 SP France
Tel: +33 (0) 1 4568 1571
Fax: +33 (0) 1 4568 5570
E-mail: wh-info@unesco.org
www: http: //whc.unesco.org/

7，place de Fontenoy
75352 Paris 07 SP France
Tel：+33（0）1 4568 1571
Fax：+33（0）1 4568 5570
E–mail：wh–info@unesco.org
www：http：//whc.unesco.org

27. The World Heritage Committee is assisted by a Secretariat appointed by the Director-

27. 由联合国教科文组织总干事指定的秘书处协助世界遗产委员会工作。1992 年创建了世

General of UNESCO. The function of the Secretariat is currently assumed by the World Heritage Centre, established in 1992 specifically for this purpose. The Director-General designated the Director of the World Heritage Centre as Secretary to the Committee. The Secretariat assists and collaborates with the States Parties and the Advisory Bodies. The Secretariat works in close co-operation with other sectors and field offices of UNESCO.

界遗产中心，担负秘书处的职能，联合国教科文组织总干事指派世界遗产中心主任为委员会的秘书。秘书处负责协助和协调缔约国和咨询机构的工作。秘书处还与联合国教科文组织的其他部门和外地办事处密切合作。

Article 14.2 of the World Heritage Convention.

Rule 43 of Rules of Procedure of the World Heritage Committee.

Circular Letter 16 of 21 October 2003 http: // whc.unesco.org/circs/circ03-16e.pdf

《世界遗产公约》第 14 条

《世界遗产委员会议事规则》第 43 条。

2003 年 10 月 21 日《通函 16 号》，可参见以下网址：

http ：//whc.unesco.org/circs/circ03-16e.pdf

28. The Secretariat's main tasks are:

28. 秘书处主要任务包括：

a) the organization of the meetings of the General Assembly and the Committee;

a）组织缔约国大会和世界遗产委员会的会议；

Article 14.2 of the World Heritage Convention.

《世界遗产公约》第 14.2 条。

b) the implementation of decisions of the World Heritage Committee and resolutions of the General Assembly and reporting to them on their execution;

b）执行世界遗产委员会的各项决定和联合国教科文组织大会的决议，并向委员会和大会汇报执行情况；

Article 14.2 of the *World Heritage Convention* and the *Budapest Declaration on World Heritage* (2002)

《世界遗产公约》第 14 条及布达佩斯世界遗产宣言（2002）

c) the receipt, registration, checking the completeness, archiving and transmission to the relevant Advisory Bodies of nominations to the World Heritage List;

c）接收、登记世界遗产申报文件，检查其完整性，存档并呈递到相关的咨询机构；

d) the co-ordination of studies and activities as part of the Global Strategy for a Representative, Balanced and Credible World Heritage List;

d）协调各项研究和活动，作为加强《世界遗产名录》代表性、平衡性和可信性全球战略的一部分；

e) the organization of Periodic Reporting and co-ordination of Reactive Monitoring;

e）组织定期报告和协调反应性监测；

f) co-ordination and conduct of Reactive

f）协调和执行反应性监测，包括反应性监

Monitoring, including Reactive Monitoring missions[①], as well coordination of and participation in Advisory missions[②], as appropriate;

测任务[①]，必要时，协调咨询机构参与[②]

g) the co-ordination of International Assistance;

g）协调国际援助；

h) the mobilisation of extra-budgetary resources for the conservation and management of World Heritage properties;

h）调动预算外资金保护和管理世界遗产；

i) the assistance to States Parties in the implementation of the Committee's programmes and projects; and

i）协助各缔约国实施委员会的方案和项目；

j) the promotion of World Heritage and the *Convention* through the dissemination of information to States Parties, the Advisory Bodies and the general public.

j）通过向缔约国、咨询机构和公众发布信息，促进世界遗产的保护和增强对《公约》的认识。

29. These activities follow the decisions and

29. 开展这些活动要服从于委员会的各项决

---

① Reactive Monitoring missions are part of the statutory reporting by the Secretariat and the Advisory Bodies to the World Heritage Committee on the state of conservation of specific properties that are under threat (see Paragraph 169). They are requested by the World Heritage Committee to ascertain, in consultation with the State Party concerned, the condition of the property, the dangers to the property and the feasibility of adequately restoring the property or to assess progress made in implementing such corrective measures, and include a reporting back to the Committee on the findings of the mission (see Paragraph 176.e). The terms of reference of Reactive Monitoring missions are proposed by the World Heritage Centre, in line with the decision adopted by the World Heritage Committee, and consolidated in consultation with the State Party and the relevant Advisory Body(ies). The costs of the Reactive Monitoring missions are borne by the World Heritage Fund.

反应性监测任务是秘书处和咨询机构向委员会提交的处于威胁下的特定遗产保护状况的法定报告（见第169段）。世界遗产委员会要求他们与相关缔约国协商，查明遗产状况、遗产面临的威胁、充分恢复的可能性及评估纠正措施进度，包括向委员会反馈任务的结果（第176.e）。按照世界遗产中心的建议及委员会通过的决定，并综合缔约国和相关咨询机构意见，确定反应性监测任务的范围。世界遗产基金承担反应性监测任务的费用。

② Advisory missions are not part of the strict statutory and mandatory processes, as they are voluntarily initiated by States Parties and depend on the considerations and judgement of the States Parties requesting them. Advisory missions are to be understood as missions providing expert advice to a State Party on specific matters. They can concern provision of “upstream” support and advice on identification of sites, tentative lists or nomination of sites for inscription on the World Heritage List or alternatively, they can relate to the state of conservation of properties and provide advice in evaluating possible impact of a major development project on the Outstanding Universal Value of the property, advice in the preparation/revision of a management plan, or in the progress achieved in the implementation of specific mitigation measures, etc. The terms of reference of Advisory missions are proposed by the State Party itself, and consolidated in consultation with the World Heritage Centre and the relevant Advisory Bod(ies) or other organization. The entire costs of Advisory missions are borne by the State Party inviting the mission, except where the State Party is eligible for relevant International Assistance or funding from the new budget line for Advisory missions approved by Decision 38 COM 12.

咨询任务不是严格的法定性和强制性进程的一部分，因为他们缔约国是自愿发起的，他们的思考和判断，取决于缔约国要求。咨询任务可以理解为就特定事务提供专家意见。他们可在识别遗址，预备名录或遗产申报录入遗产目录或选择等问题上提供“上游”支持和建议，他们可以在遗产状况声明，评估重要开发项目对遗产突出普遍价值的影响，或实施具体缓解措施取得的成就等相关方面提建议。咨询任务的范围由缔约国提议，并综合世界遗产中心和相关咨询机构及其他组织的意见。由发出任务邀请的缔约国承担咨询任务的费用。除非缔约国获得 38 COM 12/38号决定批准的有关国际援助资金或新的项目预算。

Strategic Objectives of the Committee and the resolutions of the General Assembly of the States Parties and are conducted in close co-operation with the Advisory Bodies.

定和战略目标以及缔约国大会的各项决议，并与咨询机构密切合作。

I.G Advisory Bodies to the World Heritage Committee

I.G 世界遗产委员会咨询机构

30. The Advisory Bodies to the World Heritage Committee are ICCROM (the International Centre for the Study of the Preservation and Restoration of Cultural Property), ICOMOS (the International Council on Monuments and Sites), and IUCN - the International Union for Conservation of Nature.

Article 8.3 of the *World Heritage Convention*

30. 世界遗产委员会的咨询机构包括：ICCROM（国际文物保护和修复研究中心）、ICOMOS（国际古迹遗址理事会）以及 IUCN（世界自然保护联盟）

《世界遗产公约》第 8.3 条

31. The roles of the Advisory Bodies are to:

a) advise on the implementation of the *World Heritage Convention* in the field of their expertise;

Article 13.7 of the *World Heritage Convention*.

Decision 39 COM 11

b) assist the Secretariat, in the preparation of the Committee's documentation, the agenda of its meetings and the implementation of the Committee's decisions;

c) assist with the development and implementation of the Global Strategy for a Representative, Balanced and Credible World Heritage List, the Global Training Strategy, Periodic Reporting, and the strengthening of the effective use of the World Heritage Fund;

d) monitor the state of conservation of World Heritage properties (including through Reactive Monitoring missions at the request of the Committee and Advisory missions at the invitation of the States Parties) and review requests for International Assistance;

Article 14.2 of the World Heritage Convention.

e) in the case of ICOMOS and IUCN evaluate properties nominated for inscription on the World

31. 咨询机构的角色：

a）以本领域的专业知识指导《世界遗产公约》的实施；

《世界遗产公约》第 13.7 条。

第 39 COM11 决定

b）协助秘书处准备委员会需要的文献资料，安排会议议程以及协助委员会实施各项决定；

c）协助制定和实施加强《世界遗产名录》代表性、平衡性和可信性的全球战略、全球培训战略、定期报告，加强世界遗产基金的有效使用；

d）监督世界遗产的保护状况，（包括通过委员会要求的反应性监测任务和缔约国邀请的咨询任务）审核国际援助的申请；

《世界遗产公约》第 14.2 条。

e）由国际古迹遗址理事会和世界自然联盟评估申请列入《世界遗产名录》的遗产，在与

Heritage List, in consultation and dialogue with nominating States Parties, and present evaluation reports to the Committee; and

f) attend meetings of the World Heritage Committee and the Bureau in an advisory capacity.

Article 8.3 of the *World Heritage Convention*.

申报的缔约国协商和对话后，向委员会呈递评估报告；

f）以咨询者的身份列席世界遗产委员会及其主席团会议。

《世界遗产公约》第 8.3 条

ICCROM

国际文物保护和修复研究中心

32. ICCROM (the International Centre for the Study of the Preservation and Restoration of Cultural Property) is an international intergovernmental organization with headquarters in Rome, Italy. Established by UNESCO in 1956, ICCROM's statutory functions are to carry out research, documentation, technical assistance, training and public awareness programmes to strengthen conservation of immovable and moveable cultural heritage.

32.ICCROM，即国际文物保护和修复研究中心，是一个各国政府间组织，总部设在意大利的罗马，由联合国教科文组织于 1956 年创建，根据规定，该中心的作用是开展研究、记录，提供技术援助、培训和推行增强公众意识的项目，加强对可移动和不可移动文化遗产的保护。

ICCROM
Via di S. Michele, 13I-00153 Rome, Italy

Tel : +39 06 585531 Fax: +39 06 5855 3349
Email: iccrom@iccrom.org
http: //www.iccrom.org/

国际文物保护和修复研究中心地址：
意大利罗马（Via di S.Michele，13　I–00153 Rome，Italy）
电话：+39 06 585531　传真：+39 06 5855 3349
电子邮箱 iccrom@iccrom.org
网址 http ：//www.iccrom.org/

33. The specific role of ICCROM in relation to the *Convention* includes: being the priority partner in training for cultural heritage, monitoring the state of conservation of World Heritage cultural properties, reviewing requests for International Assistance submitted by States Parties, and providing input and support for capacity-building activities.

33. 国际文物保护和修复研究中心在《公约》中相关的特殊职责包括：文化遗产培训领域的重要合作伙伴、监督世界文化遗产保护状况、审查由缔约国提交的国际援助申请，以及为能力建设活动提供支持。

ICOMOS

国际古迹遗址理事会

34. ICOMOS (the International Council on Monuments and Sites) is a non-governmental organization with headquarters in Paris, France. Founded in 1965, its role is to promote the

34. ICOMOS，即国际古迹遗址理事会，是一个非政府组织，总部在法国巴黎，创建于 1965 年。理事会的作用在于推广建筑和考古遗产保护理论、方法和科学技术的应用。理事会

application of theory, methodology and scientific techniques to the conservation of the architectural and archaeological heritage. Its work is based on the principles of the 1964 *International Charter on the Conservation and Restoration of Monuments and Sites (the Venice Charter).*

的工作以 1964 年《国际古迹遗址保护和修复宪章》（又称《威尼斯宪章》）的原则为基准。

ICOMOS

国际古迹遗址理事会

49-51, rue de la Fédération 75015 Paris, France

Tel : +33 (0) 1 45 67 67 70 Fax : +33 (0) 1 45 66 06 22

E-mail: secretariat@icomos.org

http: //www.icomos.org/

法国巴黎（49–51，rue de la Fédération 75015 Paris，France）

电话：+33（0）1 45 67 67 70

传真：+33（0）1 45 66 06 22

电子邮箱：secretariat@icomos.org

网址 http：//www.icomos.org

35. The specific role of ICOMOS in relation to the *Convention* includes: evaluation of properties nominated for inscription on the World Heritage List, monitoring the state of conservation of World Heritage cultural properties, reviewing requests for International Assistance submitted by States Parties, and providing input and support for capacity-building activities.

35. 国际古迹遗址理事会在《公约》中相关的特殊职责包括：评估申报世界遗产的项目，监督世界文化遗产保护状况，审查由缔约国提交的国际援助申请，以及为能力建设活动献策和提供支持。

IUCN

36. IUCN-The International Union for Conservation of Nature was founded in 1948 and brings together national governments, NGOs, and scientists in a worldwide partnership. Its mission is to influence, encourage and assist societies throughout the world to conserve the integrity and diversity of nature and to ensure that any use of natural resources is equitable and ecologically sustainable. IUCN has its headquarters in Gland, Switzerland.

世界自然保护联盟

36.IUCN，即世界自然保护联盟，创建于 1948 年，为各国政府、非政府组织和科学工作者在世界范围的合作提供了平台。其使命在于影响、鼓励和协助世界各团体保护自然的完整性和多样化，并确保对自然资源的任何使用都是公平的、符合生态的并且可持续发展的。世界自然保护联盟总部设在瑞士格兰德。

IUCN - The International Union for Conservation of Nature

rue Mauverney 28

CH-1196 Gland, Switzerland

IUCN——世界自然保护联盟

瑞士格兰德（rue Mauverney 28　CH–1196 Gland，Switzerland）

Tel: + 41 22 999 0001
Fax: +41 22 999 0010
E-Mail: mail@hq.iucn.org
http: //www.iucn.org

电话：+ 41 22 999 0001
传真：+41 22 999 0010
电子邮箱：mail@hq.iucn.org
网址：http：//www.iucn.org

37. The specific role of IUCN in relation to the *Convention* includes: evaluation of properties nominated for inscription on the World Heritage List, monitoring the state of conservation of World Heritage natural properties, reviewing requests for International Assistance submitted by States Parties, and providing input and support for capacity-building activities.

37. 世界自然保护联盟在《公约》中相关的特殊职责包括：评估申报世界遗产的项目、监督世界自然遗产保护状况、审查由缔约国提交的国际援助申请，以及为能力建设活动献策并提供支持。

I.H Other organizations

I.H 其他组织

38. The Committee may call on other international and non-governmental organizations with appropriate competence and expertise to assist in the implementation of the programmes and projects, including for Reactive Monitoring missions.

38. 委员会可能号召其他具有一定能力和专业技术的国际组织和非政府组织协助各方案和项目的实施，包括反应性监测任务。

I.I Partners in the protection of World Heritage

I.I 保护世界遗产的合作伙伴

39. A partnership approach to nomination, management and monitoring provides a significant contribution to the protection of World Heritage properties and the implementation of the *Convention.*

39. 在申报、管理和监测工作中，采用合作伙伴方式，有力地促进了世界遗产的保护和《公约》的实施。

40. Partners in the protection and conservation of World Heritage can be those individuals and other stakeholders, especially local communities, governmental, non-governmental and private organizations and owners who have an interest and involvement in the conservation and management of a World Heritage property.

The Declaration on the Rights of Indigenous Peoples (2007)

Decision 39 COM 11

40. 保护和保存世界遗产的合作伙伴包括：个人和其他利益相关者，尤其是对世界遗产的保护和管理感兴趣并参与其中的当地社区、政府组织、非政府组织和私人组织以及产权人。

土著人权利声明（2007）

第 39 COM 11 决定

I.J Other Conventions, Recommendations and Programmes

41. The World Heritage Committee recognizes the benefits of closer co-ordination of its work with other UNESCO programmes and their relevant Conventions. For a list of relevant global conservation instruments, Conventions and programmes see paragraph 44.

42. The World Heritage Committee with the support of the Secretariat will ensure appropriate co-ordination and information-sharing between the *World Heritage Convention* and other Conventions, programmes and international organizations related to the conservation of cultural and natural heritage.

43. The Committee may invite representatives of the intergovernmental bodies under related Conventions to attend its meetings as observers. It may appoint a representative to observe meetings of the other intergovernmental bodies upon receipt of an invitation.

44. Selected global Conventions and programmes relating to the protection of cultural and natural heritage.

第 39COM11 决定

UNESCO Conventions and Programmes

Convention for the Protection of Cultural Property in the Event of Armed Conflict (1954)

Protocol I (1954)

Protocol II (1999)

http: //www.unesco.org/culture/laws/hague/html_eng/page1.shtml

Convention on the Means of Prohibiting and Preventing the Illicit Import, Export and Transfer of

I.J 其他公约、建议和方案

41. 世界遗产委员会认识到，密切协调好与教科文组织其他计划和相关公约的关系受益匪浅。相关的全球保护组织、公约和项目名录见 44 条。

42. 在秘书处的支持下，世界遗产委员会将保证《世界遗产公约》和其他公约、项目以及和保护文化和自然遗产有关的国际组织之间适当协调、信息共享工作。

43. 委员会可能邀请相关公约下政府间组织的代表作为观察员，参加委员会的会议。如受到其他政府间组织的邀请，委员会可能派遣代表作为观察员列席其会议。

44. 与保护文化和自然遗产相关的部分全球公约和方案。

第 39COM11 决定

联合国教科文组织公约和方案

《关于在武装冲突的情况下保护文化遗产的公约》（1954 年）

第一议定书（1954 年）

第二议定书（1999 年）

http：//www.unesco.org/culture/laws/hague/html_eng/page1.shtml

《关于采取措施禁止并防止文化遗产非法进出口和所有权非法转让公约》（1970 年）

Ownership of Cultural Property (1970)

http: //www.unesco.org/culture/laws/1970/html_eng/page1.shtml

http：//www.unesco.org/culture/laws/1970/html_eng/page1.shtml

Convention concerning the Protection of the World Cultural and Natural Heritage (1972)

http: //www.unesco.org/whc/world_he.htm

《保护世界文化和自然遗产公约》（1972 年）

http：//www.unesco.org/whc/world_he.htm

Convention on the Protection of the Underwater Cultural Heritage (2001)

http: //www.unesco.org/culture/laws/underwater/html_eng/convention.shtml

《保护水下文化遗产公约》（2001 年）

http：//www.unesco.org/culture/laws/underwater/html_eng/convention.shtml

Convention for the Safeguarding of the Intangible Cultural Heritage (2003)

http: //unesdoc.unesco.org/images/0013/001325/132540e.pdf

《保护非物质文化遗产公约》（2003 年）

http：//unesdoc.unesco.org/images/0013/001325/132540e.pdf

Man and the Biosphere (MAB) Programme

http: //www.unesco.org/mab/

"人类和生物圈"计划（MAB）

http：//www.unesco.org/mab

Other Conventions

其他公约

Convention on Wetlands of International Importance especially as Waterfowl Habitat (Ramsar) (1971)

http: //www.ramsar.org/key_conv_e.htm

《关于特别是作为水禽栖息地的国际重要湿地公约（拉姆萨尔公约）》（1971 年）

http：//www.ramsar.org/key_conv_e.htm

Convention on International Trade in Endangered Species of Wild Fauna and Flora (CITES) (1973)

http: //www.cites.org/eng/disc/text.shtml

《濒危野生动植物物种国际贸易公约》（CITES）（1973 年）

http：//www.cites.org/eng/disc/text.shtml

Convention on the Conservation of Migratory Species of Wild Animals (CMS) (1979)

http: //www.unep-wcmc.org/cms/cms_conv.htm

《野生迁徙类动物物种保护公约》（CMS）（1979 年）

http：//www.unep-wcmc.org/cms/cms_conv.htm

United Nations Convention on the Law of the Sea (UNCLOS) (1982)

《联合国海洋法公约》（UNCLOS）（1982 年）

http: //www.un.org/Depts/los/convention_agreements/texts/unclos/closindx.htm

http：//www.un.org/Depts/los/convention_agreements/texts/unclos/closindx.htm

Convention on Biological Diversity (1992)

http: //www.biodiv.org/convention/articles.asp

《生物多样性公约（1992 年）

http：//www.biodiv.org/convention/articles.asp

UNIDROIT Convention on Stolen or Illegally Exported Cultural Objects (Rome, 1995)

http: //www.unidroit.org/english/conventions/culturalproperty/c-cult.htm

《国际统一私法协会关于被盗或非法出口文物的公约》（罗马，1995）

http：//www.unidroit.org/english/conventions/culturalproperty/c-cult.htm

United Nations Framework Convention on Climate Change (New York, 1992)

http: //unfccc.int/essential_background/convention/background/items/1350.php

《联合国气候变化框架公约》（纽约，1992 年）

http：//unfccc.int/essential_background/convention/background/items/1350.php

II. THE WORLD HERITAGE LIST

II.《世界遗产名录》

II.A Definition of World Heritage

II.A 世界遗产定义

Cultural and Natural Heritage

45. Cultural and natural heritage are defined in Articles 1 and 2 of the *World Heritage Convention.*

Article 1

For the purposes of this Convention, the following shall be considered as 'cultural heritage';

- monuments: architectural works, works of monumental sculpture and painting, elements or structures of an archaeological nature, inscriptions, cave dwellings and combinations of features, which are of Outstanding Universal Value from the point of view of history, art or science;

- groups of buildings: groups of separate or connected buildings which, because of their architecture, their homogeneity or their place in the landscape, are of Outstanding Universal Value from the point of view of history, art or science;

- sites: works of man or the combined works of nature and of man, and areas including archaeological sites which are of Outstanding Universal Value

文化和自然遗产

45. 文化和自然遗产的定义见《世界遗产公约》第 1 条和第 2 条。

第 1 条

在本公约中，以下各项为“文化遗产”：

——纪念物：建筑和构筑物，从历史、艺术或科学角度看具有突出的普遍价值的建筑、纪念性雕塑和绘画、具有考古性质的构筑物或元素、铭文、洞窟以及综合体；

——建筑群：从历史、艺术或科学角度看在建筑整体性、分布和谐或与环境景色结合方面具有突出的普遍价值的独立的或连接的建筑群；

——遗址：从历史、审美、人种学或人类学角度看具有突出的普遍价值的人类作品或自然与人的共同作品以及考古遗址等。

from the historical, aesthetic, ethnological or anthropological points of view.

Article 2

For the purposes of this Convention, the following shall be considered as "natural heritage":

- natural features consisting of physical and biological formations or groups of such formations, which are of Outstanding Universal Value from the aesthetic or scientific point of view;

-geological and physiographical formations and precisely delineated areas which constitute the habitat of threatened species of animals and plants of Outstanding Universal Value from the point of view of science or conservation;

- natural sites or precisely delineated natural areas of Outstanding Universal Value from the point of view of science, conservation or natural beauty.

第 2 条

在本公约中，以下各项为“自然遗产”：

——从审美或科学角度看具有突出的普遍价值的由物理和生物结构或这类结构群组成的自然面貌；

——从科学或保护角度看具有突出的普遍价值的地质和自然地理结构以及明确划为受威胁的动物和植物栖息地；

——从科学、保护或自然美角度看具有突出的普遍价值的天然名胜或明确边界描述的自然区域。

Mixed Cultural and Natural Heritage

文化和自然混合遗产

46. Properties shall be considered as 'mixed cultural and natural heritage' if they satisfy a part or the whole of the definitions of both cultural and natural heritage laid out in Articles 1 and 2 of the *Convention.*

46. 只有同时部分满足或完全满足《公约》第 1 条和第 2 条关于文化和自然遗产定义的遗产才能认为是“文化和自然混合遗产”。

Cultural landscapes

文化景观

47. Cultural landscapes are cultural properties and represent the 'combined works of nature and of man' designated in Article 1 of the *Convention.* They are illustrative of the evolution of human society and settlement over time, under the influence of the physical constraints and/or opportunities presented by their natural environment and of successive social, economic and cultural forces, both external and internal.

47.《公约》第 1 条指出文化景观属于文化遗产，代表着“自然与人的共同作品”。它们反映了因物质条件的限制或自然环境带来的机遇，在一系列社会、经济和文化因素的内外作用下，人类社会和定居地的历史沿革。

Annex 3

见附件 3

Movable Heritage

可移动遗产

48. Nominations of immovable heritage which are likely to become movable will not be considered.

48. 对于可能发生迁移的不可移动遗产的申报将不作考虑。

Outstanding Universal Value

突出的普遍价值

49. Outstanding Universal Value means cultural and/or natural significance which is so exceptional as to transcend national boundaries and to be of common importance for present and future generations of all humanity. As such, the permanent protection of this heritage is of the highest importance to the international community as a whole. The Committee defines the criteria for the inscription of properties on the World Heritage List.

49. 突出的普遍价值指罕见的、超越了国家界限的、对全人类的现在和未来均具有普遍的重要意义的文化和自然价值。因此，该项遗产的永久性保护对整个国际社会都具有至高的重要性。世界遗产委员会规定了遗产列入《世界遗产名录》的标准。

50. States Parties are invited to submit nominations of properties of cultural and/or natural value considered to be of 'Outstanding Universal Value' for inscription on the World Heritage List.

50. 邀请缔约国申报认为具有"突出的普遍价值"的文化和自然遗产，以列入《世界遗产名录》。

51. At the time of inscription of a property on the World Heritage List, the Committee adopts a Statement of Outstanding Universal Value (see paragraph 154) which will be the key reference for the future effective protection and management of the property.

51. 遗产列入《世界遗产名录》时，世界遗产委员会会通过《突出的普遍价值声明》（见第154条），该声明将成为日后遗产有效保护与管理的重要参考文献。

52. The *Convention* is not intended to ensure the protection of all properties of great interest, importance or value, but only for a select list of the most outstanding of these from an international viewpoint. It is not to be assumed that a property of national and/or regional importance will automatically be inscribed on the World Heritage List.

52. 该《公约》不是旨在保护所有具有重大意义或价值的遗产，而只是保护那些从国际观点看具有最突出价值的遗产。不应该认为某项具有国家或区域重要性的遗产会自动列入《世界遗产名录》。

53. Nominations presented to the Committee

53. 呈递给委员会的申报文件中，应该表明

shall demonstrate the full commitment of the State Party to preserve the heritage concerned, within its means. Such commitment shall take the form of appropriate policy, legal, scientific, technical, administrative and financial measures adopted and proposed to protect the property and its Outstanding Universal Value.

该缔约国在其力所能及的范围内将全力保存该项遗产。这种承诺应该体现在采纳和提出合适的政策、法律、科学、技术、管理和财政措施，保护该项遗产以及遗产的突出的普遍价值。

II.B A Representative, Balanced and Credible World Heritage List

II.B 具有代表性、均衡性和可信性的《世界遗产名录》

54. The Committee seeks to establish a representative, balanced and credible World Heritage List in conformity with the four Strategic Objectives adopted by the Committee at its 26th session (Budapest, 2002).

Budapest Declaration on World Heritage (2002) at http: //whc.unesco.org/en/budapestdeclaration

54. 委员会根据第 26 届会议确定的四个战略目标，致力于构建一个具有代表性、均衡性和可信性的《世界遗产名录》。

（布达佩斯，2002）

《布达佩斯世界遗产宣言》见：http：//whc.unesco.org/en/budapestdeclaration

The Global Strategy for a Representative, Balanced and Credible World Heritage List

构建具有代表性、均衡性、可信性《世界遗产名录》的《全球战略》

55. The Global Strategy for a Representative, Balanced and Credible World Heritage List is designed to identify and fill the major gaps in the World Heritage List. It does this by encouraging more countries to become States Parties to the *Convention* and to develop Tentative Lists as defined in paragraph 62 and nominations of properties for inscription on the World Heritage List (see http: //whc.unesco.org/en/globalstrategy)

The report of the Expert Meeting on the Global Strategy and thematic studies for a representative World Heritage List (20-22 June 1994) was adopted by the World Heritage Committee at its 18th session (Phuket, 1994).

The Global Strategy was initially developed with reference to cultural heritage. At the request of the World Heritage Committee, the Global Strategy was subsequently expanded to also include

55. 构建具有代表性、平衡性、可信性《世界遗产名录》的《全球战略》旨在确定并填补《世界遗产名录》的主要空白。该战略鼓励更多的国家加入按《保护世界文化与自然遗产公约》第 62 条的定义编撰《预备名录》、准备《世界遗产名录》的申报文件（详见 http：//whc.unesco.org/en/globalstrategy）

关于全球战略的专家会议报告及具有代表性的世界遗产名录的主题研究报告在世界遗产委员会第 18 届大会上通过（1994 年 6 月 20–22 日）。（福克，1994）

全球战略起初是为保护文化遗产提出的。应世界遗产委员会的要求，《全球战略》随后有所扩展，包括自然遗产和文化自然混合遗产。

reference to natural heritage and combined cultural and natural heritage.

56. States Parties and the Advisory Bodies are encouraged to participate in the implementation of the Global Strategy in co-operation with the Secretariat and other partners. Regional and thematic Global Strategy meetings and comparative and thematic studies are organized for this purpose. The results of these meetings and studies are available to assist States Parties in preparing Tentative Lists and nominations. The reports of the expert meetings and studies presented to the World Heritage Committee are available at the following Web address: http: //whc.unesco.org/en/globalstrategy

56. 鼓励各缔约国和咨询团体同秘书处及其他合作方合作，参与实施《全球战略》。为此，组织召开了区域及全球战略主题会议，并开展对比研究及主题研究。会议和研究成果将有助于缔约国编撰《预备名录》和申报材料。查阅提交给世界遗产委员会的专家会议报告和研究报告，可访问网站： http ：//whc.unesco.org/en/globalstrategy，

57. All efforts should be made to maintain a reasonable balance between cultural and natural heritage on the World Heritage List.

57. 应不遗余力地保持《世界遗产名录》内文化和自然遗产的合理平衡。

58. No formal limit is imposed on the total number of properties to be inscribed on the World Heritage List.

58.《世界遗产名录》的遗产总数没有正式限制。

Other measures

其他措施

59. To promote the establishment of a representative, balanced and credible World Heritage List, States Parties are requested to consider whether their heritage is already well represented on the List and if so to slow down their rate of submission of further nominations by:

59. 要构建具有代表性、均衡性、可信性的《世界遗产名录》，缔约国须考虑其遗产在遗产名录上是否已得到充分的体现。如果是，就要采取以下措施，减缓新的申报：

Resolution adopted by the 12th General Assembly of States Parties (1999).

第 12 届缔约国会议通过的决议（1999 年）。

a) spacing voluntarily their nominations according to conditions that they will define, and/or;

a）依据自身情况，自主增大申报间隔，或；

b) proposing only properties falling into categories still under-represented, and/or;

b）只申报《世界遗产名录》内低于适当比例的遗产类别；

c) linking each of their nominations with

c）每次申报都与列入《世界遗产名录》的

a nomination presented by a State Party whose heritage is under-represented; or

d) deciding, on a voluntary basis, to suspend the presentation of new nominations.

遗产低于适当比例的缔约国的申报联系起来，或

d）自主决定暂停提交新的申报。

60. States Parties whose heritage of Outstanding Universal Value is under-represented on the World Heritage List are requested to:

Resolution adopted by the 12th General Assembly of States Parties (1999).

a) give priority to the preparation of their Tentative Lists and nominations;

b) initiate and consolidate partnerships at the regional level based on the exchange of technical expertise;

c) encourage bilateral and multilateral co-operation so as to increase their expertise and the technical capacities of institutions in charge of the protection, safeguarding and management of their heritage; and,

d) participate, as much as possible, in the sessions of the World Heritage Committee.

60. 如果缔约国的遗产具有突出的普遍价值，且在《世界遗产名录》上未能充分体现，应：

第 12 届缔约国会议通过的决议（1999 年）

a）编制《预备名录》和申报材料时优先考虑；

b）在所属区域内，寻求技术交流伙伴并巩固这种合作关系；

c）鼓励双边和多边合作以增强缔约国负责遗产保存、保护和管理机构的专业技能。

d）尽可能参加世界遗产委员会的各届会议。

61. The Committee has decided to apply the following mechanism:

Until 1 February 2018 (ind)

Decisions 24 COM VI.2.3.3, 28 COM 13.1 and 7 EXT.COM 4B.1, 29 COM 18A, 31 COM 10, 35 COM 8B.61 40 COM 11

a) examine up to two complete nominations per State Party, provided that at least one of such nominations concerns a natural property or a cultural landscape and,

b) set at 45 the annual limit on the number of nominations it will review, inclusive of nominations deferred and referred by previous sessions of the Committee, extensions (except minor modifications of limits of the property), transboundary and serial nominations,

61. 委员会决定使用以下机制：

第 24 COM VI.2.3.3 号决定、第 28 COM 13.1 号决定、第 7EXT.COM 4B.1 号决定、第 29 COM18A 号决定、第 31 COM10 决定以及第 35COM8B.61 决定。

a）最多审查每个缔约国两项完整的申报材料，其中至少有一项须与自然遗产或文化景观有关；

b）确定委员会每年审查的申报数目不超过 45 个，其中包括往届会议推迟审议的项目、补充材料后再审项目、扩展项目（遗产限制的细微变动除外）、跨界项目和系列项目，

c) the following order of priorities will be applied in case the overall annual limit of 45 nominations is exceeded:

1.nominations of properties submitted by States Parties with no properties inscribed on the List;

2. nominations of properties submitted by States Parties having up to 3 properties inscribed on the List,

3. nominations of properties that have been previously excluded due to the annual limit of 45 nominations and the application of these priorities,

4. nominations of properties for natural heritage,

5. nominations of properties for mixed heritage,

6. nominations of transboundary/transnational properties,

7. nominations from States Parties in Africa, the Pacific and the Caribbean,

8. nominations of properties submitted by States Parties having ratified the *World Heritage Convention* during the last ten years,

9. nominations of properties submitted by States Parties that have not submitted nominations for ten years or more,

10. when applying this priority system, date of receipt of full and complete nominations by the World Heritage Centre shall be used as a secondary factor to determine the priority between those nominations that would not be designated by the previous points.

d) the States Parties co-authors of a transboundary or transnational serial nomination can choose, amongst themselves and with a common understanding, the State Party which will be bearing this nomination; and this nomination can be registered exclusively within the ceiling of the bearing State Party.

c）超出每年限定的45个申报之后，其他申报的优先顺序如下：

1）尚无遗产列入《世界遗产名录》的缔约国提交的遗产申报；

2）仅有三项以下遗产列入《世界遗产名录》的缔约国提交的遗产申报；

3）由于每年45项申报数目限制未能处理且符合优先条件的遗产申报；

4）自然遗产申报；

5）混合遗产申报；

6）跨境或跨国遗产申报；

7）非洲、太平洋和加勒比地区缔约国的遗产申报；

8）最近十年加入《世界遗产公约》的缔约国的遗产申报；

9）最近十年或超过十年没有提交申报的缔约国的遗产申报；

10）采用该优先顺序机制时，若使用前面的几点无法确定申报的优先顺序，则世界遗产中心收到完整申报材料的日期，将被作为次要因素来决定它们的优先权；

d）联合编写跨境或跨国系列申报文本的缔约国可以在达成共识的前提下，自行推举一个国家提交该申报项目；此项目仅占用该缔约国的申报限额。

As from 2 February 2018:

2018 年 2 月 2 日以后

a) examine one complete nominations per State Party,

a）审查每个缔约国一项完整的申报材料；

b) set at 35 the annual limit on the number of nominations it will review, inclusive of nominations deferred and referred by previous sessions of the Committee, extensions (except minor modifications of limits of the property), transboundary and serial nominations,

b）确定委员会每年审查的申报数目不超过 35 个，其中包括往届会议推迟审议的项目、补充材料后再审项目、扩展项目（遗产限制的细微变动除外）、跨界项目和系列项目，

c) the following order of priorities will be applied in case the overall annual limit of 35 nominations is exceeded:

c）超出每年 35 个申报限定之后，其他申报的优先顺序如下：

i) nominations of properties submitted by States Parties with no properties inscribed on the List;

1）尚无遗产列入《世界遗产名录》的缔约国提交的遗产申报；

ii) nominations of properties submitted by States Parties having up to 3 properties inscribed on the List,

2）仅有三项以下遗产列入《世界遗产名录》的缔约国提交的遗产申报；

iii) resubmitted referred nominations that were not transmitted to the relevant Advisory Bodies for evaluation further to the application of paragraph 61.b)[①]

3）根据第 61.b 规定重新提交的、没有送达相关咨询机构的、需要进一步评估的申报：[①]

iv) nominations of properties that have been previously excluded due to the annual limit of 35 nominations and the application of these priorities,

4）受每年 35 项申报数目限制未能处理的遗产申报；

v) nominations of properties for natural heritage,

5）自然遗产申报；

vi)nominations of properties for mixed heritage,

6）混合遗产申报；

vii) nominations of transboundary/transnational properties,

7）跨境或跨国遗产申报；

viii) nominations from States Parties in Africa, the Pacific and the Caribbean,

8）非洲、太平洋和加勒比地区缔约国的遗产申报；

ix) nominations of properties submitted by States Parties having ratified the *World Heritage*

9）最近 20 年才加入《世界遗产公约》的缔约国提交的申报；

---

① This provision also applies in case the resubmitted referred nomination is received in the third year following the referral decision.

这一规定也适用于相关决定试运行后第三年收到重新提交的遗产申报。

Convention during the last twenty years,

x) nominations of properties submitted by States Parties that have not submitted nominations for five years or more,

xi) nominations of States Parties, former Members of the Committee, who accepted on a voluntary basis not to have anomination reviewed by the Committee during their mandate. This priority will be applied for 4 years after the end of their mandate on the Committee,

xii) when applying this priority system, date of receipt of fulland complete nominations by the World Heritage Centre shall be used as a secondary factor to determine the priority between those nominations that would not be designated by the previous points.

d) the States Parties co-authors of a transboundary or transnational serial nomination can choose, amongst themselves and with a common understanding, the State Party which will be bearing this nomination; and this nomination can be registered exclusively within the ceiling of the bearing State Party.

This decision will be implemented on a trial basis for 4 years and takes effect on 2 February 2018, in order to ensure a smooth transition period for all States Parties. The impact of this decision will be evaluated at the Committee's 46th session (2022).

The impact of this decision will be evaluated at the Committee's 39th session (2015). This paragraph takes effect on 2 February 2012, in order to ensure a smooth transition period for all States Parties l. (2022 The impact of this)

10）最近5年来没有遗产列入《世界遗产名录》的缔约国提交的遗产申报；

11）作为前委员会成员的缔约国，自愿接受在任期内不参与申报。在4年委员会成员任期结束后该缔约国的申报享有优先权；

12）采用该优先顺序机制时，若使用前面的几点无法确定申报的优先顺序，则世界遗产中心收到完整申报材料的日期，将被作为次要因素来决定它们的优先权。

d）申报跨境或跨国系列遗产的缔约国，可以在达成共识的前提下，自行推举一个国家提交该申报项目；此项目仅占用该缔约国的申报限额。

本决定自2018年2月2日生效，试运行4年，以确保所有缔约国有一个平缓过渡期。将于委员会第46届会议（2022年）评估该决定的影响。

委员会第39届会议（2015年）评估该决定的影响。本段内容自2012年2月2日生效，以确保所有缔约国有一个平缓过渡期。

II.C Tentative Lists

II.C《预备名录》

Procedure and Format

程序和格式

62. A Tentative List is an inventory of those

62.《预备名录》是缔约国认为其境内具备

properties situated on its territory which each State Party considers suitable for inscription on the World Heritage List. States Parties should therefore include, in their Tentative Lists, the names of those properties which they consider to be cultural and/or natural heritage of Outstanding Universal Value and which they intend to nominate during the following years.

列入世界遗产名录资格的遗产的详细目录，其中应包括具有突出的普遍价值的文化和自然遗产，以及今后几年内要申报的遗产的名称。

Articles 1, 2 and 11 (1) of the World Heritage Convention.

Decision 39 COM 11

《保护世界文化与自然遗产公约》第 1、2 及 11（1）条规定。

第 39 COM 11 决定

63. Nominations to the World Heritage List are not considered unless the nominated property has already been included on the State Party's Tentative List.

Decision 24COM para.VI.2.3.2

63. 如果缔约国提交申报的遗产未曾列入该国的《预备名录》，委员会将不予考虑。

第 24 号决定第六条 .2.3.2

64. States Parties are encouraged to prepare their Tentative Lists with the participation of a wide variety of stakeholders, including site managers, local and regional governments, local communities, NGOs and other interested parties and partners.

64. 鼓励缔约国编制其《预备名录》，并让遗产地管理人员、当地和地区政府、社区、非政府组织以及其他相关机构参与编制过程。

65. States Parties shall submit Tentative Lists to the Secretariat, at least one year prior to the submission of any nomination. States Parties are encouraged to re-examine and re-submit their Tentative List at least every ten years.

65. 缔约国应在遗产申报前至少一年将《预备名录》呈报至秘书处。委员会鼓励缔约国至少每十年重新审查和递交《预备名录》。

66. States Parties are requested to submit their Tentative Lists in English or French using the standard format in Annex 2A and Annex 2B (for transnational and trans-boundary future nominations), containing the name of the properties, their geographical location, a brief description of the properties, and justification of their Outstanding Universal Value.

Decision 39 COM 11

66. 缔约国需要采用附件 2A 及 2B（为未来跨境或跨界申报）所示的标准格式递交英语或法语的《预备名录》，包括遗产名称、地理位置、简短描述以及其具有突出的普遍价值申明。

第 39 COM 11 决定

67. The original duly signed version of the completed Tentative List shall be submitted by the State Party, to:

UNESCO World Heritage Centre
7, place de Fontenoy
75352 Paris 07 SP France
Tel: +33 (0) 1 4568 1136
E-mail: wh-tentativelists@unesco.org

67. 缔约国应将已签名的完整《预备名录》原件递交至：

联合国教科文组织世界遗产中心：法国巴黎（7，place de Fontenoy，Paris 07 SP）

电话：+33（0）1 4568 1136
电邮：wh–tentativelists@unesco.org

68. Upon reception of the Tentative Lists from the States Parties, the World Heritage Centre checks for compliance of the documentation with Annex 2. If the documentation is not considered in compliance with Annex 2, the World Heritage Centre refers it back to the State Party. When all information has been provided, the Tentative List is registered by the Secretariat and trans mitted to the relevant Advisory Bodies for information. A summary of all Tentative Lists is presented annually to the Committee. The Secretariat, in consultation with the States Parties concerned, updates its records, in particular by removing from the Tentative Lists the inscribed properties and nominated properties which were not inscribed.

Decision 7 EXT.COM 4A

68. 收到缔约国提交的《预备名录》后，世界遗产中心将检查文件是否符合附件 2 的要求，如认为不符合，会将文件退回缔约国。如果所有信息均已提供，秘书处会将《预备名录》登记并转呈给相关咨询机构。每年都要向委员会递交所有《预备名录》的概要。秘书处与相关缔约国协商，更新其名录，将《预备名录》上已列入《世界遗产名录》和已否决列入的申报除名。

第 27COM 4A 号决定

The Tentative Lists of States Parties are published by the World Heritage Centre at its website and/or in working documents in order to ensure transparency, access to information and to facilitate harmonization of Tentative Lists at regional and thematic levels.

Decision 41.COM 11

世界遗产中心将在其网站及工作文件中公布缔约国《预备目录》，以保证透明度、便于获取资料、和在区域内《预备目录》协调及主题研究。

第 41. COM 11 决定

The sole responsibility for the content of each Tentative List lies with the State Party concerned. The publication of the Tentative Lists does not imply the expression of any opinion whatsoever of the World Heritage Committee or of the World Heritage Centre or of the Secretariat of UNESCO

各缔约国负责其《预备目录》。公布《预备目录》并不意味着世界遗产委员会或世界遗产中心或教科文组织秘书处，对任何国家、领土、城市、地区或其边界的法律地位发表任何意见。

concerning the legal status of any country, territory, city or area or of its boundaries.

69. The Tentative *Lists* of States Parties are available at the following Web address: http: //whc.unesco.org/en/tentativelists

Decision 27 com 8A

69. 登录查阅缔约国《预备名录》：http：//whc.unesco.org/en/tentativelists，

第 27COM 8A 号决定

Tentative Lists as a planning and evaluation tool

《预备名录》作为规划与评估的工具

70. Tentative Lists are a useful and important planning tool for States Parties, the World Heritage Committee, the Secretariat, and the Advisory Bodies, as they provide an indication of future nominations.

70.《预备名录》提供未来遗产名录申报信息，是对缔约国、世界遗产委员会、秘书处及咨询机构工作有帮助的重要规划工具。

71.Tentative Lists should be drawn selectively and on the basis of evidence that supports potential Outstanding Universal Value. States Parties are encouraged to consult the analyses of both the World Heritage List and Tentative Lists prepared at the request of the Committee by ICOMOS and IUCN to identify the gaps in the World Heritage List. These analyses could enable States Parties to compare themes, regions, geo-cultural groupings and bio-geographic provinces for prospective World Heritage properties. States Parties are encouraged to seek as early as possible upstream advice from the Advisory Bodies during the development of their Tentative Lists as appropriate.

Decision 24 COM para. VI.2.3.2 (ii) Documents

WHC-04/28.COM/13.B I and II

http: //whc.unesco.org/archive/2004/whc04-28com-13b1e.pdf and

http: //whc.unesco.org/archive/ 2004/whc04-28com-13b2e.pdf

71. 在支持潜在突出普遍价值的基础上有选择的列出预备名录。鼓励缔约国参考国际古迹遗址理事会和世界自然保护联盟编制的《世界遗产名录》和《预备名录》分析报告，确定《世界遗产名录》上的缺项和空白。这些分析使缔约国能够通过比较遗产的主题、区域、地理文化群和生物地理区，更好地确定未来的世界遗产。鼓励缔约国在准备预备名录时尽早寻求咨询机构的上游建议。

第 24COM 号决定第 VI.2.3.2（ii）条文书

WHC-04/28.COM/13.B 1 和 2 详见：

http：//whc.unesco.org/archive/2004/whc04-28com-13b1e.pdf

http：//whc.unesco.org/archive/2004/whc04-28com-13b2e.pdf

72. In addition, States Parties are encouraged to consult the specific thematic studies carried out by the Advisory Bodies (see paragraph 147). These studies are informed by a review of the Tentative Lists submitted by States Parties and by reports of meetings on the harmonization of Tentative Lists, as well as by other technical studies performed by the Advisory Bodies and qualified organizations and individuals. A list of those studies already completed is available at the following Web address: http: //whc.unesco.org/en/globalstrategy

72. 另外，鼓励缔约国参考由咨询机构完成的特定主题研究报告（见 147 条）。这些研究评估了缔约国提交的《预备名录》、参考了《预备名录》协调会议报告、咨询团体以及其他有资格的团体和个人的相关技术研究。已完成的研究报告列表详见：http：//whc.unesco.org/en/globalstrategy

Thematic studies are different than the comparative analysis to be prepared by States Parties when nominating properties for inscription in the World Heritage List (see paragraph 132).

主题研究报告不同于缔约国申报遗产列入《世界遗产名录》时编撰的比较分析（见第 132 条）。

73. States Parties are encouraged to harmonize their Tentative Lists at regional and thematic levels. Harmonization of Tentative Lists is the process whereby States Parties, with the assistance of the Advisory Bodies, collectively assess their respective Tentative List to review gaps and identify common themes. The outcome of harmonization can result in improved Tentative Lists, new nominations from States Parties and cooperation amongst groups of States Parties in the preparation of nominations.

73. 鼓励缔约国在区域和主题上协调《预备名录》。在这个过程中，缔约国在咨询团体的协助下，共同评估各自的《预备名录》，审查缺项并确认相同主题。通过协调改进《预备名录》，缔约国可以更好地申报新遗产，或与其他缔约国合作申报。

Assistance and Capacity-Building for States Parties in the preparation of Tentative Lists

缔约国编撰《预备名录》过程中的援助和能力建设

74. To implement the Global Strategy, cooperative efforts in capacity-building and training may be necessary to assist States Parties to acquire and/or consolidate their expertise in the preparation, updating and harmonisation of their Tentative List and the preparation of nominations.

74. 要实施《全球战略》，就有必要共同致力于援助缔约国进行能力建设和培训，获取和增强其编制、更新和平衡《预备名录》及准备申报材料的能力。

75. International Assistance may be requested by States Parties for the purpose of preparing, updating and harmonizing Tentative Lists (see

75. 在编制、更新和协调《预备名录》方面，缔约国可以请求国际援助（见第七章）。

Chapter VII).

76. The Advisory Bodies and the Secretariat will use the opportunity of evaluation missions to hold regional training workshops to assist under-represented States in the methods of preparation of their Tentative List and nominations.

Decision 24COM VI.2.3.5 (ii)

76. 咨询机构和秘书处可在考察评估期间举办地区培训班，对《世界遗产名录》中遗产比例较低的国家在准备《预备名录》和申报方面提供帮助。

第 24COMVI.2.3.5（ii）号决定

II.D Criteria for the assessment of Outstanding Universal Value

II.D 突出的普遍价值的评估标准

These criteria were formerly presented as two separate sets of criteria - criteria (i) - (vi) for cultural heritage and (vi) - (X) for natural heritage.

The 6th extraordinary session of the World Heritage Committee decided to merge the ten criteria (Decision 6 EXT.COM 5.1)

这些标准起初分为两组，标准（i）至（vi）适用于文化遗产，标准（vi）至（X）适用于自然遗产。

世界遗产委员会第 6 届特别会议决定将这十个标准合起来（第 6EXT.COM 5.1 号决定）

77. The Committee considers a property as having Outstanding Universal Value (see paragraphs 49-53) if the property meets one or more of the following criteria. Nominated properties shall therefore :

(i) represent a masterpiece of human creative genius;

(ii) exhibit an important interchange of human values, over a span of time or within a cultural area of the world, on developments in architecture or technology, monumental arts, town-planning or landscape design;

(iii) bear a unique or at least exceptional testimony to a cultural tradition or to a civilization which is living or which has disappeared;

(iv) be an outstanding example of a type of building, architectural or technological ensemble or landscape which illustrates (a) significant stage (s) in human history;

(v) be an outstanding example of a traditional human settlement, land-use, or sea-use which is

77. 如果遗产符合下列一项或多项标准，委员会将会认为该遗产具有突出的普遍价值（见 49–53 条）。所申报遗产因而必须是：

（i）人类创造精神的杰作；

（ii）体现一段时期内或世界某一文化区域内，人类价值观的重要交流，对建筑、技术、古迹艺术、城镇规划或景观设计的发展产生重大影响；

（iii）能为延续至今或业已消逝的文明或文化传统提供独特的或至少是特殊的见证；

（iv）是一种建筑、建筑学或整体技术、景观的杰出范例，展现人类历史上一个（或几个）重要阶段；

（v）是传统人类居住地、土地使用或海洋开发的杰出范例，代表一种（或几种）文化或

representative of a culture (or cultures), or human interaction with the environment especially when it has become vulnerable under the impact of irreversible change;

人类与环境的相互作用，特别是当它面临不可逆变化的影响而变得易于损坏；

(vi) be directly or tangibly associated with events or living traditions, with ideas, or with beliefs, with artistic and literary works of outstanding universal significance. (The Committee considers that this criterion should preferably be used in conjunction with other criteria);

（vi）与具有突出的普遍意义的事件、生活传统、观点、信仰、艺术或文学作品有直接或有形的联系。（委员会认为本标准最好与其他标准一起使用）；

(vii) contain superlative natural phenomena or areas of exceptional natural beauty and aesthetic importance;

（vii）绝妙的自然现象或具有罕见自然美和美学价值的地区；

(viii) be outstanding examples representing major stages of earth's history, including the record of life, significant on-going geological processes in the development of landforms, or significant geomorphic or physiographic features;

（viii）是地球演化史中重要阶段的突出例证，包括生命记载、地貌演变中的重要地质过程或显著的地质、地貌特征；

(ix) be outstanding examples representing significant ongoing ecological and biological processes in the evolution and development of terrestrial, fresh water, coastal and marine ecosystems and communities of plants and animals;

（ix）突出代表了陆地、淡水、海岸和海洋生态系统及动植物群落演变、发展的生态和生理过程；

(x) contain the most important and significant natural habitats for in-situ conservation of biological diversity, including those containing threatened species of Outstanding Universal Value from the point of view of science or conservation.

（x）是生物多样性原址保护的最重要的自然栖息地，包括从科学和保护角度看，具有突出的普遍价值的濒危物种栖息地。

78. To be deemed of Outstanding Universal Value, a property must also meet the conditions of integrity and/or authenticity and must have an adequate protection and management system to ensure its safeguarding.

78. 只有满足完整性和真实性条件，且有足够的保护和管理机制确保遗产得到保护，此遗产才能被视为具有突出的普遍价值。

II.E Integrity and/or authenticity

II.E 完整性和 / 或真实性

Authenticity

真实性

79. Properties nominated under criteria (i)

79. 符合（i）至（vi）标准的申报遗产须满

to (vi) must meet the conditions of authenticity. Annex 4 which includes the *Nara Document on Authenticity*, provides a practical basis for examining the authenticity of such properties and is summarized below.

足真实性的条件。附件 4 中包括了关于真实性的《奈良文件》，为评估相关遗产的真实性提供了操作基础，概要如下。

80. The ability to understand the value attributed to the heritage depends on the degree to which information sources about this value may be understood as credible or truthful. Knowledge and understanding of these sources of information, in relation to original and subsequent characteristics of the cultural heritage, and their meaning as accumulated over time, are the requisite bases for assessing all aspects of authenticity.

Decision 39 COM 11

80. 理解遗产价值的能力取决于该价值信息来源的真实度或可信度。对涉及文化遗产原始及后续特征的信息来源的知识和理解，及其随时间积累的价值，是评价真实性各方面的必要基础。

见 39 COM 11 决定

81. Judgments about value attributed to cultural heritage, as well as the credibility of related information sources, may differ from culture to culture, and even within the same culture. The respect due to all cultures requires that cultural heritage must be considered and judged primarily within the cultural contexts to which it belongs.

81. 对于文化遗产价值和相关信息来源可信性的评价标准可因文化而异，甚至同一种文化内也存在差异。出于对所有文化的尊重，文化遗产的分析和判断必须首先在其所属的文化背景中进行。

82. Depending on the type of cultural heritage, and its cultural context, properties may be understood to meet the conditions of authenticity if their cultural values (as recognized in the nomination criteria proposed) are truthfully and credibly expressed through a variety of attributes including:

- form and design;
- materials and substance;
- use and function;
- traditions, techniques and management systems;
- location and setting;
- language, and other forms of intangible heritage;

82. 依据文化遗产类别及其文化背景，如果遗产的文化价值（申报标准所认可的）的下列特征真实可信，则被认为具有真实性：

- 外形和设计；
- 材料和材质；
- 用途和功能；
- 传统，技术和管理体系；
- 环境和位置；
- 语言和其他形式的无形遗产；

• spirit and feeling; and
• other internal and external factors.

83. Attributes such as spirit and feeling do not lend themselves easily to practical applications of the conditions of authenticity, but nevertheless are important indicators of character and sense of place, for example, in communities maintaining tradition and cultural continuity.

84. The use of all these sources permits elaboration of the specific artistic, historic, social, and scientific dimensions of the cultural heritage being examined. "Information sources" are defined as all physical, written, oral, and figurative sources, which make it possible to know the nature, specificities, meaning, and history of the cultural heritage.

85. When the conditions of authenticity are considered in preparing a nomination for a property, the State Party should first identify all of the applicable significant attributes of authenticity. The statement of authenticity should assess the degree to which authenticity is present in, or expressed by, each of these significant attributes.

86. In relation to authenticity, the reconstruction of archaeological remains or historic buildings or districts is justifiable only in exceptional circumstances. Reconstruction is acceptable only on the basis of complete and detailed documentation and to no extent on conjecture.

Integrity

87. All properties nominated for inscription on the World Heritage List shall satisfy the conditions of integrity.

Decision 20 COM IX.13

• 精神和感觉；
• 其他内外因素。

83. 精神和感觉这样的属性在真实性评估中虽不易操作，却是评价一个遗产地特质和场所精神的重要指标，例如，在社区中保持传统和文化连续性。

84. 采用所有这些信息时应充分考虑文化遗产在艺术、历史、社会和科学各方面的价值。"信息来源"指所有物质的、书面的、口头和图形的信息来源，从而能更好地理解文化遗产的本质、特性、意义和历史。

85. 在考虑申报遗产的真实性时，缔约国首先要确认所有适用的真实性的重要载体。真实性声明应该评估真实性在每个载体特征上的体现程度。

86. 在真实性问题上，考古遗址或历史建筑及街区的重建只有在极个别情况才予以考虑。只有依据完整、详细的档案记录，不存在任何想象成分时方可进行重建。

完整性

87. 所有申报列入《世界遗产名录》的遗产必须满足完整性条件。

第 20 COM IX.13 号决定

88. Integrity is a measure of the wholeness and intactness of the natural and/or cultural heritage and its attributes. Examining the conditions of integrity, therefore requires assessing the extent to which the property:

a) includes all elements necessary to express its Outstanding Universal Value;

b) is of adequate size to ensure the complete representation of the features and processes which convey the property's significance;

c) suffers from adverse effects of development and/or neglect.

This should be presented in a statement of integrity.

88. 完整性用来衡量自然和文化遗产及其特征的整体性和无缺憾性。因而，审查遗产完整性需要评估遗产满足以下特征的程度：

a）包括所有表现其突出普遍价值的必要因素；

b）足够大，确保能完整地体现代表遗产价值的特色和过程；

c）受到发展或忽视的负面影响。

上述条件需要在完整性陈述中进行论述。

89. For properties nominated under criteria (i) to (vi), the physical fabric of the property and/or its significant features should be in good condition, and the impact of deterioration processes controlled. A significant proportion of the elements necessary to convey the totality of the value conveyed by the property should be included. Relationships and dynamic functions present in cultural landscapes, historic towns or other living properties essential to their distinctive character should also be maintained.

Examples of the application of the conditions of integrity to properties nominated under criteria (i) - (vi) are under development.

89. 符合标准（i）至（vi）的申报遗产，其物理构造和重要特征都必须保存完好，且侵蚀退化已得到控制。能表现遗产全部价值的绝大部分必要因素，以及文化景观、历史村镇或其他现存遗产中，体现其显著特征的种种关系和动态功能均应予以保存。

将完整性条件应用于依据标准（i）至（vi）的申报的遗产之例证正在开发。

90. For all properties nominated under criteria (vii) - (x), biophysical processes and landform features should be relatively intact. However, it is recognized that no area is totally pristine and that all natural areas are in a dynamic state, and to some extent involve contact with people. Human activities, including those of traditional societies and local communities, often occur in natural areas. These activities may be consistent with the Outstanding Universal Value of the area where they

90. 所有依据标准（vii）至（x）申报的遗产，其生物物理过程和地貌特征应该相对完整。当然，任何区域都不可能完全保持天然，且所有自然区域都在变动之中，而且在某种程度上还会有人类的活动。包括传统社会和当地社区在内的人类活动在自然区域内时有发生。如果这些活动具有生态可持续性，应同自然区域突出的普遍价值一致。

are ecologically sustainable.

91. In addition, for properties nominated under criteria (vii) to (x), a corresponding condition of integrity has been defined for each criterion.

91. 另外，对于依据标准（vii）至（x）申报的遗产，每个标准又有一个相应的完整性条件。

92. Properties proposed under criterion (vii) should be of Outstanding Universal Value and include areas that are essential for maintaining the beauty of the property. For example, a property whose scenic value depends on a waterfall, would meet the conditions of integrity if it includes adjacent catchment and downstream areas that are integrally linked to the maintenance of the aesthetic qualities of the property.

92. 依据标准（vii）申报的遗产应具备突出普遍价值，且包括保持遗产美景所必须的关键地区。例如，某个遗产的景观价值在于瀑布，那么只有把能完整维持遗产美景、关系密切的近处积水潭和下游地区也被涵盖在内，才能满足完整性条件。

93. Properties proposed under criterion (viii) should contain all or most of the key interrelated and interdependent elements in their natural relationships. For example, an "ice age" area would meet the conditions of integrity if it includes the snow field, the glacier itself and samples of cutting patterns, deposition and colonization (e.g. striations, moraines, pioneer stages of plant succession, etc.); in the case of volcanoes, the magmatic series should be complete and all or most of the varieties of effusive rocks and types of eruptions be represented.

93. 依据标准（viii）申报的遗产必须包括其自然关系中所有或大部分重要的相互联系、相互依存的因素。例如，"冰川期"遗址要满足完整性条件，则需包括雪地、冰河本身和凿面样本、沉积物和植物集群（例如，条痕、冰碛层及早期植物演替等）。如果是火山，则岩浆层必须完整，且能代表所有或大部分火山岩种类和喷发类型。

94. Properties proposed under criterion (ix) should have sufficient size and contain the necessary elements to demonstrate the key aspects of processes that are essential for the long term conservation of the ecosystems and the biological diversity they contain. For example, an area of tropical rain forest would meet the conditions of integrity if it includes a certain amount of variation in elevation above sea level, changes in topography and soil types, patch systems and naturally regenerating patches; similarly a coral reef should include, for example, seagrass, mangrove or other

94. 依据标准（ix）申报的遗产必须具有足够的规模，且包含能够展示长期保护其内部生态系统和生物多样性的重要过程的必要因素。例如，热带雨林地区要满足完整性条件，需要有一定的海拔层次、多样的地形和土壤种类、群落系统和自然形成的群落；同样，珊瑚礁必须包括诸如海草、红树林和其他为珊瑚礁提供营养沉积物的临近生态系统。

adjacent ecosystems that regulate nutrient and sediment inputs into the reef.

95. Properties proposed under criterion (x) should be the most important properties for the conservation of biological diversity. Only those properties which are the most biologically diverse and/or representative are likely to meet this criterion. The properties should contain habitats for maintaining the most diverse fauna and flora characteristic of the bio-geographic province and ecosystems under consideration. For example, a tropical savannah would meet the conditions of integrity if it includes a complete assemblage of co-evolved herbivores and plants; an island ecosystem should include habitats for maintaining endemic biota; a property containing wide ranging species should be large enough to include the most critical habitats essential to ensure the survival of viable populations of those species; for an area containing migratory species, seasonal breeding and nesting sites, and migratory routes, wherever they are located, should be adequately protected.

95. 依据标准（x）申报的遗产必须是对生物多样性保护至关重要的遗产。只有最具生物多样性或代表性的申报遗产才有可能满足该标准。遗产必须包括某生物区或生态系统内，最具多样性的动植物特征的栖息地。例如：要满足完整性条件，热带草原需要具有完整的、共同进化的食草动物群和植物群；海岛生态系统则需要包括地方生态栖息地；包含多种物种的遗产必须足够大，能够包括确保这些物种生存的最重要的栖息地；如果某个地区有迁徙物种，则季节性的养育巢穴和迁徙路线，不管位于何处，都必须妥善保护。

II.F Protection and management

II.F 保护和管理

96. Protection and management of World Heritage properties should ensure that their Outstanding Universal Value, including the conditions of integrity and/or authenticity at the time of inscription, are sustained or enhanced over time. A regular review of the general state of conservation of properties, and thus also their Outstanding Universal Value, shall be done within a framework of monitoring processes for World Heritage properties, as specified within the *Operational Guidelines*①.

96. 世界遗产的保护与管理，须确保其在列入《世界遗产名录》时所具有的突出普遍价值以及完整性和真实性能继续保持或加强。为此，须按照《操作指南》中规定的，在世界遗产监测的总体框架下，对列入的遗产及其突出普遍价值的保护状况进行定期审查①。

① *The processes of monitoring specified in the Operational Guidelines are Reactive Monitoring (see paragraphs 169-176) and Periodic Reporting (see paragraphs 199-210).*

操作指南中的特定监测程序是反应性监测（见 169–176 段）和定期报告（见 199–210 段）。

97. All properties inscribed on the World Heritage List must have adequate long-term legislative, regulatory, institutional and/or traditional protection and management to ensure their safeguarding. This protection should include adequately delineated boundaries. Similarly States Parties should demonstrate adequate protection at the national, regional, municipal, and/or traditional level for the nominated property. They should append appropriate texts to the nomination with a clear explanation of the way this protection operates to protect the property.

97. 列入《世界遗产名录》的所有遗产必须有长期、充分的立法、规范、机制或传统的保护及管理，以确保遗产得到保护。保护必须包括充分的边界划定。同样，缔约国应该在国家、区域、城市和传统各个级别上对申报遗产予以足够力度的保护。申报文件的附件中明确解释具体保护措施。

Legislative, regulatory and contractual measures for protection

立法、规范和契约性的保护措施

98. Legislative and regulatory measures at national and local levels should assure the survival of the property from social, economic and other pressures or changes that might negatively impact the Outstanding Universal Value, including the integrity and/or authenticity of the property. States Parties should also assure the full and effective implementation of such measures.

Decision 39 COM 11

98. 国家和地方级的立法、规范措施应确保遗产的保存，保护遗产不因社会、经济或其他压力或变迁使其突出普遍价值包括完整性、真实性受到负面影响。缔约国还需要保证这些措施得到切实有效的实施。

第 39 COM 11 决定

Boundaries for effective protection

有效保护的边界

99. The delineation of boundaries is an essential requirement in the establishment of effective protection of nominated properties. Boundaries should be drawn to incorporate all the attributes that convey the Outstanding Universal Value and to ensure the integrity and/or authenticity of the property.

Decision 39 COM 11

99. 划定边界是对申报遗产进行有效保护的核心要求，边界划定应包括所有传递遗产突出普遍价值的特性并确保其完整性和真实性得到充分体现。

第 39 COM 11 决定

100. For properties nominated under criteria (i) - (vi), boundaries should be drawn to include all those areas and attributes which are a direct tangible expression of the Outstanding Universal Value of the property, as well as those areas which in the

100. 依据标准（i）至（vi）申报的遗产，划定的边界需要包括所有有形的、能够直接体现遗产的突出普遍价值的区域和特征，以及在将来的研究中有可能加深这种理解的区域。

light of future research possibilities offer potential to contribute to and enhance such understanding.

101. For properties nominated under criteria (vii) - (x), boundaries should reflect the spatial requirements of habitats, species, processes or phenomena that provide the basis for their inscription on the World Heritage List. The boundaries should include sufficient areas immediately adjacent to the area of Outstanding Universal Value in order to protect the property's heritage values from direct effect of human encroachments and impacts of resource use outside of the nominated area.

101. 依据标准（vii）至（x）申报的遗产，划定的边界要满足反映其成为世界遗产基本条件的栖息地、物种、过程或现象的空间要求。边界应包括与具有突出普遍价值紧邻的、足够大的区域，以保护其遗产价值不因人类的直接侵蚀和该区域外的资源开发而受到损害。

102. The boundaries of the nominated property may coincide with one or more existing or proposed protected areas, such as national parks or nature reserves, biosphere reserves or protected historic districts or other areas and territories. While such established areas for protection may contain several management zones, only some of those zones may satisfy criteria for inscription.

Decision 39 COM 11

102. 所申报遗产的边界可能会与一个或多个已存在或已建议的保护区重合，例如国家公园或自然保护区、生物圈保护区或历史保护区或其他地区和领域。虽然保护区可能包含几个管理带，但可能只有个别地带能达到世界遗产的标准。

第 39 COM 11 决定

Buffer zones

缓冲区

103. Wherever necessary for the proper protection of the property, an adequate buffer zone should be provided.

103. 如有必要，就应设立足够大的缓冲区以有效保护遗产。

104. For the purposes of effective protection of the nominated property, a buffer zone is an area surrounding the nominated property which has complementary legal and/or customary restrictions placed on its use and development to give an added layer of protection to the property. This should include the immediate setting of the nominated property, important views and other areas or attributes that are functionally important as a support to the property and its protection. The area

104. 缓冲区是为了有效保护申报遗产而设立划定的遗产周围区域，其使用和开发受到相关法律和习惯规定的限制，为遗产增加了保护层。缓冲区包括申报遗产直接所在的区域、重要景观，以及其他在功能上对遗产及其保护至关重要的区域或特征。缓冲区的构成区域应通过合适的机制来决定。申报时，需要提供有关缓冲区大小、特点、授权用途的详细信息以及一张精确标示边界和缓冲区的地图。

constituting the buffer zone should be determined in each case through appropriate mechanisms. Details on the size, characteristics and authorized uses of a buffer zone, as well as a map indicating the precise boundaries of the property and its buffer zone, should be provided in the nomination.

105. A clear explanation of how the buffer zone protects the property should also be provided.

105. 申报材料中还需明确描述缓冲区在保护申报遗产中的作用。

106. Where no buffer zone is proposed, the nomination should include a statement as to why a buffer zone is not required.

106. 如果没有提议划定缓冲区，则需要在申报材料中解释没有划定缓冲区的原因。

107. Although buffer zones are not part of the nominated property, any modifications to or creation of buffer zones subsequent to inscription of a property on the World Heritage List should be approved by the World Heritage Committee using the procedure for a minor boundary modification (see paragraph 164 and Annex 11). The creation of buffer zones subsequent to inscription is normally considered to be a minor boundary modification.①

107. 虽然缓冲区并非所申报遗产的正式组成部分，但是《世界遗产名录》内遗产的缓冲区的任何变动，都需经世界遗产委员会按照细微边界调整的程序（详见 164 条和附件 1）批准。变更后新的缓冲区设定通常被视作细微边界调整。①

Management systems

管理体制

108. Each nominated property should have an appropriate management plan or other documented management system which must specify how the Outstanding Universal Value of a property should be preserved, preferably through participatory means.

108. 每一处申报遗产都应有适宜的管理规划或其他有文可依的管理体制，其中需要详细说明将如何采取措施（最好是多方参与的方式）保护遗产突出普遍价值。

109. The purpose of a management system is to ensure the effective protection of the nominated property for present and future generations.

109. 管理体制旨在确保现在和将来对申报遗产进行有效的保护。

① In case of transnational/transboundary properties any modification will need the agreement of all States Parties concerned.

跨境或跨界遗产任何修订都需要得到全部相关缔约国的认可。

110. An effective management system depends on the type, characteristics and needs of the nominated property and its cultural and natural context. Management systems may vary according to different cultural perspectives, the resources available and other factors. They may incorporate traditional practices, existing urban or regional planning instruments, and other planning control mechanisms, both formal and informal. Impact assessments for proposed interventions are essential for all World Heritage properties.

110. 有效的管理体制的内容取决于申报遗产的类别、特点、需求以及文化和自然环境。由于文化视角、可用资源及其他因素的影响，管理体制也会有所差别。管理体制可能包含传统做法、现行的城市或地区规划手段、其他正式和非正式的规划控制机制。对所有世界遗产而言，对将采取的干预措施进行影响评估是很重要的工作。

111. In recognizing the diversity mentioned above, common elements of an effective management system could include:

Decision 39 COM 11

a) a thorough shared understanding of the property by all stakeholders; including the use of participatory planning and stakeholder consultation process;

b) a cycle of planning, implementation, monitoring, evaluation and feedback;

c) an assessment of the vulnerabilities of the property to social, economic, and other pressures and changes, as well as the monitoring of the impacts of trends and proposed interventions;

d) the development of mechanisms for the involvement and coordination of the various activities between different partners and stakeholders;

e) the allocation of necessary resources;

f) capacity-building; and

g) an accountable, transparent description of how the management system functions.

111. 考虑到上述多样性问题，有效管理体制应包括以下共同因素：

第 39 COM 11 决定

a）各利益相关者对遗产价值的透彻理解；包括使用参与计划和利益相关者咨询程序；

b）规划、实施、监测、评估和反馈的循环机制；

c）评估遗产应对社会、经济、其他压力和变化的脆弱性，同时监测影响趋势并提出干预措施；

d）开发不同合作者、各利益相关者参与和协调各类活动的参与机制；

e）必要资源的配置；

f）能力建设；

g）负责、清晰的描述管理体制的职能。

112. Effective management involves a cycle of short, medium and long-term actions to protect, conserve and present the nominated property. An integrated approach to planning and management is essential to guide the evolution of properties over time and to ensure maintenance of all aspects of their Outstanding Universal Value. This approach

112. 有效管理包括对申报遗产保存、保护和展示的短、中、长期措施。采取整体综合的规划管理方式对指导遗产长期发展至关重要，也可确保其突出普遍价值的所有方面得以维持。这一综合视角不局限于遗产本身，而是包括所有缓冲区和更广泛的背景环境。更广泛的背景环境也许与遗产的地形、自然和建筑环境及其

goes beyond the property to include any buffer zone (s), as well as the broader setting. The broader setting, may relate to the property's topography, natural and built environment, and other elements such as infrastructure, land use patterns, spatial organization, and visual relationships. It may also include related social and cultural practices, economic processes and other intangible dimensions of heritage such as perceptions and associations. Management of the broader setting is related to its role in supporting the Outstanding Universal Value.

他因素如基础设施、土地利用模式，空间组织及视觉关系相关；也许也包括相关的社会及文化实践、经济进程和其他无形遗产维度如感知和联想。广泛的背景环境管理与支持遗产的突出普遍价值的角色相关。

113. Moreover, in the context of the implementation of the *Convention*, the World Heritage Committee has established a process of Reactive Monitoring (see Chapter IV) and a process of Periodic Reporting (see Chapter V).

113. 另外，为了实施《公约》，世界遗产委员会还建立了反应监测程序（见第Ⅳ章）和《定期报告》机制（见第Ⅴ章）。

114. In the case of serial properties, a management system or mechanisms for ensuring the co-ordinated management of the separate components are essential and should be documented in the nomination (see paragraphs 137 -139).

114. 如果是系列遗产，须在申报材料中阐明能确保各个组成部分协调管理的管理体制或机制（见 137–139 条）。

115. Deleted.
Decision 39 COM11

115. 此条删除
第 39COM11 决定

116. Where the intrinsic qualities of a property nominated are threatened by action of man and yet meet the criteria and the conditions of authenticity or integrity set out in paragraphs 78-95, an action plan outlining the corrective measures required should be submitted with the nomination file. Should the corrective measures submitted by the nominating State Party not be taken within the time proposed by the State Party, the property will be considered by the Committee for delisting in accordance with the procedure adopted by the Committee (see Chapter IV.C).
Decision 39 COM 11

116. 如果遗产内在品质由于人类活动而受到威胁，且影响了满足第 78 至 95 条规定的真实性或完整性的标准和条件，则纠正措施的行动计划需要和申报材料一起提交。如果缔约国并未在拟定的时间内采取纠正措施，委员会将会考虑依据相关程序将该遗产从名单上删除。（见 IV.C 节）

第 39COM11 决定

117. States Parties are responsible for implementing effective management activities for a World Heritage property. State Parties should do so in close collaboration with property managers, the agency with management authority and other partners, and stakeholders in property management.

117. 缔约国要对境内的世界遗产实施有效的管理。在管理过程中，缔约国要同其他参与方密切合作，其中包括遗产管理人员、有管理权力的机关和其他合作者及遗产管理的利益相关者。

118. The Committee recommends that States Parties include risk preparedness as an element in their World Heritage site management plans and training strategies.

Decision 28 COM 10B.4

118. 委员会建议缔约国将风险防范机制包括在其世界遗产管理规划和培训策略中。

第 28COM10B.4 号决定

Sustainable use

可持续使用

119. World Heritage properties may support a variety of ongoing and proposed uses that are ecologically and culturally sustainable, and which may contribute to the quality of life of communities concerned. The State Party and its partners must ensure that such sustainable use or any other change does not impact adversely on the Outstanding Universal Value of the property. For some properties, human use would not be appropriate. Legislations, policies and strategies affecting World Heritage properties should ensure the protection of the Outstanding Universal Value, support the wider conservation of natural and cultural heritage, and promote and encourage the active participation of the communities and stakeholders concerned with the property as necessary conditions to its sustainable protection, conservation, management and presentation.

119. 世界遗产会有各种各样现有的、拟开发的、生态和文化可持续的使用价值，这类使用可能提高所在社区的生活质量。缔约国和合作者必须确保这些价值可持续使用，或任何其他的改变不会对遗产的突出普遍价值、完整性和真实性造成负面影响。对于有些遗产来说，人类不宜使用。世界遗产的相关立法、政策和策略措施都应确保其突出普遍价值的保护，支持对更大范围的自然和文化遗产的保护、促进和鼓励所在社区公众和利益相关者积极参与，是遗产可持续保护、保存、管理、展示的必要条件。

III. PROCESS FOR THE INSCRIPTION OF PROPERTIES ON THE WORLD HERITAGE LIST

III. 列入《世界遗产名录》的程序

III.A Preparation of Nominations

III.A 申报准备

120. The nomination document is the primary basis on which the Committee considers the

120. 申报文件是委员会考虑是否将某项遗产列入《世界遗产名录》的首要基础。所有相

inscription of the properties on the World Heritage List. All relevant information should be included in the nomination document and it should be crossreferenced to the source of information.

关信息都应该包括在申报文件中，且其信息来源须交叉引用。

121. Annex 3 provides guidance to States Parties in preparing nominations of specific types of properties.

121. 附件 3 为缔约国准备特定类型遗产的申报文件提供了指南。

122. Before States Parties begin to prepare a nomination of a Property for inscription on the World Heritage List, they should become familiar with the nomination cycle, described in Paragraph 168. It is desirable to carry out initial preparatory work to establish that a property has the potential to justify Outstanding Universal Value, including integrity or authenticity, before the development of a full nomination dossier which could be expensive and time-consuming. Such preparatory work might include collection of available information on the property, thematic studies, scoping studies of the potential for demonstrating Outstanding Universal Value, including integrity or authenticity, or an initial comparative study of the property in its wider global or regional context, including an analysis in the context of the Gap Studies produced by the Advisory Bodies. This first phase of work will help to establish the feasibility of a possible nomination at an early stage and avoid use of resources on nominations that may be unlikely to succeed. States Parties are encouraged to seek upstream advice ①

122. 缔约国在着手准备遗产申报前，应先熟悉第 168 条描述的申报周期。在提交完整、耗时耗资的申遗文本前，在初期准备工作阶段就应确定遗产的突出普遍价值，包括其完整性和真实性。这类准备工作包括收集遗产的有效信息、主题研究、关于潜在突出普遍价值证明的范围界定研究、包括完整性与真实性或关于遗产在更广泛的全球或区域背景下的初期比较研究、包括咨询机构以遗产空白研究为背景的分析。第一阶段的工作有助于在申报的早期阶段建立具有可行性的申遗战略，避免在申报中使用了不可能成功的资源。鼓励缔约国在第一阶段寻求相关咨询机构上游建议①的同时，尽早和世界遗产中心联系，以便于在申报阶段寻求有用的信息和帮助。

① Upstream Processes: In relation to the nomination of sites for inscription on the World Heritage List, "Upstream processes" include advice, consultation and analysis that occur prior to the submission of a nomination and are aimed at reducing the number of nominations that experience significant problems during the evaluation process. The basic principle of the upstream processes is to enable the Advisory Bodies and the Secretariat to provide support directly to States Parties, throughout the whole process leading up to a possible World Heritage nomination. For the upstream support to be effective, it should ideally be undertaken from the earliest stage in the nomination process, at the moment of the preparation or revision of the States Parties' Tentative Lists.

上游程序：在遗产申报录入名录时，上游程序包括在递交申报前的建议、咨询和分析，在评估程序中减少有重大问题的申报数量。上游程序的基本原则是使咨询机构和秘书处可以对缔约国提供直接支持，通过全部程序使申报可能实现。上游程序的有效性，理想情况下是在缔约国准备和修订预备名录的申遗初始阶段就开始运作。

from the relevant Advisory Body (ies) for this first phase as well as to contact the World Heritage Centre at the earliest opportunity in considering nominations to seek information and guidance.

Decision 34 COM 12 (III)

Report of the Expert meeting on 'Upstream Processes to Nominations: Creative Approaches in the Nomination Process' (Phuket: 2010)

Decision 36 COM 13.I

Decision 39 COM 11

第 34 COM 12（III）决定

专家会议报告：”申报中的上游程序：申报程序中的创意方法”

（普吉岛，2010）

第 36 COM 13.I 及第 39 COM 11 决定

123. Particiption in the nomination process of local communities, indigenous peoples, governmental, non-governmental and private organizations and other stakeholders is essential to enable them to have a shared responsibility with the State Party in the maintenance of the property. States Parties are encouraged to prepare nominations with the widest possible participation of stakeholders and to demonstrate, as appropriate, that the free, prior and informed consent of indigenous peoples has been obtained, through, inter alia making the nominations publicly available in appropriate languages and public consultations and hearings.

Decision 39 COM 11

123. 当地社区、本地居民、政府、非政府及私人组织、其他利益相关者参与申报过程中，必须使他们与缔约国共同承担保护遗产的责任。各《公约》缔约国应努力确保遗产地最广泛的利益相关者参与，并通过各种各样的宣传和展示，通过能够被充分理解的语言，通过公共咨询与听证，来达成当地群众对申遗自觉自愿的支持。

第 39 COM 11 决定

124. Preparatory Assistance, as described in Chapter VII.E, may be requested by States Parties for the preparation of nominations.

124. 如第 VII.E 章节中所述，缔约国准备申报时可以申请“筹备协助”。

125. States Parties are encouraged to contact the Secretariat, which can provide assistance throughout the nomination process.

125. 鼓励缔约国与秘书处联系，秘书处能够在整个申报过程中提供帮助。

126. The Secretariat can also provide:

a) assistance in identifying appropriate maps and photographs and the national agencies from which these may be obtained;

b) examples of successful nominations, of

126. 秘书处还能：

a）在确定合适的地图和照片以及从哪些国家机构、部门获取这些资料方面提供帮助；

b）提供成功申报案例以及管理方法和立法

management and legislative provisions;

c) guidance for nominating different types of properties, such as Cultural Landscapes, Towns, Canals, and Heritage Routes (see Annex 3)

d) guidance for nominating serial and transboundary properties (see paragraphs 134-139).

条款上的参考范例；

c）为不同类别的遗产申报提供指导，例如文化景观、城镇、运河和遗产线路（见附件 3）

d）为申报系列遗产和跨境遗产提供指导（见第 134 至 139 条）。

127. States Parties may submit draft nominations to the Secretariat for comment and review at any time during the year. However, States Parties are strongly encouraged to transmit to the Secretariat by 30 September of the preceding year (see paragraph 168) the draft nominations that they wish to submit by the 1 February deadline. This submission of a draft nomination should include maps showing the boundaries for the proposed site. Draft nominations could be submitted either in electronic format or in printed version (only in 1 copy without annexes except for maps). In both cases they should be accompanied by a cover letter.

Decision 37 COM 12.I

127. 缔约国可以在每个预备申报年度中的任何时间向秘书处提交申报文本提名草案，以获取秘书处的修改意见和建议。但建议缔约国于上一年度申报年度的的 9 月 30 日前（见 168 页），上报他们希望在来年的 2 月 1 日前提交的正式申报的草案。提交的草案应包括划定遗产的边界地图。提交的草案可以是以电子文档也可以是纸质文本（只含一个地图附件）。两种形式均要有封面。

第 37 COM 12.II

128. Nominations may be submitted at any time during the year, but only those nominations that are "complete" (see paragraph 132 and Annex 5) and received by the Secretariat on or before 1 February[①] will be considered for inscription on the World Heritage List by the World Heritage Committee during the following year. Only nominations of properties included in the State Party's Tentative List will be examined by the Committee (see paragraph 63 and 65).

Decision 37 COM 12.II, Decision 39 COM 11

128. 任何时候都可以提交申报，但只有在二月一日[①]或之前递交到秘书处且“完整”的申报（见第 132 条及附件 5）才会被世界遗产委员审核，决定次年是否列入《世界遗产名录》。委员会只审查已包含在缔约国《预备名录》上的遗产（见 63、65 条）。

第 37 COM 12.II 及第 39 COM 11 决定

III.B Format and content of nominations

III.B 申报文件的格式和内容

129. Nominations of properties for inscription on the World Heritage List should be prepared in

129.《世界遗产名录》申报应依据附件 5 所示格式提交材料。

---

① If 1 February falls on a weekend, the nomination must be received by 17h00 GMT the preceding Friday.
如果 2 月 1 日是周末，申报必须在前一个周五格林威治时间 17 : 00 前收到。

accordance with the format set out in Annex 5.

130. The format includes the following sections:
1. Identification of the Property
2. Description of the Property
3. Justification for Inscription
4. State of conservation and factors affecting the property
5. Protection and Management
6. Monitoring
7. Documentation
8. Contact Information of responsible authorities
9. Signature on behalf of the State Party (ies)

130. 格式包括如下部分：
1. 遗产的辨认
2. 遗产描述
3. 列入理由
4. 保护状况和影响因素
5. 保护和管理
6. 监测
7. 文件
8. 负责机构的联系信息
9. 缔约国代表签名

131. Nominations to the World Heritage List are evaluated on content rather than on appearance.

131.《世界遗产名录》申报是重内容轻表象的。

132. For a nomination to be considered as 'complete', the following requirements (see format in Annex 5) are to be met:

Decision 37 COM 12.II Decision 39 COM 11

Executive Summary

An Executive Summary shall include essential information (see Annex 5) extracted from the main text of the nomination including a reduced size version of the map (s) indicating the boundaries of the nominated property and of the buffer zone (where appropriate) and the draft Statement of Outstanding Universal Value (the same text presented in Section 3.3 of the nomination)

1. Identification of the Property

The boundaries of the property being proposed shall be clearly defined, unambiguously distinguishing between the nominated property and any buffer zone (when present) (see paragraphs 103-107). Maps shall be sufficiently detailed (see Explanatory Note of section 1.e in Annex 5) to determine precisely which area of land and/or water is nominated. Officially up-to-date published topographic maps of the State Party annotated to

132.“完整”申报需要满足下列要求（见附件 5 的格式）：

第 37 COM 12.II 及第 39 COM 11 决定

执行摘要

执行摘要包括从申遗文本中摘取的主要信息（见附件 5）. 包括指明申报遗产边界和缓冲区（合适）的缩版地图及突出普遍价值声明草案（与申遗文本 3.3 部分内容一致）。

1. 遗产认定

应清晰地定义申报遗产边界，清楚区分申报遗产和任何缓冲区（若存在）（见 103–107 条）的界限。地图应足够详细，能精确（见附件 5.1.e 部分的附注）标出所申报的陆地或水域。若有可能，应提供缔约国最新的官方出版的印刷版地形图，清晰标注遗产和缓冲区（如显示）的边界。如果没有清晰的边界定义，申报会被认为“不完整”。

show the property boundaries and any buffer zone (when present) shall be provided if available in printed version. A nomination shall be considered "incomplete" if it does not include clearly defined boundaries.

2. Description of the Property

The Description of the property shall include the identification of the property, and an overview of its history and development. All component parts that are mapped shall be identified and described. In particular, where serial nominations are proposed, each of the component parts shall be clearly described.

The History and Development of the property shall describe how the property has reached its present form and the significant changes that it has undergone. This information shall provide the important facts needed to support and give substance to the argument that the property meets the criteria of Outstanding Universal Value and conditions of integrity and/or authenticity.

3. Justification for Inscription

This section must make clear why the property is considered to be of Outstanding Universal Value.

The comparative analyses prepared by States Parties when nominating properties for inscription in the World Heritage List should not be confused with the thematic studies prepared by the Advisory Bodies at the request of the Committee (paragraph 148 below)

Decision 7 EXT.COM 4A

The text in sections from 3.1.a to 3.1.e should contain more detailed information to support the text of the proposed Statement of Outstanding Universal Value (section 3.3).

Section 3.1.b shall indicate the World Heritage criteria (see Paragraph 77) under which the property is proposed, together with a clearly stated argument for the use of each criterion. Statements of integrity

2. 遗产描述

遗产描述应包括遗产认定、历史及发展概述。应确认、描述地图标注的所有组成部分，如果是系列申报，应清晰描述每一组成部分。

在遗产的历史和发展中应描述遗产是如何形成现在的状态以及所经历的重大变化。这些信息应包含所需的重要事实，以证实遗产达到突出普遍价值的标准，满足完整性和真实性的条件。

3. 列入理由

本部分必须明确为何认为遗产拥有突出普遍价值。

缔约国申报遗产时提交的对比分析不可与委员会要求咨询机构做的专题研究相混淆。（见下文 148.）

第 7 EXT.COM 4A 决定

本部分第 3.1.a 至 3.1.e 将包含更多详细信息以支持拟定的突出普遍价值声明（见 3.3）。

3.1.b 部分，本部分应指出遗产申报依据的标准（见 77 条），且须明确说明依据此标准的原因。同时附上完整性（当涉及文化标准时）和真实性声明，且须展示该遗产如何满足 78–95

and (when cultural criteria are proposed) of authenticity shall be included and shall demonstrate how the property satisfies the conditions outlined in paragraphs 78-95.

条所述的条件。

In section 3.2, a comparative analysis of the property in relation to similar properties, whether or not on the World Heritage List, both at the national and international levels, shall be provided. The comparative analysis shall explain the importance of the nominated property in its national and international context.

在 3.2 部分，应提供该遗产与类似遗产的比较分析，无论用于比较分析的类似遗产是否列入《世界遗产名录》。比较分析应说明申报遗产在国内及国际范围的重要性。

In section 3.3, a proposed Statement of Outstanding Universal Value (see paragraphs 49-53 and 155) of the property prepared by the State Party shall make clear why the property is considered to merit inscription on the World Heritage List.

在 3.3 部分，缔约国应在提交的遗产《突出普遍价值声明》（见 49-53 条及 155 条）中明确说明为什么该遗产值得列入《世界遗产名录》。

4. State of conservation and factors affecting the property

4. 保护状况和影响因素

This section shall include accurate information on the present state of conservation of the property (including information on its physical condition of the property and conservation measures in place). It shall also include a description of the factors affecting the property (including threats). Information provided in this section constitutes the baseline data which are necessary to monitor the state of conservation of the nominated property in the future.

本部分应包括目前遗产保护状况的准确信息（包括遗产的物理状况和到位的保护措施）。同时，也应包括影响遗产的因素描述（包括威胁）。本部分提供的信息是将来监测该遗产保护状况必要的基线数据。

5. Protection and management

5. 保护和管理

Protection: Section 5 shall include the list of the legislative, regulatory, contractual, planning, institutional and/ or traditional measures most relevant to the protection of the property and provide a detailed analysis of the way in which this protection actually operates. Legislative, regulatory, contractual planning and/or institutional texts, or an abstract of the texts, shall also be attached in English or French.

保护：第五部分包括与遗产保护联系最为紧密的立法、规章、契约、规划、机构或传统措施，并详尽分析了实际保护措施的操作方法。立法、规章、契约、规划和机构性文本或文本摘要应以英语或法语附上。

Management: An appropriate management plan or other management system is essential and

管理：适宜的管理规划或其他管理体制很必要，应包括在申报文件中，并期待确保管理

shall be provided in the nomination. Assurances of the effective implementation of the management plan or other management system are also expected. Sustainable development principles should be integrated into the management system.

规划或其他管理体制可以得到有效执行。可持续发展原则应综合纳入管理体系。

A copy of the management plan or documentation of the management system shall be annexed to the nomination. If the management plan exists only in a language other than English or French, an English or French detailed description of its provisions shall be annexed.

管理规划或者管理体制文献的副本应附在申报文件后。如果管理规划为非英文或非法文，应附上英语或法语的条款详述。

A detailed analysis or explanation of the management plan or a documented management system shall be provided in Section 5.e of the nomination.

应在申报文件 5.e 部分提供管理规划或者管理体系的详尽分析或者说明。

A nomination which does not include the above-mentioned documents is considered incomplete unless other documents guiding the management of the property until the finalization of the management plan are provided as outlined in paragraph 115.

申报文件若不包括上述文书则被认为不完整，除非在管理规划完成之前，依据 115 条所述，提交指导遗产管理的其他文书。

6. Monitoring

6. 监测

States Parties shall include the key indicators in place and/or proposed to measure and assess the state of conservation of the property, the factors affecting it, conservation measures at the property, the periodicity of their examination, and the identity of the responsible authorities.

缔约国应在申报材料中提供衡量、评估遗产保护状况的关键指标、其影响因素、遗产保护措施、审查周期及负责机构的名称。

7. Documentation

7. 文件

All documentation necessary to substantiate the nomination shall be provided. In addition to what is indicated above, this shall include a) images of a quality suitable for printing (digital photographs at 300 dpi minimum, and, if possible, 35 mm slides, and if essential, supplementary film, video or other audio visual material; and

b) image/audiovisual inventory and authorization form (see Annex 5, point 7.a). The text of the nomination shall be transmitted in printed form as well as in electronic format (Word and/or PDF format preferred)

应提供申报所需的所有文件。除了上述文件之外，还应包括：

1）达到打印标准的照片（像素不得低于 300dpi；如可能，35mm 幻灯片；如必要，补充电影、录像或其他视听材料）；

2）图像清单以及授权表（见附件 5，7a）。申报文本应以打印形式和电子文档提交（word 或 pdf 文件为佳）

8. Contact Information of responsible authorities

Detailed contact information of responsible authorities shall be provided.

9. Signature on behalf of the State Party

The nomination shall conclude with the original signature of the official empowered to sign it on behalf of the State Party.

10. Number of printed copies required (including maps annexed)

• Nominations of cultural properties (excluding cultural landscapes) : 2 identical copies

• Nominations of natural properties and cultural landscapes: 3 identical copies

• Nominations of mixed properties: 4 identical copies

11. Paper and electronic format

Nominations shall be presented on A4-size paper (or 'letter'); and in electronic format (Word and/or PDF format).

12. Sending

States Parties shall submit the nomination in English or French duly signed, to:

UNESCO World Heritage Centre
7, place de Fontenoy 75352 Paris 07 SP
France
Tel: +33 (0) 1 4568 1136
Fax: +33 (0) 1 4568 5570
E-mail: wh-nominations@unesco.org

133. The Secretariat will retain all supporting documentation (maps, plans, photographic material, etc.) submitted with the nomination.

III.C Requirements for the nomination of different types of properties

Transboundary properties

134. A nominated property may occur:

a) on the territory of a single State Party, or

8. 负责机构的联系信息

应提供负责机构的详细联系信息。

9. 缔约国代表签名

申报材料结尾应有缔约国授权的官方原始签名。

10. 所需打印数量（含地图附件）

• 文化遗产申报文件（不包括文化景观）：2 份

• 自然遗产和文化景观申报：3 份

• 混合遗产申报：4 份

11. 文件和电子版

申报材料应使用 A4 纸张（或信纸），同时有电子版（Word 和 / 或 PDF 格式）。

12. 寄送

缔约国应提交正式签署的英语或法语申报材料，至：

法国巴黎　联合国教科文组织　世界遗产中心（7，place de Fontenoy 75352 Paris 07 SP）

电话：+33（0）1 4568 1136
传真：+33（0）1 4568 5570
Email：wh-nominations@unesco.org

133. 秘书处会保留和申报文本一起提交的所有相关资料（地图、规划、照片资料等）

III.C 各类遗产申报的要求

跨境遗产

134. 申报的遗产可能

a）位于一个缔约国境内；

Decision 7 EXT.COM 4A

b) on the territory of all concerned States Parties having adjacent borders (transboundary property).

135. Wherever possible, transboundary nominations should be prepared and submitted by States Parties jointly in conformity with Article 11.3 of the *Convention*. It is highly recommended that the States Parties concerned establish a joint management committee or similar body to oversee the management of the whole of a transboundary property.

136. Extensions to an existing World Heritage property located in one State Party may be proposed to become transboundary properties.

Serial properties

137. Serial properties will include two or more component parts related by clearly defined links:

a) Component parts should reflect cultural, social or functional links over time that provide, where relevant, landscape, ecological, evolutionary or habitat connectivity.

b) Each component part should contribute to the Outstanding Universal Value of the property as a whole in a substantial, scientific, readily defined and discernible way, and may include, inter alia, intangible attributes. The resulting Outstanding Universal Value should be easily understood and communicated.

c) Consistently, and in order to avoid an excessive fragmentation of component parts, the process of nomination of the property, including the selection of the component parts, should take fully into account the overall manageability and coherence of the property (see paragraph 114) and provided it is the series as a whole - and not necessarily the individual parts of it - which are of Outstanding Universal Value.

第 7EXT.COM 4A 号决定

b）位于几个接壤的缔约国境内（跨境遗产）。

135. 跨境遗产的申报应尽可能由几个缔约国遵照大会公约第 11.3 条要求共同准备和递交。大会强烈建议各相关缔约国建立联合管理委员会或类似组织，监督该遗产的总体管理。

136. 位于一个缔约国境内的现有世界遗产的扩展部分可以申请成为跨境遗产。

系列遗产

137. 系列遗产应包括两个或两个以上逻辑联系清晰的组成部分：

1）各组成部分应体现因长期发展而形成的文化、社会或功能性关联的相互联系，进而形成景观、生态、空间演变或栖居地上的关联性；

2）每个组成部分都应对遗产整体的突出普遍价值有实质性、科学的、可清晰界定和辨识的贡献，亦可包含无形载体。最终的突出普遍价值应该是容易理解和便于沟通的；

3）与此一致的，为避免各组成部分过度分裂，遗产申报的过程，包括对各组成部分的选择，应该充分考虑遗产整体的连贯性和管理上的可行性（见第 144 条），并作为整体系列共同提交——不必分解成独立个体——体现共同的突出普遍价值。

138. A serial nominated property may occur :

a) on the territory of a single State Party (serial national property); or

b) within the territory of different States Parties, which need not be contiguous and is nominated with the consent of all States Parties concerned (serial transnational property)

Decision 7 EXT.COM 4A

138. 申报的系列遗产可能

a）位于一个缔约国境内（本国系列遗产）；

b）位于不同缔约国境内，不必相连，同时须经所有相关缔约国同意，方可进行申报（跨国系列遗产）。

第 7EXT.COM 4A 号决定

139. Serial nominations, whether from one State Party or multiple States, may be submitted for evaluation over several nomination cycles, provided that the first property nominated is of Outstanding Universal Value in its own right. States Parties planning serial nominations phased over several nomination cycles are encouraged to inform the Committee of their intention in order to ensure better planning.

139. 如申报的第一项遗产本身具有突出普遍价值，系列遗产（无论是由一国或是多国提起的）可历经数个申报周期，递交申报文件并接受评估。计划在数轮周期中分阶段进行系列申报的缔约国可向委员会说明此意向，以确保计划更加完善。

III.D Registration of nominations

III.D 申报登记

140. On receipt of nominations from States Parties, the Secretariat will acknowledge receipt, check for completeness and register nominations. The Secretariat will forward complete nominations to the relevant Advisory Bodies for evaluation. The Secretariat will also make available the electronic format of the text of the nominations to the members of the Committee on the World Heritage Centre's website.The Secretariat will request any additional information from the State Party and when required by Advisory Bodies. The timetable for registration and processing of nominations is detailed in paragraph 168.

Decision 39 COM 11

140. 收到各缔约国递交的申报文件后，秘书处将发回执确认收到资料，核查材料是否完整，然后进行申报登记。秘书处将向相关咨询机构转交完整的申报文件进行评估。秘书处将在世界遗产中心网站上提供电子版申报文件格式给委员会成员。经咨询机构提请，秘书处将向缔约国索要补充信息。登记的时间表和申报的受理过程在第 168 条中有详细说明。

第 39 COM 11 决定

141. The Secretariat establishes and submits at each Committee session a list of all nominations received, including the date of reception, an indication of their status 'complete' or 'incomplete',

141. 秘书处在每届委员会会议时拟定并递交一份已收到的所有申报遗产的名单，包括接受草案的日期，接受官方最后提交文本的日期，申报文件“完整”与否的陈述，以及按照第 132

as well as the date at which they are considered as 'complete' in conformity with paragraph 132 and Annex 5.

条及附件 5 的要求将申报文件补充完整的日期。

Decisions 26 COM 14 and 28 COM 14B.57

第 26 COM 14 和 28 COM 14B.57 号决定

142. A nomination passes through a cycle between the time of its submission and the decision by the World Heritage Committee. This cycle normally lasts one and a half years between submission in February of Year 1 and the decision of the Committee in June of Year 2.

142. 申报周期从递交之日起到世界遗产委员会做出决定之日结束。从每年二月缔约国递交申报材料至第二年六月委员会做出决定，通常历时一年半。

III.E. Evaluation of nominations by the Advisory Bodies

III.E. 咨询机构评估

143. The Advisory Bodies will evaluate whether or not properties nominated by States Parties have Outstanding Universal Value, meet the conditions of integrity and (when relevant) of authenticity and meet the requirements of protection and management. The procedures and format of ICOMOS and IUCN evaluations are described in Annex 6.

143. 咨询机构将评估各缔约国申报的遗产是否具有突出的普遍价值，是否符合完整性（如有关系时）和真实性条件，以及是否能达到保护和管理的要求。国际古迹遗址理事会和世界自然保护联盟的评估程序和格式，在附件 6 中有详细说明。

Decision 39 COM 11

第 39 COM 11 号决定

144. Evaluations of cultural heritage nominations will be carried out by ICOMOS.

144. 对文化遗产申报的评估将由国际古迹遗址理事会完成。

145. Evaluations of natural heritage nominations will be carried out by IUCN.

145. 对自然遗产申报的评估将由世界自然保护联盟完成。

146. In the case of nominations of cultural properties in the category of 'cultural landscapes', as appropriate, the evaluation will be carried out by ICOMOS in consultation with IUCN. For mixed properties, the evaluation will be carried out jointly by ICOMOS and IUCN.

146. 作为“文化景观”类申报的文化遗产，将由国际古迹遗址理事会与世界自然保护联盟磋商之后进行评估。对于混合遗产的评估将由国际古迹遗址理事会与世界自然保护联盟共同完成。

147. As requested by the World Heritage Committee or as necessary, ICOMOS and IUCN

147. 如经世界遗产委员会要求或者在必要情况下，国际古迹遗址理事会与世界自然保护

will carry out thematic studies to evaluate proposed World Heritage properties in their regional, global or thematic context. These studies should be informed by a review of the Tentative Lists submitted by States Parties and by reports of meetings on the harmonization of Tentative Lists, as well as by other technical studies performed by the Advisory Bodies and qualified organizations and individuals. A list of those studies already completed may be found in section III of Annex 3, and on the Web addresses of the Advisory Bodies. These studies should not be confused with the comparative analysis to be prepared by States Parties in nominating properties for inscription on the World Heritage List (see paragraph 132).

ICOMOS: http: //www.icomos.org/studies/

IUCN: http: //www.iucn.org/themes/wcpa/pubs/Worldheritage.htm

联盟将开展主题研究，将申报的世界遗产置于地区、全球或主题背景中进行评估。这些研究必须建立在对各缔约国递交的预备名录的审议、关于平衡预备名录会议报告、以及由咨询机构或具备相关资质的组织或个人进行的其他技术研究的基础之上。已完成的相关研究列表，见附件 3 第三节和咨询机构的网站。这些研究不得与缔约国在申报世界遗产时准备的“比较分析”相混淆（见第 132 条）。

国际古迹遗址理事会：

http ：//www.icomos.org/studies/

世界自然保护联盟：

http ：//www.iucn.org/themes/wcpa/pubs/Worldheritage.htm

148. The following principles must guide the evaluations and presentations of ICOMOS and IUCN. The evaluations and presentations should:

Decision 28 COM 14B.57.3 Decision 30 COM 13

Decision 7 EXT.COM 4A

a) adhere to the *World Heritage Convention* and the relevant *Operational Guidelines* and any additional policies set out by the Committee in its decisions;

b) be objective, rigorous and scientific including in considering all information provided to the Advisory Bodies regarding a nomination

c) be conducted to a consistent standard of professionalism; equity and transparency throughout the evaluation process in consultation and dialogue with nominating States Parties;

d) comply to standard format, both for evaluations and presentations, to be agreed with the Secretariat and include the name of the experts who participated in the evaluation process, except desk

148. 以下为国际古迹遗址理事会和世界自然保护联盟的评估与陈述所遵循的原则。评估与陈述应：

第 28 COM 14B.57.3，第 30 COM 13 号及 7 EXT.COM 4A 决定

a）遵守《世界遗产公约》及其《操作指南》，以及委员会在决定中规定的其他政策；

b）所有提交给咨询机构的、与申报有关的信息都要做到客观、严谨和科学；

c）依照一致的专业标准；保证整个评估过程中与申遗缔约国的协商和对话公正透明；

d）遵从评估与报告的标准格式，在秘书处的认可下，列出所有参与评估过程的专家姓名，进行保密评估的专家除外；并在附件中列出评估相关开支的明细详单。

reviewers who provide confidential reviews, and, in an annex, a detailed breakdown of all costs and expenses related to the evaluation;

e) involve regional experts familiar with the subject;

f) indicate clearly and separately whether the property has Outstanding Universal Value, meets the conditions of integrity and/or authenticity, a management plan/system and legislative protection;

g) evaluate each property systematically according to all relevant criteria, including its state of conservation, relatively, that is, by comparison with that of other properties of the same type, both inside and outside the State Party's territory;

h) include references to Committee decisions and requests concerning the nomination under consideration;

i) not take into account or include any information submitted by the State Party after 28 February, in the year in which the nomination is considered. The State Party should be informed when information has arrived after the deadline and is not being taken into account in the evaluation. This deadline should be rigorously enforced; and

j) provide a justification for their views through a list of references (literature) consulted, as appropriate.

e）需要熟悉项目的区域专家；

f）清晰、明确地指出所申报遗产是否具有突出普遍价值，是否符合完整性和真实性的标准，是否拥有管理规划、管理系统和立法保护；

g）根据所有相关标准，对每处遗产（包括其保护状况），进行系统的对比性的评估，即需与缔约国境内或境外其他同类遗产进行比较；

h）应注明所引用的与被审议的申报项目相关的委员会决定和要求；

i）不考虑或计入缔约国于申报审议当年的2月28日后递交的任何信息。同时应通知缔约国，因收到的信息已逾期，所以不纳入考虑之列。必须严格遵守最后期限；

j）适时提供支持他们论点的参考书目（文献）。

149. The Advisory Bodies are requested to forward to States Parties, with copy to the World Heritage Centre for distribution to the Chair of the World Heritage Committee, by 31 January of each year a short interim report outlining the status and any issues relevant to evaluations, and detailing any requests for supplementary information, in one of the two working languages of the Convention.

Decision 7 EXT.COM 4B.1, Decision 39 COM 11

149. 咨询机构向缔约国提供评估报告，副本送世界遗产中心及委员会主席，在每年的1月31日以前，以一或两种公约要求的工作语言，提交简短的临时状况概要及与评估相关的问题、需要补充的详细信息报告。

第7 EXT.COM 4B.1 及 39 COM 11 号决定

150. Letters from the concerned States Parties, submitted in the appropriate form in Annex 12,

150. 相关缔约国应邀在委员会大会开幕至少14天前，按附件12提供的格式，致信世界

detailing the factual errors that might have been identified in the evaluation of their nomination made by the Advisory Bodies, must be received by the World Heritage Centre no later than 14 days before the opening of the session of the Committee with copies to the relevant Advisory Bodies. The letters shall be made available as an annex to the documents for the relevant agenda item, and no later than the first day of the Committee session. The World Heritage Centre and the Advisory Bodies may add their comments to the letters, in the relevant section of the form, before they are made available.

Decision 7 EXT.COM 4B.1

Decision 37 COM 12.II

遗产中心，详细说明咨询机构在其关于申报的评估意见中发现的事实性错误。该信副本抄送咨询机构。此信件作为相关议程文件的有效附件，将在委员会会议第一天提交。世界遗产中心和咨询委员会将按相关格式在该信件提交前提出他们的意见。

第 7 EXT.COM 4B.1、37 COM 12.II 号决定

151. ICOMOS and IUCN make their recommendations under three categories:

a) properties which are recommended for inscription without reservation;

b) properties which are not recommended for inscription;

c) nominations which are recommended for referral or deferral

151. 国际古迹遗址理事会和世界自然保护联盟的意见分三类：

a）建议无保留列入《世界遗产名录》的遗产；

b）建议不予列入《世界遗产名录》的遗产；

c）建议发还待议或推迟申报《世界遗产名录》的遗产。

III.F Withdrawal of nominations

III.F 撤销申报

152. A State Party may withdraw a nomination it has submitted at any time prior to the Committee session at which it is scheduled to be examined. The State Party should inform the Secretariat in writing of its intention to withdraw the nomination. If the State Party so wishes it can resubmit a nomination for the property, which will be considered as a new nomination according to the procedures and timetable outlined in paragraph 168.

152. 缔约国可以在委员会召开会议审核申报之前任何时候撤销所递交的申报，但必须以书面形式向秘书处说明意图。如某缔约国希望撤回申报，它可以重新递交一份遗产的申报，根据第 168 条所列程序和时间表，该申报将会被作为一项新申报。

III.G Decision of the World Heritage Committee

III.G 世界遗产委员会的决定

153. The World Heritage Committee decides whether a property should or should not be

153. 世界遗产委员会决定一项遗产是否应被列入《世界遗产名录》、待议或推迟申报。

inscribed on the World Heritage List, referred or deferred.

Inscription

154. When deciding to inscribe a property on the World Heritage List, the Committee, guided by the Advisory Bodies, adopts a Statement of Outstanding Universal Value for the property.

155. The Statement of Outstanding Universal Value should include a summary of the Committee's determination that the property has Outstanding Universal Value, identifying the criteria under which the property was inscribed, including the assessments of the conditions of integrity and, for cultural and mixed properties, or authenticity. It should also include a statement on the protection and management in force and the requirements for protection and management for the future. The Statement of Outstanding Universal Value shall be the basis for the future protection and management of the property.

Where necessary, the protection and management part of the Statement of Outstanding Universal Value may be updated by the World Heritage Committee, in consultation with the State Party and further to a review by the Advisory Bodies. Such updates could be made periodically further to the outcomes of Periodic reporting cycles, or at any Committee session, if required.

The World Heritage Centre will automatically keep the Statements of Outstanding Universal Value updated further to subsequent decisions taken by the Committee concerning a change of name of the property and change of surface further to minor boundary modifications and correct any factual errors as agreed with the relevant Advisory Bodies.

列入名录

154. 决定将遗产列入《世界遗产名录》时，在咨询机构的指导下，委员会将通过该遗产的《突出普遍价值声明》。

155. 突出普遍价值声明》应包括委员会确定该遗产具有突出普遍价值的决定摘要，明确遗产列入《世界遗产名录》所遵循的标准，包括完整性，文化或混合遗产的真实性状况。也包括有效保护和管理的声明及未来遗产保护、管理的要求。突出普遍价值声明将作为未来该遗产的保护和管理的基础。

必要时，突出普遍价值声明中的保护管理部分，在世界遗产委员会与缔约国协商并经咨询机构审核后更新。这类更新日后将作为定期报告的周期成果或根据委员会的要求定期进行。

世界遗产中心将根据委员会后续决定自动保持突出普遍价值声明的更新，如有关遗产名称或表面的变化，细微的边界调整或经咨询机构认可的对事实性错误的修正。

In the framework of the Gender Equality Priority of UNESCO, the use of gender-neutral language in the preparation of Statements of Outstanding Universal Value is encouraged.

在联合国教科文组织社会属性平等优先的框架下，鼓励使用中性语言准备突出普遍价值声明。

156. At the time of inscription, the Committee may also make other recommendations concerning the protection and management of the World Heritage property.

156. 列入《世界遗产名录》时，委员会也可就该世界遗产的保护和管理提出其他的建议。

157. The Statement of Outstanding Universal Value (including the criteria for which a specific property is inscribed on the World Heritage List) will be set out by the Committee in its reports and publications.

157. 委员会将在其报告和出版物中公布《突出普遍价值声明》（包括某具体遗产列入《世界遗产名录》的标准）。

Decision not to inscribe

决定不予列入

158. If the Committee decides that a property should not be inscribed on the World Heritage List, the nomination may not again be presented to the Committee except in exceptional circumstances. These exceptional circumstances may include new discoveries, new scientific information about the property, or different criteria not presented in the original nomination. In these cases, anew nomination shall be submitted.

158. 如委员会决定某项遗产不予以列入《世界遗产名录》，除非在极特殊情况下，否则该项申报不可重新向委员会提交。这些例外情况包括新发现的、有关该遗产新的科学信息或者之前申报时未提出的不同标准。在上述情况下，允许提交新的申报。

Referral of Nominations

发还待议的申报

159. Nominations which the Committee decides to refer back tothe State Party for additional information may be resubmitted to the following Committee session for examination. The additional information must be received by the Secretariat by 1 February ① of the year in which examination by the Committee is desired. The Secretariat will

159. 委员会决定发还缔约国补充信息的申报材料，可以在下一次委员会会议上重新递交并接受审议。补充信息须在委员会拟定审议当年的 2 月 1 日前①呈交秘书处。秘书处将直接转交相关咨询机构进行评估。发还的申报材料如在原委员会决定下达三年内不曾反馈给委员会，再次递交审议时将被视为新申报，依据第 168

① If 1 February falls on a weekend, the nomination must be received by 17h00 GMT the preceding Friday.
如 2 月 1 日恰为周末，申报材料需于前一周的周五格林威治时间 17 点前递交至秘书处

immediately transmit it to the relevant Advisory Bodies for evaluation. A referred nomination which is not presented to the Committee within three years of the original Committee decision will be considered as a new nomination when it is resubmitted for examination, following the procedures and timetable outlined in paragraph 168. States Parties might seek advice from the relevant Advisory Body (ies) and/ or the World Heritage Centre to discuss how the recommendations of the Committee might be addressed.

Decision 39 COM 11

条所列程序及时间表进行。缔约国从相关咨询机构或世界遗产中心处寻求建议以讨论如何处理委员会的要求。

第 39 COM 11 号决定

Deferral of Nominations

推迟申报

160. The Committee may decide to defer a nomination for more in depth assessment or study, or a substantial revision by the State Party. Should the State Party decide to resubmit the deferred nomination in any subsequent year, it must be received by the Secretariat by 1 February ① . These nominations will then be reevaluated evaluated again by the relevant Advisory Bodies during the course of the full year and a half evaluation cycle including an evaluation mission according to the procedures and timetable outlined in in paragraph 168. States Parties are encouraged to seek advice from the relevant Advisory Body and/ or the World Heritage Centre to discuss how the recommendations of the Committee might be addressed. Where required, the State Parties may wish to consider inviting an Advisory mission.

Decision 39 COM 11

160. 为了进行更深入的评估和研究，或便于缔约国对申报材料进行重大修改，委员会可能会做出推迟申报的决定。如果该缔约国决定重新递交被推迟的申报，应于 2 月 1 日①之前向秘书处提起。届时相关咨询机构将根据第 168 条所列程序和时间表对这些申报重新进行周期为一年半的包括评估任务的评估。鼓励缔约国从相关咨询机构或世界遗产中心处寻求建议以讨论如何处理委员会的要求。必要时，缔约国也可以考虑发起一个咨询邀请。

第 39 COM 11 决定

III.H Nominations to be processed on an emergency basis

III.H 紧急受理的申报

161. The normal timetable and definition of

161. 通常的时间表和其定义完整的申报材

① If 1 February falls on a weekend, the nomination must be received by 17h00 GMT the preceding Friday.
如 2 月 1 日恰为周末，申报材料需于前一周的周五格林威治时间 17 点前递交至秘书处。

completeness for the submission and processing of nominations will not apply in the case of properties which would be in Danger, as a result of having suffered damage or facing serious and specific dangers from natural events or human activities, which would constitute an emergency situation for which an immediate decision by the Committee is necessary to ensure their safeguarding, and which, according to the report of the relevant Advisory Bodies, may unquestionably justify Outstanding Universal Value. Such nominations will be processed on an emergency basis and their examination is included in the agenda of the next Committee session. These properties may be inscribed on the World Heritage List. They shall, in that case, be simultaneously inscribed on the List of World Heritage in Danger (see paragraphs 177-191).

Decision 37 COM 12.II

料的提交和受理过程不可用于：在遗产处于危机状态，因自然或人类活动受到损害或面临严重或特别威胁，需要委员会立刻做出决定以保护其安全的紧急状态，或根据相关咨询机构的报告，无可非议的具有突出普遍价值时。这类申报将被紧急受理并在下次委员会会议议程中包含对该类遗产的审查。该遗产会被列入《世界遗产名录》，同时可能被列入《濒危世界遗产名录》（见第 177–191 条）

162. The procedure for nominations to be processed on an emergency basis is as follows:

162. 紧急受理申报的程序如下：

a) A State Party presents a nomination with the request for processing on an emergency basis. The State Party shall have already included, or immediately include, the property on its Tentative List.

a）缔约国呈交申报材料并要求紧急受理。该缔约国此前已将该项遗产列入《预备名录》，或立即将其纳入《预备名录》。

b) The nomination shall:

i) describe the property and identify precisely its boundaries;

ii) justify its Outstanding Universal Value according to the criteria;

iii) justify its integrity and/or authenticity;

iv) describe its protection and management system;

v) describe the nature of the emergency, and the nature and extent of the damage or specific danger and showing that immediate action by the Committee is necessary to ensure the safeguarding

b）该项申报应

i. 描述遗产及精确的定义边界；

ii. 根据标准论证其具有突出普遍价值；

iii. 证实其真实性 / 完整性

iv. 描述其保护和管理体制

v. 描述紧急状态的性质，损害的性质和程度或具体危险，以证明委员会需即刻采取的行动方可保证该遗产的存续。

of the property.

c) The Secretariat immediately transmits the nomination to the relevant Advisory Bodies, requesting an assessment of the qualities of the property which may justify its Outstanding Universal Value, of the nature of the danger and the urgency of a decision by the Committee. A field visit may be necessary if the relevant Advisory Bodies consider it appropriate and if the time allows.

c）由秘书处直接将该项申报转交相关咨询机构，要求对遗产品质中证明其突出普遍价值、对紧急情况或危险的性质及委员会的紧急决定进行评估。如相关咨询机构认为有必要且时间允许时，须进行实地勘查。

d) When reviewing the nomination the Committee will also consider:

d）如果重新审查申报文件委员会将考虑：

i) allocation of International Assistance to complete the nomination; and

i. 分配国际援助以完成该申报。

ii) follow-up missions as necessary by the Secretariat and the relevant Advisory Bodies as soon as possible after inscription to fulfill the Committee's recommendations.

ii. 必要时由秘书处和相关咨询机构组织后续工作，在遗产录入名录后尽快落实委员会的建议。

III.I Modifications to the boundaries, to the criteria used to justify inscription or to the name of a World Heritage property

III.I 修改世界遗产的边界、原列入标准或名称

Minor modifications to the boundaries

边界的细微调整

163. A minor modification is one which has not a significant impact on the extent of the property nor affects its Outstanding Universal Value.

163. 细微调整是指对遗产的范围进行不影响其突出普遍价值的非重大改动。

164. If a State Party wishes to request a minor modification to the boundaries of a property already on the World Heritage List, it must be prepared in compliance with the format of Annex 11 and must be received by 1 February [①] by the Committee through the Secretariat, which will seek the evaluation of the relevant Advisory Bodies on whether this can be considered a minor modification or not. The Secretariat shall then

164. 如某缔约国要求对已列入世界遗产名录的遗产边界进行细微调整，可于 2 月 1 日[①]前按照附件 11 要求的格式准备并通过秘书处向委员会递交申请。在征询相关咨询机构的意见之后，委员会或批准该申请，或认定足以构成重大边界修改，在后一种情况下适用新申报程序。

① If 1 February falls on a weekend, the nomination must be received by 17h00 GMT the preceding Friday.
如 2 月 1 日恰为周末，申报材料需于前一周的周五格林威治时间 17 点前递交至秘书处。

submit the Advisory Bodies' evaluation to the World Heritage Committee. The Committee may approve such a modification, or it may consider that the modification to the boundary is sufficiently significant as to constitute a significant boundary modification of the property, in which case the procedure for new nominations will apply.

Decision 39 COM 11

第 39 COM 11 决定

Significant modifications to the boundaries

边界重大修改

165. If a State Party wishes to significantly modify the boundary of a property already on the World Heritage List, the State Party shall submit this proposal as if it were a new nomination (including the requirement to be previously included on the Tentative List - see paragraph 63 and 65). This re-nomination shall be presented by 1 February [①] and will be evaluated in the full year and a half cycle of evaluation according to the procedures and timetable outlined in paragraph 168. This provision applies to extensions, as well as reductions.

Decision 39 COM 11

165. 如某缔约国提出对已列入世界遗产名录的遗产边界进行重大修改，该缔约国应将其视为新申报并提交申请（包括先列入预备名录的要求—见 63–65 条）。新的申报材料应于 2 月 1 日[①]以前递交，并根据第 168 条所列程序和时间表接受周期为一年半的评估。对遗产边界的扩大和缩小同时适用该规定。

第 39 COM 11 决定

Modifications to the criteria used to justify inscription on the World Heritage List

《世界遗产名录》所依据标准的修改

166. Where a State Party wishes to have the property inscribed under additional, fewer or different criteria other than those used for the original inscription, it shall submit this request as if it were a new nomination (including the requirement to be previously included on the Tentative List - see paragraph 63 and 65). This re-nomination must be received by 1 February [①] and

166. 当某缔约国希望增加或减少原列入标准，或选择补充标准或不同于原列入标准的其他标准，该国应将其视为新的申报项目提交申请（包括先列入预备名录的要求——见 63–65 条）。再次申报应于 2 月 1 日[①]以前递交，并根据第 168 条所列程序和时间表接受周期为一年半的评估。所推荐遗产将只依照新的标准接受评估。即使最后对补充标准不予认定，该项遗

① If 1 February falls on a weekend, the nomination must be received by 17h00 GMT the preceding Friday.
如 2 月 1 日恰为周末，申报材料需于前一周的周五格林威治时间 17 点前递交至秘书处。

② If 1 February falls on a weekend, the nomination must be received by 17h00 GMT the preceding Friday.
如 2 月 1 日恰为周末，申报材料需于前一周的周五格林威治时间 17 点前递交至秘书处。

will be evaluated in the full year and a half cycle of evaluation according to the procedures and timetable outlined in paragraph 168. Properties recommended will only be evaluated under the new criteria and will remain on the World Heritage List even if unsuccessful in having additional criteria recognized.

产仍将保留在《世界遗产名录》上。

Decision 39 COM 11

第 39 COM 11 决定

Modification to the name of a World Heritage property

世界遗产名称的更改

167. A State Party[①] may request that the Committee authorize a modification to the name of a property already inscribed on the World Heritage List. A request for a modification to the name shall be received by the Secretariat at least 3 months prior to the meeting of the Committee.

167. 缔约国[①]可提请委员会批准对已列入世界遗产名录的遗产名称进行更改。更名申请应至少在委员会会议前三个月递交秘书处。

168. III.J Timetable - overview
Decision 39 COM 11

168. 时间表概览
第 39 COM 11 决定

168.TIMETABLE	PROCEDURES
30 September (before Year 1)	Voluntary deadline for receipt of draft nominations from States Parties by the Secretariat.
15 November (before Year 1)	Secretariat to respond to the nominating State Party concerning the completeness of the draft nomination, and, if incomplete, to indicate the missing information required to make the nomination complete.
1 February Year 1	Deadline by which complete nominations must be received by the Secretariat to be transmitted to the relevant Advisory Bodies for evaluation. Nominations shall be received by 17h00 GMT, or, if the date falls on a weekend by 17h00 GMT the preceeding Friday. Nominations received after this date will be examined in a future cycle.

① *In case of transnational/trans-boundary properties any modification will need the agreement of all States Parties concerned.*
如果是跨境或跨界遗产，任何更改都要得到所有相关缔约国的同意。

续表

168.TIMETABLE	PROCEDURES
1 February - 1 March Year 1	Registration, assessment of completeness and transmission to the relevant Advisory Bodies. The Secretariat registers each nomination, acknowledges receipt to the nominating State Party and inventories its contents. The Secretariat will inform the nominating State Party whether or not the nomination is complete. Nominations that are not complete (see paragraph 132) will not be transmitted to the relevant Advisory Bodies for evaluation. If a nomination is incomplete, the State Party concerned will be advised of information required to complete the nomination by the deadline of 1 February of the following year in order for the nomination to be examined in a future cycle. Nominations that are complete are transmitted to the relevant Advisory Bodies for evaluation. The Secretariat will also make available the electronic format of the text of the nominations to the Members of the Committee on the World Heritage Centre's website.
1 March Year 1	Deadline by which the Secretariat informs the State Party of the receipt of a Nomination, whether it is considered complete and whether it has been received by 1 February.
March Year 1 - May Year 2	Evaluation by the Advisory Bodies
31 January Year 2	The Advisory Bodies are requested to forward to States Parties with copy to the World Heritage Centre for distribution to the Chair of the World Heritage Committee by 31 January of each year a short interim report outlining the status of and any issues relevant to evaluations, and detailing any requests for supplementary information, in one of the two working languages of the Convention. Deadline by which additional information requested by the relevant Advisory Bodies shall be submitted by the State Party to them via the Secretariat.
28 February Year 2	Additional information shall be submitted in the same number of copies and electronic formats as specified in Paragraph 132 to the Secretariat. To avoid confusing new and old texts, if the additional information submitted concerns changes to the main text of the nomination, the State Party shall submit these changes in an amended version of the original text. The changes shall be clearly identified. An electronic version (CD-ROM or diskette) of this new text shall accompany the paper version.
Six weeks prior to the annual World Heritage Committee session Year 2	The relevant Advisory Bodies deliver their evaluations and recommendations to the Secretariat for transmission to the World Heritage Committee as well as to States Parties.
At least 14 working days before the opening of	Correction of factual errors by States Parties. The concerned States Parties can send, at least 14 working days before the opening of the session of the Committee, a letter to the Chairperson, with copies to the Advisory Bodies, detailing the factual errors they might have identified in the evaluation of their nomination made by the Advisory Bodies.
Annual session of the World Heritage Committee (June/July) Year 2	The Committee examines the nominations and makes its decisions.
Immediately following the annual session of the World Heritage Committee	Notification to the States Parties The Secretariat notifies all States Parties whose nominations have been examined by the Committee of the relevant decisions of the Committee. Following the decision of the World Heritage Committee to inscribe a property on the World Heritage List, the Secretariat writes to the State Party and site managers providing a map of the area inscribed and the Statement of Outstanding Universal Value (to include reference to the criteria met) .

续表

168.TIMETABLE	PROCEDURES
Immediately following the annual session of the World Heritage Committee	The Secretariat publishes the updated World Heritage List every year following the annual session of the Committee. The name of the States Parties having nominated the properties inscribed on the World Heritage List are presented in the published form of the List under the following heading: "Contracting State having submitted the nomination of the property in accordance with the Convention".
In the month following the closure of the annual session of the World Heritage Committee	The Secretariat forwards the published report of all the decisions of the World Heritage Committee to all States Parties.

时间表	程序 第 39 COM 11 决定
9 月 30 日（前一年）	为各缔约国自愿向秘书处提交下年度申报文本初稿的最后期限。
11 月 15 日（前一年）	秘书处就申报材料初稿完整与否答复相关缔约国，如不完整，注明要求补充的信息。
第一年 2 月 1 日前	秘书处收到完整的申报材料以便转交相关咨询机构评估的最后期限。 申报材料必须在格林威治时间 17 点以前送达，如当天为周末则必须在前一个星期五的 17 点（格林威治时间）以前送达。 在此日期后收到的申报材料将进入下一周期审议。
第一年 2 月 1 日—3 月 1 日	登记、评估完整性及转交相关咨询机构。 秘书处对各项申报进行登记，向提交申报的缔约国下发回执并将申报内容编目。秘书处将通知提交申报的缔约国申报材料是否完整。 不完整的申报材料（见第 132 条）不予转交相关咨询机构进行评估。如材料不完整，相关缔约国将被通知于第二年 2 月 1 日最后期限以前补齐所缺信息以便参与下一周期的审议。 完整的申报材料由秘书处转交相关咨询机构进行评估。 秘书处将在世界遗产中心网站上给委员会成员提供申报文件电子格式。
第一年 3 月 1 日	秘书处告知各缔约国申报材料接收情况的最后期限，说明材料是否完整以及是否于 2 月 1 日以前收讫。
第一年 3 月—第二年 5 月	咨询机构的评估
第二年 1 月 31 日	咨询机构向缔约国进行征询，副本送世界遗产中心及委员会主席，在每年的 1 月 31 日以前，以一或两种公约要求的工作语言，提交简短的临时状况概要及与评估相关问题、需要补充的详细信息报告。 相关咨询机构要求缔约国补充的信息需在最后期限前通过秘书处提交。
第二年 2 月 28 日	向秘书处呈交的补充信息应依照第 132 条中具体列出的数量准备复印件和电子版。为了避免新旧文本的混淆，如所递交的补充信息中包含对申报材料主要内容的修改，缔约国应将修改部分作为原申报文件的修正版提交，修改的部分应标示清楚。新文本除印刷版外还应附上电子版（光盘或软盘）。
第二年世界遗产委员会年会前 6 周	相关咨询机构向秘书处递送评估意见和建议，由秘书处转发给世界遗产委员会及各缔约国。
第二年世界遗产委员会年会开幕前至少 14 个工作日	缔约国更正事实性错误。 相关缔约国可在委员会大会开幕前至少 14 个工作日致信大会主席，副本送咨询机构，详细说明在咨询机构关于申报材料的评估意见中发现的事实性错误。

续表

时间表	程序 第 39 COM 11 决定
第二年世界遗产委员会年会期间	委员会审议申报材料并做出决定。
第二年世界遗产委员会年会结束前	通知各缔约国。 凡经委员会审议的申报，秘书处将通知该缔约国有关委员会的相关决定。 在世界遗产委员会决定将某处遗产列入《世界遗产名录》之后，由秘书处书面通知该缔约国及遗产管理方，并提供列入名录区域的地图及《突出的普遍价值声明》（注明适用标准）。
第二年世界遗产委员会年会结束	每年委员会会议结束之后，秘书处随即公布最新的《世界遗产名录》。 公布的《世界遗产名录》将注明申报项目列入《名录》的缔约国名称，标题为："缔约国根据《公约》递交遗产申报"。
世界遗产委员会年会闭幕一个月后	秘书处将向各缔约国下发世界遗产委员会全部决定的公告。

IV. PROCESS FOR MONITORING THE STATE OF CONSERVATION OF WORLD HERITAGE PROPERTIES

IV. 对世界遗产保护状况的监测程序

IV.A Reactive Monitoring

IV.A 反应性监测

Definition of Reactive Monitoring

反应性监测的定义

169. Reactive Monitoring is the reporting by the Secretariat, other sectors of UNESCO and the Advisory Bodies to the Committee on the state of conservation of specific World Heritage properties that are under threat. To this end, the States Parties shall submit specific reports and impact studies each time exceptional circumstances occur or work is undertaken which may have an effect on the Outstanding Universal Value of the property or its state of conservation. Reactive Monitoring is also foreseen in reference to properties inscribed, or to be inscribed, on the List of World Heritage in Danger as set out in paragraphs 177-191.Reactive Monitoring is foreseen in the procedures for the eventual deletion of properties from the World Heritage List as set out in paragraphs 192-198.

Decision 39 COM 11

169. 反应性监测是指由秘书处、联合国教科文组织其他部门和咨询机构向委员会递交的有关具体世界遗产保护状况受到的威胁的报告。为此，每当出现异常情况或开展可能影响遗产突出普遍价值及保护状况的活动时，缔约国都须递交具体报告和影响研究。反应性监测也涉及已列入及待列入濒危世界遗产名录的遗产如第 177–191 条所述。同时如第 192–198 条所述，从《世界遗产名录》中彻底剔除某些遗产之前须进行反应性监测。

第 39 COM 11 决定

These reports shall be submitted to the World Heritage Committee through the Secretariat, using the standard format in Annex 13, in English or French:

a) by 1 December of the year preceding the examination of the property by the Committee, for the properties inscribed on the World Heritage List,

b) by 1 February of the year of examination of the property by the Committee, for the properties inscribed on the List of World Heritage in Danger, and for specific cases of utmost urgency.

这个报告需使用附件 13 中的标准格式，用英语或法语准备，经秘书处向世界遗产委员会提交：

a）在遗产申报世界遗产名录前委员会进行遗产检查程序的当年的 12 月 1 日，

b）在将遗产列入濒危名录或遗产面临特别危急情况下委员会进行遗产检查程序的当年 2 月 1 日。

Objective of Reactive Monitoring

反应性监测的目标

170. When adopting the process of Reactive Monitoring, the Committee was particularly concerned that all possible measures should be taken to prevent the deletion of any property from the List and was ready to offer technical co-operation as far as possible to States Parties in this connection.

Article 4 of the Convention: "Each State Party to this Convention recognizes that the duty of ensuring the identification, protection, conservation, presentation and transmission to future generations of the cultural and natural heritage referred to in Articles 1 and 2 and situated on its territory, belongs primarily to that State...".

170. 实施反应性监测程序时，委员会特别关注的是如何采取一切可能的措施，避免从《世界遗产名录》中移除任何遗产。因此，只要情况允许，委员会愿意向缔约国提供相关的技术合作。

《公约》第 4 条

“本公约缔约国均认同，保证第 1 条和第 2 条中提及的、本国领土内的文化和自然遗产的确定、保护、保存、展示和传承后世是有关国家的主要职责…”

171. The Committee recommends that States Parties co-operate with the Advisory Bodies which have been asked by the Committee to carry out monitoring and reporting on its behalf on the progress of work undertaken for the preservation of properties inscribed on the World Heritage List.

171. 委员会建议缔约国与委员会指定的咨询机构合作，这些咨询机构受命代表委员会对列入《世界遗产名录》的遗产的保护工作进展进行监督和汇报。

Information received from States Parties and/or other sources

来自缔约国和 / 或其他渠道的信息

172. The World Heritage Committee invites the States Parties to the *Convention* to inform the Committee, through the Secretariat, of their

172. 如《公约》缔约国将在受《公约》保护地区开展或批准开展有可能影响到遗产突出普遍价值的大规模修复或建设工程，世界遗产

intention to undertake or to authorize in an area protected under the *Convention* major restorations or new constructions which may affect the Outstanding Universal Value of the property. Notice should be given as soon as possible (for instance, before drafting basic documents for specific projects) and before making any decisions that would be difficult to reverse, so that the Committee may assist in seeking appropriate solutions to ensure that the Outstanding Universal Value of the property is fully preserved.

委员会促请缔约国通过秘书处向委员会转达该意图。缔约国必须尽快（例如，在起草具体工程的基本文件之前）在做出任何难以逆转的决定之前发布通告，以便委员会及时帮助寻找合适的解决办法，保证继续维护遗产的突出的普遍价值。

173. The World Heritage Committee requests that reports of missions to review the state of conservation of the World Heritage properties include:

Decision 27 COM 7B.106

a) an indication of threats or significant improvement in the conservation of the property since the last report to the World Heritage Committee;

b) any follow-up to previous decisions of the World Heritage Committee on the state of conservation of the property;

c) information on any threat or damage to or loss of Outstanding Universal Value, integrity and/or authenticity for which the property was inscribed on the World Heritage List.

173. 世界遗产委员会要求检查世界遗产保护状况的工作报告必须包括：

第 27 COM 7B.106 决定

a）说明自世界遗产委员会收到上一份报告以来，遗产所面临的威胁或保护工作取得的重大进步；

b）世界遗产委员会此前关于遗产保护状况的决定的后续执行工作；

c）有关遗产列入《世界遗产名录》的突出的普遍价值、完整性和真实性受到威胁、破坏或减损的信息。

174. When the Secretariat receives information that a property inscribed has seriously deteriorated, or that the necessary corrective measures have not been taken within the time proposed, from a source other than the State Party concerned, it will, as far as possible, verify the source and the contents of the information in consultation with the State Party concerned and request its comments.

174. 一旦秘书处从相关缔约国以外的渠道获悉，已列入《名录》的遗产严重受损或在拟定期限内未采取必要的调整措施，秘书处将与有关缔约国磋商、证实消息来源和内容的真实性并要求该国对此做出解释。

Decision by the World Heritage Committee

世界遗产委员会的决定

175. The Secretariat will request the relevant Advisory Bodies to forward comments on the information received.

175. 秘书处将要求相关咨询机构评价获取的信息。

176. The information received, together with the comments of the State Party and the Advisory Bodies, will be brought to the attention of the Committee in the form of a state of conservation report for each property, which may take one or more of the following steps:

Decision 39 COM 11

a) it may decide that the property has not seriously deteriorated and that no further action should be taken;

b) when the Committee considers that the property has seriously deteriorated, but not to the extent that its restoration is impossible, it may decide that the property be maintained on the List, provided that the State Party takes the necessary measures to restore the property within a reasonable period of time. The Committee may also decide that technical co-operation be provided under the World Heritage Fund for work connected with the restoration of the property, proposing to the State Party to request such assistance, if it has not already been done; in some circumstances States Parties may wish to invite an Advisory mission by the relevant Advisory Body (ies) or other organizations to seek advice on necessary measures to reverse deterioration and address threats.

176. 将获取的信息与相关缔约国和咨询机构的评价一起以遗产保护状况报告的形式呈交委员会审阅。委员会可采取以下一项或多项措施：

第 39 COM 11 决定

a）委员会可能认定该遗产未遭受严重损害，无须采取进一步行动；

b）当委员会认定该遗产确实遭受严重损害，但损害不至于不可修复，那么只要有关缔约国采取必要措施在合理时间期限内对其进行修复，该遗产仍可保留在《世界遗产名录》上。同时委员会也可能决定启动世界遗产基金对遗产修复工作提供技术合作，并建议尚未提出类似要求的缔约国提出技术援助申请；某些情况下缔约国也许会考虑向咨询机构或相关组织发出咨询邀请以寻求必要的措施来抵制退化或解决威胁。

c) when the requirements and criteria set out in paragraphs 177-182 are met, the Committee may decide to inscribe the property on the List of World Heritage in Danger according to the procedures set out in paragraphs 183-189;

d) when there is evidence that the property has deteriorated to the point where it has irretrievably lost those characteristics which determined its inscription on the List, the Committee may decide

c）当满足第 177–182 条中所列要求与标准时，委员会可决定依照第 183–189 条所列程序将该遗产列入《濒危遗产名录》；

d）如证据表明，该遗产所受损害已使其不可挽回地失去了列入世界遗产名录的诸项特征，委员会可能会做出决定将该遗产从《世界遗产名录》中剔除。在采取任何措施之前，秘书处

to delete the property from the List. Before any such action is taken, the Secretariat will inform the State Party concerned. Any comments which the State Party may make will be brought to the attention of the Committee;

都将通知相关缔约国。该缔约国做出的任何回应都将上呈委员会；

e) when the information available is not sufficient to enable the Committee to take one of the measures described in a), b), c) or d) above, the Committee may decide that the Secretariat be authorized to take the necessary action to ascertain, in consultation with the State Party concerned, the present condition of the property, the dangers to the property and the feasibility of adequately restoring the property. such measures may include the sending of a Reactive Monitoring mission or the consultation of specialists, or through an Advisory mission. The Secretariat shall report to the Committee on the results of its action. In case an emergency action is required, the Committee may authorize its financing from the World Heritage Fund through an emergency assistance request.

e）当获取的信息不足以支持委员会采取上述 a)，b)，c)，d）项中的任何一种措施时，委员会可能会决定授权秘书处采取必要手段，在与相关缔约国磋商的情况下，确定遗产当前状态、所面临的危险及充分修复该遗产的可行性。此类措施包括派遣反应性监测任务、召集专家会谈或通过一个咨询任务。秘书处将向委员会报告行动结果。当需要采取紧急措施时，委员会可批准通过世界遗产基金的紧急援助筹措所需资金。

IV.B The List of World Heritage in Danger

IV.B《濒危世界遗产名录》

Guidelines for the inscription of properties on the List of World Heritage in Danger

列入《濒危世界遗产名录》的指导原则

177. In accordance with Article 11, paragraph 4, of the *Convention*, the Committee may inscribe a property on the List of World Heritage in Danger when the following requirements are met:

a) the property under consideration is on the World Heritage List;

b) the property is threatened by serious and specific danger;

c) major operations are necessary for the conservation of the property;

d) assistance under the *Convention* has been requested for the property; the Committee is of the view that its assistance in certain cases may most

177. 依照《公约》第 11 条第 4 条，当一项遗产满足以下要求时，委员会可将其列入《濒危世界遗产名录》。

a）该遗产已列入《世界遗产名录》；

b）该遗产面临严重的、具体的危险；

c）该遗产的保护需要实施重大举措；

d）已依据《公约》申请为该遗产提供援助。委员会认为，在某些情况下对遗产表示关注并传递这一信息可能是其所能够提供的最有效的

effectively be limited to messages of its concern, including the message sent by inscription of a property on the List of World Heritage in Danger and that such assistance may be requested by any Committee member or the Secretariat.

援助（包括将遗产列入《濒危世界遗产名录》所传递的信息）；此类援助申请可能由委员会成员或秘书处提起。

Criteria for the inscription of properties on the List of World Heritage in Danger

列入《濒危世界遗产名录》的标准

178. A World Heritage property - as defined in Articles 1 and 2 of the *Convention* - can be inscribed on the List of World Heritage in Danger by the Committee when it finds that the condition of the property corresponds to at least one of the criteria in either of the two cases described below.

178. 当委员会查明一项世界遗产（如《公约》第 1 和第 2 条所定义）符合以下两种情况中至少一种时，该遗产可被列入《濒危世界遗产名录》。

179. In the case of cultural properties:

a) ASCERTAINED DANGER - the property is faced with specific and proven imminent danger, such as:

i) serious deterioration of materials;

ii) serious deterioration of structure and/or ornamental features;

iii) serious deterioration of architectural or town-planning coherence;

iv) serious deterioration of urban or rural space, or the natural environment;

v) significant loss of historical authenticity;

vi) important loss of cultural significance.

b) POTENTIAL DANGER - the property is faced with threats which could have deleterious effects on its inherent characteristics. Such threats are, for example:

i) modification of juridical status of the property diminishing the degree of its protection;

ii) lack of conservation policy;

iii) threatening effects of regional planning projects

iv) threatening effects of town planning;

179. 如属于文化遗产：

a）已确知的危险 – 该遗产面临着具体的且确知即将来临的危险，例如：

i）材料严重受损

ii）结构特征或装饰特色严重受损；

iii）建筑和城镇规划的统一性严重受损；

iv）城市或乡村空间，或自然环境严重受损；

v）历史真实性严重丧失；

vi）文化意义严重丧失。

b）潜在的危险 – 该遗产面临可能会对其固有特性造成损害的威胁。此类威胁包括：

i）该遗产法律地位的改变造成保护力度的削弱；

ii）缺乏保护政策；

iii）区域规划项目的威胁影响；

iv）城镇规划的威胁影响；

v) outbreak or threat of armed conflict;

vi) threatening impacts of climatic, geological or other environmental factors

v）武装冲突的爆发或威胁

vi）地质、气候或其他环境因素导致的威胁影响。

180. In the case of natural properties:

Decision 39 COM 11

a) ASCERTAINED DANGER The property is faced with specific and proven imminent danger, such as:

i) A serious decline in the population of the endangered species or the other species of Outstanding Universal Value for which the property was legally established to protect, either by natural factors such as disease or by man made factors such as poaching.

ii) Severe deterioration of the natural beauty or scientific value of the property, as by human settlement, construction of reservoirs which flood important parts of the property, industrial and agricultural development including use of pesticides and fertilizers, major public works, mining, pollution, logging, firewood collection, etc.

iii) Human encroachment on boundaries or in upstream areas which threaten the integrity of the property.

b) POTENTIAL DANGER - The property is faced with threats which could have deleterious effects on its inherent characteristics. Such threats are, for example:

i) a modification of the legal protective status of the area;

ii) planned resettlement or development projects within the property or so situated that the impacts threaten the property;

iii) outbreak or threat of armed conflict;

iv) the management plan or management system is lacking or inadequate, or not fully implemented.

v) threatening impacts of climatic, geological

180. 如属于自然遗产：

第 39 COM 11 决定

a）已确知的危险 该遗产面临着具体的、且确知即将来临的危险，例如：

i）作为确立该项遗产法定保护地位依据的濒危物种或其他具有突出普遍价值物种的数量，由于自然因素（例如疾病）或人为因素（例如偷猎）锐减。

ii）遗产的自然美景和科学价值由于人类的定居、淹没遗产重要区域的水库的兴建、工农业的发展包括杀虫剂和农药的使用，大型公共工程、采矿、污染、采伐等，而遭受重大损害；

iii）人类活动对保护范围或上游区域的侵蚀，威胁到遗产的完整性。

b）潜在的危险 该遗产面临可能会对其固有特性造成损害的威胁。此类威胁包括：

i）该地区的法律保护地位发生变化

ii）在遗产范围内实施的，或虽在其范围外但足以波及和威胁到该遗产的移民或开发计划；

iii）武装冲突的爆发或威胁；

iv）管理规划或管理体系缺失、不完善或贯彻不彻底。

V）气候，地质或其他环境因素造成的威胁。

or other environmental factors.

181. In addition, the threats and/or their detrimental impacts on the integrity of the property must be those which are amenable to correction by human action. In the case of cultural properties, both natural factors and man made factors may be threatening, while in the case of natural properties, most threats will be man made and only very rarely a natural factor (such as an epidemic disease) will threaten the integrity of the property. In some cases, the threats and/or their detrimental impacts on the integrity of the property may be corrected by administrative or legislative action, such as the cancelling of a major public works project or the improvement of legal status.

Decision 39 COM 11

181. 另外，威胁遗产完整性的因素多是人力可以补救的因素。对于文化遗产，自然因素和人为因素都可能构成威胁，而对于自然遗产来说，威胁其完整性的大多是人为因素，只有少数情况是由自然因素造成的（例如传染病）。某些情况下，对遗产完整性造成威胁的因素可通过行政或法律手段予以纠正，如取消某大型公共工程项目、加强法律地位等。

第 39 COM 11 决定

182. The Committee may wish to bear in mind the following supplementary factors when considering the inclusion of a cultural or natural property in the List of World Heritage in Danger:

a) Decisions which affect World Heritage properties are taken by Governments after balancing all factors. The advice of the World Heritage Committee can often be decisive if it can be given before the property becomes threatened.

b) Particularly in the case of ascertained danger, the physical or cultural deteriorations to which a property has been subjected should be judged according to the intensity of its effects and analyzed case by case.

c) Above all in the case of potential danger to a property, one should consider that:

i) the threat should be appraised according to the normal evolution of the social and economic framework in which the property is situated;

ii) it is often impossible to assess certain threats such as the threat of armed conflict as to their effect on cultural or natural properties;

182. 审议是否将一项文化或自然遗产列入《濒危世界遗产名录》时，委员会可能要考虑到下列额外因素：

a）政府是在权衡各种因素后才做出影响世界遗产的决定。世界遗产委员会如能在遗产遭到威胁之前给予建议的话，该建议往往具有决定性。

b）尤其是对于已确知的危险，对遗产所遭受的物理和文化损害的判断应基于其影响程度，并应具体问题具体分析。

c）对于潜在的危险必须首先考虑：

i）结合遗产所处的社会和经济环境的常规进程，对其所受到的威胁进行评估；

ii）有些威胁对于文化和自然遗产的影响难以估量，例如武装冲突的威胁；

iii) some threats are not imminent in nature, but can only be anticipated, such as demographic growth.

iii）有些威胁在本质上不会立刻发生，而只能预见，例如人口的增长。

d) Finally, in its appraisal the Committee should take into account any cause of unknown or unexpected origin which endangers a cultural or natural property.

d）最后，委员会在进行评估时应将所有未知或无法预料的但可能危及文化或自然遗产的因素纳入考虑范围。

Procedure for the inscription of properties on the List of World Heritage in Danger

列入《濒危世界遗产名录》的程序

183. When considering the inscription of a property on the List of World Heritage in Danger, the Committee shall develop, and adopt, as far as possible, in consultation with the State Party concerned, a desired state of conservation for the removal of the property from the List of World Heritage in Danger, and a programme for corrective measures

183. 在考虑将一项遗产列入《濒危世界遗产名录》时，委员会应尽可能与相关缔约国磋商，确定或采纳将该遗产从濒危名录中移除的理想保护状况，和一套补救方案。

184. In order to develop the programme of corrective measures referred to in the previous paragraph, the Committee shall request the Secretariat to ascertain, as far as possible in co-operation with the State Party concerned, the present condition of the property, the dangers to the property and the feasibility of undertaking corrective measures. The Committee may further decide to send a Reactive Monitoring mission from the relevant Advisory Bodies or other organizations to visit the property, evaluate the nature and extent of the threats and propose the measures to be taken. In some circumstances, the State Party may wish to invite an Advisory mission to provide advice and guidance.

Decision 39 COM 11

184. 为了制订前段所述补救方案，委员会应要求秘书处尽可能与相关缔约国合作，弄清遗产的现状，查明其面临的危险并探讨补救措施的可行性。此外委员会还可能决定派遣来自相关咨询机构或其他组织的反应性监测任务进行实地勘查，鉴定威胁的本质及程度，并对补救措施提出建议。某些情况下缔约国也许会考虑向咨询机构或相关组织发出咨询邀请以寻求建议和指导。

第 39 COM 11 决定

185. The information received, together with the comments as appropriate of the State Party and the relevant Advisory Bodies or other organizations, will be brought to the attention of the Committee by the Secretariat.

185. 获取的信息及相关缔约国和咨询机构或其他组织的评论，将经秘书处送交委员会审阅。

186. The Committee shall examine the information available and take a decision concerning the inscription of the property on the List of World Heritage in Danger. Any such decision shall be taken by a majority of two-thirds of the Committee members present and voting. The Committee will then define the programme of corrective action to be taken. This programme will be proposed to the State Party concerned for immediate implementation.

186. 委员会将审议现有信息，并对是否将该遗产列入《濒危世界遗产名录》做出决定。出席的委员会成员须以三分之二多数表决通过此类决定。之后委员会将确定补救方案，并建议相关缔约国立即执行。

187. The State Party concerned shall be informed of the Committee's decision and public notice of the decision shall immediately be issued by the Committee, in accordance with Article 11.4 of the *Convention*.

187. 依照《公约》第 11 条第 4 条，委员会应将决定通告相关缔约国，并随即就该项决定发表公告。

188. The Secretariat publishes the updated List of World Heritage in Danger in printed form and is also available at the following Web address: http: // whc.unesco.org/en/danger

188. 由秘书处印发最新的《濒危世界遗产名录》，同时电子版也可在以下网站上获取：http://whc.unesco.org/en/danger

189. The Committee shall allocate a specific, significant portion of the World Heritage Fund to financing of possible assistance to World Heritage properties inscribed on the List of World Heritage in Danger.

189. 委员会将从世界遗产基金中特别划拨一笔相当数量的资金，为列入《濒危世界遗产名录》的遗产提供可能的援助。

Regular review of the state of conservation of properties on the List of World Heritage in Danger

对于《濒危世界遗产名录》上遗产保护状况的定期检查

190. The Committee shall review annually the state of conservation of properties on the List of World Heritage in Danger. This review shall include

190. 委员会每年将对《濒危世界遗产名录》上遗产的保护状况进行例行检查。检查的内容包括委员会可能认为必要的监测程序和专家考察。

such monitoring procedures and expert missions as might be determined necessary by the Committee.

191. On the basis of these regular reviews, the Committee shall decide, in consultation with the State Party concerned, whether:

a) additional measures are required to conserve the property;

b) to delete the property from the List of World Heritage in Danger if the property is no longer under threat;

c) to consider the deletion of the property from both the List of World Heritage in Danger and the World Heritage List if the property has deteriorated to the extent that it has lost those characteristics which determined its inscription on the World Heritage List, in accordance with the procedure set out in paragraphs 192-198.

191. 在定期检查的基础上，委员会将与有关缔约国磋商，决定是否：

a）该遗产需要额外的保护措施；

b）当该遗产不再面临威胁时，将其从《濒危世界遗产名录》中移除；

c）当该遗产由于严重受损而丧失列入《世界遗产名录》的特征时，考虑依照第 192–198 条所列程序将其从《世界遗产名录》和《濒危世界遗产名录》中移除。

IV.C Procedure for the eventual deletion of properties from the World Heritage List

Ⅳ .C《世界遗产名录》中遗产彻底除名的程序

192. The Committee adopted the following procedure for the deletion of properties from the World Heritage List in cases:

Decision 39 COM 11

a) where the property has deteriorated to the extent that it has lost those characteristics which determined its inclusion in the World Heritage List; and

b) where the intrinsic qualities of a World Heritage site were already threatened at the time of its nomination by action of man and where the necessary corrective measures as outlined by the State Party at the time, have not been taken within the time proposed (see paragraph 116).

192. 在以下情况下，委员会采取下述步骤，将遗产从《世界遗产名录》中除名：

第 39 COM 11 决定

a）遗产严重受损，丧失了其作为世界遗产的决定性特征；

b）遗产在申报时便由于人为因素导致其内在特质受到威胁，而缔约国在规定时间内又没有采取必要的补救措施（见第 116 条）。

193. When a property inscribed on the World Heritage List has seriously deteriorated, or when the necessary corrective measures have not been taken

193.《世界遗产名录》内遗产严重受损，或缔约国没有在限定的时间内采取必要的补救措施，此遗产所在缔约国应该把这种情况通知秘

within the time proposed, the State Party on whose territory the property is situated should so inform the Secretariat.

书处。

194. When the Secretariat receives such information from a source other than the State Party concerned, it will, as far as possible, verify the source and the contents of the information in consultation with the State Party concerned and request its comments.The Secretariat will request the relevant Advisory Bodies to forward comments on the information received.

194. 如果秘书处从缔约国之外的第三方得到了这种信息，秘书处会与相关缔约国磋商，尽量核实信息来源与内容的可靠性，并且听取缔约国的意见。秘书处将要求相关咨询机构提交对所收到信息的意见。

195. The Secretariat will request the relevant Advisory Bodies to forward comments on the information received.

195. 秘书处将要求相关咨询机构进一步评估收到的信息。

196. The Committee will examine all the information available and will take a decision. Any such decision shall, in accordance with Article 13 (8) of the Convention, be taken by a majority of two-thirds of its members present and voting. The Committee shall not decide to delete any property unless the State Party has been consulted on the question.

196. 委员会将审查所有可用信息，做出处理决定。根据《公约》第 13（8）条的规定，委员会与会委员三分之二以上投票同意，该决定方能通过。在未就此事宜与缔约国协商之前，委员会不应做出把遗产除名的决定。

197. The State Party shall be informed of the Committee's decision and public notice of this decision shall be immediately given by the Committee.

197. 应将委员会的决定传达给缔约国，同时尽快将决定公布于世。

198. If the Committee's decision entails any modification to the World Heritage List, this modification will be reflected in the next updated List that is published.

198. 如果委员会的决定变更了目前的《世界遗产名录》，变更内容将体现在下一期的《世界文化遗产名录》中。

V. PERIODIC REPORTING ON THE IMPLEMENTATION OF THE WORLD HERITAGE CONVENTION

V. 有关《世界遗产公约》实施情况的《定期报告》

V.A Objectives

V .A 目标

199. States Parties are requested to submit

199. 要求缔约国经由世界遗产委员会，将

reports to the UNESCO General Conference through the World Heritage Committee on the legislative and administrative provisions they have adopted and other actions which they have taken for the application of the Convention, including the state of conservation of the World Heritage properties located on their territories.

其通过的法律和行政条款以及实施《世界遗产公约》采取的其他行动报告提交教科文组织大会，其中包括其领土内世界遗产的保护状况。

Article 29 of the World Heritage Convention and Resolutions of the 11th session of the General Assembly of States Parties (1997) and the 29th session of the UNESCO General Conference.

《世界遗产公约》第 29 条，缔约国第 11 届大会（1997 年）以及联合国教科文组织第 29 届大会决议

200. Periodic Reporting is a self-reporting process and should be led as far as possible by the States Parties in each region. The Secretariat coordinates and facilitates the Periodic Reporting Process at the global level. States Parties may request expert advice from the Advisory Bodies and the Secretariat, which may also (with agreement of the States Parties concerned) commission further expert advice.

200. 定期报告是一种自我报告过程，应尽可能由缔约国领导在其各自区域内完成。秘书处在全球层面协调和促进定期报告进程。如果缔约国需要咨询机构和秘书处的专家意见，咨询机构和秘书处也可能（在相关缔约国同意的前提下）进一步寻求专家意见。

201. Periodic Reporting serves four main purposes:

a) to provide an assessment of the application of the World Heritage Convention by the State Party;

b) to provide an assessment as to whether the Outstanding Universal Value of the properties inscribed on the World Heritage List is being maintained over time;

c) to provide up-dated information about the World Heritage properties to record the changing circumstances and state of conservation of the properties;

d) to provide a mechanism for regional co-operation and exchange of information and experiences between States Parties concerning the implementation of the Convention and World Heritage conservation.

201.《定期报告》主要有以下四个目的：

a）评估缔约国《世界遗产公约》的执行情况；

b）评估《世界遗产名录》内遗产的突出的普遍价值是否得到长期的保持；

c）提供世界遗产的相关更新信息，记录遗产所处环境的变化以及遗产的保护状况；

d）就《世界遗产公约》实施及世界遗产保护事宜，为缔约国提供一种区域间合作以及信息分享、经验交流的机制。

202. Periodic Reporting is important for more

202.《定期报告》不仅为更有效的对遗产实

effective long term conservation of theproperties inscribed, as well as to strengthen the credibility of the implementation of the Convention. It is also an important tool for assessing the implementation by States Parties and World Heritage properties of policies adopted by the World Heritage Committee and the General Assembly.

施长期保存起到了至关重要的作用，也提高了《世界遗产公约》实施的可信性。同时也是评估缔约国和遗产地执行世界遗产委员会和世界遗产大会的政策情况的重要工具。

Decision 41 COM 11

第 41. COM 11 决定

V.B. Procedure and Format

V .B. 程序和格式

203. Every six years, States Parties submit periodic reports for examination by the World Heritage Committee. During the six-year Periodic Reporting cycle, States Parties report region by region in the following order:

203. 缔约国每六年提交一次《定期报告》供世界遗产委员会检查。六年中缔约国按以下顺序，按区域递交定期报告：

Decision 22 COM VI.7

Decision 41 COM 11

- Arab States
- Africa
- Asia and the Pacific
- Latin America and the Caribbean
- Europe and North America

第 22. COM VI.7 决定

第 41. COM 11 决定

- 阿拉伯国家
- 非洲
- 亚太地区
- 拉丁美洲和加勒比地区
- 欧洲和北美洲

204. The sixth year of each cycle is a period for reflection and evaluation. This pause will allow the periodic reporting mechanism to be assessed and revised as appropriate before a new cycle is initiated. The World Heritage Committee may also decide to use the reflection to initiate the development and publication of a Global World Heritage Report.

204. 每个周期的第六年是反思和评估阶段。新周期开始前，利用这个阶段对定期报告机制进行评估和修正。世界遗产委员会也决定利用这次反思机会，公开发布和出版一份全球世界遗产报告。

Decision 41 COM 11

第 41. COM 11 决定

205. At appropriate intervals, and whenever deemed necessary, the World Heritage Committee adopts and revises Monitoring Indicators and an Analytical Framework for Periodic Reporting.

205. 世界遗产委员会在适当的时间间隔，并在必要时，通过并修订定期报告的监测指标和分析框架。

205bis. The Periodic Reporting process is used as an opportunity for regional exchange and

205 注 . 定期报告过程也为地区交流和合作、加强缔约国间、特别是跨境跨国遗产间的协调

cooperation and to enhance active co-ordination and synchronization between States Parties, particularly in the case of transboundary and transnational properties.

Decision 41 COM 11

和统一，提供了机会。

第 41. COM 11 决定

206. The Periodic Reporting questionnaire is an online tool to be completed by the respective National Focal Points and Site Managers of the World Heritage properties, as appropriate.

206. 定期报告问卷是线上工具，在恰当时由国家重点代表和遗产地管理人员根据情况完成。

This format was reviewed further to the second cycle of Periodic Reporting and was adopted by the World Heritage Committee at its 41st session (Krakow, 2017).

世界遗产委员会在第二次定期报告周期后的第 41 次大会上通过本格式。（2017 年，克拉科夫）

a) Section I refers to the legislative and administrative provisions which the State Party has adopted and other actions which it has taken for the application of the Convention, together with details of the experience acquired in this field. This particularly concerns the general obligations defined in specific articles of the Convention.

a）第一部分包括缔约国执行《公约》时所采取的法律和行政条款及其他行动，以及在这一领域获得的相关经验的详细内容，特别是与《公约》中具体条款所规定义务的相关情况。

b) Section II refers to the state of conservation of specific World Heritage properties located on the territory of the State Party concerned. This Section should be completed for each World Heritage property.

b）第二部分阐述在缔约国领土内特定世界遗产的保护状况。本部分应完整说明每处世界遗产的情况。

Explanatory Notes are provided with the Format in Annex 7.

附录 7 中提供了格式及注解。

206bis. The Periodic Reporting Format may be reviewed following each cycle of Periodic Reporting. An outline of the Format is contained in Annex 7 to the Operational Guidelines.

Decision 41 COM 11

206 注 . 本定期报告格式可循环使用。格式大纲见《操作指南》附件 7。

第 41. COM 11 决定

207. In order to facilitate management and analysis of information, States Parties are requested to submit reports, in English or French, using the online tool provided on the website of the World Heritage Centre. The online tool of the full questionnaire can be accessed here:

207. 为了便于信息管理，缔约国应同时在世界遗产中心网站上提交电子版和打印版的报告，英语或法语均可。线上问卷调查工具可登陆：

http://whc.unesco.org/en/periodicreporting/
Decision 41 COM 11

http://whc.unesco.org/en/periodicreporting/
第 41. COM 11 决定

V.C Evaluation and Follow Up

Ⅴ .C 评估和后续工作

208. The Secretariat consolidates national reports into Regional State of the World Heritage reports, which are available in electronic format at the following Web address http: //whc.unesco.org/en/publications and in paper version (series World Heritage Papers).

208. 秘书处将国家报告整理成世界遗产区域性报告。该《报告》有电子版（http：//whc.unesco.org/en/publications）及打印版（世界遗产论文系列）。

209.The World Heritage Committee carefully reviews issues raised in Periodic Reports and advises the States Parties of the regions concerned on matters arising from them.

209. 世界遗产委员会认真审查《定期报告》所述议题，并就其中的问题向相关区域的缔约国提出建议。

2210. States Parties, working in partnership with the Secretariat and the Advisory Bodies, develop long-term regional follow-up programmes structured according to the Committee's Strategic Objectives and submit them for examination. These Programmes are adopted as follow up to Periodic Reports and regularly reviewed by the Committee based on the needs of States Parties identified in Periodic Reports. They should accurately reflect the needs of World Heritage in the Region and facilitate the granting of International Assistance.
Decision 36 COM 13.I
Decision 41 COM 11

210. 缔约国与秘书处、咨询机构进行磋商，根据其《战略目标》制定长期《区域性计划》，并提交委员会审议。这计划由委员会对定期报告中确定的、缔约国的需要进行定期审查，是定期报告的后续行动。该《计划》应该能准确地反映当地世界遗产的需求，并协助提供国际援助。

第 36 COM 13.I 决定
第 41. COM 11 决定

VI. ENCOURAGING SUPPORT FOR THE WORLD HERITAGE CONVENTION

Ⅵ . 鼓励对《世界遗产公约》的支持

VI.A Objectives
Article 27 of the World Heritage Convention
The

Ⅵ .A 目标
《世界遗产公约》第 27 条

211. objectives are:
a) to enhance capacity-building and research;
b) to raise the general public's awareness,

211. 目标如下：
a）加强能力建设与研究；
b）提高民众意识，使其逐渐理解并重视保

understanding and appreciation of the need to preserve cultural and natural heritage;

c) to enhance the function of World Heritage in the life of the community; and

Article 5 (a) of the World Heritage Convention

d) to increase the participation of local and national populations in the protection and presentation of heritage.

护文化与自然遗产的重要性；

c）加强世界遗产在社会生活中的作用；

《世界遗产公约》第 5（a）条

d）提高地方及全国民众参与遗产的保护与展示。

VI.B Capacity-building and research

Ⅵ .B 能力建设与研究

212. The Committee seeks to develop capacity-building within the States Parties in conformity with its Strategic Objectives.

Budapest Declaration on World Heritage (2002)

212. 委员会根据《战略目标》，致力于缔约国内的能力建设。

《布达佩斯世界遗产宣言》（2002 年）

The Global Training Strategy

全球培训战略

213. Recognizing the high level of skills and multidisciplinary approach necessary for the protection, conservation, and presentation of the World Heritage, the Committee has adopted a Global Training Strategy for World Cultural and Natural Heritage. The primary goal of the Global Training Strategy is to ensure that necessary skills are developed by a wide range of actors for better implementation of the Convention. In order to avoid overlap and effectively implement the Strategy, the Committee will ensure links to other initiatives such as the Global Strategy for a Representative, Balanced and Credible World Heritage List and Periodic Reporting. The Committee will annually review relevant training issues, assess training needs, review annual reports on training initiatives, and make recommendations for future training initiatives.

Global Training Strategy for World Cultural and Natural Heritage adopted by the World Heritage Committee at its 25th session (Helsinki,

213. 委员会认识到在世界遗产的保存、保护和展示领域，高技能以及多学科的方法是必不可少的，为此，委员会通过了“世界文化和自然遗产的全球培训战略”。“全球培训战略”的首要目标是确保相关领域工作者获得必要的技能，以便更好地实施《公约》。为了避免重复，同时有效实施该策略，委员会将确保其与《构建具有代表性、均衡性、可信性的〈世界遗产名录〉的全球战略》、“定期报告”等倡议之间的联系。委员会将每年评审相关培训议题、评估培训需求、审阅年度报告并为进一步的培训提供建议。

“世界文化和自然遗产的全球培训策略”于世界遗产委员会第 25 届会议通过（芬兰赫尔辛基，2001 年）（见文书 WHC–01/CONF.208/24 附

Finland, 2001) (see ANNEX X of document WHC-01/CONF.208/24).

件 X）.

National training strategies and regional co-operation

国家培训策略和区域性合作

214. States Parties are encouraged to ensure that their professionals and specialists at all levels are adequately trained. To this end, States Parties are encouraged to develop national training strategies and include regional co-operation for training as part of their strategies.

214. 鼓励缔约国对其专家及其从业人员进行适当的培训。为此，鼓励缔约国制定国家培训策略，并把区域合作培训作为战略的一部分。

Research

研究

215. The Committee develops and coordinates international co-operation in the area of research needed for the effective implementation of the Convention. States Parties are also encouraged to make resources available to undertake research, since knowledge and understanding are fundamental to the identification, management, and monitoring of World Heritage properties.

215. 委员会在有效实施《公约》所需的研究领域开展并协调国际合作。由于知识和理解对于世界遗产的认定、管理和监测起着至关重要的作用，还鼓励缔约国提供开展研究所需的资源。

International Assistance

国际援助

216. Training and Research Assistance may be requested by States Parties from the World Heritage Fund (see Chapter VII).

216. 缔约国可向世界遗产基金申请培训和研究援助（见第Ⅶ章）。

VI.C Awareness-raising and education

Ⅵ .C 提高认识与教育

Awareness-raising

提高认识

217. States Parties are encouraged to raise awareness of the need to preserve World Heritage. In particular, they should ensure that World Heritage status is adequately marked and promoted on-site.

217. 鼓励缔约国提高对世界遗产保护需求的认识，尤其应确保在遗产地对世界遗产的地位进行有效的标识和宣传。

218. The Secretariat provides assistance to States Parties in developing activities aimed at raising public awareness of the Convention and informing the public of the dangers threatening World Heritage. The Secretariat advises States Parties regarding the preparation and implementation of on-site promotional and educational projects to be funded through International Assistance. The Advisory Bodies and appropriate State agencies may also be solicited to provide advice on such projects.

218. 秘书处向缔约国提供援助，开展活动，以提高公众对《公约》的认识，并告知公众世界遗产所面临的威胁。秘书处将就如何筹划及开展“国际”资助的现场推广与教育项目向缔约国提出建议，也会征求咨询机构和国家有关部门关于此类活动的建议。

Education

教育

219. The World Heritage Committee encourages and supports the development of educational materials, activities and programmes.

219. 世界遗产委员会鼓励并主持编撰教材，开展和实施各种教育活动和项目。

International Assistance

国际援助

220. States Parties are encouraged to develop educational activities related to World Heritage with, wherever possible, the participation of schools, universities, museums and other local and national educational authorities.

Article 27.2 of the World Heritage Convention

220. 鼓励缔约国开展世界遗产相关教育活动，如有可能，让中小学校、大学、博物馆以及其他地方或国家的教育机构也参与其中。

《世界遗产公约》第 27.2 条

221.The Secretariat, in co-operation with the UNESCO Education Sector and other partners, produces and publishes a World Heritage Educational Resource Kit, *"World Heritage in Young Hands"*, for use in secondary schools around the world. The Kit is adaptable for use at other educational levels.

"World Heritage in Young Hands" is available at the following Web address

http: //whc.unesco.org/education/index.htm

221. 秘书处与联合国教科文组织教育部及其他伙伴合作，开发并出版世界遗产教育培训教材：“世界遗产掌握在年轻人手中”。此教材供全世界的中学使用，也可调整用于其他教育水平的人群。

可访问：

http：*//whc.unesco.org/education/index.htm*

查阅“世界遗产掌握在年轻人手中”

222. International Assistance may be requested by States Parties from the World Heritage Fund

222. 缔约国可向世界遗产基金申请国际援助，以提升遗产保护意识，开展教育活动与方

for the purpose of developing and implementing awareness-raising and educational activities or programmes (see Chapter VII).

案（见第Ⅶ章）。

VII. THE WORLD HERITAGE FUND AND INTERNATIONAL ASSISTANCE

Ⅶ. 世界遗产基金和国际援助

VII.A The World Heritage Fund

Ⅶ.A 世界遗产基金

223. The World Heritage Fund is a trust fund, established by *the Convention* in conformity with the provisions of the Financial Regulations of UNESCO. The resources of the Fund consist of compulsory and voluntary contributions made by States Parties to the *Convention*, and any other resources authorized by the Fund's regulations.

Article 15 of the World Heritage Convention.

223. 世界遗产基金是信托基金，是《公约》依据《联合国教科文组织财务条例》的规定建立的。此基金由《公约》缔约国义务或者自愿的捐献及基金规章授权的其他来源组成。

《世界遗产公约》第 15 条

224. The financial regulations for the Fund are set out in document WHC/7 available at the following Web address: http: //whc.unesco.org/en/financialregulations

224. 基金的财务管理条例见文件 HC/7，可登录以下网址查阅：http：//whc.unesco.org/en/financialregulations

VII.B. Mobilization of other technical and financial resources and partnerships in support of the *World Heritage Convention*

Ⅶ.B. 调动其他技术及财务资源，展开合作支持《世界遗产公约》

225. To the extent possible, the World Heritage Fund should be used to mobilize additional funds for International Assistance from other sources.

225. 应尽可能发挥世界遗产基金的作用，开发更多资金来源，促进国际援助。

226. The Committee decided that contributions offered to the World Heritage Fund for international assistance campaigns and other UNESCO projects for any property inscribed on the World Heritage List shall be accepted and used as international assistance pursuant to Section V of the *Convention*, and in conformity with the modality established for carrying out the campaign or project.

226. 委员会决定，根据《公约》第 V 部分的规定，在符合活动或项目开展的情况下，世界遗产基金收到的捐款应用于国际援助活动和其他联合国教科文组织《世界遗产名录》遗产保护项目。

227.States Parties are invited to provide support to the *Convention* in addition to obligatory contributions paid to the World Heritage Fund. This voluntary support can be provided through additional contributions to the World Heritage Fund or direct financial and technical contributions to properties.

Article 15 (3) of the World Heritage Convention

227. 除了向世界遗产基金义务捐款之外，还鼓励缔约国为《公约》提供自愿支持。自愿支持包括向世界遗产基金提供额外捐款，或者直接对遗产提供财政或技术援助。

《世界遗产公约》第 15（3）条

228. States Parties are encouraged to participate in international fund-raising campaigns launched by UNESCO and aimed at protecting World Heritage.

228. 鼓励缔约国参与联合国教科文组织发起的、旨在保护世界遗产的国际资金筹募活动。

229. States Parties and others who anticipate making contributions towards these campaigns or other UNESCO projects for World Heritage properties are encouraged to make their contributions through the World Heritage Fund.

229. 委员会鼓励希望为上述国际资金筹募活动或联合国教科文组织其他的世界遗产保护项目提供支持的缔约国、其他组织或个人通过世界遗产基金捐款。

230. States Parties are encouraged to promote the establishment of national, public and private foundations or associations aimed at raising funds to support World Heritage conservation efforts.

Article 17 of the World Heritage Convention

230. 鼓励缔约国创立国家、社会和私人基金或机构，用来筹资支持世界遗产保护工作。

《世界遗产公约》第 17 条

231. The Secretariat provides support in mobilizing financial and technical resources for World Heritage conservation. To this end, the Secretariat develops partnerships with public and private institutions in conformity with the Decisions and the Guidelines issued by the World Heritage Committee and UNESCO regulations.

231. 秘书处支持调动财政或技术资源保护世界遗产。为此，秘书处在遵守世界遗产委员会和联合国教科文组织相关指南和规定的前提下，与社会或私人组织发展伙伴关系。

232. The Secretariat should refer to the "UNESCO's Comprehensive Partnership Strategy" to govern external fund-raising in favour of the World Heritage Fund. This documents are available at the following Web address: *http: //en.unesco.org/partnerships.*

232. 秘书处在为世界遗产基金进行外部筹资时，应该援引："联合国教科文组织全面合作伙伴关系战略"。这些文件可以在以下网站获 http ：//en.unesco.org/partnerships

"Comprehensive Partnership Strategy" including "Separate strategies for engagement with individual categories of partners" 192 EX/5.INF

Decision 30 COM 13.13

"联合国教科文组织全面合作伙伴关系战略"包括"与特定合作伙伴约定的独立战略"192 EX/5.INF

第 30 COM 13.13 号决定

VII.C International Assistance

Ⅶ.C 国际援助

233. The *Convention* provides International Assistance to States Parties for the protection of the world cultural and natural heritage located on their territories and inscribed, or potentially suitable for inscription on the World Heritage List. International Assistance should be seen as supplementary to national efforts for the conservation and management of World Heritage and Tentative List properties when adequate resources cannot be secured at the national level.

See Articles 13 (1&2) and 19-26 of the World Heritage Convention.

233.《公约》向各缔约国提供国际援助，保护其领土内的世界文化和自然遗产、《世界遗产名录》内遗产以及符合《名录》要求的潜在世界遗产。当国家不能确保足够的资金时，国际援助辅助该缔约国保护、管理世界遗产及《预备名录》内遗产。

见《世界遗产公约》第 13 条（1&2）和第 19–26 条

234. International Assistance is primarily financed from the World Heritage Fund, established under the *World Heritage Convention*. The Committee determines the budget for International Assistance on a biennial basis.

Section IV of the World Heritage Convention

234. 国际援助主要来自世界遗产基金，世界遗产基金是依据《世界遗产公约》建立的。委员会每两年决定一次国际援助的预算。

《世界遗产公约》第Ⅳ部分。

235. The World Heritage Committee co-ordinates and allocates types of International Assistance in response to State Party requests. These types of International Assistance, described in the summary table set out below, in order of priority are:

Decision 30 COM 14A

a. Emergency assistance

b. Conservation and Management assistance (incorporating assistance for training and research, technical co-operation and promotion and education)

c. Preparatory assistance.

235. 世界遗产委员会应缔约国的请求，协调分配各种国际援助。国际援助有以下几种，按照优先性依次排列如下：

第 30 COM 14A 号决定

a）紧急援助

b）保护与管理援助（包括培训与研究援助、技术合作援助以及宣传和教育援助）

c）筹备性援助

VII.D Principles and priorities for International Assistance

Ⅶ .D 国际援助的原则和优先顺序

236. Priority is given to International Assistance for properties inscribed on the List of World Heritage in Danger. The Committee created a specific budget line to ensure that a significant portion of assistance from the World Heritage Fund is allocated to properties inscribed on the List of World Heritage in Danger.

Article 13 (1) of the World Heritage Convention.

236. 国际援助将优先给予《濒危世界遗产名录》内的遗产。委员会规定了具体的预算线，确保世界遗产基金中相当大的一部分资金用来救援《濒危世界遗产名录》内的遗产。

《世界遗产公约》第 13（1）条

237. States Parties in arrears of payment of their compulsory or voluntary contributions to the World Heritage Fund are not eligible for international assistance, it being understood that this provision does not apply to requests for emergency assistance.

Decision 13 COM XII.34

237. 拖欠世界遗产基金必付款项或无自愿捐款的缔约国，没有资格享受国际援助，但是这一条不适用于紧急援助。

第 13 COM XII.34 号决定

238. To support its Strategic Objectives, the Committee also allocates International Assistance in conformity with the priorities set out in its decisions and in the Regional Programmes it adopts as a follow up to Periodic Reports (see para. 210).

Decisions 26 COM 17.2,
26 COM 20 and 26 COM 25.3

238. 委员会也会根据区域计划的优先顺序分配国际援助，以支持其战略目标。区域计划是《定期报告》的后续措施，委员会将根据《定期报告》中缔约国的需求，定期评审区域计划（见第 210 节）。

第 26 COM 17.2 号、26 COM 20 号 和 26 COM 25.3 号决定

239. In addition to the priorities outlined in paragraphs 236-238 above, the following considerations govern the Committee's decisions in granting International Assistance:

Decisions 26 COM 17.2, 26 COM 20 and 26 COM 25.3

a) the likelihood that the assistance will have a catalytic and multiplier effect ("seed money") and promote financial and technical contributions from other sources;

b) when funds available are limited and a selection has to be made, preference is given to:

Decision 31 COM 18B

• a Least Developed Country or Low Income

239. 委员会在分配国际援助时，除按上述 236–238 条规定的优先性顺序外，还会考虑以下因素：

第 26 COM 17.2 号、26 COM 20 号 和 26 COM 25.3 号决定

a）带来催化和倍增效应的援助（“种子基金”），可能会吸引其他资金或技术贡献；

b）由于资金有限，必须做出抉择时，将优先考虑符合下列条件的国家：

第 31COM 18B 号决定

• 联合国经济社会发展政策委员会所定义的

Economy as defined by the United Nations Economic and Social Council's Committee for Development Policy, or

• a Lower Middle Income Country as defined by the World Bank, or

• a Small Island Developing State (SIDS),

• a State Party in a post-conflict situation;

c).the urgency of the protective measures to be taken at World Heritage properties;

d).whether the legislative, administrative and, wherever possible, financial commitment of the recipient State Party is available to the activity;

e).the impact of the activity on furthering the Strategic Objectives decided by the Committee;

Paragraph 26 of Operational Guidelines

f).the degree to which the activity responds to needs identified through the reactive monitoring process and/or the analysis of regional Periodic Reports;

Decision 20 COM XII

g).the exemplary value of the activity in respect to scientific research and the development of cost effective conservation techniques;

h). the cost of the activity and expected results; and

i). the educational value both for the training of experts and for the general public.

240. A balance will be maintained in the allocation of resources between cultural and natural heritage and between Conservation and Management and Preparatory Assistance. This balance is reviewed and decided upon on a regular basis by the Committee and during the second year of each biennium by the Chairperson of the World Heritage Committee. 65% of the total International Assistance budget is set aside for cultural properties and 35% for natural properties

Decision 31 COM 18B

VII.E Summary Table

最不发达国家或低收入国家；

• 世界银行定义的低水平中等收入国家

• 小岛屿或发展中国家（SIDS）；

• 冲突后缔约国；

c）对世界遗产采取保护措施的紧急程度；

d）受益缔约国是否有法律、行政措施或（在可能情况下）用来开展活动财务承诺；

e）活动对于进一步达到委员会制定的“战略目标”的影响；

《操作指南》第 26 条

f）活动满足反应监测过程和 / 或《定期报告》地区分析所定需求的程度

第 20 COM XII 号决定

g）该活动对科学研究以及开发高效低、成本的保护技术的示范价值；

h）该活动的成本和预期结果；

i）对专业培训和大众的教育价值。

240. 对文化与自然遗产的资源及保护和管理及援助之间平衡分配。委员会将定期检查这种平衡。并在每两年周期的第二年由主席或世界遗产委员会决定。国际援助总预算的 65% 用于文化遗产，35% 用于自然遗产。

第 31 COM 18B 号决定

Ⅶ.E 总表

VII.E Summary Table

241.

Type of international assistance	Purpose	Budget ceilings per request	Deadline for submission of request	Authority for approval
Emergency Assistance	This assistance may be requested to address ascertained or potential threats facing properties included on the List of World Heritage in Danger and the World Heritage List which have suffered severe damage or are in imminent danger of severe damage due to sudden, unexpected phenomena. Such phenomena may include land subsidence, extensive fires, explosions, flooding or man-made disasters including war. This assistance does not concern cases of damage or deterioration caused by gradual processes of decay, pollution or erosion. It addresses emergency situations strictly relating to the conservation of a World Heritage property (see Decision 28 COM 10B 2.c) . It may be made available, if necessary, to more than one World Heritage property in a single State Party (see Decision 6 EXT. COM 15.2) . The budget ceilings relate to a single World Heritage property. The assistance may be requested to : (i) undertake emergency measures for the safeguarding of the property; (ii) draw up an emergency plan for the property.	Up to US$ 5, 000 Between US$ 5, 001 and 75, 000 Over US$ 75, 000	At any time At any time At any time before the Committee	Director of the World Heritage Centre Chairperson of the Committee Committee
Preparatory assistance	This assistance may be requested to (in order of priority) : (i) prepare or update national Tentative Lists of properties suitable for inscription on the World Heritage List; a commitment will be required from the State Party to nominate in priority on these lists sites recognized in approved thematic advice, such as the thematic studies prepared by the Advisory Bodies, as corresponding to gaps on the List; (ii) organize meetings for the harmonization of national Tentative Lists within the same geo-cultural area; (iii) prepare nominations of properties for inscription on the World Heritage List (including preparatory work such as collection of basic information, scoping studies of the potential for demonstration of Outstanding Universal Value, including integrity or authenticity, comparative studies of the property in relation to other similar properties (see 3.2 of Annex 5) , including analysis in the context of the Gap Studies produced by the Advisory Bodies. Priority will be given to requests for sites recognized in approved thematic advice as corresponding to gaps on the List and/or for sites where preliminary investigations have shown that further inquiries would be justified, especially in the case of States Parties whose heritage is un-represented or under-represented on the World Heritage List; (IV) prepare requests for Conservation & Management assistance for consideration by the World Heritage Committee.	Up to US$ 5, 000 Between US$ 5, 001 and 30, 000	At any time 31 October	Director of the World Heritage Centre Chairperson of the Committee

续表

Type of international assistance	Purpose	Budget ceilings per request	Deadline for submission of request	Authority for approval
Conservation and Management Assistance (incorporating Training and Research assistance, Technical co-operation assistance and Promotion and education assistance)	This assistance may be requested for: (i) the training of staff and specialists at all levels in the fields of identification, monitoring, conservation, management and presentation of World Heritage, with an emphasis on group training; (ii) scientific research benefiting World Heritage properties; (iii) studies on the scientific and technical problems of conservation, management, and presentation of World Heritage properties. Note: Requests for support for individual training courses from UNESCO should be submitted on the standard "Application for fellowship" form available from the Secretariat. (iv) provision of experts, technicians and skilled labour for the conservation, management, and presentation of properties inscribed on the List of World Heritage in Danger and the World Heritage List; (v) supply of equipment which the State Party requires for the conservation, management, and presentation of properties inscribed on the List of World Heritage in Danger and the World Heritage List; (vi) low-interest or interest-free loans for undertaking activities for the conservation, management, and presentation of properties inscribed on the List of World Heritage in Danger and the World Heritage List, which may be repayable on a long-term basis. (vii) At the regional and international levels for Programmes, activities and the holding of meetings that could: -help to create interest in the Convention within the countries of a given region; -create a greater awareness of the different issues related to the implementation of the *Convention* to promote more active involvement in its application; -be a means of exchanging experiences; -stimulate joint education, information and promotional programmes and activities, especially when they involve the participation of young people for the benefit of World Heritage conservation. (viii) At the national level for: -meetings specifically organized to make the *Convention* better known, especially amongst young people, or for the creation of national World Heritage associations, in accordance with Article 17 of the Convention; -preparation and discussion of education and information material (such as brochures, publications, exhibitions, films, multimedia tools) for the general promotion of the *Convention* and the World Heritage List and not for the promotion of a particular property, and especially for young people.	Only for requests falling under items (i) to (vi) : Up to US$ 5, 000 Between US$ 5, 001 and 30, 000 Over US$ 30, 000 Only for requests falling under items (vii) and (viii) : Up to US$ 5, 000 Between US$ 5, 001 and 10, 000	Only for requests falling under items (i) to (vi) : At any time 31 October 31 October Only for requests falling under items (vii) and (viii) : At any time 31 October	Only for requests falling under items (i) to (vi): Director of the World Heritage Centre Chairperson of the Committee Committee Only for requests falling under items (vii) and (viii) : Director of the World Heritage Centre Chairperson of the Committee

240. 一览表

国际援助种类	目的	最高预算额	提交请求的截止期限	核准机关
紧急援助	该援助用于《濒危世界遗产名录》内遭受已确知及潜在威胁的遗产及《世界遗产名录》内遭受严重损坏的遗产，或由于突然、不可预料的事件使遗产遭受迫切威胁及重大损失。这些不可预料的现象包括土地沉陷、大火、爆炸、洪水和战争等的人为灾难。此类援助不用于由渐进的腐蚀、污染和侵蚀造成的遗产损害和蜕化，只严格用于救助那些与保护世界遗产有关的紧急情况（见第 28 COM 10B 2.c 号）。如有需要，该援助可以拨付给同一缔约国的多处遗产（见第 6EXT.COM 15.2 号决定）。最高预算额为单项世界遗产的预算限额。 援助可用于： （i）采取紧急措施保护遗产； （ii）为遗产制定紧急方案。	5,000 美元 5,001–75,000 美元 75,000 美元以上	随时 随时 委员会会议前任一时间	世界遗产中心主任 委员会主席 委员会
筹备性援助	援助可用于（优先顺序）： （i）准备或更新适合列入《世界遗产名录》的国家《预备名录》内的遗产；缔约国承诺应先推荐目录中经过研究确认的需要援助的遗产点，并找出与咨询机构的研究间的差距。 （ii）在同一地理文化区域内组织会议，协调各国家《预备名录》； （iii）准备列入《世界遗产名录》遗产的申报文件（其中包括申报遗产准备工作例如基本信息收集，证明其突出普遍价值的潜在范围研究，完整性，真实性以及与其他类似遗产的比较分析）（见附录 5 的 3.2）；包括咨询机构提出的差距研究的环境分析。优先考虑经过主题研究后认为在目录中相应缺少的遗产类型，以及那些初步调查后认为应该进行进一步研究的遗产，特别是没有遗产或仅有很少遗产列入名录的缔约国的申请。 （iv）世界遗产委员会考虑的保护与管理援助准备要求。	5,000 美元 5,001–30,000 美元	随时 10 月 31 日前	世界遗产中心主任 委员会主席
保护与管理援助（包括培训和研究援助、技术合作援助以及宣传和教育援助）	要求援助： （i）在世界遗产的认定、监测、保护、管理以及展示领域培训各个级别的工作人员和专家，以团体培训为主； （ii）对世界遗产有利的科学研究； （iii）致力于解决世界遗产保护、管理与展示问题的研究； 注：如果向联合国教科文组织提出个人培训的请求，首先要填写由秘书处准备的“奖学金申请”表格。 （iv）对于列在《濒危世界遗产名录》和《世界遗产名录》上的遗产给予专家、技术支持，以保护、管理、展示遗产； （v）缔约国为保护、管理、展示《濒危世界遗产名录》和《世界遗产名录》内遗产所需要的设备； （vi）为保护、管理、展示《濒危世界遗产名录》和《世界遗产名录》内遗产所需的低利率或零利率贷款，这些贷款可能是可长期偿还的。	仅限于第（i）至（vi）项： 5,000 美元 5,001–30,000 美元	仅限于第（i）至（vi）项： 随时 10 月 31 日前	仅限于第（i）至（vi）项： 世界遗产中心主任 委员会主席

续表

国际援助种类	目的	最高预算额	提交请求的截止期限	核准机关
保护与管理援助（包括培训和研究援助、技术合作援助以及宣传和教育援助）	（vii）用于地区和国际级别的计划、活动和会议：– 帮助在特定地区的国家内激起对《世界遗产公约》的兴趣； – 提高与实施《世界遗产公约》相关的不同议题的认识，推动更积极地参与《公约》的实施。 – 经验交换的渠道； – 帮助开展联合教育、信息、以及宣传活动，特别是让年轻人参加到世界遗产保护活动中来。 （viii）用于国家级别的会议： – 组织特别会议，让《公约》得到更好的了解，特别是组织有年轻人参加的会议；根据《世界遗产公约》第 17 条，创立国家世界遗产协会； – 为宣传《公约》和《世界遗产名录》，准备、讨论教育和信息资料（例如：宣传手册、出版物、展览会、电影、大众传媒工具），有年轻人参加尤为重要。本援助不用于某项特定遗产的宣传。	30,000 美元以上 仅限于第（vii）至（viii）项： 5,000 美元 5,001–10,000 美元	10 月 31 日前 仅限于第（vii）至（viii）项： 随时 10 月 31 日	委员会 仅限于第（vii）至（viii）项： 世界遗产中心主任 委员会主席

VII.F Procedure and format

242. All States Parties submitting requests for international assistance are encouraged to consult the Secretariat and the Advisory Bodies during the conceptualization, planning and elaboration of each request. To facilitate States Parties' work, examples of successful international assistance requests may be provided upon request.

243. The application form for International Assistance is presented in Annex 8 and the types, amounts, deadlines for submission and the authorities responsible for approval are outlined in the summary table in Chapter VII.E.

244. The request should be submitted in English or French, duly signed and transmitted by the National Commission for UNESCO, the State Party Permanent Delegation to UNESCO and/or appropriate governmental Department or Ministry to the following address:

UNESCO World Heritage Centre
7, place de Fontenoy
75352 Paris 07 SP
France
Tel: +33 (0) 1 4568 1276
Fax: +33 (0) 1 4568 5570
E-mail: wh-intassistance@unesco.org

245 Requests for international assistance may be submitted by electronic mail by the State Party but must be accompanied by an officially signed hard copy or be filled-in using the online format on the World Heritage Centre's Website at the following address: http: //whc.unesco.org

246.It is important that all information requested in this application form is provided. If appropriate or necessary, requests may be

Ⅶ .F 程序和格式

242. 鼓励所有申请国际援助的缔约国在构想、计划和拟定申请期间，向秘书处和咨询机构进行咨询。为方便缔约国的工作，委员会可应缔约国的要求提供国际援助的成功申请案例。

243. 国际援助的申请表格可参阅附录 8，第Ⅶ .E 章的总表概述了提交的种类、金额以及截止期限和核准批准机构。

244. 用英语或法语提出申请，联合国教科文组织国家委员会、缔约国常驻联合国教科文组织代表团和 / 或相关政府部门签字后提交至下列地址：

联合国教科文组织世界遗产中心
法国巴黎（7，place de Fontenoy 75352 Paris 07 SP France）

电话：+33（0）1 4568 1276
传真：+33（0）1 4568 5570
电邮：wh–intassistance@unesco.org

245. 缔约国可用电子邮件申请国际援助，但必须同时提交一份官方签字的书面申请，或使用世界遗产中心网站（http：//whc.unesco.org）提供的电子格式。

246. 必须提供申请表中要求填写的一切信息。在适当或必要的时候，可以随申请表附上相关信息、报告等。

supplemented by additional information, reports, etc.

VII.G Evaluation and approval of International Assistance requests

Ⅶ.G 国际援助的评估和核准

247. Provided that a request for assistance from a State Party is complete, the Secretariat, with the assistance of the Advisory Bodies, for requests above US$ 5, 000, will process each request in a timely manner, as follows.

247. 如果缔约国的国际援助申请信息完整，秘书处在咨询机构的帮助下会通过以下方式及时处理每一份金额超过 5,000 美元的申请。

248. All requests for international assistance for cultural heritage are evaluated by ICOMOS and ICCROM, except requests up to and including US$ 5, 000.

Decision 13 COM XII.34
Decision 31 COM 18B

248. 所有关于文化遗产的国际援助申请均由国际古迹遗址理事会和国际文物保护与修复研究中心评估，申请金额低于 5,000 美元的除外。

第 13 COM XII.34 号决定
第 31 COM 18B 号决定

249. All requests for international assistance for mixed heritage are evaluated by ICOMOS, ICCROM and IUCN, except requests up to and including US$ 5, 000.

Decision 31 COM 18B

249. 所有关于混合遗产的国际援助申请均由国际古迹遗址理事会、国际文物保护和修复研究中心和世界自然保护联盟评估，申请金额低于 5,000 美元的除外。

第 31 COM 18B 号决定

250. All requests for international assistance for natural heritage are evaluated by IUCN, except requests up to and including US$ 5, 000.

Decision 31 COM 18B

250. 所有自然遗产国际援助的申请都将由世界自然保护联盟做出评估，申请金额低于 5,000 美元的除外。

第 31 COM 18B 号决定

251. The evaluation criteria used by the Advisory Bodies are outlined in Annex 9.

Decision 31 COM 18B

251. 咨询机构所使用的评估标准在附录 9 中列明。

第 31 COM 18B 号决定

252. All requests for International Assistance of more than US$ 5,000, except those of Emergency Assistance, are evaluated by a panel composed of representatives of the World Heritage Centre Regional Desks and the Advisory Bodies, and if possible the Chairperson of the World Heritage Committee or,

252. 所有金额超过 5,000 美元的国际援助申请，除紧急援助外，均需要进行小组评估，小组成员包括世界遗产中心区域代表、咨询机构代表、如有可能，世界遗产委员会主席或由主席指派的观察员。小组至少每年召开一到两次会议，之后由主席或委员会做出决策。所有提

in observer capacity, a person designated by the Chairperson, meeting once or twice a year before action by the Chairperson and/or Committee. Requests for Emergency Assistance can be submitted at anytime to the Secretariat and will be submitted to the Chairperson or to the Committee at its next session for decision after comments by the Advisory Bodies and without examination by the pane

交给主席批准的紧急申请都可以随时提交给秘书处，并在咨询机构评议后交主席或委员会在下次会议决定，而不需要小组会议检查。

Decision 31 COM 18B

第 31 COM 18B 号决定

253. The Chairperson is not authorized to approve requests submitted by his own country. These will be examined by the Committee.

253. 主席不能批准来自本国的申请，这些申请将由委员会进行审查。

254. All requests for Preparatory Assistance or Conservation and Management Assistance of more than US$ 5, 000 should be received by the Secretariat on or before 31 October. Incomplete forms which do not come back duly completed by 30 November will be sent back to the States Parties for submission to a next cycle. Complete requests are examined by a first panel held in January during the meeting between the Secretariat and the Advisory Bodies. Requests for which the panel issues a positive or a negative recommendation will be submitted to the Chairperson/ Committee for decision. A second panel may be held at least eight weeks before the Committee session for requests which were revised since the first panel. Requests sent back for a substantial revision will be examined by the panel depending on their date of receipt. Requests requiring only minor revision and no further examination by the panel must come back within the year when they were examined first; otherwise they will be sent again to a next panel. The chart detailing the submission process is attached in Annex 8.

254. 秘书处将于每年 10 月 31 日前受理所有金额超过 5，000 美元的筹备援助或修复管理援助。未在 11 月 30 日补全表格内容的申请将退回缔约国，进入下一轮申请。完整的申请文件将于 1 月的秘书处与咨询机构会议期间进行小组讨论。小组讨论意见将交主席或委员会决定。在第一次小组会议提出修改意见、委员会会议前 8 周召开第二次小组会议，根据意见反馈时间决定修改意见是否合格。通过小组检查需要轻微修改的申请必须在一年内反馈，否则将进入下一周期。详细的提交程序表见附件 8.

VII.H Contractual Arrangements

VII.H 合同安排

255. Agreements are established between

255. 联合国教科文组织与相关缔约国政府

UNESCO and the concerned State Party or its representative (s) for the implementation of the approved International Assistance requests in conformity with UNESCO regulations, following the work plan and budget breakdown described in the originally approved request.

或代表要达成协议：在使用国际援助的时候，必须要遵守联合国教科文组织规章，同时要与之前批准的申请中所描述的工作计划和预算明细保持一致。

VII.I Evaluation and follow-up of International Assistance

Ⅶ.I 国际援助的评估和后续跟踪

256. The monitoring and evaluation of the implemention of the International Assistance requests will take place within 3 months of the activities' completion. The results of these evaluations will be collated and maintained by the Secretariat in collaboration with the Advisory Bodies and examined by the Committee on a regular basis.

256. 在活动结束 3 个月之内，将开始对国际援助申请进行监测和评估。秘书处和咨询机构会对评估结果进行比较，委员会将对这些结果定期进行检查。

257. The Committee reviews the implementation, evaluation and follow-up of International Assistance in order to evaluate the International Assistance effectiveness and to redefine its priorities.

257. 委员会将对国际援助的实施、评估和后续工作进行审查，以便评估国际援助的使用效果并重新定义国际援助的优先顺序。

VIII. THE WORLD HERITAGE EMBLEM

VIII. 世界遗产标志

VIII.A Preamble

VIII.A 前言

258. At its second session (Washington, 1978), the Committee adopted the World Heritage Emblem which had been designed by Mr. Michel Olyff. This Emblem symbolizes the interdependence of cultural and natural properties: the central square is a form created by man and the circle represents nature, the two being intimately linked. The Emblem is round, like the world, but at the same time it is a symbol of protection. It symbolizes the *Convention*, signifies the adherence of States Parties to the *Convention*, and serves to identify properties inscribed in the World Heritage List. It is associated

258. 在世界遗产委员会第二届大会上（华盛顿，1978 年），采用了由米歇尔·奥利夫先生设计的遗产标志。该标志表现了文化与自然遗产之间的相互依存关系：代表大自然的圆形与代表人类创造的方形紧密相连。标志是圆形的，代表世界的形状，同时也是保护的象征。标志象征《公约》，代表缔约国将遵守《公约》，同时指明了列入《世界遗产名录》中的遗产。它与大众对《公约》的了解相互关联，是对《公约》可信度和威望的认可。总而言之，它是《公约》所代表的突出普遍价值的集中体现。

with public knowledge about the *Convention* and is the imprimatur of the *Convention's* credibility and prestige. Above all, it is a representation of the universal values for which the *Convention* stands.

259. The Committee decided that the Emblem proposed by the artist could be used, in any colour or size, depending on the use, the technical possibilities and considerations of an artistic nature. The Emblem should always carry the text "WORLD HERITAGE. PATRIMOINE MONDIAL". The space occupied by "PATRIMONIO MUNDIAL" can be used for its translation into the national language of the country where the Emblem is to be used.

259. 委员会决定，根据具体的使用、技术水平和艺术考虑，该艺术家提交的标志可采用任何颜色或尺寸。标志上必须带有"WORLDHERTAGE（英语"世界遗产"）.PATRIMOINE MONDIAL"（法语"世界遗产"）的字样。各国在使用该标志时，可用本国的语言来代替中间部分的"PATRIMONIO MUNDIAL"（西语）字样。

260. In order to ensure the Emblem benefits from as much visibility as possible while preventing improper uses, the Committee at its twenty-second session (Kyoto, 1998) adopted 'Guidelines and Principles for the Use of the World Heritage Emblem' as set out in the following paragraphs. In addition, a 'Table of Uses' (Annex 14) provides complementary guidance.

260. 为了保证标志尽可能地引人注目，同时避免误用，委员会在第22届会议（京都，1998年）上通过了《世界遗产标志使用指南和原则》，内容在后续段落有所说明。附件14中的"使用表"提供了完整的指导。

261. Although there is no mention of the Emblem in the *Convention*, its use has been promoted by the Committee to identify properties protected by the *Convention* and inscribed on the World Heritage List since its adoption in 1978.

261. 尽管《公约》并未提到标志，自1978年采用该标志以来，委员会一直在推动使用该标志来标示受《公约》保护的遗产以及列入《世界遗产名录》的遗产。

262. The World Heritage Committee is

261. 世界遗产委员会负责决定世界遗产标

responsible for determining the use of the World Heritage Emblem and for making policy prescriptions regarding how it may be used. Since the adoption by the UNESCO General Conference in October 2007 of the Directives concerning the Use of the Name, Acronym, Logo and Internet Domain Names of UNESCO ①, it is strongly encouraged to use the World Heritage Emblem as part of a linked logo block accompanied by UNESCO's logo, whenever feasible. The use of the World Heritage Emblem alone remains however possible, in line with the present *Guidelines* and with the Table of Uses (Annex 14)

Decision 39 COM 11

识的使用，同时负责制定如何使用标识的政策规定。自采纳 2007 年 10 月联合国教科文组织大会《关于使用国教科文组织名称、缩写、标识及联合互联网域名的方针》以来①，极力鼓励在可行的情况下同时使用世界遗产标识和联合国教科文组织标识。也可按操作指南附件 14 中“使用表”的指导单独使用世界遗产标识。

第 39 COM 11 号决定

263. As requested by the Committee at its 26th session (Budapest, 2002), the World Heritage Emblem, with and without its surrounding text, has been notified and accepted on 21 May 2003 by the Paris Union Member states under Article 6t of the Paris Convention for the Protection of Industrial Property, adopted in 1883 and revised at Stockholm in 1967. Therefore UNESCO has recourse to Paris Convention Member States' domestic systems to prevent the use of the World Heritage Emblem where such use falsely suggests a connection with UNESCO, the *World Heritage Convention*, or any other abusive use.

Decision 26 COM 15

Decision39 COM 11

263. 按照委员会第 26 届大会（布达佩斯，2002 年）的要求，世界遗产标识，无论周围是否有多语的“世界遗产”文字环绕，均于 2003 年 5 月 21 日根据保护工业产权的巴黎公约第 6 条之规定，得到保护工业产权联盟成员国正式认可。该公约于 1883 年通过并于 1967 年在斯德哥尔摩得到修订。因此联合国教科文组织借助助于巴黎公约成员国内部系统，禁止任何组织及个人利用该标识欺骗和误导他人理解其与联合国教科文组织、《世界遗产公约》的相关性，或其他滥用行为。

第 26 COM 15 号决定

第 39 COM 11 号决定

264. The Emblem also has fund-raising potential that can be used to enhance the marketing value of products with which it is associated. A balance is needed between the Emblem's use to further the aims of the *Convention* and optimize knowledge of the *Convention* worldwide and the need to prevent its

264. 该标志还具有筹集基金的潜力，可以用于提高相关产品的市场价值。在使用该标志的过程中，要注意在以下两者之间保持平衡，即正确使用标志促进《公约》目标的实现，并在世界范围内最大限度地普及《公约》知识，但同时要避免不正确、不恰当、以及未经授权、

① The most recent version of the *Directives concerning the Use of the Name, Acronym, Logo and Internet Domain Names of UNESCO* is found in the annex to Resolution 86 of the 34th session of the General Conference (34 C/Resolution 86) or at http://unesdoc.unesco.org/images/0015/001560/156046e.pdf

最新版本的《关于使用国教科文组织名称、缩写、标志及联合互联网域名的方针》见 34 次大会第 86 号决议附件 (34 C/Resolution 86) 或登录 http://unesdoc.unesco.org/images/0015/001560/156046e.pdf

abuse for inaccurate, inappropriate, and unauthorized commercial or other purposes.

出于商业或其他目的滥用标志。

265. The Guidelines and Principles for the Use of the Emblem and modalities for quality control should not become an obstacle to co-operation for promotional activities. Authorities responsible for reviewing and deciding on uses of the Emblem may base their decisions on the parameters developed below and those contained in the Table of Uses (Annex 14).

Decision 39 COM 11

265.《世界遗产标志使用指南和原则》以及质量控制的手段不应成为合作开展宣传活动的障碍。负责审定标志使用的权威机构（见下文），在做出决定时需要参照下列参数及附件 14“使用表”中包含的内容。

第 39 COM 11 号决定

VIII.B Applicability

VIII.B 适用性

266. The Guidelines and Principles proposed herein cover all proposed uses of the Emblem by:

Decision 39 COM 11

A. The World Heritage Centre;

B. The UNESCO Publishing Office and other UNESCO offices;

C. Agencies or National Commissions, responsible for implementing the Convention in each State Party;

D. World Heritage properties;

E. Other contracting parties, especially those operating for predominantly commercial purposes.

266. 本文所述的《指南和原则》涵盖了以下各方使用标志的所有可能情况：

第 39 COM 11 号决定

a. 世界遗产中心；

b. 联合国教科文组织出版处和联合国教科文组织其他机构；

c. 各个缔约国负责实施《公约》的机构或国家委员会；

d. 世界遗产；

e. 其他签约合作方，尤其是主要进行商业运营的机构。

VIII.C Responsibilities of States Parties

VIII.C 缔约国的责任

267. States Parties to the *Convention* should take all possible measures to prevent the use of the Emblem in their respective countries by any group or for any purpose not explicitly recognized by the Committee. States Parties are encouraged to make full use of national legislation including Trade Mark Laws.

267. 缔约国政府应该采取一切可能的措施，防止未经委员会明确承认的任何组织或出于未经授权的任何目的使用该标志。鼓励缔约国充分利用包括《商标法》在内的国家立法。

VIII.D Increasing proper uses of the World Heritage Emblem

VIII.D 增加对世界遗产标志的正确使用

268. Properties inscribed on the World

268. 列入《世界遗产名录》的遗产应设立

Heritage List should be marked with the emblem jointly with the UNESCO logo, which should, however, be placed in such a way that they do not visually impair the property in question.

该标志和联合国教科文组织标识，但要以不破坏遗产为前提。

Production of plaques to commemorate the inscription of properties on the World Heritage List

制作纪念遗产列入《世界遗产名录》的标牌。

269. Once a property is inscribed on the World Heritage List, the State Party should place a plaque, whenever possible, to commemorate this inscription. These plaques are designed to inform the public of the country concerned and foreign visitors that the property visited has a particular value which has been recognized by the international community. In other words, the property is exceptional, of interest not only to one nation, but also to the whole world. However, these plaques have an additional function which is to inform the general public about the *World Heritage Convention* or at least about the World Heritage concept and the World Heritage List.

269. 一旦遗产列入《世界遗产名录》，该缔约国将尽可能设立标牌来纪念这一事件。标牌应向本国公众及外国游客说明该遗产具有特殊且已得到国际社会认可的价值。换言之，该遗产无论对该国还是世界来说，都具有非同寻常的意义。此外，该标牌还有另外一个作用，即向公众介绍《世界遗产公约》，或者至少是世界遗产概念和《世界遗产名录》。

270. The Committee has adopted the following Guidelines for the production of these plaques:

A. the plaque should be so placed that it can easily be seen by visitors, without disfiguring the property;

B. the World Heritage Emblem should appear on the plaque;

C. the text should mention the property's Outstanding Universal Value; in this regard it might be useful to give a short description of the property's outstanding characteristics. States Parties may, if they wish, use the descriptions appearing in the various World Heritage publications or in the World Heritage exhibit, and which may be obtained from the Secretariat;

D. the text should make reference to the *World Heritage Convention* and particularly to the World

270. 委员会就标牌的制作采用以下指导方针：

a. 标牌应放置在参观者容易看到的地方，但不能影响遗产外观；

b. 标牌上应带有世界遗产标志；

c. 标牌上的内容应体现遗产的突出普遍价值；考虑到这一点，内容中应对遗产的突出特点加以描述。如果愿意的话，缔约国政府可以使用各种世界遗产出版物或世界遗产展览中对相关遗产的说明。这些内容可直接从秘书处获得。

d. 标牌上的内容应提及《保护世界文化和自然遗产公约》，尤其是《世界遗产名录》及国

Heritage List and to the international recognition conferred by inscription on this List (however, it is not necessary to mention at which session of the Committee the property was inscribed); it may be appropriate to produce the text in several languages for properties which receive many foreign visitors.

际社会对列入《名录》的遗产的承认（但无需指出是在委员会的哪届会议上通过的）。如遗产有大量外国游客参观，标牌上的内容应使用多种语言。

271. The Committee proposes the following text as an example:

'(Name of property) has been inscribed upon the World Heritage List of *the Convention concerning the Protection of the World Cultural and Natural Heritage*. Inscription on this List confirms the Outstanding Universal Value of a cultural or natural property which deserves protection for the benefit of all humanity.'

271. 委员会提供了下段文字作为范例：

"（遗产名称）已根据《保护世界文化和自然遗产公约》列入《世界遗产名录》。遗产列入《名录》说明该项文化或自然遗产具有突出的普遍价值，对它的保护符合全人类的利益。"

272. This text could be then followed by a brief description of the property concerned.

272. 在这段话的后面，可对该遗产进行简要介绍。

273. Furthermore, the national authorities should encourage World Heritage properties to make a broad use of the Emblem such as on their letterheads, brochures and staff uniforms.

273. 此外，国家主管机构应该鼓励世界遗产在诸如信笺抬头、宣传手册，以及员工的工作服等物品上广泛使用世界遗产标志。

274. Third parties which have received the right to produce communication products related to the *World Heritage Convention* and World Heritage properties must give the Emblem proper visibility. They should avoid creating a different Emblem or logo for that particular product.

274. 授权负责推广《保护世界文化和自然遗产公约》和世界遗产相关产品的第三方应突出显示世界遗产标志，而且应避免在特定产品上使用不同的标志或标识。

VIII.E Principles on the use of the World Heritage Emblem

VIII.E 世界遗产标志的使用原则

275. The responsible authorities are henceforth requested to use the following principles in making decisions on the use of the Emblem:

Decision 39 COM

275. 有关权威机构在决定使用标志的过程中，应遵循以下原则：

第 39 COM 11 号决定

a).The Emblem should be utilized for all projects substantially associated with the work of the *Convention*, including, to the maximum extent technically and legally possible, those already approved and adopted, in order to promote the *Convention*.

b) A decision to approve use of the Emblem should be linked strongly to the quality and content of the product with which it is to be associated, not on the volume of products to be marketed or the financial return expected. The main criterion for approval should be the educational, scientific, cultural, or artistic value of the proposed product related to World Heritage principles and values. Approval should not routinely be granted to place the Emblem on products that have no, or extremely little, educational value, such as cups, T-shirts, pins, and other tourist souvenirs. Exceptions to this policy will be considered for special events, such as meetings of the Committee and ceremonies at which plaques are unveiled.

c) Any decision with respect to authorizing the use of the Emblem must be completely unambiguous and in keeping with the explicit and implicit goals and values of the World Heritage Convention.

d) Except when authorized in accordance with these principles it is not legitimate for commercial entities to use the Emblem directly on their own material to show their support for World Heritage. The Committee recognizes, however, that any individual, organization, or company is free to publish or produce whatever they consider to be appropriate regarding World Heritage properties, but official authorization to do so under the World Heritage Emblem remains the exclusive prerogative of the Committee, to be exercised as prescribed in these Guidelines and Principles and in the Table of Uses.

e) Use of the Emblem by other contracting parties should normally only be authorized

a）标志应用于所有与《公约》的工作密切相关的项目（包括在技术和法律许可的最大范围内，应用于已得到批准或已通过的项目上），以推广《公约》。

b）在决定是否授权使用标志时，应首先考虑相关产品的质量和内容，而非投入市场的产品数量或预期的经济回报。审核通过与否的主要标准是所申请产品与世界遗产的原则和相关的教育、科学、文化艺术价值。对于没有教育意义或教育意义很小的产品，如茶杯、T恤、别针，和其他旅游纪念品等等，应不予批准。以上规定的例外情况包括委员会会议、标牌揭幕仪式等。

c）所有涉及授权该标志使用的决定都应该非常明确，同时必须与《保护世界文化和自然遗产公约》明确表示和隐含的目标和价值保持一致。

d）除非依照这些原则得到授权，任何商业机构都不得直接在其产品上使用该标志，以此表示对世界遗产的支持。虽然委员会承认，任何个人、组织或公司都可以自由出版或生产它们认为对世界遗产有利的产品，但委员会是唯一有权授予世界遗产标志使用权的官方机构，且其授权必须遵守上述指南和原则及“使用表”的要求。

e）只有当该标志的使用与世界遗产直接相关时，其他签约合作方才能得到使用该标志的

when the proposed use deals directly with World Heritage properties. Such uses may be granted after approval by the national authorities of the countries concerned.

授权。而且，申请机构只有在其所在国的主管机构批准后才能获得使用授权。

f) In cases where no specific World Heritage properties are involved or are not the principal focus of the proposed use, such as general seminars and/or workshops on scientific issues or conservation techniques, use may be granted only upon express approval in accordance with these Guidelines and Principles with the Table of Uses. Requests for such uses should specifically document the manner in which the proposed use is expected to enhance the work of the *Convention*.

f）如果标志的使用不涉及具体的世界遗产，或具体的世界遗产不是核心内容，例如一般性的学术研讨会和有关科学问题或保存技术的讨论会，必须要根据上述指南和原则及“使用表”，得到明确批准。申请使用该标志时，要明确体现标志的使用方式，而且这种方式预计能够促进《公约》的工作。

g) Permission to use the Emblem should not be granted to travel agencies, airlines, or to any other type of business operating for predominantly commercial purposes, except under exceptional circumstances and when manifest benefit to the World Heritage generally or particular World Heritage properties can be demonstrated. Requests for such use should require approval in accordance with these Guidelines and Principles and the concurrence of the national authorities of countries specifically concerned.

g）通常标志的使用权不能授予旅行社、航空公司或任何其他商业机构的商业用途，除非在某些特殊情况以及世界遗产或特定的世界遗产项目能明确从中获益的情况下。这类使用申请需遵循《指南和原则》并得到相关权威机构的批准。

The Secretariat is not to accept any advertising, travel, or other promotional considerations from travel agencies or other, similar companies in exchange or in lieu of financial remuneration for use of the Emblem.

秘书处不会因为报酬接受旅行社或其他类似机构的任何广告、旅游或其他促销计划。

'Comprehensive Partnership Strategy' including 'Separate strategies for engagement with individual categories of partners' 192 EX/5. INF and PACT Strategy (Document WHC-13/37. COM/5D)

“全面战略伙伴关系”包括“与个别类别合作伙伴接触的独立战略”192 EX/5.INF and PACT 战略（文件 WHC–13/37.COM/5D）

Decision 37 COM 5D

第 37 COM 5D 决定

h) When commercial benefits are anticipated, the Secretariat should ensure that the World Heritage Fund receives a fair share of the revenues and conclude a contract or other agreement that

h）如果在标志的使用过程中产生了商业利益，秘书处应该确保世界遗产基金也从中分得部分收益。秘书处应该与相关方签订合同或其他协议，以确定协议的性质、管理项目和收

documents the nature of the understandings that govern the project and the arrangements for provision of income to the Fund. In all cases of commercial use, any staff time and related costs for personnel assigned by the Secretariat or other reviewers, as appropriate, to any initiative, beyond the nominal, must be fully covered by the party requesting authorization to use the Emblem.

益分配。对于所有将标志用于商业目的的情况，秘书处和其他审议者在批准使用标志申请的过程中，发生的高于常规的一切人力或物力的成本，都应该由提出申请方支付。

National authorities are also called upon to ensure that their properties or the World Heritage Fund receive a fair share of the revenues and to document the nature of the understandings that govern the project and the distribution of any proceeds.

国家权威机构也要确保该国的遗产或者世界遗产基金能够得到相应的收益，确定协议性质、管理项目和收益分配。

i) If sponsors are sought for manufacturing products whose distribution the Secretariat considers necessary, the choice of partner or partners should be consistent, at a minimum, with the criteria set forth in the Comprehensive Partnership Strategy including ‘Separate strategies for engagement with individual categories or parners’ 192 EX/5.INF and PACT Strategy (Document WHC-13/37.COM/5D) and with such further fund-raising guidance as the Committee may prescribe. The necessity for such products should be clarified and justified in written presentations that will require approval in such manner as the Committee may prescribe.

i）如果秘书处因需要制造产品进行分发而寻找赞助商，合作伙伴（或多个合作伙伴）的选择至少应与全面战略伙伴关系包括“与个别类别合作伙伴接触的独立战略”192 EX/5.INF and PACT 战略（WHC–13/37.COM/5D 文件）以及其他委员会规定的资金筹措规定保持一致。对于生产这些商品的必要性，必须做出书面声明并得到委员会的批准。

j) The sale of goods or services bearing the name, acronym, logo and/or Internet domain name of UNESCO combined with the World Heritage Emblem chiefly for profit shall be regarded as “commercial use” for the purpose of the Operational Guidelines. Such use must be expressly authorized by the Director-General, under a specific contractual arrangement.

j）以盈利为目的销售的商品或服务，联合国搭载了教科文组织名称、缩略词、徽标 / 或互联网域名和世界遗产标志，在《操作指南》中被视为“商业用途”。该用途须根据特定合同安排，得到总干事的明确授权。

(definition adapted from 2007 UNESCO Logo Directives. Art III.2.1.3)

（根据 2007 年《教科文组织标志指导》艺术 III.2.1.3 定义）

VIII.F Authorization procedure for the use of the World Heritage Emblem

Simple agreement of the national authorities

276. National authorities may grant the use of the Emblem to a national entity, provided that the project, whether national or international, involves only World Heritage properties located on the same national territory. National authorities' decision should be guided by the Guidelines and Principles and by the Table of Uses.

Decision 39 COM 11

277. States Parties are invited to provide the Secretariat with the names and addresses of the authorities in charge of managing the use of the Emblem.

Circular letter dated 14 April 1999 http: //whc.unesco.org/circs/circ99-4e.pdf

Agreement requiring quality control of content

278. Any other request for authorization to use the Emblem should adopt the following procedure:

a). A request indicating the objective of the use of the Emblem, its duration and territorial validity, should be addressed to the Director of the World Heritage Centre.

b) The Director of the World Heritage Centre has the authority to grant the use of the Emblem in accordance with the Guidelines and Principles. For cases not covered, or not sufficiently covered, by the Guidelines and Principles and by the Table of Uses, the Director refers the matter to the Chairperson who, in the most difficult cases, might wish to refer the matter to the Committee for final decision. A yearly report on the authorized uses of the Emblem will be submitted to the World Heritage Committee.

VIII.F 使用世界遗产标志的授权程序

国家权威机构的初步认定

276. 如果国家或国际项目只涉及本国的世界遗产，国家权威机构可授权本国企业使用标志。国家权威机构的决定应遵守《指南和原则》。及“使用表”。

第 39 COM 11 号决定

277. 缔约国需要向秘书处提供负责管理标志使用的权威机构的名称和地址。

1999 年 4 月 14 日通函 http：//whc.unesco.org/circs/circ99–4e.pdf

要求对内容进行质量控制的协议

278. 任何关于授权使用标志的申请都需遵循以下步骤：

a）申请应该说明使用标志的目的、使用时间、使用地域并上交给世界遗产中心主任。

b）世界遗产中心主任有权根据《指南和原则》批准使用标志。遇到《指南和原则》及“使用表”尚未涉及或完全涵盖的情况，主任应将申请提交给主席，如果是很难处理的情况，主席会将该申请提交委员会做最后决定。有关授权使用标志的年度报告应提交给世界遗产委员会。

c) Authorization to use the Emblem in major products to be widely distributed over an undetermined period of time is conditional upon obtaining the manufacturer's commitment to consult with countries concerned and secure their endorsement of texts and images illustrating properties situated in their territory, at no cost to the Secretariat, together with the proof that this has been done. The text to be approved should be provided in either one of the official languages of the Committee or in the language of the country concerned. A draft model to be used by States Parties to authorize the use of the Emblem to third parties appears below.

c）如授权在不确定的时期内在广泛行销的主要产品上使用标志，生产商应承诺与相关国家协商，就有关其境内遗产的图片和文字取得其同意，同时生产商还应提供获取同意的证明，且秘书处不承担任何费用。报批的文书须以委员会任意一种正式语言或相关国家的语言书写。缔约国用于批准第三方使用标志的草拟范本应按以下格式填写：

Content Approval Form:

[Name of responsible national body], officially identified as the body responsible for approving the content of the texts and photos relating to the World Heritage properties located in the territory of [name of country], hereby confirms to [name of producer] that the text and the images that it has submitted for the [name of properties] World Heritage property (ies) are [approved] [approved subject to the following changes requested] [are not approved]

(delete whatever entry does not apply, and provide, as needed, a corrected copy of the text or a signed list of corrections).

Notes:

It is recommended that the initials of the responsible national official be affixed to each page of text.

内容批准表：

作为负责批准使用［国家名称］世界遗产图文的官方机构，［国家主管机构的名称］在此向［生产商名称］证实，它提交的世界遗产［遗产名称］图文已［通过审批］、［如做出以下变更便可通过审批］、［未通过审批］。

（删除不适用的条目，并按需要提供校正后文字或经签名的变更后清单的副件）。

注释：

建议在文本的每一页上都注明国家主管人员姓名的首字母。

The National Authorities are given one month from their acknowledged receipt in which to authorize the content, following which the producers may consider that the content has been tacitly approved, unless the responsible National Authorities request in writing a longer period.

自收到申请之日起一个月内，国家主管机构应该做出答复，批准文本内容。如未接到答复，生产商可视为该内容已得到默许，除非该国家主管机构书面要求延长批准时限。

Texts should be supplied to the National

提交给国家主管机构的申请所使用的语言

Authorities in one of the two official languages of the Committee, or in the official language (or in one of the official languages) of the country in which the properties are located, at the convenience of both parties.

应按照双方的需要，可选用委员会的两种官方语言之一或遗产所在国的官方语言（或其中一种官方语言）。

d) After having examined the request and considered it as acceptable, the Secretariat may establish an agreement with the partner.

d）在审阅并认为可批准申请后，秘书处应该与合作伙伴签订协议。

e) If the Director of the World Heritage Centre judges that a proposed use of the Emblem is not acceptable, the Secretariat informs the requesting party of the decision in writing.

e）如果世界遗产中心主任没有批准标志的使用，秘书处会以书面形式通知申请方。

VIII.G Right of States Parties to exert quality control

VIII.G 缔约国政府有权进行质量控制

279. Authorization to use the Emblem is inextricably linked to the requirement that the national authorities may exert quality control over the products with which it is associated.

279. 国家主管机构对授权使用标志的相关产品实施密切的质量控制。

a. The States Parties to the *Convention* are the only parties authorized to approve the content (images and text) of any distributed product appearing under the World Heritage Emblem with regard to the properties located in their territories.

a.《公约》的缔约国是唯一授权批准带有世界遗产标志并在其境内行销与遗产内容（图文）相关的产品的机构。

b. States Parties that protect the Emblem legally must review these uses.

b. 合法保护标志的缔约国必须审查标志的使用情况。

c. Other States Parties may elect to review proposed uses or refer such proposals to the Secretariat. States Parties are responsible for identifying an appropriate national authority and for informing the Secretariat whether they wish to review proposed uses or to identify uses that are inappropriate. The Secretariat maintains a list of responsible national authorities.

c. 其他缔约国也可决定审查所申请的使用方式，或者将提议提交给秘书处。缔约国政府负责指定相应的国家机构，并通知秘书处是否希望审查所申请的使用方式，或明确指出使用方式不适当。秘书处持有国家主管机构清单。

IX. INFORMATION SOURCES

IX. 信息来源

IX.A Information archived by the Secretariat

IX.A 秘书处存档的信息

280. The Secretariat maintains a database of

280. 秘书处将所有世界遗产委员会和《保

all documents of the World Heritage Committee and the General Assembly of States Parties to the *World Heritage Convention*. This database is available at the following Web address: http: //whc.unesco.org/en/statutorydoc

护世界文化和自然遗产公约》缔约国大会的资料存入数据库。该数据库可在以下网址访问：http：//whc.unesco.org/en/statutorydoc

281. The Secretariat ensures that copies of Tentative Lists, World Heritage nominations, including copies of maps and relevant information received from States Parties are archived in hard copy and in electronic format where possible. The Secretariat also arranges for the archiving of relevant information relating to inscribed properties, including evaluations and other documents developed by the Advisory Bodies, any correspondence and reports received from States Parties (including Reactive Monitoring and Periodic Reports) and correspondence and material from the Secretariat and World Heritage Committee.

281. 秘书处将确保《预备名录》和世界遗产申报文件副本（包括地图和缔约国提交的相关信息副本）已通过硬拷贝纸质形式存档，同时在可能的情况下保存电子版本。秘书处也安排对已列入《世界遗产名录》的遗产的相关信息进行存档，其中包括咨询机构发表的评估报告和其他文件、任何缔约国提交的信件和报告（包括反应性监测和定期报告），以及秘书处和世界遗产委员会发出的信件和材料。

282. Archived material will be kept in a form appropriate to long-term storage. Provisions will be made for the storage of paper copies and electronic copies, as relevant. Provision will be made for copies to be provided to States Parties as requested.

282. 存档材料的格式应适宜长期保存。将提供保存纸制和电子文件的相关设备。相关规定也将按要求提供给缔约国。

283. Nominations of those properties inscribed on the World Heritage List by the Committee will be made available for consultation. States Parties are urged to place a copy of the nomination on their own Web addresses and inform the Secretariat of this action. States Parties preparing nominations may wish to use such information as guides for identifying and elaborating nomination of properties within their own territories.

283. 委员会将妥善保存列入《世界遗产名录》的遗产申报文件，方便查阅。敦促缔约国将申报材料的电子版发布在本国的网站上，并通知秘书处。其他预备申报的国家可以利用这些信息确认并完善本国境内遗产的申报材料。

284. Advisory Body evaluations for each nomination and the decision of the Committee concerning each nomination are available at the following Web address : http: //whc.unesco.org/en/

284. 咨询机构对于每一项申报的评估意见和委员会所做的决定都可以在以下网站获取：http：//whc.unesco.org/en/advisorybodies

advisorybodies

IX.B Specific Information for World Heritage Committee members and other States Parties

IX.B 世界遗产委员会成员国和其他缔约国的详细信息

285. The Secretariat maintains two electronic mailing lists: one for Committee members (wh-committee@unesco.org) and one for all States Parties (wh-states@unesco.org). States Parties are requested to supply all appropriate email addresses for the establishment of these lists. These electronic mailing lists, which supplement but do not replace the traditional means of notifying States Parties, allow the Secretariat to communicate, in a timely manner, announcements about the availability of documents, changes to meeting schedules, and other issues relevant to Committee members and other States Parties.

285. 秘书处保存了两份电子邮件清单：一份是委员会成员联系方式（wh–committee@unesco.org），另一份是缔约国联系方式（wh–states@unesco.org）。缔约国必须提供所有相关邮箱地址，以供秘书处建立清单。电子邮件清单是补充而不会取代传统的邮寄方式，但秘书处可通过电子邮件及时发布有关文件的实用性、会议计划的变更，以及其他与委员会成员和其他缔约国相关的事宜。

286. Circular letters to the States Parties are available at the following Web address: http: //whc.unesco.org/en/circularletters

Another Web address, linked to the public Web address through restricted access, is maintained by the Secretariat and contains specific information targeted at Committee members, other States Parties and Advisory Bodies.

286. 发给缔约国的通函可以在以下网址获取：http：//whc.unesco.org/en/circularletters。

还可登录另一个网站链接到公共网址，但其访问权限受到严格限制。该网站由秘书处负责维护，包括委员会委员、缔约国和咨询机构的详细信息。

287.The Secretariat maintains also a database of decisions of the Committee and resolutions of the General Assembly of States Parties. These are available at the following Web address: http: //whc.unesco.org/en/decisions

Decision 28 COM 9

287. 秘书处还同时维护另外一个有关委员会决议、缔约国大会决议的数据库。可通过以下网址登录：http：//whc.unesco.org/en/decisions。

第 28 COM9 号决议

IX.C. Information and publications available to the public

IX.C. 向大众公开的信息和出版物

288. The Secretariat provides access to information labeled as publicly available and

288. 在可能的情况下，秘书处提供标注为面向公众且不受版权限制的关于世界遗产和其

copyright free on World Heritage properties and other relevant matters, wherever possible.

他相关问题的信息。

289. Information on issues related to World Heritage is available at the Secretariat's Web address (http: //whc.unesco.org), on the Web addresses of the Advisory Bodies and in libraries. A list of databases accessible on the web and links to relevant web addresses can be found in the Bibliography.

289. 与世界遗产有关的信息能在秘书处网站（http：//whc.unesco.org）、咨询机构网站和图书馆中获取。参考书目中提供了可在线访问的数据库清单以及相关网站链接。

290. The Secretariat produces a wide variety of World Heritage publications, including the World Heritage List, the List of World Heritage in Danger, Brief Descriptions of World Heritage properties, World Heritage Papers series, newsletters, brochures and information kits. In addition, other information materials aimed specifically at experts and the general public are also developed. The list of World Heritage publications can be found in the Bibliography or at the following Web address: http: //whc.unesco.org/en/publications.

290. 秘书处出版了大量有关世界遗产的出版物，包括《世界遗产名录》、《濒危世界遗产名录》、《世界遗产简要介绍》、《世界遗产论文》系列、简报、宣传册和信息工具包。此外，其他专门为专家和大众准备的信息也得到了发展。参考书目中列出了世界遗产出版物的名单，也可通过以下网址获取：http：//whc.unesco.org/en/publications。

These information materials are distributed to the public directly or through the national and international networks established by States Parties or by World Heritage partners.

这些信息资料将直接分发给公众，或通过缔约国或世界遗产合作伙伴建立的国家或国际网络向大众公开。

ANNEXES

Annex 1A
MODEL INSTRUMENT OF RATIFICATION/ACCEPTANCE

WHEREAS the Convention concerning the Protection of the World Cultural and Natural Heritage was adopted on 16 November 1972 by the General Conference of UNESCO at its seventeenth session;

NOW THEREFORE the Government of .... having considered the aforesaid *Convention*, hereby [*ratifies* the same and undertake faithfully to carry out [*accepts* the stipulations therein contained.

IN WITNESS WHEREOF, I have signed and sealed this instrument.

Done at ....this ....day of ....20....... .

(Seal)

Signature of Head of State,
Prime Minister or
Minister of Foreign Affairs

The model instrument of ratification/acceptance is available from the UNESCO World Heritage Centre and at the following Web address: http: //whc.unesco.org/en/modelratification

The original signed version of the completed form should be sent, preferably with an official translation in English or French, to: Director-General, UNESCO, 7 place de Fontenoy, 75352 Paris 07 SP, France

附件

附件 1A
批准函或同意书示范文本

1972 年 11 月 16 日，联合国教科文组织第 17 届大会上通过了《保护世界文化与自然遗产公约》。

因此，现在 ________________________________ 政府已考虑上述公约，同意 / 接受并将忠实地执行上述公约中包含的各项规定。

上述公约中包含的各项规定。

特此证明，本人已在本文件上签字盖章。
20 年 __________ 月 __________ 地点 __________

（盖章）

国家首脑，
总理或
外交部长签字

登录联合国教科文组织世界遗产中心网站 http：//whc.unesco.org/en/modelratification 获取接受和正式批准的模板

填好的表格原件应发送至 Director–General，UNESCO，7 place de Fontenoy，75352 Paris 07 SP，France，最好附有英语或法语的正式翻译件

Annex 1B
Model Instrument Of Accession

WHEREAS the Convention concerning the Protection of the World Cultural and Natural Heritage was adopted on 16 November 1972 by the General Conference of UNESCO at its seventeenth session;

NOW THEREFORE the Government of .... having considered the aforesaid *Convention*, hereby accedes the same and undertake faithfully to carry out the stipulations therein contained.

IN WITNESS WHEREOF, I have signed and sealed this instrument.

Done at ....this ....day of ....20....... .

(Seal)

Signature of Head of State,
Prime Minister or
Minister of Foreign Affairs

The model instrument of accession is available from the UNESCO World Heritage Centre and at the following Web address: http: //whc.unesco.org/en/modelratification

The original signed version of the completed form should be sent, preferably with an official translation in English or French, to: Director-General, UNESCO, 7 place de Fontenoy, 75352 Paris 07 SP, France

附件 1B
同意书示范文本

1972 年 11 月 16 日，联合国教科文组织第 17 届大会通过了《保护世界文化与自然遗产公约》。

现在 ______________________________ 政府经考虑同意加入并忠实地执行上述公约。

特此证明，本人已在本文件上签字盖章。

20 年 __________ 月 __________ 地点 __________

（盖章）

国家首脑签字，

总理或

外交部长

登录联合国教科文组织的世界遗产中心网站 http：//whc.unesco.org/en/modelratification 获取此正式批准的模板

填好的表格原件应发送至 Director-General，UNESCO，7 place de Fontenoy，75352 Paris 07 SP，France，最好附有英语或法语的正式翻译件

Annex 2A
TENTATIVE LIST SUBMISSION FORMAT

STATE PARTY: DATE OF SUBMISSION:

Submission prepared by:

Name: E-mail:

Address: Fax:

Institution: Telephone:

NAME OF PROPERTY:

State, Province or Region:

Latitude and Longitude, or UTM coordinates

DESCRIPTION:

Justification of Outstanding Universal Value:

(Preliminary identification of the values of the property which merit inscription on the World Heritage List)

Criteria met [see Paragraph 77 of the *Operational Guidelines*]:

(Please tick the box corresponding to the proposed criteria and justify the use of each below)

(i)	(ii)	(iii)	(iv)	(v)	(vi)	(vii)	(viii)	(ix)	(x)

Statements of authenticity and/or integrity [see Paragraphs 78-95 of the *Operational Guidelines*]:

Comparison with other similar properties:

(The comparison should outline similarities with other properties on the World Heritage List or not, and the reasons that make the property stand out)

The Tentative List submission format is available from the UNESCO World Heritage Centre and at the following Web address: http: //whc.unesco.org/en/tentativelists

Further guidance on the preparation of Tentative Lists can be found in Paragraphs 62-67 of the

Operational Guidelines.

An example of a completed Tentative List submission format can be found at the following Web address: http: //whc.unesco.org/en/tentativelists

All Tentative Lists submitted by States Parties are available at the following Web address: http: //whc.unesco.org/en/tentativelists

The original signed version of the completed Tentative List submission format should be sent in English or French to: UNESCO World Heritage Centre, 7 place de Fontenoy, 75352 Paris 07 SP, France

States Parties are encouraged to also submit this information in electronic format (diskette or CD-Rom) or by e-mail to wh-tentativelists@unesco.org

附件 2A
《预备名单》提交格式

缔约国：　　　　　　　　　　　　提交日期：
提交准备机构：
名称：　　　　　　　　　　　　　电子邮件：
地址：　　　　　　　　　　　　　传真：
机构：　　　　　　　　　　　　　电话：

遗产名称：

国家、省份或地区：

经纬度或 UTM 坐标：

描述：

突出普遍价值申明：
（初步确认应列入《世界遗产名录》的遗产价值）

符合标准［参见《操作指南》第 77 条］：
（请勾选与提议的标准相对应的文本框，并给出选择理由）

(i)	(ii)	(iii)	(iv)	(v)	(vi)	(vii)	(viii)	(ix)	(x)

完整性和真实性声明［参见《操作指南》第 78–95 条］：

与其他类似遗产的比较分析：
（比较分析应体现出该遗产与《世界遗产名录》中遗产或其他遗产的相似性以及该遗产卓尔不群的原因）

登录 http：//whc.unesco.org/en/tentativelists 网站可获得完整的《预备名录》提交格式样板。

《操作指南》第 62–67 条中含有《预备名单》准备工作的详细指导。

完整地预备目录提交表格范例可在 http：//whc.unesco.org/en/tentativelists 下载。

缔约国提交的预备目录可在下列网站查询；
http：//whc.unesco.org/en/tentativelists

填好的《预备名录》原件应发送至 Director–General，UNESCO，7 place de Fontenoy，75352 Paris 07 SP，France，最好附有英语或法语的正式翻译件。

鼓励缔约国同时提交电子版表格（磁盘或 CD）或发送电子邮件至；
wh–tentativelists@unesco.org

Annex 2B
TENTATIVE LIST SUBMISSION FORMAT FOR TRANSNATIONAL AND TRANSBOUNDARY FUTURE NOMINATIONS

STATE PARTY: DATE OF SUBMISSION:

Submission[①] prepared by:

Name: E-mail:

Title:

Address: Fax:

Institution: Telephone:

1.a Name of the transnational/trans-boundary future nomination[②]: 1.b Other States Parties participating:

1.c Name (s) of the national component part (s) : 1.d State, Province or Region: 1.e Latitude and Longitude, or Universal Transverse Mercator (UTM) coordinates:

2.a Brief Description of the transnational/trans-boundary future nomination[③]:

2.b Description of the component part (s) :

3.JUSTIFICATION FOR OUTSTANDING UNIVERSAL VALUE[④] OF THE FUTURE NOMINATION AS A WHOLE

(Preliminary identification of the values of the future nomination as a whole which merit inscription on the World Heritage List)

3.a Criteria met [⑤][see Paragraph 77 of the *Operational Guidelines*]:

(Please tick the box corresponding to the proposed criteria and justify the use of each below)

---

① This submission will be valid only when all the States Parties indicated in Section 1.b have sent their submissions.

② The text provided in this section should be identical in all submissions of the States Parties involved in the presentation of the same transnational / trans-boundary future nomination.

③ In case of transnational/trans-boundary properties any modification will need the agreement of all States Parties concerned.

④ In case of transnational/trans-boundary properties any modification will need the agreement of all States Parties concerned.

⑤ In case of transnational/trans-boundary properties any modification will need the agreement of all States Parties concerned.

(i)	(ii)	(iii)	(iv)	(v)	(vi)	(vii)	(viii)	(ix)	(x)

3.b Statements of authenticity and/or integrity [see Paragraphs 79-95 of the *Operational Guidelines*]:

3.c.1 Justification of the selection of the component part (s) in relation to the future nomination as a whole:

3.c.2 Comparison with other similar properties[①]:

(This comparison should outline the similarities with other properties inscribed or not on the World Heritage List, and the reasons for the exceptional character of the future nomination).

① In case of transnational/trans-boundary properties any modification will need the agreement of all States Parties concerned.

附件 2B
跨国和跨境遗产申报
《预备名单》提交格式

缔约国：　　　　　　　　　　　　提交日期：
提交[①]准备机构：
名称：　　　　　　　　　　　　　电子邮件：
地址：　　　　　　　　　　　　　传真：
机构：　　　　　　　　　　　　　电话：

1.a　未来申报跨国或跨境遗产名称[②]：
1.b　其他参与缔约国：

1.c　本国构成部分的名称：
1.d　国家、省份或地区：
1.c　经纬度或 UTM 坐标：

2.a　跨国或跨境遗产申报的简介[③]：
2.b　各组成部分描述：

3. 申报遗产整体的突出普遍价值[④]声明
（对遗产整体赖以列入《世界遗产名单》的突出普遍价值的初步认定）

3.a　符合标准[⑤][参见《操作指南》第 77 条]：
（请勾选与提议的标准相对应的文本框，并给出选择理由）

(i)	(ii)	(iii)	(iv)	(v)	(vi)	(vii)	(viii)	(ix)	(x)

3.b　完整性和真实性声明 [参见《操作指南》第 78–95 条]：
3.c.1　对整体申报项目中各构成部分的选择加以解释：

---

① 只有当 1.b 中涉及的所有缔约国都提交后该提交方被认可。
② 本部分提交的文本与相关缔约国展示的跨境、跨界或未来申报完全一致。
③ 对跨境、跨界遗产的任何修改都需要全体相关缔约国的一致同意。
④ 对跨境、跨界遗产的任何修改都需要全体相关缔约国的一致同意。
⑤ 对跨境、跨界遗产的任何修改都需要全体相关缔约国的一致同意。

3.c.2 与其他类似遗产的比较分析[1]：

（比较分析应体现出该遗产与《世界遗产名录》中遗产或其他遗产的相似性以及该遗产卓尔不群的原因）

① 对跨境、跨界遗产的任何修改都需要全体相关缔约国的一致同意。

Annex 3 Guidelines on the inscription of specific types of properties on the World Heritage List[①]

The ICOMOS List of thematic studies is available at the following address:

http://www.icomos.org/studies

The IUCN List of thematic studies is available at the following address:

http://www.iucn.org/about/work/programmes/wcpa_worldheritage/wheritage_pub/

INTRODUCTION

1. This annex provides information on specific types of properties to guide States Parties in preparing nominations of properties for inscription on the World Heritage List. The following information constitutes guidelines that should be used in association with Chapter II of the *Operational Guidelines*, which contains the criteria for inscription of properties on the World Heritage List.

① *Guidelines by the World Heritage Committee at its 16th session (Santa Fe 1992) (see document WHC-92/CONF.002/12).*

附件 3 特定类型遗产列入《世界遗产名录》指南[①]

ICOMOS 主题研究详细目录可见于：http://www.icomos.org/studies

IUCN 主题研究详细目录可见于：

http://www.iucn.org/about/work/programmes/wcpa_worldheritage/wheritage_pub/

序言

1. 该附件提供了特定类型遗产的相关信息以便指导缔约国申报遗产列入《世界遗产名录》的准备工作。下列信息可与《操作指南》第二章联合使用，其中包含遗产列入《世界遗产名录》应满足的标准。

① 委员会会为遗产未来开发提供附加指导。世界遗产委员会第 16 届大会操作指南（Santa Fe 1992）（WHC-92/CONF. 002/12 文件）。

2.The Committee has endorsed the findings of expert meetings on the subject of cultural landscapes, towns, canals and routes (Part I, below).

2. 委员会已经批准了文化景观、城镇、运河和文化线路召开的专家会议所做的决议（参见下文第一部分）。

3. The reports of other expert meetings requested by the World Heritage Committee, in the framework of the Global Strategy for a representative, balanced and credible World Heritage List, are referred to in Part II.

3. 应世界遗产委员会的要求，在具代表性、均衡性和可信性《世界遗产名录》的全球战略大框架下的其他专家会议报告（参见第二部分）。

4. Part III lists various comparative and thematic studies prepared by the Advisory Bodies.

4. 第三部分列出了咨询团体完成的各种比较和主题研究。

I. Cultural Landscapes, Towns, Canals and Routes

I. 文化景观、城镇、运河与文化线路

5. The World Heritage Committee has identified and defined several specific types of cultural and natural properties and has adopted specific guidelines to facilitate the evaluation of such properties when nominated for inscription on the World Heritage List. To date, these cover the following categories, although it is likely that others may be added in due course:

a) Cultural Landscapes;
b) Historic Towns and Town Centres;
c) Heritage Canals;
d) Heritage Routes.

5. 世界遗产委员会已经认定并定义了几种特殊的文化与自然遗产类型，并制定了具体的指南以便对这些遗产申报列入《世界遗产名录》进行评估。到目前为止，这些遗产包括以下种类，当然未来也可能会有其他类型被适时列入：

1）文化景观；
2）历史城镇和城镇中心；
3）遗产运河；
4）遗产线路。

CULTURAL LANDSCAPES[①]

文化景观[①]

Definition

定义

6. Cultural landscapes are cultural properties and represent the 'combined works of nature and

6. 文化景观属于文化遗产，正如《公约》第一条所述，它们是"人类与大自然的共同杰作"。文化景观见证了人类社会和聚落在自然限制或自然环境的影响下，随着时间的推移而产

① This text was included in the January 1987 version of The Operational Guidelines following the discussion by the Committee at its 8th session (Buenos Aires, 1984) which met in Paris from 5 to 7 September 1984 organized by ICOMOS

① 本部分内容见 1987 年 1 月的操作指南，经国际古迹遗址理事会于 1984 年 9 月 5—7 日在巴黎召开的。第 8 次（Buenos Aires, 1984）大会讨论通过。

of man' designated in Article 1 of the *Convention*. They are illustrative of the evolution of human society and settlement over time, under the influence of the physical constraints and/or opportunities presented by their natural environment and of successive social, economic and cultural forces, both external and internal.

生的进化，也展示了社会、经济和文化外部和内部的发展力量。

7. They should be selected on the basis both of their Outstanding Universal Value and of their representativity in terms of a clearly defined geo-cultural region and also for their capacity to illustrate the essential and distinct cultural elements of such regions.

7. 文化景观选择的依据包括其突出普遍价值、在特定地理文化区域中的代表性，以及体现这些地区核心和独特文化元素的能力。

8. The term 'cultural landscape' embraces a diversity of manifestations of the interaction between humankind and its natural environment.

8. “文化景观”一词包含了人类与其所在的自然环境之间互动的多种表现。

9. Cultural landscapes often reflect specific techniques of sustainable land use, considering the characteristics and limits of the natural environment they are established in, and a specific spiritual relation to nature. Protection of cultural landscapes can contribute to modern techniques of sustainable land use and can maintain or enhance natural values in the landscape. The continued existence of traditional forms of land use supports biological diversity in many regions of the world. The protection of traditional cultural landscapes is therefore helpful in maintaining biological diversity.

9. 考虑到其所处自然环境的局限性和特点，文化景观通常能够反映可持续土地利用的特殊技术，反映了与大自然特定的精神关系。保护文化景观有利于用现代技术保持土地可持续使用或提升景观的自然价值。传统土地使用形式的持续存在支持了世界大多数地区的生物多样性，因此，对传统文化景观的保护也有益于保持生物多样性。

Definition and Categories

定义和种类

10. Cultural landscapes fall into three main categories, namely:

(i) The most easily identifiable is the clearly defined landscape designed and created intentionally by man. This embraces garden and parkland landscapes constructed for aesthetic

10. 文化景观有三种主要的类型，即：

（i）最易识别的一类是明确定义的、人类刻意设计及创造的景观。其中包含出于美学原因建造的园林和公园景观，它们经常（但不总是）与宗教或其他纪念性建筑物或建筑群相结合。

reasons which are often (but not always) associated with religious or other monumental buildings and ensembles.

(ii) The second category is the organically evolved landscape. This results from an initial social, economic, administrative, and/or religious imperative and has developed its present form by association with and in response to its natural environment. Such landscapes reflect that process of evolution in their form and component features. They fall into two sub-categories:

（ii）第二类是有机演进的景观。它们产生于最初始的一种社会、经济、行政以及宗教需要，并通过与周围自然环境的联系或相适应而发展到目前的形式。这种景观反映了其形式和重要组成部分的进化过程。它们又可分为两类：

- a relict (or fossil) landscape is one in which an evolutionary process came to an end at some time in the past, either abruptly or over a period. Its significant distinguishing features are, however, still visible in material form.

– 文物（或化石）景观，它代表过去某一时间内已经完成的进化过程，它的结束或为突发性的或渐进式的。然而，它的显著特征在实物上仍清晰可见。

- a continuing landscape is one which retains an active social role in contemporary society closely associated with the traditional way of life, and in which the evolutionary process is still in progress. At the same time it exhibits significant material evidence of its evolution over time.

– 另外一种是延续性景观，它在当今社会与传统生活方式的密切交融中持续扮演着一种积极的社会角色，演变过程仍在持续，同时，它也是历史演变发展的重要物证。

(iii) The final category is the associative cultural landscape. The inscription of such landscapes on the World Heritage List is justifiable by virtue of the powerful religious, artistic or cultural associations of the natural element rather than material cultural evidence, which may be insignificant or even absent.

（iii）最后一种景观是关联性文化景观。将这一景观列入《世界遗产名录》是因为这类景观体现了强烈的与自然因素、宗教、艺术或文化的关联性，而不仅仅是实体的文化物证，后者对它来说并不重要，甚至是可以缺失的。

Inscription of Cultural Landscapes on the World Heritage List

将文化景观列入《世界遗产名录》

11. The extent of a cultural landscape for inscription on the World Heritage List is relative to its functionality and intelligibility. In any case, the sample selected must be substantial enough to adequately represent the totality of the cultural landscape that it illustrates. The possibility of designating long linear areas which represent

11. 文化景观能否列入《世界遗产名录》取决于其功能性和可理解性。无论如何，被选的要素必须能够充分代表该种文化景观所要表达的全部内容的实质。不排除申报具有文化意义的长距离的代表交通和交流网络的线性区域的可能性。

culturally significant transport and communication networks should not be excluded.

12. General criteria for protection and management are equally applicable to cultural landscapes. It is important that due attention be paid to the full range of values represented in the landscape, both cultural and natural. The nominations should be prepared in collaboration with and the full approval of local communities.

12. 总的保护和管理的一般标准同样适用于文化景观。应重视景观所表现的文化与自然所有方面的价值。申报应取得当地社区的同意并在他们的协同合作下进行。

13. The existence of a category of 'cultural landscape', included on the World Heritage List on the basis of the criteria set out in Paragraph 77 of the *Operational Guidelines*, does not exclude the possibility of properties of exceptional importance in relation to both cultural and natural criteria continuing to be inscribed (see definition of mixed properties as set out in Paragraph 46). In such cases, their Outstanding Universal Value must be justified under both sets of criteria.

13.“文化景观”现存的类别，包括根据《操作指南》的第 77 条标准已列入《世界遗产名录》的景观，不排除继续吸收能展现文化和自然特殊重要性的遗产的可能性（参见第 46 条落中对混合遗产的定义）。在这种情况下，可同时根据两套标准对其突出普遍价值进行评定。

HISTORIC TOWNS AND TOWN CENTRES[①]

历史城镇和城镇中心[①]

Definition and Categories

定义和种类

14. Groups of urban buildings eligible for inscription on the World Heritage List fall into three main categories, namely:

(i) towns which are no longer inhabited but which provide unchanged archaeological evidence of the past; these generally satisfy the criterion of authenticity and their state of conservation can be relatively easily controlled;

(ii) historic towns which are still inhabited

14. 符合列入《世界遗产名录》标准的城区包括下列三种：

（i）无人居住但城镇原始状态保存完好的城镇，这些城镇一般符合真实性的评价标准且保护状况相对易于控制；

（ii）沿用至今的历史城镇，这些城镇在社会经济和文化的变化中不断发展并将持续发展，

① Expert meeting on "Heritage Canals" (Canada, 15-19 September 1994) (see document WHC-94/CONF.003/INF.10) discussed by the World Heritage Committee at its 19th session (Berlin, Germany, 1995) (see document WHC-95/CONF.203/16).

① 世界遗产委员会在第 19 届大会（1995 年德国柏林）（WHC–95/CONF.203/16 文件）上讨论了“遗产运河”专家会议报告（加拿大 1994 年 9 月 15–17）（见 WHC–94/CONF.003/INF.10 文件

and which, by their very nature, have developed and will continue to develop under the influence of socio economic and cultural change, a situation that renders the assessment of their authenticity more difficult and any conservation policy more problematical;

(iii) new towns of the twentieth century which paradoxically have something in common with both the aforementioned categories: while their original urban organization is clearly recognizable and their authenticity is undeniable, their future is unclear because their development is largely uncontrollable.

这种情况致使对它们真实性的评估更加困难，保护政策存在的问题也较多；

（iii）二十世纪的新镇，这类城镇与上述两种城镇都有相似之处：一方面它最初的城市组织结构仍清晰可见，其历史真实性不容置疑，另一方面它的未来是不明确的，因为它的发展基本是不可控的。

Inscription of Historic Towns and Town Centres on the World Heritage List

将历史城镇和城镇中心列入《世界遗产名录》

15. The significance of Historic Towns and Town Centres can be examined under the factors outlined below:

(i) Towns no longer inhabited

The evaluation of towns that are no longer inhabited does not raise any special difficulties other than those related to archaeological properties in general: the criteria which call for uniqueness or exemplary character have led to the choice of groups of buildings noteworthy for their purity of style, for the concentrations of monuments they contain and sometimes for their important historical associations. It is important for urban archaeological sites to be listed as integral units. A cluster of monuments or a small group of buildings is not adequate to suggest the multiple and complex functions of a city which has disappeared; remains of such a city should be preserved in their entirety together with their natural surroundings whenever possible.

(ii) Inhabited historic towns

In the case of inhabited historic towns the difficulties are numerous, largely owing to the fragility of their urban fabric (which has in

15. 历史城镇和城镇中心的价值可以通过下列因素评估：

（i）废弃无人居住的城镇

对无人居住的城镇的评估除了有关的考古遗产的一般性问题，不会产生其他特殊困难：要求独特性或典范性的评价标准致使人们在选择建筑群时更关注其风格纯粹性，所含历史遗迹的集中程度，有时甚至包括与重要历史事件的关联性。列入时把城市里的文物古迹作为一个整体单位这一点很重要。几个纪念性建筑和建筑群不足以说明一个已消失城市复杂多样的功能，对于这种城市的遗迹，应尽可能地保留它们的完整性，包括它们周围的自然环境。

（ii）沿用至今的历史城镇

评估尚有人居住的历史城镇困难较多，这在很大程度上是因为城市构造的脆弱性（其中大多数的发展进程在工业时代到来后被打乱），

many cases been seriously disrupted since the advent of the industrial era) and the runaway speed with which their surroundings have been urbanized. To qualify for inscription, towns should compel recognition because of their architectural interest and should not be considered only on the intellectual grounds of the role they may have played in the past or their value as historical symbols under criterion (vi) for the inscription of cultural properties on the World Heritage List (see Paragraph 77 (vi) of the *Operational Guidelines*). To be eligible for inscription in the List, the spatial organization, structure, materials, forms and, where possible, functions of a group of buildings should essentially reflect the civilization or succession of civilizations which have prompted the nomination of the property. Four categories can be distinguished:

周围环境以近乎失控的速度不断被城市化。要想列入《世界遗产名录》，这些城镇的建筑价值应该得到认可，不应该仅仅依赖它们在历史中曾经的重要角色和作为历史象征的价值（将文化遗产列入《世界遗产名录》的标准（vi）（参见《操作指南》第77（vi）条内容）。要达到列入《世界遗产名录》的要求，空间组织、结构、材料、形式，甚至建筑群的功能应从本质上反映遗产所在地区文明社会的文明和文明演进的过程。这类城镇可分为以下四类：

a) Towns which are typical of a specific period or culture, which have been almost wholly preserved and which have remained largely unaffected by subsequent developments. Here the property to be listed is the entire town together with its surroundings, which must also be protected;

a）突出代表了某一特定时期或文化的城镇，保存完整且未受到后续发展的影响。这种城镇将作为一个整体申报，其周围环境也要受到保护；

b) Towns that have evolved along characteristic lines and have preserved, sometimes in the midst of exceptional natural surroundings, spatial arrangements and structures that are typical of the successive stages in their history. Here the clearly defined historic part takes precedence over the contemporary environment;

b）城镇具有明显的演进进化脉络并在特殊的自然环境中时常保存了各个历史时期中的典型空间安排和结构的城镇。这种情况下，明确定义的历史城区比当代环境更具价值；

c) 'Historic centres' that cover exactly the same area as ancient towns and are now enclosed within modern cities. Here it is necessary to determine the precise limits of the property in its widest historical dimensions and to make appropriate provision for its immediate surroundings;

c）与原来古镇的分布区域几乎完全相同但今天处于现代城市中的“历史中心”，这种情况下，有必要在最宽泛的历史维度下确定遗产范围并为它的周边环境制定适当的规定；

d) Sectors, areas or isolated units which, even in the residual state in which they have survived,

d）城区、地域或一些孤立的城市空间单元，即使残破不堪，也为一个已消失的历史城镇的

provide coherent evidence of the character of a historic town which has disappeared. In such cases surviving areas and buildings should bear sufficient testimony to the former whole.

特征提供统一连贯的证明。这种情况下遗存空间和建筑蕴含的证据必须能充分见证原有整体地区。

Historic centres and historic areas should be listed only where they contain a large number of ancient buildings of monumental importance which provide a direct indication of the characteristic features of a town of exceptional interest. Nominations of several isolated and unrelated buildings which allegedly represent, in themselves, a town whose urban fabric has ceased to be discernible, should not be encouraged. However, nominations could be made regarding properties that occupy a limited space but have had a major influence on the history of town planning. In such cases, the nomination should make it clear that it is the monumental group that is to be listed and that the town is mentioned only incidentally as the place where the property is located. Similarly, if a building of clearly Outstanding Universal Value is located in severely degraded or insufficiently representative urban surroundings, it should, of course, be listed without any special reference to the town.

只有当历史中心和历史区域包含了大量具有重大意义的古建筑，能直接显示一个具备极高价值的城镇的典型特征时，才可以被列入《世界遗产名录》。如果只是若干孤立和毫无关联的建筑群，无法再现历史城市的原有格局，则不应申报。

可以申报空间有限但却对城镇规划的历史影响重大的遗产，这种情况下，需明确申报的是文物古迹，城镇只是作为其所在区域被申报。同样，如果一座具有明确的突出普遍价值的建筑坐落在已严重退化或不具有充分的代表性的城市环境中，则应被独立申报，不必专门申报城镇。

(iii) New towns of the twentieth century

（iii）二十世纪的新城

It is difficult to assess the quality of new towns of the twentieth century. History alone will tell which of them will best serve as examples of contemporary town planning. The examination of the files on these towns should be deferred, save under exceptional circumstances. Under present conditions, preference should be given to the inscription in the World Heritage List of small or medium sized urban areas which are in a position to manage any potential growth, rather than the great metropolises, on which sufficiently complete information and documentation cannot readily be provided that would serve as a satisfactory basis for their inscription in their entirety. In view of

评定二十世纪新城镇的品质比较困难。历史本身会说明哪座城镇最能代表当代城镇规划的典范。对这些城镇资料的审核可推后，某些特殊情况除外。

在现行条件下，《世界遗产名录》应优先选择能够控制发展的中小型城区而不是大都市，大城市也很难为其整体申报提供完整的信息和文献资料作为满意的依据。

考虑到将一座城镇列入《世界遗产名录》对其未来发展的影响，应被视为特殊情况处理。申报列入《名录》意味着已经有相应的立法和行政手段确保对建筑群及其背景环境的保护。

the effects which the inscription of a town on the World Heritage List could have on its future, such entries should be exceptional. Inscription in the List implies that legislative and administrative measures have already been taken to ensure the protection of the group of buildings and its environment. Informed awareness on the part of the population concerned, without whose active participation any conservation scheme would be impractical, is also essential.

提高当地居民的保护意识也很重要，没有他们的积极参与，任何保护方案都是不切实际的。

HERITAGE CANALS

运河遗产

16. The concept of 'canals' is discussed in detail in the Report of the Expert Meeting on Heritage Canals (Canada, September 1994) ①

16. 关于运河遗产概念的专家会议（加拿大，1994 年 9 月）报告中对 " 运河 " 这一概念进行了详细的讨论 ①。

Definition

定义

17. A canal is a human-engineered waterway. It may be of Outstanding Universal Value from the point of view of history or technology, either intrinsically or as an exceptional example representative of this category of cultural property. The canal may be a monumental work, the defining feature of a linear cultural landscape, or an integral component of a complex cultural landscape.

17. 运河是人类设计并修建的水路。从历史或技术角度看，运河本质上或作为这种文化遗产类型的一个特例都可能具有突出普遍价值。历史运河可以被看作一个文物古迹，一个具有典型特征的线性文化景观，或是一个复杂的文化景观中的一个组成部分。

Inscription of Heritage Canals on the World Heritage List

将运河列入《世界遗产名录》

18. Authenticity depends holistically upon values and the relationships between these values. One distinctive feature of the canal as a heritage element is its evolution over time. This is linked

18. 真实性整体上取决于价值和这些价值之间的关系。运河作为一种遗产要素，其特征在于动态的演变过程。这与它在不同时期的用途和它所经历过的技术改变相关，这些改变可能构成重要的遗产要素。

① Expert meeting on "Heritage Canals" (Canada, 15-19 September 1994) (see document *WHC-94/CONF.003/INF.10*) discussed by the World Heritage Committee at its 19th session (Berlin, Germany, 1995) (see document *WHC-95/CONF.203/16*).

① 世界遗产委员会在第 19 届大会（1995 年德国柏林）（*WHC-95/CONF.203/16* 文件）上讨论了"遗产运河"专家会议报告（加拿大 1994 年 9 月 15–17）（见 *WHC-94/CONF.003/INF.10* 文件）

to how it was used during different periods and the associated technological changes the canal underwent. The extent of these changes may constitute a heritage element.

19. The authenticity and historical interpretation of a canal encompass the connection between the real property (subject of the *Convention*), possible movable property (boats, temporary navigation items) and the associated structures (bridges, etc) and landscape.

19. 一条运河的真实性和历史阐释包含真实的遗产（本《公约》主题）、与之相关的可移动遗产（船只、临时航运设施）以及相关构造（桥等）和景观之间的关系。

20. The significance of canals can be examined under technological, economic, social, and landscape factors as outlined below:

20. 运河的意义可从技术、经济、社会和景观等方面考虑：

(i) Technology

Canals can serve a variety of purposes: irrigation, navigation, defence, water-power, flood mitigation, land-drainage and water-supply. The following are areas of technology which may be of significance:

a) The lining and waterproofing of the water channel;

b) The engineering structures of the line with reference to comparative structural features in other areas of architecture and technology;

c) The development of the sophistication of construction methods; and

d) The transfer of technologies.

（i）技术

运河功能众多，包括：灌溉、航运、防御、水力发电、泄洪、地面排水和给水。以下从技术方面考虑可能具有重要意义：

a）水渠的衬砌和防水；

b）具有与其他建筑和技术领域结构特征相比较的水道工程结构；

c）综合建造方法的开发；

d）技术转移

(ii) Economy

Canals contribute to the economy in a variety of ways, e.g. in terms of economic development and the conveyance of goods and people. Canals were the first man-made routes for the effective carriage of bulk cargoes. Canals played and continue to play a key role in economic development through their use for irrigation. The following factors are important:

a) Nation building;

b) Agricultural development;

（ii）经济

运河以多种形式为经济做出贡献，如在经济发展、货物和人员运输方面。运河是人类开发最早的有效运输大批货物的线路；运河通过发挥灌溉功能在经济发展中扮演了并将继续扮演重要角色。下列因素很重要：

a）国家建设；

b）农业发展；

c) Industrial development;

d) Generation of wealth;

e) Development of engineering skills applied to other areas and industries; and

f) Tourism.

(iii) Social Factors

The building of canals had, and their operation continues to have, social consequences:

a) The redistribution of wealth with social and cultural results; and

b) The movement of people and the interaction of cultural groups.

(iv) Landscape

Such large-scale engineering works had and continue to have an impact on the natural landscape. Related industrial activity and changing settlement patterns cause visible changes to landscape forms and patterns.

c）工业发展；

d）传递财富；

e）可应用于其他领域和产业中的工程技术的发展；

f）旅游

（iii）社会因素

开凿运河及其持续使用具有社会影响：

a）具有社会和文化效应的财富再分配；

b）人口流动以及文化群组间的交互作用。

（iv）景观

大规模的工程曾经并将继续对自然景观造成影响。相关的工业活动和不断变换的聚居形式使景观的形式和格局发生了显著的变化。

HERITAGE ROUTES

遗产线路

21. The concept of 'routs' or cultural itineraries was discussed by the expert meeting on "Routes as a Part of our Cultural Heritage" (Madrid, Spain, November 1994)[①]

21.“将线路作为文化遗产的一部分”的专家会议（西班牙马德里，1994 年 12 月）上讨论了“线路”或文化线路的概念[①]。

Definition

定义

22. The concept of heritage routes is shown to be a rich and fertile one, offering a privileged framework in which mutual understanding, a plural approach to history and a culture of peace can all operate.

22. 遗产线路的概念丰富多彩，它提供了一种有效的构架，相互理解、多种历史观及和平文化能在其中共同发挥作用。

23. A heritage route is composed of tangible

23. 遗产线路由各种有形的要素构成，这些

① *Expert Meeting on "Routes as part of Our Cultural Heritage" (Madrid, 24-25 November 1994) (see document WHC-94/CONF.003/INF.13) discussed by the World Heritage Committee at its 19th session (Berlin, 1995) (see document WHC-95/CONF.203/16).*

① 世界遗产委员会在第 19 届大会（1995 年柏林）（WHC–95/CONF.203/16 文件）上讨论了在西班牙马德里举办的“将线路作为文化遗产的一部分”的专家会议报告（1994 年 11 月 24–25 日，马德里）（见文件 WHC–94/CONF.003/INF.13） elements of which the cultural significance comes from exchanges and a multi-dimensional dialogue across countries or regions, and that illustrate the interaction of movement, along the route, in space and time.

要素的文化意义来自于跨国界和跨地区的交流和多维对话，说明了沿这条线路上展开的时空的交流互动。

Inscription of Heritage Routes on the World Heritage List

将遗产线路列入《世界遗产名录》

24. The following points should be considered when determining whether a heritage route is suitable for inscription on the World Heritage List:

24. 在决定一条遗产线路是否具备列入《世界遗产名录》的资格时，下列几点应予以考虑：

(i) The requirement to hold Outstanding Universal Value should be recalled.

（i）重新考虑具有突出普遍价值的相关要求。

(ii) The concept of heritage routes:

（ii）遗产线路的概念：

- is based on the dynamics of movement and the idea of exchanges, with continuity in space and time;

– 基于动态的迁徙、思想的交流、空间和时间上具有的连续性；

- refers to a whole, where the route has a worth over and above the sum of the elements making it up and through which it gains its cultural significance

– 涉及一个整体，因此线路的整体价值要远远大于组成要素价值之和，也因此获得了其文化意义；

- highlights exchange and dialogue between countries or between regions;

– 强调国家间或地区间交流和对话；

- is multi-dimensional, with different aspects developing and adding to its prime purpose which may be religious, commercial, administrative or otherwise.

– 应是多维的，不同方面的发展，不断丰富和补充其主要用途，可能是宗教的、商业、行政的或其他用途。

(iii) A heritage route may be considered as a specific, dynamic type of cultural landscape, just as recent debates have led to their acceptance within the *Operational Guidelines*.

（iii）遗产线路可被视为一种特殊的动态的文化景观（近期这种争论使其被纳入《操作指南》）。

(iv) The identification of a heritage route is based on a collection of strengths and tangible elements, testimony to the significance of the route itself.

（iv）对遗产线路的认定基于各种物质和有形要素的集合，以见证线路本身重大意义的。

(v) The conditions of authenticity are to be applied on the grounds of its significance and other elements making up the heritage route. It will take into account the duration of the route, and

（v）真实性条件也将基于线路的重要性和其他组成要素。线路的使用时间也要考虑在内，可能还需考虑其现今使用的频率和受其影响的族群对其发展的合理意愿。

perhaps how often it is used nowadays, as well as the legitimate wishes for development of peoples affected.

These points will be considered within the natural framework of the route and its intangible and symbolic dimensions.

以上几点需放在线路的自然框架及其无形的和象征性层面考虑。

II. REPORTS OF REGIONAL AND THEMATIC EXPERT MEETINGS

II. 地区和主题专家会议报告

25. The World Heritage Committee, in the framework of the Global Strategy for a representative, balanced and credible World Heritage List has requested a number of regional and thematic expert meetings on different types of properties. The results of these meetings may guide States Parties in preparing nominations. The reports of the expert meetings presented to the World Heritage Committee are available at the following Web address: http://whc.unesco.org/en/globalstrategy

25. 在构建具有代表性、均衡性和可信性的《世界遗产名录》的全球战略构架指导下，世界遗产委员会要求为不同遗产类型开展一系列地区和主题专家会议。这些会议的结果将指导缔约国的申报准备工作。可通过下列网址获取已呈递给世界遗产委员会的会议报告：http://whc.unesco.org/en/globalstrategy

III. THEMATIC AND COMPARATIVE STUDIES BY THE ADVISORY BODIES

III. 咨询团体的主题和比较研究

26. To fulfil their obligations concerning evaluations of nominations of cultural and natural properties, the Advisory Bodies have undertaken comparative and thematic studies, often with partner organizations, in different subject areas in order to provide a context for their evaluations.

26. 为了履行评估文化与自然遗产申报的责任，咨询团体与合作伙伴组织对不同主题进行了各种比较研究和主题研究，旨在提供评估依据。

These reports, most of which are available on their respective Web addresses, include:

大部分相关报告可通过各有关网站获取，这些报告包括：

Earth's Geological History - A Contextual Framework for Assessment of World Heritage Fossil Site Nominations (September 1996)

《地球地质史——评估化石遗址世界遗产申报的背景框架》（1996 年 9 月）

International Canal Monuments List (1996)
http://www.icomos.org/studies/canals-toc.htm

《国际运河纪念碑名录》（1996 年）
http://www.icomos.org/studies/canals-toc.htm

World Heritage Bridges (1996)

http://www.icomos.org/studies/bridges.htm

《世界遗产中的桥梁》(1996年)

http://www.icomos.org/studies/bridges.htm

A Global Overview of Forest Protected Areas on the World Heritage List (September 1997)

http://www.unep-wcmc.org/wh/reviews/forests/

《〈世界遗产名录〉中的全球森林保护区概览》(1997年9)

http://www.unep-wcmc.org/wh/reviews/forests/

A Global Overview of Wetland and Marine Protected Areas on the World Heritage List (September 1997)

http://www.unep-wcmc.org/wh/reviews/wetlands/

《〈世界遗产名录〉中的全球湿地和海洋保护区概览》(1997年9月)

http://www.unep-wcmc.org/wh/reviews/wetlands/

Human Use of World Heritage Natural Sites (September 1997)

http://www.unep-wcmc.org/wh/reviews/human/

《人类对世界自然遗产的利用》(1997年9月)

http://www.unep-wcmc.org/wh/reviews/human/

Fossil Hominid Sites (1997)

http://www.icomos.org/studies/hominid.htm

《原始人类化石遗址》(1997年)

http://www.icomos.org/studies/hominid.htm

The Urban Architectural Heritage of Latin America (1998)

http://www.icomos.org/studies/latin-towns.htm

《拉丁美洲的城市建筑遗产》(1998年)

http://www.icomos.org/studies/latin-towns.htm

Les Théâtres et les Amphithéâtres antiques (1999)

http://www.icomos.org/studies/theatres.htm

《古剧院和古剧场》(1999年)

http://www.icomos.org/studies/theatres.htm

Railways as World Heritage Sites (1999)

http://www.icomos.org/studies/railways.htm

《铁路作为世界遗产》(1999年)

http://www.icomos.org/studies/railways.htm

A Global Overview of Protected Areas on the World Heritage List of Particular Importance for Biodiversity (November 2000)

http://www.unep-wcmc.org/wh/reviews/

《〈世界遗产名录〉中具有特殊意义的全球生物多样性保护区概览》(2000年11月)

http://www.unep-wcmc.org/wh/reviews/

Les villages ouvriers comme éléments du

《作为工业遗产组成要素的村镇工厂》(2001年)

patrimoine de l'industrie (2001)

http://www.icomos.org/studies/villages-ouvriers.htm

http://www.icomos.org/studies/villages–ouvriers.htm

A Global Strategy for Geological World Heritage (February 2002)

《世界地质遗产的全球战略》（2002 年 2 月）

Rock-Art Sites of Southern Africa (2002)

http://www.icomos.org/studies/sarockart.htm

《南非的岩石艺术遗址》（2002 年）

http://www.icomos.org/studies/sarockart.htm

AUTHENTICITY IN RELATION TO THE WORLD HERITAGE CONVENTION

《保护世界文化与自然遗产公约》相关的真实性

Annex 4 Autheuticity in Relation to the World Heritage Convention

Introduction

This Annex reproduces the Nara Document on Authenticity, drafted by the 45 participants to the Nara Conference on Authenticity in Relation to the World Heritage Convention, held at Nara, Japan, from 1-6 November 1994. The Nara Conference was organized in co-operation with UNESCO, ICCROM and ICOMOS.

The World Heritage Committee examined the report of the Nara meeting on Authenticity at its 18th session (Phuket, Thailand, 1994) (see document WHC-94/CONF, 003/16).

Subsequent expert meetings have enriched the concept of authenticity in relation to the *World Heritage Convention* (see Bibliography of the *Operational Guidelines*).

I. THE NARA DOCUMENT ON AUTHENTICITY

Preamble

1. We, the experts assembled in Nara (Japan), wish to acknowledge the generous spirit and intellectual courage of the Japanese authorities

附件 4 关于世界遗产的真实性

导言

本附件使用了《奈良真实性文件》。1994 年 11 月 1 日至 6 日，《世界遗产公约》相关真实性会议在日本奈良召开，与会的 45 位代表起草了《奈良真实性文件》。奈良会议由联合国教科文组织、国际文化遗产保护与修复研究中心和国际古迹遗址理事会联合主办。

世界遗产委员会第 18 届会议（泰国普吉岛，1994 年）上审核了奈良会议中关于真实性的报告（见文件 WHC–94/CONF，003/16）。

此后的专家会议丰富了《世界遗产公约》相关的真实性的概念（见《操作指南》的参考文献）。

I.《奈良真实性文件》

导言

1. 作为参与奈良（日本）会与会专家，我们在此感谢日本当局的慷慨精神与学术勇气，为我们适时提供了此论坛，使我们得以挑战遗

in providing a timely forum in which we could challenge conventional thinking in the conservation field, and debate ways and means of broadening our horizons to bring greater respect for cultural and heritage diversity to conservation practice.

产保护领域的传统思想，通过辩论的方式和手段拓展我们的视野，使我们在遗产保护的实践中更加尊重文化与遗产的多样性。

2. We also wish to acknowledge the value of the framework for discussion provided by the World Heritage Committee's desire to apply the test of authenticity in ways which accord full respect to the social and cultural values of all societies, in examining the outstanding universal value of cultural properties proposed for the World Heritage List.

2. 借此机会，我们对世界遗产委员会所提供的讨论的价值框架的表示感谢。该框架在尊重全社会的社会与文化价值的基础上验证真实性，并检验被列入《世界遗产名录》的文化遗产的突出普遍价值。

3. The Nara Document on Authenticity is conceived in the spirit of the Charter of Venice, 1964, and builds on it and extends it in response to the expanding scope of cultural heritage concerns and interests in our contemporary world.

3.《奈良真实性文件》是基于 1964 年《威尼斯宪章》的精神，并加以延伸，以应对当代世界对文化遗产的关注与兴趣的不断拓展。

4. In a world that is increasingly subject to the forces of globalization and homogenization, and in a world in which the search for cultural identity is sometimes pursued through aggressive nationalism and the suppression of the cultures of minorities, the essential contribution made by the consideration of authenticity in conservation practice is to clarify and illuminate the collective memory of humanity.

4. 在一个日益受到全球化以及同质化力量影响的世界，有时通过侵略性民族主义和压制少数民族文化以获取文化认同的世界，在保护实践中纳入真实性考虑具有重要的作用，可厘清并阐明人类的集体记忆。

Cultural Diversity and Heritage Diversity

文化多样性和遗产多样性

5. The diversity of cultures and heritage in our world is an irreplaceable source of spiritual and intellectual richness for all humankind. The protection and enhancement of cultural and heritage diversity in our world should be actively promoted as an essential aspect of human development.

5. 整个世界的文化与遗产多样性对所有人类而言，都是一项无可替代的丰富的精神与知识源泉。我们必须积极推动世界文化与遗产多样性的保护和强化，将其作为人类发展不可或缺的一部分。

6. Cultural heritage diversity exists in time and

6. 文化遗产的多样性存在于时间与空间之

space, and demands respect for other cultures and all aspects of their belief systems. In cases where cultural values appear to be in conflict, respect for cultural diversity demands acknowledgment of the legitimacy of the cultural values of all parties.

中，需要对其他文化及其信仰系统的各个方面予以尊重。在文化价值出现冲突的情况下，对文化多样性的尊重则意味着需要认可所有各方的文化价值的合理性。

7. All cultures and societies are rooted in the particular forms and means of tangible and intangible expression which constitute their heritage, and these should be respected.

7. 所有的文化与社会都根植于以有形与无形所表现出来的特殊形式和方法，这些形式和方法构成了他们的遗产，应该受到尊重。

8. It is important to underline a fundamental principle of UNESCO, to the effect that the cultural heritage of each is the cultural heritage of all. Responsibility for cultural heritage and the management of it belongs, in the first place, to the cultural community that has generated it, and subsequently to that which cares for it. However, in addition to these responsibilities, adherence to the international charters and conventions developed for conservation of cultural heritage also obliges consideration of the principles and responsibilities flowing from them. Balancing their own requirements with those of other cultural communities is, for each community, highly desirable, provided achieving this balance does not undermine their fundamental cultural values.

8. 至关重要的是强调任何一种文化遗产都是所有人类的共同遗产，这是联合国教科文组织的基本原则。对文化遗产的责任和管理首先应该是归属于其所产生的文化社区，接着是照看这一遗产的文化社区。然而，除这些责任之外，在决定相关原则与责任时，还应该遵守为文化遗产保护而制订的国际公约与宪章。所有社区都需要在尽量不损坏其基本文化价值的情况下，在自身的要求与其他文化社区的要求之间达成平衡。

Values and authenticity

价值与真实性

9. Conservation of cultural heritage in all its forms and historical periods is rooted in the values attributed to the heritage. Our ability to understand these values depends, in part, on the degree to which information sources about these values may be understood as credible or truthful. Knowledge and understanding of these sources of information, in relation to original and subsequent characteristics of the cultural heritage, and their meaning, is a requisite basis for assessing all aspects of

9. 对文化遗产的所有形式与历史时期的信息加以保护是遗产价值的根本。我们理解价值的能力部分的取决于有关价值的信息来源的真实或可靠的程度。对这些与文化遗产的最初与后续特征有关的信息来源及其意义的认识与了解是全面评估真实性的必备基础。

authenticity.

10. Authenticity, considered in this way and affirmed in the Charter of Venice, appears as the essential qualifying factor concerning values. The understanding of authenticity plays a fundamental role in all scientific studies of the cultural heritage, in conservation and restoration planning, as well as within the inscription procedures used for the *World Heritage Convention* and other cultural heritage inventories.

10.《威尼斯宪章》所探讨及认可的真实性是与价值相关的基本要素。对于真实性的了解在与文化遗产相关的科学研究、保护与修复规划以及《世界遗产公约》与其他遗产名单收录程序中都起着至关重要的作用。

11. All judgements about values attributed to cultural properties as well as the credibility of related information sources may differ from culture to culture, and even within the same culture. It is thus not possible to base judgements of values and authenticity within fixed criteria. On the contrary, the respect due to all cultures requires that heritage properties must be considered and judged within the cultural contexts to which they belong.

11. 一切有关文化项目价值以及相关信息来源可信度的判断都可存在文化差异，即使在相同的文化背景下，也可出现不同标准。因此不可基于固定的标准来评判价值和真实性。反之，出于对所有文化的尊重，必须在相关文化背景之下来对遗产项目加以考虑和评判。

12. Therefore, it is of the highest importance and urgency that, within each culture, recognition be accorded to the specific nature of its heritage values and the credibility and truthfulness of related information sources.

12. 因此，在每一种文化内部就其遗产价值的具体性质以及相关信息来源的真实性和可靠性达成共识就变得极其重要和迫切。

13. Depending on the nature of the cultural heritage, its cultural context, and its evolution through time, authenticity judgements may be linked to the worth of a great variety of sources of information. Aspects of the sources may include form and design, materials and substance, use and function, traditions and techniques, location and setting, and spirit and feeling, and other internal and external factors. The use of these sources permits elaboration of the specific artistic, historic, social, and scientific dimensions of the cultural heritage being examined.

13. 文化遗产的性质、文化语境、时间演进等方面的真实性评判可能会与信息来源有关。这些来源可包括很多方面，譬如形式与设计、材料与物质、用途与功能、传统与技术、地点与背景、精神与感情以及其他内在或外在因素。使用这些来源可对文化遗产的特定艺术、历史、社会和科学的维度加以详尽考察。

Appendix 1: Suggestions for follow-up (proposed by Herb Stovel)

1. Respect for cultural and heritage diversity requires conscious efforts to avoid imposing mechanistic formulae or standardized procedures in attempting to define or determine authenticity of particular monuments and sites.

2. Efforts to determine authenticity in a manner respectful of cultures and heritage diversity requires approaches which encourage cultures to develop analytical processes and tools specific to their nature and needs. Such approaches may have several aspects in common:

- efforts to ensure assessment of authenticity involve multidisciplinary collaboration and the appropriate utilisation of all available expertise and knowledge;
- efforts to ensure attributed values are truly representative of a culture and the diversity of its interests, in particular monuments and sites;
- efforts to document clearly the particular nature of authenticity for monuments and sites as a practical guide to future treatment and monitoring;
- efforts to update authenticity assessments in light of changing values and circumstances.

3. Particularly important are efforts to ensure that attributed values are respected, and that their determination included efforts to build, as far as possible, a multidisciplinary and community consensus concerning these values.

4. Approaches should also build on and facilitate international co-operation among all those with an interest in conservation of cultural heritage, in order to improve global respect and understanding for the diverse expressions and

附录 1：后续建议（由 H. Stovel 提议）

1. 对文化与遗产多样性的尊重，需要有意识的努力避免在试图界定或判断特定纪念物或历史场所的真实性时，套用机械化的公式或标准化的程序。

2. 尊重文化与遗产多样性来判断真实性需要采取一定的方法，鼓励不同文化针对其性质和需求制定出特定的分析过程与工具。这些方法可能会有以下共同点：

– 努力确保在真实性评估中纳入跨学科合作，合理使用所有专业技术和知识；

– 努力确保相关价值真正代表了一个文化和利益的多样性，尤其是纪念物与历史场所；

– 努力清晰记录有关纪念物与历史场所的真实性的特殊性质，作为未来保护与监测的实用指南；

– 努力根据不断的变化，对价值和环境真实性评估加以更新。

3. 尤其重要的是努力确保相关价值受到尊重，且尽量在决策中形成与这些价值有关的跨学科及社区统一意见。

4. 这些方法还应该建立在有志于文化遗产保护的所有各方的国际合作基础上，并进一步推动这一合作，以促进全世界对每一种文化的多样化表达和价值的尊重与理解。

values of each culture.

5. Continuation and extension of this dialogue to the various regions and cultures of the world is a prerequisite to increasing the practical value of consideration of authenticity in the conservation of the common heritage of humankind.

5. 将此对话延伸并拓展到全世界不同区域与文化之间，是提升人类共同遗产保护的真实性的实用价值的必要前提。

6. Increasing awareness within the public of this fundamental dimension of heritage is an absolute necessity in order to arrive at concrete measures for safeguarding the vestiges of the past. This means developing greater understanding of the values represented by the cultural properties themselves, as well as respecting the role such monuments and sites play in contemporary society.

6. 增进公众对遗产的了解对于获得保护历史遗迹的切实措施很有必要。这意味着在增进对这些文化资产自身价值的了解的同时，也要尊重这些纪念物与历史场所在当代社会所扮演的角色。

Appendix 2: Definitions

附录 2：定义

Conservation: all efforts designed to understand cultural heritage, know its history and meaning, ensure its material safeguard and, as required, its presentation, restoration and enhancement. (Cultural heritage is understood to include monuments, groups of buildings and sites of cultural value as defined in Article 1 of the *World Heritage Convention*).

保护：是指所有旨在理解遗产，掌握其历史和意义，确保其自然形态，根据需要，在展示、修复和提升过程中所付出的所有努力。（文化遗产包括《世界遗产公约》第一条所定义的具有文化价值的纪念物、建筑群与历史场所）。

Information sources: all material, written, oral and figurative sources which make it possible to know the nature, specifications, meaning and history of the cultural heritage.

信息源：可使人了解文化遗产的性质、规范、意义与历史的所有物质的、书面的、口述的与图像。

II. Chronological BIBLIOGRAPHY - on authenticity

II. 按年代顺序排列的关于真实性的参考文献

Publications which preceded the Nara meeting and which helped prepare the ground for the authenticity discussion which took place in Nara:

Larsen, Knut Einar, A note on the authenticity

奈良会议召开前的出版物和有助于奈良的真实性讨论的出版物包括：

《关于木质历史建筑（尤指日本）的真实性

of historic timber buildings with particular reference to Japan, Occasional Papers for the World Heritage Convention, ICOMOS, December 1992.

的注解》，作者 Larsen, Knut Einar,《世界遗产公约》的学术论文，国际古迹遗址理事会，1992 年 12 月；

Larsen, Knut Einar, Authenticity and Reconstruction: Architectural Preservation in Japan, Norwegian Institute of Technology, Vols. 1-2, 1993.

《真实性和重建：日本建筑的保护》作者 Larsen, Knut Einar, 挪威理工学院学报第 1–2 卷，1993 年。

Preparatory meeting for the Nara Meeting, held in Bergen, Norway, 31 January - 1 February 1994:

1994 年 1 月 31 日至 2 月 1 日在挪威卑尔根召开的奈良会议的预备会议：

Larsen, Knut Einar and Marstein, Nils (ed.), Conference on authenticity in relation to the World Heritage Convention Preparatory workshop, Bergen, Norway, 31 January - 2 February 1994, Tapir Forlag, Trondheim 1994.

《关于〈世界遗产公约〉中真实性的预备工作会议》，作者 Larsen, Knut Einar 和 Marstein, Nils (ed.), 1994 年 1 月 31 日至 2 月 1 日挪威卑尔根，Tapir Forlag 特隆赫姆，1994 年。

The Nara meeting, 1-6 November 1994, Nara, Japan:

1994 年 11 月 1–6 日在日本奈良召开的奈良会议：

Larsen, Knut Einar with an editorial group (Jokilehto, Lemaire, Masuda, Marstein, Stovel), Nara conference on authenticity in relation to the World Heritage Convention. Conférence de Nara sur l'authenticité dans le cadre de la Convention du Patrimoine Mondial. Nara, Japan, 1-6 November 1994, Proceedings published by UNESCO - World Heritage Centre, Agency for Cultural Affairs of Japan, ICCROM and ICOMOS, 1994.

《与世界遗产公约相关的奈良真实性会议》，（法语名：*Conférence de Nara sur l'authenticité dans le cadre de la Convention du Patrimoine Mondial*），作者 Larsen 和 Knut Einar 领导的编辑组（包括 Jokilehto, Lemaire, Masuda, Marstein 和 Stovel)，日本奈良，1994 年 11 月 1–6 日，会议论文集，联合国教科文组织世界遗产中心、日本文化部、国际文化遗产保护与修复研究中心和国际古迹遗址理事会，1994 年。

The Nara meeting brought together 45 experts from 26 countries and international organizations from around the world. Their papers are contained in the volume cited above, as is the Nara document prepared in a working group of 12 meeting participants and edited by Raymond Lemaire and Herb Stovel. This volume of Proceedings invites members of ICOMOS and others to extend the discussions of the Nara Document issues to other

奈良会议汇聚了来自 26 个国家和国际组织的 45 名专家。和由 12 个参会者组成的工作组准备的并由 Raymond Lemaire 和 Herb Stovel 编辑的奈良文件一样，这 45 名专家的论文也包含在上述引用的会议论文集中。该论文集邀请国际古迹遗址理事会成员和其他有关专家一起将奈良文件问题相关讨论扩大到世界其他地区。

regions of the world.

Significant post-Nara regional meetings (as of January 2005):

奈良会议后具有重大意义的地区性会议（截至 2005 年 1 月）：

Authenticity and Monitoring, October 17-22, 1995, Cesky Krumlov, Czech Republic, ICOMOS European Conference, 1995.

《真实性和遗产监测，1995 年 10 月 17–22 日》，捷克共和国契斯基库伦隆，国际古遗址理事会欧洲会议，1995 年。

The European ICOMOS Conference of 17-22 October, 1995 which took place in Cesky Krumlov, Czech Republic brought together 18 European members of ICOMOS to present national views of the application of authenticity concepts from 14 countries. A synthesis of presentations affirmed the importance of authenticity within the analytical processes we apply to conservation problems as a means of assuring truthful, sincere and honest approaches to conservation problems, and gave emphasis to strengthening the notion of dynamic conservation in order to apply authenticity analysis appropriately to cultural landscapes and urban settings.

1995 年 10 月 17–22 日，欧洲国际古遗址理事会欧洲会议在捷克共和国契斯基库伦隆召开。会议聚集了 18 位国际古迹遗址理事会欧洲成员，提出了来自 14 国的关于应用真实性概念的观点。这种综合阐述证实了真实性作为一种确保真实和诚实的手段在处理保护问题分析过程中的重要性，而这种分析过程是处理保护问题中确保信任、真诚和诚实的手段，并强调加强动态保护观念，以便在文化景观和城市遗产中恰当地应用真实性分析。

Interamerican symposium on authenticity in the conservation and management of the cultural heritage, US/ICOMOS, The Getty Conservation Institute, San Antonio, Texas 1996.

《关于文化遗产保护和管理中真实性的研讨会》，美国及国际古迹遗址理事会，美国德克萨斯州圣安东尼，盖蒂保护研究所，1996 年。

This Authenticity meeting which took place in San Antonio, Texas, USA in March 1996, brought together participants from ICOMOS national committees of North, Central and South America to debate the application of the concepts of Nara. The meeting adopted the Declaration of San Antonio, which discussed the relationship between authenticity and identity, history, materials, social value, dynamic and static sites, stewardship and economics, and contained recommendations extending 'proofs' of authenticity to include reflection of its true value, integrity,

1996 年 3 月在德克萨斯州圣安东尼奥召开的真实性会议，汇聚了来自北美、中美和南美国际古遗址理事会国家委员会的参会者，共同商讨了奈良概念的应用。该会议通过了《圣安东尼奥宣言》，该宣言讨论了真实性和身份认同、历史、材料、社会价值、动态和静态遗产、管理和经济学之间的关系，包含了扩充真实性"证据"的相关建议，包括对真实价值、完整性、背景环境、身份特性、使用和功能的反映，以及针对不同类型遗产的相关建议。

context, identity, use and function, as well as recommendations pertinent to different typologies of sites.

Saouma-Forero, Galia, (edited by), Authenticity and integrity in an African context: expert meeting, Great Zimbabwe, Zimbabwe, 26-29 May 2000, UNESCO - World Heritage Centre, Paris 2001.

《非洲文化背景下遗产保护的真实性和完整性：大津巴布韦专家会议》，Saouma–Forero, Galia,（编辑），津巴布韦，2000年5月26–29日，联合国教科文组织世界遗产中心，2001年，巴黎。

The Great Zimbabwe meeting organised by the World Heritage Centre (26-29 May 2000) focused attention on both authenticity and integrity in an African context. Eighteen speakers looked at issues arising in management of both cultural and natural heritage properties. The meeting resulted in the publication cited above, which includes a set of recommendations coming from meeting participants. Among recommendations were suggestions to include management systems, language, and other forms of intangible heritage among attributes expressing authenticity, and an emphasis given to the place of local communities in the sustainable heritage management process.

大津巴布韦会议由世界遗产中心组织召开（2000年5月26–29日），会议重点强调非洲遗产的真实性和完整性。18位发言人讨论了文化与自然遗产管理面临的问题。该会议后发表了上述出版物，其中包含了参会人员提出的建议。这些建议包括建议将管理体系、语言和其他形式的非物质遗产纳入真实性的表达，并强调当地社区在可持续遗产管理过程中的作用。

Reconstruction discussions in the context of the *World Heritage Convention* (as of January 2005):

《世界遗产公约》中关于重建问题的讨论（截止至2005年1月）：

The Riga Charter on authenticity and historical reconstruction in relationship to cultural heritage adopted by regional conference, Riga, 24 October 2000, Latvian National Commission for UNESCO - World Heritage Centre, ICCROM.

里加地区会议通过的《关于文化遗产相关真实性和历史重建问题的里加宪章》，2000年10月24日，联合国教科文组织世界遗产中心拉脱维亚委员会，国际文化遗产保护与修复研究中心。

Incerti Medici, Elena and Stovel, Herb, Authenticity and historical reconstruction in relationship with cultural heritage, regional conference, Riga, Latvia, October 23-24 2000: summary report, UNESCO - World Heritage

2000年10月23–24日拉脱维亚里加地区会议《关于文化遗产相关真实性和历史重建问题的地区会议总结报告》，起草人 Incerti Medici, Elena 和 Stovel, Herb, 2001年，巴黎联合国教科文组织世界遗产中心，国际文化遗产保护与修复

Centre, Paris, ICCROM, Rome 2001.

研究中心。

Stovel, Herb, The Riga Charter on authenticity and historical reconstruction in relationship to cultural heritage, Riga, Latvia, October 2000, in Conservation and management of archaeological sites, Vol. 4, n. 4, 2001.

2000 年 10 月拉脱维亚里加地区会议通过的《关于考古遗址保护和管理中的文化遗产相关真实性和历史重建问题的里加宪章》，起草人 Stovel, Herb，《考古遗址保护和管理》2001 年第 4 卷。

Alternatives to historical reconstruction in the World Heritage Cities, Tallinn, 16-18 May 2002, Tallinn Cultural Heritage Department, Estonia National Commission for UNESCO, Estonia National Heritage Board.

《避免世界遗产城市中历史建筑重建的选择》2002 年 5 月 16–18 日，塔林文化遗产部，联合国教科文组织爱沙尼亚国家委员会，爱沙尼亚国家遗产部。

Format for the nomination of properties for inscription on the World Heritage List

《世界遗产名录》遗产申报材料格式

Annex 5 A

FORMAT FOR THE NOMINATION OF PROPERTIES
FOR INSCRIPTION ON THE WORLD HERITAGE LIST

This Format must be used for all nominations
submitted after 2 February 2005

The Nomination Format is available at the following Web address:

http: //whc.unesco.org/en/nominationform

Further guidance on the preparation of nominations can be found in Section III of the *Operational Guidelines*

The original signed version of the completed Nomination Format should be sent in English or French to

UNESCO World Heritage Centre
7, place de Fontenoy
75352 Paris 07 SP
France
Telephone: +33 (0) 1 4568 1571
Fax: +33 (0) 1 4568 5570

附件 5A
《世界遗产名录》遗产申报材料格式

2005 年 2 月 2 日后提交的所有申报材料均须遵循此格式

登录以下网址可获取本申报材料格式：http ：//whc.unesco.org/en/nominationform

有关申报材料编写的更多指导请参见《操作指南》的第三部分

按申报格式编写，有原始签名的英语或法语完整版本寄送至以下地址：

联合国教科文组织世界遗产中心

法国巴黎（7，place de Fontenoy

75352 Paris 07 SP France）

电话：+33（0）1 4568 1571

传真：+33（0）1 4568 5570

电邮：wh–nominations@unesco.org

Annex 5 B
Executive Summary

This information, to be provided by the State Party, will be updated by the Secretariat following the decision by the World Heritage Committee. It will then be returned to the State Party confirming the basis on which the property is inscribed on the World Heritage List.

State Party	
State, Province or Region	
Name of Property	
Geographical coordinates to the nearest second	
Textual description of the boundary (ies) of the nominated property	
A4 or A3 size map (s) of the nominated property, showing boundaries and buffer zone (if present)	Attach A4 or A3 size map (s) which should be the reduced size version of the original copies of topographic or cadastral maps showing the nominated property and buffer zone (if present) at the largest scale available included or annexed to the nomination.
Criteria under which property is nominated (itemize criteria) (see Paragraph 77 of the Operational Guidelines)	
Draft Statement of Outstanding Universal Value (text should clarify what is considered to be the Outstanding Universal Value embodied by the nominated property, approximately 1-2 page format)	According to the paragraph 155, the Statement of Outstanding Universal Value should be composed of: Brief synthesis Justification for Criteria Statement of Integrity (for all properties) Statement of authenticity for properties nominated under criteria (i) to (vi) Requirements for protection and management See format in Annex 10
Name and contact information of official local institution/ agency	Organization: Address: Tel: Fax: E-mail: Web address:

附件 5B
执行摘要

以下信息由缔约国提供，由秘书处根据世界遗产委员会的决定进行更新。之后将返还给缔约国，确认遗产列入《世界遗产名录》的依据。

缔约国	
国家、省份或地区	
遗产名称	
精确到秒的地理坐标	
遗产申报保护范围的文字说明	
A4 纸或 A3 大小的申报遗产地图，显示遗产保护范围和缓冲区（如果有）	附原始地形或地籍图的 A4 或 A3 纸大小的最大规格、指明申报遗产边界和缓冲区（如有）的缩版图，作为申报文件的附件。
遗产申报符合的标准 （列举标准） （见《操作指南》第 77 条）	
《突出普遍价值声明》 （正文应说明申报遗产所包含的突出普遍价值，约 1–2 页篇幅）	根据第 155 条，《突出普遍价值声明》应包含： 1）简要综述 2）符合标准的理由 3）完整性声明（适用所有遗产） 4）真实性声明（适用按照标准 i–vi 条申报的遗产） 5）保护和管理要求 见附件 10 中的格式
当地官方机构 / 组织的名称及联系方式	机构： 地址： 电话： 传真： 电邮： 网址：

Annex 5C
Properties for inscription on the World Heritage List

Note: In preparing the nomination, States Parties should use this format but delete the explanatory notes.

NOMINATION Format	Explanatory Notes
1. Identification of the Property	Together with Section 2, this is the most important section in the nomination. It must make clear to the Committee precisely where the property is located and how it is geographically defined. In the case of serial nominations, insert a table that shows the name of the component part, region (if different for different components) , coordinates, area and buffer zone. Other fields could also be added (page reference or map number, etc.) that differentiate the several components.
1.a Country (and State Party if different)	
1.b State, Province or Region	
1.c Name of Property	This is the official name of the property that will appear in published material about World Heritage. It should be concise. Do not exceed 200 characters, including spaces and punctuation. In the case of serial nominations (see Paragraphs137-139 of the *Operational Guidelines*) , give a name for the ensemble (e.g., Baroque Churches of the Philippines) . Do not include the name of the components of a serial nomination, which should be included in a table as part of 1.d and 1.f.
1.d Geographical coordinates to the nearest second	In this space provide the latitude and longitude coordinates (to the nearest second) or UTM coordinates (to the nearest 10 metres) of a point at the approximate centre of the nominated property. Do not use other coordinate systems. If in doubt, please consult the Secretariat. In the case of serial nominations, provide a table showing the name of each component part, its region (or nearest town as appropriate) , and the coordinates of its centre point. Coordinate format examples: N 45° 06' 05" W 15° 37' 56" or UTM Zone 18 Easting: 545670 Northing: 4586750

Id n°	Name of the component part	Region (s) / District (s)	Coordinates of the Central Point	Area of Nominated component of the Property (ha)	Area of the Buffer Zone (ha)	Map N°
001						
002						
003						
004						
Etc.						
Total area (in hectares)				ha	ha	

续表

NOMINATION Format	Explanatory Notes
1.e Maps and plans, showing the boundaries of the nominated property and buffer zone	Annex to the nomination, and list below with scales and dates: (i) Original copies of topographic maps showing the property nominated, at the largest scale available which shows the entire property. The boundaries of the nominated property and buffer zone should be clearly marked. The boundaries of zones of special legal protection from which the property benefits should be recorded on maps to be included under the protection and management section of the nomination text. Multiple maps may be necessary for serial nominations (see table in 1.d) . The maps provided should be at the largest available and practical scale to allow the identification of topographic elements such as neighbouring settlements, buildings and routes in order to allow the clear assessment of the impact of any proposed development within, adjacent to, or on the boundary line. The choice of the adequate scale is essential to clearly show the boundaries of the proposed site and shall be in relation to the category of site that is proposed for inscription: cultural sites would require cadastral maps, while natural sites or cultural landscapes would require topographic maps (normally 1: 25 000 to 1: 50 000 scale) . Utmost care is needed with the width of boundary lines on maps, as thick boundary lines may make the actual boundary of the property ambiguous. Maps may be obtained from the addresses shown at the following Web address http: //whc.unesco.org/en/mapagencies. All maps should be capable of being geo-referenced, with a minimum of three points on opposite sides of the maps with complete sets of coordinates. The maps, untrimmed, should show scale, orientation, projection, datum, property name and date. If possible, maps should be sent rolled and not folded. Geographic Information in digital form is encouraged if possible, suitable for incorporation into a GIS (Geographic Information System) . however, this may not substitute the submission of printed maps. In this case the delineation of the boundaries (nominated property and buffer zone) should be presented in vector form, prepared at the largest scale possible. The State Party is invited to contact the Secretariat for further information concerning this option. (ii) A Location Map showing the location of the property within the State Party, (iii) Plans and specially prepared maps of the property showing individual features are helpful and may also be annexed. To facilitate copying and presentation to the Advisory Bodies and the World Heritage Committee A4 (or 'letter') size reduction and a digital image file of the principal maps should also be included in the nomination text if possible. Where no buffer zone is proposed, the nomination must include a statement as to why a buffer zone is not required for the proper protection of the nominated property.
1.f Area of nominated property (ha.) and proposed buffer zone (ha.) Area of nominated property: ________ ha Buffer zone________ ha Total ________ ha	In the case of serial nominations (see Paragraphs 137-140 of the *Operational Guidelines*), insert a table that shows the name of the component part, region (if different for different components) , coordinates, area and buffer zone. The serial nomination table should also be used to show the size of the separate nominated areas and of the buffer zone (s) .

续表

NOMINATION Format	Explanatory Notes
2. Description	
2.a Description of Property	This section should begin with a description of the nominated property at the date of nomination. It should refer to all the significant features of the property. In the case of a cultural property this section will include a description of whatever elements make the property culturally significant. It could include a description of any building or buildings and their architectural style, date of construction, materials, etc. This section should also describe important aspects of the setting such as gardens, parks etc. For a rock art site, for example, the description should refer to the rock art as well as the surrounding landscapes. In the case of an historic town or district, it is not necessary to describe each individual building, but important public buildings should be described individually and an account should be given of the planning or layout of the area, its street pattern and so on. In the case of a natural property the account should deal with important physical attributes, geology, habitats, species and population size, and other significant ecological features and processes. Species lists should be provided where practicable, and the presence of threatened or endemic taxa should be highlighted. The extent and methods of exploitation of natural resources should be described. In the case of cultural landscapes, it will be necessary to produce a description under all the matters mentioned above. Special attention should be paid to the interaction of people and nature. The entire nominated property identified in section 1 (Identification of the Property) should be described. In the case of serial nominations (see Paragraphs 137-140 of the *Operational Guidelines*) , each of the component parts should be separately described.
2.b History and Development	Describe how the property has reached its present form and condition and the significant changes that it has undergone, including recent conservation history. This should include some account of construction phases in the case of monuments, sites, buildings or groups of buildings. Where there have been major changes, demolitions or rebuilding since completion they should also be described. In the case of a natural property, the account should cover significant events in history or pre-history that have affected the evolution of the property and give an account of its interaction with humankind. This will include changes in the use of the property and its natural resources for hunting, fishing or agriculture, or changes brought about by climatic change, floods, earthquake or other natural causes. Such information will also be required in the case of cultural landscapes, where all aspects of the history of human activity in the area needs to be covered..
3. Justification for Inscription①	The justification should be set out under the following sections. This section must make clear why the property is considered to be of 'Outstanding Universal Value'. The whole of this section of the nomination should be written with careful reference to the requirements of the *Operational Guidelines*. It should not include detailed descriptive material about the property or its management, which are addressed in other sections, but should convey the key aspects that are relevant to the definition of the Outstanding Universal Value of the property.
3.1.a Brief synthesis	The brief synthesis should comprise (i) a summary of factual information and (ii) a summary of qualities. The summary of factual information sets out the geographical and historical context and the main features. The summary of qualities should present to decision-makers and the general public the potential Outstanding Universal Value that needs to be sustained, and should also include a summary of the attributes that convey its potential Outstanding Universal Value, and need to be protected, managed and monitored. The summary should relate to all stated criteria in order to justify the nomination. The brief synthesis thus encapsulates the whole rationale for the nomination and proposed inscription.

① See also paragraphs 132 and 133

续表

NOMINATION Format	Explanatory Notes
3.1.b Criteria under which inscription is proposed (and justification for inscription under these criteria)	See Paragraph 77 of the *Operational Guidelines*. Provide a separate justification for each criterion cited. State briefly how the property meets those criteria under which it has been nominated (where necessary, make reference to the 'description' and 'comparative analysis' sections of the nomination, but do not duplicate the text of these sections) and describe for each criterion the relevant attributes.
3.1. c Statement of Integrity	The statement of integrity should demonstrate that the property fulfils the conditions of integrity set out in Section II.D of the *Operational Guidelines*, which describe these conditions in greater detail. The *Operational Guidelines* set out the need to assess the extent to which the property: • includes all elements necessary to express its Outstanding Universal Value; • is of adequate size to ensure the complete representation of the features and processes which convey the property's significance; • suffers from adverse effects of development and/or neglect (Paragraph 88) . The *Operational Guidelines* provide specific guidance in relation to the various World Heritage criteria, which is important to understand (Paragraphs 89-95) .
3.1.d Statement of Authenticity (for nominations made under criteria (i) to (vi)	The statement of authenticity should demonstrate that the property fulfils the conditions of authenticity set out in Section II.D of the *Operational Guidelines*, which describe these conditions in greater detail. This section should summarise information that may be included in more detail in section 4 of the nomination (and possibly in other sections) , and should not reproduce the level of detail included in those sections. Authenticity only applies to cultural properties and to the cultural aspects of 'mixed' properties. The *Operational Guidelines* state that 'properties may be understood to meet the conditions of authenticity if their cultural values (as recognized in the nomination criteria proposed) are truthfully and credibly expressed through a variety of attributes' (Paragraph 82) . The *Operational Guidelines* suggest that the following types of attributes might be considered as conveying or expressing Outstanding Universal Value: • form and design; • materials and substance; • use and function; • traditions, techniques and management systems; • location and setting; • language and other forms of intangible heritage; • spirit and feeling; and • other internal/external factors.
3.1.e Protection and management requirements	This section should set out how the requirements for protection and management will be met, in order to ensure that the Outstanding Universal Value of the property is maintained over time. It should include both details of an overall framework for protection and management, and the identification of specific long term expectations for the protection of the property. This section should summarise information that may be included in more detail in section 5 of the nomination document (and also potentially in sections 4 and 6) , and should not reproduce the level of detail included in those sections.

续表

NOMINATION Format	Explanatory Notes
3.1.e Protection and management requirements	The text in this section should first outline the framework for protection and management. This should include the necessary protection mechanisms, management systems and/or management plans (whether currently in place or in need of establishment) that will protect and conserve the attributes that carry Outstanding Universal Value, and address the threats to and vulnerabilities of the property. These could include the presence of strong and effective legal protection, a clearly documented management system, including relationships with key stakeholders or user groups, adequate staff and financial resources, key requirements for presentation (where relevant) , and effective and responsive monitoring. Secondly this section needs to acknowledge any long-term challenges for the protection and management of the property and state how addressing these will be a long-term strategy. It will be relevant to refer to the most significant threats to the property, and to vulnerabilities and negative changes in authenticity and/or integrity that have been highlighted, and to set out how protection and management will address these vulnerabilities and threats and mitigate any adverse changes. As an official statement, recognised by the World Heritage Committee, this section of the Statement of Outstanding Universal Value should convey the most important commitments that the State Party is making for the long-term protection and management of the property.
3.2 Comparative Analysis	The property should be compared to similar properties, whether on the World Heritage List or not. The comparison should outline the similarities the nominated property has with other properties and the reasons that make the nominated property stand out. The comparative analysis should aim to explain the importance of the nominated property both in its national and international context (see Paragraph 132) . The purpose of the comparative analysis is to show that there is room on the List using existing thematic studies and, in the case of serial properties, the justification for the selection of the component parts.
3.3 Proposed Statement of Outstanding Universal Value	A Statement of Outstanding Universal Value is the official statement adopted by the World Heritage Committee at the time of inscription of a property on the World Heritage List. When the World Heritage Committee agrees to inscribe a property on the World Heritage List, it also agrees on a Statement of Outstanding Universal Value that encapsulates why the property is considered to be of Outstanding Universal Value, how it satisfies the relevant criteria, the conditions of integrity and (for cultural properties) authenticity, and how it meets the requirements for protection and management in order to sustain Outstanding Universal Value in the long-term. Statements of Outstanding Universal Value should be concise and are set out in a standard format. They should help to raise awareness regarding the value of the property, guide the assessment of its state of conservation and inform protection and management. Once adopted by the Committee, the Statement of Outstanding Universal Value is displayed at the property and on the UNESCO World Heritage Centre's website. The main sections of a Statement of Outstanding Universal Value are the following: Brief synthesis Justification for Criteria Statement of Integrity (for all properties) Statement of authenticity for properties nominated under criteria (i) to (vi) Requirements for protection and management

续表

NOMINATION Format	Explanatory Notes
4. State of Conservation and factors affecting the Property	
4.a Present state of conse-rvation	The information presented in this section constitutes the base-line data necessary to monitor the state of conservation of the nominated property in the future. Information should be provided in this section on the physical condition of the property, any threats to the Outstanding Universal Value of the property and conservation measures at the property (see Paragraph 132). For example, in a historic town or area, buildings, monuments or other structures needing major or minor repair works, should be indicated as well as the scale and duration of any recent or forthcoming major repair projects. In the case of a natural property, data on species trends or the integrity of eco-systems should be provided. This is important because the nomination will be used in future years for purposes of comparison to trace changes in the condition of the property. For the indicators and statistical benchmarks used to monitor the state of conservation of the property see section 6 below.
4.b Factors affecting the property	This section should provide information on all the factors which are likely to affect or threaten the Outstanding Universal Value of a property. It should also describe any difficulties that may be encountered in addressing such problems. Not all the factors suggested in this section are appropriate for all properties. They are indicative and are intended to assist the State Party to identify the factors that are relevant to each specific property.
(i) Development Pressures (e.g., encroachment, adaptation, agriculture, mining)	Itemize types of development pressures affecting the property, e.g., pressure for demolition, rebuilding or new construction; the adaptation of existing buildings for new uses which would harm their authenticity or integrity; habitat modification or destruction following encroaching agriculture, forestry or grazing, or through poorly managed tourism or other uses; inappropriate or unsustainable natural resource exploitation; damage caused by mining; the introduction of exotic species likely to disrupt natural ecological processes, creating new centres of population on or near properties so as to harm them or their settings.
(ii) Environmental pressures (e.g., pollution, climate change, desertification)	List and summarize major sources of environmental deterioration affecting building fabric, flora and fauna.
(iii) Natural disasters and risk preparedness (earthquakes, floods, fires, etc.)	Itemize those disasters which present a foreseeable threat to the property and what steps have been taken to draw up contingency plans for dealing with them, whether by physical protection measures or staff training.
(iv) Responsible visitation at World Heritage sites	Provide the status of visitation to the property (notably available baseline data; patterns of use, including concentrations of activity in parts of the property; and activities planned in the future). Describe projected levels of visitation due to inscription or other factors. Define the carrying-capacity of the property and how its management could be enhanced to meet the current or expected visitor numbers and related development pressure without adverse effects. Consider possible forms of deterioration of the property due to visitor pressure and behaviour including those affecting its intangible attributes.

续表

NOMINATION Format	Explanatory Notes
(v) Number of inhabitants within the property and the buffer zone; Estimated population located within: Area of nominated property ___________ Buffer zone___________ Total ___________ Year ___________	Give the best available statistics or estimate of the number of inhabitants living within the nominated property and any buffer zone. Indicate the year this estimate or count was made.
5. Protection and Management of the Property	This section of the nomination is intended to provide a clear picture of the legislative, regulatory, contractual, planning, institutional and/ or traditional measures (see Paragraph 132 of the *Operational Guidelines*) and the management plan or other management system (Paragraphs 108 to 118 of the *Operational Guidelines*) that is in place to protect and manage the property as required by the *World Heritage Convention*. It should deal with policy aspects, legal status and protective measures and with the practicalities of day-to-day administration and management.
5.a Ownership	Indicate the major categories of land ownership (including State, Provincial, private, community, traditional, customary and non-governmental ownership, etc.) .
5.b Protective designation	List the relevant legal, regulatory, contractual, planning, institutional and/ or traditional status of the property: For example, national or provincial park; historic monument, protected area under national law or custom; or other designation. Provide the year of designation and the legislative act (s) under which the status is provided. If the document cannot be provided in English or French, an English or French executive summary should be provided highlighting the key provisions.
5.c Means of implementing protective measures.	Describe how the protection afforded by its legal, regulatory, contractual, planning, institutional and/ or traditional status indicated in section 5.b. actually works.
5.d Existing plans related to municipality and region in which the proposed property is located (e.g., regional or local plan, conservation plan, tourism development plan)	List the agreed plans which have been adopted with the date and agency responsible for preparation. The relevant provisions should be summarized in this section. A copy of the plan should be included as an attached document as indicated in section 7.b. If the plans exist only in a language other than English or French, an English or French executive summary should be provided highlighting the key provisions.
5.e Property management plan or other management system	As noted in Paragraphs 132 of the *Operational Guidelines*, an appropriate management plan or other management system is essential and shall be provided in the nomination. Assurances of the effective implementation of the management plan or other management system are also expected. Sustainable development principles should be integrated into the management system. A copy of the management plan or documentation of the management system shall be annexed to the nomination, in English or French as indicated in section 7.b. If the management plan exists only in a language other than English or French, an English or French detailed description of its provisions shall be annexed. Give the title, date and author of management plans annexed to this nomination. A detailed analysis or explanation of the management plan or a documented management system shall be provided. A timetable for the implementation of the management plan is recommended.

续表

NOMINATION Format	Explanatory Notes
5.f Sources and levels of finance	Show the sources and level of funding which are available to the property on an annual basis. An estimate could also be given of the adequacy or otherwise of resources available, in particular identifying any gaps or deficiencies or any areas where assistance may be required.
5.g Sources of expertise and training in conservation and management techniques	Indicate the expertise and training which are available from national authorities or other organizations to the property.
5.h Visitor facilities and infrastructure	The section should describe the inclusive facilities available on site for visitors and demonstrate that they are appropriate in relation to the protection and management requirements of the property. It should set out how the facilities and services will provide effective and inclusive presentation of the property to meet the needs of visitors, including in relation to the provision of safe and appropriate access to the property. The section should consider visitor facilities that may include interpretation/explanation (signage, trails, notices or publications, guides) ; museum/exhibition devoted to the property, visitor or interpretation centre; and/or potential use of digital technologies and services (overnight accommodation; restaurant; car parking; lavatories; search and rescue; etc.)
5.i Policies and programmes related to the presentation and promotion of the property	This section refers to Articles 4 and 5 of the *Convention* regarding the presentation and transmission to future generations of the cultural and natural heritage. States Parties are encouraged to provide information on the policies and programmes for the presentation and promotion of the nominated property.
5.j Staffing levels and expertise (professional, technical, maintenance)	Indicate the skills and qualifications available needed for the good management of the property, including in relation to visitation and future training needs.
6. Monitoring	This section of the nomination is intended to provide the evidence for the state of conservation of the property which can be reviewed and reported on regularly so as to give an indication of trends over time.
6.a Key indicators for measuring state of conservation	List in table form those key indicators that have been chosen as the measure of the state of conservation of the whole property (see section 4.a above) . Indicate the periodicity of the review of these indicators and the location where the records are kept. They could be representative of an important aspect of the property and relate as closely as possible to the Statement of Outstanding Universal Value (see section 2.b above) . Where possible they could be expressed numerically and where this is not possible they could be of a kind which can be repeated, for example by taking a photograph from the same point. Examples of good indicators are the: (i) number of species, or population of a keystone species on a natural property; (ii) percentage of buildings requiring major repair in a historic town or district; (iii) number of years estimated to elapse before a major conservation programme is likely to be completed; (iv) stability or degree of movement in a particular building or element of a building; (v) rate at which encroachment of any kind on a property has increased or diminished.

Indicator	Periodicity	Location of Records

NOMINATION FORMAT	EXPLANATORY NOTES
6.b Administrative arrangements for monitoring property	Give the name and contact information of the agency (ies) responsible for the monitoring referenced in 6.a.
6.c Results of previous reporting exercises	List, with a brief summary, earlier reports on the state of conservation of the property and provide extracts and references to published sources (for example, reports submitted in compliance with international agreements and programmes, e.g., Ramsar, MAB) .
7. Documentation	This section of the nomination is the check-list of the documentation which shall be provided to make up a complete nomination.
7.a Photographs and audiovisual image inventory and authorization form	States Parties shall provide a sufficient number of recent images (prints, slides and, where possible, electronic formats, videos and aerial photographs) to give a good general picture of the property. Slides shall be in 35mm format and electronic images in jpg format at a minimum of 300 dpi (dots per inch) resolution. If film material is provided, Beta SP format is recommended for quality assurances. This material shall be accompanied by the image inventory and photograph and audiovisual authorization form as set out below. At least one photograph that may be used on the public web page illustrating the property shall be included. States Parties are encouraged to grant to UNESCO, in written form and free of charge, the non exclusive cession of rights to diffuse, to communicate to the public, to publish, to reproduce, to exploit, in any form and on any support, including digital, all or part of the images provided and license these rights to third parties. The non exclusive cession of rights does not impinge upon intellectual property rights (rights of the photographer / director of the video or copyright owner if different) and that when the images are distributed by UNESCO a credit to the photographer / director of the video is always given, if clearly provided in the form. All possible profits deriving from such cession of rights will go to the World Heritage Fund.

PHOTOGRAPHS AND AUDIOVISUAL IMAGE INVENTORY AND AUTHORIZATION FORM

Id. No	Format (slide/ print/ video)	Caption	Date of Photo (mo/yr)	Photographer/ Director of the video	Copyright owner (if different than photographer/director of video)	Contact details of copyright owner (Name, address, tel/fax, and e-mail)	Non exclusive cession of rights

NOMINATION FORMAT	EXPLANATORY NOTES
7.b Texts relating to protective designation, copies of property management plans or documented management systems and extracts of other plans relevant to the property	Attach the texts as indicated in sections 5.b, 5.d and 5.e above.
7.c Form and date of most recent records or inventory of property	Provide a straightforward statement giving the form and date of the most recent records or inventory of the property. Only records that are still available should be described.
7.d Address where inventory, records and archives are held	Give the name and address of the agencies holding inventory records (buildings, monuments, flora or fauna species) .
7.e Bibliography	List the principal published references, using standard bibliographic format.
8. Contact Information of responsible authorities	This section of the nomination will allow the Secretariat to provide the property with current information about World Heritage news and other issues.
8.a Preparer Name: Title: Address: City, Province/State, Country: Tel: Fax: E-mail:	Provide the name, address and other contact information of the individual responsible for preparing the nomination. If an e-mail address cannot be provided, the information must include a fax number.
8.b Official Local Institution/Agency	Provide the name of the agency, museum, institution, community or manager locally responsible for the management of the property. If the normal reporting institution is a national agency, please provide that contact information.
8.c Other Local Institutions	List the full name, address, telephone, fax and e-mail addresses of all museums, visitor centres and official tourism offices who should receive the free *World Heritage Newsletter* about events and issues related to World Heritage.
8.d Official Web address http: // Contact name: E-mail:	Please provide any existing official web addresses of the nominated property. Indicate if such web addresses are planned for the future with the contact name and e-mail address.
9. Signature on behalf of the State Party	The nomination should conclude with the signature of the official empowered to sign it on behalf of the State Party.

附件 5C
申报列入《世界遗产名录》的遗产

注：准备申报材料时，各缔约国应该使用本格式，但应把填报须知注释内容删除。

申报材料格式	填报须知
1. 遗产的身份证明	本部分和下面的第 2 部分是申报材料中最重要的内容，必须向委员会准确说明遗产的位置和地理界限。 如果是系列申报，插入一个表格，说明各组成部分的名称、所处地域（如果不同部分处于不同地域）、坐标、面积和缓冲区。也可列示其他表栏项目（页码说明或地图编号）以区别不同部分。
1.a 国家（缔约国，如果不同）	
1.b 国家、省份或地区	
1.c 遗产名称	是该遗产出现在世界遗产出版物上的正式名称，应简洁，不超过 200 个字符，包括空格和标点符号。 如果是系列申报（见《 操作指南》的第 137–139 条），应是整体名称（ 比如，菲律宾巴洛克大教堂）。无需说明系列申报内各组成部分的名称，这些名称应该包括在 1.d 和 1.f 的表格内。
1.d 精确到秒的地理坐标	在此处提供申报遗产的中心纬度和经度坐标（精确到秒），或 UTM 坐标（精确到 10 米）。不要用其他坐标体系。如有疑问，请咨询秘书处。 如果是系列申报，列表说明各遗产的名称、地域（或最近的城镇）、遗产中心点的坐标。 坐标格式如下： 北纬 45° 06' 05"　西经 15° 37' 56" 或者 UTM　区　18 东：545670 北：4586750

编号	地区 / 城区	中心点坐标	申报部分面积（公顷）	缓冲区面积（公顷）	地图编号
001					
002					
003					
……					
总面积（公顷）			公顷	公顷	

申报材料格式	填报须知
1.e 地图和平面图，显示申报遗产和缓冲区的范围	附在申报材料后，标上比例和日期： 用于申报遗产的地形图原件，尽可能用最大的比例显示整个遗产。应明确标明申报遗产及缓冲区的范围。可在此图或另附地图上，记录有利于遗产的受特别法律保护的遗产边界区域的范围。系列申报可能需要多种地图（见 1.d 中表格）。应尽可能提供最大比例的实用地图，以便清晰辨认如周边聚落、建筑和道路等地形要素，以便对遗产范围内或邻近或位于遗产边界上的开发计划对遗产地的影响有清晰的评估。适当比例的地图必须包括清晰的遗产边界线并与计划要申报的遗产类别相关：文化遗产应有地籍图，自然遗产或景观需要地形图（一般比例为 1 : 25000 至 1 : 50000） 对地图上的边界线条的宽度处理需极其谨慎，因为使用粗线可能会导致对遗产地边界的辨认模糊。

续表

申报材料格式	填报须知
1.e 地图和平面图，显示申报遗产和缓冲区的范围	登录以下网址，可获取地图：http：//whc.unesco.org/en/mapagencies 所有的地图都必须能够进行地理参照，地图上必须至少有三个点，点点相对，每个点都有完整的坐标。地图不能缩减，应该显示比例、方位、投影、数据、遗产名称和日期。如果可能，递送地图时应将其卷起，而不是折叠。 如果可能，建议提供数字地理信息，便于纳入地理信息系统，尽管这些信息不能替代纸质地图。在这种情况下，范围的划分（申报遗产和缓冲区）应以向量形式提供，以尽可能大的比例编制。相关详情缔约国可联系秘书处。 （ii）一张位置图，显示该遗产在缔约国的位置。 （iii）展示遗产各项特征的平面图和特殊地图也很有帮助，可以随附于申报材料后面。 为了便于向咨询机构和世界遗产中心抄送和呈报，如果可能，A4 纸（或“信纸”）大小缩略图和主要地图的电子图像文件应该包括在申报材料之中。 如果没有划分缓冲区，申报材料中必须说明对申报遗产的适当保护不需要缓冲区的原因。
1.f 申报遗产和建议的缓冲区的面积（公顷） 申报遗产的面积：__公顷 缓冲区 ___ 公顷 共 ___ 公顷	如果是系列申报（见《操作指南》第 137–140 条），插入一张表格，显示组成部分的名称、所处地域（如果不同部分处于不同地域）、坐标、面积和缓冲区。 该系列申报表还应显示各个申报区及各缓冲区的大小。
2. 描述	
2.a 遗产描述	本部分首先描述申报时遗产的情况，应涉及该项遗产的各项显著特色。 如果是文化遗产，本部分应描述使该项遗产在文化方面具有重要意义的任何因素。可描述某个或多个建筑及其建筑风格、建筑日期、所用材料等。还可以描述重要环境因素，如花园、公园。 比如，对某岩画遗址来说，描述内容应既包括岩画，还应包括其周围的景观。如果是历史名城或历史街区，没有必要描述每座建筑单体，但是应逐个描述重要的公共建筑，及该地区的规划和布局，街巷格局等等。 如果是自然遗产，应该说明重要的物理属性、地质情况、栖息地、物种及种群数量、其他重要的生态特色和进程。应尽可能提供物种列表，并突出濒危物种或地方特有的生物分类。应该描述自然资源开发的程度和方法。 如果是文化景观，有必要描述上文所提的各项内容。应特别关注人与自然之间的关系。 应该描述第 1 部分（遗产的身份证明）说明的整个申报遗产。如果是系列申报（见《操作指南》第 137–140 条），应单独描述遗产的各组成部分。
2.b 历史沿革	描述该项遗产形成和发展的历程及当下的形式和状态，经历了什么样的重大变化，包括近期的保护情况。 如果是古迹、遗址、建筑或建筑群，应该描述其发展变化的不同阶段。如果在建成后曾有过重大的变化、拆除或重建，应对这些事件进行描述。 如果是自然遗产，应该描述历史上或史前曾影响过该项遗产演化的重要事件，及该项遗产与人类之间的关系。包括遗产使用及用于狩猎、捕鱼或农业的自然资源发生的变化，以及天气变化、洪水、地震或其他自然现象带来的影响。 如果是文化景观，也要求提供这些信息其中应包括这个地区人类活动史的所有方面。
3. 列入理由①	理由陈述应按照以下顺序。 这部分必须明确为什么认为遗产具有“突出普遍价值”。 本部分遗产的描述应该严格参考《操作指南》中的相关要求。不应该包括详细的描述性的遗产情况说明和遗产管理情况说明，这些内容在其他部分提供，这部分应该着重传达与遗产突出普遍价值相关的各方面的关键信息。
3.1.a 简要综述	简要综述应包含（1）事实性信息概述（2）品质概述。事实性信息总结列出遗产的地理和历史背景及主要特征。品质概述应向决策者和公众展示遗产需要被维持的潜在的突出普遍价值，也应包括体现其突出普遍价值、并因此需要得到妥善保护管理和监测的价值载体的概述。这部分应结合所有依据的标准以解释申报理由。因此简要概述是遗产申报和建议列入的全部原理阐述的浓缩。

① 见第 132–133。

续表

申报材料格式	填报须知
3.1.b 提议遗产列入所依据的标准（和根据这些标准的列入理由）	见《操作指南》第 77 条。 分别说明引用每个标准的理由。 简述该项遗产如何满足申报标准，（如有必要，参考“描述”和“比较分析”部分，但不要重复这些部分的文字内容），并描述符合每项标准的相关价值载体。
3.1.c 完整性声明	完整性声明应证实该项遗产满足《操作指南》第 II.D 部分列出的完整性条件，《操作指南》详细描述了这些条件。 《操作指南》列出了对遗产符合以下各项范围进行评估的必要： – 包含表现遗产突出普遍价值所需的所有要素； – 规模、范围足够大以确保传递遗产重要性的所有特征和过程的完整性； – 因开发或废弃带来的负面影响（第 88 条）； 《操作指南》提供了对应不同世界遗产标准的具体指导，理解这一点很重要（89–95 条）。
3.1.d 真实性声明（适用于建议以标准 i–vi 列入的遗产申报）	真实性的声明应证实该项遗产满足：《操作指南》第 II.D 部分列出的真实性条件，《操作指南》详细描述了这些条件。 这部分应简要总结申报文本第四部分（也可能其他部分）详述的一些内容，但详略程度不应和其他章节重复。 真实性仅适用于文化遗产和混合遗产中的文化部分。 《操作指南》指出：“如果遗产的文化价值（申报标准所认可的）是通过多个载体得到真实可信的表现，则被认为符合真实性条件”（见第 82 条）。 根据《操作指南》，以下类型载体可被认为传递或表现突出普遍价值： • 外形和设计 • 材料和质地 • 用途和功能 • 传统、技术和管理体系 • 环境和位置 • 语言和其他形式的非物质遗产 • 精神和感觉 • 其他内外因素
3.1.e 保护和管理要求	这部分应包含如何达到了保护管理的各项要求，从而确保遗产的突出普遍价值得到长期的维持。内容应包括对保护管理整体框架体系的详细描述，和对遗产管理长期具体的目标的预期。 这部分应简要总结申遗文本第五部分（也可能在第四和第六部分）详述的一些内容，但详略程度不应和其他章节重复。 本部分文字应首先概述保护管理框架。其中包括保护遗产突出普遍价值载体、应对威胁和自身脆弱性的必要的保护机制、管理体系或管理规划（已存在或尚需制定）。具体包括健全有效的法律保护、记录明晰的管理体系，与主要利益相关方使用群体的必要沟通，足够的人员和财政资源，符合展示要求，有效而灵敏的监测等。 此外，这部分需要写明遗产保护管理面临的长期挑战，以及应对这些挑战的长期战略。有必要提及对遗产最重大的威胁因素，其真实性和完整性中发现的脆弱性和负面变化，并列举出如何针对这些威胁实施保护管理措施，减小负面影响。 作为受世界遗产委员会认可的官方声明，突出普遍价值声明部分将重申缔约国为遗产的长期保护和管理所做出的最重要的承诺。
3.2　比较分析	该项遗产应与类似遗产（无论是否列入《世界遗产名录》）进行比较。比较时应该罗列该项遗产与其他遗产之间的类似点，说明该项遗产之所以突出的原因。比较分析旨在解释申报遗产在本国及在国际上的重要性。（见第 132 条）。 比较分析的目的在于通过现有主题研究显示其列入名录的合理性，对系列遗产申报，则是选择其构成部分的依据。

续表

申报材料格式	填报须知
3.3 建议的《突出普遍价值声明》	《突出普遍价值声明》是世界遗产委员会在遗产列入名录时通过的官方声明。世界遗产委员会同意将某项遗产列入《世界遗产名录》，就意味着认可其声明中解释的为何该遗产被认为具有突出普遍价值，它如何符合了相关标准、完整性和（对文化遗产来说）真实性，以及它满足了确保突出普遍价值得以长期保存的保护管理条件。 《突出普遍价值声明》应力求简明，并遵循标准格式。应有助于提高公众对遗产价值的认识，指导现状评估和保护管理。一经委员会通过，该声明将在遗产地和联合国教科文世界遗产中心网站上公布。 《突出普遍价值声明》主要包含以下章节： 1）简要综述 2）对应标准的列入理由 3）完整性声明（所有遗产） 4）真实性声明（按照标准 i–vi 申报的遗产） 5）保护和管理要求
4. 保护情况和影响遗产的因素	
4.a 保护现状	本部分信息是监测所申报遗产未来保护情况的基线数据。本部分内容应包括：该项遗产的自然条件、其突出普遍价值面临的威胁和采取的保护措施（见第 132 条）。 比如，应该指出历史城镇或区域内，建筑、古迹或其他构筑物所需的大大小小修缮工作，以及近期主要修缮项目的规模和持续时间。 如果是自然遗产，应该提供物种演化趋势或生态系统完整性的数据。这很重要，因为在未来几年，对比并跟踪遗产状态变化时会用到这些申报材料。 至于监测遗产保护情况的指标和统计基准，请参见下文第 6 部分。
4.b 影响遗产的因素	本部分应说明可能影响或威胁遗产突出普遍价值的所有因素。还应该说明在解决这些问题时会面临的困难。在此罗列的各项因素并非适用于所有遗产。它们只是标示性的，旨在协助缔约国确认与各自遗产相关的因素。
（i）开发压力（比如：侵占、改建、农业和采矿）	列举影响遗产的开发压力，比如，拆除、重建或新建项目的压力；将现有建筑改作他用而损害其真实性和完整性；由于农林牧活动的扩张、管理不善的旅游业或其他原因而对栖息地进行改造和破坏；不当或非持续性自然资源开发；采矿带来的损害；引进可破坏自然生态进程的外来物种，在遗产内部或附近形成新的栖息中心，对遗产及其环境造成损害。
（ii）环境压力（比如，污染、气候变化、沙化）	列出并总结影响建筑结构、动植物环境恶化的主要根源。
（iii）自然灾害和防灾情况（地震、洪水、火灾等）	列举对遗产产生威胁的可预见的灾害，制定的应急方案中采取了哪些步骤来应对这些灾害，是否为此采取了物理保护措施，或开展了员工培训。
（iv）对世界遗产地负责任的旅游参观	提供遗产地参观状况信息（尤其是现有的基线数据，使用格局，包括遗产地各部分活动分布以及未来规划的活动等）。 描述由于列入世界遗产名录或其他因素引发的参观数量的变化。 描述遗产的“承载能力”，以及如何管理使其能接纳当前或一定数量参观者，应对开发压力而不产生负面影响
（v）遗产及缓冲区内的居民数量以下区域内的估计人口： 申报遗产区 ________ 缓冲区 ________ 总计 ________ 年份 ________	给出申报遗产及缓冲区内居民人数的现有最准确数据或估计数。标明进行人数统计或估测的年份。

续表

申报材料格式	填报须知
5. 遗产的保护与管理	本部分旨在清晰地说明法律、监管、契约、规划、机构或传统措施（见《操作指南》第132条）、以及已确立的管理规划或其他管理体系（见《操作指南》内的段落），按照《世界遗产公约》的要求保护、管理遗产。应该包括政策、法律地位和保护措施，以及日常管理的实际情况。
5.a 所有权	说明遗产范围内土地所有类型（包括国家、地方、私人、社区、传统、约定俗成和非政府所有权等）。
5.b 保护性称号	列出遗产相关的法律、监管、合同、规划、制度或传统地位，比如，国家或省级公园；依据国家法律或习俗确立的历史古迹、保护区以及其他指定称号。 说明指定称号宣布的年份及规定遗产地位的法律。 如果文件所用语言不是英语或法语，应提供一份英语或法语的执行摘要，说明文件内容要点。
5.c 保护措施执行手段	描述第5.b.条所列法律、监管、合同、规划、制度或传统地位提供的保护具体生效方式。
5.d 申报遗产所在市或地区的现有规划（比如，地区或地方规划、保护、旅游开发规划）	列出通过的各种规划，标出制定日期和负责机构。其重要条款应在本部分概述。规划副本应作为附件（如第7.b.条所示）附后。 如果规划所用语言既非英语也非法语，应提供一份英语或法语的执行摘要，说明其内容要点。
5.e 遗产管理规划或其他管理制度	如《操作指南》第132段所示，一份适宜的管理规划或其他管理制度必不可少，应该收录在申报材料内。最好也能提供该管理规划或其他管理制度有效实施的保证。 如第7.b.条所示，英语或法语文本的管理规划或者管理制度文件应附在申报材料之后。 如果管理规划所用语言既非英语也非法语，应提供英语或法语的规划条款详述，附在申报材料之后。列出管理规划（附在申报材料后）的名称、日期和编制机构或个人。 应提供该管理规划或成文管理制度的详细分析或说明。 建议提供管理规划实施时间表。
5.f 资金来源和水平	说明遗产每年的资金来源和水平。还应估计可用资金是否充足，特别要明确指出缺口、差额或其他需要援助的领域。
5.g 专业知识来源和保护与管理技术的培训	指出国家当局或其他组织提供的有关遗产的专业知识和培训。
5.h 旅游参观基础设施	本部分应描述遗产地现有的参观设施，并说明符合的保护管理要求。应具体列出这些设施和服务如何能够为遗产地提供有效展示，满足游客需要，包括提供安全、适当的到达和进入遗产地的形式。本部分的考虑范围包括阐释与展示（指示牌、路径设置、通知公告或出版物、导游讲解等）；博物馆或现场展示，游客或阐释中心；利用可能的数码技术和其他服务（住宿、参观、停车、洗手间、搜救等）
5.i 遗产展示和宣传相关的政策和方案	本部分援引《公约》的第4条和第5条，这两条阐述了文化及自然遗产的展示和传承事宜。鼓励缔约国提供申报遗产的展示和宣传政策及方案信息。
5.j 人员配置水平（专业、技术、维修）	说明良好的遗产管理所需的技能和资质，包括客流和未来培训相关的需求。
6. 监测	本部分旨在提供说明遗产保护现状的证据，可用回访、定期报告、审查等方式，以明确遗产的变化趋势。
6.a 衡量保护状况的主要指标	以表格形式列出用于衡量整个遗产保护情况的主要指标（见上文第4.a条）。指出审核发这些指标的周期，以及记录保存地点。这些指标可代表遗产的某个重要方面，并尽可能地与《突出普遍价值声明》挂钩（见上文第2.b条）。如果可能，用数字表示，不能用数字的话，以可重复的方式表现，比如，在同一地点拍照。有效指标的实例有： 1. 自然遗产内物种种类或主要物种种群的数目； 2. 历史城镇或历史街区内需要大规模修缮的建筑比例； 3. 估计完成主要保护方案需要的时间； 4. 某个建筑或建筑要素的稳定性或活动程度； 5. 对遗产侵蚀的消长速度。

指标	周期	记录保存地点

申报材料格式	填报须知
6.b 遗产监测的行政安排	负责监测（如第 6.a 条所示）的机构名称和联系方式。
6.c 前期实践结果报告的	列出遗产保护状况的前期报告，并进行简要总结，提供报告摘要和参考文献（比如，根据国际协议和方案，如《拉姆萨湿地公约》,《人与生物圈计划》，提交的报告）。
7. 文献	本部分列出了完备的申报材料所需的文献。
7.a 照片、视听影像材料的清单和授权表	缔约国应提供一定数量的近期影像资料（印制品、幻灯片，如果可能的话，还可提供电子格式、录像和航拍照片），以便对该遗产有清晰的整体的印象。 幻灯片应为 35mm 格式，电子图像是 jpg 格式，其分辨率不应低于 300dpi（每英寸点数）。如果有影像材料，为确保质量，建议使用 Beta SP 格式。 这类材料应配有影像清单和照片，以及下文列出的视听材料授权表。 至少有一张照片可用于公共网页，说明该遗产被列为世界遗产。 鼓励缔约国以书面形式，向教科文组织独家免费转让传播、公示、出版、复制及利用（以各种方式，基于各种手段，包括数字形式）全部或部分图像的权利，并准予教科文组织把这些权利授予第三方。 上述权利转让不得侵犯知识产权（摄影师、录像导演以及其他所有人的权利），另外，教科文组织在发行图像时，如果表格中有明确的说明，教科文组织通常会提供摄影师、录像导演的姓名。 此类权利转让所产生的收益将纳入世界遗产基金。

照片、图像视听材料清单及授权表

编号	格式（幻灯片 / 印制品 / 录像）	图片说明	照片日期（年 / 月）	摄影师、录像导演	版权所有人（如果不是摄像师 / 导演）	版权所有人的详细联系信息（姓名、地址、电话 / 传真和电邮）	独家权利转让

申报材料格式	填报须知
7.b 与保护性称号、遗产管理规划或成文管理制度相关的正文、其他遗产规划摘要	把上文第 5.b，5.d 和 5.e 条所示文件正文附后。
7.c 遗产近期记录或列表的格式和日期	明确阐述遗产近期记录或列表的格式和日期。仅涉及手头现有的记录。
7.d 列表、记录和档案的保存地址	提供保存这些记录（建筑、古迹、动植物种群）的机构名称和地址。
7.e 参考文献	列出已出版主要的参考文献，用标准的参考文献格式。
8. 负责机构的联系方式	秘书处可通过该联系方式，把世界遗产的最新消息和其他相关事宜通知给该遗产负责机构。
8.a 编纂人员 名字： 职称（头衔）： 地址： 国家、州 / 省、市： 电话：	提供申报材料编纂人员的名称、地址和其他联系信息。如果没有电子邮箱，则联系信息中必须包括传真号码。
8.b 地方管理机构	提供负责遗产管理的地方机构、博物馆、组织、社区或管理人员的名称。如果常规报告提供组织是国家机关，请提供该国家机关的联系方式。
8.c 其他地方机构	应列出接收免费《世界遗产时事通讯》（讨论关于世界遗产的事件和议题）的所有博物馆、游客中心和官方旅游办公室的全称、地址、电话、传真和电子邮件地址。
8.d 官方网站 http：// 联系人姓名： 电子邮件：	请提供申报遗产的现有官方网站。说明今后是否计划设立该类网站，并提供联系人姓名和电子邮件地址。
9. 缔约国代表签名	申报材料末尾应由缔约国的正式授权代表签字。

Annex 6 EVALUATION PROCEDURES OF THE ADVISORY BODIES FORNOMINATIONS

附件 6 咨询机构对申报材料的评估程序

This Annex includes:

A. THE ICOMOS PROCEDURE FOR THE EVALUATION OF CULTURAL PROPERTIES

B. THE IUCN PROCEDURE FOR THE EVALUATION OF NATURAL PROPERTIES

C. ADVISORY BODY COLLABORATION - PROCEDURE FOR THE EVALUATION OF CULTURAL AND NATURAL PROPERTIES AND OF CULTURAL LANDSCAPES

本附件包括：

A. 国际古迹遗址理事会的文化遗产评估程序

B. 世界自然保护联盟的自然遗产评估程序

C. 咨询机构合作 – 对文化和自然遗产及文化景观的评估程序

For further information please also refer to Paragraphs 143-151 of *the Operational Guidelines*.

了解更多信息，请参阅《操作指南》第 143–151 条。

A. THE ICOMOS PROCEDURE FOR THE EVALUATION OF CULTURAL PROPERTIES

A. 国际古迹遗址理事会的文化遗产评估程序

In carrying out its evaluation of nominations of cultural properties ICOMOS (the International Council of Monuments and Sites) is guided by the *Operational Guidelines*; (see Paragraph 148).

Once new nominations have been checked for completeness by the UNESCO World Heritage Centre, the nomination dossiers that are deemed as complete are delivered to ICOMOS, where they are handled by the ICOMOS World Heritage Unit. From this point, dialogue and consultation with the nominating States Parties may begin and will continue throughout the evaluation process.

国际古迹遗址理事会遵循《操作指南》（见第 148 条）的指导来评估文化遗产的申报材料。

一旦联合国教科文组织世界遗产中心认为一个新的申报是完整的，该完整的申报文件将递交到国际古迹遗址理事会世界遗产处。随后国际古迹遗址理事会与申报国的对话及讨论将贯穿整个评估过程。国际古迹遗址理事会将尽最大努力，公平、有效、高效的分配现有资源，与所有申遗的缔约国最大限度的进行对话。

ICOMOS will use its best endeavours to allocate its available resources equitably, efficiently and effectively to maximise the opportunity for dialogue with all nominating States Parties.

The ICOMOS evaluation process involves the following stages as illustrated in figure 1:

国际古迹遗址理事会评估程序步骤见表 1：

1. Requests for further information

When it has identified that further information or clarification of existing information is needed, ICOMOS starts a dialogue with States Parties in order to explore ways to meet the needs. This may involve letters, face-to face meetings, teleconferences or other forms of communication as agreed between ICOMOS and the State Party concerned.

1. 更多的信息需求

如果证实目前申报需要更多信息或说明，国际古迹遗址理事会与缔约国开始对话以探讨满足条件的方法。方法包括信件、面谈、电话会议或其他国际古迹遗址理事会与相关缔约国认可的方法。

2. Desk Reviews

Each nomination is assessed by up to ten experts who are knowledgeable about the property in its geo-cultural context and who advise on the proposed “Outstanding Universal Value” of the nominated property. This is essentially a “library” exercise undertaken by specialist academics within the membership of ICOMOS, its National and International Committees, or by individuals within many other specialist networks or institutions with which it is linked.

2. 案头审查

每项申报需经过最多10位了解遗产地缘文化背景或建议了申报遗产的“突出普遍价值”的专家的评估。这主要是专家学者的“图书馆”式运作，包括国际古迹遗址理事会会员、国家或国际委员会、其他相关专家网络或机构的特殊个人。

3. On-site missions

These are carried out by experts who have practical experience of the management, conservation, and authenticity aspects of individual properties. The process of selecting these experts makes full use of the ICOMOS network. The advice of International Scientific Committees and individual members is sought, as is that of specialist bodies with whom ICOMOS has partnership agreements, such as The International

3. 现场考察

实施这项任务的专家是那些在单项遗产管理、保护和真实性方面具有实践经验的专家。在选择专家时，会充分利用国际古迹遗址理事会的网络。国际古迹遗址理事会将征询国际科学委员会和独立会员、及以与国际古迹遗址理事会签有伙伴协议的专家团体的建议。这些专家团体包括：国际工业遗产保护协会、国际景观设计师联合会、国际现代建筑文献组织等。

Committee for the Conservation of the Industrial Heritage (TICCIH), the International Federation of Landscape Architects (IFLA), and the International Committee for the Documentation and Conservation of Monuments and Sites of the Modern Movement (DoCoMoMo).

In selecting experts to carry out on-site missions, the policy of ICOMOS is wherever possible to choose someone from the region in which the nominated property is located. Such experts are required to be experienced in heritage management and conservation of the type of property: they are not necessarily high academic experts. They are expected to be able to talk to site managers on a basis of professional equality and to make informed assessments of management plans, conservation practices, visitor handling, etc. They are provided with detailed briefings, which include copies of the relevant information from the dossiers. The dates and programmes of their visits are agreed in consultation with States Parties, who are requested to ensure that ICOMOS evaluation missions are given a low profile so far as the media are concerned. ICOMOS experts submit their reports in confidence on practical aspects of the properties concerned, and may also comment in their reports on other aspects of the nomination.

在选择执行现场考察的专家时，国际古迹遗址理事会的政策是尽可能选择申报遗产所在地区的专家。这些专家必须具有遗产管理与保护的经验，但无需是该类遗产的资深学术专家。他们需要在专业平等的基础上与遗址管理人员进行专业交流，对管理规划、保护政策和游客管理等事宜进行评估。相关人员将向这些专家简要介绍情况，其中包括申报材料中相关信息的复印本。这些专家到访的时间和日程会与缔约国进行协商，以达成一致。理事会要求缔约国确保媒体对国际古迹遗址理事会的评估团报道真实低调。国际古迹遗址理事会专家把关于遗产的实际问题如实上报，也可能会在报告中评论申报的其他方面。

3.bis Other sources of information

Other relevant institutions, such as UNESCO Chairs, universities and research institutes may also be consulted during the evaluation process, and listed, as appropriate, in the evaluation report.

3. 注 . 其他信息来源

其他相关机构例如联合国教科文组织主席，大学或研究机构在评估过程中也可能会参与讨论，适当时，会列入评估报告。

4. Review by the ICOMOS Panel

The ICOMOS World Heritage Panel comprises individual ICOMOS members who collectively represent all regions of the world and possess a wide range of relevant cultural heritage skills and experience. Some of these members serve on the

4. 国际古迹遗址理事会专家小组评估

国际古迹遗址理事会世界遗产专家小组，由国际古迹遗址理事会中能代表世界各个地区、并拥有相关文化遗产技巧和经历的特别会员组成。部分成员定期为专家小组工作，另一些则根据需要检查的申报遗产的特点进行为期一年

Panel for a fixed term while others are appointed for one year only according to the characteristics of the nominated properties to be examined. ICOMOS will include within its Panel membership some experts who have past experience as members of State Parties delegations, but who are no longer serving as members of the World Heritage Committee. These experts will serve in a personal and professional capacity.

的工作。国际古迹遗址理事会专家小组成员包括有经验的、但不再是世界遗产委员会委员的缔约国代表。这些专家以个人身份和专业能力进行工作。

The Panel meets twice, first in December and then in March. At the first meeting, the Panel evaluates each nomination, based on the reports of Desk experts and of the site missions.

专家小组开两次会，一次在12月，一次在来年3月。第一次会议，小组在案头评审和现场考察基础上评估每项申报。

The Panel aims to reach its recommendations on nominations by consensus.

专家小组的目标是达成推荐申报的共识。

The first Panel may come to final collective recommendations on some nominations while for others further dialogue with States Parties may be agreed related to the need for more information or the need for adjustments to the approach of the nomination. In cases where the Panel has concluded that the nomination has no potential to justify Outstanding Universal Value, ICOMOS will contact States Parties at this stage. A short interim report for each nomination, in one of the two working languages of the *Convention*, outlining the status and any issues relevant to the evaluation process, and any further requests for supplementary information, will be provided in January to the nominating States Parties and copied to the World Heritage Centre for distribution to the Chair of the World Heritage Committee.

第一次会议将对部分申报形成集体意见，另外部分申报需要与相关缔约国协商以提供更多信息或需要调整申报方法。如果会议认为申报不具备潜在的突出普遍价值，国际古迹遗址理事会将与缔约国联系。每项申报都要用公约要求的一或两种工作语言，编制一个简短的临时报告，简要描述遗产状况及与评估程序相关的问题、及要求进一步补充的信息，于1月交给提出申报的缔约国并将副本交世界遗产中心以派送给世界遗产委员会主席。

The second Panel undertakes further evaluation of nominations for which a recommendation has not yet been reached based on the receipt of further information or the outcome of dialogue with States Parties. The Panel then agrees the remaining collective recommendations. Following the second Panel meeting, the text of all evaluations is finalised and sent to the World

第二次会议将根据收到的更多信息和与缔约国协商的结果，对未达成共识的申报进行进一步评估。进而达成共识。第二次会议后所有最终评估将送交世界遗产中心以便于分送至缔约国。参会人员的姓名、资质将提交给世界遗产中心并在国际古迹遗址理事会网站上公布。

Heritage Centre for distribution to States Parties. The names and qualifications of the members of the Panel are then provided to the World Heritage Centre and published on the ICOMOS web site.

The ICOMOS evaluations provide an assessment of Outstanding Universal Value, including the applicability of the criteria and the requirements of integrity and authenticity, assessment of the adequacy of legislative protection, management, and the state of conservation, and finally draft recommendations to the World Heritage Committee with respect to inscription.

国际古迹遗址理事会的评估将对突出普遍价值包括适用的标识和完整性、真实性要求，评估是否有充分的立法保护、管理、保护状况声明等做出评估报告，最终推荐草案提交给世界遗产委员会作为录入名录的参考。

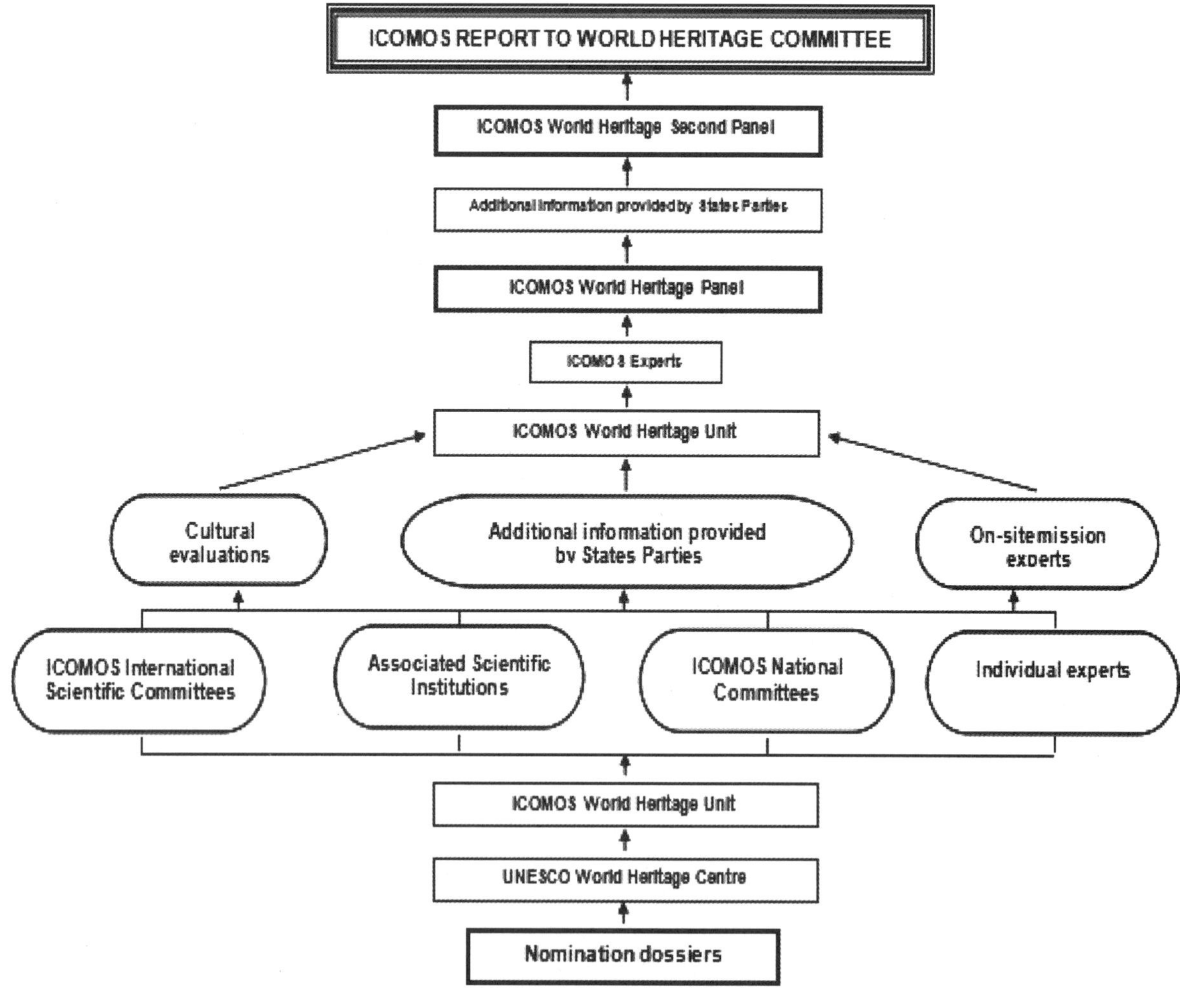

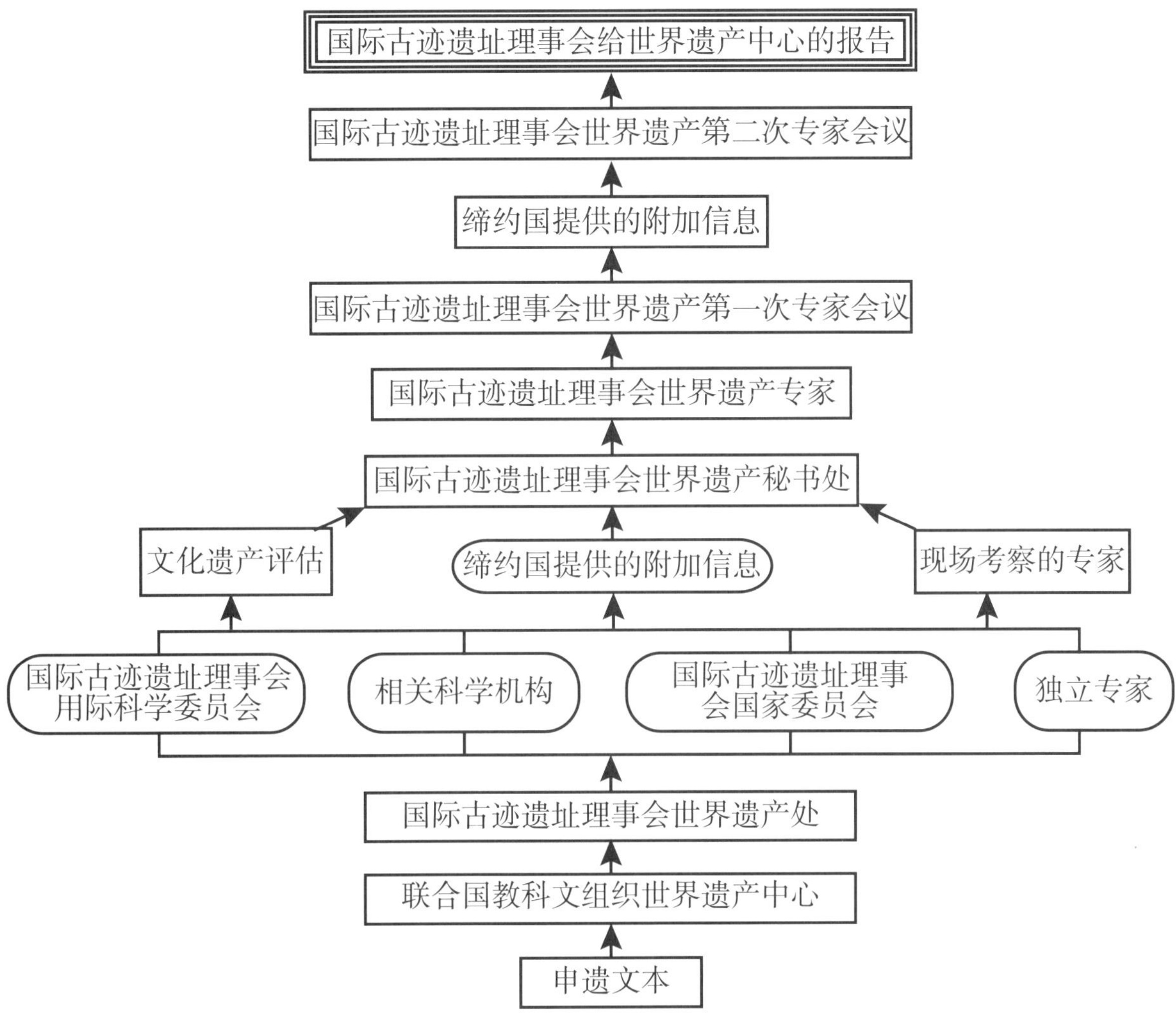

B. THE IUCN PROCEDURE FOR THE EVALUATION OF NATURAL PROPERTIES

1. In carrying out its evaluation of nominations of natural properties, IUCN (the International Union for Conservation of Nature) is guided by the *Operational Guidelines* (see Paragraph 148). The evaluation process (see Figure 2) involves five steps:

(i) Data Assembly. Following receipt of the nomination dossier from the World Heritage Centre, a standardised analysis is compiled on the property using the World Database on Protected Areas and other IUCN global databases and thematic studies. This may include comparative analyses on

B. 世界自然保护联盟的自然遗产评估程序

1. 世界自然保护联盟遵循《操作指南》（见第 148 条）的指导对自然遗产的申报材料进行评估。评估程序（见图 2）包括五个步骤：

（i）搜集数据：接到世界遗产中心递交的申报材料之后，使用世界保护区数据库和世界自然保护联盟全球数据库及专题研究中的数据，编制遗产的标准化分析。这可能包括与联合国环境规划署世界保护监测中心合作的生物多样性对比分析（UNEP–WCMC）。关键数据分析的

biodiversity values undertaken in partnership with the UNEP-World Conservation Monitoring Centre (UNEP-WCMC). Key findings of data analysis are the subject of dialogue with the State Party during the evaluation mission, and at other stages of the process.

结果是评估任务和程序中其他阶段与缔约国对话的主题。

(ii) External Review. The nomination is sent for desk review to independent experts knowledgeable about the property and/or the values that are the subject of the nomination, who are primarily members of IUCN's specialist Commissions and networks, or expert members of partner organisations of IUCN. The documents used to guide IUCN desk reviews are publicly available on the IUCN website: www.iucn.org/worldheritage

（ii）外部评审：申报文件送达参与案头审查的、具备关于该项遗产的渊博知识、并且是世界自然保护联盟专家委员会及网络成员或世界自然保护联盟合作组织成员的独立专家。指导世界自然保护联盟案头审查的文件在世界自然保护联盟网站上发布。www.iucn.org/worldheritage

(iii) Evaluation mission to the property. One or two appropriately qualified IUCN experts visit each nominated property to clarify details about the area, to evaluate site management and to discuss the nomination with relevant authorities and stakeholders. IUCN experts, selected for their global perspective on conservation and natural history as well as their knowledge of the *Convention,* are usually members of the IUCN World Commission on Protected Areas. (This field inspection is undertaken jointly with ICOMOS in certain situations - see Part C below). The format of IUCN field evalution mission reports is publicly available on the IUCN website: www.iucn.org/worldheritage.

（iii）遗产评估任务：一至两名有合格资质的世界自然保护联盟专家，对每一处申报遗产进行考察，以明确该区域的详细情况，评估遗址管理，与相关当局和利益相关者讨论申报情况。挑选世界自然保护联盟专家的标准，是根据专家对保护自然、历史的全球视角及对《公约》的了解，通常是世界自然保护联盟保护区遗产专家。（在某些情况下与国际古迹遗址理事会共同展开现场调查——见下文 C 部分）。世界自然保护联盟的现场评估任务报告的格式可网上下载：：www.iucn.org/worldheritage.

(iv) Other sources of information. IUCN may also consult additional literature and receive comments from local NGOs, communities, indigenous peoples and other interested parties in the nomination. Where relevant IUCN will also coordinate with other international conservation instruments such as the Ramsar Convention, the Man and Biosphere Programme and the Global Geoparks Network, and will consult with universities and research institutes as appropriate.

（iv）其他信息来源：世界自然保护联盟也可参考其他文献，接受地方非政府组织、社区、当地居民及其他利益方的意见和建议。世界自然保护联盟也会参照其他国际保护文件如拉姆萨尔湿地公约、人与生物圈计划、世界地质公园网络工程，并与大学及研究机构酌情磋商。

(v) IUCN World Heritage Panel Review. The IUCN World Heritage Panel is established by the Director General of IUCN to provide high quality and independent technical and scientific advice to IUCN on its work as an Advisory Body to the World Heritage Committee and strategic advice to IUCN's work on World Heritage throughout the IUCN Programme. Specific Tasks of the World Heritage Panel are to conduct a rigorous evaluation of all nominations of natural and mixed properties to the World Heritage List, leading to a panel recommendation on the IUCN position in relation to each new nomination, in line with the requirements established in *The Operational Guidelines of the World Heritage Convention*. The Panel also provides comment where relevant to ICOMOS in relation to nominations of cultural landscapes to the World Heritage List. The Panel normally meets at least twice in the evaluation process, once in December (year 1) and a second meeting in March/April (year 2);

（v）世界自然保护联盟世界遗产专家小组评审：世界自然保护联盟世界遗产专家小组由世界自然保护联盟总干事设立，为世界自然保护联盟作为世界遗产委员会咨询机构，提供高质、独立的技术和科学指导及世界遗产整体自然联盟保护项目提供建议和战略咨询。世界自然保护联盟世界遗产专家小组的特别任务，是对所有提交申报的自然和混合遗产进行严格的评估，按照《世界遗产公约操作指南》的要求，以世界自然保护联盟的立场为每个新的申报提供意见。专家小组还会对国际古迹遗址理事会与文化遗产相关的申报提供建议。专家小组在每个评估过程中至少开两次会，一次在 12 月（第一年），一次在来年 3 月或四月（第二年）。

The members of the Panel comprise senior IUCN staff, IUCN Commission members and external experts selected for their high level of experience and recognised leading expertise and knowledge relevant to IUCN's work on World Heritage, including a balance of particular thematic and/or regional perspectives. It includes some experts who have past experience as members of State Party delegations, but are not current serving members of the World Heritage Committee. These experts will serve in a personal and professional capacity. The IUCN World Heritage Panel reviews all field evaluation reports (and normally hears direct feedback from the mission team), reviewers' comments, the UNEP-WCMC and other analyses and all other background material before finalising the text of the IUCN evaluation report for each nominated property. The membership, terms of reference and working methods of the IUCN World

专家小组由世界自然保护联盟资深职员、世界自然保护联盟委员会成员、与世界自然保护联盟世界遗产工作相关的拥有高超经验、及公认的、领先的、专业技术和知识的外部专家，包括平衡特殊主题和区域观点的专家组成。专家小组成员包括有经验的，但不再是世界遗产委员会委员的缔约国代表。这些专家以个人身份和专业能力进行工作。在每份遗产的评估报告定稿以前，世界自然保护联盟的专家小组将评审所有的现场评估报告（通常直接听取任务团队的反馈）、评论人员的评论、联合国环境规划署世界保护监测中心的数据和其他背景材料。世界自然保护联盟的世界遗产专家小组的成员资质、职权范围和工作方法，将在世界自然保护联盟网站上公布并提交给世界遗产中心。

Heritage Panel are publicly available on the IUCN website, and are provided to the World Heritage Committee.

Each evaluation report presents a concise summary of the Outstanding Universal Value of the property nominated, a global comparative analysis with other similar sites (including both World Heritage properties and other protected areas) and a review of integrity and management issues. It concludes with the assessment of the applicability of the criteria, and a clear recommendation to the World Heritage Committee. The names of all experts involved in the evaluation process are included in the final evaluation report, except in the case of reviewers who have provided confidential reviews.

每份评估报告包括简明摘要的申报遗产的突出普遍价值与类似遗址（包括世界遗产及其他保护区域）的全球对比分析、完整性和管理议题的评论。最后，评估报告会评估标准的应用情况，并向世界遗产委员会提供明确的建议。除了那些提供机密审核的专家，参与评估程序的所有专家的姓名将出现在最终评估报告中。

IUCN undertakes dialogue with the nominating States Party/ies at all stages of the nomination process. IUCN will use its best endeavours to allocate its available resources equitably, efficiently and effectively, to maximise the opportunities for dialogue with all nominating States Parties. Dialogue starts early in the evaluation process and intensifies after the meeting of the IUCN World Heritage Panel in December, and includes the following:

世界自然保护联盟在整个申报程序的各个阶段与申报缔约国保持对话。世界自然保护联盟将尽力公平有效地分配可用资源，并最大程度保持与申报缔约国的对话机会。在评估程序的初期就开始对话，在 12 月的世界自然保护联盟专家小组会议后更为频繁，对话包括：

i) Prior to the evaluation mission, IUCN may request additional information on questions in the nomination document that require clarification, and will always contact the State Party to prepare for the evaluation mission.

1）在评估任务前，世界自然保护联盟可能会对申报文件中需要澄清的问题向缔约国提出更多的信息要求，并经常与缔约国联系准备评估任务。

ii) During the evaluation mission the IUCN mission team is able to undertake in-depth discussions on site with representatives of the State Party and with stakeholders.

2）在评估过程中，世界自然保护联盟任务团队能在现场与缔约国代表及利益相关者进行深入讨论。

iii) After the evaluation mission, IUCN may discuss issues that have been identified by the mission team, and request further information from the State Party as required.

3）评估任务后，世界自然保护联盟会讨论任务团队确定的问题，并要求缔约国按要求提供更多的信息。

iv) After IUCN's first World Heritage Panel

4）在世界自然保护联盟第一次专家会议后，

meeting, normally held in December, IUCN will discuss issues raised by the Panel, and request further information from the State Party as required. A short interim report outlining the status, and any issues relevant to the evaluation, and detailing any requests for supplementary information, in one of the two working languages of the *Convention*, is sent to the nominating State Party/ies, and copied to the World Heritage Centre, for transmission to the Chairperson of the World Heritage Committee. Dialogue and consultation takes place either through teleconference and/or face-to-face meetings, as mutually agreed.

通常在 12 月举行，世界自然保护联盟将讨论专家会议提出的问题，并要求缔约国按要求提供更多的信息。用一或两种公约要求的工作语言准备一个简短的临时报告，概述状况、与评估相关的问题、需要补充信息的详细要求，送达申报缔约国同时副本送世界遗产中心以递交世界遗产委员会主席。对话或商谈按约定可以通过电话会议或面对面会议进行。

IUCN takes into account in its evaluation all information that is officially submitted by the State Party in writing to the World Heritage Centre by the specified deadline (see paragraph 148 of the *Operational Guidelines*). However, at all of the above stages any stakeholder in the nomination is also at liberty to contact IUCN to provide information if they wish.

世界自然保护联盟评估缔约国按期提交给世界遗产中心的官方书面文件中的所有信息（见操作指南第 148 条）。然而，在上述各个阶段申报的利益相关者，如果愿意，可以自由向世界自然保护联盟联系提供信息。

IUCN also always considers fully all past decisions of the World Heritage Committee relevant to the nomination, such as in cases of nominations that have been previously referred or deferred by the Committee, or where the Committee has taken any position in relation to issues of policy.

世界自然保护联盟也始终关注世界遗产委员会以往与申报相关的决定，如以前被委员会提及或推迟的申报，或委员会在相关政策问题上的立场。

In the case of renominations, extensions and boundary modifications to an existing World Heritage property, IUCN also considers all matters regarding the state of conservation of that property that have been previously reported to the World Heritage Committee. IUCN may also consider bringing to the attention of the Committee, through the state of conservation reporting process, any significant matters regarding the state of conservation of that property, when such are identified for the first time during the evaluation process.

对再次申报、现有世界遗产边界的扩展或调整的申报，世界自然保护联盟也将考虑以前报告给世界遗产委员会的所有与遗产保护状况相关事项。世界自然保护联盟也将提请委员会注意评估过程中，在保护状况报告程序首次发现的、与保护状况相关的任何重大事项。

Biogeographic classification systems as a basis for comparison

2. In the evaluations, IUCN uses biogeographic classification system such as Udvardy's 'Biogeographical Provinces of the World' (1975) and the more recent terrestrial, freshwater marine ecoregions of the world as a central element of its approach to the global comparative analysis. These systems provide an objective means of comparing nominated properties with sites of similar climatic and ecological conditions.

3. It is stressed, however, that these biogeographical classification systems are used as a measure for comparison only and do not imply that World Heritage properties are to be selected solely on this basis, nor that the representation of all such classification systems is the basis for the selection process. The guiding principle is that World Heritage properties must be of Outstanding Universal Value.

Systems to identify priority areas for conservation

IUCN also uses systems which identify priority areas for conservation such as the Worldwide Fund for Nature's (WWF) Global 200 Ecoregions, WWF/IUCN's Centres of Plant Diversity, Conservation International's Biodiversity Hotspots and High-Biodiversity Wilderness Areas, and Birdlife International's Endemic Bird Areas and Important Bird Areas. and other Key Biodiversity Areas such as Alliance for Zero Extinction sites. These systems provide additional information on the significance of the nominated properties for biodiversity conservation; however it is not assumed that all such sites should be included on the World Heritage List. The guiding principle is that World Heritage properties must be of Outstanding Universal Value.

生物地理分类体系作为比较的基础

2. 评估时，世界自然保护联盟使用生物地理分类体系如乌德瓦尔第（Udvardy）“世界生物地理区域”（1975 年）对最近的陆地区域、世界淡水海洋生态区域作为核心元素进行全球对比分析。该体系提供客观手段将申报遗产与具有类似天气与生态条件的遗产进行比较。

3. 但是，需要强调的是，生物地理分类体系只是作为比较的方法，而不是选择世界遗产的唯一基础，也不代表此类分类体系是选择程序的基础。一个指导性的原则是世界遗产必须具有突出普遍价值。

确认优先保护区的体系

4. 世界自然保护联盟同时使用确认优先保护区的体系，比如，世界自然基金会（WWF）全球 200 个生态区、世界自然基金会及世界自然保护联盟植物多样性中心、保护国际的生态多样性热点地区、高生物多样性荒原、国际爱鸟联盟特有鸟类区和重要鸟类区、及其他关键多样性区域如零绝种联盟网站等。这些体系为申报遗产多样性保护提供重要附加信息；然而这不是假设所有此类遗产都要录入世界遗产名录。指导原则是世界遗产必须具备突出普遍价值。

Systems to evaluate properties for earth science value

评估遗产地球科学价值的体系

5. In evaluating properties which have been nominated for their geological value, IUCN consults with a range of specialised organisations such as the UNESCO Earth Sciences Division, International Association of Geomorphologists, the International Union of Speleology and the International Union of Geological Sciences (IUGS).

5. 评估申报遗产的地质价值时，世界自然保护联盟会咨询一些专业组织，比如联合国教科文组织的地球科学部、国际地貌学家协会、国际洞穴研究会和国际地质科学联合会的意见。

Additional reference publications used in the evaluation process

评估时使用的附加参考出版物

6.The evaluation process also includes consideration of key reference publications on the world's protected areas published by IUCN and a range of international conservation organisations. These documents together provide system-wide overviews which allow comparison of the conservation importance of protected areas throughout the world. IUCN has also undertaken a range of thematic studies to identify gaps in natural World Heritage coverage and properties of World Heritage potential. These can be viewed on the IUCN website at www.iucn.org/worldheritage.

6. 评估程序也包括参考、引用的世界自然保护联盟和其他国际保护机构关于世界保护区的关键、主要出版物。这些文件共同提供了全系统的概览，便于对全球保护区的重要性进行比较。世界自然保护联盟也进行一系列主题研究以找出世界自然遗产覆盖范围的差异和潜在世界遗产。这些可登录世界自然保护联盟网站查询。www.iucn.org/worldheritage.

IUCN also draws upon references specific to the nominated properties in order to gain insights into site values and conservation issues.

世界自然保护联盟也为申报遗产指定特殊参考，以便于了解遗产价值和保护问题。

Evaluation of Cultural Landscapes (see also Annex 3)

文化景观评估（另请见附件三）

7. IUCN has an interest in many cultural properties, especially those nominated as cultural landscapes. For that reason, it will on occasion participate in joint field inspections to nominated cultural landscapes with ICOMOS (see Part C below).

7. 世界自然保护联盟对很多文化遗产都感兴趣，特别是作为文化景观申报的遗产。因此，联盟有时会与国际古迹遗址理事会合作，对申报的文化景观进行现场调查（见下文的 C 部分）。

8. In accordance with the natural qualities of certain cultural landscapes identified in Annex 3, Paragraph 11, IUCN 's evaluation is concerned with the following factors:

(i) C onservation of natural and semi-natural systems, and of wild species of fauna and flora;

(ii) Conservation of biodiversity within sustainable use systems (farming, traditional fisheries, forestry);

(iii) Sustainable land and water use;

(iv) Enhancement of scenic beauty;

(v) Ex-situ collections, such as botanic gardens or arboreta;

(vi) Outstanding examples of humanity 's inter-relationship with nature;

(vii) Historically significant discoveries.

The following table sets each of the above list in the context of the categories of cultural landscapes in Annex 3, thereby indicating where each consideration is most likely to occur (the absence of a consideration does not mean that it will *never* occur, only that this is unlikely) :

8. 根据附件三第 11 条确认的某些文化景观遗产的自然特性，世界自然保护联盟的评估主要涉及以下几个因素：

（i）自然、半自然体系以及野生动植物的保护；

（ii）可持续利用系统内生物多样性的保护（农业、传统渔业、林业）；

（iii）可持续土地和水利用；

（iv）景色美感的提升；

（v）异地移植的植物，如植物园或树木园；

（vi）人类与自然关系的杰出范例；

（vii）具有重大历史意义的发现。

下表把上文所提每个类别均放在附件三的文化景观类型的背景之内，藉此指出哪项内容最可能出现（没提到的内容并不意味着永远不会出现，只是可能性不太大）：

Cultural Landscape type (see also Annex 3)	Natural considerations most likely to be relevant (see Paragraph 16 above)						
Designed landscape					(v)		
Organically evolving landscape - continuous	(i)	(ii)	(iii)	(iv)			
Organically evolving landscape - fossil	(i)					(vi)	
Associative landscape							(vii)

文化景观类型（另见附件三）	最可能与自然相关的内容（见上文第 16 条）						
人工设计的景观					（v）		
有机演变的景观——持续	（i）	（ii）	（iii）	（iv）			
有机演变的景观——化石	（i）					（vi）	
关联性景观							（vii）

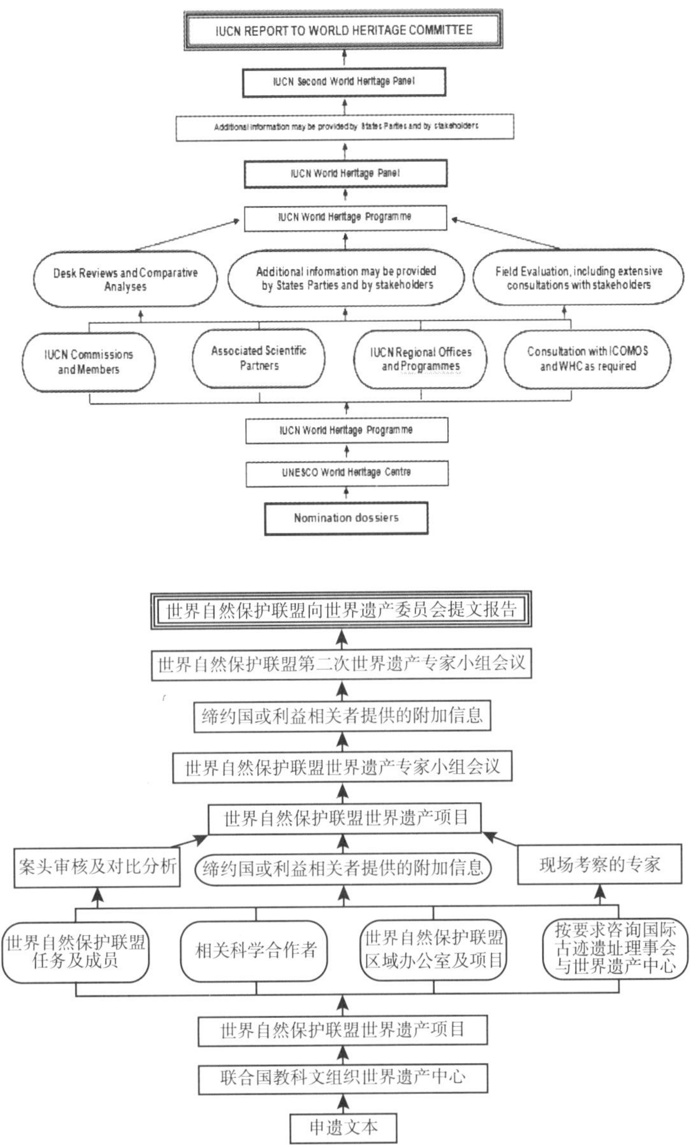

C. ADVISORY BODY COLLABORATION

Nominations of mixed properties

1. Properties that are nominated under both natural and cultural criteria entail a joint IUCN and ICOMOS mission to the nominated property. Following the mission, IUCN and ICOMOS prepare separate evaluation reports of the property under the relevant criteria (see above), and harmonise and coordinate their evaluations to the extent possible.

Cultural Landscapes

C. 咨询机构的合作评估程序

混合遗产的申报

1. 遗产在自然和文化双重标准下申报，需要世界自然保护联盟和国际古迹遗址理事会共同实施该申报遗产的评估任务。共同任务之后，世界自然保护联盟和国际古迹遗址理事会将根据相关标准，编制各自的遗产评估报告（见上文），并尽可能使评估和谐协调。

文化景观

2. Properties nominated as Cultural Landscapes are evaluated by ICOMOS under criteria (i) - (vi) (see Paragraph 77 of the *Operational Guidelines*). IUCN may provide advice when relevant on the natural values and the conservation and management of the nominated property, and addresses any questions that are raised by ICOMOS. In some cases, a joint mission is required.

2. 作为文化景观申报的遗产由国际古迹遗址理事会根据标准（i）–（vi）（见《操作指南》第 77 条）进行评估。世界自然保护联盟将对相关申报遗产的自然价值及保护和管理提供评估意见，特别是国际古迹遗址理事会提出的问题。在有些情况下，需要共同行动。

Linkages between nature and culture

自然与文化的联系

1. As most properties nominated to the World Heritage List include aspects of management related to the interaction of nature and culture, IUCN and ICOMOS, to the extent possible, discuss any such interactions during their evaluation processes.

1. 因为多数申报世界遗产名录的遗产包括与自然和文化相互影响的相关管理，世界自然保护联盟和国际古迹遗址理事会尽可能在评估过程中讨论这种相互影响。

Annex 7

Format for the periodic reporting on the application of the *World Heritage Convention*

附件 7

《世界遗产公约》实施的定期报告的格式

The Format for Periodic Reporting is available at the following Web address: http: //whc.unesco.org/en/periodicreporting

登录以下网址，可获取定期报告的格式：http：//whc.unesco.org/en/periodicreporting

Further guidance on Periodic Reporting can be found in Section V of the *Operational Guidelines*

In order to facilitate management of information, States Parties are requested to submit reports, in English or French, in electronic as well as in printed form to :

UNESCO World Heritage Centre
7, place de Fontenoy
75352 Paris 07 SP
France
Telephone: +33 (0) 1 4568 1571
Fax: +33 (0) 1 4568 5570
E-mail through: http: //whc.unesco.org/en/contacts

定期报告的更多指导意见，请参见《操作指南》的第 5 部分

为了便于信息的管理，要求缔约国提交英语或法语报告，应同时提交报告的电子版本和印刷版本，提交地址如下：

联合国教科文组织世界遗产中心
法国巴黎（7，place de Fontenoy
75352 Paris 07 SP France）

电话：+33（0）1 4568 1571
传真：+33（0）1 4568 5570
电邮：http：//whc.unesco.org/en/contacts

Annex 7 FORMAT PERIODIC REPORTING ON THE APPLICATION OF THE *WORLD HERITAGE CONVENTION*

附件 7 格式 实施《世界遗产公约》定期报告的格式

This Annex presents an outline of the Periodic Reporting questionnaire. The full questionnaire can be accessed at http://whc.unesco.org/en/periodicreporting/.

附件为定期报告问卷大纲。登录以下网址，可获取完整的问卷调查：http://whc.unesco.org/en/periodicreporting

General Requirements

总体要求

Information should be as precise, specific and concise as possible. It should be quantified where possible and fully referenced. Opportunities for comment are provided in each chapter.

信息应该尽可能地精确、具体，应尽量量化，并提供完整的参考文献。

Expressions of opinion should be supported by reference to the authority on which they are made and the verifiable facts which support them.

观点陈述应得到当局的支持，并具备能够支持该观点的确切事实。

SECTION I:
APPLICATION OF THE WORLD HERITAGE CONVENTION BY THE STATE PARTY

第 I 部分：
缔约国实施《世界遗产公约》的情况

Section I requests that the State Party provide information or validate existing information on the legislative and administrative provisions which they have adopted and other action which they have taken for the application of this Convention, together with details of the experience acquired in this field (Article 29.1 of the World Heritage Convention).

第一部分要求缔约国提供为实施《公约》通过的法律、行政条款及其他举措的相关信息及现有资料，以及在该领域获得的具体经验（《世界遗产公约》第 29.1 条）。

1. INTRODUCTION

Chapter 1 lists the name of the State Party and the year of ratification or acceptance of the Convention and seeks information on the groups and institutions involved in the preparation of Section I of the report.

1. 介绍

列出缔约国的名称、批准或接受《公约》的年份、负责编制本报告第一部分的组织或单位的信息。

2. SYNERGIES WITH OTHER CONVENTIONS, PROGRAMMES AND RECOMMENDATIONS FOR THE CONSERVATION OF THE NATURAL AND CULTURAL HERITAGE

Chapter 2 aims to gather information on existing and potential synergies between Multilateral Environmental Agreements, as well as other UNESCO conventions, programmes, and recommendations. The State Party is also invited to provide information on the extent to which it has implemented relevant policies adopted by the World Heritage Committee.

2. 与保护自然遗产和文化遗产有协同作用的其他公约、方案和建议

收集当前或未来有协同作用的多边环境协定、联合国教科文组织其他公约、方案和建议的相关信息。要求缔约国提供其执行世界遗产委员会相关政策的范围和程度的信息。

3. TENTATIVE LIST

Chapter 3 aims to gather information on the process of preparing the tentative list, the tools and guidance used, potential synergies with other conventions of properties on the tentative list as well as the sustainability of the process in line with the World Heritage and Sustainable Development Policy (2015).

3. 预备目录

收集缔约国准备《预备名录》的过程、使用的工具和指南、与其他公约或预备目录上的遗产有潜在协同作用、符合世界遗产可持续发展战略（2015）的可持续进程等信息。

4. NOMINATIONS

Chapter 4 aims to gather information on the process of nominating properties for inscription on the World Heritage List, the tools and guidance used, as well as the sustainability of the process in line with the World Heritage and Sustainable Development Policy (2015).

4. 监测

收集准备申报世界遗产过程的信息，使用的工具和指南、符合世界遗产可持续发展战略（2015）的可持续进程等信息。

5. GENERAL POLICY DEVELOPMENT

Chapter 5 aims to gather information on the legal framework for the protection, conservation

5. 总体发展政策

收集文化和自然遗产保护、修复、展示相关的法律框架及其成效等信息。

and presentation of the cultural and/or natural heritage and its effectiveness.

6. INVENTORIES/LISTS/REGISTERS OF CULTURAL AND NATURAL HERITAGE

Chapter 6 aims to gather information on the status of inventories /lists /registers of cultural and natural heritage of national significance and the processes used to compile them.

6. 清查、列表、登记文化和自然遗产

收集对境内有国家意义的文化和自然遗产状况的清查、列表、登记等程序的信息。

7. STATUS OF SERVICES FOR PROTECTION, CONSERVATION AND PRESENTATION

Chapter 7 aims to gather information on services within the territories of the State Party for the identification, protection, conservation and presentation of the cultural and natural heritage and on cooperation between the stakeholders involved.

7. 为保护、修复和展示提供服务的情况

收集缔约国为识别、保护、修复和展示境内文化和自然遗产提供服务的情况、与相关利益相关者合作的信息。

8. FINANCIAL STATUS AND HUMAN RESOURCES

Chapter 8 aims to gather information on the availability and adequacy of financial resources for the conservation and protection of cultural and natural heritage.

8. 财政状况和人力资源

收集可用而充足的文化和自然遗产修复及保护的财政资源。

9. CAPACITY DEVELOPMENT

Chapter 9 aims to gather information on capacity building in heritage conservation, protection, presentation

and management, in line with World Heritage Capacity Building Strategy (2011).

9. 发展能力

收集遗产在保护、修复、展示及管理方面的能力建设、符合世界遗产能力建设战略（2011）的信息。

10. POLICY AND RESOURCING OF WORLD HERITAGE PROPERTIES

Chapter 10 aims to gather information on specific legislation, policies and measures for the protection, conservation, presentation and management of World Heritage.

10. 世界遗产政策和资源

收集为保护、修复、展示及管理世界遗产而采用的特别法律、政策和措施等信息。

11. INTERNATIONAL CO-OPERATION

11. 国际合作及资金支持

AND FUND RAISING

Chapter 11 aims to gather information on the co-operation with other States Parties in the field of cultural and natural heritage.

收集与其他缔约国间，在文化和自然遗产保护领域开展合作的信息。

12. EDUCATION, INFORMATION AND AWARENESS BUILDING

Chapter 12 aims to gather information on steps taken to raise the awareness of decision-makers, property owners and the general public, and in particular the youth, about the protection and conservation of cultural and natural heritage.

12. 教育、信息和意识提升

收集为提升决策者、遗产所有者、大众特别是年轻人的文化和自然遗产保护意识而采取行动的信息。

13. CONCLUSIONS AND RECOMMENDED ACTIONS

Chapter 13 automatically generates the main conclusions under each of the items of Section I based on the answers provided in the questionnaire. States Parties should also provide information about the actions they have taken regarding their implementation of the World Heritage Convention.

13. 结论和建议的行动

在第一部分问卷调查的答案中自动生成结论。缔约国应提供他们为执行《世界遗产公约》而采取的行动的信息。

14. GOOD PRACTICES IN THE IMPLEMENTATION OF THE WORLD HERITAGE CONVENTION

Chapter 14 offers the opportunity to provide an example of a good practice in World Heritage protection, identification, conservation or management implemented at national level.

14. 实施《世界遗产公约》中好的实践

在国家层面为世界遗产保护、识别、修复、管理的优秀案例提供展示机会。

15. ASSESSMENT OF THE PERIODIC REPORTING EXERCISE

Chapter 15 assesses the format, content and process of the Periodic Reporting exercise, including the degree to which it meets the objectives of Periodic Reporting, how the data generated is used and the training and guidance available to respondents.

15. 评估定期报告

评估定期报告的格式、内容和程序，包括其满足定期报告目标的程度、数据生成方式、及对相关答卷者进行有效的培训和指导。

SECTION II:
STATE OF CONSERVATION OF SPECIFIC WORLD HERITAGE PROPERTIES

第二部分
具体世界遗产的保护

Section II gathers information on the implementation of the Convention at site-level and must be completed for each individual World Heritage property. The preparation of this report should involve those who are responsible for the day-to-day management of the property. For transboundary properties, it is recommended that reports be prepared jointly by or with close collaboration between the agencies concerned.

第二部分收集遗产地层面执行公约的信息，必须由各遗产地完成。负责遗产日常管理的人员应参与编制保护状况的定期报告。如果是跨国遗产，建议相关机构共同编制报告，或在编制报告的过程中紧密合作。

1. WORLD HERITAGE PROPERTY DATA

Chapter 1 requires that information be provided or existing information validated with regards to the basic data of the property (name, year of inscription, geographic coordinates, maps, social media presence), and also gathers information on the organizations or entities involved in the preparation of Section I of the report.

1. 世界遗产数据库

要求提供现有的、有关遗产的基础信息（名称、列入时间。地理坐标、地图、媒体展示等），同时收集参与准备本报告第一部分有关组织或单位的信息。

2. OTHER CONVENTIONS/PROGRAMMES UNDER WHICH THE WORLD HERITAGE PROPERTY IS PROTECTED

Chapter 2 gathers information relating to synergies with other conventions and programmes (UNESCO and others) relevant to the property and on the extent of cooperation and integration existing between these conventions and programmes (where applicable).

2. 其他保护世界遗产的公约或项目

收集其他与该遗产有协同作用的（教科文组织或其他组织）公约或项目，及相互间合作和整合程度的信息。

3. STATEMENT OF OUTSTANDING UNIVERSAL VALUE AND DEFINING OF ATTRIBUTES

Chapter 3 gathers information on the attributes of Outstanding Universal Value (OUV), their current condition and the trend in that condition since the last cycle of Periodic Reporting.

3. 突出普遍价值声明及确定的属性

收集遗产与突出普遍价值相关的属性、当前状况、上次定期报告以来的发展趋势等信息。

4. FACTORS AFFECTING THE PROPERTY

Chapter 4 gathers information on the range of factors that are currently affecting or have strong potential to affect the property, both positively and negatively.

4. 影响遗产的因素

收集当前正在及未来严重影响遗产的、积极和消极的因素及其范围等信息。

5. PROTECTION AND MANAGEMENT OF THE PROPERTY

Chapter 5 gathers information on practical issues of management, and the effectiveness of protection, management and monitoring of the property and its Outstanding Universal Value.

5. 遗产保护及管理

收集有关管理实践中的问题及其对遗产和遗产突出普遍价值的保护、修复、管理和监测造成的影响等信息。

6. FINANCIAL AND HUMAN RESOURCES

Chapter 6 gathers information on the sources of funding available, the adequacy of budget for management needs, as well as the availability of human resources and levels of capacity building at the property.

6. 财政和人力资源

收集有关可用资金来源、满足管理需求的足额预算、可用的人力资源及遗产地层面能力建设等信息。

7. SCIENTIFIC STUDIES AND RESEARCH PROJECTS

Chapter 7 gathers information on the adequacy of available knowledge (both scientific and traditional) regarding the values and attributes of the World Heritage property and the existence of research programmes directed towards management needs and/or the improvement of the understanding of the Outstanding Universal Value.

7. 科研项目

收集有关世界遗产价值和属性可用而充足的知识（科学的和历史的）、与满足管理需求、推进对突出普遍价值理解相关的、现有研究项目的信息。

8. EDUCATION, INFORMATION AND AWARENESS BUILDING

Chapter 8 gathers information on the existence and effectiveness of heritage education and awareness programmes at the property as well as general services dedicated to education, information, interpretation and awareness building.

8. 教育、信息和意识提升

收集行之有效的遗产教育、信息和意识提升项目以及服务于教育、信息、阐释和意识建设的相关信息。

9. VISITOR MANAGEMENT

Chapter 9 gathers information on tourism activities and visitor management at the property

9. 游客管理

收集遗产地旅游活动及游客管理的相关信息。

10. MONITORING

Chapter 10 gathers information on the existence of monitoring programmes and indicators for the property as well as on the implementation of property-related Committee Decisions (where applicable).

10. 监测

收集遗产现有监测项目、指标、遗产地执行相关委员会（适用）决定的信息。

11. IDENTIFICATION OF PRIORITY MANAGEMENT NEEDS

Chapter 11 automatically lists all the management needs requiring further action which have been highlighted in this Section of the Periodic Report.

11. 确定优先管理需求

自动罗列本期定期报告关注的、需要进一步采取行动的管理需求信息。

12. SUMMARY AND CONCLUSIONS

Chapter 12 highlights the most important positive and negative factors (up to ten of each) which have been highlighted in this Section of the Periodic Report.

12. 总结和结论

重点关注本期定期报告中强调的、最主要的、积极或消极的影响因素（每项不超过 10 个）的信息。

13. IMPACT OF WORLD HERITAGE STATUS

Chapter 13 gathers information regarding the impact of World Heritage status in relation to various topics, with a particular focus on the World Heritage and Sustainable Development Policy (adopted in 2015).

13. 对世界遗产地位的影响

收集影响世界遗产地位的不同话题，特别聚焦世界遗产和可持续发展（2015）论题的信息。

14. GOOD PRACTICES IN THE IMPLEMENTATION OF THE WORLD HERITAGE CONVENTION

Chapter 14 offers the opportunity to provide an example of a good practice in World Heritage protection, identification, conservation and preservation implemented at the property level.

14. 实施《世界遗产公约》好的实践

在遗产地层面为世界遗产保护、识别、修复、管理的优秀案例提供展示机会。

15. ASSESSMENT OF THE PERIODIC REPORTING EXERCISE

Chapter 15 assesses the format, content and process of the Periodic Reporting exercise, including how the data generated is used and the training and guidance available to respondents.

15. 评估定期报告

评估定期报告的格式、内容和程序，包括如何收集数据、及对相关答卷者进行的有效培训和指导。

Annex 8 INTERNATIONAL ASSISTANCE REQUEST FORM

• The International Assistance request form is available at the following Web address: http: //whc.unesco.org/en/intassistance , and can be filled at the same address.

• Further guidance on International Assistance can be found in Section VII of the *Operational Guidelines*

• See attached Explanatory Notes on completing this Request form

• The original signed version of the completed International Assistance request form should be sent in English or French to:

UNESCO World Heritage Centre
7, place de Fontenoy
75352 Paris 07 SP
France
Telephone: +33 (0) 1 45 68 12 76
Fax: +33 (0) 1 45 68 55 70
E-mail: wh-intassistance@unesco.org

1. STATE PARTY____________________

2. TITLE OF PROJECT____________________

3. TYPE OF assistance____________________

附件 8 《国际援助申请表》

• 登录以下网址下载《国际援助申请表》：http：//whc.unesco.org/en/intassistance

• 更多有关国际援助的指导说明，请参阅《操作指南》的第七节。

• 参见所附的申请表填报须知。

• 应将完整填写的英语或法语的国际援助申请表原件递交至：

联合国教科文组织世界遗产中心
地址：7，place de Fontenoy
75352 Paris 07 SP France

电话：+33（0）1 45 68 12 76
传真：+33（0）1 45 68 55 70
电子邮箱：wh–intassistance@unesco.org

1. 缔约国____________________

2. 项目名称____________________

3. 援助类型____________________

	Emergency Assistance	*Preparatory Assistance*	*Conservation and management*
Culture			
Nature			
Mixed			

	紧急援助	筹备性援助	保护与管理
文化			
自然			
混合			

4. PROJECT LOCATION:

a) Will the project be implemented at a World Heritage property?

□ - yes □ - no

If yes, give the name of the property__________

____

____

b) Will the project include a field component?

□ - yes □ - no

If yes, where and how?__________

____

____

c) If the project is being implemented at a World Heritage property, indicate whether it will also benefit other World Heritage properties, and if so, which ones and how?

____

____

5.TIMEFRAME FOR THE IMPLEMENTATION OF THE PROJECT (indicate whether estimated or fixed)

Dates: ______________________________

____

Duration: ______________________________

4. 项目地点：

a）该项目是否会在一处世界遗产地实施？

□是　□否

如果答案为“是”，提供遗产名称：__________

____

____

b）该项目是否包括野外活动部分？

□是　□否

如果答案为“是”，提供地点和方式：__________

____

____

c）如果该项目在世界遗产地实施，请说明其他世界遗产是否也能受益。如果是，请说明受益的遗产以及具体受益方式？

____

____

5. 项目实施时间表（请说明是预计或确切时间表）

日期：______________________________

____

持续时间：______________________________

6. THE PROJECT IS:

□ - local

□ - national

□ - sub regional involving a few States Parties from a region

□ - regional involving most States Parties from a region

□ - international involving States Parties from different regions

If the project is national, sub-regional, regional or international, please indicate the countries/ properties which will participate/benefit from the project:

____

____

____

____

7. JUSTIFICATION OF THE PROJECT

a) Explain why this project is needed

(for Emergency Assistance, please fill in item 8 below instead).

____

____

____

____

b) List all supporting documents submitted, if applicable.

____

____

____

____

8. FOR EMERGENCY ASSISTANCE ONLY

a) Describe the actual or potential threat/ danger affecting the property

____

____

____

____

____

6. 项目为：

地方性活动

国家性活动

涉及某一区域少数几个缔约国的次区域性活动

涉及某一区域的多数缔约国的区域性活动

涉及不同地区的众多缔约国的国际性活动

如果该项目为国家级、次区域性、区域性或国际性活动，请明确说明哪些国家将参加该项目以及哪些遗产将从该项目中收益：

____

____

____

____

7. 项目原因

a）说明需实施该项目的理由（如申请紧急援助，请忽略此项，填写第八项）

____

____

____

____

b）如有可能，请列举已提交的能支持项目实施的文件

____

____

____

____

8. 仅限于紧急援助申请

a）描述遗产面临的已知或潜在威胁

____

____

____

____

____

b) Indicate how it might affect the property's Outstanding Universal Value

____

____

____

____

b）指出这种威胁对遗产突出普遍价值的影响

____

____

____

____

c) Explain how the proposed project will address the threat/danger

____

____

____

____

c）解释该项目消除这种威胁或危险的方法

____

____

____

____

9. OBJECTIVES OF THE PROJECT

Clearly set out the specific objectives of the project

9. 项目目标

详细说明该项目的具体目标。

10. EXPECTED RESULTS

a) Clearly state the results expected from the project

____

____

____

____

10. 预期结果

a）清晰说明项目的预期结果

____

____

____

____

b) Define the indicators and means of verification which can be used to assess the achievements of these results:

____

____

____

____

b）确定能够评估预期结果的指标和验证方法

____

____

____

____

Expected Results	Indicators	Means of verification

预期结果	指标	验证方法

11. WORK PLAN (including specific activities and timetable)

11. 项目计划（包括具体活动和时间表）

Activities	*Timeframe (in months)*						
Activity							
Activity							
Activity							
Activity							

活动	时间表（月份）						
活动							
活动							
活动							
活动							

12. EVALUATION AND REPORTING

(to be submitted to the World Heritage Centre within three months after the project is completed)

12. 评估与报告

（应在项目结束后三个月之内提交给世界遗产中心）

13. Profiles of specialists, trainers, technicians and/or skilled labour, if the PROJECT foresees the participation of such PEOPLE

(if the identity of the specialists, trainers, technicians, and/or skilled labourers is already known, please state their names and include a brief CV if possible)

13. 可能参加此项活动的专家、培训人员、技术人员或技工的简介

（如果已知上述人员身份，请陈述其姓名。如有可能，应提供个人简历）

14. KEY TARGET AUDIENCES, INCLUDING Profiles of trainees/participants, if the PROJECT foresees the participation of such PEOPLE

14. 项目主要受众（包括受训人员和参与者的简介）

15. BUDGET BREAKDOWN

a) Provide, in the following table (in United States dollars), a detailed breakdown of costs of the individual elements of the project including, if possible, unit costs and show how these will be shared between the different funding sources.

15. 详细预算

a）请在下表中（以美元为单位）提供项目各个组成部分所需的详细预算。如有可能，提供单位成本，并展示分担这些费用的不同资金来源的情况。

b) Specify whether or not resources from the State Party or other sources are already available or when they are likely to become available.

b）指明是否已经或可能从缔约国或其他渠道获取资源

16. IN KIND CONTRIBUTIONS FROM THE STATE PARTY AND OTHER AGENCIES

16. 缔约国或其他机构的实物捐赠

a) National agency(ies)

a）国家机构

b) Other bi/multi lateral organizations, donors, etc

b）其他双边或多边组织、捐赠机构等

17. Agency(ies) responsible for the implementation of the PROJECT

17. 负责项目实施的机构

18. Signature on behalf of State Party

Full name ______

Title ______

Date ______

18. 缔约国代表签字

全名 ______

职务 ______

日期 ______

19. ANNEXES

______(number of annexes attached to the request)

19. 附件

______（附件编号）

figure 1

Items (choose items as applicable to the project)	Detail US$ (for applicable items)	State Party Funds US$	Amount requested to the World Heritage Fund US$	Other Sources US$	Total US$
Organization venue office expenses secretarial assistance translation simultaneous interpretation audio-visual equipment other	 US$ __ / day for __ days = US$ __ US$ __ US$ __/ day for __ days - US$ __ US$ __ / page for __ pages = US$ US$ __ / hour for __ hours = US$ US$ __ / day for __ days = US$ __ US$ __				
Personnel / consultancy service (fees) international expert national expert coordinator other	US$ __ / week for __ weeks = US$ _ US$ __ / week for __ weeks = US$ _ US$ __ / week for __ weeks = US$ _ US$ __ / week for __ weeks = US$ _ US$ _				
Travel international travel cost domestic travel costs other	 US$ __ US$ __ US$ __				
Daily subsistence allowance accommodation board	 US$ __ / day for __ persons = US$ __ US$ __ / day for __ persons = US$ __				
Equipment	 US$ __ / unit for __ units = US$ __ / unit for __ units =				
Evaluation, Reporting and Publication evaluation reporting editing, layout printing distribution other	 US$ __ US$ __ US$ __ US$ __ US$ __ US$ __				
Miscellaneous visas other	 US$ __ for __ participants = US$ __ US$ __				
TOTAL					

表 1

项目 （选择适用的项目）	具体金额（美元） （选择适用的项目）	缔约国资金 （美元）	向世界遗产基金申请数额 （美元）	其他资金来源 （美元）	小计 （美元）
组织 活动场所 办公费用 文书助理费 笔译费 同声传译费 影音设备费 其他	 每天 ___ 美元，共 __ 天 =__ 美元 __ 美元 每天 ___ 美元，共 __ 天 =__ 美元 每页 ___ 美元，共 __ 页 =__ 美元 每小时 __ 美元，共 __ 小时 =__ 美元 每天 ___ 美元，共 __ 天 = __ 美元 __ 美元				
人员 / 咨询服务费 国际专家 国内专家 协调人员 其他	 每周 ___ 美元，共 __ 周 = ___ 美元 每周 ___ 美元，共 __ 周 = ___ 美元 每周 ___ 美元，共 __ 周 = ___ 美元 每周 ___ 美元，共 __ 周 = ___ 美元 __ 美元				
差旅费 国际旅行费用 国内旅行费用 其他	 ___ 美元 ___ 美元 ___ 美元				
每日生活补助 餐饮 住宿	 每日 ___ 人 ___ 美元 = ___ 美元 每日 ___ 人 ___ 美元 = ___ 美元				
设备 …… ……	 每台 ___ 美元，共 __ 台 = ___ 美元 每台 ___ 美元，共 __ 台 = ___ 美元				
评估、报告与出版 出版 评估 报告 编辑、排版 印刷 发行 其他	 ___ 美元 ___ 美元 ___ 美元 ___ 美元 ___ 美元 ___ 美元 ___ 美元				
其他杂费 签证 其他费用	 共 ____ 人参加 ___ 美元 = ___ 美元 共 ____ 人参加 ___ 美元 = ___ 美元				
合计					

figure 2 EXPLANTORY NOTES

<table>
<tr><th></th><th>INTERNATIONAL ASSISTANCE APPLICATION FORM</th><th>EXPLANATORY NOTES</th></tr>
<tr><td>1.</td><td>STATE PARTY</td><td>Name of the State Party presenting the International Assistance request</td></tr>
<tr><td>2.</td><td>TITLE OF THE PROJECT</td><td></td></tr>
<tr><td>3.</td><td>TYPE OF assistance
<table>
<tr><th></th><th>Emergency Assistance</th><th>Preparatory Assistance</th><th>Conservation and Management*</th></tr>
<tr><td>Culture</td><td></td><td></td><td></td></tr>
<tr><td>Nature</td><td></td><td></td><td></td></tr>
<tr><td>Mixed</td><td></td><td></td><td></td></tr>
</table>
* Please note that « Conservation and Management » now includes the previous categories :
- Training, Research Assistance
-Technical Cooperation
- Assistance for education, information and awareness raising</td><td>See Paragraph 241 of the Operational Guidelines for details.

Indicate the type of assistance you are requesting, as well as the type of heritage covered by the project.

Please, tick only one box in the table.
For example:

- Training project on rock paintings:
<table>
<tr><th></th><th>Emergency Assistance</th><th>Preparatory Assistance</th><th>Conservation and Management</th></tr>
<tr><td>Culture</td><td></td><td></td><td>X</td></tr>
<tr><td>Nature</td><td></td><td></td><td></td></tr>
<tr><td>Mixed</td><td></td><td></td><td></td></tr>
</table>
- Preparation of a nomination file for a mixed property:
<table>
<tr><th></th><th>Emergency Assistance</th><th>Preparatory Assistance</th><th>Conservation and Management</th></tr>
<tr><td>Culture</td><td></td><td></td><td></td></tr>
<tr><td>Nature</td><td></td><td></td><td></td></tr>
<tr><td>Mixed</td><td></td><td>X</td><td></td></tr>
</table>
- Emergency assistance request following a tropical storm which affected a protected forest area:
<table>
<tr><th></th><th>Emergency Assistance</th><th>Preparatory Assistance</th><th>Conservation and Management</th></tr>
<tr><td>Culture</td><td></td><td></td><td></td></tr>
<tr><td>Nature</td><td></td><td></td><td></td></tr>
<tr><td>Mixed</td><td>X</td><td></td><td></td></tr>
</table></td></tr>
</table>

续表

	INTERNATIONAL ASSISTANCE APPLICATION FORM	EXPLANATORY NOTES
4.	PROJECT LOCATION a) Will the project be implemented at a World Heritage property? □ - yes □ - no If yes, give the name of the property b) Will the project include a field component? □ - yes □ - no If yes, where and how? c) If the project is being implemented at a World Heritage property, indicate whether it will also benefit other World Heritage properties, and if so which ones and how?	
5.	TIMEFRAME FOR THE IMPLEMENTATION OF THE PROJECT (indicate whether estimated or fixed)	Indicate the proposed starting date for the project as well as its duration.
6.	THE PROJECT IS: □ local □ national □ sub-regional involving a few States Parties from a region □ regional involving most States Parties from a region □ international involving States Parties from different regions If the project is national, sub-regional, regional or international, please indicate the countries/properties which will participate/benefit from the project.	If other countries benefit from the project, please state whether their support for the project has been obtained. Also note if a transboundary property is involved.
7.	JUSTIFICATION OF THE PROJECT	
	a) Explain why the project is needed (for Emergency Assistance, please fill in item 8 below instead)	Set out the problems or issues to be discussed/addressed. This should include, where appropriate, the degree of urgency of the activities to be undertaken where appropriate. If relevant, give details, in no more than 2 pages, of ascertained or potential threat to the property (ies) . Explain how the project contributes to the implementation of: - decisions of the World Heritage Committee; - recommendations of international expert missions undertaken at the request of the Committee, Chairperson or UNESCO; - recommendations of the Advisory Bodies; - recommendations of UNESCO World Heritage Centre or other UNESCO Divisions; - management plans for the property; - recommendations from previous activities supported by the World Heritage Fund. Clearly indicate which documents you are referring to (World Heritage Committee's decision number, Mission dates, etc…)

续表

	INTERNATIONAL ASSISTANCE APPLICATION FORM	EXPLANATORY NOTES
	b) List all supporting documents submitted, if applicable.	Whenever possible, support the justification with documentary evidence, such as reports, photographs, slides, maps, etc...
8.	FOR EMERGENCY ASSISTANCE ONLY	
	a) Describe the actual or potential threat/danger affecting the property	Emergency Assistance funds will not be automatically granted after a major disaster has occurred. This type of assistance will be provided only in cases when an imminent danger related to a natural or human-made disaster is threatening the overall Outstanding Universal Value of a World Heritage property and its authenticity and/or integrity, to prevent or at least significantly mitigate its possible negative impact on the property. Emergency Assistance may also be provided to assess whether or not imminent danger is present, for example as a result of a major disaster. When, on the contrary, due to a disaster, a certain loss of heritage has already taken place, but there is no more imminent threat or risk that needs to be addressed as a matter of urgency, other forms of assistance would appear to be more appropriate (e.g. conservation and management assistance) .
	b) Indicate how it might affect the property's Outstanding Universal Value	In establishing priorities for granting Emergency Assistance, consideration will be given to whether the threat/danger to be addressed has the potential, if not mitigated, to affect the Outstanding Universal Value of the World Heritage property and its authenticity and/or integrity.
	c) Explain how the proposed project will address the threat/danger	Proposals for funding under the Emergency Assistance programme should set out how the scope of the project and its activities will assess the threat/danger to the World Heritage property and show how it will be effectively mitigated.
9.	OBJECTIVE (S) OF THE PROJECT Clearly set out the specific objectives of the project	What are the objectives you want to achieve through the implementation of this particular project?
10.	EXPECTED RESULTS	
	a) Clearly state the results expected from the project proposed.	The expected results should be concrete and measurable. Each expected result will be measured by a set of indicators (see Paragraph 10b).

续表

<table>
<tr><th></th><th>INTERNATIONAL ASSISTANCE APPLICATION FORM</th><th>EXPLANATORY NOTES</th></tr>
<tr><td></td><td>
b) Define the indicators and means of verification which can be used to assess the achievements of these results:
<table>
<tr><th>Expected Results</th><th>Indicators</th><th>Means of verification</th></tr>
<tr><td></td><td></td><td></td></tr>
<tr><td></td><td></td><td></td></tr>
<tr><td></td><td></td><td></td></tr>
</table>
</td><td>
Indicators are used to measure the results achieved and to determine the progress towards the objective of the project. They are based on the expected results defined in Paragraph 10, and will serve as the base for the evaluation of the project after its completion.

These indicators should be objective, measurable and expressed in quantifiable terms such as numeric values, or percentages.

For example:

Preparatory Assistance

Objective:
To prepare a complete nomination file for submission to the World Heritage Centre.
<table>
<tr><th>Expected Results</th><th>Indicators</th><th>Means of verification</th></tr>
<tr><td>The completed nomination file submitted to the World Heritage Centre by 1 February 200x.</td><td>Nomination submitted by the deadline</td><td>Postal record of sending the file Report from the WHC/POL to the State Party</td></tr>
<tr><td>The completed management plan to be submitted along with the nomination file</td><td>Management plan submitted by the deadline</td><td>Postal record of sending the file Report from the WHC/POL to the State Party</td></tr>
<tr><td>The nomination file is judged complete by the World Heritage Centre and Advisory Bodies</td><td>Successful examination by the World Heritage Centre and Advisory Bodies for completeness</td><td>Letter from the World Heritage Centre to the State Party informing them the file is considered complete</td></tr>
</table>
Emergency Assistance

Objective:
To stabilize the structure of a building that has just been damaged due to flooding or an earthquake.
</td></tr>
</table>

续表

	INTERNATIONAL ASSISTANCE APPLICATION FORM	EXPLANATORY NOTES
		(see tables and text below)

Expected Results	Indicators	Means of Verification
The structure of the building would have been stabilized	Emergency structural problems identified Plans for emergency works finalized Temporary stabilization measures carried out	Report of a structural engineer on the emergency state of the structure Costed proposal for emergency works to be carried out Final report of the stabilization work implemented
Plans for further conservation work would have been developed for future implementation	Overall structural analysis carried out Costed plans for further necessary conservation work prepared	Report of a structural engineer on the overall state of conservation of the structure Costed proposal for necessary conservation works to be carried out

Conservation and Management Assistance

Objective:
To improve management at a property inscribed on the World Heritage List with special attention to community involvement

Expected Results	Indicators	Means of Verification
An integrated management plan for the property	Setting up of a management planning team for the development of the management plan with participants from the necessary sectors including the local community	Monthly reports of the management planning team meetings Discussion papers produced by team members of each of the key issues faced in the management of the property

续表

<table>
<tr><th></th><th>INTERNATIONAL ASSISTANCE APPLICATION FORM</th><th>EXPLANATORY NOTES</th></tr>
<tr><td></td><td></td><td>
<table>
<tr><th>Expected Results</th><th>Indicators</th><th>Means of Verification</th></tr>
<tr><td></td><td>Completion of a Statement of Outstanding Universal Value for the property
Analysis of the conservation and management problems affecting the property
Existence of clear objectives and strategies for achieving them</td><td>Final management plan document</td></tr>
<tr><td>A management committee including some members of the local community</td><td>Appointment of members of the management committee including at least two members of the local community
At least 3 regular monthly meetings of the Management Committee</td><td>Statutes and rules of procedure for the Management Committee approved by appropriate authorities
Monthly reports of the Management Committee</td></tr>
<tr><td>Management plan approved with appropriate legal status</td><td>Approval by the local government authority</td><td>Decree placed in the “National Gazette” establishing the management plan as a local regulation.</td></tr>
</table>
</td></tr>
<tr><td>11.</td><td>WORK PLAN
(including specific activities and timetable)</td><td>Describe the work plan of the activity(ies) to be undertaken with specific reference to the expected results mentioned in Paragraph 10 above. Indicate dates, duration of each activity. For meetings and training activities, tentative programmes should be provided including the themes, issues and problems to be discussed.

For example:

For Expected Result No. 1:</td></tr>
</table>

续表

<table>
<tr><th></th><th>INTERNATIONAL ASSISTANCE APPLICATION FORM</th><th>EXPLANATORY NOTES</th></tr>
<tr><td></td><td>
<table>
<tr><td>Activities</td><td colspan="7">Timeframe (in months)</td></tr>
<tr><td>Activity</td><td></td><td></td><td></td><td></td><td></td><td></td><td></td></tr>
<tr><td>Activity</td><td></td><td></td><td></td><td></td><td></td><td></td><td></td></tr>
<tr><td>Activity</td><td></td><td></td><td></td><td></td><td></td><td></td><td></td></tr>
<tr><td>Activity</td><td></td><td></td><td></td><td></td><td></td><td></td><td></td></tr>
</table>
</td><td>
<table>
<tr><td>Activities</td><td colspan="7">Timeframe (in months)</td></tr>
<tr><td>Activity</td><td bgcolor="gray"></td><td bgcolor="gray"></td><td bgcolor="gray"></td><td bgcolor="gray"></td><td bgcolor="gray"></td><td></td><td></td></tr>
<tr><td>Activity</td><td></td><td></td><td></td><td bgcolor="gray"></td><td bgcolor="gray"></td><td bgcolor="gray"></td><td bgcolor="gray"></td></tr>
<tr><td>Activity</td><td></td><td bgcolor="gray"></td><td bgcolor="gray"></td><td bgcolor="gray"></td><td></td><td></td><td></td></tr>
<tr><td>Activity</td><td></td><td></td><td></td><td bgcolor="gray"></td><td bgcolor="gray"></td><td></td><td></td></tr>
</table>
For Expected Result No. 2:
<table>
<tr><td>Activities</td><td colspan="7">Timeframe (in months)</td></tr>
<tr><td>Activity</td><td bgcolor="gray"></td><td bgcolor="gray"></td><td bgcolor="gray"></td><td></td><td></td><td></td><td></td></tr>
<tr><td>Activity</td><td></td><td></td><td></td><td></td><td bgcolor="gray"></td><td bgcolor="gray"></td><td bgcolor="gray"></td></tr>
<tr><td>Activity</td><td bgcolor="gray"></td><td bgcolor="gray"></td><td bgcolor="gray"></td><td bgcolor="gray"></td><td bgcolor="gray"></td><td bgcolor="gray"></td><td bgcolor="gray"></td></tr>
<tr><td>Activity</td><td></td><td></td><td bgcolor="gray"></td><td bgcolor="gray"></td><td bgcolor="gray"></td><td></td><td></td></tr>
</table>
</td></tr>
<tr><td>12.</td><td>EVALUATION AND REPORTING
(to be submitted to the World Heritage Centre within three months after the implementation of the project is completed)</td><td>Final Report:
The final report should be prepared by the authority/person in charge of the implementation of the project.
The final report should be structured according to the expected results defined in Paragraph 10.

Evaluation:
The evaluation should focus on the results achieved and their impact on (for example):
- the inscription of a property on the World Heritage List following a preparatory assistance,
- the Periodic Report and the State of conservation,
- the removal of a property from the List of World Heritage in danger following an emergency assistance,
- the implementation of the World Heritage Convention, including its Strategic Objectives ("4Cs") and other strategies (e.g. Global Strategy, …),
- the national and/or local institutions,
- the capacity building of local staff,
- the awareness raising of the general public,
- the participants to the project,
- attracting other resources,
- etc…

Indicate who will be responsible for the evaluation of the project.</td></tr>
</table>

续表

	INTERNATIONAL ASSISTANCE APPLICATION FORM	EXPLANATORY NOTES
13.	Profiles of specialists, trainers, technicians and/or skilled labour, if the PROJECT foresees the participation of such people (if the identity of the specialists, trainers, technicians, and/or skilled labourers is already known, please state their names and include a brief CV if possible)	Indicate the precise field of specialization and the work to be undertaken by each specialist as well as the duration required. The World Heritage Centre and the Advisory Bodies are available to recommend resource persons / trainers, should the State(s) Party(ies) concerned so request. Please include the names of any specialists, if already known, who will be taking part in the project and send a short CV if possible as an annex to the request form.
14.	KEY TARGET AUDIENCES, INCLUDING Profiles of trainees / participants, if the PROJECT foresees the participation of such people	Indicate the target groups and beneficiaries of the project, their professions, institutions, or field(s) of specialization.
15.	BUDGET BREAKDOWN	
	a) Provide, in the following table (in United States dollars), a detailed breakdown of costs of the individual elements of the project including, if possible, unit costs and show how these will be shared between the different funding sources:	Indicate in the table the breakdown of all expenses related to the project, also indicating the cost-sharing between the various donors (State Party, World Heritage Fund, others).
	(i) Organization	Items within this section could include the cost of a venue, office expenses, secretarial assistance, translation, simultaneous interpretation, audio-visual equipment, or other organizational costs necessary for the successful implementation of the project.
	(ii) Personnel and Consultancy Services	Items within this section could include the cost of international experts, national experts, a local or international coordinator, or other personnel necessary for the successful implementation of the project.
	(iii) Travel	Items within this section could include the cost of international or domestic travel necessary for the successful implementation of the project.
	(iv) Daily Subsistence Allowance	Items within this section could include the cost of accommodation, meals, and incidentals necessary for the successful implementation of the project.
	(v) Equipment	Items within this section could include any equipment necessary for the successful implementation of the project.
	(vi) Evaluation, Reporting and Publication	Items within this section could include the cost of evaluation, reporting, editing and layout, printing, distribution, and other costs necessary for the successful implementation of the project.
	(vii) Miscellaneous	Items within this section could include the cost of visas or other small costs that are necessary for the successful implementation of the project.

续表

	INTERNATIONAL ASSISTANCE APPLICATION FORM	EXPLANATORY NOTES
	b) Specify whether or not resources from the State Party or other sources are already available or when they are likely to become available	If the resources are not already available, indicate whether they will be before the beginning of the project.
16.	IN KIND CONTRIBUTIONS FROM THE STATE PARTY AND OTHER AGENCIES	
	a) National agency(ies)	Specify in detail
	b) Other bi/multi lateral organizations, donors, etc	Specify in detail
17.	agency(ies) responsible for the implementation of the PROJECT	Please provide the name, title, address and all contact details of the person/agency(ies) who will be responsible for the implementation of the project as well as those of any other participating agencies. Please, indicate whether the legislative and administrative commitment of the State Party is available for the project (see Paragraph 239d of the Operational Guidelines).
18.	Signature on behalf of State Party	Full name Title Date
19.	ANNEXES	In this section, list the number of annexes attached to the request and titles of each annex.

表 2　填报须知

<table>
<tr><th></th><th>国际援助申请格式</th><th>填报须知</th></tr>
<tr><td>1</td><td>缔约国</td><td>提出国际援助申请的缔约国名称</td></tr>
<tr><td>2</td><td>项目名称</td><td></td></tr>
<tr><td>3</td><td>援助类型
<table><tr><th></th><th>紧急援助</th><th>预备援助</th><th>保护与管理 *</th></tr><tr><td>文化</td><td></td><td></td><td></td></tr><tr><td>自然</td><td></td><td></td><td></td></tr><tr><td>混合</td><td></td><td></td><td></td></tr></table>
* 请注意，保护与管理一项包括之前下列类别：
– 培训与研究援助
– 技术合作援助
– 教育、信息与意识提升援助</td><td>具体内容请参见《操作指南》第 241 条。
应指明所申请援助类型以及该项目涉及的遗产类型。
仅选择表格中的一项内容，如：
– 岩画培训项目
<table><tr><th></th><th>紧急援助</th><th>预备援助</th><th>保护与管理</th></tr><tr><td>文化</td><td></td><td></td><td>X</td></tr><tr><td>自然</td><td></td><td></td><td></td></tr><tr><td>混合</td><td></td><td></td><td></td></tr></table>
– 编制混合遗产的申报文件
<table><tr><th></th><th>紧急援助</th><th>预备援助</th><th>保护与管理</th></tr><tr><td>文化</td><td></td><td></td><td></td></tr><tr><td>自然</td><td></td><td></td><td></td></tr><tr><td>混合</td><td></td><td>X</td><td></td></tr></table></td></tr>
<tr><td>4</td><td>项目地点
a）该项目是否会在一处世界遗产地实施？
□ 是　　　　□ 否
如果答案为“是”，提供遗产名称：

b）该项目是否包括野外活动部分？
□ 是　　　　□ 否
如果答案为“是”，提供地点和方式：

c）如果该项目在世界遗产地实施，请说明其他世界遗产是否也能受益。如果是，请说明受益遗产以及具体受益方式？</td><td>– 由于热带风暴影响了保护林区而申请紧急援助
<table><tr><th></th><th>紧急援助</th><th>预备援助</th><th>保护与管理</th></tr><tr><td>文化</td><td></td><td></td><td></td></tr><tr><td>自然</td><td>X</td><td></td><td></td></tr><tr><td>混合</td><td></td><td></td><td></td></tr></table></td></tr>
<tr><td>5</td><td>项目时间表（请说明是预计或确切时间表）</td><td>说明项目计划开始的日期及持续时间。</td></tr>
<tr><td>6</td><td>项目类型为：
地方性活动
国家性活动
涉及某一区域少数几个缔约国的次区域性活动
涉及某一区域的多数缔约国的区域性活动
涉及不同地区的众多缔约国的国际性活动
如果项目是国家性，次区域性，区域性或国际性，请说明参与或从项目中获益的国家，遗产点</td><td>如果其他国家也能从中受益，说明是否已经获得它们对项目的支持。
同时说明是否涉及跨境遗产。</td></tr>
</table>

续表

	国际援助申请格式	填报须知
7	项目原因	
	a）说明需实施该项目的理由（如申请紧急援助，请省略此项，填写第八项）	阐明将要讨论或解决的问题。应尽量说明举办这些活动的合适地点及紧迫程度。 如有涉及，应详细描述遗产面对的已知或潜在威胁，篇幅不超过两页。 解释此项活动将如何有益于执行： - 世界遗产委员会的决议； - 委员会、主席或联合国教科文组织委派的国际专家工作组的建议； - 咨询机构的建议； - 联合国教科文组织世界遗产中心以及其他部门的建议； - 与遗产有关的管理规划建议； - 世界遗产基金支持的、在世界遗产地或缔约国举行的以往活动中制定出的指导方针。 应明确指出所参考的文件（世界遗产委员会的决定号码、代表团日期等等）
	b）如有可能，请列举已提交的能支持项目实施理由的文件	如有可能，提供各种形式文献说明如报告、照片、幻灯片、地图册等。
8	仅用于紧急援助申请	
	a）描述遗产面对的已知或潜在的威胁或危险	并非发生了重大灾难就会自动拨付紧急救助基金。只有当自然或人为灾难对世界遗产的突出普遍价值、真实性和完整性带来紧急威胁时，才会提供这种援助，用以避免或大幅降低可能对遗产造成的负面影响。 紧急援助也可用来评估重大灾难等是否带来了紧急威胁。 如果灾难已经给遗产带来了一定损失，但目前没有需要紧急处理的威胁或危险，申请其他类型的援助更为恰当（如保护与管理援助）。
	b）指出这种威胁对遗产突出的普遍价值的影响	在决定优先给予紧急援助时，应考虑如果该威胁、危险得不到缓解，是否有可能影响世界遗产突出普遍价值、完整性和真实性。
	c）解释该项目消除这种威胁或危险的方法	申请紧急援助时，应阐明项目及其范围并评估世界遗产面临的威胁、危险的方式，以及有效缓解该威胁、危险的方法。
9	项目目标 清晰说明该项目的具体目标	希望通过实施该项目达成什么目标？
10	预期结果	
	a）清晰说明该项目的预期结果	预期结果应该具体且可衡量。每个预期结果都需要通过一组指标来衡量（见 10b 条）。

续表

<table>
<tr><th></th><th>国际援助申请格式</th><th>填报须知</th></tr>
<tr><td></td><td>
b）定义能够评估预期结果的指标和验证方法
<table>
<tr><th>预期结果</th><th>指标</th><th>验证方法</th></tr>
<tr><td></td><td></td><td></td></tr>
<tr><td></td><td></td><td></td></tr>
<tr><td></td><td></td><td></td></tr>
</table>
</td><td>
指标用于衡量取得的成果并判断项目目标的进展。这些指标基于第 10 条定义的预计结果，并将作为项目完成后评估的基础。
指标应客观、可衡量，以数值或百分比等量化的方式表示。例如：
筹备性援助
目标：编制完整的申报文件提交给世界遗产中心
<table>
<tr><th>预期结果</th><th>指标</th><th>验证方法</th></tr>
<tr><td>于 20XX 年 2 月 1 日前向世界遗产中心提交完整的申报文件</td><td>在截至日期前提交申报文件</td><td>– 提交文件的邮政记录
– 世界遗产中心、政策及法律咨询部门给缔约国的报告</td></tr>
<tr><td>同时提交完整的管理规划</td><td>在截至日期前提交管理规划</td><td>– 提交文件的邮政记录
– 世界遗产中心、政策及法律咨询部门给缔约国的报告</td></tr>
<tr><td>世界遗产中心及咨询机构判定申报文件完整</td><td>世界遗产中心及咨询机构判定申报文件完整</td><td>– 世界遗产中心发给缔约国的信件，通知缔约国文件完整</td></tr>
</table>
紧急援助
目标：
因洪水或地震受损的建筑物结构进行加固
<table>
<tr><th>预期结果</th><th>指标</th><th>验证方法</th></tr>
<tr><td>加固建筑物的结构</td><td>– 确定紧急出现的结构问题
– 制定紧急工作计划
– 实施临时稳定措施</td><td>– 结构工程师关于结构紧急情况的报告
– 包含所需紧急工作预算的报告
– 加固工作实施的最终报告</td></tr>
<tr><td>制定未来保护修复工作计划</td><td>– 完成全面的结构分析
– 制定包含未来所需保护修复工作预算价格的计划</td><td>– 结构工程师关于结构整体保护状况的报告
– 包含未来所需保护工作预算的报告</td></tr>
</table>
</td></tr>
</table>

续表

<table>
<tr><th></th><th>国际援助申请格式</th><th>填报须知</th></tr>
<tr><td></td><td></td><td>保护与管理援助
目标：改善世界遗产的管理，尤其注重社区参与
<table>
<tr><th>预期结果</th><th>指标</th><th>验证方法</th></tr>
<tr><td>制定遗产管理综合规划</td><td>–成立管理规划编制团队，成员包括当地社区等各相关领域的人员
–编制完成遗产的《突出的普遍价值声明》
–分析影响遗产的保护与管理的问题
–拥有清晰的目标以及实现目标的策略</td><td>–项目规划团队会议的月报
–团队成员编制的关于遗产管理中各关键问题的讨论文件
–管理规划文件定稿</td></tr>
<tr><td>成立包括当地社区人员的管理委员会</td><td>–指定管理委员会成员，其中至少两名成员来自当地社区
–至少召开三次管理委员会月度会议</td><td>–管理委员会的法律法规被相关机构批准
–管理委员会的月报</td></tr>
<tr><td>管理规划获得适当的法律地位</td><td>–获当地政府机构批准</td><td>–国家公报刊载政令，确立该管理规划为当地法规</td></tr>
</table></td></tr>
<tr><td>11</td><td>项目计划（包括具体活动和时间表）
<table>
<tr><th>活动</th><th colspan="7">时间表（月份）</th></tr>
<tr><td>活动</td><td></td><td></td><td></td><td></td><td></td><td></td><td></td></tr>
<tr><td>活动</td><td></td><td></td><td></td><td></td><td></td><td></td><td></td></tr>
<tr><td>活动</td><td></td><td></td><td></td><td></td><td></td><td></td><td></td></tr>
<tr><td>活动</td><td></td><td></td><td></td><td></td><td></td><td></td><td></td></tr>
</table></td><td>描述活动的计划，标明上文第 10 条中的预期结果。说明每一项活动的日期及持续时间。如果是会议、培训活动，应提供主题、议题等内容。如：

旨在取得第一项预期结果的活动：
<table>
<tr><th>活动</th><th colspan="7">时间表（月份）</th></tr>
<tr><td>活动</td><td></td><td></td><td></td><td></td><td></td><td></td><td></td></tr>
<tr><td>活动</td><td></td><td></td><td></td><td></td><td></td><td></td><td></td></tr>
<tr><td>活动</td><td></td><td></td><td></td><td></td><td></td><td></td><td></td></tr>
<tr><td>活动</td><td></td><td></td><td></td><td></td><td></td><td></td><td></td></tr>
</table>
旨在取得第二项预期结果的活动：
<table>
<tr><th>活动</th><th colspan="7">时间表（月份）</th></tr>
<tr><td>活动</td><td></td><td></td><td></td><td></td><td></td><td></td><td></td></tr>
<tr><td>活动</td><td></td><td></td><td></td><td></td><td></td><td></td><td></td></tr>
<tr><td>活动</td><td></td><td></td><td></td><td></td><td></td><td></td><td></td></tr>
<tr><td>活动</td><td></td><td></td><td></td><td></td><td></td><td></td><td></td></tr>
</table></td></tr>
</table>

续表

	国际援助申请格式	填报须知
12	评估与报告 （应在项目完成三个月内提交给世界遗产中心）	总结报告： 总结报告应由项目实施负责人编写， 报告结构应遵循第 10 条中的预期结果。 评估： 评估应主要针对所取得的成果及产生的影响，如对下列内容的影响： – 申请预备援助后，遗产列入《世界遗产名录》； – 定期报告及保护状况； – 申请紧急援助后，遗产从《濒危世界遗产名录》中移出； –《世界遗产公约》及其战略目标（5C）和其他战略（如全球战略）实施的情况； – 国家或当地机构； – 当地人员的能力建设； – 大众的意识提升； – 项目参与者； – 吸引其他资源，等 指定项目评估负责人。
13	可能参加此项活动的专家、培训人员、技术人员或技工的简介 （如果已知上述人员身份，请提供其姓名。如有可能，应提供个人简历）	明确说明各个专家的专业领域、承担的工作以及所需工作时间。如缔约国发出请求，世界遗产中心与专家咨询机构可以为活动推荐专家顾问、培训人员。 请提供任何已确定参加该项目的专家的姓名。如有可能，将其简历以附件形式与申请表一并提交。
14	项目主要受众（包括受训人员和参与者的简介）	说明项目的目标群体与受益人以及他们的职业、所属机构或专业领域。
15	详细预算	
	a）提供下列各项目的费用（以美元为单位），如可能，应包括单位成本以及不同资金来源分担这些成本的情况：	请在表中提供项目全部费用的详细预算，并说明不同资金来源（缔约国、世界遗产基金会、其他）分担这些费用的情况。
	（i）组织	该项包括活动地点、办公费用，如影印费、文具费、文书助理费用、笔译费、口译费、影音设备费用以及项目实施所需的其他必要的组织费用。
	（ii）人员与咨询服务	该项包括支付给国际、国内专家、协调人员费用以及项目实施所需的其他人员费用。
	（iii）差旅费	该项包括项目实施所需的国际或国内旅行费用。
	（iv）每日生活补助	该项包括项目实施所需的住宿、餐饮杂费等相关费用。
	（v）设备	该项包括项目实施所需的设备费用。
	（vi）评估、报告与出版	该项包括项目实施所需的评估、报告、编辑、排版、印刷、发行等费用。
	（vii）其他费用	该项包括项目实施所需的签证费等小额费用。
	b）详细说明缔约国或其他来源的资源是否已到位或在争取中	如果资源目前仍未到位，说明在项目开始实施时是否可以到位。

续表

	国际援助申请格式	填报须知
16	缔约国或其他机构的实物捐赠	
	a）国家机构	请详细说明。
	b）其他双边或多变组织、捐赠机构等	请详细说明。
17	负责项目实施的机构	请提供负责项目实施的人员或机构的姓名、职位、地址、详细联系信息以及其他参与机构的详细信息。 请说明缔约国是否对该项目提供了立法或行政方面的支持（见《操作指南》第239d条）。
18	缔约国代表签字	姓名： 职位： 日期：
19	附件	列出援助申请附件的编号及名称。

Process of submission for International Assistance requests for Conservation & Management Assistance and Preparatory Assistance above US$5,000

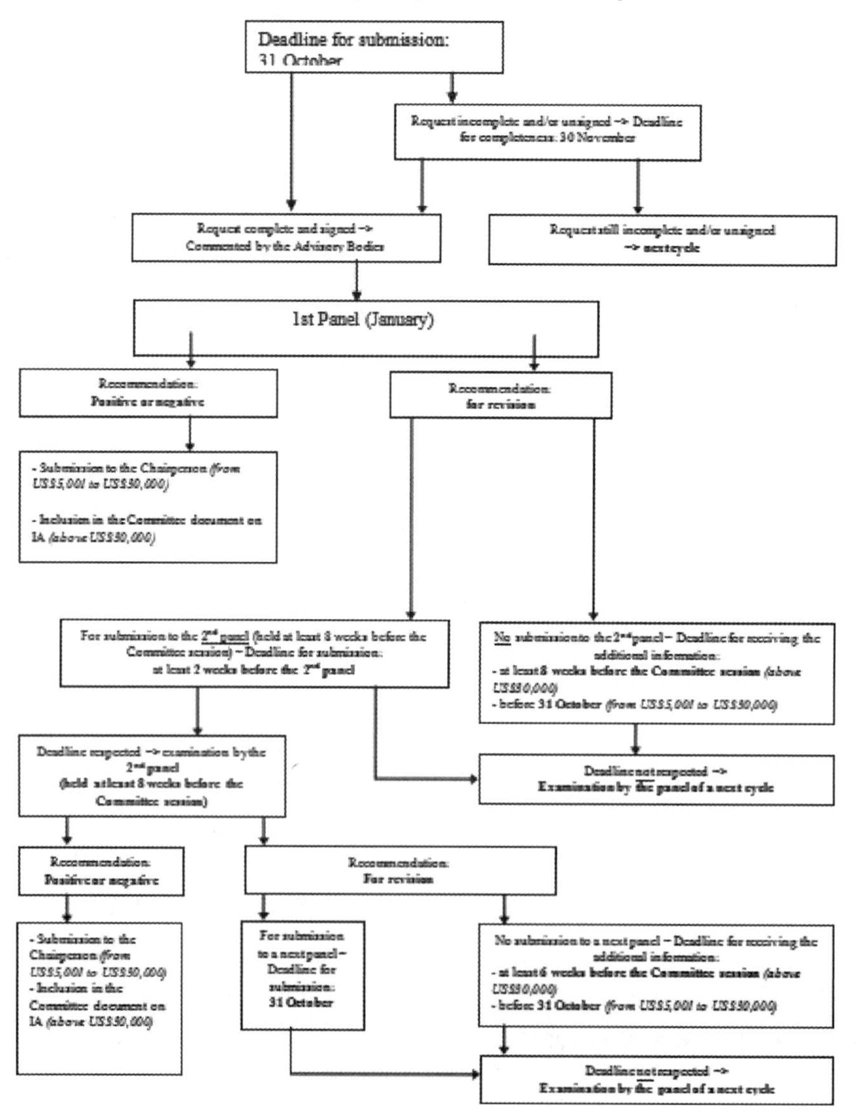

提交5000美元以上申请国际援助管理和预备援助的程序

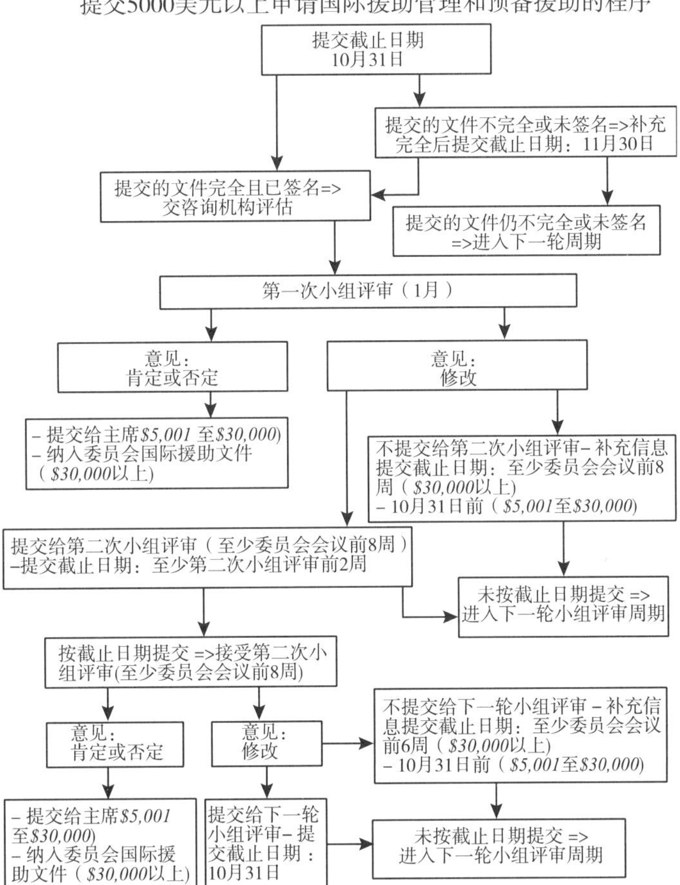

Annex 9 Evaluation Criteria of the Advisory Bodies for International Assistance Requests

附件 9 专家咨询机构评估国际援助申请的标准

The following considerations are to be taken into account by the Advisory Bodies, World Heritage Centre, and the relevant Decision-maker (the Chairperson of the World Heritage Committee, the World Heritage Committee or the Director of the World Heritage Centre) when assessing International Assistance requests.

专家咨询机构，世界遗产中心和相关决策人（世界遗产委员会主席、世界遗产委员会或世界遗产中心董事）在评估国际援助申请时将会考虑下列因素：

These items do not constitute a checklist, and not every item will be applicable to every International Assistance Request. Rather the appropriate items are to be considered together in an integrated manner in making balanced judgments concerning the appropriateness of allocating the limited financial support available through the World Heritage Fund.

这些条目不构成一个清单，并不是每个条目都适合于每一个国际援助申请。在做合理性判断时，考虑到从世界遗产基金获取有限资金支持的适宜性，一些合适的条目将会作为整体考虑。

A. Eligibility requirements

A. 资格要求

1. Is the State Party in arrears for payment of its contribution to the World Heritage Fund?

1. 缔约国是否拖欠给世界遗产基金的付款？

2. Is the request coming from an authorized organization/institution of the State Party?

2. 申请是否来自于缔约国授权的组织或机构？

B. Priority considerations

B. 优先考虑

3. Is the request from a State Party on the list of the Least Developed Countries (LDCs), Low Income Economies (LIEs), Small Island Developing

3. 提交申请的缔约国是否是最不发达国家（LDCs）、低收入国家（LIEs）、小岛屿发展中国家（SIDS）或冲突后国家？

States (SIDS) or post-conflict countries?

4. Is the property on the List of World Heritage in Danger?

5. Does the request further one or more of the Strategic Objectives of the World Heritage Committee (Credibility, Conservation, Capacity building, and Communication)?

6. Does the request respond to needs identified through the Periodic Reporting process at the property and/or regional levels?

7. Is the request linked to a regional or sub-regional capacity building programme?

8. Is there a capacity building aspect to the activity (no matter what type of assistance sought)?

9. Will the lessons learned from the activity provide benefits to the larger World Heritage system?

4. 遗产是否列入《濒危世界遗产名录》？

5. 申请能否进一步实现世界遗产委员会的一个或多个战略目标？（公信力，保护，能力建设和交流）

6. 申请是否通过遗产或区域层面的定期报告得以认定？

7. 申请是否涉及区域或次区域的能力建设规划？

8. 是否有能力建设方面的活动（不论是哪类寻求援助类型）？

9. 从活动中学习的经验是否有益于促进世界遗产系统的扩展？

C. Considerations linked to the specific content of the proposed activity

C. 拟议活动具体内容需考虑的事项

10. Are the objectives of the request clearly stated and achievable?

11. Is there a clear work plan for achieving the results, including a timeline for its implementation? Is the work plan reasonable?

12. Does the agency/organization responsible for implementing the proposal have the capacity to do so, and is there a responsible person identified for ongoing contacts?

13. Are the professionals proposed to be used (whether national or international) qualified to carry out the work being requested? Are there clear terms of reference for them, including adequate period of their involvement?

14. Is the involvement of all relevant parties taken into account in the proposal (for example stakeholders, other institutions, etc.)?

15. Are the technical requirements clearly expressed and are they reasonable?

10. 申请的目标是否清晰且切实可行？

11. 是否有一个清晰的工作计划包括时间表来完成业绩？工作计划是否合理？

12. 负责执行计划的机构或组织是否有能力完成计划？是否有保持长期联络的负责人？

13. 建议负责执行申请的专业工作人员（不论国内的还是国际的）是否合格？他们是否有明确的证明，包括他们长期从事该专业工作的证明？

14. 是否所有参与的相关各方在提议中都要有所考虑？（例如利益相关者或其他机构等等）

15. 技术要求是否都清晰表述且合理？

16. Is there a clear plan for reporting the results and for continued monitoring, including appropriate indicators for success?

16. 对于汇报结果和持续监测，包括成功的适当指标，是否有一个清晰的计划？

17. Is there a commitment of the State Party for appropriate follow-up after the activity is completed?

17. 缔约国是否有在活动后适时随访的承诺？

D. Budgetary/Financial considerations

D. 预算或财务的注意事项

18. Is the overall budget reasonable for the work that is proposed to be carried out?

18. 执行工作的总体预算是否合理？

19. Is the budget detailed sufficiently to ensure that the unit costs are reasonable and in line with local costs and/or UNESCO norms and rules as appropriate?

19. 预算是否详细到能确保单位花费合理，并且与地方费用或与联合国教科文组织的规范法则相适应？

20. Does the request act as a catalyst (multiplier) for other funding (are other sources of funding, either cash or in-kind clearly specified)?

20. 申请是否能促进其他资金积存（其他资金来源，不论现金还是实物都详细表述清晰）？

E. Considerations for specific types of International Assistance

E. 国际援助具体类型的注意事项

a). *Emergency Assistance Requests*

a）紧急援助申请

21. Does the threat or disaster covered by the request conform to the definition of an emergency within *The Operational Guidelines* (unexpected phenomena)?

21. 申请中包含的威胁或灾难是否与《操作指南》中定义的紧急情况（意外现象）一致？

22. Can the proposed intervention be carried out with reasonable safety for those involved with its implementation?

22. 提议的干预措施能否在安全合理的情况下实现？

23. Does the intervention respond to the most critical issues related to the protection/conservation of the property?

23. 干预是否解决了与遗产保护保存相关的关键问题？

b). *Preparatory Assistance Requests*

b）筹备性援助申请

For requests for preparation of nomination files

准备申报文件的申请

24.Is the property on the State Party's Tentative List?

24. 遗产是否已列入缔约国《预备名录》？

25. Does the State Party already have

25. 缔约国是否有已经列入《世界遗产名录》

properties inscribed on the World Heritage List? If yes, how many?

的遗产？如果有，数量是多少？

26. Is the type of property proposed for World Heritage listing un-represented or under-represented in the World Heritage List?

26. 被列入的遗产类型是否在《世界遗产名录》没有代表性或代表性不足？

27. Is sufficient attention paid to necessary elements, such as the preparation of the management plan, comparative analysis, Statement of Outstanding Universal Value, mapping, etc.?

27. 对一些必要元素，如管理规划的筹备、对比分析、突出普遍价值的声明、绘图等是否给予足够关注？

28. Is sufficient attention given to community involvement?

28. 对社会参与是否给予足够关注？

For requests for preparation of Tentative Lists

准备《预备名录》的申请

29. Is the process designed to include all the necessary stakeholders and points of view?

29. 过程是否包含了所有必要的利益相关者和观点？

30. Are both natural and cultural heritage professionals proposed to be involved?

30. 提议中是否自然和文化遗产都包括在内？

31. Is the State Party new to the *World Heritage Convention*?

31. 是否是新加入《世界遗产公约》的缔约国？

32. If the request is for harmonization of Tentative Lists, are representatives from all the necessary States Parties in the region or sub-region involved?

32. 为协调《预备名录》，申请是否涵盖了必要缔约国的区域或次区域的所有代表？

For requests for preparation of other types of assistance

准备其他援助类型的申请

33. If the request is for the preparation of a request for other assistance, is the need for the eventual request well documented?

33. 如果申请是为其他援助申请做准备，最后申请的需要是否被记录？

c).*Conservation and Management Assistance Requests*

c）保护与管理援助申请

For requests for conservation work or the preparation of a management plan

保护工作或准备筹备计划的申请

34. Is the property on the World Heritage List?

34. 遗产是否列入《世界遗产名录》？

35. Is the work being proposed a priority for protecting or safeguarding the property?

35. 是否遗产保护与安全工作享有优先权？

36. Does the work being proposed conform to best practice?

36. 提议的工作是否符合最佳实践？

For requests for training activities

培训活动的申请

37. Is it clearly related to the implementation of the *World Heritage Convention*?

37. 与《世界遗产公约》的执行是否明确相关？

38. Does it take place on a World Heritage property or involve a visit/case study of a World Heritage property?

38. 是否在世界遗产地举行或是否包含对世界遗产地的研究、访问？

39. Does it involve those responsible for conservation at a World Heritage property as trainees or resource persons?

39. 是否包含实习生或资源专家对遗产地的保护责任？

40. Does it respond to well-defined training needs?

40. 是否满足了明确的培训需求？

41. Are the training methods appropriate to ensure that the learning objectives will be met?

41. 培训方式是否能很好的实现学习目标？

42. Does it strengthen a local and/or regional training institution?

42. 是否加强了当地或区域的培训机构的实力？

43. Is it linked with practical applications in the field?

43. 是否与实际应用领域相关联？

44. Is there a provision for disseminating results and related training materials to other organizations in the World Heritage system?

44. 给世界遗产体系内的其他机构宣传成果和相关培训资料是否有明确规定？

For requests related to scientific research

相关科研的申请

45. Can it be demonstrated that the subject matter is of a priority nature for better protection and safeguarding of World Heritage properties?

45. 能否说明该主题对保护遗产地有优先权？

46. Can it be demonstrated that the results will be concrete and applicable widely within the World Heritage system?

46. 是否说明结果会在世界遗产体系内被大量细化且应用？

For requests for educational or awareness activities

教育或意识提升活动的申请

47. Will it help make the *World Heritage Convention* better known or create a stronger interest in it amongthe target audience?

47. 是否会提高《世界遗产公约》知名度且强化目标群体对公约的兴趣？

48. Will it create a greater awareness of the different issues related to the implementation of the *World Heritage Convention*?

48. 是否会提升与《世界遗产公约》实施相关的不同问题的认识？

49. Will it promote more involvement in *World Heritage Convention* related activities?

49. 是否会增强与《世界遗产公约》相关活动的参与？

50. Will it be a means of exchanging experiences or stimulate joint educational and information programmes, especially amongschool children?

50. 尤其是对于学校学生，是否会成为一种交换经验的方式或促进联合教育或信息程序发展？

51. Will it produce appropriate awareness materials for the promotion of the World Heritage Convention for use by the target audience?

51. 是否会给目标群体提供促进利用《世界遗产公约》意识的适合材料？

Annex 10 STATEMENT OF OUTSTANDING UNIVERSAL VALUE

附件 10 突出普遍价值声明

Format of a Statement of Outstanding Universal Value, and of a retrospective Statement of Outstanding Universal Value.

The retrospective Statement of Outstanding Universal Value should be submitted either in English or in French. An electronic version (Word or .pdf format) should also be submitted.

A Statement of Outstanding Universal Value should respect the following format (2 A4 pages max) :

a) Brief synthesis

b) Justification for Criteria

c) Statement of integrity (for all sites)

d) Statement of Authenticity (for sites under criteria i-vi)

e) Requirements for protection and management

Deadline

1 February [①] of the year preceding the one in which the approval of the Committee is requested.

突出普遍价值声明及突出普遍价值回顾的声明的格式。

对突出普遍价值回顾声明应当以英语或法语提交。电子版应以 Word 或 pdf 格式一同附上。

突出普遍价值的声明应当遵照以下格式（两页 A4 纸大小）：

a）简单的综述

b）符合标准的理由

c）完整性声明（对于所有遗址）

d）真实性声明（对符合标准 i–vi 的遗址）

e）保护与管理的要求

截止日期

要求委员会批准申请的前一年的 2 月 1 日[①]。

① If 1 February falls on a weekend, the nomination must be received by 17h00 GMT the preceding Friday.
如果 2 月 1 日是周末，申报文件必须于前一周的周五下午格林威治时间 17：00 前送达。

Annex 11 MODIFICATIONS TO WORLD HERITAGE PROPERTIES

附件 11 世界遗产的变动

MINOR MODIFICATIONS TO THE BOUNDARIES OF WORLD HERITAGE PROPERTIES

世界遗产范围的轻微变动

Boundary modifications should serve better identification of World Heritage properties and enhance protection of their Outstanding Universal Value.

轻微的变动应更有利于识别世界遗产并加强遗产突出普遍价值的保护。

A proposal for a minor boundary modification, submitted by the State Party concerned, is subject to the review of the relevant Advisory Body (ies) and to the relevant Advisory Body (ies) and to the approval of the World Heritage Committee.

由相关缔约国提交的轻微变动，是鉴于相关咨询机构的评审并需得到世界遗产委员会的批准。

A proposal for a minor boundary modification can be approved, not approved, or referred by the World Heritage Committee.

对于轻微变动的提议，世界遗产委员会可以批准，也可以不批准，或不予理会。

Documentation requested

要求的文件材料：

1) Area of the property (in hectares) : please indicate a) the area of the property as inscribed and b) the area of the property as proposed to be modified (or the area of the proposed buffer zone). (Note that reductions can be considered as minor modifications only under exceptional circumstances).

1. 遗产的面积（用公顷表示）：请指明：a）已登记遗产的面积；b）提出要修订遗产的面积（或是提出的缓冲区面积）。（注意只有在特殊情况下缩小范围可视作轻微变动）。

2) Description of the modification: please provide a written description of the proposed change to the boundary of the property (or a written description of the proposed buffer zone).

2. 变动修改的描述：请提供一份遗产范围提议变动的书面说明（或提议的缓冲区变动的书面说明）。

3) Justification for the modification: please provide a brief summary of the reasons why the boundaries of the property should be modified (or why a buffer zone is needed), with particular emphasis on how such modification will improve the conservation and/or protection of the property.

3. 变动的理由：请简要概括遗产范围需要修改的原因（或为什么需要缓冲区），尤其要强调这样的变动将如何提高对遗产的保护。

4) Contribution to the maintenance of the Outstanding Universal Value: please indicate how the proposed change (or the proposed buffer zone) will contribute to the maintenance of the Outstanding Universal Value of the property.

4. 对维护突出普遍价值的贡献：请指出提议的变动（或提议的缓冲区变动）将如何对维护遗产突出普遍价值做贡献。

5) Implications for legal protection: please indicate the implications of the proposed change for the legal protection of the property. In the case of a proposed addition, or of the creation of a buffer zone, please provide information on the legal protection in place for the area to be added and a copy of relevant laws and regulations.

5. 合法保护的影响：请指出提议的变动对遗产法律保护的影响。至于提议增加或新建一个缓冲区，请提供要增加区域已实施的法律保护和相关的法律法规的信息。

6) Implications for management arrangements: please indicate the implications of the proposed change for the management arrangements of the property. In the case of a proposed addition, or of the creation of a buffer zone, please provide information on the management arrangements in place for the area to be added.

6. 管理安排的影响：请指出提议的变动对遗产管理安排的影响。至于提议增加或新建一个缓冲区，请提供要增加区域已实行的管理安排的信息。

7) Maps: please submit two maps, one clearly showing both delimitations of the property (original and proposed revision) and the other showing only the proposed revision. In the case of the creation of a buffer zone, please submit a map showing both the inscribed property and the proposed buffer zone.

7. 地图：请提供两份地图，一份清晰显示遗产的两种界线（原始的和拟修订的），另一份仅显示拟修订的。如需新建缓冲区，请提供一份同时显示已列入的遗产及拟修订的缓冲区的地图。

Please make sure that the maps:

请确定该地图：

—are either topographic or cadastral;

——是地形地籍图；

—are presented at a scale which is appropriate to the size in hectares of the property and sufficient to clearly show the detail of the current boundary and the proposed changes (and, in any case, the largest available and practical scale);

——以公顷为单位，以适当规模显示遗产并清晰详细显示目前遗产的界线，及拟修订的更改（在任何情况下采用最大规模显示）；

—have the title and the legend/key in English or French (if this is not possible, please attach a

——有标题、英文或者法文的图例及关键词（如不可能完成，请附加翻译件）；

translation);

—mark the boundaries of the property (current and proposed revision) through a clearly visible line that can be distinguished from other features on the maps;

——用清晰可见的线条标示遗产界线（当前的和拟修订的），以与地图的其他特征区别；

—bear a clearly labeled coordinate grid (or coordinate ticks);

——带有清晰标记的坐标网格（或坐标记号）；

—clearly refer (in the title and in the legend) to the boundary of the World Heritage property (and to the buffer zone of the World Heritage property, if applicable). Please clearly distinguish the boundary of the World Heritage property from any other protected area boundaries.

——明白的指示（标题或图例）出世界遗产的边界（及世界遗产缓冲区，如有）。请明确区分世界遗产边界和其他保护区的边界。

8) Additional information: In the case of a proposed addition, please submit some photographs of the area to be added that provide information on its key values and conditions of authenticity/integrity.

8. 附件信息：在附件信息中，请提交相关增加区域的照片，添加有关其价值和完整性真实性的信息。

Any other relevant document can be submitted such as thematic maps (e.g. vegetation maps), summaries of scientific information concerning the values of the area to be added (e.g. species lists), and supporting bibliographies.

可提交其他相关文件如：主题地图（如植被图），可添加与区域价值有关的科学信息总结（如物种目录）、及配套的参考目录。

The above-mentioned documentation should be submitted in English or French in two identical copies (three for mixed properties). An electronic version (the maps in formats such as .jpg, .tif, .pdf) should also be submitted.

以上文件以英语或法语提交两个相同的副本（混合遗产需三个副本）。同时提交电子版文件（地图以 JPG，TIF，PDF 格式提交）

Deadline

期限

1 February of the year in which the approval of the Committee is requested.

委员会审批前一年的 2 月 1 日。

Annex 12
FORM FOR THE SUBMISSION OF FACTUAL ERRORS IN THE ADVISORY BODIES EVALUATIONS

(*in compliance with Paragraph 150 of the* Operational Guidelines)

STATE(S) PARTY(IES):

EVALUATION OF THE NOMINATION OF THE SITE:

RELEVANT ADVISORY BODY'S EVALUATION[①] :

Page, column, line of the Advisory Body Evaluation	Sentence including the factual error (the factual error should be highlighted in bold)	Proposed correction by the State Party	Comment (if any) by the Advisory Body and/or the World Heritage Centre

• The Factual Errors submission form, as well as an example of such a completed form, are available from the UNESCO World Heritage Centre and at the following Web address: http: //whc.unesco.org/en/factualerrors.

• Further guidance on the submission of Factual Errors can be foundin Paragraph 150 of the Operational Guidelines.

States Parties are requested to immediately submit this information in electronic format or by e-mail to wh-nominations@unesco.org.

• The original signed version of the completed Factual Errors submission form should be received in English or French by the UNESCO World Heritage Centre, at the following address: 7 place de Fontenoy, 75352 Paris 07 SP, France, no later than 14 days before the opening of the session of the Committee.

① For nominations of mixed sites, if there are errors in both the Evaluations of the Advisory Bodies, separate forms should be submitted for each Advisory Body indicating which Advisory Body 's Evaluation each submission is referring to.

附件 12
咨询机构提交的评估中事实错误表格

（依照操作指南第 150 条要求）

缔约国：

对申报遗产的评估

相关咨询机构的评估[①]：

咨询机构评估报告 第　页，栏　行	包含事实错误的句子 (事实错误需用黑体字标注)	缔约国的修改	（如有）咨询机构或世界遗产中心意见

• 事实错误例表见世界遗产中心网站：
http：//whc.unesco.org/en/factualerrors.

• 其他标准参见操作指南第 150 条。
要求缔约国立刻以电子表格或通过电子邮件提交相关信息至：wh-nominations@unesco.org.

• 有正式签名的、完全的、有事实错误的版本，应以英语或法语形式，在下次委员会会议前 14 天交至下列地址：7 place de Fontenoy，75352 Paris 07 SP，France

① 对于混合遗产等等，如果两个咨询机构的评估都认为有错误，则应向每个咨询机构提交单独的表格，说明提交的每个表格对应的咨询机构的评估。

Annex 13 FORMAT FOR THE SUBMISSION OF STATE OF CONSEVETION REPORTS BY THE STATES PARTIES

(in compliance with Paragraph 169 of the *Operational Guidelines*)

Name of World Heritage property (State (s) Party (ies)) (Identification number)

1. Executive Summary of the report

[*Note: each of the sections described below should be summarized. The maximum length of the executive summary is 1 page.*]

2. Response to the Decision of the World Heritage Committee

[Note: The State (s) Party (ies) is/are requested to address the most recent Decision of the World Heritage Committee for this property, paragraph by paragraph.]

If the property is inscribed on the List of World Heritage in Danger, Please also provide detailed information on the following:

a) Progress achieved in implementing the corrective measures adopted by the World Heritage Committee.

[Note: please address each corrective measure individually, providing factual information, including exact dates, figures, etc.]

If needed, please describe the success factors or difficulties in implementing each of the corrective measures identified.

b) Is the timeframe for implementing the corrective measures suitable? If not, please propose

附件 13 缔约国提交保护状况报告表格

（依照操作指南第 169 条要求）

世界遗产名称（缔约国）（鉴别号）

1. 报告执行摘要

（注：概述下列各部分描述，执行摘要最长不超过一页纸。）

2. 回应世界遗产委员会决定

（注：要求缔约国重点、逐段关注世界遗产委员会关于该遗产的最新决定。）

如果遗产被列入世界遗产濒危名录，请提供以下详细信息：

a）得到世界遗产委员会认可的整改措施在执行中已取得的成果。

（注：独立说明每一项整改措施，提供实际信息，包括准确的日期、数据等。）

如果需要，描述每项确定的整改措施在执行中的成功或困难因素。

b）整改措施实施时间表是否合适？如果不合适，请提出一个替代的时间表并解释为何需

an alternative timeframe and an explanation why this alternative timeframe is required.

要这个替代的时间表。

c) Progress achieved towards the Desired state of conservation for the removal of the property from the List of World Heritage in Danger (DSOCR).

c）为了达到理想的保护状况以便将遗产从濒危遗产名录中移出而取得的成就。

3. Other current conservation issues identified by the State (s) Party (ies) which may have an impact on the property's Outstanding Universal Value.

3. 目前缔约国认定的、可能影响遗产突出普遍价值的其他保护问题。

[Note: this includes conservation issues which are not mentioned in the Decision of the World Heritage Committee or in any information request from the World Heritage Centre]

（注：包括世界遗产委员会决定中没有提及的保护问题或世界遗产中心要求的任何信息。）

4. In conformity with Paragraph 172 of *the Operational Guidelines*, describe any potential major restorations, alterations and/or new construction (s) intended within the property, the buffer zone (s) and/or corridors or other areas, where such developments may affect the Outstanding Universal Value of the property, including authenticity and integrity.

4. 按操作指南第 172 条，描述任何在遗产内、缓冲区或廊道及其他地区，潜在的主要修复、改建或新建等有可能影响遗产的突出普遍价值，包括影响遗产真实性与完整性的开发。

5. Public access to the state of conservation report.

5. 公众访问保护状况报告

[Note: this report will be uploaded for public access on the World Heritage Centre's State of conservation Information System (http: //whc.unesco.org/en/soc). Should your State Party request that the full report should not be uploaded, only the 1-page executive summary provided in point (1.) above will be uploaded for public access].

（注：报告将上传世界遗产中心保护状况信息系统以供公众访问（http：//whc.unesco.org/en/soc）。应缔约国要求，不上传报告全文，仅按第一条要求上传一页执行摘要供公众访问。）

6. Signature of the Authority

6. 官方签名

Annex 14 Table of uses of the World Heritage Emble

附件 14 世界遗产标识使用表

This table was prepared on the basis of Chapter VIII of *The Operational Guidelines of the World Heritage Convention* and the *Directives Concerning the Use of the Name, Acronym, Logo and Internet Domain Names of UNESCO* (Resolution 34C/86).

本表在世界遗产公约操作指南第 8 章和《关于使用联合国教科文组织名称、缩写、标识和互联网域名》的方针的基础上编制（34C/86 决定）。

Reminder concerning the authority and delegation of authority for the use of the World Heritage Emblem according to Chapter VIII of the *Operational Guidelines*:

操作指南第 8 章关于使用世界遗产标识的权利和授权的提示：

Para. 262: 'The World Heritage Committee is responsible for determining the use of the World Heritage Emblem and for making policy prescriptions regarding how it may be used.'

262. 世界遗产委员会负责决定世界遗产标识的使用，同时负责制定如何使用标识的政策规定。

Para. 276: 'National authorities may grant the use of the Emblem to a national entity, provided that the project, whether national or international, involves only World Heritage properties located on the same national territory. National authorities' decision should be guided by the Guidelines and Principles.'

276. 如果国家或国际项目只涉及本国的世界遗产，国家权威机构可授权国家实体使用标识。国家权威机构的决定应遵守《指南和原则》。

Para. 278: Any other request must be adressed to the Director of the World Heritage Centre, who has the authority to grant the use of the Emblem in accordance with the Guidelines and Principles.

278. 任何申请应送达世界遗产中心主任——主任有权根据《指南和原则》批准使用标识。

For cases not covered, or not sufficiently covered, by the Guidelines and Principles and by the Table of Uses, the Director refers the matter to the Chairperson who, in the most difficult cases, might wish to refer the matter to the Committee for final decision.

遇到《指南和原则》及“使用表”尚未涉及或完全涵盖的情况，如果是很难处理的情况，主任应将申请提交给主席，主席会将该申请提交委员会做最后决定。

Reminder concerning the use of the linked logo and of the stand alone Emblem:

有关使用链接标识及独立标识的提示：

Para. 262: Since the adoption by the UNESCO General Conference in October 2007 of the *Directives Concerning the Use of the Name, Acronym, Logo and Internet Domain Names of UNESCO*, it is strongly encouraged to use the World Heritage Emblem as part of a linked logo block accompanied by UNESCO's logo, whenever feasible. The use of the World Heritage Emblem alone remains however possible, in line with the present Guidelines and with the Table of Uses (Annex 14 of the Guidelines).

262. 自采纳 2007 年 10 月联合国教科文组织大会《关于使用联合国教科文组织名称、缩写、标识及联合国互联网域名的方针》以来，强烈鼓励在可行的情况下同时使用世界遗产标识和联合国教科文组织标识。也可按操作指南附件 14 中的“使用表”单独使用世界遗产标识（见指南附件 14）。

Reminder concerning the graphic charter:

关于使用图文特许的提示：

The graphic charter of the UNESCO logo is available here:

http: //www.unesco.org/new/en/name-and-logo/graphics/

联合国教科文组织标识图文特许可在网站找到：

http : //www.unesco.org/new/en/name–and–logo/graphics/

According to the Preamble of Chapter VIII of the *Operational Guidelines*, the stand alone World Heritage Emblem can be used in any colour or size.

按照操作指南第 8 章导言，单独的世界遗产标识不限颜色和规格。

The logos are provided by the authorizing entities (as detailed in the following table) in digital format which cannot be modified by the users in any way.

数字化的标识由授权机构提供（详情见下表）用户不得做任何修改。

It is obligatory to submit the draft layout of the intended use to the authorizing entity for validation before production.

在确认制作前授权使用的机构必须递交版面设计草案。

Definition of commercial use:

The sale of goods or services bearing the name, acronym, logo and/or Internet domain name of UNESCO combined with the World Heritage Emblem chiefly for profit shall be regarded as "commercial use" for the purpose of the Operational Guidelines. Such use must be expressly authorized by the Director-General, under a specific contractual arrangement (definition adapted from UNESCO Logo Directives 2007. Art III.2.1.3)

商业用途的定义：

在提供商品或服务时使用联合国教科文组织名称、缩写、标识及联合国互联网域名及世界遗产标识并以盈利为目的，操作指南认定为“商业用途”。此类用途必须在具体合同下由秘书长明确授权（定义摘自联合国教科文组织标识方针，2007 年 .Art III.2.1.3）。

World Heritage Centre

Uses and purposes	Uses		Authorization		Graphic illustrations
World Heritage Centre - WHC (for international content)	Type of Logo the WHC can use	Use of the Logo by the WHC is authorized by	WHC can authorize the Logo for	Type of Logo the WHC can authorize	Logo to be used and/or authorized by the WHC
1) Publications 2) Communication materials 3) Website, social media, apps, etc. 4) Working documents 5) Communication products (such as T-shirts, bags, umbrellas), for special events 6) Stationery	UNESCO/World Heritage Convention logo	Statutory use	State Party hosting a Committee	UNESCO/World Heritage Convention logo	United Nations Educational, Scientific and Cultural Organization · World Heritage Convention
1) Publications 2) Communication materials 3) Website, social media, apps, etc. 4) Working documents 5) Communication products (such as T-shirts, bags, umbrellas), for special events 6) Stationery	UNESCO/World Heritage Centre logo	Statutory use			United Nations Educational, Scientific and Cultural Organization · World Heritage Centre
1) Publications 2) Communication materials 3) Website, social media, apps, etc. 4) Small-size communication products (such as pens, key-rings etc), for special events 5) Stationery	World Heritage Emblem	Statutory use	1) World Heritage Site Management Authority 2) State Party hosting a Committee	World Heritage Emblem	or
Committee session	UNESCO/World Heritage logo + "XXth/st/rd/nd World Heritage Committee session"	Statutory use	State Party hosting a Committee	UNESCO/World Heritage logo + "XXth/st/rd/nd World Heritage Committee session"	United Nations Educational, Scientific and Cultural Organization · 39th session of the World Heritage Committee

续表

Uses and purposes	Uses		Authorization		Graphic illustrations
Partnership with external entities (private and public sector)	UNESCO/World Heritage Centre logo with text "With the support of", "In cooperation with", or "In partnership with"	Statutory use	Entities in the framework of contractual arrangements	UNESCO/World Heritage Centre logo with text "With the support of", "In cooperation with", or "In partnership with"	In partnership with United Nations Educational, Scientific and Cultural Organization · World Heritage Centre With the support of United Nations Educational, Scientific and Cultural Organization · World Heritage Centre
	UNESCO/World Heritage Centre or Convention logo + Partner's logo and/or text			UNESCO/World Heritage Centre or Convention logo + Partner's logo and/or text	Panasonic supports sustainable development through UNESCO World Heritage conservation and education

世界遗产中心

用途及目的	使用		授权		图形图例
世界遗产中心（国际内容）	世界遗产中心可使用的标识类型	世界遗产中心使用标识的授权	世界遗产中心可授权以下单位使用标识	世界遗产中心可授权的标识类型	世界遗产中心可使用或授权的标识
出版物 交流材料 网站、社会媒体、应用程序等 工作文件 为特别活动生产的交流产品（如T恤，包，伞等） 文具	联合国教科文组织或世界遗产公约标识	依法使用	缔约国为主的委员会	联合国教科文组织或世界遗产公约标识	UNESCO United Nations Educational, Scientific and Cultural Organization · World Heritage Convention
出版物 交流材料 网站、社会媒体、应用程序等 工作文件 为特别活动生产的交流产品（如T恤，包，伞等） 文具	联合国教科文组织或世界遗产中心标识	依法使用			UNESCO United Nations Educational, Scientific and Cultural Organization · World Heritage Centre
1）出版物 交流材料 3）网站、社会媒体、应用程序等 4）为特别活动生产的小型交流产品（如钢笔、钥匙扣等） 5）文具	世界遗产徽章	依法使用	1. 世界遗产管理机构 2. 缔约国为主的委员会	世界遗产徽章	or
委员会会议	联合国教科文组织或世界遗产标识"XX届世界遗产委员会会议"	依法使用	缔约国为主的委员会	联合国教科文组织或世界遗产标识"XX届世界遗产委员会会议"	UNESCO United Nations Educational, Scientific and Cultural Organization · 39th session of the World Heritage Committee

续表

用途及目的	使用		授权		图形图例
与外部机构的合作关系（私人或公共部门）	联合国教科文组织或世界遗产中心标识加“得到支持”、“合作”、“伙伴”等文字	依法使用	合同框架下的机构	联合国教科文组织或世界遗产中心标识加“得到支持”、“合作”、“伙伴”等文字	UNESCO United Nations Educational, Scientific and Cultural Organization · In partnership with World Heritage Centre UNESCO United Nations Educational, Scientific and Cultural Organization · With the support of World Heritage Centre
	联合国教科文组织或世界遗产中心或公约标识加合作者标识或文字			联合国教科文组织或世界遗产中心或公约标识加合作者标识或文字	UNESCO United Nations Educational, Scientific and Cultural Organization · World Heritage Convention · Panasonic supports sustainable development through UNESCO World Heritage conservation and education

NATIONAL COMMISSIONS OR AGENCIES

Uses and purposes	Uses		Authorization		Graphic illustrations
1 - National Commission (for national content)	Type of Logo the NatCom can use	Use of the Logo by the NatCom is authorized by	NatCom can authorize the use of the Logo for	Type of Logo the NatCom can authorize	Logo to be used and/or authorized by the NatCom
1) Non-commercial publications 2) Communication materials 3) Website, social media, apps, etc. 4) Communication products such as T-shirts, bags, umbrellas (non-merchandising, exceptionally for special events) 5) Stationery	UNESCO/World Heritage logo with text "World Heritage in…[Country name]"	Statutory use	Local government authorities and site managing authorities	UNESCO/World Heritage logo with text 'World Heritage in +country'	United Nations Educational, Scientific and Cultural Organization · World Heritage in Switzerland
1) Website, social media, apps, etc. when space is limited 2) Communication products as a graphic element or when space is limited 3) Stationery 4) Any other applicable case according to the *Operational Guidelines*	World Heritage Emblem	Statutory use	World Heritage site management authority	World Heritage Emblem	or
Road signs, highway signs	Choice of the logo according to the kind of sign and its location: UNESCO/World Heritage logo in full or simplified with site's name underneath	Statutory use	World Heritage site management authority	UNESCO/World Heritage logo in full or simplified with site's name underneath	United Nations Educational, Scientific and Cultural Organization · Shark Bay, Western Australia inscribed on the World Heritage List in 1991 Stonehenge, Avebury and Associated sites inscribed on the World Heritage List in 1986 Text under the name of the site is optional. Possibility to replace 'inscribed on the World Heritage List in' by 'World Heritage since'
	World Heritage Emblem	Statutory use	World Heritage site management authority	World Heritage Emblem	or

续表

Uses and purposes	Uses		Authorization		Graphic illustrations
1 - National Commission (for national content)	Type of Logo the NatCom can use	Use of the Logo by the NatCom is authorized by	NatCom can authorize the use of the Logo for	Type of Logo the NatCom can authorize	Logo to be used and/or authorized by the NatCom
Commercial use	UNESCO/World Heritage logo with text 'World Heritage in... [Country name]	Director-General of UNESCO			United Nations Educational, Scientific and Cultural Organization · World Heritage in Switzerland
	World Heritage Emblem	Statutory use	National entity	World Heritage Emblem	or
Committee session	UNESCO/World Heritage + 'XXth/st/rd/nd World Heritage Committee Session'	World Heritage Centre	Organizing authority	UNESCO/World Heritage + 'XXth/st/rd/nd World Heritage Committee session'	United Nations Educational, Scientific and Cultural Organization · 39th session of the World Heritage Committee
Patronage for World Heritage related one-off events (ex: conferences, publications or audio-visual production activity on national or local level)			Organizing entities	UNESCO/World Heritage logo with text 'Under the patronage of the National Commission of xxx for UNESCO'	United Nations Educational, Scientific and Cultural Organization · Under the patronage of the National Commission of Xxxxx for UNESCO
World Heritage related partnership with national organisations			National organisation having established a partnership with the National Commission	UNESCO/World Heritage logo with text 'With the support of the xxx National Commission for UNESCO', or 'In cooperation with the xxx National Commission for UNESCO', or 'In partnership with the xxx National Commission for UNESCO'	United Nations Educational, Scientific and Cultural Organization · With the support of the National Commission of Xxxxxx for UNESCO

续表

Uses and purposes	Uses		Authorization		Graphic illustrations
2 - Agency - designated national authority (continued)	Type of Logo the agency can use	Use of the Logo by the agency is authorized by	Agency can authorize the use of the Logo to	Type of Logo the agency can authorize	Logo to be used and/or authorised by the agency
1) Non-commercial publications 2) Communication materials 3) Website, social media, apps, etc. 4) Communication products (such as T-shirts, bags, umbrellas) non-merchandising, for special events 5) Stationery	UNESCO/World Heritage logo with text 'World Heritage in... [Country name]'	National Commission or World Heritage Centre			United Nations Educational, Scientific and Cultural Organization · World Heritage in Switzerland
1) Non-commercial publications 2) Communication materials 3) Website, social media, apps, etc. when space is limited 4) Communication products (such as T-shirts, bags, umbrellas) non-merchandising, for special events 5) Stationery	World Heritage Emblem	Statutory use	World Heritage site management authority	World Heritage Emblem	or
Road signs, highway signs	Choice of the logo according to the kind of sign and its location: UNESCO/World Heritage logo in full or simplified with site's name underneath	National Commission or World Heritage Centre	World Heritage site management authority	UNESCO/World Heritage logo in full or simplified with site's name underneath	Stonehenge, Avebury and Associated sites inscribed on the World Heritage List in 1986 Text under the name of the site is optional. Possibility to replace 'inscribed on the World Heritage List in' by 'World Heritage since'
	World Heritage Emblem	Statutory use	World Heritage site management authority	World Heritage Emblem	or

续表

Uses and purposes	Uses		Authorization		Graphic illustrations
Commercial use	UNESCO/World Heritage logo with text "World Heritage in... [Country name]"	Director-General of UNESCO			United Nations Educational, Scientific and Cultural Organization · World Heritage in Switzerland
	World Heritage Emblem	Statutory use			or

国家委员会或机构

用途及目的	使用		授权		图形图例
1– 国家委员会（国家内容）	可使用的标识类型	国家委员会使用标识的授权	国家委员会可授权的标识	国家委员会可授权的标识类型	国家委员会可使用的标识类型
1）非商业出版物 2）交流材料 3）网站、社会媒体、应用程序等 4）交流产品如 T 恤，包，伞等（非商业用途，为特别活动生产） 5）文具	联合国教科文组织或世界遗产标识加“国名 + 遗产名”	依法使用	地方政府机构 遗产管理机构	联合国教科文组织或世界遗产标识加“国名 + 遗产名”	United Nations Educational, Scientific and Cultural Organization World Heritage in Switzerland
1）网站、社会媒体、应用程序等空间有限时 2）交流产品作为图形元素或空间有限时 3）文具 4）依照操作指南的其他应用案例	世界遗产徽章	依法使用	世界遗产管理机构	世界遗产徽章	or
路标，高速公路路标	根据路标种类或位置选择标识：完整的联合国教科文组织或世界遗产标识或在下面加上遗产点简称	依法使用	世界遗产管理机构	完整的联合国教科文组织或世界遗产标识或在下面加上遗产点简称	遗产名称下文字可替换。 可以用“自…年起成为世界遗产”替换“…年录入世界遗产” United Nations Educational, Scientific and Cultural Organization Shark Bay, Western Australia inscribed on the World Heritage List in 1991 Stonehenge, Avebury and Associated sites inscribed on the World Heritage List in 1986
	世界遗产徽章	依法使用	世界遗产管理机构	世界遗产徽章	or

续表

用途及目的	使用		授权		图形图例
商业用途	联合国教科文组织或世界遗产标识加“国名＋遗产名”	联合国教科文组织总干事			United Nations Educational, Scientific and Cultural Organization : World Heritage in Switzerland
	世界遗产徽章	依法使用	国家机构	世界遗产徽章	or
委员会会议	联合国教科文组织或世界遗产＋“XX 届世界遗产委员会会议”	世界遗产中心	权威组织	联合国教科文组织或世界遗产＋“XX 届世界遗产委员会会议”	United Nations Educational, Scientific and Cultural Organization : 39th session of the World Heritage Committee
赞助与世界遗产相关的一次性活动（如国家或地区层面的会议、出版物或音响发行活动）			权威组织	联合国教科文组织或世界遗产标识加文字“由联合国教科文组织 XXX 国家委员会赞助”	United Nations Educational, Scientific and Cultural Organization : Under the patronage of the National Commission of Xxxxx for UNESCO
与世界遗产相关的国家机构的合作			国家机构要建立与国家委员会的合作关系	联合国教科文组织或世界遗产标识＋文字“由联合国教科文组织 XXX 国家委员会支持”、“与联合国教科文组织 XXX 国家委员会合作”或“联合国教科文组织合作伙伴 XXX 国家委员会”	United Nations Educational, Scientific and Cultural Organization : With the support of the National Commission of Xxxxxx for UNESCO
2– 机构国家委员会 – 指定的国家主管机构（国家内容）	机构可使用的标识类型	机构使用标识的授权	机构可授权的标识	机构可授权的标识类型	机构可使用的标识类型

续表

用途及目的	使用		授权		图形图例
1）非商业出版物 2）交流材料 3）网站、社会媒体、应用程序等 4）交流产品（如T恤，包，伞）等非商业用途，为特别活动生产 5）文具	联合国教科文组织或世界遗产标识加“国名＋遗产名”	国家委员会或世界遗产中心			United Nations Educational, Scientific and Cultural Organization · World Heritage in Switzerland
1）非商业出版物 2）交流材料 3）网站、社会媒体、应用程序等 4）交流产品（如T恤，包，伞）等非商业用途，为特别活动生产 5）文具	世界遗产徽章	依法使用	世界遗产管理机构	世界遗产徽章	or
路标，高速公路路标	根据路标种类或位置选择标识：完整的联合国教科文组织或世界遗产标识或在下面加上遗产点简称	国家委员会或世界遗产中心	世界遗产管理机构	完整的联合国教科文组织或世界遗产标识或在下面加上遗产点简称	遗产名称下文字可替换 可以用“自…年起成为世界遗产”替换“…年录入世界遗产” United Nations Educational, Scientific and Cultural Organization · Shark Bay, Western Australia inscribed on the World Heritage List in 1991 Stonehenge, Avebury and Associated sites inscribed on the World Heritage List in 1986
	世界遗产徽章	依法使用	世界遗产管理机构	世界遗产徽章	or
商业用途	联合国教科文组织或世界遗产标识加“国名＋遗产名”	联合国教科文组织总干事			United Nations Educational, Scientific and Cultural Organization · World Heritage in Switzerland
	世界遗产徽章	依法使用			or

WORLD HERITAGE SITE MANAGEMENT AUTHORITY

Uses and purposes	Uses		Authorization		Graphic illustrations
World Heritage site management authority (for site-related content)	Type of Logo the WH site can use	Use of the Logo by the WH site is authorized by	WH Site can authorize the Logo for	Type of Logo the WH Site can authorize	Logo to be used and/or authorized by the WH site
1) Non-commercial publications 2) Communication materials 3) Website, social media, apps, etc. 4) Communication products (such as T-shirts, bags, umbrellas) non-merchandising, for special events 5) Stationery 6) Plaque, flag, banner	UNESCO/World Heritage site-specific logo	National Commission or World Heritage Centre			United Nations Educational, Scientific and Cultural Organization : Shark Bay, Western Australia Inscribed on the World Heritage List in 1991 可以用“自…年起成为世界遗产”替换“…年列入世界遗产名录”
1) Non-commercial publications 2) Communication materials 3) Website, social media, apps, etc. when space is limited 4) Communication products (T-shirts, bags, umbrellas, key-rings, pens etc.) non-merchandising, for special events 5) Plaque, flag, banner	World Heritage Emblem	National Commission or agency or World Heritage Centre			or
Road signs, highway signs	Choice of the logo according to the kind of sign and its location: UNESCO/World Heritage logo in full or simplified with site's name underneath	National Commission or World Heritage Centre			United Nations Educational, Scientific and Cultural Organization : Shark Bay, Western Australia Inscribed on the World Heritage List in 1991 Stonehenge, Avebury and Associated sites Inscribed on the World Heritage List in 1986 遗产名称下文字可用“自…年起成为世界遗产”替换“…年列入世界遗产名录”

续表

Uses and purposes	Uses		Authorization		Graphic illustrations
World Heritage site Management Authority (continued)	Type of Logo the WH site can use	Use of the Logo by the WH site is authorized by	WH site can authorize the Logo for	Type of Logo the WH site can authorize	Logo to be used and/or authorized by the WH site
	World Heritage Emblem	National Commission or World Heritage Centre			or
Commercial use	UNESCO/World Heritage site-specific logo	Director-General of UNESCO			可用“自…年成为世界遗产”替换“…年列入世界遗产名录”
	World Heritage Emblem	National Commission			or

世界遗产管理机构

用途及目的	使用		授权		图形图例
世界遗产管理当局（与遗产相关内容）	世界遗产点可使用的标识类型	世界遗产点使用标识的授权	世界遗产点可授权的标识	世界遗产点可授权的标识类型	世界遗产点可使用的标识类型
1）非商业出版物 2）交流材料 3）网站、社会媒体、应用程序等 4）交流产品（如T恤，包，伞）等非商业用途，为特别活动生产 5）文具 6）匾额，旗帜，横幅	联合国教科文组织或世界遗产－特别标识	国家委员会或世界遗产中心			UNESCO United Nations Educational, Scientific and Cultural Organization : Shark Bay, Western Australia inscribed on the World Heritage List in 1991 可以用“自…年起成为世界遗产”替换“…年录入世界遗产”
非商业出版物 交流材料 网站、社会媒体、应用程序等 交流产品（如T恤，包，伞）等非商业用途，为特别活动生产 匾额，旗帜，横幅	世界遗产徽章	国家委员会或机构或世界遗产中心			or
路标，高速公路路标	根据路标种类或位置选择标识：完整的联合国教科文组织或世界遗产标识或在下面加上遗产点简称	国家委员会或世界遗产中心			UNESCO United Nations Educational, Scientific and Cultural Organization : Shark Bay, Western Australia inscribed on the World Heritage List in 1991 UNESCO : Stonehenge, Avebury and Associated sites inscribed on the World Heritage List in 1986 遗产点名称下文字看替换． 可以用“自…年起成为世界遗产”替换“…年录入世界遗产”
	世界遗产徽章	国家委员会或机构或世界遗产中心			or

续表

用途及目的	使用		授权		图形图例
世界遗产管理当局（与遗产相关内容）	世界遗产点可使用的标识类型	世界遗产点使用标识的授权	世界遗产点可授权的标识	世界遗产点可授权的标识类型	世界遗产点可使用的标识类型
商业用途	联合国教科文组织或世界遗产–特别标识	联合国教科文组织总干事			UNESCO United Nations Educational, Scientific and Cultural Organization · Shark Bay, Western Australia inscribed on the World Heritage List in 1991 可以用“自…年起成为世界遗产”替换“…年录入世界遗产”
	世界遗产徽章	国家委员会			or

Specific case: serial sites or very large sites including several/various elements/monuments/places

Uses and purposes	Uses		Authorization		Graphic illustrations
World Heritage site management authority (continued)	Type of Logo the WH site can use	Use of the Logo by the WH site is authorized by	WH site can authorize the Logo for	Type of Logo the WH site can authorize	Logo to be used and/or authorized by the WH site
1) Non-commercial publications 2) Communication materials 3) Website, social media, apps, etc. 4) Communication products(T-shirts, bags, umbrellas, key-rings, pens etc)non-merchandising, for special events 5) Stationery 6) Plaque, flag, banner	UNESCO/World Heritage site-specific logo, preceded by the mention 'Xxxx [name of the element/ monument/place], part of'	National Commission or World Heritage Centre			Xxxx part of United Nations Educational, Scientific and Cultural Organization Route of Santiago de Compostela inscribed on the World Heritage List in 1993

特殊情况系列遗产或包含几个或不同原系或纪念地或地方

用途及目的	使用		授权		图形图例
世界遗产管理当局（读）	世界遗产点可使用的标识类型	世界遗产点使用标识的授权	世界遗产点可授权的标识	世界遗产点可授权的标识类型	世界遗产点可使用的标识类型
1. 非商业出版物 2. 交流材料 3. 网站、社会媒体、应用程序等 4. 交流产品（如T恤，包，伞）等非商业用途，为特别活动生产 5. 文具 6. 匾额，旗帜，横幅	联合国教科文组织或世界遗产－特别标识，加上前述“××××”（元素、纪念地、地方的名称）等部分	国家委员会或世界遗产中心			United Nations Educational, Scientific and Cultural Organization Shark Bay, Western Australia inscribed on the World Heritage List in 1991 “××遗产”之“××××”部分，××年列入世界遗产名录

World Heritage Advisory Bodies

Uses and purposes	Uses		Authorization		Graphic illustrations
Advisory Bodies	Type of Logo the Advisory Bodies can use	Use of the Logo by Advisory Bodies is authorized by	Advisory Bodies can authorize the Logo for	Type of Logo the Advisory Bodies can authorize	Logo to be used by the Advisory Bodies
1) Non-commercial publications 2) Non-commercial communication materials 3) Website 4) Non-commercial stationery	UNESCO/World Heritage Convention logo	World Heritage Centre			United Nations Educational, Scientific and Cultural Organization · World Heritage Convention
1) Publications 2) Communication materials 3) Website 4) Stationery	World Heritage Emblem	World Heritage Centre			or

世界遗产咨询机构

用途及目的	使用		授权		图形图例
咨询机构	咨询机构可使用的标识类型	咨询机构可使用的标识授权	咨询机构可授权的标识	咨询机构可授权的标识类型	咨询机构可使用的标识
1. 非商业出版物 2. 非商业交流材料 3. 网站 4. 非商业文具	联合国教科文组织及世界遗产公约标识	世界遗产中心			United Nations Educational, Scientific and Cultural Organization · World Heritage Convention
1. 非商业出版物 2. 交流材料 3. 网站 4. 文具	世界遗产徽章	世界遗产中心			or

PATRONAGE

Uses and purposes	Uses		Authorization		Graphic illustrations
Patronage			UNESCO Director-General can authorize	Type of Logo Director-General can authorize	Logo to be authorized
One-off activities (conferences, exhibitions, festivals, publications or audio-visual productions)			Organizing authorities	UNESCO/World Heritage logo with text ‘Under the patronage of’	UNESCO United Nations Educational, Scientific and Cultural Organization Under the patronage of World Heritage

赞助

用途及目的	使用		授权		图形图例
赞助			联合国教科文组织总干事授权	联合国教科文组织总干事可授权的标识类型	可授权的标识
赞助与世界遗产相关的一次性活动（国家或地区层面的会议、出版物或影像发行活动）			权威组织	联合国教科文组织或世界遗产标识加文字“由XXX赞助”	由XXX赞助 UNESCO United Nations Educational, Scientific and Cultural Organization Under the patronage of World Heritage

Select world heritage Bibliography

世界遗产相关的参考书目

World Heritage Centre Documents Database
http: //whc.unesco.org/statutorydoc

世界遗产中心文件数据库
http：//whc.unesco.org/statutorydoc

The UNESCO World Heritage Centre "Official Records" searchable online document collection permits the retrieval of information contained in the reports of the World Heritage Committee and General Assembly of States Parties to the Convention

世界遗产中心在线检索文件集"官方数据"获许对世界遗产委员会和缔约国大会报告中的信息进行检索。

Basic Texts

基础文件

UNESCO. 1972. *Convention concerning the Protection of the World Cultural and Natural Heritage*. (World Heritage Convention).
http: //whc.unesco.org/en/conventiontext

联合国教科文组织，1972 年，《保护世界文化与自然遗产公约》（世界遗产公约）

http：//whc.unesco.org/en/conventiontext

UNESCO General Assembly of States Parties to the Convention concerning the Protection of the World Cultural and Natural Heritage. 2014. *Rules of Procedure*. WHC-14/GA/1 Rev. 4 (as of 14 November 2014)
http: //whc.unesco.org/en/ga/

联合国教科文组织保护世界文化与自然遗产缔约国大会，2014 年，《程序规则》，WHC–14/GA/1 Rev.4（2014 年 11 月 14 日起）

http：//whc.unesco.org/en/ga/

UNESCO Intergovernmental Committee for the Protection of the World Cultural and Natural Heritage. 1995. *Financial Regulations for the World Heritage Fund*, Paris. (WHC/7, August 1995).
http: //whc.unesco.org/en/committeerules

联合国教科文组织保护世界文化与自然遗产政府间委员会，1995 年。《世界遗产基金财务规则》，巴黎（WHC/7，1995 年 8 月）

http：//whc.unesco.org/en/committeerules

UNESCO Intergovernmental Committee for the Protection of the World Cultural and Natural Heritage. 2013. *Rules of Procedure*, WHC-2013/5
http: //whc.unesco.org/en/committee

联合国教科文组织保护世界文化与自然遗产政府间委员会，2013 年。《程序规则》，WHC–2013/5
http：//whc.unesco.org/en/committee

UNESCO World Heritage Centre. 2017. *Basic Texts of the 1972 World Heritage Convention* (2017 Edition). Paris, UNESCO.

联合国教科文组织世界遗产中心，2017 年。《1972 年世界遗产公约的基础文件》（2017 版）。巴黎，联合国教科文组织。http：//whc.unesco.

http: //whc.unesco.org/en/basictexts/

UNESCO World Heritage Centre. *Properties inscribed on the World Heritage List*.

http: //whc.unesco.org/en/list

UNESCO World Heritage Centre. Tentative Lists.

http: //whc.unesco.org/en/tentativelists/

Strategic Documents

UNESCO World Heritage Committee, 1992. *Strategic Orientations*, in Annex II of the Report of the 16th Session of the World Heritage Committee, Santa Fe, 1992, (WHC-92/CONF.002/12).

http: //whc.unesco.org/en/documents/940

UNESCO World Heritage Committee. 1994. *Nara Document on Authenticity*.

http: //whc.unesco.org/archive/nara94.htm

UNESCO World Heritage Committee. 1996. *Report of the Expert Meeting on Evaluation of General Principles and Criteria for Nominations of Natural World Heritage sites*. (WHC-96/CONF.202/INF.9).

http: //whc.unesco.org/archive/1996/whc-96-conf202-inf9e.htm

http: //whc.unesco.org/archive/global94.htm

World Heritage Committee, Global Training Strategy for World Cultural and Natural Heritage, adopted by the World Heritage Committee at its 25th session (Annex X of WHC-01/CONF.208/24) - Update of the Global Training Strategy (Doc WHC-09/33.COM/10B). http: //whc.unesco.org/archive/2001/whc-01-conf208-24e.pdf

http: //whc.unesco.org/archive/2009/whc09-

org/en/basictexts/

联合国教科文组织世界遗产中心，《世界遗产名录》http ：//whc.unesco.org/en/list

联合国教科文组织世界遗产中心，《世界遗产预备名录》http ：//whc.unesco.org/en/tentativelists/

战略性文件

联合国教科文组织世界遗产委员会，1992年，《战略定位》，世界遗产委员会第16次会议报告附件2，圣达菲（WHC–92/CONF.002/12）.

http ：//whc.unesco.org/en/documents/940

联合国教科文组织世界遗产委员会，1994年，《奈良真实性文件》

http ：//whc.unesco.org/archive/nara94.htm

联合国教科文组织世界遗产委员会，1996年，《申报世界自然遗产一般原则和标准评估的专家会议报告》（WHC–96/CONF.202/INF.9）.

http ：//whc.unesco.org/archive/1996/whc–96–conf202–inf9e.htm

http ：//whc.unesco.org/archive/global94.htm

世界遗产委员会，《世界文化与自然遗产全球培训战略》，世界遗产委员会第25次会议通过（参见WHC–01/CONF.208/24附件10）–更新的全球培训战略（Doc WHC–09/33.COM/10B）.http ：//whc.unesco.org/archive/2001/whc–01–conf208–24e.pdf

http ：//whc.unesco.org/archive/2009/whc09–

33com-10Be.pdf

World Heritage Committee, 2002, *Budapest Declaration on World Heritage* (Doc WHC-02/CONF.202/5)

http: //whc/unesco.org/en/budapestdeclaration

UNESCO World Heritage Committee. 2004. Evaluation of the Global Strategy for a representative, balanced and credible World Heritage List (1994-2004). (Doc WHC-04/28.COM/13)

http: //whc.unesco.org/archive/2004/whc04-28com-13e.pdf

UNESCO World Heritage Comittee. 2005. Vienna Memorandum on World Heritage and Contemporary Architecture - Managing the Historic Urban Landscape. (Doc WHC-05/15.GA/INF.7).

http: //whc.unesco.org/archive/2005/whc05-15ga-inf7e.pdf

UNESCO World Heritage Committee. 2007. Strategy for Reducing Risks from Disasters at World Heritage Properties. (Doc WHC-07/31.COM/7.2)

http: //whc.unesco.org/archive/2007/whc07-31com-72e.pdf

UNESCO World Heritage Committee. 2007. *The 'fifth C' for 'Communities'*. (Doc WHC-07/31.COM/13B).

http: //whc.unesco.org/archive/2007/whc07-31com-13be.pdf

UNESCO World Heritage Centre. 2008. Policy Document on the Impacts of Climate Change on World Heritage Properties. Paris, UNESCO World Heritage Centre.

33com–10Be.pdf

世界遗产委员会，2002 年，《世界遗产布达佩斯宣言》，（文件 WHC–02/CONF.202/5）

http：//whc/unesco.org/en/budapestdeclaration

联合国教科文组织世界遗产委员会，2004，《有代表代表性、均衡性、可信性的世界遗产全球战略评估》（1994–2004）

（Doc WHC–04/28.COM/13）

http：//whc.unesco.org/archive/2004/whc04–28com–13e.pdf

联合国教科文组织世界遗产委员会，2005，《越南世界遗产和当代建筑——历史城镇景观管理备忘录》（Doc WHC–05/15.GA/INF.7）.

http：//whc.unesco.org/archive/2005/whc05–15ga–inf7e.pdf

联合国教科文组织世界遗产委员会，2007，《世界遗产减少灾害风险战略》。（Doc WHC–07/31.COM/7.2）

http：//whc.unesco.org/archive/2007/whc07–31com–72e.pdf

联合国教科文组织世界遗产委员会，2007，《社区的 5 “C”》（Doc WHC–07/31.COM/13B）.

http：//whc.unesco.org/archive/2007/whc07–31com–13be.pdf

联合国教科文组织世界遗产中心，2008，《气候变化对世界遗产影响的政策文件》。巴黎，

http：//whc.unesco.org/uploads/activities/documents/activity–397–2.pdf

UNESCO World Heritage Committee. 2010. *Reflection on the Trends of the State of Conservation*. (Doc WHC-10/34.COM/7C).

http: //whc.unesco.org/archive/2010/whc10-34com-7Ce.pdf

联合国教科文组织世界遗产委员会，2010，《保护状况趋势反思》。(Doc WHC–10/34.COM/7C）.

http：//whc.unesco.org/archive/2010/whc10–34com–7Ce.pdf

UNESCO World Heritage Committee. 2011. *World Heritage Convention and Sustainable Development*. (Doc WHC-11/35.COM/5E).

http: //whc.unesco.org/archive/2011/whc11-35com-5Ee.pdf

联合国教科文组织世界遗产委员会，2011，《世界遗产公约与可持续发展》。(Doc WHC–11/35.COM/5E）.

http：//whc.unesco.org/archive/2011/whc11–35com–5Ee.pdf

UNESCO World Heritage Committee. 2011. *Presentation and adoption of the World Heritage strategy for capacity building*. (Doc WHC-11/35.COM/9B).

http: //whc.unesco.org/archive/2011/whc11-35com-9Be.pdf

联合国教科文组织世界遗产委员会，2011，《展示和采纳世界遗产能力建设战略》。(Doc WHC–11/35.COM/9B）.

http：//whc.unesco.org/archive/2011/whc11–35com–9Be.pdf

UNESCO World Heritage Committee. 2012. *World Heritage Tourism Programme*. (Doc WHC-12/36.COM/5E).

http: //whc.unesco.org/archive/2012/whc12-36com-5E-en.pdf

联合国教科文组织世界遗产委员会，2011，《世界遗产旅游项目》(Doc WHC–12/36.COM/5E）.

http：//whc.unesco.org/archive/2012/whc12–36com–5E–en.pdf

UNESCO World Heritage Committee. 2013. *Revised Partnerships for Conservation (PACT) Initiative Strategy*. (Doc WHC-13/37.COM/5D).

http: //whc.unesco.org/archive/2013/whc13-37com-5D-en.pdf

联合国教科文组织世界遗产委员会，2013，《修订保护伙伴关系的战略倡议》。(Doc WHC–13/37.COM/5D）.

http：//whc.unesco.org/archive/2013/whc13–37com–5D–en.pdf

World Heritage Resource Manuals

http: //whc.unesco.org/en/resourcemanuals/

世界遗产资源手册

http：//whc.unesco.org/en/resourcemanuals/

UNESCO, ICCROM, ICOMOS and IUCN. 2010. *Managing Disaster Risks for World Heritage*. Paris, UNESCO World Heritage Centre.

http: //whc.unesco.org/en/managing-disaster-risks/

联合国教科文组织，国际文物保护与修复研究中心，国际古迹遗址理事会，世界自然保护联盟，2010，《世界遗产灾害风险管理》。巴黎，世界遗产中心。http：//whc.unesco.org/en/managing–disaster–risks/

UNESCO, ICCROM, ICOMOS and IUCN. 2011. *Preparing World Heritage Nominations.* (Second edition). Paris, UNESCO World Heritage Centre.

http: //whc.unesco.org/en/preparing-world-heritage-nominations/

联合国教科文组织，国际文物保护与修复研究中心，国际古迹遗址理事会，世界自然保护联盟，2011，《世界遗产申报》（第 2 版）。巴黎，世界遗产中心。http：//whc.unesco.org/en/preparing–world–heritage–nominations/

UNESCO, ICCROM, ICOMOS and IUCN. 2012. *Managing Natural World Heritage.* Paris, UNESCO World Heritage Centre.

http: //whc.unesco.org/en/managing-natural-world-heritage/

联合国教科文组织，国际文物保护与修复研究中心，国际古迹遗址理事会，世界自然保护联盟，2012，《世界自然遗产管理》。巴黎，世界遗产中心。http：//whc.unesco.org/en/managing–natural–world–heritage/

UNESCO, ICCROM, ICOMOS and IUCN. 2013. *Managing Cultural World Heritage.* Paris, UNESCO World Heritage Centre.

http: //whc.unesco.org/en/managing-cultural-world-heritage/

联合国教科文组织，国际文物保护与修复研究中心，国际古迹遗址理事会，世界自然保护联盟，2013，《世界文化遗产管理》。巴黎，世界遗产中心。

http：//whc.unesco.org/en/managing–cultural–world–heritage/

World Heritage Review

http: //whc.unesco.org/en/review/

《世界遗产》回顾

http：//whc.unesco.org/en/review/

World Heritage is a quarterly review produced in English, French and Spanish by the UNESCO World Heritage Centre, featuring in-depth articles on world heritage-related issues and inscribed sites. 76 issues published since 1996.

《世界遗产》由世界遗产中心用英语、法语和西班牙语制作的季刊，发行有特点有深度的文章 – 与世界遗产相关问题或录入名录的遗产。自 1996 起已发行 76 期。

World Heritage Paper Series

http: //whc.unesco.org/en/series/

世界遗产论文系列

http：//whc.unesco.org/en/series/

UNESCO, World Heritage Centre, Paris 2002. *Managing Tourism at World Heritage Sites: a Practical Manual for World Heritage site managers, Paris, UNESCO World Heritage Centre. (World Heritage Manual 1.)*

http: //whc.unesco.org/en/series/1/

联合国教科文组织世界遗产中心，巴黎，2002 年《世界遗产地旅游管理：世界遗产地管理实践手册》，（世界遗产手册 1.）

http：//whc.unesco.org/en/series/1/

UNESCO World Heritage Centre. 2002.

联合国教科文组织世界遗产中心，巴黎，

Investing in World Heritage: Past Achievements, Future Ambitions, World Heritage Paper No. 2, UNESCO, World Heritage Centre, Paris 2002.
http: //whc.unesco.org/en/series/2/

2002 年《投资世界遗产：过去的成果，未来的希望》世界遗产论文集 2，
http ：//whc.unesco.org/en/series/2/

UNESCO World Heritage Centre. 2003. *Periodic Report Africa*, World Heritage Report No. 3, UNESCO, World Heritage Centre, Paris 2003.
http: //whc.unesco.org/en/series/3

联合国教科文组织世界遗产中心，巴黎，2003 年，《非洲定期报告》，世界遗产报告 3，http ：//whc.unesco.org/en/series/3

Hillary, A., Kokkonen, M. and Max, L., (edited by), 2003. *Proceedings of the World Heritage Marine Biodiversity Workshop*, UNESCO World Heritage Centre.World Heritage Paper No. 4,
http: //whc.unesco.org/en/series/4/

Hillary，A.，Kokkonen，M. 与 Max，L.（编辑）《世界遗产海洋生物多样性研讨会论文集》，联合国教科文组织世界遗产中心，2003 年，世界遗产论文 4，
http ：//whc.unesco.org/en/series/4/

UNESCO, World Heritage Centre, 2003. *Identification and Documentation of Modern Heritage*, Paris. UNESCO, World Heritage Centre, (World Heritage Paper No. 5,)
http: //whc.unesco.org/en/series/5/

联合国教科文组织世界遗产中心，2003 年，《现代遗产的确认与文献记录》，（世界遗产论文 5，）
http ：//whc.unesco.org/en/series/5/

Fowler, P. J., (edited by), *World Heritage Cultural Landscapes 1992-2002*, UNESCO, World Heritage Centre, Paris. (World Heritage Paper No. 6,)
http: //whc.unesco.org/en/series/6/

Fowler，P.J.（编辑）《1992–2002 年世界遗产文化景观》，巴黎，联合国教科文组织世界遗产中心，（世界遗产论文 6）
http ：//whc.unesco.org/en/series/6/

UNESCO, World Heritage Centre, 2003. *Cultural Landscapes: the Challenges of Conservation*, Paris, UNESCO, World Heritage Centre 2003. (World Heritage Paper No. 7,)
http: //whc.unesco.org/en/series/7/

联合国教科文组织世界遗产中心，巴黎，2003 年，《文化景观：遗产保护的挑战》，（世界遗产论文 7，）http ：//whc.unesco.org/en/series/7/

UNESCO, World Heritage Centre, 2003. *Mobilizing Young People for World Heritage*, Paris , UNESCO, World Heritage Centre, (World Heritage Paper No. 8,)
http: //whc.unesco.org/en/series/8/

联合国教科文组织世界遗产中心，巴黎，2003 年《动员年轻人保护世界遗产》，（世界遗产论文 8，）
http ：//whc.unesco.org/en/series/8/

UNESCO, World Heritage Centre, 2004.

联合国教科文组织世界遗产中心，巴黎，

Partnerships for World Heritage Cities: Culture as a Vector for Sustainable Urban Development, Paris UNESCO, World Heritage Centre, (World Heritage Paper No. 9,)

http: //whc.unesco.org/en/series/9/

2004 年《世界遗产城市合作：文化作为城市可持续发展之桥梁》,（世界遗产论文 9,）

http：//whc.unesco.org/en/series/9/

Stovel, H. (ed). 2004.*Monitoring World Heritage*, UNESCO, World Heritage Centre, Paris 2004. (World Heritage Paper No. 10,)

http: //whc.unesco.org/en/series/10/

Stovel，H.（ed）.《世界遗产监测》，联合国教科文组织世界遗产中心，巴黎，2004 年 .（世界遗产论文 10,）

http：//whc.unesco.org/en/series/10/

UNESCO, World Heritage Centre, Paris 2004. *Periodic Report and Regional Programme Arab States 2000-2003*, UNESCO, World Heritage Centre. (World Heritage Paper No. 11,)

http: //whc.unesco.org/en/series/11/

联合国教科文组织世界遗产中心，巴黎，2004 年《2000–2003 年定期报告与地区项目 – 阿拉伯国家》,（世界遗产报告 11,）

http：//whc.unesco.org/en/series/11/

UNESCO, World Heritage Centre, 2004.T*he State of World Heritage in the Asia-Pacific Region - 2003*, UNESCO, World Heritage Centre, Paris. (World Heritage Paper No. 12,)

http: //whc.unesco.org/en/series/12/

联合国教科文组织世界遗产中心，巴黎，2004 年《2003 年亚太地区世界遗产状况》，联合国教科文组织世界遗产中心，巴黎，（世界遗产论文 12）

http：//whc.unesco.org/en/series/12/

de Merode, E., Smeets, R. and Westrik, C. 2004. *Linking Universal and Local Values: Managing a Sustainable Future for World Heritage*, UNESCO, World Heritage Centre, Paris, (World Heritage Paper No. 13,)

http: //whc.unesco.org/en/series/13/

de Merode，E.，Smeets，R.and Westrik，C.2004.《全球与地区价值观的结合：管理世界遗产可持续发展的未来》，联合国教科文组织世界遗产中心，巴黎，（世界遗产论文 13）

http：//whc.unesco.org/en/series/13/

UNESCO World Heritage Centre. 2005. *Caribbean Archaeology and World Heritage Convention*. Paris, UNESCO World Heritage Centre. (World Heritage Papers 14.)

http: //whc.unesco.org/en/series/14/

联合国教科文组织世界遗产中心，2005.《加勒比海地区考古与世界遗产公约》。巴黎，（世界遗产论文 14）

http：//whc.unesco.org/en/series/14/

UNESCO World Heritage Centre. 2005. *Caribbean Wooden Treasures*. Paris, UNESCO World Heritage Centre. (World Heritage Papers 15.)

http: //whc.unesco.org/en/series/15/

联合国教科文组织世界遗产中心，2005.《加勒比海地区木质瑰宝》巴黎。（世界遗产论文 15）

http：//whc.unesco.org/en/series/15/

UNESCO World Heritage Centre. 2005. *World Heritage at the Vth IUCN World Parks Congress*. Paris, UNESCO World Heritage Centre. (World Heritage Reports 16.)

http: //whc.unesco.org/en/series/16/

联合国教科文组织世界遗产中心，2005.《世界自然保护联盟第五届世界公园大会之世界遗产》。（世界遗产报告 16）

http ： //whc.unesco.org/en/series/16/

UNESCO World Heritage Centre. 2005. *Promoting and Preserving Congolese Heritage*. Paris, UNESCO World Heritage Centre. (World Heritage Papers 17.)

http: //whc.unesco.org/en/series/17

联合国教科文组织世界遗产中心，2005.《促进和维护刚果遗产》，巴黎，（世界遗产论文 17）

http ： //whc.unesco.org/en/series/17/

UNESCO World Heritage Centre. 2006. *Periodic Report 2004- Latin America and the Caribbean*. Paris, UNESCO World Heritage Centre. (World Heritage Papers 18.)

http: //whc.unesco.org/en/series/18

联合国教科文组织世界遗产中心，2006.《拉丁美洲及加勒比海地区 2004 年定期报告》。巴黎，（世界遗产论文 18）

http ： //whc.unesco.org/en/series/18/

UNESCO World Heritage Centre. 2006. *American Fortifications and the World Heritage Convention*. Paris, UNESCO World Heritage Centre. (World Heritage Papers 19.)

http: //whc.unesco.org/en/series/19/

联合国教科文组织世界遗产中心，2006.《美洲防御要塞与世界遗产公约》，巴黎，（世界遗产论文 19）

http ： //whc.unesco.org/en/series/19/

UNESCO World Heritage Centre. 2006. *Periodic Report and Action Plan, Europe 2005-2006*. Paris, UNESCO World Heritage Centre. (World Heritage Reports 20.)

http: //whc.unesco.org/en/series/20/

联合国教科文组织世界遗产中心，2006.《2005–2006 年欧洲定期报告与行动计划》，巴黎，（世界遗产报告 20）

http ： //whc.unesco.org/en/series/20/

UNESCO World Heritage Centre. 2007. *World Heritage Forests - Leveraging Conservation at the Landscape Level*. Paris, UNESCO World Heritage Centre. (World Heritage Reports 21.)

http: //whc.unesco.org/en/series/21/

联合国教科文组织世界遗产中心，2007.《森林世界遗产 – 景观层面的利用保护》。（世界遗产报告 21）

http ： //whc.unesco.org/en/series/21/

UNESCO World Heritage Centre. 2007. *Climate Change and World Heritage*. Paris, UNESCO World Heritage Centre. (World Heritage

联合国教科文组织世界遗产中心，2007.《气候变化与世界遗产》。巴黎，（世界遗产报告 22）

Reports 22.)

http: //whc.unesco.org/en/series/22/

http：//whc.unesco.org/en/series/22/

Hockings, M., James, R., Stolton, S., Dudley, N., Mathur, V., Makombo, J., Courrau, J. and Parrish, J. 2008. *Enhancing our Heritage Toolkit. Assessing management effectiveness of Natural World Heritage sites*. Paris, UNESCO World Heritage Centre. (World Heritage Papers 23.)

http: //whc.unesco.org/en/series/23/

Hockings，M.，James，R.，Stolton，S.，Dudley，N.，Mathur，V.，Makombo，J.，Courrau，J.and Parrish，J.2008 年，《优化遗产管理工具包。世界自然遗产管理有效性评估》。联合国教科文组织世界遗产中心，巴黎，（世界遗产论文 23）http：//whc.unesco.org/en/series/23/

UNESCO World Heritage Centre. 2008. *Rock Art in the Caribbean*. Paris, UNESCO World Heritage Centre. (World Heritage Papers 24.)

http: //whc.unesco.org/en/series/24/

联合国教科文组织世界遗产中心，2008.《加勒比海地区岩画艺术》，巴黎，（世界遗产论文 24）。

http：//whc.unesco.org/en/series/24/

Martin, O. and Piatti, G. (eds). 2009. *World Heritage and Buffer Zones, International Expert Meeting on World Heritage and Buffer Zones*, Davos, Switzerland, 11-14 March 2008. Paris, UNESCO World Heritage Centre. (World Heritage Papers 25.)

http: //whc.unesco.org/en/series/25/

Martin，O.and Piatti，G.（eds）.2009 年，《世界遗产及缓冲区，世界遗产及缓冲区国际专家会议》，瑞士，达沃斯，2008 年 3 月 11——14 日。巴黎，联合国教科文组织世界遗产中心（世界遗产论文 25）http：//whc.unesco.org/en/series/25

Mitchell, N., Rössler, M. and Tricaud, P-M. (authors/eds). 2009. *World Heritage Cultural Landscapes: A handbook for Conservation and Management*. Paris, UNESCO World Heritage Centre. (World Heritage Papers 26.)

http: //whc.unesco.org/en/series/26/

Mitchell，N.，R ssler，M.and Tricaud，P–M.（Authors/eds）.2009 年，《世界遗产文化景观：管理与保护手册》巴黎，联合国教科文组织世界遗产中心（世界遗产论文 26）http：//whc.unesco.org/en/series/26/

UNESCO World Heritage Centre. 2010. *Managing Historic Cities*. Paris, UNESCO World Heritage Centre. (World Heritage Papers 27.)

http: //whc.unesco.org/en/series/27/

联合国教科文组织世界遗产中心，2010 年。《历史城市管理》。巴黎，（世界遗产论文 27）http：//whc.unesco.org/en/series/27/

UNESCO World Heritage Centre. 2011. *Navigating the Future of Marine World Heritage*. Paris, UNESCO World Heritage Centre. (World Heritage Papers 28.)

http: //whc.unesco.org/en/series/28/

联合国教科文组织世界遗产中心，2011 年.《海洋世界遗产未来航向》，巴黎，（世界遗产论文 28）

http：//whc.unesco.org/en/series/28/

UNESCO World Heritage Centre. 2011. *Human Evolution: Adaptations, Dispersals and Social Developments* (HEADS). Paris, UNESCO World Heritage Centre. (World Heritage Papers 29.)

http: //whc.unesco.org/en/series/29/

联合国教科文组织世界遗产中心，2011 年《人类进化：适应，分散及社会发展》(HEADS)，巴黎，（世界遗产论文 29）

http：//whc.unesco.org/en/series/29/

UNESCO World Heritage Centre. 2011. *Adapting to Change: the State of Conservation of World Heritage Forests in 2011*. Paris, UNESCO World Heritage Centre. (World Heritage Papers 30.)

http: //whc.unesco.org/en/series/30/

联合国教科文组织世界遗产中心，2011 年，《适应变化：2011 年世界森林遗产保护状况》，巴黎，（世界遗产论文 30）http：//whc.unesco.org/en/series/30/

Albert, M.-T., Richon, M., Viňals, M.J. and Witcomb, A. (eds). 2012. *Community development through World Heritage*. Paris, UNESCO World Heritage Centre. (World Heritage Papers 31.)

http: //whc.unesco.org/en/series/31/

Albert，M.–T.，Richon，M.，Viňals，M.J.and Witcomb，A.（eds），2012 年，《世界遗产社区发展》，巴黎，联合国教科文组织世界遗产中心（世界遗产论文 31）

http：//whc.unesco.org/en/series/31/

Church, J., Gabrié, C., Macharia, D., Obura, D. 2012. *Assessing Marine World Heritage from an Ecosystem Perspective*. Paris, UNESCO World Heritage Centre. (World Heritage Papers 32.)

http: //whc.unesco.org/en/series/32/

Church，J.，Gabrié，C.，Macharia，D.，Obura，D.2012.《从生态系统观点评估海洋世界遗产》巴黎，联合国教科文组织世界遗产中心（世界遗产论文 32）

http：//whc.unesco.org/en/series/32/

UNESCO World Heritage Centre. 2012. HEADS 2: *Human Origin Sites and the World Heritage Convention in Africa*. Paris, UNESCO World Heritage Centre. (World Heritage Papers 33.)

http: //whc.unesco.org/en/series/33/

联合国教科文组织世界遗产中心，2012 年 HEADS2，:《人类起源地和非洲世界遗产公约》，巴黎，（世界遗产论文 33）http：//whc.unesco.org/en/series/33/

UNESCO World Heritage Centre. 2012. *World Heritage in a Sea of Islands - Pacific 2009 Programme. Paris*, UNESCO World Heritage Centre. (World Heritage Papers 34.)

http: //whc.unesco.org/en/series/34/

联合国教科文组织世界遗产中心，2012 年。《海洋和岛屿世界遗产 –2009 年太平洋项目》，巴黎，（世界遗产论文 34）

http：//whc.unesco.org/en/series/34/

Dingwall, P., Kawakami, K., Weise, K. 2012. *Understanding World Heritage in Asia and the Pacific - The Second Cycle of Periodic Reporting 2010-2012*. Paris, UNESCO World Heritage Centre.

Dingwall，P.，Kawakami，K.，Weise，K.2012.《理解亚洲太平洋地区世界遗产 –2010–2012 年第二轮定期报告》，巴黎，联合国教科文组织世界遗产中心，（世界遗产论文 35）

(World Heritage Papers 35.)

http: //whc.unesco.org/en/series/35/

http ：//whc.unesco.org/en/series/35/

Joffroy, T., Eloundou, L. (eds.). 2013. *Earthern Architecture in Today's World*. Paris, UNESCO World Heritage Centre. (World Heritage Papers 36.)

http: //whc.unesco.org/en/series/36/

Joffroy，T.，Eloundou，L.（eds.）.2013.《当今世界的土建筑》，巴黎，联合国教科文组织世界遗产中心，（世界遗产论文 36）

http ：//whc.unesco.org/en/series/36/

Falzon, C., Perry, J. 2014. *Climate Change Adaptation for Natural World Heritage Sites*. Paris, UNESCO World Heritage Centre. (World Heritage Papers 37.)

http: //whc.unesco.org/en/series/37/

Falzon，C.，Perry，J.2014.《世界自然遗产气候变化适应性》，巴黎，联合国教科文组织世界遗产中心，（世界遗产论文 37）

http ：//whc.unesco.org/en/series/37/

UNESCO World Heritage Centre. 2014. *Safeguarding Precious Resources for Island Communities*. Paris, UNESCO World Heritage Centre. (World Heritage Papers 38.)

http: //whc.unesco.org/en/series/38/

联合国教科文组织世界遗产中心，2014，《保护岛屿区域珍稀资源》巴黎，（世界遗产论文 38）

http ：//whc.unesco.org/en/series/38/

UNESCO World Heritage Centre. 2014. HEADS 3: *Human Origin Sites and the World Heritage Convention in Asia*. Paris, UNESCO World Heritage Centre. (World Heritage Papers 39.)

http: //whc.unesco.org/en/series/39/

联合国教科文组织世界遗产中心，2012 年 HEADS3，：《人类起源地和亚洲世界遗产公约》，巴黎，（世界遗产论文 39）

http ：//whc.unesco.org/en/series/39/

Brown, J., Hay-Edie, T. 2014. *Engaging Local Communities in Stewardship of World Heritage*. Paris, UNESCO World Heritage Centre. (World Heritage Papers 40.)

http: //whc.unesco.org/en/series/40/

Brown，J.，Hay-Edie，T.2014.《吸引社区参与遗产管理》巴黎，联合国教科文组织世界遗产中心，（世界遗产论文 40）

http ：//whc.unesco.org/en/series/40/

General and Thematic References

一般及主题研究参考

Badman, T., Bomhard, B. and Dingwall, P. 2008. *World Heritage Nominations for Natural Properties: A Resource Manual for Practitioners*. Gland, Switzerland, IUCN.

Badman，T.，Bomhard，B.and Dingwall，P.2008.《申报世界自然遗产：实践者资源手册》，瑞士格兰德，世界自然保护联盟。

Batisse, M., Bolla, G. 2005. *The Invention of*

Batisse，M.，Bolla，G.2005.《创造世界遗

World Heritage. Paris, UNESCO.

产》，巴黎，联合国教科文组织。

Cameron, C. 2005. *Background Paper for the Special Expert Meeting of the World Heritage Convention: The Concept of Outstanding Universal Value*. Kazan, Republic of Tatarstan, Russian Federation.

http: //whc.unesco.org/archive/2005/whc05-29com-inf09Ae.pdf

Cameron，C.2005《世界遗产公约特别专家会议背景论文：突出普遍价值概念》。喀山，俄罗斯联邦鞑靼斯坦共和国。

http：//whc.unesco.org/archive/2005/whc05-29com-inf09Ae.pdf

Cameron, C., Rössler, M. 2013. *Many Voices, One Vision: The Early Years of the World Heritage Convention*. Farnham, Ashgate.

Cameron，C.，Rössler，M.2013.《不同声音，一个愿景：早期世界遗产公约》法纳姆，阿什盖特。

Galla, A. (ed.). 2012. *World Heritage - Benefits Beyond Borders. Paris/Cambridge,* UNESCO Publishing/Cambridge University Press.

Galla，A.（ed.）.2012.《世界遗产－跨国界优势》巴黎及剑桥，联合国教科文组织出版，剑桥大学出版社。

Feilden, B.M. and Jokilehto, J. 1993. *Management Guidelines for World Cultural Heritage Sites*. (First edition). Rome, ICCROM.

Feilden，B.M.and Jokilehto，J.1993.《世界文化遗产管理指南》（第一版），罗马，国际文物保护与修复研究中心。

Francioni, F. (ed). 2008. *The 1972 World Heritage Convention: A Commentary*. Oxford Commentaries on International Law, UK.

Francioni，F.（ed）.2008.《1972年世界遗产公约评注》。牛津国际法评注，英国。

ICOMOS. 1965. *International Charter for the Conservation and Restoration of Monuments and Sites* (The Venice Charter 1964). Paris, ICOMOS.

http: //www.icomos.org/venice_charter.html

国际古迹遗址理事会，1965，《关于古迹遗址保护与修复的国际宪章》（1964年威尼斯宪章）。巴黎，

http：//www.icomos.org/venice_charter.html

ICOMOS. 2004. *ICOMOS Analysis of the World Heritage List and Tentative Lists and Follow-Up Action Plan*. Paris, ICOMOS.

国际古迹遗址理事会，2004，《国际古迹遗址理事会世界遗产名录、预备名录及后续行动计划分析》。

ICOMOS. 2005. *The World Heritage List: Filling the Gaps - An Action Plan for the Future*. Paris, ICOMOS.

http: //www.international.icomos.org/world_heritage/gaps.pdf

国际古迹遗址理事会，2005，《世界遗产名录：缩小差距－未来行动计划》。巴黎

http：//www.international.icomos.org/world_heritage/gaps.pdf

ICOMOS. 2005. *Xi'an Declaration on the Conservation of the Setting of Heritage Structures, Sites and Areas*.

http: //www.international.icomos.org/charters/xian-declaration.pdf

国际古迹遗址理事会，2005，《保护遗产及遗产结构周边环境的西安宣言》

http：//www.international.icomos.org/charters/xian–declaration.pdf

ICOMOS. 2008. *Compendium on Standards for the Inscription of Cultural Properties to the World Heritage List*.

http: //whc.unesco.org/en/sessions/32COM/documents/

国际古迹遗址理事会，2008.《文化遗产录入世界遗产名录的标准概要》

http：//whc.unesco.org/en/sessions/32COM/documents/

ICOMOS. 2011. *Guidance on Heritage Impact Assessments for Cultural World Heritage Properties*. Paris, ICOMOS.

http: //openarchive.icomos.org/266/1/ICOMOS_Heritage_Impact_Assessment_2010.pdf

国际古迹遗址理事会，2011，《世界文化遗产影响评估指导》。巴黎

http：//openarchive.icomos.org/266/1/ICOMOS_Heritage_Impact_Assessment_2010.pdf

ICOMOS technical and thematic studies

http: //www.icomos.org/en/documentation-center

国际古迹遗址理事会技术和主题研究 http：//www.icomos.org/en/documentation–center

IUCN. 2006. *Enhancing the IUCN Evaluation Process of World Heritage Nominations: A Contribution to Achieving a Credible and Balanced World Heritage List*.

https: //portals.iucn.org/library/efiles/documents/2006-059.pdf

世界自然保护联盟，2006，《强化世界自然保护联盟的世界遗产申报评估程序：对实现世界遗产名录可信性和平衡性的贡献》https：//portals.iucn.org/library/efiles/documents/2006–059.pdf

IUCN. 2006. *The World Heritage List: Guidance and Future Priorities for Identifying Natural Heritage of Potential Outstanding Universal Value*.

http: //cmsdata.iucn.org/downloads/ouv2006_english.pdf

世界自然保护联盟，2006，《世界遗产名录：指导和未来优先辨别自然遗产的潜在突出普遍价值》。

http：//cmsdata.iucn.org/downloads/ouv2006_english.pdf

IUCN. 2008. *Outstanding Universal Value - Standards for Natural World Heritage, A Compendium on Standards for Inscriptions of Natural Properties*

世界自然保护联盟，2008，《突出普遍价值–世界自然遗产标准，自然遗产录入世界遗产名录标准概要》

on the World Heritage List.

http: //cmsdata.iucn.org/downloads/ouv_compendium_english.pdf

http：//cmsdata.iucn.org/downloads/ouv_compendium_english.pdf

IUCN Technical and Thematic Studies:

http: //www.iucn.org/knowledge/publications_doc/

世界自然保护联盟技术和主题研究

http：//www.iucn.org/knowledge/publications_doc/

Pressouyre, L. 1993. *The World Heritage Convention, twenty years later*. UNESCO, Paris.

http: //whc.unesco.org/en/280/? id=564&

Pressouyre，L.1993.《世界遗产公约 20 年》。联合国教科文组织，巴黎。

http：//whc.unesco.org/en/280/？ id=564&

Stovel, H. 1998. *Risk Preparedness: A Management Manual for World Cultural Heritage*. Rome, ICCROM.

http: //www.iccrom.org/pdf/ICCROM_17_RiskPreparedness_en.pdf

Stovel，H.1998.《风险准备：世界文化遗产管理手册》。罗马，国际文物保护与修复研究中心。

http：//www.iccrom.org/pdf/ICCROM_17_RiskPreparedness_en.pdf

UNESCO World Heritage Centre. Education Kit. 2002. *World Heritage in Young Hands*. Paris, UNESCO World Heritage Centre.

http: //whc.unesco.org/en/educationkit/

联合国教科文组织世界遗产中心，教育配套，2002，《世界遗产在年轻人手中》。巴黎。

http：//whc.unesco.org/en/educationkit/

UNESCO World Heritage Centre. 2003. *World Heritage 2002 - Shared Legacy, Common Responsibility*. Paris, UNESCO World Heritage Centre.

http: //whc.unesco.org/en/activities/563/

联合国教科文组织世界遗产中心，2003，《2002 年的世界遗产：共同的遗产，共同的责任》。巴黎。

http：//whc.unesco.org/en/activities/563/

UNESCO World Heritage Centre. 2007. *World Heritage - Challenges for the Millenium*. Paris, UNESCO World Heritage Centre.

http: //whc.unesco.org/en/challenges-for-the-Millennium/

联合国教科文组织世界遗产中心，2007，《世界遗产 – 千年挑战》。巴黎。

http：//whc.unesco.org/en/challenges–for–the–Millennium/

UNESCO World Heritage Centre. 2007. *Case Studies on Climate Change and World Heritage*. Paris, UNESCO World Heritage Centre.

http: //whc.unesco.org/en/activities/473/

联合国教科文组织世界遗产中心，2007。《气候变化与世界遗产研究案例》。巴黎。http：//whc.unesco.org/en/activities/473/

UNESCO World Heritage Centre. 2012. African World Heritage - A Remarkable Diversity. Paris, UNESCO World Heritage Centre.

联合国教科文组织世界遗产中心，2012.《非洲世界遗产 – 显著的多样性》。巴黎。

UNESCO World Heritage Centre. 2013. *Celebrating 40 years of the World Heritage Convention*. Paris, UNESCO World Heritage Centre.

http: //whc.unesco.org/en/celebrating-40-years

联合国教科文组织世界遗产中心，2013.《庆祝世界遗产公约 40 周年》。巴黎。

http：//whc.unesco.org/en/celebrating–40–years

UNESCO World Heritage Centre. 2013. *Report of the 40th Anniversary of the World Heritage Convention*. Paris, UNESCO World Heritage Centre.

http: //whc.unesco.org/en/report-40th-Anniversary

联合国教科文组织世界遗产中心，2013。《世界遗产 40 周年报告》。巴黎。

http：//whc.unesco.org/en/report–40th–Anniversary

UNESCO World Heritage Centre. *Patrimonito's World Heritage Adventures*. Paris, UNESCO World Heritage Centre.

http: //whc.unesco.org/en/patrimonito/

联合国教科文组织世界遗产中心。《帕特里莫尼托（世界遗产青年保护者）世界遗产探秘》

http：//whc.unesco.org/en/patrimonito/

von Droste, B., Plachter, H. and Rössler, M. (eds.). 1995. *Cultural Landscapes of Universal Value: Components of a Global Strategy*, Jena (Germany), Fischer Verlag.

von Droste，B.，Plachter，H.and Rössler，M.（eds.）.1995.《文化景观的普遍价值：全球战略的组成部分。》Jena（Germany），Fischer Verlag 出版。

von Droste, B., Rössler, M. and Titchen, S. (eds.). 1999. *Linking Nature and Culture*, Report of the Global Strategy Natural and Cultural Heritage Expert Meeting, 25-29 March 1998, Amsterdam, The Netherlands, UNESCO/ Ministry for Foreign Affairs/Ministry for Education, Science, and Culture, The Hague.

http: //whc.unesco.org/archive/amsterdam98.pdf

von Droste，B.，Rössler，M.and Titchen，S.（eds.）.1999.《联系自然与文化》，自然与文化遗产全球战略专家会议报告 1998 年 3 月 25–29 日），荷兰阿姆斯特丹，联合国教科文组织及海牙外交部、教育、科学、文化部。http：//whc.unesco.org/archive/amsterdam98.pdf

World Commission on Protected Areas (WCPA) Best Practice Guidelines

www.iucn.org/about/union/commissions/wcpa/

世界保护区委员会（WCPA）
最佳实践指南

www.iucn.org/about/union/commissions/wcpa/

wcpa_puball/wcpa_bpg/

• National System Planning for Protected Areas, 1998

• Economic Values of Protected Areas: Guidelines for Protected Area Managers, 1998

• Guidelines for Marine Protected Areas, 1999

• Indigenous and Traditional Peoples and Protected Areas, 2000

• Financing Protected Areas: Guidelines for Protected Area Managers, 2000

• trans-boundary Protected Areas for Peace and Co-operation, 2001

• Sustainable Tourism in Protected Areas: Guidelines for Planning and Management, 2002

• Management Guidelines for IUCN Category V Protected Areas: Protected Landscapes/ Seascapes, 2002

• Guidelines for Management Planning of Protected Areas, 2003

• Indigenous and Local Communities and Protected Areas: Towards Equity and Enhanced Conservation, 2004

• Forests and Protected Areas: Guidance on the use of the IUCN protected area management categories, 2006

• Sustainable Financing of Protected Areas: A global review of challenges and options, 2006

• Evaluating Effectiveness: A Framework for Assessing Management Effectiveness of Protected Areas, 2006

• Identification and Gap Analysis of Key Biodiversity Areas, 2007

• Sacred Natural Sites: Guidelines for Protected Area Managers, 2008

Web Addresses

UNESCO

http: //www.unesco.org

wcpa_puball/wcpa_bpg/

• 国家保护区系统规划，1998

• 保护区经济价值：保护区管理者指南，1998

• 海洋保护区指南，1999

• 原住民和保护区，2000

• 保护区经济：保护区管理者指南，2000

• 跨界保护区的和平与合作，2001

• 保护区可持续旅游：规划管理指南，2002

• 世界自然保护联盟5类保护区管理指南：保护陆地和海洋景观，2002

• 保护区管理规划指南，2003

• 原住民和当地社区及保护区：趋于平等和强化保护，2004

• 森林和保护区：世界自然保护联盟保护区管理分类应用指导》，2006

• 保护区的可持续经济：全球挑战和选择述评，2006

• 有效性评估：保护区管理有效评估框架，2006

• 主要生物多样性地区辨别和差异分析，2007

• 自然圣境：保护区管理者指南，2008

网址

联合国教科文组织 http ：//www.unesco.org

UNESCO World Heritage Centre
http: //whc.unesco.org

联合国教科文组织世界遗产中心 http：//whc.unesco.org

UNESCO World Heritage Centre publications
http: //whc.unesco.org/en/publications/

联合国教科文组织世界遗产出版物 http：//whc.unesco.org/en/publications/

UNESCO World Heritage Review
http: //whc.unesco.org/en/review/

联合国教科文组织世界遗产审核 http：//whc.unesco.org/en/review/

UNESCO World Heritage Map
http: //whc.unesco.org/en/map/

联合国教科文组织世界遗产地图 http：//whc.unesco.org/en/map/

ICCROM
http: //www.iccrom.org

国际文物保护与修复研究中心 http：//www.iccrom.org

ICCROM publications
http: //www.archivalplatform.org/resources/entry/iccrom_publications/

国际文物保护与修复研究中心出版物
http：//www.archivalplatform.org/resources/entry/iccrom_publications/

ICOMOS
http: //www.icomos.org

国际古迹遗址理事会
http：//www.icomos.org

ICOMOS publications
http: //www.icomos.org/en/documentation-center

国际古迹遗址理事会出版物 http：//www.icomos.org/en/documentation–center

IUCN
http: //www.iucn.org
IUCN publications
http: //www.iucn.org/knowledge/publications_doc/

世界自然保护联盟 http：//www.iucn.org

世界自然保护联盟出版物 http：//www.iucn.org/knowledge/publications_doc/

World Commission on Protected Areas (WCPA) Best Practice Guidelines
www.iucn.org/about/union/commissions/wcpa/wcpa_puball/wcpa_bpg/

世界保护区委员会（WCPA）
最佳实践指南
www.iucn.org/about/union/commissions/wcpa/wcpa_puball/wcpa_bpg/

POSTSCRIPT

The United Nations Educational, Scientific and Cultural Organization (UNESCO) was founded on 16 November 1945. We are celebrating the 70th Anniversary of UNESCO in 2015. Since its inception, the preservation of the world's cultural heritage is one of its essential functions laid on the Organization by its *Constitution*. It calls for '*Maintaining, increasing and disseminating knowledge: By assuring the conservation, protection and inheritance of the world's books, works of art and monuments of history, and appealing state parties to develop relevant international standard instruments*".

As the only UN agency responsible for international cultural cooperation, the preservation of cultural heritage is one of its core functions. In 1948, UNESCO set up an International Expert Committee and an International Found to support the protection of monuments and sites of historical significance. During the 1950s, the Organization adopted the *Convention for the Protection of Cultural Property in the Event of Armed Conflict (the 1954 Hague Convention)*, established an International Centre for the Study of the Preservation and Restoration of Cultural Property (ICCROM, 1956), organized the 2nd International Congress of Architects and Technicians of Historic Monuments (Venice, 1964) and adopted the *Venice Charter*, and hence established the International Council on Monuments and Sites (ICOMOS, 1965). Importantly, UNESCO launched the *International Campaign to Safeguard the Monuments of Nubia* (1960-1968), an event that promoted the protection of the national heritage of different countries at international level, and thus the concept of world cultural heritage was formulated. As a result, UNESCO has become a driving force

in the field of heritage conservation and protection worldwide. Based on these achievements, the *Convention Concerning the Protection Of the World Cultural and Natural Heritage* (the 1972 *World Heritage Convention*) was adopted in Paris on 16 November 1972, at the 17th session of the General Conference of UNESCO.

Cultural and natural heritage properties are invaluable and irreplaceable common treasures to humanity. The 1972 *World Heritage Convention* aims for the identification, protection, conservation and presentation of the cultural and natural heritage sites which are posses 'Outstanding Universal Value'. It calls for the protection and transmission of these heritage properties for future generations. According with purpose and spirit of the 1972 *Convention*, the World Heritage Committee formulated *the Operational Guidelines for the Implementation of the World Heritage Convention (the Operational Guidelines*) in 1977. The aim of *the Operational Guidelines* is to help the State Parties understand the World Heritage Committee's decision-making procedures in determining the *World Heritage List* and the *List of World Heritage in Danger*, reviewing the statue of conservation of the World Heritage properties, and in granting international assistance under the World Heritage Fund. The July July 2013 edition of *the Operational Guideline* states that '*Outstanding Universal Value means cultural and/or natural significance which is so exceptional as to transcend national boundaries and to be of common importance for present and future generations of all humanity. As such, the permanent protection of this heritage is of the highest importance to the international community as a whole.*'

For more than 40 years, the implementation of the *World Heritage Convention* has facilitated the international community to realize ideals and concepts such as cultural diversity, cultural exchange, culture of peace and sustainable development. From this point of view, safeguarding World Heritage is making a great contribution to the peace and sustainable development of human society.

The definition and concept of cultural heritage in the *World Heritage Convention* has enriched and extended the concept of historic monuments in the 1964 *Venice Charter*, and also influenced a number of charters and recommendations adopted by ICOMOS in definition of cultural heritage. The evolution of the concept of cultural heritage is also keeping pace with the time, and is thus pushing forward the development of cultural heritage conservation.

World Heritage is a flagship programme of UNESCO. After more than 40 years of development and practice, the *World Heritage Convention* has achieved significant influence and has become the most successful international cultural cooperation project of UNESCO. The *Convention* has covered almost all Member States of the United Nations system, and 191 countries have joined the international cultural heritage protection movement.

The protection of World Heritage reflects the awareness and understanding of humanity to their living environment, history and culture, This knowledge is not only based on the sustainable protection of cultural and natural resources, but also based on the philosophical idea of cultural diversity. The protection object, especially for cultural heritage, is constantly evolving and updating in typology, concept and methods of protection. The Global Strategy adopted in 1994, symbolizes the stakeholders' reflection on the future developing direction for cultural and natural heritage protection. In fact, a great number of challenges faced by the World Heritage properties are also mirrors of the common threats to humanity, such as political and security issues that faced by international communities together. It is clearly evidenced in the current crisis in Iraq, Syria and other countries in Middle East. Through the joint efforts of World Heritage protection, international communities are thinking ahead and exploring a way forward for sustainable development of humankind. This has also had a significant influence on the dimensions of cultural exchanges, on the eradication of poverty, on social and economic development, and on environment protection.

China ratified the 1972 World Heritage Convention in December 1985. Since then, it has accumulated very rich experiences of cultural heritage protection, and has gained considerable competence. In terms of World Heritage theoretical application and cultural heritage practice, China has truly become a great power. In the collaboration of *the Serial Transnational World Heritage Nomination of the Silk Roads*, Chinese government actively responds to the initiative of the UNESCO World Heritage Centre, cooperates with UNESCO, ICOMOS and Central Asian as well as other Asian countries to promote mutual understanding, strengthen and improve the protection of cultural heritage. The firmly support from China's National Cultural Heritage Administration has assured the full success of this trans-cultural project. The ICOMOS International Conservation Centre-Xi'an (IICC-X), as a partner of this inter-cultural cooperation project, has offered strong technical support for the preparation of this serial transnational nomination of World Heritage in its first phase. During the nomination period of the project, IICC-X has also provided a great deal of inter-state coordination and technical assistance.

On 22 June 2014, at the 38th session of the World Heritage Committee in Doha, Qatar, the '*Silk*

Roads: Routes Network of Chang'an-Tianshan Corridor' submitted by China, Kazakhstan, Kyrgyzstan, was inscribed on UNESCO's *World Heritage List*. It became a new member of the World Heritage family. More than ten years hard work for the Silk Roads World Heritage nomination had achieved a result. The successful inscription of '*Silk Roads: the Routes Network of Chang'an-Tianshan Corridor'* is a testament to the tremendous progress made in China for the protection of large-scale and complex cultural heritage sites. In the Long march of the nomination process, we have experienced all kinds of emotional moments such as joy, pain, debate, misunderstanding and regret. But when we are finally celebrating the success, we can clearly feel that cultural heritage protection has beyond boundaries and nationalities. It becomes a shared heritage for humanity.

The Silk Roads is a large-scale, complex cultural route that connected the Eurasia, Africa continent and Arabian Peninsula which linked the most important ancient civilizations together. It is the most important cultural, economic and political communication channel of people before the Great Maritime age. This ancient cultural exchange system is renewing its great influence on cultural and economic exchange in the world today. During the Silk Roads World Heritage nomination process, Chinese Government has proposed the strategic developing concept of'One Belt and One Road', which refers to the 'Silk Road Economic Belt' and the '21st Century Maritime Silk Road' which extended the concept of the Silk Roads far beyond cultural heritage protection. Rather, it formulates the Great Silk Roads as a powerful driver for economic development, an important platform for trans-cultural dialogue and common regional prosperity. The silk road heritage protection has become an integral part of the regional development strategy, which will effectively promote the common development of the countries along the silk road. The Silk Roads is no longer just a cultural heritage corridor composed of monuments and sites, but also endowed with more profound meaning for connotation of sustainable development.

For more than 20 years, throughout my work in China and in UNESCO, I've always been engaged in research and study on World Heritage conservation. In my practical work, I had accumulated rich experiences of World Heritage protection and management, and directly witnessed all major World Heritage international cooperation projects in China. As UNESCO's Chief Coordinator of the Serial Transnational World Heritage Nomination of the Silk Roads, I have had first-hand communication and working relations with IICC-X. This team is from my hometown, led by Mr. Feng Jian, has impressed me for their professional dedications and persistence: a virtue always seen in people from northwest China.

In May 2007, the UNESCO World Heritage Center, ICOMOS, ICCROM and China's National Administration of Cultural Heritage jointly organized the International Symposium: *Concept and Practice of Conservation of Historic Buildings in East Asia* in Beijing. On that occasion, the first volume of *Selected Documents of International Cultural Heritage Protection* was produced. Eight years have passed and the

protection of World Heritage has become even more important. The awareness of heritage protection has been consistently increasing in different countries and communities, World Heritage inscription has become a well-known phenomenon in the world. Meanwhile, the theories and concepts of World Heritage conservation and protection have fully developed in the past four decades, and have become the landmark of cultural and natural heritage.

Under such background, IICC-X has collected and translated variety of legal documents, recommendations, international charters and operational guidelines that concerning management and conservation of cultural heritages which were published during 2007 - 2017, and compiled the 2nd volume of *Selected Documents of International Cultural Heritage Protection*. This is, truly, a valuable work for tracing the records and researching the development of World Heritage conservation.

An ancient Chinese poet wrote these wise words: '*Stone from other places may be used as a jade polisher*' (learning from others makes us success). Do these '*stones*' still work even to day and that are what we should consider while we reading. In any event, these documents included achievements of research on safeguarding the common heritages of humanity, reflection and thoughts of experts from UNESCO, ICOMOS and professionals of the international community. It could be of great value to the current practices. The year 2015 marks 70th Anniversary of UNESCO, 50th Anniversary of ICOMOS and the 30th anniversary of China ratifying the *World Heritage Convention as well as* 10th Anniversary of establishment of IICC-X. Publishing this book composed of nearly all fundamental works of World Heritage conservation is an excellent way to celebrate these important events. The publication also has very positive meaning for strengthening the soft power of Chinese culture, increase peoples' awareness of revitalizing Chinese traditional cultural heritage and building a peaceful and sustainable planet.

I sincerely hope that the work of IICC-Xi'an on cultural heritage will reach a new era in the future. I also wish that more readers of this publication will dedicate themselves to World Heritage conservation.

Finally, I wish you an enjoyable reading.

Feng JING
Chief, Asia and the Pacific Section
UNESCO World Heritage Centre
January 2018, Paris

后 记

联合国教育、科学和文化组织（简称 UNESCO 或教科文组织）成立于 1945 年 11 月 16 日，今年正好庆祝其 70 周年。自成立之日起，依照教科文组织的《组织法》，国际社会提出保世界范围护有“重要性”的文物。该《组织法》阐述了教科文组织“应该保持、增加和传播知识，以便世界的书籍，艺术品和古迹能够得以保护并呼吁各国政府制定相关的国际准则文书”。

作为联合国系统唯一的国际文化合作机构，教科文组织的职责使其在成立之初就确定保护文化遗产为主要业务领域。1948 年，该组织决定成立国际专家委员会并组建国际基金对保护“具有历史价值的纪念物和遗址”予以资助。20 世纪 50 年代，教科文组织通过了《海牙公约》（1954），成立了国际文化财产保护与修复研究中心（ICCROM，1956），组织了 1964 年的第 2 届历史性建筑保护国际会议（通过《威尼斯宪章》）并借此成立了国际古迹遗址理事会（ICOMOS，1965）。特别值得一提的是，教科文组织发起了努比亚古迹遗址国际保护运动（1960-1968）。这次活动首次将国家遗产推向世界，世界文化遗产保护的理念逐步诞生。也正是因为努比亚古迹遗址国际保护运动的成就，确立了教科文组织在世界文化遗产保护领域的主导地位。在此基础上，1972 年 11 月 16 日，教科文组织的第 17 届大会通过了《保护世界文化和自然遗产公约》（简称《世界遗产公约》）。

无论对世界各国还是对全世界人民而言，文化和自然遗产都是无可估价且无法替代的人类共同遗产。1972 年联合国教科文组织通过的《世界遗产公约》，目的就是对具有“突出的普遍价值”（Outstanding Universal Value）的文化和自然遗产进行鉴定、保护、保存和展示，并将其完好地传承给子孙后代。根据《公约》的宗旨与精神，世界遗产委员会在 1977 年制定了《实施公约的操作指南》。《操作指南》主要是为了帮助会员国了解世界遗产委员会在确定《世界遗产名录》和《濒危世界遗产名录》，在审议世界遗产的保护状况，以及在批准国际合作援助项目等事宜的决策程序。2013 年 7 月版的《操作指南》中规定：“突出的普遍价值指遗产自身文化和自然的价值是如此罕见，超越了国家的界限，对全人类的现在和将来均具有普遍的重要意义。因此，该项遗产的永久性保护对整个国际社会都具有至高的重要性。”

《世界遗产公约》实施 40 多年来，国际社会逐步接受了其所倡导文化多样性、文明间对话、和平文化、可持续发展等理念。从这个意义上讲，保护世界遗产也正是对和平与发展、人类对可持续发展的积极贡献。

《世界遗产公约》对文化遗产的定义和理念拓宽了 1964《威尼斯宪章》中的历史性建筑的概念，影响了 ICOMOS 若干宪章中对文化遗产的定义。这种理念随着时代发展逐渐被拓展，推进着文化遗产保护事业的发展。

世界遗产是联合国教科文组织的旗舰项目。《世界遗产公约》历经四十多年的发展，在全球范围内产生了巨大影响，也成为教科文组织迄今为止最为成功的国际文化合作项目。《世界遗产公约》几乎覆盖了所有联合国成员国，现在已经有 191 个国家，参与到这项国际文化遗产保护运动中。

世界遗产保护反映了人类对于自身所处的环境和历史、文化的认识，这种认识不仅基于资源角度的可持续保护，也基于文化多样性和哲学的思考。它对于保护对象，特别是文化遗产，无论在类型、保护观念和保护方法上都在不断的变化和更新。1994 年世界遗产全球战略的提出，标志着《世界遗产公约》的利益相关者对世界遗产保护发展方向的反思。事实上，世界遗产所面临的问题在很多情况下也是人类共同面对的政治和安全的问题，从当前叙利亚和伊拉克文化遗产的保护就可见一斑。通过世界遗产的保护，国际社会也在不断思考，探索人类可持续发展的途径。在当代社会的文化交流、消除贫困、社会经济发展和环境保护方面都产生了重要的影响。

中国自 1985 年 12 月加入《世界遗产公约》以来，积累了非常丰富的文化遗产保护经验，也具有了相当的遗产保护实力。无论在理论层面还是实践方面，中国都逐步成为名副其实的世界遗产大国。比如，在丝绸之路系列跨境申遗国际合作上，中国政府积极响应教科文组织世界遗产中心的倡议，与中亚和亚洲各国通力合作，联合申遗，以促进相互了解，提高文化遗产保护水平。中国国家文物局强有力支持使世界遗产中心提出的这项跨文化合作项目真正落在了实处。国际古迹遗址理事会西安国际保护中心（IICC-Xi'an）作为丝路申遗项目的合作伙伴，为中国和中亚国家首期申遗材料的准备提供了有力的支持。并在中选期间提供了大量国家间的协调与技术帮助。

2014 年 6 月 22 日，在卡塔尔首都多哈召开的第 38 届世界遗产委员会大会上，“丝绸之路：长安——天山廊道的路网”被列入了《世界遗产名录》，成为世界遗产大家庭的新成员。至此，十多年的申遗之路终于有了结果。“丝绸之路：长安——天山廊道的路网”和中国的大运河成功列为世界文化遗产，见证了中国在大型文化遗产保护方面所取得的巨大进步。这些年，在漫长的申遗过程中，我们有欢乐、有痛苦、有争议、有误解、也留下一些遗憾。当我们欢庆胜利的时候，我们也看到遗产保护已经远远地超出了国界，超出了民族，成为人类的一个共同事业。

丝绸之路作为沟通了欧亚非三大洲和阿拉伯半岛、把古代世界最为重要文明联系在一起的巨形遗产线路，构成了在大航海时代之前，人类最重要的文化、经济、政治交流通道。这一源于古代世界的文化交流系统，对于今天人类的文化、经济交流同样具有重要的意义。在丝绸之路申报世界遗产的过程中，中国提出了“一带一路”，即丝绸之路经济带和 21 世纪海上丝绸之路的战略发展构想，这使得丝绸之路的概念已经远远超出了遗产保护的范畴，而成为地区经济发展新的推动力量，成为地区文化对话、共同发展的重要平台。丝绸之路的遗产保护已经成为地区发展战略的一个组成部分，将有力地促进沿线国家的共同发展。丝绸之路已不再仅仅是一个由历史遗址和古代建筑构成的文化遗产，它已经被赋予了更为丰富的社会可持续发展的内涵。

二十多年来，无论是在国内还是后来进入联合国教科文组织工作，我一直从事世界遗产保护方面的研究与探索。在实际工作中，积累了一定的世界遗产保护和管理经验，也见证了中国几乎全部的世界遗产国际合作项目。作为丝绸之路系列跨境申遗项目的总负责人，我与国际古迹遗址理事会西安国际保护中心有了直接的交流与合作。同为乡党，冯健带领的 IICC-X 团队西北人淳朴的敬业精神让我感动。

2007 年 5 月，教科文组织世界遗产中心（WHC）、国际古迹遗址理事会（ICOMOS）、国际文化财产保护与修复研究中心（ICCROM）与中国国家文物局在北京联合召开了“东亚地区文物建筑保护理念与实践国际研讨会”。当时看到了 IICC-X 出版的《国际文化遗产保护文件选编》第一辑。8 年来，世界遗产保护的重要性不断增强。世界各国政府和民众遗产保护意识空前提高，申遗已成为潮流。同时，世界遗产保护理念在过去几十年当中也得到了充分的发展，成为遗产保护事业的理论前沿和风向标。

在这样的背景下，IICC-Xi' an 收集、整理、翻译了 2007~2017 年新出版的部分世界文化遗产保护和管理的法律文件、建议书、《操作指南》、宪章等，编辑成《国际文化遗产保护文件选编》第二辑，对于反映、跟踪、研究这一热门课题的最新动向，是大好事，也是件功德无量的事。

古代诗人曾谆谆教导我们：“它山之石，可以攻玉”。在当今的时代大潮下，它山之石，还可以攻玉吗？这也是我们阅读时需要考虑的问题。无论怎样，这些参考资料汇集了教科文组织、

ICOMOS 和世界各国在保护人类共同遗产方面的反思及其成果，对指导当下的工作很有帮助。2015 年是联合国以及教科文组织成立 70 周年、ICOMOS 也年届知天命、中国参加《世界遗产公约》30 周年，IICC–Xi'an 成立 10 周年。借着庆祝的机会，搞个“串烧”，汇编几乎所有涉及世界文化遗产的基本文件，对于弘扬中华民族的文化软实力，提高人们复兴中国传统文化遗产，构建可持续发展的世界，还是很有益处的。

我衷心祝愿 IICC–Xi'an 的工作在文化遗产保护领域芝麻开花节节高，更上一层楼！也祝愿有更多的读者投身世界遗产保护事业！

景峰

联合国教科文组织世界遗产中心

亚洲和太平洋部　主任

2018 年 1 月 15 日于巴黎

Editor’s words

In 2006, under the promotion of ICOMOS executive members such as Mr.Michael Petzet, Mr.Dinu Bumbaru, Mr.Giolar Solar, Madam Gaia Jungeblod, and Xi’an Municipal government, under the leadership of The National Cultural HeritageAdministration of China(NCHA), and Shaanxi Cultural Heritage Administration, the ICOMOS International Conservation Centre-Xi’an (hereinafter as IICC-X) was set up. IICC-X is a unique business and service centre of International Council on Monuments and Sites(ICOMOS), which is devote to international and regional cooperation for conservation of monuments, sites as well as surrounding settings in Asia-Pacific regions. Also it is an international organization which is devote to the cultural heritage protection and conservation, management, presentation; the arrangement and coordination of international and domestic academic training, provide assistance and consultancy for heritage conservation and planning projects as well as communication and legal advisory.

In 2015, with the process of ‘Silk Roads: the Routes Network of Chang’an--Tianshan Corridor’ of the Serial Transnational Nomination of Silk Road into World Heritage List, IICC-X, as the secretariat of the Nomination Committee of the Serial Transnational Nomination of Silk Road into World Heritage List (15 countries along silk roads are: China, Kazakhstan, Kyrgyzstan, Turkmenistan, Tajikistan, Uzbekistan, Japan, South Korea, India, Afghanistan, Nepal, Iran, Pakistan, Turkey, Bhutan) and the secretariat of the working group of steering committee of Kazakhstan, Kyrgyzstan and China, assisted and organized a serials meeting which were related to the Serial Transnational Nomination of Silk Road into World Heritage List, contributed positive force to the first bitch of its inscription; at the same time, participated in several thematic conferences on Silk Road serial nomination which was organized by UNESCO World Heritage Center; authorized by theworking group of NCHA, IICC-X designed and established the on-line Silk Roads Archive and Information Management System (AIMS); conveyed special technical requirements to the nominated sites in China, and assisted the serial nomination work of Shaanxi and Xi’an region, provided technical and consulting services, effectively transmitted ICOMOS’ theory and experience of scientific protection of archaeological sites as well as the requirements and standards of the world cultural heritage in the view of the world heritage center.

However, with the continuous strengthening of the nomination for World Heritage and the protection, management, utilization and research of world heritage, scholars all over the world have shown their concern and demand for world heritage and international protection documents. In 2007, IICC-X brought together a group of young cultural heritage scholars and, under the auspices of National Cultural Heritage Administration, translated and edited <Collection of International Documents on Cultural Heritage Protection>. The publication gained widespread high praise and recognition, and being an important document for world heritage nomination and cultural heritage protection study.

In 2007, during their inspection tour to IICC-X, National Cultural Heritage Administration, ICOMOS Chairman Gustavo Araoz, secretary-general Benedicte Selfslagh, and Madam Hae Un Rii, fully affirmed the <Collection of International Documents on Cultural Heritage Protection>, and believed that the compilation of IICC-X was of great importance not only to Chinese scholars, but also to ICOMOS and researchers of cultural heritage worldwide, and suggestedIICC-X continue the project in future.

In later 2013, IICC-X arranged staffs start the project of <Collection of International Documents on Cultural Heritage Protection 2006-2017>. This time, we followed the suggestion of ICOMOS executive committee, finished the compilation in bilingual, and keep some of the relevant background information of the document, so as to restore the authenticity and integrity of the document as far as possible. In order to accomplish this important task, IICC-X arranged special personnel to collect and sort out new documents related to cultural heritage protection laws and regulations, international charter and declaration, Operation Guideline WHC17/01 etc. from 2006 to 2017, organized and coordinated professionals from Northwest University of China and other units to jointly promote the compilation and translation work, which took 20 months to complete the first draft. But still, proofreading was a huge undertaking. The form of English-Chinese translation requires higher accuracy and readability of literal translation. In repeated discussions, we realized our insufficiency in translation as well as the lack of accurate cultural heritage protection concept and knowledge. But we still insisted to employ the format of mutual translations for, first, the conducive to redaction and proofreading; second, for convenient the vast number of readers be able to compare with the original document then get the original meaning as considering the level of our readers are far above us; and third, for conducive to pointing out the existing errors and facilitating to correct, so as to jointly promote our accurate understanding and dissemination of the spirit of UNESCO, ICOMOS Charter and international documents.

Here, let me on behalf of all colleagues involved in the compilation work, sincerely thanks to Dr. Feng Jing, Chief of Asia and the Pacific Section of World Heritage Centre for his kindly review of our <Collection of Documents> and writing a postscript during his busy business; sincerely thanks to sincerely thanks to Madam Zhou Jianhong and her group from the North-west University for their great support during our compilation; thanks to Xi'an Institute of Archaeology for providing publishing funds; thanks to Mr. Xu Mingfei, Ms. Wang Qinghua of Xi'an city for their support and guidance to the compilation work, thanks to colleagues of IICC-X for their professional and enthusiastic work spirit, thanks to IICC-X translation team member such as Madam Li Tongxian, Madam Zhao Fengyan, Mr. Gong Tian, Mr. Li Erwu etc.for their years hard work.

At the same time, thanks to Doctor Sun Fuxi, Sir Michael Petzet, Mr. John Hurd, and Mr. Henry Cleere whom were the late ICOMOS experts, for contact and exchange with you, we had learnt a lot, not only solved our confusion on the charters, but also deepened our understanding of the conceptual context of ICOMOS, and cultivated our love and persistence of cultural heritage, as well as protection and inheritance cultural heritage across countries, across different ethnic groups and regions. I would like to take this opportunity to express my heartfelt thanks and deep memory to you.

Due to the limit of time and language ability, please understanding any errors or omissions in collection, translation and edition.

Wish our efforts better for protection of humanity's common cultural heritage!

Executive Deputy Director of IICC-X

Feng Jian

November 11, 2019

编者的话

2006 年 10 月，在 ICOMOS 前主席 Michael Petzet, 前秘书长 Dinu Bumbaru, 前司库 Giolar Solar, 秘书处主任 Gaia Jungeblodt 等 ICOMOS 执行委员和西安市政府的共同推动下，在中国国家文物局、陕西省文物局的指导和支持下，国际古迹遗址理事会西安国际保护中心在西安成立（以下简称 IICC-X）。IICC-X 是国际古迹遗址理事会（ICOMOS）在全球范围内设立的唯一业务中心，致力于支持亚太地区的古迹、遗址及周边环境保护的国际和区域合作；也是致力于文化遗产保护、管理、展示、相关技术人员交流与培训，文化遗产保护和规划项目的研究与开发，提供文化遗产项目咨询的国际组织。

2015 年，随着“丝绸之路：长安 - 天山廊道的路网”申遗工作的不断推进，IICC-X 作为丝绸之路跨国系列申报世界文化遗产协调委员会秘书处（2009 年 11 月）（协调委员会目前由中国、哈萨克斯坦、吉尔吉斯斯坦、土库曼斯坦、塔吉克斯坦、乌兹别克斯坦、日本、韩国、印度、阿富汗、尼泊尔、伊朗，巴基斯坦、土耳其、不丹组成）和“丝绸之路：长安和天山廊道的路网”申遗协调委员会工作组秘书处（2011 年 12 月）（中国、哈萨克斯坦、吉尔吉斯斯坦三国），协助中、哈、吉三国，多次组织、举办与丝绸之路跨国系列申报世界遗产相关的工作会议，为丝绸之路系列遗产首批列入世界遗产名录贡献了积极力量；多次参加联合国教科文组织世界遗产中心组织的商讨丝绸之路系列申报的专题会议；接受中国工作组的委托，搭建丝绸之路档案信息管理系统（AIMS）；根据《实施保护世界自然与文化遗产公约的操作指南》精神，支持、协助陕西省、西安市各申遗点的工作，并持续提供技术支持及咨询等服务。

但随着申遗工作与世界遗产保护、管理、利用、研究工作的不断加强，各国学者都表现出对世界遗产、国际保护文件的关注与需求。2007 年，IICC-X 集合一批年轻的文化遗产学者，在国家文物局资助下，编译《国际文化遗产保护文件选编》，出版发行后得到社会各界广泛好评和认可，成为申报世界遗产、学习文化遗产保护的重要文献。

2007 年，国家文物局以及时任 ICOMOS 主席 Gustavo Araoz，秘书长 Benedicte Selfslagh, 执委 Hae Un Rii 一行视察 IICC-X 工作期间，对《国际文化遗产保护文件选编》给予充分肯定，认为 IICC-X 的编译工作不仅对中国学者极为重要，对 ICOMOS 及全世界文化遗产研究者同样重要，建议以中英双语形式，继续编译后续出台的宪章、文件。

2013 下半年，IICC-X 着手汇编《国际文化遗产保护文件选编（2006-2017）》，充分采纳 ICOMOS 执委建议，并保留部分文件的相关背景资料，借此尽量还原文件的真实性和完整性。为完成这项重要任务，IICC-X 安排专人收集、整理 2006 年至 2013 年文化遗产保护法规、国际宪章及宣言、2017《操作指南》等相关的新文献，并组织协调专业人员、中国西北大学等多方力量，共同推动汇编、翻译工作，历时 1 年 8 个月完成初稿。但校译工作仍然海量。英汉互译的形式，对直译准确性和意译可读性上提出了更高要求。经过反复讨论，在感慨水平不足的同时，也充分认识到自身缺乏精准文化遗产保护理念与知识的现状。因此，我们仍然决定，坚持对照互译的形式，这样，一来有利于编校、检查；二来考虑到广大读者的水平远在我们之上，方便各位能够对照原文，得其本意；三来有利于指出存在的谬误，便于更正，以共同推动我们对 UNESCO、ICOMOS 宪章、国际文件精神的精准把握与传播。

在此，我仅代表参与编译工作的所有同事，感谢联合国教科文组织世界遗产中心亚太部主任景峰先生，在百忙中抽出时间为我们审核文件，并撰写后记；感谢中国西北大学周剑虹女士和她的团队对编译工作的鼎力支持；感谢西安市文物保护考古研究院提供出版经费；感谢西安市的徐明非先生、王庆华女士对编译工作的大力支持与指导；感谢 IICC-X 同事专业、热情的工作精神，并向参与文件选编资料收集及翻译的李同仙、赵凤燕、龚天、李尔吾等同事和编译团队，道声辛苦啦！

同时，感谢已故的孙福喜先生，Michael Petzet，John Hurd，及 Henry Cleere 等 ICOMOS 专家，与您们的接触与交流，不仅解答了我们对各宪章精神的困惑，加深了我们对 ICOMOS 的理念脉络的理解，更培养了我们对文化遗产的热爱与执着，以及对跨国家、跨民族、跨地区的文化遗产保护与传承。借此，也向您们表示衷心的谢意和深切的缅怀。

因时间、能力、水平有限，文件选择中的遗漏和编译中的不足之处，敬请谅解。

愿我们的努力能为人类共同的文化遗产保护事业添砖加瓦，锦上添花！

IICC-X 执行副主任　冯健

2019 年 11 月 12 日